D0924721

Califor[illegible] Practic[illegible] Guide

CIVIL PROCEDURE BEFORE TRIAL

Chapters 8-9

ORIGINAL AUTHORS

JUDGE ROBERT I. WEIL (Ret.)
Los Angeles Superior Court

JUDGE IRA A. BROWN, JR. (Ret.)
San Francisco Superior Court

CURRENT EDITION AUTHORS

PRESIDING JUSTICE LEE SMALLEY EDMON
Calif. Court of Appeal, 2nd Dist., Div. 3

JUDGE CURTIS E.A. KARNOW
San Francisco Superior Court

2020

CONTINUING LEGAL EDUCATION 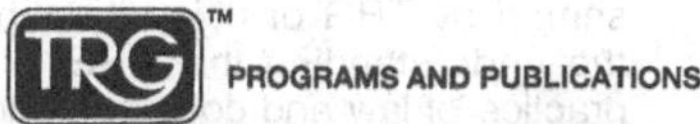 PROGRAMS AND PUBLICATIONS

THE RUTTER GROUP™
A DIVISION OF THOMSON REUTERS

© 2020 Thomson Reuters/The Rutter Group Mat #42623347

ATTORNEY EDITORS

FOUNDERS

William A. Rutter

Linda Diamond Raznick

Kathleen K. Andrews

Kathleen J. Atwater

Amy M. Hinkley

Christina J. Imre

Morgan W. McCall

Erin L. Miller

Andriy R. Pazuniak

Lorie Dewhirst Porter

Lisa K. Rozzano

Cynthia L. Sletto

Lisa E. Ward

Michael L. Woods

© Copyright 1983, 1984, 1985, 1986, 1987, 1988, 1989, 1990, 1991, 1992, 1993, 1994, 1995, 1996, 1997, 1998, 1999, 2000, 2001, 2002, 2003, 2004, 2005, 2006, 2007, 2008, 2009, 2010, 2011, 2012, 2013, 2014, 2015, 2016, 2017, 2018, 2019, 2020 by THE RUTTER GROUP, A DIVISION OF THOMSON REUTERS

Permission is hereby granted for the copying of pages or portions of pages of this book by photocopy, Xerox or other similar process, or by manual transcription, by or under the direction of licensed attorneys for use in the practice of law. Otherwise, all rights reserved; no copying for in-house training distribution or other use is permitted which will infringe the copyright without the express written consent of The Rutter Group, a Division of Thomson Reuters.

To contact us: Phone (800) 747-3161; or fax (310) 491-7293; or visit our website, www.ruttergroup.com.

This book should be cited as Weil & Brown et al., CAL. PRAC. GUIDE: CIV. PRO. BEFORE TRIAL (The Rutter Group 2020).

Please note: Programs and publications by The Rutter Group (TRG), a Division of Thomson Reuters, are intended to provide attorneys with current and accurate information about the subjects covered. However, such information may not be sufficient in dealing with a client's particular legal problem, and TRG does not warrant or represent its suitability for such purpose. Attorneys attending programs presented by TRG or using its publications do so with the understanding that TRG is not engaged in the practice of law and does not render legal, accounting or other professional services; and that the information published by TRG should not be relied upon as a substitute for independent research to original sources of authority.

TABLE OF CONTENTS

See front of each chapter for detailed summaries of contents

© 2020 Thomson Reuters/The Rutter Group

CHAPTER 8

DISCOVERY

CONTENTS

See front of each chapter for detailed summaries of contents

© 2020 Thomson Reuters/The Rutter Group

RESERVED

CHAPTER 8A

INTRODUCTION

CONTENTS

© 2020 Thomson Reuters/The Rutter Group

INTRODUCTION

1. [8:1] **Purpose of Discovery:** The basic purpose of discovery is to take the "game" element out of trial preparation by enabling parties to obtain the evidence necessary to evaluate and resolve their dispute beforehand. [*Greyhound Corp. v. Sup.Ct. (Clay)* (1961) 56 C2d 355, 376, 15 CR 90, 99 (superseded by statute on other grounds); *Emerson Elec. Co. v. Sup.Ct. (Grayson)* (1997) 16 C4th 1101, 1107, 68 CR2d 883, 886]

   Discovery can accomplish the following important objectives:

   - **Preserving evidence for trial:** Special procedures are available for avoiding loss of physical evidence and testimony of witnesses who may become unavailable (because of death, illness, leaving the state, etc.).
   - **Providing basis for pretrial motions:** Information obtained through discovery may provide the basis for motions for summary judgment or adjudication, and sanctions (which may include the striking of meritless causes of action and defenses; *see* ¶*9:1217 ff.*).
   - **Narrowing issues for trial:** Through effective discovery, parties may find that some claims or defenses are entirely without merit or so lacking in credible evidence that they are not worth pursuing. They may then be induced to stipulate to such matters, narrowing the issues to be tried, conserving court time and reducing client costs.
   - **Promoting settlement:** Through discovery, each side can obtain better information regarding the opponent's case, and thereby better evaluate the strengths *and weaknesses* of its own case. This increases the potential for pretrial settlement.
   - **Avoiding surprises at trial:** Effective discovery eliminates the need for guesswork as to the adversary's case. Each side can find out a great deal about the contentions and evidence the other side will offer. There is less chance of some "surprise" evidence or claim necessitating a continuance. And, there is also less chance for fabrication or forgetfulness by the witnesses who testify, because their trial testimony can be checked against the answers obtained through pretrial depositions, interrogatories, etc. [*Greyhound Corp. v. Sup.Ct. (Clay)*, supra, 56 C2d at 376, 15 CR at 99]

2. [8:2] **Drawbacks and Disadvantages of Discovery:** Discovery has its disadvantages. There is always the risk of "educating" your opponents by focusing attention on evidence or issues of which they were unaware. Also, experience has shown various problems with discovery. [*Kravitz v. Sup.Ct. (Milner)* (2001) 91 CA4th 1015, 1020, 111 CR2d 385, 389 (citing text)]

© 2020 Thomson Reuters/The Rutter Group

- **Costs:** Discovery was conceived as a cost-savings mechanism, but has become increasingly expensive. Fees and costs relating to certain forms of discovery (e.g., depositions, medical examinations) are often more than can be justified in routine litigation. Also, failure to use discovery procedures *efficiently* may increase discovery costs (e.g., using depositions to obtain information that could be obtained through interrogatories or document requests).
- **Discovery "overkill":** There is always a tension between the need to explore every avenue in discovery and the cost of doing so. Failure to conduct necessary discovery may expose the lawyer to malpractice liability, while excessive discovery often leads to clients dissatisfied with the cost incurred (or, in contingent fee cases, excessive expense to the lawyer). Because of this tension, it is important to develop a discovery plan and discuss with the client why certain discovery is necessary and why the cost of other potential discovery exceeds its utility.
- **Discovery disputes:** Where the lawyers and parties fail to cooperate, the result is unnecessary motions and court hearings. Petty bickering runs up the costs to all concerned, burdens the courts, and defeats the purposes of discovery.
- **Discovery abuses:** Some parties try to use discovery as a financial bludgeon. They take more depositions than necessary and send out excessive discovery requests in an attempt to wear down the opposing party by making the litigation too expensive to continue. Other parties practice the "art of obfuscation" in responding to discovery requests, making it as difficult as possible for the opposing party to get full and complete answers. These practices subvert the purposes of discovery and give wealthy litigants an unfair advantage over less wealthy adversaries. The Discovery Act of 1986 (¶*8:4 ff.*) addresses some of these abuses.

⇨ [8:2.1] ***PRACTICE POINTER:*** Lawful investigations sometimes can accomplish as much as formal discovery and at less cost. For example, evidence may be obtained from public records or Internet databases, or by interviewing nonparty witnesses, or by inspecting physical objects or public places. Such investigations are not subject to discovery limitations (*see* ¶*8:39.10*) and may yield evidence of which the opposing party is unaware. [See *Pullin v. Sup.Ct. (Vons Cos., Inc.)* (2000) 81 CA4th 1161, 1165, 97 CR2d 447, 450—property open to the public can be examined without recourse to formal discovery provided examination is conducted lawfully]

3. **Civil Discovery Act**

a. [8:3] **Background:** The first Civil Discovery Act was enacted in 1957 and served as the framework for California's discovery law for almost 30 years. However, it was awkwardly organized and unclear in certain areas, and case law increasingly was required to fill in the gaps.

b. [8:4] **Civil Discovery Act of 1986:** As a result of these deficiencies as well as perceived abuses in the discovery process, a new California Civil Discovery Act was enacted in 1986, with clean-up amendments in 1987 (former CCP §§2016-2036). [See *Terry v. SLICO* (2009) 175 CA4th 352, 356, 95 CR3d 900, 902 (citing text)]

(1) [8:4.1] **Legislative history:** The Discovery Act of 1986, as originally proposed, was the product of a "blue ribbon" commission of lawyers and judges appointed by the State Bar and the Judicial Council. In general, the aim was to embody former statutes and case law and, at the same time, make the California rules correspond more closely to the Federal Rules. [See *Terry v. SLICO*, supra, 175 CA4th at 356, 95 CR3d at 902 (citing text)]

However, few provisions of the Act were adopted intact. Most were extensively rewritten during the legislative process and there is little commentary available explaining the reasons for these changes.

(2) [8:4.2] **Relation to Federal Rules:** As originally enacted in 1957, the California Discovery Act was modeled on the discovery provisions of the Federal Rules of Civil Procedure (FRCP 26-37) then in effect.

Over the years, both the California and federal discovery rules were substantially amended, although there was little similarity in the amendments. The result was ever-increasing differences in discovery practice in California and federal courts.

(3) [8:4.3] **Liberally construed in favor of disclosure:** Like the federal rules, the California rules of civil discovery are "liberally construed in favor of disclosure." In addition, trial courts are "vested with wide discretion in granting or denying discovery." [*Emerson Elec. Co. v. Sup.Ct. (Grayson)* (1997) 16 C4th 1101, 1107, 68 CR2d 883, 886; *Williams v. Sup.Ct. (Marshalls of CA, LLC)* (2017) 3 C5th 531, 541, 220 CR3d 472, 480]

c. [8:5] **Civil Discovery Act of 2004:** In 2004, the Legislature enacted a new Civil Discovery Act *effective 7/1/05.* The new Act basically rewrote the 1986 Act to make it more readable; i.e., lengthy provisions have been divided into shorter sections and renumbered. The changes, however, are *not intended to have any substantive effect* on the law of civil discovery. [See Stats. 2004, Ch. 182, §61; and *Biles v. Exxon Mobil Corp.* (2004) 124 CA4th 1315, 1325, 22 CR3d 282, 289, fn. 7; *Terry v. SLICO*, supra, 175 CA4th at 356, 95 CR3d at 902 (citing text)]

(1) [8:5.1] **2009 Amendments:** In 2009, the Legislature enacted the "Electronic Discovery Act," amending the Discovery Act to address discovery of electronically-stored information. [Stats. 2009, Ch. 5, §4 et seq.; CCP §§1985.8 (*see ¶8:596.50 ff.*) and 2031.010 et seq. (*see ¶8:1427.5 ff.*)]

© 2020 Thomson Reuters/The Rutter Group

NOTE: Except where otherwise stated, *all further references in this Chapter to "the Discovery Act" are to the Civil Discovery Act of 2004 (as amended).*

[8:6] *Reserved.*

d. [8:7] **Structure of Discovery Act:** The broad outline of the Discovery Act is as follows:

(1) [8:8] **General provisions:** First, there are some general provisions applicable to any discovery method:

- **Scope of permissible discovery** (CCP §2017.010 et seq.).
- **Work product limitation** (CCP §2018.010 et seq.).
- **Protective orders generally** (CCP §2019.030).

  This sets forth broad grounds for limiting discovery in any case: "unreasonably cumulative or duplicative," or "unduly burdensome or expensive."

  Each discovery method (¶*8:9*) has its own provision indicating particular *kinds* of protective orders courts may grant as to that discovery method.
- **Nonparty discovery** (CCP §2020.010 et seq.).
- **Discovery misuses** (CCP §2023.010 et seq.): Sanctions may be imposed for numerous "misuses" of discovery as set forth in CCP §2023.010 et seq. (*see* ¶*8:1901*).
- **Discovery sanctions** (CCP §2023.030): The following *types* of sanctions are authorized for discovery violations:
  — monetary sanctions;
  — issue sanctions (designating facts as established);
  — evidence sanctions (barring introduction of evidence);
  — terminating sanctions (striking pleadings, ordering dismissal or entering default); and
  — contempt. [CCP §2023.030]

  Discovery sanctions are discussed at ¶*8:1900 ff.*

(2) [8:9] **Discovery methods:** The Act then contains detailed procedures for each discovery method:

- Oral and Written Depositions (CCP §§2025.010-2028.060).
- Interrogatories (CCP §2030.010 et seq.).
- Inspection, Testing and Sampling of Documents, Things, Places or Electronically-Stored Information (CCP §2031.010 et seq.).
- Physical and Mental Exams (CCP §2032.010 et seq.).
- Requests for Admissions (CCP §2033.010 et seq.).

- Simultaneous Exchange of Expert Trial Witness Information (CCP §2034.010 et seq.).
- Subpoenas to Nonparty Deponents or Business Records Custodians (CCP §§2020.010-2020.510).
- Foreign Subpoenas (CCP §2029.100 et seq.).

(3) [8:10] **Enforcement procedures:** As stated previously, each section contains its own provisions for protective orders, motions to compel and sanctions. The general pattern is as follows:

- [8:10.1] **Attempt to resolve informally:** Before filing a motion for protective order or to compel further responses, the moving party must have made "a reasonable and good faith attempt at informal resolution" of whatever issues are involved. [See, e.g., CCP §§2016.040, 2023.010(i); *and* ¶*8:1158 ff., 8:2100 ff.* (failure to attempt to resolve informally as basis for sanctions)]

  When unnecessary: The propounding party may move to compel without attempting informal resolution when the opposing party has *failed to timely respond* to a discovery demand. [See, e.g., CCP §2030.290(b)]

  [8:10.1a] **Informal conferences:** A party may request, or the court on its own motion may set, an informal conference before a discovery motion is filed. [CCP §2016.080; *see* ¶*8:787.1*]

- [8:10.2] **Monetary sanctions on motion to compel:** Normally, absent a prior court order, only monetary sanctions may be imposed on a motion to compel. But such sanctions "shall" be imposed against the losing party *unless* the court finds "substantial justification" for that party's position or other circumstances rendering sanctions "unjust." *See discussion at* ¶*8:1920 ff.*

  Mandatory vs. discretionary: There are a couple of situations where monetary sanctions on a motion to compel are *mandatory:*

  — for failure to respond to RFAs (CCP §2033.280(c), *see* ¶*8:1376 ff.*); or

  — for failure to "meet and confer" as required by statute, *notwithstanding the outcome* of the motion (CCP §2023.020, *see* ¶*8:2100 ff.*).

- [8:10.3] **Broader sanctions for failure to obey court order:** Once the court has entered an order compelling discovery, a broader range of sanctions is available for failure to make discovery. *See discussion at* ¶*8:2145 ff.*

  [8:10.4] *Reserved.*

© 2020 Thomson Reuters/The Rutter Group

(4) [8:10.5] **Relief from failure to comply:** The court has power to relieve parties from the consequences of their failure to comply with discovery. That power exists under either the Discovery Act itself or CCP §473(b) (which authorizes relief from "a judgment, dismissal, order, or other proceeding" resulting from "mistake, inadvertence, surprise, or excusable neglect"; *see ¶5:282 ff.*).

(a) [8:10.6] **Relief under Discovery Act:** The Discovery Act authorizes relief in the following situations:

1) [8:10.7] **Relief from waiver of objections resulting from failure to respond:** The court may grant relief from the waiver of objections that results from a party's delay or failure in responding to discovery requests:

- [8:10.7a] For example, failure to serve a timely response to interrogatories *waives the right to object* to the interrogatories (*see ¶8:1030*). The court may relieve the party from such waiver (i.e., allow late objections) upon finding that:
  — substantially compliant responses were subsequently served; and
  — the delay in response "was the result of *mistake, inadvertence or excusable neglect.*" [CCP §2030.290(a) (emphasis added); *see ¶8:1032*]

- [8:10.7b] Similar provisions apply to relief from waiver of the right to object as the result of delay in responding to inspection demands and requests for admissions. [CCP §2031.300(a)(2), *see ¶8:1465 ff.;* and CCP §2033.280(a)(2), *see ¶8:1369 ff.*]

2) [8:10.8] **Relief from erroneous admission:** The court may permit a party to withdraw or amend an admission made in response to RFAs based on a determination that it was made as the result of "*mistake, inadvertence or excusable neglect.*" [CCP §2033.300(b) (emphasis added), *see ¶8:1386.1*]

(b) [8:10.9] **Relief under CCP §473:** The grounds for relief under the Discovery Act provisions above (*¶8:10.6 ff.*) are similar to those of CCP §473(b) ("mistake, inadvertence, surprise, or excusable neglect").

1) [8:10.10] **No CCP §473 relief where Discovery Act applies:** But *where the Discovery Act provisions apply*, relief cannot be obtained under CCP §473(b). Rationale: The Legislature's use of §473 language indicates its intent that relief be obtained under these provisions and *not* under CCP §473(b).

[*Zellerino v. Brown* (1991) 235 CA3d 1097, 1107, 1 CR2d 222, 228; *Scottsdale Ins. Co. v. Sup.Ct. (Spyglass Homeowners Ass'n)* (1997) 59 CA4th 263, 274, 69 CR2d 112, 119]

2) [8:10.11] **CCP §473 available where no analogous Discovery Act provision:** On the other hand, where there is no analogous Discovery Act provision, relief may be obtained under CCP §473(b). The broad language of §473(b) ("judgment, dismissal, order, or *other proceeding*") includes discovery proceedings. [*Zellerino v. Brown,* supra, 235 CA3d at 1105, 1 CR2d at 226]

- [8:10.12] D's demand for exchange of expert witness reports was untimely under CCP §2034.210 et seq. (*see* ¶*8:1641*). Because the Discovery Act does not authorize relief for untimely demands, relief is available under §473(b). [*Zellerino v. Brown,* supra, 235 CA3d at 1105, 1 CR2d at 226]

3) [8:10.13] **Relief from discovery sanctions:** Similarly, relief may be available under CCP §473(b) where an attorney's failure to comply with discovery has resulted in the court ordering a dismissal, default or other sanction against a party; however, where the party was a contributing cause, it is not clear whether §473(b) mandates that the dismissal or default be set aside. *See discussion at* ¶*5:295.5 ff., 8:2300 ff.*

(c) [8:10.14] **Significance of distinction:** It is often *easier to obtain relief under CCP §473(b)* than under the Discovery Act:

- [8:10.15] Under the Discovery Act provisions, relief is *discretionary* upon an affirmative showing of "mistake, inadvertence or excusable neglect" (¶*8:10.7a, 8:10.8*). There may also be *additional requirements:* discovery responses tendered in substantial compliance with the Discovery Act; and *no substantial prejudice* to the propounding party from granting relief (*see* ¶*8:1386.1, 8:1465*).

- [8:10.16] Under CCP §473(b), there is no requirement that the discovery responses be supplied at the time of the application for relief (except where §473(b) relief is sought from a terminating sanction due to failure to provide discovery, ¶*5:305.11*); and although prejudice to the propounding party is a consideration, it is not an absolute bar to relief (*see* ¶*8:1386.2*).

© 2020 Thomson Reuters/The Rutter Group

4. [8:11] **Role of Case Law in Discovery:** California appellate courts have played an active role in developing the law of discovery.

The 1986 Discovery Act embodied many rules originally developed by case law, and expressly deferred to case law in others (e.g., for definition of "work product," and who may be present during a court-ordered mental exam). Since the 1986 Act was not intended to displace prior law (except where substantive changes were made), prior case law may be relied upon for interpretation of the Act. The 2004 Civil Discovery Act expressly provides it was *not* intended to change prior law (*see* ¶*8:5*).

a. [8:12] **No inherent judicial power to create new methods of discovery:** The only discovery permissible in civil actions is that provided by statute. California courts have no inherent power to expand the methods of discovery beyond those authorized by the Discovery Act. [See *San Diego Unified Port Dist. v. Douglas E. Barnhart, Inc.* (2002) 95 CA4th 1400, 1405, 116 CR2d 65, 68—no power to order parties to pay for destructive testing or any other discovery they do not wish to pursue; *Holm v. Sup.Ct. (Misco)* (1986) 187 CA3d 1241, 1247, 232 CR 432, 436—no power to exhume corpse to settle probate dispute over testamentary capacity; *Edmiston v. Sup.Ct. (Lagomarsino)* (1978) 22 C3d 699, 704, 150 CR 276, 278-279; *Roe v. Sup.Ct. (Hollister School Dist.)* (2015) 243 CA4th 138, 144, 196 CR3d 317, 322]

b. [8:12.1] **Compare—judicial power to control discovery:** On the other hand, courts clearly have power to *limit* discovery to prevent abuse and unfair burdens in particular cases (e.g., by protective orders, *see* ¶*8:41*); and to control the timing and sequence of discovery pursuant to their *case management* powers (*see* ¶*12:6 ff.*).

But there may be constitutional limitations on a court's power to control discovery. [See *Maggi v. Sup.Ct. (Alkosser)* (2004) 119 CA4th 1218, 1224-1225, 15 CR3d 161, 166—order prohibiting counsel and parties from contacting third party witnesses violated 1st Amendment; *San Francisco Unified School Dist. ex rel. Contreras v. First Student, Inc.* (2013) 213 CA4th 1212, 1238, 153 CR3d 583, 604-605]

c. [8:12.2] **Compare—judicial power to aid discovery:** In addition, courts have inherent power to grant *relief in aid of discovery* where appropriate; e.g., injunctions to preserve evidence (*see* ¶*8:1799*).

d. [8:13] **Role of trial vs. appellate courts in discovery:** As a practical matter, law and motion judges exercise more day-to-day control over discovery than appellate courts. This is because there is usually no right to immediate appeal of discovery rulings (except a sanctions order in excess of $5,000; CCP §904.1(a)(11)). Immediate appellate review is available only by petitioning the appellate court for a writ of mandamus or prohibition.

(The aggrieved party can, of course, wait until after judgment to appeal. But at that stage, it may be impossible to show that claimed error in a pretrial ruling was "prejudicial"; and without such showing, there is no chance for reversal on appeal. See Cal. Const. Art. VI, §13.)

(1) [8:14] **Appellate review seldom granted:** Appellate courts are usually reluctant to grant extraordinary writs to review pretrial discovery rulings: "The trial judge's application of discretion in discovery matters is *presumed correct,* and the complaining party must show how and why the court's action constitutes an *abuse of discretion* in light of the particular circumstances involved." [*Obregon v. Sup.Ct. (Cimm's, Inc.)* (1998) 67 CA4th 424, 432, 79 CR2d 62, 67 (emphasis added)]

Moreover, the party seeking extraordinary writ relief must show that denial will cause *irreparable harm* (rare unless privileged material involved). [See *Roden v. AmerisourceBergen Corp.* (2005) 130 CA4th 211, 219, 29 CR3d 810, 816]

(a) [8:15] **Application—discovery ordered over relevancy objection:** This is particularly true as to orders *granting* discovery where the only objection is on *relevancy* grounds. A writ will not issue in such cases if there is even "a reasonable *possibility*" that the information could lead to discovery of admissible evidence or be "helpful in preparation of trial." [*Colonial Life & Accident Ins. Co. v. Sup.Ct. (Perry)* (1982) 31 C3d 785, 790, 183 CR 810, 813]

(b) [8:15.1] **Alternatives following denial of writ:** If a writ is denied, and the matter is truly crucial, the losing party has no choice but to *disobey* the discovery order and suffer the sanction of dismissal or an adverse judgment on the merits in order to obtain appellate review. [*Hurtado v. Western Med. Ctr.* (1990) 222 CA3d 1198, 1204, 272 CR 324, 327, fn. 3]

➪ [8:15.2] ***PRACTICE POINTER:*** This is a dangerous choice. If you're wrong, you may have forfeited the client's case and exposed yourself to a malpractice claim. The risk involved usually counsels disclosure of the information sought to be protected.

(2) [8:16] **Cases in which writ review more likely:** Extraordinary writs are more likely to be granted on questions of "general importance to the trial courts and to the [legal] profession, and where *general guidelines* can be laid down for future cases." [*Oceanside Union School Dist. v. Sup.Ct.* (1962) 58 C2d 180, 185-186, 23 CR 375, 378, fn. 4 (emphasis added); *Toshiba America Electronic Components, Inc. v. Sup.Ct. (Lexar Media, Inc.)* (2004) 124 CA4th 762, 767, 21 CR3d 532, 537; *Regents of Univ. of Calif. v. Sup.Ct. (Aquila Merchant Services, Inc.)* (2008) 165 CA4th 672, 677, 81 CR3d 186, 189—writ review

© 2020 Thomson Reuters/The Rutter Group

appropriate where issue is one of first impression, is "of some public importance," and is otherwise likely to escape review]

(a) [8:17] **Discovery ordered over claim of privilege:** Writ review may also be granted more readily where the trial court has ordered discovery over claims of *privilege*, because once privileged information is disclosed, later appellate review would be meaningless (*see* ¶*8:193*). [*Costco Wholesale Corp. v. Sup.Ct. (Randall)* (2009) 47 C4th 725, 740-741, 101 CR3d 758, 770-771—party claiming privilege need not show its case would be harmed by disclosure of privileged evidence; *National Football League Properties, Inc. v. Sup.Ct. (Oakland Raiders)* (1998) 65 CA4th 100, 108-109, 75 CR2d 893, 898; *O'Grady v. Sup.Ct. (Apple Computer, Inc.)* (2006) 139 CA4th 1423, 1439, 44 CR3d 72, 83]

(b) [8:17.1] **Evidence withheld on basis of privilege:** Conversely, immediate writ review may be appropriate where a discovery ruling withholding relevant evidence on the basis of privilege effectively prejudices a party's ability to fairly present his or her case. (Review by appeal is inadequate because, not having seen the withheld evidence, the challenging party cannot carry its burden on appeal to show prejudice; ¶*8:13*.) [See *Citizens for Open Government v. City of Lodi* (2012) 205 CA4th 296, 308, 140 CR3d 459, 469—trial court ruling improperly excluding evidence from administrative record on basis of privilege should have been challenged by immediate writ petition]

(3) [8:18] **Compare—appellate review of sanctions:** *See discussion at* ¶*8:2040 ff., 9:1286 ff.*

Cross-refer: Writ review of discovery rulings is treated in detail in Eisenberg, *Cal. Prac. Guide: Civil Appeals & Writs* (TRG), Ch. 15.

e. [8:19] **Role of federal case law:** Absent contrary precedent under state law, California courts have found federal decisions "persuasive" in interpreting similar provisions of the California Act. [See *Greyhound Corp. v. Sup.Ct. (Clay)* (1961) 56 C2d 355, 401, 15 CR 90, 115; *Vasquez v. California School of Culinary Arts, Inc.* (2014) 230 CA4th 35, 42-43, 178 CR3d 10, 15]

5. [8:19.1] **Statutory Procedures Outside Discovery Act:** The Discovery Act does *not* provide the exclusive framework for obtaining evidence in a legal action. [*Dodge, Warren & Peters Ins. Services, Inc. v. Riley* (2003) 105 CA4th 1414, 1419, 130 CR2d 385, 389]

Other statutory procedures may be available in certain types of cases; e.g., a demand for bill of particulars in actions on an account (CCP §454, *see* ¶*8:1765 ff.*) or a request for statement of damages in personal injury cases (CCP §425.11, *see* ¶*8:1758 ff.*).

See further discussion in Ch. 8K (¶8:1805.5 ff.).

[8:19.2-19.4] *Reserved.*

6. [8:19.5] **Duty to Preserve Evidence Before Discovery Request?** The Discovery Act *does not* specifically prohibit the intentional destruction of relevant evidence ("spoliation") before a lawsuit has been filed or before a discovery request. [See *Dodge, Warren & Peters Ins. Services, Inc. v. Riley*, supra, 105 CA4th at 1419, 130 CR2d at 389]

   a. [8:19.6] **Case law unclear:** Courts disagree whether spoliation is sanctionable under the Discovery Act:

      - [8:19.7] Some cases authorize discovery sanctions for spoliation absent any discovery request: "Destroying evidence in response to a discovery request after litigation has commenced would surely be a misuse of discovery within the meaning of section 2023 *as would such destruction in anticipation of a discovery request.*" [*Cedars-Sinai Med. Ctr. v. Sup.Ct. (Bowyer)* (1998) 18 C4th 1, 12, 74 CR2d 248, 254 (dictum) (emphasis added); see *Williams v. Russ* (2008) 167 CA4th 1215, 1227, 84 CR3d 813, 823—*terminating sanction imposed* for allowing destruction of relevant records (¶*8:1502.5*)]

      - [8:19.8] Other courts reject sanctions for spoliation on the ground that the Discovery Act authorizes sanctions only "[t]o the extent *authorized by the chapter governing any particular discovery method* or any other provision of this title," and *no discovery method* applies to spoliation before a discovery request. [CCP §2023.030 (emphasis added); *New Albertsons, Inc. v. Sup.Ct. (Shanahan)* (2008) 168 CA4th 1403, 1430-1431, 86 CR3d 457, 478]

      [8:19.9] *Reserved.*

   b. [8:19.10] **Compare—federal practice:** Federal courts recognize an "uncompromising duty to preserve" relevant evidence whenever litigation is pending or probable, even though no discovery request or order to preserve evidence exists. Sanctions, including striking claims or dismissal, may be imposed under the *court's inherent power* to manage litigation. [See *Kronisch v. United States* (2nd Cir. 1998) 150 F3d 112, 130; and detailed discussion in Phillips & Stevenson, *Rutter Group Prac. Guide: Federal Civ. Pro. Before Trial* (TRG), Ch. 11]

   c. [8:19.11] **Compare—other remedies for spoliation:** Even if discovery sanctions are unavailable, there are certain restraints on destruction of relevant evidence:

      (1) [8:19.12] **Court may order preservation:** A court may issue an injunction in aid of discovery, requiring a party to preserve relevant evidence in its possession for discovery purposes. [*Dodge, Warren & Peters Ins. Services, Inc. v. Riley*, supra, 105 CA4th at 1419, 130 CR2d at 389—court has *inherent power* to issue "freeze" order enjoining party from destroying

© 2020 Thomson Reuters/The Rutter Group

electronically-stored data so that it would be available for future discovery; *see discussion at ¶8:1799 ff.*]

(2) [8:19.13] **Adverse inference jury instruction:** Where there is evidence of willful suppression, the court may instruct the jury: "You may consider whether one party intentionally concealed or destroyed evidence. If you decide that a party did so, you may decide that evidence would have been unfavorable to that party." [CACI 204; see also BAJI 2.03; see *Cedars-Sinai Med. Ctr. v. Sup.Ct. (Bowyer)* (1998) 18 C4th 1, 11-12, 74 CR2d 248, 254]

[8:19.14] ***PRACTICE POINTER:*** Courts may be reluctant to give the adverse inference jury instruction for evidence destroyed before litigation commences. Therefore, if there is a possibility that a potential adversary will destroy documents, electronic data, or other evidence that you may need in the contemplated litigation, consider filing suit promptly and seeking an immediate order for preservation of such evidence (*see ¶8:19.22*).

d. **Compare—special problems with electronically-stored information (ESI)**

(1) [8:19.15] **Federal precedent persuasive:** There is little California case law regarding discovery of ESI. However, "[b]ecause of the similarity of California and federal discovery law, federal decisions have historically been considered persuasive absent contrary California decisions." [*Ellis v. Toshiba America Information Systems, Inc.* (2013) 218 CA4th 853, 862, 160 CR3d 557, 566, fn. 6 (internal quotes omitted)]

(2) [8:19.16] **Duty to preserve?** Although there is no known California authority in point, under federal precedent, "parties are subject to a general duty to preserve such things as deleted data, backup tapes, and metadata that constitute unique, relevant evidence that might be useful to an adversary." [*Ellis v. Toshiba America Information Systems, Inc.*, supra, 218 CA4th at 862, 160 CR3d at 566, fn. 6 (internal quotes omitted); see *Victor Stanley, Inc. v. Creative Pipe, Inc.* (D MD 2010) 269 FRD 497, 523-524; *Fujitsu Ltd. v. Federal Express Corp.* (2nd Cir. 2001) 247 F3d 423, 436 (general duty to preserve evidence)]

[8:19.17-19.19] *Reserved.*

[8:19.20] ***PRACTICE POINTERS:*** Because of the importance of ESI in litigation, special consideration should be given to the following:

[8:19.20a] ***Ethical issues:*** California Rule of Professional Conduct 1.1 requires that every attorney perform legal services "with competence" (CRPC 1.1(a) (formerly CRPC 3-110(A))). In light of evolving technology, this duty of competence mandates that attorneys have at least a basic understanding of ESI issues and clients' e-discovery needs (or associate with counsel or experts who have skill in these areas). [Cal. State Bar Form.Opn. 2015-193 (construing former CRPC)—"higher level of technical knowledge and ability" may be required on a case-by-case basis; see detailed discussion in Tuft, Peck & Mohr, *Cal. Prac. Guide: Professional Responsibility* (TRG), Ch. 6]

[8:19.21] ***Preserving your client's ESI Data:*** Whenever litigation appears likely, consider the following:

— *Learn about your client's electronic data systems:* Talk to your client's information technology (IT) personnel. Learn the capabilities and limits of your client's electronic data systems (e.g., personal computers, laptops, PDAs, cellphones, etc.), and the costs associated with data production from these systems (e.g., in response to discovery requests).

— *Advise client to suspend data deletion policies with respect to relevant ESI:* Clients often have electronic data retention and deletion policies. To avoid exposure to sanctions and other risks resulting from destroying relevant documents, advise the client to suspend its data deletion policies regarding any data that is potentially relevant to the matter.

— *Advise client to send "litigation hold" letter to its personnel:* The client should identify the users of its electronic data systems that may contain relevant ESI and to send a letter instructing them to preserve all information related to the subject matter of the litigation.

— *Advise client to retrieve relevant deleted data where possible:* Relevant electronic data shown as "deleted" on the client's data server may still be retrievable at little cost. (The computer hard drive or server hard drive may still contain areas assigned to the deleted data that have not yet been overwritten; or backup tapes may be available.)

— *Create "mirror" images of stored data:* To enable the client to continue business while preserving relevant electronic evidence, it is generally a good idea to have the client create a "mirror" image of the hard drive of each computer and peripheral storage device.

[8:19.22] ***Preserving opposing party's ESI:*** Similarly, whenever litigation appears likely, consider the following:

— *Send "freeze" letter:* At the very outset of a contested matter, even before filing suit, send opposing counsel or an unrepresented party, a formal letter stating that it must preserve relevant ESI for possible use in litigation, and demand that it suspend any routine deletion practices that would result in the loss of relevant data.

© 2020 Thomson Reuters/The Rutter Group

(Cite CCP §2023.010 et seq., ¶*1:569*.)

Request "native format" with "metadata intact": Your "freeze" letter should request that the opposing party's ESI be preserved in its "native format" with "metadata intact." ("Native format" means as stored and used in the ordinary course of business. "Metadata" may show how, when and by whom the document was created, accessed or modified.)

FORM: Electronic Data Preservation Letter, *see Form 8:27* in Rivera, *Cal. Prac. Guide: Civ. Pro. Before Trial FORMS* (TRG).

— Seek order permitting immediate discovery: If you have reason to believe your preservation request will go unheeded (or, even worse, that it will actually trigger the destruction of evidence), consider filing suit and immediately moving for an ex parte order permitting you to serve a CCP §2031.010 inspection demand (to avoid the 10-day "hold" on discovery; *see* ¶*8:39.6*).

— Seek "freeze" order: In extraordinary cases where there is evidence that ESI will be lost or destroyed before discovery can be initiated, courts may be willing to grant injunctive relief to preserve relevant evidence. *See discussion at* ¶*8:1799*.

7. **Discovery in Nonjudicial Proceedings**

a. [8:20] **Discovery in administrative proceedings:** Discovery procedures are available in administrative hearings involving state agencies. The Administrative Procedure Act contains rules governing discovery in proceedings subject to that Act (see Gov.C. §11507.5 et seq.). For other administrative proceedings, the discovery rules are generally part of the special statutes governing the particular agency's hearing procedures. (Treatment of discovery in administrative proceedings is beyond the scope of this Practice Guide.)

b. [8:21] **Discovery in contractual arbitration proceedings:** Unless specifically provided in the agreement to arbitrate (including any ADR provider's rules incorporated by the agreement), there is generally *no* right to discovery in *contractual* arbitration proceedings. [See CCP §1283.1(b)]

But there are some statutory exceptions:

- [8:21.1] *Wrongful death, personal injury claims:* Parties agreeing to arbitrate wrongful death or personal injury claims have the same discovery rights and obligations as in civil actions, *except* that depositions may not be taken without prior leave of the arbitrator. [See CCP §§1283.1(a), 1283.05]

- [8:21.2] *Uninsured motorist claims:* Full discovery rights apply in arbitration of uninsured motorist (and underinsured motorist) coverage claims between insureds and their insurers. [See

Ins.C. §11580.2(f)] (Note: The statute excludes mental and physical exams under CCP §2019.010(d); but a separate provision requires that arbitration proceedings be *stayed* if the insured refuses to submit to a physical exam requested by the insurer. See Ins.C. §11580.2(o).) Discovery motions in uninsured motorist cases are heard in superior court, *not* by the arbitrator. [*Miranda v. 21st Century Ins. Co.* (2004) 117 CA4th 913, 926, 12 CR3d 159, 165-166]

— Service of a discovery motion in an uninsured motorist case is made in the same fashion as a motion in a civil suit. Service may be made by mail pursuant to CCP §1015. [*Miranda v. 21st Century Ins. Co.*, supra, 117 CA4th at 927-928, 12 CR3d at 168-169]

— The superior court has authority *to dismiss* uninsured motorist cases for discovery abuses. [*Miranda v. 21st Century Ins. Co.*, supra, 117 CA4th at 929, 12 CR3d at 170]

- [8:21.3] *Certain employment claims:* Under a preemployment arbitration agreement, the employer is deemed to *impliedly consent* to *sufficient* discovery to enable employees *to* vindicate certain statutory and common law claims. [*Armendariz v. Foundation Health Psychcare Services, Inc.* (2000) 24 C4th 83, 105, 99 CR2d 745, 761 (employment discrimination claim under FEHA); *Mercuro v. Sup.Ct. (Countrywide Secur. Corp.)* (2002) 96 CA4th 167, 180, 116 CR2d 671, 680 (discrimination claim under Lab.C. §970 and claim for time off under Lab.C. §230.8); see also *Little v. Auto Stiegler, Inc.* (2003) 29 C4th 1064, 1081, 130 CR2d 892, 905-906—claim for wrongful termination in violation of public policy, under arbitration agreement that *expressly provided* for discovery]

  The discovery required, however, may be "something *less than* the full panoply of discovery provided in CCP §1283.05." [*Armendariz v. Foundation Health Psychcare Services, Inc.*, supra, 24 C4th at 105, 99 CR2d at 761]

Cross-refer:

— Discovery in contractual arbitration proceedings is discussed in Knight, Chernick, Flynn & Quinn, *Cal. Prac. Guide: Alternative Dispute Resolution* (TRG), Ch. 5.

— Discovery in uninsured motorist arbitration proceedings is discussed in Haning, Flahavan, Cheng & Wright, *Cal. Prac. Guide: Personal Injury* (TRG), Ch. 7.

— Discovery in employment arbitrations is discussed in Chin, Wiseman, Callahan & Lowe, *Cal. Prac. Guide: Employment Litigation* (TRG), Ch. 18.

[8:22] *Reserved.*

© 2020 Thomson Reuters/The Rutter Group

RESERVED

CHAPTER 8B

THE RIGHT TO DISCOVERY

CONTENTS

© 2020 Thomson Reuters/The Rutter Group

© 2020 Thomson Reuters/The Rutter Group

RESERVED

THE RIGHT TO DISCOVERY

1. [8:23] **Leave of Court Generally NOT Required:** Most discovery procedures are available as a matter of right. No showing of "good cause" or court order is usually required to take a deposition or to serve discovery requests on the opposing party.

   a. [8:24] **Exceptions—matters discoverable only by prior court order:** For policy reasons, there are a few matters as to which discovery is allowed only by leave of court:

      (1) [8:25] **Physical and mental exams:** A court order is required to compel a party to submit to a mental or physical examination except as stated below (¶*8:26*). [CCP §2032.310(a); *see* ¶*8:1546 ff.*]

         (a) [8:26] **Exception—defense physical in personal injury cases:** Defendants in personal injury cases may compel plaintiff to submit to a physical examination simply by serving a demand for it. [CCP §2032.220(b); *see* ¶*8:1527*]

      (2) [8:27] **Defendant's financial condition in punitive damage cases:** A court order is required to obtain discovery of defendant's financial condition in actions seeking punitive damages. Such order will be granted only if the court finds "substantial probability" that plaintiff will prevail on the punitive damage claim. [Civ.C. §3295(c); *see* ¶*8:337 ff.*]

         • ***FORM:*** Motion for Order Permitting Discovery of Financial Information, *see Form 8:1* in Rivera, *Cal. Prac. Guide: Civ. Pro. Before Trial FORMS* (TRG).

      (3) [8:28] **Plaintiff's sex life in sexual harassment cases:** In civil cases alleging conduct constituting "sexual harassment, sexual assault or sexual battery," a court order is required for discovery as to plaintiff's sexual conduct with individuals other than the alleged perpetrator. [CCP §2017.220(a)]

      This applies both to consensual sexual activity and to prior sexual assaults against the plaintiff. [*Knoettgen v. Sup.Ct. (Transit Mixed Concrete)* (1990) 224 CA3d 11, 14, 273 CR 636, 638]

         (a) [8:29] **Compare—privacy protection:** A person's sex life is also protected by the constitutional right of *privacy* (*see* ¶*8:310*). But privacy protection is not absolute; a balancing of interests is required in each individual case (*see* ¶*8:323*). CCP §2017.220(a) provides *more stringent safeguards* in this area: "[I]n the majority of sexual harassment suits, a separate weighing of privacy against discovery will not be necessary [if the requirements of §2017.220(a) are satisfied]." [*Vinson v. Sup.Ct. (Peralta*

© 2020 Thomson Reuters/The Rutter Group

Comm. College Dist.) (1987) 43 C3d 833, 844, 239 CR 292, 300]

"The filing of a sexual harassment suit, even one which also alleges severe emotional distress, does not operate as an implicit waiver of the complainant's right to privacy in sexual matters." [*Mendez v. Sup.Ct. (Peery)* (1988) 206 CA3d 557, 566, 253 CR 731, 736 (disapproved on other grounds by *Williams v. Sup.Ct. (Marshalls of CA, LLC)* (2017) 3 C5th 531, 557, 220 CR3d 472, 494 & fn. 8); see also *Barrenda L. v. Sup.Ct. (Los Angeles County)* (1998) 65 CA4th 794, 801, 76 CR2d 727, 731—waiver construed narrowly where it is claimed that party waives protection by filing suit]

(b) [8:30] **Procedural requirements:** In order to obtain discovery of such information, defendants must:

- Proceed by noticed motion (no ex parte orders);
- Attach declarations showing a good faith attempt to resolve the matter informally ("meet and confer" requirement; *see* ¶*8:1158*); and
- Establish *both:*
  — *specific facts* showing *good cause* for such discovery; *and*
  — that the information sought is "*relevant* to the subject matter of the action and reasonably calculated to lead to the discovery of admissible evidence." [CCP §2017.220(a) (emphasis added)]

1) [8:31] **Relevancy:** A *higher standard* of relevancy may be required in this area. Discovery is not allowed where "[t]he claimed relevancy appears extremely speculative, obtuse and remote." [See *Mendez v. Sup.Ct. (Peery)*, supra, 206 CA3d at 578, 253 CR at 744]

2) [8:32] **Specific facts showing good cause:** To obtain discovery regarding plaintiff's sex life with others, defendant in a sexual harassment case must show specific facts justifying *that particular inquiry.* "Extraordinary circumstances" are required; i.e., a *stronger showing of "good cause"* than required for a general physical or mental examination under CCP §2032.020 (¶*8:1509*). [*Vinson v. Sup.Ct. (Peralta Comm. College Dist.)* (1987) 43 C3d 833, 843, 239 CR 292, 299-300, fn. 8]

a) [8:32.1] **Emotional distress claims not enough:** The mere fact that plaintiff claims extreme mental and emotional distress arising out of alleged sexual harassment is *not* by itself "good cause" for discovery of other sexual conduct. [*Vinson* *v. Sup.Ct. (Peralta Comm. College Dist.)*, supra, 43 C3d at 841-842, 239 CR at 298; *Barrenda L. v. Sup.Ct. (Los Angeles County)* (1998) 65 CA4th 794, 800, 76 CR2d 727, 730]

b) [8:32.2] **Counsel's declarations usually insufficient:** Declarations by *mental health professionals* may be required to establish the relevance of other sexual conduct. Defense counsel's declarations are insufficient absent proof of psychological training that would qualify counsel to demonstrate a nexus between other sexual conduct and the nature of the damages claimed. [*Barrenda L. v. Sup.Ct. (Los Angeles County)*, supra, 65 CA4th at 802, 76 CR2d at 731-732]

(c) [8:33] **Sanctions:** The court "shall" impose a monetary sanction against the losing party on the motion *unless* it finds that party acted "with substantial justification" or other circumstances making imposition of sanctions "unjust." [CCP §2017.220(b)] (Monetary sanctions are discussed at ¶*8:1921 ff.*)

(4) [8:34] **Plaintiff's sex life in action against psychotherapist for sexual contact:** Similar restrictions limit discovery of a patient's sexual history in a suit against a psychotherapist for sexual contact during therapy (or 2 years thereafter or by "therapeutic deception"). [See Civ.C. §43.93(d)—discovery allowed only if patient claims damage to his or her sexual functioning; defendant must prove relevance; court must find probative value outweighs prejudicial effect, and must detail the information or conduct subject to discovery]

b. [8:35] **Initial disclosures:** Effective January 1, 2020, California law allows the court, with the agreement of the parties, to order initial disclosures of specified information (except in unlawful detainer or small claims actions). Within 45 days of the order, the parties exchange witness contact information, descriptions of documents including electronic data which may support a claim or defense, and relevant insurance or indemnity agreements. Unlike other court discovery responses, these initial disclosures must be supplemented if and when the disclosing party knows they are incorrect or incomplete. [CCP §2016.090 (added eff. 1/1/20)]

2. [8:36] **Right to Discovery Liberally Construed:** Courts have construed the discovery statutes broadly, so as to *uphold the right to discovery.* [*Williams v. Sup.Ct. (Marshalls of CA, LLC)* 3 C5th 531, 541, 220 CR3d 472, 480—disclosure a matter of right unless statutory or public policy considerations clearly prohibit it; *Emerson Elec. Co. v. Sup.Ct. (Grayson)* (1997) 16 C4th 1101, 1108, 68 CR2d 883, 886; see *Obregon v. Sup.Ct. (Cimm's, Inc.)* (1998) 67 CA4th 424, 434, 79 CR2d 62, 69 (citing text)]

- [8:37] For example, even where the statutes require a showing of "good cause" to obtain discovery (e.g., for court-ordered mental

© 2020 Thomson Reuters/The Rutter Group

examinations), this term is *liberally* construed—to permit, rather than to prevent, discovery wherever possible. [*Greyhound Corp. v. Sup.Ct. (Clay)* (1961) 56 C2d 355, 377-378, 15 CR 90, 100 (decided under former law)]

- [8:37.1] Similarly, where the Act empowers courts to order a deponent to "answer" a deposition question, it is construed to authorize nonverbal as well as verbal responses (e.g., witness may be compelled to draw a diagram or demonstrate conduct; *see ¶8:708.1*). [*Emerson Elec. Co. v. Sup.Ct. (Grayson),* supra, 16 C4th at 1106-1108, 68 CR2d at 885-886]

3. [8:38] **Limitations on Right to Discovery:** Although very broad, the right to discovery is not absolute. There are several important limitations to consider—some contained in the Discovery Act itself, and others resulting from other laws:

a. [8:39] **Limit on scope of discovery:** The information sought must be (1) "not privileged," (2) "relevant to the subject matter" of the action, and (3) either itself admissible or "reasonably calculated to lead to the discovery of admissible evidence." [CCP §2017.010; *see ¶8:65 ff.*]

Courts also may restrict discovery based on the burden on the producing party. [*Williams v. Sup.Ct. (Marshalls of CA, LLC)*, supra, 3 C5th at 549, 220 CR3d at 487 (citing CCP §2017.020(a)); *see ¶8:42, 8:73 ff.*]

b. [8:39.1] **Limits on when discovery may be sought:** There are several limitations on the time when discovery may be sought:

(1) [8:39.2] **Requirement that action be "pending":** First of all, a "pending action" is required. [CCP §2017.010; *Department of Fair Employment & Housing v. Sup.Ct. (Young)* (1990) 225 CA3d 728, 732, 275 CR 156, 159]

(a) [8:39.3] **Compare—*before* suit filed:** Special procedures exist for perpetuation of testimony or other evidence prior to filing suit. However, a prior court order is required to obtain such discovery. [CCP §2035.010 et seq., *¶8:422*]

(b) [8:39.4] **Compare—*pending appeal:*** Similar procedures allow perpetuation of evidence while an appeal is pending. Again, a prior court order is required. [CCP §2036.010 et seq., *¶8:431*]

(c) [8:39.5] **Compare—after judgment, in aid of money judgment enforcement:** The Enforcement of Judgments Law (EJL, CCP §680.010 et seq.) allows judgment creditors to serve judgment debtors with *written interrogatories* and *requests for inspection and copying* "to aid in enforcement of the money judgment." No prior court order is required; but there are limits on how often such discovery may be propounded. [CCP §§708.020,

708.030; see *SCC Acquisitions, Inc. v. Sup.Ct. (Western Albuquerque Land Holdings, LLC)* (2015) 243 CA4th 741, 752, 196 CR3d 533, 542—§708.030 permits judgment creditor to compel production of third party's documents in judgment debtor's possession, custody or control]

In addition, a subpoena duces tecum may be issued to a third party for production of records in its possession to be used in connection with a judgment debtor examination. [CCP §§708.110, 708.130; *Shrewsbury Mgmt., Inc. v. Sup.Ct. (Boucher)* (2019) 32 CA5th 1213, 1226-1228, 244 CR3d 595, 603-605]

Cross-refer: CCP §§708.020 and 708.030 postjudgment discovery is discussed in detail in Ahart, *Cal. Prac. Guide: Enforcing Judgments & Debts* (TRG), Ch. 6G.

1) [8:39.5a] **Not nonmoney judgments:** The above EJL postjudgment discovery procedures (¶*8:39.5*) are unique because they apply although there is no pending action; but they apply only in aid of enforcing a *money judgment* and are *not* available for the enforcement of a *nonmoney judgment* until a proceeding is commenced to enforce that judgment. [CCP §§708.010(a), 708.020(a), 708.030(a); see *Department of Fair Employment & Housing v. Sup.Ct. (Young)*, supra, 225 CA3d at 732, 275 CR at 159—absent judgment creditor's initiation of *contempt* proceeding to enforce judgment for *injunctive relief, "there is no action pending*" and thus no right to obtain discovery in aid of enforcing the judgment (emphasis added)]

(2) [8:39.6] **Discovery "hold" at outset of action:** Plaintiffs (but not defendants) must obtain a court order based on a showing of "good cause" to initiate various forms of discovery during the first 10 days (20 days for depositions; 5 days for other forms of discovery in unlawful detainer cases) after defendant is served with summons or has appeared in the action. [CCP §§2025.210(b) & 2025.270(b), (d) (depositions), §2030.020(b), (c), (d) (interrogatories), §2031.020(b), (c), (d) (demands for documents, etc.), §2033.020(b), (c), (d) (requests for admission)] (*See discussion at ¶8:439, 8:906.*)

Every section of the Discovery Act pertaining to any method of discovery enumerated in §2019.010 et seq. is subject to a holding period after service on a defendant (or requires that the party to whom the discovery is directed has been served with the summons and complaint). [*California Shellfish, Inc. v. United Shellfish Co.* (1997) 56 CA4th 16, 22, 64 CR2d 797, 799]

© 2020 Thomson Reuters/The Rutter Group

(3) [8:39.6a] **Discovery "hold" while anti-SLAPP motion pending:** A special motion to strike can be used to challenge SLAPP lawsuits (CCP §425.16; *see* ¶*7:500 ff.*). Filing such motion *automatically stays* all discovery proceedings until the court's ruling, unless (for good cause shown on noticed motion) the court allows specified discovery limited to issues raised by the motion in the interim. [CCP §425.16(g); see *Britts v. Sup.Ct. (Berg & Berg Enterprises, LLC)* (2006) 145 CA4th 1112, 1125, 52 CR3d 185, 192—stay applies to discovery motions pending when anti-SLAPP motion filed; *and further discussion at* ¶*7:1095 ff.*]

(4) [8:39.7] **Discovery "cut-off" after judicial arbitration:** If a trial de novo is demanded after an arbitration award in a case that was *ordered* to arbitration, the only additional discovery permitted without a court order or stipulation is an exchange of expert witness lists and expert witness depositions under CCP §2034.210 et seq. (*see* ¶*8:1624 ff.*). [CCP §1141.24; *see* ¶*13:152*]

This limitation on postarbitration discovery does not apply, however, where judicial arbitration was by stipulation or election, rather than by court order (*see* ¶*13:152.2*).

(5) [8:39.8] **Discovery "cut-offs" before trial:** Subject to some exceptions, a court order is required to conduct most types of discovery within 30 days before trial or to have discovery motions heard within 15 days before trial. [CCP §2024.020(a); *see* ¶*8:445*]

There are, however, other pretrial cut-off deadlines for certain types of actions (*see* ¶*8:446 ff.*); and special pretrial cut-offs for expert witness discovery in any civil action (15 days before trial for discovery and 10 days before trial for discovery motions to be heard; CCP §2024.030, *see* ¶*8:447*).

(6) [8:39.9] **Time constraints on discovery before summary judgment motion:** Defendants contemplating a summary judgment or summary adjudication motion need to conduct discovery *early* in the action because most lawsuits must be resolved within 365 days after filing, and a summary judgment or summary adjudication motion generally must be heard at least 30 days prior to trial (*see* ¶*10:71*) after at least 75 days' notice of hearing (*see* ¶*10:77*).

The time available for discovery before seeking summary judgment may be further curtailed if defendant files an *anti-SLAPP motion* because discovery is automatically stayed until the ruling (*see* ¶*8:39.6a*); or a *motion to quash service of summons* (*see* ¶*3:376*) because defendants may refuse to engage in nonjurisdictional-related discovery while the motion is pending.

(7) [8:39.10] **Compare—time limits on discovery no bar to informal investigation:** The discovery "hold" and "cut-offs" do not affect a party's right to conduct informal investigations; e.g., to interview nonparty witnesses, to visit premises open to the public, to obtain copies of public records, etc. [See *Pullin v. Sup.Ct. (Vons Cos., Inc.)* (2000) 81 CA4th 1161, 1165, 97 CR2d 447, 450, fn. 4; *County of Los Angeles v. Sup.Ct. (Axelrad)* (2000) 82 CA4th 819, 829, 98 CR2d 564, 571]

c. [8:40] **Geographic limits:** There are some geographic limits on discovery: e.g., a witness cannot be compelled to travel more than a certain distance to give deposition testimony. [CCP §2025.250(a)-(d); *see ¶8:621 ff.*]

d. [8:41] **Protective orders:** The court is authorized to limit discovery through protective orders. Such orders may be granted on motion of any party or other person affected by the discovery sought (but *not* on the court's own motion). [CCP §§2017.020(a), 2019.020(b), 2019.030(a)]

(1) [8:42] **To limit scope of discovery:** Even if the information sought is "relevant to the subject matter," the court shall limit the scope of discovery if it determines that the "burden, expense or intrusiveness . . . *clearly outweighs* the likelihood that the information sought will lead to the discovery of admissible evidence." [CCP §2017.020(a) (emphasis added); *see ¶8:73*]

(2) [8:43] **To limit frequency or extent of use of any discovery method:** A protective order may also be granted to restrict the frequency or extent of use of any discovery method, on any of the following grounds:

- "The discovery sought is *unreasonably cumulative* or duplicative . . .;
- "[It] is *obtainable from some other source* that is more convenient, less burdensome or less expensive;
- "The selected method of discovery is *unduly burdensome* or expensive, taking into account the needs of the case, the amount in controversy, and the importance of the issues at stake in the litigation." [CCP §2019.030(a)(1)-(2) (emphasis added)]

(a) [8:43.1] **Comment:** Thus, regardless of relevancy considerations, the statute allows courts to cut off discovery that is too expensive or inconvenient, or simply unnecessary.

(3) [8:44] **To limit particular procedures:** The statutes authorizing the various discovery procedures (depositions, interrogatories, etc.) also provide for protective orders limiting such procedures in particular ways. Such orders may be granted as "justice requires" to protect any party or person from "*unwarranted annoyance, embarrassment or oppression*, or undue burden and expense." (For example, protective orders re de-

© 2020 Thomson Reuters/The Rutter Group

positions are authorized by CCP §2025.420; *see ¶8:501 ff., 8:642, 8:1008.1.*)

(4) [8:45] **Procedure:** The procedure to obtain protective orders is discussed at *¶8:685 ff. and 8:1013 ff.* (The moving party must show "a good faith attempt" to resolve the matter informally; and sanctions may be imposed against the losing party.)

[8:45.1-45.4] *Reserved.*

(5) [8:45.5] **Limits on stipulated protective orders in elder abuse cases:** In actions for abuse of an elder or dependent adult under Welf. & Inst.C. §15600 et seq., information acquired through discovery that is *evidence of abuse* may be filed with the court and made part of the public record despite a stipulated protective order. [See CCP §2017.320]

This prevents secret agreements to hide patterns of abuse by health care providers and the alleged abusers' identities from regulatory agencies and residents' families.

Limited to Welf. & Inst.C. §15600 et seq. actions: This provision (CCP §2017.320) applies *only* in actions for elder abuse under Welf. & Inst.C. §15600 et seq. It does *not* apply to information obtained through discovery in *professional negligence* actions against a health care provider. [CCP §2017.320(h)]

(a) [8:45.6] **Procedures required for public disclosure:** Before evidence subject to a stipulated protective order may be made part of the public record, however, the following procedures are required:

- At least one week *before filing* the information with the court, the party proposing to file it must offer to "*meet and confer*" with the party from whom the information was obtained (presumably to seek agreement re public disclosure);
- If a document is involved, information not evidence of elder abuse must be *redacted;*
- The party filing the information with the court must give concurrent notice of the filing "and its basis" (e.g., statutory and policy reasons for disclosure) to the party from whom the information was obtained;
- Any affected party then has 30 days within which to seek a protective order, based on a showing of good cause, to prevent the evidence of elder abuse from becoming part of the public record (the information remains confidential during the 30-day period). [CCP §2017.320(b)-(e)]

1) [8:45.6a] **Comment:** The parties are free to stipulate *not* to file the papers. (CCP §2016.030 permits the parties to "modify the procedures" in §2017.320.) The propounding party may not be interested in such

© 2020 Thomson Reuters/The Rutter Group

a stipulation, however, if it plans to use the information as evidence.

(b) [8:45.7] **Ruling on application to prevent public disclosure:** Confidential settlement agreements are *disfavored* in elder abuse cases (CCP §2017.310). A stipulated protective order will not prevent public disclosure of information filed with the court *unless* the court finds either:

— the information is *not evidence of elder abuse;*
— the information is *privileged;* or
— the party seeking to prevent public disclosure has demonstrated a *substantial probability that prejudice will result* from such disclosure and that party's interest cannot adequately be protected through redaction. [CCP §2017.320(f)]

1) [8:45.8] **Redacting required where public discourse allowed:** If the court denies the petition to prevent public discourse, the court must *redact* any part of the filed information it finds is *not* evidence of elder abuse. [CCP §2017.320(g)]

However, the name of the defendant should *not* be redacted from any information made available to the public. [CCP §2017.320(g)]

e. [8:46] **Limit on discovery from foreign nationals—international comity:** International comity requires American courts to exercise "special vigilance" to protect foreign litigants or witnesses from unnecessary or unduly burdensome discovery that might put them in a disadvantageous position. Their objections to discovery should receive "most careful consideration" to demonstrate "due respect for any special problem confronted by the foreign litigant on account of its nationality or the location of its operations, and for any sovereign interest expressed by a foreign state." [*Societe Nationale Industrielle Aerospatiale v. United States Dist.Ct.* (1987) 482 US 522, 546, 107 S.Ct. 2542, 2557]

(1) [8:47] **Location of evidence not controlling:** The fact that the evidence is located in this country, or that it is under the "control" of a party, is not determinative. I.e., the fact that an American court may have the *power* to order a foreign national to produce evidence does not mean such power should be exercised in every case. [See *Societe Nationale Industrielle Aerospatiale v. United States Dist.Ct.*, supra, 482 US at 546, 107 S.Ct. at 2557]

(2) [8:48] **Case-by-case determination:** The exact line between "reasonable" and "abusive" discovery must be drawn by the trial court based on the particular facts of the case and the foreign interests involved. [*Societe Nationale Industrielle Aerospatiale v. United States Dist.Ct.*, supra, 482 US at 546, 107 S.Ct. at 2557]

© 2020 Thomson Reuters/The Rutter Group

(a) [8:49] **"Intrusiveness" as factor:** However, the Supreme Court has noted that some discovery procedures are "much more intrusive than others." For example, in a wrongful death case against a foreign airplane manufacturer, an *interrogatory* asking the manufacturer simply to *identify* its test pilots, or *requests to admit* that certain advertising claims were *authorized*, were "certainly less intrusive than a request to produce all of the design specifications, line drawings and engineering plans . . ." [*Societe Nationale Industrielle Aerospatiale v. United States Dist.Ct.*, supra, 482 US at 545, 107 S.Ct. at 2556 (internal quotes omitted)]

(3) [8:50] **Hague Evidence Convention procedures optional:** The U.S. and various other countries (including Germany, France, Italy and the United Kingdom) have signed the "The Hague Convention on Taking of Evidence Abroad in Civil or Commercial Matters." (The Convention and a list of signatories, together with suggested forms, can be found following 28 USC §1781.)

The Hague Convention authorizes a judicial authority in one signatory country to send "letters of request" through government channels to a "central authority" in any other signatory country (with translations and detailed descriptions of whatever documents or information are sought). That "central authority" then determines what methods and procedures may be used to obtain the information sought. [See "Legal Resources" on the U.S. Department of State website, *https://travel.state.gov*]

However, the Hague Convention is merely a *permissive supplement*—not a replacement—for other means of discovery. It is up to American courts to decide whether parties should be required to use these procedures in lieu of regular discovery methods. [*Societe Nationale Industrielle Aerospatiale v. United States Dist.Ct.*, supra, 482 US at 536, 107 S.Ct. at 2551-2552; *American Home Assur. Co. v. Societe Commerciale Toutelectric* (2002) 104 CA4th 406, 425, 128 CR2d 430, 445]

(a) [8:50.1] **Burden of persuasion:** The foreign litigant bears the burden of persuading the court that comity considerations require use of the Hague Convention discovery procedures. [*American Home Assur. Co. v. Societe Commerciale Toutelectric*, supra, 104 CA4th at 428, 128 CR2d at 447]

[8:50.2-50.4] *Reserved.*

(b) [8:50.5] **Waiver:** The foreign litigant's failure to raise a "formal objection" or to seek a protective order waives its right to compel reliance on the Hague Convention procedures. [*American Home Assur. Co. v. Societe Commerciale Toutelectric*, supra, 104 CA4th at 429, 128 CR2d at 448]

(c) [8:51] **Discovery from nonparties:** The Hague Convention is particularly helpful in cases involving foreign witnesses or custodians of record who are not otherwise subject to personal jurisdiction in the U.S. [*Societe Nationale Industrielle Aerospatiale v. United States Dist.Ct.*, supra, 482 US at 536, 107 S.Ct. at 2551-2552]

(d) [8:52] **Orders facilitating:** The party seeking discovery may seek appropriate court orders facilitating compliance with the Hague Convention "letters of request" procedure. E.g., it may order the opposing party to provide the necessary translations and descriptions of particular documents or evidence sought.

[8:52.1] ***PRACTICE POINTER:*** The Hague Convention allows participating countries to refuse to grant "letters of request" designed to obtain *pretrial discovery* of documents. Accordingly, when you draft the "letter of request," avoid using the term "pretrial discovery" and emphasize that the requested discovery will be used for trial purposes.

(e) [8:53] **Comment:** As a practical matter, the Hague Convention procedures are more cumbersome than federal and state discovery rules. In addition, because each signatory country applies its own rules and procedures, discovery results may be unpredictable. As a result, courts are not likely to require the Hague Convention procedures except where there is no other way to obtain the information sought.

(4) [8:54] **Inter-American Convention:** Similar procedures are found in the "Inter-American Convention on Letters Rogatory" entered into between the U.S. and many Latin American countries (plus Spain).

The Inter-American Convention and list of signatories, together with sample forms, can be found following 28 USC §1781.

[8:54.1-54.4] *Reserved.*

f. [8:54.5] **Federal highway safety reports:** Surveys, studies and reports for the purpose of federal highway safety improvements "*shall not be subject to discovery* or admitted into evidence in a Federal *or State court* proceeding." [23 USC §409 (emphasis added); see *Pierce County, Wash. v. Guillen* (2003) 537 US 129, 145-146, 123 S.Ct. 720, 730-731—auto accident reports privileged if obtained by road department for *highway safety purposes*, but not if collected by sheriff for law enforcement purposes]

g. [8:54.6] **Emails stored on ISP facilities:** Subject to enumerated exceptions, the Stored Communications Act (SCA) prohibits Internet service providers (ISPs) from disclosing the *content* of emails stored on their facilities (18 USC §2702(a)(1)). This provision has been

© 2020 Thomson Reuters/The Rutter Group

held to excuse an ISP from disclosing, in response to a discovery subpoena, both the contents of an email *and the author's identity.* [*O'Grady v. Sup.Ct. (Apple Computer, Inc.)* (2006) 139 CA4th 1423, 1447-1448, 44 CR3d 72, 89-90; but see *Negro v. Sup.Ct. (Navalimpianti USA, Inc.)* (2014) 230 CA4th 879, 889, 899, 179 CR3d 215, 222, 230—ISP required to produce emails in response to subpoena under SCA's "lawful consent" exception (18 USC §2702(b)(3)); *Facebook, Inc. v. Sup.Ct. (Hunter)* (2018) 4 C5th 1245, 1274, 233 CR3d 77, 99—social media communications configured by social media user to be "public" fall within "lawful consent" exception, "presumptively permitting disclosure" by ISP]

h. [8:55] **Limited discovery in limited civil cases:** Economic litigation rules limit discovery in limited civil cases. *See discussion at ¶8:1806 ff.*

i. [8:56] **No discovery in small claims actions or appeals:** No discovery at all is permitted in small claims actions, nor in trial de novo proceedings in superior court on appeal of a small claims judgment. [CCP §§116.310(b), 116.770(b)]

j. [8:56.1] **No discovery where prohibited by federal law:** Where federal law clearly and expressly prohibits discovery of specific information, state discovery rules are preempted. [*Department of Transp. v. Sup.Ct. (Tate)* (1996) 47 CA4th 852, 855, 55 CR2d 2, 4—preemption denied because Cal Trans failed to establish information requested was compiled or collected pursuant to federal statute barring discovery re hazard elimination program]

(1) [8:56.2] **No subpoena against nonparty federal agency or employee:** Sovereign immunity prohibits state courts from enforcing subpoenas against federal agencies or instrumentalities. Similarly, a state court subpoena cannot be enforced against a federal employee where the federal agency has adopted regulations *prohibiting* the employee from testifying or producing records. [*Houston Bus. Journal, Inc. v. Office of Comptroller of Currency, U.S. Dept. of Treasury* (DC Cir. 1996) 86 F3d 1208, 1211-1212]

[8:56.3] ***PRACTICE POINTER:*** If you seek documents from a nonparty federal agency that refuses to provide them voluntarily, your remedy is to file a collateral action against the agency in federal court under the Federal Administrative Procedure Act (see 5 USC §§701-706); or possibly a mandamus action against the agency head. [See *Houston Bus. Journal, Inc. v. Office of Comptroller of Currency, U.S. Dept. of Treasury*, supra, 86 F3d at 1212, fn. 5]

[8:56.4] *Reserved.*

(2) [8:56.5] **Federal court may enjoin discovery in securities fraud action in state court:** The Private Securities Litigation Reform Act (15 USC §§77z-1, 78u-4) empowers federal courts to enjoin discovery in state court securities fraud actions (class or nonclass actions) while a motion to dismiss

similar claims is pending in federal court. [15 USC §78u-4(b)(3)(D); see *Newby v. Enron Corp.* (5th Cir. 2003) 338 F3d 467, 472]

k. [8:57] **Effect of foreign injunction limiting discovery:** The parties' discovery rights *cannot* be limited by an injunction, issued by an out-of-state court in unrelated proceedings to which they were not parties, that *seeks to suppress discoverable evidence.* Such an injunction is *not* entitled to full faith and credit in California litigation brought by strangers to the out-of-state proceedings; the California court is free to determine for itself that witnesses are competent to testify and what evidence is discoverable in the California proceeding. [*Baker by Thomas v. General Motors Corp.* (1998) 522 US 222, 237-238, 118 S.Ct. 657, 666; *Smith v. Sup.Ct. (General Motors)* (1996) 41 CA4th 1014, 1025, 49 CR2d 20, 26]

- [8:57.1] GM sued discharged Engineer in Michigan for misappropriation of trade secrets. As part of the settlement, the Michigan court permanently enjoined Engineer from testifying as an expert witness against GM in any other litigation, either at deposition or at trial. Plaintiff sought to depose Engineer in unrelated litigation in California. The Michigan injunction did not limit discovery in the California proceeding. [*Smith v. Sup.Ct. (General Motors)*, supra, 41 CA4th at 1025, 49 CR2d at 26]

4. [8:58] **Status of Pleadings Affecting Right to Discovery:** The right to discovery generally does *not* depend on the status of the pleadings. I.e., the case need not be "at issue." [*Mattco Forge, Inc. v. Arthur Young & Co.* (1990) 223 CA3d 1429, 1436, 273 CR 262, 265—sanctions upheld for refusal to make discovery because demurrer pending]

a. [8:59] **Discovery after demurrer sustained:** Deficiencies in the pleadings generally do not affect either party's right to conduct discovery. Thus, for example, discovery may continue after a demurrer has been sustained with leave to amend, although no amended complaint has yet been filed—i.e., no valid complaint need be on file. [*Budget Finance Plan v. Sup.Ct. (McDowell)* (1973) 34 CA3d 794, 797, 110 CR 302, 304]

Plaintiff may *need* discovery in such a case in order to draft the amendment. (And, defendant may wish to pin down the nature of plaintiff's claim without waiting until the amended complaint is filed.) [See *Union Mut. Life Ins. Co. v. Sup.Ct. (Scott)* (1978) 80 CA3d 1, 12, 145 CR 316, 322]

However, the court likely has discretion to disallow discovery without a valid complaint (*see ¶8:76 ff.*).

(1) [8:59.1] **Court's discretion to stay:** The result may be different where plaintiff has already had opportunity for discovery, and there is *no showing further discovery would enable* plaintiff to state a valid claim. Under those circumstances, the court *may* (discretionary) stay discovery pending amendment of

© 2020 Thomson Reuters/The Rutter Group

the complaint (*see* ¶*8:76.1*). [*Terminals Equip. Co. v. City & County of San Francisco* (1990) 221 CA3d 234, 247, 270 CR 329, 337]

b. [8:60] **Exception re trade secrets litigation:** A party claiming misappropriation of a trade secret under the Uniform Trade Secrets Act (Civ.C. §3426) must *identify* it "with reasonable particularity" *before commencing discovery* relating to the trade secret. [CCP §2019.210; see *Advanced Modular Sputtering, Inc. v. Sup.Ct. (Sputtered Films, Inc.)* (2005) 132 CA4th 826, 834-835, 33 CR3d 901, 907]

[8:60.1] ***PRACTICE POINTER:*** If the complaint does not describe the trade secret adequately, plaintiff must provide a *separate statement* containing the requisite description. Before serving the separate statement, plaintiff may seek a protective order under Civ.C. §3426.5 (e.g., "confidential—for attorneys' eyes only" and "disclosure to defendants prohibited").

Although plaintiff cannot commence discovery until such description is provided, *defendant's right to proceed with discovery is not affected.*

(1) [8:60.2] **Purpose:** CCP §2019.210 was enacted to prevent the party from conducting "fishing expeditions" into competitors' business files by unfounded claims of trade secret misappropriation. It also assists the court in framing the appropriate scope of discovery and the defendant in framing its defenses. [*Advanced Modular Sputtering, Inc. v. Sup.Ct. (Sputtered Films, Inc.)*, supra, 132 CA4th at 833-834, 33 CR3d at 906; *Computer Economics, Inc. v. Gartner Group, Inc.* (SD CA 1999) 50 F.Supp.2d 980, 985 (applying Calif. law); see *Diodes, Inc. v. Franzen* (1968) 260 CA2d 244, 253, 67 CR 19, 24]

[8:60.3-60.4] *Reserved.*

(2) [8:60.5] **"Reasonable particularity":** The trade secret must be described "*with sufficient particularity to separate it from* matters of general knowledge in the trade . . . and *to permit the defendant to ascertain* at least the boundaries within which the secret lies." [*Brescia v. Angelin* (2009) 172 CA4th 133, 144, 90 CR3d 842, 848 (emphasis added; internal quotes omitted); see also *Advanced Modular Sputtering, Inc. v. Sup.Ct. (Sputtered Films, Inc.)*, supra, 132 CA4th at 835-836, 33 CR3d at 908]

Any reasonable doubt regarding adequacy of the description is resolved in favor of *allowing* discovery to proceed. [*Brescia v. Angelin*, supra, 172 CA4th at 145, 90 CR3d at 849]

(a) **Application**

- [8:60.6] The more complex the field, the more exacting level of description may be required. Where the secret consisted of incremental advances in the state of the art in a highly specialized technical field, a greater degree of particularity was required *to distinguish the alleged trade secrets from matters already known* to persons skilled in that field. [*Advanced Modular Sputtering, Inc. v. Sup.Ct. (Sputtered Films, Inc.)*, supra, 132 CA4th at 836, 33 CR3d at 908; *Perlan Therapeutics, Inc. v. Sup.Ct. (Nexbio, Inc.)* (2009) 178 CA4th 1333, 1350, 101 CR3d 211, 225-226]

- [8:60.7] On the other hand, the trade secret claimant *need not particularize* how the alleged secret differs from matters already known to skilled persons in the field *where the description given is adequate* to permit the defendant to ascertain the boundaries of the claimed secret so as to prepare available defenses, and to permit the court to determine the scope of relevant discovery. [*Brescia v. Angelin*, supra, 172 CA4th at 145-146, 90 CR3d at 849-850]

[8:60.8-60.9] *Reserved.*

(b) [8:60.10] **Determining sufficiency of description:** The trial court may consider expert witness declarations (and other relevant evidence) to determine whether the trade secrets are adequately described and distinguished from prior art. [*Advanced Modular Sputtering, Inc. v. Sup.Ct. (Sputtered Films, Inc.)*, supra, 132 CA4th at 836, 33 CR3d at 908; *Perlan Therapeutics, Inc. v. Sup.Ct. (Nexbio, Inc.)*, supra, 178 CA4th at 1351, 101 CR3d at 227]

5. [8:61] **Compare—Right to Discovery Under Federal Rules:** Discovery proceedings are subject to much stricter control in federal courts:

a. [8:62] **Discovery conferences:** Discovery conferences are generally held at the outset of each case, at which time the federal judge orders what kinds of discovery will be permitted, and sets a schedule for its completion. [FRCP 26(f), 16(b)]

b. [8:63] **Restrictions on use of discovery:** In addition to granting protective orders to control discovery (as state judges are authorized to do, ¶*8:41 ff.*), a federal judge, on a party's or his or her own motion, *must restrict* the *use* of discovery procedures where:

- The information sought is unreasonably *cumulative*, or could be obtained less expensively, more conveniently, or with less burden from some other source; or
- The party seeking discovery has had ample *opportunity* to obtain such information in earlier discovery in the action; or
- The discovery is unduly *burdensome* or expensive, taking into account whether the burden is "proportional to the needs

© 2020 Thomson Reuters/The Rutter Group

of the case," based on consideration of "the importance of the issues at stake in the action, the amount in controversy, the parties' relative access to relevant information, the parties' resources, the importance of the discovery in resolving the issues, and whether the burden or expense of the proposed discovery outweighs its likely benefit." [FRCP 26(b)(1), (2)(C), (c)]

c. [8:64] **Certification by counsel:** Every discovery request or response must be *signed by counsel* (and also by the party, where required). Counsel's signature acts as a *certification* that the paper "is well-grounded in fact and is warranted by existing law or a good faith argument" for change in the law, and that it is not interposed "for any improper purpose, such as to harass or to cause unnecessary delay or needless increase in the cost of litigation." The attorney is subject to sanctions if this certification proves false. [FRCP 11]

d. [8:64.1] **Initial disclosures:** In most civil cases, parties in federal court must make initial disclosures of contact information for witnesses, descriptions of documents including electronic data which may support a claim or defense, computations of damages and relevant insurance agreements. [FRCP 26(a)]

(1) [8:64.2] **Compare—California law:** Effective January 1, 2020, California law allows the court, with the agreement of the parties, to order a similar procedure (except in unlawful detainer or small claims actions). *See ¶8:35.*

Cross-refer: For detailed discussion, see Phillips & Stevenson, *Rutter Group Prac. Guide: Federal Civ. Pro. Before Trial* (TRG), Ch. 11.

CHAPTER 8C

SCOPE OF DISCOVERY

CONTENTS

© 2020 Thomson Reuters/The Rutter Group

© 2020 Thomson Reuters/The Rutter Group

© 2020 Thomson Reuters/The Rutter Group

SCOPE OF DISCOVERY

[8:65] **Statute:** "Unless otherwise limited by order of the court . . . any party may obtain discovery regarding *any matter, not privileged*, that is *relevant to the subject matter* involved . . . if the matter either is itself admissible in evidence or appears *reasonably calculated to lead to the discovery of admissible evidence* . . ." [CCP §2017.010 (emphasis added)]

Thus, the permissible scope of discovery depends on three factors:

- Is the information sought *relevant* to the *subject matter* involved? (*See ¶8:66 ff.*)
- Is it admissible or *reasonably calculated to lead to discovery of admissible evidence? (See ¶8:67 ff.*)
- Is it *privileged? (See ¶8:109 ff.*)

The discovery statutes should be construed liberally in favor of discovery. [*Williams v. Sup.Ct. (Marshalls of CA, LLC)* (2017) 3 C5th 531, 540-541, 220 CR3d 472, 479-480]

1. [8:66] **"Relevant to Subject Matter":** The first and most basic limitation on the scope of discovery is that the information sought must be relevant to the "subject matter" of the pending action or to the determination of a motion in that action. [CCP §2017.010]

   The phrase "subject matter" does not lend itself to precise definition. It is *broader* than relevancy to the *issues* (which determines admissibility of evidence at trial). [*Bridgestone/Firestone, Inc. v. Sup.Ct. (Rios)* (1992) 7 CA4th 1384, 1392, 9 CR2d 709, 713]

   a. [8:66.1] **Purpose:** For discovery purposes, information should be regarded as "relevant" to the subject matter if it might reasonably assist a party in *evaluating* the case, *preparing* for trial, or facilitating *settlement.* [*Gonzalez v. Sup.Ct. (City of San Fernando)* (1995) 33 CA4th 1539, 1546, 39 CR2d 896, 901 (citing text); *Lipton v. Sup.Ct. (Lawyers' Mut. Ins. Co.)* (1996) 48 CA4th 1599, 1611, 56 CR2d 341, 347 (citing text); *Stewart v. Colonial Western Agency, Inc.* (2001) 87 CA4th 1006, 1013, 105 CR2d 115, 120 (citing text)]

   b. [8:66.2] **Size of case as factor:** "Relevancy" may vary with size and complexity of the case and must be considered with regard to the *burden and value* of the information sought (among other factors). [See *Bridgestone/Firestone, Inc. v. Sup.Ct. (Rios)*, supra, 7 CA4th at 1391, 9 CR2d at 712 (citing text)]

      As noted by the Supreme Court: "[I]n a small case dealing with facts and issues of moderate quantity, the trial court could adopt a very relaxed view of relevancy and still keep the discovery under control; in a large, complex case dealing with numerous and diverse issues, a court could adopt more restrictive standards to contain

© 2020 Thomson Reuters/The Rutter Group

discovery within manageable limits." [*Pacific Tel. & Tel. Co. v. Sup.Ct. (Duke)* (1970) 2 C3d 161, 173, 84 CR 718, 726, fn. 15]

2. [8:67] **"Reasonably Calculated to Lead to Discovery of Admissible Evidence":** This phrase is more helpful in defining the scope of permissible discovery. It makes it clear that discovery extends to any information that reasonably might lead to other evidence that would be admissible at trial. Thus, the scope of permissible discovery is one of *reason, logic and common sense.* [*Lipton v. Sup.Ct. (Lawyers' Mut. Ins. Co.)* (1996) 48 CA4th 1599, 1611, 56 CR2d 341, 348 (citing text)]

   a. [8:68] **Admissibility NOT the test:** Admissibility at trial is *not* required. Rather, the test is whether the information sought might reasonably lead to *other evidence* that *would* be admissible. [CCP §2017.010; see *Davies v. Sup.Ct. (State of Calif.)* (1984) 36 C3d 291, 301, 204 CR 154, 161; *Volkswagen of America, Inc. v. Sup.Ct. (Rusk)* (2006) 139 CA4th 1481, 1490-1491, 43 CR3d 723, 728]

   The court ruling on a discovery motion cannot determine whether the information sought will in fact be relevant and admissible at trial: "It can only attempt to foresee whether it is *possible* that information in a particular subject area *could* be relevant or admissible at the time of trial." [*Maldonado v. Sup.Ct. (ICG Telecom Group, Inc.)* (2002) 94 CA4th 1390, 1397, 115 CR2d 137, 142-143 (emphasis added)]

   (1) [8:69] **Hearsay:** Thus, discovery cannot be refused on the ground that the information sought is inadmissible hearsay. The question is whether the hearsay might reasonably *lead* to other evidence that *would* be admissible. [*Smith v. Sup.Ct. (Alfred)* (1961) 189 CA2d 6, 11-12, 11 CR 165, 169]

   (2) [8:70] **Stipulated matters:** Nor can a party prevent discovery by stipulating to whatever issue is involved. While such stipulation may render evidence on the issue inadmissible at trial, that is *not* the test for discovery purposes.

   - [8:70.1] For example, defendants in auto accident suits cannot avoid answering questions as to their driving by stipulating that they were negligent. Their stipulation may remove this as an issue at trial, but the information sought is still discoverable because it *may* lead to *other* admissible evidence (e.g., excessive speed may show force of impact, establishing causation of injuries and property damage).

   [8:70.2-70.4] *Reserved.*

   (3) [8:70.5] **Cumulative evidence:** It is immaterial that the party seeking discovery already has extensive other evidence of the same fact: A party "is entitled to discover any non-privileged information, cumulative or not . . ." [*TBG Ins. Services Corp. v. Sup.Ct. (Zieminski)* (2002) 96 CA4th 443, 448, 117 CR2d 155, 160; *City of King City v. Community Bank of Central Calif.* (2005) 131 CA4th 913, 933, 32 CR3d 384, 398]

b. [8:71] **Policy favoring discovery:** The "relevance to the subject matter" and "reasonably calculated to lead to discovery of admissible evidence" standards are applied *liberally.* Any doubt is generally resolved in favor of *permitting* discovery, particularly where the precise issues in the case are not yet clearly established. [*Colonial Life & Accident Ins. Co. v. Sup.Ct. (Perry)* (1982) 31 C3d 785, 790, 183 CR 810, 813, fns. 7-8]

c. [8:72] **"Fishing trips" permissible:** Lawyers sometimes make the objection that opposing counsel are on a "fishing expedition." But this is *not* a valid ground for refusal to make discovery. The plain and simple answer is that "fishing expeditions" are expressly authorized by statute—i.e., the Discovery Act provides for discovery of matters "reasonably calculated to *lead* to discovery of admissible evidence." [CCP §2017.010 (emphasis added); see *Greyhound Corp. v. Sup.Ct. (Clay)* (1961) 56 C2d 355, 384-385, 15 CR 90, 104 (superseded by statute as stated in *Coito v. Sup.Ct. (State of Calif.)* (2012) 54 C4th 480, 497-498, 142 CR3d 607, 620)—"The method of 'fishing' may be, in a particular case, entirely improper . . . . But the possibility that it may be abused is not of itself an indictment of the fishing expedition *per se*"; see also *Gonzalez v. Sup.Ct. (City of San Fernando)* (1995) 33 CA4th 1539, 1546, 39 CR2d 896, 901]

(1) [8:72.1] **Compare—improper "fishing trips":** Nevertheless, there are limits on "fishing expeditions." For example, courts may intervene to control discovery requests that:

— contain *insufficient identification* of the requested information to acquaint the other party with the nature of information desired;

— attempt to place the *burden and cost* of supplying information equally available to both solely upon the adversary;

— place more burden upon the adversary than the *value* of the information warrants. [*Greyhound Corp. v. Sup.Ct. (Clay)*, supra, 56 C2d at 384-385, 15 CR at 104; *Calcor Space Facility, Inc. v. Sup.Ct. (Thiem Indus., Inc.)* (1997) 53 CA4th 216, 225, 61 CR2d 567, 573]

(2) [8:72.2] **Compare—discovery from nonparty:** "Fishing expeditions" are more likely to be held improper where discovery is being sought from a nonparty witness, records custodian, etc. The costs and burdens of discovery should be placed on nonparties only where the litigating parties *do not possess* the material sought to be discovered; or where the material in their possession is *unreliable* and subject to impeachment by material in possession of the nonparty. [*Calcor Space Facility, Inc. v. Sup.Ct. (Thiem Indus., Inc.)*, supra, 53 CA4th at 225, 61 CR2d at 573]

d. [8:73] **Protective orders as limitation:** The trial court has discretion to narrow the broad scope of discovery on a case-

© 2020 Thomson Reuters/The Rutter Group

by-case basis by *protective orders* (¶*8:41*). Such orders may be granted on motion of any party or other affected person where "the burden, expense, or intrusiveness of that discovery *clearly outweighs* the likelihood that the information sought will lead to the discovery of admissible evidence." [CCP §2017.020(a) (emphasis added)]

(1) [8:74] **"Benefits vs. burdens approach":** This recognizes the court's inherent power to *balance the benefits vs. the burdens* of the proposed discovery. Courts can simply cut off discovery that has reached the point of diminishing returns; i.e., becoming too time-consuming, too expensive, etc. for the value of the information likely to be obtained. Or, where "sensitive" information is sought, because the need for discovery is *outweighed* by the privacy rights of the person to whom the information pertains (*see* ¶*8:323 ff.*).

(a) [8:74.1] **Comment:** As part of this balancing, the court may take into account:

— the *stakes* in the case (because a given cost of production may be reasonable in a large case but not a smaller one);

— the availability of less burdensome, *alternative sources* of the proposed discovery;

— *materiality* of the information sought (i.e., how peripheral or collateral it is to a claim or defense in the case); and

— *utility* of the information (i.e., how useful it will be to prove a material issue in the case).

e. [8:75] **Application:** The following illustrates problems commonly encountered in applying the "relevant to subject matter" and "reasonably calculated to lead to discovery of admissible evidence" standards:

(1) [8:76] **Claims or defenses of either party:** "Discovery may relate to the claim or defense of the party seeking discovery, or of any other party to the action." [CCP §2017.010]

Such information is clearly within the scope of permissible discovery ("relevant to subject matter," etc.), and thus enables a party to use discovery both to establish his or her own case and to attack the adversary's.

(a) [8:76.1] **Where demurrer sustained and no amended pleading filed:** Relevancy may be impossible to determine where a demurrer has been sustained to an earlier pleading and before an amended pleading has been filed from which to determine a party's claims or defenses.

- [8:76.2] Discovery of privileged information was sought on the basis that the privilege had been *waived.* Discovery could not be compelled where there was "no viable claim on file" because a demurrer had been sustained to the earlier complaint and no amended complaint had been filed: "Put simply, prior to any finding on the question of waiver, [plaintiff] must file an acceptable complaint." [*Wellpoint Health Networks, Inc. v. Sup.Ct. (McCombs)* (1997) 59 CA4th 110, 129, 68 CR2d 844, 856]

(2) [8:77] **Contentions:** A party may discover its opponent's contentions on some issue, although they are merely opinions which would be inadmissible at trial. Again, admissibility is *not* the test. Contentions are discoverable because they are relevant to the "subject matter" and may reasonably *lead* to discovery of admissible evidence. This is true whether the contentions relate to issues of fact or law. [*West Pico Furniture Co. of Los Angeles v. Sup.Ct. (Pacific Finance Loans)* (1961) 56 C2d 407, 416-417, 15 CR 119, 123]

(a) [8:78] **Evidence supporting contentions:** In addition, a party may be compelled to disclose the *evidence* supporting each such claim or contention. E.g., "State all facts, grounds and evidence which you claim supports your contention that . . ." [*Burke v. Sup.Ct. (Fidelity & Deposit Co. of Maryland)* (1969) 71 C2d 276, 281-282, 78 CR 481, 487-488]

(b) [8:79] **Discovery method?** The choice of discovery method may affect discoverability:

- Contentions are discoverable through *interrogatories* because interrogatory responses are prepared with the assistance of counsel (CCP §2030.010(b); *see ¶8:984 ff.*).
- And, *requests for admission* (RFAs) may ask a party to admit or deny its contentions: A party may be requested to "admit . . . the truth of specified matters of fact, *opinion* relating to fact, *or application of law to fact.*" [CCP §2033.010 (emphasis added); *see ¶8:1299*]
- But contention questions may be improper in *oral depositions* (*see ¶8:723*).

(3) [8:80] **Description of physical evidence:** "Discovery may be obtained of the . . . existence, description, nature, custody, condition, and location of any *document, electronically stored information, tangible thing, or land or other property.*" [CCP §2017.010 (emphasis added)]

(4) [8:81] **Witnesses:** "Discovery may be obtained of the *identity* and *location* of persons *having knowledge of any discoverable matter* . . ." [CCP §2017.010 (emphasis added); see *Puerto v. Sup.Ct. (Wild Oats Markets, Inc.)* (2008) 158 CA4th 1242, 1249-1250, 70 CR3d 701, 705-706]

© 2020 Thomson Reuters/The Rutter Group

Examples: The eyewitness to the accident; the doctor who examined the victim; the person who made the entries in the hospital records; the person who supplied plaintiff with certain records or information. [See *Gonzalez v. Sup.Ct. (City of San Fernando)* (1995) 33 CA4th 1539, 1546-1547, 39 CR2d 896, 901]

(a) [8:82] **"Any discoverable matter":** Section 2017.010 et seq. includes witnesses with "knowledge of any discoverable matter"—i.e., fact or opinion. [*Gonzalez v. Sup.Ct. (City of San Fernando)*, supra, 33 CA4th at 1546, 39 CR2d at 901 (citing text)]

(b) [8:83] **Credibility:** Information regarding the credibility of witnesses is also discoverable: e.g., grounds for impeachment, evidence of bias, etc. The credibility of their statements or testimony is itself "relevant to the subject matter."

(c) [8:84] **Compare—which witnesses to testify NOT discoverable:** On the other hand, a party is *not* generally required to disclose which witnesses the party intends to call at trial, or the sequence in which they will testify, or the substance of their expected testimony. [*City of Long Beach v. Sup.Ct. (Henderson)* (1976) 64 CA3d 65, 72-75, 134 CR 468, 473-475]

1) [8:85] **Rationale:** Such information is protected as "*work product*," reflecting the pretrial preparations and tactics of opposing counsel (*see ¶8:236.2*).

2) [8:86] **Different rule as to expert trial witnesses:** However, the identities and opinions of *experts* who have been designated as trial witnesses are discoverable. Otherwise, counsel would have no way of preparing to counter their expert opinion testimony. A special statutory procedure is available for this purpose (CCP §2034.010 et seq., *discussed at ¶8:1624 ff.*).

a) [8:86.1] **No discovery until designation:** But the opinions of experts retained by the opposing party are *not* discoverable unless and until they have been designated as testifying experts under CCP §2034.010 et seq. Otherwise, one party could obtain a "free ride" at the expense of the other. [*County of Los Angeles v. Sup.Ct. (Martinez)* (1990) 224 CA3d 1446, 1457, 274 CR 712, 719; *Hernandez v. Sup.Ct. (Acheson Indus., Inc.)* (2003) 112 CA4th 285, 296-297, 4 CR3d 883, 892-893—although early disclosure may be ordered upon good cause; *see ¶8:1644*]

However, it may be possible to depose an expert whose declaration has been used in a motion for summary judgment or adjudication. *See* ¶*10:66.1*.

b) [8:86.2] **Not applicable to treating physicians:** In contrast, the identities and opinions of treating physicians are subject to no special discovery restrictions: "Indeed, defendants have a strong incentive to depose treating physicians well prior to the exchange of expert information to ascertain whether their observations and conclusions support the plaintiff's allegations." [*Schreiber v. Estate of Kiser* (1999) 22 C4th 31, 38, 91 CR2d 293, 299]

3) [8:87] **Different rule in limited civil cases:** In limited civil cases, either party may serve on the other a request to identify the witnesses who will testify at trial, other than for impeachment (and also to describe any physical or documentary evidence that will be offered). Witnesses not identified in response to such request will not be permitted to testify. [CCP §96(a); *see* ¶*8:1821*]

4) [8:88] **Superior court rules may require exchange of witness lists before trial:** Some superior courts have local rules requiring parties to exchange, shortly before trial, lists of all witnesses who will testify on direct. Witnesses not listed are barred from testifying unless "good cause" is shown. (E.g., L.A. Sup.Ct. Rule 3.25(f)(1), applicable to unlimited civil cases, requires such exchange at least five days before the final status conference; Orange Sup.Ct. Rule 317 requires counsel to meet and prepare a *joint* witness list, except for impeachment or rebuttal witnesses, at least 14 days before trial; San Diego Sup.Ct. Rule 2.1.15 requires disclosure (in "Joint Trial Readiness Conference Report" form provided by court) of all witnesses to be called (this form must be presented at trial readiness conference held approximately four weeks before trial, *see* ¶*12:85.5 ff.*); S.F. Sup.Ct. Rule 20.3(B) requires witness lists in asbestos cases two court days after the case is assigned to a trial department.)

These rules have been *upheld* against claims they conflict with the work product doctrine; *see* ¶*8:237.8*.

(5) [8:89] **Other accidents:** Reports of other accidents at the same location (or involving the same instrumentality) are within the scope of permissible discovery because they may show *knowledge* of a dangerous condition or a *common contributory factor*. [See *Davies v. Sup.Ct. (State of Calif.)* (1984) 36 C3d 291, 300, 204 CR 154, 160]

© 2020 Thomson Reuters/The Rutter Group

(But the identities of the persons involved in the other accidents may be protected under *right of privacy* limitations; *see* ¶*8:313*.)

(a) [8:89.1] **Accidents at other locations:** In certain cases, accidents at other locations may also be "relevant to the subject matter."

[8:89.2] Example: Plaintiffs were injured when an out-of-control vehicle crashed into a State DMV building. They claimed the building was negligently designed because there was no protection from vehicles in the adjacent parking lot. State was required to furnish information on car accidents at *other DMV buildings having the same design* and parking lot layout: "Their relevance would be based on the fact that the State knew or should have known of the unusual risk associated with DMV parking lots." [*Morfin v. State of Calif.* (1993) 12 CA4th 812, 817, 15 CR2d 861, 864]

[8:90] *Reserved.*

(6) [8:91] **Defendant's insurance coverage:** A party may obtain discovery of the *existence* and *contents* of a defendant's liability insurance coverage. This includes the identity of the carrier and the nature and limits of the coverage. [CCP §2017.210]

Production of the *insurance policy itself* may be compelled by request for production under CCP §2031.010. [*Irvington-Moore, Inc. v. Sup.Ct. (Jordan)* (1993) 14 CA4th 733, 741, 18 CR2d 49, 53]

(a) [8:91.1] **Coverage disputes:** A party may also discover whether the defendant's insurance carrier is disputing coverage of the claim involved in the action *but not the nature and substance of the dispute.* [CCP §2017.210]

For example, D may be required to disclose whether its carrier has admitted coverage or is defending on a reservation of rights basis. But D *cannot* be compelled to disclose the *reasons* the carrier is denying coverage. (P cannot use D's insurance carrier to prove D was acting "willfully" in injuring P.)

(b) [8:92] **Rationale for discovery:** Insurance information is essential because it allows settlement to be "worked out on the basis of realities." [*Smith v. Sup.Ct. (Alfred)* (1961) 189 CA2d 6, 11, 11 CR 165, 169; see *Laddon v. Sup.Ct.* (1959) 167 CA2d 391, 396, 334 P2d 638, 640—insurance policy "relevant to the subject matter" of personal injury action]

But discovery is allowed only *after* a lawsuit is filed against the insured. I.e., injured parties cannot compel disclosure without filing suit. [*Griffith v. State Farm Ins. Co.* (1991) 230 CA3d 59, 69, 281 CR 165, 170]

(c) [8:92.1] **Compare—defendant's other assets:** Arguably, a defendant's financial ability to pay an adverse judgment is as relevant to settlement as insurance coverage (¶*8:91*). But such information generally is *not* discoverable. Rationale: A qualified *right of privacy* protects a person's financial affairs (*see* ¶*8:303*). [See *Doak v. Sup.Ct.* (1968) 257 CA2d 825, 827-828, 65 CR 193, 194]

However, financial information may be discoverable to prove alter ego allegations, which may depend on proof of, e.g., commingling of funds, failure to adequately capitalize and the absence of corporate assets. [See *Leek v. Cooper* (2011) 194 CA4th 399, 417, 125 CR3d 56, 69; *Sonora Diamond Corp. v. Sup.Ct. (Sonora Union High School Dist.)* (2000) 83 CA4th 523, 538-539, 99 CR2d 824, 836; *see also* ¶*8:337 ff.*]

(d) [8:92.2] **Compare—liability insurer's financial condition?** Plaintiffs probably *cannot* obtain discovery regarding a liability insurance company's financial ability to pay whatever judgment may be obtained against an insured defendant.

1) [8:92.3] **Reinsurance not discoverable:** Plaintiffs are not entitled to discover whether defendant's liability insurer has *reinsured* the risk with another insurer: "Because a contract of reinsurance is . . . made for the benefit of the liability insurer . . ., it has *no relevance* in an underlying tort action brought against an insured under the policy of liability insurance." [*Catholic Mut. Relief Soc. v. Sup.Ct. (Roman Catholic Archdiocese of San Diego)* (2007) 42 C4th 358, 368, 64 CR3d 434, 440 (emphasis added)]

Cross-refer: Reinsurance is discussed in Croskey, Heeseman, Ehrlich & Klee, *Cal. Prac. Guide: Insurance Litigation* (TRG), Ch. 8.

2) [8:92.4] **Comment:** This holding strongly suggests that a liability insurer's financial condition generally is not discoverable by plaintiffs in a tort case against an insured.

(e) [8:93] **Compare—third party's insurance coverage:** Whether a *nonparty* is insured is generally *irrelevant* for discovery purposes. It usually has no effect on liability between the parties or on settlement prospects. [*Snell v. Sup.Ct. (Marshall Hosp.)* (1984) 158 CA3d 44, 50-51, 204 CR 200, 203-204]

© 2020 Thomson Reuters/The Rutter Group

1) **Application**

- [8:94] In a suit alleging Hospital's negligence in screening and evaluating the *competency* of doctors on its staff, whether staff doctors carried malpractice insurance was not discoverable. Hospital's duty to exercise care in evaluating its doctors' competence "has palpably little to do with whether" doctors were insured. [*Snell v. Sup.Ct. (Marshall Hosp.),* supra, 158 CA3d at 50, 204 CR at 204]

- [8:94.1] *Contra view:* The result is different where the Hospital's *own rules require* staff doctors to carry malpractice insurance. In such cases, their lack of insurance is relevant for discovery purposes: "Failure of Hospital to inquire . . . when its own rules require the coverage, *demonstrates a willingness* to ignore that the physician is *not coverable* for reasons that may go to the physician's *medical competency.*" [*Brown v. Sup.Ct. (West Hills Med. Ctr.)* (1985) 168 CA3d 489, 502, 214 CR 266, 275 (emphasis added) (rejecting *Snell*'s reasoning)]

2) [8:95] **Compare—third party's insurance relevant to damages in present case:** A nonparty's liability insurance may be discoverable where relevant to issues of causation and damages in the present case. [*Hecht, Solberg, Robinson, Goldberg & Bagley v. Sup.Ct. (Panther)* (2006) 137 CA4th 579, 597-598, 40 CR3d 446, 459-460]

- [8:95.1] Client sued Attorney for malpractice in settling a claim against Third Party for less than it was worth. Third Party's insurance coverage was discoverable "to show how much money could have been collected from the [Third Party] if a substantial judgment had been entered against it, as opposed to the settlement amount." [*Hecht, Solberg, Robinson, Goldberg & Bagley v. Sup.Ct. (Panther),* supra, 137 CA4th at 598, 40 CR3d at 459]

[8:95.2-95.4] *Reserved.*

(f) [8:95.5] **Compare—insurer's loss reserves in bad faith case:** Where an insured sues its insurer for bad faith failure to settle a liability claim against the insured, the existence and amount of the insurer's loss reserves on that claim are discoverable: "Without doubt, such information would assist [insured] in *evaluating* his bad faith case and in *preparing* it for trial. That is enough to justify discovery." [*Lipton v. Sup.Ct. (Lawyers' Mut.*

Ins. Co.) (1996) 48 CA4th 1599, 1616, 56 CR2d 341, 350 (emphasis in original)]

(7) [8:96] **Plaintiff's compensation from "collateral sources":** Normally, an injured party need not disclose compensation received from a "collateral source" for injuries caused by the defendant, because such evidence is *not admissible to mitigate* damages. (The "collateral source" may be plaintiff's own insurance, or wages or disability pay from plaintiff's employer, etc.) The rationale is that defendant should not benefit from plaintiff's foresight in obtaining insurance or other sources of compensation. [See *Helfend v. Southern Calif. Rapid Transit Dist.* (1970) 2 C3d 1, 6, 84 CR 173, 175]

(a) [8:97] **Compare—settlement terms:** Although plaintiff's settlement with its own insurer may be inadmissible at trial under the "collateral source" rule, the settlement terms with the insurer *may* lead to discovery of admissible evidence: e.g., plaintiffs' motives in pursuing the litigation, "or their bias and credibility as witnesses." [*Norton v. Sup.Ct. (Ein)* (1994) 24 CA4th 1750, 1761, 30 CR2d 217, 224]

(b) [8:98] **Compare—medical malpractice actions:** The Medical Injury Compensation Reform Act (MICRA) permits evidence of collateral source payments in professional negligence actions against health care providers. [See Civ.C. §3333.1(a)]

(c) [8:99] **Compare—negotiated amount paid for medical expenses:** Where a medical provider has agreed to accept discounted payments by a health insurer as full payment for a patient's medical care, the injured party is limited to recovery of the amount paid for the medical services (*Howell v. Hamilton Meats & Provisions, Inc.* (2011) 52 C4th 541, 559, 129 CR3d 325, 338). Defendant should be able to discover the negotiated amount that was accepted as full payment.

(d) [8:100] **Compare—insured plaintiff who chooses to be treated outside medical plan:** However, an insured plaintiff who has chosen to be treated by providers outside his or her insurance plan is considered "uninsured" for purposes of determining economic damages. [*Pebley v. Santa Clara Organics, LLC* (2018) 22 CA5th 1266, 1277-1278, 232 CR3d 404, 412-413—plaintiff who was treated outside his insurance plan was permitted to introduce evidence of full medical bills incurred and evidence of his insured status was inadmissible]

Cross-refer: See further discussion in Wegner, Fairbank, Epstein & Chernow, *Cal. Prac. Guide: Civil Trials & Evidence* (TRG), Ch. 8E; and Haning, Flahavan, Cheng & Wright, *Cal. Prac. Guide: Personal Injury* (TRG), Ch. 3.

© 2020 Thomson Reuters/The Rutter Group

[8:101-106] *Reserved.*

(8) [8:107] **Settlement offers or negotiations:** Settlement offers or negotiations are generally inadmissible to prove liability for the loss or injury involved (Ev.C. §1152). Nor is such evidence likely to lead to discovery of admissible evidence because *no logical inference* of liability can be drawn therefrom; i.e., defendants often settle even frivolous lawsuits in order to "buy peace." [*Covell v. Sup.Ct. (Drasin)* (1984) 159 CA3d 39, 43, 205 CR 371, 374—plaintiff claiming earlier suit against him was maliciously prosecuted could not be asked whether he had offered to settle earlier suit]

But settlement offers and negotiations may be relevant to the subject matter for *other purposes:*

(a) [8:108] **Compare—"good faith" settlement proceedings:** Where plaintiff settles with one of several joint tortfeasors and the settlor then seeks a "good faith" determination under CCP §877.6 (to block indemnity claims from the other tortfeasors), the nonsettling tortfeasors have the right to discover the terms and conditions of the settlement. *See discussion at ¶12:875 ff.*

(b) [8:108.1] **Compare—"bad faith" by insurer:** Where an insured has made a claim for policy benefits, the insurer's *unreasonably low* settlement offers may be admissible to show a breach of its duty of good faith and fair dealing with the insured. [See *White v. Western Title Ins. Co.* (1985) 40 C3d 870, 885, 221 CR 509, 517]

Other offers or counteroffers by the insured may be admissible to rebut the inference of "bad faith" in such cases, and to show the insurer's good faith efforts to settle the case. [Ev.C. §1152(b)]

(c) [8:108.2] **Compare—attorney's failure to communicate settlement offer to client:** Attorneys must promptly advise their clients of written settlement offers from opposing parties. Such offers and communications with clients are discoverable where the *existence or communication* of the offer is at issue; e.g., in a malpractice action against the attorney for failing to communicate the offer to the client. [See Bus. & Prof.C. §6103.5]

[8:108.3-108.5] *Reserved.*

(9) [8:108.6] **"Reasonableness" of attorney fees:** When attorney fees are recoverable by either statute or contract, discovery is often directed at attorney time records showing the hours worked and services performed. But hours are not the only areas for discovery relating to attorney fee motions. For example, the Rules of Professional Conduct enumerate various factors relevant to determining whether a claimed legal fee is "unconscionable" (e.g., results involved, degree of skill

required, etc.), and most of those topics are relevant for fee motions, as well. [See CRPC 1.5(b) (formerly CRPC 4-200(B))]

[8:108.6a] ***PRACTICE POINTER:*** Production of attorney time and billing records often raises questions of attorney-client privilege or attorney work product. Any potential problems resulting from such production can usually be avoided by redacting protected information. (*But see ¶8:146.15* (privilege claims re attorney bills sought under California Public Records Act).)

(a) [8:108.7] **Firm's profit margins irrelevant:** A law firm's profit margins and cost of providing its services (e.g., salaries paid its contract attorneys) are *not* among the enumerated factors and are irrelevant to determination of "reasonableness" of the firm's fees. [*Shaffer v. Sup.Ct. (Simms)* (1995) 33 CA4th 993, 1002-1003, 39 CR2d 506, 512-513]

Rationale: "[I]t would place courts in the position of supervising attorney's fees on the basis of individual profit margins instead of the going market price for given services." [*Shaffer v. Sup.Ct. (Simms)*, supra, 33 CA4th at 1003, 39 CR2d at 513]

[8:108.8-108.9] *Reserved.*

(10)[8:108.10] **Immigration status generally not discoverable:** Except as required to comply with federal law, a person's immigration status is "irrelevant" for purposes of *enforcing California's labor, employment, civil rights, consumer protection and housing laws.* I.e., undocumented workers are entitled to the same protection, rights and remedies as citizens under state wages and hours laws. [Civ.C. §3339; Gov.C. §7285; Lab.C. §1171.5]

(a) [8:108.11] **Other civil actions:** This protection from discovery of immigration status extends to actions for personal injury or wrongful death (Ev.C. §351.2(a)), as well as state labor, employment, civil rights, consumer protection and housing cases. A court may allow discovery of the status only if there is clear and convincing evidence that the inquiry is necessary to comply with federal immigration law. [Civ.C. §3339(b)]

(b) [8:108.12] **Immigration status of minor child:** The immigration status of a minor child seeking recovery under any law is "irrelevant" to the issues of liability or remedy, "except for employment-related prospective injunctive relief that would directly violate federal law." [Civ.C. §3339.5(a)]

Also, no discovery is allowed in any civil action regarding a minor child's immigration status except where the minor's

© 2020 Thomson Reuters/The Rutter Group

claim places his or her immigration status "directly in contention" or the person seeking discovery of the status shows by "clear and convincing evidence" the discovery is necessary to comply with federal immigration law. [Civ.C. §3339.5(b)]

3. [8:109] **"Not Privileged":** The third major limitation on the scope of permissible discovery is that the information sought be "not privileged." I.e., discovery is permitted of "any matter, *not privileged*, that is relevant to the subject matter," etc. [CCP §2017.010 (emphasis added)]

   a. [8:110] **Privileges—in general:** Any matter protected against disclosure at trial under an evidentiary privilege is generally protected against discovery. This applies to any of the "standard" privileges enumerated in the Evidence Code:

      - Self-incrimination (Ev.C. §940)
      - Attorney-client (Ev.C. §950 et seq.)
      - Lawyer referral service-client (Ev.C. §965 et seq.)
      - Spousal (Ev.C. §§970 et seq. (not to testify against spouse), 980 et seq. (protecting confidential marital communications))
      - Physician-patient (Ev.C. §990 et seq.)
      - Psychotherapist-patient (Ev.C. §1010 et seq.) and educational psychologist-patient (Ev.C. §1010.5 et seq.)
      - Clergy-penitent (Ev.C. §1030 et seq.)
      - Sexual assault counselor-victim (Ev.C. §1035 et seq.)
      - Domestic violence counselor-victim (Ev.C. §1037 et seq.)
      - Human trafficking caseworker-victim (Ev.C. §1038 et seq.)
      - Official records (Ev.C. §1040 et seq.)
      - Secrecy of political ballot (Ev.C. §1050)
      - Trade secrets (Ev.C. §1060 et seq.)

      Cross-refer: See Wegner, Fairbank, Epstein & Chernow, *Cal. Prac. Guide: Civil Trials & Evidence* (TRG), Ch. 8E.

      (1) [8:110a] **Courts cannot create new privileges:** The privileges contained in the Evidence Code are *exclusive* and courts cannot create new ones. [See Ev.C. §911; *Valley Bank of Nevada v. Sup.Ct. (Barkett)* (1975) 15 C3d 652, 656, 125 CR 553, 555]

         - [8:110b] Thus, for example, the *privilege for "self-critical analysis"* (protecting a party's investigations and critique of its own operations), recognized in some federal courts, is *not* recognized in California because it is not among the privileges enumerated in the Evidence Code. [*Cloud v. Sup.Ct. (Litton Indus., Inc.)* (1996) 50 CA4th 1552, 1558-1559, 58 CR2d 365, 369]

(2) [8:110c] **Courts cannot create exceptions to statutory privileges:** Nor can courts create exceptions to statutory privileges beyond those provided by the statute. [*University of Southern Calif. v. Sup.Ct. (Comeau)* (1996) 45 CA4th 1283, 1290, 53 CR2d 260, 264]

(3) [8:110d] **Effect of claiming privilege:** A party claiming a privilege to avoid disclosing facts essential to a claim or defense may be *barred* from asserting that claim or defense at trial. [*Steiny & Co., Inc. v. California Elec. Supply Co.* (2000) 79 CA4th 285, 292, 93 CR2d 920, 925—by invoking trade secrets privilege to avoid disclosing proprietary information relevant to its damage calculations, plaintiff was barred from proceeding with damages claims; *Fremont Indem. Co. v. Sup.Ct. (Sharif)* (1982) 137 CA3d 554, 560, 187 CR 137, 140—court could order dismissal of suit against fire insurance company where plaintiff invoked 5th Amendment privilege to preclude questioning as to whether he started fire; *see ¶8:133*]

b. [8:110.1] **Where privilege absolute:** Information within the scope of certain of the above privileges (e.g., attorney-client, *¶8:110*) is absolutely protected from disclosure (unless the privilege is *waived*; *see ¶8:199 ff.*). This means the court *cannot* "weigh" or "balance" the privilege against the need for the information: "As a general rule, privileged communications are protected regardless of their relevancy to the issues in the litigation, and despite any private or public interest in disclosure." [*Rittenhouse v. Sup.Ct. (Board of Trustees of Leland Stanford Jr. Univ.)* (1991) 235 CA3d 1584, 1590, 1 CR2d 595, 598; see *Doe 2 v. Sup.Ct. (Calkins)* (2005) 132 CA4th 1504, 1517, 34 CR3d 458, 466—court cannot compel disclosure even if protective order imposed]

With certain privileges, such as the attorney-client privilege, a court may not require disclosure of information claimed to be privileged in order to rule on the claim of privilege (*see ¶8:192.1*). [Ev.C. §915(a); *Southern Calif. Gas. Co. v. Public Utilities Comm'n* (1990) 50 C3d 31, 45, 265 CR 801, 809, fn. 19; *Costco Wholesale Corp. v. Sup.Ct. (Randall)* (2009) 47 C4th 725, 736-738, 101 CR3d 758, 767; *Clark v. Sup.Ct. (Verisign, Inc.)* (2011) 196 CA4th 37, 50-51, 125 CR3d 361, 371-372]

[8:110.2-110.4] *Reserved.*

c. [8:110.5] **Where privilege qualified:** Certain other information receives only *qualified* protection from pretrial discovery, including:

— information protected by the "right of privacy" under the State Constitution (*see ¶8:293 ff.*);

— a news reporter's sources and unpublished information protected under the U.S. Constitution, First Amendment, as well as under state law (*see ¶8:340 ff.*);

— "official information" under Ev.C. §1040(b) (*see ¶8:125 ff.*);

— police personnel files under Ev.C. §1043 (*see ¶8:126 ff.*);

— trade secrets under Ev.C. §1060 (*see* ¶*8:129 ff.*); and
— *certain types* of "attorney work product" (other types receive absolute protection; *see* ¶*8:213 ff.*).

"Qualified protection" means disclosure may be compelled if the court finds the interests of justice in obtaining the information *outweigh* the interests sought to be protected. Where there is a prima facie showing of *relevance*, the party claiming a qualified privilege bears the burden of *establishing the preliminary facts* essential to the claim of privilege. [*Gonzalez v. Sup.Ct. (City of San Fernando)* (1995) 33 CA4th 1539, 1548, 39 CR2d 896, 902—speculation and conclusions not enough]

d. [8:111] **Particular privileges:** Certain privileges have special importance in discovery proceedings.

(1) [8:112] **Tax returns:** Taxpayers are privileged to withhold disclosure of copies of both their federal and state tax returns and the information contained therein. The privilege is implied from the policy of confidentiality re *state* income tax returns expressed in Rev. & Tax.C. §19542 (misdemeanor for public officials to reveal contents of tax returns). [*Webb v. Standard Oil Co. of Calif.* (1957) 49 C2d 509, 513-514, 319 P2d 621, 624]

(a) [8:113] **Purpose:** The purpose of the privilege is to facilitate collection of taxes. Allowing discovery could discourage taxpayers from making full and truthful tax returns, out of concern their returns could be used against them for other purposes. [*Sav-On Drugs, Inc. v. Sup.Ct. (Botney)* (1975) 15 C3d 1, 6, 123 CR 283, 286-287]

(b) [8:113.1] **Protection *not* absolute:** Unlike the statutory privileges listed above (¶*8:110*), the privilege for tax returns is *not* absolute. [*Schnabel v. Sup.Ct. (Schnabel)* (1993) 5 C4th 704, 721, 21 CR2d 200, 210]

1) [8:113.2] **Waiver exception:** The privilege cannot be asserted where a party has intentionally *or impliedly* waived it. [*Schnabel v. Sup.Ct. (Schnabel)*, supra, 5 C4th at 721, 21 CR2d at 210]

An implied waiver exists where the gravamen of the lawsuit is "so inconsistent with the continued assertion of the taxpayer's privilege as to compel the conclusion that the privilege has in fact been waived" (e.g., suing an accountant for malpractice in preparing the return). [*Schnabel v. Sup.Ct. (Schnabel)*, supra, 5 C4th at 721, 21 CR2d at 210 (internal quotes omitted)]

a) [8:113.3] **Waiver by disclosure to third persons?** Ev.C. §912(a) provides that various statutory privileges are waived by voluntary disclosure of the privileged information to a third party (*see* ¶*8:199 ff.*). Although the tax return privilege is not enumerated in §912(a), the statutory privileges and their exceptions "may provide analogous reasoning in the appropriate case." [*Fortunato v. Sup.Ct. (Ingrassia)* (2003) 114 CA4th 475, 480, 8 CR3d 82, 85, fn. 3]

b) [8:113.4] **Privacy right as limitation on waiver:** Waiver is determined on a case-by-case basis. Thus, the fact that a party's tax return is also protected by a constitutional right of privacy (*see ¶8:303*) "has bearing upon the question of whether the tax-return privilege was waived in this case." [*Fortunato v. Sup.Ct. (Ingrassia)*, supra, 114 CA4th at 481, 8 CR3d at 86]

c) [8:113.4a] **Involuntary relinquishment not waiver:** Waiver requires a *voluntary* relinquishment. Thus, for example, producing a tax return under court order is not a voluntary relinquishment and does not waive the privilege. [See *Thomas B. v. Sup.Ct. (Sherry H.)* (1985) 175 CA3d 255, 263, 220 CR 577, 581]

1/ [8:113.4b] **Disclosure to bank involuntary?** One case states disclosure of tax returns and financial affairs to a bank (e.g., in connection with a loan application) "is not entirely volitional, since it is impossible to participate in the economic life of contemporary society without maintaining a bank account." [*Fortunato v. Sup.Ct. (Ingrassia)*, supra, 114 CA4th at 481, 8 CR3d at 86 (internal quotes omitted)]

[8:113.4c] *Comment:* Other courts may disagree with this result because it appears to expand the scope of evidentiary privileges and protections. [See *McKesson HBOC, Inc. v. Sup.Ct. (State of Oregon)* (2004) 115 CA4th 1229, 1236-1238, 9 CR3d 812, 817-819—attorney-client and work product privileges waived by disclosure to government despite confidentiality agreement; *see ¶8:199.14*]

2) [8:113.5] **Public policy exception:** The tax return privilege cannot be asserted where a public policy *greater* than that of confidentiality of tax returns is involved. [*Schnabel v. Sup.Ct. (Schnabel)*, supra, 5 C4th at 721, 21 CR2d at 210]

[8:113.6] *Reserved.*

- [8:113.7] The privilege does not shield the tax returns of a *closely-held corporation* in which a spouse is a shareholder, or the payroll tax returns of the shareholder spouse. The public policy favoring full disclosure between spouses and fair division of community property (see Fam.C. §§2100, 2120(a)) outweighs any interest in confidentiality of tax returns. [*Schnabel v. Sup.Ct. (Schnabel)*, supra, 5 C4th at 721, 21 CR2d at 210]

- [8:113.8] Similarly, a defendant found liable for punitive damages in the first phase of a bifurcated trial was ordered to produce her tax returns after she engaged in conduct that frustrated discovery and prevented plaintiffs from obtaining relevant financial information. A public policy "greater than confidentiality of the tax return [was] involved. . . ." [*Weingarten v. Sup.Ct. (Pointe San Diego Residential Comm.)* (2002) 102 CA4th 268, 274, 125 CR2d 371, 376; see *Li v. Yan* (2016) 247 CA4th 56, 67-68, 201 CR3d 772, 780—judgment debtor required to disclose tax returns in judgment debtor exam due to strong public policy to prevent fraud against creditors, lenders and court]

  Compare: But the mere fact that a party's liability for punitive damages has been established is *not* enough. Nor is the fact that a party's financial records are difficult to obtain and the tax return would facilitate establishing net worth. [*Weingarten v. Sup.Ct. (Pointe San Diego Residential Comm.)*, supra, 102 CA4th at 276, 125 CR2d at 377]

(c) [8:114] **Application:** The privilege has been broadly construed. It applies to:

- [8:115] Both personal and corporate taxpayers. [See *Sav-On Drugs, Inc. v. Sup.Ct. (Botney)* (1975) 15 C3d 1, 7, 123 CR 283, 287]

- [8:116] All kinds of tax returns—i.e., income taxes, employment taxes, sales taxes, estate taxes, etc. [See *Sav-On Drugs, Inc. v. Sup.Ct. (Botney)*, supra, 15 C3d at 6, 123 CR at 287; *Deary v. Sup.Ct. (Hendrick)* (2001) 87 CA4th 1072, 1078, 105 CR2d 132, 136]

- [8:117] Returns filed either by parties to the action *or by nonparties*. [*Rifkind v. Sup.Ct. (Rifkind)* (1981) 123 CA3d 1045, 1050, 177 CR 82, 84 (disapproved on other grounds by *Schnabel v. Sup.Ct. (Schnabel)* (1993) 5 C4th 704, 21 CR2d 200)—in a marital dissolution action, H could not be compelled to produce tax returns of partnerships and corporations in which he had interest]

- [8:118] The return itself and any information entered thereon (e.g., amounts of income reported or deductions claimed). [See *Sav-On Drugs, Inc. v. Sup.Ct. (Botney)*, supra, 15 C3d at 6, 123 CR at 287]

- [8:119] Other documents or information that are an *"integral part"* of the tax return—such as W-2 forms (withholding tax statements received by the taxpayer from employer, showing earnings). [*Brown v. Sup.Ct. (Executive Car Leasing)* (1977) 71 CA3d 141, 142, 139 CR 327, 328—personal injury plaintiff, claiming earnings loss, could not be compelled to produce W-2 forms received from employer]

(d) [8:120] **Limitation—support proceedings:** By statute, different rules apply in child or spousal support proceedings: A party's *state and federal* income tax returns—including joint returns with another person—are discoverable by the other party to such proceedings. (If deemed relevant to the disposition of the case, the court may order such returns sealed and retained as a confidential court record.) [Fam.C. §3552; see Hogoboom & King, *Cal. Prac. Guide: Family Law* (TRG), Ch. 11]

(e) [8:121] **Limitation—foreign tax returns:** The privilege for tax returns is limited to federal and California tax returns. It does *not* apply to tax returns filed in foreign countries. [*Firestone v. Hoffman* (2006) 140 CA4th 1408, 1419, 45 CR3d 534, 542—Canadian tax returns not privileged]

(f) [8:122] **Compare—taxpayer's records not protected:** Only the tax return and information that is an "integral part" thereof is protected. The records and data upon which the return is based (i.e., the party's checkbooks, journals and ledgers) are still subject to discovery. (Such information, however, may be protected by a party's *constitutional right to privacy* in confidential financial information; *see* ¶*8:303*.)

(g) [8:123] **Compare—accountants' work papers:** It is an *open question* whether accountants' work papers *used in preparing* a tax return are discoverable. Arguably, if the accountant's work papers were prepared expressly for the tax return (e.g., as "back up" for entries in the return itself), they might be considered an "integral part" of the return and thus be protected against discovery. However, no known case has so held.

© 2020 Thomson Reuters/The Rutter Group

1) [8:124] **No "work product" privilege for accountants:** There is no "work product" privilege for accountants' papers analogous to the attorneys' work product privilege (*see ¶8:213 ff.*). [See *United States v. Arthur Young & Co.* (1984) 465 US 805, 816, 104 S.Ct. 1495, 1502]

[8:124.1-124.4] *Reserved.*

2) [8:124.5] **Compare—federal law prohibiting voluntary disclosure:** It is a federal crime for any tax preparer to disclose "information furnished to him for, or in connection with, the preparation of" a federal tax return. [26 USC §§6713(a), 7216(a)]

Although an exception is provided for information ordered by a court (26 USC §7216(b)(1)(B)), federal courts have been cautious in ordering disclosure of taxpayer records. A showing of relevancy to the matters at issue is required, plus a *compelling need* for the information, and that the information is not otherwise readily obtainable. [See *Mitsui & Co. (U.S.A.) Inc. v. Puerto Rico Water Resources Auth.* (D PR 1978) 79 FRD 72, 81-82]

[8:124.6] ***PRACTICE POINTER:*** If served with a subpoena for taxpayer records, an accounting firm is likely to assert the federal statute (*¶8:124.5*) as the basis for a motion for protective order or order quashing the subpoena. The party seeking the records should be prepared to show a *compelling need* for the information and that it is not readily obtainable from any other source.

(2) [8:125] **Official records and information:** Various types of official records and information may be protected from discovery to some degree:

(a) [8:125.1] **Disclosure against public interest:** Information acquired "in confidence" by public employees is privileged where its disclosure would be "against the public interest." This requires a finding that the need for confidentiality *outweighs* the interest of justice in full disclosure of relevant information. [Ev.C. §1040(b)]

In determining whether disclosure is "against the public interest," the public entity's interest, if any, in the outcome of the action (e.g., where it is a party) is *not* considered. [Ev.C. §1040(b)(2)]

[8:125.2-125.4] *Reserved.*

1) [8:125.5] **Police investigative files:** Evidence gathered as part of an ongoing criminal

investigation is by its nature confidential. Police investigative files are therefore privileged so long as the need for confidentiality *outweighs* the benefits of disclosure in the particular case. [*County of Orange v. Sup.Ct. (Wu)* (2000) 79 CA4th 759, 765, 94 CR2d 261, 264]

- [8:125.6] An alleged rape victim's confidential statement to police was held discoverable by the *accused* in a subsequent defamation action, where the need for the evidence outweighed the rape victim's privacy interest. [*Rider v. Sup.Ct. (L.F.P., Inc.)* (1988) 199 CA3d 278, 284-285, 244 CR 770, 773-774]
- [8:125.7] But the parents of a murdered child were *not* entitled to discovery of sheriff's investigative files in a defamation action against the sheriff where the *investigation was ongoing.* For a reasonable period of time, the public interest in apprehending the killer outweighed the parents' need for discovery. [*County of Orange v. Sup.Ct. (Wu)*, supra, 79 CA4th at 768, 94 CR2d at 266]

(b) [8:126] **Police personnel files:** Subject to certain exceptions and limitations, information contained in a peace officer's or custodial officer's personnel file is protected from discovery or disclosure under Pen.C. §832.7 and Ev.C. §1043 et seq. Motions to secure this information are often referred to as "*Pitchess* motions" (*see ¶8:127.1 ff.*).

These provisions take precedence over the general discovery rules. [*Davis v. City of Sacramento* (1994) 24 CA4th 393, 400, 29 CR2d 232, 234]

This protection applies in civil, criminal and administrative proceedings. [*Copley Press, Inc. v. Sup.Ct. (County of San Diego)* (2006) 39 C4th 1272, 1284, 48 CR3d 183, 190-191 (police officer's administrative appeal of a disciplinary matter)]

The protection extends to *records and findings of governmental agencies that investigate* complaints against peace officers (e.g., police review commissions). [*Berkeley Police Ass'n v. City of Berkeley* (2008) 167 CA4th 385, 404-405, 84 CR3d 130, 146-147; *but see ¶8:127*]

1) [8:126.1] **Matters protected:** The protection extends to *any* information of a private nature, including complaints and investigations of the officer and information concerning the officer personally (e.g., home address; marital status; education and employment history; employee advancement, appraisal and discipline, etc.). [See Pen.C. §§832.7(a), 832.8]

© 2020 Thomson Reuters/The Rutter Group

It is immaterial that the latter could be obtained from other sources. [*Hackett v. Sup.Ct. (Glin)* (1993) 13 CA4th 96, 100, 16 CR2d 405, 407—officer's home address, telephone number, date of birth and similar data protected]

On the other hand, the mere fact that a document is included in a police officer's personnel file does not, by itself, preclude discovery. To be protected as a "personnel record," a complaint or investigation of a complaint "must both concern an event that *involved the officer as a participant* or witness and pertain to the officer's performance of his or her duties." [*Zanone v. City of Whittier* (2008) 162 CA4th 174, 189, 75 CR3d 439, 450 (emphasis added)]

a) [8:126.2] **Personal recollection of records also protected:** Absent a court order, police officers cannot be compelled to answer interrogatories or deposition questions regarding contents of their personnel files. The same protections against discovery of the file itself apply to the officer's knowledge of the file's contents. [*City of San Diego v. Sup.Ct. (Pallonetti)* (1981) 136 CA3d 236, 239, 186 CR 112, 113]

b) [8:126.3] **Protection not waived by failure to respond to discovery requests:** Most privileges are waived if not timely raised (¶*8:200*). However, the Evidence Code provides the *exclusive* means for discovery of peace officer personnel records. Thus, no response is required to demands for production under the Discovery Act (CCP §2031.010 et seq.); and failure to respond is *not* a waiver of the Evidence Code protection. [*County of Los Angeles v. Sup.Ct. (Uhley)* (1990) 219 CA3d 1605, 1611, 269 CR 187, 190]

c) [8:126.4] **Compare—no bar to agency's review of own files:** But the statute does not prevent a law enforcement agency from reviewing its own personnel files for relevant purposes. Such a review is not "discovery or disclosure" within the meaning of Pen.C. §832.7 and Ev.C. §1043 et seq. [*Michael v. Gates* (1995) 38 CA4th 737, 744, 45 CR2d 163, 167—city attorney reviewed retired police officer's personnel records seeking information that could be used to impeach his testimony as expert witness in action against City]

d) [8:126.5] **Compare—no bar to discovery re names, dates of employment, official photos or salaries:** The names, dates of employment, employing agencies, official photos *and salaries* of peace officers do not constitute "peace officer personnel records" under Pen.C. §§832.7 and 832.8. Such information is subject to disclosure under the California Public Records Act (CPRA, Gov.C. §6250 et seq.) and is also therefore subject to discovery. [See *Commission on Peace Officer Standards & Training v. Sup.Ct. (Los Angeles Times Communications LLC)* (2007) 42 C4th 278, 293-294, 64 CR3d 661, 671-672; *International Federation of Professional & Technical Engineers, Local 21, AFL-CIO v. Sup.Ct. (Contra Costa Newspapers, Inc.)* (2007) 42 C4th 319, 346, 64 CR3d 693, 712; *Ibarra v. Sup.Ct. (Tillman)* (2013) 217 CA4th 695, 704-705, 158 CR3d 751, 758-759 (authorizing production of current photographs of officer in personnel file but requiring protective order re use to protect officer safety)]

e) [8:126.6] **Compare—marital dissolution proceedings:** A police officer's *payroll records* are *not* protected from disclosure in a marital dissolution proceeding: "[T]here is no good reason to force the spouse of a peace officer to jump through the *Pitchess* hoop to obtain financial information he or she is entitled to by law." [*Slayton v. Sup.Ct. (Slayton)* (2006) 146 CA4th 55, 59-60, 52 CR3d 731, 735 (internal quotes omitted)]

On the other hand, personnel records of *complaints of violence or brutality* received against an officer *are* protected and subject to the following procedures when sought to be introduced on custody and visitation issues in the dissolution proceedings. [*Slayton v. Sup.Ct. (Slayton)*, supra, 146 CA4th at 60-61, 52 CR3d at 735-736]

2) [8:127] **Procedure for disclosure:** There is a special two-step procedure for securing disclosure of most peace officer personnel records. [*Warrick v. Sup.Ct. (City of Los Angeles Police Dept.)* (2005) 35 C4th 1011, 1019, 29 CR3d 2, 7; *California Highway Patrol v. Sup.Ct. (Luna)* (2000) 84 CA4th 1010, 1019, 101 CR2d 379, 386]

However, commencing July 1, 2019, audio or video recordings relating to a police officer's discharge of a firearm at a person, or use of force resulting

© 2020 Thomson Reuters/The Rutter Group

in death or great bodily injury, are discoverable under certain circumstances pursuant to the CPRA. [Gov.C. §6254(f)(4); *see* ¶*8:1805.18 ff.*]

In addition, other records relating to the report, investigation or findings of shootings or serious uses of force by police officers, as well as sustained findings of sexual assault involving a member of the public, or dishonesty directly relating to the reporting, investigation or prosecution of a crime must be made available for public inspection under the CPRA. [Pen.C. §832.7(b)(1); *see* ¶*8:1805.1 ff.*]

a) [8:127.1] **First step—a "*Pitchess* motion":** The party seeking disclosure must file a motion that identifies the peace officer, the agency in possession of the records, a description of the records, who is seeking the records, as well as time and place of the hearing. [Ev.C. §1043(b)(1)]

(This is a so-called *"Pitchess* motion," derived from *Pitchess v. Sup.Ct. (Echeveria)* (1974) 11 C3d 531, 113 CR 897). The motion *must* be accompanied by a declaration:

— showing "good cause" for disclosure of the records;

— setting forth the materiality of the records; and

— stating upon reasonable belief that the governmental agency has the requested documents. [Ev.C. §1043(b)(3)]

1/ [8:127.2] **"Good cause" declaration:** The Ev.C. §1043(b) "good cause" declaration must be sufficiently specific "to preclude the possibility of a defendant's simply casting about for any helpful information." [*People v. Mooc* (2001) 26 C4th 1216, 1226, 114 CR2d 482, 491]

[8:127.3] **Hearsay:** Since the party seeking disclosure usually does not know the contents of the records, it may be difficult to establish "good cause" for disclosure. Declarations on information and belief (i.e., hearsay) have been held sufficient in criminal cases. [*City of Santa Cruz v. Mun.Ct. (Kennedy)* (1989) 49 C3d 74, 88, 260 CR 520, 527]

[8:127.4] **"Good cause" showing:** The moving party need show only a "plausible factual foundation" for discovery—i.e., a scenario of officer misconduct that *might occur or could have occurred.* [*Warrick v. Sup.Ct. (City of Los Angeles Police Dept.)*, supra, 35 C4th at 1026, 29 CR3d at 13]

This is a "relatively low threshold." [*City of Santa Cruz v. Mun.Ct. (Kennedy)*, supra, 49 C3d at 83, 260 CR at 525]

[8:127.4a] **May be filed under seal:** The trial court has *discretion* to permit the declaration in support of the request for disclosure to be filed under seal, and to have the opposing party served with a redacted copy omitting privileged information. [*Garcia v. Sup.Ct. (City of Santa Ana)* (2007) 42 C4th 63, 72, 63 CR3d 948, 954]

2/ [8:127.5] **Where excessive force alleged:** If the party seeking disclosure alleges excessive force by a peace officer during an arrest, a copy of the arrest report must be attached to the motion. [Ev.C. §1046]

3/ [8:127.6] **Notice requirements:** Notice must be served in compliance with CCP §1005(b) (*see* ¶*9:31*) on the parties and *on the governmental agency* having the records. [Ev.C. §1043(a)]

The *agency* is required to notify the individual officer whose records are sought. [Ev.C. §1043(a)]

[8:127.7-127.9] *Reserved.*

4/ [8:127.10] **Hearing:** A hearing is held in open court, where counsel for the agency or the peace officer typically appears. The court must determine whether good cause exists for disclosure, which, if found, leads to an in camera hearing (¶*8:127.15*). [*City of Los Angeles v. Sup.Ct (Brandon)* (2002) 29 C4th 1, 9, 124 CR2d 202, 208]

[8:127.11-127.14] *Reserved.*

b) [8:127.15] **Second step—in camera hearing:** If the court finds good cause (¶*8:127.10*), an in camera hearing must be held. [*Slayton v. Sup.Ct. (Slayton)* (2006) 146 CA4th 55, 61, 52 CR3d 731, 736; *Brown v. Valverde* (2010) 183 CA4th 1531, 1541, 108 CR3d 429, 435 (citing text)]

1/ [8:127.16] **Persons present:** The parties to the lawsuit are not allowed to be present

© 2020 Thomson Reuters/The Rutter Group

in chambers. Only the judge, the custodian of records for the agency, sometimes the attorney for both the agency and the officer, and a court reporter participate in this second phase of the disclosure process. [Ev.C. §915(b); *People v. Mooc* (2001) 26 C4th 1216, 1226, 1229, 114 CR2d 482, 491, 493]

[8:127.17-127.19] *Reserved.*

c) [8:127.20] **Applicable in administrative proceedings:** The same "*Pitchess* motion" procedure is available before the hearing officer in most administrative proceedings. "[T]he Legislature, by expressly allowing *Pitchess* motions to be filed with an appropriate administrative body under Evidence Code section 1043, contemplated administrative *Pitchess* motions from the very beginning of the scheme." [*Riverside County Sheriff's Dept. v. Stiglitz* (2014) 60 C4th 624, 647, 181 CR3d 1, 20—*Pitchess* motion procedure applicable where personnel files sought on administrative appeal from discipline of correctional officer]

Limitation—"per se" driver's license suspension: The "*Pitchess* motion" procedure for discovery of peace officer personnel records is not available in a DMV "per se" hearing involving a driver's license suspension. [*Brown v. Valverde* (2010) 183 CA4th 1531, 1552, 108 CR3d 429, 444; see also *Riverside County Sheriff's Dept. v. Stiglitz*, supra, 60 C4th at 641, 181 CR3d at 14—"precedential value of *Brown* is limited to its facts involving a driver's license suspension"]

3) [8:128] **Order for disclosure of "relevant" records:** After personally examining the records in camera, the trial court shall order disclosure of peace officer personnel records that are "relevant to the subject matter involved in the pending litigation." [Ev.C. §1045(a); *People v. Mooc*, supra, 26 C4th at 1226, 114 CR2d at 491]

a) [8:128.1] **Compare—information available from other agency records:** When the litigation involves the employing *agency's* "policies or pattern of conduct," the court must consider whether the information sought may be obtained from other agency records, to avoid the need for disclosure of individual personnel records. [Ev.C. §1045(c)]

b) [8:128.2] **Mandatory order limiting use to present case:** Even when no protective order is sought, if disclosure is ordered, the court must also order that the disclosed information may not be used "for any purpose other than a court proceeding pursuant to applicable law." [CCP §1045(e); see *Alford v. Sup.Ct. (People)* (2003) 29 C4th 1033, 1039-1040, 130 CR2d 672, 677]

c) [8:128.3] **Protective order:** In addition, the court may, on motion by the officer or employing agency showing "good cause," issue a protective order to protect the agency or officer from "unnecessary annoyance, embarrassment or oppression." [Ev.C. §1045(d)]

[8:128.4-128.7] *Reserved.*

4) [8:128.8] **Limited initial disclosure in excessive force cases:** Some cases hold the *initial* disclosure of complaints in excessive force cases should consist only of the name and address of the complainant. [See *Alvarez v. Sup.Ct. (People)* (2004) 117 CA4th 1107, 1112, 12 CR3d 252, 255-256]

If the complainant refuses to speak to counsel, is unavailable or cannot remember the incident, the trial court is *required* to order disclosure of the complainant's statement contained in the peace officer personnel records. [*Alvarez v. Sup.Ct. (People)*, supra, 117 CA4th at 1113, 12 CR3d at 256]

a) [8:128.9] *Compare:* One case holds the trial judge has *discretion* to order disclosure of a report containing a complainant's allegations when directly relevant to the issues at hand *without* first only directing revelation of witnesses' names and addresses. [*Haggerty v. Sup.Ct. (Guindazola)* (2004) 117 CA4th 1079, 1090-1091, 12 CR3d 467, 476-477]

5) [8:128.10] **Limitations on disclosure:** The court may *not* order disclosure of:

— complaints against the officer for conduct occurring *more than five years* before the event or transaction that is the subject of the litigation; [Ev.C. §1045(b)(1); see *City of Los Angeles v. Sup.Ct. (Brandon)* (2002) 29 C4th 1, 12, 124 CR2d 202, 216; *Riske v. Sup.Ct. (City of Los Angeles)* (2018) 22 CA5th 295, 305-309, 231 CR3d 367, 374-377—only complaints, not all information related to complaints, are subject to 5-year ban, so documents that simply related to older complaints were discoverable]

© 2020 Thomson Reuters/The Rutter Group

— facts "so *remote* as to make disclosure of little or no practical benefit"; [Ev.C. §1045(b)(3)]

— personnel records of *officers not present* at the time of the arrest (or conduct alleged to have occurred within a jail) or who have had no contact with the party seeking disclosure; [Ev.C. §1047]

— records *protected by the official information privilege* (disclosure against public interest because need for preserving confidentiality outweighs need for disclosure in interest of justice; *see ¶8:125.1*); [Ev.C. §1040(b)(2); see *Davis v. City of Sacramento* (1994) 24 CA4th 393, 401, 29 CR2d 232, 235]

— an officer's *opinions* concerning an investigation. [*Haggerty v. Sup.Ct. (Guindazola)*, supra, 117 CA4th at 1088-1089, 12 CR3d at 474]

(3) [8:129] **Trade secrets:** The owner of a trade secret has a privilege to prevent disclosure *if* allowance of the privilege "will not tend to conceal fraud or otherwise work injustice." [Ev.C. §1060]

Thus, unlike other privileges where protection is absolute, the court *has* power to order disclosure of a trade secret if necessary to prevent fraud or injustice. [*Bridgestone/Firestone, Inc. v. Sup.Ct. (Rios)* (1992) 7 CA4th 1384, 1390, 9 CR2d 709, 712]

An *injunction* prohibiting disclosure of a trade secret must be evaluated under First Amendment (free speech) standards. The injunction may be upheld only if it is "content neutral" (without reference to the content of regulated speech) and imposes no greater burden on speech than necessary to serve "significant governmental interests embodied in the trade secret law." [*DVD Copy Control Ass'n, Inc. v. Bunner* (2003) 31 C4th 864, 879, 4 CR3d 69, 83]

(a) [8:129.1] **Burdens on parties**

- The party claiming the privilege has the burden of establishing its existence (i.e., that the information involved is a "trade secret" and the party is its owner).
- Thereafter, the party seeking discovery must make a *prima facie* showing that the information is "relevant and necessary to proof of, or defense against, a material element of a cause of action" and that it is essential to a fair resolution of the lawsuit.
- At this point, the trade secret claimant must demonstrate any claimed disadvantages of a protective order.

  He or she ultimately must demonstrate why an alternative to disclosure "will not be unduly burdensome to the opposing side and . . . will maintain the same fair balance in the litigation that would have been achieved by disclosure." [*Bridgestone/Firestone, Inc. v. Sup.Ct. (Rios)*, supra, 7 CA4th at 1393, 9 CR2d at 714—disclosure order reversed because no showing information *necessary* to prove moving party's case; *Citizens of Humanity, LLC v. Costco Wholesale Corp.* (2009) 171 CA4th 1, 14, 89 CR3d 455, 466 (disapproved on other grounds by *Kwikset Corp. v. Sup.Ct. (Benson)* (2011) 51 C4th 310, 337, 120 CR3d 741, 763) (same))]

(4) [8:130] **Self-incrimination:** Any party or *witness* in a discovery proceeding may claim the Fifth Amendment privilege against disclosure of information that might tend to incriminate him or her under either federal or state law. [*Zonver v. Sup.Ct. (Zonver)* (1969) 270 CA2d 613, 620-621, 76 CR 10, 14-15; *Warford v. Medeiros* (1984) 160 CA3d 1035, 1043, 207 CR 94, 99—nonparty witness]

It also protects against incrimination under *foreign law* if the foreign country recognizes a similar privilege. [*Klein v. Sup.Ct. (Thomas)* (1988) 198 CA3d 894, 903-905, 244 CR 226, 230-232—privilege against incrimination under Swiss law]

(a) [8:131] **"Testimonial compulsion":** The privilege extends to compelled testimony in whatever form. Thus, it may properly be invoked in response to deposition questions or to interrogatories. [See *Marriage of Hoffmeister ("Hoffmeister I")* (1984) 161 CA3d 1163, 1171, 208 CR 345, 350]

(b) [8:132] **Document production:** However, the Fifth Amendment privilege rarely extends to documents or records *voluntarily* prepared (no "testimonial compulsion"), even if the contents are incriminatory—e.g., *business records* of a sole proprietor showing illegal transactions. [See *United States v. Doe* (1984) 465 US 605, 610, 104 S.Ct. 1237, 1241]

Yet, the privilege may apply where *production* of the documents would *itself* be "testimonial" and incriminatory—e.g., where by producing the documents sought, a party would effectively admit their existence and *authenticate* them as his or hers, thus supplying a link in the chain of evidence needed for prosecution. [*United States v. Doe*, supra, 465 US at 612, 104 S.Ct. at 1242]

1) [8:132.1] **Corporations vs. sole proprietors:** Although a sole proprietor may be able to claim the privilege (where the document production is "testimonial"), a corporation *cannot* because a corporation has no Fifth Amendment privilege. [*Braswell v. United States* (1988) 487 US 99, 104, 108 S.Ct. 2284, 2288]

© 2020 Thomson Reuters/The Rutter Group

Further, the custodians (officers, directors or shareholders) of corporate records hold them only in a *representative* capacity and may be compelled to produce them even if the records will *personally incriminate* such custodians. Because the custodian acts as a representative, the production is deemed *by the corporation*; hence, no Fifth Amendment claim lies. [*Braswell v. United States*, supra, 487 US at 109-110, 108 S.Ct. at 2291]

2) [8:132.2] **Records required by law:** There is no Fifth Amendment protection for *records required by law to be kept* when sought by a regulatory agency responsible for enforcing that law. (E.g., Lab.C. §1174 requires employers to maintain wage and hour records for inspection by Labor Commission.) Rationale: The state's need to verify compliance with valid police power regulations *outweighs* concerns re implicating the records-keeper in criminal conduct. [*Craib v. Bulmash* (1989) 49 C3d 475, 489, 261 CR 686, 696]

[8:132.3] **Effect:** State agencies can enforce their regulations by criminal prosecutions based wholly on compelled self-incrimination.

(c) [8:133] **Effect of claiming privilege:** No "punishment" can be imposed against a party or witness for claiming the privilege against self-incrimination. But, at the same time, a *party* is not permitted to take advantage of his or her adversary by invoking the Fifth Amendment; i.e., the party "may be required either to waive the privilege or accept the civil consequences of silence if he or she does exercise it." [*Blackburn v. Sup.Ct. (Kelso)* (1993) 21 CA4th 414, 425-426, 27 CR2d 204, 209; *see* ¶*8:110d*]

In any case, a blanket claim of "self-incrimination" is insufficient. The court must have the opportunity to determine *whether specific questions* pose a threat of self-incrimination. [*Fuller v. Sup.Ct. (IPC Int'l Corp.)* (2001) 87 CA4th 299, 305, 104 CR2d 525, 530]

1) [8:134] **Plaintiff claiming privilege risks dismissal:** Commencing a lawsuit *waives* the privilege as to factual issues tendered by the complaint. ("Plaintiff cannot have his cake and eat it too.") A plaintiff who persists in refusal to answer *risks dismissal* of the lawsuit. [*Fremont Indemnity Co. v. Sup.Ct. (Sharif)* (1982) 137 CA3d 554, 557, 187 CR 137, 138-139—P sued to collect fire insurance proceeds on his restaurant, but refused to answer discovery requests because under indictment for arson of the restaurant; *see* ¶*8:204*]

[8:134.1] Alternatively, lesser sanctions may be imposed: e.g., P may be barred from introducing evidence at trial on issues relating to discovery questions he or she refused to answer. [*Dwyer v. Crocker Nat'l Bank* (1987) 194 CA3d 1418, 1432-1433, 240 CR 297, 305]

[8:134.2] A court has *discretion* to stay the proceedings until the criminal prosecution against P terminates (or the statute runs). But a stay is properly *denied* where it would prejudice the opposing party—e.g., by creating a risk that cross-actions against P would be subject to dismissal for failure to bring them to trial within 5 years. [See *Dwyer v. Crocker Nat'l Bank*, supra, 194 CA3d at 1432, 240 CR at 304; see also *Fisher v. Gibson* (2001) 90 CA4th 275, 284, 109 CR2d 145, 151—threat of criminal prosecution does not itself mandate continuance of summary adjudication motion]

2) [8:135] **Defendant claiming privilege risks being barred from testifying at trial:** A defendant claiming the privilege against self-incrimination to avoid discovery risks the court excluding his or her testimony as to such matters at time of trial. [See *Marriage of Hoffmeister ("Hoffmeister I")* (1984) 161 CA3d 1163, 1169, 208 CR 345, 348]

Alternatively, plaintiff may seek a *protective order* prior to trial to bar defendant from testifying to such matters when the case comes to trial. [*Pacers, Inc. v. Sup.Ct. (Needham)* (1984) 162 CA3d 686, 688-689, 208 CR 743, 745]

However, preclusion of testimony is only one tool available to the trial court in fashioning a fair resolution for the competing interests involved (including plaintiff's interests). [*Fuller v. Sup.Ct. (IPC Int'l Corp.)* (2001) 87 CA4th 299, 307-308, 104 CR2d 525, 531-532]

a) [8:135.1] **Court may grant immunity:** To facilitate discovery, the court may grant the defendants immunity against use of their deposition answers or evidence derived from these answers in any criminal prosecution. [*Fuller v. Sup.Ct. (IPC Int'l Corp.)*, supra, 87 CA4th at 308-310, 104 CR2d at 532-533; see also *People v. Sup.Ct. (Kaufman)* (1974) 12 C3d 421, 428-429, 115 CR 812, 817—court in consumer fraud action could compel deposition after granting deponent immunity against criminal prosecution based on use of information disclosed in deposition or facts derived therefrom]

b) [8:136] **Court may stay discovery until criminal prosecution barred:** Alternatively, the court may stay discovery until disposition of any pending criminal proceedings or until the statute of limitations has run on criminal prosecution, so that defendant can no longer claim a Fifth Amendment privilege. [*Pacers, Inc. v. Sup.Ct. (Needham),* supra, 162 CA3d at 689, 208 CR at 745-746—depositions postponed for one year, at which time criminal prosecution would be barred]

Such a stay is *discretionary;* defendant has *no right* to a blanket stay on Fifth Amendment grounds. [*Klein v. Sup.Ct. (Thomas)* (1988) 198 CA3d 894, 905, 224 CR 226, 232; see *Avant! Corp. v. Sup.Ct. (Nequist)* (2000) 79 CA4th 876, 885, 94 CR2d 505, 510-511 (enumerating various factors to be considered)]

And a stay is not favored where the statute of limitations on criminal prosecution has years to run. [*Fuller v. Sup.Ct. (IPC Int'l Corp.),* supra, 87 CA4th at 309, 104 CR2d at 533]

[8:136.1-136.4] *Reserved.*

1/ [8:136.5] **Corporations not entitled to discovery stay:** A corporation has no Fifth Amendment rights and therefore is not entitled to a stay of discovery. [*Avant! Corp. v. Sup.Ct. (Nequist),* supra, 79 CA4th at 886-887, 94 CR2d at 511-512]

2/ [8:136.6] **Compare—corporate employees:** But if *individual employees* are joined as a defendants and assert Fifth Amendment rights, they may seek such a stay. [See *Fuller v. Sup.Ct. (IPC Int'l Corp.),* supra, 87 CA4th at 309, 104 CR2d at 533]

[8:136.7-136.9] *Reserved.*

c) [8:136.10] **Court may impose pretrial deadline for waiver of privilege:** To avoid a party testifying at trial on matters as to which it had previously asserted the privilege, the court may impose a pretrial deadline for any waiver of the privilege. The deadline should allow sufficient time for the opposing party to conduct depositions and other necessary discovery. [See *Fuller v. Sup.Ct. (IPC Int'l Corp.),* supra, 87 CA4th at 310, 104 CR2d at 533]

Even if the party waives the privilege, the court cannot impose evidentiary restrictions on the party's testimony without a prior motion to compel discovery or motion in limine by the opposing party. [See *People ex rel. City of Dana Point v. Holistic Health* (2013) 213 CA4th 1016, 1030-1032, 153 CR3d 810, 820-822 (summary judgment motion)]

(d) **Procedure on claiming self-incrimination**

1) [8:137] **Specific objection required:** The party or witness must assert the privilege as to *particular questions* asked or other evidence sought. A blanket refusal to appear or testify is *not* sufficient. [*Warford v. Medeiros* (1984) 160 CA3d 1035, 1045, 207 CR 94, 101]

Blanket objections, including repeating the same boilerplate objection, are insufficient. [*Siry Investment, L.P. v. Farkhondehpour* (2020) 45 CA5th 1098, 1125, 259 CR3d 466, 486-487]

Further, the objecting party must establish that "injurious disclosure could result" by showing a nexus between the information requested and the risk of criminal prosecution. [*Siry Investment, L.P. v. Farkhondehpour*, supra, 45 CA5th at 1125-1126, 259 CR3d at 487 (internal quotes omitted)]

2) [8:138] **Waived if not timely raised:** Delay or failure to assert the privilege may result in waiver. [CCP §2030.290(a)—interrogatories; CCP §2033.280(a)—requests for admission; CCP §2025.460(a)—depositions; CCP §2031.300(a)—inspection demands; and see *Brown v. Sup.Ct. (Boorstin)* (1986) 180 CA3d 701, 712, 226 CR 10, 16]

3) [8:139] **Burden on motion to compel:** If the discovering party moves to compel answers, the burden is on the party or witness to show that the testimony or other evidence could tend to incriminate him or her. [*Warford v. Medeiros*, supra, 160 CA3d at 1045, 207 CR at 101; *Marriage of Sachs* (2002) 95 CA4th 1144, 1151-1152, 116 CR2d 273, 280 (citing text)]

4) [8:140] **Court must make findings:** The court must make a "particularized inquiry" as to whether the claimant has met such burden with respect to each claim of privilege. It may be required to conduct "in camera" hearings (outside the jury's presence) to assist such inquiry. It must make findings on the record as to whether the privilege claim is valid as to each question or document. [*Warford v. Medeiros*, supra, 160 CA3d at 1045, 207 CR at 101]

© 2020 Thomson Reuters/The Rutter Group

(e) [8:141] **No privilege if immunity granted:** The privilege against self-incrimination cannot be claimed if the party or witness is granted immunity against criminal prosecution based on *use* of the information disclosed. ("Use immunity" is sufficient. The witness or party can still be prosecuted on the basis of information obtained from *other* sources.) [*People v. Sup.Ct. (Kaufman)* (1974) 12 C3d 421, 428-429, 115 CR 812, 816-817]

[8:141.1] ***PRACTICE POINTER:*** If the client's conduct violates both state and federal criminal laws, *federal* "use immunity" will also have to be obtained.

1) [8:142] **Example:** In a civil proceeding brought by the county to establish paternity and compel child support payable to the county (Fam.C. §17402), the alleged father can claim the Fifth Amendment privilege as to questions re sex with the child's mother and his financial ability to pay. Such information could be used to prosecute him criminally for failure to provide support (Pen.C. §270). But, once the court grants immunity against such prosecution, the information becomes discoverable in the civil proceeding. [*Gonzales v. Sup.Ct. (County of Orange)* (1980) 117 CA3d 57, 69-70, 178 CR 358, 364-365]

2) [8:143] **Procedure to obtain immunity:** The grant of immunity is authorized by *protective order* (limiting use of evidence obtained through discovery). Therefore, the party seeking immunity should file a motion for protective order.

A noticed motion is required (no ex parte orders). The moving papers must show:

— defendant is being compelled to testify;

— the possibility of criminal prosecution is *actual* rather than speculative;

— the substance of each question is such that answering it could be incriminating; and

— notice has been given to the prosecuting authority (*see* ¶*8:144*). [*Blackburn v. Sup.Ct. (Kelso)* (1993) 21 CA4th 414, 425, 27 CR2d 204, 209]

a) [8:144] **Notice required to prosecutor:** In addition to notice to all parties to the action, notice must be given to the appropriate prosecuting authority that a grant of immunity is being sought. [*Daly v. Sup.Ct. (Duncan)* (1977) 19 C3d 132, 148, 137 CR 14, 24]

The notice must be sufficient to enable the prosecuting agency to *make an informed judgment on whether to object* to the immunity request. It must disclose the subject matter of the questions to which immunity is sought; and if it appears the statute of limitations has run on the crime, why the defendant still needs to be immunized. [*Blackburn v. Sup.Ct. (Kelso)*, supra, 21 CA4th at 432, 27 CR2d at 213—D must disclose why he or she believes statute of limitations may be tolled]

b) [8:145] **Prosecutor's objection bars grant of immunity:** If the prosecutor objects (by declaration that the proposed immunity might unduly hamper prosecution of a criminal proceeding), immunity *must* be denied. There is an irrebuttable presumption that the prosecutor's objection is not groundless. [*Philibosian v. Sup.Ct. (Coalition Against Police Abuse)* (1983) 149 CA3d 938, 941, 197 CR 208, 210]

(5) [8:146] **Attorney-client privilege:** Communications between client and counsel are presumed to have been made in confidence and are broadly privileged against discovery. This promotes effective pretrial preparation by encouraging full disclosure between attorney and client. It makes no difference that the communications relate to "factual information" as opposed to "legal advice." [*Mitchell v. Sup.Ct. (Shell Oil Co.)* (1984) 37 C3d 591, 601, 208 CR 886, 891—client could not be questioned about facts she said she learned from her attorney; see *Costco Wholesale Corp. v. Sup.Ct. (Randall)* (2009) 47 C4th 725, 734, 101 CR3d 758, 764—attorney's confidential communication to client protected even if it includes unprivileged material (recitation of witness statements); *DP Pham, LLC v. Cheadle* (2016) 246 CA4th 653, 665, 200 CR3d 937, 946]

"[T]he privilege applies not only to communications made in anticipation of litigation, but also to legal advice when no litigation is threatened." [*Roberts v. City of Palmdale* (1993) 5 C4th 363, 371, 20 CR2d 330, 334—governmental entity may claim privilege]

The privilege applies in *any proceeding in which testimony may be compelled*, thus including administrative as well as judicial proceedings. [*Southern Calif. Gas Co. v. Public Utilities Comm'n* (1990) 50 C3d 31, 38, 265 CR 801, 804]

The privilege is not limited to parties. A *nonparty* may assert the attorney-client privilege in response to a discovery request (no need to intervene and become a party to the action to assert privilege). [*Mylan Laboratories Inc. v. Soon-Shiong* (1999) 76 CA4th 71, 80, 90 CR2d 111, 117]

© 2020 Thomson Reuters/The Rutter Group

Cross-refer: The attorney-client privilege is discussed in detail in Wegner, Fairbank, Epstein & Chernow, *Cal. Prac. Guide: Civil Trials & Evidence* (TRG), Ch. 8E.

(a) [8:146.1] **Confidential communication:** The privilege applies to confidential communications between lawyer and client as well as to legal opinions formed by counsel even if the opinions have not been transmitted to the client. Accordingly, confidential communications between attorneys within a law firm on a client's behalf (or presumably between attorneys of different firms on the same client's behalf) are covered by the attorney-client privilege. [*Fireman's Fund Ins. Co. v. Sup.Ct. (Front Gate Plaza, LLC)* (2011) 196 CA4th 1263, 1273-1274, 127 CR3d 768, 776—it is an "everyday reality that attorneys, working together and practicing law in a professional association, share each other's, and their clients', confidential information" (internal quotes omitted)]

There is no protection, however, for conversations in the presence of others whose presence was not essential to further the client's interests. [Ev.C. §952]

1) [8:146.2] **Electronic communications:** A privileged communication does not lose its confidential character solely because it is communicated "by electronic means" (e.g., email, cellular telephone, etc.); or because persons involved in the delivery, facilitation or storage of the electronic transmission system have access to the communication. [Ev.C. §917(b)]

2) [8:146.3] **Compare—using employer's computer:** There is no privilege, however, for a client's emails to his or her attorney using an employer's computer, which the client knew was to be used *exclusively for business purposes* and that his or her communications might be monitored by the employer. Under such circumstances, the client's emails could not be considered a "confidential communication between client and lawyer." [*Holmes v. Petrovich Develop. Co., LLC* (2011) 191 CA4th 1047, 1051, 119 CR3d 878, 882]

3) [8:146.4] **Attorney's communications with nonattorney agents:** The attorney-client privilege extends to an attorney's confidential communication with a nonattorney agent retained by the attorney to assist with the representation. [See Ev.C. §952; *Fireman's Fund Ins. Co. v. Sup.Ct. (Front Gate Plaza, LLC)* (2011) 196 CA4th 1263, 1274, 127 CR3d 768, 776—such agents fall into the category of "those to whom disclosure is reasonably necessary for the transmission of the information or the accomplishment

of the purpose for which the lawyer is consulted" (internal quotes omitted)]

But the privilege does not extend to communications among attorney, client and public relations personnel not needed to facilitate attorney communication to client, nor to litigate the case. [*Behunin v. Sup.Ct. (Charles R. Schwab)* (2017) 9 CA5th 833, 849, 215 CR3d 475, 487-488]

4) [8:146.5] **Attorney hired by insurer:** Counsel retained by an insurer to defend an insured or to prosecute the insured's claims has an attorney-client relationship with *both the insurer and the insured*, and both are holders of the privilege. Communications between counsel and *either* the insurer or insured are privileged. [*Bank of America, N.A. v. Sup.Ct. (Pacific City Bank)* (2013) 212 CA4th 1076, 1083, 1093-1096, 151 CR3d 526, 531, 539-541]

[8:146.6-146.9] *Reserved.*

5) [8:146.10] **Compare—disclosure to attorney-litigant's counsel:** An attorney-litigant in a wrongful termination action against her former law firm was entitled to disclose to her counsel confidential and arguably privileged communications between the attorney and her former clients (nonparties) in order to assess how to litigate the case. This limited disclosure furthers the attorney-client privilege because it allows counsel to evaluate whether the information is privileged and if so, how to protect it. [*Chubb & Son v. Sup.Ct. (Lemmon)* (2014) 228 CA4th 1094, 1109-1110, 1116, 176 CR3d 389, 400-402, 406; see also *Fox Searchlight Pictures, Inc. v. Paladino* (2001) 89 CA4th 294, 308, 106 CR2d 906, 918—in-house counsel could disclose former employer's confidential and privileged information to her attorney in wrongful discharge case]

[8:146.11-146.14] *Reserved.*

6) [8:146.15] **Compare—attorney fee bills:** Whether an attorney's fee bill is protected by the attorney-client privilege depends on whether the information in the billing invoice is conveyed "for the purpose of legal representation." [*Los Angeles County Bd. of Supervisors v. Sup.Ct. (ACLU of Southern Calif.)* (2016) 2 C5th 282, 297, 212 CR3d 107, 117—attorney-client privilege does not categorically shield entire billing invoice from disclosure under Calif. Public Records Act, Gov.C. §6254(k) (*see* ¶*8:1805.18 ff.*)]

For example, information in the billing invoice that informs the client of the amount or nature of work

© 2020 Thomson Reuters/The Rutter Group

in connection with a pending or active issue "lies in the heartland of the attorney-client privilege," whereas a cumulative fee total for a matter that concluded long ago and does not reflect the substance of the legal consultation would likely not be protected. [*Los Angeles County Bd. of Supervisors v. Sup.Ct. (ACLU of Southern Calif.)*, supra, 2 C5th at 297-298, 212 CR3d at 117]

(b) [8:147] **Client communications with attorney's agents:** Information disclosed to an agent of the attorney for transmission to the attorney is also privileged. [See Ev.C. §952]

1) [8:148] **Includes expert consultant employed to examine client:** An expert (e.g., physician) employed by the attorney to examine the client and evaluate the client's condition (and not to provide treatment), may be treated as the attorney's "agent" for this purpose. Thus, any disclosures made by the client to the expert are protected as communications to an "agent" of the attorney. [*People v. Gurule* (2002) 28 C4th 557, 594, 123 CR2d 345, 375-376]

The expert's reports to the attorney regarding the client's condition are protected as communications on behalf of the client. Such reports *enable the client to interpret and communicate* the client's condition to the attorney. [*City & County of San Francisco v. Sup.Ct.* (1951) 37 C2d 227, 238, 231 P2d 26, 31-32]

- [8:148.1] The fact that the client put his or her mental or physical condition in issue in the litigation is immaterial. I.e., there is *no* "client litigant" exception to the attorney-client privilege (as there is with the doctor-patient privilege). [*City & County of San Francisco v. Sup.Ct.*, supra, 37 C2d at 237-238, 231 P2d at 31-32]

2) [8:149] **Effect of designating expert as trial witness:** However, if the expert is later designated under CCP §2034.010 et seq. to testify as an expert witness at trial (*see ¶8:1624 ff.*), the attorney-client privilege is *waived* and *earlier reports* from that expert become discoverable: "[T]he confidential nature of the communication is gone once it is determined that the expert is to be a witness—the client having impliedly, if not actually, consented to the disclosure of the information given to the attorney by way of the expert." [*National Steel Products Co. v. Sup.Ct. (Rosen)* (1985) 164 CA3d 476, 484, 210 CR 535, 539]

[8:150] *Reserved.*

(c) [8:150.1] **Attorney communications with client's agents:** Attorney communications with agents and employees of a client (e.g., a corporate client) are likewise protected by the attorney-client privilege. The attorney is free both to *give* and *receive* information from the client's agents.

The agent need *not* be a member of the client's "control group" (e.g., a managing officer or director) . . . because such limitation on the privilege "would largely destroy the ability of corporate counsel to freely communicate." [See *Upjohn Co. v. United States* (1981) 449 US 383, 391-393, 101 S.Ct. 677, 683-684; *Continental Ins. Co. v. Sup.Ct. (Commercial Bldg. Maint.)* (1995) 32 CA4th 94, 114, 37 CR2d 843, 855]

The privilege extends to lower level persons *who reasonably need to know of the communication* in order to act for the organization, even if they had no direct contact with the lawyer. [*Zurich American Ins. Co. v. Sup.Ct. (Watts Indus., Inc.)* (2007) 155 CA4th 1485, 1499-1500, 66 CR3d 833, 842-843]

(d) [8:151] **Report to third party for transmission to attorney:** The attorney-client privilege may apply where the dominant purpose of a witness' report to a third party, such as an insurer or employer, is the eventual transmission of the report to an attorney.

[8:151.1-151.4] *Reserved.*

1) [8:151.5] **Reports to insurers:** An accident report by insureds to their insurers may be protected by the attorney-client privilege if the insurer is obligated to defend the insured. It does not matter that the attorney has not yet been retained as long as the communication was intended to help whichever attorney the insurer ultimately hires to handle the defense. [See *Travelers Ins. Cos. v. Sup.Ct. (Becknell)* (1983) 143 CA3d 436, 448-450, 191 CR 871, 879-880]

It is immaterial that no lawsuit has yet been filed; it is sufficient that litigation is a "threat on the horizon." [*Soltani-Rastegar v. Sup.Ct. (Brinzo)* (1989) 208 CA3d 424, 427, 256 CR 255, 257]

2) [8:151.6] **Reports to employers:** Where an employer requires employees to prepare a report with the dominant purpose of eventual transmission to the employer's lawyers, the attorney-client privilege may protect the report from disclosure to opposing parties. [*Scripps Health v. Sup.Ct. (Reynolds)* (2003) 109 CA4th 529, 534, 135 CR2d 126, 129—confidential "occurrence report" prepared by hospital employees

© 2020 Thomson Reuters/The Rutter Group

in anticipation of litigation protected by attorney-client privilege]

(e) [8:152] **"Crime-fraud" exception:** There is no attorney-client privilege where a lawyer's services are sought "to enable or aid" anyone to commit or plan to commit a crime or fraud. [Ev.C. §956]

1) [8:152.1] **"Fraud":** The *attempt* to defraud is all that need be shown to avoid the privilege. I.e., the other party *need not have been deceived:* "[B]ecause section 956 applies where an attorney's services are sought *to enable* a party to plan to commit a fraud," the party seeking discovery need not show justifiable reliance or damages. [*BP Alaska Exploration, Inc. v. Sup.Ct. (Nahama)* (1988) 199 CA3d 1240, 1263, 245 CR 682, 697 (emphasis added)]

2) [8:152.2] **Misrepresentations to dissuade suit:** The "crime-fraud" exception applies where, after consulting with an attorney, clients misrepresent facts to an opposing party in an attempt to dissuade suit. [*BP Alaska Exploration, Inc. v. Sup.Ct. (Nahama)*, supra, 199 CA3d at 1263, 245 CR at 697]

a) [8:152.3] **Example:** TP threatened to sue Client. Client consulted with Attorney and then sought to deter TP from suing by misrepresenting certain facts. TP was not misled and sued anyhow. Client's consultation with Attorney was discoverable: "*[I]t is entirely possible that [Client] could have planned to commit a fraud when it investigated and sought legal advice* from its attorneys . . . *If this is shown,* then [Client] has forfeited the benefits of the attorney-client privilege for discovery purposes even though [TP] has not shown at this stage of the proceedings that it relied on and suffered damages from the misrepresentations . . ." [*BP Alaska Exploration, Inc. v. Sup.Ct. (Nahama)*, supra, 199 CA3d at 1263, 245 CR at 697 (emphasis added)]

3) [8:153] **Fraud on court:** An attempted fraud on the court (e.g., giving knowingly false testimony) may be sufficient to invoke the crime-fraud exception to the attorney-client privilege. [*State Farm Fire & Cas. Co. v. Sup.Ct. (Taylor)* (1997) 54 CA4th 625, 648-649, 62 CR2d 834, 850]

- [8:153.1] Defendant's former employee, who coordinated its litigation strategy with outside counsel, gave a declaration stating her supervisors instructed her to conceal the truth at her deposition, to cover up forgeries and to withhold relevant documents in response to document demands. This evidence justified disclosure of communications otherwise protected by the attorney-client privilege. [*State Farm Fire & Cas. Co. v. Sup.Ct. (Taylor),* supra, 54 CA4th at 648-649, 62 CR2d at 850]

4) [8:154] **Proof required to defeat privilege:** Most courts require the party claiming the crime-fraud exception to provide "a factual basis *adequate to support a good faith belief* by a reasonable person" that a crime or fraud has been committed or that there was a plan to do so. [See *United States v. Zolin* (1989) 491 US 554, 572, 109 S.Ct. 2619, 2631 (emphasis added)]

[8:155] *Reserved.*

a) [8:156] **"Independent" evidence required?** Usually, the only way of proving the attorney and client were planning a crime or fraud is by testimony of persons who were present or had access to the attorney-client communications (typically, a disaffected employee or associate).

The California rule is unclear, but federal law *allows* such testimony (if the communication to such persons was not itself privileged) to prove the crime-fraud exception. I.e., the evidence need *not* be "independent" of the attorney-client communications. [*United States v. Zolin* (1989) 491 US 554, 574, 109 S.Ct. 2619, 2632—dissident church member obtained tapes of conversations between church officials and their attorney]

5) [8:156.1] **Procedure in determining whether exception applies:** *See discussion at ¶8:191 ff.*

[8:156.2-156.4] *Reserved.*

(f) [8:156.5] **"Prevention of criminal act" exception:** No attorney-client privilege exists where the lawyer knows or reasonably should know disclosure of a confidential communication is necessary to prevent a criminal act that is likely to result in death or substantial bodily harm. [See Ev.C. §956.5; *People v. Dang* (2001) 93 CA4th 1293, 1296-1299, 113 CR2d 763, 766-767]

(g) [8:156.6] **Other exceptions:** Other important exceptions to the attorney-client privilege include:

— "joint client" exception (Ev.C. §962);
— "breach of duty" exception (e.g., in malpractice actions) (Ev.C. §958); [See *Anten v. Sup.Ct. (Weintraub Tobin Chediak Coleman Grodin, Law Corp.)* (2015) 233

CA4th 1254, 1259-1260, 183 CR3d 422, 425-426—in legal malpractice action brought by one of three former joint clients, nonsuing clients cannot assert attorney-client privilege to prevent discovery of otherwise privileged attorney-client communications made in course of former joint representation]

— "deceased client" exception (Ev.C. §§957 (claim through deceased client), 960 (re intent to transfer), 961 (re validity of transfer instrument)). [See *DP Pham, LLC v. Cheadle* (2016) 246 CA4th 653, 669-673, 200 CR3d 937, 949-952—exception limited to disputes between parties claiming *through* deceased client's estate (or information attesting witness could provide) and not applicable to competing purchasers of property with claims *against* estate]

Cross-refer: The attorney-client privilege is discussed in detail in Wegner, Fairbank, Epstein & Chernow, *Cal. Prac. Guide: Civil Trials & Evidence* (TRG), Ch. 8E.

(6) [8:156.7] **Lawyer referral service-client privilege:** California also recognizes a lawyer referral service-client privilege that is similar to (but not entirely identical with) the attorney-client privilege. [See Ev.C. §§912, 965-968]

[8:156.8] **Comment re interpretation:** With some exceptions (¶*8:156.20*), the lawyer referral service-client privilege is nearly identical to the attorney-client privilege. Courts can therefore be expected to rely on attorney-client privilege cases in interpreting the new privilege.

(a) [8:156.9] **Lawyer referral service:** To be covered by the privilege, a lawyer referral service must be "certified under, and operating in compliance with," Bus. & Prof.C. §6155. [Ev.C. §965(d)]

The privilege extends to an "enterprise" the client *reasonably believes to be* a lawyer referral service under Bus. & Prof.C. §6155. [Ev.C. §965(d)]

1) [8:156.10] **Comment re proof:** Since most lay clients will be unaware of the existence of Bus. & Prof.C. §6155, it is unclear what evidence will be necessary to enable the client to claim the privilege for communications with uncertified referral organizations.

2) [8:156.11] **Includes staff:** The privilege applies to "anyone employed by the lawyer referral service to render services" to clients. [Ev.C. §966(b)]

[8:156.12-156.14] *Reserved.*

(b) [8:156.15] **Confidential communication:** The definition of "confidential communication" is virtually identical to the definition for the attorney-client privilege (see Ev.C. §965(b); compare Ev.C. §952 (*discussed at ¶8:146.1 ff.*)). Unlike the attorney-client privilege definition, however, it does not expressly include "a legal opinion formed and the advice given" in the course of the relationship. [Ev.C. §952; compare Ev.C. §965(b)]

(c) [8:156.16] **Client:** The client is a person who contacts a lawyer referral service for the purpose of "retaining, or securing legal services or advice from, a lawyer in his or her professional capacity." There is no limitation as to whether the client intends to pay for the services or is seeking pro bono representation. As with the attorney-client privilege, the communication may be through an "authorized representative" or by a person lacking decision-making capacity or a conservator or guardian on that person's behalf. [Ev.C. §965(a)]

1) [8:156.17] **Entities as clients:** The client may be a partnership, corporation, limited liability company, association or other group or entity. [Ev.C. §966(b)]

(d) [8:156.18] **Crime-fraud exception:** The privilege is subject to a crime-fraud exception if the client seeks the services of the lawyer referral service "to enable or aid" anyone to commit or plan to commit a crime or fraud. [Ev.C. §968(a); *see discussion at ¶8:152 ff.*]

(e) [8:156.19] **"Prevention of criminal act" exception:** No privilege exists where a staff member of a lawyer referral service receives a confidential communication in processing a request for legal services and reasonably believes that disclosure of that communication is necessary to prevent a criminal act that is likely to result in death or serious bodily harm. [Ev.C. §968(b); *see discussion at ¶8:156.5*]

(f) [8:156.20] **Compare—attorney-client privilege subject to additional exceptions:** Several of the exceptions to the attorney-client privilege do *not* apply to the lawyer referral service-client privilege. [See Ev.C. §968; compare Ev.C. §§957-962; *and ¶8:156.6*]

(7) [8:157] **Spousal privileges:** Confidential marital communications are generally privileged (Ev.C. §980).

On the other hand, the privilege *not to testify* against a spouse (Ev.C. §970) does not apply in an action *by or against* either spouse for the "immediate benefit" of the other or for both of them (Ev.C. §973).

- [8:158] For example, in an action brought by Husband for personal injuries, Wife can be compelled to give deposition testimony. Husband's action is deemed brought for Wife's "immediate benefit," because his claim for personal injuries during marriage implicates community property interests. [*Hand v. Sup.Ct. (Boles)* (1982) 134 CA3d 436, 442, 184 CR 588, 591]

[8:159-170] *Reserved.*

(8) [8:171] **Medical board proceedings:** Subject to certain exceptions (*see ¶8:189 ff.*), the "proceedings" and "records" of hospital staff committees *responsible for evaluating care rendered* by staff physicians, etc. are not subject to discovery. Persons who attended such meetings cannot be compelled to testify as to what transpired. [Ev.C. §1157(a), (b); see *Pomona Valley Hosp. Med. Ctr. v. Sup.Ct. (Cabana)* (2012) 209 CA4th 687, 694, 147 CR3d 376, 380-381—§1157 applies to records of institutional review board despite inclusion on board of lay people not affiliated with hospital]

Likewise protected are proceedings and records of similar committees in local medical professional societies—e.g., county medical associations, dental associations, etc. (Ev.C. §1157(a)); in mental health departments (Ev.C. §1157.6); in nonprofit medical care foundations or professional standards review organizations (Ev.C. §1157.5); and in local governmental agencies monitoring certain health care services (see Ev.C. §1157.7).

Peer review bodies in various other health service facilities described in Bus. & Prof.C. §805 are similarly protected. [Ev.C. §1157(a); see *County of Los Angeles v. Sup.Ct. (Gavira)* (2006) 139 CA4th 8, 14, 42 CR3d 390, 395—quality assurance committee of county jail mental health services division was "peer review body" covered by statutory privilege]

Note: Ev.C. §1157 does not apply to *criminal* proceedings. [See Ev.C. §1157(e); *People v. Sup.Ct. (Memorial Med. Ctr.)* (1991) 234 CA3d 363, 375, 286 CR 478, 484]

Nor does it apply to *investigative subpoenas* issued by the State Medical Board; they are not "discovery" within the meaning of §1157. [*Arnett v. Dal Cielo* (1996) 14 C4th 4, 24, 56 CR2d 706, 719]

(a) [8:172] **Purpose of protection:** Allowing discovery would "stifle candor and inhibit objectivity" by hospital medical staff in evaluating patient care, which in turn could endanger the quality of in-hospital medical practice. [*Alexander v. Sup.Ct. (Saheb)* (1993) 5 C4th 1218, 1228, 23 CR2d 397, 402 (disapproved on other grounds by *Hassan v. Mercy American River Hosp.* (2003) 31 C4th 709, 3 CR3d 623); *Fox v. Kramer* (2000) 22 C4th 531, 539, 93 CR2d 497, 502-503]

1) [8:172.1] **Not limited to malpractice actions:** The quality of care rendered by a hospital includes *risks to employees* and visitors as well as to patients. Ev.C. §1157 thus bars discovery of medical board

"records" and "proceedings" in actions by hospital employees, as well as in malpractice actions by patients. [*Willits v. Sup.Ct. (Health Dimensions, Inc.)* (1993) 20 CA4th 90, 102, 24 CR2d 348, 355—nurse who became HIV positive after needle stick could not compel discovery of relevant medical staff reports]

(b) [8:173] **Bar to compelled disclosure:** By its terms, Ev.C. §1157 creates only a limitation against discovery *from medical staff committees.* It does *not* create a bar against introduction of evidence obtained from other sources (e.g., where medical committee records somehow come into plaintiff's hands). [*Alexander v. Sup.Ct. (Saheb),* supra, 5 C4th at 1223, 23 CR2d at 400, fn. 4]

"Literally, section 1157 establishes an immunity from discovery but not an evidentiary privilege in the sense that medical staff records are excluded from evidence." [*Fox v. Kramer* (2000) 22 C4th 531, 539, 93 CR2d 497, 502 (internal quotes omitted)]

1) [8:173.1] **No bar to discovery from other sources:** Nor does §1157 prevent plaintiff from discovering relevant information by deposing the defendant doctors, nurses, etc. or reviewing public records (e.g., to determine whether the doctor has suffered a malpractice judgment or disciplinary action). [*Alexander v. Sup.Ct. (Saheb),* supra, 5 C4th at 1223, 23 CR2d at 400, fn. 4]

[8:173.2-173.4] *Reserved.*

2) [8:173.5] **No bar to voluntary testimony:** A member of the hospital staff committee may testify *voluntarily* as to matters discussed at committee meetings. The statute only protects against compelled disclosure of such matters. [*West Covina Hosp. v. Sup.Ct. (Tyus)* (1986) 41 C3d 846, 851, 226 CR 132, 134]

a) [8:173.6] **Rationale:** One of the purposes of Ev.C. §1157 was to protect doctors who participate in such committees from the burdens of discovery and court appearances in malpractice actions against their peers. This purpose does not apply where a doctor is *willing* to testify. [*West Covina Hosp. v. Sup.Ct. (Tyus),* supra, 41 C3d at 852, 226 CR at 135]

b) [8:173.7] **Effect of agreement *not* to testify?** Physicians serving on peer review committees may be asked to agree in writing to maintain confidentiality and *not* to testify voluntarily. It is unclear whether such agreements to suppress testimony are enforceable.

© 2020 Thomson Reuters/The Rutter Group

c) [8:173.7a] **Compare—testimony re "remedial measures" barred by Ev.C. §1151:** Ev.C. §1151 excludes evidence of "remedial measures" to show negligence. Thus, in appropriate cases, even *voluntary* testimony by a participant in peer review proceedings about the hospital's taking remedial measures (e.g., suspending errant doctors, etc.), although admissible under §1157, could be excluded under §1151. [*Fox v. Kramer* (2000) 22 C4th 531, 545, 93 CR2d 497, 506, fn. 2]

But note: Medical peer review *investigations and reports* are *not* "remedial measures" within the meaning of Ev.C. §1151—even if such investigations and reports may later serve as the basis for disciplinary or other corrective action. [*Fox v. Kramer*, supra, 22 C4th at 543, 93 CR2d at 506]

3) [8:173.8] **Bar to compelled disclosure at any time:** The records protected from discovery by Ev.C. §1157 also cannot be subpoenaed. The statute's purpose of preserving confidentiality "would clearly be undermined if [plaintiff] could obtain through a trial subpoena the same evidence it was *prohibited* from obtaining through a pretrial discovery request . . . The Legislature could not have intended such an absurd result." [*Fox v. Kramer* (2000) 22 C4th 531, 542, 93 CR2d 497, 504-505 (emphasis in original)]

4) [8:173.9] **Bar to expert testimony based on protected records:** Malpractice plaintiffs cannot obtain the equivalent of discovery of the contents of hospital peer review records by offering testimony by an expert witness whose opinions are based on his or her review of those records in the course of his or her official duties for a public agency. [*Fox v. Kramer*, supra, 22 C4th at 541, 93 CR2d at 503—State Medical Board investigator, who reviewed records as part of official investigation, could not testify based thereon as to whether plaintiff had received proper care]

(c) [8:173.10] **Waiver of protection?** Ev.C. §1157 is *not* one of the privileges enumerated in Division 8 of the Evidence Code. Rather, it is one of the "extrinsic policies for exclusion of evidence" enumerated in Division 9 (Ev.C. §§1150-1159).

The distinction is important because the privilege *waiver* provisions (Ev.C. §912) *do not apply* to §1157's discovery exemption. [*University of Southern Calif. v. Sup.Ct. (Comeau)* (1996) 45 CA4th 1283, 1292, 53 CR2d 260, 266—leaving open what kind of waiver doctrine, if any, does apply]

1) [8:173.11] **Compliance with medical board subpoena not waiver:** Ev.C. §1157 protection is not waived by the hospital's turning its records over to the State Medical Board (Department of Health Services) because the hospital's cooperation is mandatory. [*Fox v. Kramer* (2000) 22 C4th 531, 540-541, 93 CR2d 497, 503-504]

Thus, even if the State Medical Board discloses the hospital's records to plaintiffs, there is *no waiver by the hospital* and the content remains inadmissible at trial. [*Fox v. Kramer*, supra, 22 C4th at 540, 93 CR2d at 503]

(d) [8:174] **Impact on claims against hospitals based on negligent selection or supervision of staff:** The prohibition on discovery of the proceedings and records of hospital staff committees frequently precludes actions against hospitals for negligent selection or retention of staff physicians. [See, e.g., *West Covina Hosp. v. Sup.Ct. (Tyus)* (1984) 153 CA3d 134, 136-138, 200 CR 162, 164]

(e) [8:175] **Which committees:** Hospital staff committees may be medical, medical-dental, psychological, marriage and family therapists, licensed clinical social workers, registered dietitians, podiatrists, even veterinarians. Committees of local professional societies include all of these plus chiropractors and dental hygienists. [See Ev.C. §1157(a)]

Also protected are records and proceedings of committees *established by private foundations* to review health care services; and *by governmental agencies* to oversee mental health care facilities and "specialty health care services" in acute hospitals. [See Ev.C. §§1157.5-1157.7]

1) [8:175.1] **Formalities not required:** No "committee" as such need be appointed. Nor need minutes be kept or other formalities observed. [*County of Los Angeles v. Sup.Ct. (Martinez)* (1990) 224 CA3d 1446, 1448, 274 CR 712, 714—weekly meetings of *all* physicians in Obstetrics Department held privileged where purpose was to improve patient care]

© 2020 Thomson Reuters/The Rutter Group

2) [8:175.2] **Committee may include nonphysicians:** The privilege is not affected by the fact that nonphysician members of the hospital staff (e.g., nursing supervisors, hospital administrators, technicians) participate in the "committee" meeting. [*County of Los Angeles v. Sup.Ct. (Martinez)*, supra, 224 CA3d at 1449, 274 CR at 714]

3) [8:176] **Responsibility delegated to other committees:** Hospital medical staffs often appoint committees to supervise particular operations within the hospital (e.g., pharmacy, laundry, dietary, infection control, etc.). Whether reports and proceedings of such committees are protected depends on whether they have "responsibility for evaluation and improvement of the quality of care rendered in the hospital." If so, they are immune from discovery under Ev.C. §1157, the same as a medical staff committee. [See *Santa Rosa Memorial Hosp. v. Sup.Ct. (Leary)* (1985) 174 CA3d 711, 715, 220 CR 236, 238]

[8:177-178] *Reserved.*

(f) [8:179] **Which "records" or "proceedings" protected:** By its terms, the statute protects only the "records" and "proceedings" of physician peer review committees. But these terms are *broadly* construed in order to limit external access to the medical peer review process. [*Alexander v. Sup.Ct. (Saheb)* (1993) 5 C4th 1218, 1224, 23 CR2d 397, 401, fn. 6 (disapproved on other grounds by *Hassan v. Mercy American River Hosp.* (2003) 31 C4th 709, 3 CR3d 623)]

Protection extends to documents submitted to a medical staff committee from outside sources (e.g., letters of reference or complaint) as well as to documents prepared by the committee. [*Alexander v. Sup.Ct. (Saheb)*, supra, 5 C4th at 1227-1228, 23 CR2d at 403]

1) [8:179.1] **Committee member identities protected:** In order not to discourage candid evaluations, the identities of the physicians serving on the peer review committee are protected. [*Cedars-Sinai Med. Ctr. v. Sup.Ct. (Schwartz)* (1993) 12 CA4th 579, 588, 16 CR2d 253, 258]

2) [8:179.2] **Product evaluations protected:** Proceedings to determine the safety or efficacy of any product (e.g., drugs) being used at the hospital are protected. [*Mt. Diablo Hosp. Dist. v. Sup.Ct. (Stella)* (1986) 183 CA3d 30, 34-35, 227 CR 790, 793-794]

3) [8:179.3] **Applications for staff privileges:** A physician's application (or reapplication) for staff privileges is privileged because the information provided

pertains to the investigative and evaluative functions of peer review committees. [*Alexander v. Sup.Ct. (Saheb)*, supra, 5 C4th at 1227, 23 CR2d at 402]

It is immaterial that the application is *generated by the physician* rather than the committee. Both are "records" of the committee within the meaning of Ev.C. §1157. [*Alexander v. Sup.Ct. (Saheb)*, supra, 5 C4th at 1227, 23 CR2d at 402]

[8:179.4] *Reserved.*

4) [8:179.5] **Compare—information placed in committee's file *not necessarily* protected:** Information developed by hospital administrators or others does not become privileged by being placed in a medical staff's committee files. I.e., a hospital administrator or other staff member cannot protect damaging information simply by disclosing to a medical staff committee. [*Santa Rosa Memorial Hosp. v. Sup.Ct. (Leary)* (1985) 174 CA3d 711, 724, 726-727, 220 CR 236, 245, 247]

(g) [8:180] **Matters *not* protected:** Matters that are not "records" or "proceedings" of a peer review committee are not protected from discovery under Ev.C. §1157.

1) [8:180.1] **Fact of evaluation not privileged:** A medical malpractice plaintiff is entitled to discover *whether* Hospital has evaluated the competency of a doctor on its staff (e.g., by investigating the doctor's application for staff privileges or later reviewing the doctor's performance). Indeed, Hospital might appear to be negligent if it never evaluated doctors on its staff.

Allowing such disclosure "stimulates the evaluation process without permitting penetration of the content of committee discussions" protected under Ev.C. §1157. [*Brown v. Sup.Ct. (West Hills Med. Ctr.)* (1985) 168 CA3d 489, 501, 214 CR 266, 274]

a) [8:180.2] **Compare:** However, the hospital need not disclose whether a *particular patient's records* have been reviewed by the committee evaluating the doctor. That disclosure might "itself be prejudicial and therefore inhibit the candor and objectivity of the committee discussion." [See *Santa Rosa Memorial Hosp. v. Sup.Ct. (Leary)*, supra, 174 CA3d at 729, 220 CR at 248]

[8:181] *Reserved.*

© 2020 Thomson Reuters/The Rutter Group

2) [8:182] **Hospital administrative records not protected:** Only the records of hospital staff committees responsible for evaluating medical care at the hospital are protected under Ev.C. §1157. Files of the *hospital administration* itself are not. [*Alexander v. Sup.Ct. (Saheb)* (1993) 5 C4th 1218, 1224, 23 CR2d 397, 400 (disapproved on other grounds by *Hassan v. Mercy American River Hosp.* (2003) 31 C4th 709, 3 CR3d 623); *Matchett v. Sup.Ct. (Petway)* (1974) 40 CA3d 623, 628, 115 CR 317, 319-320]

Nor can hospital administrators shield such records from discovery simply by turning them over to a medical staff committee (*see* ¶*8:179.5*).

a) [8:183] **Personnel action taken by hospital administration:** Nor is there any immunity from discovery for the "plain fact (as opposed to the underlying facts of the investigation and evaluation) of *denial, suspension or termination* of staff privileges," at least where such action was taken by the *hospital administration* rather than by a medical staff committee. [*Hinson v. Clairemont Comm. Hosp.* (1990) 218 CA3d 1110, 1128-1129, 267 CR 503, 514 (emphasis added) (disapproved on other grounds by *Alexander v. Sup.Ct. (Saheb)*, supra, 5 C4th at 1225, 23 CR2d at 401, which was disapproved on other grounds by *Hassan v. Mercy American River Hosp.* (2003) 31 C4th 709, 724, 3 CR3d 623, 633, fn. 4)]

(The result may be contra as to personnel files *maintained exclusively* by a peer review committee. See *Snell v. Sup.Ct. (Marshall Hosp.)* (1984) 158 CA3d 44, 48, 204 CR 200, 202).

1/ [8:184] **Possible privacy limitations:** Apart from Ev.C. §1157, there may be privacy limitations on disclosure of information in hospital personnel files (*see* ¶*8:308*).

For example, the court may refuse to order production of the personnel files of *all* persons on a hospital staff who rendered medical care—e.g., *nonparty* nurses, therapists, etc. The court has to balance the privacy interests of the nonparties before disclosure can be compelled. [*Saddleback Comm. Hosp. v. Sup.Ct. (Harvey By & Through Harvey)* (1984) 158 CA3d 206, 209, 204 CR 598, 600]

b) [8:185] **Compare—information generated by peer review committees protected:** On the other hand, hospital administrative records *are* privileged to the extent they contain *information resulting from investigations* of a medical review committee. [See *Brown v. Sup.Ct. (West Hills Med. Ctr.)* (1985) 168 CA3d 489, 495, 214 CR 266, 270]

1/ [8:186] **Burden on hospital:** The burden is on the hospital, as the party resisting discovery, to establish that the information falls within the class of material protected under Ev.C. §1157. [*Santa Rosa Memorial Hosp. v. Sup.Ct. (Leary)* (1985) 174 CA3d 711, 724, 726-727, 220 CR 236, 245, 247]

A positive showing must be made. It is *not* enough that the hospital's files "may include" materials generated by a medical review committee. [*Brown v. Sup.Ct. (West Hills Med. Ctr.)*, supra, 168 CA3d at 495, 214 CR at 270]

2/ [8:187] **Court must inspect before allowing discovery:** To prevent disclosure of privileged information, the trial court must conduct an *ex parte, in camera inspection* of hospital administrative records that are claimed to contain such information. [*Saddleback Comm. Hosp. v. Sup.Ct. (Harvey By & Through Harvey)* (1984) 158 CA3d 206, 209, 204 CR 598, 600]

c) [8:188] **Compare—communications to hospital privileged:** A separate privilege protects communications to a hospital or its medical staff for the purpose of aiding in the evaluation of a medical practitioner's qualifications or fitness. [Civ.C. §43.8; see *Hassan v. Mercy American River Hosp.* (2003) 31 C4th 709, 717, 3 CR3d 623, 627—privilege is qualified, not absolute]

(h) [8:189] **Exceptions:** The statute specifies various situations in which the records and proceedings of hospital staff committees are discoverable:

1) [8:189.1] **Statement by person in attendance who is party to action:** Statements made at a hospital staff committee meeting by a committee member who is a *party* to litigation "the subject matter of which was reviewed at that meeting" are discoverable. [Ev.C. §1157(c)]

a) [8:189.1a] **Narrowly interpreted:** This applies only to statements made *about the lawsuit* itself.

© 2020 Thomson Reuters/The Rutter Group

It does *not* allow disclosure of statements previously made about matters which occurred before the lawsuit was filed. Otherwise, the exception would apply whenever a lawsuit was filed and render meaningless the prohibition on discovery of such statements. [*University of Southern Calif. v. Sup.Ct. (Comeau)* (1996) 45 CA4th 1283, 1291, 53 CR2d 260, 264-265]

b) [8:189.2] **Not applicable to negligence actions:** The "statement by person in attendance" exception has been held *not* to apply where a staff doctor is being sued for *malpractice*; nor where the *hospital* is being sued for negligence in screening or retention of such staff person. Rationale: Otherwise, the statutory immunity from discovery would be meaningless in most cases. [See *West Covina Hosp. v. Sup.Ct. (Tyus)* (1984) 153 CA3d 134, 137, 200 CR 162, 164]

2) [8:189.3] **Persons requesting hospital staff privileges:** Nor does the statute apply to statements made "to a person requesting hospital staff privileges." [Ev.C. §1157(c)]

Such persons can thus compel *others in* attendance at the meeting to testify to what was said notwithstanding §1157. [See *Matchett v. Sup.Ct. (Petway)* (1974) 40 CA3d 623, 629, 115 CR 317, 321]

a) [8:189.4] **"Request" for staff privileges:** This exception applies both where doctors initially *apply* for staff privileges and also where their staff privileges were *terminated* and they request reinstatement. [*Roseville Comm. Hosp. v. Sup.Ct. (Physicians Consulting Lab.)* (1977) 70 CA3d 809, 814, 139 CR 170, 172]

b) [8:189.5] **Narrowly interpreted:** The exception is limited primarily to mandamus actions where doctors seek to obtain or retain hospital staff privileges:

- [8:189.6] The exception does *not* allow discovery of peer review committee proceedings in malpractice actions or in a *damages* action brought by a doctor against the hospital for restriction of his or her staff privileges. [*California Eye Institute v. Sup.Ct. (Kaye)* (1989) 215 CA3d 1477, 1485, 264 CR 83, 87-88]

- [8:189.7] Nor does it apply to a hospital's evaluation of postgraduate resident doctors who have been terminated from the hospital's training programs. Seeking *readmission to a training program* is *not* the same as applying for "staff privileges." [*University of Southern Calif. v. Sup.Ct. (Comeau)* (1996) 45 CA4th 1283, 1290, 53 CR2d 260, 264]

[8:189.8-189.9] *Reserved.*

3) [8:189.10] **Bad faith actions against insurers:** Nor does Ev.C. §1157 apply in "bad faith" actions against an insurance company alleging unreasonable refusal to settle a claim within its policy limits. [Ev.C. §1157(c)]

For example, plaintiffs who have recovered a judgment against Hospital in excess of its liability insurance limits may take an assignment of Hospital's claim against its insurer for "bad faith" refusal to settle plaintiffs' claims within the policy limits. At this point, plaintiffs' need for discovery is deemed to outweigh any risk of compromising the "candor and objectivity" of the hospital committee meetings.

4) [8:190] **Medical society committee meetings:** Another exception allows discovery of "medical society" (not hospital) committee meetings when reviewing the conduct or practice of a committee member. [Ev.C. §1157(d)]

[8:190.1-190.2] *Reserved.*

(9) [8:190.3] **Clergy-penitent privilege:** "Penitential communications" between clergy and penitent are privileged and not subject to disclosure. The privilege applies even though the penitent is not a member of any particular church nor of the same faith as the clergy. [Ev.C. §§1033, 1034; *Doe 2 v. Sup.Ct. (Calkins)* (2005) 132 CA4th 1504, 1517, 34 CR3d 458, 467]

(a) [8:190.4] **"Penitential communication":** A privileged "penitential communication" is a communication made *in confidence*, in the presence of *no third persons* (so far as the penitent is aware), to a *clergy member* who, incident to the tenets of his or her religious denomination, is *authorized to hear or accustomed to hearing* such communications *and* has a *duty* to keep them secret. [Ev.C. §1032]

There is no requirement that the communication be a confession of a "flawed act." The privilege encompasses any confidential communication by a penitent made to the cleric in the cleric's capacity as such. [*Doe 2 v. Sup.Ct. (Calkins)*, supra, 132 CA4th at 1518-1519, 34 CR3d at 467-468]

© 2020 Thomson Reuters/The Rutter Group

Cross-refer: The clergy-penitent privilege is discussed in greater detail in Wegner, Fairbank, Epstein & Chernow, *Cal. Prac. Guide: Civil Trials & Evidence* (TRG), Ch. 8E.

(10)[8:190.5] **Mediation:** Settlement offers and negotiations generally are not admissible in evidence or discoverable (Ev.C. §1152, *see ¶8:107*). Similarly, admissions or statements made in mediation briefs or in the course of mediation, as well as any findings made by the mediator, are confidential and neither admissible in evidence nor discoverable. [Ev.C. §§1119, 1121; see *Foxgate Homeowners' Ass'n, Inc. v. Bramalea Calif., Inc.* (2001) 26 C4th 1, 15, 108 CR2d 642, 653-654; *Doe 1 v. Sup.Ct. (Roman Catholic Archbishop of Los Angeles)* (2005) 132 CA4th 1160, 1165-1170, 34 CR3d 248, 251-255; *Wimsatt v. Sup.Ct. (Kausch)* (2007) 152 CA4th 137, 158-159, 61 CR3d 200, 215—allegedly unauthorized settlement demand made in mediation briefs]

Also protected are communications made by any participant before the end of mediation *outside the mediator's presence* that are materially related to the purpose of the mediation. [*Eisendrath v. Sup.Ct. (Rogers)* (2003) 109 CA4th 351, 364, 134 CR2d 716, 725; *Wimsatt v. Sup.Ct. (Kausch)*, supra, 152 CA4th at 159, 61 CR3d at 215—emails to opposing counsel that quoted from mediation brief; *Cassel v. Sup.Ct. (Wasserman, Comden, Casselman & Pearson, L.L.P.)* (2011) 51 C4th 113, 127, 119 CR3d 437, 448—settlement discussions *between lawyer and client* in preparation for and during mediation inadmissible in client's malpractice action against lawyer]

(a) [8:190.6] **Includes "writings" prepared for mediation:** In addition, "writings" prepared for or in the course of mediation (Ev.C. §1119(b)) are protected, including briefs, photographs and summaries of evidence prepared for the mediator. [*Rojas v. Sup.Ct. (Coffin)* (2004) 33 C4th 407, 416, 15 CR3d 643, 649]

But *physical* materials, like an air sample, are not "writings" within the meaning of Ev.C. §1119(b) and thus are outside the scope of the mediation confidentially protection. [*Rojas v. Sup.Ct. (Coffin)*, supra, 33 C4th at 416, 15 CR3d at 649]

1) [8:190.7] **Compare—written settlement agreements:** A written settlement agreement reached through mediation is not made inadmissible or protected from disclosure by Ev.C. §1115 et seq. if it is *signed* by the settling parties *and* any of the following conditions apply:

— the agreement provides that it is admissible or subject to disclosure (or words to that effect); or

— the agreement provides that it is enforceable or binding (or words to that effect); or

— all parties to the agreement expressly agree in writing (or orally pursuant to Ev.C. §1118) to its disclosure; or

— the agreement is used to show fraud, duress or illegality that is relevant to an issue in dispute. [Ev.C. §1123(b); *see discussion at ¶12:967.1 ff.*]

2) [8:190.8] **Compare—documents required by statute:** Documents required to be exchanged by statute are not shielded from discovery simply because they are exchanged during mediation. [*Lappe v. Sup.Ct. (Lappe)* (2014) 232 CA4th 774, 785, 181 CR3d 510, 518—financial declarations of disclosure mandated by Family Code in marriage dissolution actions not subject to Ev.C. §1115 et seq. protection simply because exchanged by spouses during mediation ("they were prepared for the purpose of complying with" the Family Code, not for the purpose of mediation)]

3) [8:190.8a] **Compare—document re attorney's compliance with disclosure requirement:** Except in class or other representative actions, an attorney representing a client in mediation must provide the client with a written disclosure advising the client that all communications in the course of a mediation are confidential and obtain the client's written acknowledgement that the client has read and understood the confidentiality restrictions. [Ev.C. §1129(a)]

That document is not made inadmissible or protected from disclosure by Ev.C. §1115 et seq. [Ev.C. §1122(a)(3)]

(b) [8:190.9] **Waiver:** Any waiver of confidentially in mediation must be *express;* i.e., no implied waivers. [See Ev.C. §1122; *Simmons v. Ghaderi* (2008) 44 C4th 570, 588, 80 CR3d 83, 97; *Eisendrath v. Sup.Ct. (Rogers),* supra, 109 CA4th at 364, 134 CR2d at 725]

(c) [8:190.9a] **No exception for lawsuits between attorney and client:** There is no exception to the mediation confidentiality statutes for lawsuits between attorney and client (unlike the attorney-client privilege, ¶*8:156.6*). [*Cassel v. Sup.Ct. (Wasserman, Comden, Casselman & Pearson, L.L.P.),* supra, 51 C4th at 117-118, 132-133, 138, 119 CR3d at 440-441, 452-453, 457; see *Amis v. Greenberg Traurig LLP* (2015) 235 CA4th 331, 333, 338-339, 185 CR3d 322, 323, 327-328—"malpractice plaintiff cannot circumvent mediation confidentiality by advancing inferences about his former attorney's supposed acts or omissions during an underlying mediation"]

Cross-refer: Mediation confidentiality protection is discussed in greater detail in Wegner, Fairbank, Epstein & Chernow, *Cal. Prac. Guide: Civil Trials & Evidence* (TRG), Ch. 8E; and Knight, Chernick, Flynn & Quinn, *Cal. Prac. Guide: Alternative Dispute Resolution* (TRG), Ch. 3.

(11) [8:190.10] **Governmental "deliberative process privilege":** Under the "deliberative process privilege," senior officials of all three branches of government—legislative, executive and judicial—enjoy a qualified, limited privilege not to disclose *or be examined* concerning:

— the *mental processes* by which a given decision was reached; or

— "the substance of conversations, discussions, debates, deliberations and like materials reflecting advice, opinions, and recommendations by which governmental policy is processed and formulated." [*Regents of Univ. of Calif. v. Sup.Ct. (Molloy)* (1999) 20 C4th 509, 540, 85 CR2d 257, 276; see *San Joaquin Local Agency Formation Comm'n v. Sup.Ct. (South San Joaquin Irrig. Dist.)* (2008) 162 CA4th 159, 167, 76 CR3d 93, 99-100—privilege extends to members of quasi-legislative administrative agency]

(a) [8:190.11] **Includes testimony by others:** Nor can nonlegislators be questioned on matters reflecting the thought processes of legislators or factors that may have led to their votes. [*City of Santa Cruz v. Sup.Ct. (Bombay Corp.)* (1995) 40 CA4th 1146, 1155, 48 CR2d 216, 222—City Planning Director could not be asked whether City Council members had agreed to refuse alternative zoning proposals for certain property regardless of facts presented]

(b) [8:190.12] **Burden on government to establish privilege:** The party (govermental body) asserting the "deliberative process privilege" bears the burden of showing (i) what the "public's *specific* interest in nondisclosure" is in the case and (ii) why that interest clearly outweighs the public interest in disclosure. [*Citizens for Open Government v. City of Lodi* (2012) 205 CA4th 296, 307, 140 CR3d 459, 468-469 (emphasis added)—city failed to meet burden by relying solely on general policy behind privilege rather than proving specific public interest in nondisclosure of city staff emails from administrative record]

[8:190.13-190.14] *Reserved.*

(12) [8:190.15] **Internet anonymity:** The First Amendment protects the right to speak anonymously, which includes the right to use a pseudonym in posting messages on an Internet bulletin board. [*Krinsky v. Doe 6* (2008) 159 CA4th 1154, 1163, 72 CR3d 231, 238]

Internet anonymity is also protected under the California constitutional right of privacy (Cal. Const. Art. 1, §1; *see* ¶*8:293 ff.*). [*Digital Music News LLC v. Sup.Ct. (Escape Media Group, LLC)* (2014) 226 CA4th 216, 228, 171 CR3d 799, 809 (disapproved on other grounds by *Williams v. Sup.Ct. (Marshalls of CA, LLC)* (2017) 3 C5th 531, 557, 220 CR3d 472, 494 & fn. 8) (also noting right to speak anonymously "draws its strength" from *both* 1st Amendment freedom of speech *and* California constitutional right of privacy)]

(a) **Application**

- [8:190.16] A corporation defending a fraud suit served a subpoena on an Internet Service Provider to disclose the identity of the person who (using a pseudonym) had posted messages critical of the corporation on an Internet bulletin board. The anonymous poster was allowed to appear anonymously in court (as "Doe") to move to quash the subpoena. [*Doe v. 2TheMart.com Inc.* (WD WA 2001) 140 F.Supp.2d 1088, 1092—motion to quash granted]

- [8:190.17] Plaintiff in a copyright infringement lawsuit sought to obtain the identity of an anonymous writer who posted an online message claiming to have worked for defendant and that defendant regularly encouraged copyright infringement. Even if reasonably calculated to lead to the discovery of admissible evidence, the anonymous speaker's identity was protected by the California constitutional right of privacy, which in this case was held to outweigh plaintiff's need for the information. [*Digital Music News LLC v. Sup.Ct. (Escape Media Group, LLC)*, supra, 226 CA4th at 228, 171 CR3d at 809]

  [8:190.18-190.19] *Reserved.*

(b) [8:190.20] **Limitation—disclosure may be ordered where plaintiff makes prima facie showing:** The First Amendment right to publish anonymously is not absolute, however. Thus, an Internet Service Provider (ISP) may be ordered to identify the person responsible for an anonymous posting where plaintiff makes a prima facie showing, by admissible evidence, that the poster's *tortious conduct* has resulted in *actual harm* to plaintiff. [*Columbia Ins. Co. v. seescandy.com* (ND CA 1999) 185 FRD 573, 578—ISP could be ordered to identify owner of website infringing plaintiff's trademark; see *Krinsky v. Doe 6*, supra, 159 CA4th at 1172, 72 CR3d at 245—discovery denied because postings *not* actionable]

Plaintiff "seeking compulsory disclosure of an allegedly libelous speaker's identity must state a legally sufficient cause of action against the defendant, and must

© 2020 Thomson Reuters/The Rutter Group

make a prima facie showing of the elements of that cause of action," including proof of false statements. [*ZL Technologies, Inc. v. Does 1-7* (2017) 13 CA5th 603, 613, 220 CR3d 569, 580 (agreeing with *Krinsky v. Doe 6*, supra, 159 CA4th at 1172-1179, 72 CR3d at 245-251); *Glassdoor, Inc. v. Sup.Ct. (Machine Zone, Inc.)* (2017) 9 CA5th 623, 634-635, 215 CR3d 395, 405-406—discovery denied because no prima facie case of breach of confidentiality agreement]

(c) [8:190.21] **Who may object:** A third party website publishing anonymous speech has standing to object to the disclosure on behalf of the speaker. [*Glassdoor, Inc. v. Sup.Ct. (Machine Zone, Inc.)*, supra, 9 CA5th at 634, 215 CR3d at 405]

[8:190.22-190.24] *Reserved.*

(d) [8:190.25] **Sanctions on quashing subpoena served on ISP for "personally identifying information":** The court *must* award the moving party his or her expenses, including reasonable attorney fees, incurred in moving to quash a subpoena served on an ISP for the moving party's "personally identifying information" if:

— the information was sought *for use in an action pending outside California*; and

— the motion was granted because the *respondent failed to make a prima facie showing* of a cause of action. [CCP §1987.2(c); *see* ¶*8:602.10*]

e. [8:191] **Procedure for claiming privilege generally:** A claim of privilege can be asserted simply by *objecting* and stating the specific privilege that bars discovery. This shifts the burden to the party seeking discovery: He or she must then file a *motion to compel answers* to the discovery request (*see* ¶*8:737, 8:787 ff.*). On hearing the motion, the judge will rule on the validity of the privilege claim.

Alternatively, the party claiming privilege could seek a *protective order* excusing response, before the response was due. But as a practical matter this is rarely done because simply objecting raises the issue and shifts the burden of going to court to the other party. [See *Monarch Healthcare v. Sup.Ct. (Cassidenti)* (2000) 78 CA4th 1282, 1290, 93 CR2d 619, 625 (citing text)]

(1) [8:192] **Burden of establishing privilege:** In response to a motion to compel answers (¶*8:191*), the burden is on the party claiming a privilege to establish whatever *preliminary facts* are essential to the claim. [See Ev.C. §§402, 405; *Lopez v. Watchtower Bible & Tract Soc. of New York, Inc.* (2016) 246 CA4th 566, 596, 201 CR3d 156, 181]

For example, upon asserting the attorney-client privilege, the client, or the attorney in the client's absence, must prove that the attorney-client relationship existed when the communication was made. Once this showing is made (typically through declarations), the communications between lawyer and client are *presumed* to have been made in confidence. [*Clark v. Sup.Ct. (Verisign, Inc.)* (2011) 196 CA4th 37, 51, 125 CR3d 361, 372; *Citizens for Ceres v. Sup.Ct. (City of Ceres)* (2013) 217 CA4th 889, 911, 159 CR3d 789, 803 (citing text); *DP Pham, LLC v. Cheadle* (2016) 246 CA4th 653, 664-665, 200 CR3d 937, 945-946—whether attorney-client privilege applies is question of fact for court to determine]

Upon such showing, the burden shifts to the party seeking discovery to disprove those facts or to prove some applicable statutory exception (e.g., that the privilege has been waived, *see ¶8:199 ff.*). [*Lopez v. Watchtower Bible & Tract Soc. of New York, Inc.*, supra, 246 CA4th at 596, 201 CR3d at 181; *DP Pham, LLC v. Cheadle*, supra, 246 CA4th at 659-660, 200 CR3d at 941-942; *Uber Technologies, Inc. v. Google LLC* (2018) 27 CA5th 953, 967, 238 CR3d 765, 777-778]

(a) [8:192a] **Effect of privilege log:** A privilege log (*¶8:192.10*) that identifies communications between the attorney and client that have not been disclosed to any third party may satisfy this preliminary burden. This is true even if the privilege log is *unverified*. [*Bank of America, N.A. v. Sup.Ct. (Pacific City Bank)* (2013) 212 CA4th 1076, 1100-1101, 151 CR3d 526, 544-545; compare *Lopez v. Watchtower Bible & Tract Soc. of New York, Inc.*, supra, 246 CA4th at 596, 201 CR3d at 181—defendant failed to meet burden where *no* privilege log produced and *no* specific confidential communications identified]

(2) [8:192.1] **Court cannot require in camera disclosure of contents:** Subject to certain exceptions (*¶8:192.2*), a court cannot require disclosure of information claimed to be attorney-client privileged in order to rule on the claim. [Ev.C. §915(a); *Southern Calif. Gas Co. v. Public Utilities Comm'n* (1990) 50 C3d 31, 45, 265 CR 801, 809, fn. 19; *Costco Wholesale Corp. v. Sup.Ct. (Randall)* (2009) 47 C4th 725, 736-738, 101 CR3d 758, 767; *Clark v. Sup.Ct. (Verisign, Inc.)*, supra, 196 CA4th at 50-51, 125 CR3d at 371-372]

A disclosure order is no less intrusive because it only requires "in camera" inspection of privileged documents. There is no statutory or other provision allowing such inspection. [*Southern Calif. Gas Co. v. Public Utilities Comm'n*, supra, 50 C3d at 45, 265 CR at 809, fn. 19; *Bank of America, N.A. v. Sup.Ct. (Pacific City Bank)* (2013) 212 CA4th 1076, 1100, 151 CR3d 526, 544—documents on privilege log not subject to disclosure for in camera inspection]

(a) [8:192.2] **Exceptions:** In camera disclosure may be required in ruling on privilege claims for *trade secrets*

© 2020 Thomson Reuters/The Rutter Group

(Ev.C. §1060), or *official information* and identity of informers (Ev.C. §1040), where necessary to decide the claim. [Ev.C. §915(b)]

(b) [8:192.2a] **Compare—attorney work product:** Courts may order in camera inspection of material subject to protection as *qualified* attorney work product; it is unclear if a court may order such an inspection of materials claimed to be *absolutely* protected under the doctrine. *See ¶8:267.*

(3) [8:192.3] **Court may determine *facts upon which privilege rests:*** The ban on reviewing contents of allegedly privileged communications does not preclude the court from determining the *facts* asserted as the basis for the privilege (e.g., whether the communication was intended to be confidential, whether made in the course of an attorney-client relationship, etc.). [See *Moeller v. Sup.Ct. (Sanwa Bank)* (1997) 16 C4th 1124, 1135, 69 CR2d 317, 324; *Cornish v. Sup.Ct. (Capital Bond & Ins. Co.)* (1989) 209 CA3d 467, 480, 257 CR 383, 390]

To do so, the court may conduct an Ev.C. §402 "preliminary fact" hearing (in camera or otherwise) on whether the privilege exists. If the facts are in dispute, the court may require live testimony.

(a) [8:192.4] **Court may determine whether exception applies:** Similarly, the court may conduct in camera hearings to determine whether an exception to a claimed privilege applies (e.g., whether third persons were present; whether privilege waived, etc.). [See *Cornish v. Sup.Ct. (Capital Bond & Ins. Co.)*, supra, 209 CA3d at 480, 257 CR at 390; *Costco Wholesale Corp. v. Sup.Ct. (Randall)*, supra, 47 C4th at 737, 101 CR3d at 768—hearing may be held to determine validity of claim of privilege *without requiring disclosure* of communication claimed to be privileged]

[8:192.5] *Reserved.*

☞ [8:192.6] ***PRACTICE POINTER:*** If the parties stipulate to in camera review, the party asserting the privilege should make clear in the stipulation, and obtain a court order, that if the court rules the information is privileged, the agreement to submit the information for in camera review does not constitute a *waiver* of the privilege. However, it is not clear that this will thwart a *third party's* claim that the voluntary submission of the documents to the court for review effectively waived the privilege (*see ¶8:113.4c*).

[8:192.7-192.9] *Reserved.*

(4) [8:192.10] **Privilege log generally required:** If a party objects to document production based on a claim of privilege

or work product protection, "the response shall provide sufficient factual information for other parties to evaluate the merits of that claim, including, if necessary, a privilege log." [CCP §2031.240(c)(1); see also CCP §2031.240(c)(2)—Legislature's intent to codify concept of privilege log as used in California case law]

The purpose of a privilege log is to make a record of the documents withheld and the privilege claim asserted as to each. [*Wellpoint Health Networks, Inc. v. Sup.Ct. (McCombs)* (1997) 59 CA4th 110, 130, 68 CR2d 844, 857; *Best Products, Inc. v. Sup.Ct. (Granatelli Motorsports, Inc.)* (2004) 119 CA4th 1181, 1188-1189, 15 CR3d 154, 159]

Cross-refer: See more detailed discussion at ¶8:1474.5 ff.

(5) [8:193] **Appellate court review:** Normally, appellate courts will not entertain interlocutory review of pretrial discovery orders (¶*8:14*). But an exception may be made where the order requires disclosure of information claimed to be privileged. Here, immediate *writ review* (by mandamus or prohibition) is often granted because redress after disclosure of privileged information would, of course, be impossible. [*Sav-On Drugs, Inc. v. Sup.Ct. (Botney)* (1975) 15 C3d 1, 5, 123 CR 283, 285-286; *Costco Wholesale Corp. v. Sup.Ct. (Randall)* (2009) 47 C4th 725, 740-741, 101 CR3d 758, 770-771—even if disclosure of attorney's opinion letter would not impair client's ability to present its case, writ review granted to preserve confidential attorney-client relationship; see *Bank of America, N.A. v. Sup.Ct. (Pacific City Bank)* (2013) 212 CA4th 1076, 1102, 151 CR3d 526, 546—writ review warranted since order denying motion to quash would result in production of privileged materials, threatening attorney-client relationship]

[8:194] ***PRACTICE POINTER:*** If you plan to seek appellate review and need additional time, *ask for a temporary stay* of the discovery order (i.e., until such time as the writ is disposed of or as the court of appeal otherwise directs) to allow you to prepare your petition without risking sanctions for violation. Most judges will grant such requests. Also, it may be appropriate to ask the appellate court to stay the discovery order while considering the writ petition.

[8:195-198] *Reserved.*

f. **Waiver of privileges**

(1) [8:199] **Waiver by disclosure:** A statutory privilege may be waived if the holder of the privilege has voluntarily *disclosed* a "significant" part of the communication to a third party or *consented* to such disclosure. Failure to timely claim the privilege (i.e., failure to object) constitutes "consent" to disclosure. [Ev.C. §912(a); see *People v. Hayes* (1999) 21 C4th 1211, 1265, 91 CR2d 211, 248]

© 2020 Thomson Reuters/The Rutter Group

(a) [8:199.1] **What constitutes "significant" part:** The disclosure must reveal enough *substantive information* so that the specific content of the communication has been disclosed. [See *Southern Calif. Gas Co. v. Public Utilities Comm'n* (1990) 50 C3d 31, 49, 265 CR 801, 812]

1) [8:199.2] **Conclusions not enough:** Merely disclosing the *conclusions* arrived at by the lawyer does *not* waive the attorney-client privilege as to the *content* of the communications. [*Southern Calif. Gas Co. v. Public Utilities Comm'n*, supra, 50 C3d at 49, 265 CR at 812]

[8:199.3] **Example:** Client disclosed it had consulted with its lawyer regarding enforceability of a certain contract, and that its lawyer had concluded the contract was enforceable. This was *not* such a "significant" part of the attorney-client communication to constitute a waiver. [*Southern Calif. Gas Co. v. Public Utilities Comm'n*, supra]

[8:199.4-199.9] *Reserved.*

(b) [8:199.10] **Waiver by disclosure to coparty ("common interest" doctrine)?** There is *no* "joint defense" *privilege* as such under California law. However, under the "common interest" (or "joint defense") doctrine, disclosures made in confidence to third persons do not waive the attorney-client privilege or attorney work product protection if "*reasonably necessary* for the accomplishment of the purpose for which the lawyer . . . was consulted." [Ev.C. §§912(d) (emphasis added), 952; see *Citizens for Ceres v. Sup.Ct. (City of Ceres)* (2013) 217 CA4th 889, 914-915, 159 CR3d 789, 805 (citing text)—although Ev.C. §§912(d) and 952 relate specifically to attorney-client privilege, the "same considerations apply to waiver or nonwaiver of the work-product doctrine"]

Arguably, cooperation with coparties in defense (or prosecution) of a lawsuit may be one of the purposes for which an attorney is consulted. If so, and if mutual disclosure of client confidences is "reasonably necessary" to accomplish that purpose, there would be no waiver. [See *Raytheon Co. v. Sup.Ct. (Renault)* (1989) 208 CA3d 683, 687, 256 CR 425, 428; *STI Outdoor LLC v. Sup.Ct. (Eller Media Co.)* (2001) 91 CA4th 334, 340-341, 109 CR2d 865, 869]

The "joint defense" or "common interest" doctrine requires a showing of the following:

— the information shared with a coparty would otherwise be protected from disclosure (e.g., as a confidential client communication or as an attorney's mental impressions and theories);

— the participants in the exchange had a reasonable expectation that the information disclosed would remain confidential; and

— the disclosure was made to advance their shared interest in securing legal advice on a common matter. [*OXY Resources Calif. LLC v. Sup.Ct. (Calpine Natural Gas LP)* (2004) 115 CA4th 874, 890, 9 CR3d 621, 636; *Meza v. H. Muehlstein & Co.* (2009) 176 CA4th 969, 981, 98 CR3d 422, 431; *Seahaus La Jolla Owners Ass'n v. Sup.Ct. (La Jolla View Ltd., LLC)* (2014) 224 CA4th 754, 770, 169 CR3d 390, 401-402]

[8:199.10a] ***PRACTICE POINTER:*** If you intend to rely on the common interest doctrine in sharing information with co-counsel, ask the court to include in its case management order, or a stipulated protective order, a provision that counsel may exchange information regarding their common interests without waiving the attorney-client privilege and work product protection. That way, if a waiver question is ever raised, there will be little question as to your reasonable expectation that the information disclosed would remain confidential. [See *Meza v. H. Muehlstein & Co.*, supra, 176 CA4th at 982, 98 CR3d at 433]

1) [8:199.10b] **Compare—possible common interest in future:** If the parties do not yet have a common interest, their communications are not protected by the common interest doctrine, even if they may develop a common interest in the future. [*Citizens for Ceres v. Sup.Ct. (City of Ceres)*, supra, 217 CA4th at 917-922, 159 CR3d at 807-812—prior to City completing its CEQA review and approving development project, City and developer did not have common interest in creating an EIR that would withstand challenge]

2) [8:199.11] **Comment:** As a practical matter, it will be difficult for the party seeking the information to show it was *not* "reasonably necessary" for coparties to share their client confidences. The fact that they also have claims against each other does *not* mean there was no need to cooperate. I.e., their shared desire to see the opposing party lose should be enough to make their sharing of client confidences "reasonably necessary."

3) [8:199.12] **In camera review:** The protection afforded by the common interest doctrine is qualified because it depends on the content of the shared information. In camera review may be required to

© 2020 Thomson Reuters/The Rutter Group

determine whether the disclosed communications advance the common interest, *not* whether the underlying information is privileged. [*OXY Resources Calif. LLC v. Sup.Ct. (Calpine Natural Gas LP)*, supra, 115 CA4th at 895-896, 9 CR3d at 640-641; see also *Costco Wholesale Corp. v. Sup.Ct. (Randall)* (2009) 47 C4th 725, 739-740, 101 CR3d 758, 770]

[8:199.13] *Reserved.*

(c) [8:199.14] **Waiver despite confidentiality agreement:** Disclosure to a third person (other than a coparty, ¶*8:199.10*) waives the privilege as to everyone else *even if that person agreed to keep the information confidential.* [*McKesson HBOC, Inc. v. Sup.Ct. (State of Oregon)* (2004) 115 CA4th 1229, 1236-1238, 9 CR3d 812, 817-819—target of government investigation waived attorney-client privilege and work product protection for documents disclosed to government, despite confidentiality agreement with government, allowing others to obtain documents; see *In re Pacific Pictures Corp.* (9th Cir. 2012) 679 F3d 1121, 1128-1129 (applying federal law)—voluntary compliance with government subpoena, without asserting privilege or redacting confidential information, waived attorney-client privilege despite purported agreement by government to keep documents confidential]

(d) [8:199.15] **No waiver by attorney's inadvertent disclosure during discovery:** The privilege belongs to the client, not the attorney. Therefore, absent evidence of the client's intent to waive the privilege, the attorney's inadvertent disclosure of confidential communications during discovery does *not* constitute a waiver. [*State Comp. Ins. Fund v. WPS, Inc.* (1999) 70 CA4th 644, 652-654, 82 CR2d 799, 804-805—privileged documents accidentally included in large stack of documents delivered in response to inspection demand]

1) [8:199.16] **Ethical obligation:** Attorneys are obligated not only to protect their client's interests *but also to respect the legitimate interests of fellow members of the bar*, the judiciary, and the administration of justice. [*Rico v. Mitsubishi Motors Corp.* (2007) 42 C4th 807, 818, 68 CR3d 758, 767]

Therefore, upon receiving material that "obviously appears" to be confidential and privileged (or attorney work product) and not intentionally produced by the holder of the privilege, a lawyer must:

— *refrain from examining* the materials any more than is essential to ascertain if the materials are privileged;

— *immediately notify the sender* that he or she possesses material that appears to be privileged;

— proceed to resolve the situation by agreement with the sender or resort to the court for guidance with the benefit of protective orders and other judicial intervention as may be justified. [*Rico v. Mitsubishi Motors Corp.*, supra, 42 C4th at 817-818, 68 CR3d at 766-767; see CRPC 4.4; see also State Bar California Attorney Guidelines of Civility and Professionalism §9.b.3; *Clark v. Sup.Ct. (Verisign, Inc.)* (2011) 196 CA4th 37, 51, 125 CR3d 361, 372—above-stated obligations extend to situation where lawyer obtains opposing party's privileged documents from his or her own client]

Failure to comply with this ethical standard is ground for *disqualification*. [*Rico v. Mitsubishi Motors Corp.*, supra, 42 C4th at 819, 68 CR3d at 767—lawyers disqualified for using and disseminating opposing counsel's inadvertently disclosed work product; *McDermott Will & Emery LLP v. Sup.Ct. (Hausman)* (2017) 10 CA5th 1083, 1120, 217 CR3d 47, 79-80—disqualification of third party counsel who received and used inadvertently disclosed privileged material]

Additionally, failure to comply with these obligations may result in attorney discipline. [CRPC 4.4]

(e) [8:199.17] **No waiver by agent's disclosure without client's consent:** Because the holder of the attorney-client privilege is the client, there is no waiver where the client's agent discloses a privileged communication without the client's authorization. [*DP Pham, LLC v. Cheadle* (2016) 246 CA4th 653, 668, 200 CR3d 937, 948—court erred in reviewing contents of communication to determine whether privileged (*see ¶8:192.1*)]

[8:199.18-199.19] *Reserved.*

(f) [8:199.20] **No waiver by electronic communication:** Confidential communications between attorney-client, lawyer referral service-client, physician-patient, psychotherapist-patient, clergy-penitent, marital or domestic partnership, sexual assault victim-counselor, domestic violence victim-counselor, or human trafficking caseworker-victim do not lose their privileged status because communicated electronically (e.g., email or fax or because persons involved in the delivery, facilitation or storage of electronic communication may have access to the content of the communication). [Ev.C. §917(b)]

[8:199.21-199.24] *Reserved.*

© 2020 Thomson Reuters/The Rutter Group

(g) [8:199.25] **No waiver where disclosure coerced by threat of governmental sanctions:** If made under threat of indictment or regulatory sanctions, disclosure of attorney-client privileged documents to a governmental agency is not "voluntary" and does not waive the privilege: "The law does not require that the holder of the privilege take 'strenuous or Herculean efforts' to resist disclosure." [*Regents of Univ. of Calif. v. Sup.Ct. (Aquila Merchant Services, Inc.)* (2008) 165 CA4th 672, 683, 81 CR3d 186, 194]

1) [8:199.26] **Compare—waiver by disclosure pursuant to "solicited" government subpoena:** A crime victim's compliance with a subpoena he solicited (as part of his request that the U.S. Attorney's Office investigate the crime) was deemed voluntary since there was no threat of contempt and the victim made no attempt to assert the attorney-client privilege or redact confidential information in the documents produced. [*In re Pacific Pictures Corp.* (9th Cir. 2012) 679 F3d 1121, 1130 (applying federal law)]

(2) [8:200] **Waiver by *failure to object* to discovery requests:** Failure to make a *timely* and *specific* objection to a discovery request waives any objection thereto (Ev.C. §912(a)). This specifically *includes* claims of privilege or work product protection. [See CCP §2025.460 (a)—depositions; CCP §2030.290(a)—interrogatories; CCP §2031.300(a)—inspection demands; and CCP §2033.280(a)—RFAs] (However, an objection to the production of electronically stored information (ESI) on the basis of burden preserves other objections. *See ¶8:1475.10 ff.*)

This waiver rule applies both where there is a complete failure to respond to discovery as well as where the objection is not raised in the *original* response. [*Scottsdale Ins. Co. v. Sup.Ct. (Spyglass Homeowners Ass'n)* (1997) 59 CA4th 263, 273, 69 CR2d 112, 118]

Not much is required to prevent waiver, however. Even a "general and nonspecific" reference to the "attorney-client privilege" in the original response has been held sufficient. [*Korea Data Systems Co. Ltd. v. Sup.Ct. (Aamazing Technologies Corp.)* (1997) 51 CA4th 1513, 1516, 59 CR2d 925, 926; *Best Products, Inc. v. Sup.Ct. (Granatelli Motorsports, Inc.)* (2004) 119 CA4th 1181, 1189, 15 CR3d 154, 159—"boilerplate" objections sufficient]

(a) [8:200.1] **Compare—police personnel records:** Ev.C. §§1043, 1045 provide the *exclusive means* for discovery of most peace officer personnel records (*see ¶8:126*), and the police need not respond to CCP §2031.010 demands for such records. Thus, their failure to do so is not a waiver of the Evidence Code protection. [*County of Los Angeles v. Sup.Ct. (Uhley)* (1990) 219 CA3d 1605, 1611, 269 CR 187, 190; *see* ¶*8:126.3*]

(b) [8:200.2] **Includes attorney-client privilege:** The attorney-client privilege may be waived *either* by voluntary disclosure as provided in Ev.C. §912(a) or by *failure to object* as provided in the Discovery Act. [*Scottsdale Ins. Co. v. Sup.Ct. (Spyglass Homeowners Ass'n)*, supra, 59 CA4th at 273, 69 CR2d at 118]

(c) [8:201] **Compare—noncompliance with discovery order not waiver:** Once privilege has been timely claimed, however, a party's delay or failure to comply with a court order for discovery does *not* waive the privilege. Sanctions for the delay may be appropriate, but a "compelled waiver" of the privilege is not. [See *Motown Record Corp. v. Sup.Ct. (Brockert)* (1984) 155 CA3d 482, 492, 202 CR 227, 233-234—before Discovery Act, compelled waiver of privilege *too drastic* a remedy for delay in response to discovery request]

[8:202] *Reserved.*

(3) [8:203] **Implied waiver ("fundamental fairness" exceptions):** An *implied waiver* of the privilege may occur where the party claiming the privilege has placed the privileged communication "directly at issue and . . . disclosure is essential for a fair adjudication of the action." [*Kaiser Found. Hosps. v. Sup.Ct. (Smee)* (1998) 66 CA4th 1217, 1226, 78 CR2d 543, 548]

If the communication goes to the *heart of the claim* in controversy, "fundamental fairness" may require that privileged matters be disclosed in order for the litigation to proceed. [See *Mitchell v. Sup.Ct. (Shell Oil. Co.)* (1984) 37 C3d 591, 604, 208 CR2d 886, 893—recognizing general proposition; *Steiny & Co. v. California Elec. Supply Co.* (2000) 79 CA4th 285, 292, 93 CR2d 920, 925]

(a) [8:204] **Plaintiff's complaint as waiver of self-incrimination on factual issues tendered:** Plaintiff may waive his or her constitutional privilege against self-incrimination by commencing a lawsuit raising factual issues to which the privileged information relates. "Plaintiff cannot have his cake and eat it too." [*Fremont Indem. Co. v. Sup.Ct. (Sharif)* (1982) 137 CA3d 554, 560, 187 CR 137, 140; *see* ¶*8:134*]

(b) [8:205] **Plaintiff's complaint as waiver of patient-physician privilege:** The physician-patient privilege is waived if the patient tenders an issue in the litigation regarding his or her medical condition. [See Ev.C. §996(a); *Karen P. v. Sup.Ct. (Andres P.)* (2011) 200 CA4th 908, 913, 133 CR3d 67, 71—privilege not waived by

© 2020 Thomson Reuters/The Rutter Group

child's disclosure of sexual abuse to authorities and submitting to forensic medical exam before dependency litigation was filed because child did not file the litigation and did not tender her medical condition *in the litigation*]

(c) [8:206] **Client's claiming "advice of counsel" as implied waiver of attorney-client privilege:** The attorney-client privilege is *not* waived by the client filing suit or placing in issue the matter to which the privileged communication relates (unlike the doctor-patient privilege; see Ev.C. §996).

Nor is the privilege waived merely by revealing that one has *consulted* an attorney. [*Mitchell v. Sup.Ct. (Shell Oil Co.)*, supra, 37 C3d at 603, 208 CR at 893]

But there may be circumstances under which the attorney-client privilege is *impliedly waived* by the claims or defenses raised by the client. [See *Mitchell v. Sup.Ct. (Shell Oil Co.)*, supra, 37 C3d at 604, 208 CR at 893]

Waiver is established "by demonstrating that *the client has put the otherwise privileged communication directly at issue* and that disclosure is essential for a fair adjudication of the action." [*Southern Calif. Gas Co. v. Public Util. Comm'n* (1990) 50 C3d 31, 40, 265 CR 801, 806 (emphasis added)]

1) [8:207] **Where client puts attorney's state of mind in issue:** "Fundamental fairness" may require disclosure of otherwise privileged communications where the client places in issue the *decisions, conclusions and mental state of the attorney* when he or she advised the client. [See *Mitchell v. Sup.Ct. (Shell Oil Co.)*, supra, 37 C3d at 605, 208 CR at 894]

a) [8:208] **Example:** P claimed Insurance Co. had acted in bad faith in earlier lawsuit by furnishing inaccurate information that had "confused" P's then-lawyer. *By tendering the issue* as to the lawyer's mental state (i.e., whether he was "confused" by the information supplied), P waived the attorney-client privilege as to advice received from the lawyer. [*Merritt v. Sup.Ct.* (1970) 9 CA3d 721, 730, 88 CR 337, 342]

2) [8:209] **Where client puts substance of "advice" in issue:** Arguably, "fundamental fairness" may also require disclosure of a privileged communication between attorney and client where the client has placed in issue the *substance* of the communication. In such cases, "disclosure is essential to a fair

adjudication of the action." [See *Wellpoint Health Networks, Inc. v. Sup.Ct. (McCombs)* (1997) 59 CA4th 110, 128, 68 CR2d 844, 856]

a) **Application**

- [8:209.1] Where an employer defends an employment discrimination lawsuit on the ground that it took reasonable corrective action, it thereby puts in issue the *adequacy of its investigation* of the employee's claims. Where that investigation was *undertaken by an attorney or law firm,* the employer's defense "must result in waiver of the attorney-client privilege and work product doctrine . . . The defendant cannot have it both ways." [*Wellpoint Health Networks, Inc. v. Sup.Ct. (McCombs),* supra, 59 CA4th at 128, 68 CR2d at 855-856]

- [8:209.2] *Compare—investigation by nonattorney:* Where the in-house investigation was performed by a *nonattorney* (e.g., personnel manager or human resources specialist) and the employer *produced* the investigator's reports *except specified communications* between the investigator and the employer's attorneys, there was no waiver of the attorney-client privilege as to those communications. [*Kaiser Found. Hosps. v. Sup.Ct. (Smee)* (1998) 66 CA4th 1217, 1228, 78 CR2d 543, 549]

b) [8:210] **Waiver by verifying pleading alleging facts learned from privileged communications?** A client's verification of a pleading *alleging facts* learned through privileged communications or attorney work product apparently does not waive the privilege, at least where the verification is on "information and belief" and the allegations are "vague, conclusional and lack factual depth." [*Alpha Beta Co. v. Sup.Ct. (Sundy)* (1984) 157 CA3d 818, 831, 203 CR 752, 758-759]

[8:210.1-210.4] *Reserved.*

3) [8:210.5] **Compare—no discovery to show client *ignored* advice:** Opposing parties *cannot* discover privileged communications to show the client *ignored* advice of counsel. Thus, the mere fact the client claims it acted "reasonably" or "prudently" does *not* permit discovery of attorney-client communications to *disprove* such claims. [*Southern Calif. Gas Co. v. Public Utilities Comm'n* (1990) 50 C3d 31, 42-43, 265 CR 801, 807-808]

© 2020 Thomson Reuters/The Rutter Group

(d) [8:211] **Compare—no waiver by raising claim for emotional distress:** The result is different where the client has *not* itself placed the privileged communication in issue, but has simply raised an issue to which such communication may relate—e.g., the *client's knowledge or state of mind.* In such cases, "fundamental fairness" does not require waiver of the attorney-client privilege. The party seeking discovery must obtain other evidence. [*Mitchell v. Sup.Ct. (Shell Oil Co.)*, supra, 37 C3d at 603-610, 208 CR at 892-898]

Thus, plaintiff's filing suit for emotional distress does *not* render discoverable the substance of all communications plaintiff has had with his or her lawyer regarding emotional distress. Even if information obtained from the lawyer contributed to the client's distress (and thus might be relevant to the "genuineness" of the claim), the *client has not placed such communications in issue.* [*Mitchell v. Sup.Ct. (Shell Oil Co.),* supra, 37 C3d at 603-610, 208 CR at 892-898]

1) [8:212] **Example:** P sued Chemical Co. for emotional distress based on its contamination of water and air in vicinity of P's home. Chemical Co. was not entitled to discover what warnings or information P had obtained from her lawyer regarding the contamination. The substance of the warnings was *not* in issue—only their effect on P—and this could be proved by other evidence. [*Mitchell v. Sup.Ct. (Shell Oil Co.)*, supra]

[8:212.1-212.4] *Reserved.*

(4) [8:212.5] **Waiver by one joint holder not waiver by others:** Where two or more persons are joint holders of an attorney-client, lawyer referral service-client, physician-patient, psychotherapist-patient, sexual assault victim-counselor, domestic violence victim-counselor, or human trafficking caseworker-victim privilege, a waiver by one does not affect the other's right to claim the privilege. Likewise, a spouse's waiver of the right to claim the marital privilege does not waive the other's right to do so. [Ev.C. §912(b)]

Similarly, if one joint holder brings a motion for a protective order in response to a subpoena, the other holder need not bring its own motion; and its failure to do so is not a waiver for either party. [*Bank of America, N.A. v. Sup.Ct. (Pacific City Bank)* (2013) 212 CA4th 1076, 1096-1097, 151 CR3d 526, 541-542]

4. [8:213] **Attorney Work Product Protection:** CCP §2018.030 restates the attorney "work product" doctrine. Although "work product" is not defined, the statute limits the conditions under which it is discoverable.

Unlike privileged information, which generally receives absolute protection, many types of work product receive only *qualified* protection from discovery (*see* ¶*8:222*) and a court may order disclosure of work product under certain circumstances (*see* ¶*8:248 ff.*).

a. [8:214] **Purpose of protection:** "It is the policy of the state to do both of the following:

"(a) Preserve the rights of attorneys to prepare cases for trial with that degree of privacy necessary to encourage them to prepare their cases thoroughly and to *investigate not only the favorable but the unfavorable aspects* of those cases;

"(b) *Prevent attorneys from taking undue advantage* of their adversary's industry and efforts." [CCP §2018.020 (emphasis added)]

(1) [8:214.1] **Includes nonlitigation matters:** "The protection afforded by the privilege is not limited to writings created by a lawyer in anticipation of a lawsuit. It applies as well to writings prepared by an attorney while acting in a nonlitigation capacity." (E.g., memos prepared by lawyers negotiating business deals reflecting their opinions; *see* ¶*8:226*.) [*State Comp. Ins. Fund v. Sup.Ct. (People)* (2001) 91 CA4th 1080, 1091, 111 CR2d 284, 292; *County of Los Angeles v. Sup.Ct. (Axelrad)* (2000) 82 CA4th 819, 833, 98 CR2d 564, 574]

b. [8:215] **Protection limited to work product of attorneys or pro pers:** The Discovery Act refers only to the "work product" of *attorneys* acting on a client's behalf. [CCP §2018.010 et seq.]

However, *pro per* litigants may also assert work product protection. [*Dowden v. Sup.Ct. (Dowden)* (1999) 73 CA4th 126, 136, 86 CR2d 180, 187—result supported by policy of promoting diligence by each party in preparing its own case rather than relying on adversary's efforts]

(1) [8:216] **Includes attorney's agents and consultants:** However, "work product" of an attorney's employees or agents (investigators, researchers, etc.) is treated as the "work product" of the attorney. [See *Rodriguez v. McDonnell Douglas Corp.* (1978) 87 CA3d 626, 647-648, 151 CR 399, 410 (disapproved on other grounds by *Colto v. Sup.Ct. (State of Calif.)* (2012) 54 C4th 480, 499, 142 CR3d 607, 621-622)]

The "work product" of experts consulted by the attorney and who will *not* testify at trial is likewise treated as the attorney's "work product." [*Scotsman Mfg. v. Sup.Ct.* (1966) 242 CA2d 527, 530, 51 CR 511, 514] (Compare: Experts who testify may be compelled to disclose all reports they have prepared; *see* ¶*8:255 ff.*)

(2) [8:217] **Compare—party's or insurer's consultants:** But a party's or insurer's consultations with an expert *before hiring counsel* are *not* protectible as "attorney work product." Nor can an attorney later "by retroactive adoption convert the independent work of another, already performed, into his own."

© 2020 Thomson Reuters/The Rutter Group

[*Jasper Const., Inc. v. Foothill Junior College Dist. of Santa Clara County* (1979) 91 CA3d 1, 16, 153 CR 767, 776 (internal quotes omitted) (disapproved on other grounds by *Los Angeles Unified School Dist. v. Great American Ins. Co.* (2010) 49 C4th 739, 753, 112 CR3d 230, 240)]

[8:217.1] *Reserved.*

(3) [8:217.2] **Compare—attorney hired for nonlegal work:** "Work product" protection may not be available where the client hires an attorney to perform *nonlegal* services—for example, attorneys hired *solely* to investigate or adjust a claim, or to negotiate a contract, rather than to provide legal advice. (Nor would the attorney-client privilege be available in such cases.) [See *Aetna Cas. & Sur. Co. v. Sup.Ct. (Pietrzak)* (1984) 153 CA3d 467, 475-476, 200 CR 471, 476; *2022 Ranch, L.L.C. v. Sup.Ct. (Chicago Title Ins. Co.)* (2003) 113 CA4th 1377, 1394, 7 CR3d 197, 210 (citing text) (disapproved on other grounds by *Costco Wholesale Corp. v. Sup.Ct. (Randall)* (2009) 47 C4th 725, 739, 101 CR3d 758, 769)] (Compare: But any *writings* they prepare reflecting their *opinions, research*, etc. are entitled to absolute protection; *see ¶8:226.*)

Where an attorney is hired *both to investigate and to advise* the client, the court may have to review the attorney's file in camera to determine which documents reflect investigative work and which reflect the rendering of legal advice. [*Aetna Cas. & Sur. Co. v. Sup.Ct. (Pietrzak)*, supra, 153 CA3d at 475-476, 200 CR at 476; see also *Wellpoint Health Networks, Inc. v. Sup.Ct. (McCombs)* (1997) 59 CA4th 110, 122-124, 68 CR2d 844, 852-853] (In camera examination can be compelled with respect to qualified work product claims, whereas it *cannot* be compelled where a *privilege* is claimed; *see ¶8:192.1.*)

➪ [8:217.3] ***PRACTICE POINTER:*** This can be a particular problem for *in-house legal counsel* who are often asked to "investigate" or "handle" a matter without knowing whether legal advice is required.

If sensitive information is likely to be encountered, it may be a good idea to consider hiring *outside* counsel or an independent investigator to do the investigation. That way, in-house counsel will be free to maintain *separate files*, and can evaluate the case and advise the client without fear that those files will be discoverable by the opposing party.

c. [8:218] **What constitutes "work product":** The Discovery Act does not define "work product" (beyond the provision requiring greater protection for attorneys' mental impressions, *¶8:223*). The definition of "work product" is thus left to case law.

(1) [8:219] **Test—"derivative" vs. "nonderivative" material:** Work product protection covers "derivative" materials—i.e., materials created by or derived from an attorney's work on behalf of a client that reflect the *attorney's evaluation or interpretation* of the law or the facts. "Nonderivative" materials are those that are only *evidentiary* in character, and are not protected even if attorney "work" went into obtaining the materials. [See *Mack v. Sup.Ct. (State of Calif.)* (1968) 259 CA2d 7, 10, 66 CR 280, 283]

(2) [8:220] **Examples of "derivative" material:** Under this test, "work product" includes material that *evaluates or interprets* the facts or the law, or reflects a party's trial strategy. For example:

- Charts and diagrams prepared for trial;
- Audit reports or compilations of entries in documents and records;
- Appraisals, opinions and reports of experts employed as consultants (and not yet designated as trial witnesses; *see ¶8:246 ff.*). [See *Williamson v. Sup.Ct. (Shell Oil Co.)* (1978) 21 C3d 829, 834, 148 CR 39, 42; and *Mack v. Sup.Ct. (State of Calif.)*, supra, 259 CA2d at 10, 66 CR at 283]

(3) [8:221] **Examples of "nonderivative" (evidentiary) matters:** The following would be regarded as merely "evidentiary" in nature, and hence not "work product" despite whatever "work" was invested by counsel in obtaining or locating same:

- The *identity and location of physical evidence* (e.g., the defective product in a products liability case).
- The *identity and location of witnesses* (persons having knowledge of relevant facts). Such information is discoverable regardless of how much attorney "work" went into locating them. [*Aerojet-General Corp. v. Transport Indem. Ins.* (1993) 18 CA4th 996, 1004, 22 CR2d 862, 866; *Huffy Corp. v. Sup.Ct. (Winterthur Swiss Ins. Co.)* (2003) 112 CA4th 97, 109, 4 CR3d 823, 834 (citing text)]

d. [8:222] **Scope of protection:** A distinction is drawn as to the type of "work product" involved:

— *Attorney opinions absolutely protected:* Writings containing an attorney's impressions, conclusions, opinions, etc. are absolutely protected from discovery (CCP §2018.030(a); *see ¶8:223 ff.*).

— *Qualified protection for other "work product":* All other "work product" is entitled to only qualified protection, meaning the court may order disclosure if it determines that "denial of discovery will unfairly prejudice the party seeking discovery in preparing that party's claim or defense or will result in an injustice." [CCP §2018.030(b)]

© 2020 Thomson Reuters/The Rutter Group

(1) [8:223] **Absolute protection for attorney's mental processes:** "A writing that reflects an attorney's impressions, conclusions, opinions or legal research or theories is not discoverable under any circumstances." [CCP §2018.030(a)]

(a) [8:223.1] **Purpose:** As explained in the leading federal case: "Were such materials open to opposing counsel on mere demand, much of what is now put down in writing would remain unwritten. An attorney's thoughts . . . would not be his own. Inefficiency, unfairness and sharp practices would inevitably develop in the giving of legal advice and in the preparation of cases for trial. The effect on the legal profession would be demoralizing. And the interests of the clients and the cause of justice would be poorly served." [*Hickman v. Taylor* (1947) 329 US 495, 511, 67 S.Ct. 385, 393-394 (construing similar provision of FRCP 26(b)(3))]

(b) [8:224] **Protects both written and unwritten opinion work product:** The absolute protection applies when the attorney's mental impressions, etc. are reflected in a "writing." [CCP §2018.030(a)]

"Writing" is broadly defined by the Discovery Act to include *any recorded information*—e.g., letters, photographs, graphs, pictures, audio or videotape, computer data, etc. [CCP §2016.020(c); Ev.C. §250]

But the work product doctrine protects the attorney's mental processes even where the opinions have not yet been reduced to a writing. [*Fireman's Fund Ins. Co. v. Sup.Ct. (Front Gate Plaza, LLC)* (2011) 196 CA4th 1263, 1281-1282, 127 CR3d 768, 782—attorney was not required to respond to deposition questions because her unwritten opinion work product was entitled to absolute work product protection]

1) [8:224.1] **Includes oral communications among law firm members:** Confidential oral communications among members of a law firm on a client's behalf, which involve sharing of opinion work product, are absolutely protected even if not reduced to writing. [*Fireman's Fund Ins. Co. v. Sup.Ct. (Front Gate Plaza, LLC)*, supra, 196 CA4th at 1281, 127 CR3d at 782] Presumably the same rule would obtain where attorneys in different law firms are representing the same client.

(c) [8:225] **Writings "reflecting" attorney work:** To receive absolute protection as "work product," the writing must "reflect" the attorney's impressions, conclusions, research, etc. [CCP §2018.030(a)]

1) [8:225.1] **Documents reviewed with client in preparation for deposition?** It is unclear whether documents reviewed with a client in preparation for the client's deposition are protected as "opinion work product." (The argument for protection is that the documents selected by the lawyer are "writings" reflecting counsel's impressions as to what is and is not important. *See discussion at ¶8:724.3.*)

However, documents used to *refresh* the deponent's memory are discoverable (¶*8:724.3*).

(d) [8:226] **Protects nonlitigating lawyers as well as litigators:** The absolute work product protection is not limited to writings created by a lawyer in anticipation of a lawsuit or preparation for trial. It applies as well to writings prepared while acting in a nonlitigation legal capacity (e.g., memos prepared by lawyers negotiating business deals reflecting their opinions, research, etc.). Thus, if the deal goes sour and the parties sue each other, the attorney's drafts and memos reflecting his or her thought processes in connection with the deal are absolutely protected from discovery. [*Rumac, Inc. v. Bottomley* (1983) 143 CA3d 810, 815, 192 CR 104, 107; *Laguna Beach County Water Dist. v. Sup.Ct. (Woodhouse)* (2004) 124 CA4th 1453, 1460, 22 CR3d 387, 392-393]

(e) [8:227] **No "crime-fraud" exception:** The absolute protection shields even writings prepared to enable a client to commit a crime or fraud. I.e., the "crime-fraud" exception to the attorney-client privilege (Ev.C. §956) does not apply to documents protected as attorney work product under CCP §2018.030(a). [*BP Alaska Exploration, Inc. v. Sup.Ct. (Nahama)* (1988) 199 CA3d 1240, 1249-1250, 245 CR 682, 688-689]

1) [8:227.1] **Compare—criminal prosecution against attorney:** No claim of attorney work product protection is allowed, however, in an official law enforcement investigation or criminal proceeding against a lawyer suspected of knowingly participating in a crime or fraud "if the services of the lawyer were sought or obtained to enable or aid anyone to commit or plan to commit a crime or fraud." [CCP §2018.050; see also Pen.C. §1524(h); and *Rico v. Mitsubishi Motors Corp.* (2007) 42 C4th 807, 820, 68 CR3d 758, 768]

2) [8:227.2] **Compare—communications with client:** Communications to and from the client to enable the client to commit a crime or fraud are discoverable. Such communications are not protected as "work product" and they are not privileged because the "crime-fraud" exception applies to the attorney-

© 2020 Thomson Reuters/The Rutter Group

client privilege (*see* ¶*8:152*). [*BP Alaska Exploration, Inc. v. Sup.Ct. (Nahama),* supra, 199 CA3d at 1262, 245 CR at 697]

a) [8:227.3] **Comment:** This may undo any work product protection. Absent attorney-client privilege, the attorney and client can be questioned on what facts were told to the attorney as the basis for the memorandum or writing. That will probably yield the same information as allowing discovery of the memorandum or writing itself.

(f) [8:228] **Protection not lost by delivery to client:** The attorney's absolute work product protection is not lost by the attorney's delivering copies of his or her writing to the client. [*Wells Fargo Bank, N.A. v. Sup.Ct. (Boltwood)* (2000) 22 C4th 201, 214, 91 CR2d 716, 726]

1) [8:228.1] **Rationale:** This is because the client has an interest in the confidentiality of the work product; and so do other attorneys representing the client. [*Wells Fargo Bank, N.A. v. Sup.Ct. (Boltwood),* supra, 22 C4th at 214, 91 CR2d at 726]

Moreover, the attorney's need for privacy as to his or her writings does not cease upon their delivery to the client. [*BP Alaska Exploration, Inc. v. Sup.Ct. (Nahama)* (1988) 199 CA3d 1240, 1260, 245 CR 682, 695]

(g) [8:229] **Limitation—no protection in litigation with client:** No work product protection exists in litigation between an attorney and client (or former client) on matters "relevant to an issue of breach by the attorney of a duty to the client arising out of the attorney-client relationship." [CCP §2018.080]

1) [8:229.1] **Effect:** Lawyers sued for malpractice or any other "breach of duty" may not withhold their research notes or other documents as "work product."

Moreover, the statute is not limited to malpractice actions. Even fee disputes or actions involving business dealings between attorney and client may involve "duties" owed by the attorney arising out of the attorney-client relationship (e.g., duty not to charge "unconscionable" fees; CRPC 1.5 (formerly CRPC 4-200)).

➪ [8:229.2] ***PRACTICE POINTER:*** If a dispute with a client arises, reject any thought of "trashing" your research notes, etc. to avoid their discovery. First of all, you may need your notes to prove a defense. Next, failure to keep notes could be regarded as evidence of substandard practice. Finally, severe spoliation sanctions may be imposed. *See, e.g.,* ¶*8:2236.*

(h) [8:230] **Protection absolute in other litigation:** In any other litigation, the absolute protection belongs to the attorney alone. Not even the client or former client can compel disclosure of writings reflecting the attorney's impressions, theories, conclusions, etc. [*Lasky, Haas, Cohler & Munter v. Sup.Ct. (Getty)* (1985) 172 CA3d 264, 279, 218 CR 205, 214; see *State Farm Fire & Cas. Co. v. Sup.Ct. (Taylor)* (1997) 54 CA4th 625, 650, 62 CR2d 834, 851]

1) **Application**

- [8:230.1] Third Party sued Lawyer for malicious prosecution of client's earlier lawsuit against Third Party. Lawyer could properly refuse to disclose inter-office memos concerning the earlier suit. The memos were absolutely protected because they contained Lawyer's opinions and conclusions. It made no difference that Lawyer's defense was that there was "probable cause" for the earlier suit (and the memos were relevant to that issue). [*Popelka, Allard, McCowan & Jones v. Sup.Ct. (Coster)* (1980) 107 CA3d 496, 500, 165 CR 748, 751]

- [8:230.2] Lawyer who had represented Client in business transaction could not be compelled to disclose his "opinion" work product in lawsuit between Client and Third Party *even though both parties demanded* such disclosure. The work product protection belonged to the attorney alone. [*Rumac, Inc. v. Bottomley* (1983) 143 CA3d 810, 812, 192 CR 104, 105]

- [8:230.3] Lawyer who formulated opinion in the course of representing Trustee but had not communicated it to Trustee, could not be compelled to disclose that opinion in Beneficiaries' suit to remove Trustee for mismanagement. Lawyer could not be forced to disclose "opinion" work product (no issue of breach of duty by Lawyer involved). [*Lasky, Haas, Cohler & Munter v. Sup.Ct. (Getty)*, supra, 172 CA3d at 273, 218 CR at 210]

(i) [8:231] **Compare—liability to client for refusal to disclose?** That the work product protection belongs to the attorney does not necessarily mean the attorney can withhold information needed by the client with impunity (for example, where the client or former

© 2020 Thomson Reuters/The Rutter Group

client needs the attorney's research notes in order to perfect a claim or defense against a third party).

Under such circumstances, the attorney may be liable to the client for damages proximately resulting from the attorney's assertion of the work product privilege and refusal to disclose the information sought by the client. [See *Rumac, Inc. v. Bottomley* (1983) 143 CA3d 810, 812, 192 CR 104, 105, fn. 3; and *Lasky, Haas, Cohler & Munter v. Sup.Ct. (Getty)* (1985) 172 CA3d 264, 273, 218 CR 205, 210]

Also, a Rule of Professional Conduct requires attorneys, upon termination of employment, to release to their clients "all . . . [c]lient materials and property," including "other items reasonably necessary to the client's representation, whether the client has paid for them or not" (CRPC 1.16(e)(1) (formerly CPRC 3-700(D)(1))). Whether the quoted phrase includes an attorney's written impressions, conclusions, opinions, etc. is presently unclear. [See *Metro-Goldwyn-Mayer, Inc. v. Sup.Ct. (Tracinda Corp.)* (1994) 25 CA4th 242, 249, 30 CR2d 371, 375, fn. 8 (decided under former rule)]

(j) [8:232] **Waiver:** The absolute protection provided for an attorney's impressions, conclusions and research, is subject to waiver under the same conditions as the attorney-client privilege. [*Wells Fargo Bank, N.A. v. Sup.Ct. (Boltwood)* (2000) 22 C4th 201, 214, 91 CR2d 716, 726]

1) [8:233] **Attorney's disclosure to third party as waiver:** Waiver may be found where an attorney discloses his or her impressions and opinions to someone who has no interest in maintaining confidentiality. Such disclosure would be "wholly inconsistent with the purpose of the privilege." [*Laguna Beach County Water Dist. v. Sup.Ct. (Woodhouse)* (2004) 124 CA4th 1453, 1459, 22 CR3d 387, 392 (internal quotes omitted)]

- [8:233.1] No waiver was found, however, where an attorney's opinions were disclosed to the client's auditor in response to an inquiry from the auditor. Both the attorney and auditor intended to retain the confidentiality and the disclosure was made to assist the auditor in preparing the client's financial statements. [See *Laguna Beach County Water Dist. v. Sup.Ct. (Woodhouse)*, supra, 124 CA4th at 1461, 22 CR3d at 393]

(k) [8:234] **Estoppel:** In appropriate cases, attorneys may be estopped to assert work product protection for their opinions, conclusions, etc. [*Metro-Goldwyn-Mayer, Inc. v. Sup.Ct. (Tracinda Corp.)*, supra, 25 CA4th at 249,

30 CR2d at 375-376—attorneys who formerly represented both parties cannot choose sides in litigation between those parties and withhold information from one side]

(2) [8:235] **Qualified protection for other "work product":** All work product other than an attorney's mental impressions, etc. is entitled only to qualified protection; i.e., the court may order disclosure by finding the denial of discovery will either:

— "*unfairly prejudice*" the party seeking discovery in preparation of a claim or defense, or

— "*result in an injustice.*" [CCP §2018.030(b)]

e. **Application**

(1) [8:236] **Tactical information re witnesses:** The *identity* of persons having knowledge of relevant facts is clearly discoverable (*see ¶8:81*). But tactical information regarding the witnesses (e.g., which witnesses will testify or what their testimony will be) may be protected as work product.

(a) [8:236.1] **Which witnesses interviewed:** A list of witnesses whom counsel has chosen to interview may be entitled to absolute or qualified work product protection, depending upon the circumstances. [*Coito v. Sup.Ct. (State of Calif.)* (2012) 54 C4th 480, 502, 142 CR3d 607, 624 (disagreeing with *Nacht & Lewis Architects, Inc. v. Sup.Ct. (McCormick)* (1996) 47 CA4th 214, 217, 54 CR2d 575, 576—such lists "necessarily reflect counsel's evaluation of the case")]

If the choice of witnesses to be interviewed would reveal counsel's tactics or evaluation of the case, *absolute* protection may apply. On the other hand, the list may be entitled to *qualified* protection if it reflects the attorney's industry and effort in selecting witnesses. However, where the attorney interviews all (or almost all) known witnesses, disclosure of the list would be "unlikely to violate the work product privilege." [*Coito v. Sup.Ct. (State of Calif.)*, supra, 54 C4th at 502, 142 CR3d at 624; *see further discussion at ¶8:238 ff.*]

(b) [8:236.2] **Which witnesses to testify:** A party is not required to disclose in advance of trial which witnesses he or she intends to call at trial (except expert witnesses, *see ¶8:237.5*). Such tactical information is entitled to qualified protection as "work product." [*City of Long Beach v. Sup.Ct. (Henderson)* (1976) 64 CA3d 65, 73, 134 CR 468, 473]

(c) [8:237] **What testimony to be given:** Likewise, the testimony which each witness is expected to give at trial is "work product." Even a description of the "nature" of the witness' testimony (e.g., eyewitness, expert, rep-

© 2020 Thomson Reuters/The Rutter Group

utation, etc.) is subject to qualified work product protection. [*City of Long Beach v. Sup.Ct. (Henderson)*, supra, 64 CA3d at 80, 134 CR at 478]

- [8:237.1] An *interrogatory* asking for such information is also objectionable because a response would require disclosure of matters known to the responding party's attorney (¶*8:1088*); and writings containing the *attorney's mental impressions*, conclusions and opinions are *absolutely* privileged under CCP §2018.030(a) (*see* ¶*8:223*). [*City of Long Beach v. Sup.Ct. (Henderson)*, supra, 64 CA3d at 80, 134 CR at 478]

  [8:237.2-237.4] *Reserved.*

(d) [8:237.5] **Compare—procedure for discovery of expert trial witnesses:** Because of the special need for preparation as to opposing expert testimony, a party may demand an exchange of expert witness lists before trial (CCP §2034.010 et seq.; *see* ¶*8:1624 ff.*). But no such procedure exists for other witnesses.

(e) [8:237.6] **Compare—permitted in limited civil cases:** In limited civil cases, either party may serve on the other a request to identify the witnesses who will testify at trial, other than for impeachment. Witnesses not identified may not testify. [CCP §96(a); *see* ¶*8:1821*]

(f) [8:237.7] **Compare—superior court rules requiring exchange of witness lists before trial:** Some superior courts also have local rules or policies requiring each side to serve on the other, shortly before trial, a list of all witnesses who will testify on direct examination, including lay as well as expert witnesses (*see* ¶*8:88, 12:85 ff.*).

1) [8:237.8] **Validity upheld:** Such rules do not conflict with the work product doctrine. That doctrine applies only to compelled disclosure *during discovery* and "does not preclude an ordered exchange of witness lists *shortly before trial.*" [See *In re Jeanette H.* (1990) 225 CA3d 25, 36, 275 CR 9, 16 (citing text)]

2) [8:237.9] **Compare—during discovery:** A local court "General Order" requiring plaintiffs in asbestos cases to file a "case report" *shortly after filing suit* identifying each (nonexpert) witness they intend to call and each document they intend to rely on at trial, was held invalid because it conflicted with the absolute work product protection set forth in CCP §2018.030. [*Snyder v. Sup.Ct. (Caterpillar, Inc.)* (2007) 157 CA4th 1530, 1537, 69 CR3d 600, 604]

(2) [8:238] **Witness statements:** All witness statements from attorney-directed interviews are entitled to at least *qualified*

work product protection. [*Coito v. Sup.Ct. (State of Calif.)* (2012) 54 C4th 480, 499, 142 CR3d 607, 621-622 (disapproving prior cases "to the extent they suggest that a witness statement taken by an attorney does not, as a matter of law, constitute work product")]

Such statements are entitled to *absolute* work product protection if their disclosure would reveal the attorney's mental processes (*see ¶8:223*)—i.e., when the witness statements are "inextricably intertwined" with counsel's comments or notes about the witness or the case. [*Coito v. Sup.Ct. (State of Calif.)*, supra, 54 C4th at 495, 142 CR3d at 618]

(a) [8:238.1] **Procedure on claim of work product protection:** A party seeking disclosure of an attorney-directed witness statement over a claim of work product protection has the burden to establish that withholding disclosure would unfairly prejudice the party in preparing its claim or defense. [*Coito v. Sup.Ct. (State of Calif.)*, supra, 54 C4th at 499-500, 142 CR3d at 622]

The party resisting the discovery on the basis of *absolute* work product protection must make a preliminary showing that disclosure would reveal the attorney's "impressions, conclusions, opinions, or legal research or theories" (per CCP §2018.030(a)). Upon an adequate showing, the trial court should determine, by means of an in camera review if necessary, whether some or all of the material is entitled to absolute protection (*Coito v. Sup.Ct. (State of Calif.)*, supra, 54 C4th at 499-500, 142 CR3d at 622). But such an inspection is not permitted when, in addition to work product protection, the attorney-client privilege is invoked. [*Bank of America, N.A. v. Sup.Ct. (Pacific City Bank)* (2013) 212 CA4th 1076, 1100, 151 CR3d 526, 544]

(b) [8:239] **Compare—independent witness statements:** Statements independently prepared by witnesses are *not* entitled to either qualified or absolute work product protection, even if subsequently turned over to counsel. [*Coito v. Sup.Ct. (State of Calif.)*, supra, 54 C4th at 500-501, 142 CR3d at 623]

(c) [8:240] **Surreptitious recordings?** Witness statements recorded without the witness' consent may be *unlawful.* Pen.C. §632(a) prohibits recording a conversation if either party had a reasonable expectation it was not being overheard or recorded. [See *Flanagan v. Flanagan* (2002) 27 C4th 766, 774, 117 CR2d 574, 579-580; compare *Smith v. LoanMe, Inc.* (2019) 43 CA5th 844, 848, 257 CR3d 61, 63—Pen.C. §632.7 prohibits third party eavesdroppers (not parties to the call) from intentionally recording calls involving at least one cellular or cordless telephone]

© 2020 Thomson Reuters/The Rutter Group

Because such recordings violate the attorney's duty to uphold the law (Bus. & Prof.C. §6068(a)), they may not be protectible as "work product."

(d) [8:241] **"Good cause" required for discovery of witness statements:** Witness statements obtained by counsel are usually work product (*Coito v. Sup.Ct. (State of Calif.)*, supra, 54 C4th at 494, 142 CR3d at 617) and so discoverable only for "good cause" shown. The "good cause" requirement comes from the statute governing inspection demands (CCP §2031.010 et seq.); i.e., where a demand for inspection of a witness statement has been refused, the demanding party must show "*specific facts showing good cause justifying the discovery*" to obtain a court order compelling production. [CCP §2031.310(b)(1) (*¶8:1495 ff.*); and see *Greyhound Corp. v. Sup.Ct. (Clay)* (1961) 56 C2d 355, 387-388, 15 CR 90, 106-107 (superseded by statute as stated in *Coito v. Sup.Ct. (State of Calif.)* (2012) 54 C4th 480, 497-498, 142 CR3d 607, 620) (dealing with similar provision under former law); *People v. Hunter* (2017) 15 CA5th 163, 181, 223 CR3d 113, 129 (citing text)]

1) [8:241.1] **Rationale:** The rationale for the "good cause" requirement is simple fairness: Each side is expected to do its own investigation and trial preparation; neither should be allowed to "ride free on the opponent's industry." [*Greyhound Corp. v. Sup.Ct. (Clay)*, supra, 56 C2d at 401, 15 CR at 115; see *People v. Hunter*, supra, 15 CA5th at 181, 223 CR3d at 129 (citing text)]

2) [8:241.2] **What constitutes "good cause" for discovery of witness statement:** Not much has been required to establish "good cause" for production of such witness statements. "Good cause" has been found to exist where the party seeking discovery shows:

— a special need for discovery (e.g., to refresh witness' memory, to resist potential impeachment); and

— the inability to obtain a similar statement or deposition testimony (e.g., because the witness cannot be located or no longer remembers the details). [See *Christy v. Sup.Ct. (Mazzie Farms)* (1967) 252 CA2d 69, 71-72, 60 CR 85, 86-87; *and ¶8:1495*]

3) [8:241.3] **Compare—attorney work product protection:** A bare showing of "good cause" is *not enough* to compel production of materials constituting attorney work product. A court will order disclosure of such materials only if the party seeking discovery

can demonstrate *injustice or unfair prejudice*, a much heavier burden. [CCP §2018.030(b); *People v. Hunter*, supra, 15 CA5th at 182, 223 CR3d at 129 (citing text); *see* ¶*8:235*]

[8:242] *Reserved.*

(3) [8:243] **Photos, videos, surveillance films:** Surprisingly, there is no recent authority dealing with claims of work product protection for photos, videos, etc. prepared under an attorney's direction. (Again, the Discovery Act is not helpful because it leaves the definition of "work product" to case law.)

- [8:243.1] Photographs of *physical evidence* taken by the attorney or attorney's agents (e.g., the damaged vehicle, the accident scene, the injuries, etc.) may be treated as "nonderivative" material; and thus discoverable as "mere evidence."
- [8:243.2] But photos or films *reflecting counsel's strategies and tactics* in preparation for trial should be treated as "qualified work product" (e.g., a video or surveillance film impeaching plaintiff's claim of disabling injury). It would be basically unfair to allow the other side free access to such material. That party should have to show a *special need* for discovery and *inability to obtain similar information*, etc. [See *Suezaki v. Sup.Ct. (Crawford)* (1962) 58 C2d 166, 177-178, 23 CR 368, 374 (decided before attorney "work product" received statutory protection)]
- [8:243.3] Indeed, certain photos or films "reflecting" counsel's "impressions, conclusions (or) theories" may be "writings" entitled to *absolute* protection (e.g., photos taken from a particular angle or viewpoint, photographic *enlargements*, that show counsel's theory of liability).

(4) [8:244] **Litigation data bases?** In large-scale litigation, attorneys often create enormous data bases of everything they deem potentially relevant; e.g., correspondence, documents, exhibits, witness statements, deposition transcripts, etc. Search mechanisms make this information instantly retrievable by topic, names, dates, etc.

(a) [8:244.1] **Comment:** These data bases appear to be "derivative" work product. However, no known case has yet decided whether, or to what extent, such data bases are protected.

[8:245] *Reserved.*

(5) [8:246] **Consultants' reports:** The identities and opinions of experts retained by counsel *solely* as a consultant—to help evaluate the case or to prepare for trial, and *not* as a trial witness—are entitled to qualified "work product" protection. And, so are "derivative" materials created by such consultants to

© 2020 Thomson Reuters/The Rutter Group

explain or interpret their findings to the attorney (e.g., diagrams, reports and communications to the attorney). [*Williamson v. Sup.Ct. (Shell Oil Co.)* (1978) 21 C3d 829, 834, 148 CR 39, 42]

(a) [8:247] **Rationale for protection:** Protecting such information encourages parties to seek expert advice in evaluating the case. They need not worry about having to disclose unfavorable opinions expressed by the expert; or even the *identity* of such expert (to prevent opposing counsel subpoenaing the expert to testify). Such protection also *encourages experts to serve as consultants*, knowing that doing so will not subject them to subpoenas, depositions, etc. [*Williamson v. Sup.Ct. (Shell Oil Co.)*, supra]

(b) [8:248] **"Good cause" justifying discovery:** As with other qualified work product, the court could order disclosure if denial would "unfairly prejudice" the party seeking discovery or otherwise result in an "injustice." [CCP §2018.030(b); *see ¶8:222*]

However, such disclosure will be ordered only under *exceptional* circumstances. For example:

- [8:249] The consultant is the *only* expert qualified on the particular subject; or one side has consulted with *all* the experts in the vicinity ("cornering the expert market"). [See *Kenney v. Sup.Ct. (Casillas)* (1967) 255 CA2d 106, 113, 63 CR 84, 90 (superseded by statute on other grounds as stated in *California Eye Institute v. Sup.Ct. (Kaye)* (1989) 215 CA3d 1477, 1483, 264 CR 83, 86)]
- [8:250] The consultant inspected and tested an object which is now lost or destroyed and thus not available for inspection and testing by the opponent's experts; or the consultant's testing so altered the object tested that the opponent cannot make like tests. [See *Grand Lake Drive In, Inc. v. Sup.Ct. (Bateman)* (1960) 179 CA2d 122, 132, 3 CR 621, 628]
- [8:250.1] Numerous plaintiffs sued Toxic Waste Facility for damages. Plaintiffs' Attorney hired Doctors to conduct a study on health effects of persons living near the facility. State Health Director (whose job it was to enforce pollution laws) tried to conduct similar study but plaintiffs refused to cooperate because of the pending litigation. "Good cause" was shown for discovery by the State Health Director because he was *not a party* to the action and there was *no showing the opposing party* (toxic waste facility) *would gain access thereto*. [*Kizer v. Sulnick* (1988) 202 CA3d 431, 441, 248 CR 712, 718]

- [8:250.2] In return for a codefendant's promise of indemnification, D withdrew an expert witness it had previously designated in order to suppress the expert's testimony. Plaintiff was entitled to discovery of the expert's reports: "[N]o policy underlying the work product doctrine justifies . . . [purchased] suppression of evidence." [*Williamson v. Sup.Ct (Shell Oil Co.)* (1978) 21 C3d 829, 838, 148 CR 39, 45; *see ¶8:262*]

(c) [8:251] **Compare—no discovery where consultant's report also protected by attorney-client privilege:** The report of an expert retained by the attorney to examine the client and evaluate the client's condition may also be protected under the attorney-client privilege. It may be treated as a *communication on behalf of the client* to the attorney (*see ¶8:148*). If such privilege applies, of course, no showing of "good cause" would justify disclosure.

(d) [8:252] **Compare—no discovery where consultation was for purpose of filing certificate of merit in malpractice action:** In malpractice actions against certain professionals (architects, engineers, etc.), plaintiff's attorney is required to certify that he or she consulted with a qualified expert before filing the action and believes the case to be meritorious. [CCP §411.35, *discussed at ¶1:874 ff.*]

This consultation is privileged, and plaintiff's attorney cannot be required to disclose the identity of the expert consulted. Exception: If plaintiff *loses* the case (but not a settlement), the court may order plaintiff's attorney to identify the expert consulted in order to "verify compliance" with the certificate of merit requirement. (Such identification is made in camera and defendant may not be present.) [CCP §411.35; see *Korbel v. Chou* (1994) 27 CA4th 1427, 1431-1433, 33 CR2d 190, 192-193; *see also ¶1:892*]

[8:253] *Reserved.*

(e) [8:254] **Waiver by demanding copy of opposing medical examiner's report:** In personal injury cases, plaintiff must submit to a defense medical exam on demand, but has the right to request a copy of the examiner's report. Doing so, however, obligates plaintiff to furnish copies of his or her *own* medical reports to the defendant, including reports of doctors previously engaged on a *consultant* basis whose work would otherwise be shielded as "work product." [CCP §2032.630; *see ¶8:1611*]

© 2020 Thomson Reuters/The Rutter Group

1) [8:254.1] **Includes consultants not designated as trial witnesses:** Whether plaintiff's doctors are going to testify as experts at trial is irrelevant: "To conclude otherwise would permit [plaintiff] to arrange unlimited medical examinations and reports and suppress those he might think unfavorable merely by characterizing the doctors who prepared them as advisers to counsel and promising not to call them as witnesses." [*Queen of Angels Hosp. v. Sup.Ct. (Jones)* (1976) 57 CA3d 370, 374-375, 129 CR 282, 285]

2) [8:254.2] **But not identity of experts who made no written reports:** But plaintiff need not disclose the identity of doctors who examined plaintiff and *never put their reports in writing.* This prevents plaintiff from having to disclose unfavorable evaluations from doctors he or she would not call to testify. [See CCP §2032.640, ¶*8:1616*]

☞ [8:254.3] ***PRACTICE POINTER:*** Obviously, if you represent plaintiff and ask a doctor or other expert to examine plaintiff and evaluate the injuries, instruct the doctor *to report to you orally* after the examination. Only if the evaluation is favorable should a written report be requested. (*See further discussion at ¶8:1616 ff.*)

(f) [8:255] **Waiver by designating consultant as trial witness:** "Work product" protection may terminate when a consultant is designated *to testify as an expert witness under CCP §2034.010 et seq.* (statutory procedure for exchange of expert witness information before trial, *see ¶8:1624 ff.*). Upon such designation, the expert's identity, opinions and reports may be discovered to the extent discussed below (¶*8:256 ff.*).

1) [8:256] **Reports "in capacity of expert witness" fully discoverable:** When an expert witness demand is made, reports containing "findings and opinions that go to the establishment or denial of a principal issue in the case" must be turned over to the opposing party. [*National Steel Products Co. v. Sup.Ct. (Rosen)* (1985) 164 CA3d 476, 489, 210 CR 535, 543]

"[O]nce a defendant physician is designated as an expert for trial . . . her present and previous opinion about the medical procedures at issue . . . would be proper subjects of discovery, *notwithstanding any communications she may have had with counsel,* retained experts, or [others]." [*County of Los Angeles v. Sup.Ct. (Martinez)* (1990) 224 CA3d 1446, 1458, 274 CR 712, 720 (emphasis added)]

© 2020 Thomson Reuters/The Rutter Group

2) [8:257] **"Advisory" reports still protected as "work product":** However, reports previously rendered in a *consultant* capacity do *not* automatically lose their protected status as "work product." (E.g., reports rendered to assist the attorney in such matters as preparation of pleadings and discovery requests, manner of proof and cross-examination of opposing expert witnesses.) These remain protected after an expert witness demand because they are often "reflective of the mental processes of the attorney under whose direction the expert works." [*National Steel Products Co. v. Sup.Ct. (Rosen)*, supra, 164 CA3d at 489, 210 CR at 543]

The advice in the report given by the expert in a consulting capacity on trial preparation, etc. remains subject to conditional work product protection. The trial court may conduct an in camera review to separate the information (¶*8:264*). [*DeLuca v. State Fish Co., Inc.* (2013) 217 CA4th 671, 690, 158 CR3d 761, 775—report may be redacted and partially disclosed]

a) [8:258] **Possible impeachment as "good cause" for discovery of "advisory" reports:** As with other qualified work product, however, disclosure may be ordered where denial of discovery would "unfairly prejudice" the party or result in an "injustice" (CCP §2018.030(b), *see* ¶*8:222*). This may be the case where the expert's prior reports as a consultant contain information that could be used for *potential impeachment* purposes. In such cases, "a court [must] *weigh carefully* the power of impeachment as a valuable tool in the process of truth ascertainment against the benefits of protecting the privilege of 'work product.' " [*Jasper Const., Inc. v. Foothill Junior College Dist. of Santa Clara County* (1979) 91 CA3d 1, 17, 153 CR 767, 776 (emphasis added) (disapproved on other grounds by *Los Angeles Unified School Dist. v. Great American Ins. Co.* (2010) 49 C4th 739, 753, 112 CR3d 230, 240)]

1/ [8:259] **Rationale:** The need for discovery to prepare for cross-examination and rebuttal of an expert is the same or greater than for lay witnesses. And there is *no adequate substitute* for the expert's prior report: "[T]he potential impeachment value . . . lies in the fact that it was prepared by the expert identified as a witness . . . and may include

© 2020 Thomson Reuters/The Rutter Group

inconsistent prior statements of that witness." [*National Steel Products Co. v. Sup.Ct. (Rosen)*, supra, 164 CA3d at 491-492, 210 CR at 544]

2/ [8:260] **Example:** After exchange of expert witness lists, P demanded production of a report D's expert had prepared for D in prior, *unrelated* litigation. D's expert gave a declaration stating he had *not* relied on his prior report in formulating his opinion in the present case. But it was "reasonable to infer that the expert *considered* his prior" report because both had been prepared for the same client and related to the same type of problem. Therefore, it was discoverable for possible impeachment. [*National Steel Products Co. v. Sup.Ct. (Rosen)*, supra, 164 CA3d at 491, 210 CR at 544 (emphasis added)]

[8:260.1-260.4] *Reserved.*

[8:260.5] ***PRACTICE POINTERS:*** Expect your opponent to claim "potential impeachment" in order to get at your experts' earlier "advisory" reports.

Some lawyers instruct experts whom they plan to call to testify at trial to report *orally* so there will be no reports to turn over. However, there is a risk in this: Opposing counsel may argue to the jury that any responsible expert would have prepared a written report (*see ¶8:1685.1*).

In any event, if you have written reports from a consulting expert, be sure to review those reports *before* designating him or her as a trial witness under CCP §2034.260. And don't attempt to "turn" an expert who has initially given you an unfavorable written report. The earlier report will surely surface and will destroy the value of any testimony given at trial.

3) [8:260.6] **Protection lost once reasonably clear expert will testify:** Once "it becomes reasonably certain an expert will give his professional opinion as a witness on a material matter in dispute, then his opinion has become a factor in the cause. At that point the expert has ceased to be merely

a consultant" and the work product protection ceases (*but see ¶8:261*). [*DeLuca v. State Fish Co., Inc.* (2013) 217 CA4th 671, 689-690, 158 CR3d 761, 775 (internal citation omitted)—point where reasonably certain expert will testify is "bright line" with work product protection before but not after; see *Williamson v. Sup.Ct. (Shell Oil Co.)* (1978) 21 C3d 829, 834-835, 148 CR 39, 42-43]

At that point, work product protection is waived for all past reports and communications. [*DeLuca v. State Fish Co., Inc.,* supra, 217 CA4th at 689, 158 CR3d at 774]

4) [8:261] **Right to withdraw designated expert:** A party has the right to withdraw an expert designated under CCP §2034.010 who has not yet been deposed. Work product protection is *reinstated* if the expert is retained in a consultant capacity. [*County of Los Angeles v. Sup.Ct. (Hernandez)* (1990) 222 CA3d 647, 656, 271 CR 698, 704; *see ¶8:1687.5*]

   a) [8:262] **Limitation—no paid-for suppression of expert testimony:** Once experts have been designated as potential witnesses, their opinions and reports are discoverable to the extent indicated above (*¶8:255 ff.*). The party employing such experts cannot "withdraw" them and return them to consultant status (shielded from discovery) *in return for a pay-off* from another party likely to be harmed by the experts' testimony. [See *Williamson v. Sup.Ct. (Shell Oil Co.)* (1978) 21 C3d 829, 838, 148 CR 39, 45 (decided under former statute for expert witness identification)]

5) [8:263] **Opposing party's right to call expert as witness?** While there is no known authority in point, nothing in CCP §2034.010 et seq. precludes the opposing party from calling as a witness at trial a person who may be a consultant for the opposing party. I.e., the attorney work-product doctrine limiting *discovery* of a consultant's identity and opinions should not affect admissibility of relevant testimony at trial. [See *Riley v. Dow Chemical Co.* (ND CA 1989) 123 FRD 639, 640]

   a) [8:263.1] **Ex parte interview with consultant?** Before calling the expert to testify, counsel usually wants to know what the expert will say. But it may be *ethically improper* to interview an expert *knowing* he or she is a consultant to the opposing party. Indeed, *counsel risks disqualification* if confidential or privileged information is disclosed

© 2020 Thomson Reuters/The Rutter Group

by the expert. [See *County of Los Angeles v. Sup.Ct. (Hernandez)*, supra, 222 CA3d at 657-658, 271 CR at 704; *Shadow Traffic Network v. Sup.Ct. (Metro Traffic Control, Inc.)* (1994) 24 CA4th 1067, 1087-1088, 29 CR2d 693, 705—law firm disqualified for retaining expert whom it *knew* had previously been consulted by opposing counsel]

b) [8:263.2] **Hiring opposing party's expert in a subsequent trial?** As a general rule, the conditional protection for any work product conveyed to a consulting expert ceases "once the expert is likely to testify" (*see ¶8:260.6*). Thus, after an expert has testified, the other side may be able to use the expert in a retrial or subsequent proceeding. [*DeLuca v. State Fish Co., Inc.*, supra, 217 CA4th at 692-693, 158 CR3d at 777; *see ¶1:89.5 ff.*]

However, "[e]ven if attorney work product conveyed to a consulting expert remains subject to work product protection after the expert has been designated as a testifying expert," opposing counsel would be subject to disqualification for later retaining that expert *only if* confidential information materially relevant to the present proceedings was conveyed to the expert. [*DeLuca v. State Fish Co., Inc.*, supra, 217 CA4th at 686, 692, 158 CR3d at 771-772, 777—order disqualifying counsel reversed where showing not made]

[8:263.3-263.9] *Reserved.*

(g) [8:263.10] **Waiver by sharing work product with others?** Sharing with others information that is entitled to qualified work product protection does not waive the protection unless the circumstances are *inconsistent with safeguarding* the privacy of the attorney's trial preparations. [See *Raytheon Co. v. Sup.Ct. (Renault)* (1989) 208 CA3d 683, 689, 256 CR 425, 429]

1) [8:263.11] **Work product shared with retained expert:** Attorney work product protection is not lost by the attorney delivering copies to experts retained by the attorney or in discussions relating to retention of the expert, even if the expert is not subsequently retained. [*Shadow Traffic Network v. Sup.Ct. (Metro Traffic Control, Inc.)*, supra, 24 CA4th at 1079, 29 CR2d at 699]

2) [8:263.12] **Work product shared with counsel for collaborating parties:** Where parties collaborate on creating or obtaining work product, waiver of the protection by one of them does not bar the other from asserting it: "Where work product is the result of collaboration by counsel, all holders of the attorney work-product privilege must consent to waiver of the privilege." [*Armenta v. Sup.Ct. (James Jones Co.)* (2002) 101 CA4th 525, 532, 124 CR2d 273, 278—party's willingness to waive attorney work product protection for test results by expert jointly retained with coparty did not affect coparty's right to prevent disclosure of those results]

(h) [8:264] **Three-step analysis required:** To rule on claims of "work product" protection, it will often be necessary for the trial judge to conduct an in camera inspection of the reports in question and to make the following determinations:

- First, if the report reflects in whole or in part the *attorney's impressions, conclusions, opinions or theories*, such information is *absolutely* protected and cannot be reviewed in camera (Ev.C. §915(a), *but see* ¶*8:267*) or discovered under any circumstances (*see* ¶*8:223 ff.*).
- Second, as to portions not absolutely privileged, was the report made by an expert designated as a trial witness (i.e., fully discoverable) or was it merely *advisory* to the attorney? (If only advisory, it is conditionally privileged and cannot be discovered unless "unfair prejudice" to the party seeking discovery is shown; *see* ¶*8:246 ff.*)
- Third, as to advisory reports, does "good cause" for discovery *outweigh* the policies supporting work product protection? Particularly, could the report serve as possible impeachment of the expert's testimony at trial? [*National Steel Products Co. v. Sup.Ct. (Rosen)* (1985) 164 CA3d 476, 489-492, 210 CR 535, 543-544]

(i) [8:265] **Comment:** This remains a difficult area, and numerous problems are still unresolved:

- For example, it may be difficult to determine whether a particular report was rendered in an "advisory" capacity or in the expert's capacity as a prospective witness. Its *timing* is certainly significant (whether before or after the expert was designated as a trial witness); but should not be controlling (even a report prepared on the day of trial might be held "advisory").
- Issues may also arise as to *how much* of the expert's

© 2020 Thomson Reuters/The Rutter Group

file is discoverable: Are the expert's *rough drafts* and preliminary reports discoverable on the theory they may conflict with final conclusions and thus potentially impeach the expert? Are *oral* communications with counsel discoverable on the same ground? Does all or any portion of the report reflect the *attorney's* impressions, etc. so that it is absolutely protected? (As a result, courts may be required to "cut and paste"; i.e., to separate the report into discoverable and nondiscoverable parts.)

f. **Procedural matters**

(1) [8:266] **Who may assert:** The *attorney*, rather than the client, is the holder of work product protection (*Wells Fargo Bank, N.A. v. Sup.Ct. (Boltwood)* (2000) 22 C4th 201, 215, 91 CR2d 716, 726, fn. 5). As between a law firm and its individual attorneys, the firm is the holder of the right. [*Tucker Ellis LLP v. Sup.Ct. (Nelson)* (2017) 12 CA5th 1233, 1245, 220 CR3d 382, 391]

But, if the attorney is not present, the client may assert it. [*Mylan Laboratories Inc. v. Soon-Shiong* (1999) 76 CA4th 71, 81, 90 CR2d 111, 118, fn. 2]

(a) [8:266.1] **Limitation:** Attorneys cannot assert work product protection *against* their clients when sued for malpractice or other "breach of duty"; *see ¶8:229.*

Nor can attorneys who formerly represented both parties assert work product protection in later litigation between the parties; *see ¶8:234.*

(b) [8:266.2] **In pro pers:** A litigant in pro per may also assert work product protection. [*Dowden v. Sup.Ct. (Dowden)* (1999) 73 CA4th 126, 136, 86 CR2d 180, 187; *see ¶8:215*]

[8:266.3-266.4] *Reserved.*

(2) [8:266.5] **Methods for claiming "work product" protection:** The "work product" limitation can be raised in various ways:

- By *specific objection* to a demand for document production (CCP §2031.210(a)(3), *¶8:1474*);
- By motion for *protective order* (CCP §2031.060, *¶8:1452*); or
- By *motion to quash* a subpoena duces tecum (*see ¶8:601*).

(3) [8:267] **In camera inspection may be required for qualified work product:** In order to rule on a claim of work product protection, the court may order disclosure or inspection in camera (in chambers) of material sought to be protected as "qualified" work product (*see ¶8:222*). [Ev.C. §915(b)]

It is not clear if under *Coito v. Sup.Ct. (State of Calif.)* (2012) 54 C4th 480, 499-500, 142 CR3d 607, 622, a court may also make an in camera inspection to determine an absolute work product claim. *Coito* states that the "trial court should . . . make an in camera inspection to determine whether absolute work product protection applies to some or all of the material," but does not discuss Ev.C. §915(a) which appears to *bar* court review of material claimed to be protected under the absolute attorney work product doctrine.

g. [8:268] **Work product protection available at trial?** There is a split of authority on whether "work product" is ground for excluding otherwise admissible evidence at trial:

- [8:269] One view is that "work product" is only a limitation on pretrial discovery and *not* on evidence at trial. (Rationale: The limitation is part of the Discovery Act, not the Evidence Code.) Thus, if the opposing party somehow obtains access to the evidence, it is admissible over any objection based on work product. [*Jasper Const., Inc. v. Foothill Junior College Dist. of Santa Clara County* (1979) 91 CA3d 1, 16, 153 CR 767, 775 (disapproved on other grounds by *Los Angeles Unified School Dist. v. Great American Ins. Co.* (2010) 49 C4th 739, 753, 112 CR3d 230, 240)—expert witness testimony could not be excluded on ground that witness had originally been retained as consultant for opposing party; *In re Jeanette H.* (1990) 225 CA3d 25, 37, 275 CR 9, 16—local rules requiring exchange of witness lists shortly before trial do not conflict with work product doctrine, which applies only *during discovery*]

- [8:270] But there is also authority contra, on the rationale that the policy of preventing parties from taking "unfair advantage" of their adversaries' efforts is just as important at trial as during pretrial discovery. [*Rodriguez v. McDonnell Douglas Corp.* (1978) 87 CA3d 626, 648, 151 CR 399, 410 (disapproved on other grounds by *Coito v. Sup.Ct. (State of Calif.)* (2012) 54 CA4th 480, 499, 142 CR3d 607, 621-622)—notes taken by attorney's investigator during witness interview could not be introduced by opposing party as impeachment evidence; *Kizer v. Sulnick* (1988) 202 CA3d 431, 440, 248 CR 712, 717 (dictum)]

h. [8:271] **Work product protection in later lawsuit:** The protection is *not* limited to the lawsuit for which the information was prepared or obtained. It continues *indefinitely* and may be asserted in later litigation. [*Fellows v. Sup.Ct. (Allstate Ins. Co.)* (1980) 108 CA3d 55, 61, 166 CR 274, 278 (disapproved on other grounds by *Coito v. Sup.Ct. (State of Calif.)* (2012) 54 CA4th 480, 499, 142 CR3d 607, 621-622)]

Even so, under appropriate circumstances, qualified-protection work product may be discoverable in the later lawsuit. I.e., if a "substantial need" is shown for discovery of work product from the earlier suit (e.g., for impeachment purposes), and the information is not reasonably obtainable from other sources, the

© 2020 Thomson Reuters/The Rutter Group

work product protection may be pierced and discovery allowed. [*National Steel Products Co. v. Sup.Ct. (Rosen)* (1985) 164 CA3d 476, 491, 210 CR 535, 544; *see ¶8:258*]

(1) [8:271.1] **Limitation re attorney-client litigation:** There is *no* work product protection in litigation between attorney and a former client involving claims of breach of duty by the attorney (assuming the work product-protected material is relevant to the issues in the later action). [CCP §2018.080; *see ¶8:229*]

i. [8:272] **No work product protection in State Bar disciplinary proceedings:** The State Bar may discover the work product of an attorney against whom disciplinary charges are pending if relevant to issues of breach of duty by the lawyer. Discovery is allowed only with the client's approval (which is implied where the client has initiated the proceedings against the attorney). Upon showing "good cause," the attorney may obtain a protective order to assure confidentiality of the work product and limit its use to the disciplinary investigations. [CCP §2018.070(a), (b)]

[8:273-292] *Reserved.*

5. [8:293] **Privacy Protection:** Even highly relevant, nonprivileged information may be shielded from discovery if its disclosure would impair a person's "inalienable right of privacy" provided by Calif. Const. Art. 1, §1. [*Britt v. Sup.Ct. (San Diego Unified Port Dist.)* (1978) 20 C3d 844, 855-856, 143 CR 695, 702; *Pioneer Electronics (USA), Inc. v. Sup.Ct. (Olmstead)* (2007) 40 C4th 360, 370, 53 CR3d 513, 520—right of privacy "protects the individual's *reasonable* expectation of privacy against a *serious* invasion" (emphasis in original)]

The right to privacy is also guaranteed by the U.S. Constitution. [*Griswold v. State of Connecticut* (1965) 381 US 479, 484, 85 S.Ct. 1678, 1681; *Palay v. Sup.Ct. (County of Los Angeles)* (1993) 18 CA4th 919, 931, 22 CR2d 839, 847 (disapproved on other grounds by *Williams v. Sup.Ct. (Marshalls of CA, LLC)* (2017) 3 C5th 531, 557, 220 CR3d 472, 494 & fn. 8)]

Privacy protection is recognized in administrative as well as civil proceedings. [*Sehlmeyer v. Department of Gen. Services* (1993) 17 CA4th 1072, 1079, 21 CR2d 840, 843]

Privacy protection in filed documents: Only the last four digits in an individual's *social security number* or *financial accounts* may be used in documents filed with the court. [CRC 1.201(a); *see discussion at ¶6:13.10 ff.*]

New laws effective January 1, 2020, including the California Consumer Privacy Act (Civ.C. §1798.100 et seq. (amended eff. 1/1/20)), provide an array of new privacy protections for consumers, creating rights over data ownership, broad definitions of personal information, rights to know what data is collected and to ask for deletion of personal data, as well as other rights. While these new laws do not expressly amend privacy interests in the civil discovery context, they are likely to have some effect. [See also Civ.C. §§1798.29, 1798.81.5, 1798.82, 1798.130, 1798.145 (all amended eff. 1/1/20)]

a. [8:294] **Protection not absolute:** Unlike privilege, the protection afforded is qualified, not absolute. In each case, the court must *carefully balance* the right of privacy against the need for discovery (*see ¶8:323 ff.*). The showing required to overcome the protection depends on the nature of the privacy right asserted; in some cases, a simple balancing test is sufficient, while in others, a compelling interest must be shown. "Only *obvious invasions of interests fundamental to personal autonomy* must be supported by a compelling interest." [*Williams v. Sup.Ct. (Marshalls of CA, LLC)*, supra, 3 C5th at 557, 220 CR3d at 494 (emphasis added); *Hill v. National Collegiate Athletic Ass'n* (1994) 7 C4th 1, 34-35, 26 CR2d 834, 856; *Kirchmeyer v. Phillips* (2016) 245 CA4th 1394, 1403, 200 CR3d 515, 522; *Lewis v. Sup.Ct. (Medical Bd. of Calif.)* (2017) 3 C5th 561, 572-573, 220 CR3d 319, 328-329—medical board obtaining doctor's prescribing history did not intrude on fundamental autonomy right, so balancing test applied]

The burden is on "the party asserting a privacy interest to establish its extent and the seriousness of the prospective invasion," and then the court must "weigh the countervailing interests the opposing party identifies." [*Williams v. Sup.Ct. (Marshalls of CA, LLC)*, supra, 3 C5th at 557, 220 CR3d at 493-494]

In almost every case, disclosure may be ordered if a "compelling public interest" would be served thereby. [*Britt v. Sup.Ct. (San Diego Unified Port Dist.)*, supra, 20 C3d at 855-856, 143 CR at 702; *Cross v. Sup.Ct. (Kidane)* (2017) 11 CA5th 305, 326-327, 217 CR3d 569, 585—compelling interest in investigation of improper prescribing of controlled substances overcame patients' privacy right in psychiatric records; *John B. v. Sup.Ct. (Bridget B.)* (2006) 38 C4th 1177, 1199, 45 CR3d 316, 332—compelling state interest in preventing spread of AIDS virus; *see ¶8:305 ff.*]

Moreover, "[t]he particular context, i.e., the specific kind of privacy interest involved and the nature and seriousness of the invasion and any countervailing interests, remains the critical factor in the analysis." [*Hill v. National Collegiate Athletic Ass'n*, supra, 7 C4th at 34, 26 CR2d at 855—involving drug testing of college athletes with reduced expectation of privacy; see *Kirchmeyer v. Phillips*, supra, 245 CA4th at 1403, 200 CR3d at 522]

⇨ [8:294.1] ***PRACTICE POINTER:*** A balancing of privacy versus need does not necessarily result in an absolute ruling to either permit discovery or not permit it. Rather, *Williams v. Sup.Ct. (Marshalls of CA, LLC)*, supra, 3 C5th at 557, 220 CR3d at 493-494, seems to suggest that the balancing often results in the following: if the privacy interests can be accommodated with conditions (such as a protective order, limits on dissemination, redactions of social security numbers, and the like), give the discovery with the conditions. In other

© 2020 Thomson Reuters/The Rutter Group

words, the court may try to accommodate both the need for discovery and the interests that inhibit it. If you are trying to obtain discovery over privacy objections, consider suggesting appropriate conditions that will persuade the court that they accommodate the privacy interests.

(1) **Application**

- [8:295] As part of an investigation of Physician for billing irregularities and standard of care violations, Medical Board issued an administrative subpoena for his patients' medical records. The court's order requiring production of the records was affirmed on grounds the state's interest in quality medical care, and a factual showing that the specific records sought were likely to be material to the investigation, were sufficiently compelling to overcome the patients' privacy rights. [*Fett v. Medical Bd. of Calif.* (2016) 245 CA4th 211, 221, 199 CR3d 196, 204 (*see* ¶*8:306*)]

  [8:295.1] *Reserved.*

- [8:295.2] *Compare:* During an investigation of a complaint alleging Psychiatrist improperly had sex with Patient, Medical Board issued an administrative subpoena and moved to compel production of Psychiatrist's notes of his sessions with Patient. The court's order *denying* production was affirmed because the therapy session notes were protected by the psychotherapist-patient privilege, which is based on a constitutional right of privacy. The Board failed to show a compelling interest to warrant production of those specific records. [*Kirchmeyer v. Phillips*, supra, 245 CA4th at 1403-1404, 200 CR3d at 522-523; see also *Grafilo v. Wolfsohn* (2019) 33 CA5th 1024, 1037, 245 CR3d 564, 574—insufficient evidence of doctor abuse in prescribing pain medication and thus no good cause to release patient files]

  [8:295.3-295.4] *Reserved.*

(2) [8:295.5] **Effect of contract for confidentiality:** Parties may be bound by an agreement not to seek disclosure of certain confidential information. Where it would affect the privacy of a noncontracting party, he or she may have standing to enforce the agreement as a third-party beneficiary. [See *Johnson v. Sup.Ct. (Calif. Cryobank, Inc.)* (2000) 80 CA4th 1050, 1064-1065, 95 CR2d 864, 873 (disapproved on other grounds by *Williams v. Sup.Ct. (Marshalls of CA, LLC)* (2017) 3 C5th 531, 557, 220 CR3d 472, 494 & fn. 8)—parties purchasing sperm for artificial insemination agreed not to seek information re sperm donor]

Conversely, parties may contract for a waiver of privacy rights. [*TBG Ins. Services Corp. v. Sup.Ct. (Zieminski)* (2002) 96

CA4th 443, 452, 117 CR2d 155, 163—employment contract waived employee's privacy as to information stored on computer furnished by employer]

(a) [8:295.6] **Public policy limitation:** A confidentiality agreement may be held unenforceable, however, where it is contrary to a statute or public policy. [*Johnson v. Sup.Ct. (Calif. Cryobank, Inc.)*, supra, 80 CA4th at 1065, 95 CR2d at 873—agreement prohibiting information re sperm donor violated statute authorizing disclosure upon court order and public policy protecting children conceived through artificial insemination (information re donor's genetic and medical history needed for important medical decisions re child conceived with donor's sperm); see also *Crab Addison, Inc. v. Sup.Ct. (Martinez)* (2008) 169 CA4th 958, 974, 87 CR3d 400, 413—public policy favoring class actions to enforce employees' statutory wage and overtime rights required employer to disclose contact information for employees who were potential class members *even if they had signed a form* stating they did *not consent* to release of such information]

b. [8:296] **Whose privacy protected:** The privacy protected may be either that of one of the parties to the action or of some *third person* (nonparty) to whom the information pertains.

(1) [8:297] **Business entities:** The right of privacy contained in the California Constitution (Art. 1, §1) is limited to "people," meaning natural persons: "[T]he constitutional provision simply does not apply to corporations." [*Roberts v. Gulf Oil Corp.* (1983) 147 CA3d 770, 791, 796-797, 195 CR 393, 406, 411-412; see *SCC Acquisitions, Inc. v. Sup.Ct. (Western Albuquerque Land Holdings, LLC)* (2015) 243 CA4th 741, 755-756, 196 CR3d 533, 544-545—"While corporations do have a right to privacy, it is not a constitutional right"]

Although the issue is unsettled, some privacy protection may exist for business entities, apart from its members or shareholders, depending on the circumstances: "Two critical factors are the strength of the nexus between the artificial entity and human beings and the context in which the controversy arises." [*Roberts v. Gulf Oil Corp.*, supra, 147 CA3d at 796-797, 195 CR at 411-412—corporation cannot prevent County Tax Assessor from obtaining corporate financial records for tax assessment purposes, but 14th Amendment limits extent of possible intrusion into corporate records; see *Ameri-Medical Corp. v. WCAB* (1996) 42 CA4th 1260, 1286-1289, 50 CR2d 366, 383-385—professional medical corporation retained privacy interest in financial and employment information *unrelated* to preparation of medical reports sought by workers' compensation insurers]

[8:297.1-297.4] *Reserved.*

© 2020 Thomson Reuters/The Rutter Group

(a) [8:297.5] **Balancing required:** Assuming a business entity has a right of privacy, courts must determine whether it is outweighed by the relevance of the information sought to the subject matter in the pending action. "[D]oubts as to relevance should generally be resolved in favor of permitting discovery." [*Hecht, Solberg, Robinson, Goldberg & Bagley v. Sup.Ct. (Panther)* (2006) 137 CA4th 579, 593, 40 CR3d 446, 456 (internal quotes omitted); see *SCC Acquisitions, Inc. v. Sup.Ct. (Western Albuquerque Land Holdings, LLC)*, supra, 243 CA4th at 755-756, 196 CR3d at 545—since corporate privacy right not constitutionally protected, discovery determined by balancing test]

- [8:297.6] Client sued Attorney for malpractice for allegedly settling Client's claim against Partnership for less than it was worth. Partnership's privacy interest in its financial records was outweighed by their relevancy in determining causation and damages in the malpractice case (i.e., whether Partnership had the ability to pay more than its settlement with Client). [See *Hecht, Solberg, Robinson, Goldberg & Bagley v. Sup.Ct. (Panther)*, supra, 137 CA4th at 595-596, 40 CR3d at 457-458]

(2) [8:298] **Nonparties:** Information pertaining to a third person may be within the recognized "zone of privacy" protected from discovery (¶*8:301 ff.*) in an action between other parties. [See *Coito v. Sup.Ct. (State of Calif.)* (2012) 54 C4th 480, 502, 142 CR3d 607, 624 (citing text)]

(a) [8:299] **Identity of nonparties (contact information):** Where nonparties' identity is relevant to the action (e.g., because they have suffered similar injuries), a party may be compelled to disclose their *names, addresses and phone numbers, provided* the nonparties are notified and given an opportunity to *object* to disclosure of their contact information. [See *Pioneer Electronics (USA), Inc. v. Sup.Ct. (Olmstead)* (2007) 40 C4th 360, 367, 53 CR3d 513, 516-517—in order to determine suitability of *potential class action,* manufacturer of allegedly defective DVD players could be compelled to disclose identities of purchasers who had complained to manufacturer, after they were notified and given an opportunity to object to such disclosure; but see *Life Technologies Corp. v. Sup.Ct. (Joyce)* (2011) 197 CA4th 640, 655, 130 CR3d 80, 92 (disapproved on other grounds by *Williams v. Sup.Ct. (Marshalls of CA, LLC)* (2017) 3 C5th 531, 557, 220 CR3d 472, 494 & fn. 8)—where providing third parties' contact information would necessarily disclose confidential information in which third parties had right of privacy, third parties had substantial interest in the privacy of contact information; *see also* ¶*14:135.3 ff.*]

[8:299.1-299.4] *Reserved.*

1) [8:299.5] **Compare—percipient witnesses:** Although disclosure may invade their privacy, there is generally no protection for the identity, addresses and phone numbers of percipient witnesses. Thus, a court may not require the party seeking discovery to obtain the witnesses' consent to disclosure: "[A] percipient witness's willingness to participate in civil discovery has never been considered relevant—witnesses may be compelled to appear and testify whether they want to or not." [*Puerto v. Sup.Ct. (Wild Oats Markets, Inc.)* (2008) 158 CA4th 1242, 1251-1252, 70 CR3d 701, 708—error to require plaintiff to secure witnesses' consent to disclosure of their names and addresses]

   a) [8:299.6] **Limitations:** The above rule (¶*8:299.5*) is subject to certain limitations:

      - [8:299.7] A protective order may issue where disclosure of a witness' identity or contact information could subject the witness to *physical danger.* [*Puerto v. Sup.Ct. (Wild Oats Markets, Inc.),* supra, 158 CA4th at 1254, 70 CR3d at 710]
      - [8:299.8] Moreover, a protective order may limit the discovering party's use and dissemination of a witness' contact information. [*Puerto v. Sup.Ct. (Wild Oats Markets, Inc.),* supra, 158 CA4th at 1259, 70 CR3d at 714-715; *Life Technologies Corp. v. Sup.Ct. (Joyce)*, supra, 197 CA4th at 655, 130 CR3d at 92]
      - [8:299.9] The court may require other procedural safeguards, such as requiring defendant's attorney, rather than plaintiff's attorney, to give notice to the nonparties before the nonparties' contact information is released. Or the court may require nonparties be given a simple objection form on which they can object to disclosure of all or specific categories of their information. [*Life Technologies Corp. v. Sup.Ct. (Joyce),* supra, 197 CA4th at 654-655, 130 CR3d at 91]
      - [8:299.10] Insurance companies are not required to disclose personal information

© 2020 Thomson Reuters/The Rutter Group

collected or received in connection with an insurance transaction without *written authorization* from the person involved. [Ins.C. §791.13; see *Puerto v. Sup.Ct. (Wild Oats Markets, Inc.),* supra, 158 CA4th at 1257, 70 CR3d at 713]

(b) [8:300] **Private information of nonparties:** In addition, a party may be entitled to discover confidential personal information of nonparties (e.g., the age of other employees where age discrimination is claimed). [See *Alch v. Sup.Ct. (Time Warner Entertainment Co.)* (2008) 165 CA4th 1412, 1423, 82 CR3d 470, 479]

1) [8:300.1] **Showing of need for discovery:** Nonparties must be given notice and opportunity to object to disclosure of their private information (¶*8:300.5 ff.*). Upon objection, the party seeking discovery must show a need for the nonparty information that overrides the party's privacy interest. A compelling need is demonstrated where the information is "directly relevant" and "essential to the fair resolution" of the lawsuit. [*Britt v. Sup.Ct. (San Diego Unified Port Dist.)* (1978) 20 C3d 844, 859, 143 CR 695, 704; *Alch v. Sup.Ct. (Time Warner Entertainment Co.),* supra, 165 CA4th at 1427, 82 CR3d at 483—demographic and work history information of Screen Writers Guild members ordered disclosed as necessary to prove plaintiffs' claim of industry-wide age discrimination; *see* ¶*8:326.2*]

For each category of information sought, the trial court must determine whether the need for the information outweighs the third party's privacy interests, taking into consideration whether less intrusive means exist to obtain the information. [*Life Technologies Corp. v. Sup.Ct. (Joyce)* (2011) 197 CA4th 640, 655-656, 130 CR3d 80, 92 (disapproved on other grounds by *Williams v. Sup.Ct. (Marshalls of CA, LLC)* (2017) 3 C5th 531, 557, 220 CR3d 472, 494 & fn. 8)]

2) [8:300.2] **Balancing required:** The court employs a balancing test in determining whether the privacy rights are outweighed by the need shown for disclosure. [*In re Clergy Cases I* (2010) 188 CA4th 1224, 1235, 116 CR3d 360, 368—protecting children from molestation outweighed individual friars' privacy interest in psychotherapist records]

[8:300.3-300.4] *Reserved.*

3) [8:300.5] **Notice and opportunity to object required:** The person whose privacy is involved must be given notice of the discovery request and an opportunity to object to the invasion of his or her privacy prior to disclosure. [*Valley Bank of Nevada v. Sup.Ct. (Barkett)* (1975) 15 C3d 652, 658, 125 CR 553, 556; *see ¶8:304; Life Technologies Corp. v. Sup.Ct. (Joyce)*, supra, 197 CA4th at 656, 130 CR3d at 92]

Alternatively, the court may order the party from whom disclosure is sought to ask the third persons for their permission to disclose confidential information. Disclosure is then permitted only as to those who give permission; and counsel are barred from contacting those who do not. [See *Colonial Life & Accident Ins. Co. v. Sup.Ct. (Perry)* (1982) 31 C3d 785, 794-795, 183 CR 810, 815]

The court must decide which notice method is appropriate in a particular case. [*Olympic Club v. Sup.Ct. (City & County of San Francisco)* (1991) 229 CA3d 358, 364-365, 282 CR 1, 4]

a) [8:300.6] **Special notice required when "personal records" of "consumer" or "employment records" subpoenaed:** Special notice must be given upon subpoenaing the "personal records" of a "consumer" or "employment records" (unless the subpoenaing party is the consumer or employee whose records are sought). The person whose records are being subpoenaed is entitled to a hearing before delivery of the records. [See CCP §§1985.3, 1985.6, 1985.7 (*discussed at ¶8:580 ff.*)]

4) [8:300.7] **Provisions for maintaining confidentiality required:** The trial court should make provisions for maintaining the confidentiality of disclosed information by sealing it or limiting its use or dissemination. [*Life Technologies Corp. v. Sup.Ct. (Joyce)*, supra, 197 CA4th at 655-656, 130 CR3d at 92]

c. [8:301] **What information is protectible:** Several "zones" of privacy have been recognized, as discussed below (¶*8:302 ff.*).

Note: This does not necessarily mean the information is nondiscoverable. As stated above (¶*8:294*), privacy protection is qualified, not absolute. A "balancing" is required: i.e., the need for discovery in each case must be *weighed* against the interests sought to be protected by the privacy right recognized (*see* ¶*8:323 ff.*).

(1) [8:302] **Membership in associations:** The constitutional right to freedom of association requires protection of a person's

© 2020 Thomson Reuters/The Rutter Group

membership in associations, whether they pertain to religious, political, economic or even purely social matters. [*Britt v. Sup.Ct. (San Diego Unified Port Dist.)* (1978) 20 C3d 844, 852, 143 CR 695, 699; *Pacific-Union Club v. Sup.Ct. (State Franchise Tax Bd.)* (1991) 232 CA3d 60, 71, 283 CR 287, 292]

These interests are also protected by federal law. [*National Ass'n for Advancement of Colored People v. State of Ala. ex rel. Patterson* (1958) 357 US 449, 462, 78 S.Ct. 1163, 1171-1172]

(2) [8:303] **Personal finances:** A right of privacy exists as to a party's confidential financial affairs, even when the information sought is admittedly relevant to the litigation. [*Cobb v. Sup.Ct. (Tleel)* (1979) 99 CA3d 543, 550, 160 CR 561, 566—privacy as limit on discovery of defendant's net worth where punitive damages sought; and see Civ.C. §3295(c), ¶*8:337 ff.*]

(a) **Application**

- [8:303.1] The will and estate planning documents of a *living person* are protected by a right of privacy in litigation in which he or she is a party. [*Estate of Gallio* (1995) 33 CA4th 592, 597, 39 CR2d 470, 472-473]
- [8:303.2] Confidential financial information given to a bank by a customer is protected by the right to privacy: "[T]here is a right to privacy in confidential customer information *whatever* form it takes, whether that form be tax returns, checks, statements, or other account information." [*Fortunato v. Sup.Ct. (Ingrassia)* (2003) 114 CA4th 475, 481, 8 CR3d 82, 86 (emphasis in original)—protection for tax returns submitted in connection with loan application]

(b) [8:304] **Finances of third parties:** Moreover, the confidential financial affairs of *third persons* (nonparties) are entitled to privacy. This may limit—but does not necessarily preclude—discovery, whether directed at a party or the third persons themselves. [See *Valley Bank of Nevada v. Sup.Ct. (Barkett)* (1975) 15 C3d 652, 658, 125 CR 553, 556—nonparty bank customers whose loan files were sought by borrower suing bank were entitled to prior notice and opportunity to object; and *Hecht, Solberg, Robinson, Goldberg & Bagley v. Sup.Ct. (Panther)* (2006) 137 CA4th 579, 595-596, 40 CR3d 446, 457-458—legal malpractice plaintiff could obtain discovery of third party's finances where relevant to causation and damages in malpractice action; *see* ¶*8:297.6*]

(c) [8:304.1] **Party's confidential settlement with nonparty:** Likewise, the constitutional right of privacy applies to a party's confidential settlement of a prior lawsuit with a nonparty. [*Hinshaw, Winkler, Draa, Marsh & Still v. Sup.Ct. (Kauffman)* (1996) 51 CA4th 233, 241, 58 CR2d 791, 795 (disapproved on other grounds by *Williams v. Sup.Ct. (Marshalls of CA, LLC)* (2017) 3 C5th 531, 557, 220 CR3d 472, 494 & fn. 8)—redacting nonparties' names would *not* provide sufficient protection]

The court must analyze the privacy issues under the test set forth in *Hill v. National Collegiate Athletic Ass'n* (1994) 7 C4th 1, 26 CR2d 834. [See *Williams v. Sup. Ct. (Marshalls of CA, LLC)*, supra, 3 C5th at 552-558, 220 CR3d at 489-495—party asserting privacy must establish a legally protected privacy interest, an objectively reasonable expectation of privacy and a threatened intrusion that is serious to be balanced against allegedly legitimate and important countervailing interests in discovery; *see ¶8:294*]

1) [8:304.2] **Compare—documents in court file:** But settlement documents that are part of a court file are generally open to the public for inspection and copying. [See CRC 2.550(c)]

A court may order records sealed only on finding an overriding public interest in confidentiality. [See CRC 2.550(d); *In re Providian Credit Card Cases* (2002) 96 CA4th 292, 297-298, 116 CR2d 833, 837; *and detailed discussion at ¶9:416 ff.*]

☞ [8:304.3] ***PRACTICE POINTERS:*** If your client wants to enter into a confidential settlement, *avoid filing the settlement agreement* in court. Otherwise, in subsequent litigation or if disclosure is requested by a journalist or other member of the public, the terms of the settlement will probably be unsealed.

Therefore, if you need a court determination that the settlement is in good faith under CCP §877.6 (*see ¶12:760*), you cannot guarantee the terms of the settlement will be protected from disclosure (*see ¶12:892*). You also risk disclosure of the agreement if you are party to a motion to enforce the agreement under CCP §664.6 (*see ¶12:950 ff.*).

(3) [8:305] **Medical records:** The constitutional right of privacy applies to a party's medical records. [*John B. v. Sup.Ct. (Bridget B.)* (2006) 38 C4th 1177, 1198, 45 CR3d 316, 332]

"An individual's right of privacy encompasses not only the state of his mind, but also his viscera . . ." [*Board of Med.*

© 2020 Thomson Reuters/The Rutter Group

Quality Assur. v. Gherardini (1979) 93 CA3d 669, 679, 156 CR 55, 61 (disapproved on other grounds by *Williams v. Sup.Ct. (Marshalls of CA, LLC)* (2017) 3 C5th 531, 557, 220 CR3d 472, 494 & fn. 8); *Pettus v. Cole* (1996) 49 CA4th 402, 441, 57 CR2d 46, 72—a "quintessential zone of human privacy"; see also Civ.C. §56.10 ff. and 42 USC §1320d et seq. (HIPPA) (health care providers generally may not disclose medical information without patient's authorization or court order)]

(a) **Application**

- [8:305.1] Although a plaintiff suing for personal injuries waives the physician-patient privilege (Ev.C. §996), plaintiff still has a right of privacy in his or her medical records. Disclosure thereof depends upon *balancing* the need for discovery against the need for confidentiality. Ordinarily, discovery of *relevant* medical history is allowed because defendants have no other means by which to obtain this information. [*Palay v. Sup.Ct. (County of Los Angeles)* (1993) 18 CA4th 919, 933-934, 22 CR2d 839, 848 (disapproved on other grounds by *Williams v. Sup.Ct. (Marshalls of CA, LLC)* (2017) 3 C5th 531, 557, 220 CR3d 472, 494 & fn. 8)]

- [8:305.2] But this does *not* make discoverable plaintiff's "lifetime" medical history. Plaintiff's right of privacy is protected as to physical and mental conditions *unrelated* to the claim or injury sued upon. [See *Britt v. Sup.Ct. (San Diego Unified Port Dist.)* (1978) 20 C3d 844, 864, 143 CR 695, 708]

- [8:305.3] Where plaintiff makes *no claim* of mental or emotional distress, a "garden variety" personal injury action seeking damages for "pain and suffering" does *not* place plaintiff's mental condition in issue. Plaintiff's right to privacy in his or her postinjury psychotherapeutic records outweighs any need for discovery thereof. [*Davis v. Sup.Ct. (Williams)* (1992) 7 CA4th 1008, 1016, 9 CR2d 331, 336]

(b) [8:306] **Third party's medical records:** Privacy protection extends to medical records pertaining to *third persons*. [*Board of Med. Quality Assur. v. Gherardini*, supra, 93 CA3d at 679, 156 CR at 61; *Binder v. Sup.Ct. (Neufeld)* (1987) 196 CA3d 893, 901, 242 CR 231, 235 (disapproved on other grounds by *Williams v. Sup.Ct. (Marshalls of CA, LLC)* (2017) 3 C5th 531, 557, 220 CR3d 472, 494 & fn. 8)]

However, "the state's interest in ensuring that the public receives medical care that conforms with the standard of care is a compelling interest" that may overcome the patient's privacy rights. [*Fett v. Medical Bd. of Calif.* (2016)

245 CA4th 211, 221, 199 CR3d 196, 204, fn. 2—disclosure of medical records upheld based on detailed facts showing good cause to believe doctor deviated from standard of care]

1) [8:306.1] **Compare—patient anonymity preserved:** Also, the right of privacy does *not* prevent disclosure of medical records where the patient's identity and identifying medical information has been redacted. [*Snibbe v. Sup.Ct. (Gilbert)* (2014) 224 CA4th 184, 194-196, 168 CR3d 548, 557-559—production of redacted postoperative orders did not infringe patients' privacy rights; *see also ¶8:307.7*]

2) [8:307] **Who may object:** A nonparty's privacy rights may be asserted by any party to the action. [*Wood v. Sup.Ct. (Board of Med. Quality Assur.)* (1985) 166 CA3d 1138, 1145, 212 CR 811, 817-818 (disapproved on other grounds by *Williams v. Sup.Ct. (Marshalls of CA, LLC)* (2017) 3 C5th 531, 557, 220 CR3d 472, 494 & fn. 8)—doctor accused of writing unlawful prescriptions may assert patients' right to privacy in refusing to produce their medical records; *Lewis v. Sup.Ct. (Medical Bd. of Calif.)* (2017) 3 C5th 561, 570, 220 CR3d 319, 326—where doctor's and patients' interests are aligned, doctor may assert patients' privacy rights]

   The privacy right may also be asserted by the nonparty whose privacy is at issue. [*In re Clergy Cases I* (2010) 188 CA4th 1224, 1233, 116 CR3d 360, 367—nonparty friars had standing to appeal order for disclosure of their personal and medical records; *Kirchmeyer v. Phillips* (2016) 245 CA4th 1394, 1403, 200 CR3d 515, 521—both patient and psychotherapist may assert privilege]

   [8:307.1-307.4] *Reserved.*

(c) [8:307.5] **Physician-patient privilege distinguished:** A person's right to maintain the privacy of his or her medical records exists *in addition to* the statutory physician-patient and psychotherapist-patient privileges (Ev.C. §§994, 1014). Thus, even if the evidentiary privilege has been *waived* (e.g., by testimony in an earlier proceeding), the witness' right to privacy may preclude discovery of his or her medical records. [See *San Diego Trolley, Inc. v. Sup.Ct. (Kinder)* (2001) 87 CA4th 1083, 1092, 105 CR2d 476, 481 (disapproved on other grounds by *Williams v. Sup.Ct. (Marshalls of CA, LLC)* (2017) 3 C5th 531, 557, 220 CR3d 472, 494 & fn. 8)—witness' deposition testimony admitting she was under psychiatric care may have waived psychotherapist-patient privilege but did not waive her right to privacy of her psychiatric records (*see* ¶*8:315.8*); *Manela v. Sup.Ct. (Manela)* (2009) 177 CA4th 1139, 1151, 99 CR3d 736, 745—where H's health was at issue in child custody proceedings, H waived physician-patient privilege by permitting W to sit in on doctor's exam, but not privacy objection]

1) [8:307.6] **Privilege inapplicable to nurses and other medical staff:** For purposes of the physician-patient privilege, "physician" is limited to a person authorized to practice medicine (Ev.C. §990) and does not extend to a nurse or other medical staff. [*Duronslet v. Kamps* (2012) 203 CA4th 717, 736, 137 CR3d 756, 771]

2) [8:307.7] **Privilege not violated by disclosure of redacted medical records:** Compelled disclosure of medical records with patient-identifying information redacted does not violate the physician-patient privilege (or the right of privacy, *see* ¶*8:306.1*). [*Snibbe v. Sup.Ct. (Gilbert)* (2014) 224 CA4th 184, 192-194, 168 CR3d 548, 555-557—no "blanket prohibition" against disclosure of redacted medical records in California]

[8:307.8-307.9] *Reserved.*

(4) [8:307.10] **Employment history:** A person's work history (e.g., names of employers, dates of employment, job titles, full or part-time) is protected by a right of privacy. But where work history of third persons was "directly relevant" and "essential to the fair resolution" of the suit, the court could order disclosure. [*Alch v. Sup.Ct. (Time Warner Entertainment Co.)* (2008) 165 CA4th 1412, 1426-1427, 82 CR3d 470, 482-483—in order to determine whether work history of nonparty members of Screen Writers Guild should be ordered disclosed, the court was required to evaluate invasion of privacy against extent to which it furthered "legitimate and important competing interests" of allowing discovery; see also *Life Technologies Corp. v. Sup.Ct. (Joyce)* (2011) 197 CA4th 640, 652-653, 130 CR3d 80, 89-90 (disapproved on other grounds by *Williams v. Sup.Ct. (Marshalls of CA, LLC)* (2017) 3 C5th 531, 557, 220 CR3d 472, 494 & fn. 8)—although confidential personnel records were arguably directly relevant to plaintiff's age discrimination suit, trial court erred by failing to evaluate each category of information to determine whether plaintiff's need for the information outweighed the third parties' privacy interests]

(5) [8:308] **Personnel records:** Confidential personnel files at a person's place of employment are within a zone of privacy. [*Board of Trustees of Leland Stanford Jr. Univ. v. Sup.Ct. (Dong)* (1981) 119 CA3d 516, 528-530, 174 CR 160, 166-167 (disapproved on other grounds by *Williams v. Sup.Ct. (Marshalls*

of CA, LLC) (2017) 3 C5th 531, 557, 220 CR3d 472, 494 & fn. 8)]

- [8:309] Again, the privacy protected may be that of some *third person*, rather than that of the employee. For example, the personnel file may contain confidential letters regarding the employee written by outsiders. Disclosure would impair the confidentiality they expected would be accorded to their communications. [*Board of Trustees of Leland Stanford Jr. Univ. v. Sup.Ct. (Dong)*, supra, 119 CA3d at 528-530, 174 CR at 166-167—outsiders' communications to university committee investigating faculty member]
- [8:309a] It was error to order discovery of the names, residential addresses and telephone numbers of Planned Parenthood's staff and volunteers in litigation regarding the scope of the right to protest by anti-abortion groups. The discovery order implicated the *First Amendment rights* of nonparties to freely and privately associate with Planned Parenthood. [*Planned Parenthood Golden Gate v. Sup.Ct. (Foti)* (2000) 83 CA4th 347, 358, 99 CR2d 627, 637 (disapproved on other grounds by *Williams v. Sup.Ct. (Marshalls of CA, LLC)* (2017) 3 C5th 531, 557, 220 CR3d 472, 494 & fn. 8)]

(6) [8:309.1] **Faculty selection proceedings:** Discussions at faculty meetings re appointment or granting tenure to proposed faculty members are intended to be confidential. Although there is no statutory privilege, the *privacy rights of those present* limit discovery of their comments regarding a proposed candidate. They are free to express candid appraisals of the candidate without fear of disclosure. [*Kahn v. Sup.Ct. (Davies)* (1987) 188 CA3d 752, 769, 233 CR 662, 673 (disapproved on other grounds by *Williams v. Sup.Ct. (Marshalls of CA, LLC)* (2017) 3 C5th 531, 557, 220 CR3d 472, 494 & fn. 8); *Scharf v. Regents of Univ. of Calif.* (1991) 234 CA3d 1393, 1408, 286 CR 227, 237—privacy rights of those providing information in peer review process justify denying professor's demand for disclosure]

[8:309.2] *Compare—federal courts:* No such protection is provided in federal courts in employment discrimination cases. [See *University of Penn. v. Equal Employment Opportunity Comm'n* (1990) 493 US 182, 189, 110 S.Ct. 577, 582]

[8:309.3-309.4] *Reserved.*

(7) [8:309.5] **Marital relationship:** "There can be no doubt that the marital relationship serves as a foundation for assertion of the right to privacy." [*Tylo v. Sup.Ct. (Spelling Entertainment Group, Inc.)* (1997) 55 CA4th 1379, 1388, 64 CR2d 731, 736]

© 2020 Thomson Reuters/The Rutter Group

But a plaintiff who tenders her psychological condition (e.g., claims of emotional distress) may be questioned as to her marital relationship *as it relates to the claim sued upon.* [*Tylo v. Sup.Ct. (Spelling Entertainment Group, Inc.)*, supra, 55 CA4th at 1388, 64 CR2d at 736]

(a) [8:309.6] **Showing required:** The burden is on the defendant seeking discovery of such information to:

— *identify* the specific emotional injuries which plaintiff claims resulted from defendant's acts; and

— *demonstrate a "nexus"* between those injuries and emotional distress that may arise out of the marital relationship. [*Tylo v. Sup.Ct. (Spelling Entertainment Group, Inc.),* supra, 55 CA4th at 1388, 64 CR2d at 736—moving party's assertion that there are "other stressors that *might* have caused, or contributed to, [petitioner's] alleged emotional injuries" was clearly *not* sufficient (brackets and emphasis in original)]

(8) [8:310] **Sexual relations:** A party's sexual practices are protected by the California Constitution's right of privacy. [Cal. Const. Art.I, §1; *Vinson v. Sup.Ct. (Peralta Comm. College Dist.)* (1987) 43 C3d 833, 841, 239 CR 292, 298; *John B. v. Sup.Ct. (Bridget B.)* (2006) 38 C4th 1177, 1198, 45 CR3d 316, 332]

The right to privacy is not absolute and must be balanced against other important interests. Any compelled disclosure, however, "must be *narrowly drawn* to assure maximum protection of the constitutional interests at stake." [*John B. v. Sup.Ct. (Bridget B.)*, supra, 38 C4th at 1200, 45 CR3d at 333 (emphasis added)—where wife alleged husband infected her with AIDS, discovery of husband's sexual history limited to date when husband could have been first infected through date when couple last had sexual relations; *see also ¶8:325.2*]

[8:311] *Reserved.*

(a) [8:312] **Waiver issues:** A party may waive his or her right of privacy as to sexual relations by asserting certain claims. However, the concept of "waiver" is construed *narrowly.* [*Barrenda L. v. Sup.Ct. (County of Los Angeles)* (1998) 65 CA4th 794, 800, 803, 76 CR2d 727, 730, 732]

1) [8:312.1] **Sexual harassment:** By claiming *emotional distress* from sexual harassment, plaintiff may *waive* his or her privacy as to his or her present mental or *emotional* condition (i.e., so as to be subject to a CCP §2032.010 mental exam). [*Vinson v. Sup.Ct. (Peralta Comm. College Dist.)*, supra, 43 C3d at 839-840, 239 CR at 297]

But such claims do *not* waive his or her privacy as to past or present *sex practices*, absent any claim of damage to his or her present sexuality. [*Vinson v. Sup.Ct. (Peralta Comm. College Dist.)*, supra, 43 C3d at 842, 239 CR at 299]

2) [8:312.2] **Pregnancy as basis for employment termination:** Employer fired Actress from television series when she became pregnant, relying on contract provision allowing termination for "change in appearance." Actress claimed Employer negligently failed to disclose that this provision included pregnancy. Questions as to whether she was *trying* to become pregnant at the time the contract was negotiated were permissible because they tended to refute her claimed reliance on Employer's alleged nondisclosure. [*Tylo v. Sup.Ct. (Spelling Entertainment Group, Inc.)* (1997) 55 CA4th 1379, 1391, 64 CR2d 731, 738-739]

(9) [8:313] **Auto accident reports to CHP:** Drivers involved in auto accidents are required by statute to file reports with the California Highway Patrol or local police department (Veh.C. §20008). Such reports are for the "confidential use" of the DMV, although persons with a "proper interest" can obtain copies (Veh.C. §20012). The statute is designed to protect the *privacy* of the reporting parties from persons not having a "proper interest" in the reports. [*Davies v. Sup.Ct. (State of Calif.)* (1984) 36 C3d 291, 299, 204 CR 154, 159]

Reports to the California Highway Patrol by investigative officers following such accidents are likewise "confidential." [Veh.C. §20014; *Nelson v. Sup.Ct. (State of Calif.)* (1986) 184 CA3d 444, 450-451, 229 CR 94, 98-99]

(a) [8:313.1] **What portions confidential:** Only the names and addresses of the reporting parties are confidential. Other portions of the report (e.g., name of investigating officer, time and place of accident) may be disclosed: "A construction which limits confidentiality of accident reports to the *reports themselves* and to *identifying data* is consistent with the need for careful balancing of the rights of parties seeking discovery and those of the party or persons for whose benefit confidentiality is created." [*Davies v. Sup.Ct. (State of Calif.)*, supra, 36 C3d at 300, 204 CR at 160 (emphasis added)]

(b) [8:314] **Persons having "proper interest" may obtain discovery:** The parties involved in the accident may obviously obtain copies of the report. So may other persons having a "proper interest" therein. [Veh.C. §20012; *California ex rel. Dept. of Transp. v. Sup.Ct. (Hall)* (1985) 37 C3d 847, 855, 210 CR 219, 224, fn. 10]

- [8:314.1] Persons involved in later accidents at the same location may have a "proper interest" in obtaining

© 2020 Thomson Reuters/The Rutter Group

earlier accident reports because the reports may disclose *highway conditions causing* their accident. [See *California ex rel. Dept. of Transp. v. Sup.Ct. (Hall)*, supra, 37 C3d at 855, 210 CR at 224, fn. 10]

- [8:314.2] An accused facing criminal charges resulting from an accident was held to have a "proper interest" in discovering earlier accident reports at the same location (with names and addresses of persons involved in those accidents deleted). Such evidence may indicate that highway conditions or other factors were the cause of the accident, rather than his or her conduct. [*California ex rel. Dept. of Transp. v. Sup.Ct. (Hall)*, supra—confidential identifying data deleted pursuant to stipulation]

(10)[8:315] **Newsperson's confidential sources:** A news reporter's confidential sources have a reasonable expectation of privacy when they disclose information to the reporter. The reporter has standing to assert *their* rights in refusing to disclose their identities. (As with other zones of privacy, however, their rights are not absolute, and may give way where a compelling state interest is shown.) [*Dalitz v. Penthouse Int'l, Ltd.* (1985) 168 CA3d 468, 482, 214 CR 254, 263]

Compare: A news reporter may also have a *First Amendment* right to withhold disclosure of his or her sources (*see ¶8:342*), as well as rights under state law (*see ¶8:341*).

(11)[8:315.1] **Insurance claims files:** Insurance company files regarding an insured or claimant are protected by statute ("Insurance Information and Privacy Protection Act"; Ins.C. §791.01 et seq.). Disclosure of "any *personal or privileged information* about an individual collected or received in connection with an insurance transaction" is restricted. [Ins.C. §791.13 (emphasis added)]

- [8:315.1a] The statute provides, however, for disclosure upon *written consent* of the person to whom the file relates. Thus, where insurance claims files become relevant in litigation involving *other parties*, discovery may be conditioned on obtaining the written consent of the persons to whom those files relate. [See *Mead Reinsurance Co. v. Sup.Ct. (City of Laguna Beach)* (1986) 188 CA3d 313, 321-322, 232 CR 752, 757]

(12)[8:315.2] **Juvenile court records:** A party's juvenile court records are confidential and a court order is required for their release to third persons (Welf. & Inst.C. §827). But this is not an absolute privilege, and such records *may* be discoverable under appropriate conditions:

(a) [8:315.3] **Relevancy:** First of all, the juvenile records must be relevant to the present litigation. [*Navajo Express* *v. Sup.Ct. (Russo)* (1986) 186 CA3d 981, 986, 231 CR 165, 168]

For example, where a personal injury plaintiff claims brain damage causing violent behavior, his juvenile records are relevant because they may reveal such behavior *before* the accident. [*Navajo Express v. Sup.Ct. (Russo)*, supra]

However, there is no requirement that the minor be a party to the action or even that there be a pending action. [See *R.S. v. Sup.Ct. (M.L.)* (2009) 172 CA4th 1049, 1056, 91 CR3d 546, 551—disclosure of records ordered to assist prelawsuit settlement negotiations with insurance company]

(b) [8:315.4] **Guidelines for disclosure:** The California Judicial Council has adopted the following guidelines for disclosure of juvenile court records:

- In determining whether to authorize inspection or release of juvenile case files, the court must balance the interests of the child and the other parties, the interests of the petitioner and of the public.
- The confidentiality of juvenile case files is to protect the privacy rights of the child. If the court grants the petition, it must find that the need for discovery outweighs the policy considerations favoring confidentiality.
- The court may permit disclosure only to the extent necessary, and only if petitioner shows by a preponderance of the evidence that the records are necessary and have *substantial relevance* to the legitimate need of the petitioner.
- If, after an in camera review and consideration of objections, the court orders all or a portion of the file may be disclosed, the court must make orders regarding what will be disclosed and the procedure for providing access to it.
- The court may issue protective orders with respect to the information. [CRC 5.552(d)(4)-(8)]

[8:315.4a] ***PRACTICE POINTER:*** Unless local rules provide otherwise, a petition for disclosures of juvenile court records should be directed to the presiding judge of the *juvenile court*.

(c) [8:315.5] **Compare—records pertaining to defendants:** It is doubtful that a *defendant's* juvenile court records would ever be discoverable by a civil plaintiff. [See *Parmett v. Sup.Ct. (Chrystal B.)* (1989) 212 CA3d 1261, 1269, 262 CR 387, 391—"a civil plaintiff has little basis upon

© 2020 Thomson Reuters/The Rutter Group

which to claim entitlement to invade the privilege of the sealing statute"]

(13)[8:315.6] **Arrest records:** Release of arrest records or information about arrests implicates the arrestees' right of privacy. [See *Kilgore v. Younger* (1982) 30 C3d 770, 794, 180 CR 657, 671; *Denari v. Sup.Ct. (Kern County)* (1989) 215 CA3d 1488, 1498, 264 CR 261, 266]

(a) [8:315.7] **Third persons' privacy protected:** Litigants receiving discovery demands for the arrest records of third persons have standing to assert those persons' privacy rights.

Example: P sued County for violating her civil rights while in jail. She demanded the names and addresses of other prisoners in jail at the same time. County could assert their privacy rights in refusing discovery. [*Denari v. Sup.Ct. (Kern County)*, supra, 215 CA3d at 1499, 264 CR at 266—state law privacy rights not affected by suit on federal claim]

(14)[8:315.8] **Communications between patient and psychotherapist:** Confidential communications between a patient and his or her psychotherapist are protected *both* by statutory privilege (Ev.C. §1014) *and* by the patient's constitutional right of privacy. [*Roe v. Sup.Ct. (Roe)* (1991) 229 CA3d 832, 837, 280 CR 380, 382]

Thus, even if an exception to the statutory privilege applies (e.g., child abuse reporting cases; see Pen.C. §11171(b)), constitutional privacy considerations may still limit disclosure (*Roe v. Sup.Ct. (Roe)*, supra, 229 CA3d at 837, 280 CR at 382). Even so, discovery may be ordered if the need for disclosure *outweighs* the patient's privacy interest. [*Cross v. Sup.Ct. (Kidane)* (2017) 11 CA5th 305, 325-326, 217 CR3d 569, 584-585; *see ¶8:323*]

[8:315.9] *Reserved.*

(15)[8:315.10] **Statements made in confidence to ombudsman:** Employers sometimes provide ombudsmen (neutrals) to mediate employee disputes. Disclosures to an ombudsman may be protected *both* by the *mediation privilege* (see Ev.C. §1119) and by the participants' constitutional right of privacy, at least where the employees had a reasonable expectation their statements would be kept confidential. [See *Garstang v. Sup.Ct. (Calif. Institute of Tech.)* (1995) 39 CA4th 526, 532, 46 CR2d 84, 87 (disapproved on other grounds by *Williams v. Sup.Ct. (Marshalls of CA, LLC)* (2017) 3 C5th 531, 557, 220 CR3d 472, 494 & fn. 8)—employer had assured those participating in ombuds process their statements would be kept confidential]

Cross-refer: The Ev.C. §1119 privilege for statements made during mediation is discussed further in Wegner, Fairbank,

Epstein & Chernow, *Cal. Prac. Guide: Civil Trials & Evidence* (TRG), Ch. 8E; and Knight, Chernick, Flynn & Quinn, *Cal. Prac. Guide: Alternative Dispute Resolution* (TRG), Ch. 3.

[8:315.11-315.14] *Reserved.*

(16)[8:315.15] **Private investigators:** Private investigators are prohibited by law from divulging information developed during the course of an investigation for a client (subject to certain statutory exceptions). [See Bus. & Prof.C. §7539(a)]

But no privilege or right of privacy protects the *identity* of the investigator's employer or client. A private investigator therefore may be compelled to disclose the client's identity in discovery proceedings. [*Flynn v. Sup.Ct. (Bolling)* (1997) 57 CA4th 990, 995-996, 67 CR2d 491, 494]

[8:315.16-315.19] *Reserved.*

(17)[8:315.20] **Client's identity:** The *identity* of an attorney's client is generally not protected by the attorney-client privilege. (Exceptions are recognized where disclosure would implicate the client in unlawful activities or betray confidential information regarding the client.) Even if there is no privilege, however, the identity of an attorney's clients, before any public disclosure thereof, is "sensitive personal information that implicates the *clients' rights of privacy*." [*Hooser v. Sup.Ct. (Ray)* (2000) 84 CA4th 997, 1005, 101 CR2d 341, 347 (emphasis added) (disapproved on other grounds by *Williams v. Sup.Ct. (Marshalls of CA, LLC)* (2017) 3 C5th 531, 557, 220 CR3d 472, 494 & fn. 8); see also *Tien v. Sup.Ct. (Tenet Healthcare Corp.)* (2006) 139 CA4th 528, 539, 43 CR3d 121, 128]

d. [8:316] **Procedure for raising privacy objection:** The party asserting privacy may either *object* and refuse to answer on this ground; or, if there is time, seek a *protective order* excusing the duty to answer (*see ¶8:328*).

Nonparties: Where the information sought pertains to third persons, they must be given notice and an opportunity to object; *see ¶8:300.5.*

☞ [8:317] ***PRACTICE POINTER:*** The most practical procedure is simply to object. This shifts the burden to the party seeking discovery to file a motion to compel answers (*¶8:787*).

Of course, at the hearing on the motion, you will have to justify the privacy claim. But even if the court overrules your objection, it is unlikely to impose sanctions if there was a *reasonable* basis for your claim.

[8:318-319] *Reserved.*

(1) [8:319.1] **Waiver by delay or failure to object?** According to the Discovery Act, failure to respond *timely* to discovery requests may waive "*any objection* . . . including one based

on privilege or on the protection for work product." [CCP §2030.290(a) (emphasis added) (applicable to interrogatories, but similar waiver provisions apply to other discovery procedures)]

(a) [8:319.2] **Comment:** Whether these provisions apply to a party's failure to object on privacy grounds is unclear. Arguably, privacy rights are *constitutional* in nature and cannot be waived by a "technical shortfall." [See *Boler v. Sup.Ct. (Everett)* (1987) 201 CA3d 467, 472, 247 CR 185, 187-188, fn. 1 (dictum because third persons' rights involved; *see ¶8:319.8*)]

(b) [8:319.3] **No waiver by failure to raise simultaneously with other objections:** One case suggests that if the responding party timely objected on *other* grounds (e.g., relevancy), the privacy objection *can be raised later* if the other objections are overruled. I.e., there is *no waiver* by failure to assert it in the initial response. [*Heda v. Sup.Ct. (Davis)* (1990) 225 CA3d 525, 529, 275 CR 136, 138; *see further discussion at ¶8:1101.1 ff.*]

Burden objections to the production of electronically stored materials may preserve all other objections. *See ¶8:1475.12.*

[8:319.4-319.6] *Reserved.*

(c) [8:319.7] **Compare—effect of failure to challenge subpoena for "personal records" of "consumer" or "employment records":** Subpoenas directed to "personal records" of a "consumer" or "employment records" are subject to special requirements, *including a "notice of privacy rights"* and opportunity to object to disclosure. [CCP §§1985.3(e), 1985.6(e); *see ¶8:588, 8:596.16*]

The affected party's failure to challenge the subpoena before his or her records are turned over to the subpoenaing party *may* waive privacy rights. However, there is no known authority in point. [See *Inabnit v. Berkson* (1988) 199 CA3d 1230, 1239, 245 CR 525, 531—failure to object waived psychotherapist-patient privilege; *Colleen M. v. Fertility & Surgical Assocs. of Thousand Oaks* (2005) 132 CA4th 1466, 1479, 34 CR3d 439, 447]

(2) [8:319.8] **Compare—no waiver of *third persons'* privacy:** A party's failure to object cannot impair privacy rights of nonparties who have no notice of the proceedings in which the question is asked. Their rights may be asserted for the first time in opposition to a motion to compel: "An inflexible waiver rule would . . . infringe upon the constitutional privacy rights of citizens not participating in the lawsuit." [*Boler v. Sup.Ct. (Everett),* supra, 201 CA3d at 472, 247 CR at 187, fn. 1]

©2020 Thomson Reuters/The Rutter Group

(a) [8:319.9] **Example:** Deponent was asked about his extramarital affairs. He objected only on grounds of *relevancy* (failing to raise privacy). Even if the questions were relevant, a court could not compel answers that would impair D's privacy rights *and those of his unnamed sexual partners*. [*Boler v. Sup.Ct. (Everett)*, supra]

Cross-refer: See further discussion of waiver at ¶8:726.5.

e. **Burden on party seeking discovery**

(1) [8:320] **Directly relevant to issue in case:** The party seeking discovery must show a particularized need for the confidential information sought. The broad "relevancy to the subject matter" standard is *not* enough here. The court must be convinced that the information is *directly relevant* to a cause of action or defense, i.e., that it is *essential* to determining the truth of the matters in dispute. [*Britt v. Sup.Ct. (San Diego Unified Port Dist.)* (1978) 20 C3d 844, 859-862, 143 CR 695, 704-706; *Harris v. Sup.Ct. (Smets)* (1992) 3 CA4th 661, 665, 4 CR2d 564, 567 (citing text) (disapproved on other grounds by *Williams v. Sup.Ct. (Marshalls of CA, LLC)* (2017) 3 C5th 531, 557, 220 CR3d 472, 494 & fn. 8)]

- [8:320.1] **Example:** P sued Doctor for failing to diagnose skin cancer that caused decedent's death. P sought discovery of Doctor's photos of *other patients* with conditions similar to decedent's (disclosure of which would violate their privacy). It was error to grant discovery because the photos were *not directly relevant* to P's claims against Doctor. It was *not enough* that they might lead to discoverable evidence (reflecting on Doctor's knowledge re skin cancers). [*Binder v. Sup.Ct. (Neufeld)* (1987) 196 CA3d 893, 901, 242 CR 231, 235 (disapproved on other grounds by *Williams v. Sup.Ct. (Marshalls of CA, LLC)* (2017) 3 C5th 531, 557, 220 CR3d 472, 494 & fn. 8)]

(2) [8:321] **No alternative means for obtaining information:** Discovery will not be ordered if the information sought is available from other sources or through less intrusive means. [*Allen v. Sup.Ct. (Sierra)* (1984) 151 CA3d 447, 449, 198 CR 737, 741; and see *Britt v. Sup.Ct. (San Diego Unified Port Dist.)* (1978) 20 C3d 844, 856, 143 CR 695, 702—discovery "cannot be pursued by means that broadly stifle fundamental personal liberties when the end can be more narrowly achieved"]

- [8:321.1] **Example:** The amount of income a personal injury defense doctor receives from insurance companies may be relevant in a personal injury action (showing possible bias); but it is protected by the doctor's right of privacy. Thus, the doctor cannot be compelled to produce records showing the amounts and sources of his or her income if *less intrusive means* are available; e.g., a de-

© 2020 Thomson Reuters/The Rutter Group

position can be used to determine what percentage of the doctor's practice is devoted to defense medical exams. (Also, such information may be available from commercial publications reporting cases in which defense doctors testify.) [*Allen v. Sup.Ct. (Sierra)*, supra, 151 CA3d at 449, 198 CR at 741]

f. [8:322] **In camera review:** If so requested, the court should review the information in camera before production to assess its value to the discovering party and the harm disclosure might cause the party whose privacy is threatened. [*Schnabel v. Sup.Ct. (Schnabel)* (1993) 5 C4th 704, 714, 21 CR2d 200, 205]

(1) [8:322.1] **Party opposing discovery should provide declarations explaining records:** The party seeking in camera review of documents has the burden of showing good cause for the review. Even if good cause is shown for an in camera review, the court should not be asked to sift through a "melange" of financial records to determine what is and is not discoverable. Rather, the burden is on the party seeking to prevent discovery to provide declarations explaining the details of the transactions involved (e.g., the source and expenditure of the funds in question). This will facilitate the court's determination of the records' relevance. [*Babcock v. Sup.Ct. (DiGiovanni)* (1994) 29 CA4th 721, 727-728, 35 CR2d 462, 465-466]

g. [8:323] **Court must balance interests:** The court must then "carefully balance" the interests involved: i.e., the claimed right of privacy versus the *public interest in obtaining just results in litigation.* [*Valley Bank of Nevada v. Sup.Ct. (Barkett)* (1975) 15 C3d 652, 657, 125 CR 553, 555; *Alch v. Sup.Ct. (Time Warner Entertainment Co.)* (2008) 165 CA4th 1412, 1422, 82 CR3d 470, 478; *Life Technologies Corp. v. Sup.Ct. (Joyce)* (2011) 197 CA4th 640, 653, 130 CR3d 80, 90 (disapproved on other grounds by *Williams v. Sup.Ct. (Marshalls of CA, LLC)* (2017) 3 C5th 531, 557, 220 CR3d 472, 494 & fn. 8)]

Considerations should include:

— the *purpose* of the information sought;

— the *effect* that disclosure will have on the parties and the trial;

— the *nature of the objections* urged by the party resisting disclosure; and

— the "ability of the court to make an *alternative order* which may grant partial disclosure, disclosure in another form, or disclosure only in the event that the party seeking the information undertakes certain specified burdens which appear just under the circumstances." [*Valley Bank of Nevada v. Sup.Ct. (Barkett),* supra, 15 C3d at 658, 125 CR at 556 (emphasis added; internal quotes omitted); see *Pioneer Electronics (USA), Inc. v. Sup.Ct. (Olmstead)* (2007) 40 C4th 360, 371, 53 CR3d 513, 521]

(1) [8:324] **"Sensitive" information:** The more "sensitive" the information (e.g., personal financial information, customers'

lists, trade secrets, etc.), the greater the need for discovery must be shown. [*Hoffman Corp. v. Sup.Ct. (Smaystrla)* (1985) 172 CA3d 357, 362, 218 CR 355, 357; *Tien v. Sup.Ct. (Tenet Healthcare Corp.)* (2006) 139 CA4th 528, 540, 43 CR3d 121, 129]

Some types of personal information are more "sensitive" than others. Thus, where several types of personal information are sought, the court must consider the possibility of requiring partial disclosure rather than denying discovery outright *with regard to each category* of protected information. [*Alch v. Sup.Ct. (Time Warner Entertainment Co.)*, supra, 165 CA4th at 1437, 82 CR3d at 491]

(a) **Examples**

- [8:325] In a products liability action, P demanded Manufacturer's confidential list of customers in order to contact them regarding their experiences with the product which caused his injuries. The list was admittedly relevant (evidencing prior accidents or complaints). But P's need for discovery had to be *weighed against the potential commercial embarrassment* to Manufacturer. Partial discovery having already been obtained (Manufacturer had disclosed all prior complaints and accidents), it was an *abuse of discretion* to require disclosure of the customers list. [*Hoffman Corp. v. Sup.Ct. (Smaystrla)*, supra, 172 CA3d at 363-364, 218 CR at 358-359]

- [8:325.1] P sought discovery of D's medical records in an effort to show D's health was so precarious that the case was entitled to immediate trial setting under CCP §36(d) (*see* ¶*12:251.2*). Discovery was denied because the need for privacy of sensitive matters in medical records *outweighed* the opposing party's need to obtain trial priority, particularly where *other means* of presenting D's testimony were available (e.g., videotape deposition). [*Heda v. Sup.Ct. (Davis)* (1990) 225 CA3d 525, 528-529, 275 CR 136, 137-138]

- [8:325.2] Wife alleged Husband infected her with AIDS, and sought discovery of Husband's sexual history before he met Wife and after the couple stopped having sex. Husband's constitutional right of privacy regarding his sexual history had to be balanced against Wife's need for information relevant to her claim. Therefore, Wife's discovery was limited to the period between when Husband could have been first infected and the date the couple last had sex. [*John B. v. Sup.Ct. (Bridget B.)* (2006) 38 C4th 1177, 1200-1201, 45 CR3d 316, 333-335; *see also* ¶*8:310*]

© 2020 Thomson Reuters/The Rutter Group

(b) [8:326] **Compare—disclosure ordered:** Even sensitive personal information may be ordered disclosed if it is shown to be "directly relevant" and "essential to a fair determination" of the action. [*Alch v. Sup.Ct. (Time Warner Entertainment Co.)* (2008) 165 CA4th 1412, 1431-1432, 82 CR3d 470, 486-487]

- [8:326.1] Husband's extramarital sexual relations were found "directly relevant" and "essential to a fair determination" of the issue of damages in his suit for Wife's wrongful death. [*Morales v. Sup.Ct. (Smith)* (1979) 99 CA3d 283, 288, 160 CR 194, 197]
- [8:326.2] The *work history* and *demographic information* (age, gender, race, etc.) of thousands of members of the Screen Writers Guild was "directly relevant" and "essential to a fair determination" of industry-wide age discrimination claims. [*Alch v. Sup.Ct. (Time Warner Entertainment Co.),* supra, 165 CA4th at 1432-1434, 82 CR3d at 487-489—demographic data and work history records are "not especially sensitive" information]

(2) [8:327] **Special protection in trade secret actions:** In actions for misappropriation of trade secrets, courts are required to preserve secrecy of the alleged trade secret "by reasonable means, which may include granting protective orders in connection with discovery proceedings, holding in camera hearings, sealing the records of the action, and ordering any person involved in the litigation not to disclose an alleged trade secret without prior court approval." [Civ.C. §3426.5]

(3) [8:327.1] **Presumption in favor of protective order where financial information sought:** In certain cases, a presumption is recognized in favor of granting a protective order to limit disclosure of confidential financial information:

(a) [8:327.1a] **Third party's finances:** A *third party* witness or deponent is presumptively entitled to a protective order to limit disclosure of his or her financial information. [*Schnabel v. Sup.Ct. (Schnabel)* (1993) 5 C4th 704, 714, 21 CR2d 200, 205; *Harris v. Sup.Ct. (Smets)* (1992) 3 CA4th 661, 668, 4 CR2d 564, 569 (disapproved on other grounds by *Williams v. Sup.Ct. (Marshalls of CA, LLC)* (2017) 3 C5th 531, 557, 220 CR3d 472, 494 & fn. 8)]

(b) [8:327.2] **Defendant's finances in punitive damages cases:** Discovery of defendant's finances in punitive damage cases is limited to start off with (*see ¶8:339*). But even where discovery is ordered, the presumption is that disclosure of defendant's confidential financial information should be *limited to opposing counsel* and solely *for the purposes of the lawsuit.* [See *Richards v. Sup.Ct. (Lee)* (1978) 86 CA3d 265, 272, 150 CR 77,

81, ¶*8:339.11*] (If the information is used in court (e.g., during a punitive damages phase at trial), it may be further disclosed.)

(c) [8:327.3] **Other cases?** Whether this presumption is limited to punitive damage cases is unclear.

- [8:327.4] Some courts hold a party is presumptively entitled to a protective order against disclosure of confidential financial information in any case even where the information is *germane to the claim sued upon*. [*Moskowitz v. Sup.Ct. (Zerner, Sims & Cibener)* (1982) 137 CA3d 313, 318, 187 CR 4, 8 (disapproved on other grounds by *Williams v. Sup.Ct. (Marshalls of CA, LLC)* (2017) 3 C5th 531, 557, 220 CR3d 472, 494 & fn. 8)—legal malpractice plaintiff claimed losses resulting from alleged financial inability to post an execution bond; his finances were germane to his damage claim; but he was *presumptively entitled to protective order* limiting disclosure of confidential financial information disclosed at his deposition; burden on opposing parties to show such relief not warranted]

- [8:327.5] But there is also authority contra. [*GT, Inc. v. Sup.Ct. (Santa Cruz Sentinel Publishers, Inc.)* (1984) 151 CA3d 748, 754, 198 CR 892, 896—*no presumption* in favor of protective order in unfair competition action between competitors although on showing of "good cause," court can restrict dissemination of confidential information obtained through discovery to counsel for discovering party]

[8:327.6-327.9] *Reserved.*

(4) [8:327.10] **Compare—CCP §877.6 "good faith" settlement proceedings:** A settling tortfeasor's finances are discoverable in CCP §877.6 "good faith settlement" proceedings (*see* ¶*12:835 ff.*). The settlor's right to financial privacy is held *outweighed* by the need for this important evidence affecting whether the settlement was made in "good faith." [*City of Grand Terrace v. Sup.Ct. (Boyter)* (1987) 192 CA3d 1251, 1260, 238 CR 119, 124; *discussed at* ¶*12:877; and see* ¶*8:1805.7*]

(5) [8:327.11] **Civil rights actions:** In actions *to enforce civil rights* statutes, the need to discover the identity of *persons discriminated against* may *outweigh* any interest in protecting their privacy. [See *Olympic Club v. Sup.Ct. (City & County of San Francisco)* (1991) 229 CA3d 358, 363-364, 282 CR 1, 3]

- [8:327.12] **Example:** City sued to enforce civil rights statute against Private Club. City's need for the *names of rejected applicants* outweighed their privacy rights.

© 2020 Thomson Reuters/The Rutter Group

Nor was City required to obtain the applicants' permission for such disclosure; victims of discrimination may be reluctant to come forward voluntarily. [*Olympic Club v. Sup.Ct. (City & County of San Francisco)*, supra, 229 CA3d at 363-364, 282 CR at 3]

- [8:327.13] **Compare—tax enforcement proceedings:** Members' privacy rights are more likely to be upheld where their identity is sought in connection with *tax enforcement* proceedings. [See *Pacific-Union Club v. Sup.Ct. (State Franchise Tax Bd.)* (1991) 232 CA3d 60, 78, 283 CR 287, 297—State sought membership list in order to test member's compliance with statute prohibiting members of private clubs that discriminate from deducting club-related business expenses on state income tax return]

  [8:327.14-327.19] *Reserved.*

[8:327.20] ***PRACTICE POINTER:*** Because the court must balance competing interests, if both sides insist on an "all or nothing" approach, at least one side will be unhappy with the decision. Counsel opposing discovery may be able to minimize the impact of an adverse decision by pointing out the most sensitive information and suggesting alternative means to provide the information needed by the party seeking discovery.

Some trial courts, particularly in complex cases, encourage counsel to discuss these issues with the court *before* making discovery motions. Counsel may seek, or the court on its own motion may require, such pre-motion conferences. [See, e.g., CCP §2016.080; *and further discussion at ¶8:787.1*]

[8:327.21] ***FURTHER PRACTICE POINTER:*** Before filing a motion for a *protective order*, ask opposing counsel to stipulate to the relief you seek. Sample forms for stipulated protective orders are available on the Los Angeles Superior Court website (*www.lacourt.org*). If opposing counsel refuses to stipulate, that fact can be included in your declaration showing a "reasonable and good faith attempt" was made to informally resolve the issues (*see ¶8:1015*).

h. [8:328] **Discovery orders narrowly drawn:** If discovery is ordered, the order will preserve the right of privacy involved to the greatest extent possible. Any discovery order should be carefully tailored to protect the interests of the party seeking discovery while not unnecessarily invading the privacy of the party whose privacy is threatened. Upon request, the court should consider appropriate protective orders. [*Schnabel v. Sup.Ct. (Schnabel)* (1993) 5 C4th 704, 714, 21 CR2d 200, 205; *Life Technologies Corp. v. Sup.Ct. (Joyce)* (2011) 197 CA4th 640, 654, 130 CR3d 80, 92 (disapproved on other grounds by *Williams v. Sup.Ct. (Marshalls of CA, LLC)* (2017) 3 C5th 531, 557, 220 CR3d 472, 494 & fn. 8)]

(1) [8:329] **Protecting identities of third persons:** Where the privacy rights of third persons are involved, the court may order their names deleted from the records disclosed (*Davies v. Sup.Ct. (State of Calif.)* (1984) 36 C3d 291, 204 CR 154); or that answers identifying them be sealed or disclosed only in in camera hearings. [*Valley Bank of Nevada v. Sup.Ct. (Barkett)* (1975) 15 C3d 652, 658, 125 CR 553, 556]

- [8:329.1] An order can be fashioned that maintains the confidentiality of a nonparty deponent's identity and that of his or her family. For example, attendance at the deposition can be limited to the parties' counsel and the deposition transcript might refer simply to the deponent as "John Doe." [*Johnson v. Sup.Ct. (Calif. Cryobank, Inc.)* (2000) 80 CA4th 1050, 1072, 95 CR2d 864, 879 (disapproved on other grounds by *Williams v. Sup.Ct. (Marshalls of CA, LLC)* (2017) 3 C5th 531, 557, 220 CR3d 472, 494 & fn. 8)—sperm donor deposed to determine information re his genetic and medical history needed for medical decisions re child conceived with his sperm]

(2) [8:330] **Allowing only partial disclosure:** If the competing interests can be "accommodated" by allowing *partial disclosure* of the confidential information, the court will limit its order accordingly. [*Valley Bank of Nevada v. Sup.Ct. (Barkett),* supra, 15 C3d at 658, 125 CR at 556]

- [8:331] Persons involved in auto accidents have a right of privacy as to the "confidential" accident reports they file with the DMV (*see ¶8:313*). Victims of other accidents at the same location may need access to such reports to show causal similarities. These conflicting interests can be accommodated by *partial* disclosure: i.e., releasing data generated from such reports (date, place, diagrams of accidents, etc.), but withholding the reporting parties' *identities* so as to protect their privacy rights. [*Davies v. Sup.Ct. (State of Calif.)*, supra, 36 C3d at 300, 204 CR at 160]

- [8:332] Husband's extramarital sex relations may be discoverable in his suit for wrongful death of Wife (*see ¶8:326.1*). But an order requiring Husband to provide the names and addresses of his sex partners goes too far. The order should be *limited* to asking him to admit such relationships without revealing their identities. [*Morales v. Sup.Ct. (Smith)* (1979) 99 CA3d 283, 291, 160 CR 194, 199]

- [8:332.1] Female workers sued Employer, claiming job discrimination in favor of male coworker (not a party to action). An order allowing discovery of the male coworker's *entire* personnel file was error. The court should have considered whether the information sought could be

© 2020 Thomson Reuters/The Rutter Group

obtained by less intrusive means (e.g., deposing the male coworker). Even if inspection of the file is necessary, the court should first examine it in camera and order disclosure only of those *parts relevant* to the lawsuit. [*El Dorado Sav. & Loan Ass'n v. Sup.Ct. (Savoca)* (1987) 190 CA3d 342, 346, 235 CR 303, 305 (disapproved on other grounds by *Williams v. Sup.Ct. (Marshalls of CA, LLC)* (2017) 3 C5th 531, 557, 220 CR3d 472, 494 & fn. 8)]

(3) [8:333] **Limiting disclosure to counsel for discovering party:** Instead of denying discovery, the court may restrict who may inspect confidential information and conditions under which such inspection will be allowed. Typically, disclosure is limited to counsel for the party seeking discovery; and that counsel is ordered to use such information only for purposes of the lawsuit. [*Moskowitz v. Sup.Ct. (Zemer, Sims & Cibener)* (1982) 137 CA3d 313, 318-319, 187 CR 4, 8 (disapproved on other grounds by *Williams v. Sup.Ct. (Marshalls of CA, LLC)* (2017) 3 C5th 531, 557, 220 CR3d 472, 494 & fn. 8); see *Elmore v. Sup.Ct. (Valley Nitrogen Producers, Inc.)* (1967) 255 CA2d 635, 638-639, 63 CR 307, 310]

Indeed, an "attorney's eyes only" provision is common in stipulated protective orders.

(a) [8:334] **Example:** In an unfair competition suit between business competitors, the court may properly order that financial data obtained through discovery be *restricted to counsel* for the discovering party and used solely for purposes of trial preparation. Counsel may be *ordered not to disclose* such information to their own clients so as to avoid unfair use of the information obtained. [*GT, Inc. v. Sup.Ct. (Santa Cruz Sentinel Publishers, Inc.)* (1984) 151 CA3d 748, 755, 198 CR 892, 896]

(b) [8:335] **Validity of order prohibiting counsel from disclosing to own client?** Prohibiting counsel from disclosing to their own clients information obtained through discovery arguably impairs counsel's right to communicate with the client.

However, such an order appears to be valid. I.e., upon a showing of good cause, the public policy protecting defendant's right to privacy may prevail over the need for communication between attorney and client. [See *GT, Inc. v. Sup.Ct. (Santa Cruz Sentinel Publishers, Inc.)*, supra, 151 CA3d at 755-756, 198 CR at 896-897—good cause shown by danger of misuse of information due to animus between parties]

(c) [8:336] **Order allowing disclosure to counsel in similar cases:** Public policy *favors* sharing discovered information with litigants in other cases involving the same subject matter. (It reduces the costs to all involved and forces the responding party to be consistent in each suit.) Therefore, a protective order *permitting* disclosure of trade secrets or other confidential information to *counsel* in similar cases will be upheld, provided there is protection from disclosure to the general public. This can be accomplished by requiring counsel receiving the information to stipulate not to further disseminate or disclose it. [*Raymond Handling Concepts Corp. v. Sup.Ct. (Zuelzke)* (1995) 39 CA4th 584, 590, 45 CR2d 885, 888]

[8:336.1-336.4] *Reserved.*

(4) [8:336.5] **No prior restraints:** A discovery order cannot support a prior restraint on speech, even to prevent disclosure of information that invades a person's privacy: "[S]paring citizens from embarrassment, shame, or even intrusions into their privacy has never been held to outweigh the guarantees of free speech in our federal and state constitutions." [*Hurvitz v. Hoefflin* (2001) 84 CA4th 1232, 1244-1245, 101 CR2d 558, 567-568—order barring parties and counsel from disclosing sensitive information regarding cosmetic surgeon's patients was unconstitutional prior restraint]

However, First Amendment concerns generally do not affect pretrial discovery (*see* ¶*8:681*) and parties routinely enter into stipulated protective orders barring dissemination of discovery materials.

i. [8:337] **Punitive damage claims:** Where plaintiff's cause of action includes a claim for punitive damages, defendant's financial condition is certainly "relevant to the subject matter": i.e., defendant's *net worth* and the *profits* derived from its wrongful conduct reflect on the "sting" necessary to punish defendant.

But unlimited discovery of defendant's finances encourages "games playing"—creating a situation in which plaintiffs, by alleging a punitives claim, could force defendant to settle simply in order to protect its financial privacy. [See *Rawnsley v. Sup.Ct. (Pioneer Theaters)* (1986) 183 CA3d 86, 90, 227 CR 806, 808 (citing text); *Jabro v. Sup.Ct. (Hill)* (2002) 95 CA4th 754, 757, 115 CR2d 843, 845]

Special rules have been adopted to avoid this:

(1) [8:338] **Limit on evidence at trial:** For "good cause," the trial judge may grant defendant a protective order: Plaintiff may be required to prove a *prima facie* case of liability for punitive damages *before* any evidence of defendant's net worth or its profits from the allegedly wrongful conduct will be admitted. [Civ.C. §3295(a)]

In addition, on defendant's motion, the *amount* of punitives is tried separately from liability issues. Evidence of defendant's

© 2020 Thomson Reuters/The Rutter Group

profits and net worth cannot be considered until *after* the jury first returns a verdict for plaintiff on the underlying tort claim and finding defendant guilty of "oppression, fraud or malice" in accordance with Civ.C. §3294. [Civ.C. §3295(d)]

(2) [8:339] **Limit on pretrial discovery:** Moreover, the right to pretrial discovery of defendant's net worth and wrongful profits is limited:

(a) [8:339.1] **Document and witness identification permitted:** Plaintiff may require defendant to *identify documents* in its possession that are *admissible* (not merely relevant) on the issue of its profits or financial condition. Defendant may also be required to identify "*witnesses* employed by or related to the defendant who would be most competent to testify" to its financial condition. [Civ.C. §3295(c) (emphasis added)]

Also, plaintiff may *subpoena* these documents or witnesses to be available at trial for purposes of establishing defendant's financial condition. [Civ.C. §3295(c); see *Soto v. BorgWarner Morse TEC Inc.* (2015) 239 CA4th 165, 193, 191 CR3d 263, 284-285—traditional subpoena process protects defendant's privacy interests while affording plaintiff some assurance defendant's financial information will be ready if and when necessary]

(b) [8:339.2] **Court order required for further discovery:** Beyond the foregoing, *no* pretrial discovery by plaintiff is permitted without a court order; and such order can be granted only if the court finds there is a "*substantial probability that the plaintiff will prevail*" on his or her claim for punitive damages. [Civ.C. §3295(c) (emphasis added); see *Kerr v. Rose* (1990) 216 CA3d 1551, 1565, 265 CR 597, 605]

1) [8:339.3] **Procedure:** To obtain such an order, plaintiff must file a motion supported by "appropriate affidavits" (i.e., affidavits sufficient to establish "oppression, fraud or malice" under Civ.C. §3294). [Civ.C. §3295(c)]

Defendant must be given the opportunity to present opposing declarations. [Civ.C. §3295(c)]

The court has discretion whether to hold a formal hearing. (As a practical matter, such a hearing is almost always held.) [Civ.C. §3295(c)]

FORM: Motion for Order Permitting Discovery of Financial Information, *see Form 8:1* in Rivera, *Cal. Prac. Guide: Civ. Pro. Before Trial FORMS* (TRG).

2) [8:339.4] **Findings required:** To allow discovery of defendant's financial condition, the court must

find "on the basis of the supporting and opposing affidavits" that plaintiff has "established a substantial probability" of prevailing on the punitive damages claim. [Civ.C. §3295(c)]

3) [8:339.5] **Weighing of affidavits:** Section 3295(c) has been interpreted to mean that the court must (1) *weigh the evidence presented by both sides* "and (2) make a finding that it is *very likely* the plaintiff will prevail on his claim for punitive damages." [*Jabro v. Sup.Ct. (Hill)* (2002) 95 CA4th 754, 758, 115 CR2d 843, 845 (emphasis added)—relying on legislative history]

   a) [8:339.6] **Prima facie showing not enough?** Under this interpretation, it is *not* enough for plaintiff merely to present evidence that would support a finding (prima facie proof) of "oppression, fraud or malice." [*Jabro v. Sup.Ct. (Hill)*, supra, 95 CA4th at 759, 115 CR2d at 846-847]

   b) [8:339.7] **Comment:** Civ.C. §3295(c)'s requirement that plaintiff establish a "substantial probability" of prevailing on a punitive damages claim *mirrors similar language in CCP §425.13* (dealing with amendments to allege punitive damage claims against health care providers). Yet, the Supreme Court has interpreted CCP §425.13 to require only *prima facie proof*. [*College Hosp., Inc. v. Sup.Ct. (Crowell)* (1994) 8 C4th 704, 719-720, 34 CR2d 898, 907; *see ¶6:340*]

4) [8:339.8] **Compare—discovery at trial:** Instead of conducting pretrial discovery, plaintiff may wait until liability for punitive damages is established and then request that defendant produce the financial records. [Civ.C. §3295(c)—court "may at any time enter an order permitting" discovery; see *Soto v. BorgWarner Morse TEC Inc.*, supra, 239 CA4th at 193, 191 CR3d at 284-285]

   However, waiting is risky because the court may be unwilling to hold a jury after a liability verdict to allow plaintiff to conduct discovery. The court is likely to want to immediately go into the punitive damages phase and thus, may deem the request untimely. [See *I-CA Enterprises, Inc. v. Palram Americas, Inc.* (2015) 235 CA4th 257, 283-284, 185 CR3d 24, 45-46—party's request made on eve of punitive damages trial phase deemed too late; *Soto v. BorgWarner Morse TEC Inc.*, supra, 239 CA4th at 197-198, 191 CR3d at 288—court "not obligated to accommodate

© 2020 Thomson Reuters/The Rutter Group

plaintiffs' last-minute attempt to obtain" information it could have discovered earlier]

[8:339.9-339.10] *Reserved.*

(c) [8:339.11] **Presumption in favor of limiting disclosure to opposing counsel:** Even if discovery is ordered, defendant is "*presumptively entitled to a protective order*" limiting disclosure of the evidence obtained *solely to opposing counsel* and solely for the purposes of the lawsuit. [*Richards v. Sup.Ct. (Lee)* (1978) 86 CA3d 265, 272, 150 CR 77, 81; *see* ¶*8:327.2, 8:333 ff.*]

(3) [8:339.12] **Compare—defendant's finances germane to cause of action:** Civ.C. §3295(c) does not bar pretrial discovery where defendant's finances are *directly related to the substantive claim involved.* In such cases, the fact that punitive damages are or are not being sought does not prevent discovery on elements of the substantive claim. [*Rawnsley v. Sup.Ct. (Pioneer Theaters)* (1986) 183 CA3d 86, 91, 227 CR 806, 809]

(a) [8:339.13] **Example:** P sued D for misappropriating funds from a partnership. P sought to recover both compensatory and punitive damages. Information as to D's *profits and finances* was discoverable because it went "to the heart of the action itself" (the misappropriation claim) as distinguished from discovery on D's *net worth*, which was relevant only for punitive damages purposes. [*Rawnsley v. Sup.Ct. (Pioneer Theaters)*, supra, 183 CA3d at 91, 227 CR at 809 (internal quotes omitted)—but questions were overbroad and unreasonably invasive]

(b) [8:339.14] **Presumption favoring protective order?** Even without a punitive damages claim, discovery of confidential financial information is still subject to *privacy protection* (¶*8:303*). Therefore, upon timely objection, disclosure may be ordered only after the balancing test discussed previously (¶*8:323*).

Courts are presently split on whether there is any *presumption favoring* protective orders in such cases limiting disclosure to opposing counsel (*see* ¶*8:327.3*).

6. [8:340] **Protection for News Media:** There are several separate bases upon which news media may resist discovery demands:

a. [8:341] **"Shield law" against contempt:** California has a "shield law" that protects news reporters, editors, publishers, broadcasters, etc. *against punishment for contempt* for refusing to disclose either:

- Their *sources*, or
- *Unpublished* information obtained in the course of gathering, receiving or processing information for communication to the

public (e.g., interview notes, "outtakes," etc.). [Cal. Const. Art. I, §2; and Ev.C. §1070]

Testimony or other evidence given by a member of the news media under subpoena *does not waive* these immunity rights provided by the Constitution. [CCP §1986.1(a)] (Subpoenas to news media are subject to a special notice requirement; *see ¶8:571.5.*)

(1) [8:341.1] **Covered persons:** The protection extends to "a publisher, editor, reporter, or other person connected with or employed upon a newspaper, magazine, or other periodical publication . . ." [Cal. Const. Art. I, §2(b)]

(a) [8:341.2] **Internet website operators:** The operator of a news-oriented Internet website that is open to the public has been held to be a "publisher" for purposes of the shield law. [*O'Grady v. Sup.Ct. (Apple Computer, Inc.)* (2006) 139 CA4th 1423, 1459-1460, 44 CR3d 72, 99—news-oriented websites are "like a newspaper or magazine for these purposes"]

[8:341.3-341.4] *Reserved.*

(2) [8:341.5] **Information gathered for communication to the public:** The phrase "information for communication to the public" requires that the person or entity invoking the shield law be engaged in "legitimate journalistic purposes, or have exercised judgmental discretion in such activities." [See *Rancho Publications v. Sup.Ct. (Downey Comm. Hosp.)* (1999) 68 CA4th 1538, 1545, 81 CR2d 274, 278]

(a) [8:341.6] **"Legitimate journalism":** What constitutes "legitimate journalism" is presently unclear. [See *O'Grady v. Sup.Ct. (Apple Computer, Inc.)*, supra, 139 CA4th at 1457, 44 CR3d at 97—"We can think of no workable test or principle that would distinguish 'legitimate' from 'illegitimate' news"]

(b) [8:341.7] **No protection for advertisements:** The shield law does *not* protect the identity of advertisers. [*Rancho Publications v. Sup.Ct. (Downey Comm. Hosp.)*, supra, 68 CA4th at 1544, 81 CR2d at 278]

Compare—other protections: However, the advertiser's identity may be protected under the First Amendment (free speech) and California's constitutional right of privacy. [*Rancho Publications v. Sup.Ct. (Downey Comm. Hosp.)*, supra, 68 CA4th at 1547, 81 CR2d at 279-280]

[8:341.8-341.9] *Reserved.*

(3) [8:341.10] **Information need not be "confidential":** *Any* unpublished information is protected under the shield law. The information need not have been obtained in confidence by a newsperson. For example, unpublished photographs and *eyewitness observations* by a newsperson are protected.

© 2020 Thomson Reuters/The Rutter Group

[*Delaney v. Sup.Ct. (Kopetman)* (1990) 50 C3d 785, 805, 268 CR 753, 764; *Miller v. Sup.Ct. (People)* (1999) 21 C4th 883, 897, 89 CR2d 834, 843—unbroadcast portions of a defendant's confession]

(4) [8:341.11] **Protection absolute in civil cases:** At least where no constitutional right is involved, the shield law provides *absolute* immunity against contempt in civil cases. I.e., *no balancing test* can be applied to determine whether a party's "need" for the information outweighs the media's right to withhold it. [*New York Times v. Sup.Ct. (Sortomme)* (1990) 51 C3d 453, 461, 273 CR 98, 102—trial court *cannot* require in camera disclosure of unpublished information]

(a) [8:341.12] **Compare—criminal cases:** The result may be contra in criminal cases. A criminal defendant's federal constitutional right to a *fair trial* must be *balanced* against the shield law immunity provided by the California Constitution. [*Delaney v. Sup.Ct. (Kopetman)*, supra, 50 C3d at 805, 268 CR at 764]

(5) [8:341.13] **Protection continues after story published:** The nonpublished material retains its protection even *after* the story has been published. It makes no difference that the published story purports to paraphrase or summarize the nonpublished material. [*Playboy Enterprises, Inc. v. Sup.Ct. (Greene)* (1984) 154 CA3d 14, 23-24, 201 CR 207, 215]

(6) [8:341.14] **Protection continues after employment:** The "shield law" covers persons formerly connected with or employed by a news organization, as well as those presently employed. [See Calif. Const. Art. I, §2; and Ev.C. §1070(a)]

(7) [8:341.15] **Discovery sanctions other than contempt may be imposed:** While the "shield law" protects newspersons against punishment for contempt, it is not a privilege against discovery. Thus, where newspersons are *parties* to civil litigation, *other sanctions* may be imposed against them for refusal to comply with discovery orders (including entry of judgment against them). [*Mitchell v. Sup.Ct. (Synanon Church)* (1984) 37 C3d 268, 274, 208 CR 152, 155]

Compare: Where they are *not* parties to the litigation, newspersons are subject only to *monetary sanctions* for disobeying discovery orders. But this may be a "virtually ineffectual" remedy because CCP §1992 limits monetary sanctions for disobedience to a subpoena to a $500 forfeiture plus whatever damages the subpoenaing party can prove in a separate lawsuit. [*New York Times v. Sup.Ct. (Sortomme)*, supra, 51 C3d at 464, 273 CR at 105; *see ¶8:618*]

[8:341.16-341.19] *Reserved.*

b. [8:341.20] **News sources' right of privacy:** Persons disclosing facts in confidence to a news reporter have a protectible right of privacy. The news reporter has standing to raise the privacy rights of his or her sources in resisting discovery. [*Dalitz v. Penthouse Int'l, Ltd.* (1985) 168 CA3d 468, 482, 214 CR 254, 263; *see* ¶*8:315*]

However, as previously discussed, the right of privacy is not absolute. A balancing of interests is required (¶*8:323*); and, in appropriate cases, discovery may be ordered. [*Dalitz v. Penthouse Int'l, Ltd.*, supra, 168 CA3d at 482, 214 CR at 263]

In any event, a publisher or reporter cannot raise "privacy" objections where it is the *plaintiff* in the action. If it wants to protect its sources, it cannot sue: "The law simply does not provide for using the same privilege for both printing and suing." [*Dalitz v. Penthouse Int'l, Ltd.*, supra, 168 CA3d at 482, 214 CR at 263]

c. [8:342] **First Amendment privilege:** A reporter, editor or publisher may also have a constitutional privilege to withhold both his or her sources and unpublished information obtained from such sources in civil litigation. This privilege is designed to protect investigative reporting, and is based on the "free press" guarantees of the First Amendment and correlative provisions of the California Constitution. [*Mitchell v. Sup.Ct. (Synanon Church)*, supra, 37 C3d at 274, 208 CR at 155]

(1) [8:342a] **What is privileged:** The First Amendment protects the news media's *confidential sources* and any *unpublished* information ("outtakes") from such sources. [*Mitchell v. Sup.Ct. (Synanon Church)*, supra, 37 C3d at 274, 208 CR at 155]

(a) [8:342b] **Compare—no "editorial privilege":** Discovery of a newspaper's editorial processes does not pose the same risk of inhibiting investigative reporting as disclosure of confidential sources. Therefore, an editor *can* be compelled to answer questions relating to his or her *thought processes*— e.g., what information he or she decided to include or omit from a published story. [*Herbert v. Lando* (1979) 441 US 153, 99 S.Ct. 1635; *Mitchell v. Sup.Ct. (Synanon Church)*, supra, 37 C3d at 279, 208 CR at 158]

(2) [8:342.1] **Privilege not absolute:** Unlike attorney-client and other privileges, the First Amendment privilege is qualified, not absolute. Whether discovery will be allowed depends on the facts of each case. The interests sought to be protected must be *balanced* against the interests of the litigants to full disclosure of relevant information. [*Mitchell v. Sup.Ct. (Synanon Church)*, supra, 37 C3d at 276, 208 CR at 156]

(3) [8:342.2] **Determinative factors:** The scope and effect of the First Amendment privilege is determined in each case by weighing the following factors: [*Mitchell v. Sup.Ct. (Synanon Church)*, supra, 37 C3d at 279-280, 208 CR at 159]

- *Nature of the litigation*, and whether the reporter is a

© 2020 Thomson Reuters/The Rutter Group

party. (The privilege will more likely be upheld in criminal proceedings than civil, and where the newsperson is *not* a party to the litigation.)

- Whether the *information "goes to the heart"* of plaintiff's claim (i.e., mere relevance is not enough).
- Whether plaintiff has *exhausted all alternative sources* for obtaining the information sought (compulsory disclosure being "the last resort").
- Any *public interest* in protecting confidentiality of the source. (E.g., there is a strong public interest in revelation of wrongdoing in public affairs, and in protecting the "whistleblower" from retaliation.)
- Finally, the court may require plaintiff to make a *prima facie showing* that the alleged defamatory statements were false before requiring disclosure. (While not a prerequisite, it may "tip the balance" in favor of discovery.) [*Mitchell v. Sup.Ct. (Synanon Church)*, supra, 37 C3d at 283, 208 CR at 161; see also *O'Grady v. Sup.Ct. (Apple Computer, Inc.)* (2006) 139 CA4th 1423, 1468-1479, 44 CR3d 72, 106-115]

Of the foregoing factors, the most important is whether the information sought "goes to the heart of the claim." [*Dalitz v. Penthouse Int'l, Ltd.* (1985) 168 CA3d 468, 477, 214 CR 254, 260]

(4) [8:342.3] **Application:** The following are typical situations in which the First Amendment may be claimed in civil discovery.

(a) [8:342.4] **Libel action against newspaper:** Disclosure of confidential sources will generally be ordered in libel actions by a public figure against a news reporter or publication. Reason: Plaintiff's burden is to prove defendants acted with "actual malice," and this may be impossible if defendants can withhold identity of their informant. I.e., to allow the privilege in such cases might immunize news media against civil liability for libel. [*Mitchell v. Sup.Ct. (Synanon Church)*, supra, 37 C3d at 279-280, 208 CR at 159]

(b) [8:342.5] **Publisher's cross-action:** Disclosure of confidential sources will also generally be ordered where the publisher asserting the privilege is itself a protagonist, seeking judicial relief. [*Dalitz v. Penthouse Int'l, Ltd.*, supra, 168 CA3d at 477, 214 CR at 260]

- [8:342.6] Upon being sued for defamation, Publisher cross-complained for slanders uttered by the parties whom it had allegedly defamed. Under such circumstances, it was proper to order Publisher to disclose the sources for its defamatory publication, and to strike its cross-complaint for refusal. It could not "use the First Amendment simultaneously as a sword *and* a shield." [*Dalitz v. Penthouse Int'l, Ltd.*, supra, 168 CA3d at 479, 214 CR at 260 (emphasis added)]

[8:342.7-342.9] *Reserved.*

(c) [8:342.10] **Invasion of privacy:** In an action against a publisher for invasion of privacy (as to a nonpublic figure), the "prima facie" showing required to overcome the journalist's privilege is that the defendant intentionally disclosed information otherwise not public regarding the plaintiff. In order to make this showing, plaintiff may be entitled to *discovery* from the publisher-defendant as to what nonpublic information it had, and to whom it was disclosed. [*Anti-Defamation League of B'Nai B'Rith v. Sup.Ct. (Shabbas)* (1998) 67 CA4th 1072, 1096-1097, 79 CR2d 597, 612]

(5) [8:343] **Publisher's duty to find out reporter's confidential sources?** If disclosure of confidential sources is otherwise required, it is no excuse that Publisher does not know its reporters' sources. If it has made no effort to retract or disassociate itself from the defamatory article, Publisher may be under a *duty* to *acquire knowledge* of the sources, and is subject to sanctions if it refuses. [*Dalitz v. Penthouse Int'l, Ltd.*, supra, 168 CA3d at 474-475, 214 CR at 258]

Such sanctions may include an order barring Publisher from claiming at trial that there was any source at all for the story; and an order striking Publisher's cross-complaint for defamation (¶*8:342.6*). [*Dalitz v. Penthouse Int'l, Ltd.*, supra, 168 CA3d at 474-475, 214 CR at 258]

[8:344-345] *Reserved.*

© 2020 Thomson Reuters/The Rutter Group

RESERVED

CHAPTER 8D

DISCOVERY PRACTICE—PRESERVING EVIDENCE—CREATING DISCOVERY PLAN

CONTENTS

© 2020 Thomson Reuters/The Rutter Group

DISCOVERY PRACTICE—PRESERVING EVIDENCE—CREATING DISCOVERY PLAN

1. [8:346] **Discovery Plan—Reasons for Plan:** There should be a discovery plan in *every* case, even if the "plan" is to conduct *no* discovery.

- [8:346.1] There are disadvantages as well as advantages to discovery (*see* ¶*8:2*). Among other drawbacks are the cost, time and possibility of "educating" your adversary. Moreover, in some cases, you may want to avoid discovery in the hope that it will lull your adversary into inaction or failure to prepare the case properly for trial.
- [8:347] But any decision *not* to undertake discovery should be deliberate—after carefully balancing any potential disadvantages against the benefits available through discovery (i.e., better evidence, avoidance of surprise, enhanced settlement potential, etc.).
- [8:348] **Caution:** Keep in mind that failure to conduct discovery may be a "red flag" for claims of *legal malpractice.* If the case is lost, or the client is unhappy with the result, your failure to conduct thorough pretrial discovery may have to be explained in a negligence action or even in disciplinary proceedings. Consequently, this risk also has to be evaluated in any decision not to proceed with discovery.

  Another risk: If you're representing the plaintiff, the defendant may *move to dismiss for failure to prosecute* (CCP §583.410). Defendant may argue that your failure to conduct discovery demonstrates lack of diligence in preparing the case for trial.

[8:348.1] ***PRACTICE POINTERS:*** Be sure to consult with the client in preparation of your discovery plan. In approprlate cases, a budget for discovery should be prepared and presented to the client for approval.

Helping the client evaluate the cost of discovery in relation to the economic potential of the case may avoid later malpractice or fee dispute problems.

To avoid misunderstandings, confirm in writing the client's agreement to the discovery plan and budget, including any agreed-upon limitations. Likewise, confirm in writing any changes to the plan that may be required after consulting with the client.

2. [8:349] **What a Discovery Plan Can Accomplish:** In addition to serving as "preventive medicine" against legal malpractice claims, an effective discovery plan can posture the case for settlement or trial.

It should serve the following functions (each of which is discussed in detail below, ¶*8:350 ff.*):

© 2020 Thomson Reuters/The Rutter Group

- *Obtaining proof* of your claims or defenses;
- *Pinning down your opponent* at an early stage;
- *Selecting the proper discovery tools* to obtain the information needed;
- *Determining the sequence* in which discovery should proceed; and
- *Timing your discovery* so you have what you need at various stages in the litigation—e.g., settlement, summary judgment and trial.

3. [8:350] **Obtaining Proof:** The first step in creating a discovery plan is to determine what needs to be proved—both with respect to your own case and your opponent's.

a. **Analysis of your own case**

(1) [8:351] **Determine legal elements required to establish your own case:** If you are representing the plaintiff, determine the precise elements of the cause of action sued upon (the "prima facie case"). Likewise, if you're representing the defendant, determine the specific elements of any affirmative defense.

(a) [8:352] **Comment:** This may sound rather obvious, but *legal research* is usually the indispensable first step in any discovery plan. "Hitting the books" is often required to tie down exactly what *are* the elements of the claim or defense involved.

☞ [8:353] ***PRACTICE POINTER:*** If your case is covered by CACI (Judicial Council of California Civil Jury Instructions) or BAJI (Book of Approved Jury Instructions), use the applicable CACI or BAJI instructions as a checklist of the elements of your claim or defense.

Cross-refer: The essential elements of many claims and defenses are discussed in detail in Gaab & Reese, *Cal. Prac. Guide: Civ. Pro. Before Trial—Claims & Defenses* (TRG).

(2) [8:354] **Determine facts necessary to establish each element:** The next step is to determine *what facts* are necessary to prove *each element* of your claim or defense. In short, how are you going to prove each element of your claim?

(3) [8:355] **Determine sources of proof:** In some cases, all the proof you need will be in your control or the control of your client; and your only concern will be to preserve the evidence for trial. In other cases, however, much of the proof will have to be obtained from your opponent or third parties; and a discovery plan prepared for obtaining such evidence.

Each crucial fact has to be linked to a *competent* source: if a document, where it is located, who has control of it, etc.; if a witness, his or her name and address, and any problems relating to said witness (bias, reluctance to testify, etc.).

☞ [8:355.1] ***PRACTICE POINTER:*** Consider sending *written demands to preserve* specified evidence to the opposing party *and any third party* who may have such evidence. (For example, security videotapes may be in the opposing party's possession or in the possession of a nonparty business in the vicinity of an accident.) This is particularly important with respect to electronically-stored information (ESI), which may be routinely discarded or recorded over. If you wait for formal discovery to attempt to obtain that evidence with a subpoena, it may no longer exist. *See also ¶8:19.20 ff.*

(a) [8:356] **Investigations vs. discovery:** Obviously, you don't need to employ discovery devices to obtain proof of every fact in the case. Usually, your client will be able to provide records or competent testimony for much of your own case. Or, such facts may be obtained from friendly witnesses who will give interviews and witness statements, and who will testify willingly if the case goes to trial. Or, such facts may be obtained from other sources without the necessity of formal discovery—e.g., matters of public record can be proved by obtaining authenticated copies of the record (marriage certificates; birth certificates; death certificates; transfers of title to real property, etc.).

Don't overlook the Internet as a valuable investigative tool.

☞ [8:356.1] ***PRACTICE POINTER:*** Social media sites, such as Facebook and Twitter, can provide valuable information about opposing parties and witnesses. Sometimes people comment on their "pages" about their reaction to the litigation or about their personal lives in ways relevant to the litigation (e.g., where claims of severe emotional distress are contradicted or linked to other causes).

However, there may be ethical limitations for an attorney to consider before accessing an adverse party's "pages": Seeking to become a "friend" in order to access information for litigation purposes may be challenged, if the adverse party is represented by counsel, as an *improper communication with a represented person* (violating CRPC 4.2 (formerly CRPC 2-100)).

(4) [8:357] **Consider costs of discovery:** The various discovery procedures involve varying cost considerations, in terms of both actual out-of-pocket expense and attorney time (¶*8:2*). The size of the case and the client's financial ability must be taken into consideration. The "best" discovery procedures may have to be set aside where they cannot be afforded.

© 2020 Thomson Reuters/The Rutter Group

(5) [8:357.1] **Consider complexity of case:** If your case has many parties and/or is likely to involve numerous difficult discovery issues, consider seeking complex designation (*see* ¶*12:47 ff.*) to have the case assigned to a single, experienced judge who may stay, bifurcate or otherwise control discovery and thereby reduce its burden.

b. **Analysis of your opponent's case**

(1) [8:358] **Determine exactly what claims or defenses are being asserted:** First and foremost, you need to be sure you know exactly what causes of action or defenses are being asserted by your adversary. The pleadings will usually indicate the major theories, but not always. Consequently, in every case, you must make sure that you know exactly *what* legal theories your adversary is relying on, and utilize appropriate discovery tools to accomplish this (*see* ¶*8:377 ff.*).

(2) [8:359] **Consider elements, facts, sources of proof, etc.:** After you are satisfied that you know exactly what causes of action or defenses are being asserted by your opponent, go through the same analysis as with your own case: i.e., determine the legal *elements* of the opponent's claim or defense; what *facts* are necessary to prove each such element; and the probable *sources* of proof as to such facts—keeping in mind the *costs* of discovery.

Cross-refer: The essential elements of many claims and defenses are discussed in detail in Gaab & Reese, *Cal. Prac. Guide: Civ. Pro. Before Trial—Claims & Defenses* (TRG).

(3) [8:360] **Determine proof necessary to counter:** With the opponent's probable "game plan" before you, it is your job to determine what evidence will be required to overcome the opponent's case; and to come up with a discovery plan to accomplish this.

c. [8:361] **"Nailing down" uncontested facts or issues:** In most cases, there will be some facts that are not in real dispute; e.g., dates, places, persons present, etc. But this does not mean such facts can be safely ignored until trial. There is always the risk that proof may then be unavailable or costly to obtain, or that the opposing party may raise some last-minute dispute or denial of the facts.

(1) [8:362] **Determine whether stipulation available:** It will not be necessary to utilize any discovery procedure if the other side will stipulate as to such facts or issues. Thus, before implementing discovery, it is wise to propose a stipulation thereto.

⇨ [8:363] ***PRACTICE POINTER:*** *This kind of stipulation should always be in writing.* This will avoid any chance that opposing counsel may forget or disagree as to the matters stipulated; or that such counsel may withdraw from the case and new counsel refuse to honor the stipulation.

As a practical matter, opposing counsel is not likely to stipulate to anything really important or controversial. But even relatively unimportant facts (dates, places, etc.) may have to be proved at trial. And, if you are going to rely on stipulations as to such matters, you want to avoid any unexpected "surprises" at trial.

(2) [8:364] **Early discovery recommended if stipulation refused:** If your adversary refuses to stipulate to matters that you believe to be beyond controversy, you should then implement appropriate discovery procedures to establish such matters in admissible form: e.g., requests for admissions, interrogatories or depositions. And, you should do so at an *early* stage of the litigation, when memories are clearest and when you will have ample time to follow up with further discovery if your adversary continues to deny such matters.

d. [8:365] **Laying foundation for evidence:** Also, consider the documentary evidence that may be needed at trial and what facts will be required to lay a foundation for each document. (Examples: genuineness of signatures, correctness of copies, etc.) By establishing the foundational facts early in the case, you will not find yourself on the eve of trial desperately trying to persuade an unwilling witness with crucial foundation testimony to testify.

(1) [8:366] **Foundational facts for deposition testimony:** If you plan to use a witness' deposition because the witness will be unavailable at trial, you may need to establish the *source of the witness' knowledge* for some statement of fact made in the deposition. Otherwise, *even if no objection was raised at the deposition*, you may run into a hearsay objection at trial. (This "trap" is discussed at *¶8:730*.)

(a) [8:367] The proper foundational facts should appear *in the deposition itself*, rather than attempting to prove same by extrinsic evidence.

(2) [8:368] **Determine whether stipulation available:** *See discussion at ¶8:362 ff.*

[8:369] *Reserved.*

4. [8:370] **"Pinning Down" Your Opponent:** Discovery should be utilized at an early stage to determine the nature and extent of your opponent's claims or defenses.

a. [8:371] **Plaintiff's claims:** Plaintiff's complaint will usually be broadly worded. As a result, defendants may need to conduct discovery to refine responsive pleadings, to fully evaluate the claims, and to prepare for trial.

(1) [8:372] **Defenses to claim:** Discovery of the details (dates, times, places) may disclose pertinent defenses (e.g., running of the statute of limitations, jurisdictional problems).

(2) [8:373] **Contentions:** The complaint may be so broadly worded that the underlying nature of the claim is concealed

© 2020 Thomson Reuters/The Rutter Group

(e.g., suit on a common count for tortious injury). Discovery will be essential to pleading and proving proper defenses.

(3) [8:374] **Damages:** The nature and extent of damages may be pleaded generally or not at all (e.g., in a personal injury or wrongful death case). Discovery will enable defendant to determine and evaluate the damages claimed.

(a) [8:375] **Compare—CCP §425.11 request:** In a personal injury or wrongful death action, the amount of damages claimed is not pleaded (CCP §425.10; *see* ¶*6:279*). Instead, the defendant is entitled, on 15 days' request, to a statement detailing the nature and extent of damages claimed (CCP §425.11; ¶*8:1758*). But the §425.11 statement *need not contain the details* and back-up information that may be obtained through effective discovery.

b. [8:376] **Defendant's defenses:** Defendants sometime plead every conceivable defense "on information and belief"—even those for which there are no facts. (Example: Pleading contributory negligence and assumption of the risk as defenses in every negligence or product liability action, regardless of the facts.)

When faced with such answers, plaintiffs will usually want to force defendants to "fish or cut bait" at an early stage. Through discovery, plaintiff can force defendants to divulge what, if any, *facts* underlie each defense pleaded. And, if there are no such facts, to admit this, in order to approach a realistic evaluation of the case.

[8:376.1] ***PRACTICE POINTER:*** Consider serving a set of "*Official Form Interrogatories*" (Judicial Council form DISC-001) shortly after receiving the answer to your pleading, checking "*Interrogatory 15.0 Denials and Special or Affirmative Defenses.*" This interrogatory asks for all the facts, witnesses and documents supporting each affirmative defense, allowing you to distinguish between defenses that the defendant is serious about and those pleaded just so counsel would not overlook a possible defense.

5. [8:377] **Selecting Proper Discovery Tools:** Designing a discovery plan also involves selecting the *proper* discovery method to do the job. These devices are designed to be used in a coordinated fashion; i.e., what one method cannot get, another generally can. But each also has its own limitations and *cost* considerations.

a. [8:378] **Discovery tools—an overview:** The Discovery Act enumerates the various methods by which discovery may be obtained:

— oral and written depositions (*see Ch. 8E*);
— interrogatories to a party (*see Ch. 8F*);
— inspection of documents, things and places (*see Ch. 8H*);
— physical and mental examinations (*see Ch. 8I*);
— requests for admissions (*see Ch. 8G*); and
— simultaneous exchange of expert trial witness information (*see Ch. 8J*). [CCP §2019.010]

The paragraphs below (¶*8:379 ff.*) briefly describe each method, plus some additional procedures for discovery found *outside* the Discovery Act:

- [8:379] **Depositions:** The examination of a witness, under oath, with the opportunity for cross-examination, including both:

  [8:380] **Depositions on oral questions in California [CCP §2025.010 et seq.]:** This is the most common form of deposition. It consists of oral questioning of the witness before a notary public (who is usually also the deposition reporter). The questions and answers are recorded and transcribed and may be admissible at trial under certain conditions.

  [8:381] **Depositions on written questions [CCP §2028.010 et seq.]:** Although rarely used, a deposition may be taken on written questions as well. The opposing party gets to see the questions in advance and may submit cross questions (followed by redirect and recross, etc.). The witness appears before a notary public and answers the questions orally. The answers are then recorded and transcribed, and may be admissible at trial under the same conditions as an oral deposition. (*See* ¶*8:757 ff.*)

- [8:382] **Interrogatories [CCP §2030.010 et seq.]:** Written questions directed to a party, who must answer them under oath, in writing.

- [8:383] **Requests for Admissions [CCP §2033.010 et seq.]:** A request to a party to admit the truth of some fact or the genuineness of some document. The party must respond to the request under oath and in writing, either by admitting the request, denying it, or setting forth factual reasons why the request cannot be either admitted or denied.

- [8:384] **Demands for Production of Documents or Things [CCP §2031.010 et seq.]:** A party may demand the right to inspect, copy, test or sample documents or other physical evidence or electronically-stored information in the possession or custody of the opposing party.

- [8:385] **Requests for Physical, Mental or Blood Examination [CCP §2032.010 et seq.]:** Whenever the mental or physical condition of a party is in controversy, the other party may, on a showing of good cause, seek a court order for such an examination. (Exception: In personal injury cases, defendant may demand a medical exam of plaintiff *without* leave of court or showing good cause; CCP §2032.220(b), ¶*8:1516.*)

- [8:386] **Demand to Exchange List of Expert Witnesses [CCP §2034.010 et seq.]:** Forces disclosure of identity of expert witnesses the other side intends to have testify at trial, and pertinent facts re their qualifications and opinions.

© 2020 Thomson Reuters/The Rutter Group

[8:387] Special rules apply in *condemnation cases* for exchange of lists of expert witnesses and the *statements of valuation data* on which they intend to testify at trial. [See CCP §1258.210 et seq.]

- [8:388] **Bill of Particulars [CCP §454]:** The bill of particulars is not part of the Discovery Act, and was originally thought of as a pleading device, rather than a discovery device. However, its function is one of discovery: In certain types of contract actions (particularly those pleaded on common counts), it forces the pleader to set forth the specifics on which the claim is based.

- [8:389] **Request for Statement re Damages [CCP §425.11]:** This is also not part of the Discovery Act, but serves discovery purposes: It is used to compel plaintiffs in personal injury or wrongful death actions to set forth the *nature* and *amount* of damages claimed (often before interrogatories or other discovery). *See ¶8:1758 ff.*

- [8:390] **"Business Records" Subpoena [CCP §2020.410]; or "Records and Testimony" Subpoena [CCP §2020.510]:** These are not really separate discovery devices, but rather are used in conjunction with or in lieu of a deposition. They require the witness to produce for copying or bring to the deposition the documents described in the subpoena. *See ¶8:537 ff.*

- [8:391] **Injunctions to Prevent Destruction of Physical Evidence:** The Discovery Act does not specifically authorize orders for preservation of physical evidence for discovery purposes. (E.g., an automobile involved in an accident case about to be scrapped.)

  The Act's provisions for protective orders do not apply; they are for the protection of *parties*, not physical evidence. [*Northpoint Homeowners Ass'n v. Sup.Ct.* (1979) 95 CA3d 241, 244, 157 CR 42, 44]

  However, some cases recognize an *inherent judicial power to enjoin* destruction of physical evidence needed for discovery in pending civil litigation. [*Northpoint Homeowners Ass'n v. Sup.Ct.*, supra, 95 CA3d at 244, 157 CR at 44; *see discussion at ¶8:1799 ff.*]

b. [8:392] **Consider advantages vs. disadvantages of each device:** Each of the above discovery tools (*see ¶8:378 ff.*) has its own strengths and limitations. Consequently, choosing the proper tool to do the job requires weighing the advantages and disadvantages of the various tools available.

These will be discussed in greater detail in later sections of this volume. But the following observations generally apply:

(1) [8:393] **Depositions** will usually be:

- The most effective form of examination (through follow-up

questions, etc.) and the most likely to provide the witness' unvarnished responses (rather than responses worded by opposing counsel to interrogatories and requests for admissions);

- The quickest method of discovery, because the information is obtained at the time of the deposition;
- The best way of evaluating a witness' credibility and demeanor;
- The only way of obtaining information or documents from a nonparty witness (*see ¶8:397*);
- The only way of presenting evidence at trial from witnesses who are unavailable to testify (ill, dead, out of state, etc.);
- Less helpful, however, in obtaining details which the witness may not have at his or her fingertips (e.g., addresses, telephone numbers, dates, amounts, etc.);
- Very expensive and time-consuming;
- Not useful in obtaining information supporting a party's *contentions* ("legal contention questions"). [See *Rifkind v. Sup.Ct. (Good)* (1994) 22 CA4th 1255, 1263, 27 CR2d 822, 827—improper to ask deponent to "state all facts, list all witnesses, and identify all documents that support or pertain to a particular contention"]

(2) [8:394] **Interrogatories** will usually be:

- Less costly and time-consuming than depositions, at least when the opposing party provides complete answers (but the cost savings vanish if the opposing party is recalcitrant, because obtaining a court order compelling further answers is burdensome and time-consuming, *see ¶8:1136 ff.*);
- Better suited to discovery of detailed information that a witness may not remember at deposition but that is available to the witness (e.g., dates, telephone numbers, addresses, lists of witnesses, specific dollar amounts, etc.);
- More effective in obtaining adverse party's contentions and nonprivileged information known to opposing counsel;
- Less likely to provide helpful information because answers usually will be drafted by opposing counsel;
- Not available for obtaining information from nonparty witnesses.

(3) [8:395] **Requests for Admissions** will usually be:

- Helpful in establishing the genuineness of documents or signatures;

© 2020 Thomson Reuters/The Rutter Group

- Helpful in isolating *undisputed* facts and issues (especially when combined with Form Interrogatory 17.1, *see* ¶*8:412.1*);
- Less helpful in establishing *controverted* facts because admissions can be artfully avoided in many cases ("unable to admit or deny based on information presently known").

(4) [8:396] **Demands for Production of Documents, etc.** will usually be:

- Least expensive way of obtaining documents or records from opposing party (but discovery of electronically-stored information can be very expensive);
- Unavailing where records or evidence held by nonparty witness.

(a) [8:397] **Compare—"Business Records" Subpoena or "Records and Testimony" Subpoena:** These deposition subpoenas will usually be the only way to compel *nonparty witnesses* to produce documents (*see* ¶*8:537 ff.*).

c. [8:398] **Practical considerations:** The choice of the appropriate discovery tool is inevitably determined by practical considerations in each particular case, including:

(1) [8:399] **Value of case:** From the plaintiff's standpoint, how much is the claim really worth; is it likely to settle without the necessity of further discovery expense; is discovery likely to enhance the value of the claim?

From the defendant's standpoint, what is the real *exposure*; is the proposed discovery justified by the amount at stake; is it likely to reflect on the strengths or weaknesses of the plaintiff's claim?

(2) [8:400] **Costs of discovery:** Is the particular discovery device justified by its cost? Often, the attorney will have to forego the "optimum" or "best" discovery tools for those that can be afforded in light of the value of the case (¶*8:399*) and/or the client's willingness or ability to pay.

- [8:400.1] **Caution:** Cost considerations alone may not justify failure to engage in discovery *reasonably required* for trial preparation. Such failure may violate the attorney's duties to the client regardless of cost.

☞ [8:400.2] ***PRACTICE POINTER:*** This is something to think about *before accepting* low-end cases. If you've already accepted the case, get express client approval to limit your discovery. (Bear in mind, however, that such approval does not excuse your obligation to satisfy the applicable standard of care.)

(3) [8:401] **Adversary's capability:** The more experienced your adversary, the more careful you will want to be in the discovery stage. This may affect your decision as to how much discovery to conduct and what discovery tools to utilize.

➪ [8:401.1] ***PRACTICE POINTER:*** Particularly when dealing with experienced and reputable adversaries, explore whether some discovery can be done informally or on a streamlined basis without formal discovery procedures. E.g., discuss early what electronically-stored information each side will need to produce and agree upon the format for production, the search terms to be used, etc. Such agreements may result in more effective discovery, as well as tremendous cost savings.

Even though it appears that you and your opponent agree about informal discovery methods, be sure to document (by stipulation, letter agreement or otherwise) precisely what you have agreed to. That way, in the event of a later dispute, you will have a basis to enforce the agreement and your client will be protected.

6. [8:402] **Determining Sequence of Discovery Procedures:** Determining which discovery tool to use *first* is another problem. For example, do you send out interrogatories, or a notice of deposition? The answer will vary with the facts of the case, but the following observations are generally true:

a. [8:403] **Clarify claims and contentions:** Often, the pleadings are general and fail to reveal the precise nature of the claims involved. Discovery devices should be used in such cases to pin down the adversary's position as soon as possible.

(1) [8:404] **Example:** A complaint for medical malpractice alleges "negligence" in general terms, and seeks an unspecified amount of damages. Defense counsel can immediately (a) send a *request for statement re damages* (CCP §425.11) to force plaintiff to disclose the nature and amount of damages claimed, and (b) send *interrogatories* asking for the facts upon which plaintiff's contentions re negligence are based. The information obtained will pin down the plaintiff's claim and will be essential to preparing for depositions.

(2) [8:405] **Example:** A complaint is filed on a common count for "services rendered." This is not enough to show whether plaintiff is suing on an express or implied contract, or whether he or she is claiming full performance or that performance was excused. Defense counsel can immediately: (a) serve a *demand for bill of particulars* (CCP §454) to get an itemization of the claim; and (b) follow up with *interrogatories* asking for details regarding each of the items so disclosed. Then, once these details are known, other discovery (e.g., depositions) may be utilized.

© 2020 Thomson Reuters/The Rutter Group

b. [8:406] **Obtain documents early:** Document production should be sought very early in the case. The other side's documents often will provide the foundation for deposition questions of witnesses. They often are helpful in determining individuals who played significant roles in the events in dispute.

If your case involves substantial *electronically-stored information (ESI),* you may need an extra amount of lead time to resolve issues regarding the scope of the search and manner of production (*see ¶8:1427.5 ff.*).

c. [8:407] **Depositions following other discovery:** Depositions can be a wasted effort if the examiner does not know enough about the case to ask the proper questions. And, there is no right to take "follow up" depositions of natural persons without leave of court (CCP §2025.610(a)-(b), *¶8:478*). Therefore, it is usually better to utilize other discovery devices (interrogatories, requests to produce documents, etc.) *before* taking depositions.

- Of course, there are cases where depositions should be taken at the *outset* regardless: e.g., to determine jurisdictional facts in connection with motions to quash service of summons; or for injunctions or to certify a class action; or where a key witness is mortally ill or about to leave the state and may be "unavailable" at trial.
- Moreover, in some cases it may be advisable to depose the opposing parties early in order to "freeze" their testimony before it can be "shaped" by information they learn through later discovery.
- Early depositions also may be needed to determine crucial facts about electronically-stored information, such as the identity of custodians, the types of computers and backup systems, document destruction policies, etc.

d. [8:408] **Move from the broad to the specific:** Early discovery should be painted with a "broad brush" to pick up all potential issues and facts (e.g., interrogatories asking opponent to state the facts upon which the allegations in the pleading are based). As the case progresses, discovery tools should pare down the questioning to the "meat" of the case (e.g., deposition questions directed to key matters disclosed in earlier discovery).

e. [8:409] **Coordinated use of discovery tools:** Finally, effective discovery sometimes requires a coordinated use of the various discovery devices; i.e., using one device to flush out certain information, and the other to follow up on the information obtained. For example:

(1) [8:410] **Interrogatories coordinated with demand for production:** A party can serve interrogatories on an opposing party, asking what evidence or records exist as to particular issues; and then serve a demand to produce for inspection and copying the records or evidence described in the interrogatory answers.

[8:410.1-410.4] *Reserved.*

[8:410.5] ***PRACTICE POINTER re electronic data:*** Consider serving an early set of interrogatories to determine the types of electronic records maintained by the opposing party, as well as that party's retention and destruction policy and the location of backup tapes. You can then serve a document request to obtain the relevant data and consider physically inspecting the company's computers or electronic storage units.

(2) [8:411] **Depositions coordinated with document production:** A party can notice the deposition of any other party or witness, and at the same time require the deponent or *some third person* to produce documents at the deposition. This enables the examining party to ask the deponent questions regarding the documents or explaining their contents. (However, the better practice is to time the document production so that you have a chance to review the documents *before* the deposition, and thus prepare your questioning of the witness. *See detailed discussion of document production at ¶8:1421 ff.*)

(3) [8:412] **Requests for admissions coordinated with interrogatories:** As to matters believed not to be in dispute, a party can serve requests for admission and then, if the request is denied, follow up with interrogatories. For example, "State the facts upon which you based your denial of Request for Admission No. 5; State the name and address of each person having knowledge of such facts; Describe any document or record in which such facts are contained," etc. (*see ¶8:965*).

Limitation: The interrogatories and requests for admission must be set forth in *separate documents* (requests for admission cannot be combined with any other method of discovery; see CCP §2033.060(h), ¶*8:964*).

[8:412.1] ***PRACTICE POINTER:*** Consider serving a set of "*Official Form Interrogatories*" (Judicial Council form DISC-001) along with your Requests for Admissions, checking the box in Sec. 5 marked "*Interrogatory 17.0 Responses to Request for Admissions.*" This interrogatory (17.1) asks for all facts, witnesses and documents supporting the response to each request for admission that is not an unqualified admission; and is thus a quick and inexpensive method to determine the basis for any denial. For some types of civil actions, there are specialized sets of Judicial Council Form with interrogatories similar to 17.1—e.g., DISC-002 (Employment Law) and DISC-005 (Construction Litigation).

7. [8:413] **Proper Scheduling of Discovery:** Whatever discovery devices are used, carefully consider sequence and timing so that ap-

© 2020 Thomson Reuters/The Rutter Group

plicable deadlines will be met. Bear in mind that subject to a few exceptions, all non-expert discovery must be completed by 30 days before the initial trial date (15 days before trial for expert discovery; *see* ¶*8:1690*). [CCP §2024.020(a); *see* ¶*8:445*]

a. [8:413.1] **Plan to serve supplemental interrogatories:** Because the opposing party owes no duty to update its answers to interrogatories to provide information discovered after its original answers were served (¶*8:1118*), be sure to include time in your discovery plan for serving supplemental interrogatories (*see* ¶*8:942 ff.*) before the discovery cutoff date.

b. [8:413.2] **Complete discovery needed for summary judgment motion:** If you intend to file a summary judgment motion, calendar the filing deadline as soon as the court sets the initial trial date. Remember that the motion has a 75-day notice period (¶*10:77*), the motion must be heard at least 30 days before trial (¶*10:71*) and the normal time for responding to most discovery requests (e.g., interrogatories, requests for admission, inspection demands, physical or mental exams) is a minimum of 30 days. Thus, discovery will have to be *served* early—*at least 4-1/2 months before trial*—to ensure that you have all needed responses before the motion must be filed. Absent circumstances beyond your control, the court is not likely to grant a continuance of the trial date merely to give you more time to obtain needed discovery.

[8:413.2a] ***PRACTICE POINTER:*** Plan ahead. Even 4-1/2 months may not be enough time to get the responses you need for your motion. Requests for extension of time to respond are common and generally granted. If you need to obtain further responses through either a meet and confer process or a discovery motion, several months could be added to the time schedule. As a practical matter, you may need to start *8-9 months* before trial to make sure your written discovery is completed.

[8:413.3] ***FURTHER PRACTICE POINTERS:*** In actions where case management conferences are held, discovery deadlines may be discussed at the initial conference (¶*12:77.5 ff.*). Counsel should know the applicable case disposition guidelines, and schedule sufficient time to complete discovery and make any pretrial motions. [See CRC Standards of Jud. Admin., Standard 2.2] (In some courts, clerks conduct case management conferences, in which event nothing is addressed other than trial dates.)

If the complexity of the case or unanticipated problems make completion of discovery unlikely within one year of filing the complaint, counsel should be prepared to address those issues with the trial judge at the case management conference and to argue for extended deadlines. Raising those issues with the trial judge early usually improves the chances of obtaining relief.

Consider *sequencing* discovery (limiting discovery at the outset to particular issues) if resolving one or two issues will make the case easier to settle or determine by motion. Raise your sequencing plan with the trial judge at the first case management conference because you may need more time before the scheduled trial date to allow for sequencing. The judge is likely to look positively on any reasonable plan to resolve the matter early.

Note that some courts (e.g., Los Angeles Superior Court) have eliminated case management conferences for most personal injury cases.

[8:413.4] ***CAUTION RE SCHEDULING:*** Familiarize yourself with the motion scheduling practice in your assigned department or courtroom at the outset of your case. Many courts have adopted special rules regarding the calendaring of motions, sometimes requiring that motions be scheduled several months in advance. As a precaution, practitioners should evaluate the requirements to ensure they schedule hearing dates for discovery and summary judgment motions in order to have them heard before trial. Also, counsel should promptly cancel dates that are no longer needed so that the valuable time can be used by the court on other matters.

© 2020 Thomson Reuters/The Rutter Group

RESERVED

CHAPTER 8E

DEPOSITIONS

CONTENTS

© 2020 Thomson Reuters/The Rutter Group

© 2020 Thomson Reuters/The Rutter Group

© 2020 Thomson Reuters/The Rutter Group

© 2020 Thomson Reuters/The Rutter Group

© 2020 Thomson Reuters/The Rutter Group

© 2020 Thomson Reuters/The Rutter Group

© 2020 Thomson Reuters/The Rutter Group

RESERVED

DEPOSITIONS

[8:414] **Statutes:** The following sections of the Discovery Act contain the ground rules governing depositions:

- **CCP §2025.010 et seq.:** Oral depositions in California;
- **CCP §2026.010:** Oral depositions in another state;
- **CCP §2027.010:** Oral depositions in another country;
- **CCP §2028.010 et seq.:** Written depositions; and
- **CCP §2029.100 et seq.:** Depositions in actions pending in another state or country.

Additional statutes must be consulted when depositions (or other discovery) are sought before a lawsuit has been filed or while the action is on appeal:

- **CCP §2035.010 et seq.:** Discovery before action filed; and
- **CCP §2036.010 et seq.:** Discovery pending appeal.

And, the rules governing subpoenas re depositions are found in:

- **CCP §§1985-1987** (subpoenas generally); and
- **CCP §2020.010 et seq.:** Discovery from nonparties.

[8:415] **"Deposition" Defined:** A deposition is testimony taken before trial, under oath, subject to cross-examination, and preserved in writing. Under certain circumstances, such testimony may be admissible at trial (*see* ¶*8:876 ff.*).

[8:416] **Oral vs. Written Depositions:** Although the Discovery Act provides for both oral and written depositions, this section deals primarily with depositions on *oral* examination. (Written depositions are discussed briefly at ¶*8:757 ff.*)

STRATEGIES AND TACTICS RE ORAL DEPOSITIONS

[8:417] **Advantages**

- **More Effective Questioning:** The major advantage of a deposition over any other discovery device is that oral examination permits more effective questioning. If the deponent's answers are incomplete or nonresponsive, the examiner can pursue the point with follow-up questions. Also, the deponent's credibility and memory can be tested by questions as to peripheral matters that tend to confirm or disprove earlier answers. Finally, there is a much better chance of getting spontaneous admissions than with other discovery devices (e.g., interrogatories, where the answers are usually prepared by opposing counsel).
- **Size up witness' credibility and demeanor:** Another advantage

© 2020 Thomson Reuters/The Rutter Group

STRATEGIES AND TACTICS RE ORAL DEPOSITIONS (Cont'd)

is that depositions permit the examiner to determine the impression the witness is likely to make on the jury if the case goes to trial; i.e., whether sincere, sympathetic, believable, etc. Other forms of discovery produce only written responses that shed little light on the witness' credibility and demeanor.

- **Quicker:** Depositions can usually be set on 10 or 15 days' notice to the opposing party. (However, depositions generally should not be noticed until *all* parties have appeared so the depositions will count as each party's opportunity for a deposition and thus cannot be taken again absent consent or leave of court; *see* ¶*8:878 ff.*) Documents can be inspected and answers can be obtained (orally) at the time of the deposition. This is far quicker than other discovery devices.
- **Audio or video recording:** The examiner has the option of recording the deposition by audio or video technology, which often provides a far greater impact in jury trials than any other form of discovery (*see* ¶*8:658 ff.*).

[8:418] **Disadvantages**

- **Expensive:** The major disadvantage is that depositions are costly both in terms of out-of-pocket expense and also lawyer-time (and client-time) spent in preparing for and taking the deposition.
- **Reporter fees** vary from location to location and depend to a great extent on the services requested, such as instant visual display, rough transcripts, videographers, CD of transcript and exhibits. The original and one copy of even a short deposition, without any other services, often will run hundreds of dollars; and a full day deposition with other services can cost thousands of dollars.

  (Some bar associations have negotiated discounts from providers, and many providers are willing to adjust rates for lawyers or firms that use their services frequently. *It pays to shop around.*)
- **Witness fees and service fees** may have to be paid if it is necessary to subpoena a nonparty witness to attend. And, if an *expert* witness is involved, substantial additional fees may have to be paid (¶*8:578 ff.*).
- **Travel expenses** may have to be paid if the party or witness resides out of town, since it is usually necessary to take the deposition where the deponent resides (¶*8:621 ff.*).
- **Time-consuming preparation:** The lawyer who will do the questioning has to spend as much time preparing for a deposition as to prepare for examining an adverse witness at trial; e.g., reviewing investigators' reports, witness statements, the pleadings, earlier discovery, etc. The lawyer whose client or witness is being deposed also has to spend considerable time; e.g., reviewing the same materials and meeting with the client or witness beforehand to prepare for the deposition.

STRATEGIES AND TACTICS RE ORAL DEPOSITIONS (Cont'd)

- **Elicits only deponent's personal knowledge:** "I don't know" is a satisfactory answer, even if the information sought is known to the deponent's lawyer or is otherwise available to him or her (¶*8:705 ff.*).

[8:419] **Principal Reasons to TAKE Depositions**

- **To "pin down" adverse testimony:** Depositions enable you to get a "fix" on the claims and testimony to be expected at trial from the opposing party and witnesses. Depositions are better for this purpose than interrogatories or other discovery procedures because follow-up questions can be used to get an adverse witness to commit to an answer (e.g., "Have you now described every *ache* or pain you suffered after the accident?" "Have you now told us *everything* you remember about how the accident occurred?"). In addition, the deposition yields testimony directly from the witness rather than answers shaped by opposing counsel to interrogatories or requests for admissions.
- **To question witness re contents of documents:** A party or witness can be compelled to produce documentary evidence at his or her deposition (*see* ¶*8:556*). This allows the examiner to review the documents and to question the witness then and there regarding entries therein—on a line-by-line basis, if required. (But if the documents are voluminous, it is better to demand their production beforehand under CCP §2031.010 et seq.; *see* ¶*8:1417*. Reviewing voluminous documents during a deposition may require lengthy recesses, which could subject counsel to sanctions.)
- **To obtain discovery from a nonparty witness:** Depositions are the *only* discovery procedure by which nonparty witnesses can be compelled to disclose information.
- **To lay foundation for future impeachment:** Depositions are an effective tool to demonstrate inconsistencies in an opposing party's or witness' testimony at trial.
- **To preserve favorable testimony:** If there is a chance that friendly witnesses (including your client) may be *unavailable* when the case comes to trial (e.g., because of advanced age, illness, or moving away), depositions can be taken to preserve their testimony.

  ⇨ ***PRACTICE POINTER:*** If the witness has important testimony, opposing counsel will probably depose the witness in any event. But if opposing counsel does not, you have to weigh the *costs* of the deposition and the drawback of "educating" your opponent, against the *potential harm* to your case if that witness is unavailable at trial.

  If you decide to take the deposition of a friendly witness for use at trial in lieu of live testimony, consider taking a *video* deposition. It will be far more effective at trial than reading a printed transcript.

© 2020 Thomson Reuters/The Rutter Group

STRATEGIES AND TACTICS RE ORAL DEPOSITIONS (Cont'd)

- **To move adversary toward settlement:** Often, a well-taken deposition will force your adversary to recognize the strengths of your position and the weaknesses of his or her position, which may make settlement discussions more productive.

  PRACTICE POINTERS

  - It is a good idea to bring up settlement at the end of a deposition. It will usually be a convenient time for such discussions, with opposing counsel meeting face-to-face, often for the first time. The case will be fresh in everyone's mind, and settlement proposals will therefore be more realistic.
  - If it appears you are moving toward a settlement, *instruct the deposition reporter to hold off on finalizing the transcript.* This can save a good portion of the deposition expense.

[8:420] **Principal Reasons NOT to Take Depositions**

- **Costs vs. benefits:** The costs involved may simply outweigh the potential advantages (e.g., where the amount at stake is simply too small).
- **Avoid "educating" opposing counsel:** Taking a deposition may alert opposing counsel to facts or issues of which they were unaware, taking away the advantage of surprise at trial. Or, it may simply prompt opposing counsel to prepare the case more diligently, to initiate their own discovery, etc.
- **Avoid or delay deposition of your own witnesses:** Noticing depositions of the other side's witnesses will almost invariably produce notices to depose your witnesses. Sometimes, you may want to defer or avoid depositions of your own witnesses (e.g., to try to settle, to complete document discovery, etc.). In such cases, it is better not to start the ball rolling by sending out deposition notices to the other side.
- **Avoid perpetuating adverse testimony:** If the witness is adverse, but there is a *chance that he or she may not testify* at trial (e.g., because of advanced age, illness, moving away, etc.), it may be a mistake to take his or her deposition. You run the risk of perpetuating adverse testimony that otherwise might not be available at time of trial.

1. [8:421] **When PRIOR COURT ORDER Required:** Depositions are generally available as a matter of right; i.e., without leave of court. [CCP §2025.210(a)-(b)]

   However, a prior court order based on a showing of "good cause" is required in the following situations:

   a. [8:422] **Before suit filed:** Occasionally, a deposition (or other discovery) may be sought although no lawsuit has yet been filed. Usually, it is where the person seeking discovery expects to be sued and wishes to preserve evidence that may be unavailable later on. (For example, persons may wish to perpetuate testimony of a favorable witness who is about to move overseas; or to preserve their own testimony, if they are ill and fear imminent death.) The statutory procedure for preserving evidence and perpetuating testimony in such cases requires a court order. [CCP §2035.010 et seq.]

(1) [8:423] **Discovery methods available:** The statutory procedure for prelawsuit discovery is not limited to depositions. Also available are *inspection of documents* and other physical evidence; and *physical and mental exams* (e.g., medical examination or blood tests of expected adverse party). [CCP §2035.020(b), (c)]

(a) [8:424] **Example:** A minor injured in a traffic accident has been ordered to submit to a physical examination at the request of the other driver. The minor's parents had notified the other driver that a claim would be made but refused to provide any information as to the child's injuries. Prelawsuit discovery was proper because suit might not be filed for years (statute of limitations would not begin to run until child reaches majority). [*Block v. Sup.Ct. (Shaver)* (1963) 219 CA2d 469, 478, 33 CR 205, 210]

(2) [8:425] **Procedure:** The person expecting to sue or be sued must file a *verified* petition in the superior court of the *county in which the expected adverse party resides* (or, if that party is not a California resident, in any county where venue would be proper). [CCP §2035.030(a)]

(a) [8:426] **Contents of petition:** The petition must set forth the following:

- Petitioner (or petitioner's successor in interest) *expects to be a party* to a lawsuit in California;
- Petitioner (or petitioner's successor in interest) is *presently unable* to bring that action or cause it to be brought (usually because petitioner expects to be the *defendant* in the action);
- Petitioner's involvement in the subject matter of the expected action (attaching a copy of any *written document* the validity or construction of which may be called into question or that is connected with the subject matter of the proposed discovery);
- The names or description of those whom petitioner expects to be adverse parties (so far as known);
- The discovery methods which petitioner seeks to employ (e.g., deposition to preserve testimony of key witness);
- The names and addresses of those from whom

© 2020 Thomson Reuters/The Rutter Group

discovery is sought, and the substance of the information expected to be elicited from each;

- The *facts to be established* by the proposed testimony (note that this *precludes* discovery for the purpose of ascertaining what the facts are); and
- The *reasons* why it is necessary to perpetuate testimony before the lawsuit is filed (e.g., because the witness is aged, ill or about to move out of state, etc.). [CCP §2035.030(b)]

(b) [8:427] **Service on expected adverse party:** Copies of the petition and notice of hearing thereon must be served on the expected adverse party at least *20 days* before the date set for the hearing. Service must be made in the manner provided for service of summons (i.e., personal service in most cases). [CCP §2035.040(a), (c)]

1) [8:427.1] **Service by publication:** The court may authorize service by publication where the petitioner is unable after the exercise of due diligence to locate the potential adverse party. In this event, if the potential adverse party fails to appear at the hearing on the petition, the court *must* appoint an attorney *at the petitioner's expense* to represent the adverse party throughout the prelawsuit discovery process. [CCP §2035.040(d), (e); see *California Shellfish, Inc. v. United Shellfish Co.* (1997) 56 CA4th 16, 22, 64 CR2d 797, 808]

(c) [8:428] **Order:** If satisfied that the preservation of evidence "may prevent a failure or delay of justice," the court will order the taking of the deposition (or other discovery). The deposition so authorized is then conducted in accordance with the rules governing depositions generally. [CCP §2035.050(a)-(c)]

1) [8:428.1] **Discovery by successor in interest:** Where petitioner expects a successor in interest to be a party to the action, the court must consider whether the discovery could be conducted by the successor in interest. [CCP §2035.050(a)]

[8:429] *Reserved.*

(3) [8:430] **Use as evidence:** Depositions taken pursuant to CCP §2035.010 et seq. (or under comparable laws in effect where the deposition was taken or under federal law) may be used "in any action involving the same subject matter" against any party named in the petition as an expected adverse party. [CCP §2035.060; see *N.N.V. v. American Ass'n of Blood Banks* (1999) 75 CA4th 1358, 1395-1396, 89 CR2d 885, 911-912—prelawsuit deposition inadmissible where potential adverse

party did not receive adequate notice and did not appear at deposition]

b. [8:431] **After trial, pending appeal:** A similar procedure is required for taking a deposition *after* judgment and while the case is on appeal. [CCP §2036.030(a)]

(Such discovery may become necessary, for example, in order to preserve the testimony of a newly-discovered witness whose testimony would be helpful on retrial if the judgment is reversed, but whose availability to testify is uncertain because he or she is ill, aged or about to move away, etc.)

Post-trial discovery is not limited to depositions; document inspection, and physical and mental exams may also be ordered. [CCP §2036.020]

A motion before the court that entered judgment and an order are required. But service of the motion and notice of hearing can be made on opposing counsel, rather than personal service on the adverse party. [CCP §2036.030]

c. [8:432] **Successive deposition from same person:** A natural person, including a party, cannot be examined more than once without a court order based on a showing of good cause. [CCP §2025.610(a)-(b); *see* ¶*8:478*] (An exception exists for attachment proceedings; *see* ¶*8:482.1*.)

d. [8:433] **Place of deposition beyond geographic limits:** A court order based on a showing of good cause is required to depose a witness more than 75 miles from his or her residence (if deposed *outside* the county where the action is pending), or more than 150 miles from his or her residence (if deposed *within* the county where the action is pending). [CCP §§2025.250(a), 2025.260(a); *see* ¶*8:630 ff.*]

e. [8:434] **Depositions during discovery "hold":** A court order based on a showing of good cause is required for *plaintiff* to take depositions *during the first 20 days* after service of summons. [CCP §2025.210(b); *see* ¶*8:439*]

f. [8:435] **Deposition after discovery "cut-off":** Likewise, a court order based on a showing of good cause is required for *either* party to take depositions *within 30 days before trial.* [CCP §§2024.020(a), 2024.050(a); *see* ¶*8:445 ff.*]

Other pretrial cut-off deadlines apply in certain types of actions (*see* ¶*8:446 ff.*); and there are special pretrial cut-offs for expert witness discovery in any civil action (15 days before trial for discovery and 10 days before trial for discovery motions to be heard; CCP §2024.030; *see* ¶*8:447*).

g. [8:436] **Prisoners:** Special statutes require a court order for taking the deposition of a person in jail. The court order must be based on a showing of the *materiality* of the prisoner's testimony. [See CCP §§1995-1997]

© 2020 Thomson Reuters/The Rutter Group

2. [8:437] **WHEN Depositions May be Taken:** There is a "hold" on depositions by plaintiff at the beginning of the lawsuit (¶*8:439*). And, there is a "cut-off" on discovery shortly before trial (¶*8:445*) or after judicial arbitration (¶*8:446.3*). Otherwise, depositions may be taken without leave of court at any time during the pendency of a civil action. [CCP §2025.210(b)]

⇨ [8:438] ***PRACTICE POINTERS:*** It is generally best to take depositions *as soon as possible* in the lawsuit, while memories are still fresh.

- You may wish to precede the deposition by other discovery procedures: e.g., interrogatories to flush out the adversary's claims and contentions; and demands for documents so that you will be prepared to question the deponent about them.
- But take your depositions as soon as you can. It gives you a better chance of pinning down opposing parties before they learn the theory of your case and "refine" their testimony.
- Some defense lawyers like to take plaintiff's deposition *before answering* or otherwise pleading in response to the complaint. This sometime results in obtaining admissions that prevent later amendments to the complaint when defendant demurs or moves to strike. Also, since defendant has not yet revealed its affirmative defenses, plaintiff may not be well prepared on defensive matters (e.g., facts indicating estoppel or running of statute of limitations).
- **Caution:** But don't take depositions before you are *prepared* to do so. Under the Discovery Act, a natural person cannot be deposed more than once without court permission (CCP §2025.610(a)-(b), *see* ¶*8:478*). So, if you rush into depositions without adequate preparation, you may waste your right to depose the deponent. (You can always ask the court for permission to depose the same witness again, but don't count on getting it.)

a. [8:439] **"Hold" on depositions by plaintiff at outset of case:** Defendants may serve notice of deposition any time after they are served or appear in the action. But plaintiffs may not serve deposition notices until *20 days* after service of summons or appearance of any defendant. [CCP §2025.210(b)]

Since at least 10 days' notice is required for depositions (¶*8:491*), this means no depositions can actually be taken by plaintiff without leave of court until at least 30 days after a defendant has been served or appeared in the action.

(1) [8:440] **Scope:** CCP §2025.210(b) applies to *all* discovery by deposition, including business records subpoenas to nonparties (*see* ¶*8:540*). [*California Shellfish, Inc. v. United Shellfish Co.* (1997) 56 CA4th 16, 21, 64 CR2d 797, 799—improper to serve

business records subpoena before serving any defendant with summons and complaint]

(2) [8:441] **Purpose:** This rule prevents plaintiffs from overwhelming defendants with discovery before they have a chance to obtain counsel, commence investigations, etc. [See *Waters v. Sup.Ct. (Hughes Tool Co.)* (1962) 58 C2d 885, 892, 27 CR 153, 156]

(3) [8:442] **Effect—defendant's initial priority:** As the party "attacked" in the lawsuit, defendant is given the "first crack" at taking depositions if he or she wants it. By sending out notice of deposition *promptly* after being served, defendants can set their depositions before the 20-day "hold" on plaintiff's depos expires. (Note: The mere fact that defendant *notices* a deposition first does not necessarily assure priority, however; it is the date on which the depo is set that controls; *see* ¶*8:494 ff.*)

Caution: Propounding discovery before filing a motion to quash waives a defendant's right to object to personal jurisdiction (*see* ¶*3:158.1c*).

(4) [8:443] **Expiration of "hold" after summons served on ANY defendant?** The statute says plaintiff can serve a deposition notice 20 days after the service on or appearance by "*any* defendant." [CCP §2025.210(b)]

Arguably, as long as one defendant has been served more than 20 days ago, there is no "hold" on deposing later-served defendants: i.e., P might serve D1, wait 20 days, and then serve D2 with summons, complaint *and notice of D2's deposition* 10 days later. However, a more reasonable interpretation of the statute is that the 20-day hold applies to each defendant served.

Comment: Whether the statute will be given the earlier interpretation is doubtful because it would destroy D2's initial deposition priority (¶*8:442*). In any event, a court is likely to grant a protective order in such cases.

Additionally, it has been suggested that if the complaint names *only* "Doe" defendants and is not served on anyone, the 20-day period may not commence running until someone is served. [See *Bernson v. Browning-Ferris Indus. of Calif., Inc.* (1994) 7 C4th 926, 930, 30 CR2d 440, 442, fn. 2]

(5) [8:444] **Earlier depo by leave of court:** For "good cause" shown, the court may authorize plaintiff to serve a deposition notice before expiration of the 20-day hold period. Such order may be granted on ex parte motion. [CCP §2025.210(b)]

One such situation might be where plaintiff does not know the names of all parties responsible for the injury and wants to find this out before the statute of limitations runs. [See *Bernson*

© 2020 Thomson Reuters/The Rutter Group

v. Browning-Ferris Indus. of Calif., Inc., supra, 7 C4th at 930, 30 CR2d at 442, fn. 2]

b. [8:445] **"Cut-off" on discovery before trial:** The Discovery Act imposes two separate "cut-offs" on discovery. Unless otherwise ordered:

- Discovery *proceedings* must be "completed" *30 days* before the date initially set for trial (¶*8:448*); *and*
- Discovery *motions* must be heard no later than *15 days* before the date initially set for trial. [CCP §2024.020(a)] (With respect to *retrials, see* ¶*8:451*.)

Extension for weekends, holidays: If either of these dates falls on a Saturday, Sunday or judicial holiday (see CCP §10), the last day shall be the *next court day* closer to the trial date. (E.g., where the 30-day or 15-day before trial period falls on a weekend, the cut-off date is the following Monday, not the preceding Friday.) [CCP §§2016.060, 2024.020(a); see *Pelton-Shepherd Indus., Inc. v. Delta Packaging Products, Inc.* (2008) 165 CA4th 1568, 1585, 82 CR3d 64, 76]

No earlier cut-off under local rules or court order: Local rules or court orders may *not* impose shorter time limits for discovery than provided by the Discovery Act. [Gov.C. §68616(f); see *Wagner v. Sup.Ct. (General Motors Corp.)* (1993) 12 CA4th 1314, 1319, 16 CR2d 534, 537—discovery "cut-off" invalid where no trial date had been set] (Even so, some courts at the case management conference routinely ask counsel to *stipulate* to an earlier discovery cut-off; and some case management report forms include such stipulation. Benefits of these stipulations include more time after discovery to prepare for summary judgment and expert discovery, carefully considered in limine motions, and providing time for meet and confer after formal discovery responses are provided, while still leaving time for regularly noticed motion practice (*see* ¶*8:449*).)

"Complex" cases: The court may establish special time limits and discovery schedules in cases which have been determined to be "complex." [CRC Standards of Jud. Admin., Standard 3.1(d)]

(1) [8:446] **Exceptions:** These "cut-off" dates do not apply to:

(a) [8:446.1] **Unlawful detainer actions:** (in which discovery, including depositions, must be completed *at least 5 days* before trial). [CCP §§2024.040(b)(1), 2025.270(b); *see* ¶*8:493.2*]

(b) [8:446.2] **Eminent domain proceedings:** (expert witness discovery and exchange of valuation data permitted until 20 days before trial; see CCP §1258.020). [CCP §2024.040(b)(2)]

(c) [8:446.3] **Cases set for judicial arbitration:** Court rules govern the time limit for completing discovery in cases set for judicial arbitration. These rules require that all discovery be completed *15 days* before the date set for the arbitration *hearing* (unless the court orders otherwise for good cause shown). [CCP §2024.040(a); CRC 3.822(b); *see* ¶*13:96*]

1) [8:446.4] **Limit on postarbitration discovery:** After an arbitration award in a case *ordered* to arbitration, if a trial de novo is demanded, the only additional discovery permitted without a court order or stipulation is an exchange of expert witness lists and expert witness depositions under CCP §2034.010 et seq. [CCP §§2024.040(a), 1141.24; *see* ¶*13:152*]

   (However, this does not apply where judicial arbitration was by stipulation or election, rather than by court order; *see* ¶*13:152.2*.)

[8:446.5] ***PRACTICE POINTER:*** Where it appears likely that the judicial arbitration may result in a settlement, attorneys often *stipulate to leave certain discovery open* until after the arbitration. (Such a stipulation is expressly permitted by CCP §1141.24.) When entering into such a stipulation, be sure it is in writing and identifies the scope of the remaining discovery.

(2) [8:447] **Special "cut-off" dates on expert witness discovery:** Because the expert witnesses who will testify at trial may not be disclosed until shortly before trial (through exchange of expert witness lists under CCP §2034.010 et seq.; *see* ¶*8:1639 ff.*), special rules apply:

- Discovery proceedings pertaining to expert witnesses identified under CCP §2034.010 et seq. may be "completed" until *15 days* before the initial trial date; and
- Motions concerning such discovery may be *heard* until *10 days* before the initial trial date. [CCP §2024.030]

(3) [8:448] **When proceedings "completed":** Discovery proceedings are deemed "completed" on the day a deposition *begins*. Other discovery procedures (interrogatories, RFAs, etc.) are deemed "completed" the day the *response is due*. [CCP §2024.010]

Thus, as long as depositions *commence* before the "cutoff," they may be continued and completed within the 30-day period preceding trial.

But there is *no* additional time for motions to compel if questions are not answered.

© 2020 Thomson Reuters/The Rutter Group

☞ [8:449] ***PRACTICE POINTER:*** It's very risky to schedule depositions or other discovery proceedings close to the 30-day cut-off period. If the deponent refuses to answer questions or respond, you may not be able to set a motion to compel for hearing before the 15-day cut-off on discovery hearings. You can seek a court order shortening time but don't count on the request being granted.

To be safe, serve your last round of interrogatories or requests for admission at least *90 days* before trial; and schedule your last depositions no later than *60 days* before trial. That way, you will have time to evaluate the answers and responses and, if necessary, to set a motion to compel for hearing before the 15-day cut-off on discovery motions.

(4) [8:450] **Continuance of trial does not reopen discovery:** The 30-day and 15-day "cut-offs" are measured from the *first* date set for trial of the case. A continuance or postponement of the trial does *not* operate to reopen discovery proceedings. [CCP §2024.020(b); see *Pelton-Shepherd Indus., Inc. v. Delta Packaging Products, Inc.* (2008) 165 CA4th 1568, 1575, 82 CR3d 64, 69, fn. 10]

☞ [8:450.1] ***PRACTICE POINTER:*** Whenever the trial date is continued, be sure to make an assessment of the status of your discovery. If you still need more discovery, get the other side to stipulate, or the court to order, that the discovery cutoff dates are also continued.

(5) [8:451] **Effect of mistrial, new trial or reversal of judgment:** A mistrial, new trial or reversal of the judgment on appeal automatically restarts the time limitations on discovery. Discovery is reopened and the "cut-off" dates are thereafter measured from the date set for *retrial.* [*Fairmont Ins. Co. v. Sup.Ct. (Stendell)* (2000) 22 C4th 245, 247, 92 CR2d 70, 71; *Beverly Hosp. v. Sup.Ct. (Castaneda)* (1993) 19 CA4th 1289, 1294, 24 CR2d 238, 240 (citing text); *Hirano v. Hirano* (2007) 158 CA4th 1, 6, 69 CR3d 646, 649-650]

(a) [8:451.1] **Rationale:** CCP §2024.020(a) states that the "cut-off" is measured from the "date *initially* set for trial" (emphasis added). But "initially" simply means the *first* date set for trial of the action, and when a retrial has been ordered, it means the scheduled retrial date. [*Fairmont Ins. Co. v. Sup.Ct. (Stendell)*, supra, 22 C4th at 250, 92 CR2d at 74; *Beverly Hosp. v. Sup.Ct. (Castaneda)*, supra, 19 CA4th at 1293, 24 CR2d at 240 (citing text)]

(b) [8:451.2] **Compare—discovery limits not affected:** Reopening discovery for a retrial does not change applicable limits on discovery. Thus, unless the court orders otherwise:

— persons previously deposed may not be deposed again (CCP §2025.610(a)-(b), *see* ¶*8:478*);

— including those previously served, no more than 35 specially prepared interrogatories and no more than 35 RFAs not relating to genuineness of documents may be served on an opposing party (CCP §§2030.030(b), 2033.030(a), *see* ¶*8:1269*). [*Fairmont Ins. Co. v. Sup.Ct. (Stendell),* supra, 22 C4th at 254, 92 CR2d at 77]

(6) [8:452] **Parties may stipulate to later discovery:** The parties may stipulate to extend the time for completion of discovery proceedings or for hearing discovery motions; or to reopen discovery after the trial date has been continued. Such stipulation, however, does *not* require the court to postpone or continue the trial date. [CCP §2024.060]

[8:453] ***PRACTICE POINTER:*** If your stipulation involves a hearing after the "cut-off" date, *ask the law and motion judge to approve* your stipulation upon execution. Otherwise, even if no continuance of the trial is required, the law and motion judge may simply be unwilling to hear a contested discovery matter on the eve of trial.

(a) [8:454] **All parties must consent:** The agreement is not effective unless all parties to the action have consented. [CCP §2024.060]

(b) [8:455] **Writing required:** The stipulation may be informal, but it must be *"confirmed* in a writing that *specifies* the extended date." [CCP §2024.060 (emphasis added)]

(Comment: The writing apparently need not be signed by all parties or counsel. A letter or email by counsel for one of the parties to all other counsel, setting forth the stipulation, would seem to suffice.)

1) [8:455.1] **Not filed with court:** Agreements extending time, etc. are not filed with the court unless they become relevant on a motion to compel. [See CRC 3.250(a)(7)]

(c) [8:456] **Motions to enforce stipulation subject to 15-day "cut-off"?** CCP §2024.010 et seq. is unclear on whether a motion to enforce a stipulation extending discovery is itself subject to the 15-day "cut-off" on discovery motions.

(7) [8:457] **Court may permit later discovery:** On motion of any party, the court may allow discovery proceedings to be completed, or a discovery motion to be heard, after the "cut-off" dates above (¶*8:445 ff.*); or, it may reopen discovery

© 2020 Thomson Reuters/The Rutter Group

after the trial has been continued to a new date. [CCP §2024.050(a); see *Pelton-Shepherd Indus., Inc. v. Delta Packaging Products, Inc.* (2008) 165 CA4th 1568, 1588, 82 CR3d 64, 79—court erred in hearing motion to compel after trial postponed without first deciding whether to reopen discovery, taking into consideration CCP §2024.050(b) factors (¶*8:459*)]

(a) [8:458] **Procedure:** The Discovery Act requires a "motion" to commence this procedure but does *not* specify a "noticed" motion. [See CCP §2024.050(a)]

Comment: Arguably, an ex parte motion should be permitted because of the limited period of time available (within 30 days of trial). However, many courts *restrict* ex parte motions to those *specifically authorized* by law (*see* ¶*9:347 ff.*), which this is not. The alternative is an ex parte application to shorten the time for notice and hearing on the motion.

1) [8:458.1] **Declaration requirements:** The motion should be accompanied by declarations covering the factors identified below (¶*8:459*), plus facts showing "a reasonable and good faith attempt" to resolve the matter informally. [CCP §2024.050(a)] (See "attempt to resolve informally" requirement at ¶*8:1158 ff.*)

2) [8:458.2] **Copy of proposed discovery:** Although not required by statute, it is recommended that a copy of the proposed discovery be attached to the motion to permit later discovery.

(b) [8:459] **Factors considered:** In exercising its discretion to grant or deny the motion, the court must take into consideration any relevant matter, including the following:

- The necessity and reasons for the additional discovery sought;
- The diligence or lack of diligence by the party seeking discovery, and the reasons why the discovery was not completed or the discovery motion heard earlier;
- Whether permitting the discovery or granting the discovery motion will likely prevent the case from going to trial on the date set, or otherwise interfere with the trial calendar or prejudice any party; and
- The length of time elapsed between any date previously set and the date presently set for trial. [CCP §2024.050(b); see *Sears, Roebuck & Co. v. National Union Fire Ins. Co. of Pittsburgh* (2005) 131 CA4th 1342, 1351-1352, 32 CR3d 717, 722-723—nonparty attorney-deponent who failed to appear at deposition and made evasive and dilatory responses to

document production subpoena was estopped from relying on cut-off date for resulting motion to compel]

(c) [8:460] **Monetary sanction against losing party:** The court "shall" impose a monetary sanction against the losing party on the motion *unless* it finds such party "acted with substantial justification" or "other circumstances make imposition of the sanction unjust." [CCP §2024.050(c)] (Monetary sanctions on discovery motions are discussed at ¶*8:1921 ff.*)

[8:461] *Reserved.*

3. [8:462] **WHOSE Deposition May be Taken:** "Any party may obtain discovery . . . by taking in California the oral deposition of *any person*, including any party to the action. The person deposed may be a natural person, an organization such as a public or private corporation, a partnership, an association, or a governmental agency." [CCP §2025.010 (emphasis added)]

a. [8:463] **Parties:** Thus, a party can take the deposition of any other party—adverse parties or coparties.

Parties can even take their *own* depositions; e.g., for the purpose of perpetuating testimony in the event they are unavailable to testify at trial (*see* ¶*8:422 ff.*).

b. [8:463.1] **Unnamed members in class actions:** Oral, written and business records *depositions* may be sought from unnamed class members who have not appeared in the action, through service of a subpoena and without court order. [CRC 3.768(a)]

(1) [8:463.2] **Compare—interrogatories:** Interrogatories may not be served on unnamed class members without a prior court order. [CRC 3.768(c)]

(2) [8:463.3] **Protective orders available:** A party representative or deponent or other affected person may move for an order prohibiting or limiting depositions of unnamed class members. [CRC 3.768(b)]

[8:463.4-463.9] *Reserved.*

(3) [8:463.10] **Determination by court:** In deciding whether to grant a protective order (or allow discovery by interrogatories to unnamed class members), the court must consider all relevant factors including:

— timing of the request;
— subject matter to be covered;
— materiality of the information sought;
— whether class representatives are seeking discovery on the same subject;
— likelihood that unnamed class members have such information;
— possibility of obtaining stipulations eliminating the need for such discovery; and

© 2020 Thomson Reuters/The Rutter Group

— whether discovery will result in "annoyance, oppression or undue burden or expense for the members of the class." [See CRC 3.768(d); *and discussion at ¶14:137.2 ff.*]

c. [8:464] **Nonparty witnesses:** The only methods by which someone who is not a party to the action can be compelled to provide testimony or produce other evidence are:

— an oral deposition under CCP §2020.310 (the most common method, *see ¶8:535 ff.*);

— an oral deposition with production of "business records" under CCP §2020.510 (*see ¶8:556 ff.*);

— a written deposition under CCP §2028.010 (*see ¶8:757 ff.*); or

— a "business records" subpoena under CCP §2020.410 (*see ¶8:540 ff.*). [CCP §2020.010(a)]

(1) [8:465] **Comment:** This makes it more costly and difficult to obtain certain kinds of discovery from nonparties. For example, expensive deposition proceedings may be necessary to obtain from a nonparty witness the same kind of information that could be obtained inexpensively from a *party* through interrogatories.

On the other hand, a "business records" subpoena is really no more costly or burdensome than a CCP §2031.010 et seq. inspection demand (*see ¶8:540*).

☞ [8:466] ***PRACTICE POINTER:*** It never hurts to ask the witness to produce information *voluntarily*. Often, the witness will be anxious to avoid the inconvenience of a deposition and will give you a witness statement or otherwise comply with your request. This will save you time and expense, and perhaps even the necessity of disclosing the information to your opponent.

But taking the witness' deposition is worth the cost and effort if there is a question as to the witness' *availability* at trial. (A deposition is admissible evidence if the witness is unavailable to testify; *see ¶8:885.*)

However, by obtaining documents voluntarily, you may still need formal discovery to establish a foundation for their admissibility. Also, if the records are protected by a confidentiality obligation, a right of privacy or a privilege, don't ask the witness to turn them over voluntarily. Releasing such records without a court order could subject the witness to personal liability for breach of the witness' obligations.

(2) [8:467] **Prisoners:** If the witness is a prisoner, a court order may be required to obtain his or her deposition. [See CCP §§1995-1997]

A showing of *materiality* of the prisoner's testimony is required to obtain the order (i.e., mere "relevance to the subject matter" is not enough). [CCP §1996]

(The Discovery Act expressly preserves these provisions where a deposition subpoena is served; see CCP §2020.030.)

(3) [8:467.1] **Opposing counsel:** Opposing counsel may be deposed if they have knowledge of relevant facts. However, such depositions are "*presumptively* improper, severely restricted, and require '*extremely' good cause*—a high standard." [*Carehouse Convalescent Hosp. v. Sup.Ct. (Sims)* (2006) 143 CA4th 1558, 1562, 50 CR3d 129, 131 (emphasis added); see also *Spectra-Physics, Inc. v. Sup.Ct. (Teledyne)* (1988) 198 CA3d 1487, 1496, 244 CR 258, 263; *and ¶8:1805.9*]

(a) [8:467.2] **Determinative factors:** The following factors determine whether an opposing-counsel deposition is allowable:

— whether the party seeking the deposition has *other practical means* to obtain the information sought;

— whether it is *crucial* to preparation of the case; and

— whether the information sought is subject to a *privilege* claim. [See *Carehouse Convalescent Hosp. v. Sup.Ct. (Sims)*, supra, 143 CA4th at 1563, 50 CR3d at 131-132]

(b) [8:467.3] **Burden of proof:** The party seeking the deposition has the burden of proving the first two factors (*¶8:467.2*). However, the burden of proving the third factor (information subject to a privilege claim) lies with the party *opposing* the deposition. [*Carehouse Convalescent Hosp. v. Sup.Ct. (Sims)*, supra, 143 CA4th at 1563-1564, 50 CR3d at 132]

[8:467.4] *Reserved.*

(c) [8:467.5] **Sanctions:** Counsel seeking to depose opposing counsel without prior leave of court run the risk of sanctions. [See *Estate of Ruchti* (1993) 12 CA4th 1593, 1602-1603, 16 CR2d 151, 156—sanctions upheld where attorney seeking deposition unreasonably forced opposing counsel to seek a protective order to stop deposition and failed to show information could not be obtained through interrogatories or "other discovery devices less intrusive to the attorney/client privilege and work product protection"]

[8:467.6-467.9] *Reserved.*

d. [8:467.10] **Compare—deposing expert witnesses:** Depositions of expert witnesses normally are governed by CCP §2034.010 et seq., which provides a detailed procedure for the exchange of expert witness information shortly before trial and deposing experts so disclosed. *See discussion at ¶8:1624 ff.*

(1) [8:467.11] **On summary judgment motions:** The §2034.010 et seq. procedure for deposing expert witnesses does not bar earlier depositions of experts whose opinions are filed

© 2020 Thomson Reuters/The Rutter Group

in support of or in opposition to a motion for summary judgment or summary adjudication. If an opposing party presents facts raising a legitimate question regarding the foundation of the expert's opinion, a deposition *limited to that subject* may be allowed. [*St. Mary Med. Ctr. v. Sup.Ct. (Mennella)* (1996) 50 CA4th 1531, 1539, 58 CR2d 182, 186]

(a) [8:467.12] **Discretionary:** Unlike deposing nonparty witnesses generally (¶*8:464*), such discovery is discretionary with the trial court: "[I]t would defeat the purpose of the summary [judgment] procedure were we to recognize an absolute right . . . to depose any person who provides evidence in support of or in opposition to the proceeding." [*St. Mary Med. Ctr. v. Sup.Ct. (Mennella)*, supra, 50 CA4th at 1538, 1540, 58 CR2d at 186, 188—"we caution that the process should not be utilized to turn summary proceedings into mini-trials"]

e. [8:468] **Corporations and other entities:** A deposition can be taken of any entity—corporation, partnership, governmental agency, etc.—by examining an officer or agent designated to testify on its behalf. [CCP §2025.010]

These are often referred to as person most knowledgeable (PMK) or person most qualified (PMQ) depositions.

[8:469] ***PRACTICE POINTER:*** You can also take the deposition of particular officers, directors or employees of the corporation, if so desired. But where the corporation is a party to the action, take the deposition of the *entity* as well; or, alternatively, serve the entity with *requests for admission* of facts obtained in the deposition of its officers and employees. Otherwise, their depositions may not be admissible evidence against the entity (allowing it to escape admissions obtained therein).

(Protective orders may limit depositions of "high level" officers or directors who have no direct knowledge of the matters involved (sometimes referred to as "apex" depositions); *see* ¶*8:684.6*.)

(1) [8:470] **Notice or subpoena directed to entity:** Where the deposition of a corporation or other entity is sought, the notice of deposition or subpoena is *directed to the entity itself;* e.g., "XYZ Corp., a corporation." It is the entity, not the officer or agent testifying on its behalf, that is the "deponent." (The entity will then be obligated to produce the "most qualified" person to testify on its behalf; *see* ¶*8:473*.)

(2) [8:471] **Notice or subpoena must describe matters to be asked:** A deposition notice or subpoena directed to an entity must "describe *with reasonable particularity* the matters on which examination is requested." [CCP §2025.230 (emphasis added); *see* ¶*8:487*]

(a) [8:472] **Effect of omission?** Absent such description, the entity is under no duty to designate the "most qualified" person to testify on its behalf (*see* ¶*8:473*). Whether lack of such description invalidates the notice or subpoena is unclear. (Arguably, the entity still should be required to send *someone* to testify on its behalf.)

(3) [8:473] **Entity must produce "most qualified" person to testify on its behalf:** If the notice of deposition or subpoena served on the entity describes the matters on which questions will be asked "with reasonable particularity," the entity is under a *duty to designate and produce* the officers, directors, managing agents or employees "most qualified" to testify on its behalf. [CCP §2025.230] (The deposition subpoena must advise the entity of its duty to make such a designation. CCP §2020.310(e).)

The person or persons designated by the entity must testify "to the extent of any information known *or reasonably available* to the deponent [entity]." [CCP §2025.230 (emphasis added)] Thus, the person designated must inform himself or herself as to the information known to the entity.

Moreover, when a request for *documents* is made, the witness or someone in authority "is expected to make an inquiry of *everyone* who might be holding responsive documents or everyone who knows where such documents might be held." [*Maldonado v. Sup.Ct. (ICG Telecom Group, Inc.)* (2002) 94 CA4th 1390, 1396, 115 CR2d 137, 142 (emphasis added)]

(a) [8:474] **Purpose:** The purpose of this provision is to eliminate the problem of trying to find out who in the corporate hierarchy has the information the examiner is seeking. E.g., in a product liability suit, who in the engineering department designed the defective part?

(Under former law, the entity was required only to designate "one or more" officers or employees to testify on its behalf. This permitted considerable "buck-passing" and "I don't know" answers at deposition.) [*Maldonado v. Sup.Ct. (ICG Telecom Group, Inc.)*, supra, 94 CA4th at 1395, 115 CR2d at 141]

(b) [8:475] **Effect:** If the subject matter of the questioning is clearly stated, the burden is on the entity, not the examiner, to produce the right witnesses. And if the particular officer or employee designated lacks personal knowledge of all the information sought (which frequently happens), he or she must find out from those who do.

(c) [8:475.1] **Not applicable to former officers and employees:** A corporation is not required to produce any of its *former* officers, directors, managing agents or employees even if they are far more knowledgeable about the matters specified in the deposition notice than

© 2020 Thomson Reuters/The Rutter Group

its current staff. [*Maldonado v. Sup.Ct. (ICG Telecom Group, Inc.)*, supra, 94 CA4th at 1398, 115 CR2d at 143; *see ¶8:518*]

(d) [8:476] **Sanctions?** The Act does not specify what *sanctions* (*see ¶8:819 ff.*) may be imposed against an entity for designating someone lacking knowledge of all matters specified in the notice.

Apparently, a motion would lie to *compel* the corporation to designate someone having the information requested.

And monetary sanctions no doubt could be imposed (ordering the entity to pay the costs and fees incurred by the deposing party in taking the additional depositions). (Failure to respond or making an evasive response is a "misuse of the discovery process"; see CCP §2023.010(d), (f).)

Also, a company that refused to produce a deponent able to respond to reasonable deposition topics potentially could be precluded from introducing evidence at trial on those topics from the company's witnesses.

If a deposition *subpoena* was served, additional sanctions might be appropriate (see CCP §2020.240, ¶*8:609*).

[8:477] ***PRACTICE POINTER:*** The entity's duty to designate the "most qualified" person to testify on its behalf may work better in theory than in practice.

It may be useful if all you need is to authenticate corporate records or proceedings. But it may not pin down exactly who knows what, or did what, within the organization. I.e., the witness designated as the "most qualified" by the corporation may not have the information you require. So you may have to take additional depositions to find out what you need to know.

Therefore, if the matter involved is critical to your case, *do not rely on the entity's duty to designate* the "most qualified" officer or employee. It is better practice to do your own investigation or send out *interrogatories* asking who in the organization has knowledge of the *particular facts* you seek; and take that person's deposition.

Afterwards, if the corporation is a party to the action, follow up with *requests for admission* to make sure the facts obtained are binding on the corporation (*see ¶8:1387*).

f. [8:478] **Limit on number of times person may be deposed:** Natural persons (including parties to the action) may not be deposed more than once without a court order based on a showing of good cause. [CCP §2025.610(a), (b); see *Fairmont Ins. Co. v. Sup.Ct. (Stendell)* (2000) 22 C4th 245, 254, 92 CR2d 70, 77]

This applies both to depositions by the party who took the first depo and to *any other party served with the deposition notice*. I.e., all parties are expected to examine the deponent during the first deposition. [CCP §2025.610(a)-(b)]

Cross-refer—depo examination time limit: There is also a statutory *time limit* on the total number of hours a witness can be subjected to deposition examination (CCP §2025.290). *See discussion at ¶8:702 ff.*

[8:479] *Reserved.*

(1) [8:480] **New parties not bound:** The limit on successive depositions applies only to parties who "have been served with a deposition notice" of the first deposition. Later-joined parties are entitled to depose the person again on the same or new matters, without leave of court. [CCP §2025.610(a); see also CCP §2025.290(b)(6) (exception to 7-hour limit on depo examination of a witness where party appeared in action after witness' depo concluded, ¶*8:702.8*)]

(a) [8:481] **Comment:** It is unclear under §2025.610(a) whether all other parties have the right to examine the witness at the successive deposition noticed by the later-joined party, including those who examined the witness at a previous deposition. However, if the general seven-hour limit on deposition examination of a witness (¶*8:702*) was reached in the prior deposition, §2025.290(b)(6) appears to give only the *later-joined* party additional depo examination time (¶*8:702.8*) absent court order, party stipulation or other statutorily-specified exception (*see ¶8:702.3 ff.*).

(2) [8:482] **Not applicable where first depo on behalf of entity:** The limitation against taking more than one depo from a natural person does not apply where that person was previously examined as an officer, director or employee of a corporation designated to testify on its behalf (under CCP §2025.230; *see ¶8:473*). [CCP §2025.610(c)(1)]

(Nor, presumably, is leave of court required to examine a person designated to testify on behalf of a corporation where that person was *previously* deposed as an individual.)

(3) [8:482.1] **Exception—attachment proceedings:** An additional deposition of a defendant may be taken in connection with attachment proceedings. Where a right to attach order has been issued pursuant to CCP §485.230, plaintiffs may depose a defendant for a second time "for the limited purpose of discovering . . . the identity, location, and value of property in which the deponent has an interest." [CCP §2025.610(c)(2)]

According to CCP §2025.610(c)(2), this additional deposition must be "pursuant to a court order under Section 485.230." The meaning is unclear, however, because §485.230 does

© 2020 Thomson Reuters/The Rutter Group

not provide for a court order (but instead authorizes discovery "through any means provided for").

(4) [8:482.2] **Compare—deposing nonparty records custodian:** Parties seeking to obtain document discovery must *specifically describe* each document or *reasonably particularize* each category of documents. [See CCP §2020.410(a), *discussed at ¶8:544 ff.*]

To obtain a sufficient description of documents held by *nonparties*, it may be necessary to depose them if they refuse to provide such information informally. This should not bar a subsequent deposition of the same person, if needed, after the records have been examined: "[T]rial courts should be liberal in permitting such a second deposition upon a showing the earlier deposition was made necessary by the party's refusal to cooperate in agreeing to less formal procedures." [*Calcor Space Facility, Inc. v. Sup.Ct. (Thiem Indus., Inc.)* (1997) 53 CA4th 216, 223, 61 CR2d 567, 571]

[8:482.3-482.4] *Reserved.*

g. [8:482.5] **Limitation—standards of professionalism:** Various guidelines exist to discourage abusive deposition tactics (*see ¶8:496.5*). The Los Angeles Superior Court has adopted certain of these guidelines as "civility in litigation recommendations to members of the bar":

- "Depositions should be taken only where actually needed to ascertain facts or information or to perpetuate testimony. They should never be used as a means of harassment or to generate expense." [L.A. Sup.Ct. Rule 3.26, Appendix 3.A(e)(1)]

Because local rules "relating to" discovery are preempted by CRC 3.20(a) (*see ¶9:13.2*), it is questionable whether sanctions can be imposed for violation of these professional standards. However, such conduct may also be sanctionable as a *discovery misuse* under CCP §2023.010 et seq. (*see ¶8:1901*).

4. [8:483] **Notice of Deposition:** Service of a proper Notice of Deposition serves two purposes:

- First, it constitutes notice to *all parties* of the taking of the deposition, so that they may attend and examine the deponent. (Parties who fail to do so may thereafter be barred from separate depositions of that witness; *see ¶8:478.*)
- Second, it is effective *by itself* to *compel* a *party* or *"party-affiliated" witness* to appear, to testify and to *produce* records or other evidence in his or her possession *without necessity of a subpoena*. [CCP §2025.280(a); *see ¶8:516 ff.*] (Nonparty witnesses must be subpoenaed (CCP §2025.280(b).)

a. [8:484] **To whom notice must be given:** Notice of deposition must be served on all parties who have *appeared* in the action. (I.e., notice need not be served on parties named in the pleadings but who are not yet served, who are served but have not yet responded or who are in default.) [CCP §2025.240(a)]

If the deposition will be conducted using instant visual display ("real time transcription"), a copy of the notice must also be given to the *deposition reporter.* [CCP §2025.220(a)(5); *see* ¶*8:655.1*]

[8:484.1] ***PRACTICE POINTER:*** Although not required, it may be a good idea to serve non-appearing parties with the deposition notice to limit the possibility the witness may have to be deposed more than once (*see* ¶*8:480 ff.*).

(1) [8:485] **Not filed with court:** The deposing party retains the original notice with proof of service. It is not filed with the court unless it becomes relevant in a law and motion hearing. [CRC 3.250(a)(3)]

(The same is true for *stipulations* setting or extending the time for depositions; see CRC 3.250(a)(7).)

(2) [8:486] **Where "employment records" or "personal records" of "consumer" subpoenaed:** Where an oral deposition is for the purpose of obtaining "employment records" (see CCP §1985.6, ¶*8:596.5*) or the "personal records" of a consumer (see CCP §1985.3, ¶*8:580*), the deposition notice must also be served on the "employee" or "consumer" if he or she is not already a party to the action. [CCP §2025.240(b); *see detailed discussion at* ¶*8:580 ff.*]

b. [8:487] **Content of notice:** The notice must state *all* of the following in at least 12-point type (CCP §2025.220(a)):

- The *date, time* and *place* where the deposition will be taken. [CCP §2025.220(a)(1), (2)]
- The deponent's name, and if not a party to the action, the deponent's *address* and *telephone number* (if known). [CCP §2025.220(a)(3)]

  If the deponent's name is not known, the notice should contain a description sufficient to identify the person or class to which the person belongs (e.g., "custodian of records of XYZ Bank"). [CCP §2025.220(a)(3)]
- If the deposition is to be *recorded* by *audio* or *video* technology, the notice must so state. [CCP §2025.220(a)(5)]

  Likewise, if the deposition is to be stenographically recorded by a machine using instantaneous (or "real time") transcription (i.e., instant visual display of the question and testimony), the deposition notice must so state and a copy of the notice furnished to the deposition officer. [CCP §2025.220(a)(5); *see discussion at* ¶*8:660*]

  And, if the deposing party plans to use a *video recording* of the deposition of a doctor or other *expert witness in lieu of*

© 2020 Thomson Reuters/The Rutter Group

live testimony at trial (under CCP §2025.620(d), *see* ¶*8:892*), this fact must also be stated in the notice. [CCP §2025.220(a)(6)]

- If the deponent is a corporation or other entity, the notice must describe with "reasonable particularity" the matters on which questions will be asked so that it can designate the "most qualified" persons to testify on its behalf. [CCP §2025.230; *see* ¶*8:473*]
- If the deponent (whether or not a party) is being required to produce documents at the deposition, the materials *or category* of materials, including any electronically-stored information, to be produced must be specified with "reasonable particularity." [CCP §2025.220(a)(4)]

  (If the deponent is a *party*, the notice by itself *compels production* of the documents. Otherwise, a "records and testimony" deposition subpoena must be served; *see* ¶*8:535*.)
- The notice must specify the form in which any electronically-stored information is to be produced when a particular form is desired by the requesting party. [CCP §2025.220(a)(7)]
- The notice must include a statement disclosing the existence of a contractual relationship (if known to the noticing party) between the noticing party (or third party financing any part of the litigation) and the deposition officer or entity providing the services of the deposition officer. [CCP §2025.220(a)(8)(A)]

  Also, the notice must include a statement disclosing any direction from the noticing party (or third party financing any part of the litigation) to use a particular officer or entity to provide the deposition services. [CCP §2025.220(a)(8)(B)]
- Finally, the deposition notice or the accompanying proof of service must *list all parties or attorneys* for parties on whom the deposition notice is being served. [CCP §2025.240(a)]

FORM: Notice of Deposition, *see Form 8:2* in Rivera, *Cal. Prac. Guide: Civ. Pro. Before Trial FORMS* (TRG).

(1) [8:488] **Deposition subpoenas to be attached to notice:** If the deponent's attendance is being compelled by deposition subpoena, a copy of the subpoena must be served with the notice of deposition. [CCP §2025.240(c); *and see* ¶*8:565*]

(2) [8:489] **"Business records" subpoena as substitute for depo notice:** Copies of business records maintained by a nonparty can be obtained simply by serving a "records only" subpoena on the custodian of the records (CCP §2020.020(b), *see* ¶*8:540*). The party seeking the records must serve a copy of the "records only" subpoena on all other parties to the action; and it has the same effect as a notice of deposition. [CCP §2025.220(b)]

(3) [8:490] **Weekdays vs. weekend:** Nothing in the statute prohibits noticing a deposition on other than a normal business

day. But the deponent or opposing parties may seek a protective order altering the date selected by the noticing party (¶*8:677*).

[8:490.1] ***PRACTICE POINTER:*** If it is necessary to depose someone on a weekend or holiday, good practice dictates clearing this in advance with all concerned. Failure to do so is likely to lead to ill will, probably to motions, and possibly to sanctions.

[8:490.2-490.4] *Reserved.*

(4) [8:490.5] **Effect of provision that depo "continue day to day until completed":** A notice of deposition often states that the deposition will commence on a certain date and "continue from day to day thereafter until completed." [See *Sprague v. Equifax, Inc.* (1985) 166 CA3d 1012, 1041, 213 CR 69, 88—deposition could not be used at trial where deponent's counsel refused to permit deposition to be completed on following day, because it deprived opposing counsel of opportunity to cross-examine]

(a) [8:490.6] **Comment:** It is doubtful that this boilerplate language by itself obligates a deponent to remain indefinitely. Indeed, subject to certain exceptions, CCP §2025.290 ordinarily limits the deposition of a witness by all counsel, other than the witness' counsel of record, to *seven hours* of total testimony (*see* ¶*8:702 ff.*).

[8:490.7] ***PRACTICE POINTER:*** If a deposition is likely to last more than a day, the dates should be cleared in advance with opposing counsel. Similarly, if a deposition unexpectedly cannot be completed by the end of the day and the deponent or opposing counsel is unwilling to come back the next day, a date for continuance of the deposition should be determined by agreement with the deponent and all counsel. Failing agreement, deposing counsel should seek a court order for a continued deposition based on a showing of good cause.

c. [8:491] **Amount of notice required:** The notice must be served *at least 10 days* before the date set for the deposition. [CCP §2025.270(a)]

(1) [8:492] **Longer if served by mail, overnight delivery, fax or electronically:** The regular extensions of time apply where notices are served by mail: 5 calendar days if the address *and* place of mailing are in California; 10 calendar days if either is in another state; and 20 days if either is in another country. [CCP §§2016.050, 1013(a)]

The extension is only 2 *court days* for notices served by express mail or other method providing for overnight delivery; or by fax (allowed only if agreed to in writing); or by electronic trans-

© 2020 Thomson Reuters/The Rutter Group

mission or notification (allowed only if agreed to or required by the court). [See CCP §§1010.6, 1013; CRC 2.250-2.259]

Personal service under CCP §1011 is also authorized (CCP §2016.050). If personal service is made to an attorney's office and no one is present, the papers may be left in a conspicuous place in the office between the hours of 9 a.m. and 5 p.m. If personal service is made at a party's residence, service must be made between 8 a.m. and 8 p.m. [CCP §1011]

(2) [8:493] **Longer where employment or "personal records" of "consumer" subpoenaed:** Where the deposition is for the purpose of obtaining employment records (see CCP §1985.6, ¶*8:596.5*) or "personal records" of a "consumer" (see CCP §1985.3, ¶*8:580 ff.*), it cannot proceed until *20 days after the deposition subpoena was issued.* (This allows the employee or "consumer" time to seek a protective order against invasion of his or her privacy.) [CCP §2025.270(c); *see* ¶*8:605*]

Comment: The statute says the 20 days run "from the *issuance* of the subpoena." It would make more sense to have the 20-day period run from the date the subpoena was *served.* Until the statute is changed, however, counsel should assume the statute means what it says.

(a) [8:493.1] **Compare—depo notice to party:** But a party deponent may be compelled to produce such records without a subpoena or the 20-day waiting period. The normal 10-day deposition notice compels document production by a party (*see* ¶*8:516*).

(3) [8:493.2] **Shorter in unlawful detainer actions:** In unlawful detainer actions, depos must be set at least 5 days after service of the notice but not later than 5 days before trial. [CCP §2025.270(b)]

(4) [8:493.3] **Court may alter date:** For "good cause" shown, the court may lengthen or shorten the notice or time for scheduling a deposition. And, where a motion for protective order is pending, the court may *stay* the deposition until the matter is determined. [CCP §2025.270(d)]

Such order may be granted on motion or *ex parte* application of the deponent or any party. [CCP §2025.270(d)]

d. [8:494] **Depo priority based on notice?** Ordinarily, depositions proceed in whatever order they are noticed by the parties. But questions of priority may arise where a later-served notice sets a deposition before the date set in the first-served notice.

For example, on July 1, Plaintiff serves notice of Defendant's deposition on August 15. The next day, July 2, Defendant serves notice of Plaintiff's deposition on August 14. Both notices are timely (i.e., served more than 10 days in advance of the deposition dates). Does the fact that Plaintiff's depo notice was *served* first block Defendant's right to proceed first?

(1) [8:495] **Discovery Act:** The Discovery Act does not recognize priority based on notice alone: Unless state or local court rules or local uniform written policy provide otherwise, "the fact that a party is conducting discovery, whether by deposition or another method, *shall not operate to delay the discovery of any other party.*" [CCP §2019.020(a) (emphasis added)]

(a) [8:495.1] **Local rules preempted:** Local rules relating to discovery are preempted by CRC 3.20(a).

[8:496-496.4] *Reserved.*

(2) [8:496.5] ***Civility Guidelines***

— An attorney should not use discovery to harass an opposing counsel, parties or witnesses;

— When another party notices a deposition for the near future, absent unusual circumstances, an attorney should not schedule another deposition in the same case for an earlier date without opposing counsel's agreement;

— An attorney should delay a scheduled deposition only when necessary to address scheduling problems and not in bad faith;

— An attorney should treat other counsel and participants with courtesy and civility, and should not engage in conduct that would be inappropriate in the presence of a judicial officer. [State Bar California Attorney Guidelines of Civility and Professionalism §9(a)]

— As soon as an attorney knows that a previously scheduled deposition will or will not in fact go forward as scheduled, the attorney should notify all counsel;

— An attorney who obtains a document pursuant to a deposition subpoena should, upon request, make copies of the document available to all other counsel at their expense. [State Bar California Attorney Guidelines of Civility and Professionalism §11(e), (f)]

(a) [8:496.6] **Nonparty deponents:** With respect to *nonparty witnesses:*

— An attorney should be courteous and respectful in communications with nonparty witnesses;

— Upon request, an attorney should extend professional courtesies and grant reasonable accommodations, unless to do so would materially prejudice the client's lawful objectives;

— An attorney should take special care to protect a witness from undue harassment or embarrassment and to state questions in a form that is appropriate to the witness' age and development;

— An attorney should not issue a subpoena to a nonparty witness for inappropriate tactical or strategic purposes, such as to intimidate or harass the nonparty. [State

© 2020 Thomson Reuters/The Rutter Group

Bar California Attorney Guidelines of Civility and Professionalism §11(a)-(d)]

[8:496.7] ***PRACTICE POINTER:*** Even if the witness agrees to attend voluntarily, a deposition subpoena should be served to assure the witness' attendance at the agreed-upon date. Otherwise, you run the risk of sanctions if the witness fails to show up for any reason (*see ¶8:824*).

(3) [8:497] **Comment:** Even in the absence of statutory authority or rule, many judges will order depositions to be taken and *completed* in the order noticed. Protective orders (¶*8:501 ff.*) may be granted to prevent a party from unilaterally altering the sequence of depositions (e.g., by obtaining a continuance of his or her deposition and then noticing a deposition of the opponent). [See *Young v. Rosenthal* (1989) 212 CA3d 96, 106, 260 CR 369, 374, fn. 10]

[8:498] ***PRACTICE POINTER:*** "Playing games" with deposition sequence is a poor tactic. It undermines professionalism. Equally important, it is sure to raise the antagonism level in the case, making further proceedings more costly and settlement more difficult.

[8:499-500] *Reserved.*

(4) [8:501] **Protective orders available:** If an issue as to priority of depositions arises, a protective order may be sought under either of the following provisions:

- "[F]or good cause shown, the court may establish the sequence and timing of discovery for the convenience of parties and witnesses and in the interests of justice." [CCP §2019.020(b); *see ¶8:678*]
- "The court, for good cause shown, may make any order that justice requires to protect any party . . . from unwarranted annoyance, embarrassment, or oppression, or undue burden and expense. This protective order may include . . . the following directions:

  "(1) That the deposition not be taken at all.

  "(2) That the deposition be taken at a different time . . .

  "(5) That the deposition be taken only on certain specified terms and conditions . . ." [CCP §2025.420(b); *see ¶8:677*]

(a) [8:502] **Procedure:** The procedure for obtaining protective orders is discussed at ¶*8:685 ff.* A noticed motion is required; and it must include a declaration showing a "reasonable and good faith attempt at an informal resolution" of the matters in controversy. Monetary sanctions may be imposed against the losing party. [See

CCP §2025.420(a), (h); *and further discussion at ¶8:2070 ff.*]

(b) [8:503] **Disadvantage of being deposed first not "good cause" for protective order:** As explained by the Supreme Court: "Since discovery proceedings can seldom if ever be conducted simultaneously, it is inherent in such proceedings that the party who secures discovery first may derive advantages by securing information from his adversary before he is required to reciprocate by divulging information to him . . . [T]he existence of such advantages alone will ordinarily *not* constitute good cause for changing the normal timing of discovery or justify a conclusion that such timing will result in 'annoyance, embarrassment or oppression.' " [*Rosemont v. Sup.Ct. (Turner)* (1964) 60 C2d 709, 714, 36 CR 439, 442 (emphasis added)]

(c) [8:504] **Comment:** Protective orders are, of course, discretionary. In deciding whether to alter the sequence of depositions, courts apply a *practical* judgment as to whether any real harm would result to either side from allowing the other to proceed first.

e. [8:505] **Stipulations re notice:** Unless the court orders otherwise, the statutory notice requirements for all discovery methods, including deposition notices, may be *altered by written stipulation.* [CCP §2016.030]

[8:506] ***PRACTICE POINTER:*** It is good practice to confer with other counsel in the case before setting depositions. (Indeed, this courtesy is required under "Codes of Professionalism" adopted by many bar associations.) Doing so may avoid rescheduling depositions because of unavailability of the witness or counsel and other duplication of effort and will avoid expensive and time-consuming motions.

In any event, however, *do not rely on oral stipulations.* Counsel frequently set depositions by oral stipulation, *waiving* the requirement of formal notice entirely. While this may be common, it is *not* a good practice because the statute requires a *writing* for the stipulation to be enforceable.

If counsel stipulate to a date for the deposition, a *formal notice of deposition* should be served for the agreed date. This will avoid any risk of misunderstanding as to what was agreed upon; and will assure sufficiency of notice if you have to enforce discovery. If the opposing party fails to appear for deposition, it will put you in a better position to seek *sanctions* for your expenses (*see* ¶*8:819 ff.*). And, it will avoid your being subject to sanctions for expenses incurred by other parties attending the deposition (*see* ¶*8:825 ff.*).

[8:506.1-506.4] *Reserved.*

© 2020 Thomson Reuters/The Rutter Group

(1) [8:506.5] **Effect of "notice of unavailability":** Some attorneys serve a "notice of unavailability" to indicate intended vacations, etc., to deter opposing counsel from scheduling depositions or other proceedings in their absence. Such a notice has *no legal effect*, however, and does not entitle anyone to a continuance. [See *Carl v. Sup.Ct. (Coast Comm. College Dist.)* (2007) 157 CA4th 73, 75, 68 CR3d 566, 567 (dealing with practice in appellate courts)]

☞ [8:506.6] ***PRACTICE POINTER:*** Even so, it is good practice to notify your opponents *in advance* when you will be unavailable. It is harassment for attorneys to schedule discovery *knowing* an opponent may be unable to respond, and doing so may result in *sanctions*. [See *Tenderloin Housing Clinic, Inc. v. Sparks* (1992) 8 CA4th 299, 305, 10 CR2d 371, 374]

If there is any question as to opposing counsel's willingness to accommodate your unavailability, seek a continuance from the court (by *ex parte* order, if necessary) *before* your absence. Keep in mind that properly noticed depositions may be admissible against your client even if you do not attend.

f. [8:507] **Procedure for challenging defects in deposition notice:** Errors or defects in a deposition notice are rarely critical to the outcome of the case and, for this reason, are *waived unless promptly challenged*. [CCP §2025.410(a)]

(1) [8:508] **Written objection must be served before deposition:** Any error or irregularity in the deposition notice is waived unless *written* objections are served *specifying* the defect. The objection must be served on the party noticing the deposition, and on all other parties who received such notice, *at least 3 calendar days* before the deposition. (If made on the third day preceding the deposition, personal service is required on the party noticing the deposition.) [CCP §2025.410(a), (b)]

(Such objections are *not* filed with the court when served. They may be filed later, however, if they become relevant on a motion to compel; CRC 3.250(a)(3).)

(a) [8:509] **Example:** P serves a notice of D's deposition requiring production of "all books and records of D." D believes this description is too general to require production. D must timely serve written objections *before* the deposition. If D waits until the deposition to raise the objection, it is *waived;* and D cannot refuse to produce the documents at the deposition on grounds they were not adequately described.

(b) [8:510] **Effect of timely objection:** If the objection is timely made, "[a]ny deposition taken after the service of a written objection *shall not be used against the objecting party . . . if the party did not attend* the deposition and if the court determines that the objection was a valid one." [CCP §2025.410(b) (emphasis added)]

(c) [8:511] **Waiver by attending?** This does not say that the objecting party waives any defect in the notice by attending the depo. Depending on the objection to the notice (e.g., improper address), attendance may waive that objection, particularly if the party did not incur any cost as a result of the defect in the notice. However, if parties attend after proper objections have been made, then further proceedings should take place and the parties should deal with the objection by negotiation or further motion, if necessary.

[8:512] ***PRACTICE POINTER:*** If you receive a deposition notice in time to attend, it is risky (maybe foolhardy) to stay away from the deposition because of perceived errors or defects in the notice.

If it is your client's deposition, you are exposing the client and yourself to the risk of sanctions if it turns out you are wrong.

If the deposition is of another party, information obtained by your adversary in your absence may *lead* to admissible evidence even if your objection is valid. And, the limit on number of times a natural person may be deposed (CCP §2025.610(a)-(b), ¶*8:478*) may block your later attempt to depose the same witness.

If you do not want the deposition to go forward and are willing to risk not attending, you could file a motion for protective order (¶*8:675*). Filing a motion to quash the depo notice will stay the deposition (¶*8:513 ff.*).

As a practical matter, however, the effort and expense involved in such motions are *rarely* justified. It usually makes more sense simply to contact counsel noticing the depo and *negotiate* your objections.

(2) [8:513] **Motion to quash depo notice:** After serving written objections, the objecting party may move for an order staying the deposition and quashing the deposition notice.

Such motion must be accompanied, however, by a declaration of *"reasonable and good faith attempt" to resolve the issues informally*. (This clearly requires you to call the defect to opposing counsel's attention and give him or her the opportunity to send out proper notice, as discussed (¶*8:515.*)) [CCP §2025.410(c)] (The "attempt to resolve informally" requirement is discussed in more detail at ¶*8:1158 ff.*)

© 2020 Thomson Reuters/The Rutter Group

☞ [8:513.1] ***PRACTICE POINTER:*** *Consider alternative procedures discussed at ¶8:787.1.*

(a) [8:514] **Effect—deposition automatically stayed:** Filing the motion to quash *automatically* stays the taking of the deposition until the matter is determined. No court order is required. [CCP §2025.410(c)]

Compare: A motion for *protective order* will *not* automatically stay a deposition; notice and hearing are required (*see ¶8:687*).

(b) [8:514.1] **Monetary sanction against losing party:** The court "shall" impose a monetary sanction against the losing party on the motion *unless* it determines that party acted "with substantial justification" or that other circumstances make imposition of such sanctions "unjust." [CCP §2025.410(d); see *California Shellfish, Inc. v. United Shellfish Co.* (1997) 56 CA4th 16, 25-26, 64 CR2d 797, 802] (Monetary sanctions on discovery motions are discussed at *¶8:1921 ff.*)

☞ [8:515] ***PRACTICE POINTER:*** Moving to quash the deposition notice is *not recommended* unless the defect is critical and you have *exhausted reasonable efforts* to obtain a proper notice.

Otherwise, even if you're right and you win the motion, all you will accomplish is delay. The court will not grant sanctions in your favor if you did not make a "reasonable and good faith attempt" to resolve the issues informally. Indeed, failure to do so may subject *you* to sanctions for "misuse of the discovery process"—even if you win the motion (see CCP §2023.010(i)).

5. [8:516] **Subpoena NOT Necessary for Party or "Party-Affiliated" Witnesses:** There is no need to serve a deposition subpoena on an opposing party in order to take that party's deposition. Proper service of *notice* of deposition *compels* the opposing party to appear, to testify, *and* to produce documents if requested. [CCP §2025.280(a)]

a. [8:517] **"Party-affiliated" witnesses:** Nor is a deposition subpoena required to compel the attendance and testimony of a person who, although not a named party, is either an *officer, director, managing agent or employee* of a party. [CCP §2025.280(a)]

(1) [8:517.1] **Managing agent:** A managing agent may, but need not, be an officer, director or employee of a party. For purposes of the discovery statutes, a managing agent is determined based on several factors: "(1) does the person exercise judgment and discretion in dealing with the party's matters; (2) can the person be expected to comply with the party's directive to appear; and (3) can the person be anticipated to identify himself or herself with the party's interests." [*Lopez*

v. Watchtower Bible & Tract Soc. of New York, Inc. (2016) 246 CA4th 566, 602, 201 CR3d 156, 186]

This determination is "highly dependent" on the specific facts of the case and the party seeking to compel the deposition has the initial burden to show the named deponent is a managing agent of the party. [*Lopez v. Watchtower Bible & Tract Soc. of New York, Inc.*, supra, 246 CA4th at 601, 201 CR3d at 185—member of defendant's "Governing Body" not a managing agent where no evidence defendant could compel deponent's attendance for his depo]

(2) [8:518] **Compare—former employees:** The "affiliation" must exist at the *time of deposition.* Persons *formerly* affiliated with a party (e.g., former officers or employees) are not required to attend a deposition unless subpoenaed. [*Maldonado v. Sup.Ct. (ICG Telecom Group, Inc.)* (2002) 94 CA4th 1390, 1398, 115 CR2d 137, 143 (citing text)]

(3) [8:519] **Notice does not confer jurisdiction over nonparty:** The requirement that an "officer, director, managing agent or employee" appear for deposition without necessity of subpoena does *not* mean that such persons are subject to the court's personal jurisdiction. Rather, it means that it is the responsibility of the *party* to produce such persons for deposition (or risk the sanctions discussed below, ¶*8:533 ff.*).

[8:520] ***PRACTICE POINTER:*** If there is *any* question as to the witness' present "affiliation" with a party, don't rely on a deposition notice to compel that person's attendance. *Serve a deposition subpoena* instead, or serve both the notice and a subpoena.

This will avoid any argument from opposing counsel as to the witness' status—i.e., that the witness is no longer "an officer, director, managing agent or employee" of the opposing party. (Before serving the subpoena, you can ask opposing counsel to stipulate as to the status of the witness; if the stipulation is refused, you'll *know* a subpoena is necessary.)

b. [8:521] **Production of documents, electronically-stored information, etc. at deposition:** No subpoena is required to compel a party or "party-affiliated" witnesses to produce books, records or other materials—including electronically-stored information—in their possession at the time of deposition as long as the notice of deposition specified with *reasonable particularity* the materials or category of materials (including any electronically-stored information) they are to produce. [CCP §2025.220(a)(4)]

Compare—CCP §2031.010 et seq. inspection demands: Production of documents, electronically-stored information, and other things can also be obtained through a CCP §2031.010 et seq. inspection demand (*discussed in Ch. 8H*). But these are separate

© 2020 Thomson Reuters/The Rutter Group

procedures. Absent a protective order, neither procedure bars use of the other. [*Carter v. Sup.Ct. (CSAA Inter-Insurance Bureau)* (1990) 218 CA3d 994, 997, 267 CR 290, 291-292—party who missed deadline for compelling inspection under CCP §2031.010 et seq. may compel inspection at deposition]

☞ [8:521.1] ***PRACTICE POINTERS:*** If you expect the documents to be complex or voluminous, serve an inspection demand under CCP §2031.010 et seq., scheduling the inspection *before* the deposition, rather than seeking production by deposition notice. It is difficult to examine complex or voluminous documents "under the gun" in a deposition setting and frame intelligent questions. You may have to ask for a recess or continuance, which will run up the cost to all concerned and may be opposed.

This is particularly true with regard to electronically-stored information (ESI). Unless requesting a small amount of ESI that can readily be produced in printout form (e.g., relevant emails to or from the deponent), it makes better sense to obtain the ESI through a CCP §2031.010 et seq. inspection demand *before the deposition*. Alternatively, you should agree with the producing party to obtain the ESI called for in the notice before the oral deposition.

(1) [8:522] **Location of records immaterial:** A party can be compelled to produce records located in another state or country if they are shown to be under the party's control. [See *Boal v. Price Waterhouse & Co.* (1985) 165 CA3d 806, 810-811, 212 CR 42, 44-45—Los Angeles partner in national accounting firm subpoenaed to produce records from partnership office in New York for trial in California]

(2) [8:523] **Sufficiency of description:** The materials or category of materials, including any electronically-stored information, to be produced must be described with "*reasonable particularity*" in the deposition notice. [CCP §2025.220(a)(4)]

This is an *objective* test: i.e., whether a person of average intelligence would know what items are being sought. (Thus, "I didn't realize what you wanted" may not be a valid excuse for failure to produce.)

(a) [8:524] **Compare—other document discovery methods:** The same standard—"by category" and "reasonably particularizing each category"—applies to CCP §2030.010 et seq. inspection demands (CCP §2031.030(c)(1), ¶*8:1439*) and deposition subpoenas (CCP §2020.510(a)(2), ¶*8:561*).

[8:525] *Reserved.*

(b) [8:526] **Effect:** Allowing descriptions "by category" and "with reasonable particularity" does *not* mean the responding party must bear the burden of going through all of its records to determine which records satisfy a broadly-worded discovery demand.

Particularly where discovery is sought from a *nonparty*, the burden should be placed on the party seeking discovery: The description in the deposition notice therefore should bear *some relationship to the manner in which the records are kept.* [*Calcor Space Facility, Inc. v. Sup.Ct. (Thiem Indus., Inc.)* (1997) 53 CA4th 216, 222, 61 CR2d 567, 571; *see discussion at ¶8:544.1 ff.*]

[8:527] ***PRACTICE POINTER:*** From this perspective, your deposition notice should identify the *subject matter* or *transaction* in question as *narrowly* as possible.

- Requests for "all correspondence between Jones and Smith in 2005" may suffice if the amount of correspondence between them is not too large. However, it would be better to state the subject matter you're looking for (e.g., "relating to purchase of Smith's house").
- But requests for "all financial records of XYZ Co." or "all documents relating to XYZ's liability to Jones" would seem too broad. They could embrace many subcategories completely unrelated to the litigation. A protective order (¶*8:531.3*) might be granted.

[8:528] *Reserved.*

(3) [8:529] **Challenges to production:** A party may challenge the demand for production of materials described in a deposition notice by various methods:

(a) [8:529.1] **Inadequate description:** Where the description in the deposition notice is so broad that the deponent cannot identify the documents to be produced, the deponent may serve written *objections* at least *3 days before* the deposition and may file a motion to stay the deposition and quash the notice. [CCP §2025.410(a), (c), *discussed at ¶8:508 ff.*]

(b) [8:530] **Unjustly burdensome:** Where compliance with the demand would involve an unreasonable effort and expense, the party or party-affiliated deponent may apply to the court for a protective order under CCP §2025.420 (*see ¶8:675 ff.; and ¶8:692.5 ff.* re special rules for ESI protective orders).

Alternatively, the deponent can simply *object* on these grounds at the time of the deposition.

(c) [8:531] **Not permissible discovery:** If the documents described are privileged, attorney work product,

© 2020 Thomson Reuters/The Rutter Group

or not "relevant to the subject matter," the deponent may seek a protective order; or may raise these grounds as an objection at the deposition. The examiner will then have to file a motion to compel (¶*8:787*).

[8:531.1] ***PRACTICE POINTER:*** A protective order is the only safe procedure to prevent production of documents by a *coparty* or nonparty deponent. Merely objecting at the deposition won't prevent the deponent from turning over the documents.

(4) [8:531.2] **Challenges by coparty or nonparty:** Even if the deponent does not seek to avoid production of the documents, another party or a nonparty to whom the records pertain may have standing to do so. (E.g., Former Wife sues Husband and Bank for conspiring to conceal community assets. She serves Bank with depo notice demanding production of Husband's personal financial records at depo. Husband may seek to prevent disclosure even if Bank does not.)

(a) [8:531.3] **By protective order:** Any party to the action or any person to whom the records pertain has standing to seek a protective order against disclosure of the records. [CCP §2025.420(a)-(b); *see* ¶*8:685*]

(b) [8:531.4] **By motion to quash?** CCP §§1985.3(g) and 1987.1 authorize a motion to quash or limit a "subpoena" where a party's personal records are sought from a records custodian (whether it is a party to the action or not). By their terms, those sections do not apply to depo notices; however, CCP §2025.410(c) permits an objection to the notice and a motion to quash for failure to comply with the consumer notice requirements of CCP §2025.240(b). *See* ¶*8:601 ff.*

c. [8:532] **Enforcement procedure:** The party noticing the deposition may move for an order compelling discovery from a party deponent who fails to appear or answer questions or to produce materials requested in the deposition notice, and who has not served a valid objection under §2025.410(a). [CCP §2025.450(a); *see* ¶*8:787*]

[8:532a] ***PRACTICE POINTER:*** *Consider alternative procedures discussed at* ¶*8:787.1.*

(1) [8:532.1] **"Good cause" for production:** The motion to compel must "set forth specific facts showing good cause" justifying the production for inspection of the requested document, ESI or tangible thing. [CCP §2025.450(b)(1)] ("Good cause" is discussed in connection with CCP §2031.010 et seq. inspection demands; *see* ¶*8:1495 ff.*)

(a) [8:532.2] **Effect:** The party noticing the deposition need not show "good cause" for inspection in the deposition notice. But he or she must be prepared to do so if the deponent refuses to produce the documents, ESI or things requested. This effectively limits pure "fishing expeditions."

(b) [8:532.3] **Compare—depo questions:** No showing of "good cause" is required on a motion to compel answers to *deposition questions*. (It makes no difference that the questioner was on a "fishing trip" if the question was reasonably calculated to lead to admissible evidence; *see ¶8:72.*) But production of documents, ESI or things may involve a greater intrusion than testimonial compulsion. Hence, the discovery standards are more rigid.

[8:532.4-532.9] *Reserved.*

(2) [8:532.10] **Separate statement of disputed matters:** A motion to compel (or to quash) production of documents or tangible things at a deposition must be accompanied by a separate statement setting forth the particular documents or demands at issue, the responses received, and the reasons why production should be compelled. However, a separate statement is not required if no response was provided to the requested discovery. [CRC 3.1345(a)(5), (b)]

(a) [8:532.11] **Form and content of statement:** *See detailed discussion at ¶8:1151 ff.*

(b) [8:532.12] **Compare—concise outline:** In lieu of a separate statement, the court may direct the parties to file a "concise outline" of the discovery demands and responses in dispute. [CRC 3.1345(b)(2) (amended eff. 1/1/20)—no separate statement needed "[w]hen a court has allowed the moving party to submit—in place of a separate statement—a concise outline of the discovery request and each response in dispute"; see CCP §§2030.300(b)(2) (re interrogatories), 2031.310(b)(3) (re demands for inspection, copying and testing), 2033.290(b)(2) (re requests for admissions) (all amended eff. 1/1/20)]

These outlines are designed to be shorter than separate statements, and presumably would include reasons for requested court action only once, as opposed to in connection with every demand at issue as is usually provided in a separate statement.

[8:532.13-532.14] *Reserved.*

(3) [8:532.15] **Special rules and procedures re motions to compel ESI production:** On a motion to compel production of electronically-stored information (ESI), the party objecting to or opposing the request on the ground that the requested ESI is from a source not "reasonably accessible" because of "undue burden or expense" bears the burden of

© 2020 Thomson Reuters/The Rutter Group

demonstrating the ESI is in fact not from a reasonably accessible source because of undue burden or expense. [CCP §2025.450(c)]

Upon a "good cause" showing by the demanding party, however, the court may grant the motion to compel even if the resisting party meets this burden. But the court may also set conditions for the discovery (including allocating the discovery expense); and, in any event, even if it finds the ESI is from a reasonably accessible source, the court must *limit the frequency or extent* of the ESI discovery upon determining that any of four statutorily-specified conditions exist (¶*8:692.8*). [CCP §2025.450(d)-(f)]

Cross-refer: The CCP §2025.450 provisions concerning enforcement of ESI are the mirror image of the CCP §§1985.8 and 2020.220 provisions concerning burdens and procedures on objection to subpoenas for production of ESI, explained in greater detail at ¶*8:596.65 ff.*; and of the CCP §2025.420 provisions concerning ESI discovery protective orders, explained in greater detail at ¶*8:692.5 ff.*

(4) **Sanctions**

(a) [8:533] **Monetary sanctions:** If the motion to compel is granted, a monetary sanction *must* be imposed against the deponent or the party with whom the deponent is affiliated unless the court determines the failure to comply was "substantially justified." [CCP §2025.450(g)(1)]

(b) [8:534] **Further sanctions after order compelling discovery:** If the failure to appear at deposition, answer questions or produce requested materials continues after the court orders discovery, additional sanctions may be imposed against a party deponent or the party with whom the deponent is affiliated. [CCP §2025.450(h)] (See discussion of "issue sanction," "evidence sanction" and "terminating sanction" at ¶*8:2175 ff.*)

(c) [8:534.1] **"Safe harbor" against sanctions where ESI lost or destroyed due to computer system:** Absent exceptional circumstances, sanctions may not be imposed against a party or party's attorney for failure to provide ESI that has been lost, damaged, altered or overwritten as a result of the "routine, good faith operation of an electronic information system." [CCP §§2025.450(i)(1), 2025.480(*l*)(1)]

But this provision does not alter any obligation to *preserve* discoverable information. [CCP §§2025.450(i)(2), 2025.480(*l*)(2)]

6. [8:535] **SUBPOENA to Nonparty Deponent or Business Records Custodian:** Where the witness whose deposition is sought is *not* a party (or a "party-affiliated" witness), a subpoena must be served to compel his or her attendance, testimony, or production of documents. [CCP §§2020.010(b), 2025.280(b); see *Terry v. SLICO* (2009) 175 CA4th 352, 357, 95 CR3d 900, 903 (citing text)] (CCP §1985 et seq. dealing with subpoenas generally also apply to deposition subpoenas except as modified by §2020.010 et seq.; see CCP §2020.030.)

The clerk of the court in which the action is pending issues the deposition subpoena forms in blank, already signed and sealed. Or, attorneys may prepare and sign their own deposition subpoena forms (without the court's seal). [CCP §2020.210]

Subject to certain geographical limitations (*see ¶8:621 ff.*), personal service of a deposition subpoena requires a person who is a resident of California to appear, testify and produce whatever documents or things are specified in the subpoena; and *also* to appear in any *proceedings to enforce* discovery. [CCP §2020.220(c)(3)]

The original subpoena and proof of service are retained by the subpoenaing party. They are *not* filed with the court unless relevant to a motion to compel. [CRC 3.250(a)(1)]

[8:536] ***PRACTICE POINTER:*** It is risky to rely on a nonparty witness' promise to appear voluntarily, without subpoena. If he or she fails to appear for any reason, the court may impose a monetary sanction against the party noticing the deposition to reimburse other parties for their expenses, including attorney fees, in showing up for the aborted deposition (see CCP §2025.440(a), ¶*8:832*).

This applies even as to "friendly" witnesses. You may want to explain in advance the necessity for serving the deposition subpoena; but follow up with service in any event.

One *caveat* is where the witness lives beyond the court's subpoena power (e.g., in another state). In such a case, you'd have to obtain a subpoena from a court where the witness resides, and this may be complex and costly (requiring filing of some sort of proceedings in the other state; *see ¶8:636 ff.*). Therefore, you may want to weigh the risk of the witness' breaking a promise to appear voluntarily against the costs you're likely to incur if the witness does not appear.

a. [8:537] **Three types of deposition subpoena:** A deposition subpoena may command either:

- Only the attendance and testimony of the deponent ("testimony only" subpoena);
- Only the production of business records for copying ("business records" subpoena); or
- The attendance and testimony of the deponent, *and* the pro-

© 2020 Thomson Reuters/The Rutter Group

duction of business records, other documents, electronically-stored information, and tangible things ("records and testimony" subpoena, officially called "deposition subpoena for personal appearance and production of documents and things"; formerly called a "subpoena duces tecum"). [CCP §2020.020(a)-(c); see *Terry v. SLICO*, supra, 175 CA4th at 357-358, 95 CR3d at 903 (citing text)]

(1) [8:538] **"Testimony only" subpoena:** A deposition commanding the witness to appear and testify must meet the following requirements:

- It must state the *time* and *place* where the deponent is commanded to appear;
- It must set forth a *summary* of (1) the nature of a deposition; (2) the deponent's rights and duties; and (3) the penalties for disobedience to a deposition subpoena (see CCP §2020.310(b));
- The deposition subpoena must state if the deposition is to be *video-recorded, audio-recorded, or conducted using instant digital display* (see CCP §2020.310(c)-(d)); and
- If the deponent is a corporation or other entity, both a description "with reasonable particularity" of the matters on which examination is requested, and a statement of its *duty to designate* its "most qualified" officers or employees to testify (CCP §2020.310(e); *see ¶8:473*).

FORM: Deposition Subpoena for Personal Appearance (Judicial Council form SUBP-015).

See Form 8:3 in Rivera, *Cal. Prac. Guide: Civ. Pro. Before Trial FORMS* (TRG).

[8:539] While attorneys may sign and issue their own deposition subpoenas (CCP §2020.210(a)-(b)), they *must* use this subpoena form. [CRC 1.31(b)]

(2) [8:540] **"Business records" subpoena:** A deposition subpoena may command only the production of *business* records for *copying—without attendance at a deposition*. [See CCP §2020.020(b)]

[8:540.1] **Compare—"records and testimony" subpoena:** Alternatively, business records may be obtained by use of a "records and testimony" subpoena (*discussed at ¶8:556 ff.*), requiring the custodian both to produce the records *and to attend and testify* at a deposition. But that is a more expensive and complicated procedure (*¶8:558*).

[8:540.2] **Compare—CCP §2031.010 et seq. inspection demands to party:** The "business records" subpoena procedure is designed for discovery from *nonparties* (CCP §2020.020(b)). An opposing party's records (business or otherwise) can be obtained by a CCP §2031.010 et seq.

inspection demand (¶*8:1417 ff.*). However, *it is easier to obtain discovery from a nonparty* using a "business records" subpoena than to obtain discovery from an opposing *party* under CCP §2031.010 et seq.:

— The "business records" subpoena requires production more quickly (e.g., 15 days after service or 20 days after issuance whichever is later (*see* ¶*8:545*), as opposed to 30 days for §2031.010 et seq. inspection demands).

— If the opposing party refuses to comply with a §2031.010 et seq. inspection demand, the burden is on the demanding party to file a motion to compel and show "good cause" for production. *No such showing is required to enforce a "business records" subpoena.* Moreover, the burden is usually on the person seeking to prevent disclosure to show grounds to quash or for a protective order (*see* ¶*8:597 ff.*).

(a) [8:540.3] **"Business records" only:** The Discovery Act does not define "business records," but the term includes every kind of *record maintained by* every kind of business, governmental activity, profession or occupation, whether carried on for profit or not. [See Ev.C. §§1270, 1560(a)]

As used in CCP §2020.410 et seq. (concerning business records subpoenas), "business records" means things like journals, account books, reports and the like—i.e., an item, collection or grouping of information *about* a business entity (*Urban Pac. Equities Corp. v. Sup.Ct. (Steiner & Libo)* (1997) 59 CA4th 688, 692-693, 69 CR2d 635, 638); it also includes business records in the form of *electronically-stored information* (see CCP §2020.410(a)).

Compare: It does *not* include records which are the *product* of its business. [*Urban Pac. Equities Corp. v. Sup.Ct. (Steiner & Libo),* supra, 59 CA4th at 692, 69 CR2d at 638—business records subpoena could *not* be used to obtain copy of deposition reporter's transcript, which is its *product*, not a record of its business]

1) [8:540.4] **Records outside California?** It is unclear whether service of a "business records" subpoena on a *nonparty* corporation in California compels production of its records located *outside* the state. (As noted in ¶*8:522*, *parties*, in contrast to *nonparties*, can be compelled to produce their records no matter where located.) CCP §2020.410(c) requires that the subpoena be directed to the records "custodian" (or someone authorized to certify the records). Whether "custodian" requires *actual custody* of the records is unclear. If it does, serving an officer or agent in California would not compel production of business records located elsewhere.

© 2020 Thomson Reuters/The Rutter Group

2) [8:540.5] **Limitation—records "prepared by" subpoenaed business:** Even where the subpoena describes the correct *type* of documents, it may not be enforceable where the business records sought were prepared or generated by entities *other than* the subpoenaed business. [See Ev.C. §1561(a)—records custodian must attest records were "prepared by" subpoenaed business; *Cooley v. Sup.Ct. (Greenstein)* (2006) 140 CA4th 1039, 1041, 45 CR3d 183, 184; *and ¶8:543, 8:550.2*]

3) [8:540.6] **Compare—"records and testimony" subpoena (CCP §2020.510):** The result is different where a "records and testimony" subpoena is used. That procedure extends to records in *control* of the subpoenaed party, not merely in his or her custody. [See CCP §1985(a)—witness subpoenaed to attend hearing must bring "any books, documents, electronically stored information, or other *things under the witness's control*" (emphasis added) (applicable to deposition subpoenas under CCP §2020.030)]

4) [8:540.7] **Comment:** It is unclear whether the Legislature intended this distinction between "business records" subpoenas and "records and testimony" subpoenas. But the distinction seems dictated by the language of the respective statutes. (There is no known case authority in point.)

[8:541] *Reserved.*

(b) [8:541.1] **Notice to other parties required:** Copies of the "business records" subpoena must be served on all other parties who have appeared in the action. In such cases, the copies of the subpoena serve as the notice of deposition. [CCP §2025.220(b)]

(If the other parties want copies of the subpoenaed records, they will have to make arrangements with whoever is doing the photocopying; *¶8:554.*)

Where personal records of a "consumer" (CCP §1985.3, *¶8:580 ff.*) or an employee's employment records (CCP §1985.6, *¶8:596.5 ff.*) are subpoenaed, the "deposition" (or records turnover) cannot take place until *at least 20 days after* the subpoena is "issued." [CCP §2025.270(c)] (Comment: This apparently assumes the subpoena will be promptly *served;* if service is delayed, there may not be enough time for protective orders and motions.)

(c) [8:542] **Content of "business records" subpoena:** The statutory requirements below (*¶8:543 ff.*) are best reviewed in conjunction with the Official Form Subpoena.

FORM: Deposition Subpoena for Production of Business Records (Judicial Council form SUBP-010).

See Form 8:4 in Rivera, *Cal. Prac. Guide: Civ. Pro. Before Trial FORMS* (TRG).

While attorneys may sign and issue their own deposition subpoenas (CCP §2020.210(a)-(b)), they *must* use this subpoena form. [CRC 1.31(b)]

1) [8:543] **Person to whom directed:** The subpoena must be directed to the "custodian of records" or some other person qualified to authenticate the records. [CCP §2020.410(c)]

   A nonparty's possession of records by itself does not necessarily make him or her the "custodian" of those records. The subpoena must be delivered to someone able to *attest to the authenticity and trustworthiness* of those records (as required by Ev.C. §1561, *see* ¶*8:550.2*). This is "more than simply a clerical task." [*Cooley v. Sup.Ct. (Greenstein)* (2006) 140 CA4th 1039, 1045, 45 CR3d 183, 186—error to serve subpoena on District Attorney because not "custodian" of records generated by *other* entities]

2) [8:544] **Description of records:** The business records to be produced must be designated either by:

   — "*specifically describing* each individual item"; or

   — "reasonably particularizing each *category*." [CCP §2020.410(a) (emphasis added)]

   a) [8:544a] **Items specifically described:** The subpoena must provide a "specific description" of each item. But it need *not* provide *information obtainable only from the records themselves* or from the deponent's record system, "like a policy number or the date when a consumer interacted with the witness." [CCP §2020.410(b)]

   b) [8:544b] **Form of electronically-stored information (ESI):** The subpoena must specify the form in which ESI is to be produced if the subpoenaing party desires a particular form. [CCP §2020.410(a); *see* ¶*8:1445.5 ff.*]

   c) [8:544.1] **"Reasonably particularized" categories:** The categories of documents to be produced must be "reasonably" particularized *from the standpoint of the party on whom the demand is made.* [*Calcor Space Facility, Inc. v. Sup.Ct. (Thiem Indus., Inc.)* (1997) 53 CA4th 216, 222, 61 CR2d 567, 571—CCP §2020.410

© 2020 Thomson Reuters/The Rutter Group

should *not* be used to determine whether documents exist]

[8:544.2] A description of document categories may be held *unreasonable* where it bears *no relationship to the manner in which the records are kept*, and imposes on the subpoenaed party the *burden of searching extensive files* at many locations to see what it can find to fit the categories in the demand. [*Calcor Space Facility, Inc. v. Sup.Ct. (Thiem Indus., Inc.)*, supra, 53 CA4th at 222, 61 CR2d at 571]

- [8:544.3] The categories of documents described in a business records subpoena were so broad that they in effect asked for *everything in the custodian's possession* relating to the subject of litigation. The subpoena was unduly burdensome and unenforceable. [*Calcor Space Facility, Inc. v. Sup.Ct. (Thiem Indus., Inc.)*, supra, 53 CA4th at 223, 61 CR2d at 572]

  [8:544.4] *Reserved.*

d) [8:544.5] **Improper use of "definitions" and "instructions":** An otherwise permissible description of categories in a deposition subpoena may become burdensome if combined with detailed "definitions" and "instructions" that expand and complicate the demand. [*Calcor Space Facility, Inc. v. Sup.Ct. (Thiem Indus., Inc.)*, supra, 53 CA4th at 223, 61 CR2d at 572—detailed "definitions" and "instructions" turned each of 32 document requests into a complicated "category" described in more than 6 pages; held "particularly obnoxious" and "grossly excessive"]

[8:544.6] *Compare—interrogatories:* No "preface" or "instruction" at all is permitted in a set of interrogatories. [CCP §2030.060(d); *see* ¶*8:967*]

[8:544.7-544.9] *Reserved.*

e) [8:544.10] **Preliminary discovery to determine description:** For documents held by parties, interrogatories may be used to determine the existence and categories of documents sought. For documents held by nonparties, however, a preliminary deposition may be required if they refuse to provide such information informally. *See discussion at* ¶*8:482.2.*

3) [8:545] **Time for compliance:** The subpoena must command compliance by the custodian of

records with the duties described at ¶*8:548 ff.* on a specific date—no sooner than 20 days after the subpoena's issuance, or 15 days after service, whichever is later. [CCP §2020.410(c)]

The party serving the subpoena and the custodian may, however, agree on a different compliance date. [Ev.C. §1560(b)(3)]

a) [8:545.1] **Warning where delivery to deposition officer required:** A special notice must be affixed to the subpoena where delivery to a deposition officer is required, warning against early delivery of the record. *See* ¶*8:549.2.*

4) [8:546] **Special rules for §1985.3 and §1985.6 subpoenas:** Special rules apply to subpoenas for the "personal records" of a "consumer" (CCP §1985.3) or "employment records" of an "employee" (CCP §1985.6).

- [8:546.1] The deposition subpoena *cannot be served* on the records custodian until *at least* 5 days after copies of the subpoena and a "Notice of Privacy Rights" have been served on the "consumer" or "employee" (*see* ¶*8:588 ff., 8:596.15 ff.*).
- [8:546.2] When served on the records custodian, the deposition subpoena must be accompanied by either a written release from the "consumer" or "employee" or proof that he or she has been served with copies of the subpoena and "Notice of Privacy Rights" (*see* ¶*8:593 ff., 8:596.35 ff.*). [CCP §2020.410(d)]

[8:546.3] *Cross-refer:*

— CCP §1985.3 requirements are discussed in detail at ¶*8:580 ff.*

— CCP §1985.6 requirements are discussed at ¶*8:596.5 ff.*

5) [8:547] **Designation of person responsible for copying—deposition officer OR subpoenaing attorney:** The subpoenaing attorney may *either* engage a registered professional photocopier (see Bus. & Prof.C. §22450 et seq.), *or may assume responsibility for the copying.* [CCP §2020.420; Ev.C. §1560(e)]

[8:547.1] **Professional photocopier:** In the former case, the professional photocopier must be named in the "Deposition Officer" box in the subpoena, and either item "1.a." or "1.b." should be checked.

Limitation: The officer must *not* be a relative or employee of any attorney and must have no financial

© 2020 Thomson Reuters/The Rutter Group

interest in the lawsuit. Any objection to the officer's qualifications is waived unless raised prior to the time set for production of the documents; or as soon thereafter as could be discovered with reasonable diligence. [CCP §2020.420]

[8:547.2] **Subpoenaing attorney:** If the subpoenaing attorney wishes to assume responsibility for the inspection and copying, he or she may do so by *leaving the "Deposition Officer" blank,* and checking item "1.c." on the Deposition Subpoena form:

"1. You are ordered to produce the business records described in Item 3 as follows:

. . .

c. [X] by making the original business records described in Item 3 available for inspection at your business address by the attorney's representative and permitting copying at your business address under reasonable conditions during normal business hours."

[8:547.3-547.4] *Reserved.*

6) [8:547.5] **No "good cause" affidavit required:** A subpoena for the production of business records need *not* be accompanied by an affidavit or declaration showing good cause for production of the records. [CCP §2020.410(c)]

(d) [8:548] **Duties of custodian of records:** The duties of the person served with a "business records" subpoena depend on what the subpoena requires:

1) [8:549] **Where custodian directed to mail copies to professional photocopier:** If item "1.a." on the "business records" subpoena form is checked, the custodian must mail to the deposition officer (professional photocopier):

- A "true, legible and durable copy" of the business records; and
- An affidavit *authenticating* the copies and the records (see Ev.C. §1561).

These documents must be mailed in a *sealed envelope*, with the records enclosed in an inner envelope marked with the name and number of the lawsuit, the custodian's name, and the date of subpoena written thereon (see Ev.C. §1560(c)). [CCP §2020.430(b)]

a) [8:549.1] **Early delivery prohibited:** To allow time for protective orders and motions, the custodian "shall not" deliver the records involved before the time specified in the subpoena . . . unless the parties stipulate otherwise. (If "personal records . . . of a consumer" are involved (*see* ¶*8:580 ff.*), the "consumer" must join the stipulation.) [CCP §2020.430(d)]

b) [8:549.2] **Special warning required:** Where the subpoena requires delivery to a *deposition officer*, the following legend must appear in *boldface type* immediately following the date and time specified for production:

— **"Do not release the requested records to the deposition officer prior to the date and time stated above."** [CCP §2020.430(d)]

c) [8:549.3] **Comment:** None of this is required, however, where the *subpoenaing attorney assumes responsibility* for copying the records (so that no delivery to a "deposition officer" is involved); *see* ¶*8:550.1*. But the subpoenaing attorney must still notify all other parties by serving copies of the business records subpoena (CCP §2025.220(b); *see* ¶*8:541.1*), allowing time for protective orders and motions.

2) [8:550] **Where custodian required to deliver copies to professional photocopier at custodian's address:** If item "1.b." on the "business records" subpoena form is checked, the custodian may either:

- Allow the deposition officer *to photocopy* the records at the custodian's office; *or*
- Allow the deposition officer to *pick up* at the custodian's office photocopies prepared by the custodian upon paying for the reasonable costs thereof (see Ev.C. §1563). [CCP §2020.430(c)]

The custodian must also furnish an *affidavit authenticating* the records (Ev.C. §1561). [CCP §2020.430(a)(2); *see* ¶*8:550.2*]

3) [8:550.1] **Where subpoenaing attorney assumes responsibility for inspection and copying:** As an alternative to the procedures described above (¶*8:550*), the subpoenaing attorney may direct the custodian to make the records available for inspection and copying by the attorney or the attorney's representative at the custodian's business address during normal business hours. [Ev.C. §1560(e); CCP §2020.430(c)(1)] (If given at least 5 days' prior notice, the custodian must designate a time period of at least 6 hours on a date certain for this purpose.)

© 2020 Thomson Reuters/The Rutter Group

Where this method is utilized, *two separate affidavits* (declarations) must be obtained:

a) [8:550.2] **Custodian's affidavit:** The custodian must furnish an affidavit stating in substance that:

- affiant is the duly authorized custodian of the records (or other qualified witness and has authority to certify the records);
- the records were prepared by personnel of the business in the ordinary course of business at or near the time of the events recorded;
- the records were delivered to the attorney or the attorney's representative for copying pursuant to Ev.C. §1560(e);
- the identity of the records; and
- a description of the mode of preparation of the records. [Ev.C. §1561(a)]

FORM: Declaration of Custodian of Records, *see Form 8:5* in Rivera, *Cal. Prac. Guide: Civ. Pro. Before Trial FORMS* (TRG).

1/ [8:550.2a] **Impact of affidavit on admissibility of records at trial:** *See discussion at ¶8:555 ff.*

☞ [8:550.2b] ***PRACTICE POINTER:*** Consider including a cover letter to the records custodian with the subpoena, explaining the Ev.C. §1561 requirements and the importance of completing the affidavit truthfully and accurately.

b) [8:550.3] **Subpoenaing attorney's affidavit:** In addition to the custodian's affidavit, copies of the records must be accompanied by an affidavit from the subpoenaing attorney stating these are true copies of all records delivered to him or her for copying. [Ev.C. §1561(c)]

FORM: Declaration of Attorney Issuing Subpoena, *see Form 8:6* in Rivera, *Cal. Prac. Guide: Civ. Pro. Before Trial FORMS* (TRG).

(e) [8:551] **Custodian's fee and costs:** The business records custodian does not have to attend a deposition and therefore is *not* entitled to the witness and mileage fees payable to deponents. [CCP §2020.230(b); *see ¶8:579*]

Instead, the following costs and fees are payable to the custodian:

1) [8:552] **If custodian furnishes copies:** If the custodian furnishes copies of the subpoenaed records, the custodian is entitled to be paid the "reasonable costs" incurred. Payment may be demanded simultaneously with delivery of the records. [CCP §2020.430(c)(2); Ev.C. §1563(b)(2)]

   a) [8:552.1] **"Reasonable costs":** "Reasonable costs" includes, but is *not limited* to, the following:
      — the custodian's clerical expense in locating the records and making them available (billed at a maximum rate of $24 per hour per person, computed at $6 per quarter hour or fraction thereof);
      — actual costs charged by a third party for retrieving them and returning them to storage;
      — copying costs (computed at $.10 per page; $.20 from microfilm); and
      — actual postal charges. [Ev.C. §1563(b)(1)]

   b) [8:552.2] **Remedy for excess charges:** The subpoenaing party can petition the court to recover excess charges paid to obtain such records. The court can award costs and fees against the custodian if it finds "bad faith" (and, conversely, against the subpoenaing party if the charges are found *not* excessive). [Ev.C. §1563(b)(4)]

2) [8:553] **If custodian delivers records to attorney for copying:** Where records are delivered to the subpoenaing attorney or attorney's representative for copying at the custodian's place of business, the custodian must be paid:

   • a fee not to exceed $15 "for complying with the subpoena"; plus

   • any sums actually paid by the custodian to a third person (e.g., storage company) for retrieval and return of records held offsite or on microfilm. [CCP §2020.230(b); Ev.C. §1563(b)(6)]

(f) [8:554] **Other parties must be allowed to purchase copies:** If the copies of the business records are delivered to a professional photocopier, it is that officer's responsibility to furnish the records to the party at whose instance the deposition subpoena was served; and to *all other parties* who then or thereafter *notify* the officer that they desire to purchase a copy of those records. [CCP §2020.440]

© 2020 Thomson Reuters/The Rutter Group

Where (as will frequently be the case), the *subpoenaing attorney* has assumed responsibility for inspecting and copying the records: "It shall be the responsibility of the attorney's representative to deliver any copy of the records as directed in the subpoena." [Ev.C. §1560(e)]

1) [8:554.1] **Comment:** Unfortunately, the Judicial Council form SUBP-010 subpoena provides no "directions" as to delivery of copies. Presumably, therefore, the attorney is under the same duties as the deposition officer (professional photocopier) to notify opposing parties and allow them to purchase copies upon request. [See CCP §2020.440]

2) [8:554.2] **Caution—no "shortcuts":** Using a deposition subpoena to obtain business records without giving opposing counsel the required notice or allowing them to obtain copies thereof, would appear to be a "misuse" of the discovery process (CCP §2023.010(b)). Appropriate sanctions may be imposed against the subpoenaing party and counsel. It may also constitute *unethical conduct* by such counsel.

(g) [8:555] **Admissibility at trial:** Copies of business records obtained in accordance with this procedure may be used at trial in lieu of the originals; and the custodian's (or attorney's) affidavit (¶*8:550.2 ff.*) may authenticate both the records and the copies. [CCP §2020.430(f); Ev.C. §§1560-1562; see *People v. Blagg* (1968) 267 CA2d 598, 609-610, 73 CR 93, 101]

However, the records involved (whether copies or originals) are not necessarily admissible as evidence unless they qualify as "business records" under the Ev.C. §1271 hearsay exception. This requires, among other things, that the source of information, method and time of preparation of the record "were such as to indicate its trustworthiness." [Ev.C. §1271(d)]

[8:555.1] ***PRACTICE POINTER:*** If you intend to rely on a records custodian's affidavit for a deposition subpoena under Ev.C. §1560 to establish admissibility at trial, make sure the custodian also attests to the manner and mode of preparation or the sources of information in the record.

Cross-refer: For a detailed discussion of the admissibility of business records, see Wegner, Fairbank, Epstein & Chernow, *Cal. Prac. Guide: Civil Trials & Evidence* (TRG), Ch. 8D.

(3) [8:556] **"Records and testimony" subpoena:** The deponent may be commanded to attend and testify *and* to produce described business records, documents, electronically-

© 2020 Thomson Reuters/The Rutter Group

stored information, and/or tangible things at his or her deposition. [CCP §2020.510(a)]

A mandatory official form subpoena is provided for this purpose. (It is *not* the same form used to compel personal attendance at the deposition.)

FORM: Deposition Subpoena for Personal Appearance and Production of Documents and Things (Judicial Council form SUBP-020).

See Form 8:7 in Rivera, *Cal. Prac. Guide: Civ. Pro. Before Trial FORMS* (TRG).

[8:557] **Compare—"business records" subpoena:** Copies of *business records* can also be obtained by use of a "business records" subpoena (¶*8:540*). But this is available only for *business* records. And, it will not provide the opportunity to question the records custodian. [CCP §2020.410(a), ¶*8:540*]

[8:557.1] **Compare—records located outside California:** A "records and testimony" subpoena *apparently* compels production of records under the deponent's *control*; *see* ¶*8:540.4*.

[8:557.2] **Compare—subpoena duces tecum for trial:** An entirely different form is used to obtain production of documents and things at trial.

FORM: Civil Subpoena (Duces Tecum) for Personal Appearance and Production of Documents and Things at Trial or Hearing and Declaration (Judicial Council form SUBP-002) (adopted for *mandatory* use).

[8:558] **PROCEDURE:** This is probably the most complicated discovery procedure. Here is a checklist of the various steps that must be taken:

- *Prepare subpoena. See* ¶*8:560.*
- *Serve subpoena. See* ¶*8:568.*
- *Pay witness fees. See* ¶*8:572.*
- *Serve notice of deposition* (with copy of subpoena attached). *See* ¶*8:565.*
- *Additional requirements where "personal records" of a "consumer" are subpoenaed:*
  — *Serve notice of rights on consumer. See* ¶*8:590.*
  — *Furnish custodian with proof of service. See* ¶*8:593.*

(a) [8:559] **No "good cause" affidavit required:** The Discovery Act provides that a records and testimony subpoena "need not be accompanied by an affidavit or declaration showing good cause for the production." [CCP §2020.510(b); see *Terry v. SLICO* (2009) 175 CA4th 352, 359, 95 CR3d 900, 904 (citing text)—CCP §2020.510(b) controls over contrary provisions in CCP

§§1985(b) & 1987.5 (*requiring* affidavits showing good cause for production)]

(b) [8:560] **Prepare subpoena:** Under the Discovery Act, the subpoenaing party can simply check and fill in the appropriate boxes on the Judicial Council form Deposition Subpoena (SUBP-020) (¶*8:556*). (Use of this form is mandatory.)

1) [8:560.1] **Notice provisions:** To start off with, it must include the same notice and requirements as for a "testimony only" subpoena (CCP §2020.310, ¶*8:538*)—all of which are covered in the Judicial Council form.

2) [8:561] **Description of materials to be produced:** The subpoena must contain either a specific description of each individual item to be produced or a *"reasonably particularizing"* of *each category* of item (*see* ¶*8:561.1*). And, if testing or sampling of the materials is being sought, the subpoena must so state. [CCP §2020.510(a)(2)-(3)]

Additionally, as with a "business records" subpoena (¶*8:544b*), if ESI is sought, the "records and testimony" subpoena must specify the *form* in which the ESI is to be produced when the subpoenaing party desires a particular form. [CCP §2020.510(a)(4); *see* ¶*8:1445.5 ff.*]

a) [8:561.1] **"Reasonably particularizing" categories:** The Discovery Act applies the same description standard to depo subpoenas as to CCP §2031.010 et seq. demands (¶*8:1439*) and deposition notices (¶*8:523*): i.e., the records sought may either be described individually or "*by reasonably particularizing* each category." [CCP §2020.510(a)(2) (emphasis added)]

The categories must be "reasonably" particularized *from the standpoint of the party on whom the demand is made*. [*Calcor Space Facility, Inc. v. Sup.Ct. (Thiem Indus., Inc.)* (1997) 53 CA4th 216, 222, 61 CR2d 567, 571; *see discussion at* ¶*8:544.1 ff.*]

- [8:561.2] If the records are so extensive that a request for "all documents" on a broad and complicated subject would be improper, a subpoena describing documents by categories that *bear no relationship to the manner in which the documents are kept* may not meet the "reasonable particularity" standard. Such a request might require the subpoenaed party to determine (at risk of sanctions) which of its extensive records fit a demand that asks for everything in its possession relating to a specific topic. [See *Calcor Space Facility, Inc. v. Sup.Ct. (Thiem Indus., Inc.),* supra, 53 CA4th at 222, 61 CR2d at 571; *and* ¶*8:544.2*]

b) [8:562] **Compare—subpoena duces tecum at trial:** CCP §1985(b), still applicable to civil trial subpoenas, requires description of the "*exact matters or things desired to be produced*" (emphasis added). And, cases interpret this requirement literally (see *Flora Crane Service, Inc. v. Sup.Ct.* (1965) 234 CA2d 767, 785-787, 45 CR 79, 89-90—condemning "omnibus descriptions" and "blanket" subpoenas). However, deposition subpoenas are now governed by the more flexible standard above (¶*8:561 ff.*).

[8:563] *Reserved.*

[8:564] ***PRACTICE POINTER:*** Usually, it is not difficult to describe accurately the documents you are seeking: e.g., telephone records relating to a specific telephone number; medical records relating to a particular patient; correspondence relating to a *specific transaction* or with a *specific person.*

However, sometimes you simply don't know enough about what records the nonparty witness has to describe them accurately. In such cases, the solution usually is to *ask the witness,* or *find out from other parties* to the action (through interrogatories, if necessary), what records the nonparty witness is supposed to have. If the witness refuses to cooperate, it may be necessary to *depose* the witness in order to determine the existence of the documents and a sufficient description for a subpoena. *See discussion at* ¶*8:482.2.*

(c) [8:565] **Attach subpoena copy to notice of deposition:** A copy of the subpoena (describing the materials to be produced at the deposition) must be attached to the notice of deposition. [CCP §§1987.5, 2025.240(c); *and see* ¶*8:488*]

(d) [8:566] **Added requirements where "personal records" of "consumer" subpoenaed (CCP §1985.3):** Service of a deposition subpoena for the "personal records" of a "consumer" (CCP §1985.3, ¶*8:581*) must be accompanied by *either:*

© 2020 Thomson Reuters/The Rutter Group

— the "consumer's" written release of the records, or
— proof of service of a special notice to the "consumer" that the records are being subpoenaed. (The purpose is to give the "consumer" a chance to seek appropriate orders protecting the privacy of such records.) [CCP §§2020.510(c), 1985.3(e), *discussed at* ¶*8:580 ff.*]

1) [8:567] **Similar requirements for "employment records":** The same notice and proof of service requirements apply where the business records described in the subpoena are employment records pertaining to an employee. [CCP §2020.510(d)]

FORM: Notice to Consumer or Employee and Objection (Judicial Council form SUBP-025).

See Form 8:8 in Rivera, *Cal. Prac. Guide Civ. Pro. Before Trial FORMS* (TRG).

b. [8:568] **Service of subpoena:** The second step is to serve the subpoena on the deponent or records custodian. Personal service is required, *not* service by mail. [CCP §2020.220(b)-(c)]

Service on a business entity may be made by delivering the subpoena to any officer, director *or custodian of records* (or any agent or employee authorized to accept service). [CCP §2020.220(b)(2)]

Service on a *law enforcement officer* may be made by *either* serving the officer personally or delivering two copies to his or her immediate supervisor (or an agent designated by the supervisor to receive service). [See Gov.C. §68097.1]

(1) [8:568a] **Who may serve:** *Any* person may serve a subpoena. [CCP §1987(a)]

Compare—service of process: Unlike a subpoena, a summons may be served only by a person at least 18 years old and not a party to the action. [CCP §414.10; *see* ¶*4:110*]

➪ [8:568b] ***PRACTICE POINTER:*** Persons under age 18 or who are parties to the action may serve a deposition subpoena. But their declarations of service and/or testimony might be given less weight if the deponent denies service.

[8:568c-568e] *Reserved.*

(2) [8:568f] **Service in gated communities:** Guards at gated communities must allow the following persons access for the purpose of serving a subpoena, upon proper identification: a county sheriff or marshal, licensed process servers and licensed private investigators. The same access must be provided to investigators employed by: an office of the Attorney General, a county counsel, a city attorney, a district attorney or a public defender. [CCP §415.21; *see* ¶*4:189*]

(3) [8:568.1] **Where served:** If the deponent is a California resident, he or she can be served anywhere in the state. [CCP §1989]

However, CCP §2025.250 sets geographic limits on where a deposition may be *taken* (*see ¶8:621*), the effect of which is to limit the distance persons must travel in response to the subpoena.

(4) [8:568.2] **When served:** Where personal appearance is required (i.e., "testimony only" or "records and testimony" subpoenas), service must be effected a "*reasonable time*" before the deposition. [CCP §2020.220(a)]

Compare: A "business records" subpoena must be served *at least 15 days* before the date set for production of the records. [CCP §2020.410(c); *¶8:545*]

(a) [8:569] **"Reasonable time":** The subpoena must be served "a sufficient time in advance of the deposition to provide the deponent a *reasonable opportunity* to locate and produce any designated business records, documents, electronically stored information, and tangible things . . . and . . . a *reasonable time* to travel to the place of deposition." [CCP §2020.220(a) (emphasis added)]

⇨ [8:570] ***PRACTICE POINTER:*** Although there is no fixed minimum number of days required by statute, try to serve a deposition subpoena *at least 10 days* before the deposition (the same length of time as required for the notice of deposition). This usually should foreclose objections and motions to quash for inadequate time to prepare and travel.

(b) [8:571] **Special time requirements where "personal records" of "consumer" subpoenaed (CCP §1985.3):** Special rules apply to issuance and service of subpoenas requiring production of "personal records" of a "consumer." [CCP §1985.3; *¶8:581 ff.*]

1) [8:571.1] **Also applicable to "employment records" (CCP §1985.6):** *See discussion at ¶8:567.*

[8:571.2-571.4] *Reserved.*

(c) [8:571.5] **Five days' notice required to subpoena "journalist's" records:** Important constitutional rights are implicated when a "journalist" (i.e., a news reporter, broadcaster, publisher or editor; see CCP §1986.1(d)) who is not a party to the action is subpoenaed to testify in discovery proceedings (or at trial). The First Amendment of the U.S. Constitution protects investigative reporting; and the California Constitution immunizes such persons against punishment for contempt for refusing to disclose their confidential sources and unpublished information. *See discussion at ¶8:340 ff.*

© 2020 Thomson Reuters/The Rutter Group

Accordingly, absent "circumstances that pose a clear and substantial threat to the integrity of the criminal investigation or present an imminent risk of death or serious bodily harm," a journalist subpoenaed in a civil or criminal proceeding must be given *at least five days' notice* by the party issuing the subpoena that his or her appearance will be required. [CCP §1986.1(b)(1)] (The apparent purpose is to assure an opportunity to seek a protective order.)

Likewise, and subject to the same exception, a party issuing a subpoena to a third party that seeks a journalist's records must provide *at least five days' advance notice* to the journalist and the publisher or station operations manager that employs or contracts with the journalist. That notice must include, "at a minimum," an explanation why the records being sought will be of "material assistance" to the party seeking them and why other sources of information are not sufficient to avoid the need for the subpoena. [CCP §1986.1(b)(2)]

c. [8:572] **Payment of witness fees:** The deposing party *must* pay a deponent who is required to appear for deposition the same witness fees and mileage payable to witnesses who appear in court. Such payment must be made *whether or not* requested by the deponent. [CCP §2020.230]

[8:573] **Compare—trial witnesses:** Under CCP §1987(a), fees are payable only *if demanded* by the witness *at time of service* of the subpoena. But §2020.230(a) supersedes this as to depositions.

(1) [8:574] **When payment due:** Payment can be made (at the option of the subpoenaing party) *either* at the time the subpoena is served or at the time of the deposition. [CCP §§2020.230, 1986.5]

(2) [8:575] **Amount:** The amount payable currently is $35 per day plus $.20 per mile to and from the place of deposition. [CCP §2020.230(a); Gov.C. §68093]

(3) [8:576] **Special rules for law enforcement officers:** Where a "peace officer" (police, sheriff, highway patrol, etc.) is sought to be deposed on matters investigated in the course of his or her official duties, the party requesting the subpoena must reimburse the public entity for the officer's salary and travel expenses; and must tender to the person accepting the subpoena $275 for each day the officer's presence is required. [See Gov.C. §68097.2(b); *Nick v. Department of Motor Vehicles* (1993) 12 CA4th 1407, 1415, 16 CR2d 305, 309—subpoena properly refused absent tender of required fee]

The court may relieve indigent parties of such payments. [Gov.C. §68097.55]

(a) [8:577] **Not applicable where government party to action:** No such payment is required where the police officer's employer is a *party* to the action (e.g., P sues City for personal injuries arising out of collision with police car). In such cases, the police officer receives the same witness fee and mileage payable to other deponents, and *not* the special compensation under Gov.C. §68097.2. [*Patterson v. Sharp* (1967) 253 CA2d 838, 841, 61 CR 517, 519; *Fox v. State Personnel Bd.* (1996) 49 CA4th 1034, 1042-1043, 57 CR2d 279, 283-284]

(4) [8:578] **Special rules for expert trial witnesses under CCP §2034.010 et seq.:** No deposition subpoena is required, and hence no statutory witness fee need be paid, to depose an *employed or retained expert designated as a trial witness* by the opposing party under CCP §2034.460(a). The designating party must produce such expert for deposition upon notice. [CCP §2034.460(a), ¶*8:1688*]

But the deposing party must pay an *expert witness fee:* i.e., the expert's "reasonable and customary" fees for the time spent in deposition. The anticipated expert witness fee must be tendered *with the deposition notice* or at commencement of the deposition. [CCP §§2034.430(b), 2034.450(a); *see* ¶*8:1697 ff.*; see also *True v. Shank* (2000) 81 CA4th 1250, 1256, 97 CR2d 462, 466 (citing text)]

(5) [8:579] **No witness fee or mileage on "business records" subpoena:** A person served with a "business records" subpoena (¶*8:540*) is not obliged to attend a deposition; therefore, no mileage or witness fee is payable. [CCP §§2020.230(b), 1986.5]

(The custodian is entitled, however, to "reasonable costs" for furnishing copies; or a $15 fee for delivering the records to the subpoenaing attorney for copying. See Ev.C. §1563(b), *discussed at* ¶*8:552 ff.*)

d. [8:580] **Additional requirements for subpoenaing "personal records" of "consumer" or employee:** Special notice and procedures are required for production of the "personal records" of a "consumer" or employee, to protect that person's *right of privacy.* The purpose is to give that person the opportunity to seek a court order to quash or limit the subpoena before the records are disclosed. [See CCP §§1985.3(e), 1985.6(e)]

These requirements apply where production is sought from a *nonparty.* By contrast, personal records held by an *opposing party* can be obtained without subpoena by a CCP §2031.010 inspection demand (¶*8:1421 ff.*). (However, even under CCP §2031.010, privacy rights are protectible; *see* ¶*8:293.*)

(1) [8:581] **Records subject to requirements:** The additional requirements below (¶*8:586 ff.*) apply whenever "personal records" of a "consumer" are subpoenaed from a nonparty custodian. [CCP §1985.3]

© 2020 Thomson Reuters/The Rutter Group

The quoted phrases have special statutory meanings:

(a) [8:582] **"Personal records":** This term means records or electronic data pertaining to a "consumer" (¶*8:584*) *maintained* either by a:

- Physician;
- Psychotherapist (as defined in Ev.C. §1010);
- Dentist;
- Ophthalmologist or optometrist;
- Chiropractor;
- Physical therapist;
- Acupuncturist;
- Podiatrist;
- Hospital, medical center, clinic, radiology or MRI center, clinical or diagnosis laboratory;
- Pharmacy or pharmacist;
- Attorney;
- Accountant;
- Bank, savings and loan association;
- Credit union or member of Federal Credit System;
- Securities brokerage;
- Mortgage loan broker;
- Escrow agent;
- Private or public school or community college;
- Title company or insurance company;
- Trust company;
- Telephone company; or
- Veterinarian or veterinary hospital or clinic. [See CCP §1985.3(a)(1)]

1) [8:583] **Includes records held for safekeeping:** The term "personal records" includes not only the custodian's own records pertaining to its dealings with the "consumer," but also to documents and records held for safekeeping on behalf of the "consumer." [*Sasson v. Katash* (1983) 146 CA3d 119, 124, 194 CR 46, 48—lease held by Bank in safekeeping for Landlord]

(b) [8:584] **"Consumer":** This term means basically any *noncorporate* party; i.e., an individual, partnership of 5 or fewer persons, association or trust. [CCP §1985.3(a)(2)]

(c) [8:585] **Also applies to "personal information" in government files:** The same subpoena and notice requirements below (¶*8:586 ff.*) are also required where "personal information" is subpoenaed from government files. (This applies, however, only where the "consumer" is a *natural person*.) [CCP §1985.4]

"Personal information" includes information that identifies or describes an individual (e.g., name, address, phone number, social security number, physical description, etc.); or his or her education, financial matters, and medical or employment history. It also includes *statements made by or attributed to* the individual. [Civ.C. §1798.3; see *Jennifer M. v. Redwood Women's Health Ctr.* (2001) 88 CA4th 81, 89, 105 CR2d 544, 549-550—§1798.3 not applicable to records of *private* entity]

(2) [8:586] **Special procedural requirements:** Several special rules apply to deposition subpoenas seeking production of such records:

[8:587] *Reserved.*

(a) [8:588] **Documents to be served on "consumer" or employee:** CCP §1985.3(b) requires that the following documents be served on the person to whom the records relate (unless the subpoenaing party is the consumer and is the only subject of the subpoenaed records; see CCP §§1985.3(*l*), 2025.240(b)):

- [8:588.1] **Copy of subpoena:** A copy of the deposition subpoena and affidavit, if any, supporting its issuance;
- [8:589] **"Notice of privacy rights":** The person to whom the records pertain must be notified that:
  - — Records about him or her are being sought from the records custodian named in the subpoena;
  - — If the "consumer" objects to the records custodian furnishing such records, he or she must file papers with the court prior to the date set for production of the documents (*see* ¶*8:601 ff.*) except that a *nonparty* "consumer" may instead serve *written* objections by that date on the records custodian, the deposition officer and the party requesting the records (*see* ¶*8:603 ff.*); and
  - — If not already represented by counsel, legal advice should be sought about protecting his or her right to privacy. [CCP §1985.3(e)]

  FORM: Notice to Consumer or Employee and Objection (Judicial Council form SUBP-025).

  See Form 8:8 in Rivera, *Cal. Prac. Guide: Civ. Pro. Before Trial FORMS* (TRG).

© 2020 Thomson Reuters/The Rutter Group

[8:589.1] **Alternative method for parties:** If the "consumer" is a party to the action, the separate "Notice of Privacy Rights" can be dispensed with. The notice elements (¶*8:589*) may be included in the "Notice of Deposition" served on the "consumer." [CCP §1985.3(e); *Inabnit v. Berkson* (1988) 199 CA3d 1230, 1236, 245 CR 525, 529]

- [8:589.2] **Proof of Service:** A proof of service showing the documents (¶*8:588 ff.*) were served on the "consumer" (party or nonparty) either in person or by mail. [CCP §1985.3(b)] (A proof of service form is on page 2 of the Judicial Council form SUBP-025 Notice to Consumer, ¶*8:589.*)

1) [8:589.3] **Not filed with court:** The documents (¶*8:588 ff.*) are not filed with the court unless they become relevant on a motion to compel. [See CRC 3.250(a)(4)]

2) [8:590] **How served:** If the "consumer" is already a party to the action, service may be made upon his or her attorney of record. [CCP §1985.3(b)(1)] (For parties in pro per, see CCP §1011(b).)

   Otherwise, the documents must be served on the "consumer" either:

   - *personally;*
   - "*or* at his or her *last known address*," suggesting they can be left with someone else [but the matter is unclear];
   - "or in accordance with [CCP §§1010 ff.]," which includes service *by mail* (CCP §1012). [CCP §1985.3(b)(1) (emphasis added)]

   (Special rules apply where the "consumer" is a *minor;* see CCP §1985.3(b)(1).)

3) [8:590.1] **When served; 10-day/5-day rules:** Service must be completed:

   - at least 10 days before the date set for production of the records; *and*
   - at least 5 days *before service on the records custodian.* [CCP §1985.3(b)(2), (3)]

   Effect of time for service on records custodian: As a practical matter, this means the depo subpoena and privacy notice must be served on the consumer *at least 20 days* before the date set for production because the depo subpoena must be served on the records custodian *at least 15 days* before that date (CCP §2020.410(c); *see* ¶*8:545*).

[8:590.2] *Reserved.*

a) [8:590.3] **Extended for service by mail, Express Mail, fax or electronically:** If the documents are served *by mail* (*see ¶8:590*), these time limits are extended under CCP §1013(a); e.g., if the place of mailing and the address are both in California, they must be served at least 15 calendar days before the deposition and 10 days before service on the records custodian. [CCP §1985.3(b)(2), (3)]

The extension is only 2 *court days* for notices served by *express mail* or other method providing for *overnight delivery*, by *fax* (allowed only where so agreed to in writing), or by *electronic transmission* or notification (allowed only where agreed to or required by the court). [See CCP §§1010.6, 1013; CRC 2.250-2.259; *see ¶9:87 ff.*]

(The extensions provided by §1013 apply to any method of discovery; see CCP §2016.050.)

b) [8:590.4] **Orders shortening time available:** The subpoenaing party is "entitled" to an order shortening time or waiving the notice requirement altogether "upon good cause shown and provided that the rights of witnesses and consumers are preserved." [CCP §1985.3(h)]

[8:590.5] **Comment:** The term "entitled" does *not* mean that such orders are automatic. The court must determine whether "good cause" and "due diligence" have been shown.

4) [8:590.6] **Exception—records with identifying information redacted:** The notice requirements of CCP §1985.3(b) do not apply where a records custodian is required to delete all information that would identify the consumer whose records are sought. [CCP §1985.3(i); see *Snibbe v. Sup.Ct. (Gilbert)* (2014) 224 CA4th 184, 197, 168 CR3d 548, 559—notice to patients not required prior to disclosure of redacted postoperative orders]

(b) [8:591] **Documents to be served on records custodian:** Finally, the following must be served on the custodian of the records:

1) [8:592] **Deposition subpoena:** First of all, CCP §1985.3 refers only to a "subpoena duces tecum." But it applies as well to deposition subpoenas (see CCP §2020.030).

The deposition subpoena may be either a "business records" subpoena (CCP §§2020.410 ff.) or a "records and testimony" subpoena (CCP §2020.510).

© 2020 Thomson Reuters/The Rutter Group

a) [8:592.1] **Time for service:** The deposition subpoena (whether for records only or for records and testimony) must be served in sufficient time to allow the witness a "reasonable time" to locate and produce the records or copies thereof. "Reasonable time" means the date set for production may be no sooner than *15 days after the subpoena was served* or 20 days after it was issued, whichever is later. [CCP §1985.3(d) (incorporating CCP §2020.410(c) time limit; ¶*8:545*); see *Rosenfeld v. Abraham Joshua Heschel Day School, Inc.* (2014) 226 CA4th 886, 903, 172 CR3d 465, 479-480 (citing text)]

b) [8:592.2] **Prior service on "consumer" required:** The deposition subpoena may not be served on the records custodian until *at least 5 days after* the "consumer" was served with a copy of the subpoena and notice of privacy rights (*see* ¶*8:588*). [CCP §1985.3(b)(3)]

Comment: Those documents will have to be served on the "consumer" at least *20 days* before the date set for production in order to accommodate the time allowed for service on the records custodian (*see* ¶*8:590.1*).

2) [8:593] **Proof that consumer notified:** Along with the deposition subpoena, the subpoenaing party must serve the records custodian with *either:*

- [8:593.1] **Written release:** A *written release* of the records signed by the "consumer" or his or her attorney of record. (If signed by an attorney, the custodian may presume the attorney has authority from the "consumer" and that any objection to release of the records is waived.) [CCP §§1985.3(c), 2020.410(d)]
- [8:593.2] **Proof of service:** More commonly, *proof of service* on the "consumer" or his or her attorney of record of a copy of the depo subpoena and notice of privacy rights, described above (¶*8:590*). [CCP §§1985.3(c), 2020.410(d)]
- [8:593.3] **Exception—telephone records:** Proof of service is *not* sufficient to obtain telephone company records pertaining to a customer. A consent to release *signed by the customer* (not an attorney) is required. [CCP §1985.3(f); Pub.Util.C. §2891]

[8:593.4] The release or proof of service on the "consumer" must *accompany* the depo subpoena served on the records custodian. [CCP §2020.410(d)—business records subpoena; CCP §2020.510(c)—records and testimony subpoena]

[8:593.5-593.9] *Reserved.*

(3) [8:593.10] **Procedure for "consumer" to object:** The "consumer" may object to production of the subpoenaed records by either filing a *motion to quash* the subpoena, or simply *serving written objections* on the requesting party, the proposed deponent and the deposition officer (*see ¶8:601 ff.*).

(4) [8:594] **Effect of noncompliance:** Failure to comply with any of the foregoing requirements *by itself* invalidates the service, so that the custodian is under no duty to produce the records sought by the subpoena. [CCP §1985.3(k)]

Moreover, even if the custodian voluntarily produces the records, it is ground for *objection* to admission of such records by the person whose records were subpoenaed. [*Sasson v. Katash* (1983) 146 CA3d 119, 125, 194 CR 46, 49]

(a) [8:595] **Compare—certain defects may be excused:** Minor defects in the documents *served on the "consumer"* (not the records custodian) may be cured for "good cause" shown. As long as rights of the records custodian and the consumer are preserved, a subpoenaing party who has acted with "due diligence" is *entitled* to an order waiving defects in such documents. [See CCP §1985.3(h)]

(5) [8:596] **Exception for governmental entities:** The foregoing requirements do not apply to state or local agencies, or to certain other public entities in specified adjudicative proceedings, or to certain proceedings under the Labor Code. [See CCP §1985.3(a)(3) & (j)]

- [8:596.1] Despite its broad language, CCP §1985.3(a)(3) has been interpreted to exempt state and local governments *only* when obtaining information from financial institutions concerning their customers (for which other privacy protection already exists). Otherwise, state and local governments must comply with §1985.3 in civil litigation, the same as other litigants. [*Lantz v. Sup.Ct. (County of Kern)* (1994) 28 CA4th 1839, 1852, 34 CR2d 358, 365-366 (disapproved on other grounds by *Williams v. Sup.Ct. (Marshalls of CA, LLC)* (2017) 3 C5th 531, 557, 220 CR3d 472, 494 & fn. 8)—statute "inartfully" drafted]

[8:596.2-596.4] *Reserved.*

e. [8:596.5] **Additional requirements for subpoenaing "employment records" (CCP §1985.6):** The procedure for subpoenaing "employment records" is similar to that provided under CCP §1985.3 (¶*8:580 ff.*) for subpoenaing "personal records" of a "consumer."

© 2020 Thomson Reuters/The Rutter Group

(1) [8:596.6] **"Employment records" (present or former):** The requirements below (¶*8:596.10 ff.*) apply whenever an employer's records and electronic data "pertaining to the employment" of a present *or former* employee are sought to be subpoenaed. [CCP §1985.6(a)(3)]

Also included are records of a labor organization that represents or has represented the employee. [CCP §1985.6(a)(3)]

[8:596.7-596.9] *Reserved.*

(2) [8:596.10] **Procedure:** The following rules apply to subpoenas seeking production of such records:

[8:596.11-596.14] *Reserved.*

(a) [8:596.15] **Documents to be served on employee:** CCP §1985.6(b) requires that the following documents be served on the employee (unless he or she is the subpoenaing party and the only subject of the subpoenaed records; see CCP §1985.6(k)):

- [8:596.15a] **Copy of subpoena:** A copy of the deposition subpoena;
- [8:596.16] **"Notice of privacy rights":** The employee must be notified that:
  - — Records about him or her are being sought from the records custodian named in the subpoena;
  - — If he or she objects to the records custodian furnishing such records, he or she must file papers with the court prior to the date set for production of the documents (*see* ¶*8:601*), except that a *nonparty* employee may instead serve *written* objections by that date on the records custodian, deposition officer and the party requesting the records (*see* ¶*8:603*); and
  - — If not already represented by counsel, legal advice should be sought about protecting his or her right to privacy. [CCP §1985.6(e)]

  FORM: Notice to Consumer or Employee and Objection (Judicial Council form SUBP-025).

  See Form 8:8 in Rivera, *Cal. Prac. Guide: Civ. Pro. Before Trial FORMS* (TRG).

  [8:596.16a] **Alternative method for parties:** If the employee is a party to the action, the separate "Notice of Privacy Rights" can be dispensed with. The notice elements (¶*8:596.16*) may be included in the "Notice of Deposition" served on the employee. [CCP §1985.6(e)]

- [8:596.16b] **Proof of service:** A proof of service showing the documents (¶*8:596.15 ff.*) were served on the employee (party or nonparty) either in person or by mail. [CCP §1985.6(b)] (A proof of service form is on page 2 of the Judicial Council form SUBP-025 Notice to Employee; *see* ¶*8:596.16*.)

1) [8:596.17] **Not filed with court:** The documents (¶*8:596.15 ff.*) are not filed with the court unless they become relevant on a motion to compel. [See CRC 3.250(a)(4)]

2) [8:596.18] **How served:** If the employee-party is represented by counsel, service may be made upon his or her attorney of record. [CCP §1985.6(b)(1)] (For parties *in pro per*, see CCP §1011(b).)

   Otherwise, the documents (¶*8:596.15 ff.*) must be served on the employee either:
   — personally; or
   — "at his or her last known address" (suggesting they can be left with someone else, but the matter is not clear); or
   — in accordance with CCP §1010 et seq. (which includes service *by mail*, see CCP §1012). [CCP §1985.6(b)(1)]

   (Special rules apply where the employee is a *minor;* see CCP §1985.6(b)(1).)

3) [8:596.19] **When served:** Service of the documents (¶*8:596.15 ff.*) on the employee must be completed:
   — at least 10 days before the date *set for production* of the records; *and*
   — at least 5 days before *service* of the subpoena *on the records custodian*. [CCP §1985.6(b)(2) & (3)]

   a) [8:596.20] **Effect of time for service on records custodian:** As a practical matter, this means the depo subpoena and privacy notice must be served on the employee *at least 20 days* before the date set for production because the depo subpoena must be served on the records custodian *at least 15 days* before that date (CCP §2020.410(c); *see* ¶*8:545*).

   b) [8:596.21] **Extended for service by mail, overnight delivery, fax or electronically:** If the documents are served *by mail* (*see* ¶*8:596.18*), these time limits are extended under CCP §1013(a); e.g., if the place of mailing and the address are both in California, they must be served at least 15 calendar days before the deposition and 10 days before service on the employer. [See CCP §1985.6(b)(2) & (3)]

© 2020 Thomson Reuters/The Rutter Group

The extension is only 2 *court days* for notices served by *express mail* or other method providing for *overnight delivery*, by *fax* (allowed only where so agreed to in writing), or by *electronic transmission* or notification (allowed only where agreed to or required by the court). [See CCP §§1010.6, 1013; CRC 2.250-2.259; *see ¶9:87 ff.*]

c) [8:596.22] **Orders shortening time available:** The subpoenaing party is "entitled" to an order shortening time or waiving the notice requirement altogether "upon good cause [and due diligence] shown and provided that the rights of witnesses and employees are preserved." [CCP §1985.6(g)]

Comment: The term "entitled" is inapt. Orders shortening time are *not automatic;* the court must determine whether "good cause" and "due diligence" have been shown.

[8:596.23-596.24] *Reserved.*

(b) [8:596.25] **Documents to be served on records custodian:** Finally, the following must be served on the employer (custodian of records):

1) [8:596.26] **Deposition subpoena:** Although CCP §1985.6 refers to service of a "subpoena duces tecum," it includes a deposition subpoena (see CCP §2020.030).

The deposition subpoena may be either a "business records" subpoena (CCP §§2020.410 ff.) or a "records and testimony" subpoena (CCP §2020.510).

a) [8:596.27] **Time for service:** The deposition subpoena (whether for records only or for records and testimony) must be served in sufficient time to allow the witness a "reasonable time" to locate and produce the records or copies thereof. "Reasonable time" means the date set for production may be no sooner than *15 days after the subpoena was served* or 20 days after it was issued, whichever is later. [See CCP §1985.6(d) (incorporating CCP §2020.410(c) time limit; *see ¶8:545*)]

[8:596.28-596.29] *Reserved.*

b) [8:596.30] **Prior service on "employee" required:** A deposition subpoena may not be served on the records custodian until *at least 5 days after* the "employee" was served with a copy of the subpoena and notice of privacy rights (*see ¶8:596.19*). [CCP §1985.6(b)(3)]

Comment: Those documents will have to be served on the "employee" at least *20 days* before the date set for production in order to accommodate the time allowed for service on the records custodian (*see ¶8:596.27*).

[8:596.31-596.34] *Reserved.*

2) [8:596.35] **Proof that employee notified:** Along with the deposition subpoena, the subpoenaing party must serve the records custodian with *either:*

a) [8:596.36] **Written release:** A written release of the records signed by the employee or his or her attorney of record. (If signed by an attorney, the employer may presume the attorney has authority from the employee and any objection to release of the records is waived.) [CCP §§1985.6(c)(2), 2020.410(d)]

b) [8:596.37] **Proof of service:** More commonly, *proof of service* on the employee or his or her attorney of record of a copy of the depo subpoena and "Notice of Privacy Rights" described above (*¶8:596.15 ff.*). [CCP §§1985.6(c)(1), 2020.410(d)]

[8:596.38-596.39] *Reserved.*

(3) [8:596.40] **Effect of noncompliance:** Failure to comply with any of the foregoing requirements *by itself* invalidates the service so that the employer (records custodian) is under no duty to produce the records sought by the subpoena. [CCP §1985.6(j)]

Moreover, even if the employer voluntarily produces the records, noncompliance with §1985.6 is ground for *objection* to admission of such records by the person whose records were subpoenaed. [See *Sasson v. Katash* (1983) 146 CA3d 119, 125, 194 CR 46, 49 (dealing with CCP §1985.3 subpoena, but result should be the same under §1985.6)]

(a) [8:596.41] **Compare—certain defects may be excused:** Minor defects in the documents *served on the employee* (not the employer) may be cured for "good cause" shown. As long as the employer's and employee's rights are preserved, a subpoenaing party who has acted with "due diligence" is *entitled* to an order waiving defects in such documents. [See CCP §1985.6(g)]

[8:596.42-596.44] *Reserved.*

(4) [8:596.45] **Exception for governmental entities:** The foregoing requirements do not apply to state or local agencies or to certain other public entities in specified adjudicative proceedings, or to certain proceedings under the Labor Code. [See CCP §1985.6(a)(5) & (i)]

© 2020 Thomson Reuters/The Rutter Group

(a) [8:596.46] **Narrowly construed:** Despite this broad language, this provision may be interpreted narrowly. A companion provision (CCP §1985.3(a)(3)) has been interpreted to exempt state and local governments *only* when obtaining information from *financial institutions* concerning their customers (for which other privacy protection already exists); in all other cases, state and local governments must comply with these procedural requirements the same as other litigants. [See *Lantz v. Sup.Ct. (County of Kern)* (1994) 28 CA4th 1839, 1852, 34 CR2d 358, 365-366 (disapproved on other grounds by *Williams v. Sup.Ct. (Marshalls of CA, LLC)* (2017) 3 C5th 531, 557, 220 CR3d 472, 494 & fn. 8)—§1985.3(a)(3) "inartfully" drafted]

[8:596.47-596.49] *Reserved.*

f. [8:596.50] **Subpoenas for electronically-stored information (ESI):** A subpoena may require that electronically-stored information (ESI) "be produced and that the party serving the subpoena, or someone acting on the party's request, be permitted to inspect, copy, test, or sample the information." [CCP §1985.8(a)(1); see *Vasquez v. California School of Culinary Arts, Inc.* (2014) 230 CA4th 35, 41, 178 CR3d 10, 14-15]

The subpoenaing party, however, must take "reasonable steps" to avoid imposing "undue burden or expense" on persons subject to the subpoena. [CCP §§1985.8(k), 2020.220(k)]

The provisions governing subpoenas for ESI generally parallel those governing *inspection demands* for ESI under CCP §2031.010 et seq. (*see ¶8:1427.5 ff.*).

Compare—party deponents: CCP §1985.8 is not limited by its terms to nonparty witnesses. Even so, party deponents can be required to produce ESI by a deposition notice (CCP §2025.220(a)(4))—no subpoena is required. *See ¶8:521 ff.*

(1) [8:596.51] **ESI defined:** [CCP §2016.020] *See discussion at ¶8:1427.5.*

(2) [8:596.52] **Subpoena may specify form for producing ESI:** The party serving the subpoena for ESI may specify the form or forms in which *each type* of ESI is to be produced. (For example, the subpoena may specify one format for emails and a different format for financial spreadsheets, etc.) [CCP §§1985.8(b), 2020.410(a), 2020.510(a)(4); *see discussion at ¶8:1445.5*]

(a) [8:596.52a] **Objection to specified ESI form:** The person responding to the subpoena may object to the specified form or forms for producing the ESI and state the form or forms in which he or she intends to produce the ESI. [CCP §1985.8(c)]

1) [8:596.52b] **No objection based on availability of paper form:** The fact the requested documents already exist in paper form is not a proper objection and does not excuse the obligation to produce the documents in an electronic format. [*Vasquez v. California School of Culinary Arts, Inc.*, supra, 230 CA4th at 43, 178 CR3d at 16]

➪ [8:596.53] ***PRACTICE POINTERS—Drafting subpoenas for ESI:*** *See the Practice Pointer at ¶8:1445.6 re drafting CCP §2031.010 demands.*

(3) [8:596.54] **Where subpoena does not specify form for production:** If the subpoena does *not* specify a form for producing the ESI, it must be produced in the form "in which it is ordinarily maintained" *or* in a form "that is reasonably usable," unless the parties agree or the court orders otherwise. [CCP §§1985.8(d)(1), 2020.220(d)(1)]

(4) [8:596.55] **Same information need not be produced in more than one form:** The same ESI need not be produced in more than one form unless the parties agree or the court orders otherwise. [CCP §§1985.8(d)(2), 2020.220(d)(2)]

[8:596.56-596.59] *Reserved.*

(5) [8:596.60] **Where data translation necessary:** "If necessary, the subpoenaed person, *at the reasonable expense of the subpoenaing party,* shall, through detection devices, translate any data compilations" called for by the subpoena into a "reasonably usable form." [CCP §§1985.8(h), 2020.220(h) (emphasis added); see CCP §2025.280(c); *Vasquez v. California School of Culinary Arts, Inc.*, supra, 230 CA4th at 44, 178 CR3d at 16-17—subpoena properly required nonparty to write program to extract ESI from existing database]

(a) [8:596.61] **"If necessary":** "If necessary" presumably covers any situation in which the ESI is not reasonably usable without being translated. This includes situations where the subpoena requires production of ESI in a *different form* than that in which it is regularly maintained; or where the data is maintained in a form *not reasonably usable* by the subpoenaed party.

(6) [8:596.62] **Where ESI password protected:** A deponent producing ESI must provide access to any ESI that is password protected. [CCP §2025.280(c)]

[8:596.63-596.64] *Reserved.*

(7) [8:596.65] **Opposing production where ESI not reasonably accessible:** A subpoenaed person may oppose the production and move to quash the subpoena on the ground that the ESI sought is not reasonably accessible because of "undue burden or expense." [CCP §§1985.8(e), 1987.1, 2020.220(e)]

© 2020 Thomson Reuters/The Rutter Group

The objection preserves other objections to the production of ESI (*see* ¶*8:1475.12*).

(a) [8:596.66] **Burden shifting on motion to quash:** The person opposing production has the burden of initially proving the ESI comes from a source that is not "reasonably accessible because of undue burden or expense." [CCP §§1985.8(e), 2020.220(e); see *Vasquez v. California School of Culinary Arts, Inc.*, supra, 230 CA4th at 42, 178 CR3d at 15]

If such a showing is made, the burden *shifts* to the subpoenaing party to show "good cause" for production notwithstanding the burden or expense. [CCP §§1985.8(f), 2020.220(f)]

(8) [8:596.67] **Order for production may be conditional:** If it finds "good cause" for production of the ESI, the court may set conditions on its production, *including allocating the expenses* incurred. [CCP §§1985.8(g), 2020.220(g); *see further discussion at* ¶*8:1456.27*]

(a) [8:596.68] **Nonparties protected from undue burden or expense:** Any order requiring compliance with a subpoena for ESI shall *protect* a person who is neither a party nor a party's officer from "undue burden or expense" in complying with the subpoena. [CCP §§1985.8(*l*), 2020.220(*l*)]

[8:596.69] *Reserved.*

(9) [8:596.70] **Other grounds for challenging ESI subpoenas:** A subpoena for ESI may also be challenged on grounds applicable to deposition subpoenas generally (*see* ¶*8:598 ff.*).

For example, a motion to quash may lie for defects in form or service, or on grounds of privilege, privacy or relevancy, or because the demands are oppressive and unduly burdensome (e.g., a subpoena for all email traffic between people with no connection to the dispute).

(10)[8:596.71] **Grounds for limiting frequency or extent of discovery:** The court "shall" limit the frequency or extent of discovery of ESI—*even from reasonably accessible sources*—if *either:*

- It is possible to obtain the ESI from another source that is more convenient, less burdensome or less expensive;
- The discovery sought is unreasonably cumulative or duplicative;
- The party seeking discovery has had ample opportunity by discovery in the action to obtain the information sought; or
- The likely *burden or expense* of the proposed discovery

outweighs the likely benefit, taking into account the amount in controversy, the resources of the parties, the importance of the issues in the litigation, and the importance of the requested discovery in resolving the issues. [CCP §§1985.8(i), 2020.220(i)]

(a) [8:596.72] **Effect:** The *burden is on the party resisting discovery* to establish with admissible evidence one or more of these grounds. Each calls for a case-by-case determination within the sound discretion of the trial court.

[8:596.73-596.74] *Reserved.*

(11) [8:596.75] **"Clawback" procedures for disclosure of privileged information:** A special procedure is provided to resolve claims that documents produced in response to a subpoena for ESI are privileged or work product and should be returned. CCP §§1985.8(j) and 2020.220(j) incorporate the "clawback" procedure provided in CCP §2031.285 for such cases (*see ¶8:1481.5 ff.*).

(12) [8:596.76] **"Safe harbor" against sanctions where ESI lost or destroyed due to computer system:** Absent exceptional circumstances, sanctions may not be imposed on a person responding to a subpoena (or on that person's attorney) for failure to provide ESI that has been lost, damaged, altered or overwritten as a result of the "*routine, good faith operation* of an electronic information system." [CCP §§1985.8(m)(1), 1987.2(b)(1), 2020.220(m)(1), 2023.030(f)(1), 2025.410(e)(1) & 2025.450(i)(1) (emphasis added)]

But this "safe harbor" does not alter any obligation to *preserve* discoverable information. [CCP §§1985.8(m)(2), 1987.2(b)(2), 2020.220(m)(2), 2023.030(f)(2), 2025.410(e)(2) & 2025.450(i)(2)]

Only "good faith operation" is protected under the statute, so if you allow data to be destroyed *knowing* that materials relevant to the litigation may be lost, you may not be able to invoke the safe harbor.

g. [8:597] **Procedures for challenging deposition subpoena:** Either the nonparty witness who has been subpoenaed, or any party to the action, may challenge the deposition subpoena.

⇨ [8:597.1] ***PRACTICE POINTER:*** *Consider alternative procedures discussed at ¶8:787.1.*

(1) [8:598] **Grounds:** A deposition subpoena may be attacked for:

- Defects in form or content of the subpoena (e.g., inadequate description of requested documents in "records only" or "records and testimony" subpoenas);
- Defects in *service* of the subpoena, including tender of fees;

© 2020 Thomson Reuters/The Rutter Group

- Records sought *not within permissible scope of discovery*— i.e., privileged, privacy or attorney work product; or not "relevant to the subject matter";
- Unjustly burdensome or oppressive demands;
- With regard to requested *ESI discovery*, objection to the specified *form* for producing the ESI (CCP §1985.8(c), ¶*8:596.52a*) or objection to production on the ground that the ESI is from a source that is not reasonably accessible because of undue burden and expense (CCP §1985.8(e), ¶*8:596.65 ff.*);
- "Consumer's" right of privacy in "personal records" (CCP §1985.3(e), ¶*8:580 ff.*); or
- Employee's right of privacy in "employment records" (CCP §1985.6(e), ¶*8:596.5 ff.*).

[8:599] *Reserved.*

(2) [8:600] **Particular procedures:** The procedures that may be used depend on who is raising the challenge:

(a) [8:601] **Motion to quash deposition subpoena duces tecum:** A motion to quash (or modify) a deposition subpoena for production of documents may be made by:
— a party;
— a (nonparty) witness;
— a "consumer" whose personal records have been subpoenaed (CCP §1985.3, *see* ¶*8:580 ff.*);
— an "employee" whose "employment records" have been subpoenaed (CCP §1985.6, *see* ¶*8:596.5 ff.*); or
— a person whose "personally identifying information" (see Civ.C. §1798.79.8) is sought in connection with an action involving his or her exercise of *free speech rights* (e.g., a defamation action based on anonymous Internet postings). [CCP §1987.1(b)]

1) [8:602] **Service requirements:** A motion to quash by a "consumer" or "employee" must be served on the witness *and* the deposition officer *at least five days* before the date set for production of the subpoenaed records. (Failure to serve the deposition officer does not invalidate the motion but excuses the officer from liability for improper release of the subpoenaed records.) [CCP §§1985.3(g), 1985.6(f)]

a) [8:602.1] **Time limit not jurisdictional:** The five-day time limit for service is not jurisdictional. The court can grant a motion to quash served even *after* the date set for production. [*Slagle* *v. Sup.Ct. (Maryon)* (1989) 211 CA3d 1309, 1313, 260 CR 122, 124]

[8:602.2-602.4] *Reserved.*

2) [8:602.5] **Separate statement of disputed matters required:** A motion to quash production of documents at a deposition must be accompanied by a separate statement setting forth the particular documents or demands at issue and the factual and legal reasons why production should not be compelled. [See CRC 3.1345(a)(5)]

   a) [8:602.6] **Form and content of statement:** *See detailed discussion at ¶8:1151 ff.*

   b) [8:602.7] **Compare—concise outline:** As of January 1, 2020, the court may allow the use of a concise list of issues instead of the separate statement. *See ¶8:532.12.*

   [8:602.8-602.9] *Reserved.*

3) [8:602.10] **Monetary sanction against losing party:** The court *should* order the losing party to pay the prevailing party's expenses, including reasonable attorney fees, incurred on the motion to quash, if it finds that the motion was "made or opposed in *bad faith* or *without substantial justification* or that one or more of the requirements of the subpoena was oppressive." [CCP §1987.2(a) (emphasis added); *Vasquez v. California School of Culinary Arts, Inc.* (2014) 230 CA4th 35, 41, 178 CR3d 10, 14; *Evilsizor v. Sweeney* (2014) 230 CA4th 1304, 1311, 179 CR3d 400, 406—sanctions upheld for failing to withdraw motion to quash after it became unjustified]

   In addition, the court *must make such an award* where the subpoena was served on an Internet Service Provider (ISP) for "personally identifying information" if:

   — the information is sought for use in litigation *outside California* involving the moving party's exercise of *free speech rights* (e.g., a defamation action based on anonymous Internet postings); and

   — the motion is granted because the *respondent fails to make a prima facie showing* of a valid cause of action. [See CCP §1987.2(c), ¶*8:190.25*]

   a) [8:602.11] **"Safe harbor":** If ESI is destroyed due to the routine good faith operation of a computer system, sanctions may not be imposed. *See ¶8:596.76.*

© 2020 Thomson Reuters/The Rutter Group

(b) [8:603] **Written objections by nonparty "consumer" or "employee":** A "consumer" (CCP §1985.3) or "employee" (CCP §1985.6) who is *not a party* to the action is not required to file a motion to quash. [CCP §1987.1(c)]

Instead, he or she may serve the subpoenaing party, the records custodian and the deposition officer with *written objections* to production of the subpoenaed records, stating specific grounds on which production of the records should be prohibited (e.g., invasion of privacy). [CCP §§1985.3(g), 1985.6(f)(2)]

[8:603.1-603.4] *Reserved.*

1) [8:603.5] **Production of records automatically stayed:** Either filing a motion to quash or serving such written objections (by a nonparty "consumer" or "employee") *automatically excuses* the custodian and deposition officer from producing the subpoenaed records until the court orders their production or the parties stipulate thereto. [CCP §§1985.3(g), 1985.6(f)(3)]

2) [8:604] **Motion to enforce subpoena over written objections:** Where a nonparty "consumer" or "employee" has served written objections as stated above (¶*8:603*), the requesting party may move for an order to enforce the subpoena. (The burden of obtaining a court order is on the party seeking discovery.) [CCP §§1985.3(g), 1985.6(f)(4)]

a) [8:604.1] **Filing and service requirements:** Any such motion must be filed *within 20 days* after service of the written objections. [CCP §§1985.3(g), 1985.6(f)(4)]

The motion should be served on all parties and, although not specifically required by statute, on the "consumer" or "employee" if not a party to the action.

b) [8:604.2] **Separate statement of disputed matters required:** *See* ¶*8:602.5.*

c) [8:604.3] **Attempt to resolve informally required:** The motion must be accompanied by a declaration showing a "reasonable and good faith attempt at informal resolution of the dispute" between the party requesting the records and the "consumer" or "employee" whose records are involved or counsel for such person. [CCP §§1985.3(g), 1985.6(f)(4)]

(c) [8:605] **Protective orders:** Alternatively, any party, witness, consumer, employee or person whose personal identifying information is sought in connection with an action involving that person's right of free speech (*see ¶8:601*) may seek a protective order against the subpoena or deposition proceedings. The court may make whatever orders are appropriate to protect that person from "unreasonable or oppressive demands, including unreasonable violations of *the right of privacy of the person.*" [CCP §1987.1 (emphasis added); see CCP §2025.420(b), *¶8:675 ff.*]

(d) [8:605.1] **Objections to "records only" subpoena:** A nonparty served with a "records only" subpoena may either move to quash all or a portion of the subpoena, or merely object to the production of all or some of the documents and put the onus on the proponent to make a motion to compel. [*Monarch Healthcare v. Sup.Ct. (Cassidenti)* (2000) 78 CA4th 1282, 1290, 93 CR2d 619, 625 (citing text)]

(e) [8:606] **Objections at deposition:** Or, a party or witness may wait until the deposition and raise objections at that time to the form or content of the subpoena, or to demands for production of privileged documents, etc. [See *Monarch Healthcare v. Sup.Ct. (Cassidenti)*, supra, 78 CA4th at 1290, 93 CR2d at 625 (citing text)]

[8:607] *Reserved.*

[8:608] ***PRACTICE POINTER:*** Seek a protective order to curtail discovery from a *nonparty* witness (e.g., on the ground your client's privacy would be infringed by the witness' disclosures).

You could, of course, object at the deposition on the same grounds. But *your objection by itself will not prevent the nonparty witness from testifying*. Thus, the information you are trying to protect will be disclosed notwithstanding the validity of your objection. (The testimony may be inadmissible at trial but that is usually not the point of the objection.)

h. [8:609] **Enforcing subpoena:** Personal service of a deposition subpoena obligates any resident of California to appear, testify and produce whatever documents or things are specified in the subpoena; *and to appear in any proceedings to enforce discovery*. [CCP §2020.220(c)]

The deposition subpoena is enforceable either by:

- A *motion to compel* compliance (CCP §1987.1);
- *Contempt* proceedings (*¶8:610*); and/or
- A civil *damages* action by the aggrieved party (*¶8:618*). [CCP §2020.240]

(1) [8:609.1] **Motion to compel:** If a nonparty disobeys a depo subpoena, the subpoenaing party may seek a court order

© 2020 Thomson Reuters/The Rutter Group

compelling the nonparty to comply with the subpoena within *60 days* after completion of the *deposition record.* [CCP §2025.480(b); see *Unzipped Apparel, LLC v. Bader* (2007) 156 CA4th 123, 127, 67 CR3d 111, 112]

A nonparty opposing such motion without substantial justification is subject to *sanctions.* [CCP §§1987.2(a), 2020.030, 2025.480; see *Person v. Farmers Ins. Group of Cos.* (1997) 52 CA4th 813, 818, 61 CR2d 30, 33; *and ¶8:842*]

This rule applies to subpoenas for production of documents at a deposition and also to *business records subpoenas* (*¶8:540 ff.*). The objections or other responses to a business records subpoena are the "deposition record" for purposes of measuring the 60-day period for a motion to compel. [*Unzipped Apparel, LLC v. Bader*, supra, 156 CA4th at 132-133, 67 CR3d at 116-117; *Rutledge v. Hewlett-Packard Co.* (2015) 238 CA4th 1164, 1192, 190 CR3d 411, 434]

Such order may be sought under either:

- CCP §2025.480 (applicable to depositions generally; *see ¶8:787 ff.*); or
- CCP §1987.1 (applicable to depo subpoenas by CCP §2020.030).

⇨ [8:609.2] ***PRACTICE POINTER:*** This procedure is generally recommended over contempt (*¶8:610*). Although attorney fees may be awarded in contempt proceedings (*see ¶8:617*), such an award is more likely in connection with a motion to compel under CCP §1987.2.

Also, contempt proceedings are quasi-criminal in nature and require extensive procedural safeguards (*¶8:612 ff.*), and almost never result in actual adjudications of contempt. Therefore, many courts *discourage* OSCs re Contempt and prefer issuing OSCs re an Order to Comply.

(a) [8:609.3] **Document discovery "good cause" requirement:** A showing of "good cause" is required on motions to compel document discovery from a *party* under CCP §2025.450(b)(1) (depositions) or §2031.310(b)(1) (inspection demands). But the relevant statutes do not specify such requirement on a motion to compel a *nonparty* to comply with a deposition subpoena for document production (see CCP §§1987.1, 2025.480). At least one court has held that if there is a "good cause" showing required to compel production of party documents, such a requirement also applies to nonparty production. [*Calcor Space Facility, Inc. v. Sup.Ct. (Thiem Indus., Inc.)* (1997) 53 CA4th 216, 223-224, 61 CR2d 567, 572—"since it is unlikely the Legislature intended to place greater burdens on a nonparty than on a party to the litigation, we read a similar [good faith] requirement" into the relevant statutes]

(b) [8:609.4] **Special rules re motion to compel production of electronically-stored information:** *See discussion at ¶8:532.15.*

(2) [8:610] **Contempt:** A deponent who *disobeys* a deposition subpoena may be punished for contempt—*without the necessity of a prior court order* directing compliance by the witness or any showing of good cause. [CCP §§1209(a)(10), 1991.1, 2020.240, 2023.030(e)]

(If necessary, the court may issue a civil bench warrant for the deponent's arrest; CCP §§1993-1993.2.)

(a) [8:611] **"Disobedience":** "Disobedience" means a *conscious refusal* to attend the deposition. It must be shown that the witness had *knowledge* of the subpoena, the *ability* to comply therewith, and deliberately failed to do so. If the failure was inadvertent, ordinarily no remedy of any kind is available against the witness. [See CCP §1991; and *Chapman v. Sup.Ct.* (1968) 261 CA2d 194, 200, 67 CR 842, 846]

(b) **Procedural matters**

- [8:612] The subpoenaing party must file an *affidavit* alleging proper service of the subpoena on the witness and the witness' "disobedience" thereto (i.e., willful refusal to appear or testify, etc.).

- [8:613] The court will then issue an *order to show cause* (OSC) *re contempt.* The OSC and affidavit must be *served personally* on the witness. [*Cedars-Sinai Imaging Med. Group v. Sup.Ct. (Moore)* (2000) 83 CA4th 1281, 1286-1287, 100 CR2d 320, 324]

  (Thus, a stubborn witness has to be personally served *twice*—once with the deposition subpoena, and then again with the OSC re contempt.)

- [8:614] The hearing on the OSC is normally before the law and motion judge or department; or, where an "all purpose" or "direct calendar" assignment has been made, to the assigned judge.

  (Comment: The judge will most likely order the witness to appear for and submit to the taking of his or her deposition, and hold the contempt proceedings in abeyance pending compliance. Judges are usually more interested in compliance than in inflicting punishment.)

- [8:615] An order finding the witness guilty of contempt must recite the *specific facts* giving rise to the contempt

© 2020 Thomson Reuters/The Rutter Group

(including his or her ability to perform). Without such facts, the order is *void*. [*In re de la Parra* (1986) 184 CA3d 139, 144, 228 CR 864, 867]

(c) [8:616] **Punishment:** A person found guilty of contempt is subject to *fine* (up to $1,000) or *imprisonment* (up to 5 days), or both. [CCP §1218; see *People v. Gonzalez* (1996) 12 C4th 804, 816, 50 CR2d 74, 82]

A court could also impose civil contempt sanctions: i.e., imprisonment until the party complies (or as a practical matter, agrees to comply). [CCP §1219(a)]

(d) [8:617] **Attorney fees:** In addition, a *party or "an agent"* of a party to the action who is adjudged guilty of contempt may be ordered to pay the opposing party's reasonable attorney fees in connection with the contempt proceedings. [See CCP §1218(a)]

⇨ [8:617.1] ***PRACTICE POINTER:*** The contempt procedure is complex, time-consuming and doomed to failure unless all the procedural niceties are observed. Even if they are met, many judges are reluctant to hold a person in contempt *absent a prior court order*.

Therefore, it is usually a better idea to move first for an order compelling the deponent to attend and for an award of monetary sanctions (*see* ¶*8:617.5*). Consider contempt proceedings only if the witness disobeys a specific court order or otherwise is persistently recalcitrant.

[8:617.2-617.4] *Reserved.*

(3) [8:617.5] **Monetary sanctions:** Monetary sanctions (as well as contempt) are available against nonparties who "flout the discovery process." [*Temple Comm. Hosp. v. Sup.Ct. (Ramos)* (1999) 20 C4th 464, 476-477, 84 CR2d 852, 861 (nonparty destroyed evidence); see also *Brun v. Bailey* (1994) 27 CA4th 641, 658-659, 32 CR2d 624, 634 (superseded by statute on other grounds) (*see* ¶*8:2072*); *Sears, Roebuck & Co. v. National Union Fire Ins. Co. of Pittsburgh* (2005) 131 CA4th 1342, 1350-1351, 32 CR3d 717, 721-722 (nonparty attorney's bad faith noncompliance with deposition and document production subpoenas; *discussed at* ¶*8:459*)]

(4) [8:618] **Civil action by aggrieved party:** The subpoenaing party can also file a civil action against the witness who disobeys the subpoena to recover a forfeiture of *$500*, plus all damages sustained as a result of the witness' failure to attend (e.g., attorney fees and deposition expenses). [CCP §§2020.240, 1992]

- [8:619] **Comment:** However, as noted by the Supreme Court, this is an impractical remedy: "The simple economics of modern litigation essentially preclude such an action." [*New York Times v. Sup.Ct. (Sortomme)* (1990) 51 C3d 453, 464, 273 CR 98, 105]

(5) [8:620] **Compare—where deponent appears but refuses to answer questions:** A nonparty witness complies with a deposition subpoena by showing up at the deposition, being sworn as a witness, and producing any documents or things commanded by the subpoena. Thereafter, *no* contempt or forfeiture proceedings lie even if the witness refuses to answer any and all questions. The deposing party's remedy is to obtain a *court order directing the witness to answer* (CCP §2025.480(a); *see* ¶*8:787 ff.*). Monetary sanctions may be imposed against the witness in connection with such motion (CCP §2025.480(k); ¶*8:817*).

[8:620.1-620.4] *Reserved.*

i. [8:620.5] **Litigation privilege bars tort liability:** The Civ.C. §47(b) litigation privilege (*see* ¶*1:604 ff.*) protects a records custodian who produces records in response to a subpoena against liability for invasion of privacy or other tort liability. [*Foothill Fed. Credit Union v. Sup.Ct. (King)* (2007) 155 CA4th 632, 641-642, 66 CR3d 249, 256—§47(b) litigation privilege applied despite faulty notice (person whose records were produced had not received prior notice as required by CCP §1985.3; *see* ¶*8:593 ff.*)]

[8:620.6-620.19] *Reserved.*

7. [8:620.20] **Foreign Subpoenas:** Subpoenas issued by courts in *another state or country* ("foreign subpoenas") may be enforced in California as provided in the "Interstate and International Depositions and Discovery Act" (CCP §2029.100 et seq.), as described below (¶*8:620.21 ff.*).

a. [8:620.21] **Issuance of subpoena by California lawyer:** If a party to an out-of-state legal proceeding retains a California lawyer and provides the lawyer with the original or a copy of the foreign subpoena, the California lawyer may issue a subpoena to a local resident without prior court approval. [See CCP §2029.350(a)]

(1) [8:620.22] **Form and content:** A subpoena issued by a California lawyer must:

— be on a Judicial Council form (see CCP §2029.390);
— bear the caption and case number of the *out-of-state case* to which it relates;
— state the name of the superior court of the county in which the deposition is to be conducted;
— *incorporate the terms used in the foreign subpoena*; and
— contain or be accompanied by the names, addresses and telephone numbers of all counsel of record in the foreign proceeding (and of any party not represented by counsel). [See CCP §2029.350(b)]

© 2020 Thomson Reuters/The Rutter Group

(a) [8:620.23] **Terms of foreign subpoena:** The terms of the foreign subpoena may command the California resident to do *any* of the following:
— attend and give testimony;
— produce and permit inspection, copying, testing or sampling of designated books, documents, records, electronically-stored information, or tangible things in that person's possession, custody or control; or
— permit inspection of premises under that person's control. [See CCP §2029.200(e)]

[8:620.24] *Reserved.*

b. [8:620.25] **Issuance of subpoena by court clerk:** Otherwise, a party to the foreign proceeding may request issuance of a subpoena by the clerk of the superior court in the county where the deposition or discovery is to be conducted by:
— submitting the original or a true and correct copy of a foreign subpoena;
— submitting an application for issuance of a subpoena on a Judicial Council form (see CCP §2029.390) (no civil case cover sheet required); and
— paying a filing fee (see Gov.C. §70626(b)). [CCP §2029.300(a), (b)]

The request for issuance of a local subpoena does *not* constitute an "appearance" in California courts by the requesting party. [CCP §2029.300(a)]

(1) [8:620.26] **Form and content:** The form and content for a subpoena issued by the court clerk (¶*8:620.25*) are the same as for a subpoena issued by a California attorney as stated in ¶*8:620.22 ff.*

[8:620.27-620.29] *Reserved.*

c. [8:620.30] **Service of subpoena:** Whether issued by a California lawyer or court clerk, the subpoena must be personally served under the rules governing service of subpoenas in California actions generally (¶*8:568 ff.*). [See CCP §2029.400]

d. [8:620.31] **Enforcement of subpoena:** California statutes and rules governing depositions, production or inspection apply, including rules governing costs or sanctions. [CCP §2029.500]

Special rules apply where a California court is called upon to adjudicate disputes relating to such depositions or discovery. [See CCP §2029.600 et seq.]

8. [8:621] **PLACE of Deposition:** CCP §2025.250(a)-(d) sets geographic limits on where a deposition may be taken. These limits apply even if the witness has been *subpoenaed* to appear. (Although a subpoena has a statewide range, the Discovery Act limits the distance persons are required to travel to have their depositions taken.)

a. [8:622] **Natural persons (including parties):** Except as provided below (¶*8:625*), natural persons, including parties to the action, must be deposed within:

- *75* miles from their residence; or
- (at the option of the deposing party) in the *county* where the *action is pending* at a place within *150 miles* of the deponent's residence. [CCP §2025.250(a)]

(1) [8:623] **Example:** If a lawsuit is pending in Los Angeles County, a person living in Santa Barbara can be deposed anywhere within 75 miles of his or her residence. Or, at the option of the deposing party, the deposition could be set *anywhere* in Los Angeles County within 150 miles of the deponent's Santa Barbara residence.

[8:624] *Reserved.*

(2) [8:625] **Limits extendible for party's deposition:** By *stipulation* of all counsel, the deposition of a *party* or "party-affiliated" witness (officer, director, managing agent or employee of party) can be taken beyond the geographic limits above (¶*8:621 ff.*) unless the court orders otherwise. [CCP §2016.030]

Moreover, a court has power, in the "interests of justice," to order parties or "party-affiliated" witnesses to appear for deposition beyond those limits. [CCP §§2025.250(a), 2025.260(a)]

(3) [8:626] **Compare—nonparty's deposition cannot be extended:** However, neither stipulation nor court order can force a *nonparty* to travel beyond the geographic limits above (¶*8:621 ff.*). A stipulation between the parties or their counsel is not binding on a nonparty; and the court has no power to order a nonparty to travel beyond those limits.

➩ [8:627] ***PRACTICE POINTER:*** Thus, if you need to depose a nonparty witness who resides more than 75 miles from your office (150 miles, if your office is in the county where the suit is pending), plan to take it *where the witness resides.*

Of course, you might be able to get the nonparty witness to come to your office by agreeing to advance travel costs. But this is generally *not* a good idea because you run the risk of *sanctions* if the witness fails to appear (¶*8:832*). Thus, if you need that witness' deposition, be prepared to travel.

(4) [8:627.1] **Procedures for depositions in other states or countries:** *See ¶8:635 ff. and 8:643 ff.*

b. [8:628] **Corporations or other entities:** The place of deposition depends on whether the entity is a party to the action, and whether it has designated a principal executive or business office in California:

© 2020 Thomson Reuters/The Rutter Group

(1) [8:628.1] **Nonparty deponent:** The deposition of a corporation, partnership or association that is not a party to the action, and that has designated a principal executive or business office in California, must be taken within 75 miles of that office (unless it consents to a more distant place). [CCP §2025.250(c)]

(2) [8:628.2] **Party deponent:** If the entity is a *party* to the action, it must be deposed within:

- *75 miles* of its designated principal executive or business office in California; or
- (at the option of the deposing party) in the *county where the action is pending* at a place within *150 miles* of the entity's designated office. [CCP §2025.250(b)]

(3) [8:628.3] **Corporations not having designated office:** If the organization (party or nonparty) has not designated a principal executive or business office in California, its deposition may be taken, at the option of the deposing party, *either:*

- within 75 miles of *any business office of the organization* here; or
- *anywhere in the county where the action is pending.* [CCP §2025.250(d)]

(a) [8:628.4] **Comment:** CCP §1989 provides that a person cannot be required to testify as a witness in California unless he or she is a California resident, and one case has held that restriction applies to depositions. [*Toyota Motor Corp. v. Sup.Ct. (Stewart)* (2011) 197 CA4th 1107, 1110, 130 CR3d 131, 133; *see* ¶*8:631 ff.*] In light of that holding, it is unclear whether a party can rely on CCP §2025.250(d) to force a nonparty corporation that has no officers or employees resident in the state to testify in the county where the action is pending. (*See also* ¶*8:631 ff.*)

[8:629] *Reserved.*

c. [8:630] **Court may order party or "party-affiliated" witness to attend beyond geographic limits:** The court may order a party, or a party-affiliated witness (officer, director, managing agent or employee of a party), to appear for deposition beyond the limits stated above (¶*8:621 ff.*). [CCP §2025.260(a)]

(1) [8:631] **Limits on court discretion to set location of depositions?** It is unclear whether the court may compel a witness residing outside California to travel to California for deposition.

One court stated that, if a foreign corporation filed suit in California, members of its management who were residents of Indiana could be ordered to travel to California and give deposition testimony here. [*Glass v. Sup.Ct. (Indiana Western*

Mortg. Corp.) (1988) 204 CA3d 1048, 1052-1053, 251 CR 690, 692]

But a later case holds that CCP §1989, which provides that a person is not obliged to attend as a witness "before any court, judge, justice *or any other officer*" unless the witness is a California resident, applies to depositions pursuant to notice under CCP §2025.260; and therefore, the court may not order a nonresident of California to be deposed here. [*Toyota Motor Corp. v. Sup.Ct. (Stewart)* (2011) 197 CA4th 1107, 1110, 130 CR3d 131, 133 (disagreeing with *Glass*, supra)—Japanese residents who were employees of D corporation could not be compelled to testify at deposition in California; *I-CA Enterprises, Inc. v. Palram Americas, Inc.* (2015) 235 CA4th 257, 281-282, 185 CR3d 24, 43-44]

(a) [8:631.1] **Residence of designated corporate witness immaterial?** A corporation or other entity must designate its "most qualified" officers or agents to testify on its behalf (CCP §2025.230, ¶*8:473*). It is an open question whether the designated agent who resides outside the state can be compelled to attend in the state on the theory it is the *entity's* deposition that is being taken. This issue was expressly not addressed in *Toyota Motor Corp.*, supra. [*Toyota Motor Corp. v. Sup.Ct. (Stewart)*, supra, 197 CA4th at 1125, 130 CR3d at 146, fn. 20; see *I-CA Enterprises, Inc. v. Palram Americas, Inc.*, supra, 235 CA4th at 280-282, 185 CR3d at 43-44—by failing to address CCP §1989 and its applicability to CCP §2025.230 on appeal, party forfeited argument that trial court lacked power to compel deposition of entity's nonresident person most knowledgeable]

(b) [8:631.2] **Comment:** Where the corporation has a witness in California who could make the necessary investigation and testify to that information known to the corporation, the corporation could produce that witness in California. If the corporation wanted someone from outside California, it could make arrangements for that person to testify in California. Alternatively, California counsel may go to the deponent's state and use, e.g., the Uniform Interstate Depositions and Discovery Act, adopted by 42 states, the District of Columbia and the U.S. Virgin Islands (see *www.uniformlaws.org*).

(2) [8:632] **Procedure:** A noticed motion is required by the party seeking to take the deposition beyond the geographic limits. The motion should be supported by declarations establishing the necessity and reasons for exceeding the geographic limit, plus facts "showing a reasonable and good faith attempt" to resolve informally the issues presented by the motion. [CCP §2025.260(a)-(b)] Notice is governed by CCP §1005(b) (*see* ¶*9:31*). [CCP §1005(a)(8)]

© 2020 Thomson Reuters/The Rutter Group

(3) [8:633] **Factors considered:** In ruling on the motion, the court must consider "any factor tending to show whether the *interests of justice* will be served" by granting the order, including:

- Whether the moving party filed the suit locally;
- Whether the deponent (party or party-affiliated witness) will be present to testify at trial of the action;
- The convenience of the deponent;
- The deponent's whereabouts at the time for which the deposition is scheduled (assuming it has been scheduled);
- The feasibility of conducting the deposition by written questions or by a discovery method other than a deposition;
- The number of depositions sought to be taken beyond the geographic limits above (¶*8:621 ff.*); and
- The expense to each party in requiring them to take the deposition where the deponent resides. [CCP §2025.260(b)]

(4) [8:634] **Court may order moving party to pay deponent's travel costs:** An order compelling a party to appear for deposition beyond the geographic limits above (¶*8:621 ff.*) may be *conditioned* on the moving party advancing the deponent's reasonable costs and travel expenses in attending the deposition. [CCP §2025.260(c)]

(5) [8:634.1] **Monetary sanction against losing party:** The court "shall" impose a monetary sanction against the losing party *unless* it finds that party made or opposed the motion with "substantial justification" or other circumstances make the sanction "unjust." [CCP §2025.260(d)] (Monetary sanctions on discovery motions are discussed at ¶*8:1921 ff.*)

d. **Procedures for depositions in another state**

(1) [8:635] **Party or party-affiliated witnesses residing outside California:** The deposition of a party or party-affiliated witness (officer, director, managing agent or employee of party) who resides in another state may be noticed at a place *within 75 miles of the deponent's residence or business office.* [CCP §2026.010(b)]

The deposition notice by itself is effective to compel a party or party-affiliated witness to appear and testify. No subpoena or court order is required. [CCP §2026.010(b)]

(2) [8:636] **Nonparty witness residing in another state:** If the nonparty witness lives in another state, his or her attendance can be compelled only under the *law of the place where the deposition is to be taken.* It is the responsibility of the party seeking to depose such a witness to proceed under that law. [CCP §2026.010(c)]

The requirements for compelling a witness' attendance vary considerably from state to state:

(a) [8:637] **Under Interstate and International Depositions and Discovery Act:** In states or countries that have adopted the "Interstate and International Depositions and Discovery Act" (CCP §2029.100 et seq., *discussed at ¶8:620.20 ff.*), the clerk of the court in the other state or country is empowered to issue a subpoena (or court order, however denominated) requiring a person to:

— attend and give testimony;
— produce and permit inspection, copying, testing or sampling of designated books, documents, records, electronically-stored information, or tangible things in that person's possession, custody or control; or
— permit inspection of premises under that person's control. [See CCP §2029.200(e)]

(b) [8:638] **Other states require further showing:** Other states require a showing of "relevancy" or "materiality" of the testimony sought to be obtained from the local resident, for issuance of a deposition subpoena.

[8:639] *Reserved.*

(c) [8:640] **Some states require "commission" from court where action pending:** Still other states require, for issuance of a deposition subpoena, that the court in which the action is pending have appointed an officer to administer oaths and take the deposition.

The Discovery Act authorizes California courts, when necessary or convenient, to issue a "commission" to a deposition officer in another state. Such appointment effectively authorizes that person to administer oaths and to take testimony for use in the California action. (The appointee is usually designated by the moving party—normally a court reporter, attorney or judicial officer in the other state.) [CCP §2026.010(f)]

1) [8:640.1] **Procedure:** Upon request, the court clerk will issue a commission, to any party in a pending action, without the necessity of a noticed motion or court order. The commission may contain whatever terms are required by the foreign jurisdiction to initiate the process. [CCP §2026.010(f)]

If the foreign jurisdiction requires a court order for issuance of the commission, such an order may be obtained by *ex parte* application. [CCP §2026.010(f)]

FORMS

- Motion for Issuance of Commission or Letters

Rogatory, *see Form 8:9* in Rivera, *Cal. Prac. Guide: Civ. Pro. Before Trial FORMS* (TRG).

- Commission, *see Form 8:10* in Rivera, *Cal. Prac. Guide: Civ. Pro. Before Trial FORMS* (TRG).

[8:641] ***PRACTICE POINTER:*** If you're taking depositions in another state, *associate local counsel*. Even if you can arrange the deposition yourself (hiring court reporter, etc.), you may need local counsel's assistance in obtaining and serving a deposition subpoena. More importantly, if the witness fails to appear or problems arise in the course of the deposition, you will need orders from local courts enforcing discovery. Unless you are admitted to practice in the other state and are familiar with its procedures, it will be difficult or impossible for you to obtain such orders without local counsel's help.

(3) [8:642] **Protective orders available:** Out-of-state depositions are very expensive, and this can burden less wealthy litigants. (E.g., a wealthy party may notice depositions all over the country, or all over the world, which less wealthy adversaries cannot afford to attend.) For "good cause shown," the court can make whatever orders are appropriate to protect any party from "undue burden and expense." [CCP §2025.420(b); *see* ¶*8:675*]

Such orders may include a wide variety of directives and conditions, such as:

- That the deposition not be taken at all;
- That it be taken at a less distant place;
- That it be taken on written, rather than oral, examination;
- That counsel or a nonparty deponent be permitted to participate in the deposition by telephone or other electronic means (*see* ¶*8:649*); or
- That it be taken only upon specified conditions (e.g., that the deposing party *pay the travel expenses of the other party's lawyer*). [CCP §2025.420(b)(1)-(16)]

(4) [8:642.1] **Compare—discovery questions governed by California law:** Although the procedures for compelling attendance of a nonresident are governed by the law of the place where he or she resides, discovery disputes arising during the deposition between the parties to the California litigation are governed by California law. [*International Ins. Co. v. Montrose Chemical Corp. of Calif.* (1991) 231 CA3d 1367, 1371, 282 CR 783, 785]

Thus, for example, a California party cannot evade California's liberal discovery rules by showing documents to a witness residing in a state with more restrictive rules. To suggest another state's law governs discoverability simply because a deposition is taken there is "nonsense, pure and simple." [*International Ins. Co. v. Montrose Chemical Corp. of Calif.*, supra, 231 CA3d at 1371, 282 CR at 785]

Compare—witness privileges: Conceivably, any issue as to privileges claimed by the nonresident witness may be determined by the law of the place where the deposition is taken. [Cf. CCP §2026.010(c)—deposing party shall use "process and procedures required and available under the laws of the state . . . where the deposition is to be taken to compel the deponent to attend and testify"]

e. **Procedures for depositions in foreign country**

(1) [8:643] **Party or party-affiliated witness:** A party subject to the jurisdiction of a California court, or any officer, director, managing agent or employee of a party, can be deposed in a foreign country. Service of a deposition notice is effective by itself to compel such persons to attend and to testify, and to produce for inspection, copying, testing or sampling any document, electronically-stored information or thing described in the notice. [CCP §2027.010(b)]

The Hague Convention provides other procedures for such discovery, but those procedures are *optional. See discussion at ¶8:50 ff.*

(a) [8:644] **Example:** A defendant in a California lawsuit can be compelled to appear for deposition, or to permit depositions of its employees, in a foreign country, and to allow examination of its records and plant there. If it fails to do so, it risks sanctions in the California lawsuit. [See *Volkswagenwerk Aktiengesellschaft v. Sup.Ct. (Thomsen)* (1981) 123 CA3d 840, 856-857, 176 CR 874, 884 (abrogated on other grounds as stated in *American Home Assur. Co. v. Societe Commerciale Toutelectric* (2002) 104 CA4th 406, 409, 128 CR2d 430, 433)]

(b) [8:645] **International comity as limitation:** However, international comity requires American courts to exercise "special vigilance" to avoid subjecting foreign litigants to unreasonably burdensome discovery. American courts must give "most careful consideration" to the policies and interests of whatever country is involved, and to any special problem confronted by the foreign litigant in complying with the discovery request. [*Societe Nationale Industrielle Aerospatiale v. U.S. Dist.Ct.* (1987) 482 US 522, 546, 107 S.Ct. 2542, 2557; *see ¶8:46*]

(c) [8:645.1] **Deposition officer:** The deposition must be taken under supervision of someone authorized to administer oaths in the U.S. or the foreign nation. Normally,

© 2020 Thomson Reuters/The Rutter Group

this is a U.S. diplomatic officer (secretary of embassy or legation; consul or consular agent, etc.). Or, it may be anyone else agreed upon by all parties. [CCP §2027.010(d)]

(2) [8:646] **Nonparty witnesses:** To depose a resident of a foreign country who is *not* a party to the California action (or officer, director, managing agent or employee of a party), the party seeking discovery must proceed under the laws and procedures of the foreign country. [CCP §2027.010(c)]

(a) [8:647] **Letters rogatory:** The party seeking discovery normally makes a motion in the California action for issuance of a commission or "letters rogatory." These are basically letters of *request* to the foreign government, asking it to appoint a deposition officer and to order the witness to appear and testify before such officer. [CCP §2027.010(e)]

Letters rogatory are addressed simply: "To the Appropriate Judicial Authority in (foreign country)." The deposition officer may be designated by name or descriptive title (e.g., "secretary of U.S. Embassy in . . ."). [See CCP §2027.010(e)]

FORM: Motion for Issuance of Commission or Letters Rogatory, *see Form 8:9* in Rivera, *Cal. Prac. Guide: Civ. Pro. Before Trial FORMS* (TRG).

(b) [8:648] **Compare—Hague Convention procedures:** Where the deposition is sought to be taken in a country which has signed the Hague Convention, the deposing party may (optionally) utilize the Convention's procedures. (*See discussion at ¶8:50 ff.*)

f. [8:649] **Depositions by telephone, videoconference or other electronic means:** Any party may take an oral deposition by telephone, videoconference or other remote electronic means, *provided:*

— notice of the specific electronic means is served with the notice of deposition or the subpoena; and

— that party makes the arrangements for any other party to participate in the deposition in an equivalent manner (i.e., by telephone, videoconference, etc.). (The party utilizing the services must pay whatever expenses are incurred or properly allocated to it for those services.) [CCP §2025.310(c); CRC 3.1010(a)]

Certified court reporters may administer oaths and perform the duties of a deposition officer in depositions taken by telephone or other remote electronic means. [See CCP §2093(b)(2)]

(1) [8:649.1] **Party deponent must appear in person:** A *party* deponent must appear at his or her deposition in person and in the presence of the deposition officer. [CCP §2025.310(b); CRC 3.1010(c)]

(2) [8:649.2] **Nonparty deponent may appear at remote location:** A *nonparty* deponent, however, may seek a court order, based on a finding of good cause and no prejudice to any party, allowing him or her to appear by telephone, videoconference or other remote electronic means. The deponent must be "sworn" (but apparently need not testify) in the presence of the deposition officer, or as otherwise provided by stipulation or court order. [CCP §2025.310(b); CRC 3.1010(d)]

(3) [8:649.3] **Party's right to appear at deposition by telephone, videoconference or other remote electronic means:** Any party may participate in a deposition by telephone, videoconference or other remote electronic means by:

— serving written notice of such appearance by fax, email or personal delivery at least three court days before the deposition; and

— making all arrangements and paying all expenses incurred for the appearance. [CRC 3.1010(b)]

[8:649.4] *Reserved.*

(4) [8:649.5] **Other parties' right to attend:** Any *party* may be personally present at a deposition taken by telephone, videoconference or other remote electronic means without giving prior notice. [CRC 3.1010(a)(3), (d)]

[8:649.6-649.9] *Reserved.*

(5) [8:649.10] **Other arrangements by stipulation or court order:** Any of the above procedures (¶*8:649 ff.*) (or any other discovery procedure) may be modified by court order or written stipulation of the parties. [CCP §2016.030; see also CRC 3.1010(e) (court order)]

[8:650] ***PRACTICE POINTER:*** Telephone depositions can certainly save time and expense of long trips to depose witnesses in other states or countries. However, the arrangement has its limitations: You can't see the impact of your questions, the witness' nonverbal responses, or exactly which part of a document the witness is looking at. Sometimes, you run into inexplicable pauses between the question and answer, and you wonder who may be listening in and "coaching" the witness. Also, the deposition reporter sometimes has trouble determining who is talking. As a result, telephone depositions are not recommended for obtaining controversial testimony.

These shortcomings can be ameliorated to some extent through *video conferencing*, which enables you to observe a witness' "live" testimony without the expense of travel. Teleconferencing centers now exist in most major U.S. cities and in many foreign countries. A camera at each location allows the parties to observe each other simultaneously; and when documents are provided in advance, split-screen technology enables

© 2020 Thomson Reuters/The Rutter Group

the questioner to view the documents as the witness testifies about them. The parties should also consider stipulating to the use of free or low cost video chat services (e.g., Skype or FaceTime). (*See also Practice Pointer at ¶8:659.*)

9. [8:651] **Deposition Officer:** The deposition must be conducted under the supervision of an officer authorized to administer oaths (e.g., notary public), who is neither related to nor employed by any attorney or party, and who has no financial interest in the action. [CCP §§2025.320(a), 2093]

[8:652] ***PRACTICE POINTER:*** The most common practice is to designate someone who is both a notary public and also a certified shorthand reporter (CSR). The deposition officer thus serves the dual function of administering the oath and recording the testimony. [*Serrano v. Stefan Merli Plastering Co., Inc.* (2008) 162 CA4th 1014, 1033, 76 CR3d 559, 572 (citing text)]

If for any reason the oath is administered by one person and the testimony taken down by another, the officer administering the oath (e.g., notary public) is responsible for "supervising" the proceedings and *must remain present* during the entire proceedings.

(This rarely occurs in local practice, but is sometimes encountered with depositions on written questions to a witness residing abroad. The oath will be administered by a consular official, while the testimony will be taken down by a secretary or stenographer.)

a. [8:653] **Procedure for challenging qualifications:** Any objection to the qualifications of the deposition officer is *waived* unless made before the deposition begins or as soon thereafter as the ground for that objection becomes known or could be discovered by reasonable diligence. [CCP §2025.320(e)]

[8:653.1-653.4] *Reserved.*

b. [8:653.5] **Services available to all parties:** Any service or product provided by a deposition officer must be made available at the same time to all parties or their attorneys. [CCP §2025.320(b)]

Upon request by any party, each other party must state on the record all services and products obtained from the deposition officer. [CCP §2025.320(d)]

(1) [8:653.6] **Allocation of charges among parties:** CCP §2025.320(b)-(d) does not expressly deal with the fees a deposition reporter may charge for its services. However, the statutory requirement that such services be made "available" to all parties limits *unreasonable* charges by a court reporter or unreasonable allocation of those charges between or among the parties (*see ¶8:767 ff.*). [See *Serrano v. Stefan Merli Plastering Co., Inc.*, supra, 162 CA4th at 1039, 76 CR3d at 578]

[8:653.7-653.9] *Reserved.*

c. [8:653.10] **No investigation or evaluation of deponent:** A deposition officer may not, as a service to any party, collect information about the deponent, or provide notations or comments regarding demeanor and personal identifying data of any witness, attorney or party present at the deposition. [CCP §2025.320(c)]

d. [8:653.11] **No deposition summary by reporter:** The court reporter may not, as a service to any party, transcribe or assist in the preparation of a summary of a deposition conducted by that reporter. [See 16 CCR §2474]

10. **Preservation of Testimony**

a. [8:654] **Administration of oath:** The first step in the proceedings is for the deposition officer to put the deponent under oath (or affirmation, ¶*8:654.1*). [CCP §2025.330(a)]

(1) [8:654.1] **Form of oath:** A nonreligious oath is available as an alternative to "so help me, God." [See CCP §2094(a)—"Do you solemnly state, under penalty of perjury . . ."]

b. [8:655] **Stenographic recording:** Unless counsel stipulate or the court orders otherwise, the entire proceedings—questions, answers, objections, arguments, etc.—must be taken down stenographically (i.e., by shorthand or stenotype machine) by a *certified* deposition reporter (see Bus. & Prof.C. §8020 et seq.). [CCP §2025.330(b)]

(1) [8:655.1] **"Real time transcription":** If the deposition is to be conducted using instant visual display of questions and answers ("real time transcription"), that fact must be included in the deposition subpoena or notice (*see* ¶*8:487*) and a copy given to the deposition reporter. [CCP §§2020.310(d), 2025.220(a)(5)]

➪ [8:655.2] ***PRACTICE POINTER:*** If you are the deposing counsel, position the display screen so that it *cannot be seen by the witness.* (If the witness' attorney has plugged a laptop into the reporter's machine, make sure the witness is not reading from the attorney's laptop.) Otherwise, the witness may decide not to answer until after reading the question, providing additional time to "ponder" the question and disrupting the flow of your questioning.

(2) [8:655.3] **Rough transcripts ("dailies"):** The deposition reporter may offer to provide either party with a "dirty disk" (before clean-up) or a printout of the instant visual display or rough draft transcripts ("dailies").

If such an agreement is made with either party, the deposition officer must make the same offer to all parties in attendance at the deposition. [CCP §2025.340(d)]

© 2020 Thomson Reuters/The Rutter Group

(3) [8:656] **Stipulation "off the record":** Counsel present may stipulate that any portion of the proceedings be "off the record": i.e., not taken down by the deposition reporter.

☞ [8:657] ***PRACTICE POINTER:*** This is common practice while counsel are examining documents, arranging dates for further discovery, etc.

It can also be used to avoid taking down *arguments between counsel.* A simple statement of the ground for objection is enough to preserve any objection at trial. And, a simple statement of the reasons why the objection does not lie is enough for a court to rule on a motion to compel. The balance of arguments between counsel can very well be "off the record." This often eliminates pages and pages of transcript, reducing costs, and making the transcript itself easier to handle.

On the other hand, sometimes opposing counsel try to take advantage of being "off the record" by offensive comments or conduct. In such cases, simply tell the deposition reporter you want to go "back on the record."

Also, if you have reached any oral stipulations while "off the record," remember to repeat them *on the record* when you resume the proceedings.

[8:657.1-657.4] *Reserved.*

(4) [8:657.5] **Cost of "real time" or rough transcripts:** Any party or attorney requesting instant visual display of testimony or rough draft transcripts must pay the reasonable cost of those services, not to exceed the charges to any other party or attorney. [CCP §2025.220(a)(5)]

c. [8:658] **Audio or video recording:** *In addition* to the stenographic recording, a deposition may be recorded by audio or video technology if the parties so agree or if the deposition notice so provides. [CCP §2025.330(c)]

If the deposition is recorded both stenographically and by audio or video technology, the stenographic transcript is the official record for purposes of trial and appeal. [CCP §2025.510(g)] (The parties may stipulate to eliminate the stenographic recording; but this is rarely done.)

The conditions under which the audio or video recording may be played at trial are discussed at ¶*8:674*.

☞ [8:659] ***PRACTICE POINTER:*** Video recording depositions is extremely effective. In the past, lawyers worried that the witness might be distracted by the video camera; or that opposing counsel might engage in unnecessary theatrics. But experience with video recording generally proves otherwise. [See *Emerson Elec. Co. v. Sup.Ct. (Grayson)* (1997) 16 C4th 1101, 1109, 68 CR2d 883, 887, fn. 3 (quoting text in part)]

- First of all, video recording usually *cuts down on abuses by counsel* during the deposition (e.g., coaching the witness, unnecessary interruptions of the questioning, abusive questions or objections, etc.).
- It also tends to make the *witness more candid.* (The "eye of the camera" is upon him or her, etc.)
- It also provides a far *better record* of the examination than any transcript or audio recording. It is clearly the *best* way to preserve the testimony of a witness who is ill or feeble and may be unavailable to testify at trial; or of a key witness living in another state or country who is unwilling or unable to testify in person at trial. Additionally, it records the witness' *nonverbal* responses (e.g., shifty eyes, long pauses, facial expressions), which undeniably influence juries.
- The deponent can be requested to demonstrate or "act out" what happened. For example, in product liability cases, the plaintiff can be asked to show how he or she *used* the product (often providing invaluable evidence where misuse is claimed). (*See discussion at ¶8:708.1.*)
- If you represent the deponent, be sure to *prepare and rehearse* the client as you would for testimony at trial. If possible, make a *practice* video recording that you can critique with the client prior to the actual deposition.
- Although video recording adds an element of expense, video recording costs are generally *recoverable as court costs* if you win (see CCP §1033.5(a)(3)).
- Search and retrieve capabilities can be greatly enhanced by *obtaining the recording in a searchable electronic format.* Many reporters will generate written deposition transcripts with time stamps synced to the video recording that makes finding specific testimony (either from the video to the transcript, or vice versa) much easier.

(1) [8:660] **Deposition notice must state recording will be made:** Absent stipulation by all counsel, audio or video recording of a deposition is allowed only if the deposition notice states the deposing party's intention to record the testimony by either of these methods. [CCP §§2025.220(a)(5), 2025.330(c); *see ¶8:487*]

© 2020 Thomson Reuters/The Rutter Group

[8:660.1] ***PRACTICE POINTER:*** Many lawyers routinely include a notice of video recording in their notices of deposition. There is no known authority imposing a penalty for later deciding not to video record the deposition. However, if a party did not give his or her own notice of video recording (¶*8:662*) in reliance on the deposing party's notice, counsel should attempt to work out the consequences (e.g., suspend the deposition to make video recording arrangements).

(a) [8:661] **Special notice if expert witness video to be used at trial:** As discussed later, a video recording of an expert witness' deposition testimony may be used *in lieu of* live testimony at trial without showing the expert is unavailable to testify in person (CCP §2025.620(d), *see* ¶*8:892*). But this is allowed only if the *deposition notice* states the party's intent to do so. [CCP §2025.220(a)(6); *see* ¶*8:487*]

[8:661.1] ***PRACTICE POINTER:*** This can substantially reduce the cost of using expert testimony. And it avoids the problem of scheduling the expert's testimony at trial.

Consequently, consider using this procedure regularly for expert witness depositions. (You can always change your mind and offer expert testimony live if you choose; e.g., where opposing experts are testifying live and credibility is crucial.)

(b) [8:662] **Other parties may make own recordings; notice required:** Any other party may make a separate audio or video recording of the proceedings at his or her own expense. Notice of the intent to do so must be served on all other parties (and on the deponent if subpoenaed) at least 3 calendar days before the deposition. (If served just 3 days before the deposition, personal service is required.) [CCP §2025.330(c)]

[8:662.1-662.4] *Reserved.*

(c) [8:662.5] **Recording opposing counsel?** Whether the above statute (¶*8:662*) allows video recording *opposing counsel* instead of the witness is "questionable." [*Green v. GTE Calif., Inc.* (1994) 29 CA4th 407, 408-410, 34 CR2d 517, 518-519—sanctions upheld against counsel who, *without* providing requisite notice, brought along video camera to record opposing counsel's "intimidation tactics" (e.g., facial expressions and gestures); court stated: "If this case is an example, the term 'civil procedure' is an oxymoron"]

➪ [8:662.6] ***PRACTICE POINTER:*** If controlling opposing counsel during the deposition is a potential problem, ask the court for an order *expressly authorizing* such video recording before the deposition commences. Also consider obtaining the court's help in arranging for space at the courthouse for the deposition. Proximity to the judge may reduce bad behavior by deponents and counsel.

(2) [8:663] **Operator's qualifications:** The operator of the recording equipment must be *competent* to set up, operate and monitor the equipment involved; and must not distort the appearance or demeanor of the participants by camera or sound recording techniques. [CCP §2025.340(b), (g)]

(a) [8:664] **May be deposing attorney's employee:** The operator may be an employee of the attorney taking the deposition; but in such case may not also be the deposition officer (administering the oath). [CCP §§2025.320(a), 2025.340(b)]

(b) [8:665] **Special requirements where expert witness video recording to be used at trial:** Where an expert witness' testimony is being video recorded for use at trial in lieu of live testimony (see CCP §2025.620(d), ¶*8:892*), the operator *cannot* be a relative or employee of any attorney or party or have any financial interest in the action; and must be *authorized to administer the oath*. (These restrictions can be waived by the parties attending the deposition.) [CCP §2025.340(c)]

(3) [8:666] **Procedures:** The Discovery Act sets forth in considerable detail the procedures to be followed in an audio or video recorded deposition:

(a) [8:667] **Area:** The area used for recording must be "suitably large, adequately lighted and reasonably quiet." [CCP §2025.340(a)]

(b) [8:668] **Opening information:** The deposition must begin with an oral or written statement (on camera or on the audio recording) that includes:

- operator's name and business address;
- name and business address of the operator's employer;
- date, time and place of the deposition;
- caption of the case;
- name of the deponent;
- on which party's behalf the deposition is being taken; and
- any stipulations of the parties. [CCP §2025.340(h)]

© 2020 Thomson Reuters/The Rutter Group

Counsel for the parties must then identify themselves on camera or on the audio recording. [CCP §2025.340(i)]

(c) [8:669] **Administration of oath:** The oath must then be administered to the deponent on camera or on the audio recording. [CCP §2025.340(j)]

(d) [8:670] **Tape run-overs:** Where the deposition requires use of more than one unit of tape or electronic storage, the end of each unit and the beginning of the next must be announced on camera or on the audio recording. [CCP §2025.340(k)]

(e) [8:671] **Conclusion:** A statement must be made on camera or on the audio recording stating the examination is concluded, and setting forth any stipulations re custody of the recording and exhibits, or other matters. [CCP §2025.340(*l*)]

[8:672] *Reserved.*

(4) [8:673] **Copies of recording:** Any party (including those not attending the depo) is entitled, upon request, to review the audio or video recording and obtain a copy upon payment of reasonable costs of duplication. [CCP §2025.510(f)]

(5) [8:674] **Notice required prior to use at trial:** A party intending to offer an audio or video recording of a deposition at trial must give written notice to the court and all other parties sufficiently in advance of trial for objections to be made and ruled on *before* the trial or hearing. A stenographic transcript must accompany whatever portions of the recording are being offered. [See CCP §2025.340(m)]

(a) [8:674.1] **Includes video recording of expert witness depo:** The provision allowing use at trial of an expert witness' video recorded deposition specifically requires the proponent to comply with the above procedure (¶*8:674*) so that objections to any portion of the expert's testimony can be settled prior to trial. [CCP §2025.620(d), *discussed at* ¶*8:892*]

11. [8:675] **Protective Orders:** Before, after or even during a deposition, "for good cause shown," the court may grant a protective order to control the deposition proceedings or the information obtained thereby. [See CCP §2025.420]

[8:675.1] ***PRACTICE POINTER:*** It isn't always necessary to seek a protective order to control improper deposition questions or tactics. It is usually more practical *simply to object* than it is to adjourn the depo and seek a protective order. (See "Strategies and Tactics re Protective Orders," *discussed at* ¶*8:1022*.)

But a protective order is the *only* effective remedy where you are seeking to suppress or limit deposition testimony by an *independent witness* (e.g., on grounds his or her information is privileged). Merely objecting at the deposition won't prevent the independent witness from disregarding your objection and answering the questions.

a. [8:676] **Grounds for relief:** The court is empowered to issue whatever order "justice requires" to protect a party or deponent against "unwarranted annoyance, embarrassment, or oppression, or undue burden and expense." [CCP §2025.420(b); see *Nativi v. Deutsche Bank Nat'l Trust Co.* (2014) 223 CA4th 261, 316, 167 CR3d 173, 218—§2025.420(b) provides "*nonexclusive* list of permissible directions that may be included in a protective order" (emphasis in original)]

Generally, this requires a showing that the *burdens* involved in the deposition proceeding *clearly outweigh* whatever *benefits* are sought to be obtained thereby. [See CCP §2017.020(a), ¶*8:74*]

It is also ground for relief that the information sought is unnecessarily cumulative; or that it is obtainable elsewhere at less cost and inconvenience. [See CCP §2019.030(a), ¶*8:43*]

b. [8:677] **Relief available:** "For good cause shown," the court is empowered to make whatever orders are required, including the following:

- *Prohibiting* the deposition entirely;
- *Changing* the time or place from that stated in the deposition notice;
- *Postponing* a video deposition of an expert witness that is to be used at trial in lieu of live testimony (under CCP §2025.620(d), *see* ¶*8:892*) to allow opposing parties time to prepare for cross-examining the expert (including taking his or her deposition, if necessary);
- *Limiting scope* of questioning permitted at the deposition;
- *Limiting form* of discovery, by requiring written instead of oral questions, or interrogatories to a party instead of a deposition;
- *Denying production* or inspection of materials demanded in the deposition notice;
- *Setting conditions* for the production of *electronically-stored information;*
- *Protecting confidential information* (trade secrets, etc.) by limiting the persons to whom disclosure is to be made, and how much information must be disclosed;
- *Excluding nonparties* from the deposition;
- *Limiting public access* to the deposition transcript (by requiring it to be sealed and thereafter opened only on court order);
- *Imposing terms and conditions* on which the deposition may proceed (CCP §2025.420(b));

© 2020 Thomson Reuters/The Rutter Group

- *Appointing a referee* to preside over the deposition and rule on any objections (CCP §639(a)(5), *see* ¶*8:742 ff.*);
- *Changing* the otherwise applicable *time limit* on deposition examination of a witness (CCP §2025.290(c), *see* ¶*8:702.10*).

c. **Application**

(1) [8:678] **Control timing and priority of depositions:** Generally, depositions are allowed to proceed in the order in which they are noticed; i.e., earlier notice does not assure priority (although some courts have different policies; *see* ¶*8:494*).

But if one party is seeking an *unfair* advantage from the timing of the deposition, the other may seek a protective order. [*Poeschl v. Sup.Ct. (Fair)* (1964) 229 CA2d 383, 386-387, 40 CR 697, 699—delaying deposition until deponent had chance to review earlier tape-recorded conversation to refresh his recollection of events]

[8:678.1-678.4] *Reserved.*

(2) [8:678.5] **Control duplicative or burdensome discovery:** A court may limit or prohibit a particular discovery procedure that it finds to be "unreasonably cumulative or duplicative, or . . . unduly burdensome or expensive." [CCP §2019.030(a); *Emerson Elec. Co. v. Sup.Ct. (Grayson)* (1997) 16 C4th 1101, 1110, 68 CR2d 883, 888—in appropriate cases, court can impose conditions on video recorded depositions]

(3) [8:679] **Control conduct of deposition:** A court is empowered to terminate or limit a deposition that is being conducted in bad faith, or in such a manner as to *unreasonably* annoy, embarrass or oppress the deponent or party. [CCP §2025.420(b); *see* ¶*8:714 ff.*]

(4) [8:680] **Control dissemination of deposition testimony:** Information obtained through pretrial discovery does *not* automatically become public property. The court may, through protective orders, prohibit disclosure of deposition testimony that has not yet been introduced into evidence at a public trial. [*Seattle Times Co. v. Rhinehart* (1984) 467 US 20, 33, 104 S.Ct. 2199, 2207-2208 (decided under similar Federal Rule)]

(a) [8:681] **No First Amendment concern:** Pretrial discovery is a matter of "legislative grace." Litigants have no First Amendment right to publish information so obtained; and the public has no right to receive such information: "[P]retrial depositions and interrogatories are *not public* components of a civil trial . . . Much of the information that surfaces during pretrial discovery may be unrelated, or only tangentially related, to the underlying cause of action. Therefore, restraints placed on discovered, but not yet admitted, information are not a restriction on a traditionally public source of information." [*Seattle Times Co. v. Rhinehart*, supra, 467 US at 33, 104 S.Ct.

at 2208; *NBC Subsidiary (KNBC-TV), Inc. v. Sup.Ct. (Locke)* (1999) 20 C4th 1178, 1208, 86 CR2d 778, 802, fn. 25]

(b) **Examples**

- [8:682] A newspaper defendant in a libel suit may be enjoined from publishing confidential information regarding the plaintiff obtained through pretrial discovery. [*Seattle Times Co. v. Rhinehart*, supra, 467 US at 33, 104 S.Ct. at 2208]
- [8:683] Plaintiffs suing City for police harassment may be prohibited from disseminating information obtained through pretrial discovery from police files; and, on settlement, may be required to *return* the documents to City. (Plaintiffs were seeking to retain the documents for release to the news media and for use in other litigation against City.) [*Coalition Against Police Abuse v. Sup.Ct. (City of Los Angeles)* (1985) 170 CA3d 888, 894, 216 CR 614, 617]

(c) [8:684] **Compare—information publicly disclosed:** Once deposition testimony has been publicly disclosed, however (e.g., at a public hearing or trial), it is in the public domain, and further restraints on a party's use or republication thereof are improper. [*Coalition Against Police Abuse v. Sup.Ct. (City of Los Angeles)*, supra, 170 CA3d at 902, 216 CR at 623]

[8:684.1-684.4] *Reserved.*

(5) [8:684.5] **Protect informant's identity:** The court's power to protect "a party, deponent *or other natural person*" from embarrassment or oppression "necessarily includes the authority to protect the identity of an informant whose safety would be jeopardized by disclosure." [*John Z. v. Sup.Ct. (Swafford)* (1991) 1 CA4th 789, 791, 2 CR2d 556, 557 (emphasis added; internal quotes omitted)]

(6) [8:684.6] **Prohibit deposing unknowledgeable top executive:** A protective order prohibiting the deposition of a corporate president may be granted where it is shown he or she lacks knowledge or involvement in the litigation, and such deposition is being sought prior to plaintiff's exhaustion of less intrusive means of discovery. Such "high level" (or "apex") depositions "raise a tremendous potential for discovery abuse and harassment." [*Liberty Mut. Ins. Co. v. Sup.Ct. (Frysinger)* (1992) 10 CA4th 1282, 1287-1288, 13 CR2d 363, 366 (analogizing to federal cases and citing text)]

Similarly, heads of governmental agencies and other top officials normally are not subject to depositions involving matters on which they have no personal knowledge. It makes no difference that they are named as parties in the litigation. [*Nagle v. Sup.Ct. (Green)* (1994) 28 CA4th 1465, 1467-1468, 34 CR2d 281, 282; *Westly v. Sup.Ct. (Cates)* (2005) 125 CA4th 907, 910-911, 23 CR3d 154, 156; *Contractors' State License Bd. v. Sup.Ct. (Black Diamond Elec., Inc.)* (2018) 23 CA5th 125, 128, 232 CR3d 558, 560—head of government agency generally not subject to deposition unless he or she has "direct personal factual information pertaining to material issues in the action . . . not available through any other source" (internal quotes omitted)]

(7) [8:684.7] **Prohibit deposing opposing counsel:** *See discussion at ¶8:467.1 ff.*

d. **Procedural matters**

(1) [8:685] **Who may obtain relief:** Protective orders may be granted on motion of the deponent or any party, or any third person who could be affected by the disclosure (e.g., a nonparty whose privacy would be impaired). [CCP §2025.420(a)]

☞ [8:685.1] ***PRACTICE POINTER:*** *Consider alternative procedures discussed at ¶8:787.1.*

(a) [8:686] **Not on court's own motion:** There is no statutory authority for a court limiting discovery on its own motion. Both CCP §2017.020(a) and §2019.030(b) require a "motion" by the deponent or party or person affected. However, judges handling cases designated "complex" (¶*12:47 ff.*) may have more flexibility to manage and control discovery.

(2) [8:687] **Notice and hearing required:** A formal noticed motion and hearing are always required. A protective order *cannot* be granted ex parte. [*St. Paul Fire & Marine Ins. Co. v. Sup.Ct. (Borak)* (1984) 156 CA3d 82, 85-86, 202 CR 571, 573]

However, for good cause (e.g., a looming discovery cut-off date), the court may grant an ex parte application for an order shortening the time for *notice* of the motion; *see* ¶*9:364.*

FORM: Motion for Protective Order and for Sanctions and Proposed Order, *see Form 8:18* in Rivera, *Cal. Prac. Guide: Civ. Pro. Before Trial FORMS* (TRG).

Cross-refer: The motion is governed by the rules and procedures governing motions generally; *see Ch. 9 Part I.*

(3) [8:688] **Attempt to resolve informally required:** The motion for protective order must be accompanied by a declaration stating facts showing a "reasonable and good faith attempt" to resolve the matter outside court. [CCP §2025.420(a)] (The "attempt to resolve informally" requirement is discussed in more detail at ¶*8:1158 ff.*)

(4) [8:689] **Burden of proof:** The burden is on the moving party to establish "good cause" for whatever relief is requested: "Generally, a deponent seeking a protective order will be required to show that the burden, expense, or intrusiveness involved in . . . [the discovery procedure] clearly outweighs the likelihood that the information sought will lead to the discovery of admissible evidence." [*Emerson Elec. Co. v. Sup.Ct. (Grayson)* (1997) 16 C4th 1101, 1110, 68 CR2d 883, 888; see *Nativi v. Deutsche Bank Nat'l Trust Co.* (2014) 223 CA4th 261, 318, 167 CR3d 173, 220—burden *not* met by "entirely conclusory" declaration that "lacked any factual specificity"]

➪ [8:690] ***PRACTICE POINTER:*** Normally, the motion for protective order is based on declarations by the moving party's counsel. Such declarations must state *facts* (rather than mere conclusions) showing grounds for relief. I.e., it is *not* enough simply to repeat the statutory grounds ("unwarranted annoyance, embarrassment or oppression or undue burden and expense").

However, to be admissible, declarations generally must be based on demonstrated personal knowledge and often it is only the *client* (or others) who has first-hand knowledge of issues such as burden.

(a) [8:691] **Compare—where moving party "presumptively entitled to protective order":** Such a showing is not necessary, however, where the moving party is "presumptively entitled to a protective order"; e.g., where a defendant is asked questions regarding his or her net worth in an action for punitive damages (*see* ¶*8:327.1 ff.*).

(b) [8:691.1] **Special ESI protective order burdens of proof:** *See discussion at* ¶*8:692.5 ff.*

(5) [8:692] **Court's discretion:** Ultimately the granting or denial of a protective order rests in the judge's sound discretion. If complete relief is denied, the court may nevertheless impose terms or *conditions* upon which the deposition may proceed. [CCP §2025.420(g)]

(a) [8:692.1] **Limited appellate review:** An order granting or denying a protective order is reviewable only by writ petition (¶*8:13 ff.*) and only for abuse of discretion. [See *Meritplan Ins. Co. v. Sup.Ct. (Wexler)* (1981) 124 CA3d 237, 242, 177 CR 236, 239—abuse shown where court barred taking attorney's deposition simply because questions asked *might* be privileged (adequate procedures exist for asserting privilege, and attorney might be asked for information *not* privileged); *Nativi v. Deutsche Bank Nat'l Trust Co.*, supra, 223 CA4th at 318-319, 167 CR3d at 220—issuance of "sweeping" order that went "far

© 2020 Thomson Reuters/The Rutter Group

beyond" restricting pretrial document disclosure was abuse of discretion]

[8:692.2-692.4] *Reserved.*

(6) **Special procedural rules and conditions re ESI protective orders (ESI from not "reasonably accessible" source)**

(a) [8:692.5] **Initial burden on party resisting discovery:** The party or affected person seeking a protective order regarding production, inspection, etc. of *electronically-stored information* (ESI) on the ground that the information is *from a source that is not "reasonably accessible"* because of "*undue burden or expense*" bears the burden of demonstrating the information is in fact from a source not reasonably accessible because of undue burden or expense. [CCP §2025.420(c) (emphasis added)]

(b) [8:692.6] **Demanding party's "good cause" burden:** If the party resisting the ESI discovery establishes that the information is from a source not reasonably accessible because of undue burden or expense, the burden shifts to the demanding party to establish "good cause" for the ESI discovery nonetheless. [CCP §2025.420(d)]

(c) [8:692.7] **Conditional order for discovery:** Upon finding the demanding party has met its "good cause" burden (¶*8:692.6*), the court may order the ESI discovery *subject to certain limitations* (¶*8:692.8*) and may set *conditions* for the discovery, including allocation of the ESI discovery expense. [CCP §2025.420(d), (e)]

(d) [8:692.8] **Limitations on frequency or extent of ESI discovery:** The court "shall" limit the frequency or extent of ESI discovery—*even from a reasonably accessible source*—upon determining that *any of the following conditions exist:*

— it is possible to obtain the ESI from another source that is "more convenient, less burdensome, or less expensive";

— the ESI sought is "unreasonably cumulative or duplicative";

— the party seeking the ESI has had "ample opportunity by discovery in the action" to obtain the information; or

— the "likely burden or expense" of the proposed ESI discovery "outweighs the likely benefit, taking into account the amount in controversy, the resources of the parties, the importance of the issues in the litigation, and the importance of the requested discovery in resolving the issues." [CCP §2025.420(f)(1)-(4)]

(e) [8:692.9] **"Safe harbor" against sanctions where ESI lost or destroyed due to computer system:** Absent exceptional circumstances, sanctions "shall not" be imposed against any party, deponent or other affected person or organization, or any of their attorneys, for failure to provide electronically-stored information that has been lost, damaged, altered or overwritten as a result of the "routine, good faith operation of an electronic information system." [CCP §2025.420(i)(1)]

But this "safe harbor" provision does *not alter* any obligation to *preserve* discoverable information. [CCP §2025.420(i)(2)]

(7) [8:693] **Monetary sanction against losing party:** The court "shall" impose a monetary sanction against whichever party loses on the motion for protective order *unless* it finds that party acted "with substantial justification" or other circumstances render the sanction "unjust." [CCP §2025.420(h); *see further discussion at ¶8:2070 ff.*]

[8:694] *Reserved.*

12. [8:695] **Conduct of Deposition:** Examination and cross-examination of witnesses generally proceeds in the same manner as at trial under the Evidence Code. [CCP §2025.330(d)]

But there are some important differences:

a. [8:696] **Who may attend:** The Discovery Act does not specifically state who may or may not attend a deposition. But it recognizes that parties and their counsel have the *right* to be there. This is implicit in the statute dealing with protective orders which allows the court to exclude from a deposition "designated persons, *other than the parties to the action and their officers and counsel.*" [CCP §2025.420(b)(12) (emphasis added)]

(1) [8:697] **Parties:** Therefore, a court has no power to grant a protective order barring a party from attending another's deposition even on a showing that the deponent will feel "intimidated" by the party's presence at the deposition. [*Willoughby v. Sup.Ct. (Lui)* (1985) 172 CA3d 890, 892, 218 CR 486, 487]

(a) [8:697.1] **Compare—Federal Rule:** FRCP 26(c), dealing with protective orders, contains no exception for parties or counsel. Thus, even parties may be excluded from a deposition to prevent harassment or embarrassment to the deponent. [See *Galella v. Onassis* (2nd Cir. 1973) 487 F2d 986, 997]

(2) [8:697.2] **Officers of corporate parties:** The statute says a party's "officers" cannot be excluded. But this is given a common-sense interpretation. Not *every* officer of a corporate party is entitled to be present. To prevent discovery abuse, the court may grant a protective order excluding *some* officers.

© 2020 Thomson Reuters/The Rutter Group

[*Lowy Develop. Corp. v. Sup.Ct. (Fontenla)* (1987) 190 CA3d 317, 321, 235 CR 401, 403]

(a) [8:697.3] **Example:** Where a corporate officer's deposition is being taken, a court may exclude other officers whose depositions are to follow, to prevent their "parroting" the first officer's testimony provided, however, that at least one officer or agent *other than the deponent* is present at all times. [*Lowy Develop. Corp. v. Sup.Ct. (Fontenla)*, supra, 190 CA3d at 321-322, 235 CR at 403-404]

In addition, if there is a protective order in place barring certain documents or information from disclosure to a party (e.g., highly competitive trade secret information), presumably a party can be excluded from the room while that information and/or documents are discussed.

(3) [8:698] **Nonparties:** As the statute makes clear, for "good cause shown" the court may exclude "designated persons" from attending a deposition. [CCP §2025.420(b)(12)]

But the converse is also true: Absent a protective order, nonparties *may attend* a deposition. (Indeed, it may be necessary or efficient to have a nonparty attend: e.g., a caregiver for the deponent; or a consultant to hear the testimony of an opposing expert.)

(a) [8:699] **Comment:** As a practical matter, total strangers (e.g., the press) cannot force their way into a deposition because the proceedings are usually in private offices rather than a public courthouse.

The more difficult question is whether a party or counsel may *invite* nonparties to sit in and observe the deposition. Sometimes, deponents invite family members or staff for psychological support or to help refresh their memory during recesses. Sometimes, the lawyer conducting the deposition will invite the press or nonparties whose presence makes the deponent feel uncomfortable.

Unless counsel resolve the matter amicably, one side or the other will suspend the deposition and seek a protective order (*see ¶8:714*). A showing will have to be made that allowing such nonparties to attend would cause "*unwarranted* annoyance, embarrassment, or oppression." [CCP §2025.420(b) (emphasis added)]

[8:700] *Reserved.*

b. [8:701] **Explanation to witness:** Deposing counsel usually begins the deposition by explaining to the witness the nature of the proceedings: i.e., that the witness is under oath; that the witness should not answer unless he or she fully understands the question; that the witness will have a chance to correct the transcript, but that counsel may comment to the jury upon such corrections at time of trial, etc.

These explanations are important because they put the deponent "on notice" of the significance of the proceedings and the consequences of his or her answers. It becomes very difficult for the deponent later to claim that he or she "didn't understand" the questions, etc.

☞ [8:701.1] ***PRACTICE POINTER:*** If the deponent is represented by counsel, you probably don't need a lot of introductory explanation. You can simply ask, "Did your lawyer explain to you the nature of these proceedings and the consequences of the testimony you will be giving here today?" If the deponent answers "Yes," it is probably sufficient to overcome any later argument that he or she did not understand what was involved.

On the other hand, some lawyers prefer to go through a detailed explanation at the beginning of each deposition. It gives them a chance to "loosen up" before jumping right into the questioning. It may also put the deponent at ease and establish a climate for more responsive answers.

Also, a more detailed explanation, on the record, may be useful at trial if the witness attempts to avoid impeachment by claiming he or she did not understand the deposition process or the nature of the oath administered.

c. [8:702] **Time limitation:** Subject to exceptions noted below (¶*8:702.1 ff.*), the deposition examination of a witness by all counsel, other than the witness' counsel of record, is limited to *seven hours* of total testimony. [CCP §2025.290(a)]

(1) [8:702.1] **Additional time by court order:** Deposition examination of a witness may go beyond the seven-hour limit by court order, including a case management order. The court "shall" allow additional time "if needed to fairly examine the deponent or if the deponent, another person, or any other circumstance impedes or delays the examination." [CCP §2025.290(a); see *Certainteed Corp. v. Sup.Ct. (Hart)* (2014) 222 CA4th 1053, 1060, 166 CR3d 539, 544—7-hour time limit is "merely presumptive" and applies only if court does not order otherwise]

When necessary to fairly examine the deponent, the court may likewise extend the 14-hour time limit applicable to complex cases where the witness' survival is doubtful (or for other reasons) (¶*8:702.5*). [*Certainteed Corp. v. Sup.Ct. (Hart)*, supra, 222 CA4th at 1061-1062, 166 CR3d at 544-545]

(2) [8:702.2] **Additional time by stipulation:** The parties may stipulate that the seven-hour limit does not apply to a specific

© 2020 Thomson Reuters/The Rutter Group

deposition or to all depositions in the proceeding. [CCP §2025.290(b)(1)]

(3) [8:702.3] **Other exceptions to seven-hour limit:** The seven-hour limit does not apply in the following circumstances:

- [8:702.4] *Expert witnesses:* To the deposition of any witness designated as an expert under CCP §§2034.210-2034.310 (*see Ch. 8J*) (CCP §2025.290(b)(2));

- [8:702.5] *"Complex" cases:* To cases designated by the court as "complex" pursuant to CRC 3.400 (¶*12:47.3b*), *unless* a licensed physician attests in a declaration that a deponent's condition or illness raises substantial medical doubt about the deponent's survival beyond six months, in which case the deponent's testimony (excluding examination by his or her counsel) is limited to *two days* of no more than *seven hours each*, or 14 hours of total testimony (CCP §2025.290(b)(3));

- [8:702.5a] *Compare—certain medical conditions:* However, even in complex cases, plaintiff's deposition by opposing parties is limited to seven hours if a doctor provides a declaration that the deponent suffers from mesothelioma or silicosis, raising substantial medical doubt of the deponent's survival beyond six months. Parties can seek a court order for up to three more hours of deposition if more than 10 defendants appear at the deposition (for up to 10 hours total), or an additional seven hours of deposition if more than 20 defendants appear at the deposition (for up to 14 hours total). [CCP §2025.295 (added eff. 1/1/20)]

- [8:702.6] *Employment litigation:* To any action brought by an employee or applicant for employment against an employer "for acts or omissions arising out of or relating to the employment relationship" (CCP §2025.290(b)(4));

- [8:702.7] *Depositions of corporations and other entities:* To any deposition of a person designated as the "most qualified" to be deposed on behalf of a corporation or other entity under CCP §2025.230 (¶*8:473 ff.*) (CCP §2025.290(b)(5));

- [8:702.8] *Late-appearing parties:* To any party who had not yet appeared in the action when a witness' deposition concluded, in which case the new party may notice another deposition of the witness but subject to the §2025.290(a) seven-hour limit (absent court order or stipulation allowing a longer time, or the application of another exception under §2025.290(b)) (CCP §2025.290(b)(6)).

[8:702.9] *Reserved.*

(4) [8:702.10] **Protective orders:** The §2025.290 time limitations and exceptions thereto (¶*8:702 ff.*) do not affect any party's right to move for a protective order or the court's discretion to make orders limiting a deposition in the interest of justice to protect a party, deponent or other natural person or organization from "unwarranted annoyance, embarrassment, oppression, undue burden, or expense." [CCP §2025.290(c); *and see discussion of deposition protective orders at* ¶*8:675 ff.*]

d. [8:703] **Scope of examination:** As with discovery generally, questions may relate to "any matter, not privileged, that is *relevant* to the subject matter . . . if the matter either is itself admissible in evidence or *appears reasonably calculated to lead to the discovery of admissible evidence.*" [CCP §2017.010 (emphasis added); see *Kalaba v. Gray* (2002) 95 CA4th 1416, 1423, 116 CR2d 570, 576 (citing text); *and* ¶*8:67 ff.*]

(1) [8:704] **Comment:** Thus, the scope of questioning at a deposition is *very broad.* Objections for "irrelevancy" are difficult to sustain and instructions not to answer on that basis are never proper (unless too many pointless questions cross the line into harassment, ¶*8:734.5*). Hearsay and opinions may be freely inquired into on the theory that they "may lead to the discovery of admissible evidence."

[8:704.1] ***PRACTICE POINTER:*** Don't confine your questions to evidence admissible at trial. Use open-ended questions ("Why?" "What was the reason?") that call on the deponent to give background information and explanations. Questions calling for hearsay ("What have you heard?"), opinions or conclusions ("How did she look?" "How serious were her injuries?") are also usually proper.

[8:704.2] ***FURTHER PRACTICE POINTER:*** On each topic covered, ask "closing questions" so that the deponent cannot later claim he or she was not asked for further information. (E.g., "Was anything else said during the meeting?" "Were there any other persons present at the time?" "Do you know of any other documents relating to . . .?") Keep repeating this type of question *until the deponent acknowledges* that he or she has no other information regarding the topic.

(2) [8:705] **Deponent's own knowledge:** But a witness is required to answer only to matters within his or her own knowledge. [Ev.C. §702] A deponent is not required to speculate or guess, although he or she may be asked to give an *estimate* of matters upon which estimates are commonly made (e.g., distance, size, weight, etc.).

Thus, "I don't know" and "I can't recall" are sufficient answers to deposition questions.

© 2020 Thomson Reuters/The Rutter Group

[8:705.1] ***PRACTICE POINTER—Preparing deponent to testify:*** Some deponents assume that, because a question is asked, they must give an answer whether it is correct or not. Others react in the opposite manner; if a question makes them the least bit uncomfortable, they resort to "I don't know" or "I don't remember."

Either of these approaches may cause the deponent to be impeached or come across as less than credible at trial. Therefore, be sure to discuss these matters with your witnesses when preparing them for deposition and caution them against both extremes.

[8:705.2] ***PRACTICE POINTER—Party deponent risks summary judgment:*** Plaintiffs who provide "I don't know" answers on critical elements of their case, where the information sought is of a type that would be within their personal knowledge, risk losing the case before trial. Defendants may move for summary judgment on the ground such answers show plaintiffs' claims "cannot be established" as a matter of law. [See CCP §437c(p)(2), *discussed at ¶10:240 ff.*]

Defendants may also object should plaintiff seek to *correct the deposition transcript* to provide the answers. If plaintiff *knew* the information at the time of the deposition, a court may treat the corrections as "sham" (*see ¶8:772*).

(a) [8:706] **Compare—information known to counsel:** Only the deponent's *own* knowledge is discoverable by deposition. The deponent need not provide other information known only to his or her counsel (or others) and not by the deponent personally.

(*Interrogatories* are the correct procedure for discovery of such information; *see ¶8:1051 ff.*)

(b) [8:707] **Refreshing deponent's recollection:** If requested to do so by deposing counsel, the deponent may be required to review documents or other evidence available at the deposition for the purpose of *refreshing* his or her memory. [See *Filipoff v. Sup.Ct. (Putnam)* (1961) 56 C2d 443, 451, 15 CR 139, 143]

[8:707.1] ***PRACTICE POINTER—Dealing with "I don't know" responses:*** If you think the deponent is being evasive, you can follow up with other questions such as:

— "Where would you go to find this information?

— "What have you heard about this matter?

— "Who might know where to find this information?

— "What records exist that might contain this information?

— "Did you once know the answer to this question?
— "What might bring back your memory regarding this matter?"

On the other hand, there are sometimes reasons *not* to follow up on a deponent's "I don't know" and "I can't recall" answers. Such answers may *undermine the witness' credibility* at trial: i.e., if the witness testifies to matters he or she couldn't recall at deposition, the jury may be unfavorably impressed by his or her lapse of memory.

(3) [8:708] **Deponent asked to perform physical act at video recorded depo ("show me" questions):** The court's power to order a deponent "to *answer* any question" (CCP §2025.480(a)) includes ordering *nonverbal responses* at a video recorded deposition. [*Emerson Elec. Co. v. Sup.Ct. (Grayson)* (1997) 16 C4th 1101, 1113, 68 CR2d 883, 889]

(a) [8:708.1] **Demonstrations, reenactments, etc.:** Thus, a deponent at a video recorded deposition may be asked to *draw a diagram* showing how the accident occurred; or to *demonstrate* how he or she used the allegedly defective product; or to *reenact* the event in question (or to furnish a handwriting exemplar). [See *Emerson Elec. Co. v. Sup.Ct. (Grayson),* supra, 16 C4th at 1111-1112, 68 CR2d at 889]

(b) [8:708.2] **Protective orders as limitation:** In appropriate cases, the court may limit or prohibit reenactments or demonstrations on safety, feasibility or on other grounds. [*Emerson Elec. Co. v. Sup.Ct. (Grayson),* supra, 16 C4th at 1110, 68 CR2d at 888; *see ¶8:675 ff.*]

[8:708.3-708.9] *Reserved.*

(4) [8:708.10] **Exhibits:** If documents or other materials are shown to the deponent, they should be marked for identification by the court reporter. The court reporter normally attaches copies of such exhibits to the deposition transcript.

➪ [8:708.11] ***PRACTICE POINTER:*** Try to obtain agreement with opposing counsel to use the same exhibit numbers at deposition, for all motions and at trial. Doing so will eliminate a frequent source of confusion.

In cases involving voluminous documents and numerous parties, it is good practice to assign a *large block of numbers* to each party at the outset of the case to be used in marking exhibits. This permits the parties to assign exhibit numbers to documents prior to discovery and to use the same numbers during all phases of discovery and during the trial. Consistent reference

© 2020 Thomson Reuters/The Rutter Group

to the same exhibit numbers avoids confusion. The exhibit numbers need not be consecutive; nor need the documents be offered chronologically.

Some lawyers still follow the practice of assigning numbers to plaintiff's exhibits and letters to defense exhibits. This practice is not recommended, however, particularly where there are voluminous documents and numerous parties. There is no reason why all exhibits should not be identified by number.

e. [8:709] **Cross-examination:** All parties present at the deposition have the right to cross-examine the deponent, just as at trial. [CCP §2025.330(d)]

(1) [8:710] **When to "cross-examine" own client or witness:** Thus, counsel representing the deponent has the same right to ask questions as other counsel present. (But whether they should do so is another matter, *see* ¶*8:711*.)

➪ [8:711] ***PRACTICE POINTERS:*** Attorneys often decide *not* to ask questions at depositions of their own clients or witnesses favorable to their side. Since there is no judge or jury present, there is usually nothing to be gained by bringing out favorable testimony via "cross-examination." Moreover, it may even do harm by "educating" opposing counsel, or by allowing them to ask questions about matters they had forgotten to inquire about.

However, it is a mistake *not* to "cross-examine" your own client or witnesses if they have made statements *damaging to your case.* You need them to explain their earlier statements or state further facts to limit the damage done. This will prevent the deposing party from (a) using the deposition as the basis for a motion for summary judgment; or (b) claiming that your client's contrary testimony at trial is inherently unbelievable because it is being raised for the first time at trial. And if the harmful statements *are* used, you may be able to introduce the "corrective" testimony from your cross-examination (*see* ¶*8:891.2*).

You also may need the deposition testimony if your witness or client dies before trial.

f. [8:711.1] **Party not attending may send written questions:** In lieu of participating in the oral examination, a party may send written questions in a sealed envelope to the deposing party. The deposing party must deliver the sealed envelope to the deposition officer. *At the end of the oral examination by other parties,* the deposition officer will open the envelope and propound the written questions to the deponent. [CCP §2025.330(e)]

[8:711.2] ***PRACTICE POINTER:*** This can be a good way to keep down your client's deposition costs. But it is advisable only as to noncontroversial matters; or perhaps where a coparty can be relied upon to ask most of the questions you would ask if you were there.

Also, keep in mind, however, that a natural person cannot be deposed a second time without a court order (CCP §2025.610(a), (b)). And, if you elect to send written questions in lieu of attending, it is *unlikely* that a court would grant such an order absent extraordinary circumstances.

g. [8:712] **Controls on abusive questioning:** Occasionally, the examining lawyer may attempt to "browbeat" the deponent by argumentative or unduly repetitive questions and hostile or threatening words or gestures.

Civility Guidelines:

— An attorney should treat other counsel and (deposition) participants with courtesy and civility, and should not engage in conduct that would be inappropriate in the presence of a judicial officer;

— An attorney should remember that vigorous advocacy can be consistent with professional courtesy, and that arguments or conflicts with other counsel should not be personal. [State Bar California Attorney Guidelines of Civility and Professionalism §9(a) (available on the State Bar website, *www.calbar.org*)]

(1) [8:713] **Objections:** The first line of attack on such behavior is timely and specific *objection* to the improper questioning or conduct (*see ¶8:719 ff.*).

Compare—instructing witness not to answer: But unless the question asks for privileged information, instructing the witness not to answer is *improper* and may subject counsel to sanctions (*see ¶8:734 ff.*).

(2) [8:714] **Suspend proceedings to obtain protective order:** The deposition officer must suspend taking testimony *upon demand* of either the deponent or any party present, to enable the deponent or that party to move for a protective order terminating or limiting further examination. [CCP §2025.470]

Compare—asking to "go off the record": Otherwise, the deposition officer may *not* suspend taking testimony except by stipulation of *all parties* present; i.e., counsel may not instruct the deposition officer to go "off the record" unless *all* parties agree. [CCP §2025.470]

Comment: The *deponent's* consent is *not* required to go off-the-record. On the other hand, the deponent, as well as any party present, has the right to suspend the deposition to enable him or her to seek a protective order.

© 2020 Thomson Reuters/The Rutter Group

(a) [8:714.1] **Grounds for protective order:** A motion for protective order must be sought on the ground that the examination is being conducted in "bad faith," or in a manner that "unreasonably annoys, embarrasses or oppresses" the deponent or party seeking the protective order. [CCP §2025.470]

(b) [8:715] **Procedure:** There is no specific time limit within which the motion for protective order must be filed, although the statute indicates it should be brought "promptly." [See CCP §2025.420(a)—party "may promptly move for a protective order"]

Also, the motion must be accompanied by a "meet and confer" declaration showing a "reasonable and good faith attempt" to resolve the issues informally. [CCP §§2016.040, 2025.420(a); *see discussion at ¶8:811 ff.*]

(c) [8:716] **Notice and hearing required:** An order terminating or limiting a deposition *cannot* be granted on ex parte application by deponent's counsel. The deponent must comply with the notice and hearing requirements applicable to motions generally. [*St. Paul Fire & Marine Ins. Co. v. Sup.Ct. (Borak)* (1984) 156 CA3d 82, 85-86, 202 CR 571, 573]

However, for good cause (e.g., a looming discovery cut-off date), the court may grant an ex parte application for an order shortening the time for *notice* of the motion; *see ¶9:364.*

(d) [8:717] **Order:** If "good cause" is shown, the court may grant whatever relief is appropriate to control the abusive questioning and protect the deponent from "unwarranted annoyance, embarrassment or oppression." It may either *limit* the scope and manner of further questioning (e.g., by requiring written questions); or, it may *terminate* the deposition—in which event, the deposition may not be resumed without further court order. [CCP §2025.420(b)(16)]

(e) [8:717.1] **Monetary sanction against losing party:** The court "shall" impose a *monetary sanction* against whichever party loses the motion *unless* it finds that party acted "with substantial justification" or other circumstances render imposition of the sanction "unjust." [CCP §2025.420(h)] (Monetary sanctions on discovery motions are discussed at ¶*8:1921 ff.*)

(3) [8:718] **Motion for appointment of referee:** Alternatively, the deponent's counsel may seek (or the court on its own motion may direct) the appointment of a referee to monitor further questioning of the witness. [CCP §639(a)(5), *discussed at ¶8:742 ff.*]

(4) [8:718.1] **Compare—"team" questioning not per se abusive:** It is not a per se abuse to have two attorneys, rather than one, question the deponent. It may be improper during trial (because of a risk of confusing jurors). But nothing in California law prohibits questioning by two attorneys at a deposition. [*Rockwell Int'l, Inc. v. Pos-A-Traction Indus., Inc.* (9th Cir. 1983) 712 F2d 1324, 1325 (applying California law)]

- [8:718.2] **Comment:** This procedure may be acceptable if distinct subject matters are inquired into and each of the attorneys covers his or her particular subject matter in turn. Absent such a situation, some courts may hold "team" questioning abusive.

h. [8:719] **Objections:** Because the permissible scope of examination is so broad (¶*8:703 ff.*), the grounds for objection to deposition questioning are limited; and those that exist must be pursued properly or are *waived.* [CCP §2025.460(b); see *Boler v. Sup.Ct. (Everett)* (1987) 201 CA3d 467, 472, 247 CR 185, 187, fn. 1 (citing text)]

Civility Guidelines:

— Once a question is asked, an attorney should not interrupt a deposition or make an objection for the purpose of coaching a deponent or suggesting answers;

— An attorney questioning a deponent should provide counsel present with a copy of any document shown to the deponent before or contemporaneously with showing the document to the deponent;

— An attorney should not direct a deponent to refuse to answer a question or end the deposition without a legal basis for doing so;

— An attorney should refrain from self-serving speeches and speaking objections. [State Bar California Attorney Guidelines of Civility and Professionalism §9(a)]

(1) [8:720] **Grounds for objection:** The grounds for objection at a deposition differ from those available at trial. (For example, at trial, evidence is objectionable if irrelevant to the *issues*, or if inadmissible hearsay or opinion; but these are not valid objections at deposition.)

The following are the most commonly encountered grounds for objection to deposition questions:

- *Privilege or work product* (¶*8:109 ff.*);
- *Lack of relevancy to subject matter*—i.e., not calculated to lead to discovery of admissible evidence (although because of the broad scope of examination permitted, this is often difficult to sustain; *see* ¶*8:66 ff.*);
- *Defects in deposition notice* (¶*8:483 ff., 8:507 ff.*);
- *Defects in oath or affirmation administered* (¶*8:654 ff.*);

© 2020 Thomson Reuters/The Rutter Group

- *Misconduct by a party, counsel or deposition officer* (e.g., abusive questioning; *see* ¶*8:712 ff.*);
- *Privacy* (¶*8:293 ff., 8:726.5 ff.*).

(a) [8:721] **Objection as to FORM of questions:** Objection is permitted as to the *form* of any *question or answer* at a deposition; and, to avoid waiver, such objection must be made *on the record* at the deposition (*see* ¶*8:725*). [CCP §2025.460(b)]

Examples: Objection to a question on the ground that it:

- is ambiguous, uncertain or not readily understood;
- is compound;
- calls for narration or lengthy explanation;
- calls for speculation and conjecture;
- is argumentative;
- is leading and suggestive to questioner's own client or witness.

1) [8:722] **Compare—not valid for other discovery devices:** Such objections are generally *not* appropriate for other discovery devices (interrogatories, document demands, etc.). But they are appropriate for depositions because, unlike the other discovery devices, the witness is required to give an *immediate* answer without the aid of counsel. [*Greyhound Corp. v. Sup.Ct. (Clay)* (1961) 56 C2d 355, 392, 15 CR 90, 109]

[8:722.1] ***PRACTICE POINTER:*** Inexperienced counsel often raise objections on such grounds as "relevancy," "hearsay" or "lack of foundation." These do not go to the form of the question and, in view of the broad scope permitted in discovery, such objections are *improper*. Persistence in making such improper objections may constitute discovery abuse.

[8:722.2] ***PRACTICE POINTER:*** If you are the deposing counsel, do not quibble with opposing counsel's objections to the form of your questions. If the judge at trial finds the objections were well-taken, any answers obtained will be excluded. Therefore, if the objection appears even remotely proper, *take the time to reframe your question.*

(b) [8:723] **Objection to party's legal CONTENTIONS:** It is improper to ask a party deponent to state or explain his or her legal contentions in the case, or to des-

© 2020 Thomson Reuters/The Rutter Group

ignate documents or evidence supporting them. [*Rifkind v. Sup.Ct. (Good)* (1994) 22 CA4th 1255, 1259, 27 CR2d 822, 824]

Examples:

— "*Do you contend* X's conduct was negligent (legal conclusion)?"

— "If you do, state all facts, list all witnesses, and identify and describe all documents that *support your contention* that X was negligent." [See *Rifkind v. Sup.Ct. (Good),* supra, 22 CA4th at 1259, 27 CR2d at 824]

1) [8:724] **Rationale:** Contention questions are clearly proper in *written interrogatories* because answers to interrogatories are prepared with the assistance of counsel (*see ¶8:898 ff.*).

But such questions are objectionable at a deposition because it is *unfair* to ask a party at deposition to explain his or her lawyer's legal conclusions and contentions: "There is no legitimate reason to put the deponent to that exercise . . . This is what lawyers are for." [*Rifkind v. Sup.Ct. (Good)*, supra, 22 CA4th at 1262-1263, 27 CR2d at 826-827 (internal quotes omitted)—makes no difference party deponent is a lawyer]

[8:724.1] *Reserved.*

2) [8:724.2] **Distinguish—factual contentions:** On the other hand, it is clearly proper to ask a deponent questions about the basis for factual conclusions or assertions:

"Thus, if a deponent says that a certain event happened at a particular time or place, it is quite proper to ask the person, at deposition, how he or she became aware of it, his or her knowledge about it, and for similar information of a factual nature." [*Rifkind v. Sup.Ct. (Good),* supra, 22 CA4th at 1259, 27 CR2d at 824]

(c) [8:724.3] **Objection as to DOCUMENTS REVIEWED:** A common question in deposing an adversary is: "What documents did you review to refresh your memory in preparation for your testimony today?" Or, "Did your lawyer show you any documents to refresh your recollection for this deposition; if so, what were they?"

The first question is unobjectionable. The second question invades attorney work product and possibly attorney-client privileges.

- *Examiner's right to inspect, in general:* If a witness "either while testifying *or prior thereto*, uses a writing to refresh his memory with respect to any matter about which he testifies, *such writing must be produced* . . . at the request of an adverse party." [Ev.C. §771 (emphasis added)]

Thus, opposing counsel cannot properly refuse to produce documents shown to the deponent (party or nonparty) to refresh his or her recollection in preparation for the deposition. [*International Ins. Co. v. Montrose Chemical Corp. of Calif.* (1991) 231 CA3d 1367, 1372-1373, 282 CR 783, 786]

- *Privileged documents:* Privileged documents do not lose their protected status because reviewed by the client in advance of a deposition. [*Sullivan v. Sup.Ct. (Spingola)* (1972) 29 CA3d 64, 68, 105 CR 241, 243-244]

  Exception: If the client claims *no present memory* of the events recorded in a statement given to his or her attorney, *and uses that statement in order to testify*, it would be "unconscionable" to prevent the adverse party from seeing it. Any privilege is waived. [*Kerns Const. Co. v. Sup.Ct. (Southern Calif. Gas Co.)* (1968) 266 CA2d 405, 410, 72 CR 74, 76]

- *Attorney work product?* No known California case has considered this argument.

1) [8:724.4] **Comment:** Until California precedent is established, many judges are likely to *overrule* the "work product" objection unless, perhaps, there were literally thousands of documents involved and the selection process really reflected some analysis by the lawyer. To hold otherwise would emasculate Ev.C. §771 (allowing inspection of documents used by the witness to refresh his or her recollection; *see* ¶*8:724.3*).

[8:724.5] ***PRACTICE POINTER:*** For this reason, carefully consider whether to show documents to your clients in preparation for their depositions.

If only a few documents are at issue, it may be better to *read and discuss* with the client whatever sections of the documents are pertinent. (Your discussions will be protected under the *attorney-client privilege* even if no work product protection is available.)

Otherwise, your witness may appear evasive or unknowledgeable when questioned about the documents (particularly if the deposition is videotaped). If your witness later reviews the documents and gives detailed testimony about them at *trial*, the deposition can be powerful impeachment.

(2) [8:725] **Waiver by failure to object:** Objections as to *form* of questions *or discoverability* of information sought are generally *waived* unless properly raised (¶*8:726 ff.*). [CCP §2025.460(b)]

(a) [8:726] **Includes privilege and work product:** This includes objections on the ground of privilege or work product: i.e., they are *waived* unless a *specific* objection to disclosure is *timely made* during the deposition (*see* ¶*8:731*). [CCP §2025.460(a); *International Ins. Co. v. Montrose Chemical Corp. of Calif.* (1991) 231 CA3d 1367, 1373, 282 CR 783, 786, fn. 4]

1) [8:726.1] **Waiver at trial?** Although §2025.460(a) states only that "protection of information from discovery" is waived, *voluntary* disclosure of protected information (failure to object) may also waive any privilege at trial. [See Ev.C. §912]

Compare: But, if an objection is timely made, a subsequent *court-ordered* disclosure should not result in waiver at trial because Ev.C. §912(a) applies only to disclosures "without coercion."

[8:726.2-726.4] *Reserved.*

(b) [8:726.5] **Compare—privacy rights not necessarily waived:** A party's failure to object to questions that invade privacy rights does *not* automatically waive the privacy objection, particularly where the privacy of third persons is involved. [*Boler v. Sup.Ct. (Everett)* (1987) 201 CA3d 467, 472, 247 CR 185, 187, fn. 1; *Mendez v. Sup.Ct. (Peery)* (1988) 206 CA3d 557, 564, 253 CR 731, 734 (disapproved on other grounds by *Williams v. Sup.Ct. (Marshalls of CA, LLC)* (2017) 3 C5th 531, 557, 220 CR3d 472, 494 & fn. 8)]

1) [8:726.6] **Example:** D was asked about extramarital affairs. He objected only on grounds of *relevancy* (failing to raise privacy). On motion to compel, the court found the questions were relevant. But it could not compel answers that would impair D's privacy rights and those of his unnamed sexual partners. [*Boler v. Sup.Ct. (Everett)*, supra, 201 CA3d at 472, 474, 247 CR at 187, 189]

2) [8:726.7] **Rationale:** The waiver rule applies primarily to matters of evidentiary privilege and work product. The right of privacy is of *constitutional* dimension. Moreover, where (as here) disclosure

© 2020 Thomson Reuters/The Rutter Group

would infringe the privacy of *third persons*, their rights to object must be protected. [*Boler v. Sup.Ct. (Everett)*, supra, 201 CA3d at 472, 247 CR at 187-188, fn. 1]

3) [8:726.8] **Comment:** The fact that privacy is of constitutional origin may not be determinative. Other constitutional rights (e.g., Fifth Amendment privilege against self-incrimination) can be waived by failure to object.

(c) [8:727] **Error or irregularity in proceeding waived by failure to object:** Errors or irregularities "of any kind" *occurring at the deposition* that could be cured if then objected to are *waived* unless a timely and specific objection is made during the deposition. [CCP §2025.460(b)]

1) [8:727.1] **Application:** Such errors include, without limitation, matters relating to:

- the *manner of taking the deposition* (e.g., by video where no notice given);
- the oath or affirmation administered;
- the *conduct of any party, counsel, deponent* or the deposition officer; or
- the *form of any question or answer* (e.g., "leading," "argumentative," etc.; *see* ¶*8:721*). [CCP §2025.460(b)]

(d) [8:728] **Compare—objections to admissibility at trial not waived:** On the other hand, there is no need to object—and no waiver by failure to object—to the competency of the deponent, or to the relevancy or materiality or admissibility *at trial* of the testimony or documents produced. [CCP §2025.460(c)]

Rationale: These are not valid grounds for objection to *discovery*. (For discovery purposes, the test is whether the information might reasonably *lead* to other, admissible evidence.) Since no discovery objection lies, failure to object is not a waiver.

[8:729] ***PRACTICE POINTERS:*** This could create "traps" at a deposition, whether you're the examiner or representing the deponent:

[8:729.1] ***If you represent the deponent***, you have to be sharp with your objections as to the *form* of questioning. You can't afford to let sloppy questions slide by. Sloppy questions often evoke sloppy answers; or, even worse, answers that volunteer information. It is too late to raise your objections when the answers are introduced at trial.

- On the other hand, do *not* interpose objections on the ground of hearsay, opinion evidence, materiality, etc. Nothing is gained because these are not valid grounds for objecting to discovery (*see ¶8:720 ff.*). And, you may "educate" opposing counsel to evidentiary problems they hadn't considered (*see ¶8:730*).
- Nor should you object on the ground of privilege or work product *unless you also instruct your client or witness not to answer the question* (*see ¶8:734.1*). There is little to be gained by raising the objection and then "permitting the deponent to testify over the objection."

[8:730] ***If you're taking the deposition***, don't get "trapped" by opposing counsel's *not objecting* to your questions:

- For example, questions calling for hearsay are frequently asked at depositions. Such questions are perfectly proper for *discovery* purposes (¶*8:69*). But, of course, hearsay is generally inadmissible at trial. Opposing counsel does *not* waive the hearsay objection by failing to raise it at the deposition (*see ¶8:728*). Therefore, you may end up with wonderful hearsay testimony that will be totally useless at trial.
- Another common occurrence is for the deponent to testify to facts or opinions for which no foundation has been laid. (Example: testimony by "eyewitnesses" without showing that they were in a position to have observed what they claim to have seen.) In such a case, if you try to use the deposition as evidence at trial, you're bound to run into an objection at the time of trial that there was "no foundation" for the deponent's testimony, and the testimony is therefore incompetent.
- Bottom line: If you're just looking for "leads" to other evidence, by all means ask for hearsay (e.g., "Have you ever heard from anyone . . . ?").

  But, if you intend to use deposition testimony at trial (and you usually do), *phrase your questions to avoid all substantive objections*—i.e., hearsay, no foundation, conclusion, etc.—*even if no objection is made at the deposition.* Otherwise, you may find you have conducted a very expensive discovery procedure which does you no good at trial.

(3) [8:731] **Form of objection:** Obviously, it is not enough simply to state, "I object." To preserve any ground for objection at a deposition, the ground for objection must be:

© 2020 Thomson Reuters/The Rutter Group

- *Timely made* during the deposition (before the question is answered; if already answered, the objecting party must move the court to exclude the answer as evidence at trial or in pretrial proceedings); and
- *Specifically stated* (to give the examiner opportunity to rephrase the question and avoid the objection). [CCP §2025.460(b); and see Ev.C. §353]

[8:732] ***PRACTICE POINTER:*** Instead of objecting, opposing counsel may request a "clarification" or ask the examining lawyer, "Do you mean . . .?" Within limits, this is helpful in avoiding confusion of questions and answers.

However, it can also be overdone. Sometimes opposing counsel use this technique in an attempt to break up the flow and impact of the questioning, or to "signal" the deponent to give a desired answer.

If this happens to you while examining a witness, state on the record that you request opposing counsel to limit themselves to stating the ground for any objection—and no more. You may also warn them that if they persist, you may suspend the deposition and seek a protective order (*see ¶8:714*).

(4) [8:733] **Effect of objection alone:** All objections made are recorded by the deposition reporter. But an objection does not excuse the deponent from the duty to answer *unless* the objecting party *demands the deposition be suspended* to permit a motion for protective order. [CCP §§2025.460(b), 2025.470]

Otherwise, the deponent must answer the question and the testimony will be received, *subject to* the objection. [CCP §2025.460(b)]

This preserves objections to the *form* of questioning (which are otherwise waived by failure to object; *see ¶8:725*). Thus, if the testimony is offered at trial, the court will rule on the merits of the objection; and if the form of questioning *was* improper, the testimony can be excluded on this ground alone.

(5) [8:734] **Effect of objection coupled with deponent's refusal to answer:** As stated, an objection alone does not excuse the deponent from the duty to answer. But opposing counsel may follow up the objection with an instruction to the deponent *not* to answer the question, which usually will be effective if the deponent is represented by that counsel.

The examiner will then be faced with the deponent's *failure to answer*, the consequences of which are discussed below (*¶8:737 ff.*).

(a) [8:734.1] **Instructing witness not to answer to protect privileged information:** Where a deposition question seeks discovery of privileged information, counsel must interpose a specific objection and instruct the deponent not to answer in order to preserve the privilege or work product protection. [See CCP §2025.460(a)]

(b) [8:734.2] **Instructing witness not to answer *otherwise improper:*** It is generally improper, however, for counsel to instruct a witness not to answer on grounds other than privilege, privacy, trade secrets or other matters statutorily or constitutionally exempt from discovery. [See *Stewart v. Colonial Western Agency, Inc.* (2001) 87 CA4th 1006, 1013-1015, 105 CR2d 115, 120-121]

1) [8:734.3] **Defects in form:** Counsel must *object* to defects in the *form* that might be cured if promptly raised (e.g., ambiguous, uncertain, etc.) or the defect is waived (CCP §2025.460(b)). But such defects are not ground for instructing the witness not to answer; the witness must answer over the objection. (Of course, deposing counsel bears the risk that if the objection is valid that portion of the deposition testimony will be inadmissible at trial.) [*Stewart v. Colonial Western Agency, Inc.*, supra, 87 CA4th at 1014, 105 CR2d at 120; *see ¶8:727.1*]

2) [8:734.4] **Irrelevance:** Irrelevance alone is an insufficient ground to justify instructing a witness not to answer a deposition question: "Relevance objections should be held in abeyance until an attempt is made to use the testimony at trial." [*Stewart v. Colonial Western Agency, Inc.*, supra, 87 CA4th at 1015, 105 CR2d at 121—witnesses are expected to endure an occasional irrelevant question]

a) [8:734.5] **Compare—suspending deposition:** The deponent's counsel, however, may suspend the deposition in order to seek a protective order if deposing counsel's insistence on inquiring into irrelevant matters reaches the point of *oppression or harassment.* [CCP §2025.470; *Stewart v. Colonial Western Agency, Inc.*, supra, 87 CA4th at 1015, 105 CR2d at 121; *see ¶8:714*]

☞ *PRACTICE POINTERS*

- [8:735] ***If you're representing the deponent:*** The only situation that clearly justifies instructing a witness not to answer is where the information sought is statutorily or constitutionally protected from discovery (e.g., under a privilege, right of privacy, etc.). In such cases, when instructing the witness not to answer, state your *reasons on the*

© 2020 Thomson Reuters/The Rutter Group

record. If a motion to compel is made, this will help the judge rule on your objection; and if you lose, it may show you were proceeding in good faith and limit your exposure to sanctions.

Be careful about instructing your client not to answer on any other ground. If in fact the questions are "manifestly irrelevant" and calculated to harass, you *may* be justified in suspending the deposition and asking the court for a protective order. But this is risky: If you lose, you may be sanctioned for the cost of reopening an improperly suspended deposition *and* for improperly seeking a protective order. [See *Stewart v. Colonial Western Agency, Inc.*, supra, 87 CA4th at 1015, 105 CR2d at 121]

(On the other hand, you may want to bank on the reality that attorneys who engage in abusive questioning usually do not go to the trouble of a motion to compel with the risk that the judge will read the transcript.)

- [8:736] ***If you're taking the deposition:*** Make sure the witness' failure or refusal to answer is clearly stated *on the record.* Otherwise, later efforts at renewing the deposition may be barred by the one-deposition limit for natural persons.

  Also, if opposing counsel has made a record of his or her reasons for instructing the witness not to answer, you should *state on the record* your position as to each of these arguments.

  Finally, wherever possible, state on the record your *attempts to work out a compromise* to avoid the objection. Doing so increases your chance for a sanctions award if you win the motion to compel, and may avoid the risk of sanctions if you lose.

(6) [8:736.1] **Caution re coaching deponent during deposition:** Coaching a deponent or suggesting answers during a deposition, through unfounded objections or otherwise, may violate standards of professionalism (see L.A. Sup.Ct. Rule 3.26, Appendix 3.A(e)(8)) and be sanctionable as a *discovery misuse* under CCP §2023.010 (*see* ¶*8:1901*). [See *Tucker v. Pacific Bell Mobile Services* (2010) 186 CA4th 1548, 1561-1562, 115 CR3d 9, 18-19 (upholding sanctions imposed for coaching)]

In addition, the judge might allow the coaching sessions to be heard by the jury as impeachment.

(a) [8:736.2] **Compare—"taking a break"?** Although there is no known California authority on point, other

© 2020 Thomson Reuters/The Rutter Group

courts have disagreed over the extent to which a deponent may consult with his or her attorney during a recess. [See *Hall v. Clifton Precision, a Div. of Lifton of Litton Systems, Inc.* (ED PA 1993) 150 FRD 525, 528 (decided under Federal Rules)—conference before answering question not allowed as improper coaching except for purposes of determining whether to assert privilege; compare *In re Stratosphere Corp. Secur. Litig.* (D NV 1998) 182 FRD 614, 621—conference permitted during recess scheduled by court order; *In re Flonase Antitrust Litig.* (ED PA 2010) 723 F.Supp.2d 761, 764-766 (decided under Penn. state law)—conference protected by attorney-client privilege where deponent testified no coaching took place]

[8:736.3] ***PRACTICE POINTER:*** If confronted with such a situation, state on the record that it appears counsel is coaching the witness. If the practice continues, consider adjourning the deposition and making a motion for a protective order. In extreme situations, asking for a discovery referee to preside at the deposition may be warranted.

[8:736.4] *Reserved.*

(7) [8:736.5] ***Caution* re asking to "go off the record":** *See discussion at ¶8:714.*

i. [8:737] **Examiner's alternatives re completing examination following deponent's failure to answer:** If a deponent fails to answer a question, or to produce records or things specified in the depo notice or subpoena, the deposing party may either:

- *Complete* the depo on other matters; or
- *Adjourn* the depo and file a *motion to compel* answers. [CCP §2025.460(e)]

(In either case, the deposition reporter may be instructed to "*cite the witness*" to appear in court at the hearing on the motion to compel. *See procedure at ¶8:789.*)

(1) [8:737a] **Local practice (Los Angeles):** In Los Angeles, a form "Discovery Resolution Stipulation" is served with the complaint. If the parties sign the stipulation and the court accepts it, the parties must request an informal discovery conference before filing any discovery motion. At the conference, the court considers the parties' dispute and determines whether it can be resolved informally. The Discovery Resolution Stipulation is available on the court's website (*www.lacourt.org;* under "Civil, Tools for Litigators, Voluntary Efficient Litigation Stipulations"). (*See also ¶8:787.1.*)

© 2020 Thomson Reuters/The Rutter Group

[8:737.1] ***PRACTICE POINTER:*** Another alternative is to ask the judge to resolve the dispute immediately *by telephone or in an informal meeting.* This practice is migrating into many civil courts, particularly those with direct calendar assignments. Most judges dislike discovery motions and will take informal steps to resolve such disputes without formal hearings.

Call when the judge is not likely to be on the bench, and ask the clerk if the judge is willing to hear the matter informally. If all parties waive notice and stipulate to the precise issue, you may be able to get a ruling on the spot.

(2) [8:738] **Completing depo does not bar later motion to compel:** Completing the deposition on other matters does not waive the examining counsel's right at a later time to move for an order compelling the answer or production of information sought. [CCP §2025.460(e)]

[8:739] ***PRACTICE POINTER:*** Adjourning a deposition makes sense only if the information sought is *essential to any further questioning* of the deponent. Otherwise, use the opportunity to question the deponent on other matters in the case.

If you adjourn the deposition and *lose* on the motion to compel, you may lose the right to depose the witness again. (Remember the one-deposition limit for natural persons; CCP §2025.610(a), ¶*8:478.*) You can ask the court for permission; but it may refuse because you already had the chance.

(3) [8:740] **No need to show "refusal" to answer:** CCP §2025.460(e) uses the term "*fails* to answer" (rather than "refuses"). Thus, no showing of willful obstruction of discovery is required. All that need be shown is that the witness has in fact not answered the question.

(4) [8:741] **Effect of incomplete answer?** As long as a partial answer has been given, the witness has not "failed" to answer. It is up to the examiner to press for a complete answer at the time of deposition. Unless the examiner does so, there is no basis for a motion to compel (or ground for allowing a second deposition of the same witness).

(a) [8:741.1] **Example:** Examiner asks for "names and addresses of all doctors who treated you." Deponent gives their names but not their addresses. But Examiner was inattentive and fails to follow up on this point. Later, on reading the transcript, Examiner realizes Deponent did not fully answer the question. Most judges would probably *deny* a motion to compel further discovery in such a case on the rationale that Deponent should not be required to submit to additional questioning because of Examiner's mental lapses at the deposition.

(5) [8:741.2] **Procedure on motion to compel:** *See discussion at ¶8:787 ff.*

(6) [8:741.3] **Sanctions:** *See discussion at ¶8:819 ff.*

j. [8:742] **Appointment of discovery referees:** The court has power to appoint a referee to supervise the deposition, if necessary. The referee in a *special* reference may be ordered to hear specified discovery motions and disputes, and to report findings and make recommendations. [CCP §§638(b), 639(a); *Jogani v. Jogani* (2006) 141 CA4th 158, 176, 45 CR3d 792, 803 (citing text); *see detailed discussion at ¶8:1803 ff.*]

In a *general* reference made by the parties' agreement, the referee hears and resolves any or all disputes. [CCP §638(a); *Lindsey v. Conteh* (2017) 9 CA5th 1296, 1303, 215 CR3d 801, 806 (discussing general and special references)]

(1) [8:743] **Purpose:** Where either party anticipates that the other will try to frustrate legitimate discovery at a deposition (e.g., numerous, frivolous objections, or evasive answers), the referee's presence can curtail such conduct. Likewise, where a deposition has been suspended for abusive questioning by the examiner (*¶8:714*), the court may appoint a referee to protect the witness on resumption of the deposition.

(2) [8:744] **Procedure:** The appointment can be made on application of *either* party or on the court's own motion. [See CCP §639(a); *see detailed discussion at ¶8:1804 ff.*]

The person appointed as referee may be any third party to the litigation. If available, a court commissioner may be appointed.

- ***FORM:*** Application for Order Appointing Discovery Referee to Supervise Deposition and Proposed Order, *see Form 8:11* in Rivera, *Cal. Prac. Guide: Civ. Pro. Before Trial FORMS* (TRG).

[8:745] ***PRACTICE POINTER:*** If you anticipate numerous disputes in the course of the deposition, ask the referee to have the deposition held in some available room *at the courthouse*; e.g., a jury room adjoining the judge's courtroom. In this way, the judge may be available for immediate ruling on objections or motions, and to impose sanctions if necessary.

As a practical matter, the proximity of the judge may minimize the need for such rulings. Moreover, if a ruling *is* necessary, it will save the time, expense and delay of a formal motion and court hearing. Instead, an immediate ruling can be obtained, and the deposition may then continue uninterrupted.

Another technique to eliminate deposition disputes is to *videotape* the deposition. Obstreperous counsel often tone down their conduct when the deposition is being videotaped.

© 2020 Thomson Reuters/The Rutter Group

(3) [8:746] **Fees and costs:** The court is empowered to order a reasonable fee paid to the referee for his or her services (if the referee is not an officer (i.e., employed by) or commissioner of the court). This fee may be ordered paid in any manner the court deems just, including apportionment among all the parties. [CCP §645.1; *see* ¶*8:1805*] (Fees so paid may be recoverable as court costs after judgment by the prevailing party; CCP §1023.)

(a) [8:746.1] **Ability to pay:** The court may not appoint a discovery referee without finding that either (i) no party has established an economic inability to pay, or (ii) one or more parties have established an inability to pay a pro rata share of the referee's fees and the other party or parties have *agreed voluntarily* to pay that additional share of the fee. [CCP §639(d)(6)(A); CRC 3.922(f); *see* ¶*8:1805*]

[8:746.2] ***PRACTICE POINTER:*** Be careful what you ask for. You may find that proceedings before a discovery referee take longer to conclude than court proceedings, and that discovery referees are costly and difficult to get rid of once appointed. The best way to protect against such problems is to obtain appointment of a referee for only a *limited* assignment. The parties can then control whether that assignment should be expanded at a later date.

(4) [8:747] **Not limited to depositions:** The court's power to appoint a referee is not limited to supervising depositions. Rather, a referee may be appointed to hear and determine "any and *all* discovery motions and *disputes relevant to discovery*." [CCP §639(a)(5) (emphasis added); ¶*8:1803*]

k. [8:748] **Stipulations at deposition:** Counsel frequently enter into stipulations at the time of depositions. Such stipulations may alter any of the statutory procedures governing depositions (CCP §2016.030). The clients' consent is not required unless the stipulations relate to "substantive" matters (*see* ¶*1:314*).

[8:749] ***PRACTICE POINTERS:*** Various stipulations may be proposed during the course of a deposition:

- [8:749.1] **"The usual stipulations":** You may be asked by opposing counsel at the outset, or during the deposition, whether you agree to the "usual stipulations."

  This phrase is meaningless. There are no "usual" stipulations. What stipulations are intended vary from lawyer to lawyer. Hence, any stipulation should be carefully defined.

Some common stipulations are discussed below (¶*8:750 ff.*). But *none* is required and some of them may not be in your client's interests.

- [8:750] **"Reserve all objections until time of trial":** Sometimes counsel for the deponent (or for a third party) will propose stipulating that "all objections to questions be reserved until time of trial."

  If you are the examiner, do *not* enter into such a stipulation. *Insist that any objections to the form of questioning be raised at the deposition.* Otherwise, the trial court might exclude valuable deposition testimony simply because of the *form* of your questions (e.g., compound, complex, argumentative, speculative, etc.).

- [8:751] **"Instruction not to answer deemed a refusal to answer":** Sometimes opposing counsel will offer to stipulate that if deponent's counsel instructs the deponent not to answer, it shall be deemed a refusal to answer by the deponent.

  This stipulation is unnecessary because a motion to compel no longer requires a "refusal" to answer. (The motion is available simply for a *failure* to answer; see CCP §2025.460(e), ¶*8:787 ff.*)

  But the stipulation may be advantageous to counsel taking the deposition, because it sets up a stronger claim for *sanctions* if the motion to compel is successful.

- [8:752] **"Any notary public"?** In the past, at the end of the deposition, it was common to stipulate that the witness could sign and verify the deposition transcript before "any notary." But this stipulation is now meaningless because the Discovery Act no longer requires notarization or verification of a deposition. The deponent "approves" the transcript by signing it or noting approval in a letter mailed by registered or certified mail to the court reporter. [CCP §2025.520(b)-(c)]

- [8:753] **"Waive reading and signing":** It is sometimes agreed at the end of the deposition that the transcript need not be shown to the deponent at all, and that it may be used "*as if read and signed* by the deponent *without correction.*"

  Obviously, you will not want to so stipulate as to your client's deposition. But it may make sense with *nonparty* deponents, if their testimony is not too controversial. It eliminates the necessity of the deposition reporter having to locate the deponent, make an appointment to have the deponent read and sign it, etc.

  In any event, do not enter into such a stipulation until *after* the examination is concluded so you can determine

© 2020 Thomson Reuters/The Rutter Group

if there is any likelihood the deponent may wish to change his or her testimony.

- [8:754] **"Deponent's counsel to retain custody of transcript":** Formerly, in the absence of stipulation, the deposition reporter was required to retain custody of the original transcript. But this made it difficult for the deponent to review and correct the original; and it was cumbersome for deposition reporters. The Discovery Act now provides that the original transcript be delivered to and retained by the *attorney noticing the deposition* in all cases (see CCP §2025.550(a), ¶*8:778*).

  But a stipulation for delivery and retention by *counsel for the deponent* may still be useful because it facilitates review and correction of the deposition. (*See suggested form of stipulation at* ¶*8:777.*) [See *Urban Pac. Equities Corp. v. Sup.Ct. (Steiner & Libo)* (1997) 59 CA4th 688, 690, 69 CR2d 635, 636, fn. 2 (citing text)]

  [8:755-756] *Reserved.*

13. [8:757] **Compare—Depositions on WRITTEN Questions:** As mentioned earlier, depositions may be taken on written questions instead of by oral examination. Sometimes this is a matter of choice; sometimes, it is *required* by court order (e.g., a protective order allowing out-of-town depositions to proceed only on written questions to protect a party against undue burden and expense; see CCP §2025.420(b)(6), *discussed at* ¶*8:642*).

    In either event, depositions on written questions are governed by the rules applicable to oral depositions except as provided below (¶*8:759 ff.*). [CCP §2028.010(a)]

    [8:758] ***PRACTICE POINTER:*** Depositions on written questions are far less expensive than flying across country or overseas to take oral depositions.

    On the other hand, this method is not suited for important and controversial testimony. The deponent usually knows in advance what questions will be asked (at least on direct examination; *see* ¶*8:759*); so, there is little chance of spontaneous answers. And, of course, there is *no* chance for follow-up questioning.

    a. [8:759] **Notice:** The same deposition notice requirements (¶*8:483*) apply, except:

       - The notice must include both the name *and address* of the deposition officer;
       - The date, time and place for the deposition may be left open (to be determined by the deposition officer); and
       - The written questions to be propounded to the deponent on *direct* examination must be *attached* to the deposition notice. [CCP §§2028.020, 2028.030(a)]

b. [8:760] **Cross-questions:** Opposing parties have 30 days after receipt of the deposition notice to serve cross-questions to the deponent. [CCP §2028.030(b)]

Any *redirect* questions are due within 15 days thereafter; and any *recross questions,* within 15 days after service of the redirect. [CCP §2028.030(c)-(d)]

Each of these periods is extended for service by mail (see CCP §2016.050, ¶*8:590.3*) and may be extended or shortened by stipulation or court order (see CCP §2028.030(e); *and* ¶*8:505*).

c. [8:761] **Objections:** Objections are waived unless served on all parties within *15 days* after service of the questions (extended for service by mail). [CCP §2028.040(a) (waiver rule), CCP §2016.050 (extension by mail)]

An objection does *not* excuse the deponent from answering unless the objecting party *promptly* moves for and obtains a *court order sustaining* the objection. Otherwise, the deposition officer will propound the question *subject to* the objection. [CCP §2028.040(b)]

Exception: A different rule applies where the objection is made on the ground of *privilege* or *work product*. In such cases, the deposition officer will *not* propound the question, unless the deposing party obtains a court order *overruling* the objection. [CCP §2028.050(b)]

d. [8:762] **Protective orders:** To protect against "unwarranted annoyance, embarrassment or oppression," the court may grant whatever protective orders are just, including:

- That the deponent's testimony be taken only by *oral* examination, instead of written questions; or
- That one or more parties be permitted to attend the written deposition and to ask questions orally. [See CCP §2028.070(a)-(b)]

e. [8:763] **Deponent may preview DIRECT questions only:** The party taking the deposition on written questions may forward to the deponent for study whatever questions are to be asked on direct examination. However, "[n]o party or attorney shall permit the deponent to preview the form or the substance of any cross, redirect or recross questions." [CCP §2028.060]

(1) [8:764] **Comment:** How this provision is to be enforced is unclear (particularly where the deponent is friendly to one side in the case).

f. [8:765] **Conduct of deposition:** It is the deposing party's responsibility to forward to the deposition officer copies of the notice, plus copies of all questions to be propounded to the deponent, including the cross, redirect and recross questions.

It is then the deposition officer's responsibility to propound the questions to the deponent and to take and record the deponent's

© 2020 Thomson Reuters/The Rutter Group

answers. The questions and answers must be recorded stenographically (although they may also be recorded on audio or video if the deposition notice so states). [CCP §2028.080]

14. [8:766] **Deposition Transcript:** Unless the parties agree otherwise, the deposition reporter is under a duty to transcribe the testimony; and to certify the transcript as a true record of the testimony given by the deponent. [CCP §2025.540(a)]

The stenographic transcript is the official record of the proceedings for purposes of trial and appeal, even if an audio or video recording is also made. [CCP §2025.510(g)] (If the parties agree to forego a stenographic transcript, special provisions govern certifying the accuracy of the audio or video recording; see CCP §§2025.530, 2025.540(a).)

Audio or video recordings made by the parties or by the deposition reporter as an aid in preparing the stenographic transcript are *not* considered recordings of the proceedings. Only the stenographic transcript qualifies. [CCP §2025.510(g)]

➪ [8:766.1] ***PRACTICE POINTER:*** Most deposition reporters can also provide a transcript in an *electronic format* if you ask for it. You can then use ordinary word processing software to search for words or groups of words in the transcript. (E.g., if you want to locate every passage where Witness mentioned the XYZ Co. transaction, simply search for "XYZ.")

a. [8:767] **Costs of transcript and copies:** Unless otherwise stipulated by the parties or ordered by the court, the *party noticing the deposition* is responsible for the cost of the original transcript. [CCP §2025.510(b); see *Serrano v. Stefan Merli Plastering Co., Inc.* (2008) 162 CA4th 1014, 1033, 76 CR3d 559, 572]

The deposition reporter customarily also furnishes a copy of the transcript to the deposing party without additional charge. Any other party who wishes a copy must make arrangements with the deposition reporter. [CCP §§2025.320(b), 2025.510(c); see *Urban Pac. Equities Corp. v. Sup.Ct. (Steiner & Libo)* (1997) 59 CA4th 688, 694, 69 CR2d 635, 639, fn. 10; *Serrano v. Stefan Merli Plastering Co., Inc.*, supra, 162 CA4th at 1037, 76 CR3d at 575—§2025.510(c) *impliedly* authorizes limits on fees charged by deposition reporter to non-noticing parties]

If a party requests the original or copy on an expedited basis, the depo reporter must notify the other parties attending the deposition and, if they so request, furnish all copies *at the same time.* [See CCP §2025.510(d); *Serrano v. Stefan Merli Plastering Co., Inc.*, supra, 162 CA4th at 1033, 76 CR3d at 572-573]

It is the *requesting attorney's* (or in pro per party's) *responsibility* to "timely pay" the deposition officer's fees, *unless* the deposition officer was *notified in writing* when the services were requested that a party or other identified person would be responsible for payment. [CCP §2025.510(h)]

© 2020 Thomson Reuters/The Rutter Group

The fees charged by deposition reporters are *not* set by statute; deposition reporters are free to charge "whatever the market will bear." [*Urban Pac. Equities Corp. v. Sup.Ct. (Steiner & Libo),* supra, 59 CA4th at 691-692, 694, 69 CR2d at 637, 639—fee demanded for uncertified photocopy of depo deemed "unconscionable"]

Even so, the court's *inherent power* "to control the conduct of ministerial officers in pending actions" includes the power to protect against deposition reporters acting *unreasonably*; e.g., by refusing to deliver copies of a deposition transcript to non-noticing parties unless they agree to pay an *unreasonable fee.* [*Serrano v. Stefan Merli Plastering Co., Inc.*, supra, 162 CA4th at 1035, 76 CR3d at 574—court can order deposition reporter to deliver transcripts upon payment of *reasonable* fee determined by court]

(1) [8:767a] **Favoritism in charges prohibited:** Courts recognize that the deposition reporter is *chosen by the deposing party* and may have a close relationship with that party. Courts therefore must guard against favoritism in the deposition reporter's charges; e.g., charging deposing counsel a nominal amount for the original transcript while charging an excessive amount to opposing counsel for copies: "In light of the importance of deposition testimony in a pending action and the non-noticing party's lack of bargaining power, a trial court must be cautious not to lend assistance to overreaching by the deposition reporter." [*Serrano v. Stefan Merli Plastering Co., Inc.*, supra, 162 CA4th at 1036, 76 CR3d at 575]

(a) [8:767b] **Challenging reasonableness of rates:** Any challenge to the reasonableness of the rate charged to a non-noticing party must be brought by motion in the action in which the deposition is taken: "[A]bsent extraordinary circumstances, the court in the action in which the dispute arises *is the only court* to resolve the issue." [*Las Canoas Co. v. Kramer* (2013) 216 CA4th 96, 100, 156 CR3d 561, 564 (emphasis added); see *Serrano v. Stefan Merli Plastering Co., Inc.*, supra, 162 CA4th at 1038-1039, 76 CR3d at 577—deferring determination to later, separate proceeding "would be impractical and inefficient and would undermine the trial court's necessary authority . . . as well as imperil the due process rights of the non-noticing party"]

(2) [8:767.1] **Court may order other parties to share costs:** On motion and for "good cause" shown, the court may order some other party or parties to pay or share the cost of preparing the reporter's transcript. [CCP §2025.510(b)]

(a) [8:767.2] **"Good cause":** Such an order may be proper, for example, where another party engaged in prolonged arguments and "speeches" throughout the deposition, and refused to go "off the record" with these. Or, where after the deposing party finished, the other party engaged

© 2020 Thomson Reuters/The Rutter Group

in prolonged "cross-examination," dragging out the deposition much longer than reasonably necessary. (Under former law, there was no way to prevent this, and opposing parties often took advantage of the fact that the party noticing the deposition had to pay the entire cost of the transcript.) [*San Diego Unified Port Dist. v. Douglas E. Barnhart, Inc.* (2002) 95 CA4th 1400, 1405, 116 CR2d 65, 68, fn. 3 (citing text)]

☞ [8:767.3] ***PRACTICE POINTER:*** The court's power to order costs may help you speed up depositions and control abusive conduct by opposing counsel: If they drag out the proceedings unnecessarily, politely remind them of the court's power under CCP §2025.510(b). It may curtail even the most long-winded questioner.

(3) [8:767.4] **Effect of instructing reporter not to prepare transcript:** The deposition reporter is under a duty to transcribe the deposition testimony unless the *parties agree* otherwise. [CCP §2025.510(a)]

Thus, the deposing party *alone* cannot instruct the reporter to "hold up" on the transcript; e.g., because no relevant information was obtained at the examination. If other parties present want copies, the deposing party has to pay for the transcript. (But "on motion and for good cause shown," the court has power to order them to share the cost; see CCP §2025.510(b).)

☞ [8:767.5] ***PRACTICE POINTER:*** Settlement talks often take place at or after depositions. If settlement appears likely, the parties should *jointly instruct* the deposition reporter to "hold up" on the transcript while talks continue. (The reporter should be so instructed *the same day* as the deposition, because many reporters start transcribing immediately afterwards.)

[8:767.6-767.9] *Reserved.*

(4) [8:767.10] **Nonparty's right to obtain copy:** "Any person" may obtain a copy of the deposition transcript or audio or video recording from the deposition officer (if still in the officer's possession) by paying a reasonable charge set by the reporter. [See CCP §2025.570(a)]

(a) [8:767.11] **Protective orders:** Before providing the copy, the deposition officer must mail notice to the deponent and all parties attending the deposition of the request, to enable them to seek a protective order. If no such order is served within 30 days, the copy must be provided to the nonparty. [See CCP §2025.570(b), (c)]

b. [8:768] **Reading, correcting and signing by deponent:** Unless the parties stipulate otherwise (and they often do; *see ¶8:777*), the deposition reporter oversees the review, correcting and signing of the deposition.

(1) [8:769] **Notice by deposition reporter that transcript available for review:** Upon completing the transcript, the deposition reporter notifies the deponent and other parties attending the deposition that the original transcript is available for review and signing by the deponent. [CCP §2025.520(a); see *Serrano v. Stefan Merli Plastering Co., Inc.* (2008) 162 CA4th 1014, 1033, 76 CR3d 559, 573]

Along with this notice, the deposition reporter mails a copy of the transcript to the examining counsel and other counsel who ordered copies.

[8:769.1-769.4] *Reserved.*

(2) [8:769.5] **Notice that recording is available if no transcription:** If there is no stenographic transcription of the deposition, the deposition officer must send a written notice to the deponent and to all parties that the audio or video recording made by or at the direction of any party is available for review, unless they agreed on the record to waive hearing or viewing of the recording. [CCP §2025.530(a)]

(3) [8:770] **30-day period for corrections:** The deponent has 30 days (extended for service by mail) following receipt of the reporter's notice to review and sign the transcript and make any corrections to it. [CCP §2025.520(b); see *Serrano v. Stefan Merli Plastering Co., Inc.*, supra, 162 CA4th at 1033, 76 CR3d at 573]

The same 30-day time period applies for the deponent to change the substance of an answer when the deposition is recorded via audio or video but no transcript is prepared. [CCP §2025.530(b)]

(a) [8:770a] **Court's power to shorten:** For "good cause shown," the court may shorten (but *not lengthen, see* ¶*8:771*) the period for correcting a transcript. [See CCP §2025.520(d); *Serrano v. Stefan Merli Plastering Co., Inc.*, supra, 162 CA4th at 1033, 76 CR3d at 573]

The 30-day period for correcting audio or video depositions, however, may not be shortened. [See CCP §2025.530]

Comment: Even so, for "good cause shown," the trial court presumably retains authority to alter the time for corrections pursuant to the *protective order provisions* applicable to deposition procedures generally. [CCP §2025.420(b)]

(b) [8:770.1] **How corrections made:** The deponent can change the form or substance of any answer either:

- on the face of the transcript at the deposition reporter's office; or

© 2020 Thomson Reuters/The Rutter Group

- (more commonly) by a *letter signed by the deponent* to the deposition reporter mailed by certified or registered mail with return receipt requested. Copies of this letter must be mailed (by first class mail) to all parties attending the deposition. [CCP §2025.520(c)]
- If the deposition was audio or video recorded and there is no stenographic transcript, the deponent may change the substance of the answer to any question in person or by signed letter to the deposition officer. [CCP §2025.530(b)]

[8:770.1a] ***PRACTICE POINTER:*** Counsel representing the deponent should limit changes to those that are *essential* to the case. Opposing counsel is likely to comment to the jury at trial upon any changes made in the deposition transcript. Moreover, the changes do not preclude opposing counsel from referring to the *original* answers in attempting to impeach the deponent's testimony at trial. And the factfinder may conclude the original answers were true and the corrections (presumably made with the assistance of counsel) are not trustworthy.

(c) [8:770.2] **Where depo taken in several sessions:** If the deposition is taken in more than one session, the deposition officer must give written notice upon completing the transcript of each session. If the deponent and attending parties *agree on the record*, the reading, correcting and signing of each transcript may take place after the entire deposition has been concluded. [CCP §2025.520(a)]

(d) [8:770.3] **Effect of failure to correct or review transcript:** If no corrections are made, or if the deponent fails to review and sign the transcript within the 30-day period, "*the deposition shall be given the same effect as though it had been approved*" by the deponent *without corrections.* [CCP §§2025.520(f) (emphasis added), 2025.530(d)]

(e) [8:771] **Relief after expiration of time to correct:** The Discovery Act does not authorize any extensions of the 30-day period for corrections unless agreed to by the parties on the record or in writing (CCP §2025.520(b)). Nor does it provide any procedure for relieving a party from misstatements or errors overlooked during the 30-day period (*see* ¶*8:770*).

Therefore, after the 30-day period, relief may be sought under CCP §473(b) on the grounds of "mistake, inadvertence, surprise or excusable neglect." (CCP §473(b) relief is available where there is no analogous Discovery Act provision; *see* ¶*8:10.11.*) But this is always discretionary with the court.

1) [8:772] ***Caution re "sham" corrections:*** A court is unlikely to grant relief under §473(b) where the corrections are made in response to a motion for summary judgment or other dispositive motion and seek to avoid admissions made during the deposition. Courts may treat these as "sham corrections" similar to the "sham affidavit" rule recognized on anti-SLAPP motions and summary judgment motions (*see* ¶*7:1066 and 10:156.10*).

Federal courts have adopted this position. [See *Hambleton Brothers Lumber Co. v. Balkin Enterprises, Inc.* (9th Cir. 2005) 397 F3d 1217, 1225—"a deposition is not a take home examination"]

[8:773] ***PRACTICE POINTER:*** This can be a real trap for the unwary. Thus, if your client's deposition has been taken, make sure you and the client both read the transcript *promptly* upon receipt thereof. And, do so carefully. You have only 30 days (extended for service by mail) within which to spot any errors and make necessary corrections. If you delay, you may be stuck with inadvertent misstatements.

At the same time, don't overdo the corrections. Make only those changes that are essential. Otherwise, it may look like your client was being evasive at the deposition.

(4) [8:774] **When notice required by deposition reporter of deponent's corrections:** Deponents usually make their changes or corrections by letter to the deposition reporter, with copies to all parties who attended the deposition (*see* ¶*8:770.1*). No further notice is required in such cases.

However, where deponents make changes on the original transcript in person at the deposition reporter's office, it is the reporter's duty to notify all parties who attended the deposition of such changes. [CCP §2025.520(e)]

If the deposition was *recorded* and there is no stenographic transcript, the deponent may make changes by notifying the deposition officer in person or by signed letter. The deposition officer must then provide a letter to accompany the recording, noting any changes, plus the deponent's signed letter (if there is one), or a statement that the deponent failed to supply his or her signature or to contact the deposition officer within the allotted time. [See CCP §2025.530(c)-(d)]

[8:775] ***PRACTICE POINTER:*** In any event, the attorney who took the deposition should monitor the process to *make sure all parties receive proper notice* of changes made by the deponent. Otherwise, there may be problems in admitting the transcript at trial.

© 2020 Thomson Reuters/The Rutter Group

(5) [8:776] **Motion to suppress depo:** If the deponent has *refused* to sign a transcript (e.g., because of gross errors in reporting), the court may, upon noticed motion, *suppress* the deposition in whole or in part. There is no time limit on when the motion can be made; but it must be accompanied by a declaration showing a "reasonable and good faith attempt" to resolve the matter informally. [CCP §§2025.520(g), 2025.530(e)]

As with other discovery motions, monetary sanctions "shall" be imposed against the losing party unless the court finds the party subject to the sanction acted with "substantial justification" or other circumstances make sanctions "unjust." [CCP §§2025.520(h), 2025.530(f)]

(6) [8:777] **Stipulations changing procedure:** Stipulations relieving the deposition reporter of responsibility in this area are common (*see ¶8:753 ff.*).

For example, counsel at a deposition often stipulate that:

- The original transcript be delivered directly to counsel for the *deponent* (rather than examining counsel);
- Deponent's counsel assumes responsibility for notifying other counsel of any changes made by the deponent during the 30-day period;
- Unless such notice is given, the deposition shall have the same force and effect as though signed by the deponent without corrections;
- Deponent's counsel shall retain custody of the original transcript until after final judgment in the action or as otherwise ordered by the court; and
- Deponent's counsel will lodge the original transcript on reasonable notice for any hearing or trial.

c. [8:778] **Custody of original transcript:** After expiration of the 30-day period for corrections (*see ¶8:770*), the deposition reporter is under a duty to:

- *Certify* the transcript as a true record of the testimony given by the deponent (CCP §2025.540(a));
- *Seal it* in an envelope (marked "Deposition of . . ."); and
- *Deliver* it to the attorney who took the deposition. [CCP §2025.550(a)] (Formerly, absent stipulation, the reporter retained custody of the transcript; but this was cumbersome and created problems if the reporter was unavailable.)

(1) [8:779] **Counsel's responsibility:** The attorney to whom the transcript is delivered (examining attorney, unless counsel stipulate otherwise) must store it "under *conditions that will protect it against loss, destruction, or tampering.*" [CCP §2025.550(a) (emphasis added)]

➪ [8:780] ***PRACTICE POINTER:*** What exactly this requires remains to be determined. Arguably, anything less than a fireproof safe or locked steel cabinet would not suffice. Lawyers handling complex litigation with numerous, large depositions are likely to run out of suitable storage space.

Of course, parties can stipulate in writing to modify or excuse this duty (see CCP §2016.030). Presumably, a stipulation on the record at the time of deposition that "the original *or any copy* of the transcript be retained by *any counsel*, to be used by *any* party for any *purpose*," would accomplish this.

(2) [8:781] **Length of time transcript to be retained:** Counsel must retain the transcript until *6 months after final disposition* of the action. After then, it may be destroyed unless, for good cause shown, the court orders otherwise. [CCP §2025.550(b)]

[8:781.1-781.4] *Reserved.*

d. [8:781.5] **Custody of video or audio recording:** Where the deposition is recorded on audio or video, it is the operator's responsibility to retain custody of the recording "under conditions that will protect it against loss, destruction, or tampering, and preserve as far as practicable the quality of the recording and the integrity of the testimony and images it contains." [CCP §2025.560(a)]

As with transcripts, the recording must be retained until 6 months after final disposition of the action. [CCP §2025.560(c)]

e. [8:782] **When court orders transcript filed:** Normally, deposition transcripts are *not* filed with the court (see CCP §2025.550(a)). But there are situations in which the transcript must be provided to the court:

(1) [8:783] **Pretrial motions:** The original deposition may have to be "lodged" with the court (delivered for review) in connection with motions to compel answers (*see ¶8:802*). This is *not* a filing, however. After the hearing, the court will order the transcript returned to the party that lodged it.

The court generally will not order the original *filed* unless in connection with some motion that will be dispositive of the proceedings (e.g., a motion for summary judgment based on the deposition testimony). More commonly, the relevant portions of the transcript are appended to a declaration of an attorney who attended the deposition, authenticating it.

➪ [8:783.1] ***PRACTICE POINTER—Seeking appellate review:*** Be sure to obtain an order for filing of the transcript if you wish to preserve the right to seek appellate review of an adverse ruling based on deposition testimony. Otherwise, appellate courts will invoke

© 2020 Thomson Reuters/The Rutter Group

the presumption that any evidence that is not part of the record *supports* the ruling. (See Eisenberg, *Cal. Prac. Guide: Civil Appeals & Writs* (TRG), Chs. 4 & 8.)

(2) [8:784] **Trial:** If the case goes to trial, some judges may order all originals filed at the outset or before a deposed witness testifies. Other judges may simply order the deposition transcripts lodged with the court clerk. Other judges require neither. Because this is a matter on which local practices vary, counsel should check with the court clerk in advance of trial.

Depositions are generally *not* a part of the record on appeal. Rather, deposition testimony becomes a part of the trial record only to the extent it is *read into evidence.*

If a party presents an audio or video recording of deposition testimony at trial, and the contents of the recording are not taken down by the court reporter, the party presenting the evidence must serve and file a copy of the pages of the transcript marked to show the testimony presented or offered into evidence. [CRC 2.1040(a)]

☞ [8:785] ***PRACTICE POINTER:*** Thus, as part of your trial preparation, *make sure you can produce* the original deposition of all witnesses you intend to call or cross-examine.

If the original transcript is in the custody of opposing counsel, use a Notice to Produce to make sure it is available when you need it.

Also have copies of the transcript available for opposing counsel and the judge, as well as your own use, because once you introduce the original, you will need another to facilitate reading excerpts into the record, making objections, etc.

(3) [8:786] **Disposition of transcripts filed:** A special statutory procedure enables courts to dispose of transcripts previously ordered filed:

- The court clerk must retain the transcript until dismissal or "final determination" of the action (unless, pursuant to stipulation or good cause shown, the court orders the transcript returned to one of the parties). [CCP §1952(a)]
- After dismissal or final determination of the proceedings, deposition transcripts may be destroyed upon order of court, after at least 60 days' notice to all parties of the proposed order of destruction. [CCP §1952(c)]
- Any party may file a written request for preservation of the transcript for up to one year (to provide time for copying, etc.). In such event, the court shall not order destruction

until after the period of time stated in the request. [CCP §1952(b)]

15. [8:787] **Motion to Compel Answers:** If a deponent fails to answer a deposition question or produce documents or things designated in the deposition notice or subpoena, the examiner may either complete the examination on other matters or adjourn the deposition. [CCP §§2025.460(e), 2025.480(a); *see* ¶*8:737*]

In either event, if the examiner wants an answer to the question or the documents produced, the examiner must file a motion to compel within the time limit and in accordance with the procedures discussed below (¶*8:788 ff.*). [CCP §2025.480(b)-(k)]

a. [8:787.1] **Consider informal conference as alternative to discovery motions:** Many judges try to avoid formal discovery motions. Although counsel are required to try to resolve discovery disputes informally before filing motion papers (*see* ¶*8:811, 8:1158 ff.*), this is often unsuccessful.

To avoid the costs and delay of formal discovery motions, many civil judges with individual calendars make themselves available for an *informal conference.* Each judge has his or her own procedures. In addition, any party can request, or a judge can require, an informal discovery conference under CCP §2016.080. The party requesting a conference must file a meet and confer declaration under CCP §2016.040. Other parties may, but are not required to, file a response to the declaration. If the court is in session it has 10 days to grant, deny or schedule the request or it is deemed denied. The conference must take place within 30 days of the court agreeing to the conference and before the discovery cut-off date, and the court may toll the time for discovery motions or make other orders. If the conference is not held within 30 days, the request is deemed denied. [CCP §2016.080]

In preparation for the conference, unless otherwise ordered by the court, it is helpful for counsel to submit a short (e.g., a single page) description of the discovery dispute. The judge then meets with counsel and tries to resolve the dispute, often with a suggestion of how the court might rule if presented with a motion. For most discovery disputes, such guidance from the court is all that is necessary. (For some disputes, however (e.g., those with complicated privilege issues), counsel will want to make a motion and obtain a formal ruling to preserve the issue for appellate review.)

Counsel should consider asking the court for such an informal conference before incurring substantial costs. The judge will probably appreciate counsel's efforts to save costs and avoid delay, and the time saved for the court in reviewing and ruling on a formal discovery motion.

b. [8:788] **Alternative procedures to set court hearing:** The examiner has several alternatives in noticing a motion to compel answers to deposition questions:

© 2020 Thomson Reuters/The Rutter Group

- "*Cite the witness*" at the time of the deposition; or
- Obtain and serve an *order to show cause* (OSC) on the witness after the deposition; or
- Simply serve and file a regular *notice of motion* for the order sought.

(1) [8:789] **Oral notice at deposition ("cite the witness"):** Any time before the end of the deposition, the examiner may notify the deponent and other parties present when and where the motion to compel will be heard (the motion must be "made" within 60 days after completion of transcript; *see* ¶*8:801*). The *deposition officer* must then *direct the deponent to appear* in court at the time and place specified. [CCP §2025.480(c)]

Note that the examining counsel does not "cite" the witness personally. Counsel merely states on the record when and where the motion to compel will be heard. It is *the deposition officer* who must then "cite" the deponent (i.e., instruct the deponent to appear at the time and place specified). [See *Parker v. Wolters Kluwer U.S., Inc.* (2007) 149 CA4th 285, 296, 57 CR3d 18, 26, fn. 24]

(a) [8:790] **Written notice required for nonparty deponents:** Although the Discovery Act allows oral notice at the time of the deposition, court rules require *personal service of written notice* of motion to compel answers by a deponent who is *not* a party to the action, "unless the nonparty deponent agrees to accept service by mail or electronic service at an address or electronic service address specified on the deposition record." [CRC 3.1346]

1) [8:791] **Comment:** This does not foreclose the "cite the witness" procedure (oral notice) at the deposition; but simply requires a "follow up" written notice as well. (As discussed below, the moving papers must be *personally served* on the nonparty deponents; ¶*8:797*.)

(b) [8:792] **Written notice to other parties:** Although oral notice may be sufficient for party-deponents, a written notice of motion must be served on *all* other parties to the action even if they were present at the deposition. [See CCP §2025.480(c)]

☞ [8:793] ***PRACTICE POINTER:*** Before "citing the witness," make sure of two things:

- ***When transcript will be completed:*** Ask the deposition reporter to estimate how long it will take to complete the deposition transcript, because the hearing date must be within 60 days thereafter (*see* ¶*8:801*). Also, you will need to lodge relevant parts of the transcript, or a joint statement in lieu thereof, with the court before the hearing (*see* ¶*8:802 ff.*).

- ***Availability of date chosen:*** It's a good idea to take a short recess in the deposition and call the clerk in the department where the motion will be heard to check on availability of the date.

[8:794-795] *Reserved.*

(2) [8:796] **Mailed notice:** Another alternative is for the examiner simply to serve and file a regular notice of motion for the order sought. Such notice can be served on the deponent personally or *by mail* under the statutes governing service of notice generally (CCP §1010 et seq.). Copies must likewise be served on all other parties to the action. [CCP §2025.480(c)]

Cross-refer: The motion is governed by the rules and procedures governing motions generally; *see Ch. 9 Part I.*

(a) [8:797] **Limitation—personal service required for nonparty deponents:** Court rules require that the notice of motion to compel answers and all supporting papers be *personally served* on nonparty deponents. Service by mail alone is not sufficient, "unless the nonparty deponent agrees to accept service by mail or electronic service at an address or electronic service address specified on the deposition record." [CRC 3.1346]

c. [8:798] **Motion filed in court where action pending:** Even if the deposition was taken in another county (e.g., where deponent resides), the motion is heard in the court where the action is pending. [CCP §2025.480(c)]

d. [8:799] **Jurisdiction over nonparty deponents:** Party-deponents, of course, are already subject to the personal jurisdiction of the court where the action is pending (*see Chapter 3*). Nonparty deponents "subjected themselves to court jurisdiction" by *appearing* at the deposition and refusing to answer questions. [*Marriage of Lemen* (1980) 113 CA3d 769, 780, 170 CR 642, 647 (upholding award of *sanctions* against nonparty deponent and his lawyer based on mailed notice of motion)]

Moreover, service of a deposition *subpoena* on a California resident notifies the nonparty deponent that failure to appear is punishable as a *contempt of court.* [See Judicial Council form SUBP-015, *Form 8:3* in Rivera, *Cal. Prac. Guide: Civ. Pro. Before Trial FORMS* (TRG)]

(1) [8:800] **Compare—out-of-state depo:** However, where a *nonparty* witness' deposition is taken *out-of-state*, any motion to compel must be brought where the deposition is taken; *see* ¶*8:636 ff.*

© 2020 Thomson Reuters/The Rutter Group

e. [8:801] **Time limit on motion:** The motion to compel must be "*made* no later than *60 days* after the completion of the record of the deposition." [CCP §2025.480(b) (emphasis added)]

Notice of motion *and all supporting papers* must be filed within the mandatory 60-day period. [*Weinstein v. Blumberg* (2018) 25 CA5th 316, 321, 235 CR3d 658, 662—service of "notice of motion and motion to compel" within 60-day period, but memorandum of points and authorities, separate statement and declarations served later rendered motion untimely]

Comment: It is *unclear* whether the deposition record is "completed" when the reporter sends *notice* that the transcript is available for review (*see* ¶*8:769*) or only after the expiration of time to sign or correct the transcript (*see* ¶*8:770.3*). The safer course is to use the date of the reporter's notice.

(1) [8:801.1] **Deposition subpoena for production of documents:** Where the motion is based on a deposition subpoena for production of documents (or a business records subpoena), the 60-day time limit runs from the date objections are served because the deposition record is then complete. [*Rutledge v. Hewlett-Packard Co.* (2015) 238 CA4th 1164, 1192, 190 CR3d 411, 434; *see* ¶*8:609.1*]

f. [8:801.2] **Showing of "good cause" required for document production:** A motion to compel production of documents described in a deposition notice must be accompanied by a showing of "good cause"—i.e., declarations containing *specific facts* justifying inspection of the documents described in the notice. [CCP §2025.450(b)(1)]

(1) [8:801.3] **Liberally construed:** "Good cause" has been construed liberally in the past: Justification for discovery is found where *specific facts* show the documents are necessary for effective *trial preparation* or *to prevent surprise at trial.* [*Associated Brewers Dist. Co., Inc. v. Sup.Ct. (Jos. Schlitz Brewing Co.)* (1967) 65 C2d 583, 587, 55 CR 772, 775]

The fact that there is no alternative source for the information sought is an important factor in establishing "good cause." But it is *not* essential in every case. [*Associated Brewers Dist. Co., Inc. v. Sup.Ct. (Jos. Schlitz Brewing Co.),* supra, 65 C2d at 587-588, 55 CR at 775-776]

g. [8:802] **Transcript must be "lodged" with court:** The moving party must "lodge" with the court, at least *5 days* before the hearing on the motion, a *certified copy* of whatever *parts* of the transcript are relevant to the motion. [CCP §2025.480(h)]

[8:803] ***PRACTICE POINTER:*** Consult with your judge; most dispense with this requirement unless there is an issue of the accuracy of the copies used.

[8:804] *Reserved.*

(1) [8:805] **Certified copy:** The statute requires a "certified copy" of "any parts" of the transcript lodged. [CCP §2025.480(h)]

(2) [8:806] **Deposit and return of transcript:** The deposition transcript is merely deposited with the clerk of the court in which the motion is to be heard (*not* the main court clerk's office). It will be returned to the party that deposited it after the hearing, unless the court orders otherwise.

[8:806.1] ***PRACTICE POINTER:*** To facilitate return of the transcript, attach a stamped self-addressed envelope to the "lodged" transcript.

"Lodging" of documents with the court is discussed at *¶9:51 ff.*

(3) [8:807] **No use of "rough draft" transcript:** A "rough draft" transcript cannot be certified, nor used as a certified transcript or to rebut or contradict a certified transcript. [CCP §2025.540(b)]

h. [8:808] **Moving papers:** The motion to compel should comply with the same CRC 3.1345 format/content requirements discussed in connection with motions to compel further answers to interrogatories. *See discussion at ¶8:1151 ff.*

FORM: Motion for Order Compelling Answers to Deposition Questions (and Production of Documents and for Sanctions) and Proposed Order, *see Form 8:12* in Rivera, *Cal. Prac. Guide: Civ. Pro. Before Trial FORMS* (TRG).

(1) [8:809] **Separate statement of matters in dispute required:** The questions and answers in dispute must be set forth verbatim in a separate document (not in the notice of motion itself). This separate document must also state the factual or legal reasons why a further answer should be compelled. [CRC 3.1345(a), (c); *see discussion at ¶8:1151 ff.*]

- ***FORM:*** Separate Statement of Disputed Questions and Answers, *see Form 8:13* in Rivera, *Cal. Prac. Guide: Civ. Pro. Before Trial FORMS* (TRG).

(2) [8:810] **Declaration supporting motion:** A declaration is also required, showing a good faith attempt to resolve the dispute informally (*¶8:811*), reasonable expenses incurred as ground for sanctions (*¶8:835.2*) and, if documents are involved, "good cause" for their production (*¶8:1495*). (*See Form 8:12* in Rivera, *Cal. Prac. Guide: Civ. Pro. Before Trial FORMS* (TRG).)

i. [8:811] **Attempt to resolve informally ("meet and confer") requirement:** The motion to compel must be accompanied by a declaration stating *facts* showing "a *reasonable and good faith attempt at an informal resolution* of each issue presented by the motion." [CCP §§2016.040 (emphasis added), 2025.480(b); *see*

© 2020 Thomson Reuters/The Rutter Group

detailed discussion at ¶8:1158 ff. in connection with motions to compel further answers to interrogatories]

(1) [8:812] **Postdeposition efforts required?** The statute requires a serious effort at negotiation and informal resolution; i.e., counsel must "attempt to talk the matter over, compare their views, consult and deliberate." [*Townsend v. Sup.Ct. (EMC Mortg. Co.)* (1998) 61 CA4th 1431, 1433, 72 CR2d 333, 334—informal resolution requirement not fulfilled by bickering between counsel during deposition]

This is not always possible in the heat of a deposition; a brief cooling-off period may be necessary. But there is no absolute rule requiring that informal resolution always await conclusion of the deposition: "We leave it to the parties to determine the proper time, manner and place for such discussion." [*Townsend v. Sup.Ct. (EMC Mortg. Co.)*, supra, 61 CA4th at 1438, 72 CR2d at 337 (citing text); see *Obregon v. Sup.Ct. (Cimm's, Inc.)* (1998) 67 CA4th 424, 431, 79 CR2d 62, 66, fn. 8; *Stewart v. Colonial Western Agency, Inc.* (2001) 87 CA4th 1006, 1016, 105 CR2d 115, 122—good faith effort shown by off-the-record discussions at deposition where issue was relatively simple and no other opportunity to confer before discovery cut-off date]

(2) [8:813] **Compare—where deponent fails to appear or produce records:** No "meet and confer" is required where the deponent "fails to attend the deposition and produce the documents . . . described in the deposition notice." In such cases, all that is required is a declaration by the moving party that he or she has contacted the deponent "to inquire about the nonappearance." [CCP §2025.450(b)(2)]

(a) [8:813.1] **Failure to appear alone:** Although the statute appears to apply only if the deponent fails to both appear *and* produce documents, it has been held to apply simply on a deponent's failure to appear. [*Leko v. Cornerstone Building Inspection Service* (2001) 86 CA4th 1109, 1124, 103 CR2d 858, 869]

(b) [8:813.2] **Good-faith inquiry required:** Implicit in the requirement that counsel contact the deponent to "inquire" about the nonappearance is a requirement that counsel *listen* to the reasons offered and make a good faith attempt to resolve the issue by rescheduling the deposition. [*Leko v. Cornerstone Building Inspection Service*, supra, 86 CA4th at 1124, 103 CR2d at 869—failure to consider rescheduling depo and instead filing motion to compel resulted in sanctions against deposing counsel for filing unnecessary motion]

☞ [8:813.3] ***PRACTICE POINTER:*** To avoid slip-ups, it is always a good idea for deposing counsel to contact deponent's counsel the day before a scheduled deposition to make sure the deponent plans to appear. Doing so strengthens a motion for sanctions in event of nonappearance. (But it is still necessary to file a declaration that you contacted deponent's counsel to "inquire" about the nonappearance.)

j. [8:814] **Burden on DEPONENT to justify refusal:** A deponent who has objected to a question and refused to answer bears the burden of justifying such refusal on the motion to compel. For example, if the objection was that the question called for privileged information, the burden is on the deponent to show that the question in fact calls for information protected by a privilege.

(1) [8:815] **Factual matters:** Sometimes, the deponent will have to prove extrinsic facts in order to justify his or her objection. For example, if the objection is privilege, the deponent may have to show the *existence* of the privileged relationship (attorney-client, husband-wife, etc.). [*San Diego Professional Ass'n v. Sup.Ct. (Paderewski, Mitchell, Dean & Assocs.)* (1962) 58 C2d 194, 199, 23 CR 384, 386]

☞ [8:816] ***PRACTICE POINTER:*** Include in your moving papers arguments as to why the deponent should be ordered to answer; e.g., why the information sought is not privileged, etc. This will inform the court as to the nature of the controversy *before* the hearing. And, it won't change the rule that the ultimate burden of justifying the refusal is on the objector.

k. [8:817] **Monetary sanction against losing party on motion to compel:** The court "shall" impose a monetary sanction against the losing party *unless* it finds the losing party "acted with substantial justification" or other circumstances make imposition of the sanction "unjust." [CCP §§2025.450(g)(1), 2025.480(j); *but see also* ¶*8:534.1* (limitation against losing party sanctions for failure to produce ESI "that has been lost, damaged, altered or overwritten as a result of the routine, good faith operation of an electronic information system")]

The "substantial justification" standard is discussed at ¶*8:1964 ff.* (Monetary sanctions on discovery motions are discussed at ¶*8:1921 ff.*)

(1) [8:817.1] **Expenses and fees:** The losing party may be ordered to pay the *reasonable expenses, including attorney fees*, incurred by the party prevailing on the motion. [CCP §2023.030(a)]

l. [8:818] **Sanctions for disobedience to order to compel:** If the motion to compel is granted and the court orders the deponent to answer, further sanctions may be imposed if the deponent fails to obey the court's order:

© 2020 Thomson Reuters/The Rutter Group

- If the deponent is a party or "party-affiliated" witness (officer, director, managing agent or employee of party), "issue," "evidence" or "terminating" sanctions may be imposed against the party involved. In addition or in lieu thereof, monetary sanctions may be imposed against the deponent. [CCP §2023.030(a)-(d)]
- Alternatively, the deponent (whether or not a party to the action) may be punished for *contempt* of court. [CCP §§2025.480(k), 2023.030(e)]

(Sanctions for disobedience to court orders are discussed at ¶*8:852, 8:2145 ff.*)

16. [8:819] **Sanctions re Depositions:** Various sanctions may be imposed to enforce discovery by deposition:

a. [8:820] **Sanctions for deponent's FAILURE TO APPEAR:** The following remedies and sanctions are available where a deponent fails to attend a deposition; or appears and refuses to be sworn as a witness. (Compare: Once testimony begins, sanctions for failure to *answer* questions are awardable only in connection with a motion to compel; *see* ¶*8:835 ff.*)

(1) [8:821] **Nonparty witness fails to appear:** A witness who is not a party to the action but has been *subpoenaed* to appear for deposition, is subject to the following sanctions for failure to appear or refusal to be sworn:

- [8:822] *Contempt* proceedings for disobedience to the subpoena. (The subpoena itself is technically a court order; no other court order directing compliance is necessary.) [CCP §§2020.240, 1991.1; *Lund v. Sup.Ct.* (1964) 61 C2d 698, 713, 39 CR 891, 901; *see* ¶*8:610 ff.*]
- [8:823] *Payment of $500* to the aggrieved party, plus all *damages* resulting from the failure to appear. [CCP §§2020.240, 1992; *see* ¶*8:618*]
- [8:823.1] Compare: Alternatively, an order compelling compliance may be granted under CCP §1987.1 (¶*8:609.1*). The court can award expenses and fees to the prevailing party only if it finds the motion was made or opposed in "bad faith" or "without substantial justification," or if one or more of the subpoena requirements was "oppressive." [CCP §1987.2]

[8:824] **Compare—if no subpoena served:** If the nonparty witness was not subpoenaed *no* sanctions of any kind are available against the nonparty *witness* for failure to appear. (However, the *party noticing the deposition* may be ordered to pay reasonable expenses and attorney fees incurred by *other* parties who showed up for the deposition expecting the witness to appear; see CCP §2025.440(a), ¶*8:832.*)

(2) [8:825] **Party or person "affiliated" with party fails to appear:** Service of a proper deposition notice obligates a party or "party-affiliated" witness (officer, director, managing agent or employee of party) to attend and testify, without necessity of subpoena. [CCP §2025.280(a), ¶*8:516 ff.*]

If such party or "party-affiliated" deponent fails to appear (or to produce materials designated in the deposition notice), monetary sanctions may be imposed. [CCP §§2025.450(g)(1), 2025.480(j); *but see also* ¶*8:534.1* (limitation against sanctions for failure to produce ESI "that has been lost, damaged, altered or overwritten as a result of the routine, good faith operation of an electronic information system")]

(a) [8:826] **Who may obtain sanction:** Both the party noticing the deposition and all other parties who showed up in expectation the deponent's testimony would be taken may obtain monetary sanctions. [CCP §2025.450(g)(1), (2)]

1) [8:826.1] **Lawyers appearing *pro bono:*** Monetary sanctions in the form of fees for the reasonable value of counsel's services may be awarded even where counsel is serving free of charge. The party entitled to the award need not have incurred a fee obligation. [See *Do v. Sup.Ct. (Nguyen)* (2003) 109 CA4th 1210, 1218, 135 CR2d 855, 860-861 (decided under former statute)]

[8:826.2-826.4] *Reserved.*

(b) [8:826.5] **Against whom sanctions may be imposed:** Sanctions may be imposed against the deponent or the *party* with whom the deponent is "affiliated" (as an officer, director, managing agent or employee). [CCP §2025.450(g)(1); *see* ¶*8:836*]

(c) [8:827] **Failure to appear need not be willful:** Monetary sanctions may be imposed against a deponent party *even if his or her failure to appear was entirely inadvertent.* It is enough that the deponent "fails to appear for examination." [CCP §2025.450(a)]

[8:828-829] *Reserved.*

(d) [8:830] **Discretion to refuse sanction limited:** The court "shall" award monetary sanctions against the losing party *unless* the prevailing party failed to make a reasonable effort to resolve the issues informally, or the deponent shows an *excuse* for failure to appear:

- "Substantial justification" for his or her conduct; or
- Other circumstances making sanctions "unjust." [CCP §2025.450(g); and see CCP §2023.030(a), *discussed at* ¶*8:845 ff.*]

© 2020 Thomson Reuters/The Rutter Group

[8:831] *Reserved.*

b. [8:832] **Sanctions against PARTY NOTICING DEPOSITION for failure to proceed:** If the party noticing the deposition fails to attend or proceed with it, the court may impose a monetary sanction in favor of "any party attending in person or by attorney." [CCP §2025.430]

Likewise, monetary sanctions can be imposed against the party noticing the deposition where a *nonparty deponent fails to appear* if no deposition subpoena has been served (as required by CCP §2020.010(b)). Such sanctions can be imposed in favor of any other party who showed up for the deposition. [CCP §2025.440(a); *see* ¶*8:536*]

(1) [8:833] **Compare—no sanctions to nonparty deponents who appear:** A nonparty deponent subpoenaed to attend a deposition is entitled to a witness fee and mileage (¶*8:572*). But he or she *cannot* obtain monetary sanctions (e.g., attorney fees) against the party noticing the deposition for failing to proceed with it. [See *Poe v. Diamond* (1987) 191 CA3d 1394, 1399, 237 CR 80, 83—construing similar provision under former law]

[8:834] *Reserved.*

c. [8:835] **Sanctions for REFUSAL TO ANSWER:** If a deponent appears and is sworn as a witness, but thereafter refuses to answer any questions or to produce documents designated in the deposition notice or subpoena, the deposing party's remedy is a motion to compel (*see* ¶*8:620*). Monetary sanctions may be awarded on the motion to compel as follows:

(1) [8:835.1] **Monetary sanction only:** The only sanction authorized on a motion to compel, when there has been no prior court order to answer, is a monetary sanction pursuant to CCP §2023.030(a). [CCP §2025.480(j)]

(a) [8:835.2] **"Reasonable expenses":** Section 2023.030(a) authorizes an order for payment of the "reasonable expenses, *including attorney's fees*" incurred as a result of the conduct for which the sanctions are imposed. [CCP §2023.030(a) (emphasis added)]

1) [8:835.2a] **Lawyers appearing *pro se?*** Lawyers appearing on their own behalf *cannot* recover attorney fees as discovery sanctions. But they can recover reasonably identifiable *costs* (e.g., computer-assisted legal research, or photocopying, or transportation to and from court) even if those costs would ordinarily be included in the lawyer's hourly rate. [*Kravitz v. Sup.Ct. (Milner)* (2001) 91 CA4th 1015, 1021, 111 CR2d 385, 389 (involving inspection demands)]

2) [8:835.2b] **Lawyers appearing *pro bono?*** *See* ¶*8:826.1.*

(b) [8:835.3] **Award to moving party only?** According to one case, sanctions may be awarded only in favor of the party who noticed the deposition and moved for sanctions. Other parties who may have attended the deposition and joined the motion are "outsiders" and not entitled to sanctions. [*Townsend v. Sup.Ct. (EMC Mortg. Co.)* (1998) 61 CA4th 1431, 1438, 72 CR2d 333, 337]

But cases dealing with other forms of discovery have allowed sanctions in favor of *nonmoving* parties. [See *Trail v. Cornwell* (1984) 161 CA3d 477, 483, 207 CR 679, 681, fn. 4; *Calvert Fire Ins. Co. v. Cropper* (1983) 141 CA3d 901, 905, 190 CR 593, 594]

1) [8:835.4] **Comment:** The latter rule makes more practical sense, particularly in the case of depositions where parties other than the moving party incurred expenses for attending the aborted deposition.

[8:835.5-835.9] *Reserved.*

(c) [8:835.10] **Limited to expenses "incurred":** Sanctions are limited to costs that have been "incurred." Thus, the court may *not* award the costs of *future* follow-up depositions as a discovery sanction. [*Tucker v. Pacific Bell Mobile Services* (2010) 186 CA4th 1548, 1563, 115 CR3d 9, 19-20]

(2) [8:836] **Against whom sanctions awardable:** Monetary sanctions may be awarded against "any *party, person or attorney* who *unsuccessfully* makes or opposes a motion to compel an answer or production." [CCP §2025.480(j) (emphasis added)]

Thus, if the motion is *granted* and the deponent ordered to answer, the deponent (and any party with whom he or she is "affiliated") is subject to monetary sanctions.

Conversely, if the motion to compel is *denied*, the deposing party may end up paying sanctions for making the motion.

(a) [8:837] **Sanctions despite no opposition:** Sanctions may also be awarded against a party who *fails to oppose a motion to compel*, or who *withdraws* its opposition or furnishes the requested discovery before the motion hearing. [CRC 3.1348(a); *see discussion at ¶8:2010 ff.*]

[8:838-839] *Reserved.*

(b) [8:840] **Party or counsel or both:** Monetary sanctions for misuse of discovery may be imposed against the party engaging in such conduct, *and/or* against the attorney advising the improper conduct. [CCP §§2023.030(a), 2025.480(j)]

© 2020 Thomson Reuters/The Rutter Group

1) [8:840.1] **Right of contribution where one pays sanctions imposed against both:** Where sanctions are imposed against both attorney and client *without* apportionment of liability, whoever pays the sanction is entitled to pro rata contribution from the other. [*Young v. Rosenthal* (1989) 212 CA3d 96, 130, 260 CR 369, 390]

[8:841] *Reserved.*

(c) [8:842] **Nonparty deponents:** Monetary sanctions are authorized even against *nonparty* deponents if they "unsuccessfully oppose" a motion to compel. [CCP §2025.480(j); *Person v. Farmers Ins. Group of Cos.* (1997) 52 CA4th 813, 818, 61 CR2d 30, 33—health care provider refused to allow inspection and copying of records until patient signed lien; *see ¶8:1805.40*]

1) [8:843] **Compare:** Absent service of subpoena, no sanctions can be imposed against a nonparty who *fails to appear* for deposition (*¶8:824*).

But if the nonparty witness shows up at the deposition, whether a subpoena was served becomes immaterial at that point. *Personal service of the motion to compel* on the nonparty deponent establishes the court's power to order discovery (CRC 3.1346, *¶8:790*) and to impose sanctions for refusal to answer questions at the depo. [See *Marriage of Lemen* (1980) 113 CA3d 769, 780-781, 170 CR 642, 647 (decided under similar provision of former law)]

2) [8:844] **Moving party must attempt to resolve informally:** The nonparty deponent can always avoid sanctions by agreeing to provide the requested information. Before sanctions can be awarded, the moving party must show it made a *reasonable and good faith attempt* to resolve the issues informally. [CCP §2025.480(b); *see ¶8:811*]

(3) [8:845] **Court's discretion to refuse sanctions limited:** The statute says the court "*shall* impose" a monetary sanction against the losing party, *unless* it finds:

- The person or party against whom sanctions are sought acted "with substantial justification"; or
- Other circumstances make imposition of sanctions "unjust." [CCP §2025.480(j)]

(a) [8:846] **"Substantial justification":** *See discussion at ¶8:1964 ff.*

(b) [8:847] **Other circumstances making sanctions "unjust":** *See discussion at ¶8:1973.*

Cross-refer: Monetary sanctions on discovery motions are discussed at *¶8:1921 ff.*

[8:848-851] *Reserved.*

d. [8:852] **Sanctions for DISOBEYING discovery orders:** Once a deponent has been *ordered* to attend a deposition, or to answer questions or to produce documents at a resumed deposition, more severe sanctions are available for continued refusal to make discovery. [CCP §2023.030(b)-(d)]

"Disobeying a court order to provide discovery" is itself a "*misuse of the discovery process*" (CCP §2023.010(g), ¶*8:1901*), for which a broad range of sanctions is authorized. *See detailed discussion at ¶8:2145 ff.*

[8:853-875] *Reserved.*

17. [8:876] **Use of Depositions at Trial:** A deposition transcript may be admissible evidence at trial or other hearing in the action, as discussed below (¶*8:877*). [CCP §2025.620(a)-(b)] (Use of depositions in *judicial arbitration* proceedings is discussed at ¶*8:893*.)

In general, deposition evidence is admissible against any party present at the deposition, or who had *notice* thereof and did not serve a valid objection (*see* ¶*8:719 ff.*). [CCP §2025.620]

a. [8:877] **Deposition of party or "party affiliated" deponent admissible for any purpose:** The adverse party may use the deposition of a party or "party affiliated" deponent (officer, director, managing agent or employee of party) for *any purpose*—i.e., either:

- As *impeachment*, or
- As *substantive evidence* against such party (i.e., an admission). [CCP §2025.620]

Comment: The statute allows only an "adverse party" to use another party's deposition for "any purpose" (i.e., as substantive proof). It is not clear, however, whether a *nonadverse* party can do likewise (e.g., where D1 wants to use D2's deposition to prove a common defense).

[8:877.1] ***PRACTICE POINTER:*** This is the reason, of course, it is so crucially important to spend the time and effort necessary to *prepare your clients and witnesses thoroughly* before they testify at their depositions.

(1) [8:878] **Immaterial whether party testifies:** It is *not* ground for objection to the use of the deposition that the party deponent is present and willing to testify in person, or has already testified. [CCP §2025.620(b)]

(2) [8:878.1] **Not affected by substitution of party:** Substitution of parties does *not* affect the right to use depositions previously taken. [CCP §2025.620(f)]

- [8:878.2] This applies, for example, where deponents *transfer their interest* in the litigation after their depositions are taken. It makes no difference that the transferees

© 2020 Thomson Reuters/The Rutter Group

are substituted in as parties in place of the deponents. Their depositions are still admissible "for any purpose" by opposing parties.

(Depositions of parties now deceased or otherwise "unavailable" to testify would be admissible in any event; *see* ¶*8:885*.)

(3) [8:879] **No foundation required:** Since the deposition can be used "for any purpose," the adverse party can simply pick up the transcript and read the deposition testimony directly into evidence.

[8:880] ***PRACTICE POINTERS***

- First of all, make sure the original transcript is *lodged* with the court before attempting to read excerpts into evidence. Otherwise, the court won't permit it *over objection* by opposing counsel. (But this is not usually a problem; such objections are unusual.)
- It is often very effective to organize your cross-examination of the adverse party so that *key questions are asked in substantially the manner as they were at deposition*. Then, if the adverse party gives a different answer, simply pick up his or her deposition and read to the jury the appropriate excerpt contradicting the live testimony.

b. [8:881] **Deposition of nonparty deponent admissible to impeach testimony at trial:** The deposition of an independent witness may be used to impeach or contradict live testimony given by that witness at time of trial. [CCP §2025.620(a)]

(It may also be used for *any other* purpose permitted by the Evidence Code or under the circumstances described in ¶*8:884 ff.*)

(1) [8:882] **No foundation required:** As long as the witness is still on the witness stand, no foundation is required (i.e., the deposition need not be shown to the witness, nor need the witness be given a chance to explain any inconsistencies therein). The cross-examiner can simply read into evidence the contradictory testimony given at the time of deposition. [Ev.C. §770(b)]

(2) [8:883] **Compare—after witness excused:** However, once a witness has left the witness stand and has been excused from giving further testimony in the action, the witness cannot be impeached in this manner (without prior opportunity to explain or deny the impeaching testimony). [See Ev.C. §770(a)]

c. [8:884] **Deposition of ANY witness admissible under special circumstances:** Under the circumstances described below (¶*8:885 ff.*), the deposition of *any* deponent (including a party or someone "affiliated" with a party) may be used by *any party* (including the deponent personally) for *any purpose*. I.e., the deposition can be used as a *substitute for live testimony* at trial, either as impeachment or substantive evidence, and either *by* or *against* the party whose deposition was taken or *any other party* who was present or had notice of the deposition. [CCP §2025.620(c); see *N.N.V. v. American Ass'n of Blood Banks* (1999) 75 CA4th 1358, 1396, 89 CR2d 885, 912]

(1) [8:885] **Deponent "unavailable" to testify:** Deposition testimony is admissible where (through no fault of the party offering the deposition) the deponent is shown to be:

- Dead; or
- Unable to attend or testify because of existing physical or mental illness or infirmity; or
- Incapable of being served with subpoena despite "reasonable diligence"; or
- Exempted or precluded on ground of *privilege* from testifying concerning the matter to which the deposition testimony is related; or
- Otherwise *disqualified* from testifying. [CCP §2025.620(c)(2)(A)-(E)]

(In such cases, the deposition transcript is admissible under the "recorded testimony" exception to the hearsay rule; see Ev.C. §§1291, 240.)

(a) [8:886] **Burden of showing "unavailability":** The burden is on the party seeking to introduce the deposition to establish one or more of these factors (¶*8:885*). [See Ev.C. §240]

(2) [8:887] **Residence more than 150 miles from place of trial:** A deposition is also admissible "for any purpose" if the deponent resides more than 150 miles from the place of trial or other hearing. [CCP §2025.620(a)-(c)(1)]

(a) [8:888] **Unavailability not required:** No showing of "unavailability" is required. Thus, *any* deposition can be used in lieu of live testimony simply by showing that the deponent resides more than 150 miles from the courthouse. It makes no difference that he or she could be subpoenaed. Nor is any warning required that the deposition will be offered in lieu of live testimony. (But, of course, an opposing party may subpoena the deponent to appear in person.)

(b) [8:889] **Party's own deposition:** Parties who live more than 150 miles from the courthouse can use this provision to testify by deposition, in lieu of appearing in person at trial, if they choose. [CCP §2025.620(c)(1)]

© 2020 Thomson Reuters/The Rutter Group

[8:890] ***PRACTICE POINTER:*** Unless your client is too ill or infirm to testify in person, it is very risky to use deposition testimony in lieu of live testimony. If the opposing party appears in person, most juries (and some judges) will be predisposed to accept that party's version of any disputed facts over your client's deposition testimony. They may conclude, rightly or wrongly, that if it wasn't important enough for your client to travel to the courthouse, your client deserves to lose. Moreover, the judge may sustain objections to critical portions of the deposition transcript, leaving you with no evidence on an issue.

(3) [8:891] **Other "exceptional circumstances":** Finally, a deposition transcript may be used for any purpose where the court finds that "exceptional circumstances" justify such use. [CCP §2025.620(c)(3)]

(a) [8:891.1] **Comment:** "Exceptional circumstances" is not further defined in the statute, and this ground is rarely invoked. But it does give the trial judge discretion to admit a deposition transcript where the witness lives *less* than 150 miles from the courthouse (¶*8:887*), or the proponent cannot establish "unavailability" (¶*8:885*), and the interests of justice still make it desirable to receive deposition testimony.

d. [8:891.2] **Partial use "opens up" other parts relevant to part introduced:** Whenever a party introduces into evidence only *part* of a deposition transcript, any other party may introduce *other parts relevant* to the part introduced. [CCP §2025.620(e)]

Effect: Partial use of a deposition allows opposing parties to introduce other relevant parts that otherwise could not have been introduced (e.g., because no showing of unavailability). (Of course, appropriate evidentiary objections may still be available; e.g., hearsay, privileged, etc.)

PRACTICE POINTERS

- [8:891.3] *Think long and hard before offering excerpts from a deposition that is otherwise inadmissible.* (E.g., depositions of employees or officers of opposing corporate party who are not shown to be "unavailable" to testify.)

  The part you offer may be admissible as substantive evidence against the adverse party. But, if other parts of the deposition are harmful to your case, you are inviting their use.

- [8:891.4] And, *don't attempt to take excerpts of depositions out of context.* It probably won't work, because opposing counsel has the right to introduce other parts of the deposition to show the entire picture. This can destroy the effectiveness of your examination and the credibility of your case.

e. [8:892] **Video recording of expert witness deposition:** As discussed earlier (¶*8:661*), a video recording of an expert witness' deposition may be admissible in lieu of live testimony by that expert at trial (no showing of "unavailability" required), *provided:*

- The *deposition notice stated* the deposition would be video recorded for this purpose (CCP §2025.220(a)(6), *see* ¶*8:487*);
- If a *deposition subpoena* was served, the subpoena also stated the deposition would be video recorded (CCP §2020.310(c), *see* ¶*8:538*); and
- Before trial, the party notified the court and other parties *what portions* of the video recording would be offered so that any objections could be ruled upon (CCP §2025.340(m), *see* ¶*8:674*). [CCP §2025.620(d)]

f. [8:892.1] **Use in subsequent litigation:** Depositions taken in an earlier action between the same parties and involving the same subject matter (e.g., where earlier action dismissed before trial) can be used as if taken in the later action. (This prevents plaintiff from "burying" adverse deposition testimony by dismissing and filing a new suit.) [CCP §2025.620(g)]

Moreover, depositions in an earlier action may be admissible in a later action under the "former testimony" exception to the hearsay rule. (This usually requires showing both that the deponent is now "unavailable" to testify; and that the party against whom the evidence is offered had the opportunity to cross-examine the deponent with the same motive and interest as at present.) [See Ev.C. §1290 et seq.; see also *N.N.V. v. American Ass'n of Blood Banks* (1999) 75 CA4th 1358, 1396, 89 CR2d 885, 912]

18. [8:893] **Use of Depositions in Judicial Arbitration Hearings:** The California Rules of Court contain rules re use of depositions in judicial arbitration hearings (under CCP §1141.10 et seq.) that are even more liberal than those under the Discovery Act. Basically, depositions can be used not only to impeach live witnesses, or against a party for any purpose (*see* ¶*8:877*), but also as a *substitute for live testimony by nonparty witnesses* under the circumstances below (¶*8:894*). [CRC 3.823(b)(3)]

[8:893.1] **Superseded by Discovery Act?** CCP §2025.620 governs admissibility of depositions "at the trial *or any other hearing* in the action." Whether "other hearing" refers only to *court* hearings, or also includes judicial arbitration hearings, is unclear. So far as known, there was no legislative intent to repeal the California Rules of Court governing judicial arbitration hearings. But the wording of the statute—"any other

© 2020 Thomson Reuters/The Rutter Group

hearing"—certainly could apply. This point may have to be resolved by future case law.

a. [8:894] **Depositions in lieu of live testimony:** The deposition of *any witness* (party or nonparty) can be introduced at the judicial arbitration hearing, even if the deponent is available to testify and resides within 150 miles of the courthouse. [CRC 3.823(b)(3)(A)]

   This is particularly helpful with respect to independent witnesses (e.g., eyewitnesses to the accident). Their depositions can be introduced in lieu of having to subpoena them and obtain their live testimony. The result is considerable cost savings in these smaller cases.

b. [8:895] **Procedure:** The party who wants to use a deposition instead of live testimony must notify the opposing party of the intention to do so *at least 20 days* before the arbitration hearing. [CRC 3.823(b)(3)(A)(ii)]

c. [8:896] **Opposing party may subpoena:** The opposing party then has the option of subpoenaing the witness to be present. It is then up to the arbitrator to decide whether the deposition should be excluded in favor of live testimony from that witness; or whether the deposition should be admitted as the direct testimony, and the witness simply cross-examined by the party who subpoenaed him or her. [CRC 3.823(b)(3)(B)]

d. [8:897] **Objections:** Deposition testimony so received is subject to the same evidentiary objections (hearsay, materiality, competency, etc.) as the deponent's live testimony at trial. [CRC 3.823(b)(3)(A)]

CHAPTER 8F

INTERROGATORIES

CONTENTS

© 2020 Thomson Reuters/The Rutter Group

© 2020 Thomson Reuters/The Rutter Group

RESERVED

INTERROGATORIES

[8:898] **Statute:** CCP §2030.010 et seq. sets forth the rules and procedures governing interrogatories.

[8:899] **Defined:** An interrogatory is a written question asked by one party to another party, who must answer under oath and in writing. The answer may be used in evidence against the answering party. [See CACI 209; BAJI 2.07]

[8:900] **Compare—deposition on written questions:** As discussed earlier, depositions may be taken on *written* questions instead of orally (CCP §2028.010 et seq.; *see ¶8:757 ff.*). Written deposition questions are sometimes called "interrogatories," but the procedure is governed by the rules applicable to *depositions* and is quite different from the interrogatory method discussed below (*¶8:905 ff.*).

STRATEGIES AND TACTICS RE INTERROGATORIES

[8:901] **Advantages**

- **Inexpensive:** Interrogatories are far less costly than depositions. There are no court reporter fees, transcript costs, travel expenses, etc.
- **Less preparation:** In most cases, far less time is required to draft and serve interrogatories than to prepare for and take a deposition.
- **Obtaining information "available" to opposing party:** Interrogatories require the answering party to furnish information "available" to him or her, whereas depositions usually reach only the deponent's personal knowledge. Interrogatories thus enable the propounding party to obtain nonprivileged information known to *opposing counsel* or any other agent or employee of the opposing party (*see ¶8:1047 ff.*).
- **Obtaining details:** Interrogatories are usually better suited than depositions for obtaining data persons are not likely to have at their fingertips: e.g., exact dates, times and places; account numbers; exact costs, etc.
- **Obtaining adversary's contentions:** Interrogatories are also better than depositions for ascertaining the opinions and contentions of the opposing party (*see ¶8:984 ff.*).
- **Setting up other discovery:** Interrogatories are often used as the "opening salvo" in discovery. They can secure information necessary to prepare for deposing the adverse party, to locate witnesses, to obtain descriptions of documents or physical evidence you want to examine, etc.
- **Following up after other discovery:** They can also be used to follow up on questions not completely answered at depositions, and

© 2020 Thomson Reuters/The Rutter Group

STRATEGIES AND TACTICS RE INTERROGATORIES (Cont'd)

on leads obtained through other discovery. (This is particularly important where the one-deposition-limit for natural persons prevents renewed depositions; ¶*8:478*.)

[8:902] **Disadvantages**

- **Limited number:** There is a limit on the number of specially prepared interrogatories that may be served ("Rule of 35 Plus"; *see* ¶*8:935*). So, unlike depositions, it may be necessary to hoard your questions and avoid asking about background or marginally important matters.
- **Slower:** There is usually at least a 30-day wait between the time the questions are served and the answers are received; often, much longer. (In depositions, of course, the answers are immediate.) Also, as trial approaches, there may not be time enough to wait 30 days for answers (*see* ¶*8:1024 ff.*).
- **No spontaneity:** Answers to interrogatories are usually prepared by or with the assistance of counsel, so there is little likelihood of spontaneity or unguarded revelations as there is with depositions.
- **No chance for follow-up questions:** Interrogatories aren't suited for broad or controversial issues because there is no chance for immediate follow-up questions. If the answer fails to respond precisely to the question asked, new sets of interrogatories or motions to compel may be required.
- **No help in sizing up adversary:** The answers are faceless forms and of no help in sizing up the demeanor or credibility of the answering party as a witness if the case goes to trial.
- **Can be sent to parties only:** Depositions are the only procedure by which nonparties can be compelled to give information (*see* ¶*8:419, 8:464*).

[8:903] **Practical Considerations**

- **Costs to propounding party:** As with any discovery procedure, the attorney planning to send out interrogatories must weigh the costs involved against the importance of the information sought and the amount at stake in the lawsuit. Is it possible to obtain such information some other, less expensive way (e.g., would opposing counsel provide it *voluntarily* or *stipulate* as to the facts in question)?
- Interrogatories are usually the least expensive discovery device, and can be cost-justified even in lawsuits of moderate size.
- But that doesn't mean that you can stint on the time required to draft interrogatories. Since only a limited number of specially prepared interrogatories are allowed, you need to make each question count.
- Also, sloppy questions usually draw sloppy answers, necessitating motions to compel further answers, etc. This can run up the costs dramatically. To obtain complete answers, the propounding party may have to file a motion to compel; and this requires compliance with time-consuming meet-and-confer rules. The result may be that

STRATEGIES AND TACTICS RE INTERROGATORIES (Cont'd)

the information could have been obtained more inexpensively through a deposition. (*See ¶8:1136 ff.*)

- **Cost to responding party:** Answering interrogatories is usually more costly than sending them out. The attorney has to spend time educating the client as to the importance of the answers given, then send out the questions to the client and check to see that the answers are received back expeditiously. Further time will have to be spent to turn the raw information collected from the client into an adequate set of answers. Carelessly drawn answers usually spawn motions to compel further responses, or may end up "burning" the answering party at the time of trial.

[8:904] **Concerns Re Abuse:** There has been more abuse in this area of discovery than any other. Some lawyers use word processors to broadside their opponents with mountains of interrogatories—more for the purpose of burdening the opposition than for discovery. Evasive responses are provided in order to hinder and burden their opponents. Patently broad discovery demands and boilerplate objections are routine and many lawyers assume these are simply precursors to "meet and confer" sessions where each side will ultimately come up with reasonable positions. Such actions are discovery misuse because they delay and increase the costs to the other side.

- **Legislative reforms:** The 1986 Discovery Act, as recodified in 2004 (¶*8:5*), took steps toward curbing these abuses. It limits the number of specially prepared interrogatories that may be served (see "Rule of 35 Plus," ¶*8:935*); and spells out a broad array of sanctions for failure to make discovery.
- **Ethical considerations:** Improper use of discovery undermines public respect and confidence in the legal system. It therefore violates the attorney's fundamental duty to uphold the laws of the State of California (Bus. & Prof.C. §6068(a)).

  Civility Guidelines:
  - — An attorney should narrowly tailor special interrogatories and not use them to harass or impose an undue burden or expense on an opposing party;
  - — An attorney should not intentionally misconstrue or respond to interrogatories in a manner that is not truly responsive;
  - — When an attorney lacks a good faith belief in the merit of an objection, the attorney should not object to an interrogatory. If an interrogatory is objectionable in part, an attorney should answer the unobjectionable part. [State Bar California Attorney Guidelines of Civility and Professionalism §9(c) (available on the State Bar website, *www.calbar.org*)]
- **Dilatory tactics:** Some responding parties routinely request extensions, which are often granted as a matter of courtesy, then follow with inadequate responses, prompting a meet and confer prior to bringing a motion to compel. Because of scheduling delays in some courts

© 2020 Thomson Reuters/The Rutter Group

STRATEGIES AND TACTICS RE INTERROGATORIES (Cont'd)

due to budget cuts starting in 2008, it may take six months to a year for the motion to be heard. As a result, it can be very difficult to obtain proper responses if a party "games" the system, which minimizes the effectiveness of interrogatories. Compounding the problem, some parties do not oppose the motion to compel but instead file supplemental responses just before the hearing. While doing so may moot the motion, it does not eliminate the right to sanctions. In these circumstances, the propounding party should diligently document these abuses to help convince a busy trial judge that significant relief is warranted.

- **Practical consequences:** Discovery abuses usually lead to court hearings (motions for protective orders, to compel answers, etc.). Judges are not naive. Increasingly, they tend to come down hard on attorneys whom they perceive to be abusing discovery privileges. Substantial monetary sanctions are likely to be imposed against the attorney (rather than merely against the party represented), on the theory that a little prophylactic medicine may prevent future abuses by that attorney—and others.

1. [8:905] **WHEN Interrogatories May be Served:** Interrogatories may be served without leave of court any time during the action, except as stated below (¶*8:906 ff.*). [CCP §2030.020(a)]

   a. [8:906] **"Hold" on interrogatories by plaintiff at outset of case:** Plaintiff may not serve interrogatories on defendant within the *first 10 days* after service of summons or defendant's appearance in the action (whichever is first). [CCP §2030.020(b)] (Compare: The *deposition* "hold" period is *20* days; *see* ¶*8:439*.)

      Exception: In unlawful detainer actions, the "hold" on plaintiff's interrogatories is only *5 days* after service of summons or defendant's appearance in the action (whichever is first). [CCP §2030.020(c)]

      (1) [8:907] **Purpose:** The purpose of the 10-day "hold" is to give defendant an opportunity to employ counsel and to review the facts with counsel before having to respond to interrogatories.

      (Note that the "hold" applies only to plaintiff's interrogatories; defendant can serve interrogatories on plaintiff during this period if it chooses to do so.)

      (2) [8:908] **Court may grant leave for earlier interrogatories:** In appropriate cases, plaintiff may seek leave of court to serve interrogatories immediately. "Good cause" must be shown, but leave may be granted ex parte if necessary. [See CCP §2030.020(d)]

   b. [8:909] **"Cut-off" on discovery before trial:** There are two separate discovery "cut-off" dates to consider. Unless otherwise ordered:

      - Discovery *proceedings* must be *completed 30 days* before the initial trial date; *and*

- Discovery *motions* must be heard no later than *15 days* before the initial trial date. [CCP §2024.020(a); *see* ¶*8:445*]

(1) [8:910] **Exceptions:** These cut-off dates do not apply in:

- *Unlawful detainer* actions (CCP §2024.040(b)(1)—discovery cut-off 5 days before the initial trial date);
- *Eminent domain* proceedings (CCP §2024.040(b)(2)); or
- Cases ordered to *judicial arbitration* (an *earlier* cut-off applies in such cases; and after an arbitration award, only expert witness discovery is generally permitted), absent a stipulation or court order. [CCP §2024.040(a)]

[8:911] *Reserved.*

(2) [8:912] **When proceedings "completed":** Discovery proceedings are deemed "completed" on the day the *response* is due (or a deposition begins). [CCP §2024.010; *see* ¶*8:448*]

Thus, interrogatories must be served so that the *responses* are due no later than 30 days before the first trial date. The minimum requirement is therefore 61 days before trial; 66 days, if served by mail (to a California address). Otherwise, an order shortening time for answers is required.

Extension for weekends, holidays: See CCP §2024.020(a) and §2016.060, *discussed at* ¶*8:445*.

[8:913] ***PRACTICE POINTER:*** To avoid problems, serve your last round of interrogatories *at least 90 days* before trial so that the response is due *no later than 60 days* before trial (not just 30). That way, if the response contains objections or inadequate answers, you'll have time to make the required "attempt to resolve informally" (*see* ¶*8:1158 ff.*); and if necessary, to file a motion to compel (minimum 16 court days' notice) and have it *heard* before the cut-off on discovery hearings (15 days before trial).

Caution: Given court congestion as a result of budget cuts, 60 days may be insufficient to schedule a hearing on a motion to compel. In many courts, you will also need to apply ex parte for an early hearing date.

(3) [8:914] **Continuance of trial does not reopen discovery:** The 30-day and 15-day cut-off periods (¶*8:909*) are measured from the *first* trial date. A continuance of the trial date does *not* by itself reopen discovery. [CCP §2024.020(b); *see* ¶*8:450*]

(4) [8:915] **Parties may stipulate to later interrogatories:** [CCP §2024.060; *see* ¶*8:452 ff.*]

© 2020 Thomson Reuters/The Rutter Group

(5) [8:916] **Court may grant leave for later interrogatories:** [CCP §2024.050; *see* ¶*8:457 ff.*]

2. [8:917] **To WHOM Interrogatories May be Sent:** Interrogatories may be sent to "*any other party*" to the action. [CCP §2030.010(a) (emphasis added)]

a. [8:918] **Parties only:** Interrogatories *cannot* be served on *nonparty* witnesses. (This is a major disadvantage of interrogatories as compared to depositions; *see* ¶*8:462 ff.*)

b. [8:919] **Coparties:** There is no requirement that the party to whom interrogatories are sent be adverse to the propounding party. Thus, for example, plaintiff can, if it chooses, serve interrogatories on a coplaintiff; and defendant can serve interrogatories on a codefendant. [*Westrec Marina Mgmt., Inc. v. Jardine Ins. Brokers Orange County, Inc.* (2001) 85 CA4th 1042, 1048, 102 CR2d 673, 676 (citing text)]

c. [8:920] **Parties to complaint vs. cross-complaint:** Whether "any other party to the action" allows parties to a *cross-complaint* to serve others who are parties to the main action only is unclear.

For example, P sues D. D cross-complains against third party (TP). Can P and TP serve interrogatories on each other? Are they parties to the same "action"?

- [8:921] For *pleading* purposes, a cross-complaint is regarded as a separate proceeding, *not* the same "action" as the complaint (*see* ¶*6:503*).

- [8:922] However, for *discovery* purposes, parties to the complaint and cross-complaint should be treated as parties to the same "action," so as to permit service of interrogatories between P and TP. Otherwise, to obtain discovery from each other, depositions would be required. (Other parties are not prejudiced because answers to interrogatories are admissible at trial only against the responding party; *see* ¶*8:1245.*)

d. [8:923] **Corporations and other entities:** If the party involved is a corporation, partnership or other entity, the interrogatories must be directed to the *entity* itself rather than to an officer, director or employee thereof. I.e., the propounding party *cannot* designate who is to answer on behalf of the entity. [*Mowry v. Sup.Ct.* (1962) 202 CA2d 229, 233-235, 20 CR 698, 700-701 (disapproved on other grounds by *San Diego Professional Ass'n v. Sup.Ct. (Paderewski, Mitchell, Dean & Assocs.)* (1962) 58 C2d 194, 23 CR 384)]

(1) [8:924] **Entity must provide information known to its officers or employees:** In responding to interrogatories, the entity party is under a duty to provide whatever information is known to *any* of its officers or agents (*see* ¶*8:1056*). Thus, whoever acts on behalf of the entity must check with other persons in its employ who have the information sought.

➪ [8:925] ***PRACTICE POINTER:*** If you are seeking information from a *particular* officer, director or employee, use a *deposition* rather than interrogatories. For example, if the entity denies notice or knowledge of certain facts, you may need to take the deposition of whichever officer or employee you believe has such notice or knowledge.

(Alternatively, if the facts support a cause of action against that officer or employee individually, you can *join* him or her as a codefendant; and in that event, interrogatories could be directed to him or her individually.)

e. [8:926] **Unnamed class members in class action:** The unnamed members of the class are "parties" to a class action for discovery purposes, and therefore can be required to answer interrogatories. [See *Southern Calif. Edison Co. v. Sup.Ct. (Carlson)* (1972) 7 C3d 832, 840, 103 CR 709, 713]

However, to prevent the opposing party from harassing the class members (endangering the class action), various safeguards are imposed:

(1) [8:927] **Prior court order required:** First of all, the party seeking discovery cannot simply send out interrogatories to the class members as a matter of right. A prior court order is required. [CRC 3.768(c); see *Danzig v. Sup.Ct. (Grynberg)* (1978) 87 CA3d 604, 606, 151 CR 185, 187]

(2) [8:928] **Determination by court:** In deciding whether to allow interrogatories to unnamed class members, the court must consider all relevant factors, including:

— timing of the request;
— subject matter to be covered;
— materiality of the information sought;
— whether class representatives are seeking discovery on the same subject;
— likelihood that unnamed class members have such information;
— possibility of obtaining factual stipulations eliminating the need for such discovery; and
— whether discovery will result in "annoyance, oppression or undue burden or expense for the members of the class." [See CRC 3.768(d); *and discussion at ¶14:137.1*]

f. [8:929] **Foreign parties—international comity as limitation on discovery:** *See discussion at ¶8:46 ff.*

3. [8:930] **Propounding Interrogatories:** Various rules and policies affect the form, content and number of questions that may be asked.

a. [8:931] **Official Form Interrogatories:** Pursuant to statutory authority (CCP §2033.710), the Judicial Council has approved the following Official Form Interrogatories for optional use:

- Form Interrogatories—General (DISC-001) (primarily for use in personal injury and contract actions).

See Form 8:14 in Rivera, *Cal. Prac. Guide: Civ. Pro. Before Trial FORMS* (TRG).

- Form Interrogatories—Employment Law (DISC-002).
- Form Interrogatories—Unlawful Detainer (DISC-003/UD-106).
- Form Interrogatories—Limited Civil Cases (Economic Litigation) (DISC-004) (primarily for use in limited civil case personal injury actions; subparts eliminated).
- Form Interrogatories—Construction Litigation (DISC-005).
- Form Interrogatories—Family Law (FL-145).

(1) [8:932] **Optional only:** The Official Form Interrogatories are purely optional. The propounding party may serve different or additional interrogatories. [CCP §2033.740(a)]

(2) [8:933] **"Objection proof" as to form?** An advantage of the Official Form Interrogatories is that a judge is not likely to sustain an objection as to their *form* (which is a concern with specially-drafted interrogatories; *see* ¶*8:957 ff.*).

[8:933.1-933.4] *Reserved.*

(3) [8:933.5] **Objections as to contents:** Official Form Interrogatories asking for privileged information are, of course, objectionable. Likewise, a relevancy objection may lie where *too many boxes* on *the form are checked*, on the ground that the information sought is totally unrelated to the subject matter of the action.

In addition, the wording of several Form Interrogatories may be objectionable:

- [8:933.6] Form Interrogatory 12.2 (DISC-001) asks:

  —"Have you or ANYONE ACTING ON YOUR BEHALF interviewed any individual concerning the INCIDENT? (If so, identify them.)"

  This interrogatory *may* be objectionable on ground that the names of witnesses interviewed are attorney work product entitled to either (a) *absolute* protection (i.e., if the names of witnesses interviewed reflect counsel's evaluation of which witnesses are important) or (b) *qualified* protection (i.e., if the attorney devoted significant effort or industry in determining which witnesses to interview). [*Coito v. Sup.Ct. (State of Calif.)* (2012) 54 C4th 480, 499, 502, 142 CR3d 607, 622, 624; *see discussion at* ¶*8:236.1 ff.*]

  Similarly, Form Interrogatory 12.3 (DISC-001) (seeking the identities of persons from whom opposing counsel has obtained written or recorded statements) may be objectionable as entitled to absolute or qualified work product protection. [*Coito v. Sup.Ct. (State of Calif.)*, supra, 54 C4th at 502, 142 CR3d at 624; *see discussion at ¶8:238 ff.*]

- [8:933.7] Form Interrogatory 15.1 (DISC-001) states:

  —"Identify each denial of a *material* allegation . . . in your pleadings (and state facts upon which you base the denial)."

  The word "material" may cause problems; i.e., asking your opponent to state what is "material" may violate the protection for attorney work product.

- [8:933.8] Objections to certain Official Form Interrogatories are likely to be sustained in cases involving *complex business transactions*. For example, in a securities fraud suit:

  —"2.11 At the time of the INCIDENT, were you acting as an agent or employee for any PERSON?"

  The term "INCIDENT" may be ambiguous and confusing where the claim involved is based on multiple phone calls, letters, conversations, etc.

  ⇨ [8:933.9] ***PRACTICE POINTER—define "incident":*** Official Form Interrogatory 4(a)(2) (DISC-001) allows you to define "INCIDENT" with a *unique description*. This may avoid the ambiguous and confusing objection.

(4) [8:934] **NOT subject to "Rule of 35":** The big advantage of Official Form Interrogatories is that they are *not subject* to the "Rule of 35" applicable to specially prepared interrogatories (*see ¶8:935*). A party may ask "[a]ny additional number of official form interrogatories . . . that are relevant to the subject matter of the pending action." [CCP §2030.030(a)(2)]

(**Compare—limited civil cases:** In limited civil cases, there is a limit of 35 on *all* discovery requests—i.e., interrogatories, inspection demands and RFAs combined. See CCP §§94, 95, *discussed at ¶8:1810 ff.*)

⇨ [8:934.1] ***PRACTICE POINTER:*** Use the Official Form Interrogatories as an opening salvo wherever possible. Save your 35 specially prepared interrogatories for follow-up questions.

This applies most obviously in personal injury, contract, employment, unlawful detainer, construction and family law actions that have specially designed Official Form Interrogatories. (Use in other actions is facilitated by inserting your own definition of the term "INCIDENT"; see DISC-001, "Sec. 4 Definitions.")

© 2020 Thomson Reuters/The Rutter Group

Some of the Official Form Interrogatories (DISC-001) can be used in practically *any* lawsuit. For example:

- agency (No. 2.11);
- business entity status (No. 3);
- damages (Nos. 6-9);
- witnesses and investigations (Nos. 12-13);
- contentions re opposing party's denials or special defenses (No. 15) (plus Nos. 16.1-16.10 for personal injury defendants);
- insurance coverage (No. 4), etc.

You may get *more information per question* from the official forms than from questions you draft yourself. This is because the limitations against subparts and conjunctive and disjunctive questions (CCP §2030.060(f)) do not apply to the Official Form Interrogatories (*see ¶8:976*).

⇨ [8:934.2] ***FURTHER PRACTICE POINTER:*** Do not tinker with the Official Form Interrogatories. Retyping the questions or interspersing some of your own may make them "specially prepared" interrogatories, subject to the Rule of 35. (There is no known appellate authority on this point, but judges are likely to resent having to read through typed-out questions to see if they vary from the Form Interrogatories.)

⇨ [8:934.3] ***FURTHER PRACTICE POINTER—USE WITH RFAS:*** If you serve Requests for Admission simultaneously with the Official Form Interrogatories, you can use "Interrogatory 17.1" (DISC-001) that, in effect, *provides additional contention interrogatories* that are not included in the limit of 35:

> "17.1 Is your response to each request for admission served with these interrogatories an unqualified admission? If not, for each response that is not an unqualified admission:
>
> (a) state the number of the request;
>
> (b) state all facts upon which you base your response;
>
> (c) state the names, ADDRESSES, and telephone numbers of all PERSONS who have knowledge of those facts; and
>
> (d) identify all DOCUMENTS and other tangible things that support your response and state the name, ADDRESS, and telephone number of the PERSON who has each DOCUMENT or thing."

There are similar questions, although numbered differently, in each of the other form interrogatories (e.g., Form Interrogatories—Employment Law, Interrogatory No. 217.1 (DISC-002)).

b. [8:935] **Specially prepared interrogatories; "Rule of 35 Plus":** In addition to Official Form Interrogatories, each party has the right to propound 35 "specially prepared" interrogatories to every other party. [CCP §2030.030(a)(1)]

PLUS: The "Rule of 35" is *not* an absolute limit, however. As indicated, additional interrogatories are permissible:

- As "supplemental" interrogatories to update earlier answers (¶*8:942*); or
- By "declaration of necessity" (¶*8:949*); or
- By written stipulation (¶*8:947*).

(**Compare—limited civil cases:** CCP §§94-95 limit to 35 *all* discovery requests in such actions—interrogatories, RFAs and inspection demands combined. *See* ¶*8:1810 ff.*)

(1) [8:936] **Need not be asked simultaneously:** First of all, the 35 specially prepared interrogatories need not all be asked at the same time. "If the initial set of interrogatories does not exhaust this limit, the balance may be propounded in subsequent sets." [CCP §2030.030(b)]

The successive sets may be served without leave of court. The interrogating party may inquire about matters not covered by the earlier questions; or may follow up on information disclosed in the answers to the earlier set. (Unreasonable repetition of questioning, however, may be ground for a protective order; *see* ¶*8:1011.*)

(2) [8:937] **Separate 35-limit for each party:** The 35-limit applies to discovery by and from *each* party. "*A party* may propound to *another party*." [CCP §2030.030(a) (emphasis added)]

Thus, where a single plaintiff sues several defendants, plaintiff has the right to propound 35 specially prepared interrogatories to *each* defendant. Likewise, where there are several plaintiffs, *each* plaintiff can serve a separate set on *each* defendant. [CCP §2030.030(a); see *Demyer v. Costa Mesa Mobile Home Estates* (1995) 36 CA4th 393, 397, 42 CR2d 260, 262 (overruled on other grounds by *Wilcox v. Birtwhistle* (1999) 21 C4th 973, 983, 90 CR2d 260, 267, fn. 12)—3 defendants served separate sets of RFAs to each of 35 plaintiffs, requiring over 2200 separate responses]

(a) [8:938] **Comment:** This does not necessarily mean that separate sets of interrogatories will always be allowed in multi-party cases:

Where clients aligned in interest: If you represent several parties aligned in interest against a single opponent (e.g.,

© 2020 Thomson Reuters/The Rutter Group

Husband and Wife suing on a promissory note payable to them jointly), some judges may issue a protective order barring *separate* sets of interrogatories on behalf of each client as an evasion of the 35-limit.

Where opposing parties aligned in interest: Similarly, where the opposing parties are aligned in interest, some judges may bar separate sets of interrogatories to each such party, as an evasion of the 35-limit.

Nor can the 35-limit be evaded by asking one party to state agreement or disagreement with another's responses (e.g., asking Husband 34 questions, and then asking Wife to identify any of Husband's answers with which she disagrees and state why). Reason: Doing so *incorporates by reference* each of those interrogatories and counts accordingly; *see ¶8:979.5.*

(There is also an evidentiary risk in sending separate sets to each opposing party because answers given by one may not be admissible against the others.)

(3) [8:939] **Excess interrogatories need not be answered:** Unless a "declaration of necessity" is served (*see ¶8:949 ff.*), the party served need only respond to the *first 35* specially prepared interrogatories served. That party may simply state an *objection* to the balance on the ground the 35-limit has been exceeded. [CCP §2030.030(c)]

(a) [8:940] **Responding party may not pick and choose:** The responding party may *not* select the 35 easiest questions and then object to the balance. Rather, the objection can be used only to avoid answering those numbered 36 and up. [See CCP §2030.030(c)]

(Note: If any of the first 35 interrogatories contains subparts or compound questions, a separate objection will lie on that ground; *see ¶8:1091.*)

(b) [8:941] **Objection may be waived:** Interrogatories in excess of 35 are *not* void. Unless properly and timely raised, the objection may be waived (*see ¶8:1030*), in which event the responding party must answer the excess interrogatories regardless of the 35-limit.

(4) [8:942] **Additional "supplemental" interrogatories:** In addition to the 35-limit, a party may propound "a supplemental interrogatory" to obtain later-acquired information on *matters covered* by earlier interrogatories (but not on other topics). [CCP §2030.070(a)]

FORM: Supplemental Interrogatories, *see Form 8:15* in Rivera, *Cal. Prac. Guide: Civ. Pro. Before Trial FORMS* (TRG).

(a) [8:943] **Purpose:** A responding party has no duty to update earlier answers to interrogatories; and "continuing" interrogatories are not allowed (CCP §2030.060(g), *see* ¶*8:998*). Therefore, the only way to discover information *after* the responding party's answers were prepared is to serve "supplemental" interrogatories before trial.

(b) [8:944] **Example:** "Please review your answers to interrogatories previously served on you in this action. If, for any reason, any answer is no longer correct and complete, identify the answer and *state whatever information is necessary to make it correct and complete as of this date.*"

(c) [8:945] **Limited to topics covered:** Supplemental interrogatories cannot be used to obtain "updates" on matters *not* covered in earlier questions. They can be used only to obtain later information "bearing on all answers *previously made.*" [CCP §2030.070(a) (emphasis added)]

(If the propounding party needs discovery on additional matters, and the 35-limit is exhausted, a "declaration of necessity" can be served along with the additional interrogatories; *see* ¶*8:949*.)

(d) [8:946] **Number and times:** A supplemental interrogatory can be served *at least 3 times:*

- Twice prior to any trial setting; and
- *Once after the initial trial setting* (and before the 30-day "cut-off" on discovery proceedings before trial; *see* ¶*8:909*). [CCP §2030.070(b)]
- Further, if "good cause" is shown (e.g., lengthy continuances of the trial date), the court may permit more supplemental interrogatories. [CCP §2030.070(c)]

(5) [8:947] **Additional interrogatories by stipulation:** Parties may stipulate *in writing* that either or all may ask more than 35 interrogatories, or even that the number be *unlimited.* (CCP §2016.030 allows the parties to change any discovery method by written stipulation.)

(a) [8:948] **Not filed with court:** The parties retain their stipulation. It is not filed with the court unless it becomes relevant on a motion to compel. [CRC 3.250(a)(18)]

(6) [8:949] **Additional interrogatories by "declaration of necessity":** A party may propound more than 35 specially prepared interrogatories *simply by attaching a declaration* (in form required by statute; *see* ¶*8:949.1 ff.*) stating why more are necessary. [CCP §§2030.040(a), 2030.050]

FORM: Declaration for Additional Discovery—Interrogatories, *see Form 8:16* in Rivera, *Cal. Prac. Guide: Civ. Pro. Before Trial FORMS* (TRG).

(a) [8:949.1] **Grounds:** The declaration must show one or more of the following grounds:

© 2020 Thomson Reuters/The Rutter Group

- **Complexity:** "The complexity or the quantity of the existing and potential issues in the particular case."
- **Depos too expensive:** "The financial burden on a party entailed in conducting the discovery by oral deposition."
- **Expedience:** "The expedience of using this method of discovery [interrogatories] to provide to the responding party the opportunity to conduct an inquiry, investigation, or search of files or records to supply the information sought." [CCP §2030.040(a)]

(b) [8:950] **Whose declaration:** The declaration must be by "the attorney" for the party (or by the party personally if in pro per). [CCP §2030.050]

(c) [8:951] **Content:** The declaration must contain "substantially" the statements contained in the statutory form (*see Form 8:16* in Rivera, *Cal. Prac. Guide: Civ. Pro. Before Trial FORMS* (TRG)) including the following key provisions:

- "I am familiar with the issues and the previous discovery conducted by *all of the parties* in the case.
- "I have personally examined each of the questions in this set of interrogatories.
- "This number of questions is warranted under CCP §2030.040 because . . ." (stating which of the statutory grounds above (¶*8:949.1*) is relied upon *and the reasons* it applies in this case).
- "*None of the questions . . . is being propounded for any improper purpose*, such as to harass the party, or the attorney for the party, to whom it is directed, or to cause unnecessary delay or needless increase in the cost of litigation." [CCP §2030.050 (emphasis added)]

(d) [8:952] **Effect:** This provision is designed to soften the impact of a rigid 35-limit, and to avoid the necessity of obtaining prior court orders for additional discovery in complex cases. Its main effect is to *make the attorney personally "vouch" for the extra interrogatories.* If a court later determines they were unnecessary, the attorney personally can be *sanctioned* for "misuse of the discovery process" (CCP §2023.010(c)).

⇨ [8:953] ***PRACTICE POINTER:*** Don't let the fact that you may be "vouching" personally for the excess interrogatories deter you from full discovery. It is highly unlikely a court will impose sanctions against you for asking whatever number of questions is realistically required.

For example, to identify documents, you usually have to ask numerous questions (date? title? parties? substance? custody? etc.). In view of the limitation against subparts (*see* ¶*8:974*), each question may need to be set forth separately and counts against the 35-limit, so that if you have a number of documents, you are sure to exceed that limit. A judge is *not* likely to sanction you for asking for information you *need* in order to proceed with further discovery (document requests, etc.).

Moreover, even if your "declaration of necessity" is marginal, the risk of sanctions may be minimal because the only way the responding party can challenge your declaration is by a motion for protective order (*see* ¶*8:954*). It may be easier for the responding party to answer the excess questions than to make that effort.

(e) [8:954] **"Declaration of necessity" may be challenged by motion for protective order:** If, despite the propounding party's "declaration of necessity," the responding party deems the number of interrogatories excessive, he or she may seek a protective order under CCP §2030.090 (*see* ¶*8:1009*). Such order may be granted on the ground "[t]hat, contrary to the representations made [in the declaration of necessity] . . . the number of specially prepared interrogatories is unwarranted." [CCP §2030.090(b)(2); see *People v. Sarpas* (2014) 225 CA4th 1539, 1552-1553, 172 CR3d 25, 40—protective order upheld limiting set of over 5,300 duplicative interrogatories]

1) [8:955] **Burden on propounding party to justify number:** The motion for protective order effectively controverts the propounding party's "declaration of necessity" and *places the burden on the propounding party* to justify more than 35 questions: "If the responding party seeks a protective order on the ground that the number of specially prepared interrogatories is unwarranted, the propounding party shall have the burden of justifying the number of these interrogatories." [CCP §2030.040(b)]

(f) [8:956] **Mere objection insufficient:** The statute authorizes more than 35 interrogatories when accompanied by a "declaration of necessity," *"[s]ubject to* the right of the responding party to seek a protective order." [CCP §2030.040(a) (emphasis added)]

The clear implication is that the responding party *cannot* simply *object* to more than 35 interrogatories. Rather,

© 2020 Thomson Reuters/The Rutter Group

the responding party must seek a protective order (within the time and in the manner required by CCP §2030.090(a); ¶*8:1007 ff.*). [*Catanese v. Sup.Ct. (Ray)* (1996) 46 CA4th 1159, 1165, 54 CR2d 280, 283 (disapproved on other grounds by *Lewis v. Sup.Ct. (Green)* (1999) 19 C4th 1232, 82 CR2d 85)]

1) [8:956.1] **"Unduly burdensome" objection?** In the past, courts upheld objections to interrogatories on the ground of "*burdensome and oppressive*" (¶*8:1094*). Arguably, this is still a valid ground to challenge interrogatories, notwithstanding an accompanying "declaration of necessity." But something more than an excessive *number* of questions must be shown (*see* ¶*8:1099*).

c. [8:957] **Format requirements:** Specially prepared interrogatories must comply with the format rules discussed below (¶*8:958 ff.*).

FORMS

- Specially Prepared Interrogatories, *see Form 8:17* in Rivera, *Cal. Prac. Guide: Civ. Pro. Before Trial FORMS* (TRG).
- Supplemental Interrogatories, *see Form 8:15* in Rivera, *Cal. Prac. Guide: Civ. Pro. Before Trial FORMS* (TRG).

(1) [8:958] **First paragraph:** The first paragraph immediately below the title of the case must show:

- The identity of the propounding party;
- The identity of each party who is to respond; and
- The set number (each set to be numbered consecutively). [CCP §2030.060(a), (b)]

If these are supplemental interrogatories (¶*8:942*), the words "supplemental interrogatories" must be included. [CRC 3.1000(a)]

(a) [8:959] **Example:** "PLAINTIFF JOHN SMITH'S SECOND SET OF INTERROGATORIES TO DEFENDANT HARRY BROWN"

(2) [8:960] **Numbering of sets and questions:** Each *set* of interrogatories must be numbered consecutively ("Plaintiff's Interrogatories to Defendant Jones, Set No. 1"). [CCP §2030.060(a)]

Each *interrogatory* (question) within the set must be identified by number or letter. [CCP §2030.060(c)]

(a) [8:961] **Consecutive numbering of questions from set to set not required:** Court rules used to require that interrogatories be numbered consecutively from set to set. (E.g., if the first set contained Questions 1-10, the second set had to start with Question 11.) But these rules have been repealed and CCP §2030.060 omits this requirement.

[8:961.1] ***PRACTICE POINTER:*** Although no longer required, it is still permissible to number questions consecutively from set to set. Doing so is a good idea because it helps keep track of the 35-limit. And, it avoids having to deal with several questions in different sets bearing the same question number.

(3) [8:962] **No need to provide room for answer following question:** Neither statute nor court rules require a vacant space following each question for filling in the answer. However, many attorneys favor this format because it avoids having to work with different documents and different pages.

(a) [8:963] **Comment:** The fact that neither statute nor court rules require this format does not make it improper. Parties may modify the requirements for any discovery method by written stipulation (CCP §2016.030); their using such format should be regarded as such a stipulation.

(4) [8:964] **No combining with RFAs:** Interrogatories and requests for admission must be set forth in *separate documents.* [CCP §2033.060(h)]

[8:965] ***PRACTICE POINTER:*** Nevertheless, you can *coordinate* RFAs and interrogatories. The most efficient way is to serve your RFAs *together with* a set of the *Judicial Council Form Interrogatories* (Form DISC-001), checking Box 17.1, which requires disclosure of facts supporting denial of any RFA served with the interrogatories.

This way you do not use up your limited number of *custom* interrogatories and need not wait until receipt of the RFA responses before asking for the basis for denial.

d. [8:966] **Each question separate and complete:** Each interrogatory must be "separately set forth" and "full and *complete in and of itself.*" [CCP §2030.060(c)-(d) (emphasis added)]

Because of the 35-limit on specially prepared interrogatories, the form of questions asked is extremely important. The rules below (¶*8:967 ff.*) are designed to prevent questions worded so as to obtain more information than could be asked by 35 separate interrogatories.

(1) [8:967] **No preface or instructions:** No preface or instruction shall be included in a set of interrogatories *unless it has been approved* by the Judicial Council for use in an Official Form interrogatory. [See CCP §§2030.060(d), 2033.710]

© 2020 Thomson Reuters/The Rutter Group

(a) [8:968] **Compare—Official Form Interrogatories:** The Official Form Interrogatories contain a preface and rather elaborate "Instructions to the Answering party."

FORM: Form Interrogatories—General, Sec. 3 (DISC-001), *see Form 8:14* in Rivera, *Cal. Prac. Guide: Civ. Pro. Before Trial FORMS* (TRG).

[8:969] *Reserved.*

(2) [8:970] **Specially defined terms:** Terms used in interrogatories may be given special definitions. The terms so defined must be typed in *capital letters* every time they are used. [CCP §2030.060(e)]

(a) [8:971] **Unusual definitions:** The Discovery Act does not prohibit terms being defined in an unusual manner. For example:

- "For purposes of this interrogatory, 'DOCUMENT' means a writing, as defined in Evidence Code section 250, and includes the original or a copy of handwriting, printing, photostats, photographs, electronically stored information, and every other means of recording upon any tangible thing and form of communicating or representations, including letters, words, pictures, sounds, or symbols, or combinations of them."

However, some judges may find definitions in effect create impermissible multiple interrogatories—e.g., "IDENTIFY a witness means providing all contact information, the substance of the witness' testimony, his or her relationship to any party, the substance and location of every writing executed by the person, and . . ." etc.

(b) [8:972] **Placement:** Whether definitions may be placed at the *beginning* of specially prepared interrogatories is unclear (again, no "preface" or "instruction" is permitted unless *approved by the Judicial Council* in an Official Form Interrogatory; *see ¶8:967*).

(3) [8:973] **Objections to form:** Any defect in the form of questions is waived unless a timely and specific objection is made on this ground. Absent such objection, the interrogatory must be answered regardless of the form of the question. [CCP §2030.240(b); *see procedure for objections at ¶8:1071 ff.*]

(4) [8:974] **No subparts:** No specially prepared interrogatory may contain subparts. [CCP §2030.060(f)]

This does *not* apply to Official Form Interrogatories. [CCP §2030.060(f)]

(a) [8:975] **Example:** (Form Interrogatory 3.1, DISC-001)

"[ ] 3.1 Are you a corporation? If so, state:

"(a) the name stated in the current articles of incorporation;

"(b) all other names used by the corporation during the past 10 years and the dates each was used;

"(c) the date and place of incorporation;

"(d) the ADDRESS of the principal place of business; and

"(e) whether you are qualified to do business in California."

(b) [8:976] **Comment:** Although this format used to be commonplace, it is now permissible only in Official Form Interrogatories. In any other interrogatories, the responding party can avoid answering by objecting on the ground the interrogatory contains impermissible subparts.

[8:977] ***PRACTICE POINTERS:*** This again illustrates the big advantage to using Official Form Interrogatories wherever possible.

To avoid the "subparts" objection when drafting specially prepared interrogatories, stay away from questions that branch into "who-what-when-where," etc.

Instead, try asking single questions requiring *narrative* or descriptive answers. Use words like "State . . .," "Identify . . .," "Describe . . .," etc. For example:

- "*Identify* the persons present at the meeting by stating their names, addresses and positions in the company"; or
- "*Describe* the document by stating its title, date, parties signatory, and subject matter."

(5) [8:978] **No "compound, conjunctive or disjunctive" questions:** Unless part of an Official Form Interrogatory, an interrogatory may not contain "compound, conjunctive or disjunctive" questions. [CCP §2030.060(f)]

(a) [8:978.1] **Purpose:** The purpose again is to prevent questions worded so as to require more information than could be obtained by 35 separate questions.

How strictly this rule will be applied remains to be seen. Arguably, any question containing an "and" or "or" is compound and conjunctive. [See *Clement v. Alegre* (2009) 177 CA4th 1277, 1291, 99 CR3d 791, 802 (citing text)]

(b) [8:979] **Comment:** The rule should probably apply only where *more than a single subject* is covered by the question. Questions regarding the same subject should be allowed although they include an "and" or "or." For

© 2020 Thomson Reuters/The Rutter Group

example: "State your first name, middle name *and* last name, *and* your current address *and* telephone number." Since only one subject is involved—identification of responding party—the question should not be objectionable because of the "ands" used. [See *Clement v. Alegre*, supra, 177 CA4th at 1291, 99 CR3d at 802 (citing text)]

However, the rule against subparts may apply where two *discrete matters* are covered by the same question—i.e., where there are really two separate questions linked together by an "and" or "or." For example: "How much earnings income did you *or* your spouse receive during . . . (year), *and* from whom did you or your spouse receive it?" The rule against subparts would apply here because there are really several *separate* subjects involved—income of responding party, income of spouse, and identification of employer of each.

[8:979.1-979.4] *Reserved.*

(6) [8:979.5] **No incorporation of other materials:** The requirement that each interrogatory be "full and complete in and of itself" is violated where resort must necessarily be made to other materials in order to answer the question. [*Catanese v. Sup.Ct. (Ray)* (1996) 46 CA4th 1159, 1164, 54 CR2d 280, 283 (disapproved on other grounds by *Lewis v. Sup.Ct. (Green)* (1999) 19 C4th 1232, 82 CR2d 85); *Clement v. Alegre*, supra, 177 CA4th at 1289, 99 CR3d at 800 (citing text)]

- [8:979.6] Following his lengthy deposition (more than 10,000 questions), P served interrogatories asking *whether D contended any of P's deposition testimony was untrue;* and if so, for D to identify such testimony, and to list witnesses and documents supporting D's contentions.

  P's interrogatories were *not* "full and complete in and of [themselves]" because they required reference to transcripts of P's deposition testimony. P was effectively asking more than 10,000 separate questions (violating the Rule of 35). [*Catanese v. Sup.Ct. (Ray)*, supra, 46 CA4th at 1165, 54 CR2d at 283-284; see *Clement v. Alegre*, supra, 177 CA4th at 1290, 99 CR3d at 801 (citing text)]

- [8:979.7] *Compare:* Interrogatory No. 6 asked plaintiffs to describe "all economic damages you claim to have sustained as a result of any alleged fraudulent conduct of defendant." Interrogatory No. 8 asked "As to each item of damages identified in interrogatory No. 6, please state the date such damages were incurred." This did *not* violate the statutory requirement that interrogatories be "full and complete in and of [themselves]" because it did *not* require the responding party to go to *materials outside* the interrogatories. [*Clement v. Alegre,* supra, 177 CA4th at 1290, 99 CR3d at 801, fn. 11]

[8:980] ***PRACTICE POINTERS RE DRAFTING INTERROGATORIES:*** First of all, as stated earlier, *use the Official Form Interrogatories wherever possible.* You avoid disputes over wording, increase the number of questions you can ask, and greatly expand the amount of information discoverable via interrogatories. (*See ¶8:934.1.*)

Here are some suggestions for drafting specially prepared interrogatories:

- **Beware of old forms:** Except for the most common routine matters, draft *new* interrogatories for each case. Existing interrogatories from another case may not reach some essential element of a claim or defense applicable to your case.
- **Check format:** Remember the rules against subparts, compound or conjunctive questions, preface and instructions.
- **Use open-ended questions:** To obtain the maximum amount of information, use open-ended questions: (e.g., "Identify . . ."; "Describe . . ."; "List . . ."; "State . . ."; *see ¶8:977*). Avoid questions calling for "Yes/No" responses.
- **Keep it simple:** Long, loosely-worded questions give the opposing party room to provide useless or misleading answers, so the whole process is a wasted effort. Moreover, compound, conjunctive or disjunctive ("and/or") questions invite objections or evasive answers. Draft interrogatories as if you were asking questions at deposition or trial: I.e., *ask one question at a time*, dealing with *one specific subject*.
- **Be your own worst critic:** Test your questions by reviewing them from the standpoint of the opposing party: i.e., is there ground for objection? Is there some way to "fully" answer the question and still *avoid* disclosing the information sought? Don't hesitate to rewrite the question.

e. [8:981] **Content—what questions may be asked:** There are limits to consider whether drafting specially prepared interrogatories or checking off boxes on the Official Form Interrogatories:

(1) [8:981.1] **Standards of professionalism:** Some Bar associations and courts have adopted guidelines to discourage abusive discovery (see L.A. Sup.Ct. Rule 3.26, Appendix 3.A(g)(1)). Because court rules relating to discovery are preempted by CRC 3.20, a court may not sanction a party for violation of these guidelines. Nevertheless, the prohibited conduct may be sanctionable as a discovery abuse (CCP §2023.010(a)-(c); *see ¶8:1901*).

(2) [8:982] **Permissible scope of discovery:** As with other discovery methods, interrogatories must seek information "relevant to the subject matter involved in the pending action" and "rea-

© 2020 Thomson Reuters/The Rutter Group

sonably calculated to lead to the discovery of admissible evidence." [CCP §§2017.010, 2030.010(a); *Kalaba v. Gray* (2002) 95 CA4th 1416, 1417, 116 CR2d 570, 576 (citing text)]

This scope is broadly construed in light of "the prodiscovery policies of the statutory scheme." [*Williams v. Sup.Ct. (Marshalls of CA, LLC)* (2017) 3 C5th 531, 540, 220 CR3d 472, 479] (*See detailed discussion of scope of discovery at ¶8:65 ff.*)

[8:983] ***PRACTICE POINTER:*** In view of the 35-limit on specially prepared interrogatories (¶*8:935*), don't waste them on matters of marginal "relevancy to the subject matter." (Example: Asking a personal injury plaintiff for "lifetime" residence addresses, names of former spouses, etc.)

While such "boilerplate" might conceivably "lead" to discovery of admissible evidence, in most cases it simply wastes permissible discovery. There is also a risk that a court might view such questions as an attempt to harass the opposing party, exposing you and your client to possible sanctions for "misuse of the discovery process" (CCP §2023.010(a)-(c)).

[8:983.1] ***CAUTION re overbroad interrogatories:*** Overly broad discovery requests invite controversy and reproach by the court: "When discovery requests are grossly overbroad on their face, and hence do not appear reasonably related to a legitimate discovery need, *a reasonable inference can be drawn of an intent to harass* and improperly burden." [*Obregon v. Sup.Ct. (Cimm's, Inc.)* (1998) 67 CA4th 424, 431, 79 CR2d 62, 66 (emphasis added)]

Thus, avoid asking for "any and all" or "all matters that refer, relate, pertain, concern, allude to."

[8:983.2] ***FURTHER PRACTICE POINTER:*** Because the responding party's attorney will shape the answers to interrogatories, only inquire about information that you don't care if the attorney answers (e.g., verifiable facts, such as "Identify all invoices to X by date, number and amount") or where you *want* the attorney's answer (e.g., contention interrogatories to find *all* facts known to the party and its lawyer). If you want to know why a party did something, *depose him or her* to get the party's reasons.

(3) [8:984] **Party's CONTENTIONS:** An interrogatory may properly ask a party to state his or her contentions as to any matter or issue in the case; and the facts, witnesses or writings on which the contentions are based. [CCP §2030.010(b); see *Burke v. Sup.Ct. (Fidelity & Deposit Co. of Maryland)* (1969) 71 C2d 276, 281, 78 CR 481, 487]

(a) [8:985] **Either fact or law:** Interrogatories may require a party to state his or her contentions as to either factual or legal issues: "An interrogatory is *not objectionable* because an answer . . . relates to fact or the application of law to fact, *or would be based on* . . . *legal theories* . . ." [CCP §2030.010(b) (emphasis added)]

1) [8:986] **Example:** A contracting party may be compelled to state its contentions regarding whether it has "performed" or "breached" a contract, although these may be legal conclusions.

2) [8:986.1] **Legal theories?** Arguably, the reference in CCP §2030.010(b) to "legal theories" could be read to require disclosure of the legal reasoning behind a party's contentions, including particular statutes or cases upon which counsel is relying.

However, this interpretation seems doubtful because *writings* (interrogatory answers) reflecting an attorney's "impressions, conclusions, opinions," etc. are *absolutely* protected as "work product." [See CCP §2018.030(a), ¶*8:223*; *Sav-On Drugs, Inc. v. Sup.Ct. (Botney)* (1975) 15 C3d 1, 5, 123 CR 283, 286—improper to ask for particular statutes or administrative regulations supporting party's position]

3) [8:986.2] **Compare—deposition questions:** Parties who are being deposed may *not* be asked to state or explain their *legal* contentions; it is unfair to ask them to explain their lawyers' conclusions. [*Rifkind v. Sup.Ct. (Good)* (1994) 22 CA4th 1255, 1263, 27 CR2d 822, 827; *see* ¶*8:723 ff.*]

[8:986.3-986.4] *Reserved.*

4) [8:986.5] **Compare—layperson's lack of personal knowledge of scientific matters:** Contention interrogatories cannot be used to require a layperson to provide answers to scientific matters on which expert testimony will be required at trial. (E.g., " 'For each . . . product which you *contend* caused your multiple myeloma, *identify the mechanism*' by which it occurred.")

A layperson's "I don't know" responses to such interrogatories are *not* admissions that he or she will be unable at trial to provide expert testimony on causation. [*Bockrath v. Aldrich Chem. Co., Inc.* (1999) 21 C4th 71, 84, 86 CR2d 846, 855]

© 2020 Thomson Reuters/The Rutter Group

(b) [8:987] **Includes materials obtained through pretrial preparations:** "An interrogatory is *not objectionable* because an answer . . . would be based on information obtained or legal theories *developed in anticipation of litigation or in preparation for trial.*" [CCP §2030.010(b) (emphasis added)]

1) [8:988] **Example:** Plaintiff may be compelled to state his or her contentions as to the manner in which defendant was "negligent" and the facts supporting this contention. It makes no difference that the facts were obtained entirely through *investigations* by plaintiff's attorney. [*Southern Pac. Co. v. Sup.Ct. (Fuller)* (1969) 3 CA3d 195, 197-199, 83 CR 231, 232-233 (overruled on other grounds by *Kadelbach v. Amaral* (1973) 31 CA3d 814, 107 CR 720)]

[8:989] *Reserved.*

☞ [8:990] ***PRACTICE POINTERS:*** "Contention" interrogatories are one of the most formidable discovery tools because they can force disclosure of your adversary's case.

They are most effective when used in conjunction with "back-up" interrogatories asking:

- "State *all facts upon which you base* the contention that . . . (e.g., plaintiff was comparatively at fault). If you make no such contention, you need not answer this interrogatory."
- "State the *name and address of each person who has knowledge* of the facts upon which you base such contention."
- "Describe each *document* which you believe supports such contention."

[8:990.1] **CAUTION:** Remember the 35-limit on specially prepared interrogatories (¶*8:935 ff.*). These "contention" interrogatory and "back-up" questions (¶*8:990*) count as three separate questions.

[8:990.2] **Use Official Forms re contentions:** Some of the Official Form Interrogatories will provide information regarding the opposing party's contentions. Each *includes* the necessary "backup" questions.

For example, interrogatory 15.1 on the DISC-001 Official Form Interrogatories can be used to force disclosure of facts and theories upon which the opposing party bases each denial or affirmative defense.

And, personal injury plaintiffs can use interrogatory numbers 16.1-16.10 on the DISC-001 Official Form

Interrogatories to force disclosures re defenses ("Defendant's Contentions—Personal Injury").

[8:991] *Reserved.*

(4) [8:992] **Identification of documents or evidence:** Interrogatories can be used to find out from an opposing party what documents, records or other physical evidence exists, where it is located, etc. This is often done as a first step toward seeking discovery of such documents or evidence. [See *Hernandez v. Sup.Ct. (Acheson Indus., Inc.)* (2003) 112 CA4th 285, 292, 4 CR3d 883, 890]

(a) [8:993] **Cannot force production:** Interrogatories cannot be used, however, to force a party to produce documents or records in his or her possession for inspection and copying. Other discovery procedures (e.g., CCP §2031.010 demands, *see* ¶*8:1421*) must be utilized for that purpose, based on information obtained through the interrogatories.

☞ [8:994] ***PRACTICE POINTER:*** Even so, in drafting interrogatories, you can ask the adverse party *voluntarily* to attach copies of any document identified in his or her answers. The worst that can happen is that he or she will refuse. And, the answering party often will comply voluntarily, because the documents can usually be obtained by other means anyhow (¶*8:995*).

(b) [8:995] **Compare—documents held by nonparties:** Interrogatories of course cannot be used to obtain documents from a nonparty. But interrogatories to a party may be used to obtain a *description* and *location* of documents or other physical evidence held by third parties. (E.g., interrogatories may ask *what* physical evidence exists and *who* has it—whether a party to the action or not.) The information obtained can then be used to subpoena documents held by nonparties (¶*8:535 ff.*).

(c) [8:996] **Sufficiency of description:** Where interrogatories are used for document identification, they should call for a description *in sufficient detail* so that the answers can be used as the basis for a deposition subpoena or notice or inspection demand.

For example: "Describe . . . (document sought) by stating:

- The type of document (letter, contract, deed, memo, etc.);
- Date;
- Author or parties signatory;
- Addressee or recipients;

© 2020 Thomson Reuters/The Rutter Group

- Number of pages;
- Subject matter;
- Name and address of each person having possession of original or any copy."

[8:997] **Comment:** Arguably, the above form (¶*8:996*) is objectionable on the ground that it is "compound, conjunctive or disjunctive." Also, the responding party can respond by simply making the documents available for inspection (*see* ¶*8:1065*).

It remains to be seen how strictly courts will enforce this rule (*see* ¶*8:978*). Arguably, all of the above relates to a *single subject*—identification of the document.

In any event, without such detail, the propounding party may be unable to describe the document sufficiently for further discovery. Consequently, these questions *need* to be asked. If this results in exceeding the 35-limit, the attorney for the propounding party should utilize a "declaration of necessity" under CCP §2030.050 (¶*8:949*).

(5) [8:998] **No "continuing" interrogatories:** The Discovery Act specifically prohibits so-called "continuing interrogatories"—i.e., asking the responding party to provide both information now known and acquired in the future. [CCP §2030.060(g)]

(a) [8:999] **Example:** "State the name and address of each physician who is treating or has treated you for the injuries described in the complaint. If you are treated by any other physician *in the future*, please amend your response accordingly."

The responding party has no duty to provide anything beyond identifying the doctors who have treated him or her *to date*. [CCP §2030.060(g)]

Distinguish: A question that asks, "State the name of all physicians *you plan to see* in the future" is *not* a continuing interrogatory. To the extent the answer to this question is presently known, a truthful response is required.

(b) [8:1000] **Compare—supplemental interrogatories:** The Discovery Act authorizes "supplemental interrogatories" to *update earlier* answers (CCP §2030.070; ¶*8:942 ff.*). The difference, of course, is that the burden is on the *propounding party* to *initiate the updating process* rather than on the responding party to update its answers.

☞ [8:1001] ***PRACTICE POINTER:*** Never count on a responding party to amend or update earlier answers voluntarily. As a matter of routine, send out *supplemental interrogatories* in every case approaching trial. (They can be sent out twice prior to trial setting and once after the first setting, in addition to the 35-limit; *see* ¶*8:946*.)

(c) [8:1002] **Compare—Federal Rules:** The Federal Rules *require* a party to *amend* answers to interrogatories to:

- *Correct wrong or misleading information* in the original answers;
- Disclose newly-acquired information re *percipient witnesses;* and
- Disclose the names of *experts* engaged to testify at trial and the substance of their testimony. [FRCP 26(e)]

(d) [8:1002.1] **Compare—interrogatories re collateral source providers:** Government entity defendants may serve interrogatories to obtain information re "collateral source" benefits obtained by plaintiff (insurance proceeds, etc.). A special statute requires plaintiffs to *update their answers* as new "collateral source provider" information is obtained. [Gov.C. §985(c), *discussed at* ¶*8:1805.16*]

(e) [8:1002.2] **Compare—continuing duty to furnish data in Family Code dissolution proceedings:** Each party in a Family Code dissolution, legal separation or nullity action must make a full and accurate disclosure of all assets and liabilities that affect the property rights of the other party (including but not limited to, investment opportunities, business interests, etc.). Each party also has a *continuing duty* "to update and augment that disclosure." [See Fam.C. §2100(c)]

Cross-refer: See detailed discussion in Hogoboom & King, *Cal. Prac. Guide: Family Law* (TRG), Ch. 11.

f. [8:1003] **Signature:** Interrogatories customarily have been signed by the attorney of record for the propounding party. However, such signature is *not required* by statute. (Note: There is no signature block on the Official Form Interrogatories.)

[8:1003.1] Nor is any verification required, except that if more than 35 questions are asked, the attorney must attach a separate declaration to "vouch" for the necessity of the excess questions (CCP §2030.050; *see* ¶*8:949*).

(1) [8:1004] **Compare—Federal Rules:** In federal practice, the attorney's signature on a discovery request constitutes a *certificate by the attorney* that he or she has read it; that the request is warranted by law; that it is not interposed for delay, harassment or other improper purpose; and that it is not unduly burdensome given the needs of the case. If the certificate proves false, *sanctions* may be imposed against the attorney. [See FRCP 26(g)]

© 2020 Thomson Reuters/The Rutter Group

g. [8:1005] **Service of interrogatories:** Copies of the interrogatories must be served on the party to whom directed, plus all other parties who have appeared in the action. (If this is unduly burdensome or expensive, an order may be obtained excusing such service by ex parte application or motion.) [CCP §2030.080]

(1) [8:1006] **Not filed with court:** The propounding party retains the original interrogatories. They are *not* filed with the court. (Custody of interrogatories and answers is discussed at ¶*8:1130*.)

4. [8:1007] **Protective Orders:** The party to whom interrogatories are directed may "promptly" move for a protective order. [CCP §2030.090(a)]

a. [8:1008] **Grounds for relief:** The fact that the information sought is "relevant to the subject matter" does not preclude relief. A court may make any order that justice requires to protect a party or other natural person from "unwarranted annoyance, embarrassment, or oppression or undue burden and expense." [CCP §2030.090(b)]

(1) [8:1008.1] **"Undue" burden:** The discovery burden is "undue" only if the inconvenience and expense of responding *clearly outweigh* the benefits *likely* to be obtained if the interrogatories are answered. [CCP §§2019.030(a), 2030.090(b); *see* ¶*8:42*]

The objecting party must supply evidence to support its claim of undue or excessive burden, showing the quantum of work required. Absent such evidence, the trial court has nothing "upon which to base a comparative judgment that any responsive burden would be undue or excessive, relative to the likelihood of admissible evidence being discovered." [*Williams v. Sup.Ct. (Marshalls of CA, LLC)* (2017) 3 C5th 531, 549-550, 220 CR3d 472, 487]

(2) [8:1009] **To challenge "declaration of necessity" for additional interrogatories:** A motion for protective order can also be used to challenge a "declaration of necessity" which is required to justify *more than 35* interrogatories (under CCP §2030.050, ¶*8:949*). [See CCP §2030.090(b)(2)]

b. [8:1010] **Relief available:** For "good cause" shown, the court may make whatever orders "justice requires," including:

- *Excusing* answers to any or all interrogatories;
- Finding the number of specially prepared interrogatories "unwarranted" despite the representations made in the "declaration of necessity" (thus excusing the duty to answer the excess number);
- Setting *terms and conditions* upon which answers will be required;
- *Extending time* within which to respond;
- Requiring oral depositions (or other discovery methods) in lieu of interrogatories;

- Protecting certain information (e.g., trade secrets or other confidential research) from disclosure or ordering it disclosed only in a certain way;
- Requiring that some or all of the answers be sealed and thereafter opened only on order of court. [CCP §2030.090(b)]

c. **Application**

(1) [8:1011] A protective order may be granted to limit the number or sets of interrogatories that a party may be required to answer; or to limit the scope of particular questions. But it is an abuse of discretion to *strike* an entire set of interrogatories if *any* question therein is proper. [*West Pico Furniture Co. of Los Angeles v. Sup.Ct. (Pacific Finance Loans)* (1961) 56 C2d 407, 417, 15 CR 119, 124]

(2) [8:1012] A protective order may be granted against "boilerplate" interrogatories that would require "thousands of hours" to answer and that are served in an apparent last-minute effort to stall trial. [*Day v. Rosenthal* (1985) 170 CA3d 1125, 1172, 217 CR 89, 119—"It is difficult to imagine a scenario in which a court would be more justified in saying, 'Enough!' "]

d. **Procedure**

(1) [8:1013] **Must be sought "promptly":** If a protective order is to be obtained, relief must be sought:

- "Promptly" (CCP §2030.090(a)); and
- *Before* expiration of the 30-day period within which to respond to the interrogatories (CCP §2030.260(a)), because otherwise the grounds for objection may be *waived* (CCP §2030.290(a), ¶*8:1030*).

(2) [8:1014] **Noticed motion:** Protective orders may be issued only "pursuant to a motion" by an interested party or person. [CCP §§2017.020(a), 2019.030(b)]

"Motion" means a formal, noticed motion; i.e., protective orders cannot be issued ex parte. (But a court can grant an ex parte order shortening the notice required on the motion; see CCP §1005(b).)

Cross-refer: The motion is governed by the rules and procedures governing motions generally; *see Ch. 9 Part I.*

➪ [8:1014.1] ***PRACTICE POINTER:*** *Consider alternative procedures discussed at* ¶*8:787.1.*

(3) [8:1015] **Attempt to resolve informally required:** The motion for protective order must be accompanied by a declaration showing the moving party made a "reasonable and good faith attempt" to resolve the issues outside of court. [CCP §2030.090(a)]

(See further discussion of this requirement in connection with motions to compel at ¶*8:1158 ff.*)

(4) [8:1016] **Burden of proof on motion:** The burden is on the party seeking the protective order to show "good cause" for whatever order is sought. [*Fairmont Ins. Co. v. Sup.Ct. (Stendell)* (2000) 22 C4th 245, 255, 92 CR2d 70, 77]

The concept of "good cause" requires a showing of *specific facts* demonstrating "undue burden," etc., and justifying the relief sought. [See *Goodman v. Citizens Life & Cas. Ins. Co.* (1967) 253 CA2d 807, 819, 61 CR 682, 690]

(a) [8:1017] **Admissible evidence:** The facts are established in declarations on behalf of the party seeking the protective order. These declarations must contain admissible evidence—i.e., first-hand knowledge of the facts. Hearsay allegations or those made "on information and belief" do not suffice. Nor do conclusory statements that particular relief is "necessary." [*Goodman v. Citizens Life & Cas. Ins. Co.*, supra, 253 CA2d at 819-820, 61 CR at 690]

[8:1017a] ***PRACTICE POINTER:*** When the basis for the desired protective order is undue burden and expense or embarrassment, usually only the client or its representatives will be able to provide admissible evidence of the facts justifying the protective order. However, be careful about using a key witness for this purpose if doing so will prematurely identify the witness and make him or her a target of further discovery. In addition, you may not want an important witness to testify before you have had a chance to gather all the facts, since an early mistake could be used at trial to impeach the witness' credibility.

Declarations of counsel may be admissible on matters within the attorney's knowledge, such as the burden of reviewing or producing documents, etc.

(b) [8:1017.1] **Exception—propounding party's burden to show necessity for more than 35 interrogatories:** Where more than 35 specially prepared interrogatories have been served with a "declaration of necessity," and the responding party seeks a protective order, the burden is on the *propounding party* to prove the number of questions is justified. [CCP §2030.040(b); *see ¶8:954*]

In this situation, the moving party *need not* produce competent evidence of hardship or burden. It is up to the propounding party to *prove* the allegations of his or her "declaration of necessity": i.e., complexity of the case, financial burden of depositions, expedience of interrogatory answers (*see ¶8:955*).

(5) [8:1018] **Proposed order:** The moving papers should include a proposed order, or at least specific proposals and terms of the protective order sought. If there are alternatives, each should be indicated so the court may choose the most appropriate relief.

(6) [8:1018.1] **Monetary sanction against losing party:** The court "shall" impose a monetary sanction against the losing party on the motion for protective order *unless* it finds that party made or opposed the motion "with substantial justification" or other circumstances make sanctions "unjust." [CCP §2030.090(d)]

The "substantial justification" standard is discussed at ¶*8:1964 ff.*

FORM: Motion for Protective Order and for Sanctions and Proposed Order, *see Form 8:18* in Rivera, *Cal. Prac. Guide: Civ. Pro. Before Trial FORMS* (TRG).

e. [8:1019] **Court's discretion:** Unlike various other discovery orders, a protective order may be granted simply on the court's determination that "justice so requires." The motion is directed to the court's inherent power to control the proceedings before it. The granting or denial of relief therefore lies within the sound discretion of the law and motion judge, and is reviewable only for abuse. [*Greyhound Corp. v. Sup.Ct. (Clay)* (1961) 56 C2d 355, 379-381, 15 CR 90, 101-102 (superseded by statute on other grounds)]

STRATEGIES AND TACTICS RE PROTECTIVE ORDERS

[8:1020] **Advantages:** Seeking a protective order in advance of responding (as opposed to simply objecting to the interrogatory) is advantageous in certain cases:

- **Claims of "unwarranted embarrassment, annoyance or oppression":** Such claims may draw a more sympathetic ear from the court if raised in advance by a motion for protective order than if asserted as an objection and refusal to answer (which may be seen as obstreperous and an effort to stall).
- **Claims of "sensitive" information:** Simply objecting on the ground of privacy or trade secrets, etc. may not provide the court with a sufficient record to limit or curtail discovery. It may be a better idea to seek a protective order in advance, so that the potential harm can be detailed for the court and limits on discovery suggested.
- **To limit risk of sanctions:** There is always a possibility that objections to interrogatories will lead to a motion to compel and result in sanctions against the objecting party and counsel. Seeking a protective order in advance avoids this risk, although the court can impose monetary sanctions against the moving party if relief

© 2020 Thomson Reuters/The Rutter Group

STRATEGIES AND TACTICS RE PROTECTIVE ORDERS (Cont'd)

is denied (¶*8:1018.1*). However, if the motion is made in good faith, the chances of drawing sanctions on denial are minimal.

[8:1021] **Disadvantages:** Seeking a protective order frequently entails significant burdens and disadvantages:

- **Costly and cumbersome:** A noticed motion with supporting declarations and proposed order must be filed; and a court hearing is required. Also, you may need an additional trip to court to obtain an order shortening notice or extending the time to respond (*see* ¶*8:1025 ff.*).
- **Time pressures:** Protective orders usually are sought "under the gun" because responses are due. If the opposing side is unwilling to stipulate to an extension, you may have to obtain a court order shortening the time for hearing or extending the time to respond until after the hearing on the protective order (in order to avoid waiver of any objections; *see* ¶*8:1030*).

[8:1021.1] **Informal resolution:** Before deciding whether to seek a protective order or simply object, try to avoid the problem altogether, and save substantial expense, by negotiating limitations on the interrogatories early in the process. This risks nothing: If you decide to seek a protective order, you will be required to try to resolve the dispute informally (*see* ¶*8:1158 ff.*), and some courts will make you try to work it out before they make a final ruling, even after both sides have expended substantial resources on motion papers. If appropriate, also consider an informal conference with the judge (*see* ¶*8:1158.2*).

[8:1022] ***PRACTICE POINTERS:*** It is *not necessary* to seek a protective order to avoid answering interrogatories that are truly "burdensome and oppressive." The responding party can simply *object* on this ground (¶*8:1094 ff.*).

(Keep in mind, however, that where the *only* "burden" is the *number* of questions asked, no objection lies until after 35 questions have been propounded; and if a "declaration of necessity" is attached, the only challenge then permitted is by motion for protective order; *see* ¶*8:954.*)

Where, regardless of number, the interrogatories are "burdensome and oppressive," it is usually more advantageous for a responding party simply to *object* than to seek a protective order, shifting the burden to the propounding party to file a motion to compel if he or she really wants the information. This is usually more practical for several reasons:

- First, *most objections do not result in motions to compel;* i.e., many counsel seeking discovery simply don't bother trying to enforce discovery. So, your objection will be enough by itself to do the job and will save the considerable effort

STRATEGIES AND TACTICS RE PROTECTIVE ORDERS (Cont'd)

and expense that would have been required on a motion for protective order.

- Second, if you (responding party) do seek a protective order, there's a chance you'll *lose* on some objection that might not have been followed up on by motion to compel had you simply objected and refused to respond.
- The only real risk you run by objecting is *sanctions* against you and your client if the court overrules your objection. But you can limit this risk: You can build a record showing "substantial justification" for your objection (solid declarations and points and authorities).

5. [8:1023] **Responding to Interrogatories:** Unless excused by protective order, the party to whom the interrogatories are directed is under a duty to respond to each question *separately*, *under oath*, and within the *time limits* stated below (¶*8:1024 ff.*). [CCP §2030.210(a)]

Such response may be either:

- An *answer* (¶*8:1046 ff.*);
- An *objection* (¶*8:1071 ff.*); or
- An *election to allow inspection and copying of records* (¶*8:1065 ff.*). [CCP §2030.210(a)]

A response stating "inability to respond" is legally insufficient. If the responding party lacks personal knowledge sufficient to respond, he or she may so state, but only after making *a reasonable and good faith effort to obtain the information* by inquiry to other persons or organizations. [See *Sinaiko Healthcare Consulting, Inc. v. Pacific Healthcare Consultants* (2007) 148 CA4th 390, 406, 55 CR3d 751, 762]

[8:1023.1] ***PRACTICE POINTERS:*** When dealing with inexperienced clients, be patient and thorough in explaining the importance of their responses to interrogatories. Otherwise, clients may treat them as bothersome details and may give incomplete answers which return to haunt them later.

Avoid simply mailing interrogatories to the client with requests for answers. It is better to ask the client to come into the office, so that you can explain the process and assist with the answers.

Be careful about putting your words into the client's mouth. Interrogatory answers must disclose information known either by the client or by you (*see* ¶*8:1055*). But the client is the one verifying the answers. So make sure the client understands and agrees with each answer, and knows enough about the matter to withstand cross-examination on deposition or trial.

© 2020 Thomson Reuters/The Rutter Group

a. [8:1024] **Time limit for response:** The response is due *within 30 days* from the date the *interrogatories* were *served* (extended for service by mail, overnight delivery, fax or electronically per CCP §§1010.6(a)(4), 1013; *see* ¶*9:87 ff.*). [CCP §§2030.260(a), 2016.050]

Exception: In *unlawful detainer* actions, responses are due within *5 days* after service. [CCP §2030.260(b)]

If the last day falls on a weekend or holiday, the time limit is extended to the next court day closer to the trial date. [CCP §2016.060]

(1) [8:1025] **Court may shorten or extend time:** On motion of the propounding party, the court may shorten the time for response; and conversely, on motion of the responding party, it may extend the time. [CCP §2030.260(a)]

(a) [8:1026] **Noticed motion required:** In either event a "motion" is required—apparently meaning a formal, noticed motion.

(Compare: The court may grant ex parte relief, however, limiting the parties to be served with copies of the responses; *see* ¶*8:1115.*)

(2) [8:1027] **Stipulations extending time:** Likewise, the parties may stipulate for an extension of time within which to respond to interrogatories (or to particular interrogatories within the set). [CCP §2030.270]

(a) [8:1028] **Written confirmation required:** The agreement may be informal "but it shall be confirmed in a writing that specifies the extended date for service of a response." [CCP §2030.270(b)]

Presumably, an email qualifies as a "writing" for this purpose.

(b) [8:1029] **Includes right to object:** Unless it expressly provides *otherwise*, a stipulation extending the time to "respond" applies to any form of response—i.e., objections as well as answers. [CCP §2030.270(c)]

(3) [8:1030] **Delay WAIVES objections:** Failing to respond within the time limit waives most objections to the interrogatories, including claims of privilege and "work product" protection. [CCP §2030.290(a); see *Leach v. Sup.Ct. (Markum)* (1980) 111 CA3d 902, 905-906, 169 CR 42, 43-44]

Such delay *also* waives the option to produce writings under CCP §2030.230 in lieu of information contained therein; *see* ¶*8:1065.* [CCP §2030.290(a)]

(a) [8:1031] **Example:** P served interrogatories inquiring about matters for which D was facing criminal charges. D failed to respond within the time permitted. His later attempts to avoid discovery by claiming self-incrimination were unavailing: "Defendants had ample opportunity to timely raise their Fifth Amendment objection and failed to do so, *thereby waiving their privilege.*" [*Brown v. Sup.Ct. (Boorstin)* (1986) 180 CA3d 701, 712, 226 CR 10, 16 (emphasis added)]

(b) [8:1031.1] **Exceptions to waiver:** There may be some case law exceptions to the waiver rule stated in §2030.290(a):

- [8:1031.2] *Relief through protective order:* One case holds that a party may, upon a proper showing, obtain a protective order limiting discovery of objectionable information even *after* the party has waived its right to object to discovery thereof. [See *Stadish v. Sup.Ct. (Southern Calif. Gas Co.)* (1999) 71 CA4th 1130, 1144, 84 CR2d 350, 358 (dealing with inspection demands), *discussed at ¶8:1454.2*]

- [8:1031.3] *Privacy rights:* In light of the sensitive nature of privacy rights, courts are reluctant to find a waiver and, even if a waiver is found, are likely to grant relief from it (¶*8:1032*). [*Heda v. Sup.Ct. (Davis)* (1990) 225 CA3d 525, 530, 275 CR 136, 138-139; *see ¶8:1101.1 ff.*]

(c) [8:1032] **Relief from waiver:** The court has statutory power to grant relief from such waiver in accordance with the procedures discussed below (¶*8:1033 ff.*). [CCP §2030.290(a)]

1) [8:1033] **Noticed motion required:** A noticed motion for relief from waiver is required. (I.e., such relief *cannot* be granted ex parte, or where the only motion pending is a motion to compel.) [CCP §2030.290(a)]

2) [8:1034] **Delayed responses must be served:** The party seeking belatedly to assert some objection must show that he or she has belatedly served responses "in *substantial compliance*" with that party's duty to respond under CCP §2030.210(a). [CCP §2030.290(a)(1) (emphasis added)]

a) [8:1035] **Comment:** Any form of response under §2030.210 is permissible—i.e., answer, *objection* or election to allow inspection of records. But it must be in "substantial compliance" with the duty to respond. I.e., there must be a full and fair response to each interrogatory; so that all questions are answered other than those to which the belated objections relate.

3) [8:1036] **Excuse for delayed response:** The declarations must establish that the party's failure

© 2020 Thomson Reuters/The Rutter Group

to serve a timely response resulted from "mistake, inadvertence or *excusable* neglect." [CCP §2030.290(a)(2) (emphasis added)]

a) [8:1037] **Application:** The judge has broad discretion in this area, but not every "excuse" is excusable. [See *Mannino v. Sup.Ct. (Southern Calif. Edison Co.)* (1983) 142 CA3d 776, 778-779, 191 CR 163, 164-165]

[8:1038] For example, D's attorney offered no explanation for delay in responding to P's interrogatories other than his client's failure to sign the verification on time. D's attorney had requested one extension from P's counsel, but failed to ask for another. These facts did *not* show "good cause" for relief from waiver. [See *Mannino v. Sup.Ct. (Southern Calif. Edison Co.)*, supra, 142 CA3d at 778-779, 191 CR at 164-165 (decided under former law applying CCP §473)]

(d) [8:1038.1] **No relief under CCP §473(b):** Because the Discovery Act contains specific provisions for relief for delayed responses, relief *cannot* be obtained under CCP §473(b) (authorizing relief from default generally for "mistake, inadvertence, surprise or excusable neglect"; *see* ¶*5:282 ff.*). [See *Zellerino v. Brown* (1991) 235 CA3d 1097, 1107, 1 CR2d 222, 228, *discussed at* ¶*8:10.5*]

1) [8:1038.2] **Compare:** Where there is *no analogous* Discovery Act provision, CCP §473(b) relief is available. [*Zellerino v. Brown*, supra, 235 CA3d at 1104-1106, 1 CR2d at 226-228—CCP §473 relief granted for untimely demand for expert witness exchange because no Discovery Act provision for such relief]

2) [8:1038.3] **Significance:** It is *often easier* to obtain relief under CCP §473(b). *See discussion at* ¶*8:10.14 ff.*

b. [8:1039] **Format of response:** The following rules govern the format of the response:

(1) [8:1040] **Opening paragraph:** The first paragraph immediately below the title of the case must state:

- The identity of the responding party;
- The identity of the propounding party;
- The set number of the propounding party's interrogatories being responded to. [CCP §2030.210(b)]

If the response is a supplemental or further response (answers to supplemental interrogatories, or after court order for further response), the words "supplemental responses" or "further response" must be included. [CRC 3.1000(a)]

See Form 8:18.1 in Rivera, *Cal. Prac. Guide: Civ. Pro. Before Trial FORMS* (TRG).

(a) [8:1041] **Example:** "DEFENDANT DONALD DALTON'S SUPPLEMENTAL RESPONSES TO PLAINTIFF PAUL PROCTOR'S SECOND SET OF INTERROGATORIES"

[8:1042] *Reserved.*

(2) [8:1043] **Numbering:** Each response (whether answer, objection or election to furnish documents) must be in the same order and must be identified by the same number or letter as the interrogatory to which it relates. [CCP §2030.210(c)]

(3) [8:1044] **Question need not be repeated:** The text of the interrogatory need not be repeated in the response (except as may be required with electronic exchange of interrogatories and responses, ¶*8:1045*). [CCP §2030.210(c) (amended eff. 1/1/20); CRC 3.1000(b)]

(4) [8:1045] **Electronic exchange of interrogatories and responses:** Nonetheless, it is generally desirable to have the questions and answers in a single document. Upon request, a party must provide the document *propounding* interrogatories in electronic format within three court days of the request. If this is provided, the responding party must include the text of the interrogatory preceding any response. Upon request, a party *responding* to the interrogatories must provide the responses to the propounding party in an electronic format within three court days of the request. [CCP §2030.210(d)(1), (2), (6) (all added eff. 1/1/20)]

c. [8:1046] **Answers to interrogatories:** As stated earlier, the response may consist either of answers, objections, or election to allow inspection and copying of records. [CCP §2030.210(a)]

The following rules apply to answers:

(1) [8:1047] **Duty to provide "complete" answers:** Each answer in the response must be "as *complete* and *straightforward* as the information reasonably available to the responding party permits. If an interrogatory cannot be answered completely, it shall be answered to the extent possible." [CCP §2030.220(a), (b) (emphasis added)]

(a) [8:1048] **False or evasive answers improper:** "Parties must state the truth, the whole truth, and nothing but the truth in answering written interrogatories." [*Scheiding v. Dinwiddie Const. Co.* (1999) 69 CA4th 64, 76, 81 CR2d 360, 368 (internal quotes omitted); see CCP §2023.010(f)—evasive response is ground for *sanctions* (¶*8:1920*)]

- [8:1048.1] Where the question is specific and explicit, an answer that supplies only a portion of the

© 2020 Thomson Reuters/The Rutter Group

information sought is improper. It is also improper to provide "deftly worded conclusionary answers designed to evade a series of explicit questions." [*Deyo v. Kilbourne* (1978) 84 CA3d 771, 783, 149 CR 499, 509]

- [8:1048.2] Where an interrogatory asks for the names of *all* witnesses to a particular event then known to the responding party, a response omitting the name of a known witness could subject the adversary to unfair surprise at trial and therefore may result in an order excluding that witness' testimony. [See *R & B Auto Ctr., Inc. v. Farmers Group, Inc.* (2006) 140 CA4th 327, 356, 44 CR3d 426, 450; *and* ¶*8:2390*]

(b) [8:1049] **Referencing other documents improper:** It is not proper to answer by stating, "See my deposition" or "See the complaint herein." If the question requires reference to some other document, it should be identified and its contents summarized so that the answer *by itself* is fully responsive to the interrogatory. [*Deyo v. Kilbourne*, supra, 84 CA3d at 783-784, 149 CR at 510]

Alternatively, where answering the interrogatory would require a compilation or summary of information contained in documents, the answering party may opt to allow the interrogating party to inspect the books and records that contain the information (*see* ¶*8:1065 ff.*).

[8:1050] ***PRACTICE POINTER:*** Sometimes several interrogatories appear to ask for the same information. It is usually *not* a good idea to answer, "See my answer to Question No. . . ." or "I incorporate my answer to Question No. . . ." The reason is that the questions may differ in some detail, so there is a chance that your prior answers will not be completely responsive to the present question. Take the time and trouble to provide a *full* answer to the present question.

[8:1050.1-1050.4] *Reserved.*

(c) [8:1050.5] **Responding to interrogatories re privileged documents:** An interrogatory may ask the responding party to *identify* documents as to which a privilege is claimed. The *existence* of a privileged document is not generally privileged. Therefore, an adequate response must include a description of the documents, even if the party has the right to object to a demand for their production. The responding party *need not* provide a privilege log (¶*8:192.10*) in responding to the interrogatory. [*Hernandez v. Sup.Ct. (Acheson Indus., Inc.)* (2003) 112 CA4th 285, 293, 4 CR3d 883, 890]

Compare—request for document production: A privilege log may be required, however, when objecting to a CCP §2031.010 et seq. demand for document production based on a claim of privilege or work product protection (CCP §2031.240(c)). *See ¶8:1474.5.*

[8:1050.6-1050.9] *Reserved.*

(d) [8:1050.10] ***Caution*—incomplete answers may expose responding party to summary judgment:** "Factually devoid" interrogatory answers may come back to haunt the responding party if the opposing party moves for summary judgment. The responding party's incomplete answers can be used *to satisfy the moving party's burden* on summary judgment to show there is *no evidence* of a triable issue of material fact. [See *Union Bank v. Sup.Ct. (Demetry)* (1995) 31 CA4th 573, 580-581, 37 CR2d 653, 657; *Collin v. Calportland Co.* (2014) 228 CA4th 582, 591, 176 CR3d 279, 287—factually devoid discovery responses raised inference plaintiff could not prove causation]

(2) [8:1051] **Duty to obtain information:** "If the responding party does not have personal knowledge sufficient to respond fully to an interrogatory, that party shall so state, *but shall make a reasonable and good faith effort to obtain* the information by inquiry to other natural persons or organizations, except where the information is equally available to the propounding party." [CCP §2030.220(c) (emphasis added); *Regency Health Services, Inc. v. Sup.Ct. (Settles)* (1998) 64 CA4th 1496, 1504, 76 CR2d 95, 100 (citing text)]

[8:1052] *Reserved.*

[8:1053] **Compare—depositions:** An individual deponent is required to answer only according to his or her *personal knowledge* at the time of deposition (*see* ¶*8:705*). He or she is *not* under any duty to investigate or search out information. But the rules are different for interrogatories because, unlike depositions, *interrogatory answers are prepared with the assistance of counsel.* Therefore, a broader duty of response is justified.

(a) [8:1054] **Information available from sources under party's control:** In answering interrogatories, a party must furnish information available from sources under the party's control: "[A party] cannot plead ignorance to information which can be obtained from sources under his control." [*Deyo v. Kilbourne*, supra, 84 CA3d at 782, 149 CR at 509; *Regency Health Services, Inc. v. Sup.Ct. (Settles)* (1998) 64 CA4th 1496, 1504, 76 CR2d 95, 100 (citing text)]

1) [8:1055] **Party's lawyer:** A party must disclose *nonprivileged* facts known to his or her lawyer,

© 2020 Thomson Reuters/The Rutter Group

even if the party has no personal knowledge of such facts. [*Smith v. Sup.Ct. (Alfred)* (1961) 189 CA2d 6, 11-12, 11 CR 165, 169—names of witnesses, existence of photographs, etc.]

2) [8:1056] **Agents or employees:** Interrogatories directed to a corporation or other entity require it to disclose information known to *all persons* in its employ, not merely the particular officer or agent designated to verify the responses: "While a corporation or public agency may select the person who answers interrogatories in its behalf, it has a corresponding duty to obtain information from *all sources under its control*—information which may not be personally known to the answering agent." [*Gordon v. Sup.Ct. (U.Z. Mfg. Co.)* (1984) 161 CA3d 157, 167-168, 207 CR 327, 333 (emphasis added)—corporation bound by initial, untruthful answers given by employee who answered interrogatories on its behalf]

3) [8:1057] **Family members:** In answering interrogatories, a party is expected to make good faith inquiry of his or her family members, at least where they are shown to be *cooperating* with the party in the lawsuit. [*Jones v. Sup.Ct. (Benny)* (1981) 119 CA3d 534, 552, 174 CR 148, 159 (disapproved on other grounds by *Williams v. Sup.Ct. (Marshalls of CA, LLC)* (2017) 3 C5th 531, 557, 220 CR3d 472, 494 & fn. 8)]

   - [8:1058] **Example:** Daughter sued for birth defects allegedly caused by Mother's ingestion of dangerous drug. In answering interrogatories, Daughter was under a duty to furnish information known to Mother, because Mother was closely cooperating in the suit. Mother (not a party to the action) was free, however, to decline to answer for privacy reasons or otherwise. [*Jones v. Sup.Ct. (Benny)*, supra, 119 CA3d at 552-553, 174 CR at 159]

4) [8:1059] **Expert trial witnesses:** An expert who has been retained by a party and designated as a trial witness may be treated as the agent of that party, so that, in answering interrogatories, the party may be required to furnish *facts known to the expert.* [*Sigerseth v. Sup.Ct. (Canoga Park Lutheran Church)* (1972) 23 CA3d 427, 433, 100 CR 185, 188]

   ☞ [8:1060] ***PRACTICE POINTER:*** Don't rely on interrogatories for this purpose. Expert witnesses are usually not designated until 50 days before trial (see CCP §§2034.220 ff. dealing with exchange of expert witness lists, ¶*8:1649.2*). Discovery from the designated experts may continue until 15 days before trial (see CCP §2024.030, ¶*8:1690*). However, *depositions,* rather than interrogatories, should be used at that point.

(b) [8:1061] **Information presumably available to responding party:** Another consequence of the duty to attempt to obtain information is that "I don't know" or "Unknown" are *insufficient* answers to matters presumably known to the responding party. (Example: Question asks, "What is the name and address of each physician who treated you for the injuries described in your complaint?")

The responding party must make a reasonable effort to obtain whatever information is sought; and if unable to do so, must *specify* why the information is unavailable and *what efforts he or she made to obtain it.* [See *Deyo v. Kilbourne* (1978) 84 CA3d 771, 782, 149 CR 499, 509]

(c) [8:1062] **Exception—no duty to provide information equally available to propounding party:** The duty to make reasonable efforts to obtain requested information does not apply to "information equally available to the propounding party." [CCP §2030.220(c)]

- [8:1063] Thus, there is no duty to search out matters of *public record.* [See *Bunnell v. Sup.Ct. (California Life Ins. Co.)* (1967) 254 CA2d 720, 723-724, 62 CR 458, 461]

- [8:1064] Nor is the responding party under a duty to make inquiry from *independent witnesses* (persons not his or her agents or employees) in order to answer interrogatories. [*Holguin v. Sup.Ct. (Hoage)* (1972) 22 CA3d 812, 821, 99 CR 653, 658]

d. [8:1065] **Option to allow interrogating party to inspect files and records:** If the interrogatory seeks information contained in files and records, the responding party is under a duty to provide "complete and straightforward" answers. [CCP §2030.220(a)]

However, if the answer would necessitate making a *compilation* or summary of information contained in such records, the responding party has the *option* to allow the interrogating party to inspect and copy the records in question. In effect, the responding party *may* shift the burden of compiling the information to the interrogating party. [CCP §2030.230]

Exercising the option is equivalent to a statement *under oath* that the records identified actually exist and that they contain the information necessary to provide a "complete and straightforward"

© 2020 Thomson Reuters/The Rutter Group

answer to the interrogatory. [See *Deyo v. Kilbourne* (1978) 84 CA3d 771, 784, 149 CR 499, 510]

(1) [8:1066] **Requirements:** To answer an interrogatory in this manner, the following must be shown:

- A *compilation, abstract, audit or summary* of the responding party's records is necessary in order to answer the interrogatory; *and*
- No such compilation, etc. presently exists; *and*
- The burden or expense of preparing or making it would be substantially the same for the interrogating party as for the responding party. [CCP §2030.230]

(2) [8:1067] **How option exercised:** To utilize this option, the response must:

- Be *timely* (delay waives the right to exercise the option; see CCP §2030.290(a), ¶*8:1030*); and
- *Refer to CCP §2030.230;* and
- *Specify* the documents from which the answer may be derived or ascertained. [CCP §2030.230]

(a) [8:1068] **Identification of records:** The responding party must describe the records from which the compilation or summary can be made with sufficient particularity that they can be easily located. (For example, "see my files and records" is *not* a proper response.) [*Fuss v. Sup.Ct. (Rosenthal)* (1969) 273 CA2d 807, 815-817, 78 CR 583, 588-589]

(3) [8:1069] **Inspection and copying:** Upon exercising the option, the responding party must then afford the interrogating party a "reasonable opportunity" to inspect and copy the records or documents identified. [CCP §2030.230]

➪ [8:1070] ***PRACTICE POINTER:*** If you represent the responding party, be careful about exercising this option. Its purpose supposedly is to save you (or your client) the time required to prepare a summary or compilation.

However, you should never open up your client's records to inspection by opposing counsel *unless you have already reviewed them* and *know* what's in them.

In many cases, a thorough review will require you to spend almost the same time as would be required to make the compilation sought by the interrogatory, so the time savings won't be as great as supposed.

Moreover, if the compilation could result in evidence admissible at trial, it will be *better for you to prepare the compilation yourself.*

e. [8:1071] **Objections:** In lieu of answering (¶*8:1046 ff.*) or allowing inspection of records (¶*8:1065 ff.*), the responding party may serve objections. Each objection must be stated *separately* (no objections to entire set), and must bear the same number or letter as the interrogatory to which it is directed. [CCP §2030.210(a)(3); *see* ¶*8:1045* (electronic exchange of interrogatories and responses)]

Objections must be *specific.* A motion to compel lies where objections are "too general." [CCP §2030.300(a)(3); see *Korea Data Systems Co. Ltd. v. Sup.Ct. (Aamazing Technologies Corp.)* (1997) 51 CA4th 1513, 1516, 59 CR2d 925, 926—objecting party subject to sanctions for "boilerplate" objections; *and* ¶*8:1920*]

(1) [8:1072] **As alternative to protective order:** Some grounds for objection to interrogatories would also be ground for a protective order: e.g., that the interrogatories are *burdensome and oppressive* (¶*8:1007*). [CCP §2030.090(b)]

But the responding party does *not* have to seek a protective order against "burdensome or oppressive" interrogatories. The responding party can raise this by objection to the interrogatories (*see* ¶*8:1022*).

(a) [8:1073] **Burden on propounding party to seek order compelling answer:** Once an objection is made, it is up to the propounding party to decide whether to take the matter to court. If the objection is believed to be without merit, the propounding party must file a *motion to compel answers* (¶*8:1136 ff.*). And, the motion must be filed *promptly* or the matter is waived (¶*8:1146*).

(b) [8:1074] **Burden on responding party to justify objection:** If a motion to compel answers is filed, the burden will then be on the objecting party to establish whatever facts are necessary to justify the objection. Usually, this is done by filing declarations in opposition to the motion to compel (*see* ¶*8:1179*).

[8:1075] ***PRACTICE POINTER:*** To save time and effort, the responding party may wish to set forth such facts in the *response to the interrogatories.* Doing so may dissuade the propounding party from filing a motion to compel answers. And, even if the motion is made, it may lessen the burden of preparing the requisite declarations to establish the facts.

(2) [8:1076] **Grounds for objection:** The grounds for objecting to interrogatories are even more limited than the grounds for objecting to deposition questions. There is *less concern* as to the *form* of questioning because the answering party will have the assistance of counsel in preparing responses. [*Greyhound Corp. v. Sup.Ct. (Clay)* (1961) 56 C2d 355, 392, 15 CR 90, 110, fn. 16 (superseded by statute on other grounds)]

© 2020 Thomson Reuters/The Rutter Group

➪ [8:1076.1] ***PRACTICE POINTER:*** Avoid general or "boilerplate" objections and other equivocal responses that have the effect of obstructing discovery. Judges usually will not tolerate such responses and if a motion to compel is filed, substantial sanctions are a real likelihood.

(a) [8:1077] ***Improper* objections:** In addition, the following are generally *not* valid grounds for objecting to an interrogatory:

- [8:1078] Question calls for *hearsay*. [*Greyhound Corp. v. Sup.Ct. (Clay)*, supra, 56 C2d at 392-393, 15 CR at 109-110—hearsay discoverable as long as it may lead to admissible evidence]
- [8:1079] Question calls for *opinion* or *conclusion*. [*West Pico Furniture Co. of Los Angeles v. Sup.Ct. (Pacific Finance Loans)* (1961) 56 C2d 407, 416-417, 15 CR 119, 123]
- [8:1080] Question has been *asked and answered* at deposition. [*Coy v. Sup.Ct. (Wolcher)* (1962) 58 C2d 210, 218, 23 CR 393, 397]
- [8:1081] Question *assumes facts not in evidence*. [*West Pico Furniture Co. of Los Angeles v. Sup.Ct. (Pacific Finance Loans)*, supra, 56 C2d at 421, 15 CR at 126]
- [8:1082] Interrogating party is "conducting a *fishing expedition*." [*Greyhound Corp. v. Sup.Ct. (Clay)*, supra, 56 C2d at 384, 15 CR at 104]

  [8:1083] *Reserved.*
- [8:1084] Question is "*ambiguous, confusing or overbroad*." Courts generally do *not* sustain this kind of objection unless the question is totally unintelligible. The answering party owes a duty to *respond in good faith as best he or she can*. [See *Deyo v. Kilbourne* (1978) 84 CA3d 771, 783, 149 CR 499, 509—verification of answers is "in effect a declaration that the party has disclosed *all information available* to him" (emphasis added)]

  (Compare: But if the question is so broad that it is "oppressive," an objection can be stated on that ground; *see ¶8:1094 ff.*)
- [8:1085] Question seeks "*confidential information*." Again, this is *not* a proper objection; the answering party should seek a *protective order* to excuse the duty to answer. [*Columbia Broadcasting System, Inc. v. Sup.Ct. (Rolfe)* (1968) 263 CA2d 12, 23, 69

CR 348, 355] (The court may also order the response be made, but perhaps subject to a confidentiality order.)

(Compare: If the information sought is *privileged* or protected by the constitutional *right of privacy,* rather than simply "confidential," an objection may be stated on those grounds; *see* ¶*8:1088.*)

- [8:1086] Objections to the *entire set* of interrogatories will not be sustained if *any* of the questions is proper. [*Wooldridge v. Mounts* (1962) 199 CA2d 620, 628, 18 CR 806, 811]

- [8:1086.1] Objections that do not actually apply to any responsive answer (e.g., "attorney-client privilege" when there is no such responsive material).

  [8:1086.2-1086.4] *Reserved.*

- [8:1086.5] Where an interrogatory asks about the *existence* of a document, an objection on the ground of *privilege* is improper. I.e., the document must be described although a privilege claim may later be asserted concerning its contents. [*Best Products, Inc. v. Sup.Ct. (Granatelli Motorsports, Inc.)* (2004) 119 CA4th 1181, 1190, 15 CR3d 154, 160]

(b) [8:1087] **PROPER objections:** Objections to interrogatories may be sustained on the following grounds:

- [8:1088] Question seeks information protected by privilege, work product, or right of privacy (¶*8:109 ff.*).

- [8:1089] Question exceeds *permissible scope* of discovery; i.e., it seeks information "not relevant to the subject matter of the action" (¶*8:65 ff.*).

- [8:1090] More than 35 specially prepared interrogatories have been served (in the present set or together with previous sets) *without a "declaration of necessity"* under CCP §2030.050. [See CCP §2030.040(a); *and* ¶*8:939*]

  (Compare: But where a "declaration of necessity" accompanies the interrogatories, no objection lies solely because of the number of interrogatories served. The appropriate procedure is to challenge the "declaration of necessity" by a *motion for protective order* (CCP §2030.090(b)(2)*; see* ¶*8:954*). However, a "burdensome and oppressive" objection might still lie; *see* ¶*8:1094.*)

- [8:1091] Question is improper in *form* because not "full and complete in and of itself"; or (if not an Official Form Interrogatory) because it contains:

© 2020 Thomson Reuters/The Rutter Group

- *Subparts* (CCP §2030.060(f)); or
- "*Compound, conjunctive or disjunctive*" questions (CCP §2030.060(f)); or
- A preface or instructions (CCP §2030.060(d)); or
- Special definitions of terms carried over from question to question are not capitalized. (See CCP §2030.060(e)).

- [8:1092] Question seeks *content* or *production of documents*; interrogatories cannot be used for this purpose (¶*8:993*). (But they can be used to obtain *description* and location of the documents sought.) [*West Pico Furniture Co. of Los Angeles v. Sup.Ct. (Pacific Finance Loans)* (1961) 56 C2d 407, 419, 15 CR 119, 125]

- [8:1093] Question seeks *information equally available to interrogating party* (¶*8:1062*). [*Alpine Mut. Water Co. v. Sup.Ct. (Susana Knolls Mut. Water Co.)* (1968) 259 CA2d 45, 53, 66 CR 250, 255—interrogating party cannot force answering party to search *public records* to ascertain answers to interrogatories]

- [8:1094] Question is "*burdensome and oppressive*": The court has power to issue protective orders to protect a party against "unwarranted annoyance, embarrassment or *oppression*" (CCP §2030.090(b), *see* ¶*8:1008*).

  "Oppression" may also be raised as ground for objection, in lieu of making a motion for protective order. [*West Pico Furniture Co. of Los Angeles v. Sup.Ct. (Pacific Finance Loans)*, supra, 56 C2d at 418, 15 CR at 123-124]

  But it is a *weak ground* because difficult to justify if a motion to compel answers is made.

  [8:1094.1] ***PRACTICE POINTER:*** Even so, it is a good idea to raise the objection where grounds exist. The party seeking discovery must attempt to resolve the matter with you informally before moving to compel answers (¶*8:1158*).

  You can use the opportunity to negotiate limits on the interrogatories.

1) [8:1095] **"Burdensome" by itself not enough:** The ground for objection is "oppression." Thus, it is not enough that the questions will require a lot of work to answer. It must be shown that the burden of answering is so *unjust* that it amounts to oppression.

[*West Pico Furniture Co. of Los Angeles v. Sup.Ct. (Pacific Finance Loans)*, supra, 56 C2d at 417-418, 15 CR at 124]

2) [8:1096] **"Oppression":** In determining whether the burden is unjust, a weighing process is required: It must appear that the *amount of work required to answer the questions is so great*, and the *utility of the information sought so minimal*, that it would defeat the ends of justice to require the answers. [See *Columbia Broadcasting System, Inc. v. Sup.Ct. (Rolfe)* (1968) 263 CA2d 12, 19, 69 CR 348, 352; and *West Pico Furniture Co. of Los Angeles v. Sup.Ct. (Pacific Finance Loans)*, supra, 56 C2d at 417-418, 15 CR at 124]

a) [8:1097] **Showing required:** On a motion to compel answers, the burden is on the objecting party to sustain the objection by detailed evidence showing precisely *how much* work is required to answer; conclusionary statements are not sufficient. [*West Pico Furniture Co. of Los Angeles v. Sup.Ct. (Pacific Finance Loans)*, supra, 56 C2d at 417, 15 CR at 123-124—declaration by manager that search of 78 branch offices would be required was insufficient; should show hours required]

[8:1097.1] A discovery request was held "oppressive" where uncontradicted declarations showed that response would require review of over 13,000 insurance claims files, requiring 5 claims adjusters working full time for 6 weeks each. [*Mead Reinsurance Co. v. Sup.Ct. (City of Laguna Beach)* (1986) 188 CA3d 313, 318, 232 CR 752, 754—involving document demand; *see ¶8:1475.1*]

b) [8:1098] **Contents of business records; effect of CCP §2030.230 option:** If the information sought is a compilation of entries in files and records, the answering party has the option to allow the interrogating party to inspect and copy the records (CCP §2030.230; *¶8:1065*). An answering party who has this option available, but *declines to use it* (because he or she doesn't want the adverse party inspecting his or her records), cannot rely on a "burdensome and oppressive" objection. The answering party must suffer the burden. [*Brotsky v. State Bar* (1962) 57 C2d 287, 304, 19 CR 153, 162]

© 2020 Thomson Reuters/The Rutter Group

c) [8:1099] **Number of interrogatories as factor:** Where more than 35 specially prepared interrogatories are accompanied by a "declaration of necessity" under CCP §2030.050, any challenge to the *number* of questions must be by *motion for protective order* (CCP §2030.090(b)(2); *see ¶8:954*). Therefore, a "burdensome and oppressive" objection would not lie *solely* on the basis of the number of questions asked. Other reasons must be shown.

3) [8:1100] **Court may limit questions rather than excuse answers altogether:** Discovery should not be denied if the information sought has any relevancy to the subject matter. Therefore, even if interrogatories are found to be "burdensome and oppressive," the court should *not* simply sustain the objection and thereby excuse any answer. Rather, the trial court should *limit* the question to a *reasonable scope*. [*Borse v. Sup.Ct. (Southern Pac. Co.)* (1970) 7 CA3d 286, 289, 86 CR 559, 561]

(3) [8:1101] **Failure to object as waiver:** If the party to whom the interrogatories are directed *does not timely respond*, most objections are waived. [CCP §2030.290(a); *see ¶8:1030*]

Moreover, there is no provision for filing subsequent objections. Thus, even where a timely response is made, the responding party cannot later *add* objections without a court order granting relief from the waiver. [*Scottsdale Ins. Co. v. Sup.Ct. (Spyglass Homeowners Ass'n)* (1997) 59 CA4th 263, 273, 69 CR2d 112, 118 (citing text)]

(See further discussion of waiver and relief from waiver at *¶8:1030 ff.*)

(a) [8:1101.1] **Compare—delayed privacy objection:** However, one case has permitted a party to raise a *privacy* objection *after the initial response* to the interrogatories. [*Heda v. Sup.Ct. (Davis)* (1990) 225 CA3d 525, 529-530, 275 CR 136, 138-139—D objected to questions re his medical records solely on *relevance* grounds; P moved to compel, demonstrating relevancy; D then raised privacy objection; "Plaintiff now claims that failure also to object on privacy grounds forever waives defendant's privacy rights. Plaintiff cites no persuasive authority for such a draconian rule . . . *[W]aivers of constitutional rights are not lightly found*" (emphasis added)]

[8:1101.2] **Comment:** This seems incorrect. The court did not consider or discuss CCP former §2030(k), now §2030.290(a), and later cases which hold that omitting a claim of privilege in the original discovery response *waives* the objection. [*Scottsdale Ins. Co. v. Sup.Ct. (Spyglass Homeowners Ass'n)* (1997) 59 CA4th 263, 273, 69 CR2d 112, 118; *see* ¶*8:200*]

[8:1101.3-1101.4] *Reserved.*

(4) [8:1101.5] **Standards of professionalism:** Various guidelines exist to discourage abusive discovery. The Los Angeles Superior Court has adopted certain of these guidelines as "civility in litigation recommendations to members of the bar," including the following:

- "Objections to interrogatories should be based on a good faith belief in their merit and *not be made for the purpose of withholding relevant information.* If an interrogatory is objectionable only in part, the unobjectionable portion should be answered." [L.A. Sup.Ct. Rule 3.26, Appendix 3.A(g)(3) (emphasis added)]

  Comment: Although these guidelines do not have the force of law and parties may not be sanctioned directly for violations, the conduct proscribed therein may nevertheless be sanctionable as a discovery misuse under CCP §2030.010 (*see* ¶*8:1901*).

f. [8:1102] **Signature and verification:** The responses must be signed under oath by the party to whom the interrogatories are directed. If they contain an objection, the *attorney* must also sign the response; and if it consists *entirely* of objections, only the attorney's signature is required. [CCP §2030.250(a), (c); see *Blue Ridge Ins. Co. v. Sup.Ct. (Kippen)* (1988) 202 CA3d 339, 344, 248 CR 346, 349—responses consisting entirely of objections need not be verified]

(1) [8:1102.1] **Answers and objections intermixed:** Where the response contains *both* answer and objections, there is no need to verify that portion of the response containing the objections. But the portion containing fact-specific responses must be verified. [*Food 4 Less Supermarkets, Inc. v. Sup.Ct. (Fletcher)* (1995) 40 CA4th 651, 657, 46 CR2d 925, 928; *see* ¶*8:1113.1*]

(2) [8:1103] **Form:** In practice, the responding party usually signs a verification form attached to or inserted at the end of the answers: "I certify and declare under penalty of perjury under the laws of the State of California that the foregoing answers are true and correct." [See CCP §2015.5]

(a) [8:1104] **"Information and belief" insufficient:** A verification on behalf of an individual stating "I am informed and believe that the matters stated herein are true" is insufficient. This form is acceptable for *pleadings* (see CCP §446, ¶*6:225 ff.*), but not for interrogatory answers.

Reason: Interrogatory answers must contain the responding party's personal knowledge or state the inability to provide

© 2020 Thomson Reuters/The Rutter Group

such information despite a *reasonable and good faith effort* to obtain it (see CCP §2030.220(c); ¶*8:1051*).

Answers on "information and belief" indicate the information is hearsay, not personal knowledge, and fail to state that the requisite effort has been made to obtain first-hand information.

(b) [8:1104.1] **Verification by "Doe" sufficient:** Where plaintiff files an action under a fictitious name to preserve anonymity (¶*2:136.5 ff.*), plaintiff may verify discovery responses by signing the fictitious name. [*Doe v. Sup.Ct. (Luster)* (2011) 194 CA4th 750, 756, 123 CR3d 557, 561—trial court erred in requiring plaintiff to provide verifications in her true name]

(3) [8:1105] **Verification by entity party:** If the responding party is a corporation, partnership or other entity, "one of its officers or agents" must execute the verification on its behalf. [CCP §2030.250(b)]

The usual corporate verification form is as follows: "I am an officer of XYZ, Inc. and am authorized to make this verification on its behalf. I have read the foregoing Responses to Interrogatories and know its contents. I am informed and believe that the matters stated therein are true and on that ground certify or declare under penalty of perjury under the laws of the State of California that the same are true and correct."

However, this form raises several problems:

(a) [8:1106] **Signer's knowledge of facts; use of "information and belief" form?** The person designated to verify the corporation's responses may not have personal knowledge of *all* facts stated therein. (The entity is obliged to provide facts known to *any* agent or employee, but the particular officer verifying may not have personal knowledge thereof.)

Under such circumstances, "information and belief" is the only realistic way to verify answers on behalf of the entity. Unfortunately, nothing in the Discovery Act authorizes verification of interrogatories on "information and belief."

- [8:1106.1] ***PRACTICE POINTER:*** Until the Legislature clarifies this issue, consider modifying the usual declaration form to reflect these realities. For example, a corporate secretary's declaration might state: "I certify and declare under penalty of perjury under the laws of the State of California that:
  — I am the Secretary of XYZ, Inc.; and
  — I have made reasonable efforts to review relevant documents, records and information possessed by or known to XYZ, Inc. and its officers and employees; and

— Based on such review, the facts stated herein are true and correct."

This is similar to federal practice for entity discovery verifications. See detailed discussion in Phillips & Stevenson, *Rutter Group Prac. Guide: Federal Civ. Pro. Before Trial* (TRG), Ch. 11.

(b) [8:1107] **Signer's authority?** Another problem is whether the signer's allegations that he or she is an "officer" and "authorized" to verify on behalf of the corporation establish his or her authority to do so; or whether resolutions of the board of directors, etc. are required. Again, the Discovery Act is silent on this point; and there is no known case authority.

Many judges would hold the above form (¶*8:1106.1*) sufficient *prima facie*.

(c) [8:1107a] **Compare—when no officer or agent of the party:** When a corporation has no officer or agent to verify responses due to dissolution and resignation of officers, its lawyer may verify if authorized to waive the attorney-client privilege (¶*8:1109 ff.*). If the corporation cannot or will not waive privilege, the responses must be treated as *unverified* (*see* ¶*8:1113 ff.*). [*Melendrez v. Sup.Ct. (Special Elec. Co., Inc.)* (2013) 215 CA4th 1343, 1357-1358, 156 CR3d 335, 347]

- [8:1107b] Corporation filed for bankruptcy, following which it existed only as a shell through which personal injury (asbestos) lawsuits were passed on to Insurer for resolution. In one suit, Corporation's attorney (hired by Insurer) filed substantive responses to requests for admission but stated that the responses could not be verified because Corporation had no officers, directors or agents who could do so. Because Attorney could not verify the responses without waiving the attorney-client privilege, Corporation was required to elect or appoint an officer or director to decide the waiver issue. If this was not possible because Corporation no longer existed, the privilege transferred to Insurer. If the privilege was not waived, the responses would be treated as unverified on a motion to compel. [*Melendrez v. Sup.Ct. (Special Elec. Co., Inc.)*, supra, 215 CA4th at 1357-1358, 156 CR3d at 347]

(4) [8:1107c] **Verification by minor, incompetent parties:** A guardian ad litem is authorized to verify interrogatories on behalf of a minor or incompetent ward. I.e., even lacking personal knowledge of the facts, the guardian ad litem has authority, subject to the court's ultimate supervision, to verify proper responses to interrogatories on behalf of the ward.

© 2020 Thomson Reuters/The Rutter Group

Otherwise, the ward, the real party in interest, could evade discovery altogether. [*Regency Health Services, Inc. v. Sup.Ct. (Settles)* (1998) 64 CA4th 1496, 1504, 76 CR2d 95, 100; see also Prob.C. §2462—authorizing guardians ad litem to "institute *and maintain*" actions for benefit of ward (emphasis added)]

(5) [8:1107.1] **Attorney verifying on behalf of client:** As discussed above (¶*8:1102*), an attorney *must* sign responses containing *objections*. The question here is whether an attorney may *verify* responses *on behalf of* the client.

(a) [8:1108] **Generally improper:** CCP §2030.250(a) requires verification by the responding *party*. Therefore, an attorney cannot properly verify interrogatory responses on behalf of a client. [See *Steele v. Totah* (1986) 180 CA3d 545, 550, 225 CR 635, 637—dealing with verification of RFAs, *discussed at* ¶*8:1363*]

(**Compare—pleadings:** Pleadings *can* be verified by an attorney on behalf of the client under certain circumstances. See CCP §446, ¶*6:320*.)

(b) [8:1109] **Permissible if attorney authorized agent:** However, a corporation, partnership or other entity may authorize its attorney or someone on its legal staff to sign on its behalf—i.e., as an agent of the corporation. [CCP §2030.250(b)]

1) [8:1110] **Verification must so state:** In such event, the verification should state that the signer is the *authorized agent* of the corporation to sign the responses on its behalf and not simply that the signer is the attorney for the corporation.

2) [8:1111] **Waiver of privilege or work product protection:** If an attorney signs responses as agent of a corporation or other entity, the entity waives any attorney-client privilege or work product protection with respect to subsequent discovery from the attorney concerning the sources from whom the information was obtained. [CCP §2030.250(b)]

This waiver is "narrowly circumscribed," however, and should not subject the verifying attorney to "lengthy further discovery." [*Melendrez v. Sup.Ct. (Special Elec. Co., Inc.)* (2013) 215 CA4th 1343, 1352-1353, 156 CR3d 335, 342 (noting that there is "no indication [in the statutes] that a deposition of the verifying attorney would ever be necessary in any particular case")]

Comment: The purpose of the waiver rule is to prevent a party from "hiding behind" the privileges otherwise assertable by its attorney where it has the attorney sign its interrogatory answers.

[8:1112] ***PRACTICE POINTER:*** *Avoid* verifying discovery documents (or pleadings) on behalf of a client.

- First, it is rarely necessary, because opposing counsel will normally give you an extension of time to obtain your client's verification when the client is out of town, etc. (And, if opposing counsel won't, the court almost certainly will.) Even if the client is out of town, you can *mail* the answers to him or her for verification. (Verification outside of California is valid as long as the declaration states that it is "under penalty of perjury under the laws of the State of California"; see CCP §2015.5.)
- More importantly, your verifying such documents could subject you to *being called as a witness* by the opposing party—i.e., being deposed or subpoenaed to testify at trial regarding the facts you verified and the sources of those facts. While such testimony may not be "necessary" (*see ¶8:1111*), that does not mean the opposing party won't try to obtain it or that a court might not order it. Further, if your testimony relates to a contested matter in the case, you could be *disqualified* from representing the client at trial if the client does not execute a written consent. [CRPC 3.7 (formerly CRPC 5-210)]
- Moreover, as CCP §2030.250(b) now makes clear, when your client is a corporation or other entity, your verification on its behalf constitutes a waiver of at least some privileged communications and some of your own work product.

(6) [8:1113] **Effect of unverified response:** Where a verification is required (*see ¶8:1102 ff.*), an unverified response is ineffective; it is the equivalent of no response at all. [See *Appleton v. Sup.Ct. (Cook)* (1988) 206 CA3d 632, 636, 253 CR 762, 764]

(a) [8:1113.1] **Compare—responses containing both answers and objections:** But no verification is required to preserve objections (see CCP §2030.250(a)). Therefore, an unverified response containing *both* answers and objections is effective to preserve those objections. The lack of verification renders the fact-specific *answers* untimely; but that only creates a right to move for orders and sanctions (under §2030.290(b); *see ¶8:1136*). It does not result in a waiver of the objections made. [See *Food 4 Less Supermarkets, Inc. v. Sup.Ct. (Fletcher)* (1995) 40 CA4th 651, 657, 46 CR2d 925, 928 (involving CCP §2031.010 document requests)]

© 2020 Thomson Reuters/The Rutter Group

(b) [8:1114] **Compare—may be used as impeachment:** Even unverified answers can be used *against* the answering party—i.e., as a prior inconsistent statement to impeach his or her testimony at trial. [Ev.C. §§1235, 1236; *LeGrand v. Yellow Cab Co.* (1970) 8 CA3d 125, 129, 87 CR 292, 294]

g. [8:1115] **Service of responses:** The responding party must serve the *original* responses on the propounding party, with copies on all other parties who have appeared in the action. (If this is unduly burdensome, the court may grant ex parte relief limiting the parties to be served.) [CCP §2030.260(c)]

Note that the interrogatories and responses are *not* filed with the court. Custody of these documents is discussed at ¶*8:1130.*

[8:1116-1117] *Reserved.*

h. [8:1118] **Amended responses:** The responding party has no duty to amend earlier answers, but has the option to do so, as provided below (¶*8:1119 ff.*). [CCP §§2030.060(g), 2030.310(a)]

(1) [8:1119] **No duty to amend:** The responding party need only provide such information as is available at the time the answers are prepared. There is *no* duty to update or amend the answers, either to correct errors or to include new information discovered later. [*Singer v. Sup.Ct. (Parr-Richmond Terminal Co.)* (1960) 54 C2d 318, 325, 5 CR 697, 701; *Biles v. Exxon Mobil Corp.* (2004) 124 CA4th 1315, 1328, 22 CR3d 282, 291 (citing text)]

Result: Earlier answers do not bar the responding party from introducing at trial evidence discovered after those answers were prepared: "In fact, such answers would not even prevent production of facts *now known* to defendant, but not included in the answers, upon a proper showing that the oversight was in good faith." [*Singer v. Sup.Ct. (Parr-Richmond Terminal Co.),* supra, 54 C2d at 325, 5 CR at 701 (emphasis added)]

(a) [8:1120] **Continuing interrogatories invalid:** *See discussion at ¶8:998.*

(b) [8:1121] **Supplemental interrogatories available:** *See discussion at ¶8:942.*

[8:1122] *Reserved.*

(2) [8:1123] **Right to amend:** A party wishing to amend answers to interrogatories, either to correct errors or omissions or to include subsequently-discovered facts, has the right to do so. Leave of court is *not* required. The amended answers can simply be served on the interrogating party and all others who received copies of the original answers. [CCP §2030.310(a)]

☞ [8:1124] ***PRACTICE POINTER:*** Often, the need to amend is discovered only after a motion is pending in which the answers are relevant (e.g., opposing party's motion for summary judgment). In such a case, in addition to serving the amended answers on opposing parties, submit the amended answers to the court hearing the motion with a declaration explaining that the amended answers have been served.

(a) [8:1125] **Repudiated answer as impeachment:** At trial, the interrogating party or any other party can use the original answer for impeachment (as a prior inconsistent statement), in the same manner as a changed response to a deposition question. [CCP §2030.310(a); see *Jahn v. Brickey* (1985) 168 CA3d 399, 405, 214 CR 119, 123]

(b) [8:1125.1] **Repudiated answers not binding as matter of law:** Even if the amended answer contradicts the original answer, the responding party is *not* bound as a matter of law to the original answers. [*Williams v. American Cas. Co. of Reading* (1971) 6 C3d 266, 275, 98 CR 814, 820—D served "supplemental answers" in the middle of trial which repudiated earlier answers]

(c) [8:1126] **Motion to hold repudiated answer binding:** In lieu of simply using it for impeachment, the interrogating party may seek a court order holding the original answer *binding* on the responding party for purposes of the action. (A "reasonable and good faith attempt" to resolve the matter informally must be shown.) [CCP §§2016.040, 2030.310(b)]

In effect, this is a motion to preclude the use of the *amended* answer.

The court may grant the motion if it finds:

- The initial failure to answer the interrogatory correctly has *substantially prejudiced* the interrogating party; and
- The responding party has *failed to show substantial justification* for the incorrect answer; and
- The prejudice to the interrogating party *cannot be cured* by either a *continuance* to permit further discovery or use of the initial answer as impeachment. [CCP §2030.310(c); see *Gordon v. Sup.Ct. (U.Z. Mfg. Co.)* (1984) 161 CA3d 157, 168, 207 CR 327, 333; *People ex rel. Gov. Employees Ins. Co. v. Cruz* (2016) 244 CA4th 1184, 1194-1195, 198 CR3d 566, 575-576—court erred in deeming responses binding where moving party failed to establish prejudice or that any prejudice could not be cured]

© 2020 Thomson Reuters/The Rutter Group

1) [8:1127] **Example:** P sued Driver and Employer for personal injuries. Employer answered interrogatories stating Driver had been on errand for Employer at time of accident. Employer knew this was not true, but stated this in an effort to obtain coverage under Employer's liability insurance. Relying on this answer (indicating Driver had been acting in course and scope of employment), P did not serve Driver personally. Later, the action was dismissed against Driver for delay in service of summons. Then, Employer amended the earlier answer to *deny* Driver was acting in course and scope of employment. Held: Since P could no longer proceed against Driver, Employer would not be permitted to change its earlier admission that Driver had been acting in course and scope of employment at time of accident. [*Gordon v. Sup.Ct. (U.Z. Mfg. Co.)*, supra, 161 CA3d at 167-168, 207 CR at 333]

2) [8:1127.1] **Comment:** Interrogatory responses (original and amended) are not preclusive in the way that admissions to requests for admissions are—i.e., the responses usually may be contradicted at trial.

(d) [8:1128] **Sanctions:** The court "shall" impose a *monetary* sanction against the losing party on the above motion (¶*8:1126*) *unless* it finds that party acted "with substantial justification" or other circumstances make sanctions "unjust." [CCP §2030.310(d)]

The "substantial justification" standard is discussed at ¶*8:1964 ff.*

i. [8:1129] **Supplemental and further responses:** "Supplemental responses" refer to responses to supplemental interrogatories (CCP §2030.070, ¶*8:942*). "Further responses" means *additional* answers ordered by the court when the original responses are held inadequate—e.g., on a motion to compel (*see* ¶*8:1145 ff.*).

6. [8:1130] **Custody of Interrogatories and Responses:** The propounding party *retains* the original interrogatories (¶*8:1006*) and *receives* the original responses from the responding party (¶*8:1115*). The propounding party thus ends up with both the original questions and original answers; and must retain them until 6 months after final disposition of the action. [CCP §2030.280(b)]

a. [8:1131] **NOT filed with court:** Neither the interrogatories nor answers are filed with the court. [CCP §2030.280(a); CRC 3.250(a)(8)]

(In earlier years, these documents all ended up in the court files, making the court files unwieldy.)

b. [8:1132] **Not "lodged" with court:** Neither statute nor court rules contemplate "lodging" of interrogatories and answers, even in conjunction with a motion to compel further answers (¶*8:1145 ff.*). This is because the specific questions and answers in dispute (or a concise outline of them, ¶*8:1157.3*) must be set forth in the moving papers (¶*8:1151 ff.*); and there is no need for the remaining questions and answers to be placed before the court.

(1) [8:1133] **Compare—"lodging" of deposition transcript:** On a motion to compel answers to deposition questions, the moving party must "lodge" the relevant pages of the transcript before the hearing (*see* ¶*8:802*). This is because it is often necessary for the court to read passages before and after the specific question in order to rule on the motion. But that is not the case with interrogatory questions and answers.

[8:1134-1135] *Reserved.*

7. [8:1136] **Motion to Compel Answers:** If a party to whom interrogatories are directed either *fails* to respond at all, or responds with *objections* or *incomplete answers*, the propounding party's remedy is to seek a court order compelling answers (or further answers) to the interrogatories. [CCP §§2030.290, 2030.300]

Note that the burden is on the propounding party to enforce discovery. Otherwise, no penalty attaches either for the responding party's failure to respond or responding inadequately. [*Saxena v. Goffney* (2008) 159 CA4th 316, 334, 71 CR3d 469, 483 (citing text)]

The same procedure—a motion to compel—is used to enforce discovery where parties from whom discovery is sought fail to respond at all or where they respond with objections or incomplete answers. But there are differences in the procedural requirements, as discussed below (¶*8:1137 ff.*).

Cross-refer: The motion is governed by the rules and procedures governing motions generally; *see Ch. 9 Part I.*

a. [8:1137] **For FAILURE to respond:** If a party to whom interrogatories were directed fails to serve a timely response, the propounding party may move for an order compelling responses and for a monetary sanction. [CCP §2030.290(b); see *Sinaiko Healthcare Consulting, Inc. v. Pacific Healthcare Consultants* (2007) 148 CA4th 390, 404, 55 CR3d 751, 760 (citing text)]

The motion to compel may be heard even if *tardy responses* are served *after* the motion is filed. Unless the propounding party takes the matter off calendar, the court may determine whether the responses are legally sufficient and award sanctions for the failure to respond on time. [*Sinaiko Healthcare Consulting, Inc. v. Pacific Healthcare Consultants*, supra, 148 CA4th at 410-411, 55 CR3d at 765]

(1) [8:1138] **No time limit on motion:** The statute (CCP §2030.290) contains no time limit for a motion to compel where *no* responses have been served (i.e., no objections or answers of any kind). [*Sinaiko Healthcare Consulting, Inc. v. Pacific*

© 2020 Thomson Reuters/The Rutter Group

Healthcare Consultants, supra, 148 CA4th at 410-411, 55 CR3d at 765 (citing text)] Therefore, apparently, the only limit would be the cut-off on hearing discovery motions 15 days before trial (CCP §2024.020(a); ¶*8:445*).

[8:1139] *Reserved.*

(2) [8:1140] **Moving papers:** All that need be shown in the moving papers is that a set of interrogatories was properly served on the opposing party, that the time to respond has expired, and that no response of any kind has been served. [See *Leach v. Sup.Ct. (Markum)* (1980) 111 CA3d 902, 905-906, 169 CR 42, 44] (No separate statement is required; see CRC 3.1345(b).)

(a) [8:1140.1] **Joinder of motions against several parties?** Motions to compel compliance with separate discovery requests ordinarily should be filed separately. But they may be joined where the requests are so interrelated as to make separate motions wholly inefficient (e.g., where several defendants have all failed to answer the same set of interrogatories). However, local rules so providing appear to have been preempted by CRC 3.20(a); *see* ¶*9:13.2.*

(3) [8:1141] **No attempt to resolve informally required:** The moving party is *not* required to show a "reasonable and good faith attempt" to resolve the matter informally with opposing counsel before filing the motion. [CCP §2030.290; *Sinaiko Healthcare Consulting, Inc. v. Pacific Healthcare Consultants*, supra, 148 CA4th at 411, 55 CR3d at 766 (citing text); *Leach v. Sup.Ct. (Markum)*, supra, 111 CA3d at 906, 169 CR at 44]

(a) [8:1142] **Rationale:** The failure to timely respond *waives all objections* to the interrogatories (¶*8:1030*); so there are no issues left to "resolve" with opposing counsel. [See *Leach v. Sup.Ct. (Markum)*, supra, 111 CA3d at 906, 169 CR at 44]

➪ [8:1143] ***PRACTICE POINTER:*** Even if not required, it is good practice before filing your motion to write a letter to opposing counsel, pointing out that you have not received responses to your interrogatories and stating your intent to file the motion. Your letter may induce your opponent to answer the interrogatories promptly. And, even if it does not, it will improve your chances of getting monetary sanctions at the hearing on the motion.

(4) [8:1144] **Monetary sanctions:** The court "shall" impose a *monetary* sanction against the losing party on the motion to compel *unless* it finds that party acted "with substantial justification" or other circumstances render the sanction "unjust." [CCP §2030.290(c)] (*See further discussion at* ¶*8:1921 ff.*)

b. [8:1145] **For UNSATISFACTORY responses:** A motion to compel also lies where the party to whom the interrogatories were directed gave responses deemed improper by the propounding party; e.g., objections, or evasive or incomplete answers. [CCP §2030.300; see *Best Products, Inc. v. Sup.Ct. (Granatelli Motorsports, Inc.)* (2004) 119 CA4th 1181, 1189-1190, 15 CR3d 154, 160-161—motion to compel proper to challenge "boilerplate" responses]

(1) [8:1146] **45-day limit:** In this situation, a notice of motion to compel must be served, if at all, *within 45 days* after verified responses, or any verified supplemental responses, were served (extended under CCP §§1010.6(a)(4), 1013, if served by mail, overnight delivery, fax or electronically; *see ¶9:87 ff.*), unless the parties agree in writing to extend the time. [CCP §2030.300(c)]

Delaying the motion beyond the 45-day time limit *waives* the right to compel a further response to the interrogatories. [CCP §2030.300(c); see *Vidal Sassoon, Inc. v. Sup.Ct. (Halpern)* (1983) 147 CA3d 681, 685, 195 CR 295, 298—court *lacks jurisdiction* to order further answers after 45 days]

[8:1147] ***PRACTICE POINTER:*** This is a potential malpractice "trap." Here are some suggestions:

- First, make sure you and your client *both* review the opposing party's responses to your interrogatories *promptly* upon receipt.
- If the responses are not entirely satisfactory, put a note in your tickler file to remind yourself of the 45-day limit on a motion to compel.
- If you decide to make the motion, do so *promptly*; and watch out for the "*meet and confer*" requirement (*see ¶8:1158 ff.*) that must be satisfied *before* you file the motion.

(a) [8:1148] **Stipulations to extend time for motion:** The parties may extend the 45-day limit on making a motion to compel by *written agreement specifying* a later date. [CCP §2030.300(c)]

(b) [8:1149] **Court order extending time?** The Discovery Act omits an earlier statute that gave courts authority to extend the time for making a motion to compel. This "indicates an intention by the Legislature not to vest any authority in the court to permit discovery that is not timely made." [*Sexton v. Sup.Ct. (Mullikin Med. Ctr.)* (1997) 58 CA4th 1403, 1409-1410, 68 CR2d 708, 712 (dictum)]

Presumably, however, the court has inherent power to extend the 45-day limit *before* it expires, but that issue has not been addressed in any published opinion.

(c) [8:1150] **Relief for untimely motions?** There is no authority under the Discovery Act for relief for untimely motions to compel further responses to interrogatories.

© 2020 Thomson Reuters/The Rutter Group

Relief for untimely motions may be available, however, under CCP §473(b) based on "mistake, inadvertence or excusable neglect" (*see ¶5:282 ff.*). CCP §473(b) relief is available only where the Discovery Act contains no analogous provision for relief. [See *Zellerino v. Brown* (1991) 235 CA3d 1097, 1107, 1 CR2d 222, 228, *discussed at ¶8:10.5 ff.*]

Note: The court in *Sexton,* supra, held the 45-day time limit on motions to compel was "jurisdictional." However, the court did not discuss or consider whether relief for untimely motions was available under CCP §473(b). [*Sexton v. Sup.Ct. (Mullikin Med. Ctr.),* supra, 58 CA4th at 1409-1410, 68 CR2d at 712]

[8:1150.1-1150.4] *Reserved.*

(d) [8:1150.5] **No "second chance" to ask same questions:** The party who failed to meet the 45-day deadline cannot "reset the clock" by asking the same questions again in a later set of interrogatories. The failure *waives* the right to compel answers to those questions. [*Professional Career Colleges, Magna Institute, Inc. v. Sup.Ct. (Stewart)* (1989) 207 CA3d 490, 494, 255 CR 5, 7]

[8:1150.6] ***PRACTICE POINTER:*** Although you may not ask the same questions again in interrogatories, you may be able to use *other discovery devices* to obtain the information; e.g., depositions, RFAs, document production requests and subpoenas. [See *Carter v. Sup.Ct. (CSAA Inter-Insurance Bureau)* (1990) 218 CA3d 994, 997, 267 CR 290, 291-292 (*discussed at ¶8:521*)]

(e) [8:1150.7] **Time limit applicable where only *unverified* objections received?** CCP §2030.300(c) states that the time limit for bringing a motion to compel further responses runs from the service of a *verified* response or supplemental *verified* response. It is not clear whether the statute's 45-day period also applies to a response that is made up of only objections and therefore is not verified. There is no known authority on this point.

- [8:1150.8] **Comment:** Before 2013, the statutes applicable to interrogatories (CCP §2030.300(c)), requests for admissions (CCP §2033.290(c)) and inspection demands (CCP §2031.310(c)) all provided that a motion to compel had to be brought within 45 days of service of the "response." In 2013, the Legislature added the word "verified" to clarify that, where answers were served without verification but with a promise of service of verification in the future, the time for bringing the motion does not begin to accrue until verification is received. [See AB 1183, Sen. Jud. Comm. Bill Analysis (4/8/13)]

However, a response with nothing other than objections does not need to be verified (*see* ¶*8:1102*) and is complete as of the date of service. Therefore, a court might take the position that the 45-day clock begins ticking as of the date of service of the unverified objections. Because this issue is not free from doubt, to be safe, you should serve your motion within 45 days of service of unverified objections.

(2) [8:1151] **Separate statement of objections or disputed answers:** A notice of motion for order compelling answers must be accompanied by a *separate document* setting forth the following information, unless the court permits the moving party to submit a concise outline of the matters in dispute (*see* ¶*8:1157.3*):

- Each interrogatory (or other discovery request) to which further answer is sought, numbered and set forth *verbatim*;
- The answer or objection made by the opposing party to each such discovery request, also *verbatim*;
- The *reason* why further responses should be ordered by the court (i.e., the factual or legal reason why the objection is invalid or the answer given is incomplete);
- If necessary, the text of all definitions, instructions and other matters required to understand each discovery request and the response to it;
- Other discovery requests and responses if they are relevant to why further responses are necessary to the present discovery request; and
- A summary of any pleadings or other documents on file by the party relying on them in the present discovery dispute. [CRC 3.1345(c)]

[8:1151.1] ***PRACTICE POINTER:*** Do *not* simply include this information in your notice of motion or points and authorities. Failure to include the separate statement required by CRC 3.1345 is ground for *denial* of your motion (unless the court allows a concise outline of issues; *see* ¶*8:532.12, 8:1157.3*).

Don't overlook the tactical advantage of your separate statement. This is the major document the court will look at before reviewing opposing papers. Therefore, it is the opportunity to state the argument for your client's position succinctly and convincingly. *Avoid* generalities or reference back to arguments made in earlier papers.

© 2020 Thomson Reuters/The Rutter Group

(a) [8:1152] **Interrogatories and responses quoted verbatim:** This is required because the interrogatories and answers are not on file with the court (¶*8:1131*); and there is no provision for "lodging" these documents with the court (¶*8:1132*). Similarly, if the interrogatories and responses are quoted verbatim, there is no need to append the discovery demands and responses to the attorney's declaration filed with the motion papers.

1) [8:1153] **No incorporation by reference from other documents:** If the answer to any particular interrogatory depends on the answer given to some other interrogatory, the other interrogatory and answer must be set forth *verbatim* as well. [CRC 3.1345(c)]

Incorporation by reference is *not* allowed *except* for identical responses and reasons previously stated in the same document. [CRC 3.1345(c)]

2) [8:1154] **Grouped by subject matter:** If the disputed responses are numerous, it is good practice to group them by subject matter (e.g., all questions relating to the accident, or to damages, etc.); or, alternatively to *index* them by stating the general subject matter and, immediately thereafter, the numbers of each question relating thereto.

(b) [8:1155] **Statement of reasons:** The moving party must also include reasons why further answers should be ordered: legal or factual arguments why the answers given were incomplete or nonresponsive, or the objections invalid. [CRC 3.1345(c)]

1) [8:1156] **Pleadings or other discovery documents to be summarized:** Pleadings, evidence or other discovery documents relevant to the motion must be *summarized.* They *cannot* simply be "incorporated by reference." [CRC 3.1345(c)]

[8:1157] *Reserved.*

(c) [8:1157.1] **No other statements or summaries required:** In the past, some courts required moving and responding parties to "merge" their separate statements into a single *joint statement* (containing the question, the response, the moving party's reasons why further response is necessary, and the responding party's reasons why it is not).

However, this is not required by the CRC (and any such requirement under local rules is preempted by CRC 3.20).

[8:1157.2] ***PRACTICE POINTER:*** Even so, there is no reason why counsel cannot submit a joint statement *voluntarily.* (Counsel can exchange electronic files to facilitate its preparation.)

The judge will appreciate the effort. It will be a lot easier to rule without having to flip through two large separate documents simultaneously.

(d) [8:1157.3] **Concise outline in lieu of separate statement:** *Effective January 1, 2020*, in lieu of a separate statement, the court may in its discretion allow the moving party to submit a concise outline of the discovery request and each response in dispute. [CCP §2030.300(b)(2) (amended eff. 1/1/19; operative 1/1/20)]

The California Rules of Court have been amended to allow the concise outline. [CRC 3.1345(b) (amended eff. 1/1/20)]

[8:1157.4] ***PRACTICE POINTER:*** Following the January 1, 2020 effective date, before filing your motion to compel, find out whether the court in which the matter is pending will accept a concise outline of the matters in dispute in lieu of a separate statement. If you file a concise outline and later learn that is not permitted by the judge, your motion may be denied and it may be too late for you to file a motion with a separate statement.

FORMS

- Motion to Compel (Further) Answers to Interrogatories and for Sanctions and Proposed Order, *see Form 8:19* in Rivera, *Cal. Prac. Guide: Civ. Pro. Before Trial FORMS* (TRG).
- Separate Statement of Interrogatories and Responses in Dispute, *see Form 8:20* in Rivera, *Cal. Prac. Guide: Civ. Pro. Before Trial FORMS* (TRG).

(3) [8:1158] **Attempt to resolve informally ("meet and confer") requirement:** The motion to compel must also be accompanied by a *declaration* stating facts showing a "*reasonable and good faith attempt*" to resolve informally the issues presented by the motion *before filing the motion*. [CCP §§2016.040, 2030.300(b)(1)]

Under the Discovery Act, it is clear that no in person "meeting" is required.

The attempt to resolve informally may be made *either* by conferring "*in person*, by *telephone* or *by letter* with an opposing party or attorney." [CCP §2023.010(i) (emphasis added) (failure to make such attempt constitutes "misuse of discovery process")]

[8:1158.1] ***PRACTICE POINTER:*** A face-to-face meeting between counsel with authority to resolve the dispute is usually more effective than phone calls

© 2020 Thomson Reuters/The Rutter Group

or emails. The fewer the issues the court must deal with, the more inclined it may be to resolve those issues. You are much less likely to be sent to the jury room to "work it out" before your motion is heard.

[8:1158.2] ***FURTHER PRACTICE POINTER—INFORMAL CONFERENCE PROCEDURE:*** Parties may seek, or courts may require, an informal discovery conference with the judge before a motion is filed. *See discussion at ¶8:787.1.*

(a) [8:1159] **Purpose:** The purpose of the meet and confer requirement is to force lawyers to reexamine their positions, and to narrow their discovery disputes to the irreducible minimum, before calling upon the court to resolve the matter. It also enables parties and counsel to avoid sanctions that are likely to be imposed if the matter comes before the court. [*Stewart v. Colonial Western Agency, Inc.* (2001) 87 CA4th 1006, 1016, 105 CR2d 115, 121-122]

(b) [8:1160] **Compare—not required where motion based on failure to respond:** An "attempt to resolve informally" is not required where a party has *failed* to respond within the statutory time limit. Such failure *waives all objections* to the interrogatories (¶*8:1142*), so there are no "disputed issues" left to resolve. [See *Leach v. Sup.Ct. (Markum)* (1980) 111 CA3d 902, 906, 169 CR 42, 44]

(The party who failed to respond may seek relief from waiver *after* serving proposed responses in substantial compliance with the discovery request; *see* ¶*8:1034*.)

(c) [8:1160.1] **Caution—time trap:** Efforts to "resolve informally" do *NOT* extend the 45-day limit within which the propounding party must move for further answers. [CCP §2030.300(c); *Vidal Sassoon, Inc. v. Sup.Ct. (Halpern)* (1983) 147 CA3d 681, 683-684, 195 CR 295, 296-297; *see* ¶*8:1146*]

[8:1160.2] ***PRACTICE POINTERS:*** If the conferring process takes more than 45 days, it will be too late to file a motion to compel, *unless* you obtain a stipulation extending the time.

If you anticipate your negotiations with opposing counsel may extend beyond the 45-day period, *ask for an agreement at the outset*, extending the time for filing a motion to compel. If opposing counsel refuses, you know at the outset that you have 45 days—*and no more*—within which to act. If you wait until the end of the 45-day period to request such agreement, opposing counsel may refuse and it may then be difficult or impossible to get your motion filed in time.

(d) [8:1161] **What constitutes "reasonable and good faith attempt":** The moving party's declaration must show a "reasonable and good faith attempt" to resolve the issues informally with opposing counsel. [CCP §§2016.040, 2030.300(b); see *Clement v. Alegre* (2009) 177 CA4th 1277, 1294, 99 CR3d 791, 804—reasonable and good faith attempt at informal resolution entails something more than bickering with opposing counsel]

1) [8:1161.1] **Telephone or letter may suffice:** The attempt need not be made in person; it may be by telephone or even by letter. [CCP §2023.010(i)]

2) [8:1162] **Personal animosity no excuse:** Instructing one's paralegal to discuss the matter with opposing counsel, plus uncompleted telephone calls, have been held *not* a "reasonable" attempt to resolve disputed issues. The fact that the attorneys had a strong personal dislike for each other is no excuse. [*Volkswagenwerk Aktiengesellschaft v. Sup.Ct. (Golsch)* (1981) 122 CA3d 326, 333-334, 175 CR 888, 892-893]

3) [8:1162.1] **Factors considered:** Various factors may be considered by the court in determining whether a party made a "reasonable" and "good faith" attempt to resolve the issue informally, including:

- *Size of case, complexity of discovery:* Greater effort at informal resolution may be required in larger, more complex cases;
- *Previous relations with opposing counsel:* The history of the litigation and the nature of the interaction between counsel;
- *Present dispute:* The nature of the issues, and the type and scope of discovery requested;
- *Timing:* The time available before the motion filing deadline, and the extent to which the responding party was complicit in the lapse of available time;
- *Prospects for success:* Whether, from the perspective of a reasonable person in the position of the discovering party, additional effort appeared likely to bear fruit;
- *Evidence of discovery abuse?* When discovery requests are grossly overbroad on their face, and hence do not appear reasonably related to a legitimate discovery need, a reasonable inference can be drawn of an intent to harass and improperly burden. [*Obregon v. Sup.Ct. (Cimm's, Inc.)* (1998) 67 CA4th 424, 431, 79 CR2d 62, 66-67]

© 2020 Thomson Reuters/The Rutter Group

[8:1162.2-1162.4] *Reserved.*

4) **Application**

- [8:1162.5] P's lack of a "good faith" effort at informal resolution was shown by the following:
  — P propounded grossly overbroad interrogatories (suggesting improper motives);
  — Upon receiving D's objections, P sent a single brief letter, *late in the relevant time period,* requesting informal resolution; and
  — P's motion to compel made no effort to explain why interrogatories of such breadth were proper. [*Obregon v. Sup.Ct. (Cimm's, Inc.)*, supra, 67 CA4th at 432-433, 79 CR2d at 67]

[8:1163] ***PRACTICE POINTERS RE "REASONABLE ATTEMPT":*** The following should satisfy the "reasonable attempt" requirement. They should also help position you to obtain monetary sanctions if your motion to compel is granted; or, if you lose, to resist sanctions on the basis that there was "substantial justification" for your motion.

- **First, send a letter:** Your letter should be a "script" for the arguments you plan to make on the motion. For each item in dispute, describe the deficiencies in the responses, and cite the authorities which establish your right to discovery. (If an issue of law is involved, it is a good idea to *attach copies* of the cases you are relying on.)

  If the dispute is not resolved, this letter should be included as an exhibit to your motion to show your "reasonable and good faith attempt" to resolve the issues. With this in mind, keep the tone of your letter amicable. *Demonstrate willingness to negotiate* and to avoid unnecessary court hearings. Avoid insults or the appearance of petty bickering with opposing counsel.

- **Ask for an agreement waiving the deadline on a motion to compel:** As stated above (¶*8:1160.1*), efforts to "resolve informally" do *not* extend the 45-day deadline for filing a motion to compel. Thus, ask for an agreement at the outset to eliminate this as a problem later on, and send a letter or email confirming the agreement.

- **Follow up with telephone call or personal meeting:** Where there are numerous items in dispute or the matter is complicated, a mere exchange of letters is not likely to resolve anything.

©2020 Thomson Reuters/The Rutter Group

A "reasonable and good faith" attempt may require you to seek a meeting or telephone conference with opposing counsel. Face-to-face meetings are usually more productive than telephone conferences (due to interruptions, lack of preparation, etc.). You can use your letter as the agenda for the meeting.

- **Be prepared to give and take:** Allowing opposing counsel to "score some points" usually improves your chances to resolve the dispute. So, be willing to capitulate on less important items in order to obtain discovery on the more important. A good faith effort to resolve the dispute will enhance your position if a motion becomes necessary.
- **Offer a compromise:** If there is a middle ground and one party offers a compromise while the other maintains an all-or-nothing position, the court may adopt the compromise as being more reasonable. Even if you don't get your compromise, the court may find that you acted with substantial justification and not assess sanctions.
- **Follow up with confirming letter:** Immediately following the telephone conference or meeting, send a letter to opposing counsel stating which items in your original letter have been resolved and which have not; and if further responses have been promised, the date on which they are due. Without such a follow-up letter, your opponent may deny whatever agreements were reached. If the case goes to court, the law and motion judge will never know for sure whom to believe (impairing your chances for obtaining sanctions).
- **Provide a *detailed* declaration on your motion to compel:** Your declaration should contain each fact essential to the court's understanding of your motion and request for sanctions. *As an added benefit, the declaration does not count toward the 15-page limit on points and authorities.*

[8:1164-1173] *Reserved.*

(e) [8:1174] **Sanctions for failure to make reasonable attempt to resolve informally:** Failing to make a "reasonable and good faith attempt" to resolve the issues informally before a motion to compel is filed constitutes a "misuse of the discovery process." Monetary sanctions can be imposed against whichever party is guilty of such conduct, *even if that party wins the motion*

© 2020 Thomson Reuters/The Rutter Group

to compel. [CCP §§2023.010(i), 2023.020; *see detailed discussion at ¶8:2100 ff.*]

[8:1175-1178] *Reserved.*

(4) [8:1179] **Burden on responding party to justify objections:** If a timely motion to compel has been filed, the burden is on the responding party to justify any objection or failure fully to answer the interrogatories. [*Coy v. Sup.Ct. (Wolcher)* (1962) 58 C2d 210, 220-221, 23 CR 393, 398; *Fairmont Ins. Co. v. Sup.Ct. (Stendell)* (2000) 22 C4th 245, 255, 92 CR2d 70, 77]

[8:1179.1] ***PRACTICE POINTERS:*** If you represent the responding party, you need to prepare and file declarations and/or points and authorities. It is your job to *explain clearly* the grounds for each objection or failure to answer fully. (If you lose the motion, the court will impose monetary sanctions *unless* you show "substantial justification" for your client's position or circumstances making sanctions "unjust.")

Make sure your declarations include admissible evidence of the facts on which your objection was based (i.e., no "information and belief" allegations). If your objection is based on other discovery documents or pleadings, they should be attached or quoted verbatim.

Remember that your opposing declarations and points and authorities must be served and filed with the court at least 9 court days before the hearing on the motion. [CCP §1005(b)]

If you believe there is no substantial justification for the motion, include a request for monetary sanctions against the moving party.

Your request for sanctions should contain a *notice provision* clearly stating against whom you are seeking sanctions—opposing party, or counsel, or both (¶*8:1980 ff.*). And it must be supported by factual declarations showing the amount of sanctions sought (CCP §2023.040, ¶*8:2002*).

Even if you end up losing, the stronger your showing, the less likelihood of sanctions being awarded against you: i.e., by showing there was room for a *legitimate difference of opinion as to discoverability*, you establish "substantial justification" for your client's position (*see* ¶*8:1964*).

(5) [8:1180] **Ruling on motion to compel further answers:** The granting or denial of a motion to compel rests within the court's sound discretion.

(a) [8:1181] **Factors considered:** The ruling usually is based on consideration of the following factors:

- The relationship of the information sought to the issues framed in the pleadings;
- The likelihood that disclosure will be of practical benefit to the party seeking discovery;
- The burden or expense likely to be encountered by the responding party in furnishing the information sought. [*Columbia Broadcasting System, Inc. v. Sup.Ct. (Rolfe)* (1968) 263 CA2d 12, 19, 69 CR 348, 352]

(b) [8:1182] **Each objection considered separately:** The court must rule on each objection separately. It is an abuse of discretion to fully grant a motion to compel if *any* of the objections were valid. [*Deaile v. General Tel. Co. of Calif.* (1974) 40 CA3d 841, 851, 115 CR 582, 588]

(6) [8:1183] **Appointment of referee:** Where the motion is voluminous and complex, some courts may refer the dispute to a court commissioner, if available. If not, the court has the power to appoint a referee to hear and determine "any and all discovery motions and disputes relevant to discovery" (CCP §639(a)(5)). The power of the court to appoint discovery referees is limited by very specific requirements. *See discussion at ¶8:1803 ff.*

[8:1183.1] ***PRACTICE POINTER:*** There are pros and cons involved in using a discovery referee. On the positive side, it is likely easier to arrange for time and special briefing schedules before referees and to set longer periods for the hearings. A referee is likely to have more time to dig into the facts and attend to a long series of items. If there are many discovery disputes, the referee can provide continuity in a way the trial judge (who may be handling hundreds of cases) cannot.

On the other hand, some discovery referees may set aside exorbitant amounts of time for prehearing document review and the hearing itself, substantially increasing costs. Referee rulings are generally reviewable by the trial judge, causing delay and increased costs as a second hearing on the same issue must be briefed and heard. Some judges discourage the use of referees because discovery disputes may be an important vehicle for case management.

Usually, parties should not use a referee unless court-ordered and unless they are generally willing to follow the referee's rulings (to avoid wasting time and judicial resources in having the rulings reviewed). Consider alternative procedures wherever possible. *See discussion at ¶8:787.1.*

© 2020 Thomson Reuters/The Rutter Group

8. [8:1184] **Sanctions in Enforcing Discovery:** As with discovery procedures generally, normally only monetary sanctions can be imposed on a motion to compel where there has been no prior court order compelling discovery. *See detailed discussion at ¶8:1920 ff.*

However, once an order compelling discovery is granted (or where such order would be "futile," *see ¶8:1935*), the full range of discovery sanctions is available. *See detailed discussion at ¶8:2145 ff.*

Cross-refer: Discovery sanctions are discussed in detail at ¶*8:1900 ff.*

[8:1185-1243] *Reserved.*

9. [8:1244] **Use of Interrogatories at Trial:** Admissibility of interrogatory answers depends upon the rules of evidence generally. But it is not ground for objection that the responding party is present and available to testify at trial. [CCP §2030.410]

a. [8:1244.1] **May be used BY any party:** Answers to interrogatories may be offered in evidence against the responding party *by any other party* at time of trial. Thus, for example, admissions made by P in his or her answers to D's interrogatories can be used by other defendants as well. [CCP §2030.410]

- [8:1244.2] **Comment:** This is particularly important because each party has the right to serve only a limited number of specially prepared interrogatories ("Rule of 35 Plus"; ¶*8:935 ff.*) on each opposing party. Allowing coparties to use the answers to each other's interrogatories saves duplicating questions.

b. [8:1245] **Admissible against responding party only:** Answers to interrogatories are admissible only against the party giving the answer. [CCP §2030.410]

For example, they may be offered as *admissions* by the responding party (Ev.C. §1220) or as *prior inconsistent statements* to impeach the responding party's testimony at trial (Ev.C. §1235).

(1) [8:1246] **Hearsay as to other parties:** The answers are admissible only against the responding party, and are inadmissible hearsay as to other parties. Therefore, on proper motion, the court must limit the jury's consideration of the answers accordingly. [*Castaline v. City of Los Angeles* (1975) 47 CA3d 580, 587-588, 121 CR 786, 791]

c. [8:1247] **Answering party may rebut or explain:** Interrogatory answers are *not* preclusive. The answering party may contradict or explain the answers by introducing newly-discovered evidence, etc. [*Mason v. Marriage & Family Ctr.* (1991) 228 CA3d 537, 546, 279 CR 51, 56; see *Ahn v. Kumho Tire U.S.A., Inc.* (2014) 223 CA4th 133, 146-147, 166 CR3d 852, 863]

Compare—RFAs: The evidentiary effect of answers to RFAs is discussed at ¶*8:1387 ff.*

(1) [8:1248] **Example:** P's answers to interrogatories stated she suffered sexual injury from her psychotherapist from

"September 1977 to present." Later, in opposition to summary judgment, she gave a credible explanation why this was a mistake (her treatment began September 1977, but sexual contacts were later). She was not bound by her mistaken discovery response. [*Mason v. Marriage & Family Ctr.*, supra, 228 CA3d at 545-546, 279 CR at 55-56]

(2) [8:1249] **Exception—willfully false answers:** An order barring the testimony of a witness whose name was not revealed in answer to interrogatories is proper where (1) the failure to disclose was willful; (2) the answer impeded the other party's trial preparation; (3) a trial continuance could not cure the defect; and (4) impeachment was no remedy. [*Thoren v. Johnston & Washer* (1972) 29 CA3d 270, 274, 105 CR 276, 278]

[8:1250-1251] *Reserved.*

d. [8:1252] **Other uses of interrogatory answers:** In addition to their use as substantive evidence at trial, interrogatory answers are often used in connection with:

- Motions for *summary judgment.* [CCP §437c; see *Mason v. Marriage & Family Ctr.* (1991) 228 CA3d 537, 546, 279 CR 51, 56]
- Motions to *amend the pleadings* (e.g., to reflect new claims based on information disclosed in answers). [See *Los Angeles Cemetery Ass'n v. Sup.Ct. (Thriftimart, Inc.)* (1968) 268 CA2d 492, 494, 74 CR 97, 99]
- Motions to *quash service* (e.g., to establish or defeat claims re jurisdiction). [*Brunzell Const. Co., Inc., of Nevada v. Harrah's Club* (1964) 225 CA2d 734, 737, 37 CR 659, 660-661]
- *Demurrers.* [*Bockrath v. Aldrich Chem. Co.* (1999) 21 C4th 71, 83, 86 CR2d 846, 854—court may take judicial notice of discovery responses in ruling on demurrer]

e. [8:1253] **Evidence Exclusion Sanction for False Answers:** *See detailed discussion at ¶8:2390 ff.*

© 2020 Thomson Reuters/The Rutter Group

RESERVED

CHAPTER 8G

REQUESTS FOR ADMISSIONS

CONTENTS

© 2020 Thomson Reuters/The Rutter Group

RESERVED

REQUESTS FOR ADMISSIONS

[8:1254] **Statute:** CCP §2033.010 et seq. sets forth the rules and procedures governing requests for admissions (RFAs).

[8:1255] **Defined:** A request for admissions (RFA) is the procedure whereby one party can force another party to admit or deny the truth of any relevant fact or the genuineness of any relevant document.

[8:1256] **Purpose:** Unlike other discovery devices (e.g., interrogatories, depositions, document demands), RFAs are not designed to uncover factual information. Rather, their main purpose is to set issues at rest by compelling admission of things that cannot reasonably be controverted. [*Shepard & Morgan v. Lee & Daniel, Inc.* (1982) 31 C3d 256, 261, 182 CR 351, 353; *Murillo v. Sup.Ct. (People)* (2006) 143 CA4th 730, 735, 49 CR3d 511, 515—RFAs "serve a function similar to pleadings"; see *City of Glendale v. Marcus Cable Assocs., LLC* (2015) 235 CA4th 344, 352-353, 185 CR3d 331, 336-337; *Orange County Water Dist. v. The Arnold Eng. Co.* (2018) 31 CA5th 96, 115, 242 CR3d 350, 365—primary purpose of RFAs "is to set at rest triable issues so that they will not have to be tried; they are aimed at expediting trial" (internal quotes and citation omitted)]

Even so, the Discovery Act makes clear that RFAs can also be used to *discover* evidence: "Any party may *obtain discovery* by . . . Requests for Admissions . . . ." [CCP §2019.010(e) (emphasis added)]

STRATEGIES AND TACTICS RE RFAs

[8:1257] RFAs are one of the most potent discovery weapons because whatever is admitted is *preclusive*; and denials may result in an *award of costs of proof* if they turn out to be false.

[8:1258] **Advantages**

- **Creates *preclusive* admissions:** Answers to interrogatories and deposition questions can always be changed or explained. However RFAs are *preclusive* (unless the court permits an admission to be withdrawn or "interprets" it so as to limit its effect; *see* ¶*8:1387 ff.*).

  ☞ ***PRACTICE POINTER:*** Thus, one important use of RFAs is to *solidify* information obtained through other discovery. For example, if you've obtained a damaging admission from the opposing party in a deposition or in answers to interrogatories, *follow up* with an RFA on the same point. This will prevent any changes or waffling on the point. Make sure your request uses the *exact* wording obtained in the answer to the deposition question or interrogatory (to avoid quibbles in the response and the need to send out further requests).

- **Chance for immediate win:** If your opponent admits key facts,

© 2020 Thomson Reuters/The Rutter Group

STRATEGIES AND TACTICS RE RFAs (Cont'd)

you may be in a position to move for a summary judgment (or at least a summary adjudication on the cause of action to which the facts relate).

- **Denial sets up possible shifting of costs and expenses of proof:** RFAs force your opponents to take a good hard look at whether they have the evidence to back up their claims or defenses. If they stall by refusing to admit matters that are beyond *reasonable* dispute, they run the risk of serious *shifting of costs and expenses of proof* (*¶8:1404 ff.*).

  PRACTICE POINTER: For this reason, it is a good idea to serve RFAs *even on matters you expect will be denied.* Doing so costs very little. And, if you win at trial, the burden will be on the responding party to prove "good reason" for the denial; otherwise, you will be entitled to your litigation expenses to the extent attributable to proving these matters at trial (*see ¶8:1406 ff.*).

- **May establish genuineness of documents:** RFAs may be used to have your opponent concede the genuineness of documents, an important concession that can be used in summary judgment (and other) motions, as well as at trial.

[8:1259] **Disadvantages**

- **Limited number:** Like interrogatories, RFAs are subject to the "Rule of 35 plus" (*see ¶8:1269*).
- **Rarely dispositive:** As a practical matter, the *important* facts in a case are usually legitimately disputed, so they cannot be resolved by RFAs. RFAs are useful therefore only as to matters of lesser importance (for which they may not be necessary, since unimportant matters can usually be handled by stipulation with opposing counsel).
- **Equivocal denials and stalling:** The responding party may seek to avoid an admission with an equivocal denial. This forces the requesting party to seek a court order; and courts usually give the responding party another chance to respond. This means a lot of time and effort may have to be expended to force the admission.

1. [8:1260] **WHEN RFAs May be Served:** RFAs may be served any time during the lawsuit, subject to the following limitations:

   a. [8:1261] **"Hold" on plaintiff's discovery at outset:** As with interrogatories (*¶8:906*), plaintiff is barred from serving RFAs without leave of court during the first *10 days* after service of summons on the defendant or defendant's appearance in the action. The court may grant leave to serve RFAs at an earlier time based on a showing of "good cause." [CCP §2033.020(b), (d)]

      This does not bar defendant from serving RFAs during this period. [CCP §2033.020(a)]

[8:1261.1] Exception: In *unlawful detainer actions*, the "hold" on plaintiff's discovery is only 5 days. [CCP §2033.020(c)]

b. [8:1262] **"Cut-off" at end of suit:** As with depositions and interrogatories, there is a "cut-off" on the RFA process as the case approaches trial:

- A 30-day before the initial trial date deadline on "completing" discovery (meaning responses must be due by that date); and
- A 15-day before the initial trial date deadline on the right to have motions concerning RFAs heard. [CCP §2024.020(a); *discussed at ¶8:445, 8:909*]

[8:1262.1] Exceptions: The discovery cut-off dates are earlier in cases *judicially arbitrated* and later in *unlawful detainer* actions (*see ¶8:910*). Also, of course, court orders may be obtained to complete discovery or have a motion heard after the cut-off dates shown above (¶*8:1262*). [CCP §2024.050(a); *see* ¶*8:457*]

2. [8:1263] **On WHOM RFAs May be Served:** RFAs may be served on "any other party to the action," thus including coparties, as well as adverse parties. [CCP §2033.010]

a. [8:1264] **Parties to complaint serving parties to cross-complaint?** Whether "any other party to the action" includes parties to a cross-complaint is not entirely clear. (For example, P sues D; D cross-complains against TP; can P and TP serve RFAs on each other?)

For pleading purposes, a cross-complaint is regarded as an independent proceeding, *not* part of the same "action" as the complaint (¶*6:503*). So, absent any pleading relationship, P and TP arguably should *not* have the right to serve requests upon each other.

This same issue exists with interrogatories (*see* ¶*8:922*). But there is another argument against allowing RFAs in such cases: Admissions made by D in the main action (P vs. D) are *not binding* on D in the cross-action (D vs. TP); *see* ¶*8:1394*. Presumably, therefore, P and TP are not entitled to serve RFAs on each other.

3. [8:1265] **Propounding Requests:** The following rules govern the form, content and number of RFAs that may be served:

a. [8:1266] **Official Form:** The Judicial Council has been directed to "develop and approve official form . . . requests for admission" for use in the most common civil actions: personal injury, wrongful death, property damage, breach of contract, fraud, unlawful detainer and family law. Use of this form is strictly optional and does not preclude serving different or additional requests. [CCP §2033.710 et seq.]

So far, the Judicial Council has approved only a skeleton form Request for Admissions. It is not tailored to any particular type of action. (Comment: As a practical matter, it is questionable whether meaningful RFAs *can* be devised on an "official form" basis.)

© 2020 Thomson Reuters/The Rutter Group

FORM: Official Form Request for Admissions (DISC-020), *see Form 8:22* in Rivera, *Cal. Prac. Guide: Civ. Pro. Before Trial FORMS* (TRG).

b. [8:1267] **Number of requests:** The number of RFAs permitted depends on the type of admission requested:

(1) [8:1268] **NO limit on RFAs re genuineness of documents:** There is *no* limit on the number of requests that can be made relating to the *genuineness of documents.* [CCP §2033.030(a)] (Protective orders are available for excessive requests; *see ¶8:1303.*)

(2) [8:1269] **"Rule of 35 PLUS" as to other requests:** As to matters other than the genuineness of documents, however, the "Rule of 35 PLUS" applies: A party has the *right* to serve up to 35 requests on *each* other party. These can be served in one or several sets. [CCP §2033.030(a)]

Unlike interrogatories, Official Form RFAs *do* count against the 35 limit. (Another reason they are not likely to be used.) [CCP §2033.030]

(a) [8:1269.1] **Separate limit for each party:** A separate 35 RFAs may be served *by each* coparty and *to each* opposing party. *See ¶8:937 ff.*

(b) [8:1269.2] **Effect of exceeding limit:** Unless a "declaration of necessity" is attached (*¶8:1270 ff.*), the responding party must answer the first 35 RFAs (no picking and choosing the easiest questions). An *objection* can be stated to the balance. [CCP §2033.030(b); *see ¶8:939 ff.*]

(c) [8:1270] **"Declaration of necessity" for additional RFAs:** If more than 35 RFAs (not relating to genuineness of documents) are sought, the propounding party must serve a "declaration of necessity." [CCP §2033.030(b)]

1) [8:1270.1] **Ground:** The sole ground for such declaration is that the excess RFAs are justified by the "*complexity* or the *quantity of the existing and potential issues* in the particular case." [CCP §2033.040(a) (emphasis added)]

(**Compare—interrogatories:** Excess interrogatories are authorized also on grounds of "financial burden" or "expedience"; *see ¶8:949.1.* But these grounds do *not* apply to RFAs.)

2) [8:1271] **Form and content:** Except for the statement of grounds (*¶8:1270.1*), the form and content of the "Declaration for Additional Discovery" is the same as discussed in connection with interrogatories, at *¶8:949 ff.*

3) [8:1271.1] **How challenged:** The responding party may challenge the "declaration of necessity" by motion

for protective order, on the ground the number of RFAs is unwarranted. [CCP §2033.040(a)]

Such motion places the *burden on the propounding party* to justify the number of RFAs served. [CCP §2033.040(b); *see* ¶*8:955*]

c. [8:1272] **Format of RFAs:** The requests must comply with the following rules:

(1) [8:1273] **Separate from other discovery methods:** RFAs must be set forth in a *separate document*. They may not be combined with interrogatories or any other discovery method. [CCP §2033.060(h)]

[8:1274] *Reserved.*

➪ [8:1275] ***PRACTICE POINTER:*** Although RFAs and interrogatories may not be combined in the same document, it is still good practice to serve interrogatories coordinated with RFAs (*see* ¶*8:965*).

(2) [8:1276] **Opening paragraph:** The first paragraph immediately below the title of the case must show:

- The identity of the party requesting admissions;
- The set number (each set to be numbered consecutively); and
- The identity of the party to whom the requests are directed. [CCP §2033.060(a), (b)]

(a) [8:1277] **Example:** "PLAINTIFF JOHN SMITH'S SECOND SET OF REQUESTS FOR ADMISSIONS TO DEFENDANT HARRY BROWN"

(3) [8:1278] **Question numbering:** Each RFA must be identified by letter or number. [CCP §2033.060(c)]

➪ [8:1278.1] ***PRACTICE POINTER:*** Although there is no requirement that RFAs be numbered consecutively from set to set, doing so is a good idea. For example, if the first set contained Requests 1-10, start the second set with Request 11.

FORM: Attorney-Drafted Requests for Admissions, *see Form 8:23* in Rivera, *Cal. Prac. Guide: Civ. Pro. Before Trial FORMS* (TRG).

[8:1279-1280] *Reserved.*

d. [8:1281] **Each request separate and complete:** Each RFA shall be "separately set forth" and shall be "full and complete in and of itself." [CCP §2033.060(c)-(d)]

(1) [8:1282] **No subparts:** See discussion in connection with interrogatories, ¶*8:974 ff.* [CCP §2033.060(f)]

© 2020 Thomson Reuters/The Rutter Group

(2) [8:1283] **No "compound, conjunctive or disjunctive" requests:** See discussion of "and/or" questions in connection with interrogatories, ¶*8:978 ff.* [CCP §2033.060(f)]

(3) [8:1284] **No preface or instructions:** See discussion in connection with interrogatories, ¶*8:967 ff.* [CCP §2033.060(d)]

(4) [8:1285] **Specially defined terms:** Any term with a special definition must be typed in CAPITAL LETTERS whenever the term appears. See discussion in connection with interrogatories, ¶*8:970 ff.* [CCP §2033.060(e)]

(5) [8:1286] **Documents attached:** If the request is for admission of genuineness of documents, copies of the documents must be attached to the request. [CCP §2033.060(g)]

(a) [8:1287] **Originals to be available for inspection:** The requesting party must also make the originals available for inspection by the party to whom the requests are directed. [CCP §2033.060(g)]

Comment: Of course, this would not apply where the original is held by the responding party or some third party. But counsel should establish this by interrogatories or other discovery device *before* seeking admission of the document's genuineness.

[8:1287.1] ***PRACTICE POINTER:*** Keep your RFAs *as simple as possible* so there will be no room for denial or evasion. This will avoid objections on the ground of "compound and conjunctive" (¶*8:1283*). (It may run up the *number* of RFAs you need to serve, but you can use a "declaration of necessity" for more than 35 requests if need be; ¶*8:1270 ff.*)

Keep in mind that any admission obtained will probably be construed *narrowly* (*see* ¶*8:1390.2*). So, make sure there is no room for quibbling as to what was admitted.

For example, *instead* of asking:

"You are requested to admit that . . .

"5. Defendant Mary Smith was driving an automobile registered to defendant John Jones in the course and scope of her employment by John Jones at the time of the accident" . . .

Ask the following *separate* RFAs:

"You are requested to admit that . . .

"6. Defendant Mary Smith was operating a . . . (year) Buick, California License No. 3B77024, at the time and place of the accident described in the complaint.

"7. The automobile was registered at the time of the accident to defendant John Jones.

"8. Defendant Mary Smith was an employee of defendant John Jones at the time of the accident.

"9. Defendant Mary Smith was performing acts within the course and scope of her employment by Jones at the time and place of the accident."

e. [8:1288] **Content of request:** RFAs may be used as to any matter within the permissible scope of discovery: i.e., "relevant to the subject matter of the action" (CCP §2017.010, ¶*8:66 ff.*); and not otherwise privileged or protected from discovery. [CCP §2033.010]

(1) [8:1289] **Genuineness of documents:** RFAs are commonly used to establish the genuineness of specified documents. [See CCP §2033.010]

(2) [8:1290] **Factual matters:** Likewise, RFAs are commonly used to establish the truth of specified facts: e.g., due execution of documents; ownership of vehicles; dates of transactions, etc. [CCP §2033.010]

(a) [8:1291] **To obtain discovery of facts:** The Discovery Act expressly authorizes use of RFAs for *discovery* purposes rather than merely to obtain admissions. [CCP §2019.010(e); *see* ¶*8:1256*]

1) [8:1292] Thus, properly worded RFAs may force the opposing party to *disclose* evidence. For example:

"You are requested to admit that . . .

— "Your vehicle was travelling at 65 miles per hour immediately prior to the impact";

— "Witness Jones is the only person known by you to have observed the accident other than the parties to this action"; or

— "You presently have no knowledge of any fact to support the allegations in Paragraph . . . of your complaint."

[8:1293] ***PRACTICE POINTER:*** *Use such requests.* Reason: If denied, they may set the stage for *shifting of costs and expenses of proof* for failure to admit.

They can also be used as the foundation for a *motion for summary judgment* or summary adjudication. I.e., the opponent's admissions that it has *no evidence* on a particular point may satisfy your burden of proof on a summary judgment motion to show no triable issue of fact (*see* ¶*10:223, 10:242*).

Finally, such admissions could expose the opponent to sanctions (including terminating sanctions) under CCP §128.7 for asserting a claim or defense without evidentiary support (*see* ¶*9:1135*).

© 2020 Thomson Reuters/The Rutter Group

[8:1293.1] ***FURTHER PRACTICE POINTER:*** There is even an advantage to propounding RFAs you expect will be denied. If you serve RFAs simultaneously with Official Form Interrogatories—General (DISC-001), you can use "Interrogatory 17.1" which, in effect, provides 35 additional contention interrogatories that are not included in the limit of 35 "specially prepared" interrogatories (*see ¶8:934.3*). Other specialized interrogatories (e.g., for employment law (DISC-002)) contain a similar interrogatory to be served with RFAs.

(3) [8:1294] **Opinions:** RFAs may properly be used to establish an "opinion relating to fact." [CCP §2033.010]

- [8:1295] For example, parties may be required to admit or deny the *value* of property in dispute. "The fact that the request . . . calls for an opinion is of no moment." [*Cembrook v. Sup.Ct. (Sterling Drug, Inc.)* (1961) 56 C2d 423, 430, 15 CR 127, 131]
- [8:1296] Likewise, a party may be required to admit or deny that the contours of certain land "differed" from its original contours, and that there was a "greater probability" of landsliding than previously. [*Chodos v. Sup.Ct. (Lowe)* (1963) 215 CA2d 318, 321, 30 CR 303, 305]
- [8:1296.1] Also, a party may be required to admit or deny that the boundary lines between plaintiffs' and defendants' property are "accurately described" in plaintiffs' deed. [*Bloxham v. Saldinger* (2014) 228 CA4th 729, 750, 175 CR3d 650, 667]

(4) [8:1297] **Matters in controversy:** An RFA may properly relate to a matter that is in controversy between the parties. [CCP §2033.010]

Thus, P's request that D admit that "D was driving in excess of the posted speed limit at time and place of accident" is *proper*. "The fact that the request is for the admission of a controversial matter . . . is of no moment." [*Cembrook v. Sup.Ct. (Sterling Drug, Inc.)*, supra, 56 C2d at 429, 15 CR at 130]

Indeed, requests may be served asking for matters which, if admitted or deemed true (by failure to respond), would result in the unconditional surrender of the party on whom they are served. E.g., "Admit you have absolutely no grounds to prosecute (or defend) this case." [See *Demyer v. Costa Mesa Mobile Home Estates* (1995) 36 CA4th 393, 395-396, 42 CR2d 260, 261, fn. 8 (disapproved on other grounds by *Wilcox v. Birtwhistle* (1999) 21 C4th 973, 983, 90 CR2d 260, 267, fn. 12)]

[8:1298] ***PRACTICE POINTER:*** Requests of this type are usually not made with the expectation that an admission will be made. Rather, the purpose is to set the stage for a CCP §2033.420 *shifting of costs and expenses of proof* (*discussed at ¶8:1404 ff.*), which is one of the unique advantages of this discovery tool.

(5) [8:1299] **Legal conclusions:** An RFA may also require an "application of law to fact." [CCP §2033.010]

(a) [8:1300] **Examples:** Thus, a party may be required to admit or deny who is the "owner" of property; or whether the driver of a car had the owner's "permission or consent"; or whether specified acts were "negligent"; or whether a third person was an "authorized agent" or was acting in the "course and scope of employment," etc. [See *Burke v. Sup.Ct. (Fidelity & Deposit Co. of Maryland)* (1969) 71 C2d 276, 280, 78 CR 481, 487—whether attachment levy was "regular on its face"; and *Garcia v. Hyster Co.* (1994) 28 CA4th 724, 735, 34 CR2d 283, 289—whether employer was "negligent" and whether such negligence was "legal cause" of P's injuries]

(b) [8:1301] **Purpose:** Each of the foregoing involves some legal conclusion; e.g., "ownership" may depend on the validity of deeds, inheritance rights of third parties, etc.

But if a party could not be forced to admit that another is the "owner" of property, or was "acting in the course and scope of employment," these issues would have to go to trial. Forcing such admissions often leads to early dismissals or summary judgments.

(c) [8:1301.1] **Comment:** This may pose problems if the responding party in good faith is unable to characterize the transaction as requested. E.g., a responding party can be subject to a shifting of costs and expenses of proof if he or she wrongly refuses to admit "ownership" of property—even if his or her denial was based on good faith interpretation of a deed, etc. (¶*8:1408 ff.*).

[8:1301.2] ***PRACTICE POINTER:*** If you represent the responding party in such a case, consider using a denial on the basis of *inability* to admit or deny, *stating the reasons* in detail (*see* ¶*8:1341*). It is unlikely that a shifting of costs and expenses of proof would be imposed under such circumstances *unless* there is no reasonable basis for the denial (¶*8:1408 ff.*).

f. [8:1302] **Serving RFAs:** Copies of the RFAs must be served on the party to whom directed and all other parties who have appeared in the action. [CCP §2033.070]

(Only copies are served; the originals are retained by the requesting party, just as with interrogatories. *See* ¶*8:1366*.)

© 2020 Thomson Reuters/The Rutter Group

4. [8:1303] **Protective Orders:** Instead of responding, the party to whom RFAs have been directed may promptly move for a protective order. [CCP §2033.080]

   a. [8:1303.1] **Grounds for relief:** For "good cause" shown, the court may make whatever order justice requires to protect a party against "unwarranted annoyance, embarrassment, oppression or *undue burden and expense.*" [CCP §2033.080(b) (emphasis added)]

      Stated even more simply, courts are authorized to issue protective orders "based on justice and equity." [*Brigante v. Huang* (1993) 20 CA4th 1569, 1582, 25 CR2d 354, 363 (disapproved on other grounds by *Wilcox v. Birtwhistle* (1999) 21 C4th 973, 983, 90 CR2d 260, 267, fn. 12)]

      (1) [8:1303.2] **To challenge "declaration of necessity" for additional requests:** A motion for protective order also lies to challenge a "declaration of necessity" served with more than 35 RFAs (other than relating to genuineness of documents; *see ¶8:1270*). The motion places in issue whether the additional discovery requests are justified. [CCP §2033.080(b)(2)]

      (2) [8:1303.3] **Where counsel unable to locate client:** A protective order based on "oppression" may issue to delay or excuse responses where counsel for the party to whom the RFAs are directed is unable to locate his or her client. [*Brigante v. Huang*, supra, 20 CA4th at 1583, 25 CR2d at 363]

      The court must be satisfied that (a) such party is *not evading* the lawsuit or the discovery demand and is unaware of their pendency, and (b) reasonable efforts have been made and are ongoing to find that party and apprise him or her of the litigation and the discovery obligation it entails. [*Brigante v. Huang*, supra, 20 CA4th at 1583, 25 CR2d at 363]

   b. [8:1304] **Procedure:** A noticed motion is required (no ex parte protective orders). The moving papers must include a declaration showing a "reasonable and good faith attempt" to resolve the matter outside court. [CCP §§2016.040, 2033.080(a)]

      Cross-refer: The motion is governed by the rules and procedures governing motions generally; *see Ch. 9 Part I.*

      (1) [8:1304.1] **Timeliness:** The motion must be made "*promptly*" (CCP §2033.080(a)), and *before expiration* of the 30-day period within which to respond (otherwise, grounds for objection may be waived; *see ¶8:1367 ff.*). [CCP §2033.280(a)]

      (2) [8:1304.2] **Burden of proof on motion:** As with motions generally, the burden is on the party seeking relief (moving party). Competent evidence showing "good cause" for the relief sought is required.

(a) [8:1304.3] **Exception—propounding party's burden to justify more than 35 RFAs:** Where more than 35 RFAs (other than relating to genuineness of documents) have been served with a "declaration of necessity," and the responding party seeks a protective order on the ground the number is excessive, the burden is on the propounding party to justify the number served. [CCP §2033.040(b)]

Cross-refer: See further discussion of procedure on motion for protective orders in connection with interrogatories at ¶*8:1013 ff.*

c. [8:1305] **Relief available:** For "good cause shown," the court may make whatever order justice requires, including:

- *Excusing* answers to any or all requests;
- Finding the number of RFAs (not relating to genuineness of documents) "unwarranted" despite representations made in the "declaration of necessity" (thus excusing any duty to answer some or all of the excess number served);
- *Extending time* for answering the requests;
- Excusing admission of *confidential information* (trade secrets, etc.) or providing it shall be admitted only in a certain way;
- Ordering that some or all of the answers be sealed and thereafter opened only on court order. [CCP §2033.080(b); see *Brigante v. Huang* (1993) 20 CA4th 1569, 1583, 25 CR2d 354, 363 (disapproved on other grounds by *Wilcox v. Birtwhistle* (1999) 21 C4th 973, 983, 90 CR2d 260, 267, fn. 12)—court's discretion not limited to remedies enumerated in statute]

[8:1305.1] ***PRACTICE POINTER:*** It's rare that responding to RFAs is "burdensome and oppressive." But if it is, you can simply *object* on this ground (*see* ¶*8:1355*). You do not have to move for a protective order (except to challenge a "declaration of necessity" for more than 35 requests).

Objections save the large expenditure of time and money required to obtain a protective order. They also put the burden on the propounding party to file a motion to compel.

Cross-refer: See discussion of "Strategies and Tactics re Protective Orders" in connection with interrogatories at ¶*8:1020 ff.*

d. [8:1306] **Monetary sanction against losing party:** The court "shall" impose a *monetary sanction* against the losing party on the motion for protective order, *unless* it finds that party made or opposed the motion "with substantial justification" or other circumstances render sanctions "unjust." [CCP §2033.080(d); *see* ¶*8:2070 ff.*]

5. [8:1307] **Responses to RFAs:** Unless excused by protective order (¶*8:1303 ff.*), the party to whom RFAs are directed is under a duty to respond thereto. The responses must be:

© 2020 Thomson Reuters/The Rutter Group

- Timely (¶*8:1308*);
- In the proper format (¶*8:1315 ff.*); and
- Under oath (¶*8:1360*). [CCP §§2033.210-2033.250]

a. [8:1308] **Time limit for response:** The responses are due within *30 days* from the date the RFAs were served (extended for service by mail, overnight delivery or fax or electronically per CCP §§1010.6(a)(4), 1013; *see* ¶*9:87 ff.*). [CCP §§2033.250, 2016.050]

Exception: In *unlawful detainer* actions, responses are due within *5 days* after service (unless the time is extended or shortened by court order). [CCP §2033.250]

If the last day falls on a weekend or holiday, the time limit is extended to the next court day closer to the trial date. [CCP §2016.060]

(1) [8:1309] **Court may extend or shorten time:** The court has power to extend the time for response, on motion of the party to whom the RFAs are directed. (It also has power to shorten the period, on motion of the requesting party; but this is rarely done.) [CCP §2033.250]

- [8:1310] An extension apparently *cannot* be granted *ex parte*. A noticed motion is required for this purpose. (See discussion in connection with interrogatories, ¶*8:1026*.)

  Comment: The more complex the RFAs, the more likely a court will grant an extension. (The propounding party should keep this in mind and should be prepared to stipulate accordingly.)

(2) [8:1311] **Agreements extending time:** Likewise, the propounding and responding parties may agree to extend the time for responses to some or all of the RFAs served. Where this occurs, it is the responding party's obligation to notify all other parties to the action accordingly. [CCP §2033.260(a), (d)]

(a) [8:1312] **Written confirmation required:** The agreement may be informal, but it must be confirmed in a writing (e.g., letter or email from one counsel to the other) that *specifies the extended date* for response. [CCP §2033.260(b)]

(b) [8:1313] **Includes right to object:** Unless it expressly provides *otherwise*, an agreement extending time to "respond" reserves the right to object to any request. [CCP §2033.260(c)]

(3) [8:1314] **Effect of late response:** The effect of delay or failure to respond to RFAs is discussed at ¶*8:1367*.

b. [8:1314.1] **Separate vs. joint response:** The statute requires the party to whom RFAs have been directed to respond "separately" to each request. [CCP §2033.210(a)]

© 2020 Thomson Reuters/The Rutter Group

But where *identical RFAs* are served on coparties, they may properly respond in a single document *provided each verifies* the answers. To require a separate piece of paper from each coparty would exalt form over substance. [*Tobin v. Oris* (1992) 3 CA4th 814, 829, 4 CR2d 736, 745 (disapproved on other grounds by *Wilcox v. Birtwhistle* (1999) 21 C4th 973, 90 CR2d 260)]

c. **Format of response**

(1) [8:1315] **Opening paragraph:** The first paragraph immediately below the title of the case must show:

- The identity of the responding party;
- The identity of the propounding party; and
- The set number of the party's requests being responded to (CCP §2033.210(c)); and
- If a further response, it must so state. [CRC 3.1000(a)]

(a) [8:1316] **Example:** "DEFENDANT TOM BROWN'S SUPPLEMENTAL RESPONSES TO PLAINTIFF JANET SMITH'S REQUESTS FOR ADMISSIONS, SET NO. 2"

[8:1317] *Reserved.*

(2) [8:1318] **Numbering:** Each response (whether admission, denial or objection) shall bear the same number or letter as the RFA to which it pertains. [CCP §2033.210(d)]

(3) [8:1319] **Request need not be repeated:** The text of the RFA need not be repeated in the response (except as may be required with electronic exchange of requests and responses, ¶*8:1320*). [CCP §2033.210(d) (amended eff. 1/1/20)]

(4) [8:1320] **Electronic exchange of requests and responses:** Upon request, a party must provide the document *propounding* RFAs in electronic format within three court days of the request. If this is provided, the responding party must include the text of the request preceding any response. Upon request, a party *responding* to the RFAs must provide the responses to the propounding party in an electronic format within three court days of the request. [CCP §2033.210(e)(1), (2), (6) (all added eff. 1/1/20)]

FORM: Response to Requests for Admissions, *see Form 8:24* in Rivera, *Cal. Prac. Guide: Civ. Pro. Before Trial FORMS* (TRG).

d. [8:1321] **Answers:** The response must contain either an answer or an objection to the particular RFA. [CCP §2033.210(b)]

Each answer "shall be *as complete and straightforward* as the information reasonably available to the responding party permits." [CCP §2033.220(a) (emphasis added)]

Thus, absent an objection (¶*8:1349*), the response must contain one of the following:

© 2020 Thomson Reuters/The Rutter Group

- An *admission;*
- A *denial;*
- A statement *claiming inability* to admit or deny. [CCP §2033.220(b)]

(Remember that all responses must be *under oath*, CCP §2033.240(a), ¶*8:1360*.)

(1) [8:1322] **Admissions:** If any portion of the RFA is true, the party to whom it is directed must admit that portion: "Each answer shall . . . [a]dmit so much of the matter involved in the request as is true, either as expressed in the request itself or as reasonably and clearly qualified by the responding party." [CCP §2033.220(b)(1)]

(a) [8:1323] **Answering RFAs only partially correct:** The answer must be "as complete and straightforward" as the information available *reasonably permits* and must *"[a]dmit* so much of the matter involved in the request as is true . . . or *as reasonably and clearly qualified* by the responding party." [CCP §2033.220(a), (b)(1) (emphasis added)]

1) [8:1323.1] **Example:** An RFA asked plaintiff to "Admit you attended a meeting with [Party Y] on or about January 13, 2006." She responded: "Admit. [Party X] was also present." Plaintiff's response "admitted the statement and was not improper." [*St. Mary v. Sup.Ct. (Schellenberg)* (2014) 223 CA4th 762, 781, 167 CR3d 517, 532]

2) [8:1323.2] **Example:** General Contractor served Subcontractor with RFAs that referred to a *written* contract between them requiring specified acts of performance by Subcontractor. Subcontractor admitted the matters described in the RFA, including the existence of a written contract. At trial, however, he sought to offer proof that there was no written contract. Subcontractor was bound by his admission that a written contract existed. [*Valerio v. Andrew Youngquist Const.* (2002) 103 CA4th 1264, 1271, 127 CR2d 436, 441]

Comment: If Subcontractor wanted to preserve the issue, he should have admitted the truthfulness of the specified acts of performance but denied the portion of the RFA that referred to a written contract. [See CCP §2033.220(a), (b)(1)]

3) [8:1324] **Comment:** It is unclear whether a responding party must *supply facts necessary* to make an RFA true. For example:

RFA asks Defendant to admit she was the "*owner* of the *2002 Honda* California License No. 2ABC627 involved in the accident described in the complaint."

If Defendant's car was a 2001 model (instead of 2002), she should answer by stating "Admitted, except that the car is a 2001 model, not 2002."

The harder question is whether she must volunteer facts *not directly asked* in the request; e.g., that she is not the sole "owner" and that a *third party* is a *co-owner* of the car? Future case law may flesh out the responding party's obligations in this situation.

(b) [8:1325] **Evidentiary effect of admission:** *See ¶8:1387 ff.*

(c) [8:1326] **Amending or withdrawing admission:** *See ¶8:1386 ff.*

[8:1327-1330] *Reserved.*

(2) [8:1331] **Denials:** Alternatively, the responding party may "deny so much of the matter involved in the request as is untrue." [CCP §2033.220(b)(2)]

[8:1332] **Comment:** This must be read in conjunction with the requirement that the answer be "as *complete and straightforward* as the information reasonably available to the responding party permits" (CCP §2033.220(a) (emphasis added)). The responding party should not deny based solely on quibbles with the wording of the request. It may be improper to deny an RFA outright if the request is at least *partially true* (*¶8:1324*).

(a) [8:1332.1] **Must be unequivocal:** A denial of all or any portion of the request must be unequivocal. [See *American Federation of State, County & Municipal Employees v. Metropolitan Water Dist. of Southern Calif.* (2005) 126 CA4th 247, 268, 24 CR3d 285, 300 (citing text)]

But reasonable qualifications and explanations are not improper (*St. Mary v. Sup.Ct. (Schellenberg)* (2014) 223 CA4th 762, 780-781, 167 CR3d 517, 532 (citing text)):

- [8:1333] Denial "on advice of counsel" is unequivocal, "in spite of the rather weaseling qualification." [*Holguin v. Sup.Ct. (Hoage)* (1972) 22 CA3d 812, 820, 99 CR 653, 657, fn. 9]
- [8:1334] "As framed, denied" is also unequivocal. [*Smith v. Circle P Ranch Co., Inc.* (1978) 87 CA3d 267, 275, 150 CR 828, 833]
- [8:1334.1] Denial following the "boilerplate" statement "without waiving these objections" was unequivocal, justifying cost-of-proof sanctions. [*American Federation*

© 2020 Thomson Reuters/The Rutter Group

of State, County & Municipal Employees v. Metropolitan Water Dist. of Southern Calif., supra, 126 CA4th at 268, 24 CR3d at 300]

(b) [8:1335] **Denials on "information and belief":** (Example: "D denies Request No. 3 *based on information and belief* that the matter stated is not true.")

- [8:1336] In the past at least, courts permitted this form of denial to RFAs. [*Chodos v. Sup.Ct. (Lowe)* (1963) 215 CA2d 318, 322, 30 CR 303, 305; and see *Cohen v. Sup.Ct. (Gonzalez)* (1976) 63 CA3d 184, 187, 133 CR 575, 577]
- [8:1337] Whether the Discovery Act changes this rule is unclear. Arguably, a denial based "on information and belief" is *not* "straightforward" (as required by CCP §2033.220(a), ¶*8:1321*) because no one knows what "information" the responding party was relying on.

[8:1338-1339] *Reserved.*

1) [8:1340] **Compare—denials for LACK of information and belief:** A denial based on *lack* of information and belief is, in effect, a sworn statement of *inability* to admit or deny. It is clearly proper provided it meets the requirements discussed below (¶*8:1341 ff.*).

(3) [8:1341] **Claimed inability to admit or deny; reasonable inquiry required:** In lieu of admitting or denying the RFA, a party may respond by claiming *inability* (lack of sufficient information) to admit or deny the matter stated in the request. [CCP §2033.220(c)]

But a party responding in this manner *must also state that a reasonable inquiry was made* to obtain sufficient information: i.e., "a reasonable inquiry concerning the matter in the particular request has been made, and that the information known or *readily obtainable* is insufficient to enable that party to admit the matter." [CCP §2033.220(c) (emphasis added)]

(a) [8:1342] **Reasonable inquiry from available sources:** The Discovery Act thus requires the responding party to undertake a "good faith" obligation to investigate sources *reasonably available* to him or her in formulating answers to RFAs (similar to the duty owed in responding to interrogatories; ¶*8:1054*). [CCP §2033.220(c); see *Chodos v. Sup.Ct. (Lowe)* (1963) 215 CA2d 318, 322, 30 CR 303, 305]

(b) **Application**

- [8:1343] Information known to a party's *attorney* or *expert witnesses* is deemed "obtainable" by the party. Therefore, responses to RFAs must be made in light of such information. [*Chodos v. Sup.Ct. (Lowe)*, supra, 215 CA2d at 323-324, 30 CR at 305-306—improper to deny RFA claiming lack of personal knowledge, where party's expert witness had the information; *Bloxham v. Saldinger* (2014) 228 CA4th 729, 752, 175 CR3d 650, 667—party may not necessarily avoid responding to RFA on ground it "calls for expert opinion and the party does not know the answer"]

- [8:1344] But only a "reasonable" effort to find out is required. Thus, for example, a party would not be expected to travel to a foreign country to verify a street address there (or even hire a private investigator to do so). [*Lindgren v. Sup.Ct. (Lindgren)* (1965) 237 CA2d 743, 746, 47 CR 298, 299—request asked party to admit "there was no Hotel Legunitas in Madrid, Spain"]
- [8:1344.1] Parties are often requested to admit the *genuineness of the propounding party's own documents and records* (whether prepared by the propounding party or someone else). E.g., P serves D with RFAs to admit "the attached copies of my bank statements and payroll stubs are genuine."

  [8:1344.2] **Comment:** There is no known authority in point, but arguably D may properly deny such requests on the ground D has no "reasonable" way of verifying the genuineness of P's records.

  ⇨ [8:1344.3] ***PRACTICE POINTER:*** In most cases, you don't need admissions as to the genuineness of your own records. Their contents can be proved by any otherwise admissible secondary evidence (e.g., photocopies) unless a genuine dispute exists concerning material terms, or admission of secondary evidence would be "unfair." [See Ev.C. §1521]

  However, obtaining early concessions on the genuineness of your documents may obviate the need for declarations on motion practice and also may save you time at trial.

(c) [8:1345] **Effect of hearsay information?** It is not clear whether a party can properly claim "inability to admit or deny" where hearsay information *is* available. (Example: RFA asks party to admit Third Party received notice of some condition. Third Party acknowledges the notice.)

1) [8:1346] **Comment:** Arguably, a party should be permitted to use the "inability to admit or deny" re-

© 2020 Thomson Reuters/The Rutter Group

sponse even if the Third Party acknowledges the notice. I.e., the responding party should *not* be required to make binding admissions on the basis of hearsay; nor should he or she be subject to shifting of costs and expenses of proof for denying it. However, as stated, the matter is unclear.

☞ [8:1347] ***PRACTICE POINTER:*** To be safe, your response should make reference to whatever hearsay has been obtained. For example: "Other than statements or reports from . . . , *the truth or falsity of which is unknown*, Party has no knowledge or information sufficient to admit or deny Request No. . . . A reasonable inquiry concerning this matter has been made, and the only information known or readily obtainable concerning this matter is the hearsay evidence referred to above."

(d) [8:1348] **Effect of failing to make "reasonable" investigation:** The responding party's simple statement that he or she has made a "reasonable" inquiry and is unable to admit or deny the request because insufficient information is available *may not suffice as an answer to the RFA*. The propounding party may move to compel a proper response or to have the matter ordered admitted if the answering party has not made a reasonable inquiry or has access to "readily available" information that would enable him or her to admit or deny the matter. [See *Asea, Inc. v. Southern Pac. Transp. Co.* (9th Cir. 1981) 669 F2d 1242, 1245-1246 (decided under analogous FRCP rule)]

1) [8:1348.1] **Shifting of costs and expenses of proof:** Alternatively, costs and expenses of proof may be awarded after trial against a party for failure to inform himself or herself before answering (CCP §2033.420; ¶*8:1404 ff.*). The court may find there was no "good reason" for the failure to admit. [*Smith v. Circle P Ranch Co., Inc.* (1978) 87 CA3d 267, 276, 150 CR 828, 834—proof that responding party *failed to investigate*, when the means of obtaining the information were at hand, supports finding there were *no* "good reasons" for its denial]

e. [8:1349] **Objections:** In lieu of admitting or denying the RFA, the party may serve objections to particular requests. [CCP §2033.210(b)]

If only part of a request is objectionable, the remainder must be answered. [CCP §2033.230(a)]

(1) [8:1350] **Form:** The specific ground for objection must be set forth clearly in the response (including claims of privilege and work product protection). [CCP §2033.230(b)]

(2) [8:1351] **Proper objections:** Basically, the same objections available in response to interrogatories (¶*8:1071 ff.*) are available in response to RFAs:

(a) [8:1352] **Improper form:** This objection would lie where the RFA is not "separate and complete in and of itself," or contains:

- Subparts; or
- Compound, conjunctive or disjunctive requests; or
- A preface or instructions; or
- A requirement that reference must be made to other documents in order to respond. [CCP §2033.060(d), (f); *see* ¶*8:979.5, 8:1281 ff.*]

(b) [8:1353] **Excessive number:** *Absent a "declaration of necessity"* under CCP §2033.050, an objection lies to more than 35 RFAs that do not pertain to genuineness of documents. [CCP §2033.030(a)]

- [8:1353.1] However, if a "declaration of necessity" accompanies the RFAs, then any challenge to the number served must be by *motion for protective order*. The motion effectively controverts the statement of grounds in the declaration, and places the burden on the propounding party to prove the excessive number of requests is warranted by the complexity of the case. [CCP §2033.040(b), *discussed at* ¶*8:1270*]

(c) [8:1354] **"Irrelevant":** An objection may also lie on the ground that the request is "irrelevant to the subject matter of the action"—the basic limitation on scope of permissible discovery (¶*8:66*). [*Cembrook v. Sup.Ct. (Sterling Drug, Inc.)* (1961) 56 C2d 423, 428, 15 CR 127, 130]

(d) [8:1355] **"Burdensome and oppressive":** This ground for objection might be applicable, for example, to requests that are unduly repetitive, or where preparing the responses would somehow impose an "unjust burden" on the responding party. [*Cembrook v. Sup.Ct. (Sterling Drug, Inc.)*, supra, 56 C2d at 428, 15 CR at 130 (involving "shotgun variety" RFAs, consisting of numerous subparts, no longer permissible)]

1) [8:1355.1] **Excessive number alone not ground:** A "burdensome and oppressive" objection probably does *not* lie solely because of the *number* of questions asked. The Discovery Act now provides the procedure to challenge excessive numbers (*see* ¶*8:1353*).

(3) **Improper objections**

(a) [8:1356] Absent some defect in timing or service of the RFAs, objecting to the *entire set* of RFAs, without

© 2020 Thomson Reuters/The Rutter Group

some attempt to admit or deny in part, cannot be considered a "good faith" response to RFAs. Such wholesale objections may result in imposition of *sanctions* against the responding party (¶*8:1400 ff.*). [*Cembrook v. Sup.Ct. (Sterling Drug, Inc.)*, supra, 56 C2d at 430, 15 CR at 131]

(b) [8:1357] It is *not* ground for objection that the request calls for an "opinion" (¶*8:1294*), or that the facts are known to the propounder of the requests. [*Hillman v. Stults* (1968) 263 CA2d 848, 885, 70 CR 295, 317]

(c) [8:1358] Nor is it ground for objection that the request is "ambiguous," unless it is so ambiguous that the responding party cannot in good faith frame an intelligent reply. [See *Cembrook v. Sup.Ct. (Sterling Drug, Inc.)*, supra, 56 C2d at 428-429, 15 CR at 130-131]

[8:1359] ***PRACTICE POINTER:*** If you decide to object on ground that the request is "too ambiguous to frame a response," *include a brief explanation* of what you feel is ambiguous and why it prevents any intelligent reply.

f. [8:1360] **Signature and verification of responses:** The party to whom the RFAs were directed must sign the response under oath. That party's attorney must also sign a response that contains an objection. If the response consists *entirely* of objections, then only the attorney's signature is necessary. [CCP §2033.240(a), (c)]

If the response contains *both* answers and objections, there is no need to verify that portion containing the objections. [*Food 4 Less Supermarkets, Inc. v. Sup.Ct. (Fletcher)* (1995) 40 CA4th 651, 657, 46 CR2d 925, 928]

(1) [8:1361] **Form of verification:** As with interrogatories, the common practice is for the responding party to sign a separate verification form attached to the responses (e.g., "I have read the foregoing Responses and know the contents thereof and certify that the same are true of my own knowledge").

(2) [8:1361.1] **Verification by "Doe" sufficient:** Where plaintiff files an action under a fictitious name to preserve anonymity (¶*2:136.5 ff.*), plaintiff may verify discovery responses by signing the fictitious name. [*Doe v. Sup.Ct. (Luster)* (2011) 194 CA4th 750, 756, 123 CR3d 557, 561—trial court erred in requiring plaintiff to provide verifications in her true name]

(3) [8:1362] **Problems with corporate verification:** The issues discussed in connection with verification of responses to interrogatories by a partnership, corporation or other entity apply as well here:

- May the officer designated to make the verification on behalf of the entity use the "information and belief" form

© 2020 Thomson Reuters/The Rutter Group

where he or she does not have personal knowledge of all matters in the response (*see* ¶*8:1106*)?

- Is the officer's statement that he or she is "authorized" to verify on behalf of the entity sufficient to establish such authority (*see* ¶*8:1107*)?

(4) [8:1363] **Attorney verification improper:** Responses to RFAs must be verified by the responding *party*, not by counsel. The fact the party resides in another county may allow counsel to verify *pleadings* on the party's behalf (see CCP §446, ¶*6:320*); but that does *not* apply to responses to RFAs. [*Steele v. Totah* (1986) 180 CA3d 545, 550, 225 CR 635, 637; *Brigante v. Huang* (1993) 20 CA4th 1569, 1574-1575, 25 CR2d 354, 357 (disapproved on other grounds by *Wilcox v. Birtwhistle* (1999) 21 C4th 973, 983, 90 CR2d 260, 267, fn. 12)—attorney who erroneously verifies RFAs may be deposed: attorney-client and work product privileges may have been waived]

(a) [8:1364] **Compare—attorney as agent of entity:** A corporation, partnership or other entity may appoint its attorney as its *agent* to verify responses; but this effectively waives any attorney-client or work product privilege *as to the sources of the attorney's information. See discussion in connection with interrogatories at* ¶*8:1109 ff.* [CCP §2033.240(b)]

(5) [8:1364.1] **Effect of unverified response:** Where a verification is required (*see* ¶*8:1360*), an unverified response is ineffective; it is the equivalent of no response at all. [See *Appleton v. Sup.Ct. (Cook)* (1988) 206 CA3d 632, 636, 253 CR 762, 764; *Allen-Pacific, Ltd. v. Sup.Ct. (Chan)* (1997) 57 CA4th 1546, 1550-1551, 67 CR2d 804, 807 (disapproved on other grounds by *Wilcox v. Birtwhistle* (1999) 21 C4th 973, 983, 90 CR2d 260, 267, fn. 12)]

(a) [8:1364.2] **Compare—responses containing both answers and objections:** But no verification is required to preserve objections (see CCP §2033.240(a)). Therefore, an unverified response containing *both* answers and objections is effective to preserve those objections. The lack of verification renders the fact-specific *answers* untimely; but that only creates a right to move for orders and sanctions (under §2033.280; *see* ¶*8:1378*). It does not result in a waiver of the objections made. [See *Food 4 Less Supermarkets, Inc. v. Sup.Ct. (Fletcher)* (1995) 40 CA4th 651, 657, 46 CR2d 925, 928 (involving CCP §2031.010 et seq. document requests)]

g. [8:1365] **Service of responses:** The responding party serves the *original* response on the requesting party. Copies of the response must be served on all other parties who have appeared in the action. [CCP §2033.250]

© 2020 Thomson Reuters/The Rutter Group

h. [8:1366] **Custody of originals:** The requesting party ends up with the originals of both the requests and the responses, and must retain them until six months after final disposition of the action. [CCP §2033.270(b)]

These are *not* filed or lodged with the court, unless the court so orders. (If an enforcement motion is brought, copies of disputed requests and responses are simply included in the moving papers; *see ¶8:1378 ff.*)

6. [8:1367] **Effect of Delay or Failure to Respond to RFAs:** The time for response to RFAs is discussed at ¶*8:1308 ff.* The following rules apply when this time limit expires and *no response* has been made.

(Compare: If responses *have been* timely served, but are deemed deficient by the requesting party, the remedy is a *motion to compel, discussed at ¶8:1378 ff.*)

"The law governing the consequences for failing to respond to requests for admission may be the most unforgiving in civil procedure. There is no relief under section 473. The defaulting party is limited to the remedies available in [CCP §2033.280]." [*Demyer v. Costa Mesa Mobile Home Estates* (1995) 36 CA4th 393, 394-395, 42 CR2d 260, 260 (disapproved on other grounds by *Wilcox v. Birtwhistle* (1999) 21 C4th 973, 983, 90 CR2d 260, 267, fn. 12)]

a. [8:1368] **All objections waived:** Failure to timely respond to RFAs results in *waiver* of *all objections* to the requests—including claims of privilege or work product protection. [CCP §2033.280(a)]

(1) [8:1369] **Relief from waiver:** However, the court may relieve a party who fails to file a timely response from such waiver, as follows:

(a) [8:1369.1] ***Before* "deemed admitted order":** The party in default may move for relief from waiver before the court orders the matters specified in the RFAs "deemed admitted" (*see ¶8:1370*). Such relief may be granted if the court finds:

- The party's failure to serve a timely response resulted from "mistake, inadvertence or excusable neglect"; and
- The party has *subsequently served a response* in "substantial compliance" with §2033.220. [CCP §2033.280(a); see *Brigante v. Huang* (1993) 20 CA4th 1569, 1584, 25 CR2d 354, 364 (disapproved on other grounds by *Wilcox v. Birtwhistle*, supra, 21 C4th at 983, 90 CR2d at 267, fn. 12)]

1) [8:1369.2] **Relief available even if no response filed:** Even though CCP §2033.300 refers only to withdrawal or amendment of an admission, this includes admissions *deemed* admitted for failure to respond. Therefore, upon a proper showing, relief may be granted even if no responses were served. [*Wilcox v. Birtwhistle*, supra, 21 C4th at 977, 90 CR2d at 263]

2) [8:1369.3] **No relief under CCP §473(b):** Since §2033.280 specifically sets out the conditions under which relief can be given from the waiver resulting from failure to respond to RFAs, relief is not available under CCP §473(b): "[Former] Section 2033 supersedes section 473 as the avenue to obtain default relief in a situation of failure to respond to admissions requests." [*St. Paul Fire & Marine Ins. Co. v. Sup.Ct. (Advalloy, Inc.)* (1992) 2 CA4th 843, 852, 3 CR2d 412, 417 (disapproved on other grounds by *Wilcox v. Birtwhistle* (1999) 21 C4th 973, 983, 90 CR2d 260, 267, fn. 12)]

[8:1369.4] *Reserved.*

(b) [8:1369.5] ***After* "deemed admitted order":** After a "deemed admitted order" (¶*8:1370 ff.*) has been entered, the party in default may seek relief from waiver by filing a motion to *withdraw or amend* the "deemed admission" under §2033.300 (*see* ¶*8:1386 ff.*). [*Wilcox v. Birtwhistle*, supra, 21 C4th at 979, 90 CR2d at 264]

b. [8:1370] **Motion for deemed admissions:** Failure to timely respond to RFAs does *not* result in automatic admissions. Rather, the propounder of the RFAs must "move for an order that the genuineness of any documents and the truth of any matters specified in the requests *be deemed admitted*, as well as for a monetary sanction" under §2023.010 et seq. [CCP §2033.280(b) (emphasis added)]

FORM: Motion for Order Establishing Admissions and Proposed Order, *see Form 8:25* in Rivera, *Cal. Prac. Guide: Civ. Pro. Before Trial FORMS* (TRG).

(1) [8:1371] **No attempt to resolve informally required:** Since this motion deals with a *failure* to respond, rather than inadequate responses, *no* attempt to resolve the matter informally ("meet and confer") need be shown; *see* ¶*8:1141 ff., 8:1160.* [See *Demyer v. Costa Mesa Mobile Home Estates* (1995) 36 CA4th 393, 395, 42 CR2d 260, 261, fn. 4 (citing text) (disapproved on other grounds by *Wilcox v. Birtwhistle*, supra, 21 C4th at 983, 90 CR2d at 267, fn. 12); *St. Mary v. Sup.Ct. (Schellenberg)* (2014) 223 CA4th 762, 777-778, 167 CR3d 517, 529-530 (citing text)]

(2) [8:1372] **No time limit on motion:** Unlike motions to compel under other discovery provisions, there is no time limit on a

© 2020 Thomson Reuters/The Rutter Group

motion to have matters deemed admitted. [*Brigante v. Huang* (1993) 20 CA4th 1569, 1584, 25 CR2d 354, 364 (disapproved on other grounds by *Wilcox v. Birtwhistle*, supra, 21 C4th at 983, 90 CR2d at 267, fn. 12)]

(a) [8:1373] **Equitable limitation?** But if the motion is long delayed, the responding party may object or seek a protective order upon a showing of prejudice from the delay "or other equitable basis by which it is unfair to have the RFAs admitted." [*Brigante v. Huang*, supra, 20 CA4th at 1584, 25 CR2d at 364]

(3) [8:1374] **Tardy responses defeat motion:** The court "shall" grant the motion "*unless* it finds that the party to whom the requests for admission have been directed has served, before the hearing on the motion, a proposed response . . . in substantial compliance with Section 2033.220" (¶*8:1321 ff.*). [CCP §2033.280(c) (emphasis added); *St. Mary v. Sup.Ct. (Schellenberg)*, supra, 223 CA4th at 778, 167 CR3d at 530 (citing text)]

(a) [8:1374.1] **"Substantial compliance":** It is enough that the response served "substantially" complies with §2033.220. [See *Tobin v. Oris* (1992) 3 CA4th 814, 827, 4 CR2d 736, 744 (disapproved on other grounds by *Wilcox v. Birtwhistle* (1999) 21 C4th 973, 983, 90 CR2d 260, 267, fn. 12)—"that some of the responses were less than clear or complete does not detract from that conclusion"]

To make this determination, the court must evaluate the response "in toto," rather than based on responses to individual RFAs. [*St. Mary v. Sup.Ct. (Schellenberg)*, supra, 223 CA4th at 779-780, 167 CR3d at 531]

1) [8:1374.1a] **Compare—unsworn responses:** However, unsworn responses are equivalent to "no response at all" and therefore not in "substantial compliance" with §2033.240(a). [*Allen-Pacific, Ltd. v. Sup.Ct. (Chan)* (1997) 57 CA4th 1546, 1551, 67 CR2d 804, 807 (disapproved on other grounds by *Wilcox v. Birtwhistle*, supra, 21 C4th at 983, 90 CR2d at 267, fn. 12)]

2) [8:1374.1b] **Compare—response by coparty:** However, responses to identical RFAs by one party cannot be treated as responses *by a different party;* nor can they be "amended" for this purpose after the hearing. [*Courtesy Claims Service, Inc. v. Sup.Ct. (Galvan)* (1990) 219 CA3d 52, 55-56, 268 CR 30, 32 (disapproved on other grounds by *Wilcox v. Birtwhistle*, supra, 21 C4th at 983, 90 CR2d at 267, fn. 12)—P1 answered RFAs but P2 and P3 did not: P1's answers cannot be treated as responses by P2 and P3]

(b) [8:1374.2] **Effect:** As long as responses in "substantial compliance" with §2033.220 are served *prior to the hearing*, the motion to establish admissions is defeated. *No showing of "mistake, inadvertence or excusable neglect" is required.* [*Tobin v. Oris*, supra, 3 CA4th at 828, 4 CR2d at 744; *St. Mary v. Sup.Ct. (Schellenberg)*, supra, 223 CA4th at 778, 167 CR3d at 530 (citing text)]

CCP §2033.280 thus ensures that litigants receive formal notice of the need to prepare responses and some additional time to accomplish that task before the devastating effects of failing to respond to RFAs are visited upon them. [*Demyer v. Costa Mesa Mobile Home Estates*, supra, 36 CA4th at 399, 42 CR2d at 264]

(c) [8:1374.3] **Compare—relief from waiver of objections:** Remember that all *objections* to the RFAs are now *waived* (by failure to timely respond; *see* ¶*8:1368 ff.*). Thus, the only permitted responses to the requests are admissions, denials, or statements of inability to admit or deny for lack of information (¶*8:1341*). If the responding party wants to *object* to any request, it would have to seek relief from waiver under CCP §2033.280(a) (¶*8:1369 ff.*). And, a showing of "mistake, inadvertence or excusable neglect" *is* required (*see* ¶*8:1369.1*).

(d) [8:1374.4] **Compare—where hearing on shortened notice:** Responses served within the time normally allowed for hearings (at least 16 court days) prevent the deemed admissions sanction. The court *cannot* cut off the responding party's rights prematurely by shortening time for the hearing. [*Demyer v. Costa Mesa Mobile Home Estates*, supra, 36 CA4th at 401, 42 CR2d at 265, fn. 18 (citing text)]

This is true even if there were good cause for expediting the hearing: "Even the most compelling reason to shorten time for an admissions motion—an impending trial and discovery cutoff date—does not justify eliminating the ameliorative function of [the statute]." [*Demyer v. Costa Mesa Mobile Home Estates*, supra, 36 CA4th at 401, 42 CR2d at 265]

(4) [8:1375] **Deemed admissions where no response filed:** The statute states "the court *shall* make this order" unless proposed responses "in substantial compliance" with §2033.220 are filed before the hearing. [CCP §2033.280(c) (emphasis added)]

"[W]oe betide the party who fails to serve responses before the hearing. In that instance the court has no discretion but to grant the admission motion, usually with fatal consequences for the defaulting party. One might call it 'two strikes and you're out' as applied to civil procedure." [*Demyer v. Costa*

Mesa Mobile Home Estates, supra, 36 CA4th at 395-396, 42 CR2d at 261 (disapproved on other grounds by *Wilcox v. Birtwhistle* (1999) 21 C4th 973, 983, 90 CR2d 260, 267, fn. 12)]

(a) [8:1375.1] **Effect:** "[A] deemed admitted order establishes, by judicial fiat, that a nonresponding party has responded to the requests by admitting the truth of all matters contained therein." [*Wilcox v. Birtwhistle*, supra, 21 C4th at 979, 90 CR2d at 264; see *Lattimore v. Dickey* (2015) 239 CA4th 959, 971, 191 CR3d 766, 775-776—order deeming deceased patient's daughter to have admitted doctor met applicable standard of care precluded her wrongful death claim against doctor]

(b) [8:1375.2] **Relief from deemed admissions:** But relief from such admissions may still be available by a motion to withdraw or amend the deemed admissions (*see ¶8:1369.5*). [*Wilcox v. Birtwhistle*, supra, 21 C4th at 979, 90 CR2d at 264]

(5) [8:1376] **Monetary sanction also *mandatory:*** Although delayed responses may defeat a motion to compel, they will not avoid monetary sanctions. Regardless of the reason for the delay in responding, it is *mandatory* that a monetary sanction be imposed on the party or attorney, or both, whose failure to serve a timely response necessitated the filing of the deemed-admitted motion. [CCP §2033.280(c)]

(a) [8:1377] **Comment:** This is the only place in the Discovery Act where sanctions for delay are mandatory. The purpose is to provide incentive to timely respond to RFAs: i.e., no excuses accepted.

☞ [8:1377.1] ***PRACTICE POINTER:*** Here's how to handle tardy responses served by opposing counsel after you have already filed a motion to compel: If the responses are satisfactory and the only question is sanctions, promptly send opposing counsel a letter notifying them of your costs and fees in preparing the motion to compel; and offer to accept that amount and let the motion to compel go off calendar.

Opposing counsel will be hard put to refuse. If they do, the court will in all likelihood award you a greater amount to compensate you for the appearance on the motion.

(6) [8:1377.2] **Compare—tardy response served BEFORE motion filed:** The mandatory sanction is available *only* in conjunction with a motion to establish admissions. Thus, sanctions can be avoided by serving responses *before* the motion is filed, which would eliminate the ground for the motion. I.e., *no sanctions of any kind can be imposed for mere delay* in

responding to RFAs if no motion has yet been filed. [*St. Mary v. Sup.Ct. (Schellenberg)* (2014) 223 CA4th 762, 784, 167 CR3d 517, 535 (citing text)] (But the delay would, of course, still result in *waiver* of all objections to the RFAs; *see* ¶*8:1368*.)

Problems may arise where tardy responses are served but not yet received when the motion to establish admissions is filed. Arguably, service should not affect the right to sanctions in such a case. I.e., until the responses have been *received* by the propounding party, the ground for the motion exists.

c. [8:1377.3] **Opposition as motion for protective order?** One case holds that a party who fails to respond to RFAs or to file a legally sufficient response before the hearing may still obtain relief by raising grounds for a protective order in its opposition or objections to the motion for deemed admissions. [*Brigante v. Huang* (1993) 20 CA4th 1569, 1586, 25 CR2d 354, 365 (disapproved on other grounds by *Wilcox v. Birtwhistle* (1999) 21 C4th 973, 983, 90 CR2d 260, 267, fn. 12)—court has discretion to deny motion where opposition showed client could not be located to verify responses to RFAs and opposing party knew this when propounding the RFAs]

However, a later case limited *Brigante* to its facts and refused to follow it under different circumstances. [*Allen-Pacific, Ltd. v. Sup.Ct. (Chan)* (1997) 57 CA4th 1546, 1556, 67 CR2d 804, 810 (disapproved on other grounds by *Wilcox v. Birtwhistle*, supra, 21 C4th at 983, 90 CR2d at 267, fn. 12)—if party fails to serve responses before the hearing, "the court has no discretion but to grant the admission motion, usually with fatal consequences for the defaulting party"]

7. [8:1378] **Motion to Compel Further Answers:** Where responses have been timely served but are deemed deficient by the requesting party (e.g., because of objections or evasive responses), that party may move for an order compelling a further response. [CCP §2033.290; see *Wimberly v. Derby Cycle Corp.* (1997) 56 CA4th 618, 636, 65 CR2d 532, 543—requesting party not entitled to shifting of costs and expenses of proof for responding party's objections to RFA because requesting party made no motion to compel further response]

a. [8:1379] **Compare—cannot be used to force admissions of facts denied:** No further response can be ordered to an RFA that has been *unqualifiedly* denied, even if the facts involved are unquestionably true. "[A] court [cannot] force a litigant to admit any particular fact if he is willing to risk a perjury prosecution or financial sanctions" by denying them. [*Holguin v. Sup.Ct. (Hoage)* (1972) 22 CA3d 812, 820, 99 CR 653, 658]

(1) [8:1380] Thus, for example, the responding party's denial of matters he or she had already admitted on deposition, or in answers to interrogatories, is *not* ground for a motion to compel further answers. However, the denial may entitle the requesting party to be reimbursed for the cost of proof of the denied fact, after trial (*see* ¶*8:1404 ff.*).

© 2020 Thomson Reuters/The Rutter Group

[8:1381] ***PRACTICE POINTER:*** The proper procedure in such a case is to serve *interrogatories* on the responding party asking him or her to state the *facts* upon which the denials are based (¶*8:1275*).

b. [8:1382] **Procedure:** The procedural requirements on a motion to compel are the same as those discussed previously in connection with interrogatories (*see* ¶*8:1145*).

(1) [8:1383] **45-day time limit:** The motion must be made within 45 days after service of verified responses in question, or any verified supplemental responses (longer if responses served by mail, overnight delivery or fax or electronically; see CCP §§1010.6(a)(4), 1013, ¶*9:87 ff.*). Otherwise, the right to compel further responses is waived. [CCP §§2033.290(c), 2016.050]

(a) [8:1384] **Extensions?** The parties may stipulate to an extension (CCP §2033.290(c)). But whether the court may extend this 45-day period is unclear (the Discovery Act is silent on this point). The court may have inherent power to extend the 45-day deadline *before* it expires and may be able to grant relief for untimely motions under CCP §473(b) based on "mistake, inadvertence or excusable neglect" (*see* ¶*8:1149 ff.*).

(b) [8:1384.1] **Time limit applicable where only unverified objections received?** CCP §2033.290(c) states that the time limit for bringing a motion to compel further responses runs from the service of a *verified* response or supplemental *verified* response. Although not specified in the Discovery Act, the 45-day limit probably also applies where the response is unverified and includes only objections.

Comment: Because this issue is not free from doubt, to be safe, you should serve your motion within 45 days of service of unverified objections. *See* ¶*8:1150.7 ff.*

(2) [8:1385] **Moving papers:** The same Notice of Motion procedure is followed as in connection with a motion to compel further answers to interrogatories (¶*8:1136 ff.*; and see rules and procedures governing motions generally in *Ch. 9 Part I*). *Form 8:19* (Motion to Compel Further Answers to Interrogatories and for Sanctions and Proposed Order) and *Form 8:20* (Separate Statement of Interrogatories and Responses in Dispute) in Rivera, *Cal. Prac. Guide: Civ. Pro. Before Trial FORMS* (TRG), may be modified and used to prepare motions to compel further responses to requests for admission.

Alternatively, *effective January 1, 2020,* the court may allow the moving party to file a concise outline of matters in dispute in lieu of the separate statement. [CCP §2033.290(b)(2) (amended eff. 1/1/19; operative 1/1/20); *see* ¶*8:532.12, 8.1157.3 ff.*]

(3) [8:1385.1] **"Meet and confer" required:** [CCP §2033.290(b)(1)] *See* ¶*8:1158 ff.*

(4) [8:1385.2] **Compare—informal discovery conference to resolve dispute:** Parties may seek, or courts may require, an informal discovery conference with the judge before a motion is filed. *See discussion at* ¶*8:787.1.*

8. [8:1386] **Amending or Withdrawing Admissions:** An admission cannot be amended or withdrawn except by leave of court after noticed motion. [CCP §2033.300(a); see *Valerio v. Andrew Youngquist Const.* (2002) 103 CA4th 1264, 1272, 127 CR2d 436, 442]

[8:1386a] **Compare—amending answers to interrogatories:** Interrogatory answers can be changed *without leave of court* (CCP §2030.310(a), ¶*8:1123*). But admissions serve a function similar to *pleadings* in that they are aimed primarily at setting a triable issue to rest. Thus, like pleadings, leave of court is required before admissions may be amended or withdrawn. [See *Jahn v. Brickey* (1985) 168 CA3d 399, 404, 214 CR 119, 122]

a. [8:1386b] **Includes "deemed admissions":** CCP §2033.300(a) permits amendment or withdrawal of "deemed admissions" ordered by the court under §2033.280(b) (*see* ¶*8:1369.5*), as well as admissions expressly made by a party. [*Wilcox v. Birtwhistle* (1999) 21 C4th 973, 979, 90 CR2d 260, 264]

b. [8:1386.1] **Requirements:** A party will be permitted to withdraw or amend an admission only if the court finds:

- The admission resulted from "*mistake, inadvertence or excusable neglect*" (e.g., new facts discovered contradicting earlier admission); *and*

- *No substantial prejudice* to the requesting party will result from allowing the admission to be withdrawn or amended. [CCP §2033.300(b); see *New Albertsons, Inc. v. Sup.Ct. (Shanahan)* (2008) 168 CA4th 1403, 1418, 86 CR3d 457, 468]

(1) [8:1386.2] **Required showing similar to CCP §473(b):** The requirements for relief under CCP §2033.300 are similar to those governing relief from default under CCP §473(b). The terms "mistake, inadvertence, or excusable neglect" as used in CCP §2033.300 are given the same meanings as similar terms found in CCP §473(b). [*New Albertsons, Inc. v. Sup.Ct. (Shanahan)*, supra, 168 CA4th at 1419, 86 CR3d at 469]

Although the CCP §2033.300 requirement of "no substantial prejudice" to the party requesting admissions is not express in CCP §473(b), the "absence of substantial prejudice is an important factor to consider." [*New Albertsons, Inc. v. Sup.Ct. (Shanahan)*, supra, 168 CA4th at 1420, 86 CR3d at 470]

© 2020 Thomson Reuters/The Rutter Group

c. [8:1386.3] **Policy favoring relief:** CCP §2033.300 is designed to eliminate undeserved windfalls obtained through requests for admission and to further the policy favoring resolution of lawsuits on the merits. Therefore, any doubts must be resolved in favor of the party seeking relief. [*New Albertsons, Inc. v. Sup.Ct. (Shanahan)*, supra, 168 CA4th at 1420, 86 CR3d at 470]

Denial of a motion to withdraw or amend an admission "is limited to circumstances where it is clear that the mistake, inadvertence, or neglect was *inexcusable,* or where it is clear that the withdrawal or amendment would substantially prejudice the party who obtained the admission in maintaining that party's action or defense on the merits." [*New Albertsons, Inc. v. Sup.Ct. (Shanahan)*, supra, 168 CA4th at 1420-1421, 86 CR3d at 470 (emphasis added)]

d. [8:1386.4] **Relief may be granted conditionally:** If relief is granted, the court may impose whatever *conditions* are just: e.g., reopening discovery on the matter involved; and ordering the party whose admission is involved to pay the other's costs in conducting additional discovery. [CCP §2033.300(c); see *Rhule v. Wavefront Tech., Inc.* (2017) 8 CA5th 1223, 1227-1228, 214 CR3d 586, 589—reference in §2033.300(c) to "costs" includes discretion to condition relief upon payment of attorney fees]

e. [8:1386.5] **Repudiated admission as impeachment:** Even if leave to amend or withdraw is obtained, the repudiated admission still may be used for impeachment purposes at trial (as prior inconsistent statement or party admission), just as may a changed answer to an interrogatory or deposition question. [*Jahn v. Brickey*, supra, 168 CA3d at 405, 214 CR at 123]

9. [8:1387] **Evidentiary Effect of Admissions:** Any matter admitted in response to an RFA is *preclusively established* against the party making the admission, unless the court has permitted withdrawal or amendment of the admission (*see ¶8:1386*). [CCP §2033.410(a); *Murillo v. Sup.Ct. (People)* (2006) 143 CA4th 730, 736, 49 CR3d 511, 515 (citing text)]

However, such admission is preclusive only against that party, and only for purposes of the present action. [CCP §2033.410(b)]

a. [8:1388] **Preclusive effect:** Admissions in response to RFAs are treated in effect as stipulations to the truthfulness of the matters admitted. Therefore, no other evidence is necessary to establish the point at trial and *no contrary evidence is admissible unless leave of court is obtained* to withdraw or amend the response. [CCP §§2033.300-2033.410; see *Murillo v. Sup.Ct. (People)*, supra, 143 CA4th at 736, 49 CR3d at 515 (citing text); *Scalf v. D.B. Log Homes, Inc.* (2005) 128 CA4th 1510, 1522, 27 CR3d 826, 833 (citing text); *People v. $2,709 United States Currency* (2014) 231 CA4th 1278, 1286, 180 CR3d 705, 711]

(1) [8:1389] **Compare—other discovery:** Deposition answers can be changed prior to trial within 30 days of the depo-

sition unless the parties otherwise agree (CCP §2025.520(b)) (subject, of course, to appropriate comment to the jury); *see* ¶*8:770.* Likewise, answers to interrogatories are not preclusive, because contrary evidence is admissible at trial; ¶*8:1247 ff.* But admissions to RFAs *are* preclusive in the sense that no contrary evidence is admissible.

(2) [8:1389.1] **Admission no broader than request:** By the same token, an RFA response is preclusive only to the extent required by a literal reading of the request. [*Burch v. Gombos* (2000) 82 CA4th 352, 359, 98 CR2d 119, 125]

- [8:1389.2] RFA requested that plaintiffs "Admit that you have no evidence of [certain facts]." Plaintiffs' admission did not preclude them from presenting evidence *acquired later.* Their admission was limited to their *knowledge at the time the admission was made.* [*Burch v. Gombos*, supra, 82 CA4th at 356, 359, 98 CR2d at 122, 125]

(3) [8:1390] **Trial judge's "interpretation" of admission in light of other evidence:** The court retains discretion to determine the scope and effect of a party's admission. The court may determine whether it accurately reflects the truth *in light of other evidence* in the case. This prevents requests for admission being misused as a device to hide or confuse issues. [*Fredericks v. Filbert Co.* (1987) 189 CA3d 272, 278, 234 CR 395, 398]

(a) [8:1390.1] For example, the trial judge may find an RFA deceptive because the admission is *susceptible to different meanings.* [*Fredericks v. Filbert Co.*, supra, 189 CA3d at 277-278, 234 CR at 397-398—Owner admitted he "agreed" to make certain progress payments to Contractor; court found Owner's "agreement" was dependent upon work being done by Contractor]

☞ [8:1390.2] ***PRACTICE POINTER:*** Keep this in mind *when drafting* RFAs. The narrower the language in your request, the less opportunity the court has to disregard the admission (*see* ¶*8:1287.1*).

(b) [8:1390.3] Or, the court may simply read the admission differently than the propounding party expected. [See *Milton v. Montgomery Ward & Co., Inc.* (1973) 33 CA3d 133, 138, 108 CR 726, 729—personal injury plaintiff admitted certain preexisting injuries; but court held these were merely "his opinions" and could be ignored by jury where medical evidence indicated otherwise]

[8:1390.4] *Reserved.*

(c) [8:1390.5] *Compare—unambiguous admission:* But if the response is unambiguous, there is no reason to construe it. The matter admitted must be treated as

© 2020 Thomson Reuters/The Rutter Group

"conclusively established." [*Valerio v. Andrew Youngquist Const.* (2002) 103 CA4th 1264, 1273, 127 CR2d 436, 443—plaintiff bound by admission that there was a "fully executed written agreement between the parties"]

(4) [8:1391] **Evidentiary objections:** Even if the admissions are preclusive, the trial judge may sustain objections if the matters admitted are "irrelevant" or "immaterial" to the issues at trial. [*Cembrook v. Sterling Drug, Inc.* (1964) 231 CA2d 52, 62, 41 CR 492, 498]

(5) [8:1391.1] **Compare—*denials* to RFAs generally *not* admissible:** Denials of RFAs are not admissible to impeach a party at trial except, perhaps, when there is some inconsistency between the party's RFA responses and trial testimony or in an extraordinary case where the party's litigation conduct is directly in issue. [See *Gonsalves v. Li* (2015) 232 CA4th 1406, 1415-1417, 182 CR3d 383, 391 (rejecting argument that denials were admissible to impeach credibility by showing party's "attitude toward the action in which he testifies"); *Victaulic Co. v. American Home Assur. Co.* (2018) 20 CA5th 948, 973, 229 CR3d 545, 564—denials of RFAs are inadmissible whether consistent or inconsistent with trial testimony]

b. [8:1392] **May be asserted by any party:** Admissions to one party's requests may be used by all parties to the action including parties joined *after* the admissions were made. [See *Swedberg v. Christiana Comm. Builders* (1985) 175 CA3d 138, 143-144, 220 CR 544, 547-548]

c. [8:1393] **Not preclusive in other proceedings:** Admissions to RFAs are preclusive only as to the admitting party, and only for purposes of the pending action. "It is not an admission by that party for any other purpose, and it shall not be used in any manner against that party *in any other proceeding.*" [CCP §2033.410(b) (emphasis added)]

(1) [8:1394] **Complaint and cross-complaint as separate proceedings:** A defendant's admissions in response to plaintiff's request may not be binding on the defendant in a cross-complaint against a third party. In effect, the complaint and cross-complaint may be viewed as separate actions. [*Shepard & Morgan v. Lee & Daniel, Inc.* (1982) 31 C3d 256, 259-260, 182 CR 351, 352-353; *and see* ¶*8:1264*]

(a) [8:1395] **Example:** In response to plaintiff's request, defendant admitted its *contentions re causation* of the accident in which plaintiff was injured. Such admissions did not preclude defendant from asserting different contentions on its cross-complaint for indemnity against a third party. Rationale: Defendant should have the right to proceed on alternative theories of defense (just as plaintiff has the right to proceed on alternative theories of liability). [*Shepard & Morgan v. Lee & Daniel, Inc.*, supra, 31 C3d at 259-261, 182 CR at 352-353]

(b) [8:1396] **Comment:** It is not clear, however, whether a defendant would be bound by admissions of *fact* common to both the complaint and cross-complaint. *Shepard*, supra, 31 C3d at 260, 182 CR at 352, involved admissions as to contentions and legal theories.

(c) [8:1397] **Compare—after summary judgment obtained against plaintiff:** A defendant who has obtained summary judgment against P based on admissions to RFAs (facts absolving defendant from liability) is also entitled to summary judgment on a cross-complaint for *indemnity for the same injuries.* Rationale: This is not because P's admissions are binding on the codefendant seeking indemnity, but rather because *collateral estoppel precludes relitigating* the liability issues determined on the earlier summary judgment. [*Allis-Chalmers Corp. v. Sup.Ct.* (*Mifran Boman Corp.*) (1985) 168 CA3d 1155, 1159, 214 CR 615, 617]

(2) [8:1397.1] **Criminal proceedings?** Whether CCP §2033.410 bars use of RFA admissions in *criminal* proceedings against the admitting party is unclear. If it does, that party could not assert the privilege against self-incrimination as ground for refusal to answer RFAs. (Even so, some sort of judicial determination of the immunity claim, after notice to prosecuting authorities, would probably be required; *see* ¶*8:143.*)

(3) [8:1398] **Compare—plaintiff cannot avoid admissions by dismissing and filing new lawsuit:** A plaintiff who has made admissions fatal to the case *cannot* avoid their preclusive effect by dismissing the action without prejudice and filing a new lawsuit. [*Miller v. Marina Mercy Hosp.* (1984) 157 CA3d 765, 770, 204 CR 62, 65-66]

(a) [8:1399] **Rationale:** A plaintiff's right to dismiss without prejudice ceases once "trial" has begun (CCP §581(a), (c), *see* ¶*11:17 ff.*). The determination of any issue of law or fact that *effectively disposes of the action* constitutes a "trial" for dismissal purposes, so there is no further right to dismiss the action without prejudice. [*Miller v. Marina Mercy Hosp.*, supra, 157 CA3d at 770, 204 CR at 65]

Also, the parties should be *mutually bound* by their admissions in a lawsuit. Since defendants cannot avoid the evidentiary effect of their admissions, neither should plaintiffs. [*Miller v. Marina Mercy Hosp.*, supra, 157 CA3d at 769-770, 204 CR at 65]

10. **Enforcing RFAs**

a. [8:1399.1] **MANDATORY monetary sanctions for delay or failure to respond:** See CCP §2033.280(c), ¶*8:1376 ff.*

b. [8:1400] **Monetary sanctions on motion to compel further responses:** A monetary sanction "shall" be imposed against the losing party on a motion to compel further responses to RFAs unless the court finds "substantial justification" for that party's position or other circumstances making the sanction "unjust." [CCP §2033.290(d)]

Cross-refer: See detailed discussion in connection with interrogatories at ¶*8:1184 ff.*

c. [8:1401] **"Deemed admissions" if court order disobeyed:** Once an order compelling further responses has been made, further evasion or failure to answer may have more drastic consequences: The court "may order that the matters involved in the requests be *deemed admitted*" (in addition to or in lieu of a monetary sanction against the disobedient party). [CCP §2033.290(e) (emphasis added)]

d. [8:1402] **"Terminating" sanctions for evasive responses?** One case holds a defendant's answer may be stricken and its default entered for evasive responses to RFAs even without a prior order compelling further answers. [*Collisson & Kaplan v. Hartunian* (1994) 21 CA4th 1611, 1617, 26 CR2d 786, 790—court characterized defendant's responses to discovery as "evasive and quibbling" and "lawyer game playing at its worst"]

(1) [8:1403] **Comment:** This result seems incorrect. Terminating sanctions for discovery misuse are permitted only "[t]o the extent authorized by the chapter governing any particular discovery method" (CCP §2023.030, *see* ¶*8:1901 ff.*). Although other discovery procedures clearly provide for terminating sanctions, CCP §2033.290 does *not*.

e. [8:1404] **Costs imposed for denials proved false at trial:** If the responding party is found to have *unreasonably* denied an RFA, he or she may be ordered to pay the costs and fees incurred by the requesting party in proving that matter. On the requesting party's motion, the court is *required* to make this costs and expenses award ("court *shall* make this order . . .") unless the responding party proves a statutorily-recognized excuse (¶*8:1406 ff.*). [CCP §2033.420(a) & (b) (emphasis added)]

Costs may be awarded when the requesting party proves the matter at trial or on a motion for summary judgment. [*Barnett v. Penske Truck Leasing Co., L.P.* (2001) 90 CA4th 494, 497-499, 108 CR2d 821, 823-824]

Discovery sanctions distinguished: A CCP §2033.420 award of expenses and attorney fees for proving matters that were unreasonably denied in an RFA is different from sanctions for misuse of the discovery process. "[A]n award of costs of proof under section 2033.420 is not a 'discovery sanction' or a 'penalty' for engaging in 'misuses of the discovery process' . . . Costs of proof in connection with requests for admission are awarded if the response is established to be incorrect—not for the misuse of the discovery process." [*City of Glendale v. Marcus Cable Assocs., LLC* (2015) 235 CA4th 344, 359, 185 CR3d 331, 342 (internal citations omitted)—"discovery sanctions for the nine types of discovery misconduct itemized in . . . section 2023.010 do not apply to the denial of a request for admission without a reasonable basis"; *Orange County Water Dist. v. The Arnold Eng. Co.* (2018) 31 CA5th 96, 115, 242 CR3d 350, 366—"an award of expenses pursuant to [CCP §2033.420] is not a penalty. Instead, it is designed to reimburse reasonable expenses incurred by a party in proving the truth of a requested admission where the admission sought was 'of substantial importance' such that trial would have been expedited or shortened if the request had been admitted" (internal quotes and citations omitted)]

(1) [8:1404.1] **Includes failure to investigate:** If a party who denies a request for admission lacks personal knowledge but had available sources of information and failed to make a reasonable investigation, the failure will justify a CCP §2033.420 award of costs and expenses. [*Rosales v. Thermex-Thermatron, Inc.* (1998) 67 CA4th 187, 198, 78 CR2d 861, 867-868; *Doe v. Los Angeles County Dept. of Children & Family Services* (2019) 37 CA5th 675, 691, 250 CR3d 62, 78—responding party has "duty to make a reasonable investigation of the facts"]

[8:1404.2-1404.4] *Reserved.*

(2) [8:1404.5] **"Refusal to admit" required:** Section 2033.420 shifting of costs and expenses of proof is authorized only where the responding party *refused to admit* (i.e., denied) an RFA (CCP §2033.420—"If a party fails to admit . . ."). If the responding party simply objected or gave an incomplete answer, the proponent must *first move to compel further answers* (*see* ¶*8:1378*). [*Wimberly v. Derby Cycle Corp.* (1997) 56 CA4th 618, 636, 65 CR2d 532, 543]

Failure to do so *waives* the right to further responses and bars the award of costs for proving the genuiness of the document or truth of the matter requested (since there is no refusal to admit). [See *American Federation of State, County & Municipal Employees v. Metropolitan Water Dist. of Southern Calif.* (2005) 126 CA4th 247, 268, 24 CR3d 285, 300 (finding responses constituted unequivocal denials, supporting shifting of costs and expenses of proof)]

(3) [8:1405] **Not dependent on winning at trial:** CCP §2033.420 shifting of costs and expenses of proof is designed to compensate for unnecessary expenses resulting from proving matters unreasonably denied. Thus, the propounding party may be awarded such costs and expenses even if he or she *loses* the lawsuit. [*Smith v. Circle P Ranch Co., Inc.* (1978) 87 CA3d 267, 274-275, 150 CR 828, 833]

© 2020 Thomson Reuters/The Rutter Group

☞ [8:1405a] ***PRACTICE POINTER:*** If you lose at trial, it may be difficult to establish that you proved the issue. In that case, consider using special interrogatories to the jury to establish facts (CCP §625), or questions on a special verdict form (CCP §624), in order to document your success.

(4) [8:1405.1] **Costs recoverable:** The costs and expenses award is limited to "reasonable expenses incurred . . . including reasonable attorney's fees" in *proving* matters unreasonably denied. [CCP §2033.420(a)]

(a) [8:1405.2] **Limited to expenses incurred after denial:** Only expenses resulting from the responding party's *failure to admit* the RFA are awardable. Therefore, expenses and fees incurred before the RFA was denied are not awardable under CCP §2033.420. [*Garcia v. Hyster Co.* (1994) 28 CA4th 724, 736, 34 CR2d 283, 290; *Wimberly v. Derby Cycle Corp.*, supra, 56 CA4th at 638, 65 CR2d at 544]

(b) [8:1405.3] **Limited to expenses incurred in "proving" matters denied:** "Proof" requires introduction of evidence (see Ev.C. §190). Therefore, CCP §2033.420 costs and expenses cannot be awarded where the parties have merely *stipulated* at trial to facts previously denied. [*Stull v. Sparrow* (2001) 92 CA4th 860, 867-868, 112 CR2d 239, 245; *Grace v. Mansourian* (2015) 240 CA4th 523, 529-530, 192 CR3d 551, 556 (citing text)]

But where trial has begun, the fact that the case ended with a nonsuit does not defeat a costs award. [*Doe v. Los Angeles County Dept. of Children & Family Services* (2019) 37 CA5th 675, 692, 250 CR3d 62, 78 (distinguishing *Stull,* supra)]

1) [8:1405.4] **No recovery of costs for trial preparation:** Nor may §2033.420 costs and expenses be awarded for the propounding party's expenses in *preparation* for trial (e.g., where the case is settled or dismissed before trial): "Expenses are recoverable only where the party requesting the admission 'proves . . . the truth of that matter,' not where that party merely prepares to do so." [*Wagy v. Brown* (1994) 24 CA4th 1, 6, 29 CR2d 48, 50]

Comment: Of course, the preparation expenses may be recoverable when the party ultimately proves the truth of the matter—e.g., at trial. It is essential that these costs be carefully tracked on an RFA-by-RFA basis. *See ¶8:1413.1a ff.*

2) [8:1405.5] **Compare—losing party's evidence as requisite proof:** The *losing party's evidence* may supply the "proof" required for a §2033.420 costs and expenses award to the prevailing party. [*Garcia v. Hyster Co.,* supra, 28 CA4th at 736-737, 34 CR2d at 290—where P's case-in-chief demonstrated truth of matters P had previously denied in response to RFAs, nonsuit based on these matters was equivalent of "proof" required by §2033.420]

[8:1405.6-1405.9] *Reserved.*

(5) [8:1405.10] **Awarded against client, not attorney:** Section 2033.420 costs and expenses are awardable against the client, *not* against the attorney. [*Estate of Manuel* (2010) 187 CA4th 400, 404-405, 113 CR3d 448, 451-452; *City of Glendale v. Marcus Cable Assocs., LLC* (2015) 235 CA4th 344, 354, 185 CR3d 331, 338]

(6) [8:1406] **Factors excusing denial:** Costs and expenses cannot be awarded under CCP §2033.420 if:

- An objection to the request was sustained or a response thereto was waived under CCP §2033.290 (i.e., by the discovering party's failure to file a timely motion to compel; *see* ¶*8:1383*); or
- The admission sought was "*of no substantial importance*"; or
- The party who failed to make the admission had "*reasonable ground to believe* that [he or she] would prevail on the matter"; or
- There was "*other good reason*" for the failure to admit. [CCP §2033.420(b) (emphasis added); see *Lakin v. Watkins Associated Indus.* (1993) 6 C4th 644, 650-651, 25 CR2d 109, 112; *City of Glendale v. Marcus Cable Assocs., LLC,* supra, 235 CA4th at 354, 185 CR3d at 338 (citing text); *Bloxham v. Saldinger* (2014) 228 CA4th 729, 752, 175 CR3d 650, 668]

(a) [8:1407] **Requested matter "of no substantial importance":** Section 2033.420 shifting of costs and expenses may be refused if the responding party can convince the judge that the requested admission was "of no substantial importance" (CCP §2033.420(b)(2)): "[A]s a general rule, a request for admission should have at least *some direct relationship* to one of the *central issues* in the case, i.e., an issue which, if not proven, would have *altered the results* in the case." [*Brooks v. American Broadcasting Co.* (1986) 179 CA3d 500, 509, 224 CR 838, 843 (emphasis added); *Laabs v. City of Victorville* (2008) 163 CA4th 1242, 1276, 78 CR3d 372, 401; *City of Glendale v. Marcus Cable Assocs., LLC,* supra, 235 CA4th at 354, 185 CR3d at 338]

© 2020 Thomson Reuters/The Rutter Group

- [8:1407.1] A §2033.420 costs of proof award was properly denied where, although D's RFA response failed to admit the boundary lines were accurately described in P's grant deed, accuracy of the deed's legal description was *not disputed* and was not an issue at trial; rather, the "decisive issue" was the location of the known boundary lines on the ground. [*Bloxham v. Saldinger* (2014) 228 CA4th 729, 753-754, 175 CR3d 650, 669-670]

(b) [8:1408] **"Reasonable ground to believe" in denial:** Similarly, the responding party may avoid shifting of costs and expenses by establishing that it had a *reasonable basis* for believing it would prevail on the issue at time of trial, and relied thereon in denying the RFA. [CCP §2033.420(b)(3); *Samsky v. State Farm Mut. Auto. Ins. Co.* (2019) 37 CA5th 517, 524, 250 CR3d 423, 429—burden on party seeking to prove exceptions under CCP §2033.420(b) (citing text); *Doe v. Los Angeles County Dept. of Children & Family Services* (2019) 37 CA5th 675, 691, 250 CR3d 62, 78—court need not credit self-serving testimony]

The responding party must show that at the time of denial, it held a *reasonably entertained* (i.e., based on admissible evidence) *good faith belief* that it would prevail on the issue at trial. [See *Laabs v. City of Victorville,* supra, 163 CA4th at 1276, 78 CR3d at 401; *Carlsen v. Koivumaki* (2014) 227 CA4th 879, 903-904, 174 CR3d 339, 362-363; *Grace v. Mansourian* (2015) 240 CA4th 523, 532, 192 CR3d 551, 558—party's subjective belief alone insufficient]

Where RFAs require analysis of technical, complicated or sophisticated issues, "courts are more willing to credit a party's reasonable belief that it would prevail based on expert opinion evidence." [*Orange County Water Dist. v. The Arnold Eng. Co.* (2018) 31 CA5th 96, 118, 120-121, 242 CR3d 350, 367, 370—"Where a party's position is supported by a credible opinion from a qualified expert, the mere fact that an opposing party also has a credible opinion from a qualified expert will not in most cases preclude the party from reasonably believing it would prevail"]

But relying on expert opinion may not be reasonable if the opinion is not credible and it is unclear why the party relied on the opinion. [*Samsky v. State Farm Mut. Auto. Ins. Co.*, supra, 37 CA5th at 527, 250 CR3d at 431-432]

1) **Application**

- [8:1409] At trial, D proved P's car had crossed over the center line just before the accident. P had denied an RFA on this point prior to trial, relying in part on the testimony of a witness who supported his version of the accident. Costs and expenses under CCP §2033.420 were properly denied because P showed he "reasonably entertained a good faith belief" that he would prevail on that issue at trial. [*Brooks v. American Broadcasting Co.*, supra, 179 CA3d at 511-512, 224 CR at 844-845]

[8:1409.1-1409.4] *Reserved.*

- [8:1409.5] *Compare:* In light of the substantial evidence that D ran a red light, causing the accident with P (i.e., police report, P's expert's opinion and testimony of P and an eyewitness), D's "sole reliance" on his perception that the light was yellow was *not* a reasonable basis to believe he would prevail on the issue. [*Grace v. Mansourian*, supra, 240 CA4th at 530-532, 192 CR3d at 556-558—"more than a hope or a roll of the dice" needed to avoid CCP §2033.420 costs and expenses]
- [8:1409.6] A party's reliance on a hearsay witness statement was unreasonable where the witness could not be found and there was no evidence of any effort to locate the witness. [*Samsky v. State Farm Mut. Auto. Ins. Co.*, supra, 37 CA5th at 525-526, 250 CR3d at 430]

2) [8:1410] **"Hot contest" not enough:** However, simply showing the matter was "hotly contested" at trial will not avoid a §2033.420 costs and expenses award. The responding party must also show it had a *reasonable* basis for contesting the issue. [*Brooks v. American Broadcasting Co.*, supra, 179 CA3d at 511, 224 CR at 844 (criticizing contrary language in *Haseltine v. Haseltine* (1962) 203 CA2d 48, 61, 21 CR 238, 246)]

(c) [8:1411] **"Other good reason" for failure to admit:** Finally, shifting of costs and expenses under §2033.420 may be avoided by proving there was "other good reason" for failing to admit the RFA. [CCP §2033.420(b)(4); *Brooks v. American Broadcasting Co.*, supra, 179 CA3d at 509-512, 224 CR at 843-845]

Therefore, in addition to whether the matter was "of substantial importance" and whether the responding party had a "reasonable basis" for denial, the following factors are to be considered:

- Whether *at the time the RFA was denied,* the respond-

© 2020 Thomson Reuters/The Rutter Group

ing party either knew or *should have known* (from available sources) the requested matter was of "substantial importance" and was true;

- Whether, because of *later developments*, the responding party should have realized its earlier denial was erroneous, and took steps to correct or modify it; and
- The degree to which the responding party made a good faith attempt to resolve the matter outside court (e.g., by offering stipulations as to some portion of the request). [See *Brooks v. American Broadcasting Co.*, supra, 179 CA3d at 509-511, 224 CR at 843-844; *Orange County Water Dist. v. The Arnold Eng. Co.*, supra, 31 CA5th at 115-116, 242 CR3d at 366]

1) [8:1412] **Example:** Proof that the responding party *failed to investigate* matters it was requested to admit, when the *means of obtaining the information were at hand*, supports a finding there was "no good reason" for denying the RFA and thus a §2033.420 costs and expenses award. [*Smith v. Circle P Ranch Co., Inc.* (1978) 87 CA3d 267, 275-276, 150 CR 828, 834]

(7) [8:1413] **Procedure:** The party seeking CCP §2033.420 costs and expenses may make a motion therefor *after* proving the truth of the matter (or genuineness of the document) in dispute. [CCP §2033.420(a); see *Hillman v. Stults* (1968) 263 CA2d 848, 882, 70 CR 295, 315]

(a) [8:1413.1] **Burden on moving party:** As with any other motion, the moving party must set forth *specific facts supporting the amount* of costs and expenses sought (*see ¶8:1405.1 ff. for discussion of amount awardable and limitations thereon*).

1) [8:1413.1a] **Accounting required:** An accounting is required (e.g., by declarations from moving party's counsel) setting forth the hourly fees and time spent to "prove" the specific matters denied, as opposed to time spent in preparation for trial generally or in proving other matters at trial of the case. [*Garcia v. Hyster Co.* (1994) 28 CA4th 724, 737, 34 CR2d 283, 290—conclusionary statements by counsel *not* sufficient]

[8:1413.1b] ***PRACTICE POINTER:*** Carefully track your time and costs associated with proving matters on an issue-by-issue (RFA-by-RFA) basis to facilitate granting of your motion for compensation.

(b) [8:1413.2] **Timing of motion:** In most instances, the motion will be brought *after trial*, because the conditions for a §2033.420 award generally cannot be determined until then (e.g., importance of the matter denied, reasonableness of denial).

But where a party successfully moves for summary judgment demonstrating that a denial to a request for admission was not supported by the evidence (*see ¶8:1404*), the motion may be made after summary judgment is granted. [See *Barnett v. Penske Truck Leasing Co., L.P.* (2001) 90 CA4th 494, 497-499, 108 CR2d 821, 823-824 (citing text)]

1) [8:1413.3] **Cost bill?** It is unclear whether a motion for costs and expenses under CCP §2033.420 is subject to CRC 3.1700(a)(1) (cost bill must be filed within 15 days after mailing of notice of entry of judgment or within 180 days after entry of judgment, whichever occurs first) or CRC 3.1702(b)(1) (motion for attorney fees must be filed and served within 60 days after mailing of notice of entry of judgment or within 180 days after entry of judgment, whichever occurs first).

Cross-refer: See further discussion of attorney fees and costs awards in Wegner, Fairbank, Epstein & Chernow, *Cal. Prac. Guide: Civil Trials & Evidence* (TRG), Ch. 17.

[8:1413.4] ***PRACTICE POINTER:*** To be safe, file the motion within the 15-day period after notice of entry of judgment is given.

(8) [8:1414] **Findings:** The statute does not expressly require the trial court to make written findings supporting the imposition of a CCP §2033.420 costs and expenses award—i.e., findings showing that the basic statutory requirements were satisfied and disclosing the basis for the court's computation of the amount and reasonableness of the award. But such findings may be desirable "in the interest of availing the aggrieved party of a meaningful appellate review" of those issues. [See *Smith v. Circle P Ranch Co., Inc.* (1978) 87 CA3d 267, 278-280, 150 CR 828, 836-837 (costs of proof award reversed and remanded where record on appeal was insufficient to show amount awarded was reasonably related to expenses and attorney fees necessarily incurred by propounding party and reasonably related to proving matters wrongfully denied)]

[8:1415-1416] *Reserved.*

(9) [8:1416.1] **Appeal:** An appeal lies from a postjudgment order granting *or denying* attorney fees under CCP §2033.420. [*Lakin v. Watkins Associated Indus.* (1993) 6 C4th 644, 653-654, 25 CR2d 109, 114]

© 2020 Thomson Reuters/The Rutter Group

Cross-refer: For a comprehensive treatment of appealable orders and judgments, see Eisenberg, *Cal. Prac. Guide: Civ. Appeals & Writs* (TRG), Ch. 2.

CHAPTER 8I

PHYSICAL OR MENTAL EXAMINATIONS

CONTENTS

© 2020 Thomson Reuters/The Rutter Group

© 2020 Thomson Reuters/The Rutter Group

RESERVED

PHYSICAL OR MENTAL EXAMINATIONS

[8:1509] **Statute:** CCP §2032.010 et seq. sets forth the procedure to obtain a medical examination of a person whose mental or physical condition or blood group is in controversy in the action.

STRATEGIES AND TACTICS RE PHYSICAL OR MENTAL EXAMS

[8:1510] **Advantages**

- **Best method to evaluate opponent's condition:** A physical or mental exam of an opposing party is clearly the best method of evaluating claims of injury, illness or incapacity by that party. It gives defendants in personal injury cases the opportunity to have their own doctors examine plaintiff and evaluate the claimed injury. Otherwise, the defense would be completely at the mercy of such witnesses as plaintiff might call. [See *Mercury Cas. Co. v. Sup.Ct. (Garcia)* (1986) 179 CA3d 1027, 1033, 225 CR 100, 103 (citing text)]
- **May result in access to reports otherwise protected from discovery:** When defendant obtains a medical exam of plaintiff, plaintiff's counsel will usually demand a copy of the defense medical examiner's report. Plaintiff's demand *entitles* defendant to copies of *plaintiff's* doctors' reports. This may include reports otherwise protected from discovery (*see ¶8:1611*).

[8:1511] **Disadvantages**

- **Cost:** The review of medical records, the physical examination and the examiner's report in a routine case will cost at least $1,000 (much more, in some areas). This expense may not be justified in smaller cases or where the claimant concedes full recovery. (If such cases go to trial, defendant can use expert testimony based on review of plaintiff's medical records.)
- **Need medical records first:** Unless the medical examiner knows what to look for, the examination may be a waste of time. Thus, the examiner will need to review all available hospital records, medical reports, x-rays, lab tests, etc. *prior* to the examination. Unless opposing counsel cooperates, this can take a lot of time and money: Counsel seeking the exam may have to send out interrogatories to find out what medical records exist; and then follow up with deposition subpoenas to obtain copies. This can be a very expensive procedure.
- **Report may not be helpful:** There is always a risk the examination may backfire. The examiner's report might actually support, or even amplify, the injured party's claims. Defendant's medical expert might end up having to give testimony at trial that actually *hurts* defendant's case.

© 2020 Thomson Reuters/The Rutter Group

1. [8:1512] **Examinations by Stipulation:** In lieu of the statutory procedures discussed below (¶*8:1516 ff.*), parties may stipulate in writing for a physical or mental examination on whatever terms and conditions they choose. [CCP §2016.030]

   a. [8:1513] **Comment:** As a practical matter, most medical examinations are arranged by stipulation between counsel, rather than by demand or court order. (Some judges require a showing that a stipulation was *refused* before they will find "good cause" for ordering an examination.)

   b. [8:1514] **Caution re stipulations:** Unless otherwise *expressly* provided, a stipulation for medical examination is deemed to incorporate *all* of the provisions of CCP §2032.610 et seq., including the rules for *exchange of medical reports* and *waiver of privilege* (¶*8:1611*). [See CCP §2032.610; *Grover v. Sup.Ct. (Paddock Eng. Co.)* (1958) 161 CA2d 644, 649, 327 P2d 212, 215]

   [8:1515] ***PRACTICE POINTER:*** In view of the foregoing, make sure you and your client understand the consequences of stipulating to a medical exam before doing so. If you do not intend to exchange otherwise privileged medical reports, make sure the stipulation *expressly* so provides.

   Also, make sure your stipulation clearly sets forth *each specific test and procedure* as well as *conditions* of the examination (where, when, who is to be present, etc.). This can avoid unpleasant surprises at the examination and the need for motions for protective orders and sanctions. *See* ¶*8:1538 ff.*

2. [8:1516] **Physical Examination by Demand in Personal Injury Cases:** A defendant in a personal injury case has the right to *one* physical examination of the plaintiff, without leave of court, simply by serving a written demand on plaintiff. [CCP §2032.220(a)]

   "Plaintiff" includes a cross-complainant and "defendant" includes a cross-defendant. [CCP §2032.210]

   [8:1516.1] ***PRACTICE POINTER:*** It is defense counsel's responsibility to *obtain plaintiff's medical records* for use by the examining physician—if necessary, by serving a CCP §2031.010 et seq. demand for inspection of records (*see* ¶*8:1435 ff.*) sufficiently in advance of the exam.

   a. [8:1517] **What type of examination:** Only a *physical* examination of the personal injury plaintiff is authorized by demand. [CCP §2032.220(a)]

      (1) [8:1518] **NOT mental exams:** Even if plaintiff claims "mental suffering and emotional distress" as a result of his or her personal injury, mental exams are *not* available on demand. (But a mental exam may be *ordered* by the court unless plaintiff limits what

claims and evidence of mental suffering will be made; *see* ¶*8:1567*.)

(2) [8:1519] **Limited to conditions "in controversy":** The physical exam is limited to whatever portion of plaintiff's body or conditions are "in controversy" in the lawsuit. [CCP §2032.020(a); *see* ¶*8:1552*]

(3) [8:1519.1] **Separate injuries do not entitle defendant to more than one exam:** Only a single examination can be obtained on demand despite the variety of injuries claimed.

For example, if plaintiff claims both orthopedic and neurologic injuries resulting from the accident, the medical examination will have to cover both. Plaintiff cannot be compelled by demand to submit to *separate* examinations by an orthopedist and neurologist, absent a stipulation or court order.

(a) [8:1519.2] **Comment:** Because only one examination is permitted, consider postponing it until the plaintiff's condition has stabilized. *See* ¶*8:1558*.

(4) [8:1520] **No "painful, protracted or intrusive" tests:** The defendant is entitled only to an *examination* of plaintiff's person. This does *not* include "any diagnostic test or procedure that is painful, protracted or intrusive." [CCP §2032.220(a)(1)]

(Compare: Such tests might be authorized by *court order*, although it is unlikely; *see* ¶*8:1564.1*.)

(5) [8:1520.1] **Questioning plaintiff regarding medical history?** The statute mentions only a "physical examination." Nothing is said about the right to question the plaintiff regarding his or her injuries or prior medical history.

(a) [8:1520.2] **Comment:** Although there is no known authority in point, some questioning is obviously essential to the doctor's examination (e.g., "where does it hurt?"). Beyond this, the scope of permissible questioning is unclear.

Examining doctors may properly claim they need to ask about the patient's *entire* medical history in order to evaluate other potential causes of the patient's present condition.

On the other hand, the statutory term "physical examination" might not permit questioning as to matters entitled to *privacy* protection if discovery were sought by other means (e.g., demands for production of plaintiff's "lifetime medical history"; *see* ¶*8:305*).

Counsel can protect against inappropriate questioning by exercising the right to be present to observe and record the examination. [CCP §2032.510(a); *see* ¶*8:1584*]

(6) [8:1520.3] **No vocational examination:** Because a vocational examination is not one of the methods for discovery au-

© 2020 Thomson Reuters/The Rutter Group

thorized in the Discovery Act (CCP §2016.010 et seq.), a court may not compel a vocational exam by one who is not a licensed physician (or health care professional). [*Browne v. Sup.Ct. (Reeves)* (1979) 98 CA3d 610, 615, 159 CR 669, 672—a physical examination *cannot* be conducted by a "vocational rehabilitation expert"; *Haniff v. Sup.Ct. (Hohman)* (2017) 9 CA5th 191, 208, 214 CR3d 844, 857]

b. [8:1521] **Who may demand:** "Any defendant" (or cross-defendant) may demand one physical examination of the plaintiff (or cross-complainant) in personal injury cases. [CCP §2032.220(a)]

"The choice of the examining physician generally belongs to the defendant . . ., although the plaintiff has a right to the presence of counsel during the examination." [*Pratt v. Union Pac. R.R. Co.* (2008) 168 CA4th 165, 181, 85 CR3d 321, 334 (internal citation omitted)]

(1) [8:1522] **Each of several defendants?** Under the wording of §2032.220(a) ("*any* defendant"), *each* defendant apparently has the right to demand a *separate* physical examination of plaintiff; i.e., plaintiff arguably may be compelled to submit to as many examinations as there are codefendants.

(a) [8:1523] **Comment:** This may be a "glitch" in the statute. Under former law (requiring a court order for physical exams even in personal injury cases), codefendants were generally limited to a *single* examination of plaintiff. I.e., they had to agree upon the medical examiner and split the costs. Under the present statute, each defendant apparently can demand a separate examination by its own doctor.

However, a *protective order* would clearly be appropriate to prevent repeated examinations where the injury issues are the same as to each defendant.

[8:1524] *Reserved.*

(2) [8:1525] **Third-party cross-defendant may demand examination of plaintiff:** The statute expressly provides: "As used in this subdivision, plaintiff includes a cross-complainant, and defendant includes a cross-defendant." [CCP §2032.210]

This apparently allows a third-party cross-defendant to demand a physical exam of the *plaintiff* as well as of any cross-complainant. (Example: P sues D; D cross-complains for equitable indemnity against joint tortfeasor TP. TP can apparently obtain a physical examination of P on demand.)

(a) [8:1526] **Comment:** This makes sense. A cross-defendant sued for indemnity may have as much at stake as the defendant, and therefore should have as much right to discovery as the defendant.

c. [8:1527] **When demand may be made:** The demand may be made anytime after the defendant has been served or has appeared in the action. (Thus, defendant can demand a medical exam before pleading and while plaintiff's discovery is still on "hold.") [CCP §2032.220(b); see *California Shellfish, Inc. v. United Shellfish Co.* (1997) 56 CA4th 16, 22, 64 CR2d 797, 800, fn. 5]

d. [8:1528] **Demand procedure:** The procedure is similar to that provided for document inspection under CCP §2031.010 et seq. (¶*8:1435 ff.*).

FORM: Demand for Physical Examination, *see Form 8:29* in Rivera, *Cal. Prac. Guide: Civ. Pro. Before Trial FORMS* (TRG).

(1) [8:1529] **Content of demand:** Defendant's demand must specify the following:

- *Date* and *time* of exam (date designated must be at least 30 days after service of demand; *see* ¶*8:1530*);
- *Place* of exam (within 75 miles of plaintiff's residence; *see* ¶*8:1531*);
- The examiner's *identity and specialty* (see "examiner's qualifications," ¶*8:1532*); and
- The "*manner, conditions, scope* and *nature* of the examination." [CCP §2032.220(a)(2), (c) & (d)]

Other demands are improper (e.g., demands for "a complete medical history"). Plaintiff may object and refuse compliance (¶*8:1542*).

(a) [8:1530] **Date of examination vs. date for response:** The date designated in the demand must be at least 30 days after service of the demand (extended for service by mail). The court, on motion, may shorten the time. [CCP §§2032.220(d), 2016.050]

Note, however, that the plaintiff (responding party) has *20 days* within which to *respond* to the demand (CCP §2032.230(b); ¶*8:1543*).

[8:1530.1] ***PRACTICE POINTER:*** Absent some special urgency, it may be advantageous for defense counsel to designate an exam date at least 60 days later than the demand. That way, if plaintiff's response (20 days after the demand) raises any objections, there is still time to attempt to resolve the matter informally, and to have a motion to compel heard, without rescheduling the exam.

(b) [8:1531] **Place of examination:** The examination must be conducted *within 75 miles* of plaintiff's residence. [CCP §2032.220(a)(2)]

© 2020 Thomson Reuters/The Rutter Group

- [8:1531.1] **Compare:** For examinations upon *court order*, an examinee may be compelled to travel more than 75 miles; *see ¶8:1577.1*.

(c) [8:1532] **Examiner's qualifications:** The physical exam must be conducted by a licensed physician "or other appropriate licensed health care practitioner." [CCP §2032.020(b)]

1) [8:1533] **"Licensed health care practitioner":** This wording apparently allows chiropractors, optometrists, audiologists, physical therapists, etc. to conduct the examination in "appropriate" cases.

2) [8:1534] **Comment:** Although permissible, this may not be practical. Since defendant has the right to only *one* examination on demand, it will usually select an examiner with the best possible qualifications—i.e., in most cases, a licensed physician.

[8:1535] ***PRACTICE POINTERS RE SELECTION OF DEFENSE MEDICAL EXAMINER:*** If you represent defendant and are demanding a medical examination, your choice should reflect the following considerations:

- **Competence:** First of all, choose someone whose credentials are proper for the type of examination required (i.e., a board-certified specialist in most cases).
- **Clarity:** The physician must be able to write reports that can readily be understood by lawyers, judges and insurance claims managers—in short, a report that is intelligible to *non-doctors*. Reports written in impenetrable jargon or technical verbiage create the impression the doctor is trying to "snow" opposing counsel or the judge, rather than to convey important information. The physician should also be able to testify articulately as an expert witness if the case goes to trial. Many otherwise competent physicians lack these abilities, which diminishes the value of their opinions.
- **Reliable and prompt:** Your medical examiner must be able to keep appointments and prepare reports on time. (The doctor's canceling the exam or failure to deliver a report within 30 days after the examination could expose you or your client to sanctions; *see ¶8:1608*.) Therefore do not choose doctors who appear to be too busy to meet their commitments. (Doctors who fail to return your telephone calls are not likely to be prompt on other matters.)

- **Persuading adversary:** Most personal injury cases settle before trial. Settlement possibilities are enhanced by selecting a physician whose opinion will be respected by the opposing party. Choosing an "old warhorse" doctor, who does nothing but testify for one side or the other, and who hasn't treated patients for years, won't do much for your settlement prospects. The report of a competent, articulate physician who is actively engaged in the treatment of patients will usually be much more helpful.

3) [8:1536] **Persons assisting examiner:** Although the statute does not expressly say so, medical examinations apparently may be conducted by persons working *under the general direction* of a licensed physician or health care practitioner.

- [8:1536.1] **Examples:** For example, *x-ray exams* and *lab tests* may be conducted inside or outside the physician's office, as long as under the "general direction" of a licensed physician. [See *Reuter v. Sup.Ct. (Tag Enterprises)* (1979) 93 CA3d 332, 339, 155 CR 525, 530 (decided under former law)]

[8:1537] *Reserved.*

(d) [8:1538] **Conditions of examination:** The requirement for specification of the "*manner*, *conditions*, *scope* and *nature* of the examination" apparently requires disclosure of whatever diagnostic tests and procedures will be utilized (x-rays, blood and urine samples, etc.). [See CCP §2032.220(c)]

It is not clear if the notice must disclose: e.g., observers who will be present, the examiner's intent to photograph or videotape the exam.

[8:1539] ***PRACTICE POINTER:*** To avoid problems, make your demand as specific and complete as possible. Ask the physician whom you select as the examiner to *write out* the tests and procedures he or she proposes to utilize and *include these in the demand.* Also include names of all other persons who will be present, whether photographs or videotaping is contemplated, etc.

(2) [8:1540] **Service of demand:** Defendant must serve a copy of the demand for physical examination on the plaintiff and on all other parties who have appeared in the action. [CCP §2032.220(e)]

© 2020 Thomson Reuters/The Rutter Group

Personal service under CCP §1011 is authorized (CCP §2016.050). If personal service is made to a party's residence, it must be made between the hours of 8 a.m. and 8 p.m. If personal service is made to an attorney's office and no one is in the office, the papers can be left in a conspicuous space between 9 a.m. and 5 p.m. [CCP §1011(a), (b)(1)]

(3) [8:1541] **Not filed with court:** As with discovery requests generally, the demanding party *retains* the original demand and receives the original response. These originals must be retained until 6 months after final disposition of the action. [CCP §2032.260]

e. [8:1542] **Plaintiff's response:** Plaintiff is under a duty to respond in writing to defendant's demand, either by:

- Agreeing to it outright; or
- Agreeing as modified in the response; or
- Refusing to comply for *reasons stated* in the response. [CCP §2032.230(a)]

FORM: Response to Demand for Physical Examination, *see Form 8:30* in Rivera, *Cal. Prac. Guide: Civ. Pro. Before Trial FORMS* (TRG).

(1) [8:1542.1] **Protective order unnecessary:** CCP §2032.010 et seq. contains no provision for protective orders. But such orders are unnecessary because plaintiffs can simply state their objections to the demand and *refuse* to be examined. Defendant will then have to move for an order compelling the examination.

[8:1542.2] *Reserved.*

(2) [8:1542.3] **Agreement upon conditions:** Alternatively, plaintiff may respond by *agreeing* to the examination, but only under designated conditions.

☞ [8:1542.4] ***PRACTICE POINTER:*** Such response is appropriate where defendant's demand is too general. For example, in response to a demand for a "complete physical examination," P might agree to appear for examination upon condition that:

- P's attorney or a representative designated in writing shall be permitted to be present throughout the examination, to take notes and to make an *audio* recording of the examination (*see* ¶*8:1583 ff.*);
- the physical exam be *limited to the specific parts* of the body that P has placed in controversy;
- the exam consists of those *specific procedures* set forth in the demand or otherwise agreed to;

- no X-rays shall be taken (if P has given the examining physician access to existing X-rays; *see* ¶*8:1580 ff.*); and
- *P shall not be questioned* by the examining physician or anyone in the physician's employ *other than as to present or past symptoms* relating to the injuries which are the subject of this action. (This condition may provoke controversy. *See* ¶*8:1520.1 ff.*)

(3) [8:1543] **Time limit for response:** Plaintiff's response is due within *20 days* after service of the demand (extended for service by mail, overnight delivery or fax or electronically; see CCP §§1010.6(a)(4), 1013, ¶*9:87 ff.*). [CCP §§2032.230(b), 2016.050]

If the last day falls on a weekend or holiday, the time limit is extended to the next court day closer to the trial date. [CCP §2016.060]

The court has power to shorten or lengthen the time for plaintiff's response, but a "motion" (apparently meaning a noticed motion rather than ex parte application) is required. [See CCP §2032.230(b)]

(a) [8:1543.1] **Delay waives objections:** If plaintiff fails to file a timely response, he or she *waives* any objection to the demand. [CCP §2032.240(a)]

(b) [8:1543.2] **Plaintiff may move for relief from waiver:** However, the court on noticed motion may relieve plaintiff from this waiver if it finds:

- Plaintiff has now filed a response that "substantially complies" with the statutory requirements; and
- Plaintiff's delay in responding resulted from "mistake, inadvertence, or excusable neglect." [CCP §2032.240(a)]

[8:1543.3] *Reserved.*

(c) [8:1543.4] **No relief under CCP §473(b):** Because the Discovery Act contains specific conditions for relief from waiver, relief *cannot* be obtained under CCP §473(b) (which authorizes relief generally for "mistake, inadvertence, surprise or excusable neglect"; *see* ¶*5:282 ff.*).

CCP §473(b) relief is available in discovery proceedings only where there is *no analogous provision* for relief under the Discovery Act. [See *Zellerino v. Brown* (1991) 235 CA3d 1097, 1107, 1 CR2d 222, 228, *discussed at* ¶*8:10.10*]

Comment: The significance of course is that it is *often easier* to obtain relief under CCP §473(b); *see discussion at* ¶*8:10.14 ff.*

(4) [8:1544] **Service of response:** Plaintiff's response must be served on the defendant who demanded the exam, with copies to all other parties who have appeared in the action. [CCP §2032.230(b)]

f. [8:1545] **Motion to compel:** To enforce compliance with a demand for a defense physical, defendant must file a motion to compel. [CCP §§2032.240(b) (motion to compel service of response and compliance), 2032.250(a) (after receipt of response, motion to compel compliance with the demand)]

(1) [8:1545.1] **Where NO response:** If plaintiff fails to respond at all to the demand, defendant's remedy is to move for an order compelling a response. [CCP §2032.240(b)]

(a) [8:1545.2] **No attempt to resolve informally required:** Since the motion is for a *failure to respond*, no showing of a "reasonable and good faith attempt" to resolve the matter informally is required.

[8:1545.2a] ***PRACTICE POINTER:*** Even so, it's usually better practice to call opposing counsel and attempt to get a stipulation. Doing so may save your client the considerable expense involved with a noticed motion.

(b) [8:1545.3] **Too late for plaintiff to object or refuse?** Plaintiff's failure to timely respond to the demand means any objection thereto is *waived* (*see* ¶*8:1543.1*). Thus, *unless plaintiff first obtains relief from the waiver* (¶*8:1543.2*), plaintiff cannot now raise objections to the examination. The only response plaintiff can make to defendant's motion is to agree to the examination (perhaps with modifications).

(c) [8:1545.4] **Monetary sanction against losing party:** As with other motions to compel, the court "shall" impose a monetary sanction against the losing party *unless* it finds that party had "substantial justification" for its position or other circumstances make the sanction "unjust." [CCP §2032.240(c); *see* ¶*8:1921 ff.*]

(2) [8:1545.5] **For UNSATISFACTORY response:** A motion to compel may also lie where plaintiff refuses the demanded examination or agrees only on conditions defendant finds unacceptable. [CCP §2032.250(a)]

(a) [8:1545.6] **Attempt to resolve informally required:** As with discovery motions generally based on disputed responses, the motion must be accompanied by declarations stating facts showing "a reasonable and good faith attempt" to resolve the issues informally. [CCP §§2016.040, 2032.250(a); *see discussion at* ¶*8:1158 ff.*]

1) [8:1545.6a] **Opportunity for informal conference in court to resolve dispute:** *See discussion at ¶8:787.1.*

(b) [8:1545.7] **Monetary sanction against losing party:** Same as discussed above (¶*8:1545.4*).

(3) [8:1545.8] **For disobedience to prior orders:** Once the court orders plaintiff to respond, or to comply with defendant's demand for a physical exam, plaintiff risks more severe sanctions for continued refusal to comply. The court may make whatever orders are "just" for disobedience to its order, including "issue," "evidence" or "terminating" sanctions under CCP §2023.010 et seq.; and/or additional monetary sanctions. [CCP §§2032.240(d), 2032.410; *see* ¶*8:2145 ff.*]

3. [8:1546] **Examination Upon Court Order:** Except for defense physicals in personal injury cases (¶*8:1516*) and exams arranged by stipulation (¶*8:1512*), a court order is required for a §2032.010 et seq. physical or mental examination. Such order may be made only after notice and hearing, and for "good cause shown." [CCP §2032.320(a); see *Conservatorship of G.H.* (2014) 227 CA4th 1435, 1441, 174 CR3d 536, 540]

This is the *only* procedure as to which a court order is still required *before* commencing discovery. Notice and hearing are deemed essential to protect against unreasonable examinations and to safeguard the examinee's bodily and mental privacy and other constitutional rights. [See *Reuter v. Sup.Ct. (Tag Enterprises)* (1979) 93 CA3d 332, 343, 155 CR 525, 532]

a. [8:1547] **Who may be examined:** The court may order the examination of:

- Any party to the action;
- An *agent* of any party; or
- Anyone in the *custody or control* of party. [CCP §2032.020(a)]

[8:1547.1-1547.4] *Reserved.*

(1) [8:1547.5] **Agent of party:** The court may order a physical or mental examination of a nonparty who is a party's "agent." [CCP §2032.020(a)]

- [8:1547.6] Under appropriate circumstances, a child's parent may be ordered examined as the child's "agent." [See *Cruz v. Sup.Ct. (Advanced Obgyn Med. Group)* (2004) 121 CA4th 646, 651-652, 17 CR3d 368, 372—examination and blood testing of mother ordered in child's medical malpractice action because complaint alleged negligent treatment of mother during pregnancy and delivery, and mother had definable economic interest in outcome of action]

[8:1547.7-1547.9] *Reserved.*

© 2020 Thomson Reuters/The Rutter Group

- [8:1547.10] *Compare:* In Child's suit against School District and various school employees, alleging sexual molestation by another student, §2032.020(a) did not authorize the court to order a collateral interview of Child's parents as part of School District's mental exam of Child. Although one of the parents was a party to the action, School District's motion to compel sought only a mental exam of Child and Child's parents were not "parties" for purposes of *that motion*. [*Roe v. Sup.Ct. (Hollister School Dist.)* (2015) 243 CA4th 138, 144-145, 196 CR3d 317, 322]

(2) [8:1548] **Persons "in custody or control" of party:** These words are to be given a "common sense" interpretation. [See *Holm v. Sup.Ct. (Misco)* (1986) 187 CA3d 1241, 1248, 232 CR 432, 437—dead body not a "party" or "person under control of party" in will contest case]

- [8:1548.1] **Application:** For example, the court may order physical examination of a party's *employees* (e.g., the driver of D's truck); or a *minor* in the custody of a party.

- [8:1549] **Comment:** This does *not* mean such persons can be examined against their will. Rather, if such persons *refuse* the court's order, discovery sanctions can be imposed against the *party* with whom they are affiliated (*see* ¶*8:1600*).

(3) [8:1550] **Compare—nonparty witness:** The court has *no* power to order a nonparty witness, who is neither an agent nor in the custody or control of a party, to submit to *any* examination, even if stipulated to by the parties. (Example: An eyewitness to a traffic accident cannot be compelled to submit to an eye examination to determine the competency of his or her testimony.)

b. [8:1551] **Requirement that examinee's condition be "in controversy":** The examination will be limited to whatever condition is "in controversy" in the action. [CCP §2032.020(a)]

(1) [8:1552] **"In controversy":** This means the *specific injury or condition* that is the subject of the litigation. The examination must be *directly* related thereto. [See *Roberts v. Sup.Ct. (Weist)* (1973) 9 C3d 330, 337, 107 CR 309, 313]

(a) [8:1552.1] **How determined:** Often, a party's *pleadings* put his or her mental or physical condition in controversy, as when a plaintiff claims *continuing* mental or physical injury resulting from defendant's acts: "A party who chooses to allege that he has mental and emotional difficulties can hardly deny his mental state is in controversy." [See *Vinson v. Sup.Ct. (Peralta Comm. College Dist.)* (1987) 43 C3d 833, 839, 239 CR 292, 297—plaintiff claimed ongoing emotional distress from sexual harassment by former employer]

1) [8:1552.2] **Examination of one person not supported by allegations of injury to another:** Allegations of injury to one person cannot support an order for an examination of another. [*Reuter v. Sup.Ct. (Tag Enterprises)* (1979) 93 CA3d 332, 342, 155 CR 525, 531]

   • [8:1552.3] Minor's suit claimed psychiatric trauma from an accident in which he was injured and his father killed. An order for mental examination of Minor was proper. But the court could *not* order Minor's *mother* to submit to a mental examination even though she was Minor's guardian ad litem. *Her* mental condition was *not* in controversy. [*Reuter v. Sup.Ct. (Tag Enterprises)*, supra, 93 CA3d at 340, 155 CR at 530]

   [8:1552.4] *Reserved.*

2) [8:1552.5] **Allegations regarding *opposing party's* physical or mental condition:** An examination cannot be ordered of a party who has not asserted his or her mental or physical condition in support of or in defense to a claim. For example, P's general allegations that D was "negligent" and "unfit to drive" do *not* justify an order compelling D to submit to a mental or physical exam. [See *Vinson v. Sup.Ct. (Peralta Comm. College Dist.)*, supra, 43 C3d at 839, 239 CR at 297, citing *Schlagenhauf v. Holder* (1964) 379 US 104, 119-122, 85 S.Ct. 234, 243-245]

3) [8:1553] **Allegations re *past* injury not sufficient:** A mental or physical exam cannot be compelled where *no continuing injury is claimed*; e.g., where plaintiff alleges only physical injury or emotional distress *in the past.* [*Doyle v. Sup.Ct. (Caldwell)* (1996) 50 CA4th 1878, 1886-1887, 58 CR2d 476, 481-482]

4) [8:1553.1] **Compare—careful pleading may avoid exam:** By omitting claims of physical or emotional harm, plaintiff may avoid examination under §2032.010 et seq.: "A simple sexual harassment claim asking *compensation for having to endure an oppressive work environment* or for wages lost following an unjust dismissal would *not* normally create a controversy regarding the plaintiff's mental state." [*Vinson v. Sup.Ct. (Peralta Comm. College Dist.)*, supra, 43 C3d at 840, 239 CR at 297 (emphasis added)]

© 2020 Thomson Reuters/The Rutter Group

(2) [8:1554] **Mental condition in personal injury cases:** A plaintiff claiming *only physical injury* cannot be forced to submit to a psychiatric examination even on the theory her psychiatric condition decreased her tolerance to the physical pain of which she complains. [See *Roberts v. Sup.Ct. (Weist)*, supra, 9 C3d at 337, 107 CR at 313]

But a psychiatric exam may be ordered where plaintiff also claims "great *mental* pain and suffering" resulting from physical injury. [See *Reuter v. Sup.Ct. (Tag Enterprises)*, supra, 93 CA3d at 340, 155 CR at 530]

(a) [8:1555] **Plaintiff may avoid mental exam by disclaimer:** A personal injury plaintiff can avoid a mental exam by *disclaiming* any unusual mental or emotional suffering and *agreeing not to introduce expert testimony* on these issues at trial. [See CCP §2032.320(c), *discussed at ¶8:1567 ff.*]

(3) [8:1556] **Burden on moving party:** The burden is on the moving party to show (by declarations or other evidence) that the examinee's condition is "in controversy" in the action.

(a) [8:1556.1] **Pleadings:** Often, the *pleadings* will put a party's mental or physical condition "in controversy." For example, a personal injury complaint may allege that plaintiff is suffering psychiatric conditions as a result of the personal injuries sustained. Such allegations place these conditions "in controversy" and support an order for mental examination of plaintiff. [See *Reuter v. Sup.Ct. (Tag Enterprises)*, supra, 93 CA3d at 340, 155 CR at 530]

(b) [8:1556.2] **Other discovery:** If the pleadings do not mention a party's condition, other discovery procedures may. For example, defendant's answers to interrogatories or deposition questions, "I did not see" or "I did not hear" something others saw or heard, may put defendant's vision or hearing in controversy, justifying an order for medical examination.

[8:1556.3-1556.9] *Reserved.*

c. [8:1556.10] **"Examination" including fingerprints, blood tests, DNA samples?** It is not clear whether, in order to determine a party's identity or liability, the court may order a party to submit to fingerprinting, photographing or measurements (e.g., to prove identity), or to provide blood, urine or DNA samples (e.g., to prove paternity).

Comment: Although there is no clear authority in point, such tests and samples should be held included within the meaning of "physical examination" under CCP §2032.020(a). Federal cases dealing with the comparable federal rule have reached this result. [See *Harris v. Athol-Royalston Regional School Dist. Committee* (D

MA 2002) 206 FRD 30, 33-35; *McGrath v. Nassau Health Care Corp.* (ED NY 2002) 209 FRD 55, 61-62—DNA sample ordered where reasonable possibility of match with existing DNA evidence was shown]

d. [8:1557] **Requirement of "good cause" for examination:** A court order for physical or mental examination must be based on a showing of "good cause." [CCP §2032.320(a)]

This generally requires a showing both of:

- "Relevancy to the subject matter"; and
- *Specific facts* justifying discovery: i.e., allegations showing the *need* for the information sought and *lack of means for obtaining it elsewhere.* [*Vinson v. Sup.Ct. (Peralta Comm. College Dist.)* (1987) 43 C3d 833, 840, 239 CR 292, 297]

(1) [8:1557.1] **Purpose:** The purpose is to protect an examinee's privacy by preventing annoying "fishing expeditions." I.e., one party may not compel another to undergo psychiatric testing "solely on the basis of speculation that something of interest may surface." [*Vinson v. Sup.Ct. (Peralta Comm. College Dist.)*, supra, 43 C3d at 840, 239 CR at 298]

(Caution: Do not extrapolate this ban on "fishing expeditions" to discovery procedures generally. Indeed, absent a requirement of "good cause" for discovery, "fishing trips" are entirely proper. *See* ¶*8:72.*)

(2) **Application**

(a) [8:1557.2] **Continuing injury:** "Good cause" for a mental exam was shown where P alleged *continuing mental anguish and emotional distress* as a result of prior sex harassment by D: "Because the truth of these claims is relevant to plaintiff's cause of action and justifying facts have been shown with specificity, good cause . . . has been demonstrated." [*Vinson v. Sup.Ct. (Peralta Comm. College Dist.)*, supra, 43 C3d at 840-841, 239 CR at 298]

(b) [8:1558] **Second defense medical in personal injury cases:** No court order is required for a defense medical exam in personal injury cases (one exam is available on demand; ¶*8:1516*). But, if the same defendant wants to have plaintiff examined by a *second* doctor (e.g., to examine different condition), a court order must be obtained, based on a showing of "good cause" for the second examination.

"Good cause" may be found where plaintiff claims *additional* injuries, or that his or her condition is *worsening*; or even simply because of lapse of time (e.g., if it has been 3 or 4 years since the first exam and plaintiff claims *continued* symptoms, another physical examination before trial may be proper).

© 2020 Thomson Reuters/The Rutter Group

(c) [8:1558.1] **Intrusive tests:** Under appropriate circumstances, P may be compelled to submit to tests or procedures involving administration of local anesthetics and removal of skin tissue. [See *Abex Corp. v. Sup.Ct. (Crouson)* (1989) 209 CA3d 755, 758, 257 CR 498, 499-500]

Example: P claimed warts resulted from exposure to D's product. D moved for an order compelling P to submit to a biopsy of the warts. "Good cause" existed for such order based on *uncontradicted medical evidence* that the biopsy was necessary to determine the cause of the warts and would involve little pain or danger. [*Abex Corp. v. Sup.Ct. (Crouson)*, supra, 209 CA3d at 758-759, 257 CR at 499-500—mandamus compelling granting of order]

[8:1558.2-1558.4] *Reserved.*

(3) [8:1558.5] **Number of exams:** Where plaintiff's injuries are complex, several exams may be necessary by specialists in different fields. There is no limit on the number of physical *or mental* exams that may be ordered on a showing of *good cause*. The good cause requirement checks any potential harassment of plaintiff. [*Shapira v. Sup.Ct. (Sylvestri)* (1990) 224 CA3d 1249, 1255, 274 CR 516, 519 (citing text)— second mental examination may be ordered]

e. [8:1559] **Motion procedure:** The party seeking the examination must follow the usual noticed motion procedure. *See Ch. 9 Part I.*

(1) [8:1560] **Notice of motion:** The notice of motion must state the time, place, *identity and specialty* of the examiner, *and* the "manner, conditions, scope and nature of the examination." [CCP §2032.310(b)]

[8:1561] ***PRACTICE POINTERS:***

Re selection of examiner: *See ¶8:1535.*

Re date of examination: It is your responsibility to check with the doctor *before* filing the motion to make sure that the date selected is convenient for the doctor. Otherwise, you may end up with an unenforceable examination order (or a very unhappy doctor).

Also, make sure the date you request is sufficiently after the hearing date on the motion to allow you to serve notice of the order on opposing counsel and give the examinee party adequate time to appear.

Re conditions of examination: Ask the doctor whom you designate as examiner to *write out the name and description of the tests and procedures* he or she proposes to utilize; and include these in your notice (*see ¶8:1538*).

Also include in your notice of motion whatever other conditions the examinee party is likely to request (e.g., the right to have his or her lawyer present). Doing so may forestall objections, and may even result in agreement eliminating the need for a court hearing (*see* ¶*8:1539*).

[8:1561.1-1561.4] *Reserved.*

(2) [8:1561.5] **Separate statement of disputed matters required:** The notice of motion must be accompanied by a separate document setting forth the discovery request, the objection thereto and the reasons why an examination should be compelled. [See CRC 3.1345(a)(6)]

(a) [8:1561.6] **Form and content of statement:** *See discussion at* ¶*8:1151 ff.*

(3) [8:1562] **Supporting declarations:** Since the burden is on the moving party, declarations should be filed covering the following matters:

(a) [8:1562.1] **Examinee's condition "in controversy":** *See* ¶*8:1551 ff.*

(b) [8:1562.2] **"Good cause" for examination:** *See* ¶*8:1557 ff.*

(c) [8:1563] **Attempt to resolve informally:** Declarations must state facts showing that "a reasonable and good faith attempt" to arrange the examination by stipulation was unsuccessful. [CCP §2032.310(b); *see* ¶*8:1158*]

(Comment: Judges are usually reluctant to order a medical examination without a showing that a stipulation has been *refused.*)

(d) [8:1564] **Necessity for unusual test or procedure:** A court no doubt has power to authorize whatever "diagnostic tests and procedures" are appropriate in granting an order for physical or mental exam, presumably even those that are painful or dangerous (CCP §2032.320(d), ¶*8:1570*).

Whatever diagnostic tests are contemplated should be clearly described in the moving papers. (For example, if an electroencephalogram, myelogram or X-rays are anticipated, the court and the party to be examined must be made aware.)

1) [8:1564.1] **Comment:** Even so, courts are unlikely to order an unwilling examinee to submit to painful or dangerous procedures *because few doctors will perform such tests without the patient's express consent.* The risk of malpractice or other claims by an unwilling examinee is simply too great.

© 2020 Thomson Reuters/The Rutter Group

[8:1565] ***PRACTICE POINTER:*** In seeking a court order for a physical exam, avoid disputes as to whether a desired test or procedure is "unusual," "painful" or "dangerous." Obtain a *physician's declaration* for *any* procedure beyond simple x-rays, urine or blood tests. Even treadmill and exercise tests may involve some degree of danger and discomfort.

FORM: Motion for Medical Examination, *see Form 8:31* in Rivera, *Cal. Prac. Guide: Civ. Pro. Before Trial FORMS* (TRG).

(4) [8:1566] **Service of motion:** Copies of the moving papers must be served on the person sought to be examined (if not a party) and on all parties to the action. [CCP §2032.310(c)]

f. [8:1567] **Personal injury plaintiff may avoid mental exam by offering appropriate stipulations:** Personal injury plaintiffs often allege both "physical and mental suffering." Because of this, defendants often claim plaintiff's mental condition is "in controversy" and seek an order for a mental examination (*see* ¶*8:1554*).

Where plaintiff claims unusual psychiatric symptoms, a defense mental exam is clearly proper. But where the mental suffering claimed is no different than that generally associated with physical injury, forcing plaintiff to submit to a full-blown psychiatric exam may be pure harassment.

Recognizing this, the Discovery Act permits a plaintiff to *avoid* the necessity of submitting to a mental examination by stipulating that:

- *No claim is being made* for mental and emotional distress "*over and above that usually associated* with the physical injuries claimed"; *and*
- *No psychiatric testimony will be offered* at trial in support of any claimed emotional distress. [See CCP §2032.320(c)]

(1) [8:1568] **Exceptional circumstances may still justify exam:** Where such stipulations are offered by plaintiff, the court cannot order a mental examination "except on a showing of *exceptional circumstances*." [CCP §2032.320(b)]

For example, "exceptional circumstances" might include situations where, although plaintiff offers such a stipulation, plaintiff's behavior is obviously irrational or plaintiff's physical appearance suggests a mental injury. Under these circumstances, although the stipulation precludes plaintiff from expressly making a claim for mental injury or offering evidence on the subject, the jury might conclude that plaintiff sustained such an injury and award damages accordingly.

[8:1569] *Reserved.*

g. [8:1570] **Court order:** An order for a physical or mental examination must be based on findings of "good cause" (¶*8:1557*) and compliance with other statutory requirements; and it must contain the following:

- Designation of the *examiner;*
- *Time and place* of examination;
- The "*manner*, diagnostic *tests and procedures, conditions, scope* and nature of the examination." [CCP §2032.320(d) (emphasis added)]

FORM: Order for Medical Examination, *see Form 8:32* in Rivera, *Cal. Prac. Guide: Civ. Pro. Before Trial FORMS* (TRG).

(1) [8:1571] **Designation of examiner:** First of all, the order must specify the person or persons to conduct the examination. [CCP §2032.320(d)]

(a) [8:1572] **Qualifications of examiner:** A *physical* examination must be conducted by a licensed physician "or other appropriate licensed health care practitioner." [CCP §2032.020(b); *see discussion,* ¶*8:1532 ff.*]

A *mental* examination may be conducted either by:

- A licensed *physician,* or
- A licensed clinical *psychologist* with a doctoral degree and at least 5 years' experience diagnosing mental and emotional disorders. [CCP §2032.020(c)(1)]

1) [8:1572.1] **Where action involves allegations of sexual abuse of a minor:** If the action involves allegations of sexual abuse of a minor and the examinee is less than 15 years old, the mental examination must be conducted by a licensed physician or clinical psychologist with expertise in child abuse and trauma. [CCP §2032.020(c)(2)]

(b) [8:1573] **Court generally appoints physician requested by moving party:** Theoretically, in ordering a medical examination, the court could appoint whomever it chooses. However, as a practical matter, courts almost always appoint the physician requested by the moving party. [*Edwards v. Sup.Ct. (Santa Clara Unified School Dist.)* (1976) 16 C3d 905, 912-913, 130 CR 14, 18-19]

1) [8:1574] Nonetheless, if *good cause* exists for refusing the moving party's choice, the court certainly has discretion to appoint someone else. But the examinee's mere dislike for a certain doctor is probably *not* enough to prevent his or her appointment for a physical examination. [See *Edwards v. Sup.Ct. (Santa Clara Unified School Dist.),* supra, 16 C3d at 912-913, 130 CR at 18-19]

(c) [8:1575] **Examiner need not be impartial:** Medical examiners are expected to represent the interests of

© 2020 Thomson Reuters/The Rutter Group

the parties by whom they are retained. Thus, allegations that the examiner is a "mere hireling of the insurance interests" or "always writes negative reports concerning claimants for insurance benefits" do *not* disqualify the examiner. Such matters affect only the *credibility* of the examiner's report and his or her testimony at trial. [*Mercury Cas. Co. v. Sup.Ct. (Garcia)* (1986) 179 CA3d 1027, 1034, 225 CR 100, 103]

A court-ordered examination is often referred to as an "independent medical exam." But all this means is that it is independent of plaintiff's case, *not* that the examiner is unbiased. [*Mercury Cas. Co. v. Sup.Ct. (Garcia)*, supra, 179 CA3d at 1033, 225 CR at 103]

(2) [8:1576] **Date and time:** The examination will almost always be ordered at the doctor's office on a date and time requested in the moving papers.

(3) [8:1577] **Place of examination:** Where the examination is pursuant to court order, the person to be examined may be required to travel to wherever the doctor is located. [CCP §2032.320(d)]

For example, a plaintiff living outside California may be ordered to travel here and submit to an examination by a local doctor. (Defendants usually designate a local doctor, rather than a doctor where plaintiff resides, to assure the doctor will be available to testify if the case goes to trial.)

(a) [8:1577.1] **Special requirements where examinee required to travel over 75 miles:** However, where the examinee is required to travel more than 75 miles from his or her residence, the court's order must:

- Be based on a finding of "*good cause*" for the travel involved; and
- Be conditioned on the moving party paying the examinee's *reasonable travel costs.* [CCP §2032.320(e)]

(b) [8:1577.2] **Compare—exams demanded in personal injury cases:** Where a defense physical is demanded in personal injury cases (no court order required), the place of examination must be *within 75 miles* of plaintiff's residence. [CCP §2032.220(a)(2); ¶*8:1531*]

(4) [8:1578] **Scope of examination:** The order may restrict the scope of any examination—e.g., to specified portions of the body, by not requiring party to disrobe, limiting questions to be asked, etc. [*Golfland Entertainment Ctrs., Inc. v. Sup.Ct. (Nunez)* (2003) 108 CA4th 739, 745, 133 CR2d 828, 831—trial court has "broad discretion" to limit scope of questions to be asked during mental exam]

[8:1579] ***PRACTICE POINTER:*** If you represent the party or person to be examined, be sure to raise such concerns at the hearing on the motion so the court can limit the examination accordingly.

Do not wait until the time of examination and then refuse to submit to the full examination ordered. This simply postpones the dispute until the next motion hearing, running up the costs to all concerned and possibly exposing you and your client to *sanctions* for refusing to comply with the court's order (¶*8:1598 ff.*). And, with doctor's fees, monetary sanctions may be substantial.

(5) [8:1579.1] **Exam time limit where action involves sexual abuse of a minor:** In an action involving allegations of sexual abuse of a minor, the mental examination of a child under 15 years old may not exceed three hours, including breaks, though the court may extend this time limit for good cause. [CCP §2032.340]

[8:1579.2-1579.4] *Reserved.*

(6) [8:1579.5] **Specification of diagnostic tests and procedures:** The order must *specify and list by name* the diagnostic tests and procedures to be used in the examination. [*Carpenter v. Sup.Ct. (Yamaha Motor Corp.)* (2006) 141 CA4th 249, 260, 45 CR3d 821, 827—invalidating order requiring plaintiff to submit to "standardized written psychological tests" to "test emotional and cognitive functioning"]

(7) [8:1580] **Limit on X-rays:** The Discovery Act reflects public concern regarding excessive exposure to X-rays. It allows an examinee to avoid submitting to X-ray examination by giving the examiner access to *existing* X-rays of the same portion of the examinee's body. In such event, no additional X-rays may be taken without the examinee's consent "or on order of the court for good cause shown." [CCP §2032.520]

- [8:1581] For example, "good cause" for additional X-rays might exist if the existing X-rays were of poor quality or incomplete.
- [8:1581.1] Compare: Absent a showing that X-rays pose a special risk to plaintiff, a generalized fear of X-rays does *not* justify refusal to submit to X-rays. Nor can plaintiff complain of excessive X-rays if he or she is willing to have the same X-rays taken by his or her own physician. [*Ghanooni v. Super Shuttle of Los Angeles* (1993) 20 CA4th 256, 259, 24 CR2d 501, 503]

(8) [8:1582] **Others present at exam:** Courts generally permit certain other persons to be present to observe and record a *physical* examination, but not a mental examination, as discussed below (¶*8:1593 ff.*).

© 2020 Thomson Reuters/The Rutter Group

(a) [8:1583] **Physical exams—counsel and court reporter may attend:** The examinee's attorney must be permitted to observe and record a physical examination. [CCP §2032.510(a)]

1) [8:1584] **Examinee's counsel:** The attorney for the examinee or party producing the examinee is entitled to attend and observe (in person or through a representative designated in writing) any physical exam conducted for discovery purposes. [CCP §2032.510(a), (c)]

The attorney must be permitted to observe *every phase* of the examination. The court has *no discretion to exclude* counsel from any portion of the exam. [See *Munoz v. Sup.Ct. (Goings)* (1972) 26 CA3d 643, 645-646, 102 CR 686, 687]

a) [8:1585] **Purpose:** This is to assure that the examination is restricted to the scope ordered by the court, and to *prevent improper questioning* by the examining physician. [*Sharff v. Sup.Ct. (Belfast Beverages, Inc.)* (1955) 44 C2d 508, 510, 282 P2d 896, 897]

b) [8:1585.1] **Designated representative:** Counsel may designate a third person as the observer, provided the representative's authority to so act is in writing and signed by the attorney. [CCP §2032.510(c)]

2) [8:1586] **Court reporter:** The examinee's attorney is entitled to record *stenographically* or by *audio* (but not video) technology "any words spoken to or by the examinee during any phase of the examination." [CCP §2032.510(a)]

a) [8:1587] **Purpose:** This assures an objective record of what transpired and avoids unseemly disputes at trial between the attorney and the examining physician. [See *Gonzi v. Sup.Ct. (Daily News Co., Ltd.)* (1959) 51 C2d 586, 589, 335 P2d 97, 99]

☞ [8:1587.1] ***PRACTICE POINTER:*** Instruct your court reporter to record *everything audible* during the exam (including groans, exclamations of pain, etc.). Also direct the reporter to record the time the exam started and concluded. It may prove invaluable during cross-examination of the doctor at trial.

b) [8:1588] **No videotape:** However, the statute does *not* authorize the court to order the examination videotaped. An audio recording assures an objective record; there is no need for the additional intrusion that video equipment would entail. [See *Ramirez v. MacAdam* (1993) 13 CA4th 1638, 1641, 16 CR2d 911, 912-913 (citing text)]

c) [8:1588.1] **Recording by other party?** Prior case law recognized that *either party* had the right to have a court reporter present to record a physical examination. [See *Gonzi v. Sup.Ct. (Daily News Co., Ltd.)*, supra, 51 C2d at 589, 335 P2d at 99]

CCP §2032.510(a) does not state whether anyone other than the examinee is entitled to record the examination. Whether this omission was intended to change the case law is unclear.

[8:1588.2-1588.4] *Reserved.*

3) [8:1588.5] **Interpreter:** If the examinee does not "proficiently" speak or understand English, an interpreter is *required* in any medical exam requested by the defendant or by an insurance company. [Ev.C. §755.5(a)]

4) [8:1589] **Other persons:** The presence of anyone other than the examinee's counsel and a court reporter lies within the sound discretion of the court.

a) [8:1590] Thus, for example, the examinee *cannot* insist on having his or her *personal physician* present. Whether such presence is allowed is discretionary, not a matter of right. [*Long v. Hauser* (1975) 52 CA3d 490, 493, 125 CR 125, 128]

[8:1591] ***PRACTICE POINTERS***

- If you represent the party seeking the medical examination, *make sure you select a doctor who agrees* to having the examinee's lawyer and a court reporter (plus anyone else permitted by the court) present throughout the examination. Otherwise, you may find yourself having to get another doctor at the last minute.

- If you represent the examinee, it certainly isn't necessary to be present (with or without a court reporter) in every case. Indeed, if the medical examiner is known to be an ethical and competent person, it's usually a waste of time and money. But when dealing with an examiner whose integrity is open to question, or simply unknown, and where the injuries are substantial,

© 2020 Thomson Reuters/The Rutter Group

being present with a court reporter can be cost-justified.

5) [8:1592] **Controls on abuse:** If the examinee's counsel disrupts the examination (e.g., by telling examinee how to answer questions), the doctor may *suspend* the examination. The party at whose instance the examination was ordered can move for a *protective order* to control the conduct of the examinee and counsel; and for a monetary sanction. [CCP §2032.510(e)]

Likewise, if the examining doctor becomes abusive to the examinee, or tries to utilize unauthorized tests or procedures, the examinee's counsel may suspend the examination and move for a protective order and monetary sanctions against the party at whose instance the exam was ordered. [CCP §2032.510(d)]

In either event, the burden will be on the losing party to show "substantial justification" for its conduct; or other reasons why a monetary sanction would be "unjust." [CCP §2032.510(f); and see §2023.030(a)]

(b) [8:1593] **Mental exams—no observers:** The Discovery Act defers to case law in this area: "Nothing in this title shall be construed to alter, amend, or affect existing case law with respect to the presence of the attorney for the examinee or other persons during the [mental] examination . . . ." [CCP §2032.530(b)]

Case law recognizes the special need for rapport between examiner and examinee during a mental examination. Thus, absent stipulation to the contrary, *neither counsel nor court reporters* may attend. Their presence might hinder the examiner's ability to establish rapport with the examinee and thereby impair the effectiveness of the examination. [*Edwards v. Sup.Ct. (Santa Clara Unified School Dist.)* (1976) 16 C3d 905, 910, 130 CR 14, 17; and *Vinson v. Sup.Ct. (Peralta Comm. College Dist.)* (1987) 43 C3d 833, 844-845, 239 CR 292, 300-301; *Golfland Entertainment Ctrs., Inc. v. Sup.Ct. (Nunez)* (2003) 108 CA4th 739, 747-748, 133 CR2d 828, 833]

Nevertheless, the court has *discretion* to allow counsel to attend when needed (e.g., indications of likely offensive tactics). [*Vinson v. Sup.Ct. (Peralta Comm. College Dist.*, supra, 43 C3d at 845-846, 239 CR at 301; see *Toyota Motor Sales, U.S.A., Inc. v. Sup.Ct. (Braun)* (2010) 189 CA4th 1391, 1397, 117 CR3d 321, 325—proper only if *need* for counsel's monitoring shown]

1) [8:1594] **Compare—physical exams:** There is no need for rapport between the examiner and ex-

aminee in a physical exam. Hence, the presence of counsel and court reporters does not interfere. [*Edwards v. Sup.Ct. (Santa Clara Unified School Dist.)*, supra, 16 C3d at 910, 130 CR at 16-17]

2) [8:1595] **Recording the exam:** The Discovery Act specifically authorizes recording mental exams. Both examiner and examinee have the *right* to record the entire examination by *audio* (but not video) technology. [CCP §2032.530(a)]

The court may order the examiner rather than the examinee to audiorecord the examination in its entirety because this is less likely to disrupt the exam. [*Golfland Entertainment Ctrs., Inc. v. Sup.Ct. (Nunez)*, supra, 108 CA4th at 750, 133 CR2d at 835]

[8:1596] *Reserved.*

3) [8:1597] **Other procedural safeguards:** If the examinee's counsel is concerned with the accuracy of the examiner's report or conclusions, he or she may *depose* the examiner, inspect the examiner's notes and records of the examination, and introduce contradictory evidence at trial, etc. [*Edwards v. Sup.Ct. (Santa Clara Unified School Dist.)*, supra, 16 C3d at 912, 130 CR at 18]

4. [8:1598] **Sanctions:** Failure to appear or submit to examination may result in sanctions against the examinee or whichever party was required to produce him or her for examination. [CCP §§2032.410-2032.420]

Cross-refer: Procedures re sanctions generally are discussed at ¶*8:1980 ff.*

a. [8:1599] **Sanctions against examinee party:** A broad range of sanctions can be imposed against a party who fails to appear or submit to a required mental or physical exam: "issue" sanctions, "evidence" sanctions, or even "doomsday" ("terminating") sanctions, in addition to or in lieu of monetary sanctions. [CCP §§2032.410-2032.420]

(1) [8:1599.1] **Monetary sanctions:** A monetary sanction *must* be imposed against a party who unsuccessfully opposes a motion to compel compliance with a demand for physical examination unless the court finds "substantial justification" for such refusal or that imposition of sanctions would be unjust for some other reason. [CCP §2032.250(b); see *Ghanooni v. Super Shuttle of Los Angeles* (1993) 20 CA4th 256, 260, 24 CR2d 501, 503]

(a) [8:1599.1a] **Sanctions despite no opposition:** Although the statute is silent on the matter, the CRC authorize sanctions against a party who fails to oppose a motion

© 2020 Thomson Reuters/The Rutter Group

to compel, or who *withdraws* its opposition or *furnishes the requested discovery* before the motion hearing. [CRC 3.1348(a); *see* ¶*8:2008*]

(2) [8:1599.2] **Prior court order required for nonmonetary sanctions:** Issue, evidence or terminating sanctions are appropriate where the examination was ordered by the court (or arranged by written stipulation; see CCP §§2032.410-2032.420). [See *Conservatorship of G.H.* (2014) 227 CA4th 1435, 1441, 174 CR3d 536, 541—abuse of discretion to issue terminating sanction for failure to submit to mental exam where no court order for exam]

However, no prior court order is required for a defense physical in personal injury cases (see CCP §2032.220(a), ¶*8:1516*). To enforce the demand, defendant must file a motion to compel. Only *monetary* sanctions are available on the motion to compel (see CCP §2032.240(c), ¶*8:1545*).

Of course, after the court orders plaintiff to comply, broader sanctions are available if plaintiff disobeys the order (CCP §2032.240(d), ¶*8:1545.8*).

b. [8:1600] **Sanctions against party required to produce examinee:** As discussed earlier, parties may be required to produce an agent or person in their custody or control for medical examination where that person's physical or mental condition is in controversy in the action (CCP §2032.020(a), ¶*8:1547 ff.*).

If that person fails to appear or submit to a required examination, "issue," "evidence" or "terminating" sanctions can be imposed against the *party* obligated to produce that person, "*unless* the party . . . . *demonstrates an inability to produce* that person for examination." [CCP §2032.420 (emphasis added)]

- [8:1601] Thus, for example, if the court has ordered an employer (party) to produce an employee for physical exam, no sanctions are proper if the employer *proves* its *inability to produce* the employee. (E.g., declarations showing the employee has refused to submit despite good faith efforts by the employer.)

[8:1601.1-1601.4] *Reserved.*

c. [8:1601.5] **Compare—sanctions against attorney:** Monetary sanctions against the party's attorney require a finding that the attorney *advised* the client's conduct that resulted in sanctions. [*Ghanooni v. Super Shuttle of Los Angeles* (1993) 20 CA4th 256, 261, 24 CR2d 501, 504]

(1) [8:1601.6] **Burden on attorney:** The burden is on the attorney to prove he or she had *not* advised the client to engage in the sanctionable conduct. [*Ghanooni v. Super Shuttle of Los Angeles*, supra, 20 CA4th at 261, 24 CR2d at 504]

(2) [8:1601.7] **Opposition to motion not sufficient:** Plaintiff's counsel's opposition to a motion to compel plaintiff to submit

to an examination does *not* show plaintiff was advised to refuse the examination: "They were simply doing their job as advocates to try to protect their client from sanctions." [*Ghanooni v. Super Shuttle of Los Angeles*, supra, 20 CA4th at 261, 24 CR2d at 504]

5. [8:1602] **Exchange of Medical Reports; Waiver of Privilege:** The following rules apply whether the examination was conducted by stipulation, or by defendant's demand in personal injury cases, or by court order:

   a. [8:1603] **Examinee's OPTION to demand copy of examiner's report:** The party being examined (typically, the plaintiff) will normally want a copy of the examiner's report to gauge settlement prospects and to prepare for trial. The statute provides a mechanism for doing so: The examinee (plaintiff) has the *option* of demanding in writing that defendant (party at whose instance the examination was conducted) provide the information below (¶*8:1604*). [CCP §2032.610(a)]

      Moreover, the examinee is entitled to demand such report *even if the examining physician has not prepared one:* "The trade-off is clear: If one party to personal injury litigation is required by his or her opponent to submit to a medical examination, at the very least he or she is entitled to a report of the information obtained by the adversary in litigation." [*Kennedy v. Sup.Ct. (Lucky Stores, Inc.)* (1998) 64 CA4th 674, 678, 75 CR2d 373, 375]

      (1) [8:1604] **What must be provided:** If plaintiff so demands, the defendant must provide within *30 days* after service of the demand (extended for service by mail) and in no event later than 15 days before trial, the following:

         - **Examiner's report:** "A copy of a detailed written report setting out the history, examinations, findings, *including the results of all tests made*, diagnoses, prognoses, and conclusions of the examiner"; and
         - **Other reports:** "A copy of reports of all *earlier examinations* of the same condition of the examinee made by that *or any other examiner*." [CCP §2032.610(a) (emphasis added)]

         ➪ [8:1605] ***PRACTICE POINTER FOR PLAINTIFFS:*** If your demand specifies less than indicated above (¶*8:1604*), your opponent need not provide anything more. Therefore, if you decide to exercise this option, *use the statutory language* to make sure you get everything available.

         ➪ [8:1605.1] ***PRACTICE POINTER FOR DEFENDANTS:*** Beware of this if you represent defendants. By demanding plaintiff's physical, you give plaintiff the right to obtain not only the examiner's report but *all earlier reports* as well.

© 2020 Thomson Reuters/The Rutter Group

Defense files often contain candid reports by earlier examiners (e.g., conducted while the claim was being investigated by the insurance carrier) that are devastating to the defense. By turning these over, you will be giving plaintiff a "road map" to the weaknesses in your case.

FORM: Demand for Copy of Report of Medical Exam, *see Form 8:33* in Rivera, *Cal. Prac. Guide: Civ. Pro. Before Trial FORMS* (TRG).

(a) [8:1606] **No work product protection:** Although the examiner's report and all earlier reports may have been obtained to assist defense counsel in preparation for trial, no work product objection lies. Nor can defense counsel object on this ground to plaintiff's deposing the medical examiners. [CCP §2032.610(c); see *Kennedy v. Sup.Ct. (Lucky Stores, Inc.)*, supra, 64 CA4th at 679, 75 CR2d at 375 (citing text)]

(b) [8:1606.1] **Effect of defense "withdrawing" examiner as testifying expert:** The examinee's right to a copy of the examination report is not affected by defendant's withdrawing the examiner as a testifying expert. That may affect plaintiff's right to *depose* the examiner (*see ¶8:1687.5*) but it does not affect the right to a copy of the examiner's report. [*Kennedy v. Sup.Ct. (Lucky Stores, Inc.)*, supra, 64 CA4th at 678-679, 75 CR2d at 375]

(c) [8:1606.2] **"Examiners" vs. "nonexamining consultants":** The statute requires only that "examiner" reports be exchanged. This presumably does not apply to reports by medical *consultants* who may have looked at hospital and medical records, x-rays and lab reports, but *never examined plaintiff personally.* Their reports to defense counsel, whether oral or written, are apparently still protected as work product. [See *Queen of Angels Hosp. v. Sup.Ct. (Jones)* (1976) 57 CA3d 370, 374, 129 CR 282, 284—dictum that work product claim sustainable if doctor had not physically examined plaintiff and "merely submitted a hypothetical opinion based on assumed facts"]

[8:1606.3] *Reserved.*

1) [8:1606.4] **Compare—effect of designation under §2034.010 et seq.:** However, if such "nonexamining consultants" are later designated under CCP §2034.010 et seq. to testify as expert witnesses at trial, their *reports* must then be turned over; *see ¶8:1681.*

[8:1606.5] ***PRACTICE POINTER:*** Some defense counsel are not comfortable relying on the distinction between discovery of reports by "examiners" and "nonexamining consultants." They therefore instruct even nonexamining consultants to report to them *orally*—so there will never be a "report" to exchange.

However, this is dangerous because if the consultant is later called to testify as an expert witness at trial, the failure to make a written report may undermine his or her *credibility*. Opposing counsel may forcefully argue that reasonable experts *would have made reports*.

(2) [8:1607] **Enforcing demand:** If defendant (party who obtained the examination) fails to make timely delivery of the examiners' reports, plaintiff (examinee) may file a motion to compel delivery. [CCP §2032.620(a)]

(a) [8:1607.1] **Attempt to resolve informally required:** The usual declaration showing a "reasonable and good faith attempt" to resolve the matter outside court must accompany the moving papers. [CCP §§2016.040, 2032.620(a); *see* ¶*8:1158*]

(b) [8:1608] **Monetary sanction against losing party:** A monetary sanction "shall" be imposed against the losing party on the motion to compel *unless* the court finds "substantial justification" for that party's position or other circumstances make the sanction "unjust." [CCP §2032.620(b); *see* ¶*8:1921 ff.*]

(Arguably, the examining party might be able to show it was entirely the fault of the examiner over whom it had no control.)

(c) [8:1609] **Sanctions for disobeying order:** Once an order for delivery of medical reports is made, the full range of discovery sanctions is available if the order is disobeyed. The court may impose whatever sanctions are "just," including:

- "Issue," "evidence" or "terminating" sanctions against the examining party; or
- Monetary sanctions in addition to or in lieu of the above. [CCP §2032.620(c); and see CCP §2023.030(b)-(d), *discussed at* ¶*8:2175 ff.*]

(Arguably, a *contempt* sanction could also be imposed if "just"; but §2032.620(c) et seq. does not expressly so provide.)

(d) [8:1610] **Examiner's testimony barred:** Whether or not any other sanction is imposed, an examiner whose report has not been furnished in response to court order will *not* be permitted to testify at trial: "The court *shall exclude* at trial the testimony of any health care practitioner whose report has not been provided by a party ordered to do so by the court." [CCP §2032.650(c) (emphasis added)]

Effect: Unless other examinations are permitted, the examining party will be without qualified expert testimony.

b. [8:1611] **Demand entitles examining party to examinee's reports:** Plaintiff's demand for and obtaining copies of the defense medical examiner's report has two significant consequences:

- It entitles defendant to receive in exchange (simultaneously) copies of all medical *reports by the plaintiff's doctors* and experts; and
- It *waives any privilege* that otherwise would protect such reports from discovery. [CCP §2032.630; *see* ¶*8:254 ff.*]

(1) [8:1612] **Impact—REPORTS must be turned over:** In the usual personal injury case, it would be foolhardy for plaintiff's counsel *not* to request a copy of the defense medical report. But doing so ends any claim of "privilege" or "work product" protecting the reports or testimony of plaintiff's doctors. (The doctor-patient privilege is waived in personal injury cases in any event; Ev.C. §§996, 1016.)

(a) [8:1613] **No work product protection:** Thus, even reports of doctors and experts who have examined plaintiff on a *consultant* basis (not to testify at trial), and whose reports would otherwise be protected as "attorney's work product," become discoverable by the defense. [CCP §2032.630; see *Queen of Angels Hosp. v. Sup.Ct. (Jones)* (1976) 57 CA3d 370, 374-375, 129 CR 282, 285]

(b) [8:1613.1] **Reports by nonexamining consultants?** But, presumably, reports by consultants *who have not examined* plaintiff, and who base their opinions solely on review of medical history, x-rays, hypothetical facts, etc., are still protected "work product." [See *Queen of Angels Hosp. v. Sup.Ct. (Jones)*, supra, 57 CA3d at 374, 129 CR at 284; *and* ¶*8:1606.2*]

(2) [8:1614] **Future reports must also be delivered:** The examinee is under a duty promptly to exchange copies of all existing reports *plus any later reports* relating to the same condition by the same or any other examiners. The waiver of privilege also applies to these later reports. [CCP §2032.640]

(3) [8:1615] **Deposing examiner has same result:** The examinee cannot avoid the exchange and waiver of any claim of privilege or work product by deposing the examiner instead of demanding the examiner's report. Deposing the examiner has the same effect. [CCP §2032.630]

(a) [8:1615.1] **Limitation:** This rule does not apply to depositions conducted after the examiner has been designated as a trial witness under CCP §2034.210 et seq. (At that late stage, if the examinee has not previously demanded the examiner's report—which is almost unthinkable—deposing the examiner will not obligate the examinee to exchange reports.) [CCP §2032.630]

(4) [8:1616] **No duty to disclose identity of examinee's doctors if NO WRITTEN REPORT made:** The Discovery Act allows plaintiffs to conceal the identity of doctors who examined them but made no written reports. I.e., plaintiff is required to exchange *written reports* (then existing or later produced) by any examining doctor. But the identity of examining doctors who did not submit a report is still protected "work product." [CCP §2032.630]

(a) [8:1616.1] **Purpose:** This protects plaintiffs from having to disclose examining doctors who expressed *unfavorable* opinions informally. It prevents defendants from utilizing such disclosures to argue that "plaintiff's 'own doctor' denied there was any injury," etc.

☞ [8:1616.2] ***PRACTICE POINTER:*** The moral is clear: If you represent plaintiffs, *ask any examining doctor to call you BEFORE making a written report.* If the doctor's oral evaluation is negative, instruct him or her not to make a written report. That way, the doctor's identity will remain protected as "work product" (¶*8:246*) and the unfavorable evaluation will not return to haunt you later on. [See *Schreiber v. Estate of Kiser* (1999) 22 C4th 31, 37, 91 CR2d 293, 298 (citing text)]

On the other hand, if the opinion is *favorable*, you will certainly want a written report; and you will probably want to show it to defendant (e.g., for settlement purposes).

(b) [8:1616.3] **Comment:** There is no real risk of "surprise" to defendants here. Plaintiff is not going to call a witness whose opinion is unfavorable. In any event, defendants can avoid any "surprise" by serving a CCP §2034.210 et seq. expert witness demand before trial.

(5) [8:1617] **Enforcing exchange:** If plaintiff (examinee) fails to exchange reports as stated above (¶*8:1611 ff.*), the defendant's (examining party's) remedy is to move for an order compelling the examinee to do so. [CCP §2032.650(a)]

(a) [8:1617.1] **Attempt to resolve informally required:** The usual declaration stating facts showing "a reasonable and good faith attempt" to resolve the matter informally must accompany the motion. [CCP §§2016.040, 2032.650(a); *see* ¶*8:1158 ff.*]

(b) [8:1618] **Monetary sanction against losing party:** A monetary sanction "shall" be imposed against the losing party unless the court finds "substantial justification" for that party's position or other circumstances make the sanction "unjust." [CCP §2032.650(b); *see* ¶*8:1921 ff.*]

© 2020 Thomson Reuters/The Rutter Group

(c) [8:1619] **Sanctions for disobeying order:** If after an order to compel is granted, the examinee still fails to deliver copies of his or her reports, the full range of discovery sanctions is available for disobeying the court's order: i.e., an "issue," "evidence" or "terminating" sanction against the examinee. [CCP §2032.650(c); *see* ¶*8:2145 ff.*]

1) [8:1620] **Testimony excluded:** Moreover, regardless of whether any other sanction is imposed, "[t]he court *shall exclude* at trial the testimony of any health care practitioner whose report has not been provided by a party." [CCP §2032.650(c) (emphasis added)]

[8:1621] **Comment:** By itself, however, this is not much of a sanction. For example, if plaintiff holds back a written report because it is unfavorable, excluding the doctor's testimony at trial is no real sanction because plaintiff would not call this doctor as a witness in any event.

[8:1622-1623] *Reserved.*

© 2020 Thomson Reuters/The Rutter Group

CHAPTER 8H

INSPECTION DEMANDS

CONTENTS

© 2020 Thomson Reuters/The Rutter Group

© 2020 Thomson Reuters/The Rutter Group

INSPECTION DEMANDS

[8:1417] **Statute:** CCP §2031.010 et seq. sets forth the rules and procedures governing demands for inspection, copying, testing and sampling of documents (including electronically-stored information) and other physical evidence.

[8:1418] **Purpose:** Inspection of physical evidence is often the key factor in pretrial discovery. For example, in product liability actions, inspection and testing of the allegedly defective product is crucial to pretrial preparation and to furnish the basis for expert testimony at trial. And, in many cases, document inspection is the best way to determine the sequence of events and to test the credibility of witnesses.

[8:1419] **Discovery Procedures Available:** Various discovery procedures are available to obtain inspection of physical evidence:

[8:1419.1] **Deposition Subpoena:** For evidence held by *nonparty witnesses*, a deposition subpoena is the *only* procedure available. [CCP §2025.280(b); *see* ¶*8:535*]

- **"Business records":** A "business records" subpoena may be used to obtain inspection and copying of *business records* without the necessity of a deposition hearing. [CCP §2020.020(b); *see* ¶*8:540 ff.*]
- **"Records and testimony":** But for any other type of records or evidence, a "records and testimony" subpoena (former subpoena duces tecum) is required. [CCP §2020.020(c); *see* ¶*8:556 ff.*]

[8:1420] **Deposition Notice:** A *party* or *"party-affiliated" witness* (e.g., officer, director, managing agent or employee) may be compelled to produce at deposition records or other evidence described in a deposition notice, *without* necessity of subpoena. [CCP §2025.280(a); *see* ¶*8:516 ff.*]

[8:1421] **Inspection Demand:** In addition, a *party* may be compelled to produce records or other evidence in its possession or control in response to a demand for inspection under CCP §2031.010 et seq. Such demands are the focus of this Chapter.

Note: Deposition notices and CCP §2031.010 et seq. demands are *separate* procedures. Use of one does not foreclose later use of the other (subject to court orders to prevent misuse). [See *Carter v. Sup.Ct. (CSAA Inter-Insurance Bureau)* (1990) 218 CA3d 994, 997, 267 CR 290, 291-292 (*discussed at* ¶*8:521*)]

© 2020 Thomson Reuters/The Rutter Group

STRATEGIES AND TACTICS RE INSPECTION DEMANDS

[8:1422] **Advantages**

- Allows inspection at the *convenience* of the demanding party (rather than "under the gun" at the opposing party's deposition; *see* ¶*8:1434*).
- Can compel the opposing party to produce documents, etc. at deposition of *some other* party or witness (rather than only at that party's own deposition).
- No limit on the *number* of demands that can be served (unlike interrogatories and requests for admissions).
- The *only* discovery procedure for gaining entrance onto opposing party's land (where relevant to the action).
- The *only* discovery means to obtain electronically-stored information (ESI).

[8:1422.1] **Disadvantages**

- Cannot be used to obtain inspection of documents, etc. from *nonparties*.
- If the demand is not complied with voluntarily, the court will not order production unless "good cause" is shown.
- Only monetary sanctions are available for failure to comply (unlike deposition subpoenas, which are enforceable by contempt).

[8:1422.2] **Alternative procedures**

- Do not overlook the possibility of obtaining documents or other information through informal investigation. [See *Pullin v. Sup.Ct. (Vons Cos., Inc.)* (2000) 81 CA4th 1161, 1165, 97 CR2d 447, 450—although time had expired for §2031.010 et seq. request for inspection, plaintiff was not precluded from inspecting conditions at defendant's store; *County of Los Angeles v. Sup.Ct. (Axelrad)* (2000) 82 CA4th 819, 829, 98 CR2d 564, 571—denial of discovery of certain documents did not preclude plaintiff from obtaining same documents under California Public Records Act]

[8:1422.3] **Civility Guidelines**

- Document requests should be used only to seek those documents that are reasonably needed to prosecute or defend an action;
- An attorney should not make demands to harass or embarrass a party or witness or to impose an inordinate burden or expense in responding;
- If an attorney inadvertently receives a privileged document in response to an inspection demand, the attorney should promptly notify the producing party that the document has been received (*see also* ¶*8:199.16*);
- In responding to a document demand, an attorney should not intentionally misconstrue a request in such a way as to avoid disclosure or withhold a document on the grounds of privilege;
- An attorney should not produce disorganized or unintelligible documents,

STRATEGIES AND TACTICS RE INSPECTION DEMANDS (Cont'd)

or produce documents in a way that hides or obscures the existence of particular documents;

- An attorney should not delay in producing a document in order to prevent opposing counsel from inspecting the document prior to or during a scheduled deposition or for some other tactical reason. [State Bar California Attorney Guidelines of Civility and Professionalism §9(b) (available on the State Bar website, *www.calbar.org*)]

1. [8:1423] **ON WHOM Demand May be Served:** As stated, a CCP §2031.010 et seq. demand may be served on any other party to the action. This includes coparties as well as adverse parties. [CCP §2031.010(a)]

   But the procedure cannot be used to obtain documents or evidence from a nonparty witness. A deposition subpoena must be used for this purpose. [CCP §2025.280(b)]

   a. [8:1424] **Compare—"party-affiliated" persons:** A CCP §2031.010 et seq. demand *cannot* be directed to an officer, director, managing agent or employee of a party. But the demand requires production of evidence in the party's *possession, custody or control*—which in most cases will reach evidence held by "affiliated" persons.

      [8:1424.1-1424.4] *Reserved.*

      (1) [8:1424.5] **Compare—civil enforcement actions by Attorney General:** In a civil enforcement action by the Attorney General in the name of the People of the State of California, the People are not required to produce documents from other state agencies that are not in the Attorney General's possession. Because each agency is a separate entity, nonparty discovery procedures (e.g., subpoena) must be pursued to obtain such documents. [*People ex rel. Lockyer v. Sup.Ct. (Cole Nat'l Corp.)* (2004) 122 CA4th 1060, 1076-1077, 19 CR3d 324, 336]

   b. [8:1425] **Parties to complaint vs. parties to cross-complaint?** It is unclear whether a cross-complaint is the same "action" as the complaint, so as to permit a third party cross-defendant to serve CCP §2031.010 et seq. demands on plaintiff, or vice versa (*see ¶8:920 ff.*).

2. [8:1426] **WHAT May be Inspected:** A CCP §2031.010 demand may be used to obtain inspection, copying, testing or sampling of:
   — documents;
   — tangible things;
   — land; and
   — electronically-stored information (ESI) in the possession, custody or control of another party. [CCP §2031.010(a)]

   Limitations: Of course, CCP §2031.010 demands are limited to matters

© 2020 Thomson Reuters/The Rutter Group

within the permissible scope of discovery ("relevant to subject matter," etc.) and not protected by privilege, work product, right of privacy, etc. [CCP §2031.010(a)]

Standards of professionalism as limitation: Some bar associations and courts have adopted guidelines to discourage discovery misuse (*see* ¶*8:1422.3*). Some of the conduct proscribed in those standards may be sanctioned as discovery misuse (CCP §2023.010; *see* ¶*8:1901*).

a. [8:1427] **"Documents":** "Document" means a writing as defined in Ev.C. §250. [CCP §2016.020(c)]

It thus includes handwriting, typewriting, printing, photographs, photostats, photocopies, transmissions by fax and email, "and every other means of recording upon any tangible thing, any form of communication or representation, including letters, words, pictures, sounds, or symbols, or combinations thereof, and any record thereby created, regardless of the manner in which the record has been stored." [Ev.C. §250]

(1) [8:1427.1] **Application:** Thus, drawings, graphs, charts, photographs, audio or video recordings or microfilm are "documents." So also are *data compilations* from which information may be obtained; e.g., computer data recorded on tape, discs, etc. (¶*8:1427.5 ff.*).

The party in possession of such "documents" may be required to produce such information in usable form (e.g., a computer printout); see CCP §2031.280(e), ¶*8:1472 ff.*

[8:1427.2-1427.4] *Reserved.*

b. [8:1427.5] **"Electronically-stored information" (ESI):** ESI means "information that is stored in an electronic medium." [CCP §2016.020(e)]

"Electronic" means "technology having electrical, digital, magnetic, wireless, optical, electromagnetic, or similar capabilities." [CCP §2016.020(d)]

(1) [8:1427.6] **Application:** These broad provisions are intended to cover existing technologies as well as those that may be developed in the future. [See Senate Judiciary Committee Analysis of AB 5 (Reg. Sess. 2009-2010)]

For example, ESI includes data on media such as a computer's hard drive; peripheral storage devices (disks and backup tapes); thumb or USB drives; laptops; cell phones; personal data assistants (PDAs). [See *R.S. Creative, Inc. v. Creative Cotton, Ltd.* (1999) 75 CA4th 486, 498, 89 CR2d 353, 362; *TBG Ins. Services Corp. v. Sup.Ct. (Zieminski)* (2002) 96 CA4th 443, 448, 117 CR2d 155, 159-160 (home computer)]

ESI is not limited to text stored on computers. It also includes sound recordings, video recordings, digital photographs, voice mail, text messages, records of Internet searches, and even "deleted" files if they can be recovered.

[8:1427.7-1427.9] *Reserved.*

☞ [8:1427.10] ***PRACTICE POINTER—Cooperate with opposing counsel:*** Because of the costs and complexity of enforcing ESI discovery, cooperation with opposing counsel is crucially important. Effective stipulations with opposing counsel will speed up ESI discovery, and may help avoid discovery disputes that will be costly to litigate.

- [8:1427.11] ***Utilize "meet and confer" prior to initial status conference:*** The parties must meet and confer *at least* 30 calendar days before the initial case management conference (*see* ¶*12:80*). ESI discovery is one of the issues that must be considered (see CRC 3.724(8)). Use the "meet and confer" as an opportunity to propose and negotiate stipulations with opposing counsel as to the issues likely to arise in ESI discovery in your case; e.g., what databases will be searched, in what forms or format ESI will be produced, ensuring automated archival and other processes do not delete evidence, procedures for sampling, privilege claims, and cost issues in connection with ESI production.

  [8:1427.12-1427.14] *Reserved.*

c. [8:1428] **Any tangible thing:** Tangible things may be inspected, photographed and subjected to *testing or sampling*. [CCP §2031.010(c)]

(1) [8:1428.1] **Application:** The term "tangible thing" is given a common-sense interpretation. It includes physical evidence such as handwriting, exemplars, fingerprints and written statements.

It does *not* include a *dead body* because "our society extends more respect to a dead body than to other physical evidence." [*Holm v. Sup.Ct. (Misco)* (1986) 187 CA3d 1241, 1248, 232 CR 432, 437—exhumation and autopsy of corpse could *not* be ordered as discovery in will contest case]

[8:1428.2-1428.9] *Reserved.*

(2) [8:1428.10] **Destructive testing:** Under appropriate circumstances, the court may order destructive testing of all or some portion of the physical item in question. [See *San Diego Unified Port Dist. v. Douglas E. Barnhart, Inc.* (2002) 95 CA4th 1400, 1404, 116 CR2d 65, 68]

(a) [8:1428.11] **Demanding party to pay costs:** Unless the parties agree otherwise, the party demanding such tests must pay the costs: "When a party demands discovery involving significant 'special attendant' costs beyond those typically involved in responding to routine discovery, the demanding party should bear those costs." [*San Diego Unified Port Dist. v. Douglas E. Barnhart, Inc.*, supra, 95 CA4th at 1405, 116 CR2d at 68]

© 2020 Thomson Reuters/The Rutter Group

d. [8:1429] **Land:** Demand may also be made for permission to enter upon "land or other property" in the possession or control of the party on whom the demand is made. Demand may also be made for permission to measure, survey, photograph, test or sample such land or property, or any *object or operation* thereon. [CCP §2031.010(d)]

- [8:1430] Farmer claimed Aluminum Company's operations were damaging Farmer's land, water and cattle. After Farmer refused to permit it to conduct tests on Farmer's land, Aluminum Company sued to gain entry, to take samples of water and vegetation, and to conduct other tests to show its activities had not harmed Farmer's land or cattle. [*Martin v. Reynolds Metals Corp.* (9th Cir. 1961) 297 F2d 49, 56-57 (decided under similar Federal Rule); see also *Manzetti v. Sup.Ct. (Fitzgerald)* (1993) 21 CA4th 373, 375, 25 CR2d 857, 858]

3. [8:1431] **WHEN Demand for Inspection May be Made:** A CCP §2031.010 et seq. demand may be made at any time during the lawsuit, subject to the same limitations discussed earlier:

a. [8:1432] **"Hold" on plaintiff's demands at outset:** As with interrogatories (¶*8:906*), plaintiff may not serve a CCP §2031.010 demand during the first 10 days after defendant is served or first appears in the action. (The court may shorten this period "for good cause shown.") [CCP §2031.020(b); *see* ¶*8:908*]

Exception: In *unlawful detainer* actions, the "hold" on plaintiff's demands is only 5 days after service. [CCP §2031.020(c)]

b. [8:1433] **"Cut-off" before trial:** As with other discovery procedures, there is a "cut-off" on CCP §2031.010 demands before trial:

- A 30-day before the initial trial date deadline on "completing" discovery (meaning responses must be due by that time); and
- A 15-day before the initial trial date deadline on the right to have motions to compel discovery heard. [CCP §2024.020(a); *see* ¶*8:445*]
- Exception: In *unlawful detainer* actions, the discovery "cut-off" is 5 days before the initial trial date. [CCP §2024.040(b)(1); *see* ¶*8:445*]

[8:1434] ***PRACTICE POINTER:*** It is a good idea to serve requests for documents *before* other discovery procedures. Inspecting the opposing party's documents or physical evidence in advance will enable you to ask more pertinent questions at deposition or in interrogatories. (And, you don't have to worry about "wasting" your demands, because there is no limit on the number you can serve; *see* ¶*8:1435.1.*)

Using CCP §2031.010 requests *before* a deposition is usually a better idea than noticing document production at the deposition.

It is often difficult to examine documents "under the gun" at a deposition and to propound intelligent questions based on their contents. Recesses are often required and this runs up the deposition costs. (Also, if you have the documents beforehand, you won't have to mention them in your deposition notice, and you may be able to "spring" them on an unprepared deponent.)

[8:1434.1-1434.4] *Reserved.*

c. [8:1434.5] **Supplemental demands:** Supplemental demands may be served to obtain documents or things acquired or discovered by the adverse party after earlier demands were served. [See CCP §2031.050(a)]

(1) [8:1434.6] **Timing and number of demands:** Such supplemental demands may be made:

— *twice* prior to initial setting of a trial date, and

— subject to the discovery "cut-off" date (CCP §2024.010 et seq.), *once* after the initial setting of a trial date. [CCP §2031.050(b)]

For good cause shown, the court may allow a party to propound *additional* supplemental demands for inspection. This allows for updating of previously requested information. [CCP §2031.050(c)]

(2) [8:1434.7] **Comment:** The impact of §2031.050 is unclear. It does not increase the number of permissible demands because there is *no numerical limit* on inspection demands (*see* ¶*8:1435.1*). Nor does it extend the time for such demands because supplemental demands are subject to the same discovery "cut-off" as original demands.

4. [8:1435] **Demand Procedure:** The party seeking discovery serves a *demand* for inspection on the party believed to be in possession, custody or control of the documents or property to be inspected. [See CCP §2031.040]

a. [8:1435.1] **No limit on number:** Unlike interrogatories and RFAs, there is *no limit* on the *number* of CCP §2031.010 et seq. demands that can be served. (Excessive demands are controllable by protective order; *see* ¶*8:1452.*)

(1) [8:1435.2] **Limit on number of supplemental demands:** Although the number of inspection demands is not otherwise limited, CCP §2031.050(a) apparently limits the number of supplemental demands (to pick up documents or things acquired after earlier discovery) by requiring a court order based on "good cause" for additional supplemental demands. [CCP §2031.050(c); *see discussion at* ¶*8:1434.5 ff.*]

b. [8:1436] **"Good cause" as limitation:** There is *no* requirement of "good cause" to *serve* CCP §2031.010 inspection demands. But the party seeking discovery must be prepared to show "good cause" if the demand is refused because such showing is required to obtain a court order for inspection (¶*8:1495 ff.*).

© 2020 Thomson Reuters/The Rutter Group

c. [8:1437] **Form of demand:** CCP §2031.010 demands must be in writing, and each set of demands must be numbered consecutively. [CCP §2031.030(a)]

(1) [8:1437.1] **Opening paragraph:** The first paragraph under the title of the case must show:

- Identity of the propounding party;
- Set number; and
- Identity of the party who is to respond to the demand. [CCP §2031.030(b)]

(a) [8:1437.2] **Example:** "DEFENDANT JOHN SMITH'S FIRST SET OF DEMANDS FOR DOCUMENT PRODUCTION ON PLAINTIFF ROBERTA BROWN"

(2) [8:1437.3] **Numbering:** Each demand in a set must be identified by number or letter. [CCP §2031.030(c)]

(There is no requirement that demands be numbered consecutively from set to set, although it is a good idea to do so.)

d. [8:1438] **Content:** Each demand must be separately set forth and state the following:

- **Description:** Designate the documents or other evidence to be inspected by specifically describing each item or by *"reasonably particularizing" each category* of item (CCP §2031.030(c)(1) (emphasis added));
- **Form in which ESI to be produced:** The demanding party may "specify the form or forms in which each type of electronically stored information is to be produced" (CCP §2031.030(a)(2));
- **Time for inspection:** Specify a reasonable time for the inspection that is *at least 30 days* after service of the demand (extended for service by mail, overnight delivery or fax or electronically per CCP §§1010.6(a)(4), 1013, ¶*9:87 ff.*; see CCP §2016.050) (CCP §2031.030(c)(2));
- **Place for inspection:** Specify a reasonable place for making the inspection, copying, etc. (CCP §2031.030(c)(3)); and
- **Tests, etc.:** If the demanding party intends to conduct any tests, sampling or similar activity on the evidence, the demand must so state and also state the manner in which such activity will be performed (CCP §2031.030(c)(4)).

FORM: Demand for Inspection, *see Form 8:26* in Rivera, *Cal. Prac. Guide: Civ. Pro. Before Trial FORMS* (TRG).

(1) [8:1439] **Description "by category" with "reasonable particularity":** The demanding party is often seeking documents he or she has never seen, and which may or may not exist, out of files with which he or she has no familiarity. Therefore, the demand is sufficient if the documents or things to be

produced are of a *category* described with "reasonable particularity" in the demand. [CCP §2031.030(c)(1)]

This is the *same standard* now permitted in deposition notices and deposition subpoenas; *see* ¶*8:544 and 8:561 ff.*

[8:1440-1441] *Reserved.*

(a) [8:1442] **"Reasonably particularized" categories:** The categories must be "reasonably" particularized *from the standpoint of the party on whom the demand is made.* [See *Calcor Space Facility, Inc. v. Sup.Ct. (Thiem Indus., Inc.)* (1997) 53 CA4th 216, 222, 61 CR2d 567, 571; *see* ¶*8:544.1 ff.*]

It is *not* reasonable to describe documents by categories which bear *no relationship to the manner in which the documents are kept,* and which require the responding party to determine (at risk of sanctions) which of its extensive records fit a demand that asks for everything in its possession relating to a specific topic. [See *Calcor Space Facility, Inc. v. Sup.Ct. (Thiem Indus., Inc.),* supra, 53 CA4th at 222, 61 CR2d at 571; *see* ¶*8:544.2*]

From this perspective, the requesting party should identify the *subject matter or transaction* in question as *narrowly* as reasonably possible.

1) [8:1443] Thus, requests for "all financial records" or "all correspondence" or "all documents relating to liability" may be objectionable for inadequate description. They embrace too many subcategories to have much meaning.

2) [8:1444] But requests for "all correspondence relating to (a particular subject matter)" or "all correspondence between (specific parties or specific dates)" would require response.

3) [8:1445] Likewise, a request to identify and produce "any plans or blueprints relating to (designated product)" would also apparently be sufficient to require response.

[8:1445.1-1445.4] *Reserved.*

(2) [8:1445.5] **Form in which ESI to be produced:** As stated above (¶*8:1438*), the demanding party may "*specify the form or forms*" in which each type of electronically-stored information (ESI) is to be produced. [CCP §2031.030(a)(2) (emphasis added)]

Common examples of forms in which ESI may be demanded are paper printouts ("hard copy"), PDF and TIFF.

Alternatively, a demanding party may specify that documents be produced in various "native" forms—i.e., the formats in which the data was originally created (and is likely maintained),

© 2020 Thomson Reuters/The Rutter Group

such as Microsoft Word format; or emails in Microsoft Outlook format; or financial spreadsheets in Microsoft Excel format; or graphs or images in JPEG, BMP or PNG formats (which ordinarily are easier to review). Native format usually includes "metadata" (embedded information that shows how, when and by whom the document was created, accessed or modified), whereas conversion of these files into images such as TIFF or PDF may strip out the metadata. (If the responding party keeps the ESI in another form, it can object and state the form in which it will produce the data.)

[8:1445.6] ***PRACTICE POINTERS—Formulating discovery demand:*** First of all, attempt to *negotiate stipulations* with opposing counsel as to the form or forms for ESI production (*see ¶8:1468.5 ff.*).

If you are unable to obtain effective stipulations from opposing counsel, consider the following guidelines in formulating a discovery plan and implementing discovery demands for ESI:

- [8:1445.7] *Utilize an expert:* If there will be substantial discovery involving ESI, consider retaining a forensic expert at the outset. The expert will be able to help you formulate appropriate discovery requests and estimate costs that may be involved in translating the requested data into a usable form.

- [8:1445.8] *Utilize preliminary discovery:* Before formulating a demand for discovery of ESI, use interrogatories or depositions to obtain information such as:
  — operating systems used by the responding party;
  — applications used;
  — computers and portable devices used and who uses them;
  — how information is shared and by whom;
  — name and address of system administrator (if deposition required);
  — names of databases in which the type of information sought is regularly stored on the computer;
  — passwords to obtain access to databases;
  — identity of those who have passwords;
  — whether any computer files have been deleted;
  — identity of those in the chain of command regarding storage and destruction of records;
  — retention and destruction policies and practices;
  — devices used to store records;

©2020 Thomson Reuters/The Rutter Group

— location of stored records;
— backup procedures; and
— location of any network backup media.

- [8:1445.9] *Get it right the first time:* Consult your expert about the best form for obtaining information from the particular source involved—i.e., computer database, cell phone records, voicemail, etc. If you decide after reviewing some of the ESI produced that a different format would suit you better, the court may be unwilling to order the opposing party to accommodate you. [See CCP §2031.280(d)(2)—party "need not produce the *same* electronically stored information in more than one form" (emphasis added)]

  — [8:1445.10] *Printouts vs. electronic format:* Where extensive files are involved, if you ask for a written printout, you may get reams of paper that obscure the information being sought.

  — [8:1445.11] *Searchability?* Consider whether you want electronic files produced as they are kept or in a different format. Some formats provide better searchability. (Again, consult an expert where necessary.)

  — [8:1445.12] *Readability?* Consider whether you want electronic files produced as they are regularly maintained (often native format) with metadata intact (*see ¶8:1445.5*). Files produced with metadata intact may be more difficult to read. You may need proprietary software to read or search native format.

  [8:1445.13-1445.14] *Reserved.*

- [8:1445.15] *Be careful what you ask for:* Asking for more ESI than you really need may trigger even broader ESI demands from your opponent; and your objection to the "undue expense or burden" of your opponent's demands may be undercut by your own far-reaching demands. Also, you may regret the high costs of reviewing a large data dump.

- [8:1445.16] *Consider proceeding in stages:* When dealing with large volumes of ESI, it is sometimes more cost-effective to proceed in stages by requesting files from which a *sampling* can be obtained to see whether the files contain relevant information not already available through less burdensome means. Parties also usually agree to rolling productions, spreading the burdens of production and review out over time.

© 2020 Thomson Reuters/The Rutter Group

(3) [8:1446] **"Reasonable" time and place for inspection:** The demanding party gets to choose the time, as well as the place, for the inspection. But the date chosen must be at least 30 days after the demand is served (5 days in unlawful detainer actions); and the time and place must be "reasonable." [CCP §2031.030(c)(2) & (3)]

They are subject to control by the court by protective order or on motion to compel. [CCP §2031.060]

[8:1447] **Comment:** The time, place and conditions should be worked out by stipulation between counsel wherever possible. It is usually an unnecessary imposition on the court's time to resolve disputes as to what is a "reasonable" time or place for inspection of evidence.

(a) [8:1448] **Burden of production as determinative factor:** Absent agreement, courts usually look to whatever burden is involved in producing the evidence. I.e., the more voluminous the records, the more likely inspection will be ordered where the records are usually kept.

(b) [8:1449] **Conditions may be imposed:** Where necessary, the court may make whatever orders are required to assure the evidence is not harmed or changed during the course of inspection (particularly important where tangible evidence is involved). [See CCP §2031.060(b)(4)]

(c) [8:1450] **Date for inspection vs. date response due:** The date designated in the demand for inspection must be *at least 30 days* after the demand is served (5 days in unlawful detainer actions). [CCP §2031.030(c)(2)] (The date is extended for service by mail, overnight delivery or fax, or electronic transmission, per CCP §§1010.6(a)(4), 1013 (¶*9:87.1 ff.*); see CCP §2016.050.)

The party on whom the demand is served must also *respond* to the demand, stating whether it will comply with the demand for inspection on the date demanded. That response is due *within 30 days* (5 days in unlawful detainer actions) after the demand is served (even if the date for production is later). [CCP §2031.260; *see* ¶*8:1459*]

➪ [8:1450.1] ***PRACTICE POINTER:*** When drafting CCP §2031.010 demands, consider designating an inspection date at least 60 days later (unless some urgency or discovery order requires earlier inspection). This provides an opportunity to review the responding party's response (30 days later) and to attempt to resolve any objections before the inspection date.

e. [8:1451] **Service of demand:** Copies of the CCP §2031.010 demand must be served on the party to whom it is directed and on all other parties who have appeared in the action. [CCP §2031.040]

Personal service under CCP §1011 is authorized (CCP §2016.050). If personal service is made to a party's residence, it must be made between the hours of 8 a.m. and 8 p.m. If personal service is made to an attorney's office and no one is in the office, the papers can be left in a conspicuous place between 9 a.m. and 5 p.m. [CCP §1011(a), (b)(1)]

5. [8:1452] **Protective Orders:** Instead of responding to the demand, the party to whom it is directed may seek a protective order (e.g., against overbreadth). Anyone else affected by the demand (e.g., a third person whose privacy would be infringed by disclosure of the documents) also may seek such an order. [CCP §2031.060]

☞ [8:1453] ***PRACTICE POINTER:*** You don't have to run to court for a protective order in most cases. You can simply *object* to improper inspection demands (*see ¶8:1474*). This is far less costly than a motion for protective order. And, in some cases, it will end the matter because the party seeking discovery will not follow up with a motion to compel. (See Strategies and Tactics re Protective Orders, *¶8:1022.*)

a. [8:1454] **Procedure:** A noticed motion is required, including a declaration showing a "reasonable and good faith attempt" to resolve the disputed issues outside of court. [CCP §§2016.040, 2031.060(a)] (The rules and procedures governing motions generally are discussed in *Ch. 9, Part I.*)

☞ [8:1454a] ***PRACTICE POINTER:*** *Consider alternative procedures discussed at ¶8:787.1.*

FORM: Motion for Protective Order and for Sanctions and Proposed Order, *see Form 8:18* in Rivera, *Cal. Prac. Guide: Civ. Pro. Before Trial FORMS* (TRG).

(1) [8:1454.1] **Timeliness:** The Code requires that the affected party move "promptly" for a protective order. [CCP §2031.060(a)]

(a) [8:1454.2] **After waiver of ground for objection?** Failure to object to an inspection demand within the 30-day period provided for response waives the ground for objection. [CCP §2031.300(a); *see ¶8:1463*]

But, according to one case, it does not waive the right to seek a protective order to prevent misuse of the information provided: "[U]pon a proper showing a party may—even after it has waived its right to object to the production of documents, and has produced most of the documents requested—seek a protective order restricting dissemination of the documents." [*Stadish v. Sup.Ct. (Southern Calif. Gas Co.)* (1999) 71 CA4th 1130, 1144, 84 CR2d 350, 358—protective order properly granted to restrict disclosure of trade secrets despite moving party's failure to raise trade secret privilege as ground for objection to inspection demands (*¶8:1456.8*)]

1) [8:1454.3] **Comment:** The fact that a party has waived a privilege (e.g., trade secret) by failure to object does not mean the court is powerless *to prevent misuse* of the privileged information. Although the responding party must produce the privileged document or information, the court may by protective order limit the opposing party or counsel's misuse of it (e.g., by public dissemination).

[8:1454.4-1454.9] *Reserved.*

(2) [8:1454.10] **Burden of proof:** A party seeking a protective order must show good cause for issuance of the order by a preponderance of evidence. [*Stadish v. Sup.Ct. (Southern Calif. Gas Co.)*, supra, 71 CA4th at 1145, 84 CR2d at 359]

b. [8:1455] **Relief available:** For "good cause shown," the court may make whatever order justice requires to protect against oppression, undue burden, etc. The orders may include:

- *Excusing* production of some or all of the items demanded, or setting terms and conditions on which items shall be produced;
- *Extending time* for production;
- Changing *place* for production;
- Protecting *confidential commercial information* (trade secrets, etc.) by restricting the manner in which it is disclosed;
- Ordering that items produced be *sealed* and opened only on court order (CCP §2031.060(b));
- Limiting or setting conditions for discovery of the information (CCP §2031.060(c)-(f)).

c. **Application**

(1) [8:1456] **Protecting confidential commercial information (trade secrets, etc.):** Protective orders are frequently sought to prevent disclosure of documents containing confidential commercial information (e.g., trade secrets, customers lists, etc.). [CCP §2031.060(b)(5)—protective order re "trade secret or other confidential research, development, or commercial information"; see *Fireman's Fund Ins. Co. v. Sup.Ct. (Paine Webber Real Estate Secur.)* (1991) 233 CA3d 1138, 1141, 286 CR 50, 51 (referring to protection as including "sensitive commercial information" and information containing "sensitive matter"); but see also *Lipton v. Sup.Ct. (Lawyers' Mut. Ins. Co.)* (1996) 48 CA4th 1599, 1618, 56 CR2d 341, 352, fn. 20 (declining to extend protection beyond "confidential business information")]

If "good cause" is shown, discovery of this information may be denied altogether or disclosure narrowly limited to certain persons for certain purposes. [See *In re Providian Credit Card Cases* (2002) 96 CA4th 292, 298-299, 116 CR2d 833, 838, fn. 5; *Children's Hosp. Central Calif. v. Blue Cross of Calif.* (2014) 226 CA4th 1260, 1277, 172 CR3d 861, 874; *and* ¶*8:328 ff.*]

[8:1456.1] *Reserved.*

(a) [8:1456.2] **In camera review:** The court may conduct an in camera review of the documents to determine whether they contain relevant, confidential commercial information warranting a protective order. [*Fireman's Fund Ins. Co. v. Sup.Ct. (Paine Webber Real Estate Secur.)*, supra, 233 CA3d at 1141, 286 CR at 51—abuse of discretion to order disclosure of reinsurance documents without in camera review; see *Lipton v. Sup.Ct. (Lawyers' Mut. Ins. Co.)*, supra, 48 CA4th at 1618, 56 CR2d at 352 (reinsurance documents)]

Any in camera review of privileged information in the documents would be conducted "to the extent permitted by law or the agreement of the party claiming the privilege." [*Lipton v. Sup.Ct. (Lawyers' Mut. Ins. Co.)*, supra, 48 CA4th at 1619, 56 CR2d at 352; *see* ¶*8:192.1 ff.*]

[8:1456.3-1456.4] *Reserved.*

(b) [8:1456.5] **Limiting disclosure by counsel:** A protective order permitting disclosure of trade secrets and other confidential information obtained through discovery to *other counsel handling similar cases* may be upheld where there is protection against disclosure to the general public. Such protection may be accomplished by requiring counsel receiving the information to stipulate not to further disseminate or disclose it. [*Raymond Handling Concepts Corp. v. Sup.Ct. (Zuelzke)* (1995) 39 CA4th 584, 590, 45 CR2d 885, 888; *see discussion at* ¶*8:336*]

[8:1456.6-1456.7] *Reserved.*

(c) [8:1456.8] **Showing required for trade secret protection:** A party seeking a protective order restricting disclosure of trade secrets must provide an affidavit or declaration:

— listing the declarant's qualifications to give an opinion;
— identifying the alleged trade secret;
— identifying the documents disclosing the trade secret; and
— presenting evidence that the secret qualifies as a "trade secret." [Ev.C. §§1060-1061; see CCP §2031.060(b)(5); *Stadish v. Sup.Ct. (Southern Calif. Gas Co.)* (1999) 71 CA4th 1130, 1144-1145, 84 CR2d 350, 358—procedure required by Ev.C. §1061 in criminal cases held applicable to civil cases]

Even where the trade secrets privilege has been waived, a protective order limiting disclosure of trade secrets may be available (*see* ¶*8:1454.2 ff.*).

© 2020 Thomson Reuters/The Rutter Group

1) [8:1456.9] **Balancing of interests:** In deciding whether discovery should be restricted, the court must balance the interests of the parties and any *public interest* involved in preserving access to the trade secrets (e.g., for protection of public health). [*Stadish v. Sup.Ct. (Southern Calif. Gas Co.)*, supra, 71 CA4th at 1146, 84 CR2d at 359]

2) [8:1456.10] **Determination cannot be delegated to parties:** It is *improper* for the court to delegate to the parties the responsibility of determining which items of discovery contain trade secrets. [*Stadish v. Sup.Ct. (Southern Calif. Gas Co.),* supra, 71 CA4th at 1144, 84 CR2d at 358]

[8:1456.11-1456.14] *Reserved.*

(2) [8:1456.15] **Request to seal documents:** A party may seek a protective order providing that items produced be sealed and opened only on court order. [CCP §2031.060(b)(6)]

Because these are discovery matters, the standards and procedures for sealing records do not apply (*see ¶9:418.25 ff.*).

(3) [8:1456.16] **Protecting confidential financial information:** A party's financial records, even when clearly relevant to the subject matter of the action, may be protected under the constitutional *right of privacy. See discussion at ¶8:303 ff.*

Where the *only* relevancy of a party's finances is in connection with a punitive damages claim, the party is *presumptively entitled* to a protective order. (Whether such presumption applies in other cases is unclear.) *See discussion at ¶8:337 ff.*

[8:1456.17-1456.20] *Reserved.*

(4) [8:1456.21] **Protection where source of ESI not "reasonably accessible":** A party may seek a protective order upon receiving a demand for electronically-stored information (ESI) that the party believes is from a source that is not reasonably accessible *because of* "undue burden or expense." [CCP §2031.060(c)]

This type of burden objection is unique since it may be made regarding ESI without waiving any other objection (*see ¶8:1475.12 ff.*).

☞ [8:1456.22] ***PRACTICE POINTER—Objecting in lieu of seeking protective order:*** The party resisting discovery may also raise the "not reasonably accessible" ground by objecting and refusing to respond to the discovery demand. The objection is usually preferable because:

— it allows more time to try to resolve the dispute;

— it puts the burden on the demanding party to go forward with a motion to compel showing "good cause" for discovery (*see ¶8:1495*).

(a) [8:1456.23] **"Undue burden or expense":** Although the statute indicates that *either* undue expense *or* undue burden will suffice, it provides no guidance in determining what burden or how much expense is "undue" (so as to make the source "not reasonably accessible").

1) [8:1456.24] **Comment:** Such decisions will be made on a case-by-case basis in the discretion of the trial court in exercise of its power "to manage discovery and to prevent misuse of discovery procedures." [See *Toshiba America Electronic Components, Inc. v. Sup.Ct. (Lexar Media, Inc.)* (2004) 124 CA4th 762, 768-772, 21 CR3d 532, 538-541 (predating enactment of statute)]

(b) [8:1456.25] **Burden on party seeking protective order:** The burden is on the party moving for the protective order (responding party) to demonstrate that the demand seeks ESI from sources that are *not* "reasonably accessible" because of "undue burden or expense." [CCP §2031.060(c); see also CCP §2031.310(d)—burden remains on responding party on motion to compel]

(c) [8:1456.26] **Discovery may still be ordered if "good cause" shown:** Even if "undue burden or expense" is demonstrated, the court may still order production of ESI if the demanding party shows "good cause" for the production. [CCP §§2031.060(d), 2031.310(e)]

1) [8:1456.27] **Cost-shifting as condition of discovery:** If "good cause" for production of ESI is shown, the court *may* set conditions, including the allocation of expenses of the discovery. [CCP §§2031.060(e), 2031.310(f)]

(This shifting of costs is *not* a sanction; nor does it undermine the general rule that the responding party bears the expense involved in responding to discovery requests (*Toshiba America Electronic Components, Inc. v. Sup.Ct. (Lexar Media, Inc.)*, supra, 124 CA4th at 769, 21 CR3d at 538—general rule "is that the responding party bears the expense typically involved in responding to discovery requests, such as the expense of producing documents"). Rather, these costs may be shifted as a *condition* imposed on the right to discovery; *see ¶8:1472.10 ff.*)

[8:1456.28-1456.39] *Reserved.*

© 2020 Thomson Reuters/The Rutter Group

(5) [8:1456.40] **Protection against unnecessary or unreasonably burdensome ESI demands:** The court "shall" (must) limit the "*frequency or extent of discovery*" of ESI if *any* of the following conditions exist:

- *Other sources available:* It is possible to obtain the ESI from another source that is more convenient, less burdensome or less expensive; or
- *Cumulative:* The discovery sought is unreasonably cumulative or duplicative; or
- *Lack of diligence:* The party seeking discovery has had ample opportunity by discovery in the action to obtain the information sought; or
- *Burdens outweigh benefits:* The likely *burden or expense* of the proposed discovery outweighs the likely benefit, taking into account the amount in controversy, the resources of the parties, the importance of the issues in the litigation, and the importance of the requested discovery in resolving the issues. [CCP §§2031.060(f), 2031.310(g)]

(a) [8:1456.41] **Burden on party seeking protective order:** Although the statute is not express, the burden is apparently on the party resisting discovery to establish one or more of these conditions as ground for a protective order. (CCP §2031.060(a) and (b) put the burden on the party moving for a protective order to show "good cause" for the order.)

(b) [8:1456.42] **Relief mandatory:** Unlike most protective orders as to which relief is discretionary, the court "shall" (must) grant an order limiting ESI discovery where any of the foregoing conditions exist. [See CCP §§2031.060(f), 2031.310(g)]

1) [8:1456.43] **Comment:** The *existence* of such conditions, however, is determined by the court on a case-by-case basis, in the reasonable exercise of its discretion.

(c) [8:1456.44] **Objecting in lieu of seeking protective order:** *See discussion at ¶8:1456.22.*

(6) [8:1456.45] **No "free speech" issue:** Protective orders barring parties from publishing documents obtained through pretrial discovery are proper. There is no First Amendment concern because pretrial discovery is a matter of "legislative grace"; neither the press nor public has any absolute right to such documents. *See discussion at ¶8:681 ff.*

[8:1456.46-1456.49] *Reserved.*

(7) [8:1456.50] **Protective order supersedes any secrecy agreement:** Sometimes the parties stipulate to a protective order based on a preexisting secrecy agreement covering the documents in question. In such cases, the agreement is *extinguished* upon its incorporation into a court order, so that neither party can thereafter sue the other for breach of the secrecy agreement. The only remedy is to initiate *contempt* proceedings for violation of the court's order. [*Westinghouse Elec. Corp. v. Newman & Holtzinger, P.C.* (1995) 39 CA4th 1194, 1205, 46 CR2d 151, 158]

d. [8:1457] **Monetary sanction against losing party:** The court "shall" impose a monetary sanction against the losing party on a motion for protective order *unless* it finds that party made or opposed the motion "with substantial justification" or other circumstances make the sanction "unjust." [CCP §2031.060(h)] (Monetary sanctions on discovery motions are discussed at ¶*8:1921 ff.*)

6. [8:1458] **Responding to Demand:** Unless excused by protective order (¶*8:1452 ff.*), the party to whom a CCP §2031.010 demand is directed is under a duty to respond thereto. [CCP §2031.210(a)]

Such response must be:

- Timely (¶*8:1459*);
- In the proper format (¶*8:1467*); and
- Under oath (¶*8:1477*).

a. [8:1459] **Time limit for response:** The response is due 30 days after service of the demand (extended where served by mail, overnight delivery or fax or electronically; see CCP §§1010.6(a)(4), 1013, ¶*9:87 ff.*). [CCP §§2031.260, 2016.050]

Exception: In *unlawful detainer* actions, the response is due within *5 days* after service of the demand. [CCP §2031.260]

If the last day falls on a weekend or holiday, the time limit is extended to the next court day closer to the trial date. [CCP §2016.060]

(1) [8:1460] **Compare—date for production:** The time and place for producing the documents must be stated in the demand, and that date must be *at least* 30 days after service of the demand (CCP §2031.030(c)(2); *see* ¶*8:1450*). Regardless of the date for production, the party on whom the demand is made must respond within 30 days after service, stating whether inspection is agreed to, etc. [See CCP §2031.260]

(2) [8:1461] **Extension by court order:** The court has power to extend (or shorten) the time for response on "motion" by the party affected (apparently meaning a noticed motion, rather than ex parte application; *see* ¶*8:1026*). [CCP §2031.260]

© 2020 Thomson Reuters/The Rutter Group

☞ [8:1461.1] ***PRACTICE POINTER:*** Although a noticed motion is required, as a practical matter, you will probably need to file an *ex parte* application to hear the motion on shortened notice. Otherwise, you may have to respond to the inspection demand before your motion is heard.

(3) [8:1462] **Extension by agreement:** Likewise, the parties may agree to an extension. The agreement may be informal, but *must be confirmed in writing* stating the date when the response is due. Unless the agreement provides otherwise, it extends the right to *object* to the demand. [CCP §2031.270]

(4) [8:1463] **Delay WAIVES all objections:** Failing to respond to a CCP §2031.010 demand within the time permitted *waives all objections* to the demand—including claims of privilege and work product. [CCP §2031.300(a)]

[8:1464] *Reserved.*

(a) [8:1465] **Relief from waiver available:** However, the court may grant relief from such waiver. To obtain such relief, the party to whom the demand is directed must have:

- *Belatedly served* a response that is in "substantial compliance" with CCP §§2031.210-2031.240, 2031.280; and
- Filed a noticed motion supported by declarations showing that the delay resulted from "mistake, inadvertence or *excusable* neglect." [CCP §2031.300(a)]

1) [8:1465.1] **Standard applicable:** The same standards apply as for relief from default under CCP §473(b). [*City of Fresno v. Sup.Ct. (Green)* (1988) 205 CA3d 1459, 1467, 253 CR 296, 300]

a) [8:1465.2] **Application:** Counsel's simply being busy, or mistake of law on a simple matter (the provisions of a code section), is *not* "excusable neglect" under CCP §473(b), and hence not ground for relief under CCP §2031.300. [*City of Fresno v. Sup.Ct. (Green)*, supra, 205 CA3d at 1467, 253 CR at 300—claimed mistake as to when responses were due; *Scottsdale Ins. Co. v. Sup.Ct. (Spyglass Homeowners Ass'n)* (1997) 59 CA4th 263, 276, 69 CR2d 112, 120—counsel's neglect in asserting attorney-client privilege deemed "inexcusable"]

2) [8:1465.3] **No relief under CCP §473(b):** Because the Discovery Act contains specific conditions for relief from waiver, relief *cannot* be obtained under

CCP §473(b) (which authorizes relief generally for "mistake, inadvertence, surprise or excusable neglect"; *see ¶5:282 ff.*). [*Scottsdale Ins. Co. v. Sup.Ct. (Spyglass Homeowners Ass'n)*, supra, 59 CA4th at 275, 69 CR2d at 119]

CCP §473(b) relief is available in discovery proceedings only where there is *no analogous provision* for relief under the Discovery Act. [See *Zellerino v. Brown* (1991) 235 CA3d 1097, 1107, 1 CR2d 222, 228, *discussed at ¶8:10.10*]

Comment: The significance of course is that it is *often easier* to obtain relief under CCP §473(b); *see discussion at ¶8:10.14 ff.*

(b) [8:1466] **Compare—no waiver of Pen.C. §832.7 protection:** Peace officer personnel files and records of citizen complaints regarding police officers are subject to disclosure only pursuant to Ev.C. §§1043, 1046 (so-called "*Pitchess*" motions, requiring showing of "good cause," court hearing, in camera inspection, etc.). [Pen.C. §832.7, *discussed at ¶8:126 ff.*]

This limitation on discovery *overrides* the general policy evidenced in the waiver provisions of CCP §2031.300(a). Thus, untimely response to an inspection demand does *not* by itself entitle the demanding party to records protected under Pen.C. §832.7. I.e., the objection may be raised even though the response is *untimely*. [*City of Fresno v. Sup.Ct. (Green)* (1988) 205 CA3d 1459, 1476-1477, 253 CR 296, 306]

b. [8:1467] **Format of response:** The format rules are similar to those governing responses to interrogatories (*see ¶8:1039 ff.*).

(1) [8:1467.1] **Opening paragraph:** The first paragraph below the title of the case must state:

- The identity of the responding party;
- The identity of the propounding party; and
- The set number to which the response pertains. [CCP §2031.210(b)]

(a) [8:1467.2] **Example:** "DEFENDANT MARY BROWN'S RESPONSE TO PLAINTIFF PAUL BLACK'S DEMANDS FOR DOCUMENT PRODUCTION, SET NO. 3"

(2) [8:1467.3] **Numbering:** Each item in the response must bear the same number (or letter) and be in the same sequence as the item or category in the demand to which it pertains. [CCP §2031.210(c)]

© 2020 Thomson Reuters/The Rutter Group

(3) [8:1467.4] **Demand need not be repeated:** The text of the demand itself, however, need not be repeated. [CCP §2031.210(c)]

[8:1468] ***PRACTICE POINTER:*** Although not required, many lawyers prefer to do so. It saves working with different documents and pages.

Alternatively, ask the propounding party to send you an electronic version of the inspection demand and offer to provide your responses on that version; or simply agree to always exchange electronic versions.

[8:1468.1-1468.4] *Reserved.*

(4) [8:1468.5] **Specifying form for ESI:** If the party responding to a demand for production of ESI objects to the *form specified* in the discovery demand, or if *no form* is specified in the demand, the responding party "*shall state* in its response the *form in which it intends* to produce each type of information." [CCP §2031.280(c) (emphasis added); *see* ¶*8:1445.5*]

If the demanding party objects to the form stated by the responding party, the demanding party will have to file a motion to compel to resolve the issue (subject to the "meet and confer" requirement and 45-day time limit; *see* ¶*8:1490 ff.*).

(a) [8:1468.6] **Same information need not be provided in multiple forms:** The responding party need not provide the same information in more than one form, unless the parties agree or the court orders otherwise. [CCP §2031.280(d)(2)]

(b) [8:1468.7] **If no form specified in demand, information may be produced as regularly maintained:** Where the demand does not specify a form for producing ESI, it "shall" be produced in the form "in which it is ordinarily maintained" *or in a form "that is reasonably usable,"* unless the parties agree or the court orders otherwise. [CCP §2031.280(d)(1) (emphasis added)]

(c) [8:1468.8] **"Translation" costs chargeable to demanding party:** "If necessary," the responding party shall "through detection devices" translate any electronic data included in the demand into a reasonably usable form "*at the reasonable expense of the demanding party.*" [CCP §2031.280(e) (emphasis added)]

FORM: Response to Inspection Demand, *see Form 8:26.1* in Rivera, *Cal. Prac. Guide: Civ. Pro. Before Trial FORMS* (TRG).

c. [8:1469] **Content:** The party to whom the CCP §2031.010 demand is directed must respond separately to each item in the demand by one of the following:

- **Agreement to comply:** A statement that the party will comply by the date set for inspection with the particular demand for inspection, testing, etc.; or

- **Representation of inability to comply:** A statement that the party lacks the ability to comply with the particular demand; or
- **Objections:** An objection to all or part of the demand. [CCP §2031.210(a)]

If only part of an item or category demanded is objectionable, the response must contain an agreement to comply with the remainder, or a representation of inability to comply. [CCP §2031.240(a)] (General objections to the entire request are unauthorized and constitute discovery misuse; *see* ¶*8:1071* (dealing with interrogatories).)

(1) [8:1470] **Agreement to comply:** The response must be rather specific as to what is agreed to. It must state:

- That the production and inspection demanded will be allowed (in whole or in part); and
- That the documents or things in the demanded category that are in the responding party's possession, custody or control *will be produced* (except to the extent of any objections; *see* ¶*8:1474 ff.*). [CCP §2031.220]

(a) [8:1471] **What constitutes "compliance":** Documents must be sorted and labeled to correspond with the categories in the document demand. [CCP §2031.280(a) (amended eff. 1/1/20)] (Prior law permitted production of documents as they were kept in the ordinary course of business.)

[8:1471.1-1471.4] *Reserved.*

1) [8:1471.5] **Sanctions possible for noncompliance:** Sanctions may be assessed for production of documents that are in complete disorder if the court finds that the producing party is responsible for the disordered state. [*Kayne v. Grande Holdings Ltd.* (2011) 198 CA4th 1470, 1476, 130 CR3d 751, 755—producing party ordered to pay more than $74,000 of costs incurred by opposing party to organize documents; *see* ¶*8:1508.2a*]

(b) [8:1472] **Producing electronically-stored information (ESI) in "usable form":** If necessary, the responding party must "through detection devices, *translate* any data compilations included in the demand into *reasonably usable form*" at the "*reasonable expense of the demanding party.*" [CCP §2031.280(e) (emphasis added); *see* ¶*8:1445.5*]

[8:1472.1-1472.4] *Reserved.*

© 2020 Thomson Reuters/The Rutter Group

1) [8:1472.5] **"Reasonably usable form":** Although the statute is not explicit, "reasonably usable form" presumably means the ESI must be produced in a form that a party can access and read, which in some cases may be a paper printout or in other cases may be an electronically readable and searchable file using commonly available programs.

a) [8:1472.5a] **PDF vs. native format?** Under persuasive federal precedent (*see* ¶*8:19.15 ff.*), production of ESI in PDF format "may not be sufficient if the requesting party can show that the format is not 'reasonably usable' and that the native format, with accompanying metadata, meet the criteria of reasonably usable" while the PDF format does not. [*Ellis v. Toshiba America Information Systems, Inc.* (2013) 218 CA4th 853, 862, 160 CR3d 557, 566, fn. 6 (internal quotes omitted)]

b) [8:1472.6] **Compare—demanding party may specify form:** The demanding party can ensure that the ESI will be "usable" on its computer by *specifying the form* of production in its *discovery demand* (CCP §2031.030(a)(2); *see* ¶*8:1445.5*).

[8:1472.7] ***PRACTICE POINTER:*** Where a large number of documents are required to be produced, it is usually a good idea for the parties to stipulate that the documents be produced electronically (e.g., in a document depository or cloud-based storage system) or on CD-ROM or other storage device rather than by hard copies. This is particularly helpful where numerous parties are entitled to production. An additional benefit of an electronic data exchange is that all parties have an identical record of what was produced.

[8:1472.8-1472.9] *Reserved.*

2) [8:1472.10] **"Reasonable expense" to be paid by demanding party:** The "reasonable expense" of translating the data into "reasonably usable form" must be paid by the demanding party." [CCP §2031.280(e)]

[8:1472.11] ***PRACTICE POINTER:*** What is a "reasonable" expense may give rise to lengthy disputes that will delay discovery. Therefore, be conservative in your demands for ESI. Seek expert advice on framing your requests to minimize any "translation" cost involved.

a) [8:1472.12] **Protective orders available:** The demanding party may seek a protective order (CCP §2031.060(b)(4)) if asked to pay for translations of ESI it does not deem "necessary" or if it disputes the "reasonableness" of the expenses alleged. [*Toshiba America Electronic Components, Inc. v. Sup.Ct. (Lexar Media, Inc.)* (2004) 124 CA4th 762, 772, 21 CR3d 532, 540—"Reasonableness and necessity are purely factual issues . . . which . . . are properly submitted to the discretion of the trial court"]

[8:1472.13] ***PRACTICE POINTER re expert testimony:*** The technical difficulty and the expense associated with recovering electronic data and translating it into a usable form usually requires declarations from qualified experts. Because the court may wish to inquire from the experts directly, they should be selected and prepared to answer questions in court.

If the "battle of experts" does not clarify the matters sufficiently for the court to decide, the court has the ability to appoint its own expert at the parties' expense as allocated by the court (see Ev.C. §§730, 731).

All of this is likely to be very time-consuming for counsel and expensive for the parties. It is counsel's responsibility to negotiate compromises and avoid this kind of dispute wherever possible.

[8:1472.14] *Reserved.*

3) [8:1472.15] **Searches of computer backup media:** Computer backup media (including tapes, CDs and other storage devices) provide a means of recovering lost data in the event of a system failure. The difficulty with searching backup media is that they hold a large amount of data that is difficult and often expensive to access. Consequently, finding and restoring relevant data from a large number of backup media can be an *expensive and time-consuming* process. [*Toshiba America Electronic Components, Inc. v. Sup.Ct. (Lexar Media, Inc.)*, supra, 124 CA4th at 768, 21 CR3d at 537 (decided prior to enactment of statute)]

[8:1472.16] ***PRACTICE POINTER:*** To reduce costs of producing ESI stored on backup media, parties are encouraged to "meet and confer" about translating a *sample* of the ESI before

© 2020 Thomson Reuters/The Rutter Group

full compliance. [See *Toshiba America Electronic Components, Inc. v. Sup.Ct. (Lexar Media, Inc.)*, supra, 124 CA4th at 773, 21 CR3d at 541-542]

(2) [8:1473] **Inability to comply:** A response stating inability to comply with the CCP §2031.010 demand shall state the following:

- That a *diligent search* and *reasonable inquiry* has been made in an effort to locate the item demanded; and
- The *reason* the party is unable to comply: e.g., the document:
  - — never existed; or
  - — has been lost or stolen; or
  - — has been destroyed; or
  - — is not in the possession, custody or control of the responding party, in which case, the response must state the name and address of anyone believed to have the document. [CCP §2031.230]

(3) [8:1474] **Objections:** The responding party may object to any item or category demanded in whole or in part. To be effective, the objection must:

- *Identify with particularity* the specific document or evidence demanded as to which the objection is made; and
- Set forth the *specific ground* for objection, including claims of privilege or work product protection. [CCP §2031.240(b); see *Standon Co., Inc. v. Sup.Ct. (Kim)* (1990) 225 CA3d 898, 901, 275 CR 833, 834—objections constitute implicit refusals to produce]

[8:1474.1-1474.4] *Reserved.*

(a) [8:1474.5] **Objection based on privilege; "privilege log" may be required:** When asserting claims of privilege or attorney work product protection, the objecting party must provide "sufficient factual information" to enable other parties to evaluate the merits of the claim, "including, *if necessary*, a privilege log." [CCP §2031.240(c)(1) (emphasis added); *Lopez v. Watchtower Bible & Tract Soc. of New York, Inc.* (2016) 246 CA4th 566, 596-597, 201 CR3d 156, 181—burden to show preliminary facts supporting application of privilege not met where D failed to produce privilege log or identify any specific confidential communications]

1) [8:1474.5a] **Required contents of privilege log:** As the term is commonly used by courts and attorneys, a "privilege log" identifies each document for which a privilege or work product protection is claimed, its author, recipients, date of preparation, and the

specific privilege or work product protection claimed. [*Hernandez v. Sup.Ct. (Acheson Indus., Inc.)* (2003) 112 CA4th 285, 291-292, 4 CR3d 883, 888-889, fn. 6; see CCP §2031.240(c)(2)—Legislative intent to codify concept of privilege log "as that term is used in California case law"]

"The information in the privilege log must be sufficiently specific to allow a determination of whether each withheld document is or is not [in] fact privileged." [*Wellpoint Health Networks, Inc. v. Sup.Ct. (McCombs)* (1997) 59 CA4th 110, 130, 68 CR2d 844, 857; see *Catalina Island Yacht Club v. Sup.Ct. (Beatty)* (2015) 242 CA4th 1116, 1130, 195 CR3d 694, 704 & fn. 5—privilege log deficient due to failure to describe documents or contents (other than noting they were emails with counsel) since not all communications with attorneys are privileged]

FORM: Privilege Log, *see Form 8:26.2* in Rivera, *Cal. Prac. Guide: Civ. Pro. Before Trial FORMS* (TRG).

2) [8:1474.5b] **No undue burden defense to preparing privilege log:** There is no "burden" defense to the "statutory requirement" to produce a privilege log. [*Riddell, Inc. v. Sup.Ct. (Ace American Ins. Co.)* (2017) 14 CA5th 755, 772, 222 CR3d 384, 397]

3) [8:1474.6] **May be required at time of objection:** The Code seems to indicate that if a privilege log is "necessary" to enable other parties to evaluate the merits of a privilege or work product claim, it must be provided by the objecting party *with the response* to the §2031.010 inspection demand (i.e., at the time the objection is made). [See CCP §2031.240(c)(1)—if objection is based on privilege or work product claim, "the response shall provide . . . including, if necessary, a privilege log"]

a) [8:1474.6a] **Comment:** This is not entirely clear, however: CCP §2031.240(c)(2) provides that the Legislature did not, by codifying the concept of a privilege log, intend to make any "substantive change in case law." Preexisting case law indicates a privilege log need not necessarily be served at the time a privilege or work product objection is made (*see* ¶*8:1474.8 ff.*). And at least one case confirms that a tardy privilege log (served nearly two months *after* the objections) is sufficient to preserve the privilege. [*Catalina Island Yacht Club v. Sup.Ct. (Beatty)*, supra, 242 CA4th at 1126, 195 CR3d at 700-701 (¶*8:1498.6*)]

© 2020 Thomson Reuters/The Rutter Group

☞ [8:1474.7] ***PRACTICE POINTER:*** In any event, serving a privilege log *along with the objection* often will make sense. It may make apparent to opposing parties that they would be unsuccessful in an attempt to compel disclosure. Similarly, including the log as part of an opposition to a motion to compel may permit the court to deny the motion without further proceedings.

4) [8:1474.8] **May be required by court in response to motion to compel:** In ruling on a motion to compel document production, the court may require the party who objected on the ground of privilege to prepare and serve a privilege log. The purpose is to make a record of the documents withheld and the privilege claim asserted as to each. [*Wellpoint Health Networks, Inc. v. Sup.Ct. (McCombs)*, supra, 59 CA4th at 130, 68 CR2d at 857; *Best Products, Inc. v. Sup.Ct. (Granatelli Motorsports, Inc.)* (2004) 119 CA4th 1181, 1188-1189, 15 CR3d 154, 159]

5) [8:1474.9] **May be required in connection with motion for protective order:** In ruling on a motion for protective order to prevent discovery directed at privileged documents, the court may order the moving party to prepare a privilege log to assist it in ruling on the privilege claims. [*Bank of America, N.A. v. Sup.Ct. (Pacific City Bank)* (2013) 212 CA4th 1076, 1099, 151 CR3d 526, 543—court-ordered privilege log sufficient to enable court to rule on all privilege objections]

6) [8:1474.10] **Appellate court review:** Normally, appellate courts will not review pretrial discovery orders (¶*8:14*). But an exception is frequently made where the order requires disclosure of information claimed to be privileged. Here, *writ review* (by mandamus or prohibition) is often granted because redress after disclosure of privileged information would, of course, be impossible. [*Sav-On Drugs, Inc. v. Sup.Ct. (Botney)* (1975) 15 C3d 1, 5, 123 CR 283, 285-286; *Costco Wholesale Corp. v. Sup.Ct. (Randall)* (2009) 47 C4th 725, 740-741, 101 CR3d 758, 770-771; *Palmer v. Sup.Ct. (Mireskandari)* (2014) 231 CA4th 1214, 1224, 180 CR3d 620, 627]

☞ [8:1474.11] ***PRACTICE POINTER:*** If you plan to seek writ review and need additional time, *ask for a temporary stay* of the discovery order to allow you to prepare your petition without risking sanctions for violation. Most judges will grant such requests.

(b) [8:1475] **Other grounds:** The objections most likely to be sustained to a CCP §2031.010 demand are:

- Beyond the *scope* of permissible discovery (not relevant to the subject matter or likely to lead to discovery of admissible evidence);
- Privilege, work product, or *right of privacy;*
- *Oppressive* and *burdensome* (i.e., compliance would be unreasonably difficult and expensive).

(c) **Application**

- [8:1475.1] A demand for inspection of an insurer's claims files in a bad faith action was held "oppressive" where uncontradicted declarations showed over 13,000 claims would have to be reviewed, requiring 5 claims adjusters working full time for 6 weeks each. [*Mead Reinsurance Co. v. Sup.Ct. (City of Laguna Beach)* (1986) 188 CA3d 313, 318, 232 CR 752, 754; *see* ¶*8:315.1a*]
- [8:1475.2] An objection of "vague, ambiguous and unintelligible" to a request for "any and all bills, statements and invoices" may be treated as a "nuisance" objection, exposing the responding party to sanctions. [*Standon Co., Inc. v. Sup.Ct. (Kim)* (1990) 225 CA3d 898, 903, 275 CR 833, 835; see also *Manzetti v. Sup.Ct. (Fitzgerald)* (1993) 21 CA4th 373, 377, 25 CR2d 857, 858, 859]
- [8:1475.3] In a wrongful death action, Doctor objected to production of all postoperative orders for opioid pain management signed by him over a one-year period on grounds of irrelevance, undue burden and third party privacy rights. Production was upheld because the orders were directly relevant to the action, patient-identifying information was redacted (so privacy was not violated, *see* ¶*8:306.1*) and, since only 160 orders were involved, the burden was not unreasonable. [*Snibbe v. Sup.Ct. (Gilbert)* (2014) 224 CA4th 184, 196-197, 168 CR3d 548, 558-559]
- [8:1475.4] D's claim of burden was contradicted by testimony that the requested documents had been segregated and placed in easily-identifiable envelopes, as well as expert testimony that the documents were scanned into a computer program with a search function that could extract the relevant data. Also, D made no efforts to design a search, consult with an expert qualified to conduct a search or take *any* steps to locate responsive documents or offer suggestions on how to reasonably narrow the requests. Thus, the trial court was not required to credit D's

© 2020 Thomson Reuters/The Rutter Group

burden claim. [*Lopez v. Watchtower Bible & Tract Soc. of New York, Inc.* (2016) 246 CA4th 566, 594-595, 201 CR3d 156, 179-181]

[8:1475.5-1475.9] *Reserved.*

(d) [8:1475.10] **Objection that ESI "not reasonably accessible":** In lieu of moving for a protective order (*see ¶8:1456.21*), the responding party may object to discovery of electronically-stored information (ESI) on the ground that the source is "not reasonably accessible" because of "undue burden or expense," *and may refuse to search for it* in the absence of a court order. [CCP §2031.210(d)]

1) [8:1475.11] **Must identify types or categories:** To make an effective objection on this ground, the response must *identify the types or categories* of ESI that the responding party claims are not reasonably accessible. [CCP §2031.210(d)]

2) [8:1475.12] **No waiver of other objections:** By objecting and identifying the sources not searched, the party *preserves all other objections* it may have to producing that electronically-stored information. [CCP §2031.210(d)]

3) [8:1475.13] **Either "undue" burden *or* expense:** The objection may be based on the ground that the source is not reasonably accessible because of *either* undue burden *or* undue expense. [CCP §2031.210(d)]

a) [8:1475.14] **Comment:** The statute provides no guidance for determining *how much* burden or expense is "undue." As a result, this determination will have to be made by the court on a case-by-case basis in exercise of its power "to manage discovery and to prevent misuse of discovery procedures." [See *Toshiba America Electronic Components, Inc. v. Sup.Ct. (Lexar Media, Inc.)* (2004) 124 CA4th 762, 768-772, 21 CR3d 532, 538-541 (predating enactment of statute)]

[8:1475.15] ***PRACTICE POINTER—burden on objecting party:*** Counsel should be careful in raising a "not reasonably accessible" objection to any demand for ESI from an opposing party. Keep in mind that on a motion to compel, the objecting party has the burden of proof, based on admissible evidence, on this issue. If it turns out that the data is accessible without much effort or expense, sanctions may be imposed and they could be substantial (particularly where the moving party produced expert testimony).

[8:1475.16-1475.19] *Reserved.*

(e) [8:1475.20] **Objection that ESI production unnecessary or unreasonably burdensome:** The court "shall" (must) limit the "frequency or extent of discovery" if the demanding party moves to compel and the court finds the responding party has a valid objection to production on one of the following grounds (which are also grounds for a protective order):

— the ESI demanded is available from other more convenient sources;

— the ESI is cumulative or duplicative;

— the demanding party was dilatory; or

— the burdens of producing the ESI outweigh any benefits. [CCP §2031.060(f); *discussed at ¶8:1456.40 ff. re protective orders*]

1) [8:1475.21] **Comment:** Although CCP §2031.210(d) does not state these grounds may be raised as objections to an ESI demand, that seems implicit because the court *must* limit discovery when any of these conditions are found to exist on a motion for protective order or a motion to compel. [See CCP §2031.310(g)]

[8:1476] ***PRACTICE POINTERS:*** If you are going to object to inspection, make sure there is "substantial justification" for *your* position. (Don't rely solely on the fact that the moving party will have to show "good cause" for an order compelling discovery; ¶*8:1495*.)

Blanket objections (e.g., "all documents sought are irrelevant and immaterial") are ineffective and likely to result in *waiver* of any valid ground for objection, plus *sanctions* for failure to make discovery.

Avoid raising the "burdensome and oppressive" objection unless the facts are *truly unusual* (e.g., very fragile property which could be damaged by any movement, touching, etc.). If you are going to object in such a case, *state the reasons* for your objection and *offer* to permit whatever inspection can be allowed under the circumstances.

Instead of objecting to the demand, you will usually be better off seeking *limits* on the inspection beforehand by stipulation with demanding party's counsel.

(f) [8:1476.1] **Waiver by failure to object:** A party whose response fails to set forth a particular ground for objection waives its right to raise that objection later. [*Stadish v.*

© 2020 Thomson Reuters/The Rutter Group

Sup.Ct. (Southern Calif. Gas Co.) (1999) 71 CA4th 1130, 1141, 84 CR2d 350, 356—by objecting only on ground of attorney-client privilege, D waived trade secret privilege objection (but protective order still available; *see* ¶*8:1454.2*)]

But, as discussed above (¶*8:1475.10 ff.*), this is not true in the ESI context.

[8:1476.2-1476.4] *Reserved.*

(4) [8:1476.5] **Standards of professionalism governing response:** Some bar associations and courts have adopted *guidelines* to discourage discovery misuse. [See L.A. Sup.Ct. Rule 3.26, Appendix 3.A(f)(3)—counsel should not strain to interpret document demands restrictively in order to avoid disclosure]

Because local rules relating to discovery are preempted by CRC 3.20, a court may not sanction a party for violation of these guidelines. Nonetheless, the prohibited conduct may be sanctionable as discovery misuse (CCP §2023.010; *see* ¶*8:1901*).

d. [8:1477] **Signature and verification:** The response must be signed "under oath" by the party to whom it is directed. That party's attorney must also sign if the response contains an objection. If it consists *entirely* of objections, only the attorney's signature is required. [CCP §2031.250]

(1) [8:1477.1] **Verification by "Doe" sufficient:** Where plaintiff files an action under a fictitious name to preserve anonymity (¶*2:136.5 ff.*), plaintiff may verify discovery responses by signing the fictitious name. [*Doe v. Sup. Ct. (Luster)* (2011) 194 CA4th 750, 756, 123 CR3d 557, 561—trial court erred in requiring plaintiff to provide verifications in her true name]

(2) [8:1478] **"On information and belief" permissible where officer signs on behalf of entity?** *See discussion in connection with interrogatories at* ¶*8:1106.*

(3) [8:1479] **Attorney verifying on behalf of entity:** *See discussion in connection with interrogatories at* ¶*8:1107.1 ff.*

(4) [8:1479.1] **Effect of unverified response containing responses and objections:** Where the response contains *both* agreements to comply *and* objections, the portion containing the objections *need not* be under oath. Therefore, the response is effective to *preserve* the objections stated therein even though unverified. [*Food 4 Less Supermarkets, Inc. v. Sup.Ct. (Fletcher)* (1995) 40 CA4th 651, 657, 46 CR2d 925, 928]

The other portion of the response (agreements to comply) should be verified, and the lack of verification renders the agreement to comply untimely. But that only creates a right to move for orders and sanctions (under CCP §2031.310; *see* ¶*8:1483*); there is no waiver of the stated objections. [*Food 4 Less Supermarkets, Inc. v. Sup.Ct. (Fletcher),* supra, 40 CA4th at 657, 46 CR2d at 928]

e. [8:1480] **Service of response:** The original of the response is served on the demanding party; copies are served on all other parties who have appeared in the action. [CCP §2031.260]

f. [8:1481] **Custody of demand and response:** Neither the demand nor response is filed with the court. The demanding party retains the original demand and receives the original response from the responding party. These originals must be retained by the demanding party until 6 months after final disposition of the action. [CCP §2031.290(b)]

[8:1481.1-1481.4] *Reserved.*

7. [8:1481.5] **"Clawback" Procedure Where Privileged Information Produced in ESI:** Because of the increased risk of inadvertently producing privileged information in large volumes of electronically-stored information (ESI), CCP §2031.285 provides a procedure for handling claims that ESI produced in discovery is subject to "a claim of privilege or of protection as attorney work product."

Intentional or inadvertent disclosure: The "clawback" procedure applies whether the privileged information was inadvertently or intentionally produced. Normally, a privilege is *waived by intentional disclosure* of the privileged information by a party entitled to invoke the privilege (*see* ¶*8:199 ff.*). CCP §2031.285 does not address what level of conduct ("inadvertence" or something else) is sufficient to preserve the privilege. That determination must be made under rules governing evidence generally.

a. [8:1481.6] **Demand return:** The party making the claim of privilege or work product protection may simply notify any party that received the information of the claim for protection of specific information, and of the basis for the claim. [CCP §2031.285(a)]

☞ [8:1481.7] ***PRACTICE POINTER:*** The statute does not require a written notice, so an oral notice is sufficient to invoke the protections. However, as a practical matter, a written notice is recommended to make it clear when the notice was given and when the statutory time limit (¶*8:1481.9*) begins to run. In order to eliminate disputes, if notice is given orally, counsel should immediately follow up with a written confirmation.

b. [8:1481.8] **Sequester and return or submit to court:** The receiving party must "immediately sequester the information" and either return it and all copies, or present the information to the court "conditionally under seal" for judicial determination of the privilege or work product claim. [CCP §2031.285(b)]

c. [8:1481.9] **Time limit on motion:** Any motion for judicial determination of the privilege or work product claim must be made within

© 2020 Thomson Reuters/The Rutter Group

30 days after the party received notice of the claim. [CCP §2031.285(d)]

d. [8:1481.10] **No use prior to ruling on motion:** The receiving party must not use or disclose the information before resolution of the motion (or expiration of the time limit for such motion); and if it disclosed the information before being notified of the privilege or work product claim, it must immediately take reasonable steps to retrieve the information. [CCP §2031.285(c)]

e. [8:1481.11] **Compare—ethical obligation:** An attorney who receives information that appears to be privileged and that was not intentionally produced by the holder of the privilege is also under an ethical obligation to refrain from using it. [See *Rico v. Mitsubishi Motors Corp.* (2007) 42 C4th 807, 818, 68 CR3d 758, 767 (*discussed at ¶8:199.16*); *Clark v. Sup.Ct. (Verisign, Inc.)* (2011) 196 CA4th 37, 51, 125 CR3d 361, 372; *Ardon v. City of Los Angeles* (2016) 62 C4th 1176, 1180, 199 CR3d 743, 744—same obligation applies when privileged documents inadvertently produced in response to Public Records Act request (Gov.C. §6250 et seq.) (*discussed at ¶8:1805.18 ff.*)]

Note that this ethical obligation is *not* limited to the ESI context; it applies to any production of records that appear to be privileged and inadvertently produced. *See ¶8:199.16*.

8. [8:1482] **Enforcing Demand:** A motion to compel is the procedure to enforce compliance with a CCP §2031.010 demand:

- Where *no* response at all has been made, the motion is to compel a response (CCP §2031.300, *see ¶8:1483*);
- Where responses have been made but they are not satisfactory to the demanding party, the motion is to compel further responses (CCP §2031.310, *see ¶8:1490*); and
- Where an agreement to comply has been made, but compliance is not forthcoming, the motion is to compel compliance (CCP §2031.320, *see ¶8:1503*).

a. [8:1483] **Where NO response made—motion to compel response:** Where there has been no timely response to a CCP §2031.010 demand, the first thing the demanding party must do is to seek an order compelling a response. [CCP §2031.300]

(1) [8:1483.1] **No objections:** Failure to timely respond *waives* all objections, including privilege and work product (*see ¶8:1463*). So, unless the party to whom the demand was directed obtains relief from waiver (*¶8:1465*), he or she cannot raise objections to the documents demanded.

(2) [8:1484] **No time limit:** There is no deadline for a motion to compel responses (other than the "cut-offs" on discovery before trial; *see ¶8:1262*).

(a) [8:1485] **Waiver or estoppel as limit:** But the demanding party cannot always delay a motion to compel with impunity. If the delay has resulted in "substantial prejudice" to the party to whom it was directed (e.g., documents no longer available), the court may find that the demanding party has waived the right to compel response and disclosure. [See *Crippen v. Sup.Ct. (Kaiser)* (1984) 159 CA3d 254, 260, 205 CR 477, 480—decided under former law, but principle presumably still valid]

(3) [8:1486] **No "attempt to resolve informally" required:** Likewise, for *failure* to respond, the moving party need not attempt to resolve the matter outside court before filing the motion. [See CCP §2031.300]

(4) [8:1487] **No "good cause" requirement:** Where the motion seeks only a *response* to the inspection demand, no showing of "good cause" is required (whereas such showing is required for an order compelling further responses; *see* ¶*8:1495*).

(5) [8:1488] **Monetary sanction against losing party:** If a motion to compel response is filed, the court "shall" impose a monetary sanction against the losing party *unless* it finds that party made or opposed the motion "with substantial justification" or other reasons make the sanction "unjust." [CCP §2031.300(c)]

In addition, if the court finds that a party, person or attorney did not respond in good faith to the request for production, failed to meet and confer in good faith, or produced requested documents within seven days of a hearing on the motion to compel, the court must award sanctions of $250 (unless it makes written findings that the one subject to the sanction acted with substantial justification or other circumstances make imposition of the sanction unjust) and may order the attorney to report the sanction to the State Bar. [CCP §2023.050(a)-(c) (all added eff. 1/1/20)]

(Monetary sanctions on discovery motions are discussed at ¶*8:1921 ff.*)

(a) [8:1488.1] **"Substantial justification" for refusal to comply:** *See discussion at* ¶*8:1964 ff.*

[8:1488.2-1488.4] *Reserved.*

(b) [8:1488.5] **Limitation—no sanctions ("safe harbor") where ESI lost or destroyed due to computer system:** Absent exceptional circumstances, no sanctions may be imposed for failure to produce electronically-stored information (ESI) that has been lost, damaged, altered or overwritten as a result of the *"routine, good faith operation* of an electronic information system." [CCP §§2031.300(d)(1), 2031.310(j)(1) (emphasis added)]

(6) [8:1489] **Additional sanctions if order disobeyed:** If the motion to compel is granted and the party *disobeys* the court's order to respond, additional sanctions may then be imposed:

© 2020 Thomson Reuters/The Rutter Group

i.e., an "issue sanction," "evidence sanction" or even a "terminating (doomsday) sanction"—plus additional monetary sanctions. [CCP §§2031.300(c), 2023.030(b)-(d); see also *Kravitz v. Sup.Ct. (Milner)* (2001) 91 CA4th 1015, 1020-1021, 111 CR2d 385, 389 (citing text); *Los Defensores, Inc. v. Gomez* (2014) 223 CA4th 377, 390-392, 166 CR3d 899, 910-912—terminating sanction (entry of default) justified based on party's willful failure to comply with order compelling production of documents (including evidence of concealment or destruction of records); *and ¶8:2145 ff.*]

- [8:1489.1] Following settlement of a class action lawsuit, defendant sought forensic examination of plaintiff's Attorney's hard drive in response to Attorney's statement that she would seek over $26 million in fees. The trial court ultimately ordered Attorney to allow the examination, which she refused. The court did not abuse its discretion in imposing $165,000 in sanctions, representing defendant's expenses in seeking compliance, based on Attorney's refusal to comply with the court order and to meet and confer in good faith. Attorney's contention that the trial court's order was "legally erroneous" was not a substantial justification for refusing to comply with the discovery order. Rather, "[t]he record . . . strongly indicates that the purpose [of Attorney's behavior] was to generally obstruct the self-executing process of discovery." [*Ellis v. Toshiba America Information Systems, Inc.* (2013) 218 CA4th 853, 879, 160 CR3d 557, 579-580 (internal quotes omitted); see CCP §2023.010(g), (i)]

b. [8:1490] **Where response UNSATISFACTORY—motion to compel further response:** Where a response *has* been made, but the demanding party is not satisfied with it, the remedy is a motion to compel *further responses*. [CCP §2031.310]

This motion can be utilized to attack a response containing:

- Objections; or
- An agreement to comply that is incomplete; or
- A statement of inability to comply that is incomplete or evasive. [CCP §2031.310(a)]

[8:1490.1-1490.4] *Reserved.*

[8:1490.5] ***PRACTICE POINTER—Where response states ESI does not exist:*** If the responding party claims the demanded ESI does not exist or has been destroyed, the demanding party *may,* on a showing of "good cause" (*¶8:1495*), seek an order for a *search of the responding party's computer and backup systems.*

- [8:1490.6] *Engage expert:* Courts are likely to require the demanding party to employ a forensic expert for this purpose, at the demanding party's own expense, because data on the responding party's computer may be destroyed by improper handling. The court may also order the expert not to access or copy confidential data (e.g., customers' lists, trade secrets, privileged communications, etc.). In some cases, the court may require an expert to serve as a neutral on any disputes relating to the ESI.
- [8:1490.7] *Anticipate objections:* The responding party is likely to object on grounds of "undue burden and expense" and/or "privileged matter." To deflect such objections, consider offering the following:
  - — to pay all costs associated with the information recovery;
  - — to mirror (make an exact replica of) the drive and use that, instead of the production drive in use by the party, for your examination;
  - — to schedule the search before or after normal business hours in order to minimize "down time" on the responding party's computers; and
  - — that any information recovered be reviewed initially by the responding party's attorney, with an opportunity to withhold and object to disclosure of material beyond the permissible scope of discovery.

(1) [8:1491] **45-day time limit:** This motion must be served within 45 days after service of a verified response (extended if served by mail, overnight delivery or fax or electronically; see CCP §§1010.6(a)(4), 1013, ¶*9:87 ff.*). *Otherwise, the demanding party waives* the right to compel any further response to the CCP §2031.010 demand. [CCP §§2031.310(c), 2016.050; see *Sperber v. Robinson* (1994) 26 CA4th 736, 745, 31 CR2d 659, 664]

The 45-day time limit is mandatory and "jurisdictional" (court has no authority to grant a late motion). [*Sexton v. Sup.Ct. (Mullikin Med. Ctr.)* (1997) 58 CA4th 1403, 1410, 68 CR2d 708, 712—late-filed motion to compel must be denied where objection raised at hearing even if omitted in opposition papers]

(a) [8:1491.1] **Computation:** The 45-day deadline runs *from the date the verified response is served,* not from the date originally set for production or inspection. [CCP §2031.310(c); *Standon Co., Inc. v. Sup.Ct. (Kim)* (1990) 225 CA3d 898, 903, 275 CR 833, 835]

(b) [8:1491.1a] **Extension for service by mail, overnight delivery or fax or electronically:** The 45-day deadline is extended for service by mail, overnight delivery or fax or electronically, in accordance with CCP §§1010.6(a)(4), 1013. [CCP §2016.050; *see* ¶*9:87 ff.*]

© 2020 Thomson Reuters/The Rutter Group

(c) [8:1492] **Extension by stipulation:** The deadline may be extended by *written stipulation* of the parties (CCP §2031.310(c)).

1) [8:1492.1] **Extension by court order?** There is no statutory provision for extension by court order. Presumably, the court has inherent power to extend the 45-day deadline *before* it expires. But relief thereafter is doubtful. The 45-day time limit on motions to compel has been described as "jurisdictional." [*Sexton v. Sup.Ct. (Mullikin Med. Ctr.)* (1997) 58 CA4th 1403, 1409-1410, 68 CR2d 708, 712]

However, the court in *Sexton* did not discuss or consider whether relief for untimely motions was available under CCP §473(b) based on "mistake, inadvertence, surprise or excusable neglect" (*see ¶8:1150*).

(d) [8:1492.1a] **Waiver bars later demand:** Missing the 45-day deadline waives the right to compel a further response to the demand (CCP §2031.310(c)) or to compel inspection of any documents that might have been identified in such a further response (see CCP §2031.320(a)). [*New Albertsons, Inc. v. Sup.Ct. (Shanahan)* (2008) 168 CA4th 1403, 1427-1428, 86 CR3d 457, 476]

(e) [8:1492.2] **Compare—waiver no bar to document inspection at deposition:** Despite missing the deadline to compel production under §2031.310(c), the demanding party may obtain the documents by *noticing the deposition* of the party with the documents, and including a demand for production in the deposition notice. I.e., waiver of the right to compel production under §2031.310(c) does not affect a party's right to compel inspection at a deposition. [*Carter v. Sup.Ct. (CSAA Inter-Insurance Bureau)* (1990) 218 CA3d 994, 997, 267 CR 290, 291; *see ¶8:521*]

➪ [8:1492.3] ***PRACTICE POINTER:*** Don't forget the clock is ticking while you negotiate with opposing counsel under the statutorily-required "meet and confer" procedure. You have slightly more than 6 weeks to serve a motion to compel (unless opposing counsel stipulates to an extension).

If you do miss the deadline, you can insist on production at a deposition (*see ¶8:1492.2*). But that is more expensive; and it may not be possible if you have already taken the opposing party's deposition.

(f) [8:1492.4] **Time limit applicable where only unverified objections received?** CCP §2031.310(c) states that the time limit for bringing a motion to compel further responses runs from the service of a *verified* response or supplemental *verified* response. Although not specified in the Discovery Act, the 45-day limit probably also applies where the response is unverified and includes only objections.

Comment: Because this issue is not free from doubt, to be safe, you should serve your motion within 45 days of service of unverified objections. *See ¶8:1150.7 ff.*

(2) [8:1493] **Moving papers:** The motion to compel further responses should comply with the same CRC 3.1345 format requirements discussed in connection with interrogatories (*see ¶8:1151 ff.*). *Effective January 1, 2020*, as with motions to compel responses to interrogatories, the court has discretion to permit the moving party to submit, in lieu of a separate statement, a concise outline of matters in dispute. [CCP §2031.310(b)(3) (amended eff. 1/1/19, operative 1/1/20); *see ¶8:1157.3 ff.*]

FORMS

- Motion to Compel [Further] Responses to Demands for Inspection and for Sanctions and Proposed Order, *see Form 8:28* in Rivera, *Cal. Prac. Guide: Civ. Pro. Before Trial FORMS* (TRG)

- Statement of Disputed Responses to Demands for Inspection, *see Form 8:28.1* in Rivera, *Cal. Prac. Guide: Civ. Pro. Before Trial FORMS* (TRG).

(3) [8:1494] **"Attempt to resolve informally" required:** The motion to compel further responses must be accompanied by a declaration showing "a reasonable and good faith attempt" to resolve the issues outside of court. [CCP §§2016.040, 2031.310(b)(2)]

Cross-refer: The requirement is discussed in greater detail in connection with interrogatories at ¶*8:1158 ff.*

(a) [8:1494.1] **Compare—informal discovery conference to resolve dispute:** Many judges as a matter of practice allow for or require informal conferences with the court to resolve discovery disputes. A party may request, or the court on its own motion may schedule, an informal discovery conference. [CCP §2016.080; *see discussion at ¶8:787.1*]

(4) [8:1495] **"Good cause" for production required:** The motion for order compelling further responses "shall set forth *specific facts* showing *good cause* justifying the discovery sought by the demand." [CCP §2031.310(b)(1) (emphasis

© 2020 Thomson Reuters/The Rutter Group

added); *Kirkland v. Sup.Ct. (Guess?, Inc.)* (2002) 95 CA4th 92, 98, 115 CR2d 279, 284 (citing text)]

(a) [8:1495.1] **Comment:** One rationale of the "good cause" requirement is that production of documents or other physical evidence may involve a greater intrusion on one's privacy than merely answering questions. Hence, higher standards are required for discovery.

(b) [8:1495.2] **Protects party's trial preparations:** Another purpose served by the "good cause" requirement is to protect materials obtained or created by a party or its insurer in anticipation of litigation, such as witness statements. Although not "attorney work product," such statements may only be ordered produced on a showing of "good cause." [See *Greyhound Corp. v. Sup.Ct. (Clay)* (1961) 56 C2d 355, 401, 15 CR 90, 106 (superseded by statute on other grounds)]

1) [8:1495.3] **Compare—attorney work product:** A bare showing of "good cause" is insufficient to compel production of materials constituting attorney work product. Although some work product is never discoverable (e.g., attorney opinions, conclusions, etc.), other work product may be ordered disclosed, but only if the party seeking discovery can demonstrate *injustice or unfair prejudice*, a much heavier burden. [CCP §2018.030(b); *see ¶8:222 ff.*]

[8:1495.4] *Reserved.*

(c) [8:1495.5] **Effect:** Although no showing of "good cause" is required for the inspection demand, the demanding party must be prepared to make such showing if the demand is refused. This effectively bars the use of CCP §2031.010 et seq. for purely "fishing expeditions."

(d) [8:1495.6] **Showing required:** To establish "good cause," the burden is on the moving party to show both:

- *Relevance to the subject matter* (e.g., how the information in the documents would tend to prove or disprove some issue in the case); *and*
- *Specific facts justifying discovery* (e.g., why such information is necessary for trial preparation or to prevent surprise at trial). [*Glenfed Develop. Corp. v. Sup.Ct. (National Union Fire Ins. Co. of Pittsburgh, Penn.)* (1997) 53 CA4th 1113, 1117, 62 CR2d 195, 197 (citing text); see also *Kirkland v. Sup.Ct. (Guess?, Inc.)* (2002) 95 CA4th 92, 98, 115 CR2d 279, 284 (citing text)]

The fact that there is *no alternative source* for the information sought is an important factor in establishing "good cause" for inspection. But it is *not* essential in every case. [*Associated Brewers Distrib. Co., Inc. v. Sup.Ct. (Jos. Schlitz Brewing Co.)* (1967) 65 C2d 583, 588, 55 CR 772, 775 (decided under former law)]

(e) [8:1495.7] **Evidence required:** Declarations are generally used to show the requisite "good cause" for an order to compel inspection. The declarations must contain "specific facts" rather than mere conclusions. [*Fireman's Fund Ins. Co. v. Sup.Ct. (Paine Webber Real Estate Secur.)* (1991) 233 CA3d 1138, 1141, 286 CR 50, 51—P's desire to review documents for "context" is "a patently insufficient ground" for production of sensitive commercial information]

1) [8:1495.8] **Allegations on information and belief:** The declarations may be on information and belief, if necessary. However, in such cases, the "specific facts" supporting such information and belief (the sources of the information) must also be alleged. [See *Grannis v. Board of Med. Examiners* (1971) 19 CA3d 551, 564, 96 CR 863, 873—also dealing with former "good cause" requirement in affidavit for depo subpoena duces tecum]

2) [8:1495.9] **Whose declaration:** Most declarations are made by the attorney for the moving party, who is usually more familiar with the relevancy and "specific facts" constituting "good cause" for inspection.

[8:1495.10] ***PRACTICE POINTER:*** Even so, if representing the moving party, be careful about signing such declarations. You risk being called upon (in depositions, for example) to prove the truth of whatever you allege. In turn, this could lead to your being called as a witness at trial and the possibility that this would disqualify you from representing the client.

[8:1495.11-1495.14] *Reserved.*

(5) [8:1495.15] **Where ESI sought from source "not reasonably accessible":** Where the responding party has refused to provide electronically-stored information (ESI) on the ground that its source is "not reasonably accessible," the responding party bears the burden of demonstrating this fact on a motion to compel. [CCP §2031.310(d); *see discussion at* ¶*8:1456.21*]

Even so, if the demanding party shows "good cause" for discovery, the court may still order the ESI produced on conditions, *including allocation of the expense* of discovery. [CCP §2031.310(e), (f); *see discussion at* ¶*8:1456.26*]

© 2020 Thomson Reuters/The Rutter Group

(6) [8:1496] **If "good cause" shown, responding party must justify objections:** If "good cause" is shown by the moving party, the burden is then on the responding party to justify any objections made to document disclosure (the same as on motions to compel answers to interrogatories or deposition questions; *see ¶8:1179*). [*Kirkland v. Sup.Ct. (Guess?, Inc.)* (2002) 95 CA4th 92, 98, 115 CR2d 279, 284]

- [8:1496.1] The responding party could *not* justify refusal to produce a tape recording of conversations with the demanding party on the ground the demanding party knew what he said. The tape recording is discoverable because it is the only accurate and unimpeachable source of what was discussed. [*Hartbrodt v. Burke* (1996) 42 CA4th 168, 172, 49 CR2d 562, 567]

(7) [8:1497] **Court may order description of documents to be produced:** If the CCP §2031.010 demand is for *categories* of documents and an objection is made as to certain documents, the court will need an adequate description of the documents in question to make an enforceable order.

Therefore, if the responding party *objects* to an inspection demand, the response must "identify with particularity" any document or thing falling within any category in the demand to which the objection is made, and set forth the specific ground for objection. [CCP §2031.240(b)] (*Comment:* Again, general objections are improper and may result in sanctions on a motion to compel.)

(8) [8:1497.1] **Order discretionary:** The court is not required to grant an order for document production. It may properly weigh whatever utility the records are likely to have against the *cost*, time, expenses and disruption of normal business likely to result from an order compelling production. [*Volkswagen of America, Inc. v. Sup.Ct. (Rusk)* (2006) 139 CA4th 1481, 1497, 43 CR3d 723, 733 (citing text); *Calcor Space Facility, Inc. v. Sup.Ct. (Thiem Indus., Inc.)* (1997) 53 CA4th 216, 223, 61 CR2d 567, 571; *see ¶8:544.1 ff.*]

[8:1497.2-1497.4] *Reserved.*

(9) [8:1497.5] **Limitations on orders for production of ESI:** The court must limit the frequency or scope of discovery where there are grounds for a protective order against a demand for production of electronically-stored information (ESI) if:

— the ESI can be obtained from another source that is more convenient or less expensive;

— the discovery sought is unreasonably cumulative or duplicative;

— the demanding party has been dilatory; or

— the burdens outweigh the benefits of the proposed discovery. [See CCP §§2031.310(g), 2031.060(f); *and discussion at ¶8:1456.40 ff.*]

(10)[8:1498] **Monetary sanction against losing party:** Generally only a monetary sanction against the losing party may be imposed on a motion to compel further responses. Such sanction "shall" be imposed *unless* the court finds that party made or opposed the motion "with substantial justification" or other circumstances make the sanction "unjust." [CCP §§2031.310(h) (document production statute), 2023.030(a) (general sanctions statute); see *Kravitz v. Sup.Ct. (Milner)* (2001) 91 CA4th 1015, 1021, 111 CR2d 385, 389 (citing text)]

In addition, if the court finds that a party, person or attorney did not respond in good faith to the request for production, failed to meet and confer in good faith, or produced requested documents within seven days of a hearing on the motion to compel, the court must award sanctions of $250 (unless it makes written findings that the one subject to the sanction acted with substantial justification or other circumstances make imposition of the sanction unjust) and may order the attorney to report the sanction to the State Bar. [CCP §2023.050(a)-(c) (all added eff. 1/1/20)]

(Monetary sanctions on discovery motions are discussed at ¶*8:1921 ff.*)

[8:1498.1-1498.4] *Reserved.*

- [8:1498.5] In response to document requests, P served general, "boilerplate" objections, including attorney-client privilege and work product. D moved to compel further responses and to compel P to serve a privilege log (which P did before the motion was heard). P's "boilerplate" objections were *sanctionable* (e.g., by monetary sanctions). But the sanction could *not* be a forced waiver of the attorney-client privilege because even "boilerplate" objections were *sufficient* to preserve the privilege. [*Korea Data Systems Co. Ltd. v. Sup.Ct. (Aamazing Technologies Corp.)* (1997) 51 CA4th 1513, 1516, 59 CR2d 925, 926; see *Catalina Island Yacht Club v. Sup.Ct. (Beatty)* (2015) 242 CA4th 1116, 1129-1130, 195 CR3d 694, 703-704]
- [8:1498.6] Similarly, a forced waiver of the attorney-client privilege is not an appropriate sanction for submission of a *tardy* "privilege log," so long as the privilege was invoked in a timely manner. [*Hernandez v. Sup.Ct. (Acheson Indus., Inc.)* (2003) 112 CA4th 285, 293, 4 CR3d 883, 891; *Catalina Island Yacht Club v. Sup.Ct. (Beatty)*, supra, 242 CA4th at 1126, 195 CR3d at 700-701—also, no waiver based on *inadequate* privilege log that fails to sufficiently identify documents; *see* ¶*8:1474.5 ff.*]

[8:1498.7-1498.9] *Reserved.*

© 2020 Thomson Reuters/The Rutter Group

(a) [8:1498.10] **Limitation—no sanctions ("safe harbor") where ESI lost or destroyed due to computer system:** *See ¶8:1488.5.*

(11) [8:1499] **Additional sanctions if order disobeyed:** If further responses are ordered and the responding party *fails to obey* (i.e., fails to agree to produce documents demanded, etc.), additional sanctions may be imposed: i.e., an "issue sanction," "evidence sanction" or even a "terminating (doomsday) sanction," plus additional monetary sanctions. [CCP §§2031.300(c) (order compelling responses), 2031.310(i) (order compelling *further* responses), 2023.030(b)-(d) (general sanctions statute); see *Hartbrodt v. Burke* (1996) 42 CA4th 168, 174-176, 49 CR2d 562, 567; *New Albertsons, Inc. v. Sup.Ct. (Shanahan)* (2008) 168 CA4th 1403, 1427-1428, 86 CR3d 457, 476—evidence or issue sanctions improper absent prior order compelling response; *Lopez v. Watchtower Bible & Tract Soc. of New York, Inc.* (2016) 246 CA4th 566, 605-606, 201 CR3d 156, 188-189—terminating sanctions improper where no showing court could not have obtained compliance using lesser or other sanctions]

(These sanctions are discussed in greater detail at ¶*8:2145 ff.*)

(a) [8:1499.1] **Example:** Issue preclusion is not an abuse of discretion where a party has repeatedly refused to produce records demanded; and *lesser sanctions would leave the demanding party unprepared* for trial. [*Sauer v. Sup.Ct. (Oak Indus., Inc.)* (1987) 195 CA3d 213, 230, 240 CR 489, 499—decided pre-1986 Discovery Act]

(b) [8:1500] **Failure to obey:** It is not entirely clear whether *unintentional* noncompliance is sanctionable, or whether a *willful* disobedience is required. *See discussion at ¶8:2147 ff.*

(c) [8:1501] **Even inadvertent destruction:** Where the responding party inadvertently loses or destroys material evidence, sanctions may be imposed to "even up" the score but not to put the demanding party in a better position than if the evidence had been produced. [*Puritan Ins. Co. v. Sup.Ct. (Tri-C Machine Corp.)* (1985) 171 CA3d 877, 883-884, 217 CR 602, 606-607]

- [8:1502] P was injured as the result of an allegedly defective conveyor belt drive shaft. P's expert conducted extensive tests on the shaft, but then inadvertently lost it. The court granted D's motion to compel production. To "even up" the score, it was proper to bar P's expert from testifying based on his examination or tests of the original shaft. [*Puritan Ins. Co. v. Sup.Ct. (Tri-C Machine Corp.)*, supra, 171 CA3d at 887, 217 CR at 609, fn. 11]

But it was an *abuse of discretion* to bar P from introducing *photographs* of the shaft and expert testimony *interpreting* the photographs because this placed D in a more favorable position than it would have occupied had both the shaft and photographs been available at trial. This was an *excessive* sanction for the "disobedience" involved. [*Puritan Ins. Co. v. Sup.Ct. (Tri-C Machine Corp.)*, supra, 171 CA3d at 886-887, 217 CR at 608-609]

[8:1502.1-1502.4] *Reserved.*

(12) [8:1502.5] **Sanctions absent prior court order in egregious cases:** A terminating sanction may be proper even where there has been no violation of a prior court order in egregious cases of intentional spoliation of evidence. [*Williams v. Russ* (2008) 167 CA4th 1215, 1227, 84 CR3d 813, 823]

- [8:1502.6] Former Client sued Law Firm for malpractice and demanded his files. Law Firm turned over 36 file boxes of materials. Later, Law Firm made an inspection demand for some of these materials, necessary to its defense. Former Client was unable to comply because he had placed the file boxes in commercial storage and they had been destroyed after he *failed to pay the storage charges despite repeated warnings* from the storage facility. This was tantamount to intentional destruction of the files and ground for a "terminating sanction," dismissing Former Client's action against Law Firm. [*Williams v. Russ*, supra, 167 CA4th at 1227, 84 CR3d at 823]

  [8:1502.7-1502.9] *Reserved.*

(13) [8:1502.10] **"Safe harbor" where ESI lost or destroyed due to computer system:** *See discussion at ¶8:1488.5.*

c. [8:1503] **For FAILURE TO COMPLY AS AGREED—motion to compel compliance:** If the responding party *agrees* to comply with a CCP §2031.010 demand but then fails to do so, compliance may be compelled on appropriate motion. [CCP §2031.320]

[8:1504-1507] *Reserved.*

(1) [8:1508] **Procedure to enforce compliance:** If the responding party fails to permit inspection in accordance with its agreement to comply with an inspection demand, the demanding party's remedy is to file a *motion compelling compliance.* [CCP §2031.320]

(a) [8:1508.1] **Requirements:** There is *no* fixed time limit on this motion. And, *no* "attempt to resolve informally" need be shown. All that has to be shown is the responding party's failure to comply as agreed. [CCP §2031.320(a); see *Standon Co., Inc. v. Sup.Ct. (Kim)* (1990) 225 CA3d 898, 903, 275 CR 833, 836]

© 2020 Thomson Reuters/The Rutter Group

However, the motion should be heard at least 15 days before trial. [CCP §2024.020(a); *see* ¶*8:445*]

(b) [8:1508.2] **Monetary sanction against losing party:** The court "shall" impose a monetary sanction against whichever party loses on the motion to compel compliance *unless* it finds that party made or opposed the motion "with substantial justification" or other circumstances make the sanction "unjust." [CCP §§2031.320(b) (document production statute), 2023.030(a) (general sanctions statute); *see* ¶*8:1921 ff.*]

In addition, if the court finds that a party, person or attorney did not respond in good faith to the request for production, failed to meet and confer in good faith, or produced requested documents within seven days of a hearing on the motion to compel, the court must award sanctions of $250 (unless it makes written findings that the one subject to the sanction acted with substantial justification or other circumstances make imposition of the sanction unjust) and may order the attorney to report the sanction to the State Bar. [CCP §2023.050(a)-(c) (all added eff. 1/1/20)]

- [8:1508.2a] In connection with a motion to compel compliance with the requirements that documents be produced either as they are kept in the usual course of business, or sorted and labeled to correspond with the categories in the document demand (¶*8:1471*), the producing party bore the burden of establishing the manner in which the records were kept in the usual course of business. Upon concluding the producing party was responsible for the disordered state of the documents produced, the court had discretion to order that party to bear the costs of organizing the documents. [*Kayne v. Grande Holdings Ltd.* (2011) 198 CA4th 1470, 1476, 130 CR3d 751, 755—producing party ordered to pay more than $74,000 of costs incurred by requesting party to organize documents]

1) [8:1508.2b] **Unreasonable delay:** It is not an abuse of discretion to *deny* sanctions *after* a trial in which the moving party had *won* on the issue on which discovery was sought: "Prejudice is difficult to prove in the face of victory." [*Colgate-Palmolive Co., Inc. v. Franchise Tax Bd.* (1992) 10 CA4th 1768, 1788, 13 CR2d 761, 774]

(2) [8:1508.3] **Further sanctions if order disobeyed:** As with other discovery orders, additional sanctions are available if the responding party fails to obey the inspection order. The court may make whatever orders are "just," including imposition

© 2020 Thomson Reuters/The Rutter Group

of an "issue sanction," "evidence sanction," or even a "doomsday (terminating) sanction" against the responding party; and/or additional monetary sanctions. [CCP §§2031.320(c) (document production statute), 2023.030(b)-(d) (general sanctions statute); *see ¶8:2145 ff.*]

- [8:1508.4] Plaintiff was ordered to produce all documents upon which she based her breach of contract claim. She produced a forged contract and thereafter destroyed evidence pertinent to exposure of the forgery. A terminating sanction (dismissal) was not an abuse of discretion. [*R.S. Creative, Inc. v. Creative Cotton, Ltd.* (1999) 75 CA4th 486, 497, 89 CR2d 353, 361; see also *Lang v. Hochman* (2000) 77 CA4th 1225, 1244, 92 CR2d 322, 333—striking answer and rendering default judgment not an abuse of discretion for defendant's repeated violation of court orders to produce records]

  [8:1508.5-1508.8] *Reserved.*

(3) [8:1508.9] **Attorney's "mea culpa" affidavit as bar to sanctions?** *See discussion at ¶8:2300 ff.*

d. [8:1508.10] **Evidence sanctions at trial for concealing records:** The trial court has the power to exclude documents or other physical evidence at trial that has been concealed in response to interrogatories and CCP §2031.010 requests and that would cause "unfair surprise" at trial. [See *Deeter v. Angus* (1986) 179 CA3d 241, 255, 224 CR 801, 808—exclusion of audio tape not produced in response to discovery requests; *Vallbona v. Springer* (1996) 43 CA4th 1525, 1547-1548, 51 CR2d 311, 326—exclusion of records that offering party had claimed he was unable to produce for discovery because they had been stolen; *Pate v. Channel Lumber Co.* (1997) 51 CA4th 1447, 1455, 59 CR2d 919, 924—exclusion of records that offering party had not produced in response to several discovery requests and had repeatedly stated did not exist]

(1) [8:1508.11] **No prior order required:** Documents concealed during discovery may be excluded at trial even where there was no prior order compelling production. The propounding party would have no reason to seek such an order where discovery responses falsely state such documents do not exist. [*Pate v. Channel Lumber Co.*, supra, 51 CA4th at 1456, 59 CR2d at 924; *see ¶8:10*]

[8:1508.12-1508.13] *Reserved.*

e. [8:1508.14] **Terminating sanctions for concealing or destroying documents:** A court may impose terminating sanctions (e.g., entry of default) where the evidence reveals that a party has willfully concealed or destroyed written documents. [*Los Defensores, Inc. v. Gomez* (2014) 223 CA4th 377, 390-392, 166 CR3d 899, 910-912; *see ¶8:1489*]

f. [8:1508.15] **Sanctions in post-trial proceedings:** Neither the Code nor any case law mandates that discovery sanctions

© 2020 Thomson Reuters/The Rutter Group

be imposed prior to rendering of the verdict. [See *Sherman v. Kinetic Concepts, Inc.* (1998) 67 CA4th 1152, 1163, 79 CR2d 641, 648]

- [8:1508.16] Plaintiffs did not discover defendant's nondisclosure of important documents requested in discovery until after an adverse jury verdict. The case was remanded for new trial and defendant ordered to pay *monetary sanctions* for plaintiff's costs (including attorney fees) of the first trial. [*Sherman v. Kinetic Concepts, Inc.*, supra, 67 CA4th at 1164, 79 CR2d at 649]

CHAPTER 8J

EXPERT WITNESS DISCLOSURE

CONTENTS

Page

© 2020 Thomson Reuters/The Rutter Group

© 2020 Thomson Reuters/The Rutter Group

© 2020 Thomson Reuters/The Rutter Group

RESERVED

EXPERT WITNESS DISCLOSURE

[8:1624] **Statute:** Either party may compel the *exchange* of expert witness lists and related information shortly before trial, as discussed below (¶*8:1639 ff.*). [CCP §2034.010 et seq.; see *Kalaba v. Gray* (2002) 95 CA4th 1416, 1419, 116 CR2d 570, 573 (citing text)]

The §2034.010 et seq. procedure contemplates these steps: a triggering demand for expert witness discovery (¶*8:1647 ff.*); exchange of expert witness information (¶*8:1666 ff.*); expert depositions (¶*8:1688 ff.*); and expert testimony at trial.

(Exception: CCP §2034.010 et seq. does not apply in *eminent domain* cases; special statutes govern exchange of expert witness lists and valuation data in such actions. See CCP §§2034.010, 1258.010 et seq.; *Sacramento Area Flood Control Agency v. Dhaliwal* (2015) 236 CA4th 1315, 1335, 187 CR3d 182, 197; *and* ¶*8:1788 ff.*)

[8:1625] **Background:** Much litigation relies on expert testimony. To prepare for trial, each side needs to know which experts will testify for the other side and what they will have to say. [See *Stony Brook I Homeowners Ass'n v. Sup.Ct. (Diehl)* (2000) 84 CA4th 691, 700, 101 CR2d 67, 71 (citing text)] (Compare: The identities and opinions of experts engaged *solely to consult* with counsel are normally protected as "work product"; *see* ¶*8:246.*)

[8:1626] **Special problem posed by late selection of experts to testify:** There are a number of reasons (besides "game playing") why each side may purposefully delay selecting expert witnesses to testify at trial. These include:

- The cost factor (expert testimony may cost more than all other litigation costs combined);
- Cases often settle before trial, in which event the cost can be avoided;
- Experts hired too early in the litigation may not be around to testify when needed;
- Experts may need to review percipient and documentary evidence that may not be completely produced until near trial.

[8:1627] **Other discovery procedures ineffective:** Without some procedure to discover the identities and opinions of experts hired shortly before trial, there would be flurries of last-minute discovery attempts and motions for continuance of the trial. [*Kalaba v. Gray*, supra, 95 CA4th at 1423, 116 CR2d at 576 (citing text)]

[8:1628] **Problems with interrogatories:** Interrogatories served early in the litigation asking for identity and opinions of experts who will testify usually come back answered, "We have not chosen our expert witnesses yet."

© 2020 Thomson Reuters/The Rutter Group

"Update" interrogatories can be served later, but there is a cut-off on discovery 30 days before trial (*see* ¶*8:909 ff.*). So, by waiting until then to hire experts, parties can avoid disclosure entirely. And, under the interrogatory procedure, there is no way of excluding undisclosed experts from testifying.

[8:1629] *Reserved.*

[8:1630] **Under case management rules:** Courts frequently address the issue of designation of experts and exchange of expert witness reports at a case management conference, without the necessity of a formal demand under CCP §2034.010 et seq. Counsel should be open to stipulations to have early expert disclosure (and avoid last minute crises and expert motion practice), as well as staggered expert disclosure (where the party with the burden to prove a fact discloses and presents an expert before the other side does). However, if a less formal approach is used, the record should be clear that a demand will have been deemed to have been made so that the statutory penalties (e.g., excluding experts not properly disclosed) are available.

Where there are shifting burdens (such as in Proposition 65 cases), it may be appropriate for plaintiff to first disclose and produce experts on issues as to which it has the burden (followed by defendant's experts) and then vice versa for issues as to which defendant has the burden. In complex litigation, the court probably has authority to order such modifications.

[8:1631-1635] *Reserved.*

STRATEGIES AND TACTICS RE DEMANDS FOR EXCHANGE OF EXPERT WITNESS INFORMATION

[8:1636] **Advantages**

- **Prevents "surprises":** The CCP §2034.010 et seq. procedure is effective to *bar* testimony from experts whose names and opinions were not properly disclosed. Thus, neither side can spring "surprise" expert testimony at trial for which the other is unprepared.
- **Self-executing:** A CCP §2034.010 et seq. demand entitles you to discovery of the other side's experts as a matter of right. No motion, hearing or court order is required.
- **Extensive disclosures required:** A properly worded CCP §2034.010 et seq. demand will provide you with the names and qualifications of the experts, the general substance of their testimony, and copies of their discoverable *reports and writings* (¶*8:1650*).

[8:1637] **Disadvantages:** However, CCP §2034.010 et seq. is a mixed blessing. There are significant limitations to consider:

- **Reciprocal exchange required:** Serving a CCP §2034.010 et seq. demand *obligates* you to disclose your own expert witness' identities, and opinions and reports. There may be cases where this is disadvantageous or impractical (e.g., where your experts are unwilling

STRATEGIES AND TACTICS RE DEMANDS FOR EXCHANGE OF EXPERT WITNESS INFORMATION (Cont'd)

or unable to be deposed before trial). There may also be cases where you have more to lose by disclosing your experts than to gain by discovering the opponent's experts.

- **Time pressures:** The "time window" within which to depose the experts on your opponent's list is rather limited: The list is usually not due until 50 days before trial (¶*8:1649.2*); and motions to enforce discovery relating to depositions of those experts can be heard no later than 10 days before trial (*see* ¶*8:1690*). So, you have only 40 days within which to depose the opponent's experts and follow up with whatever enforcement is necessary. (You may be able to agree with the other parties to modify these deadlines. *See* ¶*8:1691 ff.*)
- **Waiver of protection for earlier reports?** If you list an expert who has previously served as your consultant on the case, your opponent is entitled to discover *all* reports by that expert—even those previously given in "consultant" status and therefore protected as "work product." "Good cause" for discovery may lie in the need to review the prior report for potential impeachment. [See *Shadow Traffic Network v. Sup.Ct. (Metro Traffic Control, Inc.)* (1994) 24 CA4th 1067, 1079, 29 CR2d 693, 699; *National Steel Products Co. v. Sup.Ct. (Rosen)* (1985) 164 CA3d 476, 484-485, 210 CR 535, 539-540; *and discussion at* ¶*8:258 ff.*]
- **Cost factors:** The expert witness declarations are supposed to enable you to determine *whether* it is necessary to depose all the experts listed (*see* ¶*8:1669 ff.*). Yet, you will probably not want to rely on the declarations for this purpose. For safety's sake, you will probably feel compelled to depose them all. In view of the stiff costs in deposing experts (*see* ¶*8:1697 ff.*), this may prove prohibitively expensive.

  ⇨ [8:1637.1] ***PRACTICE POINTER—Prepare Client for Expert Witness Fees:*** Discuss with your client *at the outset* the amount it may cost to retain experts and cross-examine opposing expert witnesses. Expert witness fees increase the cost of litigation and reduce the amount the client may obtain from settlement. Failing to alert the client beforehand to these costs increases the chance of a fee dispute with the client.

[8:1638] **Weighing Pros and Cons:** Whether to make a CCP §2034.010 et seq. demand, and which experts to designate, are among the most difficult tactical decisions in a lawsuit.

The decision is complicated by the risk of waiving the work product protection if you designate an expert who has previously been your consultant on the case, which could result in unfavorable disclosures.

Not making a demand can work to defendant's advantage. In lengthy trials, defendants will have time to evaluate plaintiff's experts and to select opposing experts whom plaintiff will have no opportunity to depose in the absence of a prior §2034.010 et seq. demand.

© 2020 Thomson Reuters/The Rutter Group

STRATEGIES AND TACTICS RE DEMANDS FOR EXCHANGE OF EXPERT WITNESS INFORMATION (Cont'd)

Ultimately, in deciding whether to make a CCP §2034.010 et seq. demand, you will have to *weigh:*

- The likely impact of your experts' testimony if *not* disclosed in advance and (also *not* subject to possible impeachment on basis of their reports to you as consultants) *versus*
- How much damage may be done by opposing experts if you do not have the right to discover their identity and prepare for their reports (including possible discovery of earlier reports made by them as consultants to opposing counsel).

It can be a difficult call. (Of course, the decision will be taken out of your hands if any other party makes the demand; *see* ¶*8:1639.*)

1. [8:1639] **Who May Make Demand:** "Any party" may obtain discovery by serving a demand for exchange of expert witness lists. [CCP §2034.210]

2. [8:1640] **Who Must Exchange:** The demand obligates *all* parties *mutually* and *simultaneously* to exchange information concerning their expert trial witnesses. [CCP §2034.210(a)]

3. [8:1641] **Deadline for Demand:** A demand for exchange of expert witness information may be made any time after the case is initially set for trial. The deadline for the demand is *10 days* after the initial trial date has been set or *70 days before that trial* date, whichever is later. [CCP §2034.220]

   If the last day falls on a weekend or holiday, the time limit is extended to the next court day closer to the trial date. [CCP §2016.060]

   Compare—under case management rules: In some courts, the demand requirement is dispensed with under local case management rules. Instead, the court proposes dates for expert witness disclosure and discovery at a case management conference and the parties are bound by their stipulation to those dates. *See further discussion at* ¶*8:1630.*

   a. [8:1642] **Relief for untimely demand:** The Discovery Act does not expressly authorize a court to shorten or lengthen the deadline for serving a demand for exchange of expert witness information. (It does, however, authorize the court to alter the time for the *exchange* of information pursuant to such demand; *see* ¶*8:1663.*)

      Because the Discovery Act is silent on this matter, relief from the CCP §2034.230 deadline may be obtained under CCP §473(b) (which authorizes courts generally to grant relief from any "judgment, dismissal, order, or other *proceeding*" on a showing of "mistake, inadvertence, surprise or excusable neglect"; *see* ¶*5:282 ff.*). [*Zellerino v. Brown* (1991) 235 CA3d 1097, 1107, 1 CR2d 222, 228]

      (1) [8:1642.1] **Example:** D's demand for expert witness exchange was four days premature. (D erroneously thought a local rule requiring earlier demand applied to the case.) P filed "objections"

to D's demand as untimely. D's motion for relief under CCP §473(b) was properly granted and P ordered to respond even though the demand was untimely. [*Zellerino v. Brown*, supra, 235 CA3d at 1107, 1 CR2d at 228]

b. [8:1643] **No right to serve demand prior to trial setting:** CCP §2034.210 authorizes a demand for exchange of expert witness information only "*[a]fter the setting* of the initial trial date." [CCP §2034.210 (emphasis added)]

This "evinces a legislative preference" for the time when such disclosure is to be made. [See *South Tahoe Pub. Utility Dist. v. Sup.Ct. (CH2M Hill Calif., Inc.)* (1979) 90 CA3d 135, 139, 154 CR 1, 3 (involving similar provision in former statute)]

Thus, there is *no right* to serve a demand for exchange of expert witness information prior to trial setting. (And there would be no advantage either, because no exchange is due under CCP §2034.230(b) until 50 days before trial; *see ¶8:1660.*) [*County of Los Angeles v. Sup.Ct. (Martinez)* (1990) 224 CA3d 1446, 1456, 274 CR 712, 719—no right to discover opinions of consultants not yet designated as testifying experts]

(1) [8:1644] **"Good cause" for early disclosure:** But a court may order early discovery from an opposing expert based on a showing of "good cause," which may exist where:

- so many experts are likely to be called that it will be difficult to depose them within the limited period after an exchange of expert witness information; or
- the party seeking discovery cannot obtain the information elsewhere and therefore is unable to prepare its claim or defense; or
- the party seeking discovery is resisting a summary judgment motion based on the expert's opinion and a legitimate question exists regarding the foundation for that opinion. [See *Hernandez v. Sup.Ct. (Acheson Indus., Inc.)* (2003) 112 CA4th 285, 297, 4 CR3d 883, 894]

c. [8:1645] **Compare—after mistrial, new trial or reversal on appeal:** A mistrial, new trial or reversal of the judgment on appeal automatically restarts the time limitations on discovery (*see ¶8:451 ff.*). In such cases, a demand for an expert witness exchange is timely if made 70 days before the date set for retrial. [*Beverly Hosp. v. Sup.Ct. (Castaneda)* (1993) 19 CA4th 1289, 1295, 24 CR2d 238, 241]

If the retrial is scheduled within the 70-day period, a party may move for relief from the time limit "just as in any other case." [*Beverly Hosp. v. Sup.Ct. (Castaneda)*, supra, 19 CA4th at 1296, 24 CR2d at 242]

- [8:1645.1] Alternatively, a party may file a *motion* for leave to designate different expert witnesses for the retrial. Providing

© 2020 Thomson Reuters/The Rutter Group

ample time remains to depose the new witnesses, it is an abuse of discretion to refuse permission. [*Guzman v. Sup.Ct. (Lee)* (1993) 19 CA4th 705, 708, 23 CR2d 585, 586]

[8:1646] *Reserved.*

4. [8:1647] **Demand Procedure:** First of all, a demand for exchange of expert witness information is *optional,* not mandatory. (See "Strategies and Tactics re Demands for Exchange of Expert Witness Information," ¶*8:1636 ff.*)

However, once a demand is served by *any* party, *all* parties are obligated to exchange such information. [CCP §2034.260(a), ¶*8:1640*]

FORM: Demand for Exchange of Information Concerning Expert Witnesses, *see Form 8:34* in Rivera, *Cal. Prac. Guide: Civ. Pro. Before Trial FORMS* (TRG).

Compare—under case management rules: See discussion at ¶*8:1641.*

a. [8:1648] **Form of demand:** The demand must be in writing. The name of the party making the demand must appear below the title of the case. [CCP §2034.230(a)]

Note that §2034.230 does not expressly require that the demand be *signed* by anyone.

b. [8:1649] **Content of demand:** The demand must specify:

(1) [8:1649.1] **Statement designating Civil Discovery Act:** First of all, the expert witness demand must state that it is being made under Chapter 18 of the Civil Discovery Act (CCP §2034.210 et seq.). [CCP §2034.230(a)]

(2) [8:1649.2] **Date when exchange to be made:** It must also state the date on which the required information is to be exchanged. That date must be *20 days* after service of the demand, or *50 days* before trial, *whichever is later.* (As discussed below (¶*8:1663*), the court has power to modify this date.) [CCP §2034.230(b)]

(a) [8:1649.3] **Extension for service by mail, etc.:** The time for performing acts is extended where a discovery demand or notice is served by mail, overnight delivery or fax or electronic service. [See CCP §§1010.6(a)(4), 1013(a); *see* ¶*9:87 ff.*]

Thus, if an expert witness demand is served by mail, the exchange date based on service (20 days after service) must be extended accordingly (i.e., 5 calendar days for mail within California, 10 calendar days for mailing to or from outside the state, etc.). [See *Staub v. Kiley* (2014) 226 CA4th 1437, 1446, 173 CR3d 104, 110 (citing text)]

(b) [8:1649.4] **Effect of premature date?** A problem arises where the demand specifies a premature date for the exchange (e.g., does not include the extension required for service by mail). The court clearly has power, upon motion for protective order, to change the date for the exchange (*see* ¶*8:1654 ff.*). Absent court intervention, however, it is not clear whether specifying a premature date invalidates the demand. [See *Staub v. Kiley*, supra, 226 CA4th at 1446, 173 CR3d at 110 (citing text)]

In one case, however, the court held that by specifying a premature exchange date in the demand, a party failed to make a "complete and timely compliance" with the expert witness list exchange requirements and thus, under CCP §2034.300, lacked standing to seek exclusion of expert witnesses at trial who were not timely designated by the opposing party. [*Staub v. Kiley*, supra, 226 CA4th at 1446, 173 CR3d at 111; *and see discussion of testimony exclusion sanction at* ¶*8:1708 ff.*]

➪ [8:1649.5] ***PRACTICE POINTER:*** Courts favor exchange of expert witness information in substantial compliance with the statutory requirements and dislike "gamesmanship"; so, don't count on the court excusing your noncompliance based on the fact the disclosure date stated in the demand is "premature."

(3) [8:1650] **May also include demand for reports:** The demand may also require "the mutual and simultaneous production for inspection and copying of *all discoverable reports and writings*" of experts employed by the parties. [CCP §2034.210(c) (emphasis added)] (However, including such demand obligates the demanding party to *exchange* reports; *see* ¶*8:1681*.)

➪ [8:1651] ***PRACTICE POINTER:*** If you're going to make a demand for exchange of expert witness information, it's a good idea to include a demand for the opposing expert's reports and writings. While only "discoverable" reports and writings need be produced, opposing counsel may not want to risk withholding *any* documents, so you could end up with the expert's entire file. You may find memoranda, notes or even correspondence with opposing counsel disclosing strengths and weaknesses of the opposing party's case.

➪ [8:1651.1] ***PRACTICE POINTER:*** Conversely, before listing any expert with whom you have consulted, *review the expert's file* to make sure you won't be handing over tools for your self-destruction.

Because of the risk here, some lawyers *avoid written communications* with experts whom they plan to designate under §2034.260(b)(1). That way, there are no "discoverable reports and writings" to exchange. (The offsetting risk, however, is that your expert's failure to make a written report may affect the credibility of his or her testimony at trial; *see* ¶*8:1685.1*.)

c. [8:1652] **Service of demand:** A copy of the demand must be served on all parties who have appeared in the action. [CCP §2034.240]

d. [8:1653] **Custody of demand and information exchanged:** Neither the demand nor the expert witness information exchanged pursuant thereto are filed with the court. [CCP §2034.290(a); CRC 3.250(a)(13)-(16)]

Rather, the originals (with proof of service) are retained by the demanding party until 6 months after final disposition of the action. [CCP §2034.290(b)]

If their contents become relevant to an issue in the action, these documents "shall be *lodged* with the court" pending determination of that issue. (For example, to enable the trial judge to rule on an objection to expert testimony for failure to comply with enumerated statutory disclosure duties; *see* ¶*8:1708 ff.*) [CCP §2034.290(c)]

5. [8:1654] **Protective Orders:** Any party served with a demand for exchange of expert witness information may *promptly* seek a protective order to limit or excuse the exchange of expert witness information demanded. [CCP §2034.250(a)]

Compare—no objections: There is no provision in the expert witness disclosure statutes for "objection" to a demand. A motion for protective order is the *only* way to challenge a defective demand for exchange of experts. [*Zellerino v. Brown* (1991) 235 CA3d 1097, 1112, 1 CR2d 222, 231 (citing text); *Cottini v. Enloe Med. Ctr.* (2014) 226 CA4th 401, 419, 172 CR3d 4, 17]

a. [8:1655] **Grounds:** Such orders may be granted to protect any party or expert from "unwarranted annoyance, embarrassment, oppression, or undue burden and expense." [CCP §2034.250(b)]

(1) [8:1655.1] **Application:** Merely exchanging lists is rarely so "oppressive and burdensome" as to require relief by protective order (unless perhaps where one party designates many experts in total or on a given issue). But such relief may be proper where the demand was not timely (i.e., made after the CCP §2034.220 deadline), and the opposing party wishes to obtain a ruling to this effect rather than run the risk of consequences for failure to exchange (*see* ¶*8:1708 ff.*). [*Zellerino v. Brown* (1991) 235 CA3d 1097, 1110, 1 CR2d 222, 230 (citing text)]

A protective order might also be proper where one party is relying on an expert witness retained by a coparty but is having difficulty in obtaining the information required for the expert witness declaration (*see* ¶*8:1668*).

b. [8:1656] **Procedure:** A motion for protective order must be filed "promptly" after the demand; and must be accompanied by the usual declaration showing a "reasonable and good faith attempt" to resolve the matter outside court. [CCP §§2016.040, 2034.250(a)]

Cross-refer: The rules and procedures governing motions generally are discussed in *Ch. 9 Part I.*

c. [8:1657] **Relief available:** If "good cause" is shown, the court may grant whatever relief is just, including:

- Quashing the demand because it was *not timely served;*
- *Changing the date or place* for the exchange of expert witness information;
- Specifying terms and conditions for the exchange to proceed;
- *Dividing the parties into sides* on the basis of their interests in the action, and designating which retained experts shall be deemed employed by each side (for purposes of the expert witness declaration and other disclosures required; see below);
- Ordering any party or side to *reduce the number* of expert witnesses designated by that party or side. [CCP §2034.250(b)]

d. [8:1658] **Monetary sanction against losing party:** A monetary sanction "shall" be imposed against the losing party *unless* the court finds "substantial justification" for that party's position or other circumstances make the sanction "unjust." [CCP §2034.250(d); *see* ¶*8:1921 ff.*]

6. [8:1659] **Exchange Required:** The following rules govern what information must be exchanged under CCP §2034.260.

a. [8:1659.1] **Who must exchange:** The expert witness disclosure process is a "two-way street": *All parties who have appeared in the action* are under a duty to exchange information as described below (¶*8:1664 ff.*). [CCP §2034.260(a)]

b. [8:1660] **When exchange due:** The exchange must be made on or before the date specified in the demand, which must be *20 days* after service of the demand (extended for service by mail, *see* ¶*8:1649.3*) *or 50 days* before the initial trial, whichever is *later.* [CCP §2034.230(b); *see* ¶*8:1649.2*]

Compare—under case management rules: See discussion at ¶*8:1641.*

[8:1661-1662] *Reserved.*

(1) [8:1663] **Court may change date:** On motion for "good cause shown," the court may order the exchange on an earlier or later date. [CCP §2034.230(b)]

(Compare: However, the court has *no* power to alter the deadline for serving the demand for exchange of expert witness information; ¶*8:1642.*)

c. [8:1664] **How exchange made:** The exchange of expert witness information may occur either at a meeting of the attorneys involved

© 2020 Thomson Reuters/The Rutter Group

or by serving the information by any method specified in CCP §1011 or §1013 on or before the date set for the exchange. [CCP §2034.260(a)]

(1) [8:1665] **"Simultaneous" exchange required:** To prevent either party from taking advantage, the exchange of expert witness lists and documents is to be "simultaneous." [CCP §2034.210]

A party may not merely file a document "reserving the right to designate witnesses in response to the other party's disclosure." The party filing such a document may be precluded from calling expert witnesses at trial. [*Fairfax v. Lords* (2006) 138 CA4th 1019, 1026-1027, 41 CR3d 850, 855-856—defendant delayed designation of his retained expert witnesses until 20 days after plaintiff had designated his expert, violating "simultaneous" exchange requirement]

Caution: Exchanges by mail may limit time available for designation of supplemental experts since the need for such experts will not be known until the opposing expert list is received (*see ¶8:1687*).

➪ [8:1665.1] ***PRACTICE POINTER:*** To avoid the delay in mailing, it is usually to everyone's advantage to *stipulate* that expert designations and reports will be *hand delivered, faxed or served electronically* on the exchange date.

d. [8:1666] **What information must be exchanged:** The following information must be exchanged by *each* party:

(1) [8:1667] **Experts list:** A list setting forth the *name* and *address* of each person whose expert opinion that party expects to offer at trial by live or deposition testimony (or a statement that the party does not presently intend to offer any expert testimony). [CCP §2034.260(b)(1), (2); see *Kalaba v. Gray* (2002) 95 CA4th 1416, 1419, 116 CR2d 570, 576]

Note: There is *no* requirement that the list be *signed* by the attorney or anyone else.

(a) [8:1667.1] **Includes treating physicians:** Attending physicians are almost always asked to express opinions as to their patients' conditions (e.g., diagnosis, prognosis, etc.). Therefore, the physicians' names and addresses usually must be included on the list. [CCP §2034.260(b)(1)] (But expert witness *declarations* are *not* required as to treating physicians; *see ¶8:1668a ff.*)

- [8:1667.1a] An expert witness list designating "all past or present examining and/or treating physicians" (without giving their names and addresses) does *not* comply with the above requirements (¶*8:1667*). The court may exclude testimony by the nondesignated doctors. [*Kalaba v. Gray*, supra, 95 CA4th at 1418, 116 CR2d at 576]

1) [8:1667.2] **Comment:** By the time of the expert witness exchange, defendants usually will have deposed all of plaintiff's treating physicians. [See *Schreiber v. Estate of Kiser* (1999) 22 C4th 31, 38, 91 CR2d 293, 299]

But there are cases in which it may be "both unnecessary and prohibitively expensive" to depose *all* of the treating and examining physicians (e.g., medical malpractice cases). For this reason, the patient's expert witness list must designate *which* of the treating physicians he or she *intends to call as an expert* at trial. [See *Kalaba v. Gray*, supra, 95 CA4th at 1423, 116 CR2d at 576—18 nonparty physicians on witness list]

(b) [8:1667.3] **Local rules may limit number of experts:** Some courts have rules limiting the number of experts that may be designated. [See San Diego Sup.Ct. Rule 2.1.11—"It is the policy of the court that parties are limited to *one expert per field of expertise per side . . .* absent a court order to the contrary" (emphasis added)]

Comment: This appears to be a trial rule rather than a rule governing discovery and therefore not subject to CRC 3.20(a) (which generally preempts local rules governing pleadings, discovery, etc.; *see ¶9:13.2*).

(c) [8:1667.4] **Court may limit number of experts:** The court may, "at any time *before* or during the trial," limit the number of experts to be called by any party. [Ev.C. §723]

Comment: Presumably, this empowers the court to limit the number of witnesses to be designated in response to a demand for exchange of expert witness information. Alternatively, a party may seek a §2034.250 protective order where an opponent designates an oppressively large number of experts (*see ¶8:1654 ff.*).

(2) [8:1668] **Expert witness declaration:** In addition, an "expert witness declaration" (prepared and signed by the attorney, *¶8:1668.3*) must be attached, which provides information about each expert designated who is either:

— a *party* to the action;
— an *employee* of a party;
— or "*retained* by a party" for the purpose of forming and expressing an opinion. [CCP §2034.210(b)]

Effect: It thus becomes essential to determine the *status* of each expert designated in the expert witness list. Nothing more

© 2020 Thomson Reuters/The Rutter Group

than name and address is required for "independent" experts or percipient witnesses (e.g., treating physicians; *see* ¶*8:1668a*). But far more detailed information must be provided for experts who are parties or employees or who have been *retained to testify.* (Note also that the party retaining an expert to testify must produce him or her for deposition; *see* ¶*8:1688.*) [*Huntley v. Foster* (1995) 35 CA4th 753, 756, 41 CR2d 358, 360 (citing text)]

(a) [8:1668a] **Not applicable to nonparty treating physician:** A nonparty treating physician must be listed on the experts list (¶*8:1667.1*), but no expert witness declaration is required. Such a declaration is required only for an expert who is "a *party or an employee* of a party, or has been retained by a party for the purpose of forming and expressing an opinion." [CCP §2034.210(b) (emphasis added); see *Schreiber v. Estate of Kiser* (1999) 22 C4th 31, 39, 91 CR2d 293, 300—nonparty treating physician for whom no expert witness declaration submitted could testify as to his opinion re *causation* of injury; *Ochoa v. Dorado* (2014) 228 CA4th 120, 139, 174 CR3d 889, 903]

The fact that the treating physician is a percipient witness "does *not* mean that his testimony is limited only to personal observations. Rather, like any other expert, he may provide both fact *and opinion* testimony." [*Schreiber v. Estate of Kiser*, supra, 22 C4th at 35, 91 CR2d at 297 (emphasis added); see *Ochoa v. Dorado*, supra, 228 CA4th at 139, 174 CR3d at 904]

1) [8:1668b] **Scope of opinion testimony:** The expert witness treating physician is not limited to opinion testimony based on observations and treatment of plaintiff. Rather, "he may testify as to any opinions formed on the basis of facts *independently acquired* and informed by his training, skill, and experience. This may well include opinions regarding causation and standard of care because such issues are inherent in a physician's work." [*Schreiber v. Estate of Kiser*, supra, 22 C4th at 39, 91 CR2d at 300 (emphasis added); see *Ochoa v. Dorado*, supra, 228 CA4th at 140, 174 CR3d at 905—includes opinion re reasonable value of services treating physician provided]

But a treating physician may not offer testimony at trial that exceeds the scope of his or her deposition testimony if the opposing party had no notice that the expert would offer new testimony in sufficient time to re-depose the expert. [*Dozier v. Shapiro* (2011) 199 CA4th 1509, 1523, 133 CR3d 142, 155—trial court properly excluded treating physician's testimony on standard of care where physician was not designated to testify on that topic and indicated at deposition that he had not formed an opinion on that issue; *see also* ¶*8:1718.1*]

2) [8:1668c] **Declaration may be required if additional work done by treating physician:** A treating physician may become a retained expert where counsel supplies the physician with additional information (such as copies of pleadings or another physician's medical records for review) and asks him or her to testify to opinions formed on the basis of that additional information. [*Belfiore-Braman v. Rotenberg* (2018) 25 CA5th 234, 245, 235 CR3d 629, 637-638]

In that event, the treating physician should be included in the expert witness declaration.

[8:1668d] ***PRACTICE POINTER FOR DEFENDANTS:*** When deposing a treating physician, be sure to ask whether he or she holds any opinions on causation and standard of care; and if so, on what facts those opinions are based. Conceivably, some treating physicians may ultimately become *defense* witnesses. [See *Schreiber v. Estate of Kiser*, supra, 22 C4th at 39, 91 CR2d at 300]

(b) [8:1668.1] **Whose expert:** An expert witness declaration is required for each expert "retained by *a* party," not necessarily the designating party. Thus, if the designating party intends to rely on experts produced by *other parties* (e.g., codefendants), he or she must furnish an expert witness declaration for those experts. [*Zellerino v. Brown* (1991) 235 CA3d 1097, 1116, 1 CR2d 222, 234 (citing text)—by listing the experts of her opponent, P assumed burden of providing declarations as to their expected testimony]

1) [8:1668.2] **Comment:** Usually, this is done by obtaining information from the party employing that expert. If this is not possible, the designating party may need to seek a protective order; *see* ¶*8:1655.1*.

(c) [8:1668.3] **Whose declaration:** The "expert witness declaration" must be signed by the designating party's *attorney* (not by the expert).

(d) [8:1668.4] **Contents:** The expert witness declaration must contain the following information:

- **Qualifications:** A brief statement of the expert's qualifications;
- **"General substance of expected testimony":** A brief narrative statement of the general substance

© 2020 Thomson Reuters/The Rutter Group

of the testimony that the expert is expected to give (¶*8:1669 ff.*);

- **Ready to testify:** Representations that the expert:
  — *has agreed* to testify at trial; and
  — will be *sufficiently familiar* with the pending action to provide a *meaningful oral deposition* concerning the specific testimony the expert is expected to give at trial (including any opinion and its basis) (¶*8:1673*);

- **Costs and fees:** A statement of the expert's hourly and daily fee for providing deposition testimony and for consulting with the retaining attorney. [CCP §2034.260(c)]

  An expert called to give deposition testimony by an opposing party is entitled to charge his or her regular rate for deposition work, provided it is a reasonable fee. The only limitation is that such fee *cannot exceed* what the expert has charged or will charge his or her own client for testimonial work. [CCP §2034.430(d); Gov.C. §68092.5; see *Rancho Bernardo Develop. Co. v. Sup.Ct. (Oaks North Villas Condominium Ass'n)* (1992) 2 CA4th 358, 363, 2 CR2d 878, 881]

  Effect: If the party designating the expert has a "wholesale rate" from the expert, the other party gets the benefit.

FORM: Expert Witness Declaration, *see Form 8:35* in Rivera, *Cal. Prac. Guide: Civ. Pro. Before Trial FORMS* (TRG).

1) [8:1668.5] **Qualifications:** Expert witness declarations should provide enough information to enable the opposing party to *gauge the credibility* of the opinion testimony. Thus, the declarations should normally cover such matters as:

   - area of expertise;
   - relevant education;
   - relevant employment or experience; and
   - professional society memberships, publications and honors.

   ⇨ [8:1668.6] ***PRACTICE POINTER:*** Many experts have professional resumes containing all of this information. Ask for one and attach it to the declaration.

2) [8:1669] **"General substance of expected testimony" requirement:** To be meaningful, *enough* facts and opinions should be disclosed to enable the opposing party to determine *whether to depose* the expert, and to *prepare for cross-examination* and *rebuttal* at trial. [See *Bonds v. Roy* (1999) 20 C4th 140, 146-147, 83 CR2d 289, 293]

a) [8:1670] **Correct legal terms not required:** The "general substance" standard does not require that the expert's opinion be expressed in strict legal terms. [See *Castaneda v. Bornstein* (1995) 36 CA4th 1818, 1828, 43 CR2d 10, 17 (disapproved on other grounds by *Bonds v. Roy*, supra, 20 C4th at 149, 83 CR2d at 294, fn. 4)—declaration said expert would testify on matters "*leading to*" infant's death: this was sufficient to put opposing party on notice expert would testify on both breach of duty and causation]

b) [8:1671] **General description may suffice:** Even rather general descriptions of the expert's proposed testimony may be held sufficient. E.g., "medical care and treatment rendered . . . [and] diagnoses and prognoses of plaintiff's physical condition." [*Sprague v. Equifax, Inc.* (1985) 166 CA3d 1012, 1040, 213 CR 69, 87 (decided under former statute with identical language)]

However, the description must be sufficiently broad and detailed so the testimony at trial clearly comes within its scope.

[8:1672] *Reserved.*

3) [8:1673] **Representation that expert be ready to testify:** The expert witness declaration must state that each expert listed is *famlllar* with the case and *ready to be deposed*—i.e., that the expert is (or will be) sufficiently familiar with the case to provide a "meaningful oral deposition" concerning any opinion and its basis. [CCP §2034.260(c)(4)]

[8:1674] *Reserved.*

a) [8:1675] **Purpose:** This provision makes counsel "vouch" for the experts listed, thus minimizing any risk parties might designate more experts than they truly intend to call and thereby make it very expensive for opponents to depose everyone on the list to find out which of the designated experts really are going to testify. In effect, pursuant to CCP §2034.260(c)(4), counsel must *guarantee* that the designated experts have been contacted and are *prepared*

© 2020 Thomson Reuters/The Rutter Group

to testify. Counsel risk sanctions personally if these representations prove inaccurate.

(e) [8:1676] **Effect of inadequate disclosure:** Inadequate disclosure of the "general substance of expected testimony" is grounds for *exclusion* of the expert's testimony at trial under CCP §2034.300 (*see ¶8:1717.1 ff.*).

(f) [8:1677] **Effect of erroneous disclosure:** Although CCP §2034.010 et seq. do not address the matter, the court has power under CCP §2023.010 to sanction a party who provides *inaccurate* information in its expert witness exchange. It need not be shown that the errors were willful. [*Kohan v. Cohan* (1991) 229 CA3d 967, 969, 280 CR 474, 475]

- [8:1678] D's expert witness list included an expert who had died 2 years earlier. P moved to exclude that expert's declaration at trial and for evidentiary and monetary sanctions. Even though D's error was not willful, monetary sanctions were proper because P was required to expend unnecessary efforts. [*Kohan v. Cohan*, supra, 229 CA3d at 969, 280 CR at 475]

[8:1679-1680] *Reserved.*

(3) [8:1681] **Discoverable reports:** In addition, if the expert witness demand included a demand for exchange of discoverable reports and writings (*see ¶8:1650 ff.*), all parties must exchange "all discoverable reports and writings," if any, made by that expert in the course of preparing his or her opinion. These reports are to be exchanged together with the expert list and declarations at the place and on the date specified in the demand. [CCP §2034.270]

Parties may also attempt to obtain expert-related documents pursuant to a notice of deposition under CCP §2025.220; if they do, the materials, including ESI, must be produced at least 3 business days before the deposition. [CCP §2034.415]

It is therefore necessary to consider which reports are discoverable and which may still be protected as "work product."

(a) [8:1682] **Reports "in capacity of expert witness" discoverable:** *See ¶8:256.*

(b) [8:1683] **Consultants' "advisory" reports still protected as work product:** *See ¶8:257.*

(c) [8:1684] **Potential impeachment as "good cause" for discovery of advisory reports:** *See ¶8:258.*

(d) [8:1685] **Three-step analysis required to determine discoverability:** *See ¶8:264.*

[8:1685.1] ***PRACTICE POINTER:*** To avoid exchanging "discoverable reports and writings," some litigators instruct their experts *not* to prepare a formal report. This avoids giving the other side ammunition for cross-examination.

But there is a downside to this practice: You may need a written report for *settlement* purposes. And, if the case goes to trial, your opponent may be able to convince the jury that any responsible expert would have prepared a formal report, so that the absence of a report undermines your expert's credibility.

(e) [8:1685.2] **Effect of incomplete disclosure?** The expert's testimony may be excluded at time of trial if the court finds the reports withheld were discoverable. [CCP §2034.300(c)]

But the procedure to compel production *before* trial is unclear: *There is no motion to compel* provision in §2034.010 et seq.; and the protective orders provision is aimed at "burdensome *demands*" rather than incomplete responses.

1) [8:1685.3] **Comment:** If the report's existence is known before trial, it can be subpoenaed for production at the expert's deposition. But that might lead to "work product" objections, necessitating a motion to compel.

[8:1685.4] *Reserved.*

(f) [8:1685.5] **Reports created *after* exchange date:** Nothing in the Discovery Act requires experts to refrain from creating *new or additional* reports or writings after the specified date, or to voluntarily disclose them. The detailed statutory procedures for exchanging expert witness information *omit* any such requirement. [*Boston v. Penny Lane Ctrs., Inc.* (2009) 170 CA4th 936, 952, 88 CR3d 707, 720]

Nevertheless, if it appears that the opposing party is trying to manipulate the expert witness discovery rules by delaying production of such reports, the court may find the failure to produce them was unreasonable and exclude opinions contained in them. [See *Boston v. Penny Lane Ctrs., Inc.*, supra, 170 CA4th at 952, 88 CR3d at 721]

[8:1685.6] ***PRACTICE POINTERS:*** If your expert prepares a report after the date specified for exchange, *promptly* provide a copy to opposing counsel. And, if the report is prepared after your expert has been deposed, *immediately offer to* *submit him or her to a second deposition* at your expense. Failure to do so significantly increases the risk that your expert will not be permitted to testify as to matters in the late report. [See *Boston v. Penny Lane Ctrs., Inc.*, supra, 170 CA4th at 952-953, 88 CR3d at 721—fact that counsel provided expert's reports "within about a day" of receiving them was factor in court's determination that counsel acted reasonably and in permitting expert to testify]

Also, consider asking the court at the final status conference to order all parties to produce any expert reports not previously produced. And, when starting to cross-examine an opposing expert at trial, consider asking whether he or she produced any reports after the exchange date.

e. [8:1686] **Supplemental expert witness lists:** Sometimes, the exchange reveals that one party plans to call experts on subjects the opposing party assumed would *not* require expert testimony. In such cases, the opposing party has the *right* to *supplement* its expert witness exchange by adding experts *to cover subjects on which the other party indicates it plans to offer expert testimony*, and on which the opposing party had not previously retained an expert to testify. [CCP §2034.280(a); see *Fairfax v. Lords* (2006) 138 CA4th 1019, 1025, 41 CR3d 850, 854-855; *Du-All Safety, LLC v. Sup.Ct. (Krein)* (2019) 34 CA5th 485, 498, 246 CR3d 211, 219 (quoting text)]

(1) [8:1686.1] **Limited to new subjects raised by another party:** The "supplemental" list is for experts on subjects *not included in the party's original exchange* that have been raised by another party. [CCP §2034.280(a)]

Thus, a supplemental list *cannot* be used to:

— add experts on subjects designated by the party in the original exchange;

— add experts on new subjects not raised by an opposing party's designation; or

— substitute for an already-designated expert. [CCP §2034.280(a); see *Basham v. Babcock* (1996) 44 CA4th 1717, 1723, 52 CR2d 456, 460—party unhappy with designated expert's deposition testimony could not call supplementally-named expert to testify on same subjects at trial]

Compare: To add an expert on an already-designated subject or to replace an expert, a motion to augment or amend must be brought; *see discussion at ¶8:1739 ff.*

(2) [8:1687] **Procedure:** Within *20 days* after the original exchange of information, any party may serve:

- A "supplemental expert witness list" containing the names and addresses of experts who will testify on the subject designated by the other party;
- An "expert witness declaration" (*see* ¶*8:1668*) for each such supplemental expert employed or retained by a party; and
- Discoverable reports and writings, if any, made by such supplemental expert. [CCP §2034.280]

Caution: The 20 days apparently run from the date of the exchange; and where the exchange is by mail, this means the date of *mailing*, not receipt. So, you may have *fewer* than 20 days within which to find, interview and employ a supplemental expert.

(3) [8:1687.1] **Depositions after "cut-off":** The party serving such a list must make the experts available for deposition "immediately"—*even if the 15-day deadline* for deposing experts (*see* ¶*8:1690 ff.*) has *expired*. [CCP §2034.280(c)]

[8:1687.2-1687.4] *Reserved.*

f. [8:1687.5] **Right to withdraw designated expert:** Sometimes, a designated expert reverses his or her opinion (or starts "waffling") before deposition or trial. The party designating the expert has the right to withdraw him or her simply by "amending" its list pursuant to CCP §2034.260(b)-(c). *No prior notice or leave of court* is required. [*County of Los Angeles v. Sup.Ct. (Hernandez)* (1990) 222 CA3d 647, 656, 271 CR 698, 704]

Any privileged information communicated to the expert is protected as long as the expert was withdrawn before a significant part of the information was disclosed. I.e., designation of the expert as an expected trial witness is not itself an implied waiver of the privilege. [*Shooker v. Sup.Ct. (Winnick)* (2003) 111 CA4th 923, 930, 4 CR3d 334, 339-340—party had previously designated himself as testifying expert; but same rule logically should apply to withdrawing *nonparty* experts who have a *privileged relationship* with party (e.g., party's doctor or lawyer); *see also* ¶*8:216*]

If the expert has been deposed, the other party may still call that expert at trial. [CCP §2034.310(a)]

[8:1687.6] ***PRACTICE POINTER:*** Of course, withdrawing a designated expert alerts your adversary to the problem. Opposing counsel is likely to try to hire the expert to give testimony against you, although there may be ethical issues that could lead to disqualification (*see* ¶*1:89.5 ff.*).

You can avoid this problem by *retaining the expert in a consultant capacity* for the balance of the litigation. That way, his or her reports remain protected as work product (*see* ¶*8:246*); and opposing counsel can neither communicate

© 2020 Thomson Reuters/The Rutter Group

with your consultant, nor depose him or her, nor designate him or her as the opposing side's expert. [See *Kennedy v. Sup.Ct. (Lucky Stores, Inc.)* (1998) 64 CA4th 674, 679, 75 CR2d 373, 375—party may "hide" expert from deposition by withdrawing expert and dubbing him or her a "consultant," thereby reinstating work product protection]

(1) [8:1687.6a] **Exception for agreement to suppress?** When two adverse parties agree that one will withdraw an expert and the expert's report in return for indemnity against liability, the agreement may be void as against public policy. [*County of Los Angeles v. Sup.Ct. (Hernandez)*, supra, 222 CA3d at 656, 271 CR at 703 (citing *Williamson v. Sup.Ct. (Shell Oil Co.)* (1978) 21 C3d 829, 836, 148 CR 39, 43-44)]

7. [8:1688] **Deposing Opposing Experts:** Either party may depose any or all of the experts listed by the other party. [CCP §2034.410]

If the expert is one who has been *retained to testify* (*see* ¶*8:1668*), it is the responsibility of the party designating that expert to make him or her available for deposition upon service of a proper deposition notice and payment of the expert's fees by the deposing party. [CCP §§2034.410, 2034.460(a); *see* ¶*8:1695*]

If *too many* experts are designated by any party, an opposing party may *promptly* seek a *protective order* to reduce the list of opposing experts. [CCP §2034.250(b)(6)]

Regular deposition rules and procedures apply to the deposition of such experts, except as stated below (¶*8:1690 ff.*). [CCP §2034.410]

➪ [8:1689] ***PRACTICE POINTERS RE DEPOSING OPPOSING EXPERTS:*** Once the identity of opposing experts is ascertained, you have to decide *whether* to take their depositions. This decision often has to be made "under the gun" because of the time pressures noted below (¶*8:1690*). Here are the factors to consider:

- The costs involved in depositions generally; and the *special costs* in deposing an opposing expert (expert witness fees, *see* ¶*8:1697 ff.*);
- Whether *reports* of the expert's expected testimony have been provided (or can be obtained from opposing counsel);
- Whether such reports provide *enough* information to gauge what the expert is likely to say on the witness stand;
- How *important or controversial* the expert testimony is likely to be;
- How *strong or weak* a witness the expert is likely to be (reputation);
- The advantages vs. disadvantages of depositions generally.

In deposing an opposing expert, be sure to elicit each and *every* opinion he or she has regarding the subject *and the reasons* supporting them. Often, the best question to ask is "Why?" (Although dangerous in cross-examining a witness at trial, "Why?" is an excellent question in deposing an expert because it exposes the opponent's theory of the case, and how well this expert can present it.) [See *Burton v. Cruise* (2010) 190 CA4th 939, 951, 118 CR3d 613, 622 (citing text)]

At the same time, try *not* to "give away" your planned avenues of attack on the expert's opinion, particularly if deficiencies in the expert's testimony can be cured before trial. The time to "destroy" an opposing expert is at trial, not at deposition.

To avoid unpleasant surprises at trial, be sure to ask an opposing expert the following:

- *What exhibits* will you use at trial?
- What assignment were you given? *Have you completed that assignment?*
  — If not, is it possible that the part you have not completed will change the exhibits you plan to use or the opinions you plan to express at trial? (If so, *when can we continue your deposition?*)
- What are the areas in which you will be offering an opinion at trial?
- Are there any other areas relevant to this case in which you are prepared to express an opinion if asked?
- What is the basis for your opinion regarding . . .?
- What documents, reference materials, conversations, meetings or examinations support that opinion?
- What part of your education or experience qualifies you to offer that opinion?
- Ask *treating physicians* whether they hold any *opinions* on the matter on which expert testimony will be required at trial; and if so, the manner in which they obtained the factual underpinning of those opinions. [See *Schreiber v. Estate of Kiser* (1999) 22 C4th 31, 39, 91 CR2d 293, 300] (Note, however, that this question may obligate deposing counsel to pay an expert witness fee to the treating physician; *see* ¶*8:1697.5.*)
- After this deposition, do you have any plans to review more evidence, conduct more experiments or do anything else to support your opinions? (*See* ¶*8:1718.2.*)
- Do you have any opinions about any of the other experts or expert opinions in this case?
- If you had limitless time and resources, is there other work you would like to do in forming your opinions?
- (In conclusion) Do you have any opinions for trial that I have not asked you about?

© 2020 Thomson Reuters/The Rutter Group

a. [8:1690] **Time limits; discovery "cut-off" before trial:** Depositions of experts identified pursuant to CCP §2034.260 may be taken as late as *15 days* before trial—instead of the 30-day "cut-off" applicable to other depositions and discovery. [CCP §2024.030]

And, motions to enforce discovery relating to such depositions may be heard until *10 days* before trial (instead of the 15-day cut-off on other discovery motions). [CCP §2024.030]

[8:1690.1] **Exception—experts on supplemental list:** Experts designated on a "supplemental expert witness list" (covering topics designated by another party; *see* ¶*8:1686*) can be deposed even after the 15-day cut-off discussed above (¶*8:1690*). [CCP §2034.280(c)]

(1) [8:1691] **Effect:** You have only a limited time within which to depose opposing experts and follow up with whatever discovery motions are required. Your opponent's list will usually not be received until 50 days before trial (*see* ¶*8:1660*); and any motion to compel must be heard not later than 10 days before trial. So, you have only *40 days* within which to schedule and take depositions of opposing experts, and to follow up with a motion to compel answers if necessary. [See *St. Mary Med. Ctr. v. Sup.Ct. (Mennella)* (1996) 50 CA4th 1531, 1538, 58 CR2d 182, 186]

(2) [8:1692] **Waiver of discovery "cut-off"?** It may be possible to relieve the time pressure somewhat by stipulating with opposing counsel to waive the CCP §2024.030 "cut-off" dates, which would allow depositions to be taken right up until the trial date. [See CCP §2016.030]

➩ [8:1693] ***PRACTICE POINTER:*** This is a *dangerous* thing to do. Extending depositions into the days and weeks before trial of a major lawsuit will undoubtedly interfere with trial preparations.

Rather than waive these "cut-offs," try to obtain stipulations with opposing counsel on a schedule for depositions which, if necessary, extends beyond the cut-off date and may involve less than 10 days' notice. Also consider agreeing to expert disclosure and discovery *earlier* than set by applicable law.

(3) [8:1693.1] **Compare—deposing experts for summary judgment motions:** The time limits for completing expert witness depositions are even more of a problem where expert opinion testimony is utilized in connection with a summary judgment motion. (That motion can be made up to 30 days before trial; CCP §437c(a), *see* ¶*10:71*.)

Further complicating matters is the 75-day notice of motion requirement for summary judgment and adjudication motions, which may *not* be shortened. [CCP §437c(a); *see* ¶*10:77 ff.*]

If the expert witness exchange does not take place until 50 days before trial, this leaves no time to depose opposing experts *before* noticing a summary judgment motion. [See *St. Mary Med. Ctr. v. Sup.Ct. (Mennella)*, supra, 50 CA4th at 1538, 58 CR2d at 186]

For this reason, although there is no statutory right to the relief, a court may permit *earlier* depositions of expert witnesses whose opinions are filed in support of or in opposition to a motion for summary judgment or summary adjudication. [*St. Mary Med. Ctr. v. Sup.Ct. (Mennella)*, supra, 50 CA4th at 1539, 58 CR2d at 186; see *Perry v. Bakewell Hawthorne, LLC* (2017) 2 C5th 536, 538, 213 CR3d 764, 765—undisclosed expert's opinion inadmissible for summary judgment motion heard after disclosure date absent relief from failure to disclose requirement; ¶*8:1719.5*]

b. [8:1694] **Geographic limits:** The deposition of an expert retained or employed by a party must be taken *within 75 miles* of the *courthouse* where the action is pending. (On a showing of "exceptional hardship," the court may allow a deposition beyond this limit.) [CCP §2034.420]

(1) [8:1694.1] **Compare—"independent" experts:** Depositions of "independent" experts (not retained or employed by any party) can be taken only pursuant to *deposition* subpoena—i.e., these experts have to be deposed within 75 miles of *their residence* (150 miles, if deposed within the county where the action is pending). [CCP §2025.250(a); *see* ¶*8:622*]

This applies to a *treating physician* who has not been designated as an expert witness.

c. [8:1695] **No subpoena necessary for retained experts:** If the expert has been *retained to testify* ("retained by a party for the purpose of forming and expressing an opinion"), no subpoena is necessary. Service of a proper deposition notice, accompanied by an expert witness fee (*see* ¶*8:1697*), obligates the party designating such expert to produce him or her for deposition. [CCP §2034.460(a)]

(1) [8:1695.1] **Subpoena necessary for documents?** It is unclear whether a notice to depose the retained expert may be coupled with a demand the expert produce documents, or whether a subpoena is necessary. CCP §2034.410 states the deposition of a listed trial expert shall be governed by §2025.010 et seq. deposition procedures; and §2025.280(b) requires a deposition subpoena for production of a nonparty deponent's records (*see* ¶*8:535 ff.*).

But CCP §2034.300(c) *provides* for exclusion of an expert's testimony where a *party* "has unreasonably failed to . . . [p]roduce reports and writings of expert witnesses." Arguably, the party who retained the expert may control the expert's documents.

[8:1695.2] ***PRACTICE POINTER:*** Until this issue is clarified, serve a deposition subpoena to obtain the expert's documents unless the party who retained the expert agrees to make them available.

(2) [8:1696] **Compare—"independent" experts:** "Independent" experts (not retained or employed by any party) must be subpoenaed. This will require payment of a *witness* fee and mileage (see CCP §2020.230(a), ¶*8:572*). *In addition*, an expert witness fee may have to be paid; *see* ¶*8:1697 ff.*

(3) [8:1696.1] **Compare—treating physicians:** Treating physicians are regarded as *percipient witnesses* (*not* "retained for the purpose" of giving expert testimony). Thus, the party designating treating physicians on an expert witness list is *not* obligated to produce them for depositions. I.e., they must be subpoenaed by the deposing party; and an expert witness fee may be payable (*see* ¶*8:1697.4 ff.*). [*Hurtado v. Western Med. Ctr.* (1990) 222 CA3d 1198, 1203, 272 CR 324, 327]

d. [8:1697] **Payment of expert's fees:** Certain experts are entitled to be paid "reasonable and customary" fees for their time spent in the deposition, as described below (¶*8:1703 ff.*). [CCP §2034.430(b)] (Similar rules apply where experts are subpoenaed to appear at trial; see Gov.C. §68092.5.)

(1) [8:1697.1] **Who must pay:** The deposing party alone is responsible for payment of the expert's fee. [CCP §2034.430(b)]

(a) [8:1697.2] **Effect of other parties prolonging deposition:** This is true even when other parties engage in prolonged cross-examination, unreasonably extending the deposition (*see* ¶*8:1706*). The Discovery Act does not empower the court to order other parties to contribute to the expert's fees.

(Compare—deposition reporter costs: Courts do have power, for "good cause" shown, to order other parties to share the costs of the *deposition transcript*; CCP §2025.510(b), ¶*8:767.1*.)

[8:1697.3] ***PRACTICE POINTER:*** If you are the deposing party in such a situation, ask garrulous cross-examiners (on the record) to assume responsibility for a portion of the expert's fees. If they refuse, *adjourn* the deposition pursuant to CCP §2025.470 and seek a protective order against further questioning by them.

(2) [8:1697.4] **Which experts entitled to fees:** Such fees are payable to *any* expert witness listed in the exchange *other than* parties or employees of parties. [CCP §2034.430(a)]

(a) [8:1697.5] **Treating physicians if asked to express expert opinion:** Thus, expert witness fees must be paid to depose a treating physician (or other health care practitioner) who *is to be asked to express an opinion* during the deposition. This includes questions asking for opinions or *facts* regarding the patient's past or present diagnosis or future prognosis, or the *reasons* for a particular treatment decision. [CCP §2034.430(a)(2)]

But no expert fee need be paid if the doctor is asked only to read "words and symbols contained in the relevant medical records" (or if they are illegible to the deponent, to ask for an approximation of what they are). [See CCP §2034.430(a)(2)]

[8:1697.6] ***PRACTICE POINTER:*** A deposing party may still be able to obtain opinions without paying an expert witness fee by *sticking to entries in the doctor's records.* E.g., "Doctor, did you make an entry in your records regarding your diagnosis of this patient?" "Where is that entry?" "What does it say?"

But this is *not* recommended where serious injuries are involved. The deposing attorney needs much more information regarding the treating physician's opinions than can be obtained by having him or her read medical records. The deposing attorney better plan on paying a fee to the treating physician.

(b) [8:1697.6a] **Architects, engineers and surveyors:** An expert witness fee must also be paid to "[a]n architect, professional engineer, or licensed land surveyor who was involved with the original project design or survey for which that person is asked to express an opinion." [CCP §2034.430(a)(3); Gov.C. §68092.5]

(c) [8:1697.7] **Not "employees":** An expert witness fee need not be paid to an expert who is either a party or an "*employee*" of the party who designated him or her. [CCP §2034.430(a)]

(Comment: "Employee" is not defined, but presumably it covers either full or part-time employment. "Employed" experts are distinguished from those "retained" by a party on a case-by-case basis to render an opinion; see CCP §2034.210(b).)

(3) [8:1698] **When payable:** The expert witness fee may be tendered *either* on service of the deposition notice *or* at *commencement* of the expert's deposition. (In either case, the fee is delivered to the *attorney* for the party designating the expert.) [CCP §2034.450(a), (b)]

(a) [8:1699] **Effect of failure to pay:** If the expert's fee has not been paid by the time of the deposition, "the expert shall not be deposed at that time unless the parties stipulate otherwise." [CCP §2034.460(b)]

Nor can sanctions be imposed against the party designating the expert based on the expert's refusal to appear or testify. [See *Tahoe Forest Inn v. Sup.Ct. (Turney)* (1979) 99 CA3d 509, 513, 160 CR 314, 316 (decided under former law)]

(4) [8:1700] **How much:** The deposing party must *estimate* how long the deposition will take, and must tender enough to pay the expert's hourly or daily rate (as stated in the expert witness declaration; *see* ¶*8:1668.4*) for that length of time. [CCP §2034.450(a)]

(a) [8:1701] **"Anticipated length of deposition":** The fee to be tendered by the deposing party must be sufficient for the *entire* deposition, not merely the estimated time it will take deposing counsel to examine the expert. I.e., the fee must include the estimated time for reasonable cross-examination by other parties attending the deposition.

☞ [8:1701.1] ***PRACTICE POINTER:*** The remedy for controlling garrulous cross-examiners is discussed at ¶*8:1697.3*.

(b) [8:1702] **NOT preparation or travel time:** However, the expert is not entitled to fees for time spent in preparing for the deposition or for travel expenses. Any such fees or expenses are the responsibility of the *party designating* the expert. [CCP §2034.440]

(c) [8:1703] **"Reasonable and customary hourly or daily fee":** The expert's "reasonable and customary" fee is the amount disclosed in the "expert witness declaration" provided in the expert witness exchange (*see* ¶*8:1668*).

1) [8:1703.1] **Variable rates permitted:** It is not unreasonable for an expert to charge more for deposition testimony and court appearances than for ordinary services and consultation: "The process of giving formal testimony under oath is an obviously more stressful and tense activity than consulting with your client in his office." [*Rancho Bernardo Develop. Co. v. Sup.Ct. (Oaks North Villas Condominium Ass'n)* (1992) 2 CA4th 358, 362, 2 CR2d 878, 880]

2) [8:1703.2] **Includes waiting time:** The fee to be paid must include all time spent by the expert witness at the deposition, from the time noticed in the deposition subpoena (or the time of the witness'

arrival, if later) until the time he or she is dismissed. It is immaterial whether the deposition commences on time or whether the expert is even deposed. [CCP §2034.430(b)]

a) [8:1703.3] **Counsel responsible for delay must pay:** Where a deposition is delayed because an attorney representing the expert or a non-noticing party is late, that attorney must pay the expert's reasonable and customary hourly or daily fee for the period of the delay (from the time noticed in the deposition subpoena until the counsel's late arrival). [CCP §2034.430(c)]

[8:1703.4] *Reserved.*

3) [8:1703.5] **Limitation:** Such witness cannot charge more than the *rate charged the party who retained* the expert (except where his or her services were donated to a charitable or other nonprofit organization). [CCP §2034.430(d); Gov.C. §68092.5] (Effect: If the party retaining the expert is getting a "wholesale rate" for the expert's time, the deposing party also benefits.)

4) [8:1703.6] **Limitation on charging daily fee:** An expert may not charge a daily fee unless required to attend a deposition for a full day, or unless the deposing party required the expert *to be available* for a full day and the expert necessarily had to forego all business he or she would have otherwise conducted that day. [CCP §2034.430(e)]

(d) [8:1704] **If amount demanded deemed excessive:** If the deposing party deems the expert's fee to be unreasonable (e.g., the expert insists on charging a full day's rate for a deposition lasting less than an hour), the deposing party may move for an order setting the compensation of that expert. [CCP §2034.470(a)]

☞ [8:1704a] ***PRACTICE POINTER:*** There is no time limit on this motion and, therefore, it apparently can be made either *before or after* the deposition. But it may be better practice to wait until *after* the deposition. Doing so beforehand will simply ensure a hostile witness.

If you intend to file such a motion, avoid making any statement that could be construed as a promise to pay the requested fees. Otherwise, the court may hold you are estopped from later seeking a reduction.

In any event, the court's power is to set a "reasonable" fee for the expert's testimony. Therefore,

© 2020 Thomson Reuters/The Rutter Group

if you're objecting to the fee charged, be prepared with *evidence* of deposition rates charged by experts with similar qualifications. (Your own declaration may suffice if you have had sufficient experience employing expert witnesses; otherwise, get declarations from qualified experts.)

1) [8:1704.1] **Attempt at informal resolution required:** As with most other discovery motions, it must be accompanied by a declaration showing a "reasonable and good faith attempt" to resolve the matter outside court. And the court may impose a monetary sanction against the losing party unless it finds "substantial justification" for that party's position or other circumstances make the sanction "unjust." [CCP §§2016.040, 2034.470(b), (g)]

   In any such attempt, the expert or party designating the expert shall provide the other with:
   — proof of the ordinary and customary fee actually charged and received by that expert for similar services provided outside the subject litigation;
   — the number of times the expert has ever charged and received the presently demanded fee; and
   — the frequency and regularity with which the presently demanded fee has been charged and received by that expert within the two-year period preceding the hearing on the motion. [CCP §2034.470(b)]

2) [8:1704.2] **Proof required on motion:** In addition to any other evidence, the expert or party designating the expert must provide the court with the information listed in the preceding paragraph. [CCP §2034.470(d)]

3) [8:1704.3] **Court's determination:** The court's determination of the "reasonable" fee to be paid by the deposing party may be based on the foregoing proof. The court may also consider the ordinary and customary fees charged by similar experts for similar services within the relevant community "and any other factors the court deems necessary or appropriate to make its determination." [CCP §2034.470(e)]

   The factors considered as well as the amount deemed "reasonable" are within the trial court's sound discretion. [*Marsh v. Mountain Zephyr, Inc.* (1996) 43 CA4th 289, 303, 50 CR2d 493, 502]

a) [8:1704.4] **Not bound by "customary" fee:** The court is *not* bound to award the expert's "customary" fee for deposition testimony. It is merely one factor considered in determining the "reasonable" fee the deposing party must pay for deposing another party's expert. [*Marsh v. Mountain Zephyr, Inc.*, supra, 43 CA4th at 304, 50 CR2d at 503—architect's "customary" fee was $360 per hour; court set $250 as "reasonable" fee]

b) [8:1704.5] **Client's responsibility for excess:** Any fee charged by the expert in excess of what the court finds "reasonable" remains a matter of negotiation and agreement between the expert and the party designating him or her. The party deposing the expert is responsible for only the "reasonable" fee set by the court. [*Marsh v. Mountain Zephyr, Inc.*, supra, 43 CA4th at 300-301, 50 CR2d at 500]

[8:1704.6] ***PRACTICE POINTER:*** If your expert demands a greater fee than the deposing party has tendered, your client should be prepared to pay the excess.

[8:1705] *Reserved.*

(e) [8:1706] **If amount tendered insufficient:** If the expert's deposition takes longer than anticipated, the deposing party must pay the balance of the expert's fee within 5 days after receipt of an itemized statement from the expert. [CCP §2034.450(c)]

1) [8:1707] **Comment:** Thus, other parties, by prolonged questioning, can run up the cost to the deposing party. *See discussion at ¶8:1697.1 ff.*

8. [8:1708] **Exclusion of Expert Testimony for Failure to Comply:** Except as provided below (¶*8:1709 ff.*), the trial court "shall exclude" expert opinion testimony offered by a party who has "*unreasonably*" failed to comply with the exchange requirements, on objection by one who has complied. [CCP §2034.300 (emphasis added)]

Similarly (although not expressly provided by statute), if a party wishes to call an expert not included on the original list and the party has unreasonably failed to obtain permission to augment its list (under CCP §§2034.610-2034.630, ¶*8:1739*), that expert's testimony shall be excluded. [*Richaud v. Jennings* (1993) 16 CA4th 81, 85, 19 CR2d 790, 792; *Pina v. County of Los Angeles* (2019) 38 CA5th 531, 546, 251 CR3d 17, 29 (quoting text)]

a. [8:1709] **Formal objection required:** First of all, a formal objection to the opposing expert testimony is required. The objection can be made by motion in limine, or can be raised when the expert takes the stand. [CCP §2034.300; *Richaud v. Jennings*, supra, 16 CA4th at 91, 19 CR2d at 796 (motion in limine)]

[8:1709.1] ***PRACTICE POINTER:*** It is better to raise the objection to expert testimony as an in limine motion that can be carefully considered by the court before trial begins, rather than surprising the court with the objection during trial and potentially requiring hearings outside the presence of the jury.

b. [8:1710] **Objecting party must have complied with all expert witness exchange requirements:** To have standing to object to opposing expert testimony under CCP §2034.300, the objecting party must have "made a *complete and timely compliance*" with all expert witness exchange requirements. [CCP §2034.300 (emphasis added); see *Staub v. Kiley* (2014) 226 CA4th 1437, 1446, 173 CR3d 104, 110-111—party whose demand specified premature exchange date did not make "complete and timely compliance" and thus lacked standing under §2034.300; compare *Cottini v. Enloe Med. Ctr.* (2014) 226 CA4th 401, 424-425, 172 CR3d 4, 22—although party failed to make "complete and timely compliance" and thus lacked standing under §2034.300, court had inherent power to exclude opposing party's expert testimony (¶*8:1714*)]

[8:1711] ***PRACTICE POINTER:*** This means that if you want to protect your client against surprise expert testimony at trial, your *own* list, declarations and disclosures must stand up to close scrutiny. If you try to "hide the ball" regarding your own experts or their testimony, you may be opening the door to whatever sort of expert testimony the opposing party decides to spring on you at trial.

Therefore, if you know an issue will arise at trial, come prepared with a declaration that proves you fully complied with all your expert witness disclosure duties.

(1) [8:1712] **Attempts to compel opposing party to comply before trial?** There is no statutory requirement that the objecting party give the opposing party opportunity to correct the defects before trial. But failure to do so may be ground for finding that the opposing party's failure to comply was not "unreasonable" (¶*8:1719.1*). [*Boston v. Penny Lane Ctrs., Inc.* (2008) 170 CA4th 936, 954, 88 CR3d 707, 722 (citing text)]

(2) [8:1713] **Showing of prejudice required?** Nor is there any statutory requirement that the objecting party have been prejudiced from the nondisclosure in order to object to the expert testimony at trial. Again, however, absent some showing of prejudice, the court may be more likely to find that the failure to comply with the expert witness disclosure requirements was *not* "unreasonable."

(3) [8:1714] **Compare—inherent court power to exclude expert testimony for violation of exchange requirements:** Even when a party lacks standing to invoke the §2034.300 testimony exclusion sanction because of his or her own failure to make a "complete and timely compliance" with the exchange requirements, the court has *inherent power*, exercisable in its *discretion*, to exclude expert witness testimony "for an egregious violation" of those requirements. [*Cottini v. Enloe Med. Ctr.*, supra, 226 CA4th at 428-429, 172 CR3d at 25]

[8:1715-1716] *Reserved.*

c. [8:1717] **Grounds for exclusion:** The objection to the expert's testimony may be based on the offering party's:

- Failure to *list* the witness as an expert;
- Failure to *submit* an *expert witness declaration*;
- Failure to *produce discoverable reports* and writings;
- Failure to make the expert *available for deposition* [CCP §2034.300]; or
- Failure to move under CCP §§2034.610-2034.630 to augment the expert witness list where a new expert is necessary. [*Richaud v. Jennings*, supra, 16 CA4th at 90, 19 CR2d at 795]

Note: These failures to comply are *not* ground for exclusion by themselves. To exclude the offered testimony, it must also be shown that the failure to comply was "unreasonable"; *see* ¶*8:1719.1.*

(1) [8:1717.1] **Inadequate expert witness declaration as ground for exclusion:** Submitting an expert witness declaration that fails to comply with the content requirements of CCP §2034.260(b) (¶*8:1668.4 ff.*) is treated the same as failure to submit an expert witness declaration altogether. For purposes of discovery and trial preparation, "[i]t makes little practical difference whether the party proffering the expert testimony failed to submit an expert witness declaration or submitted an inaccurate one." [*Bonds v. Roy* (1999) 20 C4th 140, 147, 83 CR2d 289, 293]

(a) [8:1717.2] **Effect:** Where an expert witness declaration indicates the expert will testify on Topic A, that expert may not testify on Topic B. The party presenting the expert may seek leave to augment or amend the declaration (CCP §§2034.610-2034.630) but if leave is denied, testimony on Topic B is excluded. [*Bonds v. Roy*, supra, 20 C4th at 149, 83 CR2d at 294]

It is up to the court, however, to determine whether the testimony offered is within the "general ambit" of the topic disclosed. [*Jones v. Moore* (2000) 80 CA4th 557, 566, 95 CR2d 216, 222]

© 2020 Thomson Reuters/The Rutter Group

(b) **Application**

- [8:1717.3] Defendant in medical malpractice action submitted a declaration stating his expert would testify only as to damages. When deposed, the expert confirmed this limitation. At trial, the expert was properly precluded from testifying as to causation. [*Bonds v. Roy*, supra, 20 C4th at 143, 149, 83 CR2d at 290, 294]

  [8:1717.4-1717.9] *Reserved.*

[8:1717.10] ***PRACTICE POINTERS—for party making incomplete disclosure:*** The party whose expert witness disclosure is inadequate has several possible remedies:

- *Before trial, file supplemental witness list:* A party may file a supplemental expert witness list within 20 days after the initial exchange (CCP §2034.280; *see ¶8:1686 ff.*).

- *File motion to augment or amend declaration:* This motion must be made "at a sufficient time in advance of the time limit for the completion of [expert] discovery . . . to permit the deposition of [the] expert . . . to be taken." However, "under exceptional circumstances" the court may permit amendment or augmentation at a later time. [CCP §2034.610(b)]

Obviously, the safer course is to move for leave to amend *before* trial. The later such leave is sought, the less likely it is to be granted. [See *Bonds v. Roy*, supra, 20 C4th at 149, 83 CR2d at 294—leave sought on last day of trial where there was no practical opportunity to depose expert]

[8:1717.11] ***PRACTICE POINTERS—for opposing party:*** The party against whom the expert testimony may be offered has various remedies to challenge an expert witness declaration that fails to disclose the general substance of the proposed testimony:

- *Pretrial motion to compel further disclosures?* Unlike practically every other discovery procedure, the expert witness disclosure statute does not expressly authorize a motion to compel further disclosure. Even so, courts might allow such motion by analogy to the other discovery procedures.

- *Pretrial protective order?* The statutory provision for protective orders (§2034.250) is aimed at "burdensome" demands rather than incomplete responses. Even so, courts might assert inherent power to bar expert testimony at trial unless further disclosures were made. [See *Sanders v. Sup.Ct. (Southern Pac. Transp. Co.)* (1973) 34 CA3d 270, 279-280, 109 CR 770, 777-778]

- *Limit deposition questions to topics disclosed:* When deposing opposing experts, limit your questioning *to the specific topics disclosed* in the expert's declaration. The court may be less likely to grant leave to amend the declaration to allow testimony on other topics.
- *During trial, move to exclude:* The trial court may refuse to permit the expert to testify on the undisclosed subject.
- *If leave to augment granted, offer opposing evidence:* If the court allows the expert to testify on undisclosed topics, if time permits it will usually allow a further deposition of the witness, presumably at the expense of the offending party. The court might also permit you to recall your own witnesses to rebut the additional testimony.

(2) [8:1718] **Designated expert's "surprise" testimony NOT ground for objection:** The fact that experts disclosed under §2034.260, and deposed prior to trial, give contradictory testimony at trial is *not* ground to exclude their testimony. Such "surprises" go to the weight, not the admissibility, of their testimony. [*Williams v. Volkswagen Aktiengesellschaft* (1986) 180 CA3d 1244, 1258, 226 CR 306, 313; *Easterby v. Clark* (2009) 171 CA4th 772, 781, 90 CR3d 81, 89 (citing text)]

(a) [8:1718.1] **Compare—opinions withheld at deposition:** But where the expert testified at deposition that he or she *did not have any additional opinions,* the expert may be precluded from testifying to opinions not expressed during the deposition. [*Jones v. Moore* (2000) 80 CA4th 557, 565, 95 CR2d 216, 221; *Easterby v. Clark,* supra, 171 CA4th at 780, 90 CR3d at 89—expert may not offer testimony at trial beyond scope of his or her deposition testimony if opposing party has *no notice or expectation* that expert will offer the new testimony, or the new testimony comes at a time when deposing expert is unreasonably difficult; *Dozier v. Shapiro* (2011) 199 CA4th 1509, 1523, 133 CR3d 142, 155]

[8:1718.2] ***PRACTICE POINTERS:*** When deposing an expert witness, try to extract a statement that the opinions expressed are the *only ones* he or she expects to present at trial. If the expert cannot commit to this question, there may be ground for objection under CCP §2034.260(c)(4), requiring that the expert be familiar with the case and able to provide a "meaningful oral deposition."

© 2020 Thomson Reuters/The Rutter Group

Conversely, where your expert has been deposed and disavowed having any additional opinions, and you later discover that he or she can offer additional helpful opinions, *write opposing counsel immediately*. Offer to have the expert redeposed and to *pay for the cost* of the second deposition. If opposing counsel declines this opportunity, they risk having the court permit your expert's additional opinion testimony at trial.

(3) [8:1719] **Designated expert's reliance on opinion of unlisted expert NOT ground for objection:** Nor is a designated expert disqualified from testifying because his or her opinion at trial is based on opinions rendered by other, *non*disclosed experts. [*Williams v. Volkswagen Aktiengesellschaft*, supra, 180 CA3d at 1258-1260, 226 CR at 313-314—metallurgist, who was not a stress analyst, hired a stress test in order to render an opinion on manufacturing defect] (But note that the bases of the experts' opinions may themselves have to be admissible. *See ¶9:46.1, 10:124.5.*)

(4) [8:1719a] **Compare—substituting supplementally-named expert:** A supplemental list cannot be used to *substitute* experts on the same subject (*see ¶8:1686.1*). Thus, where the party chooses not to call the expert originally designated on a particular subject (e.g., because unhappy with opinions expressed at deposition), the court will exclude testimony on the same subject by an expert named by that party on a supplemental list. [*Basham v. Babcock* (1996) 44 CA4th 1717, 1723, 52 CR2d 456, 460]

d. [8:1719.1] **Requirement that failure to comply be "unreasonable":** The exclusion sanction applies only if the failure to comply with the expert witness exchange requirements was "unreasonable." [CCP §2034.300]

Although CCP §2034.300 does not define "unreasonable," the "operative inquiry" is whether the party's conduct compromises the purposes of the discovery statutes. [*Staub v. Kiley* (2014) 226 CA4th 1437, 1447, 173 CR3d 104, 111]

(1) [8:1719.2] **Relevant factors:** Various factors are considered in determining whether a party's failure to comply was unreasonable under CCP §2034.300. This gives courts discretion to overlook excusable delays and trivial defects in the documents exchanged.

- *Appearance of gamesmanship:* Noncompliance with the exchange requirements may be deemed unreasonable when a party's conduct "gives the appearance of gamesmanship, such as undue rigidity in responding to expert scheduling issues." [*Staub v. Kiley*, supra, 226 CA4th at 1447, 173 CR3d at 111—expert disclosure one week late due to attorney's family emergency and difficulty in reaching expert *not* unreasonable gamesmanship; compare *Boston v. Penny Lane Ctrs., Inc.* (2009) 170 CA4th 936, 952, 88 CR3d 707, 721—party's intentional manipulation to ensure expert report not created until after exchange date may constitute unreasonableness]

- *"Exacerbating" behavior of objecting party:* If any unfairness from the noncompliance was "exacerbated" by the party seeking to exclude the expert testimony, "the court is less likely to find the conduct of the party offering the expert to be unreasonable." [*Boston v. Penny Lane Ctrs., Inc.*, supra, 170 CA4th at 954, 88 CR3d at 722—objecting party's "strategic choice" not to depose opponent's experts exacerbated late disclosure; *Staub v. Kiley*, supra, 226 CA4th at 1447-1448, 173 CR3d at 112 (same)]

- *Opportunity to correct defects:* Waiting until trial to raise objections that could have been made earlier (so the opposing party would have an opportunity to correct the deficiencies) may be ground for finding the opposing party's noncompliance was *not* unreasonable. [*Stanchfield v. Hamer Toyota, Inc.* (1995) 37 CA4th 1495, 1504, 44 CR2d 565, 569—where expert testified at deposition that he needed more time to fully develop his opinions, waiting until trial to object to expert's testimony rather than conducting follow-up discovery was unreasonable; see *Boston v. Penny Lane Ctrs., Inc.*, supra, 170 CA4th at 954, 88 CR3d at 722—"opportunity for meaningful deposition" is factor]

(2) [8:1719.3] **Compare—failure to move to augment expert list:** Where a designated expert becomes unavailable to testify and a replacement expert is necessary, "unreasonableness" refers to the party's *failure to seek leave to augment* the experts list, rather than the failure to list that expert originally: "The party cannot do nothing and then insist that the replacement expert can be called at trial on the ground that the party's failure to list the replacement expert when expert information was exchanged was not 'unreasonable.' " [*Richaud v. Jennings* (1993) 16 CA4th 81, 90-91, 19 CR2d 790, 795-796]

[8:1719.4] *Reserved.*

e. [8:1719.5] **Exclusion applies to summary judgment proceedings:** When the court determines an expert opinion is inadmissible due to failure to meet the disclosure requirements (and relief has not been granted), the expert's opinion "must be excluded from consideration at summary judgment if an objection is raised" because declarations submitted in summary judgment proceedings must set forth *admissible* evidence (CCP §437c(d)). [*Perry v. Bakewell Hawthorne, LLC* (2017) 2 C5th 536, 538, 213 CR3d 764, 765; *see further discussion at ¶10:206 ff.*]

- [8:1719.6] **Comment:** This rarely happens, however, because there is usually no time for summary judgment motions after

© 2020 Thomson Reuters/The Rutter Group

an expert witness exchange unless the trial date is continued. (The expert witness exchange is keyed to the *initial* trial date; *see ¶8:1660.*)

9. [8:1720] **Exceptions to Exclusion Sanction:** The Discovery Act provides for three situations in which undisclosed experts may testify at trial.

a. [8:1721] **Experts designated by other parties and deposed after expert witness exchange:** Ordinarily, a party's "unreasonable" failure to list an expert is ground for objection to offering that expert's testimony at trial. [CCP §2034.300]

However, any party may call an expert *designated by another party, provided* that expert was thereafter *deposed* pursuant to CCP §§2034.410-2034.470. [CCP §2034.310]

[8:1722] ***PRACTICE POINTER:*** Don't rely on other parties' designations of experts. CCP §2034.310 won't help you unless the other party's experts were deposed *after* the expert witness exchange; and you never know for sure at the time of the exchange which experts will be deposed.

Unless you plan to depose every expert named by every other party, the safer practice is to include in your own expert witness list the names of all expert witnesses you may wish to call, *including* those to be called by coparties or opposing parties. (This will, however, require you to sign an "expert witness declaration" for each of those witnesses, meaning you have to "vouch" for their being ready to testify, etc.; *see ¶8:1668 ff.*)

(1) [8:1723] **Background:** This problem may arise where coparties each retain *separate* experts, or one retains experts and the other does not. (Sometimes, coparties hire separate experts to defray costs or because the expert testimony is of more concern to one party than another.)

At one time, one party generally had no right to call experts designated by another party. But this created problems where coparties were relying on each other to produce expert testimony, particularly where the party having the experts settled out before trial.

CCP §2034.310 solved the problem by allowing any party to utilize experts designated by any other party, *provided* the expert's *deposition* was taken *after* the exchange of expert witness information.

The deposition requirement protects against whatever surprise or advantage may be encountered where a *different* party offers that expert's testimony at trial. Nor is the statute limited to cases where the expert was designated by a coparty who later left the case. Thus, parties may call expert witnesses disclosed by the *opposing* party. [*Powell v. Sup.Ct. (Rosebud*

Comm. Hosp.) (1989) 211 CA3d 441, 444-445, 259 CR 390, 392 (citing text)]

(2) [8:1724] **Statement "reserving right" to call other parties' experts insufficient:** Serving an expert witness list "reserving the right to call any experts identified by other parties and not called by such parties" is *not* sufficient designation of their experts. [*Gallo v. Peninsula Hosp.* (1985) 164 CA3d 899, 903, 211 CR 27, 30]

(a) [8:1725] **Rationale:** Such a statement does not apprise the opposing party of *which* expert will be called. Nor does it disclose the "general substance of the testimony" the expert may give because the *legal theories of each coparty may differ.* It would create a trap for the unwary and reintroduce "gamesmanship" into the discovery process. [*Gallo v. Peninsula Hosp.*, supra, 164 CA3d at 903-904, 211 CR at 30]

(3) [8:1726] **Relief from exclusion sanction unlikely where coparty has designated expert:** The trial judge has discretion to permit undisclosed experts to testify if the offering party failed to designate them due to "mistake, inadvertence, surprise, or excusable neglect" (see CCP §2034.720(c)(1), ¶*8:1744 ff.*). But it will be difficult to show such excuse where the expert *was* designated by a *coparty* before trial. [*Gallo v. Peninsula Hosp.*, supra, 164 CA3d at 905, 211 CR at 31]

[8:1727] *Reserved.*

b. [8:1728] **Undisclosed expert may be called to impeach opposing experts:** An expert not previously designated may be called as a witness *to impeach* an opposing expert witness, but may *not contradict* that expert's opinion. [CCP §2034.310(b)]

(1) [8:1728.1] **Testimony disputing foundational facts:** The undisclosed expert may testify to "the *falsity or nonexistence of any fact* used as the foundation for any opinion" by the opposing expert. [CCP §2034.310(b) (emphasis added)]

For example, an undisclosed expert may testify that the *foundational facts were different* than the opposing expert supposed (e.g., speed of the car, patient's prior medical history, etc.); and the *reasons* why they were different. [*Fish v. Guevara* (1993) 12 CA4th 142, 145, 15 CR2d 329, 330]

(a) [8:1728.2] **"Foundational facts":** The term is strictly construed to prevent a party from offering a contrary opinion under the guise of impeachment. [*Fish v. Guevara*, supra, 12 CA4th at 146, 15 CR2d at 331; *Tesoro Del Valle Master Homeowners Ass'n v. Griffin* (2011) 200 CA4th 619, 641, 133 CR3d 167, 185]

- [8:1728.3] To counter D's expert opinion testimony that certain soil had a permeability rate of one inch per *year*, P called Undisclosed Expert to testify the rate was one inch *per hour.* Undisclosed Expert's testimony was inadmissible because it was an *opinion* (no test had been performed), *not a foundational fact.* [*Fish v. Guevara*, supra, 12 CA4th at 146, 15 CR2d at 331-332]

- [8:1728.4] P's medical expert testified based on his education and experience as an emergency room physician that although he detected an odor of alcohol when he treated P, this did not mean that P had consumed a significant amount of alcohol. D offered rebuttal testimony by an undisclosed medical expert that a person had to have a blood-alcohol level of at least. 08 before the odor of alcohol could be detected. The rebuttal testimony was properly excluded as a *contrary opinion*, not a contrary foundational fact underlying the opinion of P's medical expert. [*Mizel v. City of Santa Monica* (2001) 93 CA4th 1059, 1068, 113 CR2d 649, 655]

- [8:1728.5] D's expert's contrary causation opinion was not legitimate impeachment because it did not relate solely to the foundational facts on which P's expert relied. Similarly, it was not proper impeachment of expert opinion that further surgery would be needed, because D's expert supported his testimony "with matters unrelated to the factual foundations of [P's expert's] opinion, including his independent examination of" P. [*Pina v. County of Los Angeles* (2019) 38 CA5th 531, 547-548, 251 CR3d 17, 30-31]

  However, it was legitimate impeachment to offer opinion "that the MRI results did not show nerve compression" because this was "a foundational fact relevant to [P's expert's] medical opinions." [*Pina v. County of Los Angeles*, supra, 38 CA5th at 549, 251 CR3d at 32]

  [8:1728.6-1728.9] *Reserved.*

(2) [8:1728.10] **Other permissible impeachment:** Impeachment is *not* limited to disproving the foundational facts relied on by the opposing experts. [See CCP §2034.310(b)]

An undisclosed expert therefore may testify as to other matters constituting impeachment of opposing expert testimony: e.g., lack of qualifications; compensation; different standards relied on by other experts in the field, etc.

(3) [8:1729] **Rationale:** Testimony from any source should be admissible on *credibility* of the opposing expert's opinion. Thus, even an undisclosed expert may be permitted to contradict *facts* upon which opposing experts based their opinions. If their foundational facts were wrong, their opinions may not

be worthy of belief. [See *Kennemur v. State of Calif.* (1982) 133 CA3d 907, 924-925, 184 CR 393, 403; and *Sprague v. Equifax, Inc.* (1985) 166 CA3d 1012, 1040, 213 CR 69, 87]

(4) [8:1730] **Contradictory opinion not allowed:** But an undisclosed expert may *not* go further and offer a *conflicting opinion* to "rebut" that given by the opposing experts. The court shall not permit the undesignated expert to contradict the other experts' opinions. [CCP §2034.310(b); see *Kennemur v. State of Calif.*, supra, 133 CA3d at 924-925, 184 CR at 403; see also *Ellenberger v. Karr* (1982) 127 CA3d 423, 427, 179 CR 583, 584]

[8:1730.1-1730.4] *Reserved.*

c. [8:1730.5] **Undisclosed expert may be called if no triggering demand:** Where no party serves a demand for exchange of expert witness information, no experts are required to be disclosed and any expert may testify.

10. [8:1731] **Relief From Exclusion Sanction:** The exclusion sanction does not apply unless the court finds the failure to comply was "unreasonable" (CCP §2034.300, ¶*8:1708*); this gives the court considerable discretion.

In addition, under the circumstances described below (¶*8:1732 ff.*), the court may permit a party to introduce expert testimony notwithstanding failure to comply with its list exchange requirements.

Compare—no relief under CCP §473(b): Because the expert witness statute provides its own procedures for relief from exclusion (¶*8:1732 ff.*), relief cannot be obtained under CCP §473(b) on the ground of "mistake, inadvertence, surprise, or excusable neglect," including the provision for mandatory relief upon filing an attorney "affidavit of fault." [See *Gotschall v. Daley* (2002) 96 CA4th 479, 484, 116 CR2d 882, 886]

a. [8:1732] **Motion for belated submission (TARDY lists):** A party who failed to exchange under CCP §2034.260 on time (normally 50 days before trial) may seek leave to submit the required material on a later date. [CCP §2034.710]

[8:1733] *Reserved.*

(1) [8:1734] **Deadline for motion:** Absent "exceptional circumstances," the motion for permission to file a tardy list must be made early enough to permit *deposing* the experts involved *before the 15-day cut-off* on expert witness depositions. [CCP §§2034.710(b), 2024.030]

(a) [8:1735] **Effect:** This leaves a very narrow time window for relief. I.e., a party missing the exchange deadline 50 days before trial must serve a motion for relief, and have it heard and granted in time for depositions to be completed 15 days before trial. Orders shortening time for hearing on the motion and for notice of deposition are likely to be required.

(b) [8:1736] **"Exceptional circumstances" for later motion:** The statute allows the motion to be granted later, even during trial, on a showing of "exceptional circumstances" and on such "terms as may be just." [See *Plunkett v. Spaulding* (1997) 52 CA4th 114, 137, 60 CR2d 377, 390-391 (citing text) (disapproved on other grounds by *Schreiber v. Estate of Kiser* (1999) 22 C4th 31, 91 CR2d 293); *Cottini v. Enloe Med. Ctr.* (2014) 226 CA4th 401, 420-421, 172 CR3d 4, 19]

(Arguably, relief might be proper if the moving party believed honestly and in good faith that its expert witness information *had been* timely exchanged, but it was lost in the mail or never received.)

(2) [8:1737] **Showing required for relief:** The court may permit tardy submission of expert witness lists and information if the following matters are shown [CCP §2034.720]:

(a) [8:1737.1] **Excuse:** The moving party's failure to exchange expert witness information on time resulted from "mistake, inadvertence, surprise or excusable neglect." [CCP §2034.720(c)(1); see *Cottini v. Enloe Med. Ctr.*, supra, 226 CA4th at 421-422, 172 CR3d at 20—no relief where failure due to "gamesmanship" rather than §2034.720(c)(1) grounds]

1) [8:1737.1a] **Mistake of law:** An *honest* mistake of law may be a valid excuse. [See *Plunkett v. Spaulding*, supra, 52 CA4th at 137, 60 CR2d at 391—moving party's counsel mistakenly believed expert witness declaration was not required for treating physicians who were expected to give standard of care testimony; mistake not unreasonable because issue was one of first impression]

(b) [8:1737.2] **Relief sought promptly:** The motion for relief is being made promptly after learning of such excuse;

(c) [8:1737.3] **Information belatedly served on all other parties:** The moving party has already served a copy of the proposed expert witness list and declarations on all other parties to the action;

(d) [8:1737.4] **Availability for deposition:** The moving party will make the witness available *immediately* for a deposition if leave is granted;

(e) [8:1737.5] **No prejudice to opposing party:** The court must "take into account" the extent to which the opposing party has *relied* on the absence of an expert witness list from the moving party. Before granting leave to submit the tardy list, the court must determine that it will not prejudice the opposing party's ability to maintain its action or defense on the merits; and

(f) [8:1737.6] **Attempt to resolve informally:** The usual declarations are required stating a "reasonable and good faith attempt" to resolve informally each issue presented by the motion. [CCP §2034.710(c)]

(3) [8:1738] **Order:** In ruling on the motion, the court must consider *all* of the §2034.720 factors enumerated above (¶*8:1737 ff.*). [*Plunkett v. Spaulding*, supra, 52 CA4th at 135-136, 60 CR2d at 390—denial based solely on *timing* of motion an abuse of discretion]

If relief is granted, it must be conditioned on the moving party making the expert available for deposition "*immediately.*" [CCP §2034.720(d)]

The court may also impose such other terms as may be just, including:

- Allowing *opposing parties to designate additional experts* or to elicit additional opinions from previously designated experts; or
- Ordering a *continuance* of the trial and *award of costs* and litigation expenses to opposing parties;
- Ordering the moving party to pay for any additional cost to obtain an expedited deposition transcript;
- Awarding *costs and litigation expenses* to *any* party opposing the motion. [CCP §2034.720(d)]

(4) [8:1738.1] **Sanctions:** A monetary sanction "shall" be imposed against the losing party *unless* the court finds "substantial justification" for that party's position or other circumstances make the sanction "unjust." [CCP §2034.730; *see* ¶*8:1921 ff.*]

b. [8:1739] **Motion to augment or amend (DIFFERENT experts or topics):** A party may discover the need for additional expert testimony after having exchanged expert witness information.

If the additional testimony is on subjects *raised in an opponent's expert witness information*, the party has the *right* to serve a "*supplemental expert witness list*" within *20 days*. [See CCP §2034.280, ¶*8:1686 ff.*]

Where, however, the additional testimony relates to subjects disclosed in the party's original exchange, the party must seek leave of court to augment or amend the earlier information, either by:

- Adding *subsequently retained* experts to the expert witness list; or
- Amending the expert witness declaration to *expand the "general substance*" of the testimony which any previously designated expert will give. [CCP §2034.610; see *Richaud v. Jennings* (1993) 16 CA4th 81, 91, 19 CR2d 790, 796—"supplemental designation" filed without leave of court held ineffective]

© 2020 Thomson Reuters/The Rutter Group

[8:1740] **Comment:** Absent leave to amend, objections will likely be sustained to an expert testifying beyond the substance of that disclosed in his or her expert witness declaration (*see ¶8:1717.1*), *unless* the opposing party had *adequate notice* that the expert would offer new testimony. [See *Easterby v. Clark* (2009) 171 CA4th 772, 781, 90 CR3d 81, 89—P's expert allowed to testify on topic not included in expert designation because D had adequate notice and opportunity to depose P's expert in advance of trial]

(1) [8:1741] **Deadline for motion:** Absent "exceptional circumstances," this motion must be made early enough to permit *deposing* the experts involved before the 15-day "cut-off" on deposing experts. [See CCP §§2034.610(b), 2024.030]

(a) [8:1741.1] **Effect:** This again leaves a very narrow time window for relief. A party who has exchanged information 50 days before trial is not likely to realize the need for more experts and be able to file a motion, have it heard and complete depositions 15 days before trial. Again, orders shortening time on the motion and notice of deposition are likely to be required.

(b) [8:1741.2] **"Exceptional circumstances" for later motion:** The statute requires a showing of "exceptional circumstances" for the motion to be heard later.

The fact an augmentation motion is delayed until trial does *not* bar relief. Even at that late date, the motion would allow the proponent to show good cause for the delay, allow the opponent to explain the prejudice created, "and, most importantly, allow the court to minimize any continuances and disruption of the litigation." [*Richaud v. Jennings* (1993) 16 CA4th 81, 92, 19 CR2d 790, 796]

1) [8:1742] **Comment:** As a practical matter, the need to augment or amend expert witness lists and information usually arises *during trial* when shifts in the evidence disclose a sudden need for new, unlisted experts, or testimony from listed experts goes beyond the topics disclosed in their expert witness declarations.

(c) [8:1743] **Limitations:** There are some *practical* limitations, however: i.e., the undisclosed expert must be made available for deposition "immediately" (*see ¶8:1744 ff.*). And the later relief is sought, the less likely it will be granted.

(2) [8:1744] **Showing required:** To obtain permission to augment or amend the expert witness information previously furnished, the moving party must convince the court as to the following matters [CCP §2034.620]:

(a) [8:1744.1] **Excuse:** First of all, it must be shown that the moving party either:

— *could not have been expected* in the exercise of reasonable diligence to call that expert or offer the additional testimony at the time of the original exchange; *or*

— *failed* to include the expert or the additional testimony through "mistake, inadvertence, surprise or *excusable neglect*." [CCP §2034.620(c)]

For example:

- [8:1744.1a] The expert originally designated by D gave deposition testimony damaging to D. This was sufficient "surprise" to permit D to augment his expert witness list. [*Dickison v. Howen* (1990) 220 CA3d 1471, 1478, 270 CR 188, 192]
- [8:1744.1b] P timely designates an expert who dies before trial. A motion to augment the expert witness list to include a replacement is appropriate. P could not have been expected to know that a replacement would be required at the time of the original designation. [*Richaud v. Jennings* (1993) 16 CA4th 81, 90, 19 CR2d 790, 795]

(b) [8:1744.2] **Relief sought promptly:** Leave to augment or amend is being sought promptly after deciding to call the expert or offer the additional testimony. [CCP §2034.620(c)(2)(A)]

(c) [8:1744.3] **Information served on all other parties:** The moving party has now served on all other parties to the action a copy of the proposed expert witness information pertaining to such expert or testimony. [CCP §2034.620(c)(2)(B)]

(d) [8:1744.4] **Availability for deposition:** The moving party will make the witness available *immediately* for a deposition if leave is granted. [CCP §2034.620(d)]

(e) [8:1744.5] **No prejudice to opposing party:** The court *must "take into account"* the extent to which the opposing party has *relied* on the expert list furnished by the moving party. Leave to augment or amend may be granted only if the court determines it will not prejudice the opposing party's ability to maintain its action or defense on the merits. [CCP §2034.620(a), (b)]

1) [8:1744.5a] The opposing party is *not* "prejudiced" simply because the new expert will give testimony adverse to that party. Rather, the focus should be on the opposing party's *ability to respond* to the new testimony. [*Dickison v. Howen*, supra, 220 CA3d at 1479-1480, 270 CR at 193]

© 2020 Thomson Reuters/The Rutter Group

☞ [8:1744.5b] ***PRACTICE POINTER:*** To deflate the other side's claims of "prejudice," the party seeking to augment should consider *offering to stipulate to the following conditions:*

— no more than one new expert;

— the new expert is to be made available for deposition immediately at the office of opposing counsel;

— all deposition expenses are to be paid by the party seeking to augment; and

— opposing counsel is to be given a list of all cases in which the new expert has consulted or given expert testimony during the past 3 years, together with an itemization of fees paid and the names of opposing counsel in those cases. [See *Dickison v. Howen*, supra, 220 CA3d at 1480, 270 CR at 193]

(f) [8:1744.6] **Attempt to resolve informally:** Finally, with discovery motions generally, factual declarations are required showing a "reasonable and good faith attempt" to resolve informally each issue raised by the motion. [CCP §§2016.040, 2034.610(c)]

(3) [8:1745] **Factors affecting court's decision:** Granting or denial of relief in these cases lies within the court's sound discretion, and is subject to appellate review only for abuse of discretion. [See *Bonds v. Roy* (1999) 20 C4th 140, 149, 83 CR2d 289, 294]

The court is likely to focus on the following factors:

(a) [8:1746] **Disruption of trial?** Undisclosed experts may be permitted to testify where the moving party was reasonably diligent in seeking relief and *no* prejudice to the opposing party is shown, if allowing such testimony will not unreasonably complicate or disrupt the trial.

As observed by one court: "[W]e can only assume that the motion would have been granted since it involved only one witness and a limited subject matter . . . The [expert's] deposition could have been taken after court hours, thereby avoiding any disruption of trial proceedings." [*Kennemur v. State of Calif.* (1982) 133 CA3d 907, 920, 184 CR 393, 400]

(b) [8:1747] **"Game playing"?** But relief will not likely be granted where the party seeking relief made a deliberate, tactical decision not to disclose the expert earlier (e.g., keeping an expert "in the closet" until after opposing experts have testified, in an effort to "sandbag" the opposing party). [See *Kennemur v. State of Calif.*, supra, 133 CA3d at 920, 184 CR at 400-401; *Sprague* *v. Equifax, Inc.* (1985) 166 CA3d 1012, 1039-1040, 213 CR 69, 87]

[8:1747.1-1747.4] *Reserved.*

(c) [8:1747.5] **No excuse for delay:** Leave to amend an expert witness declaration was properly denied on the *last day* of testimony because there was no practical opportunity to depose the expert or to provide rebuttal testimony, and counsel had offered no excuse for failure to seek leave earlier. [*Bonds v. Roy*, supra, 20 C4th at 149, 83 CR2d at 294—expert's testimony properly limited to general substance of that described in expert witness declaration]

(d) [8:1748] **Risk of new trial?** Allowing an undisclosed expert to testify (or a disclosed expert to testify on matters not disclosed in the "expert witness declaration") creates a risk that a new trial may be granted on ground of "surprise": i.e., the opposing party may have a strong claim that it was deprived of adequate opportunity to prepare for or rebut the "surprise" expert testimony. [See *City of Fresno v. Harrison* (1984) 154 CA3d 296, 300-301, 201 CR 219, 221]

(4) [8:1749] **Order:** If relief is granted, it must be conditioned on the moving party making the expert available for deposition "immediately" and such other terms as the court deems "just." [CCP §2034.620(d)]

(a) [8:1750] **Conditioned on "immediate" availability for deposition:** The effect of this requirement is that the later relief is requested, the less likely it will be granted, particularly if trial has already commenced.

1) [8:1751] **Practical considerations:** Depositions can be taken even during trial (e.g., the court may grant a continuance or order the depositions taken after hours). [See *Kennemur v. State of Calif.*, supra, 133 CA3d at 920, 184 CR at 400]

But given the technical nature of expert testimony, the judge may decide that a few hours or a few days is not enough time to prepare for cross-examination of an undisclosed expert, and therefore might refuse to allow that expert to testify. [See *Gallo v. Peninsula Hosp.* (1985) 164 CA3d 899, 905, 211 CR 27, 31]

- [8:1751.1] Where the error in complying with CCP §2034.010 is a correctable minor infraction, the trial court may be obliged to allow the expert to be deposed during trial rather than excluding his or her testimony. [See *Fatica v. Sup.Ct. (Liljegren)* (2002) 99 CA4th 350, 353, 120 CR2d 904, 906—error to exclude opinion testimony

© 2020 Thomson Reuters/The Rutter Group

of treating physician who inadvertently neglected to review medical records prior to deposition; he should have been ordered to submit to deposition during trial]

2) [8:1752] **Deposing party must still pay expert's fee:** The moving party's obligation to make the expert "available" for deposition does not change the statutory requirement that the deposing party pay the expert's "reasonable and customary fee" for deposition testimony (CCP §2034.430(b); ¶*8:1697 ff.*). [See *Tahoe Forest Inn v. Sup.Ct. (Turney)* (1979) 99 CA3d 509, 513, 160 CR 314, 316 (decided under former §2034(i)(2))]

(b) [8:1753] **Other terms and conditions:** The order granting relief may also be conditioned on other terms the court finds "just," including:

- Allowing *opposing parties to designate additional experts* or their previously designated experts to give opinions on additional subjects;
- Ordering a *continuance* of trial and an *award of costs* and litigation expenses to opposing parties; or
- Awarding *costs and litigation expenses* to *any* party opposing the motion. [CCP §2034.620(d)]

(5) [8:1754] **Sanctions:** As with discovery motions generally, a monetary sanction "shall" be imposed against the losing party on a motion to augment or amend expert witness information *unless* the court finds "substantial justification" for that party's position or other circumstances make imposition of the sanction "unjust." [CCP §2034.630]

[8:1755-1756] *Reserved.*

CHAPTER 8K

OTHER PROCEDURES FOR DISCOVERY

CONTENTS

© 2020 Thomson Reuters/The Rutter Group

OTHER PROCEDURES FOR DISCOVERY

[8:1757] There remain to be considered several procedures *outside the Discovery Act* which may be utilized for discovery purposes. As will be seen, each serves a specific function, but has only limited application:

1. [8:1758] **Request for Statement of Damages (Personal Injury or Death Cases):** In complaints for *personal injury or wrongful death*, it is improper to allege the amount of damages sought. (The purpose is to prevent harmful publicity given to inflated claims of damages, particularly in connection with medical malpractice cases.) [CCP §425.10; *see ¶6:279 ff.*]

   Of course, defendant will want to know at the outset just how serious the claim is. Since the complaint is silent, a special procedure is provided:

   a. [8:1759] **Procedure:** Defendant may at any time request from plaintiff a written statement setting forth the *nature* and *amount* of damages being sought. Such request must be in writing and served on the plaintiff. [CCP §425.11(b) (not applicable to "limited civil cases" because damage amounts must be alleged in such cases)]

   (Defendant retains the original, along with plaintiff's response. They are *not* filed with the court. See CRC 3.250(a)(20).)

   FORM: Request for Statement of Damages, *see Form 6:8* in Rivera, *Cal. Prac. Guide: Civ. Pro. Before Trial FORMS* (TRG).

   (1) [8:1759.1] **Compare—local rules:** Although the statute makes this procedure *optional*, local rules in some courts require a statement of special and general damages to be served along with the complaint in personal injury and wrongful death actions. Failure to do so may result in sanctions. [See San Diego Sup.Ct. Rule 2.1.5] (*Comment:* This rule may be void because it seemingly "relates to" pleadings within the meaning of CRC 3.20(a) and may be preempted; *see discussion at ¶9:13.2 ff.*)

   b. [8:1760] **Timing:** The request may be made at any time during the action. [CCP §425.11(b)]

   If no such request is made, plaintiff must nevertheless serve defendant with a statement of damages before a default may be taken. [CCP §425.11(c); *see ¶5:82*]

   (1) [8:1760.1] *Compare—local rules:* Under local rules in some courts, plaintiff *must* serve such notice along with the summons and complaint. [See San Diego Sup.Ct. Rule 2.1.5, *¶8:1759.1* (as noted, this Rule may be preempted under CRC 3.20(a))]

   c. [8:1761] **Response:** Plaintiff has 15 days after receipt of such request to furnish the requested information. [CCP §425.11(b)]

© 2020 Thomson Reuters/The Rutter Group

(1) [8:1761.1] **Content:** Plaintiff is required to disclose:
— the *amount* and
— the *general nature* of the damages being sought (e.g., loss of earnings, pain and suffering, etc.). [CCP §425.11(b)]

(2) [8:1761.2] **Combined with statement of punitive damages:** Where plaintiff is seeking punitive damages in connection with a personal injury or wrongful death claim, the notice form required by CCP §425.115 may be combined with the §425.11 statement. [CCP §425.11(e)]

FORM: Statement of Damages (Judicial Council form CIV-050), *see Form 6:9* in Rivera, *Cal. Prac. Guide: Civ. Pro. Before Trial FORMS* (TRG).

☞ [8:1762] ***PRACTICE POINTER:*** Plaintiff's response normally provides only a rough idea of the damage claims made (e.g., "medical expenses, $3,500; loss of earnings, $5,000; pain and suffering, $50,000").

It is then up to defendant to utilize regular discovery procedures (document demands, interrogatories, depositions, etc.) to pin down the details of the claim; e.g., specific amounts spent for what care, by which doctors, on what dates, etc.

In short, a CCP §425.11 request is no substitute for regular discovery.

d. [8:1763] **Enforcement:** If plaintiff fails to provide the requested information, defendant's remedy is to move for an order directing plaintiff to provide such information. [CCP §425.11(b); see *Argame v. Werasophon* (1997) 57 CA4th 616, 618, 67 CR2d 281, 282 (citing text)]

Failure to make such motion *waives* defendant's right to exclude damage evidence at trial for lack of such statement. [*Argame v. Werasophon,* supra, 57 CA4th at 618, 67 CR2d at 283]

(1) [8:1764] **Costs and fees?** The statute does not provide for costs and fees in connection with such motion.

And, since this procedure is outside the Discovery Act, the Act's sanctions provision (CCP §2023.010 et seq.) *cannot* be utilized.

Nonetheless, dictum in one case supports such an award: "[D]efendants should not have been placed in a position where they were obligated to make a motion to obtain information to which they were lawfully entitled . . . [T]he court would have been justified in requiring Argame (or more appropriately her counsel) to reimburse defendants for costs incurred in making such a motion." [*Argame v. Werasophon*, supra, 57 CA4th at 618, 67 CR2d at 283, fn. 3]

2. [8:1765] **Demand for Bill of Particulars:** This is also a procedure outside the Discovery Act, but it serves a discovery purpose:

It enables defendants who have been sued generally on an *account* (certain actions in contract or quasi-contract) to force plaintiff to *itemize* the account on which the complaint is based. [CCP §454]

- This procedure dates back to early common law. When plaintiff sued on a *common count*, the pleadings gave no specifics as to the nature of the claim—i.e., whether contract, quasi-contract, etc. Therefore, courts allowed a "demand for bill of particulars" to enable defendant to discover what was being claimed and to prepare for trial. Although interrogatories and depositions can now be used for the same purpose, the bill of particulars remains an alternative procedure and it also has certain advantages (¶*8:1766*).

STRATEGIES AND TACTICS RE BILL OF PARTICULARS

[8:1766] **Advantages:** The bill of particulars has some advantages over Discovery Act procedures:

- **Inexpensive:** It is far easier and less costly to send out a simple demand for bill of particulars than it is to draft interrogatories or to prepare for and take depositions.
- **Preclusive:** Answers to interrogatories or deposition questions can be used as evidence against the answering party at trial; but they are not preclusive (contradictory evidence is also admissible). On the other hand, a bill of particulars "amplifies the pleadings to which it relates" and thus *is* preclusive as to the items and amounts claimed; i.e., *no other evidence is admissible* at trial, unless the court grants leave to amend the bill of particulars (*Meredith v. Marks* (1963) 212 CA2d 265, 269-270, 27 CR 737, 740; *see* ¶*8:1779*).
- **Does not count against "Rule of 35":** Since it is not an interrogatory, the demand does not count against the numerical limits on specially prepared interrogatories under the Discovery Act (*see* ¶*8:935*).

[8:1767] **Disadvantages:** The big disadvantage is that a bill of particulars is only available in actions on "an account" (¶*8:1768*). Therefore, it is not an alternative to depositions and interrogatories in most cases.

a. [8:1768] **Actions in which available:** A demand for bill of particulars may be served on the plaintiff only in an action on "an account." As stated in the Code: "It is not necessary for a party to set forth in a pleading the items of an account therein alleged, but he must deliver to the adverse party . . . after a demand thereof in writing, a copy of the account, or be precluded from giving evidence thereof . . ." [CCP §454]

(1) [8:1769] **"On account":** This basically means any action in contract *or quasi-contract* consisting of one or more items and pleaded in general terms. The most frequent case is where the complaint contains one or more of the *common counts:*

© 2020 Thomson Reuters/The Rutter Group

- Open book accounts;
- For labor and materials furnished under a contract;
- For monies loaned;
- For "money had and received."

(2) [8:1770] **Compare—not available where complaint for account stated:** But a bill of particulars is *not* appropriate in an action on an account stated, because an account stated is deemed to *merge the various items* on which the earlier accounts were based: i.e., there is nothing left to itemize. [*Ahlbin v. Crescent Comm'l Corp.* (1950) 100 CA2d 646, 648, 224 P2d 131, 133—plaintiff may ignore defendant's demand; *Distefano v. Hall* (1963) 218 CA2d 657, 677, 32 CR 770, 783]

b. **Procedure**

(1) [8:1771] **Defendant's demand:** In the above kinds of actions (¶*8:1768*), defendant is entitled to demand a bill of particulars as a *matter of right*; no court order or permission is required.

(a) [8:1772] **Timing:** No time is prescribed by statute. Presumably, therefore, the demand could be made as late as the time of trial.

(b) [8:1773] **Form of demand:** The demand must be in writing. But no special form is required. [See CCP §454]

- ***FORM:*** Demand for Bill of Particulars, *see Form 8:36* in Rivera, *Cal. Prac. Guide: Civ. Pro. Before Trial FORMS* (TRG).

(c) [8:1774] **Custody of original:** Defendant retains the original, along with plaintiff's response thereto. (They are *not* filed with the court.) [See CRC 3.250(a)(19)]

(2) [8:1775] **Plaintiff's response:** The "bill of particulars," itemizing the specifics of the account, must be delivered to the defendant *within 10 days* after service of the demand. [CCP §454]

(a) [8:1776] **Verification:** If the original complaint was verified, the bill of particulars must also be verified. [CCP §454]

(b) [8:1777] **Amendments:** If, after furnishing the itemization, plaintiff finds that it was incomplete or incorrect, plaintiff must seek leave of court (by noticed motion) to *amend* the bill of particulars, just as he or she would to amend a pleading. [CCP §454]

FORM: Bill of Particulars, *see Form 8:37* in Rivera, *Cal. Prac. Guide: Civ. Pro. Before Trial FORMS* (TRG).

c. [8:1778] **Information furnished limits claim:** The bill of particulars furnished by the plaintiff is treated as an "amplification" of the pleadings. As such, it has the effect of a pleading. Consequently, at trial, plaintiff is limited to the items and amounts specified in his or her bill of particulars. No additional items can be shown. [See *Baroni v. Musick* (1934) 3 CA2d 419, 421, 39 P2d 435, 436]

d. [8:1779] **Amendment of bill:** The court, however, does have authority under CCP §473(a)(1) to permit plaintiff to amend the bill of particulars under the same terms as amendment of the pleadings generally (*see ¶6:602 ff.*). Such an amendment might even be permitted at the time of trial, if no prejudice to the opposing party is shown.

e. **Enforcement of demand**

(1) [8:1780] **Defective or incomplete bill furnished:** If the information furnished is deemed too general or incomplete, the defendant may make a noticed *motion for a further bill.* [CCP §454]

(a) [8:1781] **May be waived:** If defendant fails to do so before trial, he or she *waives* any objection as to the sufficiency of the information furnished. [*Burton v. Santa Barbara Nat'l Bank* (1966) 247 CA2d 427, 433, 55 CR 529, 534]

[8:1782] *Reserved.*

(2) [8:1783] **Late bill:** Technically, furnishing the bill late (i.e., after 10 days following the demand) is a breach of the statutory duty, and hence could justify exclusion of evidence. But as a practical matter, unless defendant can show some prejudice resulting from the delay, it is unlikely that any sanction will be imposed. [*McCarthy v. Mt. Tecarte Land & Water Co.* (1896) 110 C 687, 692-693, 43 P 391, 392]

(3) [8:1784] **Failure to furnish any bill:** If plaintiff delivers no bill of particulars, the court *may* bar plaintiff from introducing evidence at trial in support of the account claimed. [CCP §454]

(a) [8:1785] **Discretionary:** CCP §454 seems to make the granting of such order automatic ("[the party] must deliver the account . . . *or be precluded* from giving evidence thereof"). But courts have interpreted this as merely giving the judge *discretion* to exclude plaintiff's evidence for failing to furnish a bill of particulars. [*McCarthy v. Mt. Tecarte Land & Water Co.*, supra, 110 C at 692, 43 P at 392]

(b) [8:1786] **Procedure:** The court has power to make such an order at trial or any time beforehand. [*Burton v. Santa Barbara Nat'l Bank*, supra, 247 CA2d at 433, 55 CR at 533-534]

© 2020 Thomson Reuters/The Rutter Group

[8:1787] ***PRACTICE POINTER:*** If you represent defendant, you may be tempted to wait until the time of trial to seek such an order in an attempt to finesse the case. But it may not work. Trial judges are usually reluctant to impose such a severe penalty for what may be only an oversight, particularly where no notice was given that such relief would be sought.

Therefore, it's better practice to *give plaintiff plenty of notice before trial:* If plaintiff fails to deliver the bill of particulars within the 10 days required, start off by sending a letter warning that you will seek an order excluding evidence if the information is not provided. If still not forthcoming, file a noticed motion *before* trial for an order excluding the evidence.

3. [8:1788] **Exchange of Valuation Data and Expert Witness Lists in Condemnation Actions:** Special discovery provisions are available in eminent domain proceedings, in *addition* to those provided under the Discovery Act. [CCP §1258.010 et seq.]

   a. [8:1789] **Demand for exchange:** Either party may serve a demand to exchange lists of *expert witnesses* and *valuation data* no later than 10 days after the trial setting conference. The demand must describe the property to which the action relates and include a statement warning of the consequences of failure to supply the requested information. [CCP §1258.210]

   b. [8:1790] **Information to be furnished:** The party upon whom the demand is served, as well as the party making such demand, must exchange:

      (1) [8:1791] **List of expert witnesses:** A list of each witness the party intends to call as an expert with respect to the *value* of the property taken and/or damage to remaining properties. The list must state the address and occupation or profession of each such witness, and subject matter of his or her testimony. [CCP §1258.240]

         (a) [8:1792] **Experts testifying on case-in-chief:** Disclosure is required only as to those experts intended to be called on direct examination on the party's case-in-chief. Experts who may be called for impeachment or *rebuttal* purposes need *not* be disclosed. [CCP §1258.280]

         (b) [8:1793] **Compare—CCP §2034.010 et seq.:** Under CCP §2034.010 et seq., disclosure is required of experts who will testify for *any* purpose (except undisclosed experts may disprove "foundational facts" testified to by opposing experts). [CCP §2034.310(b); *see* ¶*8:1728*]

      (2) [8:1794] **Valuation data:** For each witness who will give opinion evidence re valuation (including the property owner),

there must be furnished a statement of the data upon which he or she is relying (e.g., date of valuation; opinion as to "highest and best use" of property taken; comparable sales; replacement costs; income and expenses, etc.). [CCP §1258.260]

c. [8:1795] **Timing of exchange:** The lists must be deposited with the court and served on the opposing party on whatever date was agreed to by the parties; or if no such agreement, *90 days* before the date set for trial on the valuation of the property in the condemnation action. [CCP §1258.220]

d. [8:1796] **Authority to call expert witness not designated:** The court has the power to permit an unlisted expert witness to testify if there has been a "good faith" effort to comply and adequate *notice* was given the opposing party of the decision to call such expert. [CCP §1258.290]

(1) [8:1797] **Compare—CCP §2034.010 et seq.:** Unlike the procedure under CCP §2034.300 (¶*8:1688*), it is *not* required that the expert be made available for deposition before trial.

e. [8:1798] **Offer of continuance:** If an expert who has not submitted a written statement of his or her proposed testimony is allowed to testify (or if his or her testimony varies from the statement), the court may properly order a continuance to enable the opposing party to take the expert's deposition.

The fact that the court has offered to order such a continuance, and the opposing party has declined, does *not* bar such party from later seeking a new trial if disappointed with the verdict. Nor is it an abuse of discretion for the court to order a new trial on the ground of "surprise" based on the use of such expert testimony. [*City of Fresno v. Harrison* (1984) 154 CA3d 296, 300, 201 CR 219, 220-221]

4. [8:1799] **Injunctions in Aid of Discovery:** Some cases recognize an *inherent* judicial power to grant injunctive relief in furtherance of discovery *and preservation of evidence* (in addition to the power to issue protective orders under the Discovery Act). [*Northpoint Homeowners Ass'n v. Sup.Ct. (Arutunian/Kinney & Assocs.)* (1979) 95 CA3d 241, 244, 157 CR 42, 44; *Dodge, Warren & Peters Ins. Services, Inc. v. Riley* (2003) 105 CA4th 1414, 1419, 130 CR2d 385, 389]

[8:1799.1] **Compare:** There is contrary language in another case: "[C]ourts are *without power* to expand the methods of civil discovery beyond those authorized by statute." [*Holm v. Sup.Ct. (Misco)* (1986) 187 CA3d 1241, 1247, 232 CR 432, 436 (emphasis added)] But this was in connection with an order for exhumation and autopsy of a dead body in a will contest case, which involves unique considerations.

a. **Application**

- [8:1800] Owner sued Landscape Contractor for negligently planting trees in such a way that their roots interfered with underground utility lines. While the action was pending, Owner

© 2020 Thomson Reuters/The Rutter Group

decided to remove the offending trees. Landscape Contractor sought a court order preserving the trees pending trial of the action. Held: Although such relief could *not* be granted as a "protective order," the court had *inherent* power to *preserve and compel* the furnishing of evidence in a civil action. [*Northpoint Homeowners Ass'n v. Sup.Ct. (Arutunian/Kinney & Assocs.)*, supra, 95 CA3d at 244, 157 CR at 44]

- [8:1801] A court has inherent power to issue *"freeze" orders* in appropriate cases, enjoining parties from destroying *electronically-stored data* so that it will be available for future discovery. Sanctions for the destruction of such evidence may not be an adequate remedy. [*Dodge, Warren & Peters Ins. Services, Inc. v. Riley*, supra, 105 CA4th at 1419, 130 CR2d at 389]

b. [8:1801.1] **Bond required:** As with any injunction, however, an undertaking is statutorily required (CCP §529) to indemnify the party enjoined from whatever damage may be suffered if the injunction is improvidently granted. [*Northpoint Homeowners Ass'n v. Sup.Ct. (Arutunian/Kinney & Assocs.)*, supra, 95 CA3d at 246, 157 CR at 45]

[8:1802] *Reserved.*

5. [8:1803] **Appointment of Referee in Aid of Discovery:** Where the discovery matter is complex, the court has authority to appoint a referee to hear and determine the dispute with or without the parties' consent. But specific requirements must be met before the court may order a reference:

a. [8:1803.1] **Reference by agreement:** A referee may be appointed by agreement of the parties filed with the clerk, entered in the minutes or on formal motion. [CCP §638; CRC 3.901(a)]

The court "shall" appoint as referee or referees the person or persons, not exceeding three, agreed upon by the parties. [CCP §640]

Although "shall" may be read as mandatory, the court nevertheless has discretion to refuse to enforce a reference agreement where a reference may result in duplication of efforts or inconsistent rulings on a common issue. [*Tarrant Bell Prop., LLC v. Sup.Ct. (Abaya)* (2011) 51 C4th 538, 545-546, 121 CR3d 312, 316-317]

(1) [8:1803.2] **Procedure:** A written agreement and proposed order of appointment must be presented to the judge, specifying the scope of the reference. The order must state the name, business address and telephone number of the referee (and his or her State Bar number, if applicable) and bear the referee's signature consenting to serve. The order also must state whether the referee will be privately compensated and whether use of court facilities or personnel is authorized. [CRC 3.901-902, 3.904(a)]

FORM: Stipulation and Order for Reference, *see Form 1:6* in Rivera, *Cal. Prac. Guide: Civ. Pro. Before Trial FORMS* (TRG).

(2) [8:1803.3] **Limitation:** Referees appointed by consent may not hear *motions to seal records.* [CRC 3.932(a)]

b. [8:1804] **Reference by court order:** If the parties do not consent to appointment of a referee, a referee may be appointed on motion of any party or on the court's own motion where necessary "to hear and determine any and all discovery motions and disputes relevant to discovery in the action and to report findings and make a recommendation thereon." [CCP §639(a)(5); CRC 3.920(a)]

(1) [8:1804.1] **Appointment must be "necessary":** Appointment of a discovery referee is authorized, however, only where "necessary" to hear and determine such motions or disputes. [CCP §639(a)(5)]

(a) [8:1804.2] **Not proper in routine matters:** Blanket orders directing "any and all" discovery motions to a referee are improper in routine matters. [See *Hood v. Sup.Ct. (Sears, Roebuck & Co.)* (1999) 72 CA4th 446, 449, 85 CR2d 114, 116, fn. 4]

(b) [8:1804.3] **Circumstances justifying appointment:** But such orders may be upheld in "unusual" cases where a majority of the following factors exist:

— multiple issues to be resolved;

— multiple motions to be heard simultaneously;

— present motion is only one in a "continuum" of many;

— numerous and voluminous documents to be reviewed (especially in connection with issues based on assertion of a privilege) make the inquiry "inordinately time consuming." [*Taggares v. Sup.Ct. (Mitchell)* (1998) 62 CA4th 94, 105, 72 CR2d 387, 393]

[8:1804.4] *Reserved.*

(c) **Application**

- [8:1804.5] A discovery referee may be appointed *to monitor depositions* where antagonism between the parties might otherwise prolong the proceedings and frustrate discovery.
- [8:1804.6] On the other hand, there is no "necessity" for appointment of discovery referees in routine, pro forma, uncomplicated matters. [*Taggares v. Sup.Ct. (Mitchell)*, supra, 62 CA4th at 104, 72 CR2d at 392 (criticizing appointments "simply for expediency or a distaste for discovery resolution"); *Hood v. Sup.Ct. (Sears, Roebuck & Co.)*, supra, 72 CA4th at 449, 85 CR2d at 116, fn. 4—judge could resolve "dispute" in about 5 minutes]
- [8:1804.7] Nor is the appointment of a referee proper where resolution of the dispute involves complex or unsettled *legal issues*. Such matters "lie peculiarly

© 2020 Thomson Reuters/The Rutter Group

within the purview of the court." [*Taggares v. Sup.Ct. (Mitchell)*, supra, 62 CA4th at 106, 72 CR2d at 393]

- [8:1804.8] The trial court, rather than a referee, should hear discovery disputes whose *outcome may affect the rights of other parties*. The court is best able to identify such parties and ensure they receive adequate notice and protection. [*Taggares v. Sup.Ct. (Mitchell)*, supra, 62 CA4th at 106, 72 CR2d at 393]

FORM: Application for Order Appointing Discovery Referee to Supervise Deposition and Proposed Order, *see Form 8:11* in Rivera, *Cal. Prac. Guide: Civ. Pro. Before Trial FORMS* (TRG).

[8:1804.9] *Reserved.*

(2) [8:1804.10] **Procedure for appointment:** Each party may submit up to three nominees, and the court "shall" appoint the referee from the nominees against whom there is no legal objection. If the parties do not nominate a referee, the court may appoint a referee against whom there is no legal objection, or a court commissioner. [CCP §§639(a), 640]

[8:1804.11-1804.14] *Reserved.*

(3) [8:1804.15] **Order appointing referee:** The order appointing a referee must include:

- [8:1804.16] *Reasons for appointment:* All orders must state the reasons for the appointment. If the referee is appointed pursuant to CCP §639(a)(5) to hear and determine discovery motions and disputes, the order must state the exceptional circumstances (specific to the circumstances of the case) requiring the reference. [CCP §639(d)(2)]

- [8:1804.17] *Scope of reference:* The subject matter or matters included in the reference. [CCP §639(d)(3)] An order appointing a discovery referee must clearly state whether the referee is appointed for all discovery purposes (a *general* reference) or for only limited purposes (a *special* reference) (CRC 3.922(d)(2)). The distinction is critical because appealable orders of a referee appointed under a general reference (CCP §638(a)) are not heard by the trial judge and are reviewed directly by the court of appeal, unlike those under a special reference (CCP §638(b)). [*Lindsey v. Conteh* (2017) 9 CA5th 1296, 1304, 215 CR3d 801, 807]

- [8:1804.18] *Referee's name, etc.:* The name, business address and telephone number of the referee; and if a member of the State Bar, the referee's State Bar number. [CCP §639(d)(4); CRC 3.922(b)]
  — Note: It is not sufficient simply to identify an ADR provider (AAA, JAMS, etc.).

- [8:1804.19] *Referee's fees:* The maximum hourly rate the referee may charge and, at the request of any party, the maximum number of hours for which the referee may charge (the number of hours may be increased upon written application of a party and for good cause shown); the order may also state that the court may seek the referee's recommendation as to an allocation of referee's fees between the parties. [CCP §639(d)(5); CRC 3.922(f)]

- [8:1804.20] *Findings re parties' ability to pay referee's fee:* A specific finding is required that either:
  - — no party has established an economic inability to pay a pro rata share of the referee's fees, or
  - — one or more parties has established an economic inability to pay a pro rata share of the referee's fees and another party has agreed voluntarily to pay that additional share of the fees. [CCP §639(d)(6); CRC 3.922(f)]
  - — [8:1804.21] *Counsel's financial ability disregarded:* In determining whether a party has established an inability to pay, the financial ability of the party, *not* the party's counsel, to pay the fees is considered. [CCP §639(d)(6)(B)]

    A party proceeding in forma pauperis shall be *deemed* unable to pay the discovery referee's fees. [CCP §639(d)(6)(B)]

    ➪ [8:1804.21a] ***PRACTICE POINTER:*** It may be in the client's interest to have discovery disputes resolved by a referee (often a retired judge) acceptable to all parties. If so, even if a client's indigence prevents the court from appointing a referee, plaintiff's counsel may choose to advance the referee's fee and seek repayment out of a settlement or judgment.

- [8:1804.22] *Referee's powers:* The referee is granted authority to set the date, time and place for all hearings determined by the referee to be necessary, to direct the issuance of subpoenas, to preside over hearings, to take evidence, and to rule on objections, motions and other requests made during the course of the hearing. [CRC 3.922(e)]

- [8:1804.23] *Referee's report:* The referee is required to submit a written report to the parties and the court within 20 days after the hearing is complete and the matter submitted. In a *special* reference, a proposed order is provided and the report must include a recommendation on the merits, a statement of total fees charged

© 2020 Thomson Reuters/The Rutter Group

and a recommendation for allocation among the parties. [CCP §643]

- [8:1804.24] *Objections to report:* In a *special* reference, objections to the report must be served and filed no later than 10 calendar days after the report is served and filed, unless otherwise directed by the court; any response to the objections may be served and filed 10 calendar days thereafter; and copies of the objections and any responses must be served on the referee. [CCP §643(c)]

  In a *general* reference, the referee's orders (if appealable) are subject to review directly by the court of appeal. [*Lindsey v. Conteh* (2017) 9 CA5th 1296, 1304, 215 CR3d 801, 807]

  [8:1804.25-1804.29] *Reserved.*

(4) [8:1804.30] **Disclosures by referee:** A referee must disclose as soon as practicable any facts that might be grounds for disqualification. A referee who has been privately compensated in any other proceeding in the last 24 months as an attorney, expert witness, consultant, judge, referee, arbitrator, mediator or settlement facilitator by a party, attorney, law firm or insurance company in the current case must disclose the number and nature of other proceedings before the first hearing. [CRC 3.924(b)]

A *certification* by the referee that he or she is aware of and will comply with applicable provisions of the Code of Judicial Ethics must be *attached to the order* appointing the referee. [CRC 3.924(a)]

[8:1804.31-1804.34] *Reserved.*

(5) [8:1804.35] **Objections to referee:** Referees are subject to objection on the following grounds:

— interest in the event or main question involved in the action;

— formed or expressed an unqualified opinion or belief as to the merits of the action;

— state of mind evincing enmity against or bias toward either party;

— related to a party, officer of a party or the judge;

— a family member, business partner, guardian, ward, conservator, conservatee, master, servant, employer, clerk, principal or agent of any party or security on any bond or obligation for any party;

— served as a juror or witness in any trial between the same parties; or

— lack of minimum qualifications necessary to serve as a juror, except county residence requirements. [CCP §641; CRC 3.925]

In environmental actions, lack of technical qualifications with respect to the particular subject matter of the proceedings is also ground for objection. [CCP §641.2]

Participation in the referee selection process does not waive any ground for objection to a referee. [CCP §640(c)]

(a) [8:1804.36] **Procedure on objection:** Objections to a reference or referee appointed by the court must be in writing and must be heard and disposed of by the court, not the referee. [CCP §642; CRC 3.925]

Objections must be made with reasonable diligence. [CRC 3.925]

[8:1804.37-1804.39] *Reserved.*

(6) [8:1804.40] **Peremptory challenge to referee:** A referee appointed in a discovery matter may be disqualified by a party on motion made to the court, as follows:

(a) [8:1804.41] **Where referee appointed for all discovery purposes:** Where the referee is appointed to hear all discovery motions and disputes in the action, the challenge must be made within 10 days after notice of the appointment, or if the party has not yet appeared, within 10 days of appearance. [CCP §639(b)(A)]

(b) [8:1804.42] **Where referees appointed for limited discovery purposes:** Where the referee is appointed to hear a particular discovery motion or dispute, the challenge must be made at least five days before the date set for hearing if the referee is known at least 10 days before the date set for hearing. [CCP §639(b)(B)]

(7) [8:1804.43] **Open proceedings:** Proceedings before a referee that would be open to the public if held before a judge must be open to the public even if held outside the courthouse. [CRC 3.931(a)]

[8:1804.44] *Reserved.*

(8) [8:1804.45] **Referee may recommend sanctions:** Appointment of a discovery referee confers power to recommend discovery sanctions. [*Sauer v. Sup.Ct. (Oak Indus., Inc.)* (1987) 195 CA3d 213, 225, 240 CR 489, 496]

[8:1804.46-1804.49] *Reserved.*

(9) [8:1804.50] **Referee's report must be reviewed by court:** In a special reference, the discovery referee's report is *advisory,* not determinative. The trial court must independently consider the referee's findings, as well as any objections and responses to the objections, before acting upon the recommendations. [*Rockwell Int'l Corp. v. Sup.Ct. (Aetna Cas. & Sur. Co.)* (1994) 26 CA4th 1255, 1269-1270, 32 CR2d 153, 162; *Lopez v. Watchtower Bible & Tract Soc. of New York,*

© 2020 Thomson Reuters/The Rutter Group

Inc. (2016) 246 CA4th 566, 588-589, 201 CR3d 156, 175—court not required to hold hearing or conduct de novo review of underlying arguments presented to referee]

(a) [8:1804.51] **Objections to report:** Any objections by a party to the report must be filed within 10 days after the report is served. [CCP §643(c)]

Other parties have 10 days to respond to the objections. [CCP §643(c)]

(b) [8:1804.52] **Hearing not essential:** Although a hearing on the objections may be held, it is not required as a matter of law. The review may be done "in whatever manner the trial court deems appropriate." [*Marathon Nat'l Bank v. Sup.Ct. (Campbell)* (1993) 19 CA4th 1256, 1258, 24 CR2d 40, 40-41]

c. [8:1805] **Fees and costs ordered by court:** The court is empowered to order the parties to pay the referee's fees (if the referee is not an officer or employee of the court) in any manner that is "fair and reasonable," including an *apportionment* of the fees among the *parties* (not among counsel). [CCP §645.1; CRC 3.922(f)]

(1) [8:1805.1] **Ordering counsel to pay for referee?** The court does not have inherent power under CCP §128 to order counsel to pay the client's share of the referee's fees. But such an order might be justified under CCP §2023.010 et seq. (misuse of discovery process) or other discovery statutes. [*Andrews v. Sup.Ct. (Thomas)* (2000) 82 CA4th 779, 783, 98 CR2d 426, 428]

(2) [8:1805.2] **Recovery by prevailing party as court costs:** Fees paid may be recoverable by the prevailing party from opposing parties as costs of suit. [See CCP §1023]

Cross-refer: For further discussion of reference proceedings, see Knight, Chernick, Flynn & Quinn, *Cal. Prac. Guide: Alternative Dispute Resolution* (TRG), Ch. 6.

[8:1805.3-1805.4] *Reserved.*

6. [8:1805.5] **Special Statutes and Court Rules:** In certain types of cases, special statutes and Rules of Court may provide additional types of discovery, and/or a broader scope of discovery than available under the Discovery Act. For example:

a. [8:1805.6] **Suit involving limited partnership records:** California limited partnerships may be ordered to produce their records in California litigation regardless of where the records are located or the partners reside, and *whether or not the partnership is a party* to the action. The court's power is "*[i]n addition to any other discovery* rights which may exist." [Corps.C. §15901.16(e) (emphasis added)]

(Compare: Under the Discovery Act, a nonparty's records can be ordered produced only through deposition subpoena; and a subpoena cannot be served on a nonresident. *See* ¶*8:535, 8:568.*)

b. [8:1805.7] **Good faith settlement hearings (CCP §877.6):** CCP §877.6 provides a procedure for the court to determine the "good faith" of "piecemeal" settlements between plaintiff and one of several joint tortfeasors (*see* ¶*12:760 ff.*). A broader scope of discovery may be available in such proceedings:

(1) [8:1805.8] **Settlor's finances:** The settling tortfeasor's ability to pay a judgment is an important factor in determining whether the settlement was in "good faith" (*see* ¶*12:772*). Accordingly, the settling defendant's finances are discoverable in a CCP §877.6 "good faith" hearing, although confidential financial information is otherwise generally protected from discovery (*see* ¶*8:327.1*). [*City of Grand Terrace v. Sup.Ct. (Boyter)* (1987) 192 CA3d 1251, 1264, 238 CR 119, 127; *see* ¶*12:877*]

(2) [8:1805.9] **Deposing opposing counsel?** There is generally a strong policy against deposing opposing counsel. However, such depositions may be allowed in certain CCP §877.6 proceedings. Under certain circumstances, counsel for *nonsettling* defendants may be deposed to prove they had the opportunity to settle on similar terms but refused to do so. (Such proof may justify saddling the nonsettling defendants with a greater share of economic responsibility than otherwise would have been proper; *see* ¶*12:821.*)

Such depos will be allowed, however, only if it is shown that (1) counsel's testimony is not privileged; (2) the testimony is crucial to the case; and (3) there is no other way to get the information. [*Spectra-Physics, Inc. v. Sup.Ct. (Teledyne)* (1988) 198 CA3d 1487, 1496, 244 CR 258, 263; *see* ¶*12:822*]

[8:1805.10-1805.15] *Reserved.*

c. [8:1805.16] **Public entity tortfeasor defendants:** Public entity defendants in tort actions may serve plaintiff with interrogatories (or "in writing at the trial-setting conference") to obtain the names and addresses of any "*provider of a collateral source*" (private medical insurance, etc.) and the amounts plaintiff has received from such providers. [Gov.C. §985(c) (emphasis added)]

Plaintiff must produce the information within 30 days and "*shall have a continuing duty to disclose* to the public entity defendant" additional "collateral source" payments received thereafter. [Gov.C. §985(c) (emphasis added); see detailed discussion in Haning, Flahavan, Cheng & Wright, *Cal. Prac. Guide: Personal Injury* (TRG), Chs. 3 & 6]

(Compare: There is *no* continuing duty to update interrogatory answers under the Discovery Act; *see* ¶*8:1119.*)

d. [8:1805.17] **Support proceedings:** Special procedures are provided for discovery of each party's income and expenses in support proceedings (request for production of current income and expense declaration). In addition, each party's federal and state tax returns are discoverable by the other party (whereas tax returns are otherwise usually protected from discovery; *see* ¶*8:112*). [Fam.C. §§3660 et seq., 3552; see detailed discussion in Hogoboom & King, *Cal. Prac. Guide: Family Law* (TRG), Chs. 11 & 17]

e. [8:1805.18] **Public Records Act:** The California Public Records Act (CPRA, Gov.C. §6250 et seq.) permits anyone to obtain, subject to certain exemptions, "any writing containing information relating to the conduct of the public's business prepared, owned, used, or retained by any state or local agency regardless of physical form or characteristics" (Gov.C. §6252(e)). Any record, whether stored in public or *private* locations, including private electronic devices, may be subject to disclosure under the CPRA if the materials relate to public business. [*City of San Jose v. Sup.Ct. (Smith)* (2017) 2 C5th 608, 622-623, 629, 214 CR3d 274, 284-285, 290]

The CPRA was designed to provide "every person in this state" with access to such information (see Gov.C. §6250). Such access has been described as "a fundamental and necessary right." [*Michaelis, Montanari & Johnson v. Sup.Ct. (City of Los Angeles Dept. of Airports)* (2006) 38 C4th 1065, 1071, 44 CR3d 663, 667 (internal quotes omitted); see *Fredericks v. Sup.Ct. (City of San Diego)* (2015) 233 CA4th 209, 223, 182 CR3d 526, 535—CPRA "generally presumes" all documents maintained by public entity are subject to disclosure to any member of public unless exemption applies]

Disclosure is required under the CPRA even if the same or similar documents could be obtained through discovery in civil proceedings. [*Wilder v. Sup.Ct. (Metropolitan Transit Auth.)* (1998) 66 CA4th 77, 83, 77 CR2d 629, 633]

Cross-refer: The CPRA is discussed in detail in Asimow, Strumwasser, Bolz & Tuleja, *Cal. Prac. Guide: Administrative Law* (TRG), Ch. 29.

(1) [8:1805.18a] **Procedure for production:** "Each agency, upon a request for a copy of records, shall, within 10 days . . . determine whether the request . . . seeks copies of disclosable public records in the possession of the agency." [Gov.C. §6253(c)]

This raises two separate questions: (1) does the request seek public records, and (2) are the records in the possession of the public agency? [*Anderson-Barker v. Sup.Ct. (City of Los Angeles)* (2019) 31 CA5th 528, 538, 242 CR3d 724, 731]

(a) [8:1805.18b] **"Possession":** For purposes of the CPRA, "possession" of the records by the agency includes both actual and constructive possession; an agency has constructive possession if it has the right to control the records, either directly or through another person. However, the mere right of the agency to access a private entity's records does not qualify as possession of those records. [*Anderson-Barker v. Sup.Ct. (City of Los Angeles),* supra, 31 CA5th at 539-541, 242 CR3d at 732-733—where City contracted with private entities for impounding vehicles, but had no authority to manage, direct or oversee their documents, documents were not in City's possession and not discoverable under CPRA]

(2) [8:1805.19] **Request must clearly describe records sought:** A request for public records must reasonably describe an identifiable record or records. [See Gov.C. §6253(b)]

However, writings may be described *by their content.* The agency must then determine whether it has such writings under its control and the applicability of any exemption. An agency is thus obliged to search for records based on criteria set forth in the search request. [*California First Amendment Coalition v. Sup.Ct. (Wilson)* (1998) 67 CA4th 159, 166, 78 CR2d 847, 849]

(3) [8:1805.20] **Electronically-stored information:** Electronic data is subject to production under the CPRA in any format in which the agency holds the data upon payment of the "direct cost of producing a copy of a record in an electronic format." [Gov.C. §6253.9(a); *Sierra Club v. Sup.Ct. (County of Orange)* (2013) 57 C4th 157, 165, 158 CR3d 639, 645] (This does *not* include computer software; *see ¶8:1805.34f.*)

Caution: The California Supreme Court has granted review to determine whether the CPRA permits a public agency to shift the cost of redacting exempt information from electronic records to the party making the request for records although the cost of redaction cannot be required for paper records (*National Lawyers Guild v. City of Hayward* (2018) 27 CA5th 937, 238 CR3d 505, rev.grntd. 12/19/18 (Case No. S252445)).

(4) [8:1805.21] **Search required of private sources:** An agency that receives a request may develop its own policies for conducting searches. "As to requests seeking public records held in employees' nongovernmental accounts, an agency's first step should be to communicate the request to the employees in question. The agency may then reasonably rely on these employees to search *their own* personal files, accounts and devices for responsive material." [*City of San Jose v. Sup.Ct. (Smith)* (2017) 2 C5th 608, 628, 214 CR3d 274, 289 (emphasis in original)]

[8:1805.22-1805.24] *Reserved.*

(5) [8:1805.25] **Exemption for matters protected by privacy or privilege:** The CPRA specifically exempts from disclosure matters that would constitute an "unwarranted invasion of personal privacy" and matters privileged under federal or state law. [Gov.C. §6254(c), (k)]

© 2020 Thomson Reuters/The Rutter Group

(a) [8:1805.26] **Police officer personnel records:** Most police officer personnel records, including records of investigation of citizen complaints, fall within this exemption and therefore are not subject to disclosure under the CPRA. They are protected from disclosure in civil or criminal proceedings by Pen.C. §832.7 and Ev.C. §1043 (*see ¶8:126 ff.*). There would be no reason for such protection if the same information could be obtained routinely under the CPRA. [*City of Richmond v. Sup.Ct. (San Francisco Bay Guardian)* (1995) 32 CA4th 1430, 1440, 38 CR2d 632, 638; see *Pasadena Police Officers Ass'n v. Sup.Ct. (City of Pasadena)* (2015) 240 CA4th 268, 289, 192 CR3d 486, 502-503—although investigation report not exempt since *not* prepared in response to citizen complaint, parts of report may be protected (*¶8:1805.26b*)]

1) **Officer-involved shootings**

a) [8:1805.26a] **Names of officers:** The *names* of peace officers involved in on-duty shootings must be disclosed under the CPRA unless a "particularized showing" is made that the anonymity of specific officers outweighs the public interest in disclosure. [*Long Beach Police Officers Ass'n v. City of Long Beach* (2014) 59 C4th 59, 73-75, 172 CR3d 56, 65-67 (disclosure required)—"Vague safety concerns" applicable to all officers involved in shootings insufficient to prevent disclosure under Gov.C. §§6254(c) or 6255 (*¶8:1805.30*); *New York Times Co. v. Sup.Ct. (Thomas)* (1997) 52 CA4th 97, 103-104, 60 CR2d 410, 413-414; but see also *Copley Press, Inc. v. Sup.Ct. (County of San Diego)* (2006) 39 CA4th 1272, 1297-1298, 48 CR3d 183, 202-203 ("disapproving" *New York Times* as "simply incorrect")]

b) [8:1805.26b] **Report re administrative investigation of shooting:** Where a report related to an administrative investigation of an officer-involved shooting was not entirely exempt (*¶8:1805.26*), portions of the report containing exempt material may nevertheless be protected from disclosure under Gov.C. §6254(k)—e.g., the parts culled from the officers' personnel information and statements made in the course of the investigation. [*Pasadena Police Officers Ass'n v. Sup.Ct. (City of Pasadena)*, supra, 240 CA4th at 290, 192 CR3d at 503—where nonexempt materials are not "inextricably intertwined with exempt materials and are reasonably separable," segregation required]

Earlier cases found that it was proper to excise from such reports materials that relate to advancement, appraisal or discipline information, or that were derived from the administrative record (e.g., *Pasadena Police Officers Ass'n v. Sup.Ct. (City of Pasadena)*, supra, 240 CA4th at 294, 192 CR3d at 507). But such exceptions to disclosure do not appear in Pen.C. §832.7(b)(5).

c) [8:1805.26c] **Audio or video footage of shootings:** Commencing July 1, 2019, police departments must release audio or video footage of officer-involved shootings or other incidents involving serious use of force by police officers no more than 45 days after the agency "knew or reasonably should have known about the incident," unless doing so would substantially interfere with an ongoing investigation. [Gov.C. §6254(f)(4)(A)(i)]

The agency may redact portions of an audio or visual recording if it determines that release of the audio or video recording violates the "reasonable expectation of privacy" of a person depicted in the recording. [Gov.C. §6254(f)(4)(B)(i)]

d) [8:1805.26d] **Certain police records made available under CPRA:** Records relating to shootings or serious uses of force by police officers, as well as sustained findings of sexual assault or dishonest reporting or prosecution of a crime by a police officer, are discoverable under the CPRA (Pen.C. §832.7(b)(1)). This applies to records that existed prior to the January 1, 2019 effective date of the legislation. [*Walnut Creek Police Officers' Ass'n v. City of Walnut Creek* (2019) 33 CA5th 940, 941, 245 CR3d 398, 399—"Although the records may have been created prior to 2019, the event necessary to 'trigger application' of the new law—a request for records maintained by an agency—necessarily occurs after the law's effective date"]

Certain redactions may be made before the records are released. [Pen.C. §832.7(b)(5)]

(b) [8:1805.26e] **Legislative Counsel:** Communications between the Legislative Counsel and an agency concerning proposed legislation are protected by the attorney work product privilege. [*Labor & Workforce Develop. Agency v. Sup.Ct. (Fowler Packing Co., Inc.)* (2018) 19 CA5th 12, 34-35, 227 CR3d 744, 762]

(c) [8:1805.27] **Correspondence with Governor:** Correspondence to and from the Governor and members of his or her staff is exempted from the CPRA. [Gov.C. §6254(*l*); *California First Amendment Coalition v. Sup.Ct. (Wilson)*, supra, 67 CA4th at 169, 78 CR2d at 852—exemption includes records pertaining to applicants for appointment by Governor]

(d) [8:1805.28] **No waiver of privilege by inadvertent disclosure:** The inadvertent disclosure of privileged documents in response to a CPRA request does not waive the attorney-client privilege or attorney work product protection as to those documents. [*Ardon v. City of Los Angeles* (2016) 62 C4th 1176, 1183, 1189, 199 CR3d 743, 747, 752]

(e) [8:1805.29] **Outside counsel billing records:** While a legal matter is pending and active, attorney billing invoices are privileged (to the extent the billing information is conveyed for purposes of the legal representation) and thus, exempt from disclosure under the CPRA. [Gov.C. §6254(k); *Los Angeles County Bd. of Supervisors v. Sup.Ct. (ACLU of Southern Calif.)* (2016) 2 C5th 282, 295-297, 212 CR3d 107, 115-117]

(f) [8:1805.29a] **Names and addresses of vehicle owners:** CHP records containing vehicle owners' names and addresses retrieved from the DMV database constitute personal information exempt from disclosure under the CPRA. [Gov.C. §6254(k); *State of Calif. v. Sup.Ct. (Flynn)* (2016) 4 CA5th 94, 101-102, 208 CR3d 501, 506—documents ordered produced after names, addresses and other personal information exempt from disclosure redacted]

(g) [8:1805.29b] **Teacher personnel records:** Teacher personnel records, including investigations into allegations of misconduct that did not result in discipline, are exempt from disclosure under the CPRA. [*Associated Chino Teachers v. Chino Valley Unified School Dist.* (2018) 30 CA5th 530, 541-543, 241 CR3d 732, 740-742—teachers' privacy interests in personnel records reflecting results of investigation into teacher's actions as girls' volleyball coach outweighed public interest in disclosure]

(6) [8:1805.30] **Exemption for "public interest" ("catchall" exemption):** The CPRA allows a public agency to withhold information by demonstrating that the public interest served by nondisclosure "clearly outweighs" the public interest served by disclosure. [Gov.C. §6255; *Michaelis, Montanari & Johnson v. Sup.Ct. (City of Los Angeles)* (2006) 38 C4th 1065, 1071, 44 CR3d 663, 667; *Wilson v. Sup.Ct. (Los Angeles Times)* (1996) 51 CA4th 1136, 1143, 59 CR2d 537, 541—applicants for appointment by governor not discoverable; *Los Angeles*

Unified School Dist. v. Sup.Ct. (Los Angeles Times Communications LLC) (2014) 228 CA4th 222, 253, 175 CR3d 90, 113—evaluation scores of individual teachers identified by name exempt from disclosure]

(a) [8:1805.30a] **Deliberative process privilege:** "The key question in every case is whether the disclosure of materials would expose an agency's decision-making process in such a way as to discourage candid discussion within the agency and thereby undermine the agency's ability to perform its functions." [*Times Mirror Co. v. Sup.Ct. (State of Calif.)* (1991) 53 C3d 1325, 1342, 283 CR 893, 903 (internal quotes omitted); see *California First Amendment Coalition v. Sup.Ct. (Wilson)* (1998) 67 CA4th 159, 169, 78 CR2d 847, 851—staff evaluations re applicant's fitness for appointment are protected from disclosure by deliberative process privilege; *Labor & Workforce Develop. Agency v. Sup.Ct. (Fowler Packing Co., Inc.)* (2018) 19 CA5th 12, 30, 227 CR3d 744, 759—identity of persons communicating confidentially with agency acting for Governor seeking advice on pending legislation protected by deliberative process privilege]

(b) [8:1805.31] **Potential adverse consequence not enough:** In evaluating the public interest served by nondisclosure, courts may *consider potential* adverse consequences from disclosure. But "[a] mere assertion of possible endangerment does *not* 'clearly outweigh' the public interest in access to these records." [*CBS Inc. v. Block* (1986) 42 C3d 646, 652, 230 CR 362, 366 (emphasis added)]

1) [8:1805.31a] **Protection of privacy rights:** Where the agency's objection to disclosure is protection of individual privacy rights, it must demonstrate a "clear overbalance" on the side of confidentiality. The purpose of the requesting party in seeking disclosure cannot be considered. [*California State Univ. v. Sup.Ct. (McClatchy Co.)* (2001) 90 CA4th 810, 835, 108 CR2d 870, 888]

(c) [8:1805.32] **Burden of production:** Records requests inevitably impose some burden on government agencies. An agency is obliged to comply so long as the record can be located with reasonable effort. But a request that requires an agency to search an enormous volume of data for the "needle in the haystack," or that compels the production of a huge volume of material, may be objectionable as unduly burdensome. [See *California First Amendment Coalition v. Sup.Ct. (Wilson)*, supra, 67 CA4th at 166, 78 CR2d at 849]

© 2020 Thomson Reuters/The Rutter Group

(d) [8:1805.33] **Purpose for which records sought irrelevant:** The purpose for which the records are to be used is *irrelevant* in making this determination. The fact the requesting party is a commercial entity seeking the information for commercial purposes does not diminish the public interest in disclosure of public records. [*State Bd. of Equalization v. Sup.Ct. (Associated Sales Tax Consultants, Inc.)* (1992) 10 CA4th 1177, 1190-1191, 13 CR2d 342, 350; *Caldecott v. Sup.Ct. (Newport-Mesa Unified School Dist.)* (2015) 243 CA4th 212, 219, 196 CR3d 223, 230]

Likewise, it is immaterial that the information is sought by persons who are planning to sue or who have sued a governmental agency. [*Wilder v. Sup.Ct. (Metropolitan Transit Auth.)* (1998) 66 CA4th 77, 83, 77 CR2d 629, 633]

(7) [8:1805.34] **Exemption for records "pertaining to pending litigation against public agency":** The CPRA also exempts records "pertaining to pending litigation to which the public agency is a party." [Gov.C. §6254(b); *Fairley v. Sup.Ct. (City of Long Beach)* (1998) 66 CA4th 1414, 1420-1421, 78 CR2d 648, 651—arrestee who claimed damages against City was entitled to all arrest-related documents *except* those expressly prepared for litigation]

(a) [8:1805.34a] **Limited to documents prepared for use in litigation:** This exemption only applies, however, to documents *specifically prepared for use* in litigation. The exemption is not triggered by the fact the records may be *sought* for use in a pending action. [*County of Los Angeles v. Sup.Ct. (Anderson-Barker)* (2012) 211 CA4th 57, 67, 149 CR3d 324, 330—billing and payment records of county's outside counsel were prepared "as an incident to the lawsuit" rather than specifically *for use* in the litigation, and thus not covered by exemption]

If a document has been prepared for a "dual purpose," its "dominant purpose" determines whether it is protected from disclosure under the pending litigation exemption. [*City of Hemet v. Sup.Ct. (Press Enterprise Co.)* (1995) 37 CA4th 1411, 1419, 44 CR2d 532, 537—dominant purpose of police department's internal affairs report was "intradepartmental concerns" rather than pending litigation, so not exempt from disclosure to media; *County of Los Angeles v. Sup.Ct. (Anderson-Barker)*, supra, 211 CA4th at 67, 149 CR3d at 330—dominant purpose of county's outside counsel billing and payment records was "normal recordkeeping," so not exempt even though records had ancillary purpose in pending litigation (used in attorney fee request)]

(b) [8:1805.34b] **Documents prepared by other parties:** The "pending litigation exemption" is not limited to documents prepared by the public agency: The exemption also prevents persons who are not parties to the litigation from obtaining documents sent to or served on the public agency by the *opposing* party and which the parties *do not intend to be revealed outside the litigation.* [*Board of Trustees of Calif. State Univ. v. Sup.Ct. (Copley Press, Inc.)* (2005) 132 CA4th 889, 898-901, 34 CR3d 82, 88-90—correspondence between public agency's counsel and opposing parties/counsel not subject to disclosure]

(c) [8:1805.34c] **Compare—deposition transcripts:** Deposition transcripts are available to the public under CCP §2025.570, which requires a deposition officer to provide a transcript copy to "any person" upon request and payment of reasonable charges (*see* ¶*8:767.10 ff.*). Thus, there is no reason to withhold deposition transcripts under the CPRA. [*Board of Trustees of Calif. State Univ. v. Sup.Ct. (Copley Press, Inc.)*, supra, 132 CA4th at 901-902, 34 CR3d at 90]

[8:1805.34d] *Reserved.*

(8) [8:1805.34e] **Exemption for investigation records:** Records of investigations are not subject to release under the CPRA. There is no exception for "routine investigations." [Gov.C. §6254(f); *Haynie v. Sup.Ct. (County of Los Angeles)* (2001) 26 C4th 1061, 1069-1070, 112 CR2d 80, 86; see *Rackauckas v. Sup.Ct. (Los Angeles Times Communications)* (2002) 104 CA4th 169, 177, 128 CR2d 234, 240—includes investigator's opinions and conclusions regarding potential criminal conduct; *Dixon v. Sup.Ct. (Neves)* (2009) 170 CA4th 1271, 1279, 88 CR3d 847, 853—includes coroner and autopsy reports in connection with homicide investigation; *American Civil Liberties Union Found. of Southern Calif. v. Sup.Ct. (County of Los Angeles)* (2017) 3 C5th 1032, 1041-1042, 221 CR3d 832, 839-840—bulk collection of license plate data not exempt as investigation records because no concrete and definite prospect of enforcement proceedings, but release of raw data violates privacy interests]

(9) [8:1805.34f] **Exemption for computer software:** Computer software developed by an agency is not a public record under the statute. "Computer software" includes "computer mapping systems, computer programs, and computer graphics systems." [Gov.C. §6254.9(a), (b); *Sierra Club v. Sup.Ct. (County of Orange)* (2013) 57 C4th 157, 165, 158 CR3d 639, 645]

(a) [8:1805.34g] **Compare—database:** Because of the policy favoring access to public records (*see* ¶*8:1805.18*), a graphic information system (GIS)-formatted *database*

© 2020 Thomson Reuters/The Rutter Group

is not exempt from production, even though the GIS *program* itself is. [*Sierra Club v. Sup.Ct. (County of Orange)*, supra, 57 C4th at 170-171, 158 CR3d at 649—term "computer mapping systems" encompasses only computer mapping software, not databases in format compatible with mapping software]

(10)[8:1805.35] **Enforcing disclosure:** If records are improperly withheld, a party may petition for a court order compelling disclosure. [See Gov.C. §6259(a)]

The Gov.C. §6259(a) procedure is the *exclusive procedure* to enforce disclosure of public records. A complaint for declaratory or injunctive relief does not lie. [*Filarsky v. Sup.Ct. (City of Manhattan Beach)* (2002) 28 C4th 419, 423-424, 121 CR2d 844, 845—City could not seek declaratory relief regarding its obligation to disclose documents to members of public]

(a) [8:1805.35a] **Discovery allowed in petition proceeding:** A CPRA petition is a "special proceeding of a civil nature" to which the Civil Discovery Act applies. [*City of Los Angeles v. Sup.Ct. (Anderson-Barker)* (2017) 9 CA5th 272, 285, 214 CR3d 858, 869]

(b) [8:1805.36] **Fees and costs:** The court must award costs and reasonable attorney fees to a "plaintiff" who prevails in such litigation. [Gov.C. §6259(d); see *Fontana Police Dept. v. Villegas-Banuelos* (1999) 74 CA4th 1249, 1253, 88 CR2d 641, 644—"plaintiff" means the person seeking the records, whether or not denominated as such in proceedings to obtain the records; *Galbiso v. Orosi Pub. Utility Dist.* (2008) 167 CA4th 1063, 1088, 84 CR3d 788, 807; *Sukumar v. City of San Diego* (2017) 14 CA5th 451, 454, 221 CR3d 418, 420-421—plaintiff need not obtain favorable final judgment where defendant's voluntary provision of records is induced by the lawsuit because lawsuit was catalyst]

A *public agency* may recover fees and costs only if the petition is "clearly frivolous." [Gov.C. §6259(d); *Crews v. Willows Unified School Dist.* (2013) 217 CA4th 1368, 1380-1381, 159 CR3d 484, 493-494; *Bertoli v. City of Sebastopol* (2015) 233 CA4th 353, 368, 182 CR3d 308, 320]

(11)[8:1805.37] **Agency's right to object not waived by failure to comply with statutory time limits:** An agency's failure to produce or object to production of public records within the time limits provided in the CPRA does *not* waive its right to object: "[R]equiring disclosure of otherwise exempt records as a penalty for delay in complying with the Act's timing requirements is unduly harsh." [*Michaelis, Montanari & Johnson v. Sup.Ct. (City of Los Angeles Dept. of Airports)* (2006) 38 C4th 1065, 1072, 44 CR3d 663, 668]

(12)[8:1805.37a] **Appellate review:** An order granting or denying a *petition compelling disclosure* is *not* an appealable order and is reviewable only by writ. [See Gov.C. §6259(c); *Powers v. City of Richmond* (1995) 10 C4th 85, 90, 40 CR2d 839, 840 (upholding constitutionality of Gov.C. §6259(c)); *Crews v. Willows Unified School Dist.*, supra, 217 CA4th at 1378, 159 CR3d at 491]

However, an order granting or denying an *award of attorney fees* under §6259(d) may be reviewed on appeal from a final judgment in the action. [*Crews v. Willows Unified School Dist.*, supra, 217 CA4th at 1379, 159 CR3d at 492]

f. [8:1805.38] **Public access to judicial administrative records:** Subject to specified exceptions, the public has a right of access to judicial administrative records, budget and management information relating to administration of the courts. [See CRC 10.500 et seq.]

[8:1805.39] *Reserved.*

g. [8:1805.40] **Patient's own medical records:** Patients have a right of access to their own medical records under several statutes:

[8:1805.41] **Health & Saf.C. §123110:** Patients are entitled to inspect and copy a health care provider's records pertaining to the patient by:

— presenting a written request for those records;

— paying "reasonable clerical costs" incurred in making the records available; and

— paying a specified fee for each page copied (to be furnished by the provider *within 15 days* after request). [Health & Saf.C. §123110(a), (b); see *Maher v. County of Alameda* (2014) 223 CA4th 1340, 1353, 168 CR3d 56, 65—patients' attorneys are *not* "patients" or "patient representatives" entitled to obtain medical records under §123110]

[8:1805.42] **Ev.C. §1158:** Prior to filing a lawsuit or defendant's appearance therein, the patient's attorney may obtain the patient's medical records by presenting the patient's signed authorization to a medical provider. The provider may charge reasonable costs of copying, etc., but must furnish copies of the patient's records *within five days* after receipt of the signed authorization. Otherwise, it may be held liable for reasonable expenses, including attorney fees, incurred in enforcing the patient's right to such records. Ev.C. §1158 specifies the *items and amounts* that may be charged. [See *Thornburg v. El Centro Regional Med. Ctr.* (2006) 143 CA4th 198, 202, 48 CR3d 840, 843]

A statutory form (completed and signed by the patient) authorizes providers to disclose this information. [Ev.C. §1158(h)]

[8:1805.42a] **Federal HIPAA:** The federal Health Insurance Portability and Accountability Act (HIPAA, 42 USC §1320d et seq.) authorizes a health care provider to charge a "reasonable, cost-based

© 2020 Thomson Reuters/The Rutter Group

fee" for copies of his or her records. Under applicable regulations, this fee is limited to the *actual cost* of copying the records and postage (see 45 CFR §164.524(c)(4)). This fee limit applies, however, only when the *patient or the patient's personal representative* (e.g., executor or administrator) requests copies; it does not limit fees charged when the patient's *attorney* requests the records. [See *Bugarin v. ChartOne, Inc.* (2006) 135 CA4th 1558, 1564, 38 CR3d 505, 509; *Webb v. Smart Document Solutions, LLC* (9th Cir. 2007) 499 F3d 1078, 1084-1085]

FORM: HIPAA Authorization Form, *see Form 1:1.1* in Rivera, *Cal. Prac. Guide: Civ. Pro. Before Trial FORMS* (TRG).

(1) [8:1805.43] **Records not yet prepared:** The patient's right of access is normally limited to documents in existence. But a health care provider may not avoid court process by refusing to prepare records it *normally would prepare in the course of practice* (e.g., records of treatment and billing statements). If it has the raw data available to prepare the requested records, and compiling the raw data would not be unduly burdensome, it must compile and produce such records in response to a proper discovery request. [*Person v. Farmers Ins. Group of Cos.* (1997) 52 CA4th 813, 818, 61 CR2d 30, 33]

- [8:1805.44] **Comment:** But this would not obligate a health care provider to prepare and furnish records it otherwise would not normally prepare in the course of practice; e.g., a narrative medical report of findings designed to help plaintiff's counsel evaluate the case.

(2) [8:1805.45] **Medical bills unpaid or lien not signed:** The patient's right to his or her own records is not conditioned on paying outstanding medical bills to the health care provider or agreeing to a lien on recovery against third persons. [See Health & Saf.C. §123110(j); *Person v. Farmers Ins. Group of Cos.*, supra, 52 CA4th at 818, 61 CR2d at 33]

(3) [8:1805.46] **Enforcement procedures:** A *separate lawsuit* is required to enforce the patient's inspection rights under the Health & Safety Code. Costs and attorney fees incurred in such proceedings may be awarded to the prevailing party. [Health & Saf.C. §123120]

The procedure under Ev.C. §1158 is much easier: The patient's attorney simply applies to the court for an *order to the provider to show cause* why the records should not be produced. The court "shall" impose monetary sanctions pursuant to Ev.C. §1158 (*see ¶8:1805.42*) unless the provider shows "substantial justification" for its failure to produce the records or that other circumstances make sanctions "unjust." [CCP §1985.7]

[8:1805.47-1805.49] *Reserved.*

h. [8:1805.50] **Mutual benefit corporations:** Members of a mutual benefit corporation have a right to "[i]nspect and copy the record of all the members' names, addresses and voting rights." [Corps.C. §8330(a)(1); see *Worldmark v. Wyndham Resort Develop. Corp.* (2010) 187 CA4th 1017, 1032, 114 CR3d 546, 556—includes right to obtain members' email addresses]

© 2020 Thomson Reuters/The Rutter Group

RESERVED

CHAPTER 8L

DISCOVERY IN LIMITED CIVIL CASES

CONTENTS

© 2020 Thomson Reuters/The Rutter Group

RESERVED

DISCOVERY IN LIMITED CIVIL CASES

[8:1806] **Background:** "Economic Litigation Rules" (CCP §§90-98, ¶*8:1806.1 ff.*) have been adopted to reduce litigation expense and delay in limited civil cases (*see* ¶*3:70 ff.*). These rules limit the discovery procedures available in such cases.

[8:1806.1] **Exception—unlawful detainer actions:** For unknown reasons, CCP §91(b) specifically *exempts* unlawful detainer actions from the limitations on discovery (¶*8:1807 ff.*). (Comment: This appears to be a legislative oversight. There is no apparent reason why greater discovery should be permitted in unlawful detainers, which are supposed to be summary proceedings.)

1. [8:1807] **Limitations on Existing Discovery Procedures:** Except for unlawful detainer actions, only the following discovery procedures are permitted in limited civil cases:

   a. [8:1808] **One deposition:** Each party is permitted one deposition "as to each adverse party." [CCP §94(b)]

      (1) [8:1809] **Whose deposition:** The deposition that may be taken is *not* limited to the deposition of the adverse party. I.e., the rule limits the *number* of depositions each party may take as a matter of right, not whose deposition may be taken.

      (Compare: The Discovery Act does not limit the number of depositions a party may take. The only limit is that a natural person cannot be deposed more than once without a court order; CCP §2025.610.)

      (2) [8:1809.1] **Where adverse party a corporation or other entity:** When the deposition notice is addressed to a corporation or other entity party, it must designate the person *or persons* "most qualified" to testify on its behalf (CCP §2025.230; *see* ¶*8:473*). Nevertheless, the deposition of an "organization" is treated as a *single* deposition even though more than one person may be designated or required to testify. [CCP §94(b)]

   b. [8:1810] **"Grabbag Rule of 35" on interrogatories, RFAs and inspection demands:** Each party may serve on *each adverse* party no more than *35 of any combination* of interrogatories, requests for admission or demands for inspection. No subparts are allowed. [CCP §94(a)]

      (Compare: The Discovery Act does not limit the number of inspection demands under CCP §2031.010 et seq. It allows 35 RFAs and 35 specially prepared interrogatories, *plus* any greater number accompanied by a declaration of necessity, *plus* official form interrogatories, *plus* supplemental interrogatories. However, the "grabbag Rule of 35" in limited civil cases allows *only* 35 interrogatories, RFAs and CCP §2031.010 et seq. demands *combined*.)

© 2020 Thomson Reuters/The Rutter Group

(1) [8:1811] **Per adverse party:** The "Rule of 35" applies to *each* opposing party; i.e., if there are several defendants, plaintiff can serve an aggregate 35 discovery requests on *each* of them.

(2) [8:1812] **Effect of excessive requests?** It is not clear whether an excessive number voids the entire set of discovery requests or just those exceeding 35. (Under the Discovery Act, an objection lies to the excess only; see CCP §2030.030(c), ¶*8:939*.)

(3) [8:1813] **Effect of objections sustained?** Nor is it clear whether a party gets additional requests if *objections* by the opposing party are sustained to the original requests. (Presumably not, since the Code limits the number of discovery requests to be "served.")

(4) [8:1813.1] **Official Form Interrogatories:** Official Form Interrogatories are available for use in *unlawful detainer, personal injury* and *contract* actions in limited civil cases.

FORMS

- Official Form Interrogatories—Unlawful Detainer (DISC-003/UD-106).
- Official Form Interrogatories—Limited Civil Cases (Economic Litigation) (DISC-004).

(a) [8:1813.2] **Official Form for personal injury and contract:** The Judicial Council Form Interrogatories for personal injury and contract actions in limited civil cases (DISC-010) are shorter and simpler than the similar Judicial Council Form Interrogatories used for unlimited civil cases (DISC-001, *see* ¶*8:931*). All unnumbered subparts are eliminated.

The DISC-004 Form Interrogatories may also be used in unlimited civil cases (see DISC-004, §2(a)). But the Form Interrogatories otherwise used in unlimited civil cases may *not* be used in limited civil cases.

(b) [8:1813.3] **Official Form Interrogatories count against "grabbag rule of 35":** Each Official Form Interrogatory served in limited civil cases *counts* against the "grabbag rule of 35" (CCP §94(a)). (Therefore, they do not have the same advantage that Official Form Interrogatories have in unlimited civil cases; *see* ¶*8:934*.) CCP §2033.710 makes the Official Forms subject to rules promulgated by the Judicial Council. Those rules appear on the forms themselves. See Judicial Council form DISC-004.

CCP §94(a) applies to "interrogatories" under Chapter 13, commencing with §2030.010. That Chapter applies to *both* "specially prepared interrogatories" *and* "official form interrogatories" (see CCP §2030.030).

1) [8:1813.4] **Comment:** The apparent rationale is that parties in limited civil cases have additional discovery procedures available to them (e.g., case questionnaire forms and requests for statements of witnesses and evidence; *see* ¶*8:1816 ff.*).

c. **Other discovery procedures**

(1) [8:1814] Physical, mental and blood examinations (CCP §2032.010 et seq.) are permitted without limitation. [CCP §94(d)]

(2) [8:1814.1] Likewise as to discovery of the identity of opposing expert witnesses (CCP §2034.010 et seq.). [CCP §94(e)]

(3) [8:1814.2] A "subpoena duces tecum" (more accurately, a business records subpoena under CCP §§2020.410 ff.) may be served, requiring the person served to *mail* copies (along with an affidavit in compliance with Ev.C. §1561) to the party's attorney. The party who issued the subpoena must mail a copy of the records so obtained to any other party who offers to pay the copying costs. [CCP §94(c)]

d. [8:1815] **Additional discovery for "good cause" shown:** On noticed motion, the court may permit additional discovery if the moving party shows that he or she *will otherwise be unable* to prosecute or defend the action. The court will take into account whether the moving party "has used all applicable discovery in good faith and . . . has attempted to secure the additional discovery *by stipulation* or by means other than formal discovery." [CCP §95(a) (emphasis added)]

2. [8:1816] **Special Discovery Procedures Permitted:** As a tradeoff for the limitations on the regular discovery procedures (*see* ¶*8:1807 ff.*), the Legislature provided two special procedures for discovery in limited civil cases:

a. [8:1817] **Reciprocal case questionnaire:** Plaintiff has the *option* of serving a "case questionnaire" form on the defendant at the *outset* of the action. These forms are designed to elicit fundamental information about each party's case, including:

- Names and addresses of all witnesses with knowledge of any relevant fact;
- List of all documents relevant to the case;
- Statement of the nature and amount of damages;
- Information as to insurance coverages, injuries and treating physicians (where applicable). [CCP §93]

FORM: Case Questionnaire—For Limited Civil Cases (Under $25,000) (Judicial Council form DISC-010), *see Form 8:38* in Rivera, *Cal. Prac. Guide: Civ. Pro. Before Trial FORMS* (TRG).

© 2020 Thomson Reuters/The Rutter Group

[8:1818] ***PRACTICE POINTER:*** If you represent the plaintiff, use these case questionnaires *cautiously*. If the facts are at all in dispute, you may not *want* to make the kinds of disclosures required by these forms (e.g., amount of damages, names of all witnesses, etc.). Be sure to leave the door open as to later-discovered evidence, by including wording such as "To the best of my present knowledge . . ."

(1) [8:1819] **Procedure:** To utilize this procedure, plaintiff must complete his or her own questionnaire form and serve it on defendant (together with a blank form for defendant's use) *at the time of serving the complaint*. Defendant then has to complete the questionnaire and serve it on plaintiff with the answer. [CCP §93(a), (b)]

(2) [8:1820] **Sanctions:** If defendant fails to comply (or if plaintiff furnishes incomplete information), a motion may be made for an order compelling answers and for monetary sanctions under CCP §2023.010 et seq. (Continued failure to comply after a court order may result in "issue," "evidence" or "terminating" sanctions in appropriate cases.) [CCP §93(e)]

b. [8:1821] **Request for statement of witnesses and evidence:** Any party may serve on any other party, shortly before trial (*see ¶8:1823*), a request for disclosure of the witnesses and evidence intended to be introduced at trial. The party upon whom such request is served must timely respond (*¶8:1826*); and must provide full and accurate information or risk exclusion of undisclosed evidence at time of trial. [CCP §§96, 97]

FORM: Request for Statement of Witnesses and Evidence—For Limited Civil Cases (Under $25,000) (Judicial Council form DISC-015), *see Form 8:39* in Rivera, *Cal. Prac. Guide: Civ. Pro. Before Trial FORMS* (TRG).

[8:1822] *Reserved.*

(1) [8:1823] **Time for request:** The request may be served only during the period between 30 and 45 days prior to the date first set for trial. [CCP §96(b)]

[8:1824] *Reserved.*

(a) [8:1825] **Effect of trial continuance?** It remains to be decided whether continuance of the trial date "reopens" the right to file a request. (It does *not* reopen discovery; CCP §2024.020(b), *see ¶8:450.*)

(2) [8:1826] **Time for response:** The response is due within 20 days after the request is served (CCP §96(c)). But if the request was served by mail, the time for response is extended five calendar days (10 calendar days if mailed from or to another state), so that the response would be due 25 (or 30) days from date of mailing. [CCP §§96(g), 1013(a)] (An extension of two court days applies where the request is served by overnight delivery or fax; see CCP §1013(c), (e), *¶9:87.4 ff.*)

(a) [8:1827] **Relief for late responses:** No additional, amended or late statement is permitted unless by stipulation, or upon court order on *noticed motion* for "good cause" shown. [CCP §96(d)]

(3) [8:1828] **Enforcement by exclusion of evidence:** Evidence not disclosed in such response will be excluded at trial, upon timely objection by any party who has served a request for statement of witnesses and evidence in compliance with CCP §96, *except* as discussed below (¶*8:1829 ff.*). [CCP §97(a)]

The following *exceptions* are provided by statute:

(a) [8:1829] **Impeachment evidence:** Witnesses and evidence admissible "solely for purposes of impeachment" are admissible although not disclosed. [CCP §97(b)(3)]

1) [8:1830] **Not rebuttal:** "Impeachment" refers to evidence affecting the *credibility* of the opposing party's evidence, and not that which simply *rebuts* the other side's evidence. To allow rebuttal evidence as "impeaching" would effectively nullify the request procedure. [*Davis v. Chew* (1979) 95 CA3d Supp. 13, 17, 157 CR 653, 655]

(b) [8:1831] **Party testimony:** Either party may testify or call an adverse party to testify even if their names were not disclosed as witnesses. [CCP §97(b)(1), (2)]

1) [8:1832] **Not corporations:** But this applies only to individual parties. If a corporate party failed to disclose the names and addresses of its officers, employees or other witnesses, they would not be permitted to testify on its behalf. [CCP §97(b)(1)]

(c) [8:1833] **Documentary evidence:** Documents *obtained through discovery* are admissible even if not disclosed in response to pretrial request. [CCP §97(b)(4)]

(4) [8:1834] **Grounds for relief:** In appropriate cases, the court may permit a party to introduce evidence that should have been, but was not, disclosed in response to pretrial request. The court must find *either* that the party made a "good faith effort to comply" *or* that the failure to comply was the result of "mistake, inadvertence, surprise or excusable neglect" within the meaning of CCP §473(b). [CCP §97(b)(5)]

If the requisite grounds exist, the court may "*upon such terms as may be just*" permit such evidence. The "terms" may include, without limitation, continuing the trial for a reasonable period of time and awarding the other party *costs and litigation expenses.* [CCP §97(b)(5) (emphasis added)]

(a) [8:1835] **Ignorance of rules as ground for relief?** In light of the clear warning on the Request Form itself,

© 2020 Thomson Reuters/The Rutter Group

it seems unlikely that a court would grant relief simply on ground that the party or counsel was unfamiliar with the statutory requirements. In any event, refusal to grant relief on such ground is clearly within the court's discretion. [*Border v. Kuznetz* (1980) 103 CA3d Supp. 14, 17, 162 CR 881, 883 (decided under former Economic Litigation Project rules; *see* ¶*8:1806*)]

[8:1836-1899] *Reserved.*

CHAPTER 8M

DISCOVERY SANCTIONS

CONTENTS

© 2020 Thomson Reuters/The Rutter Group

© 2020 Thomson Reuters/The Rutter Group

RESERVED

DISCOVERY SANCTIONS

1. [8:1900] **Introduction:** This Chapter generally addresses discovery sanctions available under California's Civil Discovery Act; more detail concerning sanctions under specific discovery methods is included in the Chapters covering those methods (*see* ¶*8:1904*).

   a. [8:1901] **Discovery misuses generally:** CCP §2023.010 sets forth a nonexclusive catalog of "misuses" of discovery for which sanctions may be imposed, including:

   — "Persisting, over objection and *without substantial justification*, in an attempt to obtain information . . . outside the scope of permissible discovery." [CCP §2023.010(a) (emphasis added)]

   — Using a discovery method *improperly* (i.e., "in a manner that does not comply with its specified procedures"). [CCP §2023.010(b)]

   — Using a discovery method so as to cause "*unwarranted annoyance,* embarrassment, or oppression, or undue burden and expense." [CCP §2023.010(c) (emphasis added)]

   — "*Failing to respond* or to submit to an authorized method of discovery." [CCP §2023.010(d) (emphasis added)]

   — "Making, *without substantial justification,* an unmeritorious objection to discovery." [CCP §2023.010(e) (emphasis added)]

   — "Making an evasive response to discovery." [CCP §2023.010(f)]

   — "Disobeying a court order to provide discovery." [CCP §2023.010(g)]

   — Making or opposing a motion to compel or limit discovery unsuccessfully and "*without substantial justification.*" [CCP §2023.010(h) (emphasis added)]

   — Failing to meet and confer; i.e., failing to make "a *reasonable and good faith attempt to resolve informally* any dispute concerning discovery" where so required by the particular discovery method involved. [CCP §2023.010(i) (emphasis added)]

   This list is illustrative, not all-inclusive. Other forms of discovery misuse are also sanctionable. [*Mattco Forge, Inc. v. Arthur Young & Co.* (1990) 223 CA3d 1429, 1440, 273 CR 262, 268—motion for *reconsideration* of sanction award constitutes separate discovery abuse; *Cedars-Sinai Med. Ctr. v. Sup.Ct. (Bowyer)* (1998) 18 C4th 1, 12, 74 CR2d 248, 254—destroying evidence in response to, *or in anticipation of*, a discovery request "would surely be a misuse of discovery" within meaning of Discovery Act; *Palm Valley Homeowners Ass'n, Inc. v. Design MTC* (2000) 85 CA4th 553, 563-564, 102 CR2d 350, 357—participating in discovery on behalf of suspended corporation, knowing it is disabled from participating

© 2020 Thomson Reuters/The Rutter Group

in litigation, constitutes abuse of discovery; see also CCP §2023.050 (added eff. 1/1/20) (*discussed at ¶8:1928 ff.*)]

[8:1902] *Reserved.*

b. [8:1903] **Types of sanctions available—in general:** The following *types* of sanctions are authorized for discovery violations:
— monetary sanctions;
— issue sanctions (designating facts as established);
— evidence sanctions (barring introduction of evidence);
— terminating sanctions (striking pleadings, dismissal or default); and
— contempt. [CCP §2023.030]

Compare—costs imposed for unreasonable denial of RFAs: See discussion at ¶8:1404 ff.

(1) [8:1904] **Statutory provisions:** Each discovery method has its own statutory provision authorizing one or more of the types of sanctions:

- Depositions: CCP §2025.410 et seq. (*see ¶8:414 ff.*);
- Interrogatories: CCP §2030.290 et seq. (*see ¶8:898 ff.*);
- Requests for admissions: CCP §2033.280 et seq. (*see ¶8:1254 ff.*);
- Inspection demands: CCP §2031.300 et seq. (*see ¶8:1417 ff.*);
- Physical or mental examinations: CCP §2032.410 et seq. (*see ¶8:1509 ff.*).

[8:1905] *Reserved.*

c. [8:1906] **Enforcement procedures—in general:** Normally, only monetary sanctions can be imposed on a motion to compel absent a prior court order (¶*8:1920 ff.*). However, the full range of discovery sanctions is available where there is a failure to comply with a court order compelling discovery or where such an order would be "futile" (¶*8:1935 ff.*).

[8:1907] *Reserved.*

d. [8:1908] **Sanctions under court's inherent power?** Sanctions based on a court's inherent power to control the litigation before it have been upheld in some circumstances. [*Peat, Marwick, Mitchell & Co. v. Sup.Ct. (People)* (1988) 200 CA3d 272, 291, 245 CR 873, 886—includes *discretion to preclude evidence* in order to prevent disclosure of confidential information and ensure a fair trial; *Stephen Slesinger, Inc. v. Walt Disney Co.* (2007) 155 CA4th 736, 763-764, 66 CR3d 268, 290—includes *discretion to dismiss* action for deliberate and egregious misconduct if no other remedy could ensure a fair trial]

[8:1909] *Reserved.*

e. [8:1910] **No tort remedies for discovery misuse:** Discovery violations are generally *not* punishable by imposing tort liability in a separate lawsuit. [See *Cedars-Sinai Med. Ctr. v. Sup.Ct. (Bowyer)* (1998) 18 C4th 1, 17, 74 CR2d 248, 257-258—no tort remedy for intentional destruction of evidence by a litigating party; see also *Temple Comm. Hosp. v. Sup.Ct. (Ramos)* (1999) 20 C4th 464, 476-478, 84 CR2d 852, 861—no tort remedy for intentional destruction of evidence *by a nonparty* to litigation, even though only limited sanctions are available for misuse of discovery by nonparties]

[8:1911] *Reserved.*

f. [8:1912] **No CCP §§128.5 or 128.7 sanctions for discovery violation:** Sanctions are not awardable under CCP §§128.5 or 128.7 for discovery requests, responses, objections or motions. [CCP §§128.5(e), 128.7(g)]

(1) [8:1913] **Monetary sanctions under CCP §§128.5 and 128.7 compared:** The basic purpose of monetary discovery sanctions is to force parties who act unreasonably in discovery disputes to pay the extra costs incurred by other parties. On the other hand, nondiscovery monetary sanctions under CCP §§128.5 and 128.7 are designed to compensate as well as deter improper behavior. [CCP §§128.5(f)(2), 128.7(d); *see detailed discussion at ¶9:1010 ff.*]

Monetary sanctions under the Discovery Act are also easier to recover; indeed, the prevailing party on a motion to compel is *presumptively entitled* to monetary sanctions (*see ¶8:1960*). No such presumption attaches where sanctions are sought under CCP §§128.5 or 128.7.

[8:1914-1919] *Reserved.*

2. [8:1920] **Sanctions for Failure to Respond or for Inadequate Responses:** Failure to respond to discovery requests, evasive responses, and objections lacking substantial justification are "misuses of the discovery process" (CCP §2023.010(d)-(f); ¶*8:1901*). The propounding party's remedy under most discovery methods is to file a motion to compel and seek monetary sanctions pursuant to the appropriate statutory provision (¶*8:1904*).

a. [8:1921] **Monetary sanctions on motion to compel (no prior order to comply):** If the motion to compel is granted, the court "shall" order the party to whom the discovery was directed to pay the propounding party's reasonable expenses, including attorney fees, in enforcing discovery "unless it finds that the one subject to the sanction acted with substantial justification or that other circumstances make the imposition of the sanction unjust." [CCP §2023.030(a); *see* ¶*8:1964 ff.*]

Conversely, if the motion is denied, the court "shall" order the moving party to pay the responding party's expenses and fees in *resisting* discovery unless it finds the moving party acted with substantial

© 2020 Thomson Reuters/The Rutter Group

justification or circumstances make imposition of the sanction unjust. [CCP §2023.030(a)]

Cross-refer: Generally, terminating ("doomsday") sanctions are not imposed as the first sanction of choice. *See discussion at ¶8:1935 ff., 8:2235 ff.*

[8:1922] *Reserved.*

(1) [8:1923] **Limited to "reasonable expenses":** The court is authorized to award as sanctions the moving party's *reasonable* expenses including attorney fees on the motion to compel. "Reasonable expenses" include the time moving party's counsel spent in research and preparation of the motion and court time in connection with the motion. [See *Ghanooni v. Super Shuttle of Los Angeles* (1993) 20 CA4th 256, 262, 24 CR2d 501, 505]

(a) [8:1924] **Examples:** Expenses that may be awarded to the moving party as sanctions include:

- The cost of reopening a deposition that was improperly suspended. [*Stewart v. Colonial Western Agency, Inc.* (2001) 87 CA4th 1006, 1015, 105 CR2d 115, 121]
- The cost of organizing documents that were not produced as kept in the ordinary course of business or according to the categories in the document demand. [*Kayne v. Grande Holdings Ltd.* (2011) 198 CA4th 1470, 1476, 130 CR3d 751, 755 (decided under prior law)] (Note that documents now are not produced as kept in the ordinary course of business but "shall be identified with the specific request number to which the documents respond" (CCP §2031.280(a) (amended eff. 1/1/20); *see ¶8:1471 ff.*).)
- Attorney fees and costs for forensic computer experts to examine a computer hard drive for deleted files. [*Ellis v. Toshiba America Information Systems, Inc.* (2013) 218 CA4th 853, 866, 160 CR3d 557, 569]

[8:1925-1926] *Reserved.*

(b) [8:1927] **No penalty:** However, the court may *not* impose a fine or penalty for refusal to make discovery. Thus, any award in excess of the moving party's "reasonable expenses" is improper. [*Ghanooni v. Super Shuttle of Los Angeles*, supra, 20 CA4th at 262, 24 CR2d at 505—$1,000 award against P for refusing request to submit to physical examination under Discovery Act was unrelated to D's expenses on motion to compel; *Department of Forestry & Fire Protection v. Howell* (2017) 18 CA5th 154, 194, 226 CR3d 727, 761—court may not award sanctions such as attorney or expert fees not actually caused by misuse of discovery process]

1) [8:1928] **Exception:** Further sanctions of $250 *must* be imposed (unless the court in writing finds the one subject to the sanction acted with substantial justification or that other circumstances make imposition of the sanction unjust) and a report to the State Bar *may* be required:

- for not responding in good faith to a request for production of documents or an inspection demand; or
- if documents were produced within seven days of a hearing on a motion to compel the documents; or
- if there was a failure to confer in good faith to informally resolve the dispute concerning the request. [CCP §2023.050(a)-(c) (all added eff. 1/1/20)]

Self-represented litigants are presumed to act in good faith unless clear and convincing evidence shows the contrary. [CCP §2023.050(e) (added eff. 1/1/20)]

a) [8:1928.1] **Comment:** This provision appears to address, among other things, the practices of (i) initially issuing essentially vacuous responses (e.g., consisting of only objections or meaningless undertakings to comply that promise production to the extent not subject to a lengthy list of objections) with the expectation that future meet and confer will result in meaningful, substantive responses; or (ii) forcing a party to file a motion to compel only to moot the motion with production shortly before the hearing.

(c) [8:1929] **No fees recoverable by self-represented litigant:** Lawyers or other self-represented litigants (appearing on their own behalf) *cannot* recover attorney fees as discovery sanctions. [*Argaman v. Ratan* (1999) 73 CA4th 1173, 1179, 86 CR2d 917, 922-923; *Kravitz v. Sup.Ct. (Milner)* (2001) 91 CA4th 1015, 1021, 111 CR2d 385, 389 (involving inspection demands)]

But such litigants can recover reasonably identifiable *expenses incurred* (e.g., computer-assisted legal research, photocopying, or transportation to and from court) even if those costs would ordinarily be included in the lawyer's hourly rate. [*Kravitz v. Sup.Ct. (Milner)*, supra, 91 CA4th at 1021, 111 CR2d at 389]

[8:1930] *Reserved.*

© 2020 Thomson Reuters/The Rutter Group

(d) [8:1931] **Compare—fees recoverable by lawyer acting *pro bono:*** Lawyers representing clients free of charge may nevertheless obtain discovery sanctions measured by the reasonable value of their services. [*Do v. Sup.Ct. (Nguyen)* (2003) 109 CA4th 1210, 1218, 135 CR2d 855, 861]

[8:1932-1934] *Reserved.*

(2) [8:1935] **Compare—broader sanctions where order to comply "futile":** Although normally only monetary sanctions can be imposed in the absence of a prior court order compelling discovery, broader sanctions may be proper where such an order would be "futile." [*Do It Urself Moving & Storage, Inc. v. Brown, Leifer, Slatkin & Berns* (1992) 7 CA4th 27, 35-36, 9 CR2d 396, 400 (citing text) (superseded by statute on other grounds)]

(a) **Application**

- [8:1936] P obtained a continuance of trial by representing it was "totally unable" to prove its case without auditing D's records, and needed more time to complete the audit, and that D would receive copies. P later reneged, claiming an audit was "impossible." Although there was no prior court order compelling discovery, an *issue sanction* (precluding P from offering accounting evidence) was proper: "[I]t is conceded that plaintiffs are *unable* to provide the promised items of discovery. Under the circumstances . . . a warning to plaintiffs, in the form of a formal order to comply, *would have been futile.*" [*Do It Urself Moving & Storage, Inc. v. Brown, Leifer, Slatkin & Berns*, supra, 7 CA4th at 36, 9 CR2d at 400 (emphasis added)]

- [8:1937] Violation of a prior discovery order was not prerequisite to evidentiary sanctions when the offending party had engaged in a pattern of willful discovery abuse that caused the unavailability of evidence. [*Karlsson v. Ford Motor Co.* (2006) 140 CA4th 1202, 1219, 45 CR3d 265, 278-279 (persistent refusal to produce witnesses for deposition and in document production)]

- [8:1938] Self-represented Attorney threatened opposing counsel with a stun gun and pepper spray at a deposition. Attorney also filed papers that were openly contemptuous of the trial judge. The case was appropriately dismissed without a prior order under the court's inherent authority (¶*8:1908*) since Attorney's conduct "made it impossible to continue with the litigation." [*Crawford v. JPMorgan Chase*

Bank, N.A. (2015) 242 CA4th 1265, 1271, 195 CR3d 868, 873]

[8:1939-1942] *Reserved.*

[8:1943] ***PRACTICE POINTER:*** The court has greater sanctions power during trial when a false or incomplete answer or other discovery abuse is discovered. Because an order to comply is usually futile at that time, the court may order evidence or issue preclusion sanctions (*see* ¶*8:2390*). Therefore, in preparing for trial, review your client's earlier discovery responses carefully. If an error is discovered, *serve an amended response* (¶*8:1118 ff.*) as soon as possible.

[8:1944-1946] *Reserved.*

(3) [8:1947] **Sanctions against party or counsel or both:** Monetary sanctions are authorized against the party, person or attorney who unsuccessfully makes or opposes a motion to compel. [CCP §2023.030(a)]

Monetary sanctions may also be recovered against the party engaging in discovery misconduct "*or* any attorney advising that conduct, *or both.*" [CCP §2023.030(a) (emphasis added)]

[8:1948-1950] *Reserved.*

(4) [8:1951] **Apportionment of sanctions where motion granted only in part:** It often happens that a motion to compel is granted in part and denied in part so that both parties are "unsuccessful" to some extent.

Under such circumstances, the court has discretion to apportion sanctions; or it may award *any* amount "reasonable under the circumstances." [*Mattco Forge, Inc. v. Arthur Young & Co.* (1990) 223 CA3d 1429, 1437, 273 CR 262, 265 (citing text)—where motion was 80% successful, award of 25% of sanctions requested was "both fair and legally correct"]

[8:1952-1954] *Reserved.*

(5) [8:1955] **Limitation—no sanctions ("safe harbor") where ESI lost or destroyed due to good faith use of computer system:** *See* ¶*8:1488.5.*

[8:1956-1959] *Reserved.*

b. [8:1960] **Court's discretion to refuse sanctions limited:** The court "shall" impose a monetary sanction against the losing party or attorney *unless* it finds:

- "The one subject to the sanction acted with *substantial justification*"; or that
- "Other circumstances make the imposition of the sanction *unjust.*" [CCP §2023.030(a) (emphasis added)]

© 2020 Thomson Reuters/The Rutter Group

(1) [8:1961] **Effect—burden on losing party:** *See ¶8:2015 ff.*

[8:1962-1963] *Reserved.*

(2) [8:1964] **"Substantial justification":** To avoid sanctions, the losing party must show "substantial justification" for his or her position—i.e., reasonable grounds to believe an objection was valid or that the answer given was adequate. [See *Foothill Properties v. Lyon/Copley Corona Assocs., L.P.* (1996) 46 CA4th 1542, 1557-1558, 54 CR2d 488, 497-498—refusing to produce documents and opposing motion to compel was "substantially justified" where refusing party's motion for protective order was pending; *Doe v. United States Swimming, Inc.* (2011) 200 CA4th 1424, 1434, 133 CR3d 465, 473—"the phrase 'substantial justification' has been understood to mean that a justification is clearly reasonable because it is well-grounded in both law and fact"; *Diepenbrock v. Brown* (2012) 208 CA4th 743, 747-748, 145 CR3d 659, 662-663 (citing text)—sanctions assessment reversed because conflicting legal authority on unsettled issue (applicability of marital privilege) provided substantial justification for motion; *City of Los Angeles v. Sup.Ct. (Anderson-Barker)* (2017) 9 CA5th 272, 291, 214 CR3d 858, 874 (citing text)—where no prior case addressed whether Civil Discovery Act applied to action brought under Public Records Act, City acted with substantial justification in opposing motion to compel]

(a) [8:1965] **Comment:** Judges are not likely to impose monetary sanctions for discovery disputes on the "cutting edge" of the law where there is room for *legitimate difference of opinion* as to discoverability. I.e., if the point involved would be a close call for the judge to make, the judge is likely to find "substantial justification" for the losing party's position.

[8:1966-1968] *Reserved.*

[8:1969] ***PRACTICE POINTER:*** If the opposing party is seeking sanctions, you should address "substantial justification" in your papers. At the same time, you will want to avoid giving the impression you expect to lose.

[8:1970-1972] *Reserved.*

(3) [8:1973] **Other circumstances making sanctions "unjust":** This language presumably may excuse monetary sanctions where the party to be sanctioned is impoverished and monetary sanctions would cause a hardship disproportionate to the discovery misuse.

[8:1974-1979] *Reserved.*

c. [8:1980] **Procedural matters:** Sanctions for misuse of the discovery process are obtainable only "after notice to any affected party, person or attorney, and after opportunity for hearing." [CCP §2023.030]

A request for sanctions may be included as part of a motion to compel or may be filed separately. It can even be filed after the action has been tried on its merits: "[W]hile it may be advisable that a party place its request for monetary sanctions in its . . . motion to compel further response, there is no legal requirement to do so." [*London v. Dri-Honing Corp.* (2004) 117 CA4th 999, 1008, 12 CR3d 240, 247 (citing text)]

[8:1981] ***PRACTICE POINTER:*** Most lawyers raise the sanctions issue as *part* of a motion to compel (or in opposition to it) because it is the most efficient manner of dealing with the issue. A separate motion will require a second court appearance and involves more paperwork for all.

[8:1982] *Reserved.*

(1) **Notice requirements**

(a) [8:1983] **No ex parte sanctions:** No matter how clear the violation, sanctions cannot be awarded on ex parte application. This is true even if the court has warned the violating party (at some earlier hearing) of the specific consequences if its order is violated. A noticed motion and hearing are still required before sanctions can be awarded. [CCP §2023.030; see *Alliance Bank v. Murray* (1984) 161 CA3d 1, 5-6, 207 CR 233, 236; *Sole Energy Co. v. Hodges* (2005) 128 CA4th 199, 210, 26 CR3d 823, 831]

(b) [8:1984] **Notice of motion must request sanctions:** *See ¶8:2000.*

(c) [8:1985] **Notice to opposing counsel against whom sanctions sought:** Where sanctions are sought against the opposing party's counsel, the notice of motion must *expressly so state*. It is *not* enough simply to attach declarations or a transcript showing that the deponent refused to appear or answer questions on counsel's advice. [See *Blumenthal v. Sup.Ct. (Corey)* (1980) 103 CA3d 317, 320, 163 CR 39, 40; *Marriage of Fuller* (1985) 163 CA3d 1070, 1075-1076, 210 CR 73, 76-77—issue may be raised for first time on appeal because prior notice of imposition of sanctions is mandated by due process]

1) [8:1986] **Example:** Where an award is sought against the attorney for advising the opposing party not to answer or respond, the notice of motion must *identify* the opposing counsel and state that sanctions are being sought against such counsel *personally*. [See *Blumenthal v. Sup.Ct. (Corey)*, supra, 103 CA3d

© 2020 Thomson Reuters/The Rutter Group

at 320, 163 CR at 40 (dealing with failure to appear for deposition)]

[8:1987-1989] *Reserved.*

(d) [8:1990] **How much notice required:** The Discovery Act does not specify any particular notice requirement for imposition of discovery sanctions. Therefore, the notice required is the same as on motions generally (CCP §1005(b), *discussed at ¶9:87 ff.*).

(e) [8:1991] **Sanctions requested in opposition papers:** Monetary sanctions are often requested in *opposition papers* filed before the hearing on a motion to compel.

(Opposition papers must be filed at least *nine court days* before the hearing; see CCP §1005(b), ¶*9:104 ff.*)

[8:1992-1999] *Reserved.*

(2) [8:2000] **Moving papers:** The notice of motion must contain a request for sanctions and must:

- *Name all parties and attorneys* against whom sanctions are being sought;
- Specify the *type* of sanction sought;
- Cite the *authority* for such sanctions; and
- Where *monetary* sanctions are sought, the notice must be accompanied by a declaration "setting forth facts supporting the amount" of the monetary sanction sought. [CCP §2023.040]

FORMS

- Motion for Order Compelling Answers to Deposition Questions and Production of Documents and for Sanctions and Proposed Order, *see Form 8:12* in Rivera, *Cal. Prac. Guide: Civ. Pro. Before Trial FORMS* (TRG).
- Motion to Compel (Further) Answers to Interrogatories and for Sanctions and Proposed Order, *see Form 8:19* in Rivera, *Cal. Prac. Guide: Civ. Pro. Before Trial FORMS* (TRG).
- Motion to Compel (Further) Responses to Demands for Inspection and for Sanctions and Proposed Order, *see Form 8:28* in Rivera, *Cal. Prac. Guide: Civ. Pro. Before Trial FORMS* (TRG).

(a) [8:2001] **Supporting declarations:** To obtain an award of sanctions, factual declarations must show a "reasonable and good faith attempt to resolve informally" whatever issues are raised on the motion to compel. [See, e.g., CCP §2025.480(b); ¶*8:1158 ff.*]

The notice of motion must be accompanied by a declaration setting forth *facts* supporting both the motion to compel and the *amount* of any monetary sanction sought. [See CCP §2023.040]

[8:2002] ***PRACTICE POINTERS:*** As a practical matter, factual declarations are required to support *any* request for sanctions. Do not rely on the court to take judicial notice of an opposing party's failure to make discovery or to comply with earlier court orders.

Make sure your declarations meet *evidentiary* requirements—i.e., no "on information and belief" allegations or conclusions. (See requirements re declarations generally at ¶*9:57 ff.*)

Be sure to set forth the nature of the work done, time expended (including time required to reply to the opposition and estimated time to appear at the motion hearing), and the reasonable hourly rate for the services performed, together with a calculation of the amount sought.

For example, your declaration should state the following:

- you spent 'x' hours preparing a letter and speaking with opposing counsel pursuant to the meet-and-confer requirement;
- during that conversation you told opposing counsel that further responses were necessary because the responses were not complete and straightforward;
- you spent 'y' hours preparing the motion to compel further responses;
- you anticipate spending 'z' hours drafting reply papers and attending the hearing on the motion;
- the hourly rate you regularly charge for such work; and
- the total sanctions requested.

Remember that the court cannot award *more* than you ask for, so don't be shy in your request.

[8:2003-2006] *Reserved.*

(3) [8:2007] **Persons to be served:** The moving papers should show proof of service on *each person* against whom sanctions are being sought—i.e., deponent, party *and/or* attorney. Apparently, represented parties can be served through their counsel. [See CCP §2023.030]

(4) [8:2008] **Sanctions despite no opposition:** Although the statute is silent on the matter, the CRC authorize an award

© 2020 Thomson Reuters/The Rutter Group

of sanctions "even though no opposition to the motion was filed, or opposition . . . was withdrawn, or the requested discovery was provided . . . after the motion was filed." [CRC 3.1348(a)]

Also, where the motion sought production of documents and the documents are produced within seven days of the hearing (perhaps otherwise mooting the motion), sanctions of $250 must be awarded, in addition to whatever other sanctions are awarded, and the lawyer may be ordered to report the sanctions to the State Bar. [CCP §2023.050 (added eff. 1/1/20) (*see ¶8:1928 ff.*)]

(a) [8:2009] **Failure to oppose not a concession:** Failure to file a written opposition or to appear at the hearing, or voluntary provision of the requested discovery, "shall not be deemed an admission that the motion was proper or that sanctions should be awarded." [CRC 3.1348(b)]

[8:2010-2014] *Reserved.*

d. [8:2015] **Burden of proof on motion:** As with any other motion, the burden is on the moving party to show (by declarations) the facts essential to an award of sanctions: e.g., the opposing party's failure to make discovery, reasonable efforts to resolve the matter informally, etc. The burden then shifts to the party against whom sanctions are being sought to establish some excuse or justification for the conduct in question.

(1) [8:2016] **Burden of proof re excuse:** Thus, to avoid sanctions on a motion to compel, the burden is on the *losing party* to prove justification or circumstances that establish sanctions would be unjust. [*Mattco Forge, Inc. v. Arthur Young & Co.* (1990) 223 CA3d 1429, 1441, 273 CR 262, 269—losing party *presumptively* must pay monetary sanction to prevailing party; see Ev.C. §500—"a party has the burden of proof as to each fact the existence or nonexistence of which is essential to the claim for relief or defense that he is asserting"]

(2) [8:2017] **Ethical dilemma where sanctions sought against counsel:** Where sanctions are sought against a party's counsel for discovery misuse by the *party*, the burden is apparently on counsel to prove that the client's conduct was *not* on his or her advice.

For example, if sanctions are sought against both a party *and* counsel for the *party's* failure to attend a deposition or to answer a particular question, to avoid sanctions counsel would have to show he or she did not advise this conduct. *See further discussion at ¶8:2290 ff.*

But this presents an ethical dilemma: advice to the client is protected by the attorney-client privilege and counsel owes a duty of loyalty to the client, so he or she should not do anything to increase the risk of sanctions against the client (*see ¶8:2295*).

[8:2018-2024] *Reserved.*

e. [8:2025] **Findings:** Where monetary sanctions are sought in connection with discovery motions, the court is required to impose such sanctions against the losing party *unless it finds* the losing party acted with "*substantial justification*" or "other circumstances make the imposition of the sanction *unjust*." [CCP §§2023.030(a), 2025.480(j) (emphasis added); *see* ¶*8:1964 ff., 8:2339 ff.*]

Similarly, where a party, person, or attorney violates CCP §2023.050 and the court declines to award the $250 sanction, the court must make written findings that the one subject to the sanction acted with substantial justification or other circumstances make imposition of the sanction unjust. [CCP §2023.050(c) (added eff. 1/1/20)]

[8:2026] ***PRACTICE POINTER:*** If you represent the losing party, be sure to *ask the court* to make such findings. If the motion is being taken under submission for decision, and sanctions are being sought against you or your client, it is a good idea to *submit proposed findings* to the judge (reciting the facts you are relying on to show "substantial justification" for your client's position, etc.).

[8:2027-2029] *Reserved.*

f. [8:2030] **Sanctions on motion for reconsideration:** Additional sanctions are authorized where the losing party seeks reconsideration of a discovery order and loses again. The motion for reconsideration is regarded as simply a continuation of the original opposition. [*Mattco Forge, Inc. v. Arthur Young & Co.* (1990) 223 CA3d 1429, 1437-1438, 273 CR 262, 266]

Effect: Unless the court finds "substantial justification" for the motion to reconsider, additional discovery sanctions are *mandatory*. It need *not* be shown that the motion was sanctionable under CCP §§128.5 (bad faith actions or tactics, ¶*9:1010 ff.*) or 128.7 (certification of merits, ¶*9:1135 ff.*). [*Mattco Forge, Inc. v. Arthur Young & Co.*, supra, 223 CA3d at 1437-1438, 273 CR at 266]

g. [8:2031] **Enforcing sanctions order:** Sanctions orders are enforceable as money judgments unless the court orders otherwise. Thus, the remedy to enforce payment of monetary sanctions is to obtain and levy a writ of execution on assets of the debtor. [*Newland v. Sup.Ct. (Sugasawara)* (1995) 40 CA4th 608, 615, 47 CR2d 24, 28 (citing text)]

[8:2032-2039] *Reserved.*

h. [8:2040] **Appellate court review of sanctions:** Monetary sanctions orders are immediately appealable only if the amount exceeds $5,000. Lesser sanctions orders are appealable only after final judgment in the main action, or if the sanctioned counsel is no longer counsel of record in the action; otherwise, the order is reviewable only by writ. [CCP §904.1(a)(11), (12) & (b); *see further discussion at* ¶*9:1286 ff.*]

(1) [8:2041] **Application to monetary discovery sanctions:** The weight of authority applies the CCP §904.1 appealability rules to monetary discovery sanctions orders—i.e., immediately appealable only if the discovery sanctions exceed $5,000. [*Rail-Transport Employees Ass'n v. Union Pac. Motor Freight* (1996) 46 CA4th 469, 475, 54 CR2d 713, 716-717]

Indeed, appellate courts now reviewing monetary discovery sanction orders have apparently assumed their appealability under CCP §904.1(a)(11), (12) (directly appealable if exceeding $5,000) without discussion. [See *Doe v. United States Swimming, Inc.* (2011) 200 CA4th 1424, 1432, 133 CR3d 465, 472; *Tucker v. Pacific Bell Mobile Services* (2010) 186 CA4th 1548, 1560, 115 CR3d 9, 17-18; *Van v. Language Line Services, Inc.* (2017) 8 CA5th 73, 79, 213 CR3d 822, 827]

[8:2042-2044] *Reserved.*

(2) [8:2045] **Compare—sanctions against nonparty witness:** Where a nonparty is authorized to bring a discovery motion and is sanctioned upon its denial, an immediate appeal lies. The sanctions order is clearly collateral to the underlying litigation. [*Brun v. Bailey* (1994) 27 CA4th 641, 648-649, 32 CR2d 624, 628 (superseded by statute on other grounds)—sanctions upheld against nonparty chiropractor who unsuccessfully sought protective order to require defendant to pay expert witness fee for deposition]

Cross-refer: For a detailed treatment of the appealability of discovery sanctions orders, see Eisenberg, *Cal. Prac. Guide: Civil Appeals & Writs* (TRG), Ch. 2.

[8:2046-2069] *Reserved.*

3. [8:2070] **Sanctions in Connection With Motion for Protective Order:** The court "shall" impose a monetary sanction against whichever party loses on the motion for protective order *unless* it finds that party acted "with substantial justification" or other circumstances make the sanction "unjust." [CCP §2025.420(h)] (Monetary sanctions are discussed in greater detail at ¶*8:1921 ff.*)

a. [8:2071] **"Good faith" not itself an excuse:** A party moving unsuccessfully for a protective order is not immune from sanctions simply because he or she was acting in "good faith." The court has discretion to award sanctions to compensate other parties for their expense in opposing the motion. [See *Flynn v. Sup.Ct. (Molini)* (1979) 89 CA3d 491, 497, 152 CR 796, 800—compensation both for expenses in obtaining order shortening time and in seeking own protective order in response to motion]

b. [8:2072] **Sanctions against nonparty:** CCP §2025.420(h) applies to "any person," whether a party or not, who moves unsuccessfully for a protective order. Thus, a nonparty who is denied a protective order is subject to sanctions. [*Brun v. Bailey*, supra,

27 CA4th at 658-659, 32 CR2d at 634 (nonparty chiropractor who had treated P)]

[8:2073-2099] *Reserved.*

4. [8:2100] **Sanctions for Failure to Make Reasonable Attempt to Resolve Informally:** Failing to make a "reasonable and good faith attempt" to resolve the issues informally (*see ¶8:1158 ff.*) before a motion to compel is filed constitutes a "misuse of the discovery process." Monetary sanctions can be imposed against whichever party is guilty of such conduct, *even if that party wins the motion to compel.* [CCP §§2023.010(i), 2023.020; see CCP §2023.050 (added eff. 1/1/20)—additional sanction of $250 and lawyer may be ordered to report sanction to State Bar for failure to confer in good faith (*discussed at ¶8:1928 ff.*)]

   a. [8:2101] **Denial of discovery?** Courts differ on whether discovery should be denied for lack of "reasonable" and "good faith" efforts at informal resolution.

   Some courts automatically deny discovery, reasoning that any other order would be "in excess of the trial court's jurisdiction." [*Townsend v. Sup.Ct. (EMC Mortg. Co.)* (1998) 61 CA4th 1431, 1439, 72 CR2d 333, 337]

   Other courts are more flexible, and may specify additional efforts at informal resolution before turning to the merits of the discovery dispute, depending on the circumstances of the case. [*Obregon v. Sup.Ct. (Cimm's, Inc.)* (1998) 67 CA4th 424, 434-435, 79 CR2d 62, 69]

      (1) [8:2102] **Compare—egregious cases:** Even under the latter approach, the requested discovery may be denied outright in "cases of clear intent to burden or harass, cases of clear flaunting of statutory responsibilities, cases of established track records of lack of good faith, and the like." [*Obregon v. Sup.Ct. (Cimm's, Inc.)*, supra, 67 CA4th at 433-434, 79 CR2d at 68]

      [8:2103-2108] *Reserved.*

   b. [8:2109] **Monetary sanction to opposing party:** The party who fails to make a "reasonable and good faith attempt" can be ordered to pay the reasonable expenses, including attorney fees, incurred by the other party on the motion to compel. [CCP §§2023.010(i), 2023.020; see *Obregon v. Sup.Ct. (Cimm's, Inc.)*, supra, 67 CA4th at 435, 79 CR2d at 69; *and further discussion at ¶8:1921 ff.*]

   c. [8:2110] **Against whom sanctions imposed:** Sanctions may be imposed against "anyone" who engaged in such conduct—including the parties, their counsel, or both. [CCP §2023.030]

      (1) [8:2111] **Both counsel:** In a proper case, monetary sanctions may even be imposed against *both counsel* at the same time. [*Volkswagenwerk Aktiengesellschaft v. Sup.Ct. (Golsch)* (1981) 122 CA3d 326, 331-334, 175 CR 888, 891-893]

© 2020 Thomson Reuters/The Rutter Group

- [8:2112] Because of personal dislike for each other, both counsel failed to make any real effort to negotiate the disputed issues. The court could have *refused* to rule on the motion to compel because of moving party's failure to meet and confer; but in order to resolve the matter, it heard the motion, found *both* lawyers to have violated the requirement, and ordered *each* to pay $150 out of his own pocket *to the other lawyer's client*. [*Volkswagenwerk Aktiengesellschaft v. Sup.Ct. (Golsch)*, supra, 122 CA3d at 331-334, 175 CR at 891-893]

  [8:2113-2117] *Reserved.*

d. [8:2118] **Compare—no dismissal sanction:** Only *monetary* sanctions are authorized for failure to meet and confer. The court has no power to dismiss the action, even if a court order to meet and confer has been disobeyed. [*McElhaney v. Cessna Aircraft Co.* (1982) 134 CA3d 285, 288-289, 184 CR 547, 549-550]

[8:2119-2144] *Reserved.*

5. [8:2145] **Sanctions for Failure to Obey Court Order:** Once a party or witness has been *ordered* to attend a deposition, or to answer discovery, or to produce documents, more severe sanctions are available for continued refusal to make discovery. [See, e.g., CCP §§2030.290(c) (motion to compel answers), 2030.300(e) (motion to compel further answers)]

a. [8:2146] **"Disobedience" vs. "failure to obey":** Willful "disobedience" must be shown to establish contempt (¶*8:2440*). But for purposes other than contempt, "disobedience" does *not* require a showing of willfulness. Failure to obey (i.e., noncompliance with the court's order) is all that need be shown. [See *Puritan Ins. Co. v. Sup.Ct. (Tri-C Machine Corp.)* (1985) 171 CA3d 877, 884, 217 CR 602, 606 (interpreting former statute dealing with "refusal" to comply); *Societe Internationale Pour Participations Industrielles Et Commerciales, S.A. v. Rogers* (1958) 357 US 197, 208, 78 S.Ct. 1087, 1094 (interpreting Federal Rule 37)]

CCP §2023.010(g) makes "*disobeying* a court order to provide discovery" a "misuse of the discovery process." But sanctions are authorized only to the extent provided by the particular discovery procedure statute (*see* ¶*8:1904*), each of which refers to the "failure to obey" language.

(1) [8:2147] **Willfulness required for severe sanctions:** However, numerous cases hold that severe sanctions (i.e., evidence or terminating sanctions) for failure to comply with a court order are allowed only where the failure was willful. [See *R.S. Creative, Inc. v. Creative Cotton, Ltd.* (1999) 75 CA4th 486, 495, 89 CR2d 353, 360; *Vallbona v. Springer* (1996) 43 CA4th 1525, 1545, 51 CR2d 311, 324; *Biles v. Exxon Mobil Corp.* (2004) 124 CA4th 1315, 1327, 22 CR3d 282, 290]

[8:2148-2149] *Reserved.*

(2) [8:2150] **Erroneous order no excuse:** If a discovery order is erroneous, appellate court review (by appeal or writ petition) should be timely sought (see CCP §904.1(a)(11), (12) & (b), *and* ¶*8:2040 ff.*). Otherwise, the error does not excuse a failure to obey; i.e., disobedient parties may *not* avoid sanctions by challenging the validity of the order. [*Marriage of Niklas* (1989) 211 CA3d 28, 34-35, 258 CR 921, 924-925]

(a) [8:2151] **Compare—"jurisdictional" challenges:** However, a party may refuse to comply with a court order and raise as a defense to imposition of sanctions that the order was *unconstitutional* or otherwise beyond the court's "jurisdiction." (E.g., orders violating privilege against self-incrimination.) [See *Marriage of Niklas*, supra, 211 CA3d at 35-36, 258 CR at 925-926—orders violating attorney-client privilege and work product protection held *not* in excess of court's jurisdiction]

[8:2152] ***PRACTICE POINTER:*** The preferred route is to ask the court for a short stay to allow you to seek a writ and a stay pending resolution by the court of appeal.

(b) [8:2153] **Compare—review on appeal from judgment:** In any case, the aggrieved party may obtain review of the discovery order and sanctions imposed on appeal from the final judgment in the case. [See *Marriage of Niklas*, supra, 211 CA3d at 36, 258 CR at 926, fn. 4]

[8:2154-2174] *Reserved.*

b. [8:2175] **Sanctions available:** If a party fails to obey a discovery order, the court may impose whatever sanctions are just, including:

- Issue sanction (¶*8:2177*);
- Evidence sanction (¶*8:2181*);
- Terminating ("doomsday") sanction (¶*8:2185*);
- Contempt sanction (¶*8:2440*); and
- Money sanctions—in addition to or in lieu of any other sanction (¶*8:2194*).

[8:2176] *Reserved.*

(1) [8:2177] **Issue sanction:** The court may order that designated facts "*shall be taken as established*" by the party adversely affected by the discovery misuse; or it may *prohibit* the party who committed such misuse from supporting or opposing designated claims or defenses. [CCP §2023.030(b)]

Thus, for example, where a party fails to obey an order to answer deposition questions, the court may order the deposing party's claims or defenses established *without further proof;* or may prohibit the deponent from introducing any evidence

© 2020 Thomson Reuters/The Rutter Group

to the contrary. [See *Juarez v. Boy Scouts of America, Inc.* (2000) 81 CA4th 377, 387, 97 CR2d 12, 19—certain issues held established because of P's failure to answer interrogatories regarding evidence supporting claims pertaining to these issues; *NewLife Sciences v. Weinstock* (2011) 197 CA4th 676, 687, 128 CR3d 538, 547—trial court was entitled to rely on issue sanctions establishing that D breached his employment contract and noncompete clause as basis for issuing preliminary injunction, and D was precluded from presenting contrary evidence]

[8:2178-2180] *Reserved.*

(2) [8:2181] **Evidence sanction:** The court may also *prohibit* the party (or party-affiliated witness) who disobeyed the court order from introducing designated matters in evidence. [CCP §2023.030(c); *Waicis v. Sup.Ct. (Schwartz)* (1990) 226 CA3d 283, 287, 276 CR 45, 48 (citing text)—no abuse of discretion to bar expert's testimony at trial where expert was repeatedly uncooperative in scheduling his deposition and walked out before it was over to attend "personal meeting"; *Deeter v. Angus* (1986) 179 CA3d 241, 255, 224 CR 801, 808—exclusion of audio tape not produced in response to discovery requests; *Vallbona v. Springer* (1996) 43 CA4th 1525, 1547-1548, 51 CR2d 311, 326—exclusion of records offering party claimed he was unable to produce for discovery because they had been stolen]

Cross-refer: Exclusion of evidence as a sanction for false discovery answers is discussed at *¶8:2390 ff.*

[8:2182-2184] *Reserved.*

(3) [8:2185] **Terminating ("doomsday") sanction:** The court may make any of the following orders against the party disobeying the discovery order:

- *Striking* that party's pleadings or parts thereof;
- *Staying* further proceedings by that party until the order is obeyed;
- *Dismissing* that party's action, or any part thereof; or
- Entering *default judgment* against that party. [CCP §2023.030(d); see *Los Defensores, Inc. v. Gomez* (2014) 223 CA4th 377, 390-392, 166 CR3d 899, 910-912—entry of default as terminating sanction justified based on party's willful failure to comply with order compelling production of documents identified at deposition; *J.W. v. Watchtower Bible & Tract Soc. of New York, Inc.* (2018) 29 CA5th 1142, 1170-1171, 241 CR3d 62, 84—terminating sanctions warranted where court gave D notice it would likely grant terminating sanctions after 4-day period if D did not start producing documents and despite warning,

D did not comply with nearly year-old discovery order so "it was reasonable to conclude that lesser sanctions would be ineffective" in motivating D to comply]

(a) [8:2186] **Limitation on terminating sanctions in personal injury and wrongful death actions:** A separate statement of damages claimed by plaintiff in personal injury and wrongful death actions must be served on defendant *before entry of default*, including where defendant's answer is stricken as a discovery sanction. [CCP §425.11; *Morgan v. Southern Calif. Rapid Transit Dist.* (1987) 192 CA3d 976, 985, 237 CR 756, 762 (disapproved on other grounds by *Schwab v. Rondel Homes, Inc.* (1991) 53 C3d 428, 434, 280 CR 83, 86); *Van Sickle v. Gilbert* (2011) 196 CA4th 1495, 1521, 127 CR3d 542, 561; *see* ¶*5:82 ff.*]

However, the remedy for failure to serve the CCP §425.11 statement is to set aside the default; the court is *not* required to reinstate defendant's answer that was stricken as a terminating sanction. [*Department of Fair Employment & Housing v. Ottovich* (2014) 227 CA4th 706, 712, 173 CR3d 881, 885-886]

⇨ [8:2187] ***PRACTICE POINTER:*** If you represent plaintiff, make sure to serve a CCP §425.11 statement *before* seeking "doomsday" sanctions against defendant. Otherwise, the court cannot grant a default sanction.

Apparently, the CCP §425.11 statement can be served on defendant's attorney of record in such a case; i.e., there is no need to serve defendant individually as there is where the default is for failure to appear in the action.

1) [8:2188] **Compare—attorney fees awarded in connection with default terminating sanction:** Prevailing party attorney fees awarded pursuant to contract or statute are not "damages" and thus may be awarded by default judgment entered as a discovery sanction even though the amount of fees is not specified in the complaint (or a statement of damages). [*Simke, Chodos, Silberfeld & Anteau, Inc. v. Athans* (2011) 195 CA4th 1275, 1285, 1290, 128 CR3d 95, 101, 106; *see also* ¶*5:241.10*]

(b) [8:2189] **No punitive damages by default absent service of CCP §425.115 statement:** Similarly, because no complaint for punitive damages may state the amount of punitive damages sought (Civ.C. §3295(e), ¶*6:175 ff.*), punitive damages cannot be awarded by default unless defendant was first served with the notice of damages prescribed by CCP §425.115 within a reasonable period

© 2020 Thomson Reuters/The Rutter Group

of time before default was taken. [CCP §425.115(b); see *Electronic Funds Solutions, LLC v. Murphy* (2005) 134 CA4th 1161, 1178, 36 CR3d 663, 674-675—§425.115 statement served *concurrently* with motion for terminating sanctions provided sufficient notice; compare *Behm v. Clear View Technologies* (2015) 241 CA4th 1, 11-13, 193 CR3d 486, 493-495—§425.115 statement filed *after* court granted motion for terminating sanctions was untimely; *and discussion at ¶5:102 ff.*]

[8:2190-2193] *Reserved.*

(4) [8:2194] **Monetary sanction:** In addition to or in lieu of any other sanction, the court may order the disobedient party or counsel responsible or both to pay the reasonable expenses, including attorney fees, incurred as a result of the failure to obey (including fees on the sanctions motion). [CCP §2023.030(a); see *Marriage of Niklas* (1989) 211 CA3d 28, 37-38, 258 CR 921, 927—declarations did not show fees were for services related to opposing party's failure to comply with prior orders]

(a) [8:2195] **Additional money sanction to court:** In addition to the foregoing discovery sanctions, a court may impose a sanction of up to $1,500 payable to the court for violation of an order "without good cause or substantial justification." [CCP §177.5; see *Caldwell v. Samuels Jewelers* (1990) 222 CA3d 970, 978-979, 272 CR 126, 131; *People v. Hooper* (2019) 40 CA5th 685, 688, 692-694, 253 CR3d 369, 375, 377-379—sanctions of $1,500 for violation of court order as to each of 11 defendants (for total of $16,500)]

[8:2196-2199] *Reserved.*

c. [8:2200] **Court's discretion re sanctions for failure to obey:** The court "may make those orders that are just" if a party fails to obey prior orders. [See, e.g., CCP §§2030.290(c) (motion to compel answers), 2030.300(e) (motion to compel *further* answers)]

Thus, which of the various sanctions discussed above (¶*8:2175 ff.*) may be granted for disobedience to court orders (indeed, whether sanctions will be granted at all), lies entirely within the court's sound discretion. I.e., the court is *not* required to grant any particular sanction or any sanctions at all. [See *Pember v. Sup.Ct. (Young)* (1967) 66 C2d 601, 604, 58 CR 567, 569; *Sauer v. Sup.Ct. (Oak Indus., Inc.)* (1987) 195 CA3d 213, 228, 240 CR 489, 498—trial court's choice of sanctions subject to appellate review only for abuse of discretion]

In extreme situations, however, it may be an abuse of discretion *not* to impose terminating sanctions. [*Doppes v. Bentley Motors, Inc.* (2009) 174 CA4th 967, 996, 94 CR3d 802, 826—abuse of discretion to *deny* terminating sanctions for *serious discovery abuse* (at time of trial, D had still not complied with four prior discovery orders); *Crawford v. JPMorgan Chase Bank, N.A.* (2015) 242 CA4th 1265, 1271, 195 CR3d 868, 873]

(1) [8:2201] **Compare—monetary sanctions for failure to respond:** Where sanctions are sought for the initial failure to respond to discovery or insufficient responses to discovery, only monetary sanctions are authorized. [See *New Albertsons, Inc. v. Sup.Ct. (Shanahan)* (2008) 168 CA4th 1403, 1427-1428, 86 CR3d 457, 476—evidence or issue sanctions improper absent prior order compelling response]

[8:2202-2204] *Reserved.*

(2) [8:2205] **Relevant factors:** The following factors may be relevant in deciding whether and which sanctions to impose for disobedience to discovery orders (*Deyo v. Kilbourne* (1978) 84 CA3d 771, 796, 149 CR 499, 518):

- The time that has elapsed since the discovery was served;
- Whether the party received extensions of time to answer or respond;
- The number of discovery requests and the burden of replying;
- The *importance* of the information sought;
- Whether the answering party acted in good faith and with reasonable diligence—i.e., whether he or she was *aware* of the duty to furnish the requested information and had the *ability* to do so;
- Whether the answers supplied were evasive or incomplete;
- The number of questions remaining unanswered;
- Whether the unanswered questions sought information that was difficult to obtain;
- The existence of prior court orders compelling discovery and the answering party's compliance with them (see *Manzetti v. Sup.Ct. (Fitzgerald)* (1993) 21 CA4th 373, 379, 25 CR2d 857, 861);
- Whether the party was unable to comply with previous orders re discovery;
- Whether an order allowing more time to respond would enable the responding party to supply the necessary information; and
- Whether some sanction short of dismissal or default would be appropriate to the dereliction. [*Deyo v. Kilbourne*, supra, 84 CA3d at 796, 149 CR at 518]

(a) [8:2206] **Whether prior misconduct punished:** Where a party or attorney engages in continuing tactics to prevent legitimate discovery, past conduct that has *not* been punished *can contribute* to a later award of sanctions based upon a more extensive course of conduct. [*Liberty Mut. Fire Ins. Co. v. LcL Administrators, Inc.* (2008) 163 CA4th 1093, 1106, 78 CR3d 200, 209—sanctioned party's history as repeat offender "is not only relevant, but also significant, in deciding whether to impose terminating sanctions"; *Siry Investment, L.P. v. Farkhondehpour* (2020) 45 CA5th 1098, 1118, 259 CR3d 466, 481—terminating sanctions upheld based in part on party's "fulsome history of discovery abuse," including ignoring discovery demands, flouting court orders to provide discovery without objection, making multiple requests for clarification/reconsideration, and burying other party and court with "document dump[s]" (brackets in original)]

On the other hand, past conduct that has already been considered by the court in a sanctions context cannot be the basis for additional sanctions. [See *Andrus v. Estrada* (1995) 39 CA4th 1030, 1043, 46 CR2d 300, 307-308; *and ¶8:2281 ff.*]

[8:2207-2211] *Reserved.*

d. [8:2212] **Policies affecting choice of sanctions:** The court's decision on sanctions must be consistent with the following public policies regarding discovery sanctions:

(1) [8:2213] **Furthering discovery:** Sanctions are imposed in discovery cases to further one or more of the following purposes:

(a) [8:2214] **Compel disclosure:** The main purpose is to enable the interrogating party to *obtain* the information sought rather than simply to punish a disobedient party or lawyer. It is an *abuse* of discretion to impose sanctions *solely* for punishment purposes. [*Ghanooni v. Super Shuttle of Los Angeles* (1993) 20 CA4th 256, 262, 24 CR2d 501, 505]

(b) [8:2215] **Compensate for costs of enforcement:** A secondary purpose is to *compensate* the interrogating party for costs and fees incurred in enforcing discovery. [*Deyo v. Kilbourne*, supra, 84 CA3d at 796, 149 CR at 518]

(c) [8:2216] **No "windfall":** But this *does not justify a windfall* to the interrogating party. I.e., the choice of sanctions should not give that party more than would have been obtained if the interrogatories had been answered. [*Caryl Richards, Inc. v. Sup.Ct. (Klug)* (1961) 188 CA2d 300, 303, 10 CR 377, 379—striking party's pleadings because of evasive interrogatory answers is excessive (order establishing facts in question against party would accomplish purposes of discovery); *Rutledge v. Hewlett-Packard Co.* (2015) 238 CA4th 1164, 1194, 190 CR3d 411, 436—sanctions requested ("sweeping evidentiary conclusions") would have improperly provided windfall by relieving party of burden to prove theory of liability]

1) [8:2217] **Application:** Motorist injured in highway accident sought documents from defendant State that might establish State's knowledge of dangerous condition. Despite a court order and a $40,000 sanction award, State still refused to produce the documents. The court could properly decline to impose a terminating sanction and select instead an issue sanction that deemed established the State's knowledge of the dangerous condition. [*Kuhns v. State of Calif.* (1992) 8 CA4th 982, 988, 10 CR2d 773, 776]

[8:2218-2219] *Reserved.*

2) [8:2220] **Even inadvertent destruction:** Where the responding party inadvertently loses or destroys material evidence, sanctions may be imposed to "even up" the score but not to put the demanding party in a better position than if the evidence had been produced. *See discussion at ¶8:1501 ff.*

[8:2221-2225] *Reserved.*

(2) [8:2226] **Jailing rarely appropriate:** Although the Discovery Act authorizes the contempt sanction to enforce its discovery orders (*see ¶8:2440*), alternative sanctions should be used wherever possible: "Imposition of a jail sentence to enforce civil discovery against a party to the lawsuit strikes us as unnecessary and overbearing. Use of this most extreme sanction *should be reserved for situations where the court's dignity is truly compromised* and no other suitable penalty can be found." [*In re de la Parra* (1986) 184 CA3d 139, 145, 228 CR 864, 867 (emphasis added)]

Extreme discovery abuse can usually be dealt with by other remedies including "doomsday" sanctions. *See ¶8:2235 ff., 8:2275.*

[8:2227-2228] *Reserved.*

(3) [8:2229] **No forced waiver of privilege:** Where a party fails to obey an order compelling discovery, the court makes those orders that are just, including issue, evidence or terminating sanctions. But the court has no authority to find a waiver of privilege as a sanction for failing to make discovery. [*Best Products, Inc. v. Sup.Ct. (Granatelli Motorsports, Inc.)* (2004) 119 CA4th 1181, 1190, 15 CR3d 154, 161; see *Catalina Island Yacht Club v. Sup.Ct. (Beatty)* (2015) 242 CA4th 1116, 1129,

© 2020 Thomson Reuters/The Rutter Group

195 CR3d 694, 703—no waiver of privilege due to generic or boilerplate objections]

(a) [8:2230] **Includes deficient "privilege log":** Nor may a court find a waiver of a claimed privilege as a sanction for a party's production of a deficient privilege log (*see* ¶*8:1498.6*). The proper remedy in such cases is a motion to compel further response to the production demand (CCP §2031.320); and the trial court retains discretion to impose other sanctions. [*People ex. rel. Lockyer v. Sup.Ct. (Cole Nat'l Corp.)* (2004) 122 CA4th 1060, 1074-1075, 19 CR3d 324, 334-335; *Catalina Island Yacht Club v. Sup.Ct. (Beatty)*, supra, 242 CA4th at 1127, 195 CR3d at 702]

[8:2231-2234] *Reserved.*

(4) [8:2235] **Lesser sanctions first:** Before imposing a "terminating" sanction, courts should usually grant lesser sanctions: e.g., orders *staying* the action until plaintiff complies, or orders declaring matters as *admitted* or *established* if answers are not received by a specified date, often accompanied with costs and fees to the moving party. It is only when a party *persists* in disobeying the court's orders that the ultimate ("doomsday") sanctions of dismissing the action or entering default judgment, etc. are justified. [*Deyo v. Kilbourne* (1978) 84 CA3d 771, 796, 149 CR 499, 518; *Lopez v. Watchtower Bible & Tract Soc. of New York, Inc.* (2016) 246 CA4th 566, 604, 201 CR3d 156, 187—discovery statutes evince an incremental approach, *starting* with monetary sanctions and *ending* with ultimate terminating sanction; *Siry Investment, L.P. v. Farkhondehpour* (2020) 45 CA5th 1098, 1117, 259 CR3d 466, 480]

- [8:2235.1] **Example:** Terminating sanctions based on willful failure to obey court orders to produce documents and a witness for deposition were reversed where there was no showing the court could not have obtained compliance by using lesser sanctions or imposing other sanctions (e.g., issue or evidentiary). [*Lopez v. Watchtower Bible & Tract Soc. of New York, Inc.*, supra, 246 CA4th at 605, 201 CR3d at 188]

(a) [8:2236] **Compare—circumstances justifying "doomsday" sanction as first sanction:** The "lesser sanctions first" policy is not an inflexible rule of law. It is therefore not an abuse of discretion to dismiss for continuing willful discovery violations *even if no monetary or other sanctions* were first imposed. [*Laguna Auto Body v. Farmers Ins. Exchange* (1991) 231 CA3d 481, 490-491, 282 CR 530, 537 (disapproved on other grounds by *Garcia v. McCutchen* (1997) 16 C4th 469, 478, 66 CR2d 319, 326, fn. 4); *R.S. Creative, Inc. v. Creative Cotton, Ltd.*

(1999) 75 CA4th 486, 497, 89 CR2d 353, 361; *New Albertsons, Inc. v. Sup.Ct. (Shanahan)* (2008) 168 CA4th 1403, 1434, 86 CR3d 457, 481—terminating sanction appropriate in first instance "in egregious cases of intentional spoliation of evidence"]

Moreover, the "lesser sanctions first" policy may not apply where it would permit a party to *benefit* from its own stalling tactics. [See *Do It Urself Moving & Storage, Inc. v. Brown, Leifer, Slatkin & Berns* (1992) 7 CA4th 27, 37, 9 CR2d 396, 401 (superseded by statute on other grounds); see also *Collisson & Kaplan v. Hartunian* (1994) 21 CA4th 1611, 1618-1619, 26 CR2d 786, 790-791—attempt to derail trial setting of case through evasive responses to RFAs (*discussed at ¶8:1402 ff.*); *Karlsson v. Ford Motor Co.* (2006) 140 CA4th 1202, 1219, 45 CR3d 265, 278-279 (*discussed at ¶8:1937*)]

1) **Application**

- [8:2237] After a motion to compel discovery and a *stipulated* court order, P answered 27 out of 32 interrogatories and RFAs. P failed to cooperate with D in answering the remaining five questions. D noticed another motion to compel. P did not appear. Dismissal was not an abuse of discretion despite the fact *no earlier sanctions* (not even monetary) had been imposed. [*Laguna Auto Body v. Farmers Ins. Exchange*, supra, 231 CA3d at 490-491, 282 CR at 537]

  Comment: This result seems more *punitive* than an attempt to compel disclosure. As noted in the *Laguna Auto Body* dissenting opinion, issue preclusion and/or monetary sanctions would seem to be more appropriate *first sanctions.*

- [8:2238] Striking ex-Husband's response to ex-Wife's petition for marriage dissolution (and entering default judgment against him) was not an excessive sanction where ex-Husband persisted for over two and a half years in refusing to produce court-ordered documents, which interfered with the court's ability to dispose of marital property and caused the unavailability of material evidence. [*Marriage of Eustice* (2015) 242 CA4th 1291, 1309, 195 CR3d 876, 889]

- [8:2239] The trial court did not abuse its discretion in issuing a terminating sanction where plaintiff failed to comply with discovery production orders, repeatedly presented false, misleading or evasive discovery responses, committed spoliation, presented false or evasive deposition testimony,

© 2020 Thomson Reuters/The Rutter Group

and misled the trial court. [*Department of Forestry & Fire Protection v. Howell* (2017) 18 CA5th 154, 191-193, 197-198, 226 CR3d 727, 758-760, 763-764—trial court may impose terminating sanctions "as a first measure in extreme cases, or where the record shows lesser sanctions would be ineffective"]

- [8:2240] Terminating sanctions were appropriate based on a party's "fulsome history of discovery abuse," including ignoring discovery demands, flouting court orders to provide discovery without objection, making multiple requests for clarification/reconsideration, burying the other party and the court with "document dump[s]," making "feckless, last-minute offers to rummage through their files for responsive documents," deliberately calculating the risk of terminating sanctions against the party's exposure in the case, and running out the clock on discovery. [*Siry Investment, L.P. v. Farkhondehpour* (2020) 45 CA5th 1098, 1118-1119, 259 CR3d 466, 481 (brackets in original)]

[8:2241-2243] *Reserved.*

(b) [8:2244] **No conditional or ex parte dismissals:** It *may* be permissible for a court to invoke lesser sanctions automatically if its orders are disregarded—e.g., an order that certain facts stand admitted unless the discovery sought is provided by a certain date (¶*8:2235*). But the ultimate sanction of dismissing the lawsuit or entering a default judgment *cannot* be ordered automatically for failure to comply by a given date. Rather, there must be a separate motion filed to determine the willfulness of the failure to comply with the earlier order. [*Duggan v. Moss* (1979) 98 CA3d 735, 741, 159 CR 425, 429]

[8:2245-2246] *Reserved.*

(5) [8:2247] **"Sins" of attorney chargeable to client:** A number of cases have upheld dismissal or other "doomsday" sanctions against a client based solely on the attorney's errors or misconduct. The client's remedy is said to be against the attorney for malpractice. [*Bernstein v. Allstate Ins. Co.* (1981) 119 CA3d 449, 451, 173 CR 841, 842; see *Carroll v. Abbott Laboratories, Inc.* (1982) 32 C3d 892, 899, 187 CR 592, 595]

(a) [8:2248] **Application:** Dismissal has been upheld because of P's attorney's *continuing willful refusal* to cooperate in discovery: "[A]ttorneys who fail to extend common courtesies to their opposition, who fail to voluntarily comply with proper discovery requests and instead obstruct discovery, who fail to file, where appropriate, written opposition to motion to compel discovery, . . .

must be sanctioned appropriately." Dismissal of the client's case was not an abuse of discretion (even though no monetary or other sanction was imposed against the attorney). [*Laguna Auto Body v. Farmers Ins. Exchange* (1991) 231 CA3d 481, 487, 282 CR 530, 534-535 (emphasis added) (disapproved on other grounds by *Garcia v. McCutchen* (1997) 16 C4th 469, 478, 66 CR2d 319, 326, fn. 4)]

[8:2249-2251] *Reserved.*

(b) [8:2252] **Limitation—"positive misconduct" by attorney:** However, the client cannot be penalized where the attorney's conduct is so extreme (more than gross negligence) that it effectively *terminates* the attorney-client relationship. (Example: Attorney abandons client's case, leaving interrogatories unanswered.) Under such circumstances, if a default or dismissal was ordered against the client, the client would be entitled to relief under CCP §473(b). [See *Carroll v. Abbott Laboratories, Inc.*, supra, 32 C3d at 899, 187 CR at 595]

- [8:2253] An attorney's willful failure to comply with the court's discovery orders does *not* fall within the "positive misconduct" exception. [*Sauer v. Sup.Ct. (Oak Indus., Inc.)* (1987) 195 CA3d 213, 231, 240 CR 489, 500—client was not "effectually and unknowingly deprived of representation"]

[8:2254-2256] *Reserved.*

(c) [8:2257] **Limitation—attorney's failure to pay monetary sanctions not ground for dismissing client's case:** Likewise, "doomsday" sanctions cannot properly be imposed against the client because of counsel's noncompliance with an order imposing monetary sanctions. [*Jones v. Otero* (1984) 156 CA3d 754, 759, 203 CR 90, 93]

[8:2258-2260] *Reserved.*

(6) [8:2261] **Policy against excessive sanctions:** While each case is to be decided on its own merits, the sanctions imposed must not go beyond those necessary to further the purposes of discovery—i.e., to compel disclosure and to compensate for costs incurred in enforcing discovery. [See *Reedy v. Bussell* (2007) 148 CA4th 1272, 1293, 56 CR3d 216, 232]

(a) **Application—sanction deemed excessive**

1) [8:2262] **Default as sanction for failure to verify responses:** D's failure to verify responses to requests for admission as required by local rule did not justify the court's ordering the requests "deemed admitted" by default. The order was an abuse of discretion, since there was *no prejudice* to the opposing party who was on notice that D intended to deny the

© 2020 Thomson Reuters/The Rutter Group

requests. [*Cohen v. Sup.Ct. (Gonzalez)* (1976) 63 CA3d 184, 186-187, 133 CR 575, 577]

2) [8:2263] **Default as sanction for failure to attend depo or answer interrogatories:** Striking D's answer and entering his or her default may be excessive punishment for failure to appear for deposition or to answer interrogatories in an auto accident case, at least where (i) D's whereabouts were *unknown to his attorney;* and (ii) *lesser sanctions were available* (D's attorney had offered to stipulate to D's liability and to limit trial to the issue of P's damages, which would have made the deposition and interrogatory answers superfluous). [*Thomas v. Luong* (1986) 187 CA3d 76, 81-82, 231 CR 631, 634-635]

Default judgment also was an excessive sanction for Ds' failure to appear at a court-ordered deposition pertaining to their financial condition for punitive damages purposes. Since the depos had limited scope, lesser sanctions would have sufficed (e.g., instructing the jury that Ds' wealth was sufficient for the punitive damages sought). [*McArthur v. Bockman* (1989) 208 CA3d 1076, 1080-1081, 256 CR 522, 524-525]

3) [8:2264] **Dismissal as sanction for delay in serving responses:** Where a self-represented plaintiff was delinquent in serving answers to interrogatories, but no prejudice to defendant resulted from the delay, dismissal was held too severe a sanction. [*Morgan v. Ransom* (1979) 95 CA3d 664, 669-670, 157 CR 212, 215—"dismissal was not remedial, but punitive"]

4) [8:2265] **Default or dismissal as sanction for blocking discovery on portion of case:** A "doomsday" sanction may be too drastic where the discovery violation relates to *only one issue* in the case. Lesser sanctions (e.g., orders barring evidence on that issue) may be more appropriate. [*Wilson v. Jefferson* (1985) 163 CA3d 952, 958-959, 210 CR 464, 467-468]

- [8:2266] The court struck D's answer and entered his default for willful disobedience to an order to produce documents relevant to a claimed defense. This led to a default judgment against D for $50,000 compensatory and $80,000 punitive damages. The default sanction was not appropriate because *D's derelictions affected discovery only on his defense*, and did not affect P's discovery on other issues: "Accordingly, to entirely exclude [D] from the litigation based on his dereliction not only went beyond what was necessary to protect respondent's interests vis-à-vis her discovery efforts, but unjustifiably precluded him from any defense *respecting aspects of the case which . . . were [not sufficiently] connected to that dereliction.*" [*Wilson v. Jefferson*, supra, 163 CA3d at 959, 210 CR at 468 (emphasis added)—fact D neither filed opposition nor appeared at hearing on sanctions was irrelevant]

- [8:2267] *Compare:* A more recent case approved terminating sanctions even when the underlying discovery requests did not encompass all issues in the case, where the obstreperous party had steadfastly refused to comply with multiple discovery requests and orders. No prejudice to the propounding party by reason of the discovery abuse need be shown. [*Siry Investment, L.P. v. Farkhondehpour* (2020) 45 CA5th 1098, 1120-1122, 259 CR3d 466, 482-484]

[8:2268-2274] *Reserved.*

(b) [8:2275] **Compare—"doomsday" sanctions for repeated willful violations:** Where defendant continued to provide meaningless responses to interrogatories after having been ordered to fully respond three times, the court did not abuse its discretion in striking defendant's answer and cross-complaint and rendering judgment for plaintiff. [*Liberty Mut. Fire Ins. Co. v. LcL Administrators, Inc.* (2008) 163 CA4th 1093, 1106, 78 CR3d 200, 209]

(c) [8:2276] **Compare—"doomsday" sanctions for failure to pay earlier monetary sanctions:** As mentioned earlier (¶*8:2257*), "doomsday" sanctions (dismissal or default) cannot be imposed against a client solely because of his or her *attorney's* failure to pay monetary sanctions.

Nor is it proper to dismiss or impose a default sanction because the party has not paid sanctions previously ordered. [*Newland v. Sup.Ct. (Sugasawara)* (1995) 40 CA4th 608, 615, 47 CR2d 24, 28—"a terminating sanction issued solely because of a failure to pay a monetary discovery sanction is never justified"]

But "doomsday" sanctions may be appropriate where, in addition to nonpayment of monetary sanctions, the client has violated *other* discovery orders. [See *Stein v. Hassen* (1973) 34 CA3d 294, 302-303, 109 CR 321, 327; *Williams v. Travelers Ins. Co.* (1975) 49 CA3d 805, 810, 123 CR 83, 86; *Creed-21 v. City of Wildomar* (2017) 18 CA5th 690, 702-703, 226 CR3d 532, 541-542—trial

© 2020 Thomson Reuters/The Rutter Group

court justified in imposing sanctions (the equivalent of terminating sanctions) where prior orders re depositions and payment of money sanctions not obeyed and further monetary sanctions would not be effective]

[8:2277-2280] *Reserved.*

(7) [8:2281] **No "stacking" of sanctions:** A severe sanction for a relatively minor infraction *cannot* be justified by the offending party's *prior* "history of delay and avoidance." This is particularly true if that party has already been sanctioned for the earlier violations. [See *Motown Record Corp. v. Sup.Ct. (Brockert)* (1984) 155 CA3d 482, 491, 202 CR 227, 233—compelled waiver of privilege for slight delay in serving amended responses could not be justified on basis that original responses were also late or evasive]

(8) [8:2282] **Compare—prior discovery abuse as evidence of improper motive:** Past experience is often a "prime indicator" in assessing an attorney's or party's credibility and motivation: "An abuse of discovery procedures in one instance can imply a continuing intent to abuse in other instances." [*Obregon v. Sup.Ct. (Cimm's, Inc.)* (1998) 67 CA4th 424, 430-431, 79 CR2d 62, 66]

[8:2283-2289] *Reserved.*

e. [8:2290] **Sanctions against attorney for disobedient party:** Monetary sanctions may be imposed against the disobedient party's attorney for *advising* disobedience to the court's order. [CCP §2023.030(a); *Corns v. Miller* (1986) 181 CA3d 195, 200, 226 CR 247, 250]

(1) [8:2291] **Burden on attorney:** To escape sanctions, the burden is on the attorney to prove that he or she did *not* advise the client to disobey the discovery order: "An attorney's advice to a client to answer or not answer an interrogatory is a fact peculiarly within the knowledge of attorney and client. To place the burden of proof on the moving party . . . would effectually . . . frustrate the statutory purpose." [*Corns v. Miller*, supra, 181 CA3d at 201, 226 CR at 251]

- [8:2292] That the attorney for the disobedient party argued against a motion to compel is *not* evidence that he or she advised disobedience of the court's order. [*Ghanooni v. Super Shuttle of Los Angeles* (1993) 20 CA4th 256, 261, 24 CR2d 501, 504]

[8:2293-2294] *Reserved.*

(2) [8:2295] **Caution—ethical dilemma:** Attorneys owe a duty of loyalty to their clients. They must be careful not to do anything which would *increase* the risk of sanctions against the client. Therefore, it would appear to be ethically improper for attorneys to try to avoid sanctions against themselves by claiming they told the clients to obey the court's order. I.e., the *at-*

torneys should be prepared to take the blame themselves. See ¶9:1074.

[8:2296] ***PRACTICE POINTER:*** If a client persists in refusing to heed his or her attorney's advice, such as to comply with court orders, the attorney should consider withdrawing from the representation.

[8:2297-2299] *Reserved.*

f. [8:2300] **Attorney's "mea culpa" affidavit as bar to sanctioning client?** An attorney affidavit of fault is ground for relief from default or dismissal (CCP §473(b), *see ¶5:292*). And a dismissal entered as a terminating sanction for discovery misuse qualifies for mandatory relief under CCP §473(b). [*Rodriguez v. Brill* (2015) 234 CA4th 715, 725, 184 CR3d 265, 272 (noting such dismissals "in essence" result from defaults on discovery obligations); *see ¶5:299.2*]

However, an attorney's CCP §473(b) affidavit of fault may not always bar terminating or other sanctions against the client (*¶8:2301 ff.*).

(1) [8:2301] **Credibility assessment:** An attorney's affidavit swearing he or she alone is responsible for the conduct resulting in sanctions will not prevent terminating or other sanctions against the client if the court finds the affidavit lacks credibility or the attorney was not the cause. [See *Johnson v. Pratt & Whitney Canada, Inc.* (1994) 28 CA4th 613, 622, 34 CR2d 26, 31; *Lang v. Hochman* (2000) 77 CA4th 1225, 1251, 92 CR2d 322, 338—§473(b) relief denied where attorney affidavit claiming sole responsibility for discovery misconduct directly contradicted counsel's prior statements to trial court implicating clients; *Behm v. Clear View Technologies* (2015) 241 CA4th 1, 15-16, 193 CR3d 486, 495 (same)]

(2) [8:2302] **Effect of client as contributing cause?** There is a split of authority whether CCP §473(b) affidavit of fault relief is available when the client was also at fault in causing the default or dismissal. [See *Lang v. Hochman*, supra, 77 CA4th at 1248, 92 CR2d at 336—§473(b) applies "only if the party is totally innocent of any wrongdoing and the attorney was the *sole* cause of the default or dismissal"; *Rodriguez v. Brill*, supra, 234 CA4th at 730, 184 CR3d at 275 (assuming §473(b) not available where client's negligence or willful misconduct is contributory cause of terminating sanction but not deciding issue since record showed client not at fault); compare *SJP Ltd. Partnership v. City of Los Angeles* (2006) 136 CA4th 511, 519, 39 CR3d 55, 61—§473(b) mandatory relief may apply even if client "equally responsible"; *see also ¶5:295.5 ff.*]

[8:2303-2309] *Reserved.*

g. [8:2310] **Procedural matters:** The same procedural rules applicable to monetary sanctions on a motion to compel (¶*8:1980 ff.*) also apply where sanctions are sought for disobedience to court orders.

(1) [8:2311] **Noticed motion required:** Sanctions for disobedience to a court order are not automatic. A separate motion for sanctions (to dismiss, etc.) is required. [See *Duggan v. Moss* (1979) 98 CA3d 735, 742, 159 CR 425, 429]

FORM: Motion for Issue, Evidence or Terminating Sanctions and Proposed Order, *see Form 8:21* in Rivera, *Cal. Prac. Guide: Civ. Pro. Before Trial FORMS* (TRG).

(a) [8:2312] **Notice requirements:** *See discussion at ¶8:1983 ff.*

[8:2313-2315] *Reserved.*

(2) [8:2316] **Separate statement required for issue or evidentiary sanctions:** A motion for issue or evidentiary sanctions must be accompanied by a *separate document* setting forth the particular discovery requests at issue, the responses thereto, and the reasons why such sanctions should be imposed. [CRC 3.1345(a)(7)]

Effective January 1, 2020, depending on the types of discovery requests involved, the trial court may permit the moving party to file a concise outline of the disputes in issue in lieu of a separate statement. [CCP §§2030.300(b)(2), 2031.310(b)(3), 2033.290(b)(2) (all amended eff. 1/1/19, operative 1/1/20); *see discussion at ¶8:1157.3 ff.*]

(a) [8:2317] **Form and content of separate statement:** *See discussion at ¶8:1151 ff.*

(3) [8:2318] **Supporting declarations:** Declarations filed in support of the motion should show:

- The specific *order* that was made;
- The specific conduct constituting *disobedience* thereof (failure to comply, coupled with showing of *willfulness*);
- Facts showing the *relevance* of the discovery request to some issue in the case and, where applicable, *prejudice* to the moving party resulting from the opposing party's failure to comply with the prior court order (*see ¶8:2326*);
- Moving party's "reasonable and good faith attempt" to obtain compliance outside of court;

  (A good faith "meet and confer" is *not* required by statute on a motion for sanctions for disobedience to a court order. But such showing will strengthen the moving party's position and the likelihood of sanctions.)
- Recital of *any prior sanctions* imposed against the party

in default for this disobedience or any other (to show why lesser sanctions may be ineffective);

- *Time and expense* incurred by moving party in attempting to obtain compliance with court's order and in preparing motion (to justify award of monetary sanctions in addition to other sanctions).

[8:2319-2324] *Reserved.*

(4) [8:2325] **Showing required for "terminating" sanctions:** The Discovery Act does not specifically require a heightened showing for imposition of "doomsday" sanctions as opposed to other sanctions. (The Act states only that, for disobedience of earlier orders, the court may make whatever orders are "just"; see, e.g., CCP §§2030.290(c) (motion to compel answers) & 2030.300(e) (motion to compel further answers).)

[8:2326] ***PRACTICE POINTER:*** As a practical matter, however, a strong showing should be made to convince a court to exercise its *discretion* to grant "doomsday" sanctions. Your declarations should show that:

- The questions involved are *clearly relevant to the issues* raised by the pleadings (not merely "relevant to the subject matter") or are *material* to a claim or defense in the case;
- Prior sanctions (listed in declaration) have not been effective in compelling the opposing party to comply with the discovery obligations; and
- (If appropriate) the refusal to answer has *prejudiced* the propounding party's ability to prepare for trial and thereby interfered with the *court's function to ascertain the truth*. [See *Morgan v. Ransom* (1979) 95 CA3d 664, 669, 157 CR 212, 215—a pre-Discovery Act case]

(a) [8:2327] **No separate statement required:** A separate statement is not needed for a motion for terminating sanctions. [*Siry Investment, L.P. v. Farkhondehpour* (2020) 45 CA5th 1098, 1119, 259 CR3d 466, 482 (citing CRC 3.1345)]

[8:2328-2329] *Reserved.*

(5) [8:2330] **Effect of other parties' joinder in sanctions motion?** The Discovery Act does not provide a clear answer to whether parties who did not propound the discovery request may be awarded sanctions against the party who failed to respond to it. Cases are divided:

- [8:2331] One case holds that where dismissal is proper for failure to comply with discovery requests by one defendant, the action may be dismissed as to other defendants as well: "The plain implication [of the Discovery Act] is that an opposing party who did not initiate the discovery may benefit from the sanction *without even requesting relief.*" [*Calvert Fire Ins. Co. v. Cropper* (1983) 141 CA3d 901, 905, 190 CR 593, 594-595 (emphasis added)]

- [8:2332] Another case reversed monetary sanctions in favor of nonpropounding parties: "[O]utsiders [to the discovery dispute] were not entitled to be awarded sanctions." [See *Townsend v. Sup.Ct. (EMC Mortg. Co.)* (1998) 61 CA4th 1431, 1438, 72 CR2d 333, 337]

- [8:2333] A third view is that sanctions in favor of a nonpropounding party are proper "only if the nonpropounding party shows it *suffered a detriment* as the result of the sanctioned party's misuse of the discovery process." Rationale: CCP §§2030.290(c) and 2030.300(e) require the court to make "those orders that are just." [*Parker v. Wolters Kluwer U.S., Inc.* (2007) 149 CA4th 285, 301, 57 CR3d 18, 30 (emphasis added)—P's failure to respond to discovery requests by D1 did *not* justify dismissal of action against D2, D3 and D4 who failed to show any prejudice from P's failure to respond to D1]

[8:2334-2336] *Reserved.*

(6) [8:2337] **Burden of proof on motion:** The moving party need only show the failure to obey earlier discovery orders. Thereafter, the burden of proof shifts to the *party seeking to avoid sanctions* to establish a satisfactory excuse for his or her conduct. [*Corns v. Miller* (1986) 181 CA3d 195, 201, 226 CR 247, 251; *Williams v. Russ* (2008) 167 CA4th 1215, 1227, 84 CR3d 813, 823]

(7) [8:2338] **Limitation—no default sanction in personal injury or death actions unless CCP §425.11 statement served:** *See discussion at ¶8:2186 ff.*

(8) [8:2339] **Findings not required:** Unlike other statutes authorizing sanctions (e.g., CCP §128.7), the discovery statutes do not require the court to specify reasons justifying the imposition of sanctions. "Indeed, the trial court is not required to make findings at all." [*Ghanooni v. Super Shuttle of Los Angeles* (1993) 20 CA4th 256, 261, 24 CR2d 501, 504]

Comment: However, as with any exercise of discretion, the trial court's reasons for the ruling are valuable for appellate review, so the proposed order should state such a basis.

(a) [8:2339.1] **Compare—CCP §2023.050:** If a party, person, or attorney violates CCP §2023.050 and the court declines to award the $250 sanction, the court *must* make written findings that the one subject to the sanction acted with substantial justification or that other circumstances make imposition of the sanction unjust. [CCP §2023.050(c) (added eff. 1/1/20)]

(9) [8:2340] **Terminating sanction as judgment on merits:** *Dismissal* of an action for plaintiff's failure to obey discovery orders operates as a judgment on the merits. Thus, the judgment of dismissal is *res judicata* and bars any later lawsuit by plaintiff on the same cause of action. (Similarly, a *default judgment* against defendant for disobedience to discovery orders bars defendant from relitigating the same issues in another lawsuit.) [*Kahn v. Kahn* (1977) 68 CA3d 372, 381-382, 137 CR 332, 337]

(10) [8:2341] **Right of appeal:** A default judgment or judgment of dismissal is a final judgment from which the aggrieved party has the right to appeal. [CCP §904.1(a)(1)]

[8:2342-2389] *Reserved.*

6. [8:2390] **Evidence Exclusion Sanction for False Discovery Answers:** The Discovery Act does not deal explicitly with the situation where false discovery responses are not uncovered until the time of trial. Nevertheless, if the discovery responses are shown to be *willfully false,* and to have impeded the discovering party's trial preparations, the court clearly has the power to exclude contrary evidence at trial. Such exclusion can be treated either as a *protective order* (CCP §2030.090(b) empowers the court to "make any order that justice requires to protect any party . . . from . . . oppression") or as an *evidence or issue preclusion sanction* for abuse of discovery. [*Thoren v. Johnston & Washer* (1972) 29 CA3d 270, 274, 105 CR 276, 278]

If the falsity is discovered *before* trial, the court may instead impose lesser sanctions; e.g., a continuance of trial with monetary sanctions or issue preclusion sanctions with appropriate jury instructions. But if the abuse is not discovered until *during* trial, exclusion of evidence is "virtually the only viable option available." [*Pate v. Channel Lumber Co.* (1997) 51 CA4th 1447, 1455, 59 CR2d 919, 924]

a. **Application**

- [8:2391] P obtained a continuance of trial by representing it was "totally unable" to prove its case without auditing D's records, and needed more time to complete the audit, and that D would receive copies. P later reneged, claiming an audit was "impossible." Although there was no prior court order compelling discovery, an *issue sanction* (precluding P from offering accounting evidence) was proper: "[I]t is conceded that plaintiffs are *unable* to provide the promised items of discovery. Under the circumstances . . . a warning to plaintiffs, in the form of a formal order to comply, *would have been futile.*" [*Do It Urself Moving & Storage, Inc. v. Brown, Leifer, Slatkin & Berns* (1992) 7 CA4th 27, 36, 9 CR2d 396, 400 (emphasis added) (superseded by statute on other grounds)]

- [8:2392] An evidence sanction was imposed at trial excluding records that the offering party claimed he was unable to produce during discovery because they had been stolen. The court found he had *willfully* failed to comply with discovery. It was immaterial that no prior order compelling discovery had been obtained. [*Vallbona v. Springer* (1996) 43 CA4th 1525, 1545, 51 CR2d 311, 324]

  [8:2393-2395] *Reserved.*

b. [8:2396] **Undisclosed witnesses:** Precluding a witness from testifying at trial due to a "party's failure to identify the witness in discovery is appropriate only if the omission was willful or a violation of a court order compelling a response." [*Mitchell v. Sup.Ct. (Johnson)* (2015) 243 CA4th 269, 272-273, 196 CR3d 168, 171—error to impose evidence sanction where failure to disclose witness names in interrogatory response was not willful or in contravention of order; *Pina v. County of Los Angeles* (2019) 38 CA5th 531, 551-552, 251 CR3d 17, 34; *Saxena v. Goffney* (2008) 159 CA4th 316, 334, 71 CR3d 469, 483—evasive, incomplete response is insufficient basis for sanction if not willfully false]

   [8:2397-2399] *Reserved.*

c. [8:2400] **Compare—interrogatory answers that were true when made but no longer correct:** Unlike federal practice, the California Discovery Act imposes *no duty to correct or update* interrogatory answers that are no longer accurate (*see ¶8:998 ff.*). Each side has the right to serve *supplemental interrogatories* shortly before trial to verify the correctness of earlier answers (*see ¶8:1000*). If they fail to do so, their reliance on earlier answers arguably should *not* be the basis for excluding contrary evidence at trial, if the evidence was not discovered by the answering party until after the earlier responses. [*Biles v. Exxon Mobil Corp.* (2004) 124 CA4th 1315, 1328, 22 CR3d 282, 291 (citing text); *R & B Auto Ctr., Inc. v. Farmers Group, Inc.* (2006) 140 CA4th 327, 357, 44 CR3d 426, 451]

   Further, no order deeming the incorrect answer to be binding may be entered pursuant to CCP §2030.310(b), unless the court finds:

   — the opposing party has suffered *substantial prejudice* that cannot be cured by a *continuance* to permit further discovery;

   — the responding party fails to show substantial justification for the initial answer to the interrogatory; and

   — compliance with the Discovery Act's "meet and confer" provisions in an effort to resolve the dispute. [CCP §2030.310(b), (c); see *Biles v. Exxon Mobil Corp.*, supra, 124 CA4th at 1328, 22 CR3d at 290-291; *and further discussion at ¶8:1126 ff.*]

   (1) [8:2401] **Application:** D moved for summary judgment in an asbestos injury case contending P could not prove he had been exposed to asbestos on D's premises. P's opposition included a declaration from a coworker, recently located by P's counsel, providing such proof. The declaration could

not be excluded on the ground the coworker was not identified either in P's answers to earlier interrogatories, or in supplemental answers after the coworker's identity was discovered. P owed *no duty to update or amend the answers* to include new information discovered later. [*Biles v. Exxon Mobil Corp.*, supra, 124 CA4th at 1328, 22 CR3d at 291]

[8:2402-2405] *Reserved.*

[8:2406] ***PRACTICE POINTER:*** In any case, the opposing party must act promptly on discovering the falsity of the discovery responses. When contrary evidence is offered, an objection should be made on the ground that the evidence had not been disclosed in response to discovery requests. Absent timely objection on this ground, any error in admitting such evidence is waived (see Ev.C. §353(a)).

Presumably, the ground for objection is Ev.C. §352—i.e., probative value of evidence outweighed by risk of undue prejudice, confusion of issues, etc. [See *Pate v. Channel Lumber Co.* (1997) 51 CA4th 1447, 1452-1453, 59 CR2d 919, 922 (upholding objection that evidence not disclosed in response to numerous discovery requests should be excluded as "unfair")]

(2) [8:2407] **Distinguish—initial disclosures:** If the parties agree and the court orders initial disclosure of witnesses and documents (*see ¶8:35*), then the responses *must* be supplemented or corrected if the responding party knows the earlier responses are incorrect or incomplete. [CCP §2016.090(a)(3)(A) (added eff. 1/1/20)]

[8:2408-2439] *Reserved.*

7. [8:2440] **Contempt Sanction:** Willful disobedience of a court order compelling discovery (e.g., to appear or to answer questions or to produce documents) is punishable as a *contempt* of court. [CCP §2023.030(e)]

   a. [8:2441] **Procedure:** Contempt proceedings are quasi-criminal in nature and require *personal service* on the refusing party, whether or not he or she is represented by counsel. An order to show cause (OSC) is issued by the court commanding the refusing party to appear and justify the failure to obey. *See ¶8:612 ff.*

   b. [8:2442] **"Disobedience":** Although the statute does not make this clear, a contempt sanction requires proof of *willful* failure to obey. A party shown *unable* to comply (e.g., as the result of illness) is not "disobedient" and cannot be held in contempt. Also, if the failure was inadvertent, ordinarily no remedy of any kind is available against the witness. [See CCP §1991; *Chapman v. Sup.Ct.* (1968) 261 CA2d 194, 200, 67 CR 842, 846—finding of contempt reversed where no evidence of willful disobedience to subpoena; *and ¶8:611*]

© 2020 Thomson Reuters/The Rutter Group

(1) [8:2443] **Specific order required:** A finding of contempt must be based on a "clear, intentional violation of a specific, narrowly drawn order. Specificity is an essential prerequisite of a contempt citation." [*Van v. Language Line Services, Inc.* (2017) 8 CA5th 73, 82, 213 CR3d 822, 829 (internal citation omitted)—abuse of discretion to sanction party for disobeying order (mere one word denial of party's own ex parte motion for stay of deposition) that neither compelled nor prohibited any action]

[8:2444] *Reserved.*

c. [8:2445] **Advice of counsel no defense:** In a contempt proceeding, it is no defense that the witness or party was acting on the advice of counsel. [*In re Bongfeldt* (1971) 22 CA3d 465, 476, 99 CR 428, 435]

d. [8:2446] **Punishment:** The punishment for contempt is up to five days' imprisonment and/or a fine of up to $1,000 for each contempt. In addition, parties or their agents may be ordered to pay reasonable attorney fees incurred by the opposing party in connection with the contempt proceeding. [CCP §1218(a)]

The party in contempt can also be incarcerated until the ordered act is performed. [CCP §1219]

e. [8:2447] **Not preclusive of other sanctions:** Such punishment apparently does not preclude other sanctions for the same conduct. The entire range of sanctions, including contempt, is authorized for any misuse of the discovery process. [See CCP §2023.030]

f. [8:2448] **Additional money sanction payable to court:** In *addition* to imprisonment, a court has power, after notice and hearing, to order a person who has violated a court order "without good cause or substantial justification" to pay a sanction of up to $1,500 to the *court*. [CCP §177.5]

This monetary sanction can be imposed *in addition* to punishment for contempt ("notwithstanding any other provision of law"). And it can be imposed against a nonparty witness, or a party, or the party's attorney. [See CCP §177.5]

[8:2449] ***PRACTICE POINTER:*** The contempt procedure is complex, time-consuming and doomed to failure unless all the procedural niceties are observed. Even if they are met, many judges are reluctant to hold a person in contempt *absent a prior court order.*

Therefore, it is usually a better idea to move first for an order to compel and for an award of monetary sanctions (*see* ¶*8:1920 ff.*). Consider contempt proceedings only if the witness disobeys a specific court order or otherwise is persistently recalcitrant and terminating sanctions would be ineffective (e.g., because the recalcitrant person is not a party).

g. [8:2450] **Appellate review:** Contempt orders are "final and conclusive" and not directly appealable; review is available only by writ (e.g., writ of prohibition). [CCP §§904.1(a)(1)(B), 1222; *Van v. Language Line Services, Inc.*, supra, 8 CA5th at 79, 81, 213 CR3d at 827, 828—contempt findings subject to "much more rigorous review" than other sanctions]

[8:2451-2454] *Reserved.*

8. [8:2455] **Sanctions in Limited Civil Cases:** The discovery sanctions available in limited civil cases are discussed at ¶*8:1820 ff.*

© 2020 Thomson Reuters/The Rutter Group

RESERVED

CHAPTER 9

PART I

LAW AND MOTION

CONTENTS

Page

© 2020 Thomson Reuters/The Rutter Group

© 2020 Thomson Reuters/The Rutter Group

© 2020 Thomson Reuters/The Rutter Group

© 2020 Thomson Reuters/The Rutter Group

© 2020 Thomson Reuters/The Rutter Group

© 2020 Thomson Reuters/The Rutter Group

© 2020 Thomson Reuters/The Rutter Group

© 2020 Thomson Reuters/The Rutter Group

© 2020 Thomson Reuters/The Rutter Group

RESERVED

PART I

LAW AND MOTION

[9:1] STRATEGY CONSIDERATIONS RE LAW AND MOTION PRACTICE

(1) **The threshold considerations are TIME and MONEY:** Time, because there is often so little of it when preparing your papers and arguing the case in court; and because there is frequently so little time on crowded court calendars that you may not be able to schedule the motion when you want or need to have it heard. And money, because it may be extremely costly for your client to win a motion, and even more costly to lose one. In many cases, it simply may not be worth the effort (unless, perhaps, you can find some way to make your opponent pay your attorney fees and costs (*see* ¶*9:463 ff.*)).

(2) **The other major consideration is your litigation objectives:** Will winning this motion significantly advance your client's interest? Winning some motions may cause your opponent to reevaluate his or her case and lead to an early settlement. However, other motions may have no impact on the probable outcome at trial. Therefore, they simply may not be worth the time and money required. Discuss with your client the costs involved, the chances of success, and the litigation objective. If losing the motion would have a negative impact on the case, this should also be discussed with the client.

(3) **Thus, the bottom line is often a costs vs. benefits analysis:** Will obtaining the relief sought by the motion advance the client's case sufficiently to outweigh the costs and risks of making the motion?

(4) **Try "meeting and conferring":** Consider whether the result sought may be obtained by some other, less expensive means—e.g., telephoning opposing counsel and proposing a stipulation as to the matter in question. The less crucial the motion, the more likely you can obtain such stipulation, and save the client the costs and risks of a motion. (A "meet and confer" is *required* on many discovery motions. See CCP §2023.010(i); *and* ¶*8:1158 ff.*)

(5) **Caution re sanctions**

- *CCP §128.5* permits a trial court to order a party or a party's attorney to pay any reasonable expenses, including attorney fees, "incurred by another party as a result of actions or tactics, made in bad faith, that are frivolous or solely intended to cause unnecessary delay" (*see* ¶*9:1010 ff.*);
- *CCP §128.7* authorizes sanctions for violation of the certificate of factual and legal merit created by an attorney's presenting any pleading or paper to the court (*see* ¶*9:1135 ff.*).

© 2020 Thomson Reuters/The Rutter Group

A. INTRODUCTION

1. [9:2] **"Motion" Defined:** A motion is simply a request that a court make an order. [CCP §1003—"An application for an order is a motion"]

   a. [9:2.1] **Formal vs. informal motions:** Motions during trial generally may be made orally. But in *pretrial* practice, motions must be made according to the procedures discussed below (¶*9:3 ff.*). Informal requests to the court (e.g., a letter to the judge asking to postpone a hearing) are *improper* and ineffective. If time does not permit filing the necessary papers, counsel's remedy is to seek an order shortening time for making the motion (*see* ¶*9:364*).

      (1) [9:2.2] **Notice requirements:** Some statutes specifically require notice to the opposing party; others do not. But even where a statute is silent as to notice, *due process of law* requires adequate notice and opportunity to be heard on any motion that affects the rights of the opposing party. *See discussion at* ¶*9:349 ff.*

      (2) [9:2.3] **"Label" not determinative:** A trial court may disregard a motion's label (title) and construe it as a different type of motion. This is consistent with the court's inherent authority to manage and control its docket. [*Austin v. Los Angeles Unified School Dist.* (2016) 244 CA4th 918, 930, 198 CR3d 239, 249—post-judgment motion "for reconsideration" treated as motion for relief under CCP §473(b); see *Sorenson v. Sup.Ct. (People)* (2013) 219 CA4th 409, 421, 161 CR3d 794, 804, fn. 13—"request for reconsideration" treated as new motion because it did not seek modification, amendment or revocation of order resulting from earlier motion; *see also* ¶*7:158.2*]

      [9:2.4] *Reserved.*

   b. [9:2.5] **When motion "made":** A motion is complete and is "deemed to have been made" upon filing and service of the notice of motion. [CCP §1005.5]

      Therefore, even though the notice of motion may specify that it will be made (i.e., heard) on a specific date in the future, it is actually "made" *upon filing and service* of the requisite papers. [*Cromwell v. Cummings* (1998) 65 CA4th Supp. 10, 13, 76 CR2d 171, 173]

2. [9:3] **Rules Governing Motions:** Motions frequently require consideration of both the substantive law on which the motion is based, and the procedural rules for making the motion. The procedural rules may be found in any or all of the following sources:

   a. [9:4] **Statutes:** The California Code of Civil Procedure contains several statutes authorizing, or requiring, various kinds of motions at various stages of the proceeding. Examples: Motions to quash service of summons (CCP §418.10); demurrers (CCP §430.10); motions for summary judgment (CCP §437c).

In addition, the CCP contains numerous provisions governing *when, how* and *where* motions before trial shall be made. Examples:

- The *time* for noticing motions (CCP §1005, ¶*9:31*);
- When a motion is deemed made (CCP §1005.5);
- The *form* of a motion (CCP §1010);
- The *method of service* of a motion (CCP §§1010.6-1015, 1017, 1020);
- Powers of judges and commissioners to hear motions (CCP §§166, 259).

b. [9:5] **Case law:** Although most of California's procedural rules have been codified, there are still a few motions based on judicial precedent rather than statute. Examples: motion for equitable relief from judgment after time for relief under CCP §473 has expired (¶*5:435 ff.*); motion to dismiss as substitute for general demurrer (¶*7:370 ff.*); and nonstatutory motion for judgment on the pleadings (¶*7:277*).

c. [9:6] **California Rules of Court:** The Judicial Council is authorized to "adopt rules for court administration, practice and procedure, not inconsistent with statute . . ." [Cal. Const. Art. VI, §6]

The Judicial Council has adopted rules of court (CRC) governing law and motion matters in superior courts and official forms to be used on certain types of motions and proceedings. These Rules and Judicial Council forms are available on the California Courts website (*www.courts.ca.gov*). Many of the Judicial Council forms can be filled out online, saved and printed.

The CRC governing law and motion practice generally—e.g., format and filing of papers, notice, hearings, etc.—are discussed in this Chapter. Other CRC rules relating to specific motions and procedures—discovery, summary judgment, injunctions, etc.—are discussed in other Chapters of this Practice Guide.

(1) [9:6.1] **Effect as law:** The California Rules of Court have the force and effect of law, so long as not inconsistent with statute. [*In re Jermaine B.* (1994) 21 CA4th 1280, 1284, 26 CR2d 612, 615; *In re Alonzo J.* (2014) 58 C4th 924, 937, 169 CR3d 661, 670—"a [CRC] rule is inconsistent with a statute if it conflicts with either the statute's express language or its underlying legislative intent"]

A CRC rule may go beyond the provisions of a related statute so long as it reasonably furthers the statutory

© 2020 Thomson Reuters/The Rutter Group

purpose. [See *Mann v. Cracchiolo* (1985) 38 C3d 18, 29, 210 CR 762, 767 (overruled on other grounds by *Perry v. Bakewell Hawthorne, LLC* (2017) 2 C5th 536, 543, 213 CR3d 764, 768)—rule limiting time to file opposition to summary judgment motion]

But a CRC rule may not *change* statutory requirements. [*People v. Hall* (1994) 8 C4th 950, 960, 35 CR2d 432, 438; *California Court Reporters Ass'n, Inc. v. Judicial Council of Calif.* (1995) 39 CA4th 15, 33-34, 46 CR2d 44, 56 (invalidating former Rule of Court that allowed electronic recording of superior court proceedings because CCP §269 requires official shorthand record); *Carlton v. Dr. Pepper Snapple Group, Inc.* (2014) 228 CA4th 1200, 1210, 175 CR3d 909, 916 (construing CRC 3.1320(j) in manner consistent with statute (CCP §471.5) because "statute takes precedence over the rule of court")]

d. [9:7] **Local court rules:** Courts are authorized to adopt local rules to expedite court operations. Such rules are valid so long they are consistent with higher authority—i.e., statutes or case law, or the statewide rules adopted by the Judicial Council. [CCP §575.1; see Gov.C. §68070; *Marriage of Woolsey* (2013) 220 CA4th 881, 900, 163 CR3d 551, 564-565—local rule "cannot impose requirements for enforcement of mediated settlement agreements in addition to those specified by statute"]

Local rules must be adopted in accordance with procedures set forth in CCP §575.1 (e.g., proposed rules submitted to the public, including local bar associations and others, for consideration and recommendation, then approved by majority of court's judges, plus publication and filing procedures). [See *Hall v. Sup.Ct. (People)* (2005) 133 CA4th 908, 915, 35 CR3d 206, 210]

Local court rules are published by local legal newspapers and are generally available on each court's website. They can also be accessed through the California courts website (*www.courts.ca.gov*).

(1) [9:7.1] **Limitation—certain local rules preempted (CRC 3.20(a)):** Local rules relating to most pretrial proceedings, including pleadings and motions, are preempted by the CRC. [CRC 3.20(a); *see discussion at ¶9:13.2 ff.*]

(2) [9:8] **Content:** Valid local court rules typically cover such matters as the time and days of the week law and motion matters are heard or the department or courtroom in which such matters are heard. [See L.A. Sup.Ct. Rules 3.5, 3.6; S.F. Sup.Ct. Rules 3.5, 6.11, 8.1-8.2, 8.10, 9.0]

Such rules, however, *cannot* impose deadlines different from those specified in statutes or the CRC. [CRC 3.20(a)]

(3) [9:9] **Effect as law:** Local courts have *inherent power* to prescribe rules of practice and procedure before such courts. Therefore, so long as those rules are not contrary to higher authority (i.e., statutes, case law or the California Rules of Court), they have the force and effect of law. [Gov.C. §68070; see *Mann v. Cracchiolo* (1985) 38 C3d 18, 29, 210 CR 762, 767 (overruled on other grounds by *Perry v. Bakewell Hawthorne, LLC* (2017) 2 C5th 536, 543, 213 CR3d 764, 768)]

(4) [9:9a] **Interpretation:** The policies and rules of the trial court are for it to construe and apply. Except where this impairs due process, an appellate court is bound by the trial court's construction of its own rules. [*Villacampa v. Russell* (1986) 178 CA3d 906, 911, 224 CR 73, 76]

(5) [9:9.1] **Enforcement:** Violation or disregard of valid local rules (i.e., those not inconsistent with higher authority) is ground by itself for denial of a motion. [See *Wisniewski v. Clary* (1975) 46 CA3d 499, 504, 120 CR 176, 180]

(a) [9:9.1a] **Sanctions:** In addition, *if the local rules so provide*, the court on motion may:

- Strike all or any part of the pleadings of the party violating the rules; or
- Dismiss the action or enter judgment by default against such party; or
- Impose other penalties of a lesser nature as otherwise provided by law; *and*
- Order that party or his or her counsel to pay to the moving party reasonable expenses, including attorney fees, incurred in seeking enforcement of the rules. [CCP §575.2(a)]

(b) [9:9.2] **Limitation—Innocent client protected:** Any penalty for failing to comply with a local rule that is counsel's responsibility must be imposed on the *lawyer,* not the client. [CCP §575.2(b); *Garcia v. McCutchen* (1997) 16 C4th 469, 475, 66 CR2d 319, 323]

This is different from the general rule that an attorney's neglect is imputed to the client. [See *Shipley v. Sugita* (1996) 50 CA4th 320, 325, 57 CR2d 750, 752]

It is the court's duty to invoke this limitation on client liability on its own motion. [*Garcia v. McCutchen,*

© 2020 Thomson Reuters/The Rutter Group

supra, 16 C4th at 475, 66 CR2d at 323; see *Cooks v. Sup.Ct. (Cruz)* (1990) 224 CA3d 723, 727, 274 CR 113, 116—error to deny client's demand for jury trial because of counsel's violation of local rule]

e. [9:10] **Local court policies:** In addition to formal rules, courts may promulgate written "policies" regulating practice and procedure.

Any policy concerning practice or procedure in that court or by a judge is *treated as a local rule* (see CRC 10.613(a)(2)) and must be adopted and published with certain formalities (i.e., see CRC 10.613(c)); and ordinarily, it may not take effect until January 1 or July 1 at least 45 days after its filing (Gov.C. §68071). [See *Lokeijak v. City of Irvine* (1998) 65 CA4th 341, 342, 76 CR2d 429, 430, fn. 1—"a rule by any other name is still a rule"; *Hall v. Sup.Ct. (People)* (2005) 133 CA4th 908, 915, 35 CR3d 206, 209-210—"30-day motion cut-off rule" (requiring motions to be filed and heard at least 30 days before trial) was "functional equivalent" of local rule and invalid because not adopted in accordance with CCP §575.1 procedures]

Like local rules, court policies that relate to most pretrial proceedings are *preempted* by CRC 3.20(a) (*see ¶9:13.2 ff.*).

[9:11] *Reserved.*

f. [9:12] **"Local, local" rules:** In addition to local court rules (and policies), individual judges may adopt rules applicable to proceedings in their particular courtrooms. (These are often referred to as "local, local" rules.) However, such rules must now be adopted with the *same formalities* as local court rules (*see ¶9:10*). [CCP §575.1(c); CRC 10.613; *Kalivas v. Barry Controls Corp.* (1996) 49 CA4th 1152, 1158-1160, 57 CR2d 200, 204-205—local courtroom rule invalid because *not* adopted in accordance with required formalities; see *Hall v. Sup.Ct. (People)*, supra, 133 CA4th at 917, 35 CR3d at 212, fn. 18]

These "local, local rules" are also subject to the preemption provisions of CRC 3.20(a) (*see ¶9:13.2 ff.*).

(1) [9:12.1] **Comment:** Because of the formalities now required, far fewer "local, local" rules are likely to be adopted in the future, and those not published as local court rules will be unenforceable (*see ¶9:10*). However, counsel should recognize that individual judges will still have preferred methods for the presentation of materials and argument to the court.

➪ [9:13] ***PRACTICE POINTER:*** Familiarize yourself not only with the court rules but also with local policies in every court in which you practice. Judges hearing law and motion estimate that at least 25% of the cases on their calendars are tentatively denied simply for failure to comply with some applicable rule.

As an officer of the court, it is your "professional responsibility *to be aware of and knowledgeable about* duly adopted local rules." [*Annex British Cars, Inc. v. Parker-Rhodes* (1988) 198 CA3d 788, 791, 244 CR 48, 50 (emphasis added)]

Also familiarize yourself with the judge's personal preferences and idiosyncrasies. You can do this by talking to the courtroom staff (when court is not in session), talking to other lawyers who have appeared before the judge, observing the judge while court is in session, and reviewing published judicial profiles (Judge's Handbook and Daily Journal "Judicial Profile" series), and verdict reports.

Other valuable sources of information are articles (i.e., law reviews, news, the Daily Journal) about or authored by the judge. You also may want to read appellate opinions affirming or reversing the judge, as well as any appellate opinions written by the judge if he or she has sat pro tem with the court of appeal. In addition, judges are required to file Form 700 Reports on a yearly basis listing gifts and sources of other income; these reports can be reviewed on the Fair Political Practices Commission website (*www.fppc.ca.gov*).

g. [9:13.1] **Local rules, policies invalid where contra to higher authority:** Local rules and policies are invalid to the extent they conflict with the CRC, statutes, the Constitution or case law. [Gov.C. §68070(a); see *Elkins v. Sup.Ct. (Elkins)* (2007) 41 C4th 1337, 1351-1352, 63 CR3d 483, 490-491—"local courts may not create their own rules of evidence and procedure in conflict with statewide statutes"]

For example:

- [9:13.1a] A local rule requiring parties to file a *joint* statement of disputed and undisputed facts on a summary judgment motion violated CCP §437c, which requires the parties to file *separate* statements. [*Kalivas v. Barry Controls Corp.* (1996) 49 CA4th 1152, 1158, 57 CR2d 200, 204]

- [9:13.1b] A local rule authorizing summary judgment in favor of the party opposing the motion even if that party made no cross-motion violated statutory requirements for summary judgment. [*Sierra Craft, Inc. v. Magnum Enterprises, Inc.* (1998) 64 CA4th 1252, 1255, 75 CR2d 681, 683]

- [9:13.1c] A local rule providing for expedited summary judgment procedures in asbestos cases impermissibly conflicted with the statute governing summary judgment motions (CCP §437c). [*Boyle v. CertainTeed Corp.* (2006) 137 CA4th 645, 649, 40 CR3d 501, 504]

- [9:13.1d] A local rule provided 60 days from issuance of the remittitur to file a peremptory challenge to a judge

© 2020 Thomson Reuters/The Rutter Group

assigned to rehear a case following remand from the court of appeal. The rule was void to the extent it conflicted with CCP §170.6(a)(2), which requires a successful appellant to make the motion within 60 days of being notified of the assignment. [*Ghaffarpour v. Sup.Ct. (Commerce Plaza Hotel)* (2012) 202 CA4th 1463, 1470-1471, 136 CR3d 544, 549-550; *see ¶9:141.5 ff.*]

- [9:13.1e] The Presiding Judge of the Juvenile Court issued a blanket order declaring the press could not be excluded from juvenile court hearings unless an objection was made and harm to the child was shown. This order was invalid because it conflicted with Welf. & Inst.C. §346 and CRC 5.530, which gave the court broad discretion to determine who could be present on a case-by-case basis. [*In re A.L.* (2014) 224 CA4th 354, 364, 168 CR3d 589, 596]

(1) [9:13.2] **Certain local rules preempted by Judicial Council:** Local rules concerning the following fields are *null and void* because preempted by the Judicial Council:

— pretrial motions;
— demurrers;
— discovery;
— pleadings;
— ex parte applications;
— provisional remedies; and
— "form and format of papers." [CRC 3.20(a)]

(a) [9:13.3] **What constitutes local rule:** "Local rule" means "every rule, regulation, order, policy, form, or standard of general application adopted by a court to govern practice or procedure in that court or by a judge of the court to govern practice or procedure in that judge's courtroom." [CRC 10.613(a)(2); see *Volkswagen of America, Inc. v. Sup.Ct. (Adams)* (2001) 94 CA4th 695, 704, 114 CR2d 541, 547—local rules apply to all members of a class, kind or order]

(b) [9:13.4] **"All" local rules preempted?** CRC 3.20(a) says "*all* local rules" concerning the above matters (*¶9:13.2*) are "null and void." But this may not apply literally. [See *Volkswagen of America, Inc. v. Sup.Ct. (Adams)*, supra, 94 CA4th at 704, 114 CR2d at 547-548]

- [9:13.4a] Certain types of local rules concerning motions are *expressly authorized;* e.g., CRC 3.1308 authorizes local rules governing tentative rulings (*see ¶9:111 ff.*).

- [9:13.4b] Others are *impliedly* authorized. For example, CRC 3.400 governing *complex liti-*

gation (*see* ¶*12:47 ff.*) is designed to facilitate the efficient and timely resolution of such cases. To accomplish this result, it impliedly authorizes local courts "to take whatever exceptional management actions are necessary," including local rules and orders. [*Volkswagen of America, Inc. v. Sup.Ct. (Adams)*, supra, 94 CA4th at 704-705, 114 CR2d at 548—no preemption of "general order" in complex asbestos litigation allowing a "master complaint and answer" that parties could incorporate by reference to avoid duplicative pleadings]

(c) [9:13.5] **Compare—rules expressly not preempted:** The following local rules are expressly *not* preempted by CRC 3.20:

— those adopted under delay reduction rules (*see* ¶*12:48*);

— those governing trial and post-trial proceedings including *motions in limine*;

— eminent domain proceedings;

— injunction proceedings under CCP §§527.6-527.8 (involving harassment, group violence and workplace violence); and

— proceedings under the Family Code, Probate Code, Welfare and Institutions Code, and Penal Code and all other criminal proceedings. [CRC 3.20(b)]

[9:13.6-13.9] *Reserved.*

3. [9:13.10] **Civility Guidelines**

- Before filing a motion, attorneys should engage in "more than a pro forma effort" to resolve the dispute or limit the issues informally. To satisfy "meet and confer" requirements (e.g., on discovery motions, *see* ¶*8:1158*), an attorney should speak *personally* with opposing counsel;

- An attorney who has no reasonable objection to a proposed motion should promptly make this position known to opposing counsel. An attorney should not force an opponent to file a motion and then not oppose it;

- If an attorney files an opposition but then realizes that the moving party's position is correct, the attorney should promptly advise the movant and the court accordingly;

- *Monetary sanctions should not be sought unless fully justified* by the circumstances and necessary to protect a client's legitimate interests; and then only after a good faith effort to resolve the issue informally with opposing counsel. [State Bar California Attorney Guidelines of Civility and Professionalism §10]

© 2020 Thomson Reuters/The Rutter Group

B. PREPARING AND FILING MOTIONS

[9:14] ***PRACTICE POINTERS:*** Saving time is a vital consideration for law and motion practitioners. Before filing any motion, ask yourself, "Is this motion really necessary?" Try to find an alternative way to obtain the relief you seek without the time and expense of a formal motion. Often, the simplest way is to obtain a stipulation from opposing counsel—who, if your motion is well-taken, would be well-advised to agree, to save time and money for his or her client.

Therefore, as a first step before filing any motion (short of dismissal or summary judgment which you know will be opposed), try a telephone request to opposing counsel for a stipulation to the relief you seek. If you're told to "make your motion," then see that it is *done right the first time*, so as to save the maximum amount of time and money for all concerned.

Here are some common pitfalls to avoid:

- [9:15] **Timing "traps":** Make certain you allocate sufficient time in your office routine to actually prepare the motion.

  Make sure you notice your motion for hearing on a date the court hears law and motion matters (in some courts, you must also reserve the date in advance with the courtroom clerk, *see ¶9:34*); and that the date chosen allows for service and filing in compliance with applicable statutes and court rules. [See CCP §1005, *discussed at ¶9:31 ff.*]

  Also, be sure not to file your motion before or after the time permitted by statute or court rules for the particular motion. [E.g., CCP §437c(a)—60-day "hold" on filing summary judgment motions at outset of litigation, and bar on setting such motions for hearing within 30 days of trial, *¶10:56, 10:71*; and CCP §2024.020(a)—15-day "cut-off" on hearing discovery motions prior to trial, *¶8:445*]

- [9:15a] **Motions filed prematurely protected?** For most purposes, a motion is deemed "made" and pending as of the date the notice of motion is served and filed *except* where this would "deprive a party of a hearing of the motion to which he is otherwise entitled." [CCP §1005.5; *see ¶9:2.5*]

  At least one court has interpreted this to protect motions served and filed *prematurely* (while a statutory "hold" is in effect); i.e., such motion will be deemed "made" orally in court *at the time of hearing*. [*Sadlier v. Sup.Ct. (Schoenburg)* (1986) 184 CA3d 1050, 1053-1054, 229 CR 374, 376 (motion for summary judgment filed within statutory "hold" period); *see ¶10:58*]

  Comment: The result is debatable: CCP §1005.5 may protect a hearing to which a party is "otherwise entitled," but a party noticing a motion during a statutory "hold" period is arguably *not entitled* to a hearing.

- [9:15.1] **File your proof of service:** If possible, always file your proof of service along with the motion papers, or immediately thereafter. CRC 3.1300(c) requires that a proof of service of the moving papers be filed with the court no later than *5 court days* before the date set for the hearing.

  CRC 3.1300(c) is mandatory ("must be filed"). Failure to comply may result in the court ordering your motion off calendar without even looking at your papers. Most law and motion judges will not consider a motion that the court file shows was never properly served. *See further discussion at ¶9:100 ff.*

- [9:16] **Unnecessary appearances:** If law and motion calendars are published in local legal newspapers or on the Internet, check to see that your case is set for hearing. If there is any question whether opposing or reply papers have been received and filed, call the court clerk. Telephone opposing counsel the day before the hearing ("Do you intend to appear?"). If there are tentative rulings, be sure to check the tentative ruling, which many judges now post on the Internet. [See *Medix Ambulance Service, Inc. v. Sup.Ct. (Collado)* (2002) 97 CA4th 109, 112, 118 CR2d 249, 251]

  If your motion is unopposed and marked for tentative approval, you may wish to submit it without appearing (but be sure to call the clerk *before* the hearing; otherwise the matter may be placed off calendar). Or, you may find that for some reason it is not on the calendar; or that opposing counsel has some emergency that necessitates a continuance. In either event, you can save yourself a wasted trip to the courthouse.

  Many courts require counsel to give prior notice of intent to argue orally, often with fixed time deadlines for doing so. For example, some courts make tentative rulings available by telephone or on the Internet by 3:00 p.m. on the day before the scheduled hearing. These courts may require that a party wishing to argue orally *notify the court and opposing counsel* by 4:00 p.m. if they intend to appear and argue. A party's failure to comply with the court's tentative ruling procedure may result in loss of the right to argue the motion (*see ¶9:111 ff.*).

  [9:16.1-16.4] *Reserved.*

  ➪ [9:16.5] ***PRACTICE POINTER:*** Where the court requires notice to the court and opposing counsel that you intend to appear for a scheduled hearing, be sure to *confirm your call with a fax or email* and bring a copy with you to court. If you receive no call from opposing counsel and do not intend to appear, confirm the *absence* of your opponent's call with a fax or email promptly after the deadline for the telephonic notice.

© 2020 Thomson Reuters/The Rutter Group

- [9:17] **Arriving late:** Judges handling law and motion generally call the calendar promptly at the opening of court. All lawyers should have checked in and read the tentative ruling before the calendar call. If you're going to be late, call the clerk (most judges will hold the matter for a short while, until counsel's arrival). Those arriving late may find themselves at the foot of the calendar, wasting precious time; or the matter may have been decided adversely, or taken off calendar.

  Some courts have local rules requiring punctuality. [L.A. Sup.Ct. Rule 3.26, Appendix 3.A(*l*)(1)]

- [9:18] **Failing to research the judge:** No two judges handle their law and motion calendars the same way. Judges have their own ways of dealing with continuances, late papers and violation of local rules. Some judges request courtesy copies. Find out all you can about the judge before whom you are going to appear (*see* ¶*9:13*).

1. **Rules Governing Form and Content of Motion Papers**

a. [9:19] **CRC Rules:** The Judicial Council Rules assure uniformity throughout the state on the following matters:

(1) [9:20] **Form of papers presented for filing:** Precise rules govern such matters as:

— at least 12 point type with typeface essentially equivalent to Courier, Times New Roman or Arial;
— minimum paper weight (20-pound);
— size of paper (8 1/2 x 11 inches);
— only one side of each page may be used;
— hole punching at top;
— page numbering (consecutively at bottom);
— first page layout (*see* ¶*6:21 ff.*); and
— footer. [CRC 2.102-2.111]

Compare—court forms: These rules do not apply to Judicial Council forms or local court forms. [CRC 2.119]

(a) [9:20.1] **Local rules preempted:** Any local rules relating to the above matters (¶*9:20*) are clearly preempted by CRC 3.20(a); *see* ¶*9:13.2 ff.*

(b) [9:20.2] **Additional rules applicable to Judicial Council forms:** Additional rules apply where a Judicial Council form (e.g., summons) is included in the moving papers:

- [9:20.3] If a *multi-page form* is used, it may be filed on pages printed on one side only (even if the original form was printed on both sides); or it may be printed on a "tumbled" two-part sheet (printed head to foot). [CRC 2.134]

(2) [9:21] **Essential data beneath case number:** The first page of each paper must specify immediately below the number of the case:

— The *date, time and place* of the scheduled hearing;
— The *name of the hearing judge if ascertainable;*
— The nature or title of any attached document other than an exhibit;
— The date of filing of the action; and
— The trial date, if set. [CRC 3.1110(b)]

(3) [9:22] **Line numbering and spacing:** Lines on each page shall be numbered consecutively and shall be *either* double-spaced or with 1 1/2 spaces between lines. [See CRC 2.108]

☞ [9:22a] ***PRACTICE POINTER:*** Double-spacing is recommended because it is easier to read. Page limits on memoranda (*see ¶9:64.10*) may tempt you to use the denser, 1 1/2 line spacing, but this will be harder for the judge to read. Therefore, stick with double-spacing. If necessary, edit your arguments to fit within the page limits or seek leave to file a longer memorandum. *See further discussion at ¶9:64.13.*

(a) [9:22.1] **Exceptions:** Single-spacing is permitted in:

— descriptions of real property; and
— footnotes and quotations (from cases, statutes or other materials). [See CRC 2.108]

Also, where corporate surety bonds are filed (e.g., on preliminary injunctions), they may be single-spaced and the lines need not be numbered. (But the first page format requirements (¶*9:21*) still apply.) [See CRC 2.108]

(4) [9:22.2] **Footers:** Except for exhibits, each paper filed with the court must bear a "footer": The bottom of each page must display the page number, then a printed line, then the title of the document ("clear and concise" abbreviations permitted) in at least 10-point type. [CRC 2.110]

(5) [9:23] **Consecutive numbering:** Documents bound together must be consecutively paginated. [CRC 2.109, 3.1110(c)]

The nature or title of any attached document other than an exhibit must be listed on the cover page (first page). [CRC 3.1110(b)]

To the extent practicable, all supporting declarations and memoranda "must be attached" to the notice of motion. [CRC 3.1113(j)]

© 2020 Thomson Reuters/The Rutter Group

[9:23a] ***PRACTICE POINTER:*** It can be helpful to the judge to put your notice of motion, declarations, memorandum of points and authorities and proof of service under one cover and bind them together to avoid their getting separated or misfiled. List the attached papers in your notice of motion. However, if you do so, the pages must be numbered serially *throughout* the package—rather than beginning anew with each of the documents. [CRC 2.109 & 3.1110(c)]

The everything-bound-together format may not work, however, for lengthy motions (e.g., motions for summary judgment with numerous separate declarations and lengthy points and authorities). Although all such documents should be filed at the same time, many judges prefer to have each document *filed and numbered separately.*

(6) [9:23.1] **References to earlier-filed documents:** Any paper previously filed shall be referred to by *date of execution* (not filing date) and *title*. [CRC 3.1110(d)]

Example: "The following points and authorities are submitted in opposition to the 'Demurrer of Defendant Smith' executed March 15, (year)."

Parties may incorporate by reference exhibits from prior motions, but it is "prudent" to provide courtesy copies to the judge. [*Roth v. Plikaytis* (2017) 15 CA5th 283, 292, 222 CR3d 850, 857-858]

[9:23.1a] ***PRACTICE POINTER:*** It is a good idea to *include the filing date* because this makes it easier for the judge to find the document in the court file.

Where the court file consists of several file folders or is electronically stored, include a copy of the previously filed document as an exhibit to your current filing (or "lodge" a copy with the court; *see ¶9:24.2*). This will save the judge the time required to locate the earlier filed document in the court file. [*Roth v. Plikaytis,* supra, 15 CA5th at 291, 222 CR3d at 857, fn. 8 (citing text)]

(7) [9:23.2] **Points and authorities:** Special rules govern the format of points and authorities. [CRC 3.1113; *see ¶9:64 ff.*]

(8) [9:23.3] **Binding:** All pages of each document and each exhibit shall be attached together at the top by a method that permits pages to be easily turned and the entire content of each page to be read (e.g., Acco fasteners). [CRC 3.1110(e)]

[9:23.4] ***PRACTICE POINTER:*** Documents bound together should be *separately tabbed* to help the judge find each document easily. Otherwise, you make the judge go through a fat stack of stapled exhibits to locate the document to which you are referring. For courtesy copies, a stack over about 2 inches high is unwieldy.

(9) [9:23.5] **Exhibits:** Each paper exhibit (as distinct from those filed electronically, *see* ¶*9:23.10*) must be separated from preceding papers by "a hard 8-1/2 x 11 sheet with hard paper or plastic tabs extending below the bottom of the page, bearing the exhibit designation." [CRC 3.1110(f)(3)]

(a) [9:23.6] **Index required:** An "index" to exhibits must be provided. The index must "briefly describe the exhibit and identify the exhibit number or letter and page number." [CRC 3.1110(f)(1)]

(b) [9:23.7] **Deposition excerpts:** Pages from a single deposition and any exhibits associated therewith must be designated as a single exhibit. [CRC 3.1110(f)(2)]

1) [9:23.7a] **Format requirements:** *See* ¶*9:50.1.*

(c) [9:23.8] **Foreign language exhibits:** Exhibits written in a foreign language must be *accompanied by an English translation*, certified under oath by a qualified interpreter. [CRC 3.1110(g)]

[9:23.9] *Reserved.*

(d) [9:23.10] **Electronic exhibits:** Unless they are submitted by a self-represented party, exhibits filed electronically "must include electronic bookmarks with links to the first page of each exhibit and with bookmark titles that identify the exhibit number or letter and briefly describe the exhibit." [CRC 3.1110(f)(4)]

[9:23.11] ***PRACTICE POINTER:*** Free software programs are available that allow users to apply electronic bookmarks or hyperlinks to electronic documents. [See Adv. Comm. Comment to CRC 3.1110; for a helpful resource on creating electronic appellate filings, see Guide to Creating Electronic Documents/ Filings, available on the California courts website (*www.courts.ca.gov*)]

b. [9:24] **Optional procedures:** In the past, many courts had local rules governing form and content of motion papers.

Although these rules have been preempted by CRC 3.20(a) (*see* ¶*9:13.2*), many attorneys continue to follow those procedures that are not inconsistent with the CRC rules discussed above (¶*9:19 ff.*).

(1) [9:24.1] **Paragraph numbering:** Many courts prefer that paragraphs be numbered consecutively throughout a pleading or motion (rather than separately for each cause of action or defense); that Arabic numbers (rather than Roman numerals) be used for all primary paragraphs; and that any subparagraphs be designated by letters (rather than numbers).

(2) [9:24.2] **Lodge "bench book" before hearing:** Where voluminous documents are involved, it is good practice to lodge a "bench book" a few days in advance. *See* ¶*9:89.1.*

Cross-refer: "*Lodging*" documents with the court is discussed at ¶*9:51 ff.*

c. [9:24.3] **Separate vs. combined motions:** Each motion or demurrer should normally be set forth in a *separate* document. (This includes any request for sanctions under CCP §128.7; *see* ¶*9:24.7.*)

However, CRC 3.1112(c) states a motion, notice of hearing and points and authorities may be combined in a single document "if the party filing a combined pleading specifies these items separately in the caption of the combined pleading." [CRC 3.1112(c)]

Comment: Although not entirely clear, CRC 3.1112(c) simply provides that all papers relating to the *same* motion or demurrer may be combined. It should *not* be read to authorize combining papers relating to *separate motions.*

➪ [9:24.4] ***PRACTICE POINTER:*** Even if no rule expressly prohibits combining several motions in a single document, it is not recommended. The judge may not be receptive to this practice or may overlook one of the combined motions. Investigate local practices.

(1) [9:24.5] **Compare—motion to strike filed in conjunction with demurrer:** Where a motion to strike is filed in conjunction with a demurrer, courts prefer two *separately captioned documents.* They should be filed concurrently, however, and set for hearing on the same date (*see* ¶*7:162 ff.*).

Although each motion or demurrer must normally be accompanied by its own supporting papers and memorandum of authorities, some courts permit a *single points and authorities* for a jointly-filed motion to strike and demurrer.

(2) [9:24.6] **Compare—motions for summary judgment and summary adjudication:** When a motion for summary adjudication of issues is filed as an *alternative* to a motion for summary judgment, the motions generally may be combined. But both motions must be expressly called out in the papers' title.

(3) [9:24.7] **Compare—sanctions requests:** Requests for sanctions in connection with *discovery disputes* may be made as part of a motion to compel; i.e., no separate motion is required (*see ¶8:1980*).

Similarly, a request for expenses under *CCP §128.5* may be made in a party's moving or responding papers. [CCP §128.5(c)]

But a request for sanctions under *CCP §§128.5 or 128.7* (for violation of implied certificate of merit, including when the challenged conduct may be obviated by withdrawing a pleading or other paper) must be filed as a separate motion. [CCP §§128.5(f)(1)(A), 128.7(c)]

(4) [9:24.8] **Compare—combining request for dismissal on forum selection grounds with demurrer:** While it may not result in forfeiture of the forum grounds, it is risky to combine a request for dismissal with a demurrer. [*Laboratory Specialists Int'l, Inc. v. Shimadzu Scientific Instruments, Inc.* (2017) 17 CA5th 755, 760-761, 225 CR3d 494, 497-498—finding compliance with requirement that forum motion be filed before demurrer, even when filed at same time]

PRACTICE POINTERS

- [9:25] ***Make sure your staff assistants are familiar with these rules:*** Copies of the CRC and any applicable local rules or policy manuals should be mounted, framed and hung over your staff assistants' (secretaries, paralegals, etc.) desks. If you file papers deviating from these rules, you're likely to run into trouble in law and motion.

  Don't expect the judge to be sympathetic if your secretary fails to follow the rules, because the ultimate responsibility is yours. (As one judge puts it, "blaming foul-ups on one's secretary is equivalent to 'the dog ate my homework' defense.")

- [9:26] ***Make it easy for the judge to read your papers:*** It's up to you to make your paperwork as readable and accessible as possible. When dealing with lengthy and complex motions, you can help the judge (and yourself) by including an *index*, *tabs* for each exhibit or declaration, *color codes* for documents of the same kind, etc. Doing so tends to ensure your arguments will be read, rather than overlooked.

© 2020 Thomson Reuters/The Rutter Group

d. [9:27] **"Joinder" in another's motion:** It is common practice for attorneys to join in another party's motion by simply filing a pleading captioned "Joinder in Motion of . . . for . . .," stating that the joining party adopts the requests and the points and authorities contained in the joined motion. [See *Barak v. Quisenberry Law Firm* (2006) 135 CA4th 654, 660-661, 37 CR3d 688, 692-693—codefendants could join another defendant's anti-SLAPP motion; *see ¶7:1060*]

(1) [9:27.1] **Limitation—summary judgment:** A party may *not* obtain a summary judgment in its favor by joining another party's motion for summary judgment because of the requirement that *each moving party* file a *separate statement* of undisputed facts (*¶10:95.3*). [See *Barak v. Quisenberry Law Firm*, supra, 135 CA4th at 660-661, 37 CR3d at 692-693]

[9:27.2] ***PRACTICE POINTER:*** To assure your client's interests are protected, the safest course is to file and serve your own notice of motion asking for relief specific to your client. You can incorporate the evidence and points and authorities filed by the first moving party. At the hearing, make it explicit that you want the same relief sought in the moving party's papers for your client. A joinder may not be in order if you have different facts or authorities, or if the relief sought by the moving party would not, on its own terms, benefit your client.

2. [9:28] **Essential Elements of Motion—Notice, Evidence, Law:** The papers filed in support of a motion or demurrer *must* consist of at least the following:

- the *motion* or demurrer itself (*see ¶9:28.2*);
- a *notice* of hearing on the motion or demurrer (*see ¶9:29 ff.*); and
- a *memorandum of points and authorities* in support of the motion or demurrer (*see ¶9:64 ff.*). [CRC 3.1112(a)]

Other papers *may* be filed in support of a motion or demurrer, such as declarations, exhibits, appendices or other documents or pleadings. [CRC 3.1112(b)]

FORM: Notice of Motion (With Attached) Memorandum in Support and Declaration, *see Form 9A:1* in Rivera, *Cal. Prac. Guide: Civ. Pro. Before Trial FORMS* (TRG).

a. [9:28.1] **Effect of incomplete papers:** A motion filed *without* the supporting papers upon which it is based is treated as an "incomplete motion" and may be continued, placed off calendar or denied without prejudice. [*Weinstein v. Blumberg* (2018) 25 CA5th 316, 320-321, 235 CR3d 658, 661-662—filing notice of motion and motion without supporting papers does not comply with CCP §1010 and does not constitute making motion, so discovery motion was untimely even if notice was timely filed]

b. [9:28.2] **Motion—required elements:** The motion must contain the following:

— identity of the party or parties bringing the motion;
— identity of the parties to whom it is addressed;
— a brief statement of the basis for the motion and the relief sought; and
— if a pleading is challenged, the specific portion challenged. [CRC 3.1112(d)]

c. [9:29] **Notice:** A Notice of Motion must be a separate paper stating:

— the *time* and *place* of hearing (*see ¶9:30 ff.*);
— the *nature of the order* sought and the *grounds* for such an order, both of which must be stated in the *first paragraph* of the notice (*see ¶9:38 ff.*); and
— the accompanying *supporting papers* listed by caption (*see ¶9:42.1*). [See CCP §1010; CRC 3.1110]

- *Compare—application for order:* If the order is being requested by way of application rather than motion, the notice may be styled "Notice of Hearing on Application."

FORMS

- Notice of Motion, *see Form 9A:2* in Rivera, *Cal. Prac. Guide: Civ. Pro. Before Trial FORMS* (TRG).
- Notice of Hearing on Application, *see Form 9A:2.1* in Rivera, *Cal. Prac. Guide: Civ. Pro. Before Trial FORMS* (TRG).

(1) [9:30] **Time and place of hearing:** First, the notice must state the date, time and place (department of the court, room number, etc.) it will be heard and the name of the hearing judge. [CRC 3.1110(b); *see ¶9:21*]

This information must be shown as part of the caption on the first page of the notice immediately below the case number; and is also customarily repeated in the opening paragraph.

(a) [9:31] **Minimum time limit:** Absent an order shortening time, the hearing date specified in the notice must allow for service of the moving papers in compliance with CCP §1005: i.e., *at least 16 court days* before the hearing, *plus* additional time for service by mail (or by fax, email or overnight delivery); *see ¶9:87 ff.* [See *Demyer v. Costa Mesa Mobile Home Estates* (1995) 36 CA4th 393, 401, 42 CR2d 260, 265, fn. 18 (citing text) (disapproved on other grounds by *Wilcox v. Birtwhistle* (1999) 21 C4th 973, 90 CR2d 260)]

1) [9:32] **Demurrers:** Demurrers are subject to the same time requirements as motions

generally. A party filing a demurrer is required to file with it a notice of hearing specifying a hearing date in accordance with CCP §1005. [CRC 3.1320(c); *see* ¶*7:110*]

[9:32.1-32.4] *Reserved.*

2) [9:32.5] **Exceptions:** There are some important exceptions to the CCP §1005(b) minimum notice requirement:

- [9:32.5a] A *summary judgment* motion requires at least *75 days'* notice. [CCP §437c(a); *see* ¶*10:77*]
- [9:32.5b] A discretionary dismissal motion based on *delay in prosecution* requires *45 days'* notice (except when the court moves to dismiss *sua sponte*, which requires *20 days'* notice). [CRC 3.1342(a), 3.1340(b); *Sakhai v. Zipora* (2009) 180 CA4th 593, 598, 102 CR3d 691, 695; *see* ¶*11:134*]

[9:32.6-32.9] *Reserved.*

3) [9:32.10] **Computation of time:** The applicable notice period is computed by *excluding* the day service was made (date of mailing, etc.) and *including the last day* unless it is a holiday (in which event it is also excluded). [CCP §§12, 12a; CRC 1.10]

a) [9:32.11] **Exception—court closed:** If the court (other than a branch office) is closed, it is deemed a holiday for purposes of computing applicable time limits. [CCP §12b; see *Bennett v. Suncloud* (1997) 56 CA4th 91, 98-99, 65 CR2d 80, 84—earthquake closures]

b) [9:32.12] **Exception—emergency conditions:** Similarly, if an emergency condition (public calamity or danger thereof or danger to the court facility) interferes with the public's ability to file papers, it is deemed a holiday for purposes of computing time under CCP §12. [Gov.C. §68115(a)(4)]

c) [9:32.13] **Compare—time measured backwards from hearing date:** Certain acts must be performed within a specified number of days *before a hearing date* (e.g., motion papers must be served and filed at least 16 court days before hearing; *see* ¶*9:31*). The time for their performance is determined by counting backwards from the hearing date (plus any additional days required because of mailing or other method of service), excluding the day of the hearing. [CCP §12c; see *Stasz v. Eisenberg* (2010) 190 CA4th 1032, 1038, 120 CR3d 21, 26]

(b) [9:33] **Excessive notice:** Except as stated below (¶*9:33.1 ff.*), there is generally no maximum time between service of a motion and the date of hearing. (CCP §1005 requires merely "*at least*" 16 court days.)

1) [9:33.1] **Limitations on excessive notice:** Excessive notice, however, is ground for denying certain procedures:

- [9:33.1a] *Demurrers* must be noticed for hearing within *35 days* after filing or on the first date available to the court thereafter. [CRC 3.1320(d); *see* ¶*7:110 ff.*]

- [9:33.1b] A *motion to dismiss* for *delay in service* of the complaint or for *delay in bringing the action to trial* must be noticed for hearing *within 30 days* after filing the notice. [CCP §418.10(b); *see* ¶*11:110*]

- [9:33.1c] Likewise, a *motion to quash service* of summons or to stay or dismiss the complaint on *forum non conveniens* grounds must be noticed for hearing *within 30 days* after the motion is filed. [CCP §418.10(b); see *Olinick v. BMG Entertainment* (2006) 138 CA4th 1286, 1295-1296, 42 CR3d 268, 275-276—hearing date more than 30 days after motion filed did not affect court's power to rule on merits; *see also* ¶*3:381*]

- [9:33.1d] Also, a special motion to strike under the anti-SLAPP statute (CCP §425.16, ¶*7:500 ff.*) must be noticed for hearing *within 30 days* after *service* (not filing) of the motion unless the court's docket conditions require a later hearing date. [See CCP §425.16(f), ¶*7:965*]

2) [9:33.2] **Comment:** Courts generally frown on excessive notice (e.g., hearing date 60 days after service) because it may cause unnecessary delay in moving the case to trial. Also, certain motions, such as venue change requests, suspend the court's jurisdiction (*see* ¶*3:580*) and therefore should be heard as rapidly as possible.

[9:33.3-33.4] *Reserved.*

© 2020 Thomson Reuters/The Rutter Group

(c) [9:33.5] **Standards of professionalism:** The California State Bar has adopted voluntary "Guidelines of Civility and Professionalism," including standards for "Service of Papers." [Cal. State Bar, Guidelines of Civility & Professionalism §7—"The timing and manner of service of papers should not be used to the disadvantage of the party receiving the papers"]

In addition, some courts have adopted civility guidelines as recommendations in the court's local rules:

- The time and manner of service of papers should not be used to the disadvantage of the party receiving the papers. [L.A. Sup.Ct. Rule 3.26, Appendix 3.A(b)(1)]
- Papers should not be served sufficiently close to a court appearance so as to inhibit the ability of opposing counsel to prepare for that appearance or, where permitted by law, to respond to the papers. [L.A. Sup.Ct. Rule 3.26, Appendix 3.A(b)(2)]
- Papers should not be served in order to take advantage of an opponent's known absence from the office or in a time designed to inconvenience an adversary, such as late on Friday afternoon or the day preceding a secular or religious holiday. [L.A. Sup.Ct. Rule 3.26, Appendix 3.A(b)(3)]

(d) [9:34] **Selection of hearing date:** In courts that still maintain separate law and motion departments, procedures for setting hearing dates vary:

- In some courts, the moving party can set a matter for hearing on any date the court has a law and motion calendar (between the minimum and maximum time limits, ¶*9:31 ff.*). [See S.F. Sup.Ct. Rule 8.2(A)(2)(a)]

But in courts with direct calendar systems (where a single judge is assigned for all purposes), law and motion matters *may* be heard on a single day of the week, and motions must be noticed for hearing accordingly. In some courts, it is necessary to reserve a date before filing the motion.

1) [9:34a] **Procedure for reserving date:** In general, hearing dates can be reserved by telephone. But some courts have alternative procedures:

- In *San Francisco Superior Court*, if the moving party has an email address, he or she *must* obtain a hearing date and reservation number via email. [S.F. Sup.Ct. Rule 8.2(A)(2)(b)]

- In many *Los Angeles Superior Court* civil courtrooms, parties are directed to reserve hearing dates using the court's online reservation system at the Online Services section of the court's website. The court's website identifies the participating courtrooms (*www.lacourt.org*).

[9:34.1] ***PRACTICE POINTER:*** If the court hears law and motion matters on more than one day, there may be an advantage in selecting a hearing date early in the week. If you notice your hearing on a Friday, you will not have the benefit of the weekend to work on your papers. (Because reply papers are due 5 court days before the hearing, if your hearing is on a Friday, the opposition papers normally will be served and filed on a Monday (9 court days beforehand), and your reply papers will be due that Friday (5 court days before the hearing); *see ¶9:105.*) Recall that in some courts, you may not be able to obtain a hearing for months after the reservation.

(e) [9:35] **Incorrect time or department:** Occasionally, counsel will notice a law and motion matter in an improper department or at an incorrect time of day. The court clerk will generally calendar it in the proper department at the proper time (and notify counsel accordingly). If for any reason this cannot be done, the clerk will simply reject the papers.

[9:36] ***PRACTICE POINTER:*** If you're not familiar with the procedures in the court in which you plan to file a motion, always check the court's website or with the court clerk *before* filing.

[9:36.1] ***PRACTICE POINTERS:*** It is good practice to clear the hearing date with opposing counsel in advance (and in some courts, counsel are directed to do so; see, e.g., S.F. Sup.Ct. Rules 8.2(A)(2)(a), 10.0(C)). This can avoid last-minute continuances and wasted preparation.

You may also wish to avoid scheduling the hearing for a Monday or any day immediately following a holiday, because court calendars tend to be unusually heavy on those days.

© 2020 Thomson Reuters/The Rutter Group

(f) [9:37] **"Notice of unavailability" disregarded:** It is a common practice in some communities for lawyers to file a "notice of unavailability" to block out dates when they will be on vacation, engaged in trial elsewhere, etc. [See *Tenderloin Housing Clinic, Inc. v. Sparks* (1992) 8 CA4th 299, 301, 10 CR2d 371, 372—monetary sanctions imposed against counsel who scheduled a hearing and depositions after being notified of opposing counsel's unavailability on those dates; *and* ¶*8:506.5*]

Such a notice has *no effect*, however, on law and motion calendars and does not affect applicable time requirements. [*Carl v. Sup.Ct. (Coast Comm. College Dist.)* (2007) 157 CA4th 73, 75, 68 CR3d 566, 567—no authority for such notice in trial or appellate courts]

(2) [9:38] **Statement of relief sought and grounds:** The notice of motion must state in the *first* paragraph exactly *what* relief is sought and *why* (what grounds). [CCP §1010; CRC 3.1110(a); see *People v. American Sur. Ins. Co.* (1999) 75 CA4th 719, 726, 89 CR2d 422, 427 (citing text)]

The court generally cannot grant different relief, or relief on different grounds, than stated in the notice of motion. [See *People v. American Sur. Ins. Co.*, supra, 75 CA4th at 726, 89 CR2d at 427-428; *Luri v. Greenwald* (2003) 107 CA4th 1119, 1124, 132 CR2d 680, 684; compare *Kinda v. Carpenter* (2016) 247 CA4th 1268, 1277-1278, 203 CR3d 183, 191-192—court had discretion to rule on grounds not stated in motion where no objection and parties had fair opportunity to address issues]

[9:39] *Reserved.*

(a) **Application**

- [9:39.1] Where the notice of motion states that sanctions will be sought from the opposing party, the court has no power to impose sanctions also against that party's *counsel.* To justify an award against counsel, the *notice of motion* must apprise opposing counsel in advance of the hearing that sanctions will be sought against him or her as well. [*Blumenthal v. Sup.Ct. (Corey)* (1980) 103 CA3d 317, 320, 163 CR 39, 40]

- [9:39.2] Because a motion for relief from default stated it was based on "excusable neglect," a ground for *discretionary* relief, it could not be considered a motion for *mandatory* relief based on attorney fault under CCP §473(b) (*see* ¶*5:304*).

[*Luri v. Greenwald*, supra, 107 CA4th at 1125, 132 CR2d at 685]

[9:39.3-39.4] *Reserved.*

☞ [9:39.5] ***PRACTICE POINTER:*** Ask yourself whether an order that states your motion is "granted" would provide meaningful and unambiguous relief to your client. If not, revise your notice of motion to state more specifically whatever relief you are requesting.

(b) [9:40] **Grounds disclosed in accompanying papers:** It is improper to "bury" the grounds in the points and authorities or declarations. The grounds should be stated in the *first paragraph* of the notice (CRC 3.1110(a), ¶*9:38*). [See *In re Sutter Health Uninsured Pricing Cases* (2009) 171 CA4th 495, 514, 89 CR3d 615, 631—"stray citation to a rule of court . . . buried at the end of a clearly-captioned" motion did not convert motion]

1) [9:41] However, this is not an absolute requirement. Relief may be granted on grounds appearing *anywhere* in the accompanying declarations and points and authorities *provided* the notice states the motion will be made on grounds disclosed in the accompanying papers. [*Carrasco v. Craft* (1985) 164 CA3d 796, 808, 210 CR 599, 607]

2) [9:42] *Comment:* Even so, some judges may refuse to consider grounds not clearly stated in the notice of motion, particularly if opposing counsel claims lack of "fair notice."

(3) [9:42.1] **Designation of supporting papers:** Finally, the notice must describe the various declarations or other evidence, if any, on which the motion will be based. [CCP §1010; *Cromwell v. Cummings* (1998) 65 CA4th Supp. 10, 13, 76 CR2d 171, 173]

The nature or title of any such documents (other than exhibits) must also appear beneath the case number; and if the documents are bound together, they must be consecutively paginated. [CRC 3.1110(b), (c); *see* ¶*9:21 ff.*]

(4) [9:42.2] **Signature:** The notice of motion is usually signed by the attorney for the moving party. [See CCP §128.7—every notice of motion or similar court paper to be signed by at least one attorney of record, and state the signer's *address* and *telephone number*]

d. [9:43] **Evidence:** Some law and motion matters must be decided solely on the basis of the pleadings, and extrinsic

© 2020 Thomson Reuters/The Rutter Group

evidence cannot be considered (except facts judicially noticeable)—i.e., demurrers, motions to strike and motions for judgment on the pleadings.

Most other motions, however, are decided on the basis of declarations, discovery documents, or other evidence presented to the court in support of the motion.

(1) [9:44] **Must accompany moving papers:** The original or copies of all evidence that will be presented to the court at the motion hearing must be served along with the notice of motion and points and authorities. [CCP §1005(b)]

Compare—CRC 3.1113(j): CRC 3.1113(j) states that "[t]o the extent practicable, all supporting memorandums and declarations must be attached to the notice of motion."

In addition, if your motion challenges the sufficiency of a pleading already on file, you may want to supply a courtesy copy of that pleading along with your motion papers. Some local rules may require you to do so. [See, e.g., S.F. Sup.Ct. Rule 8.2(A)(2)(c)]

[9:44.1-44.4] *Reserved.*

(2) [9:44.5] **Form of evidence:** Except for OSCs re contempt (*see* ¶*9:717 ff.*), law and motion matters are almost always decided on the basis of declarations or other evidence in written form. [CRC 3.1306(a)]

(a) [9:45] **Oral testimony usually not permitted:** The court has *discretion* to receive oral testimony on a contested issue of fact in a motion hearing. [*Mutual Mortgage Co. v. Avis* (1986) 176 CA3d 799, 805, 222 CR 342, 345—oral testimony allowed on motion to set aside default]

But the court also has discretion to *refuse* to allow oral testimony (and usually does so). Appellate courts will not interfere except for a clear abuse of discretion. [*Eddy v. Temkin* (1985) 167 CA3d 1115, 1121, 213 CR 597, 601—no abuse of discretion in refusing oral testimony on issues where documentary evidence more important than demeanor of witnesses; compare *Ashburn v. AIG Fin'l Advisors, Inc.* (2015) 234 CA4th 79, 98, 183 CR3d 679, 693—abuse of discretion not to hear oral testimony to resolve "significant" factual dispute on motion to compel arbitration]

1) [9:45.1] **Procedure for seeking leave to introduce oral testimony**

a) A party seeking to introduce oral testimony (other than to rebut oral testimony presented by the opposing party) must first obtain a court order on a showing of "good cause."

b) The request must be accompanied by a statement describing the proposed testimony and the estimated time required for the hearing.

c) The request and statement must be served and filed not less than *3 court days* before the hearing (and if filed less than 5 court days beforehand, it must be served in a manner to assure receipt by all other parties at least 2 days before the hearing). [CRC 3.1306(b)]

Failure to comply with these requirements justifies denial of the request for live testimony. [*City of Crescent City v. Reddy* (2017) 9 CA5th 458, 464-465, 215 CR3d 351, 356-357]

(b) [9:46] **Declarations and affidavits:** Declarations under penalty of perjury, and affidavits with jurats attached ("subscribed and sworn to" before a notary public) are the most common forms of evidence in motion hearings. [CCP §2015.5; CRC 3.1306(a)]

Declarations and affidavits are hearsay and therefore inadmissible at trial, subject to statutory exceptions. But CCP §2009 authorizes their use in motion proceedings, creating an exception to the hearsay rule and rendering them potentially admissible evidence. (But absent some other exception to the *hearsay* rule, declarations must be based on personal knowledge rather than hearsay; *see* ¶*9:59.*) [*Elkins v. Sup.Ct. (Elkins)* (2007) 41 C4th 1337, 1345, 63 CR3d 483, 485; *United Comm. Church v. Garcin* (1991) 231 CA3d 327, 344, 282 CR 368, 380 (superseded by statute on other grounds); *North Beverly Park Homeowners Ass'n v. Bisno* (2007) 147 CA4th 762, 778, 54 CR3d 644, 656 (citing text)]

FORM: Declaration in Support of Motion, *see Form 9A:4* in Rivera, *Cal. Prac. Guide: Civ. Pro. Before Trial FORMS* (TRG).

[9:46.1] ***PRACTICE POINTERS:*** Make sure your declarations include *facts* demonstrating the declarant's personal observations or knowledge. For example, it is not enough for a declarant to state simply, "The light was green." The declaration must contain additional *facts* showing the declarant was in a position to see the light at the relevant time.

© 2020 Thomson Reuters/The Rutter Group

Take particular care in drafting *expert witness* declarations. To support an expert's opinion, the declaration must contain *facts* showing the expert's qualifications and competence to express the opinion; that the opinion is not based on speculation and rests on matters of a *type reasonably relied upon* by experts; and the *factual basis* for the opinion (*see* ¶*10:124.5*). If the expert's declaration cites case-specific hearsay, that matter must be shown by otherwise admissible evidence from another witness or document. [*People v. Sanchez* (2016) 63 C4th 665, 686, 204 CR3d 102, 119—expert cannot "relate as true case-specific facts asserted in hearsay statements, unless they are independently proven by competent evidence or are covered by a hearsay exception"]

1) [9:47] **Declarations instead of affidavits:** Declarations under penalty of perjury can be used in place of affidavits. [CCP §2015.5] They are simpler to prepare because no notarization is required, and therefore are far more common.

   Many declarations, especially from out-of-state declarants, fail to conform to §2015.5, instead stating they are made under penalty of perjury only under the laws of some *other* state or of the United States; such declarations are inadmissible in California courts (¶*9:48*).

2) [9:47.1] **Caption requirements:** The caption of any declaration must state the name of the declarant and must identify the motion or other proceeding which it supports or opposes. [CRC 3.1115]

   Example: "DECLARATION OF JANE JONES IN SUPPORT OF DEFENDANT'S MOTION FOR SUMMARY JUDGMENT."

3) [9:48] **Declarations—essential wording:** Declarations executed *anywhere* (inside or outside California) are valid if they contain the following language:

   "I declare under penalty of perjury *under the laws of the State of California* that the foregoing is true and correct.

   "__________   ____________________"
   (date)   (signature)

If this form is used, you do *not* have to show the *place* where the declaration was signed. And, the declaration is valid even if executed in a state or country whose laws do not permit declarations under penalty of perjury. [CCP §2015.5]

A declaration *executed outside* of California that fails to include the words "under the laws of the State of California" is *inadmissible* hearsay. [*Kulshrestha v. First Union Comm'l Corp.* (2004) 33 C4th 601, 612, 15 CR3d 793, 800, fn. 6 (citing text); *ViaView, Inc. v. Retzlaff* (2016) 1 CA5th 198, 217, 204 CR3d 566, 581—declaration not signed under penalty of perjury under the laws of the State of California, as required by CCP §2015.5, had "no evidentiary value" and court refused to consider it]

- [9:48.1] Although it would appear obvious, a declaration must be signed by the declarant personally, *not* by an attorney on the declarant's behalf. [*Marriage of Reese & Guy* (1999) 73 CA4th 1214, 1222-1223, 87 CR2d 339, 345]

  [9:48.2-48.5] *Reserved.*

- [9:48.6] Transcripts of telephone interviews in which witnesses stated orally that their statements were true under penalty of perjury did *not qualify* as a declaration, and therefore could not be considered in opposition to a motion. [*Stockinger v. Feather River Comm. College* (2003) 111 CA4th 1014, 1025, 4 CR3d 385, 393 (disapproved on other grounds by *Regents of Univ. of Calif. v. Sup.Ct. (Rosen)* (2018) 4 C5th 607, 634, 230 CR3d 415, 436, fn. 7)]

4) [9:49] **No verified pleadings in lieu of affidavit:** Verified pleadings are generally *not* acceptable as evidence of the matters alleged because pleadings contain allegations of "ultimate" rather than "evidentiary" fact. [*Strauch v. Eyring* (1994) 30 CA4th 181, 186, 35 CR2d 747, 750 (citing text); see *ViaView, Inc. v. Retzlaff*, supra, 1 CA5th at 217, 204 CR3d at 581—verified complaint containing *evidentiary* facts may be treated as declaration]

© 2020 Thomson Reuters/The Rutter Group

a) [9:49.1] **Exception—complaint for preliminary injunction:** A verified complaint *can* be used, however, to obtain a preliminary injunction or temporary restraining order, provided it contains sufficient *evidentiary facts*. [CCP §527(a); *see ¶9:579*]

b) [9:49.2] **Limitation:** Certain types of verified pleadings *cannot* be considered as evidence (presumably for injunctions as well): Pleadings on behalf of a corporation or public entity, verified by one of its officers, and pleadings verified by an attorney because the client is unable to verify (*see ¶6:320*) "shall not . . . be considered as an affidavit or declaration establishing the facts therein alleged." [CCP §446(a); *ViaView, Inc. v. Retzlaff,* supra, 1 CA5th at 217, 204 CR3d at 581—pleading verified by corporate officer inadmissible]

[9:49.3-49.4] *Reserved.*

5) [9:49.5] **Declarations limited to facts, not legal arguments:** It is *improper* to include legal arguments in a declaration. (E.g., "the interests of justice require . . ." or "the following matters constitute 'good cause' . . .") As noted by one court, this is "a sloppy practice which should stop . . . [I]t makes a mockery of the requirement that declarations be supported by statement made under penalty of perjury." [*Marriage of Heggie* (2002) 99 CA4th 28, 30, 120 CR2d 707, 709, fn. 3] Nor do judges appreciate legal argument in declarations as a ruse to avoid page limits in a memorandum of points and authorities.

(c) [9:50] **Discovery documents:** Motions are also frequently based on answers obtained in depositions, or to interrogatories, requests for admission, etc. In such cases, copies of the questions and answers should accompany your moving papers, except for discovery motions where the separate statement includes the summary of the question and response in dispute (*see ¶8:1151 ff.*). Parties should be prepared to lodge the executed originals of the discovery response with the court if questions arise about the authenticity of copies. (Discovery documents are not filed with the court unless the court so orders; see CCP §§2025.550(a), 2030.280(a) & 2033.270(a), *discussed in Ch. 8.*) [*Greenspan v. LADT, LLC* (2010) 191 CA4th 486, 524, 121 CR3d 118, 148 (citing text)]

[9:50a] ***PRACTICE POINTER:*** Discovery responses are not admissible unless *authenticated.* Therefore, remember to attach a declaration by counsel (or the court reporter present at a deposition) confirming that the attached responses were actually given in discovery in the case.

1) [9:50.1] **Deposition transcripts:** It is rarely necessary or proper to attach an entire deposition transcript as an exhibit to a motion. Only the title page (stating the name of the deponent and date of deposition) and the "*relevant pages*" should be included. [CRC 3.1116(a), (b)]

[9:50.2] ***PRACTICE POINTER:*** Don't read "relevant" too narrowly. It is often necessary to include a few pages leading up to critical testimony in order to give it context.

- [9:50.3] *Title page:* The first page of any such exhibit shall state the name of the deponent and the date of the deposition. [CRC 3.1116(a)]

  The title page of the deposition transcript normally contains this information as well as the case caption and other information.

- [9:50.4] *Page numbering:* The page number from the original transcript must be clearly visible at the bottom of each page of deposition excerpts. [CRC 3.1116(b)]

- [9:50.5] *Relevant passages highlighted:* The relevant portion of the testimony should be *marked in a manner that calls attention* to the testimony. [CRC 3.1116(c)]

[9:50.6] ***PRACTICE POINTER:*** The easiest way to call attention to the relevant testimony as required by the rules is to *bracket the lines* of the transcript.

In addition, because some judges prefer highlighting crucial testimony with a colored marker, it may be a good idea to add such marking to the court's copy. This should be done on all copies, including copies served on opposing counsel, and, of course, your own copy.

© 2020 Thomson Reuters/The Rutter Group

2) [9:51] **"Lodging":** When the court orders original discovery documents lodged with the court, they should be delivered to the court clerk before the hearing, together with a self-addressed, stamped envelope for return after the hearing to the party lodging the documents. [See CRC 3.1302(b)]

Alternatively, some courts permit leaving an attorney-service pick-up slip with the lodged materials. But it is counsel's responsibility to make sure the attorney service picks up the papers after the hearing without reminder from the court clerk. (Do not ask the court clerk to contact the messenger.)

If the material is lodged electronically, it must specify the electronic address to which a notice of deletion may be sent. After determination of the matter, the clerk may permanently delete the electronically lodged material after sending notice of the deletion to the party who lodged it. [CRC 3.1302(b)]

3) [9:51.1] **Notice of lodging:** As an accommodation to the court and to opposing parties, it is good practice to file and serve a "Notice of Lodging" listing all of the items lodged.

☞ [9:52] ***PRACTICE POINTER:*** Ask opposing counsel to *stipulate to using the copies attached to the moving papers in lieu of the originals.* This will avoid any necessity of "lodging" documents with the court clerk. But be sure to mention such stipulation in your moving papers, or advise the court clerk, so that the judge won't be looking for the originals when he or she is reviewing the motion.

(d) [9:53] **Other documentary evidence:** Motions may also be based on admissions made in the opposing party's *pleadings*; or on other documentary evidence generally.

When relying on evidence contained in other documents, it is good practice to set forth the full text or portion relied upon, or to attach a copy to the moving papers.

Where opposing pleadings are relied upon, they may simply be incorporated by reference into declarations supporting the motion. Where other documentary evidence is offered, a proper *foundation* should be laid for such documents in supporting declarations; and although copies may be attached to the moving papers, the *original* or *certified copy* of the document should be offered at the hearing.

1) [9:53a] **Authentication:** A writing must be authenticated by declarations or other evidence establishing that the writing is what it purports to be. [Ev.C. §§250, 1401(a); see *O'Laskey v. Sortino* (1990) 224 CA3d 241, 273 CR 674 (disapproved on other grounds by *Flanagan v. Flanagan* (2002) 27 C4th 766, 117 CR2d 574)—transcript of tape recording not enough to authenticate accuracy of tape]

   It is routine in law-and-motion practice for the moving party's attorneys, who have personal knowledge of the attached exhibits, to attach declarations establishing their authenticity (i.e., how they obtained the documents, who identified them, and their status as "true and correct" copies of the originals). [*Greenspan v. LADT, LLC* (2010) 191 CA4th 486, 523, 121 CR3d 118, 147] (Recall, however, that the mere fact that the document was produced by the other side in discovery does not mean it has been authenticated.)

2) [9:53.1] **Copies generally admissible:** The "Secondary Evidence Rule" allows use of authenticated photocopies (or other secondary evidence) of a document instead of the original, unless:
   — a genuine dispute exists concerning material terms of the document and "justice" requires exclusion of copies; or
   — admission of secondary evidence would be "unfair" under the circumstances. [See Ev.C. §1521(a)]

3) [9:53.1a] **Admissibility of contents:** It is not necessary to ask the court to take judicial notice of materials previously filed in the case; you should simply call the court's attention to such papers. But except for admissions in pleadings, those materials may not be admissible for the truth of the matter.

4) [9:53.2] **Limitation:** On motions for summary judgment on a contract or promissory note, the *original* note must still be produced upon entry of judgment, so that the court clerk may mark it "paid" or "cancelled." [CRC 3.1806; *see* ¶*10:176*]

(e) [9:54] **Judicial notice:** A party may also base a motion on undisputed facts or events of which the

© 2020 Thomson Reuters/The Rutter Group

judge may or must take judicial notice. [Ev.C. §452—matters which may be judicially noticed; Ev.C. §453—court "shall" take notice of any matter under Ev.C. §452 if proper notice given (¶*9:56.1*)]

The most common situation is where judicial notice is requested of *court files in other lawsuits* (e.g., as the basis for a claim of res judicata or abuse of process). The court may take judicial notice of the fact of the filing of a particular document in another case and of any judicial action taken in such a case. However, absent an exception to the hearsay rule, such as an admission, the court may *not* take judicial notice of the truth of allegations contained in such files. [See *Richtek USA, Inc. v. uPI Semiconductor Corp.* (2015) 242 CA4th 651, 659-660, 195 CR3d 430, 437—improper for court to judicially notice truth of allegations in foreign complaints]

The judicial notice request must be a separate document that is typically served with the moving or opposing papers. Do not bury your request in another document—e.g., memorandum of points and authorities. [See CRC 3.1113(*l*); *and* ¶*7:13 ff.*]

FORM: Request for Judicial Notice, *see Form 9A:5* in Rivera, *Cal. Prac. Guide: Civ. Pro. Before Trial FORMS* (TRG).

1) [9:55] **Files of same court:** A party requesting the court to take notice of material in another case file in the same court must: (a) file a written "Request for Judicial Notice," directing the court's attention to the part of the other file sought to be judicially noticed; and (b) make arrangements with the clerk to have the file in the courtroom at the time of the hearing or confirm with the clerk that the file is electronically accessible to the court. [CRC 3.1113(*l*), 3.1306(c)]

   If the file must be physically delivered to the courtroom, the "Request" should be filed well in advance of the hearing to enable the court staff to obtain the other file in time. [CRC 3.1113(*l*), 3.1306(c)]

   ☞ [9:55.1] ***PRACTICE POINTER:*** It is a good practice to *attach to your motion* photocopies of whatever papers from the other file you want the court to notice. That way, if that file cannot be obtained in time for the hearing, the court may still be able to proceed (assuming your photocopies are accepted as correct by the opposing party).

2) [9:56] **Files of another court:** To enable the court to take judicial notice of case files in another court, the party seeking such notice must *either* serve a subpoena duces tecum on the court clerk of the other court, or (preferably) obtain *certified copies* of the file in question, and attach them to the moving papers. [*Ross v. Creel Printing & Publishing Co., Inc.* (2002) 100 CA4th 736, 743, 122 CR2d 787, 791-792—Nevada complaint not judicially noticeable because neither certified nor produced in response to a subpoena]

3) [9:56.1] **Copies to be provided:** A party requesting judicial notice of any materials under Ev.C. §§452 or 453 must provide the court and each opposing party with copies of the material to be so noticed. [CRC 3.1306(c); see Ev.C. §453; *Creed-21 v. City of San Diego* (2015) 234 CA4th 488, 519-520, 184 CR3d 128, 152—although ordinance qualified for judicial notice under Ev.C. §452, request properly denied due to insufficient information given under Ev.C. §453]

(3) [9:57] **Admissibility of evidence:** The evidence submitted to the court must meet all statutory requirements for admissibility of evidence at trial. The standards are the same as for evidence presented by a live witness. Basically, this means the declarations must be from *competent* witnesses having *personal knowledge* of the facts stated therein, rather than hearsay or conclusions. [*Pajaro Valley Water Mgmt. Agency v. McGrath* (2005) 128 CA4th 1093, 1107, 27 CR3d 741, 751]

(a) [9:58] **Competency of declarant:** A declaration is a substitute for oral testimony, and therefore must conform to the same requirements of competency as would be applicable to testimony in court. For example, if special qualifications are necessary to allow a person to give *opinion* testimony in court, such qualifications must be set forth in detail in declarations containing such testimony. [*Ochoa v. Pacific Gas & Elec. Co.* (1998) 61 CA4th 1480, 1487, 72 CR2d 232, 236—declaration lacked sufficient foundation for opinion expressed]

1) [9:58.1] **Not established by own conclusory declaration:** Declarations often recite, "I am competent to testify to the matters contained in this declaration, which are true of my own knowledge."

© 2020 Thomson Reuters/The Rutter Group

But this is purely a legal conclusion and proves nothing. The declarant's competency must appear from the *facts* alleged in the declaration (e.g., that he or she *saw* what happened or *heard* what was said). *See ¶10:110 ff.*

(b) [9:59] **Personal knowledge of declarant:** It is *not* enough for the declaration simply to state the declarant has personal knowledge of the facts stated. Rather, the declaration itself must contain facts showing the declarant's connection with the matters stated therein, establishing the source of his or her information. Otherwise, the declarant's statement he or she has such knowledge is purely a conclusion. [See Ev.C. §702; and *Osmond v. EWAP, Inc.* (1984) 153 CA3d 842, 851, 200 CR 674, 679]

1) [9:60] **"On information and belief":** A declaration on information and belief is proper only where permitted by statute (e.g., to verify pleadings; see CCP §446) or "where the facts to be established are *incapable of positive averment.*" [*City of Santa Cruz v. Mun.Ct. (Kennedy)* (1989) 49 C3d 74, 86, 260 CR 520, 527 (emphasis added)]

"Information and belief" indicates the statement is not based on the declarant's firsthand knowledge but that person nevertheless, in good faith, believes the statement to be true. [*City of Santa Cruz v. Mun.Ct. (Kennedy)*, supra, 49 C3d at 93, 260 CR at 532, fn. 9]

Generally, this means the declaration is inadmissible. But declarations on information and belief have been held sufficient in some contexts where the facts would otherwise be difficult or impossible to establish. For example:

- [9:60.1] To allege bias, prejudice, etc. on a motion for disqualification of a trial judge. [See *Blackman v. MacCoy* (1959) 169 CA2d 873, 879-880, 338 P2d 234, 236]
- [9:60.2] To allege a third party's residence on a motion for change of venue. [See *Brown v. Happy Valley Fruit Growers* (1929) 206 C 515, 520-521, 274 P 977, 979]
- [9:60.3] To show "good cause" for discovery of peace or custodial officer personnel records under Ev.C. §1043. [See *City of Santa Cruz v. Mun.Ct. (Kennedy)*, supra, 49 C3d at 88, 260 CR at 528]

- [9:60.4] To show state of mind where that is in issue; e.g., in response to a motion for sanctions, to explain why a certain motion was made, why certain discovery was sought, etc.
- [9:60.5] To show a medical diagnosis and prognosis in support of a trial preference motion under CCP §36(a). [CCP §36.5]

[9:60.6-60.7] *Reserved.*

[9:60.8] **Compare:** Statutes may also *preclude* declarations on information and belief: e.g., CCP §437c(d) requires declarations in support of a motion for summary judgment to be made on the basis of "personal knowledge" (*not* information and belief). *See ¶10:107 ff.*

2) [9:60.9] **"To the best of my knowledge":** A declaration stating it is "to the best of my knowledge" is not defective if actually and demonstrably based on personal knowledge. But the phrase "introduces an element of uncertainty which, *under certain circumstances*, can be lethal." [*Pelayo v. J.J. Lee Mgmt. Co., Inc.* (2009) 174 CA4th 484, 494, 94 CR3d 502, 510 (emphasis in original)—upholding trial court's decision to *accept* declaration, impliedly finding no uncertainty as to declarant's knowledge]

[9:60.10] ***PRACTICE POINTER:*** Avoid this phrase and any others that raise questions about whether the declarant in fact has personal knowledge. They create a risk that the court may refuse to consider the evidence.

3) [9:61] **Declarations by counsel:** Declarations by moving party's counsel as to essential facts are generally objectionable and inadmissible as hearsay, except where the lawyer somehow has personal knowledge of the facts. [*Star Motor Imports, Inc. v. Sup.Ct. (Shake)* (1979) 88 CA3d 201, 203-204, 151 CR 721, 723]

a) [9:62] **Compare:** But if the essential facts appear in pleadings, discovery documents, etc. already on file (or otherwise before the court at the hearing), the moving party's lawyer may execute a declaration stating his or her personal knowledge of their contents, and recite (or summarize) such information to support the relief sought. [See

© 2020 Thomson Reuters/The Rutter Group

Star Motor Imports, Inc. v. Sup.Ct. (Shake), supra, 88 CA3d at 203-204, 151 CR at 723-724]

b) [9:62.1] **Not verified pleadings:** Remember, however, that *pleadings* verified by an attorney (where the client is unable to do so) are *not* admissible as evidence of the facts stated therein. [CCP §446(a); *see* ¶*9:49.2*]

(c) [9:63] **Failure to object as waiver:** If the opposing party fails to object to hearsay or other inadmissible evidence contained in the moving party's declarations, the court may consider them. I.e., the evidentiary objection is *waived* by failure to assert it. [CCP §437c(d) (summary judgment motions); *Broden v. Marin Humane Soc.* (1999) 70 CA4th 1212, 1226-1227, 83 CR2d 235, 243, fn. 13 (other motions); *Schoendorf v. U.D. Registry, Inc.* (2002) 97 CA4th 227, 240, 118 CR2d 313, 322, fn. 2 (citing text); Ev.C. §353(a)]

The court should not exclude evidence on its own motion unless it is "irrelevant, unreliable, misleading, or prejudicial." [*Gonzalez v. Santa Clara County Dept. of Social Services* (2017) 9 CA5th 162, 173, 215 CR3d 22, 32 (emphasis and internal quotes omitted)]

(d) [9:63.1] **Ruling unnecessary to preserve objections:** Evidentiary objections not ruled upon by the trial court are *presumed overruled* and preserved for appellate review. [*Reid v. Google, Inc.* (2010) 50 C4th 512, 532, 113 CR3d 327, 344; *Jolley v. Chase Home Finance, LLC* (2013) 213 CA4th 872, 890, 153 CR3d 546, 561; *Zucchet v. Galardi* (2014) 229 CA4th 1466, 1480, 178 CR3d 363, 373, fn. 7]

This rule has essentially been codified for purposes of motions for summary judgment and summary adjudication. [CCP §437c(q)—court need only rule on material objections to evidence and evidentiary objections not ruled on are preserved for appellate review; *see* ¶*10:210.4*]

[9:63.2] ***PRACTICE POINTER:*** To increase the likelihood the court will rule on your evidentiary objections, make the court's job easier. Submit objections to evidence in the format set forth in CRC 3.1354 and include a checkbox for the court to indicate whether it has sustained or overruled each objection. Also, only make truly important objections (such as those you would make at trial) and avoid making multiple objections to the same evidence.

e. [9:64] **Points and authorities:** The third essential element of any motion is supporting points and authorities. [CRC 3.1112(a); *see ¶9:28*]

Without such a memorandum, the motion is incomplete and cannot be granted (CRC 3.1112(a)). Indeed, the court may treat the failure to provide the memorandum as an *admission* that the motion is not meritorious and cause for its denial. [CRC 3.1113(a)]

(1) [9:64.1] **Must accompany notice:** A memorandum of points and authorities must accompany every notice of motion *except* those listed in CRC 3.1114 (*¶9:64.6*). [CRC 3.1113(a); see *Quantum Cooking Concepts, Inc. v. LV Assocs., Inc.* (2011) 197 CA4th 927, 932, 130 CR3d 92, 97—requirement applies to post-trial motions]

The memorandum must be served and filed along with and *physically attached to* the notice of motion "to the extent practicable." [CRC 3.1113(j)]

[9:64.2-64.5] *Reserved.*

(a) [9:64.6] **Exceptions:** No supporting memorandum is necessary in connection with the following motions *filed on Judicial Council forms:*

— Application for appointment of guardian ad litem in a civil case;
— Application for an order extending time to serve pleading;
— Motion to be relieved as counsel;
— Motion filed in small claims case;
— Petition for change of name or gender;
— Petition for declaration of emancipation of minor;
— Petition for injunction prohibiting harassment;
— Petition for protective order to prevent elder or dependent adult abuse;
— Petition for order to prevent postsecondary school violence;
— Petition of employer for injunction prohibiting workplace violence;
— Petition for order prohibiting abuse (transitional housing);
— Petition to approve compromise of claim of a minor or person with a disability;
— Petition for withdrawal of funds from blocked account. [CRC 3.1114(a)]

A party may *choose* to file a memorandum in support of any of these motions if it would further the interests

© 2020 Thomson Reuters/The Rutter Group

of justice; or the court may order such a memorandum. [See CRC 3.1114(b)]

(2) [9:64.7] **Content, generally:** The memorandum "must contain a statement of facts, a concise statement of the law, evidence and arguments relied on, and a discussion of the statutes, cases and textbooks cited in support of the position advanced." [CRC 3.1113(b); see *Quantum Cooking Concepts, Inc. v. LV Assocs., Inc.*, supra, 197 CA4th at 934, 130 CR3d at 98—trial court not required to "comb the record and the law for factual and legal support that a party has failed to identify or provide"; *and ¶9:68.5 ff.*]

FORM: Memorandum in Support of Motion, *see Form 9A:3* in Rivera, *Cal. Prac. Guide: Civ. Pro. Before Trial FORMS* (TRG).

(a) [9:64.7a] **Need not be organized on cause of action basis:** A memorandum that complies with CRC 3.1113(b) cannot be disregarded because it is not structured on a cause of action by cause of action basis favored by the trial court. [*Hope Int'l Univ. v. Sup.Ct. (Rouanzoin)* (2004) 119 CA4th 719, 731, 14 CR3d 643, 651]

(3) [9:64.8] **Style:** A memorandum must consistently follow *either* the "California Style Manual" or "The Bluebook: A Uniform System of Citation" as to such matters as citations, abbreviations, capitalization, punctuation, etc. [CRC 1.200]

[9:64.9] ***PRACTICE POINTER:*** The "California Style Manual" is available from the Reporter of Decisions, Supreme Court of California. It is also available online (*www.sdap.org*).

(4) [9:64.10] **Length:** No opening or responding memorandum of points and authorities shall exceed *15 pages* in length, *except* a *20-page* limit applies to motions:
— for summary judgment or adjudication; or
— to certify or decertify a class, or to amend or modify a class certification order. [CRC 3.1113(d), 3.764(c)(2)]

No reply or closing memorandum of points and authorities shall exceed *10 pages* in length *except* a *15-page* limit applies to class certification motions. [CRC 3.1113(d), 3.764(c)(2)]

The caption page, notice of motion, exhibits, declarations and other attachments (including tables of contents and authorities, and proof of service) are not counted as part of these page limits. [CRC 3.1113(d)]

(a) [9:64.11] **Ex parte order for longer briefs:** A party may apply to the court *ex parte* (i.e., on shortened time, *see* ¶*9:345*) for permission to file a longer memorandum. Such application must be made at least 24 hours before the brief is due and after *written notice* of the application to other parties (¶*9:64.12*). The application must state *reasons* why the argument cannot be made within the above page limit (¶*9:64.10*). [CRC 3.1113(e)]

1) [9:64.12] ***Caution—written notice required:*** Ordinarily, ex parte orders may issue after oral (e.g., telephone) notice to opposing counsel as to when and where the application will be made; *see* ¶*9:351 ff.* But CRC 3.1113(e) requires a *written* notice at least 24 hours before the memorandum is due on applications for permission to file longer briefs.

   CCP §1013 allows *service* by fax or email where parties consent to this form of service (*see* ¶*9:86.10*). In addition, where a court has adopted efiling, electronic service may take place incident to the filing (*see* ¶*9:86.25 ff.*). Although no appellate court has addressed whether fax or electronic service, instead of mail or personal service, satisfy the written notice requirement, presumably they do.

   ⇨ [9:64.12a] ***PRACTICE POINTER:*** Do not assume your request for permission to file a longer memorandum will be approved. Have a backup plan to file memoranda within the prescribed length limits.

(b) [9:64.13] **More lines per page?** CRC 2.108 permits either double-spacing *or 1 1/2 spaces* between lines (*see* ¶*9:22*). Switching to 1 1/2 spaces between lines substantially increases the amount of information on each page.

   If you are going to use 1 1/2 spacing, you will need *special 37-line paper*, because *each line must be numbered* (CRC 2.108).

   ⇨ [9:64.14] ***PRACTICE POINTER:*** Use of 1 1/2 spacing is *not recommended.* It makes your memo difficult to read and is a "turn off" to most judges. It is better to stick with double-spacing and get permission to file a longer brief.

   1) [9:64.15] **Single spacing:** Single spacing with unnumbered lines is permissible in footnotes and in quotations. [See CRC 2.108(3)]

© 2020 Thomson Reuters/The Rutter Group

☞ [9:64.16] ***PRACTICE POINTER:*** But don't try to evade the 15-page limit by using lengthy, single-spaced footnotes. They may not be read and may be understood as a deliberate attempt to avoid the page limit.

(c) [9:64.17] **Effect of violating page limit:** A memorandum exceeding the permissible page limits "must be filed and considered in the same manner as a *late-filed* paper"; i.e., the court in its discretion may refuse to consider it in ruling on the motion (*see ¶9:105.4*). [CRC 3.1113(g) (emphasis added), 3.1300(d)]

[9:65] *Reserved.*

(5) [9:66] **Tables of contents, authorities:** If the memo is over 10 pages, it must contain both a table of contents *and* a table of authorities. [CRC 3.1113(f)]

☞ [9:66.1] ***PRACTICE POINTER:*** Even for shorter memoranda, such tables are recommended. They help the court follow your arguments.

(6) [9:66.2] **Pagination:** If tables of contents and authorities are included:

— the caption page ("Points and Authorities in Support of . . . .") need not be numbered; and

— the text must be numbered consecutively using Arabic numerals. [CRC 3.1113(h)]

(7) [9:67] **Case citations:** Case citations must be to the Official Reports ("Cal." and "Cal.App.") and must include the volume, page number and year of decision. The court may not require any other form of citation. [CRC 3.1113(c)]

[9:67.1] *Reserved.*

☞ [9:67.2] ***PRACTICE POINTERS:*** Even if not required, it is good practice to include internal "jump cites" (the specific page at which the quotation or cited matter appears).

If you cite to a case decided by the court of appeal for the district in which your action is pending, you may wish to show this in the citation (e.g., "Jones v. Smith (2d Dist. 1994)." However, the opinions of the various district courts of appeal are equally binding on all trial courts. [*People v. Bullock* (1994) 26 CA4th 985, 990, 31 CR2d 850, 854]

(a) [9:67.3] **Cites to out-of-state and federal authorities:** If you cite out-of-state or federal cases, statutes or rules, the judge may require that you:

— lodge a copy of each authority with your papers (and ask the court if it would like them on a USB drive); and

— if in paper form, tab and index each authority in accordance with CRC 3.1110(f)(3) (*see* ¶*9:23.5*), and if in electronic form, electronically bookmark each authority (*see* ¶*9:23.10*). [CRC 3.1113(i)(1)]

Even if not ordered by the court to do so, you must promptly provide copies of each out-of-state or federal authority to any party upon request. [CRC 3.1113(i)(3)]

(b) [9:67.4] **Cites to cases not yet published:** If you cite a California case before it is published in the advance sheets of the Official Reports, you must include the title, case number, date of decision and the appellate district. As with out-of-state authorities, the court may require that the authorities be lodged with your papers, and tabbed and indexed (or bookmarked if filed electronically) as required by Rule 3.1110(f). [CRC 3.1113(i)(2)] (Also, it is helpful to add the Thomson Reuters Westlaw citation for such cases.)

(c) [9:67.5] **Cites to online services:** If you cite an opinion available only through an online legal service, it is good practice to handle it the same way as out-of-state authority.

(d) [9:67.6] **Citing unpublished appellate opinions:** Except as relevant to law of the case, res judicata or collateral estoppel, a California appellate opinion that is "not certified for publication or ordered published *must not be cited or relied on* by a court or a party in any other action." [CRC 8.1115(a) (emphasis added)]

Electronic databases have made it much easier to locate unpublished opinions and counsel increasingly submit copies of a favorable opinion "for the court's information." Most judges understand that attempting to persuade the court in this manner may be improper and a violation of CRC 8.1115(a).

(e) [9:67.7] **Citing state trial court opinions:** State trial court rulings have no precedential value. [*Harrott v. County of Kings* (2001) 25 C4th 1138, 1148, 108 CR2d 445, 453]

(f) [9:67.7a] **Citing state appellate division opinions:** Published opinions by appellate divisions of the Superior Court have persuasive value. [*Smith v. Hume* (1937) 29 CA2d Supp. 747, 750, 74 P2d 566, 568— decisions of other appellate departments not technically binding on another appellate division but "they are

© 2020 Thomson Reuters/The Rutter Group

persuasive"; see *Velasquez v. Sup.Ct. (People)* (2014) 227 CA4th 1471, 1477, 174 CR3d 541, 545, fn. 7—"[a]ppellate division decisions have persuasive value, but they are of debatable strength as precedents and are not binding on higher reviewing courts"; *Ayala v. Dawson* (2017) 13 CA5th 1319, 1332, 220 CR3d 917, 928 (same)]

(g) [9:67.7b] **Citing federal cases:** Except for binding authority from the U.S. Supreme Court, both published and unpublished federal decisions may be cited as "persuasive" (i.e., not precedential) authority. [*Pacific Shore Funding v. Lozo* (2006) 138 CA4th 1342, 1352, 42 CR3d 283, 289, fn. 6; see also *Ortega Rock Quarry v. Golden Eagle Ins. Corp.* (2006) 141 CA4th 969, 986, 46 CR3d 517, 529, fn. 1—predecessor to CRC 8.1115(a) expressly applies only to unpublished California cases, not to unpublished federal opinions; compare *Bolanos v. Sup.Ct. (State Dept. of Health Care Services)* (2008) 169 CA4th 744, 761, 87 CR3d 174, 186-187—"a written trial court ruling has no precedential value" and court therefore declined to take judicial notice of unpublished federal district court decision]

(h) [9:67.8] **Citing to cases in which review has been granted:** Where the California Supreme Court granted review of a published Court of Appeal decision *before July 1, 2016*, the lower court opinion was *automatically vacated* and not citable.

For cases in which the California Supreme Court granted review *after July 1, 2016,* while review is pending in the high court, the intermediate appellate court's published opinion may be cited for its persuasive value but has no binding or precedential effect. Any citation to the lower court opinion must note that review has been granted. *After* the Supreme Court has issued its opinion on review, the lower court opinion may be cited "except to the extent it is inconsistent with the decision of the Supreme Court or is disapproved by that court." [CRC 8.1115(e)]

If the Supreme Court orders a Court of Appeal case depublished, it cannot be cited (CRC 8.1115(e)). Violation of this rule may lead to sanctions (e.g., striking the brief as "defective" and/or monetary sanctions against counsel). [*Alicia T. v. County of Los Angeles* (1990) 222 CA3d 869, 885-886, 271 CR 513, 520-521 (relying on predecessor to CRC 8.1115)]

(8) [9:68] **Statute citations:** Statutes should be cited in accordance with one of the authorized style manuals (¶*9:64.8*):

— Under the California Style Manual, abbreviations are improper for citations in the *text*; e.g., "Code of Civil Procedure section 437c provides . . ." [See California Style Manual §2:6]
— Cites in parentheses may be abbreviated; e.g., "(Code Civ. Proc., §437c)." [See California Style Manual §2:6]

[9:68.1] ***PRACTICE POINTERS:*** If the statute has recently been enacted or amended, it is a good idea to include the *date* of that enactment or amendment (e.g., "Code Civ. Proc., §. . ., eff. 1/1/2017").

If you are relying on *legislative history* for statutory interpretation, be sure to file a separate *request for judicial notice* of *specific documents* from the statute's legislative history *and supply copies* of the documents (committee reports, etc.). [CRC 3.1113(*l*); see *Kaufman & Broad Communities, Inc. v. Performance Plastering, Inc.* (2005) 133 CA4th 26, 31-38, 34 CR3d 520, 523-529; *People v. Hooper* (2019) 40 CA5th 685, 693, 253 CR3d 369, 378, fn. 5 (approving judicial notice of bills and committee reports but not letters to bill's sponsor); *and further discussion at ¶7:17.10*]

[9:68.2-68.3] *Reserved.*

(9) [9:68.4] **Exhibit and declaration references:** All references to exhibits or declarations in supporting or opposing papers must reference:
— the number or letter of the exhibit;
— the specific page; and
— the paragraph or line number (if applicable). [CRC 3.1113(k)]

(10) [9:68.5] **Facts, law, evidence, argument, discussion:** A memorandum of points and authorities should contain:
— a *statement of facts*;
— a concise *statement of law*;
— *evidence and arguments* relied upon; and
— a *discussion* of the statutes, cases and texts cited in support of the position advanced. [CRC 3.1113(b)]

(a) [9:68.6] **Statement of facts:** Each fact so stated should be based on *evidence attached to* the motion, followed by a precise *reference* to such evidence ("Deposition of Jones, page 3, line 10"). [See *Smith, Smith & Kring v. Sup.Ct. (Oliver)* (1997) 60 CA4th 573, 578, 70 CR2d 507, 509—matters set forth in

© 2020 Thomson Reuters/The Rutter Group

unverified "statement of facts" are *not* evidence and cannot provide basis for granting motion]

[9:68.7-68.9] *Reserved.*

(b) [9:68.10] **Opening summary:** If the memorandum *exceeds 15 pages* (allowed only in summary judgment motions, class certification motions, or by court order), it must include "an opening summary of argument" (i.e., a paragraph or two summarizing the key points). [CRC 3.1113(f)]

Comment: Although not required, such a summary may be helpful to the judge even in shorter memoranda.

[9:69] ***PRACTICE POINTERS RE DRAFTING:*** The primary purpose of your memorandum or brief is to persuade the judge. In the process of persuasion, how you present your arguments is almost as important as what you have to say. Here are some guidelines to effective brief-writing in law and motion matters:

(a) [9:70] **Introduction:** To grab the judge's attention right away, start off with a *summary* of what the case is all about, and what order you are seeking. This will help the judge focus on the issues and comprehend your arguments. No matter how complex the case, keep your introduction short and crystal-clear, never more than a page or two in length.

Even if the judge has heard earlier motions in the case, do not assume he or she remembers everything that went before. Therefore, begin with any prior orders relevant to the present motion. Then, briefly state whatever has led up to the filing of the motion or the context in which the motion arises.

- [9:71] **Present your client's version of the facts:** Your introductory paragraphs should summarize the facts in the light most favorable to your client. At the law and motion stage, you usually are not bound by any findings of fact (unlike the situation on appeal). You are therefore free to be a true advocate, and to present the facts in the most persuasive manner you can. Obviously, you may not misstate the facts to the court (CRPC 3.3 (formerly CRPC 5-200)). But you are certainly free to argue whatever reasonable inferences you believe are supported by the facts. (Keep in mind, however, that nothing destroys credibility more quickly than exaggerating or misstating the facts.)

Moreover, your summary of the facts can be used in any later memorandum or brief you write in the same case. There is absolutely nothing wrong with using the same introductory paragraphs more than once. Indeed, doing so will aid the judge in recalling the case and getting back into focus on the issues involved.

- [9:72] **State precisely what order you seek, and why:** After you tell the judge what the case is about, state precisely what relief or order you are asking him or her to make, and on what ground or grounds. For example, "By this motion, defendant (name) seeks an order transferring this action to Alameda County on the ground that it has been filed in the wrong court; and for reimbursement for his expenses and reasonable attorney fees."

(b) [9:73] **Argument:** Following the introductory paragraph, it is your job to make relevant points (arguments), and to support them with relevant authorities.

- [9:73.1] **Use logical sequence:** The "IRAC" outline (Issue, Rule, Analysis, Conclusion) you learned in law school provides a useful sequence for memoranda of points and authorities.

- [9:74] **Avoid abstractions:** A common failing is to set forth black-letter legal principles that could apply virtually to any case in the court. (E.g., "A demurrer lies for failure to state a cause of action.")

  Instead, tie your points into the particular facts of the case. (E.g., "The complaint fails to state a cause of action for defamation against defendant newspaper, because it fails to allege a demand for retraction before suit.")

  Consider if the outcome is determined by precedent, in which event you should stress the controlling authority; or is a matter of discretion, in which case you should focus on practicalities and fairness.

- [9:75] **Use common sense re citations:** A judge is bound to follow applicable appellate decisions. Hence, a single holding *in point* is all that you need. (String cites are unnecessary, and can get you into trouble if you

© 2020 Thomson Reuters/The Rutter Group

haven't read all of the cases, and the judge has. Also, if you have a case in point, the judge may never get around to reading it if it is buried in a string of cites.)

Obviously, cite California Supreme Court decisions wherever possible; and later decisions, rather than earlier—unless the earlier is a landmark or "fountainhead" on the point involved.

Always "KeyCite" or "Shepardize" your cites to make sure they are still good law, and also possibly to pick up a later case that may be even stronger authority for the point you are making.

On recent cases, *check the subsequent histories* to make sure that the opinion has not been amended, withdrawn, depublished or had review granted.

- [9:75.1] **Avoid footnotes:** Most judges are used to seeing case citations in the text. Footnotes are distracting and may divert the judge's attention from the thrust of your arguments.

- [9:76] **Use short quotes:** Of course, you need to discuss the facts of the cases you cite to show their relevancy to the matter before the court. But don't summarize the holding. Most judges would rather read a direct quotation of the language you are relying upon than your characterization of the holding. (Indeed, if you fail to include such quotation, some judges may think either the issue is not so clear as you say, or that you may be misreading the holding of the case.)

  Be careful not to "edit" your quotation unfairly. You may safely assume that your opponent or the judge (or both) will read the whole opinion, and will jump on any distortion.

- [9:77] **Be clear about opposing authority:** If there are cases which appear to be against you, say so. Obviously, attempt to distinguish them, but in any case, be sure to cite them. There are several reasons: First, you owe a duty to the court to cite *all* relevant authority, including adverse authority (CRPC 3.3(a)(2) (formerly CRPC 5-200) prohibits lawyers from failing "to disclose to the tribunal legal authority in the controlling jurisdiction known to the lawyer to be directly adverse to the position of the client"). Second, by citing the adverse authority before your opponent does, you may take some of the "steam" out of his or her arguments. Finally, whether or not your opponent cites the case, the judge may be aware of it, and may view your failure to cite it as incompetence or an attempt to mislead the court.

- [9:78] **Make it easy for the judge:** Always cite the official reports ("Cal." and "Cal. App.") and year of decision (see California Style Manual §2:6). Although not required, be sure to *include internal page references* to help the judge locate the relevant portion of the case.

  Subsequent references to the same case may use a shortened citation form (e.g., *Flanagan,* supra, 27 C4th at 767); however, avoid using "supra" without the reporter volume (e.g., *Flanagan,* supra at 767) since it may force the judge to search for earlier citation to the case.

  If you are citing an important out-of-state or federal case or statute, it is a good idea to attach a copy to your memorandum, even if the judge does not order you to do so (*see ¶9:67.3*). The judge simply may not have the time to look it up. The same observation applies to *administrative regulations.*

- [9:79] **Keep your arguments "bite size":** Your brief will do its job better if it is easy to read. Always start a separate paragraph for each point you are making, and preface it with a caption or "headline," underlined or capitalized. Then, lay out your arguments in short paragraphs (several to a page enhance readability). Finally, avoid long convoluted sentences; the judge may simply not have the time or patience to wade through them.

- [9:80] **Don't "trash" your opponent:** Judges react negatively to name-calling in briefs or oral argument. Avoid petty remarks demeaning the opposing party or counsel.

  Standards for professionalism: "Trashing" an opponent may also violate civility guidelines in local rules. [See L.A. Sup.Ct. Rule 3.26, Appendix 3.A(c)(2)—"Neither written submissions nor oral presentations should disparage the intelligence, ethics, morals, integrity or personal behavior of one's adversaries, unless such things are directly and necessarily in issue"]

- [9:80a] **Don't argue facts not properly before the court:** Limit your arguments to facts contained in supporting affidavits and other evidence properly before the court (*see ¶9:43 ff.*). Referring to other facts is likely to undermine your credibility with the court.

  By the same token, failure to mention a declaration or other evidence in your memorandum may suggest to the judge it is not important. [See *Overstock.Com, Inc. v. Goldman Sachs Group, Inc.* (2014) 231 CA4th 471, 506, 180 CR3d 234, 264-265—exhibits not mentioned in briefs were "irrelevant"]

- [9:80.1] **Be respectful to the court:** No matter how much you may disagree with any prior rulings or remarks by the judge, keep a respectful tone in your arguments. An attack on the integrity of the court is bound to hurt your client's case. Beware of manifestations of gender and other biases. [*Briganti v. Chow* (2019) 42 CA5th 504, 510-512, 254 CR3d 909, 914-915; *Martinez v. O'Hara* (2019) 32 CA5th 853, 857-858, 244 CR3d 226, 229-230]

(c) [9:81] **Conclusion:** After you have summarized the case, summarized the motion, and presented your arguments, summarize once more: *Restate exactly what relief or order you are requesting and on what grounds.* This will make it easier for the judge to incorporate in his or her ruling.

(d) [9:81.1] **Redraft:** Good briefs are not written; they are *rewritten.* Leave enough time to redraft. Tighten up your arguments. Improve the flow. Be succinct. Search for a way to make the brief more interesting.

f. [9:81.2] **Proposed order:** If a proposed order is submitted, it must be lodged and served with the moving papers, but *not attached* to them. [CRC 3.1113(m); *see further discussion at ¶9:294*]

FORM: Proposed Order, *see Form 9A:8* in Rivera, *Cal. Prac. Guide: Civ. Pro. Before Trial FORMS* (TRG).

☞ [9:81.2a] ***PRACTICE POINTER:*** Most judges prefer that you designate a proposed order as such (e.g., "(Proposed) Order Granting . . ."). The judge signing the order will then merely strike out the word "Proposed." This avoids confusion created by documents in the court file which are denominated "Order" but which have not been adopted or signed by the court (*see* ¶*9:300*).

(1) [9:81.3] **Comment:** Proposed orders rarely work in *complicated* cases. The judge usually finds it easier to dictate a minute order than to rewrite orders proposed by counsel. Unless waived or otherwise ordered, a new attorney order is then required (CRC 3.1312; *see* ¶*9:294 ff.*).

Nevertheless, sometimes proposed orders can be helpful in that they force the moving party to spell out exactly what is being requested.

(2) [9:81.4] **Attorney designation:** The name, address, etc. of the attorney submitting the proposed order should appear on the first page of the order. [CRC 2.111(1); *see* ¶*6:21*]

3. **Service Requirements**

a. [9:82] **Papers served:** The papers served must be copies of the moving and supporting papers filed or to be filed with the court. [CCP §1005]

[9:82.1-82.4] *Reserved.*

b. [9:82.5] **Who must be served:** The moving papers must be served on *all* parties who have appeared in the action, whether or not the motion seeks relief against such parties. [See CCP §1014 as to defendants; and by analogy, most courts apply a similar rule to other parties; see also *Winikow v. Sup.Ct. (Schroeder)* (2000) 82 CA4th 719, 727, 98 CR2d 413, 419—service of notice not required on defendants who have not yet appeared]

(1) [9:83] **On counsel for party; exceptions:** Where a party has appeared through an attorney, service of papers must be made on the attorney rather than the party *except* for subpoenas, writs, OSCs to hold the party in contempt, and "other process issued in the suit." [CCP §1015]

(a) [9:83a] **Motion to vacate dismissal:** The attorney-client relationship does not go on indefinitely after a case is over. However, it continues long enough after a case has been dismissed to allow service on defense counsel of plaintiff's motion to vacate the dismissal on CCP §473 grounds (e.g., mistake). [*Maxwell v. Cooltech, Inc.* (1997) 57 CA4th 629, 632, 67 CR2d 293, 295]

© 2020 Thomson Reuters/The Rutter Group

(b) [9:83b] **Parties represented by several counsel:** Where a party is represented by *several separate* attorneys or law firms of record, notice served on any of them (presumably the first-named) is apparently effective. [See *Adaimy v. Ruhl* (2008) 160 CA4th 583, 588, 72 CR3d 926, 929—notice of judgment entry served by clerk on one of two attorneys of record triggered time for filing appeal]

[9:83c] *Comment: Adaimy* (*¶9:83b*) involved service by the *court clerk*. Logically, however, the same rule should apply to service by a party.

☞ [9:83d] ***PRACTICE POINTER:*** Avoid the uncertainty. Serve copies on *each separate attorney or law firm* of record for a party.

(2) [9:83.1] **List of parties:** To facilitate service in multiparty lawsuits, court rules require the first-named plaintiff to maintain a list of the parties and their addresses for service of notice. Such list is required in any case where more than two parties have appeared and are represented by different counsel. Each party must advise the plaintiff of any change in address, so the list is kept current. [CRC 3.254]

The list of parties must be furnished on request to the court or to any party. And, it must be served with any notice or pleading served on a party who has not yet appeared in the action. [CRC 3.254]

c. [9:84] **How served:** Service of moving and opposing papers is governed by CCP §1005. The moving papers can be served either by:

— personal delivery (*see ¶9:85*);
— mail (typically first class) (*see ¶9:86a*);
— express mail "or another method of delivery providing for overnight delivery" (*see ¶9:86.7 ff.*);
— fax transmission, where the parties have a written agreement to accept service by fax (*see ¶9:86.10*); or
— electronic service where agreed to by the recipient or authorized or required by local rules (*see ¶9:86.25 ff.*).

(1) [9:85] **Personal service on attorney:** Service may be made on a party's attorney by leaving the papers with a receptionist or anyone in charge of the office. If there is no one with whom to leave the papers, they may be left in a conspicuous place in the office between the hours of 9:00 a.m. and 5:00 p.m. [CCP §1011(a); see *National Advertising Co. v. City of Rohnert Park* (1984) 160 CA3d 614, 618-619, 206 CR 696, 698]

(a) [9:85.1] **Proof of service:** A declaration of personal service is required by the person delivering the documents.

FORM: Proof of Personal Service—Civil (Judicial Council form POS-020).

☞ [9:85.2] ***PRACTICE POINTER:*** If you are going to use a messenger to serve documents on opposing counsel or parties, the proof of service must be *by the messenger.* A declaration signed by a secretary who gave the papers to the messenger is hearsay and not sufficient.

For the same reason, a declaration by the attorney (e.g., "I *caused* to be delivered by hand") is likewise insufficient. If you are relying on personal service, the *person who actually served* the document must sign the proof of service.

(b) [9:85.2a] **Where delivery to office impossible:** If the attorney's office is not open and the attorney's residence is in the same county as the office, service may be made by leaving the papers at the attorney's residence with someone at least 18 years old. [CCP §1011(a)]

If these requirements cannot be met, the papers may be served by mailing them to the attorney's office address, if known, or otherwise to the attorney's residence address. [CCP §1011(a)]

(c) [9:85.2b] **Where attorney's address unknown:** If the attorney's office and residence are both unknown, the notice or papers for the attorney may be delivered to *either*:

— the address designated on the court papers for the attorney or party of record; or

— to the clerk of the court. [CCP §1011(a)]

(d) [9:85.3] **Compare—service on self-represented party:** Parties not represented by counsel may be served personally or by *leaving papers at their residence* (not office) between 8 a.m. and 8 p.m. with someone at least 18 years old. [CCP §1011(b)(1)]

If no one age 18 or older is found at the time of attempted service, the papers may be served by mail. If the party's residence is not known, service may be made by delivering the papers to the clerk of the court. [CCP §1011(b)(2), (3)]

Where a party has no permanent residence, papers may be served at the address the party has provided

© 2020 Thomson Reuters/The Rutter Group

the court for service. [*Sweeting v. Murat* (2013) 221 CA4th 507, 513-514, 164 CR3d 383, 388—where party's listed address was rented mailbox at UPS Store, personal service properly effected by personal delivery of papers to UPS Store]

(2) [9:86] **Service by mail:** More commonly, moving papers are served by mail, postage prepaid, to the attorney's office as shown on any document he or she filed in the action. [See CCP §§1012, 1013(a)]

(a) [9:86a] **First class mail?** Although first class mail is normally used, nothing in the statute actually requires this (perhaps a legislative oversight).

[9:86b] *Reserved.*

(b) [9:86c] **Mailing date noted on face:** The papers served are normally accompanied by an unsigned copy of the declaration of service showing the date and place of mailing. Otherwise, the date and place of mailing should be noted on the face of the papers served (e.g., "Mailed at Los Angeles, California, April 15, 2017"). [CCP §1013(b)]

But this is "directory" only (see CCP §1013(h)) so that no adverse consequence flows from failure to comply.

(c) [9:86d] **When service complete:** Service by mail is effected *upon deposit* of the papers in a post office, mailbox or similar facility maintained by the U.S. Postal Service. [CCP §1013(a)]

Although service is complete upon deposit, the notice period is extended by 5 calendar days for papers mailed in California to an address within California, and for longer periods if either the place of mailing or place of address is outside California. [CCP §1005(b); *see* ¶*9:87.1*]

1) [9:86e] **Compare—CCP §1013:** The extension periods provided in CCP §1013 do *not apply* to motion papers. [CCP §1005(b); *see further discussion at* ¶*9:87.4*]

2) [9:86f] **Establishing date of service:** A formal proof of service (¶*9:86.1*) is the most common way to establish the date of service by mail. But it is not the only method: "On the contrary, it is sufficient proof of mailing if the [paper served] . . . bears a notation of the date and place of mailing [CCP §1013(b)]." [*Berg v. Darden* (2004) 120 CA4th 721, 733, 15 CR3d 829, 838]

(d) [9:86.1] **Proof of service:** Proof of service is made by a *declaration of mailing*. [See *Preis v.*

American Indem. Co. (1990) 220 CA3d 752, 758-759, 269 CR 617, 621—postal receipt filled out by post office employee is hearsay and shows only that an *envelope* was mailed, not its contents]

The form of the declaration depends on whether the declarant *personally* deposited the document in the mail:

1) [9:86.2] **By person depositing in mail:** The declaration must state the declarant's residence or business address (in the county where mailing occurs); that the declarant is over the age of 18 and not a party to the action; the name and address of the person served; that the envelope was sealed and deposited in the mail, postage prepaid; and *the date and place of deposit* in the mail. [CCP §1013a(1); see *Katelaris v. County of Orange* (2001) 92 CA4th 1211, 1215, 112 CR2d 556, 559; *American Contractors Indem. Co. v. County of Orange* (2005) 130 CA4th 579, 583, 29 CR3d 916, 919 (citing text)]

   a) [9:86.2a] **Place of deposit:** Listing the city and state satisfies §1013a; the precise location of the mailbox is not required. [*Him v. City & County of San Francisco* (2005) 133 CA4th 437, 443-444, 34 CR3d 838, 843]

   FORMS

   - Proof of Service by First-Class Mail—Civil (Judicial Council form POS-030).
   - Proof of Service—Civil (Judicial Council form POS-040).
   - Proof of Service by Mail (By Person Depositing in Mail), *see Form 9A:10* in Rivera, *Cal. Prac. Guide: Civ. Pro. Before Trial FORMS* (TRG).

2) [9:86.3] **By person familiar with business practice for mailing:** Frequently, the secretary or other person doing the mailing declaration does not actually put the mail in the U.S. mailbox, but gives it to someone in the office for this purpose. In such cases, the declarant must state (in addition to the above, ¶*9:86.2*) *familiarity with the office's practice for depositing mail*, that correspondence would be deposited in the mail on the same day, and that the document served was placed for deposit in accordance with the office practice. [CCP §1013a(3); see *Katelaris v. County of Orange*, supra, 92

CA4th at 1215, 112 CR2d at 559—upholding declaration stating "to the best of my knowledge" declarant followed regular procedure for collecting, processing and depositing mail on date in question]

a) [9:86.3a] **Presumption of valid service:** Such declarations are sufficient to raise a rebuttable presumption that the notice has been received in the ordinary course of mail. [Ev.C. §641; *Bonzer v. City of Huntington Park* (1993) 20 CA4th 1474, 1479, 25 CR2d 278, 280—presumption dispelled by declarations denying receipt]

b) [9:86.3b] **Service presumed *invalid* if postmark delayed:** Service is presumed invalid if there is more than a one-day difference between the postmark or postage meter date and the date of service shown on the proof of service. [CCP §1013a(3)]

   However, the presumption is rebuttable, affecting the burden of producing evidence; the party seeking to invoke the presumption must file a motion to obtain its benefit. [CCP §1013a(3); *Simplon Ballpark, LLC v. Scull* (2015) 235 CA4th 660, 668, 185 CR3d 482, 488]

   Compare: This presumption applies *only* where the person signs the proof of service based on "business practice" rather than personal knowledge. No such presumption applies where the affidavit of mailing is based on *personal knowledge.* [*Tobin v. Oris* (1992) 3 CA4th 814, 826, 4 CR2d 736, 743 (disapproved on other grounds by *Wilcox v. Birthwhistle* (1999) 21 C4th 973, 90 CR2d 260)—nor does it apply where service has been admitted]

c) [9:86.3c] **Not applicable to overnight delivery:** A declaration by someone familiar with the business practice for collecting and processing mail does not apply to service by overnight delivery. [*Humane Soc. of United States v. Sup.Ct. (Regents of Univ. of Calif.)* (2013) 214 CA4th 1233, 1249-1251, 155 CR3d 93, 106-108; *and see ¶9:86.8* for proofs of service by overnight delivery]

FORMS

- Proof of Service by First-Class Mail—Civil (Judicial Council form POS-030).

- Proof of Service—Civil (Judicial Council form POS-040).
- Proof of Service by Mail (Business Practice to Entrust Deposit to Others), *see Form 9A:11* in Rivera, *Cal. Prac. Guide: Civ. Pro. Before Trial FORMS* (TRG).

[9:86.4] *Reserved.*

(e) [9:86.5] **Sufficiency of address:** A proof of service is sufficient if it shows mailing to the attorney's office address "last given . . . on any document" filed in the action. [CCP §1013(a)]

If the attorney moves while the action is pending, it is the attorney's duty to file and serve a notice of change of address. [CRC 2.200]

1) [9:86.6] **Street address alone sufficient:** A declaration of mailing is sufficient if it shows the correct *street* address of the attorney's office building—even if the floor or suite number is omitted. The street address alone is deemed "substantial compliance" with CCP §1013. [*Jackson v. Bank of America* (1983) 141 CA3d 55, 58, 190 CR 78, 80]

2) [9:86.6a] **Mail sent to former address:** Mail sent to a former address is deemed properly served *for up to one year* after the change of address because postal regulations require the U.S. Postal Service to forward first class mail at no charge during that period. [See *Lee v. Placer Title Co.* (1994) 28 CA4th 503, 509-510, 33 CR2d 572, 575-576]

But mail sent to a former address more than a year after a change of address is *not* properly served because postal regulations require such mail to be returned to the sender. [*Lee v. Placer Title Co.*, supra, 28 CA4th at 510, 33 CR2d at 576]

3) [9:86.6b] **Wrong zip code:** Service is *invalid* if the wrong zip code is used unless the serving party can prove that the document was actually received. [*Moghaddam v. Bone* (2006) 142 CA4th 283, 288, 47 CR3d 602, 606; see also *Rodriguez v. Henard* (2009) 174 CA4th 529, 537, 94 CR3d 313, 318—wrong zip code on mailing affidavit for application for entry of default (see CCP §587) was not prejudicial and was not ground for setting aside default]

(3) [9:86.7] **Service by overnight delivery service:** Papers may also be served by Express Mail (U.S. Postal Service)

© 2020 Thomson Reuters/The Rutter Group

or "another method of delivery providing for overnight delivery" (e.g., Federal Express). [CCP §1013(c)]

(a) [9:86.7a] **Method of service noted on papers served:** The papers served are normally accompanied by an unsigned copy of the declaration of service (¶*9:86.8 ff.*). Otherwise, the date and place of deposit should be noted on the face of the papers served (e.g., "Deposited with U.S. Postal Service for Express Mail at Los Angeles, California, April 15, 2017"). [CCP §1013(d)]

However, this is "directory" only (see CCP §1013(h)) so no adverse consequence flows from failure to comply.

(b) [9:86.7b] **When service complete:** Service is complete at the time the papers are *deposited* with the overnight carrier. Proof of receipt is not required. [CCP §1013(c); see *Barefield v. Washington Mut. Bank* (2006) 136 CA4th 299, 302, 38 CR3d 858, 860—service complete when papers deposited with Federal Express for overnight delivery, although papers were returned to sender after 4 unsuccessful attempts at delivery; compare *Blaich v. West Hollywood Rent Stabilization Dept.* (2011) 195 CA4th 1171, 1177, 125 CR3d 317, 321—where statute required administrative record to be "personally delivered or mailed," overnight delivery did not constitute "mail," so service was not considered complete until record was delivered, not earlier at time of deposit with overnight carrier]

(c) [9:86.8] **Proof of service:** A declaration is required stating:

- [9:86.8a] For service by Express Mail, that the papers were deposited:
  — in a sealed envelope (Express Mail postage prepaid);
  — in a post office or mailbox regularly maintained by the U.S. Postal Service for Express mail service;
  — addressed to the address last shown by that person on any document filed in the action by the person to be served (or to his or her residence). [CCP §1013(c)]

- [9:86.8b] For service by "another method of delivery providing for overnight delivery" (e.g., Federal Express), that the papers were deposited:
  — in an envelope or package designated by the express service carrier;

— in a facility regularly maintained by the express service carrier or delivered to a courier or driver authorized to receive documents on its behalf;
— with delivery fees paid or provided for;
— addressed to the address last shown by that person on any document filed in the action (or to his or her residence). [CCP §1013(c)]

FORMS

- Proof of Service—Civil (Judicial Council form POS-040).
- Proof of Service by Express Mail, *see Form 9A:12* in Rivera, *Cal. Prac. Guide: Civ. Pro. Before Trial FORMS* (TRG).
- Proof of Service by Express Service Carrier, *see Form 9A:13* in Rivera, *Cal. Prac. Guide: Civ. Pro. Before Trial FORMS* (TRG).

[9:86.9] *Reserved.*

(4) [9:86.10] **Service by fax:** Service by fax is permitted only where the parties have *agreed* to this method of service and a *written confirmation* to that effect is made. [CCP §1013(e)]

The Judicial Council has adopted rules to implement such service (CRC 2.306). Service by fax is ineffective if the transmission does not "fully conform" to these rules. [CRC 2.306(h)(5)]

[9:86.11] *Reserved.*

[9:86.12] ***PRACTICE POINTER:*** The main reason to agree to fax service is to speed up service of papers on other parties. Whether this is an advantage or disadvantage is a tactical decision in each case.

Note, however, that where there are more than two parties, if any of them refuses to agree, mail service will still be required as to that party.

(a) [9:86.13] **Signature not required:** The statute and CRC rule require only a "written confirmation" of the agreement. No signature is apparently required. Therefore, a letter from one counsel to the other confirming the agreement for fax service presumably will suffice.

(b) [9:86.14] **Court may utilize parties' agreement for fax service:** Where the parties have agreed to fax service, the court may serve notices upon the parties by fax. [CRC 2.306(c)]

[9:86.15] *Reserved.*

© 2020 Thomson Reuters/The Rutter Group

(c) **Duties of parties agreeing to fax service**

1) [9:86.16] **Service lists:** The plaintiff (or petitioner named first in the petition) must maintain a current list of the parties that includes their fax numbers for service and, on request, must furnish a copy of that list to any other party or the court. [CRC 2.306(b)(1)]

A copy of this list must be served on each new party who has not yet appeared in the action, contemporaneously with service of the order, notice, or pleading served on the new party. [CRC 2.306(b)(2)(B)]

On first appearing in the action, each party agreeing to fax service must furnish the plaintiff or petitioner named first in the complaint or petition with its fax number for service. [CRC 2.306(b)(2)(A)]

[9:86.16a-86.16d] *Reserved.*

2) [9:86.16e] **Fax machine available for reception:** A party or attorney who has agreed to fax service (¶*9:86.16*) must make his or her fax machine "generally available for receipt of served documents" from 9 a.m. to 5 p.m. on days other than court holidays. [CRC 2.306(f)]

[9:86.16f] ***PRACTICE POINTER:*** Disputes may arise where one lawyer claims the other attorney's fax line is always busy or is out of paper. If fax service is crucial, call the attorney (or his or her assistant) on another line to verify the fax machine is operating; and if it is, ask them to schedule a time for reception. (Their refusal to do so could facilitate your obtaining an order shortening time for service by other methods.) Especially for voluminous papers, consider service by means other than fax, such as the far more convenient and popular electronic service, if agreed to by the parties or ordered by the court (*see* ¶*9:86.25*).

(d) [9:86.17] **When fax service complete:** Fax service is complete when the *entire document* is received by the receiving party's fax machine. If any part of the document is received after 5 p.m., the document is deemed served the *next court* day. [CRC 2.306(g)]

(e) [9:86.18] **Method of service noted on papers served:** The papers served are normally accompanied by an unsigned copy of the proof of service (¶*9:86.19*). Otherwise, the date and place of fax transmission should be noted on the face of the papers served (e.g., "Served by facsimile transmission from Los Angeles, California on April 15, 2017, to fax number (. . .)". [CCP §1013(f)]

But this is "directory" only (see CCP §1013(h)), meaning no adverse consequence flows from failure to comply.

(f) [9:86.19] **Proof of service:** Proof of fax service may be made on the same declaration form as service by mail (CCP §1013a), modified to reflect service by fax instead of by mail. [CRC 2.306(h)]

1) [9:86.20] **Recipient's fax number required:** Fax service must be to the fax machine telephone number of the person to be served as last given by that person on any document filed in the action and served on the party making the fax service. [CCP §1013(e); CRC 2.306(a)(2)]

FORMS

- Proof of Service—Civil (Judicial Council form POS-040).
- Proof of Service by Facsimile Transmission, *see Form 9A:14* in Rivera, *Cal. Prac. Guide: Civ. Pro. Before Trial FORMS* (TRG).

(g) [9:86.21] **Signatures on fax-served documents:** A party who serves (or files) a signed document by fax *represents* that the original signed document is in his or her possession or control. [CRC 2.305(a)]

[9:86.22] ***PRACTICE POINTER:*** It is not necessary for the signature to appear on the copy transmitted. An unsigned copy can be transmitted with "/s/ (signer's name)" to indicate the original bears that person's signature.

1) [9:86.23] **Procedure to obtain production of original:** Opposing parties may at any time serve a demand for production of the original signed document; and the parties shall then arrange a meeting for this purpose. [CRC 2.305(b), (c)]

[9:86.24] *Reserved.*

(5) [9:86.25] **Electronic service:** Any document that may be served by mail, overnight delivery or fax may be served electronically if:

— the recipient has *agreed to accept* service electronically (*see ¶9:86.26*); or

— *local court rules authorize* or require electronic service

© 2020 Thomson Reuters/The Rutter Group

(*see* ¶*9:86.30*). [CCP §1010.6(a)(2), (b); CRC 2.253(b); *Insyst, Ltd. v. Applied Materials, Inc.* (2009) 170 CA4th 1129, 1138, 88 CR3d 808, 814]

"Electronic service" may consist of either *electronic transmission* of a document *or electronic notification* of where the document may be viewed and downloaded (*see* ¶*9:86.37*). [CCP §1010.6(a)(1); CRC 2.250(b)(2)]

Rules governing electronic service and filing "must be construed to authorize and permit filing and service by electronic means *to the extent feasible.*" [CRC 2.250(a) (emphasis added)]

For cases *filed on or after January 1, 2019*, electronic service is not authorized unless a party or "other person" has "expressly consented" to electronic service in that action or the court has ordered electronic service. "Express consent" is accomplished either by serving a notice on all other parties and filing it with the court, or by "manifesting affirmative consent through electronic means with the court or the court's electronic filing service provider, and concurrently providing the party's electronic address with that consent for the purpose of receiving electronic service. The act of electronic filing shall not be construed as express consent." [CCP §1010.6(a)(2)(A)(ii)]

Any person who has given express consent to electronic service may expressly withdraw that consent. [CCP §1010.6(a)(6)] The Judicial Council has promulgated an optional form for doing that.

(a) [9:86.26] **Agreement to accept electronic service:** A party's consent to accept electronic service may be shown by filing and serving a notice so stating. [CRC 2.251(b)(1)(A)]

For cases filed *before January 1, 2019*, such consent may be shown by *filing any document electronically* with the court: "[E]lectronic service . . . is . . . authorized [if] a party or other person has agreed to accept electronic service in that specific action or the court has ordered electronic service . . . ." [CCP §1010.6(a)(2)(A)(i)]

For cases filed *on or after January 1, 2019*, the "act of electronic filing shall not be construed as express consent." [CCP §1010.6(a)(2)(A)(ii)]

FORM: Consent to Electronic Service and Notice of Electronic Service Address and Attachment to Proof of Electronic Service (Judicial Council form EFS-005), *see Form 9A:14.3* in Rivera, *Cal. Prac. Guide: Civ. Pro. Before Trial FORMS* (TRG).

1) [9:86.26a] **Compare—self-represented parties:** Self-represented parties must *affimatively consent* to electronic service by serving and filing a notice so stating (¶*9:86.25 ff.*). [CRC 2.251(c)(3)(B)]

2) [9:86.27] **Electronic filing service provider as agent:** A party who uses an electronic filing service provider to *serve and file* documents, *consents to service on that provider* as its agent for service in the case. [See CRC 2.251(b)(2)]

An "electronic filing service provider" is "a person or entity that receives an electronic filing from a party or other person for *retransmission* to the court or for electronic service on other parties or other person, or both . . ." [CRC 2.250(b)(8) (emphasis added)]

[9:86.28-86.30] *Reserved.*

(b) [9:86.30] **Local rules authorizing electronic service**

1) [9:86.30a] *Permissive service:* By local rule, a court may *permit* electronic service of documents in civil actions. [CCP §1010.6(a)]

2) [9:86.30b] *Mandatory service:* The court may *require* electronic service of documents in all civil actions (CCP §1010.6(d)), or, by local rule or court order require mandatory service and filing by parties and other persons in specific categories of civil actions, such as:

— all civil cases;
— cases within particular jurisdictional limits (e.g., limited or unlimited);
— cases of a specific type (e.g., contract, personal injury, employment);
— single-assigned cases;
— cases assigned to a particular department or courtroom;
— class actions, consolidated actions, coordinated actions or actions classified as "complex" under Judicial Council Rules (*see* ¶*12:47.1*);
— any combination of cases described above. [CRC 2.253(b)(1)]

A court that adopts a rule for permissive filing may *order* electronic filing and service in any class action, consolidated action (or group of separate actions), or coordinated action or "complex" action, absent "undue hardship or significant prejudice" to any party. [CCP §1010.6(c); see CRC 2.253(c)(1); ¶*9:93*]

© 2020 Thomson Reuters/The Rutter Group

A court may combine an order for electronic service and electronic filing. [CCP §1010.6(c); CRC 2.251(d)(2)]

FORM: Order Re: Electronic Service [and Filing], *see Form 9A:14.2* in Rivera, *Cal. Prac. Guide: Civ. Pro. Before Trial FORMS* (TRG).

3) [9:86.31] **If court acts sua sponte:** In courts that have adopted a local rule permitting electronic service and filing, the court may, on the motion of any party or its own motion, enter an order requiring electronic filing. If the court acts sua sponte to require electronic service and/or filing, it must first *mail notice* to the parties and give them 10 days within which to serve and file any opposition (e.g., claiming undue hardship or prejudice). [CRC 2.251(d)(3), 2.253(c)(3)]

4) [9:86.32] **If new party joined:** If a party is joined in a case in which the court has ordered electronic service and/or filing, the court may give mailed notice to the newly-joined party as provided in the previous paragraph; or, it may order the newly-joined party to electronically serve or file documents and in its order state the party has 10 days, or until such later time as the court may specify, to object to electronic service and/or filing. [CRC 2.253(c)(4)]

5) [9:86.33] **Excludes self-represented parties:** Self-represented parties are exempt from mandatory electronic service requirements adopted by the court. Each self-represented party must be served with documents by nonelectronic means unless the party affirmatively consents to electronic service (*see ¶9:86.26a*). [CRC 2.253(b)(2), (3)]

(c) [9:86.35] **Who may serve:** Electronic service may be made by a party directly or through an electronic service provider. [CRC 2.251(f)(1)]

1) [9:86.36] **Service by court:** In addition, the court may serve any court document (e.g., notices, orders, judgments) in the same manner that parties may serve documents by electronic service. [CRC 2.251(k)(1); see *Insyst, Ltd. v. Applied Materials, Inc.* (2009) 170 CA4th 1129, 1139, 88 CR3d 808, 815—superior court clerk may electronically serve "triggering document" (notice) in any case in which electronic service is authorized]

☞ [9:86.36a] ***PRACTICE POINTER:*** Email service by the parties directly may be fraught with problems. A document emailed directly may be rejected by spam filters in use by a recipient's email service provider. Similarly, a lengthy motion for summary judgment with multiple attachments may trigger a 10 MB file size restriction in use by many email security systems. If that happens, you may be completely unaware that a pleading has been served on you, and the sender may not know the document was rejected.

Stipulating to use of an electronic service provider eliminates the risk of matters not being served or documents not being delivered. The electronic service provider also maintains a docket of all pleadings that have been served in the case that can conveniently be downloaded. Alternatively, if the parties decide to email directly, they may want to stipulate to acceptable file sizes to ensure that documents that are larger than a specified number of MB will be broken into separate, smaller documents and sent via separate emails. It is helpful to identify in the body of the email the names of the files to ensure the recipient is aware of each file being transmitted.

(d) [9:86.37] **Electronic notification as alternative to electronic transmission:** As an alternative to electronic transmission of a document, electronic service may also be effected by electronic notification of *where a document may be viewed and downloaded,* with a *hyperlink* to that location. [CCP §1010.6(a)(1)(C); CRC 2.250(b)(4)]

☞ [9:86.38] ***PRACTICE POINTER:*** This is useful in complex, multi-party cases where the parties have by agreement created a website onto which all pleadings, depositions and discovery documents are downloaded. Motion and opposition papers may then include a hyperlink to retrieve voluminous documents from that website. This avoids the necessity of attaching them as an electronic file (that may be impractical for voluminous documents).

1) [9:86.39] **Party's responsibilities:** The party using electronic notification must preserve the document served and maintain the hyperlink until the case is settled or judgment is final. [See CRC 2.251(h)]

© 2020 Thomson Reuters/The Rutter Group

Compare—parties out of case: When a party is no longer in the case, he or she may give notice to all other parties that the hyperlink to documents will be maintained for 60 days and is then relieved of the obligation to maintain the hyperlink thereafter. [CRC 2.251(h)(3)(B)]

(e) [9:86.40] **When service complete:** Electronic service is complete at the time of transmission or electronic notification of service. If an electronic filing service provider is used, service is complete at the time the provider electronically transmits the document or sends electronic notification of service. Any document that is served between 12:00 a.m. and 11:59:59 p.m. on a court day is deemed served that court day. Any document served on a noncourt day is deemed served on the next court day. [CCP §1010.6(a)(5); CRC 2.251(i)]

1) [9:86.41] **Extension following electronic service:** Except as noted below (¶*9:86.42*), any period of notice or any right or duty to act or respond within a specified period to a document served electronically is extended by *2 court days*. [CCP §1010.6(a)(4)]

a) [9:86.42] **Exceptions:** The above extension of time (¶*9:86.41*) does not apply if a statute or court rule provides otherwise; and, specifically does not apply to a notice of intent to move for *new trial* or to vacate the judgment; or a notice of *appeal*. [CCP §1010.6(a)(4)]

[9:86.43-86.44] *Reserved.*

(f) [9:86.45] **Proof of electronic service:** Proof of electronic service may be made in essentially the same manner as provided for service of papers by mail (CCP §1013a), except that the declaration of service does not need to state that the person making the service is not a party to the action, and must state:

— the electronic service address of the person making the service in addition to that person's residence or business address;
— the date of the electronic service;
— the name and electronic service address of the person served; and
— that the document was served electronically. [CCP §1013b(a), (b); CRC 2.251(j)(1)]

Motion papers: Proof of electronic service of a moving party's papers must be filed with the court at least

5 court days before the hearing. [CRC 2.251(j)(2), 3.1300(c); *see* ¶*9:100*]

FORM: Proof of Electronic Service, *see Form 9A:14.1* in Rivera, *Cal. Prac. Guide: Civ. Pro. Before Trial FORMS* (TRG).

1) [9:86.46] **Electronic filing:** The proof of electronic service may be in electronic form and may be filed electronically with the court. [CRC 2.251(j)(1); CCP §1013b(d)]

2) [9:86.47] **Custody of proof of service:** If a person signs a printed form of a proof of electronic service, the party filing must maintain the printed form of the document bearing the declarant's original signature and must make it available for review and copying upon request by the court or any party. [CRC 2.251(j)(3); CRC 2.257(a)(2)]

[9:86.48-86.49] *Reserved.*

(g) [9:86.50] **Changes of address:** The court must maintain and make available to the parties electronically a list of the electronic service addresses provided by the parties. [CRC 2.251(e)]

However, each party is obligated to notify the court promptly of any change in his or her electronic service address, and to serve this notice electronically on all other parties in the case. Until such notice is filed and served, service directed to the address on file with the court is presumed valid. [CRC 2.251(c)(4), (g)]

FORM: Notice of Change of Electronic Service Address (Judicial Council form EFS-010), *see Form 9A:14.4* in Rivera, *Cal. Prac. Guide: Civ. Pro. Before Trial FORMS* (TRG).

[9:86.51-86.59] *Reserved.*

(6) [9:86.60] **Civility Guidelines:** The timing and manner of service of papers should not be used to the disadvantage of the party receiving the papers. For example:

- An attorney should serve papers on the attorney who is responsible for the matter at his or her principal place of work and, if possible, at a time agreed upon in advance;
- An attorney should allow sufficient time for opposing counsel to prepare for a court appearance or to respond to the papers. *An attorney should not serve papers to take advantage of an opponent's*

© 2020 Thomson Reuters/The Rutter Group

absence or to inconvenience the opponent (e.g., by serving papers late on Friday afternoon or the day preceding a holiday);

- When it is likely that service by mail will prejudice an opposing party, an attorney should serve the papers by other permissible means (e.g., overnight delivery or courier). [State Bar California Attorney Guidelines of Civility and Professionalism §7]

d. **Length of notice required**

(1) [9:87] **Papers served personally:** If the moving papers are to be served personally, a motion can be noticed for hearing *16 court days or more* after the papers are served and filed. [CCP §1005(b)]

(There are a few exceptions; e.g., a motion for *summary judgment* must be served at least *75 days* before the hearing; *see* ¶*10:77*.)

(2) [9:87.1] **Extension for service by mail:** If motion papers are served by mail, the required *16 court days'* notice is *increased* as follows:

— an additional *5 calendar* (not court) days, if the papers are mailed in California to an address in California;

— an additional *10 calendar* days, if the place of mailing or address is in another state; and

— an additional *20 calendar* days, if the place of mailing or address is in another country. [CCP §1005(b)]

(3) [9:87.2] **Extension for service by fax, express mail or overnight delivery:** Where the notice is served by facsimile transmission, express mail or other method providing overnight delivery (e.g., Federal Express), the 16-court-days' notice period is extended by *2 calendar* (not court) days. [CCP §1005(b) (3rd sent.)]

The time for service and filing is computed by counting backwards 16 court days from the hearing date, excluding the day of the hearing, plus counting backward an additional 2 calendar days because of service by fax, express mail or overnight delivery. [CCP §12c]

Comment: If, by counting backwards, the 16th court day is a Monday, counting back an additional 2 calendar days would be a Saturday. Because CCP §1005(b) requires motions to be served and filed "*at least* 16 court days before the hearing" (plus 2 additional days for service by fax, express mail or overnight delivery), the motion would have to be served and filed on the preceding Friday.

Further comment: Although CRC 2.306(d) purports to extend the notice period by "two *court* days" where documents are served by fax, this appears to be invalid as to motions covered by CCP §1005 because it is in direct conflict with CCP §1005(b)'s "two *calendar days*" extension.

(4) [9:87.2a] **Extension for electronic service:** Where email service is authorized (*see* ¶*9:86.25*), the 16-court-days' notice period is extended by *2 court* (not calendar) days. [CCP §1010.6(a)(4); *see* ¶*9:86.41*]

Exceptions: This extension does not apply to motions for new trial or to vacate a judgment under CCP §663a or to a notice of appeal (*see* ¶*9:86.42*).

(5) [9:87.3] **Compare—certain motions governed by other notice periods:** CCP §1005(b) expressly does not apply where other notice periods are provided by law, including:
— motions for *summary judgment* or *summary adjudication* (CCP §437c(b)(6); *see* ¶*10:77*);
— ex parte applications for determination of good faith settlement (CCP §877.6(a)(2); *see* ¶*12:841 ff.*);
— motions for new trial (CCP §659); and
— motions to set aside judgment (CCP §663a).

(6) [9:87.4] **Compare—extension for performance of other acts (CCP §1013):** CCP §1013 extends the time in which a right may be exercised or an act performed following service of papers *other than motion papers* (see CCP §1005(b) (4th sent.)). There is no difference when the service is by mail (i.e., *5 calendar days* for service by mail within California to a California address; 10 calendar days, if mailed to or from another state; 20 calendar days, if mailed to or from another country), but CCP §1013 differs from CCP §1005(b) for service by fax, express mail or other method providing overnight delivery. Under CCP §1013, the extension is for *2 court days* (not calendar days as under CCP §1005(b)). [CCP §1013(c), (e)]

(a) [9:87.5] **Extends time periods measured from date of service:** Where a time period prescribed by statute or court rule is triggered by "service" of a document, §1013(a) extends the time accordingly. For example:

- date amended pleading due after notice of ruling on demurrer served by mail (CCP §472b);
- date responsive pleadings due after amended complaint served by mail (*Lam v. Ngo* (2001) 91 CA4th 832, 842, 111 CR2d 582, 589-590—anti-SLAPP motion (*see* ¶*7:952*));
- date responses due to interrogatories served by mail;

© 2020 Thomson Reuters/The Rutter Group

- deadline for acceptance of CCP §998 settlement offer served by mail (*Poster v. Southern Calif. Rapid Transit Dist.* (1990) 52 C3d 266, 274, 276 CR 321, 325-326);
- deadline for filing peremptory challenge to assignment of all-purpose judge where notice of assignment is mailed (*California Business Council for Equal Opportunity v. Sup.Ct. (Wilson)* (1997) 52 CA4th 1100, 1106, 62 CR2d 7, 10).

(b) [9:87.6] **Not applicable to time periods measured from other dates:** On the other hand, CCP §1013 does not apply where the prescribed time period is measured from date of *filing*, hearing, entry of order, etc. For example:

- deadline for request for trial de novo after arbitration measured from *filing* of arbitration award (*see* ¶*13:146*);
- deadline for action against governmental entities after order granting relief from claim filing requirement measured from *filing* of minute order (*see* ¶*1:814*);
- deadline for court order granting new trial is measured from entry of judgment, and is not extended by mailed notice of entry. [*Westrec Marina Mgmt., Inc. v. Jardine Ins. Brokers Orange County, Inc.* (2000) 85 CA4th 1042, 1048, 102 CR2d 673, 675-676]

e. [9:88] **Defects waived by arguing merits at hearing:** Insufficient or defective notice may be waived if opposing counsel shows up at the hearing and *argues the merits* of the motion. If they appear at all, they should limit their argument to objections based on the defective notice. Otherwise, the court will treat their opposition on the merits as a waiver of the defects. [*Alliance Bank v. Murray* (1984) 161 CA3d 1, 7, 207 CR 233, 237; *Carlton v. Quint* (2000) 77 CA4th 690, 697, 91 CR2d 844, 848]

To preserve the issue for appeal, the opposing party should *expressly object* to the defective notice in its opposition papers, request a *continuance* and demonstrate *prejudice* from the defective notice. [*Reedy v. Bussell* (2007) 148 CA4th 1272, 1288, 56 CR3d 216, 228]

⇨ [9:88.1] ***PRACTICE POINTER:*** Use common sense in raising such objections. Judges may react negatively where the defective notice has not hampered preparation of a response.

[9:88.2-88.4] *Reserved.*

f. [9:88.5] **Orders shortening time:** Except in the case of summary judgment or adjudication motions (*see* ¶*10:77*), if the relief sought by the motion needs to be obtained earlier than the minimum statutory time for the making of the motion permits, counsel may apply to the court for an order shortening notice of the hearing.

Such an application may be made *ex parte*, but the opposing party must be informed (usually by telephone) that such an application will be made. [CRC 3.1203; *see detailed discussion at* ¶*9:351 ff.*]

4. **Filing Requirements**

a. [9:89] **Where filed:** The moving papers must be filed in the office of the court clerk (*not* in the department where the matter is noticed for hearing) unless otherwise provided by local rule or court order. [CRC 3.1302(a)]

[9:89.1] ***PRACTICE POINTER:*** Some courts require courtesy copies (e.g., S.F. Sup.Ct. Rule 2.7(B); Alameda Sup.Ct. Rule 3.30(c)) and many judges appreciate them. Also, courtesy copies ensure that the judge will receive all of your papers filed in connection with a motion. Generally courtesy copies are delivered directly to the department hearing the motion.

[9:89.2] ***FURTHER PRACTICE POINTER:*** Be sure the courtesy copies are printed in the same colors as the original and that any highlighting color does not obscure the text. Consider, with the court's permission, providing a USB device for voluminous briefs or exhibits. Do not fasten a stack of papers in a way that it is not readily accessible (e.g., binding a 10-inch high stack of papers at the top with an Acco clip). Make certain that all courtesy copies are in at least by the time of the reply. Consider lodging conformed copies of all moving, opposition and reply papers with the judge. And always check local rule requirements.

b. [9:90] **When filed:** Moving papers must be filed *at least 16 court days* before the hearing date, unless an order shortening time is granted. [CCP §1005(b); CRC 3.1300(a)]

The latest a paper may be filed is at the close of business of the clerk's office on the day the paper is due. (No slipping the papers under the door or fax-filing during evening hours.) [CRC 3.1300(e); see *Rosenberg v. Sup.Ct. (Germino)* (1994) 25 CA4th 897, 900, 30 CR2d 803, 805—after hours fax deemed filed following day]

Exception for certain electronically-filed documents: The preceding rule does not apply if the document is filed electronically in a court that has adopted a local rule or court order providing

© 2020 Thomson Reuters/The Rutter Group

for electronic filing of documents. Documents received between 12:00 a.m. and 11:59:59 p.m. on a court day are deemed filed that day. [CCP §1010.6(b)(3)]

c. [9:90.1] **Appearance and filing fees:** If the notice of motion is the *first paper* filed by a party in an action, an appearance fee must accompany the moving papers. [See Gov.C. §§70611-70616 (uniform filing fees)]

After the first paper has been filed, there is a fee for filing a motion, application or any other paper requiring a hearing. [See Gov.C. §70617(a)]

(1) [9:90.1a] **Effect of bounced check:** If the appearance fee is paid by a check that is returned unpaid, the court clerk must notify the party involved to pay the fees within 20 days. If the hearing is scheduled within the 20-day period, the fee must be paid *before* the hearing; otherwise, the court must *void* the motion "and proceed as if it had not been filed." [See CCP §411.20(a), (e); *Hu v. Silgan Containers Corp.* (1999) 70 CA4th 1261, 1268, 83 CR2d 333, 337; *see also* ¶*1:950 ff.*]

If the person who tendered the check was a nonparty (e.g., an attorney's filing service), the clerk must also notify the party or party's attorney. [CCP §411.20(a)]

d. [9:90.2] **Filing by fax:** Pursuant to legislative authority (CCP §1010.5), the Judicial Council has adopted rules for filing papers with a court by fax transmission. [CRC 2.303, 2.304]

(1) [9:90.3] **Which courts:** Fax filing is permitted in any court through a third person (a "fax filing" agency; *see* ¶*9:90.9*).

"Direct filing" is permissible only in courts which have adopted a local rule authorizing such filing (*see* ¶*9:90.14*). (Such rules are not preempted by CRC 3.20(a) because they are specifically authorized by CRC 2.304(a).)

Local rules authorizing direct fax filing are in effect in several courts. [See L.A. Sup.Ct. Rule 2.22]

(2) [9:90.4] **Which papers:** Except as noted below (¶*9:90.5*), any pleading, motion or other document permitted to be filed with the court may be fax-filed.

(a) [9:90.5] **Exceptions:** No *will, codicil, bond or undertaking* may be filed by fax. [CRC 2.300(b)]

Nor may the court issue by fax any document intended to carry the original seal of the court (e.g., writs, letters testamentary, etc.). [CRC 2.300(b)]

(b) [9:90.6] **Exhibits:** Exhibits larger than 8 1/2 x 11 inches must be reduced to that size before they are transmitted. [CRC 2.302]

The court may in any case require the party to *file the original* of an exhibit filed by fax. [CRC 2.302]

(3) [9:90.7] **Signatures on fax-filed documents:** *See discussion at ¶9:86.21.*

(4) [9:90.7a] **Originals retained:** Originals of documents filed by fax must be retained by counsel for production to the court and opposing parties as may be ordered by the court. [CRC 2.305(b), (c)]

(5) [9:90.8] **Direct filing vs. fax filing agency:** Two different methods of fax filing are authorized:

(a) [9:90.9] **Through fax filing agency:** Unless local court rules authorize "direct fax filing" (*see ¶9:90.14*), papers to be filed must be faxed to a "fax filing agency." (This refers to any person or company that assumes responsibility for receiving such transmissions and filing the papers with the court.) [CRC 2.303(a), 2.304(a); see also S.F. Sup.Ct. Rule 2.7(C)]

1) [9:90.10] **Advance arrangements with fax filing agency required:** A fax filing agency is not required to accept papers for filing unless "appropriate arrangements" have been made in advance for payment of applicable fees and service charges. Absent such arrangements, the agency may *discard* any papers transmitted to it for filing. [CRC 2.303(c)]

2) [9:90.11] **Duties of fax filing agency:** Upon receipt of the fax transmission, the agency will:

- *Photocopy:* Prepare the documents for filing with the court—i.e., by photocopying the fax onto 20-lb. paper as required by CRC 2.103. [CRC 2.303(b)]

- *File with court:* Physically deliver and file the documents with the court and pay any applicable filing fee. [CRC 2.303(b)]

  The agency will also normally fax (or mail) to the sender a *proof of filing;* e.g., a file-stamped copy of the papers filed or a transmittal sheet showing this information.

- *Confidentiality:* Keep confidential all documents transmitted to it except as provided by the Rules of Court. [CRC 2.303(d)]

Note: By filing a document with the court, the fax filing agency *certifies its compliance* with the above rules and that the document filed is a full and complete copy of that received by fax. [CRC 2.303(e)]

© 2020 Thomson Reuters/The Rutter Group

3) [9:90.12] **Notation of fax filing on face of document:** Each document to be fax-filed must contain the words "BY FAX" *immediately below the title* of the document (*not* at the end). [CRC 2.303(f)]

It is the fax filing agency's responsibility to make sure the document contains such notation (and to add it if it does not). [CRC 2.303(b)]

4) [9:90.13] **Responsibility for errors in transmission:** The fax filing agency acts as agent of the filing party—*not as agent of the court.* [CRC 2.303(a)]

Thus, any error in the fax transmission or filing is charged to the filing party. It *cannot be cured by nunc pro tunc order* as in courts with direct filing procedures (¶*9:90.21*).

(b) [9:90.14] **Direct fax filing (if authorized by local rules):** Any court may, by local rule, allow direct fax filings in addition to accepting filings through fax filing agencies. [CRC 2.304(a)]

The Los Angeles Superior Court allows direct fax filings in small claims and family law (as well as filings through a fax filing agency). The court's fax machines are available 24 hours a day; but filings received after business hours are deemed filed the next court day. [See L.A. Sup.Ct. Rule 2.22]

By General Order, electronic filing of all documents in the Los Angeles Superior Court is mandatory after January 2, 2019 in all limited and unlimited civil cases except for self-represented litigants, parties who apply for and are granted an exemption, and certain exempt documents. Fax filing is not permitted for mandatory e-filed documents. [See Los Angeles Superior Court General Order re Mandatory Electronic Filing for Civil, available on the court's website (*www.lacourt.org*)]

1) [9:90.15] **Time of filing:** The rule governing *service* by fax provides that fax transmissions after 5 p.m. are deemed served the next court day. [CRC 2.306(g); *see* ¶*9:86.17*]

However, there is no comparable rule governing *fax filing* of documents. It is therefore up to each court to determine the hours during which it will accept fax filings. [*Rosenberg v. Sup.Ct. (Gemino)* (1994) 25 CA4th 897, 900, 30 CR2d 803, 805—complaint transmitted at 10 p.m. on day before expiration of statute of limitations deemed filed following day because court clerk's office closed at 5 p.m.]

2) [9:90.16] **Cover sheet mandatory:** Every document to be fax filed directly with the court must be accompanied by a "Facsimile Transmission Cover Sheet" in the form approved by the Judicial Council. [CRC 2.304(b)]

FORM: Facsimile Transmission Cover Sheet (Fax Filing) (MC-005).

a) [9:90.16a] **Accompanying processing instructions:** Processing instructions may be transmitted along with the Facsimile Transmission Cover Sheet. [See *Fry v. Sup.Ct.* (2013) 222 CA4th 475, 484, 166 CR3d 328, 333—CCP §170.6 peremptory challenge fax-filed to central filing office that had no instructions as to whom it should be delivered was improper and ineffective because it did not comply with statutory requirement that peremptory challenge be "made to" challenged judge or presiding judge]

[9:90.16b] ***PRACTICE POINTER:*** If you want the document you are fax filing to be delivered to a particular location in the courthouse other than the central filing office, be sure to transmit processing instructions along with the Facsimile Transmission Cover Sheet.

3) [9:90.17] **Notation of fax filing on face of document:** The requirements are the same as for filings through fax filing agencies (*see ¶9:90.12*).

4) [9:90.18] **Filing fees:** In addition to any other required filing fee, courts are authorized to charge a "reasonable fee not to exceed costs" for direct fax filing. This fee is to be charged on a per page basis. [CRC 10.815(b)(14)]

5) [9:90.19] **Payment of filing fees:** Filing fees are payable by Visa or Mastercard charges. The fee or discount imposed by Visa or Mastercard is added to the charge. (Account numbers, expiration dates and signatures appear on the mandatory cover sheet.) [CRC 2.304(e)]

Charges rejected by the credit card company are treated in the same manner as a returned check. [See CCP §411.20; CRC 2.304(e)]

© 2020 Thomson Reuters/The Rutter Group

6) [9:90.20] **No confirmation:** There is no requirement that the court confirm a fax filing. (Even so, many courts fax or mail back a copy of the cover sheet to show the filing date and case number assigned.)

In Los Angeles, counsel can arrange, upon payment of a fee, to have the court confirm receipt of fax filings. [See L.A. Sup.Ct. Rule 2.22(b)(4)]

7) [9:90.21] **Relief for errors in transmission or filing:** The sender's machine must print out a transmission record for each fax filing. If errors occur in transmission or in the court's process of the filing, the sender can move for an order filing the document *nunc pro tunc* based on the transmission record and proof of transmission. [CRC 2.304(d)]

8) [9:90.22] **Retain documents:** Originals of the documents transmitted by fax must be retained by counsel for production to the court or other parties, if so ordered. [CRC 2.305]

e. [9:91] **Electronic filing:** "Electronic filing" is the transmission of a document to a court in electronic form. [CRC 2.250(b)(7)]

Courts are authorized to adopt local rules permitting parties to file documents electronically in any civil action or proceeding (*see* ¶*9:92*). In addition, a court may *order* electronic filing of documents in certain types of cases (*see* ¶*9:93*); and may itself electronically file any notice, order, minute order, judgment or other document prepared by the court. [CRC 2.252(g)]

Caution: Different courts are at various stages of implementing efiling. Some do not require efiling, whereas others require most documents to be efiled. Since each court's local rules typically change as its efiling requirements change, it is always prudent to check the local rules.

FORM: Order Re: Electronic Service [and Filing], *see Form 9A:14.2* in Rivera, *Cal. Prac. Guide: Civ. Pro. Before Trial FORMS* (TRG).

(1) [9:92] **When permitted:** By local rule, a court may *permit* parties to file documents electronically in any action or proceeding, directly or through an approved electronic service provider, subject to the conditions in CCP §1010.6 and CRC 2.250 et seq. [CRC 2.253(a)]

(a) [9:92.1] **Format requirements:** An electronically-filed document must be in the format specified by the court unless it cannot be created in that format. [See CRC 2.256(b)]

The format adopted by the court must meet the following requirements:

— the software for creating and reading the documents must be in the public domain or generally available at reasonable cost;

— the printing of documents must not result in loss of text, format, or appearance; and

— the document must be text searchable when technologically feasible without impairment of the document's image. [CRC 2.256(b)]

(b) [9:92.2] **When filing of original document required:** In actions requiring the filing of an original document (e.g., the original promissory note in an action on the note), an electronic copy of the document may be filed, provided the original is filed within 10 calendar days. [CRC 2.252(e)]

(c) [9:92.2a] **Efiling sealed documents:** If you have a document you want to efile under seal, consult the court's website. Some courts have adopted special procedures for electronic filing of sealed documents (*see* ¶*9:416 ff.*). For example, San Francisco Superior Court requires that a redacted copy of the document sought to be sealed be electronically filed, together with the lodging of the sealed, unredacted paper copy of the document (*www.sfsuperiorcourt.org*).

In San Diego, documents filed or provisionally filed under seal may be filed in paper form unless the court directs otherwise, though the motion to seal itself must be electronically filed (*www.sdcourt.ca.gov*). In Los Angeles, the actual motion or application to submit documents conditionally under seal must be electronically filed, and a courtesy copy of the motion or application, along with the documents submitted conditionally under seal, must be delivered directly to the courtroom to which the case is assigned (*www.lacourt.org*).

(d) [9:92.3] **Filing through agents:** Electronic filing may be permitted by the parties directly, by an agent, or through an electronic filing service provider. [CRC 2.250(b)(6), (8)]

(e) [9:92.4] **Filing as consent to electronic service:** For cases filed before January 1, 2019, filing documents electronically with the court operates as consent to electronic service in that action of any document that may be served by mail, fax, express mail, or overnight mail. [CCP §1010.6(a)(2)(A)(i)]

For cases filed on or after January 1, 2019, the "act of electronic filing shall not be construed as express

© 2020 Thomson Reuters/The Rutter Group

consent"; rather, parties must expressly consent to electronic service either by a written notice or manifesting consent with the court's electronic service provider and concurrently providing the party's electronic address for service. [CCP §1010.6(a)(2)(A)(ii); CRC 2.251(b)(1); *see* ¶*9:86.25 ff.*]

If the filing party used an electronic filing service provider to file its documents with the court, the party consents to service on the electronic filing service provider as its agent for service. [CRC 2.251(b)(2)]

However, this does not apply to self-represented parties. Self-represented parties must *affirmatively consent* to electronic service by serving and filing a notice so stating (*see* ¶*9:86.26a*). [CRC 2.251(c)(3)(B)]

(2) [9:93] **When required:**

Permissive filing: By local rule, a court may *permit* electronic filing of documents in any type of case. [CRC 2.253(a)]

Mandatory filing: By local rule, the court may *require* electronic filing and service in all civil actions or in specified categories of civil actions, such as:

— cases of a specific category (e.g., limited or unlimited);
— cases of a specific type (e.g., contract, personal injury, employment);
— cases assigned to a judge for all purposes;
— cases assigned to a particular department or courtroom;
— class actions, consolidated actions, coordinated actions or actions classified as "complex" under Judicial Council Rules (*see* ¶*12:47.1*);
— any combination of cases described above. [CCP §1010.6(d); CRC 2.253(b)(1)]

Or, if a court has adopted a local rule permitting e-filing, the court *may order*, on motion of a party or on its own motion, all parties to file documents electronically in the following types of cases:

— class actions;
— consolidated or coordinated actions;
— "a group of actions"; or
— "complex" actions. [CCP §1010.6(c); CRC 2.253(c)(1)]

Before entering such an order, the court must make a finding that the order would not "cause undue hardship or significant prejudice to any party." [CCP §1010.6(c); CRC 2.253(c)]

The order may require that the parties:

— *file* all documents electronically; or

— *serve and file* all documents electronically, except when personal service is required by statute or rule. [CRC 2.253(c)(1), (2)]

(a) [9:93a] **Parties exempted:** *Self-represented parties* are exempt from mandatory electronic filing and service requirements. When electronic service and filing are required (by local rule or court order), each self-represented party must be served with documents by nonelectronic means unless the self-represented party affirmatively consents to electronic service (*see ¶9:86.26a*). [CRC 2.253(b)(2), (3)]

In addition, a *represented party* must be excused from mandatory electronic filing and service if the party shows *undue hardship or significant prejudice*. A court requiring electronic filing and service must provide a process for parties to apply for relief from the requirement. [CRC 2.253(b)(4)]

(b) [9:93.1] **Application:** Details of the efiling programs listed below (*¶9:93.2 ff.*) can be found on the respective court's websites and in local rules:

- [9:93.2] Ventura County Superior Court permits electronic filing in all civil actions.
- [9:93.3] The Santa Clara and Contra Costa County Superior Courts have ordered that all papers in complex civil cases be filed electronically unless specifically excused by court order.
- [9:93.4] The Sacramento, San Bernardino and San Joaquin Superior Courts have adopted efiling programs for small claims division actions.

(c) **Mandatory efiling**

1) [9:93.5] **Orange County:** With limited exceptions, *all* documents filed in *limited, unlimited and complex civil actions* in Orange County *must* be filed electronically unless the court orders otherwise. [See Orange County Sup.Ct. Rule 352 and further details on court's website (*www.occourts.org*)]

2) [9:93.6] **San Francisco:** San Francisco Superior Court requires efiling and eservice for all civil cases except unlawful detainer and small claims actions. [See S.F. Sup.Ct. Rule 2.11(A)(3)]

3) [9:93.7] **Los Angeles:** The Los Angeles Superior Court requires electronic filing in all limited and unlimited civil cases, except cases designated to be complex. Electronic filing is permitted in small claims matters. Electronic filing

© 2020 Thomson Reuters/The Rutter Group

in complex civil cases is projected for some time in 2020. (See the court's website for details and general orders re electronic filing under the "e-filing" tab on the homepage (*www.lacourt.org*).)

[9:93.8-93.9] *Reserved.*

(d) [9:93.10] **Procedure:** If the court proposes to order electronic filing on its own motion, it must mail notice to the parties who have not consented to electronic service and may e-serve parties who have consented, and allow them 10 days for any opposition. [See CRC 2.253(c)(3)]

If a new party is later joined in the action, the court may either repeat the notice process or give the newly-joined party 10 days to object to electronic service and filing of documents. [CRC 2.253(c)(4)]

1) [9:93.11] **Resubmitting documents previously filed:** The court may order that documents previously filed in paper form may be resubmitted electronically. [CRC 2.253(c)(5)(A)]

2) [9:93.12] **Confirmation of filing as service:** The court may also order that when the court sends confirmation of an electronic filing to all parties, receipt of that confirmation *constitutes service* of the filed document if it is available electronically. [CRC 2.253(c)(5)(B)]

3) [9:93.13] **Compare—where electronic filing not feasible:** When electronic filing has been ordered but it is not feasible to convert a document to electronic form by scanning, imaging or other means, the court may permit filing that document in paper form. [CRC 2.252(d)]

(3) [9:93.14] **Filing fees:** The court may authorize any method of payment for electronic filing of documents, including credit cards, debit cards, electronic fund transfers or debit accounts. [CRC 2.258(a)] (Eligible persons may seek a fee waiver; see CRC 2.258(b).)

(4) [9:94] **Effect of electronic filing:** The following are some of the important effects of electronic filing:

(a) [9:94.1] **Same effect as paper filing:** Filing a document electronically does not alter any filing deadline. [CRC 2.252(c)]

1) [9:94.2] **Compare—where filing of original document required:** If the court requires the filing of an original document, the electronic filer may file an electronic copy of the document but must file the original within 10 calendar days. [CRC 2.252(e)]

[9:94.3] *Reserved.*

(b) [9:94.4] **Time of filing:** A document received electronically by the court between 12:00 a.m. and 11:59:59 p.m. on a court day is deemed filed on that court day. A document received on a noncourt day is deemed filed on the next court day. [CCP §1010.6(b)(3)]

1) [9:94.5] **Effect of court's technical problems:** If a court's technical problem prevents acceptance during regular filing hours, and an electronic filer demonstrates he or she attempted to file on that day, the document—*other than a complaint or any other initial pleading*—is deemed filed on that day. [CRC 2.259(c)]

[9:94.6] ***PRACTICE POINTER:*** You can't blame breakdowns in the court's electronic filing system for missing a statute of limitations deadline.

[9:94.7-94.9] *Reserved.*

(c) [9:94.10] **Signatures:** Unless a document is required to be filed "under penalty of perjury," an electronically-filed copy is *deemed signed* by the party who filed it electronically. [CCP §1010.6(b)(2)(A); CRC 2.257(b)]

When a document to be filed electronically provides for a signature under penalty of perjury, the document is deemed to have been signed by that person if filed electronically, provided that: 1) the declarant has signed the document using a computer or other technology in accordance with a rule of court adopted by the Judicial Council by January 1, 2019; or 2) the declarant, before filing, has physically signed a printed form of the document. By filing it electronically, the filer certifies that he or she has the signed original and will make it available for inspection and copying upon request by the court or any party. [CCP §1010.6(b)(2)(B); CRC 2.257(a)] (If such a request is made, the filer must make the original available for inspection and copying by all other parties *within 5 days* after the request; see CRC 2.257(a)(2)(B). Alternatively, the court may order it produced at a specified time and place; see CRC 2.257(a)(2)(C).)

© 2020 Thomson Reuters/The Rutter Group

1) [9:94.11] **Compare—documents requiring signatures of opposing parties:** When a document to be filed electronically requires the signature of opposing parties (e.g., a stipulation), the party filing the document must obtain the signatures of all parties on a printed form. By filing electronically, the filer "indicates" that all parties have signed it, and the filer has the original in his or her possession and will make it available for inspection and copying (¶*9:94.10*). [CRC 2.257(c)]

2) [9:94.12] **Compare—judicial signatures:** If the signature of a judicial officer is required on the electronically-filed document, it may be electronically signed "in any manner permitted by law." [CRC 2.257(e)]

(5) [9:95] **Confirmation of filing:** The court must first send the filer a confirmation, indicating date and time of receipt. [CRC 2.259(a)(1)]

If the document complies with filing requirements and the required fees have been paid, the court will send the filer confirmation that the document has been filed. The electronically-filed document is considered received at the date and time the confirmation of receipt is created. [CRC 2.259(a)(1), (2)]

If the document was rejected for filing, the court must send the filer notice to that effect, stating the reasons why the document was rejected for filing. [CRC 2.259(b)]

⇨[9:95.1] ***PRACTICE POINTER:*** It is the *filer's responsibility to verify receipt and filing of the document.* Absent a confirmation of receipt and filing from the court, there is *no presumption* that an electronically-filed document has been received and filed. [See CRC 2.259(a)(3), (4)]

(6) [9:96] **Electronic filer's obligations:** Electronic filers must:

— comply with court requirements that are designed to ensure the integrity of the filing and to protect sensitive personal information;

— furnish information the court may require to process the case;

— take reasonable steps to ensure that the filing does not contain viruses or other computer code that may harm the electronic filing system of the court or other users of the system;

— furnish electronic addresses in a manner specified by the court (by doing so, the filer agrees to accept service);

— immediately furnish the court and parties with any changes in the filer's electronic address;

— if using an electronic filing service provider, provide the service provider with the electronic address at which the filer is to be sent all documents and immediately notify the provider of any change in that address (CRC 2.256(a)); and

— file documents in a format specified by the court (formatting requirements in other rules are superseded) unless the documents cannot be created in that format (CRC 2.256(b)).

(a) [9:96.1] **Change of electronic service address:** A party or other person whose electronic notification address changes during a pending action or proceeding must promptly file a notice of change of address with the court electronically and serve this notice on all other parties and others required to be served. A party's or other person's election to contract with an electronic service provider does not relieve the party or other person of these obligations. [CRC 2.251(g)]

Until the change of electronic notification address has been filed and served, service on the party at his or her electronic address of record is presumed valid. [CRC 2.251(g)(3)]

(7) [9:97] **Public access:** An electronically-filed document is a public document at the time it is filed unless it is sealed (*see* ¶*9:416 ff.*) or otherwise made confidential by law. [CRC 2.254(c), 2.503(a)]

(a) [9:97.1] **Courthouse electronic access:** Electronic access to electronically-filed documents must be provided at the courthouse to the extent feasible (i.e., to the extent the court has the resources and technical capacity). [CRC 2.503(b)-(d)]

[9:98-99] *Reserved.*

f. [9:100] **Filing proof of service:** Proof of service in compliance with CCP §1005 (*see* ¶*9:87*) should accompany the moving papers. If filed separately, the proof of service must be filed at least *5 court days* before the hearing. [CRC 3.1300(c); *see* ¶*9:15.1*]

[9:100.1] ***PRACTICE POINTER:*** File your proof of service *with your moving papers* whenever possible. It should be attached as the *last page* of the moving papers, where it can be easily found. Reason: The first thing the judge or law clerk working on the case will look for is this proof of service.

(1) [9:100.2] **Effect of failure to comply if opposition filed:** If an opposition has been filed, the judge may overlook the moving party's failure to file a proof of service (on the assumption that the moving papers *must* have been timely served).

(A proof of service is particularly important in *multiparty* cases. The fact one party has filed an opposition does not prove timely service was made on other parties.)

[9:100.3-100.4] *Reserved.*

[9:100.5] ***PRACTICE POINTER:*** When filing a proof of service separate from the moving papers, *be sure to attach a cover sheet* captioned "Proof of Service of (*name of paper served*)." Otherwise, there is an excellent chance it will be lost.

Also, *put the hearing date* on the cover sheet because documents are often delivered to the department that will hear the matter based on the hearing date.

g. [9:100.6] **Clerk's duty to accept filing:** So long as a pleading presented for filing substantially complies with the CRC and appropriate fees are paid (or waived), the court clerk has a ministerial duty to file the pleading and has no discretion to refuse it. [*Voit v. Sup.Ct. (Montano)* (2011) 201 CA4th 1285, 1287, 134 CR3d 381, 382—clerk had no authority to demand that moving party cite or quote precedent before motion would be filed]

C. OPPOSING THE MOTION—AND REBUTTING THE OPPOSITION

PRACTICE POINTERS

- [9:101] **Determine whether opposition necessary:** Do not assume that every time your opponent makes a motion you must oppose it. If the likelihood is that the motion will be granted, why make a trip to court to fight it? Even if the ruling might go either way, there nevertheless may be sufficient merit to the motion that you should *stipulate* to its being granted, thereby saving yourself a trip to court (and your client the cost).
- [9:101.1] **Save time by not opposing:** If you represent plaintiff and have worked hard to draft the complaint, do not necessarily insist on fighting the demurrer. Keep in mind that parties are required to meet and confer on objections raised in demurrers (CCP §430.41(a)), motions to strike (CCP §435.5), and motions for judgment on the pleadings (CCP §439). In most cases, if there is any apparent merit to the demurrer, you should *agree to amend.* The time spent in amending the complaint will be far less than the time required to draft an opposition and fight the demurrer in court.

- [9:101.2] **If opposition necessary, do it right:** On the other hand, if you have a good faith basis to oppose the motion, make sure you file whatever declarations and points and authorities are necessary to defeat it. This is true *even if the moving papers appear technically insufficient:* The judge may disagree with your assessment and treat your failure to oppose as a *waiver* of any objection to the motion.

  Caution for moving party: If your opponent chooses not to file an opposition, you should not assume the motion will be granted. Because there are no "defaults" in law and motion matters, motions that are technically insufficient or lack substantive merit may be denied notwithstanding lack of opposition.

- [9:101.3] **Adhere to standards of professionalism:** It is unprofessional to force opposing counsel to make a motion that you do not intend to oppose. [See L.A. Sup.Ct. Rule 3.26, Appendix 3.A(h)(2)—"A lawyer should not force his or her adversary to make a motion and then not oppose it"]

- [9:101.4] **Avoid sanctions:** If you decide to oppose, limit your arguments to those well supported by the facts and the law. Under CCP §128.7, presenting papers to the court creates a certificate of their legal and factual merit; and sanctions may be imposed for violation of this certificate (*see* ¶*9:1135*). In addition, a trial court could order sanctions under CCP §128.5 for the filing of a frivolous opposition. [See CCP §128.5(b)(1)—bad-faith "actions or tactics" include "the making or opposing of motions"; *see* ¶*9:1010*]

1. [9:102] **Grounds for Opposition:** There are three bases on which a motion may be opposed:

   a. [9:102.1] **Procedural challenges:** The moving party's papers fail to comply with the procedural requirements applicable; e.g., insufficient notice, failure to serve all supporting documents, improper timing of motion, etc.

      ⇨ [9:102.2] ***PRACTICE POINTER:*** In such cases, opposing counsel could choose not to file any opposition and simply request a continuance at the hearing, making record as to the inadequate notice or defective service. But to avoid the risk of a continuance being denied, it is better practice to file the best opposition possible under the circumstances—i.e., pointing out the motion's procedural defects, stating the basic points of the opposition, and explaining why a more complete opposition could not be filed. Counsel should then appear at the hearing, object to the hearing taking place, and request a continuance so that a proper response to

© 2020 Thomson Reuters/The Rutter Group

the motion can be filed. [See *Carlton v. Quint* (2000) 77 CA4th 690, 697-698, 91 CR2d 844, 848; *Robinson v. Woods* (2008) 168 CA4th 1258, 1267, 86 CR3d 241, 248 (citing text)]

[9:102.3-102.4] *Reserved.*

b. [9:102.5] **Evidentiary objections:** The motion is based on inadmissible evidence.

(1) [9:102.6] **Requirements:** Evidentiary objections should be filed in a *separate document* (rather than as part of opposing points and authorities). The objections should state:

— the language verbatim to which objection is made;

— the page and line number and document where such language appears; and

— the legal ground for objection with the same specificity as would be required at trial. [*Schoendorf v. U.D. Registry, Inc.* (2002) 97 CA4th 227, 240, 118 CR2d 313, 322, fn. 2 (citing text)]

FORM: Objections to Evidence and Objections to Evidence (Alternative Format), *see Forms 10:6 and 10:6.1* in Rivera, *Cal. Prac. Guide: Civ. Pro. Before Trial FORMS* (TRG).

(2) [9:102.7] **Time for filing:** It is good practice to file and serve such objections concurrently with the opposition papers. If the objecting party decides to wait until the hearing to raise the objections, it is important to have a court reporter present to make a record of the court's ruling (clerk's minutes may not be sufficient).

(a) [9:102.8] **Summary judgment motions:** According to the CRC, "all written objections to evidence in support of or in opposition to a motion for summary judgment . . . must be served and filed at the same time as the objecting party's opposition or reply papers are served and filed." [CRC 3.1354(a)]

However, CCP §437c also allows evidentiary objections to be made *at the hearing* on a summary judgment motion (*see ¶10:210.2*).

(b) [9:102.9] **Comment:** Even so, counsel should follow CRC 3.1354(a) *on motion hearings generally* because it permits the court to prepare for the hearing.

c. [9:102.10] **Opposition "on the merits":** Here, the opposition goes to the legal sufficiency of the motion. The opposition may argue that the moving papers inaccurately state the substantive law; or, it may distinguish the authority cited in the moving papers and present other authority that supports a different legal conclusion. Alternatively, where the moving papers are based on a factual showing, the opposition may dispute the inferences drawn by the moving party from those facts; or, may dispute the facts shown by presenting admissible evidence of other relevant facts.

2. [9:103] **Form and Content of Opposition Papers:** The same requirements applicable to the moving papers apply to the declarations and points and authorities filed in opposition to the motion (*see* ¶*9:19 ff.*).

PRACTICE POINTERS

- [9:103.1] Too often, counsel attack the moving party's declarations simply by arguing that the facts are disputed in the pleadings, or by setting forth factual arguments in the memorandum. This is not sufficient. The court is likely to accept the moving party's factual assertions as true unless you present *admissible* evidence to the contrary, and this usually means opposing declarations.

- [9:103.2] It is generally good practice to structure your opposing points and authorities to respond to each point made in the moving papers in the same order that they appear. Start off with any inaccuracies in the moving party's statement of the facts or the history of the litigation. (But again, you will need admissible evidence—i.e., declarations—to establish the contradictory facts.) Follow with each argument made in the moving papers, showing why it is not valid; make sure you respond to *each* point. Finally, add whatever other reasons for denial are shown in your own declarations or evidence.

- [9:103.3] Be sure to file *written objections* to any inadmissible evidence offered by the moving party; and if the moving party is basing his or her motion on facts not before the court, be sure to point this out in your memorandum.

  FORM: Memorandum in Opposition to Motion, *see Form 9A:1.1* in Rivera, *Cal. Prac. Guide: Civ. Pro. Before Trial FORMS* (TRG).

  [9:103.4-103.9] *Reserved.*

a. [9:103.10] **Form requirements:** *See* ¶*9:19 ff.*

b. [9:103.11] **Sanctions requests:** Where the party opposing the motion seeks sanctions against the moving party or counsel, adequate notice must be given. For sanctions under CCP §128.7, a *separate* sanctions motion is required; *see* ¶*9:1190 ff.*

[9:103.12] *Reserved.*

© 2020 Thomson Reuters/The Rutter Group

c. [9:103.13] **Proposed order:** If the responding party wants to speed up entry of the order denying the motion, he or she may prepare and submit a proposed order with the opposition papers. (This saves the time involved in preparing and serving a proposed order after the hearing; CRC 3.1312(a), *see ¶9:294 ff.*)

3. [9:104] **Service and Filing Requirements—Opposition Papers:** Papers opposing a motion must be served and filed at least *9 court* days before the hearing, unless the court permits a shorter time. [CCP §1005(b); CRC 3.1300(a)]

A document received electronically by the court between 12:00 a.m. and 11:59:59 p.m. on a court day is deemed filed on that court day. A document received on a noncourt day is deemed filed on the next court day. [CCP §1010(b)(3)]

Exceptions:

- Papers opposing a summary judgment motion must be served *not less than 14 days* before the hearing (CCP §437c(b)(2); *see ¶10:217*);
- Opposition to a *discovery motion* in an *unlawful detainer* action may be made *orally* at the hearing *or* in a writing served and filed on the *court day before* the hearing by a method reasonably calculated to ensure delivery by the close of business on that day (CRC 3.1347);
- A response to a petition to compel arbitration must be served and filed *within 10 days* after service of the petition, unless extended by an agreement in writing between the parties or by court order. [CCP §1290.6; *Correia v. NB Baker Electric, Inc.* (2019) 32 CA5th 602, 612-613, 244 CR3d 177, 182; *see ¶9:408.37a*]

a. [9:104.1] **Where filed:** Unless local rules provide otherwise, opposition papers are filed in the court clerk's office (*not* in the courtroom where the matter will be heard). [CRC 3.1302(a)] (Because expressly authorized by CRC 3.1302(a), such local rules are not preempted by CRC 3.20(a).)

But some courts have adopted local rules providing otherwise. For example, in Los Angeles Superior Court, opposition and reply papers must be electronically filed in civil matters, except for self-represented parties and parties who have obtained an exemption. In those cases, the documents must be filed at the filing window by 4:30 p.m. In small claims matters (where electronic filing is permitted) and in complex matters, electronic filing is not required. [L.A. Sup.Ct. Rule 3.4; *see ¶9:93.7*] Courtesy copies may be required by individual judges in the departments and are a good practice because the electronic filing system does not post the documents to the judges' computers immediately and may even take several days.

b. [9:105] **Time not extended because moving papers served by mail (or fax):** CCP §1013(a) generally extends the time to "respond" to papers served by mail (*see ¶9:87.4*). But this does not apply to papers opposing a motion served by mail. [CCP §1005(b); *see ¶9:87.4*]

Thus, the deadline for serving and filing opposition papers is measured backward from the date of hearing (9 court days, except on summary judgment or summary adjudication motions), regardless of whether the moving papers were served personally, or by mail, overnight delivery or fax. [See *Blake v. Ecker* (2001) 93 CA4th 728, 736, 113 CR2d 422, 428, fn. 6 (disapproved on other grounds by *Le Francois v. Goel* (2005) 35 C4th 1094, 1107, 29 CR3d 249, 260 (citing text))]

Similarly, the deadline for serving and filing a reply to the opposition is measured backward from the date of the hearing by 5 court days.

c. [9:105.1] **Manner of service:** *All* papers opposing a motion must be served by personal delivery, fax, electronically, express mail, or other means consistent with CCP §§1010-1013 (the service of notice statutes) *and* "reasonably calculated to ensure delivery . . . not later than *the close of the next business day*" after the papers are filed with the court. [CCP §1005(c) (emphasis added)]

(1) [9:105.2] **Ordinary mail?** Arguably, service by ordinary mail is "reasonably calculated to ensure delivery not later than the close of the next business day" *where the mail is addressed locally*. But the matter is unclear because the statute specifically enumerates other methods. [*Blake v. Ecker*, supra, 93 CA4th at 736, 113 CR2d at 428, fn. 6 (citing text)]

d. [9:105.3] **Proof of service:** A proof of service should accompany the opposition papers. If filed separately, it must be filed at least 5 *court* days before the hearing. [CRC 3.1300(c); *see ¶9:100*]

e. [9:105.4] **Discretion re late-filed papers:** Papers submitted after the deadline must be accepted for filing. But the court, in its discretion, *may refuse to consider* these papers in ruling on the motion (in which event, the minutes or order must so state). [CRC 3.1300(d)]

(1) [9:105.5] **Comment:** A court's decision to disregard late-filed papers may not be exercised arbitrarily. [*Kapitanski v. Von's Grocery Co., Inc.* (1983) 146 CA3d 29, 32-33, 193 CR 839, 841—court can summarily reject late-filed papers under local rules, but if it considers them at all, it must apply CCP §473 standards, and it is an abuse of discretion to refuse relief if "excusable neglect" shown]

© 2020 Thomson Reuters/The Rutter Group

However, one court has held that a court has discretion to consider late-filed papers even without a CCP §473 showing. [*Juarez v. Wash Depot Holdings, Inc.* (2018) 24 CA5th 1197, 1202, 235 CR3d 250, 253—filing 2 days late with no showing of prejudice by other side supported court's discretion in "view of the strong policy of the law favoring the disposition of cases on the merits"]

If the court decides to consider late-filed papers, a continuance may be necessitated. [See *Hobson v. Raychem Corp.* (1999) 73 CA4th 614, 623, 86 CR2d 497, 503 (dictum) (disapproved on other grounds by *Colmenares v. Braemar Country Club, Inc.* (2003) 29 C4th 1019, 130 CR2d 662)]

[9:105.6-105.9] *Reserved.*

4. [9:105.10] **Effect of Failure to File Opposition Papers:** Some courts treat a party's failure to file opposition papers as an admission that the motion is meritorious, and therefore refuse to hear oral argument from such party.

The purpose is to prevent introduction of legal theories without notice to opposing counsel and the court. [*Sexton v. Sup.Ct. (Mullikin Med. Ctr.)* (1997) 58 CA4th 1403, 1410, 68 CR2d 708, 712]

a. [9:105.11] **Compare—motion untimely as a matter of law:** However, failure to file opposition papers does *not* justify granting a motion that is untimely as a matter of law (e.g., a motion to compel further discovery under CCP §2031.310(c) must be made within 45 days after responses filed). [*Sexton v. Sup.Ct. (Mullikin Med. Ctr.),* supra, 58 CA4th at 1410, 68 CR2d at 712; *see ¶8:1491*]

5. [9:106] **Reply Papers—Rebutting the Opposition:** The moving party may file reply papers (additional declarations or points and authorities in reply to the opposition papers) subject to the requirements below (*¶9:107 ff.*):

[9:106.1] ***PRACTICE POINTER:*** Some lawyers file reply briefs routinely. But reply papers that merely repeat arguments contained in the moving papers serve no purpose and may irritate the judge. Therefore, limit any reply brief to arguments introduced in the opposing papers or to explaining why the opposing papers do not rebut the arguments made in the moving papers.

It is a serious mistake to leave key arguments for the reply brief on the theory it will give you the last word with the court. The court is likely to *refuse to consider new evidence or arguments first raised in reply papers*, or it may grant the other side time for further briefing. [See *Jay v. Mahaffey* (2013) 218 CA4th 1522, 1537-1538, 161 CR3d 700, 712—under general rule of motion practice, new evidence not permitted with reply papers and is only allowed in exceptional cases; *Balboa Ins. Co. v. Aguirre* (1983) 149 CA3d 1002, 1010, 197 CR 250, 254 (stating rule in context of appellate briefs); compare *Alliant Ins. Services, Inc. v. Gaddy* (2008) 159 CA4th 1292, 1307-1308, 72 CR3d 259, 272—court has *discretion* to accept new evidence in reply papers as long as opposing party given opportunity to respond; *Jacobs v. Coldwell Banker Residential Brokerage Co.* (2017) 14 CA5th 438, 449-450, 221 CR3d 701, 710—failure to object or seek permission to file surreply may waive objection to new matter (evidence or argument) raised in reply; *see also ¶7:122.9*]

FORM: Reply Memorandum and Declaration in Support of Motion, *see Form 9A:1.2* in Rivera, *Cal. Prac. Guide: Civ. Pro. Before Trial FORMS* (TRG).

a. [9:107] **Form requirements:** *See ¶9:19 ff.*

b. [9:108] **Service and filing requirements:** Reply papers must be served and filed *at least 5 court days* before the hearing date "unless otherwise ordered or specifically provided by law." [CCP §1005(b)]

The reply to an opposition to a *discovery motion* in an *unlawful detainer* action may be made orally at the hearing (or in writing the court day before). [CRC 3.1347]

(1) [9:109] **Manner of service:** *See ¶9:105.1.*

(a) [9:109a] **Ordinary mail?** *See ¶9:105.2.*

[9:109b] ***PRACTICE POINTER:*** There is always a risk that pleadings, particularly those filed near the hearing date, may not be delivered to the judge or uploaded to the database in a court that uses only electronic "files" in time to prepare for the hearing. Consider lodging courtesy copies with the judge hearing the motion. *See ¶9:89.1.*

c. [9:109.1] **Discretion re late-filed papers:** The court, in its discretion, *may refuse to consider* late-filed papers in ruling on the motion. In such event, the court's minutes or order must so indicate. [CRC 3.1300(d); *see ¶9:105.4*]

[9:110] ***PRACTICE POINTER:*** If you decide reply papers are necessary but cannot be filed on time, it is often better practice to contact opposing counsel and *ask for a stipulation to continue the hearing.* (If refused, the judge may grant such continuance, provided a timely request is made; *see ¶9:116 ff.*)

Having the matter continued is generally safer than late filing of reply papers. It avoids the risk the judge will *refuse* to consider your papers or that you might

© 2020 Thomson Reuters/The Rutter Group

have to fight an uphill battle at the hearing because the judge has made a tentative ruling on the basis of the opposition papers without full opportunity to consider your reply papers.

d. [9:110.1] **Due process limitation?** In some cases, 5 court days may not be enough time to review and contest reply papers that raise *new factual or legal issues.* A continuance may be required in order to provide a "fair hearing." [See *Marriage of Hoffmeister ("Hoffmeister I")* (1984) 161 CA3d 1163, 1171, 208 CR 345, 350—spousal support order apparently based on financial statements served in conjunction with reply memorandum just before hearing]

[9:110.2-110.4] *Reserved.*

D. HEARING

1. Prehearing Procedures

[9:110.5] ***PRACTICE POINTERS:*** Here are important things to do before any law and motion hearing:

- *Learn about the judge:* If you are not familiar with the judge, find out whatever you can regarding his or her attitude toward law and motion arguments generally, and your type of motion in particular (*see ¶9:13*). If the hearing is important enough, sit through one of the judge's calendars *before* your hearing date.
- *Check your filing and proof of service:* The court may refuse to consider late-filed papers. If relief is necessary, ask for it *before* the hearing date (*see ¶9:105.4*).
- *Consider lodging a "bench book" in big cases:* Where voluminous documents are involved, it is good practice to lodge a "bench book" (i.e., a looseleaf binder containing copies of all documents relating to the motion) a few days before the hearing. The judge will appreciate your saving him or her the substantial amount of time required to go through the court file to locate the papers to be considered (*see ¶9:24.2*).
- *Check with court clerk to make sure case on calendar:* Sometimes, slip-ups happen in getting a case on calendar or getting the file to the courtroom. Also, ask whether the assigned judge or someone else will be handling the calendar.
- *Check for tentative rulings:* If the judge publishes tentatives, *take them seriously* and try to save yourself unnecessary trips to court (*see ¶9:111*).
- *Check with opposing counsel:* Make sure opposing counsel is ready to go so you won't waste time preparing matters that are likely to be continued.

- *Check whether a court reporter will be provided:* Many courts no longer provide court reporters for civil hearings; others have court reporters available only certain days each week. If you will need a transcript of the hearing (for appeal or other purposes), check the court's website to determine whether a court reporter will be provided or, if not, how you may arrange for a reporter at your own expense. If a party has a fee waiver, check the court's website for any procedures for indigent parties requesting reporters. [See CRC 2.956(b) (requiring trial courts to adopt and publish local policy re provision of court reporters); *and further discussion at ¶9:171 ff.*]
- *Decide whether to draft a proposed order in advance of the hearing.* If nothing else, the exercise of drafting can help the author crystallize *precisely* what the motion is requesting (and aid the court, for the same reason).
- *Consider whether to appear in person or by phone* (unless personal appearance at the hearing is required, *¶9:159 ff.*), evaluating the costs of travel, the importance of the motion and the fact that personal appearances can be more effective than telephonic ones (*see ¶9:157.2*).

a. [9:110.6] **Requesting accommodations for persons with disabilities:** The Americans with Disabilities Act (ADA) and Civ.C. §51 et seq. require courts to provide accommodations to persons with disabilities. The Judicial Council has adopted a process for handling requests for accommodations in order "to ensure that persons with disabilities have equal and full access to the judicial system." [See CRC 1.100(b)]

Each court must designate at least one person to be the court's "ADA coordinator" to address requests for accommodations (see CRC 1.100(b)). An ex parte written request for an accommodation can be made to the court's ADA coordinator on the Judicial Council form *Request for Accommodations by Persons with Disabilities and Response* (Form MC-410).

- ***FORM:*** Request for Accommodations by Persons With Disabilities and Response, *see Form 1:23* in Rivera, *Cal. Prac. Guide: Civ. Pro. Before Trial FORMS* (TRG).

Requests for accommodations must be made no fewer than 5 court days before the hearing date (see CRC 1.100(c)(3)). The accommodation could be something as simple as an assistive listening device for a person with hearing loss or something more complicated, such as changing the location of a trial or hearing because the scheduled venue is not accessible to persons using wheelchairs. The Judicial Council has developed a Q & A handout on CRC 1.100 that contains useful information; it is downloadable at the California courts website

© 2020 Thomson Reuters/The Rutter Group

(*www.courts.ca.gov*). [See also *Marriage of James M.C. & Christine J.C.* (2008) 158 CA4th 1261, 1265, 70 CR3d 715, 716—denial of request for accommodations can only be made on grounds specified in CRC 1.100(f); *Biscaro v. Stern* (2010) 181 CA4th 702, 710, 104 CR3d 817, 823—trial court has mandatory duty to rule on request for accommodation]

☞ [9:110.7] ***PRACTICE POINTER:*** Be sure to inquire of your client well in advance of the court hearing whether any parties or witnesses who intend to attend need accommodations due to disabilities. The courts are usually able to provide accommodations, but are often unable to do so on short notice.

(1) [9:110.8] **Challenging the request for accommodation:** Where a party requests a *continuance* as an accommodation, opposing parties must be given notice and an opportunity to view any medical records or other documents on which the request is based. [*Vesco v. Sup.Ct. (Newcomb)* (2013) 221 CA4th 275, 280, 164 CR3d 341, 344 (re request for trial continuance, court may hold in camera hearing and take other steps to protect privacy)]

b. [9:111] **Tentative rulings:** Judges in many courts prepare "tentative" rulings that are available from their court clerks before the hearing. These rulings indicate the way the judge is prepared to decide the matter based on the information before him or her when the ruling was prepared. Also, the judge's approach to issuing tentative rulings may impact oral argument (¶*9:113 ff.*). [See CRC 3.1308; *Brown, Winfield & Canzoneri, Inc. v. Sup.Ct. (Great American Ins. Co.)* (2010) 47 C4th 1233, 1245, 104 CR3d 145, 155 (citing text)]

In some cases, the tentative ruling may in effect *be* the court order. E.g., where local rules require counsel who disagree with the tentative to notify the court and opposing counsel by a deadline, the failure to do so may put the tentative into effect: "When plaintiffs failed to act, the tentative ruling became the ruling of the court." [*M & R Properties v. Thomson* (1992) 11 CA4th 899, 901, 14 CR2d 579, 580]

(1) [9:112] **Announcement before hearing date:** Many judges issue tentative rulings by posting a calendar note outside the courtroom on the day of the hearing or simply announcing it at the time of argument. [See CRC 3.1308(b)]

However, some courts prefer to announce tentative rulings before the day of the hearing in order to deter unnecessary appearances. (Some courts post their tentative rulings on the Internet.) To do so, however, the court must adopt a *local rule*, binding on all judges of the court, for announcing tentative rulings. [CRC 3.1308(b), (c)]

(a) [9:113] **Impact on oral argument?** One of the following systems must be adopted:

- [9:113.1] *No oral argument unless party gives notice of intent to appear:* Tentative rulings will be made available by telephone by 3:00 p.m. on the day before the hearing. Unless a party telephones the court by 4:00 p.m., stating its intent to appear, no oral argument will be permitted (unless the court has requested it) and the tentative *automatically becomes* the ruling. [CRC 3.1308(a)(1); see *Tellez v. Rich Voss Trucking, Inc.* (2015) 240 CA4th 1052, 1060, 193 CR3d 403, 409, fn. 10]
- [9:113.2] *Right to oral argument unaffected:* Alternatively, the court may make its tentative rulings at any specified time before the hearing. The parties *need not* give notice of intent to appear at the hearing. The tentative ruling does *not* become final *until* the hearing. [CRC 3.1308(a)(2)]

(b) [9:114] **Local rule requirements:** The court's local rule must specify a telephone number to be used and time by which the rulings will be available. [CRC 3.1308(c)]

Adoption of a local rule pertaining to tentative rulings does *not* require the judge to issue such rulings. [CRC 3.1308(e)]

[9:114.1] ***PRACTICE POINTER:*** Some courts have telephone equipment that allows counsel to call in and listen to a *recording* of the tentative rulings for matters on the calendar. The recording sometimes provides only abbreviated versions of the ruling (e.g., "granted" or "denied"), in which event a call to the clerk or trip to the courthouse may still be required.

[9:114.2-114.4] *Reserved.*

(2) [9:114.5] **Generally, no dismissal of case or withdrawal of motion as tactic to avoid adverse tentative ruling:** Parties are ordinarily expected to argue against a tentative ruling if they want to avoid it. They cannot, instead, after learning of the tentative but before it becomes final, dismiss the action without prejudice or withdraw the motion in an effort to escape the adverse ruling and start all over again. Such conduct, which "smacks of gamesmanship," is not permitted. [See *Cowan v. Krayzman* (2011) 196 CA4th 907, 917-919, 126 CR3d 793, 801-803—at least regarding a case-dispositive hearing, D

not entitled to withdraw first motion to vacate default after court issued tentative ruling denying motion in order to file second version of same motion; *Groth Bros. Oldsmobile, Inc. v. Gallagher* (2002) 97 CA4th 60, 72, 118 CR2d 405, 414—P not entitled to dismiss without prejudice after court posted adverse tentative ruling; *and* ¶*11:25.2 ff.*]

(a) [9:114.6] **Comment:** The court in *Cowan* (¶*9:114.5*) also noted that "[u]nder some circumstances it *may be proper* for a party to withdraw a motion after the trial court has issued an adverse tentative ruling, but before the ruling becomes final." The *Cowan* court did not, however, elaborate on what those circumstances might be. [See *Cowan v. Krayzman*, supra, 196 CA4th at 919, 126 CR3d at 803 (emphasis added)]

c. [9:115] **Prehearing telephone calls by counsel:** Although it can be difficult to get through to a busy law and motion department, some lawyers check with the court clerk and opposing counsel before the hearing to ensure the motion has been correctly calendared, especially if the court does not issue tentative rulings.

d. [9:116] **Continuances:** If counsel agree to continue a matter, the judge will usually order a continuance without any appearance by counsel *provided* the conditions below (¶*9:116.1 ff.*) are complied with.

(1) [9:116.1] **Procedure to obtain:** Some courts will grant a continuance on counsel's oral representation he or she has spoken to opposing counsel and that opposing counsel has agreed to the continuance request.

In other courts, a law and motion matter may be continued (in the court's discretion) by the moving party by *telephoning* the court at least 5 court days before the hearing, *or* by *written stipulation* of the parties filed at least 5 court days before the hearing. In either case, the moving party must serve written notice of the continued date on the other parties.

Still other courts require a written stipulation or *ex parte application* for a continuance, either of which must be based on a *declaration establishing good cause.*

(2) [9:117] **Notice to court clerk:** Regardless of which party is requesting the continuance, it is the *moving party's* duty to notify the court "immediately" if the matter will not be heard on the scheduled date. [CRC 3.1304(b)]

(3) [9:118] **Effect of prior continuances:** In some courts, only two continuances will be granted based on agreement between counsel; thereafter, a court appearance is required and "good cause" must be shown in writing.

(4) [9:119] **Court's discretion:** By statute, the court "shall" postpone the hearing of any motion or demurrer (or trial) for up to 30 days "when all attorneys of record . . . agree in writing to such postponement." [CCP §595.2]

Despite this language, the statute is held to be "directory, not mandatory" and does *not* entitle parties to a continuance as a matter of right. [*Pham v. Nguyen* (1997) 54 CA4th 11, 15, 62 CR2d 422, 424]

Rather, the granting of a continuance is within the court's sound discretion. Thus, the court has the power to *deny* a continuance and rule on a pending motion, or to order it off calendar—even if counsel have agreed otherwise.

This is particularly true of stipulations to continue hearings on summary judgment motions within 30 days of trial, because CCP §437c(a) requires "good cause" for such a continuance (*see ¶10:71*).

(a) [9:119a] **Judicial policy:** "*Of course* continuances should not be used as a dilatory tactic, and of course good cause . . . should be present . . . But . . . [t]he law should also *encourage* professional courtesy between opposing counsel . . . When opposing counsel needs a continuance [and no substantive right is impacted thereby], courts should look to section 595.2 as a statement of policy in favor of professional courtesy, not churlishness." [*Pham v. Nguyen,* supra, 54 CA4th at 17, 62 CR2d at 425 (emphasis in original)]

(b) [9:119.1] **When denial abuse of discretion:** Under certain circumstances, denial of a continuance may be treated as an abuse of discretion. [*Lerma v. County of Orange* (2004) 120 CA4th 709, 714, 15 CR3d 609, 612]

- [9:119.2] It was an abuse of discretion to deny a continuance to a lawyer who had been *seriously* ill and had only two days after leaving the hospital to prepare opposition to a motion for summary judgment. [*Lerma v. County of Orange,* supra, 120 CA4th at 712, 15 CR3d at 610]
- [9:119.3] It was an abuse of discretion to deny a trial continuance where the lawyer was engaged in trial in another court. [*Oliveros v. County of Los Angeles* (2004) 120 CA4th 1389, 1399, 16 CR3d 638, 646]

[9:119.4-119.9] *Reserved.*

© 2020 Thomson Reuters/The Rutter Group

[9:119.10] ***PRACTICE POINTER RE STIPULATIONS:*** If you are relying on a stipulation for a continuance, make sure that your stipulation has been filed with *and accepted by* the court *before* the date set for hearing. Otherwise, you may find out later that your continuance was unexpectedly denied and adverse consequences have resulted (e.g., motion for summary judgment granted for lack of opposition).

[9:119.11] ***FURTHER PRACTICE POINTER:*** If you are relying on a court clerk's statement that a hearing has been continued, *get a copy of the order* before the hearing date: "Reliance solely on a clerk's advice regarding a continuance of a motion without ensuring that an order exists attesting to the continuance might well be reckless on the part of an experienced practitioner." [*Matter of Doran* (Rev.Dept. 1998) 3 Cal. State Bar Ct.Rptr. 871]

(5) [9:120] **Sanctions for failure to notify clerk:** Failing to timely advise the court clerk the hearing will not proceed as scheduled (for any reason) may be treated as a violation of court rules, punishable by money sanctions against counsel pursuant to CCP §575.2 (*see* ¶*9:1275*).

[9:120a] ***PRACTICE POINTER:*** Keep in mind that the judge (or his or her clerk) typically reviews the file at least one or two days before the scheduled hearing. Therefore, quite apart from the risk of sanctions, it is extremely discourteous to the court for counsel to call in on the morning of the hearing and request a continuance. This not only puts the judge to a lot of wasted effort, but it causes a stream of additional paperwork for the court clerk (new minutes are needed, new calendar entries, etc.).

e. [9:120.1] **Stipulation "off calendar":** If the parties notify the court before the hearing that they have stipulated to the matter going off calendar, the court will generally so order. Some courts require a *written* stipulation or an *ex parte* application supported by a declaration showing good cause.

[9:120.2] ***PRACTICE POINTER:*** Notify the clerk in the department where the matter is noticed for hearing well in advance of the hearing. Again, last-minute notice is discourteous to the judge who may have already "worked up" the file in preparation for the hearing. You must inform the court immediately if the case settles. [CRC 1385(a)(1); see also CRC 3.650—duty to notify court and others of stay]

FORM: Official Form Notice of Settlement of Entire Case (mandatory Judicial Council form CM-200), *see Form 12B:9* in Rivera, *Cal. Prac. Guide: Civ. Pro. Before Trial FORMS* (TRG).

(1) [9:120.3] **Effect of stipulation that demurrer go off calendar:** Under *certain circumstances*, a stipulation that a demurrer go "off calendar" may be treated as the "functional equivalent" of an order *sustaining* the demurrer. *See discussion at ¶7:123.1 ff.*

(2) [9:120.4] **Discovery responses received after motion to compel filed:** The moving party should notify the court immediately if responses to discovery requests are received after a motion to compel such responses have been filed, as that may affect the nature of the motion proceedings. The court should be advised of any issues that still must be resolved (e.g., sanction requests), so that it can work up those issues and ignore the others raised by the motion.

[9:120.5-120.9] *Reserved.*

f. [9:120.10] **Stipulation to commissioner hearing motion:** "On stipulation of the parties litigant the court may order a cause to be tried by a temporary judge . . ." [Cal.Const. Art. VI, §21]

This provision applies to pretrial motion hearings. [See *Walker v. San Francisco Housing Auth.* (2002) 100 CA4th 685, 691, 122 CR2d 758, 763]

(1) [9:120.11] **Failure to object as stipulation?** Under some local rules, the parties are *deemed to stipulate* that designated matters (e.g., case management conferences) "may be heard by a temporary judge, *by failing to file an objection in writing* within thirty (30) days after the first pleading is filed in the action by that party." [S.F. Sup.Ct. Rule 3.3(A) (emphasis added); see also S.F. Sup.Ct. Rule 10.0(B)—by failing to appear at hearing on discovery motion, parties deemed to stipulate that motion may be decided by member of State Bar acting as temporary judge; but see also *Michaels v. Turk* (2015) 239 CA4th 1411, 1416, 191 CR3d 669, 672—although local rule provides for implied stipulation in certain matters, self-represented parties must be asked on record if they so stipulate]

Cases are split on whether failure to object may constitute a stipulation. [*Elena S. v. Kroutik* (2016) 247 CA4th 570, 574-575, 202 CR3d 318, 321-322—full participation in proceeding before commissioner without objection a "tantamount stipulation"; compare *Foosadas v. Sup.Ct. (People)* (2005) 130 CA4th 649, 654-655, 30 CR3d 358, 361-362 (invalidating local rule deeming party to have

© 2020 Thomson Reuters/The Rutter Group

agreed to having matter heard by commissioner if party failed to object as "without legal foundation")]

[9:120.12-120.14] *Reserved.*

(2) [9:120.15] **Limited powers of commissioners absent stipulation:** Absent a stipulation, commissioners are statutorily authorized to perform only the following functions in civil cases:

— hear and decide small claims cases (Gov.C. §72190);

— decide ex parte motions for orders and writs (CCP §259(a)); and

— approve bonds and undertakings (CCP §259(c)). [*Foosadas v. Sup.Ct. (People)*, supra, 130 CA4th at 654, 30 CR3d at 361; *Settlemire v. Sup.Ct. (Settlemire)* (2003) 105 CA4th 666, 670, 129 CR2d 560, 563]

[9:120.16-120.19] *Reserved.*

g. [9:120.20] **Court-ordered reference by commissioner or referee:** Even absent a stipulation by the parties, the court may appoint a court commissioner or another person, not usually employed by the court, as referee to hear and decide certain issues. *See discussion at ¶8:1803 ff. re procedures relating to referees.*

(1) [9:120.21] **Issues subject to reference:** The court may order a reference in the following cases:

- When examination of a long account is necessary to resolve an issue of fact. [CCP §639(a)(1)]
- When it is necessary for the information of the court to take an account, before judgment can be entered or in order to carry a judgment or order into effect. [CCP §639(a)(2)]
- *When a question of fact arises upon a motion* or otherwise that involves the resolution of an issue outside the pleadings. [CCP §639(a)(3)]
- In a "special proceeding" (e.g., eminent domain, administrative mandamus) when it is necessary for the information of the court. [CCP §639(a)(4)]
- To hear *discovery motions*. [CCP §639(a)(5)] (But note: Special procedures and limitations govern appointment of discovery referees.

Cross-refer: For further discussion of court-appointed references, see Knight, Chernick, Flynn & Quinn, *Cal. Prac. Guide: Alternative Dispute Resolution* (TRG), Ch. 6.

2. [9:121] **Peremptory Challenges to Judge (CCP §170.6):** Lawyers may disqualify a judge by filing an affidavit (usually a declaration) known as a "peremptory challenge" in any hearing involving

a "contested issue of law or fact." [CCP §170.6(a)(1); see *Maas v. Sup.Ct. (People)* (2016) 1 C5th 962, 973, 209 CR3d 571, 575—statute liberally construed in favor of challenges, which should be denied "only if the statute absolutely forbids it"]

[9:121.1-121.4] *Reserved.*

a. [9:121.5] **Form:** This challenge is made by the party or its counsel making "an oral or written motion without prior notice supported by affidavit or declaration under penalty of perjury." [CCP §170.6(a)(2); *Fry v. Sup.Ct.* (2013) 222 CA4th 475, 482, 166 CR3d 328, 332—Los Angeles Sup.Ct. Form LACIV 015 satisfies requirements of both motion and affidavit]

The statute prescribes the form of the affidavit substantially as follows:

> ". . . (*name*) being duly sworn, deposes and says: That he or she is a party (*or attorney for a party*) to the within action . . . That (*name*) the judge, court commissioner, or referee before whom . . . a hearing in the action . . . is pending . . . is prejudiced against the party (*or his or her attorney*) or the interest of the party (*or his or her attorney*) so that affiant cannot or believes that he or she cannot have a fair and impartial trial or hearing before the judge, court commissioner, or referee." [CCP §170.6(a)(6)]

Comment: The Code also permits an *oral* statement under oath (see CCP §170.6(a)(7)).

FORM: Peremptory Challenge to Judge, *see Form 9A:9* in Rivera, *Cal. Prac. Guide: Civ. Pro. Before Trial FORMS* (TRG).

[9:121.6-121.10] *Reserved.*

b. [9:121.11] **Affidavit cannot be controverted:** Where a disqualification motion is timely filed and in proper form, the trial court is bound to accept it without further inquiry. [*Maas v. Sup.Ct. (People)* (2016) 1 C5th 962, 972, 209 CR3d 571, 575; *Stephens v. Sup.Ct. (Stephens)* (2002) 96 CA4th 54, 59, 116 CR2d 616, 620]

Lack of a good faith belief that the judge is prejudiced is *irrelevant.* An affidavit filed in "bad faith" is nonetheless effective. [*School Dist. of Okaloosa County v. Sup.Ct. (City of Orange)* (1997) 58 CA4th 1126, 1136, 68 CR2d 612, 619; *People v. Sup.Ct. (Tejeda)* (2016) 1 CA5th 892, 896, 910, 205 CR3d 200, 202-203, 222]

(1) [9:121.12] **Compare—"peremptory challenge" to prospective jurors:** A "peremptory challenge" to jurors lies where *no reason* is given (see CCP §226(b)). A §170.6 challenge to a judge is based on the ground that the judge is *prejudiced* and unable to conduct a fair trial or hearing (although that ground cannot be controverted).

[9:121.13-121.19] *Reserved.*

© 2020 Thomson Reuters/The Rutter Group

c. [9:121.20] **Disqualification effective upon acceptance by court:** If the affidavit is timely and in proper form, the challenged judge is disqualified "instantly and irrevocably." But the peremptory challenge only takes effect *when the court determines* that the motion is timely and properly made. [*Davcon, Inc. v. Roberts & Morgan* (2003) 110 CA4th 1355, 1360, 2 CR3d 782, 786-787; *Frisk v. Sup.Ct. (Northwest Surgical Develop. Co., Inc.)* (2011) 200 CA4th 402, 410-411, 132 CR3d 602, 608-609]

(1) [9:121.21] **Not affected by later events:** Once the challenge has been accepted by the court, because the disqualification takes effect instantaneously and irrevocably, later events (such as dismissal of the party who asserted the challenge) do not rescind the challenge. [*Davcon, Inc. v. Roberts & Morgan,* supra, 110 CA4th at 1362, 2 CR3d at 788; *Louisiana-Pac. Corp. v. Philo Lumber Co.* (1985) 163 CA3d 1212, 1221, 210 CR 368, 374 (abrogation on other grounds recognized by *Frisk v. Sup.Ct. (Northwest Surgical Develop. Co., Inc.*) (2011) 200 CA4th 402, 132 CR3d 602)—if one codefendant has challenged a judge, plaintiff's dismissal of that defendant will not permit judge to reassume jurisdiction of action against remaining defendants]

(2) [9:121.22] **Compare—dismissal before court accepts peremptory challenge:** Where the party exercising the challenge is dismissed from the action before the court reviews or accepts the peremptory challenge, the peremptory challenge is moot because not properly made by a "party" to the action. [*Frisk v. Sup.Ct. (Northwest Surgical Develop. Co., Inc.),* supra, 200 CA4th at 413, 132 CR3d at 611]

(3) [9:121.23] **Limitation on judge's actions after challenge accepted:** The judge cannot hear any later motion or proceeding in the case, *even with the consent of the party who disqualified the judge*, absent stipulation of all other parties. [*Brown v. Sup.Ct. (14011 Ventura Blvd. Corp.*) (1981) 124 CA3d 1059, 1061-1062, 177 CR 756, 758]

However, the disqualified judge may undertake certain actions (*see* ¶*9:148.21*).

[9:121.24] *Reserved.*

d. [9:121.25] **Limited to a single challenge:** Except as noted below (¶*9:121.30*), only *one* challenge under CCP §170.6 may be made *by each side*. [CCP §170.6(a)(4); *see* ¶*9:139 ff.*]

[9:121.26-121.29] *Reserved.*

e. [9:121.30] **Limitation—race-based challenges:** CCP §170.6 cannot be used to subvert the guarantees of Fourteenth

Amendment equal protection. Thus, it cannot be used to disqualify a judge *solely* because of his or her race. [*People v. Sup.Ct. (Williams)* (1992) 8 CA4th 688, 707, 10 CR2d 873, 884]

Cross-refer: For detailed discussion of this topic, see Wegner, Fairbank, Epstein & Chernow, *Cal. Prac. Guide: Civil Trials & Evidence* (TRG), Ch. 3.

f. [9:122] **Applies to law and motion hearings:** Many law and motion matters involve contested issues of law or fact, and thus a peremptory challenge can be filed. [*Bouchard v. Insona* (1980) 105 CA3d 768, 771, 164 CR 505, 507—motion for relief from default]

(1) [9:122.1] **Compare—effect of presiding at prior hearing:** Whether a judge who presided at an *earlier* law and motion hearing can be challenged under §170.6 depends on whether the earlier ruling involved "contested *fact* issues relating to the *merits*" of the action; *see* ¶*9:137*.

(2) [9:122.2] **Applies to referees and commissioners:** A party may exercise its one peremptory challenge to disqualify either a judge, a court commissioner or an assigned referee from hearing a motion. [*Autoland, Inc. v. Sup.Ct. (Mayers)* (1988) 205 CA3d 857, 860, 252 CR 662, 663]

Comment: The parties' consent is required for a commissioner or referee to decide most motions, and therefore a §170.6 challenge is unnecessary. But there are some matters on which a commissioner may act *without* the parties' consent (see CCP §§259, 482.060, 516.040 and 639). In those situations, the §170.6 challenge is the only method to disqualify a commissioner or referee, except for cause.

[9:122.3] ***PRACTICE POINTER:*** Keep in mind that only one challenge per side is allowed in civil cases (CCP §170.6(a)(4)). Thus, it *rarely* makes sense to waste your challenge in law and motion proceedings unless the judge has been assigned for all purposes (*see* ¶*9:128 ff.*).

The only situation which *might* justify using your challenge may be hearings on *dispositive* motions: i.e., motions for summary judgment or dismissal, or other motions that may be dispositive in a practical sense (e.g., for preliminary injunction, or to expunge lis pendens).

(However, in direct calendar assignments, it is probably too late to challenge the judge; *see* ¶*9:128.*)

[9:122.4] ***PRACTICE POINTER:*** If you decide to challenge the judge and still want the matter calendared, let the court clerk know *in advance of* the hearing. This may facilitate assignment of the case to another judge on the same hearing date. Otherwise, a continuance is inevitable.

g. [9:123] **Challenge must be timely:** Subject to the exceptions discussed below (¶*9:124 ff.*) (which tend to swallow the rule), the "general rule" is that a challenge is permitted any time before commencement of a trial or hearing. [*People v. Sup.Ct. (Lavi)* (1993) 4 C4th 1164, 1171, 17 CR2d 815, 817]

Trial or hearing pending: No peremptory challenge lies, however, unless a "civil or criminal action or special proceeding of any kind or character" involving a contested issue of law or fact is pending. [*Maas v. Sup.Ct. (People)*, supra, 1 C5th at 975, 209 CR3d at 577; see also *Grant v. Sup.Ct. (Jacobs)* (2001) 90 CA4th 518, 528, 108 CR2d 825, 832—challenge not available for judge assigned solely to conduct status or settlement conference]

Effect of untimely challenge: If the challenge is untimely, the judge may proceed to rule on the matter before the court. [*Cybermedia, Inc. v. Sup.Ct. (Brown)* (1999) 72 CA4th 910, 914, 82 CR2d 126, 128]

(1) [9:124] **"Master calendar court" exception:** In master calendar courts, a peremptory challenge is timely if exercised no later than when the case is *assigned for trial* by the master calendar judge. [CCP §170.6(a)(2); see *Grant v. Sup.Ct. (Jacobs)*, supra, 90 CA4th at 526, 108 CR2d at 829-830 (citing text)]

A court is a "master calendar" court if cases are assigned for trial from the master calendar department to a department ready to hear the case. [*Ruiz v. Appellate Division of Sup.Ct. (People)* (2004) 119 CA4th 282, 286, 14 CR3d 190, 192]

(a) [9:124.1] **Compare—trial assignment by direct calendar judge:** When a judge assigned for all purposes ("direct calendar" judge, ¶*9:125*) assigns a case to another department for trial, it does *not* function as a master calendar court *unless* the case is trial ready when assigned or the parties have notice the judge is acting as a master calendar judge. Absent one of those facts, the master calendar exception does not apply, and a §170.6 challenge made before commencement of trial (rather than upon assignment) is timely. [*Entente Design, Inc. v. Sup.Ct. (Pfeiffer)* (2013) 214 CA4th 385, 392, 154 CR3d 216, 222]

(2) [9:125] **"All-purpose assignment" exception ("direct calendar" courts):** In "direct calendar" all-purpose assignment courts, the challenge must be exercised within 15 days after the case has been assigned to an all purpose judge or, if a party has not yet appeared, within 15 days after that party's appearance. [CCP §170.6(a)(2)]

The disqualification motion "shall be made to the assigned judge or to the presiding judge." [CCP §170.6(a)(2); *Fry v. Sup.Ct.* (2013) 222 CA4th 475, 482-483, 166 CR3d 328, 332-333—peremptory challenge improper and ineffective where filed by facsimile in court's central filing office with no instructions to deliver to assigned judge or presiding judge]

Notice of the motion must be served on all parties within 5 days after making the motion. [CCP §170.6(a)(3)]

(a) [9:125.1] **When applicable:** The "all-purpose assignment" rule applies to cases assigned to a particular judge who is expected to preside at trial and to process the case in its totality from the time of the assignment. Such an assignment must be made pursuant to court order or a valid local rule. [*Jonathon M. v. Sup.Ct. (People)* (2006) 141 CA4th 1093, 1101, 46 CR3d 798, 803—order posted on counsel table sufficed to assign even-numbered cases to particular judge "for all purposes"; compare *Daniel V. v. Sup.Ct. (People)* (2006) 139 CA4th 28, 40-41, 42 CR3d 471, 478—assignment made by clerk pursuant to "an informal court practice" did not trigger 15-day rule]

The 15-day rule does not apply, however, where a judge has been assigned only to conduct a *particular hearing*, and not for all purposes including trial. [*Grant v. Sup.Ct. (Jacobs)*, supra, 90 CA4th at 527, 108 CR2d at 832]

(b) [9:126] **Procedure for assignment:** In many courts, civil cases are routinely assigned to a direct calendar department upon filing of the complaint. Such assignments are usually made by rotation or some other chance method.

A local court policy can provide a valid mechanism for all-purpose assignments within the meaning of CCP §170.6. [*Shipp v. Sup.Ct. (Shipp)* (1992) 5 CA4th 147, 151-152, 6 CR2d 685, 688]

(c) [9:126a] **Label used by court not necessarily determinative:** A court order assigning a matter "for all purposes including trial" is persuasive evidence, but not necessarily conclusive, that it is an all-purpose assignment for purposes of applying the 15-day period for filing a peremptory challenge. An all-purpose assignment is one where the judicial officer is expected to handle the case in its entirety from the time of the assignment through trial. [*D.M. v. Sup.Ct. (People)* (2011) 196 CA4th 879, 887-888, 126 CR3d 785, 791—although presiding

© 2020 Thomson Reuters/The Rutter Group

judge issued order assigning delinquency case to referee "for all purposes including trial," Welf. & Inst.C. §248 prohibited referee from hearing delinquency adjudications without a stipulation, so case could not be assigned "for all purposes"]

(d) [9:127] **Assignment by name or department number:** An assignment to a department by number, rather than to a judge by name, may constitute an all-purpose assignment "if a particular judge *regularly presides* in that department and that judge's identity is either known to the litigant or discoverable on reasonable inquiry." [*People v. Sup.Ct. (Lavi)*, supra, 4 C4th at 1180, 17 CR2d at 823, fn. 12 (emphasis added)]

(e) [9:127.1] **Challenge to newly assigned judge:** The statutory time period for filing a peremptory challenge to a newly assigned calendar judge commences when the parties receive notice of the assignment. [See *Bravo v. Sup.Ct. (Los Angeles County)* (2007) 149 CA4th 1489, 1493, 57 CR3d 910, 913]

[9:127.2-127.4] *Reserved.*

(f) [9:127.5] **Challenge by later-joined parties:** A party appearing after a case has been assigned to a judge for all purposes has the right to exercise a peremptory challenge within 15 days after appearing in the case. [CCP §170.6(a)(2)]

"Appearance in the case" has been interpreted to mean a "general appearance." "An appearance is general if it is for any purpose other than to question the court's jurisdiction," and the fact parties refer to themselves as "specially appearing" is not determinative. [*Sunrise Fin'l, LLC v. Sup.Ct. (Overland Direct, Inc.)* 32 CA5th 114, 124-126, 243 CR3d 623, 630-632—Ds who filed an opposition to a transfer/consolidation motion made a general appearance, starting 15-day time period within which to file a CCP §170.6 challenge, even though Ds referred to themselves as "Specially Appearing Defendants" in opposition papers]

1) [9:127.6] **Limitation—not after decision on contested fact issue:** But such challenge is not allowed if, prior to the party's appearance, the judge has decided a contested fact issue relating to the merits (e.g., on a preliminary injunction hearing, *see* ¶*9:137*) and the party appears in the same proceeding or in a *continuation* of the proceeding in which the contested

fact issue was decided. [See *Stephens v. Sup.Ct. (Stephens)* (2002) 96 CA4th 54, 61, 116 CR2d 616, 622; *National Fin'l Lending, LLC v. Sup.Ct. (Brewer Corp.)* (2013) 222 CA4th 262, 270, 166 CR3d 88, 92]

(g) [9:128] **Effect of transfer to new all-purpose judge:** The same 15-day rule applies where a case is transferred from one "direct calendar" judge to another; i.e., parties who have already appeared may file a peremptory challenge to the new judge within 15 days after receiving notice of the change. [*Motion Picture & Tel. Fund Hosp. v. Sup.Ct. (Lopez)* (2001) 88 CA4th 488, 494, 105 CR2d 872, 876; *Cybermedia, Inc. v. Sup.Ct. (Brown)* (1999) 72 CA4th 910, 913-914, 82 CR2d 126, 127—notice of change of judge must specify case names or case numbers of cases being transferred]

(h) [9:129] **Other change of judge:** Where a judge other than one previously assigned for all purposes will hear the matter, and the new judge is *known at least 10 days* before the date set for the trial or hearing, the challenge must be exercised at least 5 days before that date. [CCP §170.6(a)(2); *Grant v. Sup.Ct. (Jacobs)*, supra, 90 CA4th at 526, 108 CR2d at 829-830]

(3) [9:130] **Judge's identity otherwise known ("10-day/5-day rule"):** Where no all-purpose assignment has been made, but the identity of the judge who is to conduct the trial or hearing is *known at least 10 days before* the date set for trial or hearing, any peremptory challenge must be *made at least 5 days* before that date. [CCP §170.6; *People v. Sup.Ct. (Lavi)*, supra, 4 C4th at 1180, 17 CR2d at 823]

(4) [9:131] **Continued proceedings:** A peremptory challenge cannot be entertained as to subsequent hearings that are a part or continuation of the original proceedings. Moreover, a new lawsuit may be treated as continuation of a prior action if "it involves substantially the same issues and matters necessarily relevant and material to the issues involved in the [original] action." [*Bravo v. Sup.Ct. (County of Los Angeles)* (2007) 149 CA4th 1489, 1494, 57 CR3d 910, 913 (internal quotes omitted)— new complaint alleging facts occurring after prior action dismissed was *not* a "continuation of an earlier action," so plaintiff could peremptorily challenge judge who presided over earlier action; *National Fin'l Lending, LLC v. Sup.Ct. (Brewer Corp.)*, supra, 222 CA4th at 278-279, 166 CR3d at 99 (post-trial collection proceedings)]

© 2020 Thomson Reuters/The Rutter Group

(a) [9:131.1] **Effect of different parties in second suit:** The continuation rule applies only when the second action involves "the *same parties* at a *later stage of their litigation with each other, or . . . arise[s] out of conduct in or orders made during the earlier proceeding*." [*NutraGenetics, LLC v. Sup.Ct. (Cavenah)* (2009) 179 CA4th 243, 257-258, 101 CR3d 657, 667-668 (emphasis in original); *Pickett v. Sup.Ct. (99¢ Only Stores)* (2012) 203 CA4th 887, 893-895, 138 CR3d 36, 40-42]

It is not enough that the second action relates to the same incidents or events as the first action so that it is a "related case" for case assignment purposes (¶*12:38 ff.*) or that it involves a *similar party* litigating *similar claims*. If *different parties* or different causes of action are involved, the later suit is *not* a "continuation" of an earlier-filed suit for peremptory challenge purposes. [*NutraGenetics, LLC v. Sup.Ct. (Cavenah)*, supra, 179 CA4th at 257-258, 101 CR3d at 667-668 (different defendants); *Pickett v. Sup.Ct. (99¢ Only Stores)*, supra, 203 CA4th at 893, 138 CR3d at 40 (different plaintiffs)—continuation rule inapplicable unless "gravamen" of second action is "rooted in or supplementary to the initial proceeding"]

(b) [9:131.2] **Effect of disqualification in related but not consolidated cases:** If cases have been deemed "related" but not consolidated for case management purposes (¶*12:38 ff.*), a valid §170.6 challenge in one case does not require disqualification in the other. [*Rothstein v. Sup.Ct. (Rothstein)* (2016) 3 CA5th 424, 428, 207 CR3d 616, 619—challenge filed in civil case related to, but not consolidated with, earlier-filed case, in which assigned judge had resolved a disputed factual merits issue, only required transfer of later-filed case to another judge]

(5) [9:132] **Special rule in cases coordinated for trial:** "Complex" cases pending in different counties involving common issues may be coordinated for trial and a single judge assigned (CCP §404 et seq.; *see* ¶*12:370*). Any CCP §170.6 challenge to the assigned judge must be made "within *20 days after service*" of the coordination order. [CRC 3.516 (emphasis added); *see* ¶*12:380.1 ff.*]

(a) [9:133] **Extended for service by mail:** Because the time limit runs from "service," the time for challenge is extended under CCP §1013 where the service is by mail (i.e., an additional 5 days if the address and place of mailing are within California). [*Citicorp North America, Inc. v. Sup.Ct. (KF Dairies, Inc.)* (1989) 213 CA3d 563, 571, 261 CR 668, 674]

Compare: The extension is only 2 court days where notice is served by express mail, fax or electronically. [CCP §§1013, 1010.6(a)(4); *see ¶9:87.4 ff.*]

(b) [9:134] **Effect of prior ruling by judge:** A peremptory challenge within 20 days after service of the coordination order is timely even if contested issues common to the coordinated cases had been decided by that judge before coordination. The coordination order provides a new time window for §170.6 challenges. [*Farmers Ins. Exchange v. Sup.Ct. (Abutal)* (1992) 10 CA4th 1509, 1511, 13 CR2d 449, 450]

(c) [9:134.1] **Effect of precoordination challenge:** A party's exercise of a peremptory challenge *before* the case was coordinated does not affect that side's right to a second peremptory challenge to the coordination judge. [*Philip Morris Inc. v. Sup.Ct. (U.A. Local 467)* (1999) 71 CA4th 116, 123, 83 CR2d 671, 676-677; *see ¶12:369*]

(d) [9:134.2] **Cases added on to coordinated proceeding subject to same 20-day limitation:** The coordination trial judge has authority to determine that similar cases should be added on to the coordinated proceeding (CRC 3.544). A party or counsel in an "add-on case" is precluded from filing a peremptory challenge once the 20-day period has run following initial assignment of the coordinated proceeding to the coordination trial judge. [See CRC 3.532(d), 3.516; *Industrial Indem. Co. v. Sup.Ct. (Arnold)* (1989) 214 CA3d 259, 263, 262 CR 544, 546—parties in cases added on 2 years after coordination denied opportunity to file peremptory challenge (decided under former CRC Rule renumbered as CRC 3.516)]

[9:134.3-134.4] *Reserved.*

(6) [9:134.5] **Untimely challenge does not exhaust right to challenge different judge:** An untimely challenge may be stricken but does not affect the challenging party's right to peremptorily challenge a different judge to whom the case is later assigned. [*Truck Ins. Exchange v. Sup.Ct. (Park Northridge Homeowners Ass'n)* (1998) 67 CA4th 142, 148, 78 CR2d 721, 724—untimely challenge to Judge X, who later retired, did not bar challenge to Judge Y to whom case was later assigned]

(7) [9:134.6] **One-judge court deadline:** CCP §170.6(a)(2) provides that, if the court in which the action is pending is authorized to have no more than one judge, the §170.6

© 2020 Thomson Reuters/The Rutter Group

challenge must be made within 30 days of the party's first appearance in the action; that does not apply to "branches" or "divisions" of a court to which only one judge is assigned. However, the Legislature has now authorized at least two judges for every county, so there are no remaining counties for which there is only one authorized judge. [See *Jones v. Sup.Ct. (People)* (2016) 246 CA4th 390, 400-402, 200 CR3d 776, 782-783—one-judge deadline does not apply where six authorized judges for Superior Court even though only one judge assigned to branch court]

Cross-refer: Timeliness of peremptory challenges is discussed further in Wegner, Fairbank, Epstein & Chernow, *Cal. Prac. Guide: Civil Trials & Evidence* (TRG), Ch. 3.

h. [9:135] **Effect of judge having presided at prior hearing:** If the §170.6 challenge is timely, the fact the judge presided at an earlier hearing in the case does not prevent disqualification, *unless* the earlier hearing involved "contested fact issues relating to the merits" of the case. [CCP §170.6(a)(2); see *Depper v. Sup.Ct. (People)* (1999) 74 CA4th 15, 21-22, 87 CR2d 563, 569]

Allowing a challenge after the judge has ruled on contested fact issues relating to the merits would make it possible for litigants to gamble on obtaining a favorable decision and then disqualify the judge if confronted with an adverse ruling. The policy against judge-shopping precludes such a result. [See *Stephens v. Sup.Ct. (Stephens)* (2002) 96 CA4th 54, 60, 116 CR2d 616, 621]

(1) [9:136] **Hearings NOT involving "contested fact issues relating to merits":** Most pretrial motions are decided without determining contested facts related to the *merits of the case,* so that the judge hearing the motion remains subject to a CCP §170.6 challenge. [*Swift v. Sup.Ct. (Mitchell)* (2009) 172 CA4th 878, 883, 91 CR3d 504, 507]

- [9:136.1] Summary judgment motions. [*Bambula v. Sup.Ct. (White)* (1985) 174 CA3d 653, 657, 220 CR 223, 224-225]
- [9:136.2] Issuance of a temporary restraining order. [*Landmark Holding Group, Inc. v. Sup.Ct. (Calif. Bell Club)* (1987) 193 CA3d 525, 527-528, 238 CR 475, 476 (but rule may be different for hearing on preliminary injunction, *see ¶9:137.3*)]
- [9:136.3] Demurrer. [*Fight for the Rams v. Sup.Ct. (Los Angeles Rams Football Co., Inc.)* (1996) 41 CA4th 953, 957, 48 CR2d 851, 854]
- [9:136.4] A motion to quash service of summons on the ground that the court lacks personal juris-

diction over defendant. [*School Dist. of Okaloosa County v. Sup.Ct. (City of Orange)* (1997) 58 CA4th 1126, 1134, 68 CR2d 612, 617—motion to quash may involve disputed fact issues (e.g., concerning defendant's "contacts" with California) but such fact issues are *not related to merits* of case]

- [9:136.5] Discovery motions. [*Swift v. Sup.Ct. (Mitchell)*, supra, 172 CA4th at 883, 91 CR3d at 507—disputed factual issues on motions to compel discovery were *not* directly related to *merits* of action; *Guardado v. Sup.Ct. (Mariposa Gardens)* (2008) 163 CA4th 91, 99, 77 CR3d 149, 156—same on motion seeking pretrial punitive damages discovery under Civ.C. §3295(c)]

(2) [9:137] **Compare—hearings involving contested fact issues relating to merits:** The following are among the pretrial rulings that may involve a determination of the merits of the case and thus bar a subsequent §170.6 motion:

(a) [9:137.1] **Contempt:** It may be too late to challenge a judge at a contempt hearing for violations of orders previously made by the judge. [*Conn v. Sup.Ct. (Farmers Group)* (1987) 196 CA3d 774, 786, 242 CR 148, 155—"This hearing was the last in a long series of proceedings . . . . which bore on the merits of the case"]

(b) [9:137.2] **Pretrial motion to exclude evidence:** Where a judge had ruled on a pretrial motion to exclude evidence, a §170.6 challenge was untimely. [*Briggs v. Sup.Ct. (People)* (2001) 87 CA4th 312, 318, 104 CR2d 445, 449 (involving proceedings to commit defendant as sexually violent predator)]

(c) [9:137.3] **Preliminary injunctions?** Courts disagree whether a ruling on a motion for preliminary injunction involves determination of contested fact issues relating to the merits. [See *Pacific & Southwest Annual Conference of United Methodist Church v. Sup.Ct. (Barr)* (1978) 82 CA3d 72, 79, 147 CR 44, 48—ruling involves merits because judge actually weighs evidence and resolves conflicts; compare *Continental Baking Co. v. Katz* (1968) 68 C2d 512, 528, 67 CR 761, 771 (not involving CCP §170.6)—ruling does not adjudicate merits because preliminary injunction merely preserves status quo; see also *Guardado v. Sup.Ct. (Mariposa Gardens)* (2008) 163 CA4th 91, 98-99, 77 CR3d 149, 155 (opining that *Pacific* holding contradicted by *Continental*)]

[9:137.4-137.9] *Reserved.*

© 2020 Thomson Reuters/The Rutter Group

(3) [9:137.10] **Compare—"make or break" issue as test?** One case holds a §170.6 challenge untimely after the judge had ruled on *issues that "make or break" the case:* e.g., order granting summary adjudication of contract interpretation issues. [*California Fed. Sav. & Loan Ass'n v. Sup.Ct. (McClintock)* (1987) 189 CA3d 267, 271, 234 CR 413, 415-416]

However, a number of cases *reject* this "make or break" test as contrary to §170.6(a)(2), which provides that only prior rulings on "*contested fact issues* relating to the merits" preclude a later §170.6 challenge. Rulings on summary judgment motions involve *legal* issues, not contested fact issues. [*School Dist. of Okaloosa County v. Sup.Ct. (City of Orange)* (1997) 58 CA4th 1126, 1133, 68 CR2d 612, 616 (citing text); *Zilog, Inc. v. Sup.Ct. (Pacific Indem. Co.)* (2001) 86 CA4th 1309, 1322, 104 CR2d 173, 182]

☞ [9:138] ***PRACTICE POINTER:*** Even if a CCP §170.6 challenge is available, it rarely makes sense to waste your challenge on a judge hearing law and motion matters—even one who has ruled against you on a prior demurrer or motion. The judge to whom the matter is assigned may be reluctant to rule differently from the judge whom you have disqualified. And it may be more important to use your §170.6 challenge for the trial.

i. [9:139] **Only one challenge per side:** Only one CCP §170.6 challenge may be *made* by each party or side (if there is more than one plaintiff or defendant) in any one action or proceeding. [CCP §170.6(a)(4)] (Different rules apply where coparties have substantially adverse interests; *see* ¶*9:141.2*.)

Thus, a CCP §170.6 challenge by one of several coparties bars any later §170.6 challenge to the new judge by any of the other coparties, including coparties *joined after* the initial §170.6 challenge. [*School Dist. of Okaloosa County v. Sup.Ct. (City of Orange)* (1997) 58 CA4th 1126, 1135, 68 CR2d 612, 617 (citing text)]

The same rule applies where the party who exercised the challenge is later dismissed from the action. The remaining parties on the same side are not entitled to a new peremptory challenge. [See *Home Ins. Co. v. Sup.Ct. (Montrose Chemical Corp.)* (2005) 34 C4th 1025, 1033, 22 CR3d 885, 890]

(1) [9:140] **Compare—effect of coparties' waiver:** On the other hand, the fact that coparties *waived* their right to challenge the judge does not affect a *newly-joined* party's right to timely challenge that judge under §170.6: "Where, as here, no other defendant has exercised its right to disqualify a judge, a late-appearing defendant

may do so within 10 days after its appearance . . ." [*School Dist. of Okaloosa County v. Sup.Ct. (City of Orange),* supra, 58 CA4th at 1135, 68 CR2d at 617 (citing text)]

(2) [9:141] **Compare—cases consolidated for trial:** Special rules for §170.6 challenges apply where separate actions are consolidated for trial. *See discussion at ¶12:369 ff.*

[9:141.1] *Reserved.*

(3) [9:141.2] **Compare—coparties with *substantially adverse* interests:** The one-challenge-per-side limit does not apply when parties on the same side have *substantially adverse interests* (e.g., where two drivers whose vehicles collide and injure the plaintiff are jointly named as defendants). [*Home Ins. Co. v. Sup.Ct. (Montrose Chemical Corp.),* supra, 34 C4th at 1033, 22 CR3d at 891]

(a) [9:141.3] **Burden on coparty seeking second challenge:** The party seeking to exercise the second challenge must establish its interests are substantially adverse to those of the codefendant. [*Home Ins. Co. v. Sup.Ct. (Montrose Chemical Corp.),* supra, 34 C4th at 1035, 22 CR3d at 892—"substantial adverse interests are not presumed"; *Orion Communications, Inc. v. Sup.Ct. (Sameis Holdings, LLC)* (2014) 226 CA4th 152, 164, 171 CR3d 596, 606—in connection with motion to amend judgment to add purported alter ego as judgment debtor, fact that proposed new party had separate counsel from original judgment debtor due to conflicts of interest not sufficient to show its interests were "substantially adverse" to original judgment debtor]

[9:141.4] *Reserved.*

(4) [9:141.5] **Special rule after reversal on appeal:** After reversal on appeal of a trial court's decision, a party may file a §170.6 challenge if the original judge is assigned to conduct a new trial of the matter, provided *that party has not previously exercised a peremptory challenge* in the case. This addresses the concern that a judge whose ruling has been reversed might be biased against the party who successfully appealed that ruling. [CCP §170.6(a)(2) (last para.); see *Stegs Investments v. Sup.Ct. (Sprecher)* (1991) 233 CA3d 572, 575-576, 284 CR 495, 497; *People v. Sup.Ct. (Maloy)* (2001) 91 CA4th 391, 395-399, 109 CR2d 897, 900-903—challenge available whether reversal results in complete retrial, retrial of limited issues, or trial in first instance]

After reversal on appeal from a *final judgment, appellant* (but *not respondent*) may file a §170.6 challenge,

© 2020 Thomson Reuters/The Rutter Group

even if appellant has already exercised a challenge before the appeal, if the original judge is assigned to rehear the matter. [CCP §170.6(a)(2) (last para.); see *McNair v. Sup.Ct. (National Collegiate Athletic Ass'n)* (2016) 6 CA5th 1227, 1235, 211 CR3d 919, 924—second peremptory challenge not available after appeal from anti-SLAPP motion which did not result in *final judgment*]

Such a challenge must be made *within 60 days* after the party or party's attorney "has been notified" of the assignment. [CCP §170.6(a)(2) (last para.); see *Hendershot v. Sup.Ct. (Pacific Southwest Investments, Inc.)* (1993) 20 CA4th 860, 862-863, 24 CR2d 645, 647—where party never received formal notice of assignment, 60 days began to run when attorney notified of assignment through informal inquiry to clerk]

Conflicting local rules void: A local rule purporting to vary the time limits or triggering events is void. [*Ghaffarpour v. Sup.Ct. (Commerce Plaza Hotel)* (2012) 202 CA4th 1463, 1470-1471, 136 CR3d 544, 549-550 (invalidating local rule commencing 60-day period on date of issuance of appellate court remittitur); *see ¶9:13.1 ff.*]

(a) [9:141.6] **60 days allowed for challenge even in direct calendar cases:** The 15-day limit on peremptory challenges in direct calendar courts (*¶9:128*) does not apply to this situation. [*Stubblefield Const. Co. v. Sup.Ct. (City of San Bernardino)* (2000) 81 CA4th 762, 769, 97 CR2d 121, 126-127]

(b) [9:141.7] **Either party may exercise challenge:** A postappeal peremptory challenge may be made by *either* the successful appellant or the unsuccessful respondent if that party has not yet used its original §170.6 challenge. [*Pfeiffer Venice Properties v. Sup.Ct. (Bernard)* (2003) 107 CA4th 761, 764, 132 CR2d 400, 403]

1) [9:141.8] **Limit on number of challenges by unsuccessful respondent:** A successful appellant may exercise a special postappeal peremptory challenge following reversal on appeal from a final judgment despite having made a peremptory challenge earlier in the litigation (CCP §170.6(a)(2); *¶9:141.5*). However, an unsuccessful *respondent* is limited by CCP §170.6(a)(4) *to one peremptory challenge* for the *entire* litigation. [*Pfeiffer Venice Properties v. Sup.Ct. (Bernard)*, supra, 107 CA4th at 764, 132 CR2d at 403]

2) [9:141.9] **No additional challenges:** An appellant who files a postappeal peremptory

challenge to disqualify a judge may not file another §170.6 challenge to a different judge. That he or she filed no peremptory challenge before the appeal is irrelevant: "He does not get two challenges simply by virtue of being a successful appellant." [*Casden v. Sup.Ct. (Casden)* (2006) 140 CA4th 417, 426, 44 CR3d 474, 480]

(c) [9:141.10] **Reversal for "new trial" means reexamination of merits:** The right to peremptory challenge following reversal on appeal applies only where the same judge is to conduct a "new trial" of the matter. [CCP §170.6(a)(2) (last para.)]

"New trial" is interpreted broadly to include any *reexamination* of any factual or legal issue in controversy in the prior proceedings. [See *Paterno v. Sup.Ct. (People)* (2004) 123 CA4th 548, 560, 20 CR3d 282, 290; *Geddes v. Sup.Ct. (Campbell)* (2005) 126 CA4th 417, 424, 23 CR3d 857, 861]

1) [9:141.11] **Reversal of summary judgment:** Thus, a right of peremptory challenge exists where a summary judgment is reversed *on its merits* (i.e., disputed questions of material fact exist). [*Stubblefield Const. Co. v. Sup.Ct. (City of San Bernardino)*, supra, 81 CA4th at 766, 97 CR2d at 124]

But there is no further right of peremptory challenge where a summary judgment is reversed *solely* for failure to provide a statement of reasons as required by CCP §437c(c) (*see ¶10:330*). [*Geddes v. Sup.Ct. (Campbell)*, supra, 126 CA4th at 424-425, 23 CR3d at 862—remand requiring judge to complete tasks not performed in prior proceeding is *not* "new trial"]

2) [9:141.12] **Reversal of order denying attorney fees:** The right to exercise a peremptory challenge exists where an order denying attorney fees is reversed on appeal. [*Pfeiffer Venice Properties v. Sup.Ct. (Bernard)*, supra, 107 CA4th at 767-768, 132 CR2d at 405-406; *First Fed. Bank of Calif. v. Sup.Ct. (Prestige of Beverly Hills, Inc.)* (2006) 143 CA4th 310, 315, 49 CR3d 296, 299]

[9:141.13-141.19] *Reserved.*

3) [9:141.20] **Compare—remands not constituting "new trial":** A remand for action by the trial court that *does not require the court to reexamine factual or legal issues* does *not* entitle a party to a peremptory challenge. [*C.C.*

© 2020 Thomson Reuters/The Rutter Group

v. Sup.Ct. (Orange County Social Services Agency) (2008) 166 CA4th 1019, 1022, 83 CR3d 225, 227—remand to perform ministerial act; *Karlsen v. Sup.Ct. (Cannonball Acquisitions)* (2006) 139 CA4th 1526, 1530, 43 CR3d 738, 740—remand to prepare statement of decision]

[9:141.21-141.24] *Reserved.*

(d) [9:141.25] **Writ proceedings:** A litigant is entitled to timely demand a new judge if a new trial is granted as part of writ relief. [*Overton v. Sup.Ct. (People)* (1994) 22 CA4th 112, 115-116, 27 CR2d 274, 275-276; *Keith R. v. Sup.Ct. (H.R.)* (2009) 174 CA4th 1047, 1058, 96 CR3d 298, 305-306—party entitled to peremptory challenge after issuance of writ of mandate and remand for new trial on disputed facts in child custody proceedings; see *State Farm Mut. Auto Ins. Co. v. Sup.Ct. (Hill)* (2004) 121 CA4th 490, 503, 17 CR3d 146, 156—writ of mandate resolving choice of law issue did not result in a "new trial" within meaning of CCP §170.6(a)(2)]

j. [9:142] **Disqualification irrevocable:** Once an affidavit is filed under §170.6 and accepted by the court, the judge is instantaneously and irrevocably disqualified (except for limited purposes specified in CCP §170.4(a); *see ¶9:121.20*).

k. [9:143] **Dealing with adverse rulings:** A litigant whose CCP §170.6 challenge is denied must either seek reconsideration by the same judge (subject to stringent limitations, *see ¶9:324 ff.*); or promptly seek a writ of mandamus from an appellate court.

(1) [9:144] **Recourse to another judge?** There is an apparent split of authority whether the validity of the challenge can be raised again before another trial judge, at least when the first judge is still on the bench.

- One case holds that the matter *cannot* be raised before another judge. [See *MicroVest Corp. v. Sup.Ct. (Computerland Corp.)* (1984) 150 CA3d 1085, 1090, 198 CR 404, 406]
- But another case holds that a second judge *can* reconsider the matter if the original judge is no longer on the court or is otherwise "unavailable"—including when the "unavailability" is the result of the original judge's recusal. [See *Geddes v. Sup.Ct. (Campbell)* (2005) 126 CA4th 417, 426, 23 CR3d 857, 863—after first judge erroneously disqualified himself, he was "unavailable," so second judge could reconsider and rescind order disqualifying first judge; *see also ¶9:324.4*]

(2) [9:145] **Appellate review:** Appellate review may be sought by petition for writ of mandate filed and served within 10 days after service of written notice of entry of the court's order determining the disqualification issue. Where notice of entry is served by mail, the time is extended as provided by CCP §1013(a). [CCP §170.3(d); see *D.M. v. Sup.Ct. (People)* (2011) 196 CA4th 879, 885-886, 126 CR3d 785, 790; *Carl v. Sup.Ct. (Coast Comm. College Dist.)* (2007) 157 CA4th 73, 75, 68 CR3d 566, 567—writ petition untimely on its face where filed almost 2 months after service of written notice of entry of order striking statement of disqualification]

Moreover, *mandamus* is the *exclusive avenue* of appellate relief for denial of a §170.6 challenge. The error is *not* ground for appeal from the judgment. [CCP §170.3(d); *People v. Freeman* (2010) 47 C4th 993, 1000, 103 CR3d 723, 727-728]

Cross-refer: For detailed discussion of writs of mandate, see Eisenberg, *Cal. Prac. Guide: Civil Appeals & Writs* (TRG), Ch. 15.

⇨ [9:146] ***PRACTICE POINTER:*** The 10-day period to file a mandate petition runs from notice of the court's decision (which may be immediate if the challenge is denied in open court). Therefore, you generally will not have time to file and have heard a CCP §1008 motion for reconsideration (even if grounds exist; *see* ¶*9:324*).

[9:147] *Reserved.*

3. [9:148] **Challenging the Judge for Cause (CCP §170.3):** Pretrial challenges for cause are rarely encountered where a judge is assigned to a case only for a law and motion hearing. Such challenges are more likely to be encountered where the case is assigned to a judge *for all purposes,* including trial.

The grounds and procedure for such disqualification are set forth in CCP §§170.1 and 170.3, and are summarized briefly below (¶*9:148.1*).

Cross-refer: Challenges for cause are discussed in greater detail in Wegner, Fairbank, Epstein & Chernow, *Cal. Prac. Guide: Civil Trials & Evidence* (TRG), Ch. 3.

a. [9:148.1] **Grounds for disqualification:** Judges must disqualify themselves under the following circumstances:

- Judge has personal knowledge of evidentiary facts at issue before the court. [CCP §170.1(a)(1)]
- Judge served as a lawyer in the proceeding or in another proceeding involving the same issues and parties or gave

© 2020 Thomson Reuters/The Rutter Group

advice to any party to the proceeding relating to the proceeding. [CCP §170.1(a)(2)]

- Judge has a financial interest in the subject matter of the proceeding or in any of the parties to the proceeding. [CCP §170.1(a)(3)]
- Close relative or spouse of the judge is a party or an officer, director or trustee of a party. [CCP §170.1(a)(4)]
- A lawyer or the spouse of a lawyer in the proceeding is the spouse, former spouse or close relative of the judge, or is affiliated in private practice with such spouse, former spouse or close relative. [CCP §170.1(a)(5)]
- Judge believes the recusal would serve the interests of justice, judge doubts his or her ability to be impartial, or "a person aware of the facts" might reasonably entertain doubts about the judge's impartiality. [CCP §170.1(a)(6)]
- Judge has a physical impairment that interferes with his or her ability to conduct the proceeding. [CCP §170.1(a)(7)]
- The matter before the judge involves ADR (alternative dispute resolution) and the judge has discussed prospective employment with an ADR provider within the past two years. [See CCP §170.1(a)(8)]
- Judge has received a campaign contribution in excess of $1,500 within the last 6 years from a party or lawyer in the matter before the court. [CCP §170.1(a)(9)(A)] (Smaller contributions must be disclosed; see CCP §170.1(a)(9)(C).)

Comment: CCP §170.1(a) contains detailed definitions of the terms used and paraphrased above. Consult the statute carefully before proceeding.

[9:148.2-148.4] *Reserved.*

b. [9:148.5] **Procedure if judge refuses recusal:** If a judge is disqualified under CCP §170.1 but refuses to recuse himself or herself, the party seeking disqualification must file a verified written statement objecting to the judge and stating the facts that provide the basis for disqualification. The statement must be personally served on the judge, or on his or her clerk provided the judge is present in the courthouse. The statement must be filed at the *earliest practicable opportunity* after discovery of the facts. Copies must be served on all parties. [CCP §170.3(c)(1); see *Tri Counties Bank v. Sup.Ct. (Amaya-Guenon)* (2008) 167 CA4th 1332, 1338, 84 CR3d 835, 840—7-month delay before asserting disqualification made challenge untimely]

If the disqualifying facts were known before the court rules on a motion, a postruling motion to disqualify the judge is too late and must be denied. [*Alhusainy v. Sup.Ct. (People)* (2006) 143 CA4th 385, 394, 48 CR3d 914, 920]

FORM: Verified Statement Objecting to Hearing Before Judge—Disqualification for Cause, *see Form 9A:28* in Rivera, *Cal. Prac. Guide: Civ. Pro. Before Trial FORMS* (TRG).

[9:148.6-148.9] *Reserved.*

c. [9:148.10] **Judge's response:** Within 10 days of the later of filing or service of the statement, the judge may either consent to the disqualification or file a verified answer to the statement. The clerk must serve a copy of the answer upon the parties. Failure to file an answer is deemed a consent to the disqualification. [CCP §170.3(c)(3), (4)]

If the judge determines that the statement was untimely filed or if, on its face, it discloses no legal grounds for disqualification, the judge may order the statement stricken. [CCP §170.4(b); see *PBA, LLC v. KPOD, Ltd.* (2003) 112 CA4th 965, 971, 5 CR3d 532, 535; *Crawford v. JPMorgan Chase Bank, N.A.* (2015) 242 CA4th 1265, 1272, 195 CR3d 868, 874—striking statement rendered judge's answer "irrelevant"]

[9:148.11-148.14] *Reserved.*

d. [9:148.15] **Hearing on judge's disqualification:** Within 5 days, all the parties may agree on another judge to decide the issue of disqualification (although as a practical matter, this rarely happens). If the parties fail to agree, a judge is appointed by the Chief Justice. (Normally, the Chief Justice will appoint a judge from another county to hear the matter.) [CCP §170.3(c)(5)]

The decision of the hearing judge is not appealable and may only be reviewed by the appellate court on a petition for writ of mandate filed within 10 days of notice of the decision. [CCP §170.3(d)]

[9:148.16-148.19] *Reserved.*

e. [9:148.20] **Actions by disqualified judge before recusal:** Orders made by a disqualified judge are void and must be vacated regardless of a showing of prejudice. [*Rossco Holdings Inc. v. Bank of America* (2007) 149 CA4th 1353, 1362, 58 CR3d 141, 148; *Christie v. City of El Centro* (2006) 135 CA4th 767, 776, 37 CR3d 718, 725; compare *Bates v. Rubio's Restaurants, Inc.* (2009) 179 CA4th 1125, 1134, 102 CR3d 206, 213—ruling made just *prior* to disqualification not void]

It makes no difference that the judge was *unaware* of the disqualifying facts when the ruling was made. [*Tatum v. Southern Pac. Co.* (1967) 250 CA2d 40, 43, 58 CR 238, 241—judgment set aside after trustee-judge discovered trust assets included stock in defendant corporation]

© 2020 Thomson Reuters/The Rutter Group

f. [9:148.21] **Actions by disqualified judge after disqualification:** Notwithstanding disqualification, a judge may take the following limited actions in the case after disqualification:

- Issue orders necessary to maintain the court's jurisdiction pending reassignment to a judge not disqualified;
- Request another judge who has been agreed to by the parties to take over the case;
- Hear and determine default matters;
- Issue orders for possession prior to judgment in eminent domain proceedings;
- Schedule a trial or hearing date;
- Conduct a settlement conference. [CCP §170.4; see *In re Steiner, Decision and Order Imposing Censure* (Calif. Comm'n on Judicial Performance 9/2/14, available online at *http://cjp.ca.gov*)—disqualified judge may not reassign case to another judge without parties' agreement]

4. **Procedures at Law and Motion Hearing**

a. **Calendar call**

(1) [9:149] **Check-in procedures:** Counsel should check in with the bailiff, court attendant or clerk prior to the hearing.

[9:149.1] ***PRACTICE POINTERS:*** Plan to arrive in the department where the motion will be heard at least 15 minutes early.

Upon arrival, check the hearing calendar (usually posted outside the courtroom) for the calendar number of the case on which you are appearing and for any tentative rulings by the court. Then check in with the bailiff, court attendant or clerk by stating the calendar number and the party for whom you are appearing; also provide your business card (two cards if there is a court reporter).

If your client is present, take time to explain the proceedings and any tentative ruling by the court.

(2) [9:150] **Priority requests:** Judges differ in the manner in which they handle their law and motion calendars. Many ask for priority requests at the outset. Others insist that priority requests be channeled through the court clerk *before* the hearing; the court clerk will advise the judge. (Call the court clerk the day before the hearing and find out how to proceed.)

(a) [9:151] **Judicial comment:** Priority requests will generally be granted only when counsel is *engaged* *in trial*. The fact that a lawyer has a deposition scheduled back at the office at 10:00 a.m. is *not* a sufficient reason for priority, because practically every lawyer in the courtroom has other appointments as well.

Although priority occasionally will be given to an attorney having an appearance in another courtroom, such double-settings are discouraged.

(3) [9:152] **Shorter matters:** After noting priority requests, some judges simply proceed through their calendars "by the numbers," from first to last. Many, however, take time estimates at the original calendar call, and hear the shorter matters first, saving those requiring longer argument for the end of the calendar. Still others take first uncontested matters where the tentative ruling favors appearing counsel, so that the majority of the lawyers may leave the courtroom quickly after the initial calendar call.

(4) [9:153] **Parties fail to appear:** It is the *moving party's* responsibility to notify the court *immediately* if a matter will not be heard on the scheduled date. [CRC 3.1304(b)]

(a) [9:153.1] **Submitting without appearance:** Either party may notify the court he or she will not appear at the hearing and submit the matter for decision, unless the court orders otherwise. In such cases, the court will rule on the matter as if the party had appeared. [CRC 3.1304(c)]

(b) [9:153.2] **Effect of "no shows":** If neither party gives such notice and no one shows up when the calendar is called, the court may *either* order the motion off calendar or proceed to rule despite the parties' absence. [CRC 3.1304(d)]

Comment: Such a ruling is likely to be a *denial* of the motion. Likewise, where only the opposing party appears, and the moving party has not advised the court it is submitting on the tentative, the motion will likely be denied.

⇨ [9:154] ***PRACTICE POINTER:*** There is no requirement that counsel must attend the motion hearing. Frequently, the lawyer for the moving party may find out the tentative ruling and decide to submit on that basis. And, opposing counsel may do likewise, knowing no greater relief can be awarded than that specified in the notice of motion (¶*9:38*). Or, counsel may have reached some agreement prior to the hearing that disposes of the matter entirely.

© 2020 Thomson Reuters/The Rutter Group

In either case, it is incumbent upon counsel to inform the court before the hearing. If an out-of-court solution has been reached, call the court clerk and have the matter taken *off calendar.* If you decide to submit on the basis of the tentative ruling, again call the court clerk and so state. Otherwise, you run the risk of having the judge do something else entirely.

(c) [9:155] **Caution—risk of sanctions:** Where the failure to appear at a scheduled hearing violates local rules requiring prior notice to the court, counsel may be sanctioned for the local rules violation. [CCP §575.2; *see* ¶*9:1275*]

Moreover, causing delay or noncompliance with delay reduction standards may also subject counsel to sanctions. [Gov.C. §68608(b); *see* ¶*12:90 ff.*]

(d) [9:155.1] **Resetting motion:** If the court has ordered the motion off calendar (rather than ruling on it despite the parties' absence), the matter may be reset only upon motion. [CRC 3.1304(d)]

(5) [9:156] **Order "off calendar":** The court has discretion to drop any matter from its calendar for "good cause." This is frequently done where the parties so request, or where they fail to appear at the hearing; or where the court rules on one portion of a matter, making it unnecessary to rule on the balance (e.g., "demurrer sustained with leave to amend; motion to strike off calendar").

An order "off calendar" is not an appealable order. It is not a dismissal, but merely a postponement. The matter may be restored on motion by one of the parties, or on the court's own motion. [*R & A Vending Services v. City of Los Angeles* (1985) 172 CA3d 1188, 1193-1194, 218 CR 667, 670] Sometimes the phrase simply means the motion is in effect withdrawn or otherwise mooted. [*Marriage of Thornton* (2002) 95 CA4th 251, 254-255, 115 CR2d 380, 383; *People ex rel. Strathmann v. Acacia Research Corp.* (2012) 210 CA4th 487, 506, 148 CR3d 361, 374—amended complaint moots demurrer which should be off calendar]

b. [9:157] **Appearance by telephone:** In superior court, counsel may choose to appear by telephone in any conference or in "nonevidentiary" law and motion hearings, at which witnesses are not called to testify, unless the court orders otherwise. [See CCP §367.5; CRC 3.670] (Telephonic appearances are also permissible in probate hearings, and in certain case management conferences; *see* ¶*12:82.10.*)

The fact that one counsel chooses to appear by telephone does not affect the other's right to appear in person because all statements made must be audible to all participants. Each attorney must identify himself or herself so that the court and other counsel and the court reporter will know who is speaking. The proceedings are recorded to the same extent and in the same manner as if counsel appeared in person. [CRC 3.670(n), (o)]

It is the court's responsibility to obtain adequate teleconferencing equipment (CRC Standards of Jud. Admin., Standard 3.1(a)). The court may provide the telephone service or it may contract with a private vendor (CRC 3.670(j)). Statewide uniform fees must be paid by the parties to the court or the vendor for each appearance (CRC 3.670(k)). Subject to specified exceptions, an "additional late request fee" is to be charged if the request to appear by telephone is not made at least two days before the scheduled appearance (CRC 3.670(k)(2)). A party who has received a fee waiver must not be charged a fee for a telephone appearance (CRC 3.670(*l*)). Telephone appearance fees are recoverable as costs under CCP §1033.5. [CCP §367.6(c)]

(1) [9:157.1] **Information made available:** Each court must publish notice providing parties and attorneys with the information necessary for them to appear by telephone. [CRC 3.670(q)]

⇨ [9:157.2] ***PRACTICE POINTERS:*** The savings in time and money are obvious. But many attorneys are reluctant to appear by telephone. Some feel they have a better chance of winning if they can see the judge's facial expressions, etc. Others believe that if the other side is going to show up in person they had better do likewise. There is also concern that if they appear by telephone and *lose*, the client may feel the attorney did not make a sufficient effort. And telephonic appearances can be difficult especially with judges who engage counsel with frequent questions during argument.

The validity of these concerns depends on the complexity of the matter and the judge before whom you are appearing.

For example, if the judge posts tentative rulings sufficiently in advance of the hearing, you may have a better feeling as to whether anything will be gained by your presence in the courtroom.

Likewise, if you feel the judge is more likely to be influenced by written presentation than oral argument, you may decide there is less reason to attend in person. On the other hand, some judges are known for engaging in vigorous discussion at the hearing, and you should consider appearing in person.

© 2020 Thomson Reuters/The Rutter Group

If there is any doubt in your mind, *discuss the matter with the client.* (Indeed, hourly-rate clients who are aware that appearances may be made by telephone may expect you to obtain their approval before charging them for court appearances.)

(2) [9:158] **Which cases:** A party may appear by telephone in *any* civil action or proceeding, *including probate and unlawful detainer*, juvenile, small claims and certain other "civil petitions." [CRC 3.670(b), (m), 1.6(4), (5), 5.324; see CCP §367.5(b); see also CRC 5.9 (authorizing telephonic appearances in family law matters)]

(3) [9:159] **Which hearings:** All parties may appear by telephone at all conferences, hearings and proceedings except:

— specified hearings at which a personal appearance is required (*see ¶9:159.1*); and

— matters in which the court requires a personal appearance on a hearing-by-hearing basis (*see ¶9:162*). [CCP §367.5; CRC 3.670(c)]

Telephone appearances for *ex parte applications* are subject to special rules (*see ¶9:159.2*).

(a) [9:159.1] **Compare—personal appearance required:** Personal appearances are generally required at:

— any hearing in which witnesses are expected to testify;

— hearings on *TROs* (but not necessarily at preliminary injunction hearings);

— *settlement conferences*;

— motions *in limine;*

— trial management conferences; and

— hearings on petitions to confirm the sale of property under the Probate Code. [See CRC 3.670(e)]

(b) [9:159.2] **Ex parte applications:** Absent an order requiring a personal appearance (*see ¶9:162*), *parties seeking an ex parte order* may appear by telephone if the moving papers are filed and a proposed order submitted by at least 10:00 a.m. two court days before the ex parte appearance. (If required by local rule, copies must also be provided directly to the department in which the matter is to be considered.)

Parties opposing ex parte applications may appear by telephone. [CRC 3.670(d)]

1) [9:159.3] **Notice required:** An *applicant* choosing to appear by telephone must:

— place the words "Telephone Appearance" below the title of the application;
— file and serve the moving papers in a manner that ensures they will be received by the court and all parties by at least 10:00 a.m. two court days before the hearing; and
— if required by local rule, present copies of the papers directly to the department in which the matter will be heard. [CRC 3.670(h)(3)]

Even if the moving party does not comply with these requirements, the *opposing party* may appear by telephone by giving notice to all parties and the court of its intent to do so, orally or in writing, no later than 2:00 p.m. the day before the hearing.

— *Oral notice* must be given either in person or by telephone;
— *Written notice* must be given by a "Notice of Intent to Appear by Telephone" filed with the court and served on all parties by any authorized means reasonably calculated to assure delivery no later than the close of business on the court day before the hearing. [CRC 3.670(h)(4)]

(4) [9:160] **Notice required (other than ex parte applications):** A party choosing to appear by telephone must either:

— place the words "Telephone Appearance" below the title of that party's moving or opposing or reply papers; or
— notify the court and all other parties of the party's intent to appear by telephone *at least two court days* before the hearing. [CRC 3.670(h)(1)]

If a party gives notice of intent to appear by telephone, other parties may also appear by telephone by notifying the court and all other parties of an intent to do so *before noon* on the court day preceding the appearance. [CRC 3.670(h)(2)]

A party that has given notice of intent to appear by telephone may change its mind and appear in person. [CRC 3.670(h)(5)]

For "good cause" shown, the court may permit a party to appear by telephone or to appear in person even though the required notices were not given. [CRC 3.670(h)(6)]

FORMS

- Notice of Motion Indicating Telephone Appearance, *see Form 9A:6* in Rivera, *Cal. Prac. Guide: Civ. Pro. Before Trial FORMS* (TRG).

© 2020 Thomson Reuters/The Rutter Group

- Notice of Intent to Appear by Telephone, *see Form 9A:7* in Rivera, *Cal. Prac. Guide: Civ. Pro. Before Trial FORMS* (TRG).

(a) [9:160.1] **Form of notice:** The notice may be *oral* or *written*, but if oral it must be given either in person or by telephone. [CRC 3.670(h)(1)(B)] (Comment: Whether this means a lawyer-to-lawyer telephone call, as opposed to leaving a message with a secretary or on an answering machine, is unclear.)

If the notice is written, it must be given by filing and serving a "Notice of Intent to Appear by Telephone" at least 2 court days before the hearing. The notice must be served by personal delivery, fax, express mail or other means reasonably calculated to ensure delivery to the parties no later than the close of the next business day. [CRC 3.670(h)(1)(B)]

[9:161] *Reserved.*

(5) [9:162] **Court may require personal appearance:** The court may, on a hearing-by-hearing basis, require counsel to appear in person upon determining that a personal appearance would materially assist in a determination of the proceeding or in the effective management or resolution of the case. [CCP §367.5(c); CRC 3.670(f)(2)]

Similarly, if the court determines during a proceeding conducted by telephone that a personal appearance is necessary, it may continue the matter and require personal appearances. [CRC 3.670(g)]

Whenever the court determines personal appearances are required, it must give "reasonable notice" to all parties and continue the hearing if necessary to accommodate personal appearance. A court issuing telephonic tentative rulings may indicate in its tentative ruling that personal appearances are required. [CRC 3.670(i)]

[9:163] *Reserved.*

(6) [9:164] **Impact on fee awards?** In awarding attorney fees (under any applicable provision of law), courts may consider whether the attorney is claiming fees for appearing in person when he or she *could have appeared by telephone*. [CRC Standards of Jud. Admin., Standard 3.1(d)]

c. **Oral argument**

(1) [9:165] **Right to hearing on certain motions:** A right to a full hearing is recognized where required by statute and on "critical pretrial matters." [*Titmas v. Sup.Ct.*

(Iavarone) (2001) 87 CA4th 738, 742, 104 CR2d 803, 807]

The right to a "hearing" means "an *oral* hearing at which the court may take evidence, entertain and rule on evidentiary objections, and determine the merits based on written *and oral presentations*." [*Hobbs v. Weiss* (1999) 73 CA4th 76, 78, 86 CR2d 146, 147 (emphasis added)]

Effect of tentative ruling? The right to oral argument may be affected by the court's posting a telephonic tentative ruling; *see ¶9:113 ff.*

(a) [9:165.1] **When required by statute:** Statutes using the term "motion" (rather than ex parte application) may be interpreted to require both notice and an oral *hearing*. [See *Titmas v. Sup.Ct. (Iavarone)*, supra, 87 CA4th at 742-743, 104 CR2d at 807—court must determine whether "statutory scheme, read as a whole, encompasses an oral hearing"]

[9:165.2-165.4] *Reserved.*

(b) [9:165.5] **Where statute unclear:** Where the statute uses imprecise terms such as "heard" or "hearing," the court should consider the following factors in determining whether to forgo oral argument:

- whether the judge will act as a factfinder or adjudicate any issues at the hearing;
- whether the litigants are entitled to any procedural remedies at the time of the hearing (making evidentiary objections, orally moving for a continuance, etc.);
- whether the issues are so obvious and well-settled that oral argument "would amount to an empty gesture"; and
- whether the proceedings involve "*critical pretrial matters* of considerable significance to the parties." [*TJX Cos., Inc. v. Sup.Ct. (Burchard)* (2001) 87 CA4th 747, 752, 104 CR2d 810, 812 (emphasis added); see also *Titmas v. Sup.Ct. (Iavarone)*, supra, 87 CA4th at 742, 104 CR2d at 807; and *Cal-American Income Property Fund VII v. Brown Develop. Corp.* (1982) 138 CA3d 268, 273, 187 CR 703, 706, fn. 3]

[9:165.6-165.9] *Reserved.*

(c) [9:165.10] **Application:** The right to oral argument has been recognized on the following law and motion matters:

- [9:165.11] Summary judgment motions. [*Mediterranean Const. Co. v. State Farm Fire & Cas.*

Co. (1998) 66 CA4th 257, 265, 77 CR2d 781, 785]

- [9:165.12] Pretrial writs of attachment. [*Hobbs v. Weiss* (1999) 73 CA4th 76, 77-78, 86 CR2d 146, 147-148]
- [9:165.13] Appointment of a receiver or confirmation of receiver's sale of property that is the subject of the litigation. [*Cal-American Income Property Fund VII v. Brown Develop. Corp.* (1982) 138 CA3d 268, 273, 187 CR 703, 706, fn. 3]
- [9:165.14] Sanctions motions. [*Marriage of Lemen* (1980) 113 CA3d 769, 784, 170 CR 642, 649]
- [9:165.15] Motion to quash or dismiss for lack of jurisdiction. [See *Marriage of Lemen*, supra, 113 CA3d at 784, 170 CR at 649]
- [9:165.16] Attorney-client privilege claimed in opposition to a discovery motion. [*Titmas v. Sup.Ct. (Iavarone)*, supra, 87 CA4th at 744-745, 104 CR2d at 808-809]
- [9:165.17] Demurrer to a class action complaint. [*TJX Cos., Inc. v. Sup.Ct. (Burchard)* (2001) 87 CA4th 747, 751, 104 CR2d 810, 813]

(2) [9:166] **Discretionary on other motions:** In other law and motion matters, the nature and amount of argument permitted rests entirely within the judge's sound discretion. [See *Wilburn v. Oakland Hosp.* (1989) 213 CA3d 1107, 1111, 262 CR 155, 158; *Sweat v. Hollister* (1995) 37 CA4th 603, 614, 43 CR2d 399, 405 (disapproved on other grounds by *Santisas v. Goodin* (1998) 17 C4th 599, 71 CR2d 830)]

(a) [9:166.1] **Comment:** Even so, "[b]ecause of basic due process concerns, law and motion judges are always on shaky ground where they entirely bar parties from having a say." [*Titmas v. Sup.Ct. (Iavarone)* (2001) 87 CA4th 738, 742, 104 CR2d 803, 806 (internal quotes omitted)]

(b) [9:166.2] **Compare—substitute judges:** An oral hearing should be provided where the judge is filling in for the judge to whom the matter is regularly assigned: "Hearing oral argument is one of the best ways we know for substitute judges to demonstrate to the satisfaction of the parties and the public that judicial responsibility has been exercised . . ." [*TJX Cos., Inc. v. Sup.Ct. (Burchard)*, supra, 87 CA4th at 755, 104 CR2d at 815]

[9:167] *Reserved.*

(3) [9:168] **Argument not permitted unless opposition filed:** If a party fails to file *timely* written opposition to a motion or demurrer, the judge may refuse to permit oral argument against the motion. The judge, as a matter of discretion, *may* consider a request for continuance to allow filing of a written opposition. Because continuances are not favored, valid reasons will have to be shown for the failure to file or late filing of opposing papers.

If a continuance is granted, the court may require the opposing party (or counsel) to pay *fees for the appearance* incurred by other parties.

[9:169] ***PRACTICE POINTER:*** In such a case, the better practice is to seek a stipulated continuance before coming to court. If opposing counsel refuses, the judge may be sympathetic. But you'll have to have a good excuse for failure to file a timely opposition in order to get your continuance.

(4) **Effective argument techniques**

[9:170] ***PRACTICE POINTERS:*** Time for oral argument is usually limited. So make your argument meaningful. Here are some suggestions:

- *Prepare in advance.* Have key documents at your fingertips. Boil down your argument to a *few* key points.
- When the case is called, *move promptly* to the counsel table. In many courts, there is a sign indicating where counsel for the respective parties should be seated. Absent such sign, plaintiff's lawyer traditionally takes the counsel table nearest the jury box. Stand at the counsel table or, if a lectern is provided, at the lectern when addressing the court.
- When it is your turn to address the court:
  — *wait* until you have the court's attention;
  — state your name, the name of your firm and whom you represent;
  — *speak slowly* and *loudly* enough for the judge and reporter to hear;
  — stand up straight at the lectern or counsel table (avoid hands in pockets, slouching or fiddling with papers);
  — try to *establish eye contact* with the judge and to appear *confident* of your position.
- Sometimes, you will encounter a judge who attempts to preempt argument by saying: "I've read all your papers. Do you have anything

© 2020 Thomson Reuters/The Rutter Group

to add? (And, if so, why isn't it in your brief?)"

If you're the moving party and haven't had time to file a reply brief, use this as an opportunity to point out weaknesses in the opposing party's papers. Otherwise, invite questions from the court and attempt to respond to such questions and any tentative ruling.

- If the tentative ruling is in your favor, say nothing or simply respond to whatever points your opponent makes.
- If the tentative ruling is against you, address it at the outset of your argument. Do not simply argue it is "wrong." Rather, try to point out why the tentative ruling is impractical or would lead to an unfair result; why some of the facts stated or assumptions made by the court are mistaken; or why the ruling is inconsistent with cases cited in your brief.
- Do not simply rehash points in your papers. Rather, respond to whatever questions the judge has raised (directing him or her, if necessary, to the particular pages or paragraphs of your declarations or memorandum of authorities).
- Focus on your *strongest* arguments. If necessary, concede minor points that do not affect the outcome.
- Be prepared to discuss the *facts of the cases cited* by you and your opponent. Even direct quotes from cases cited in your memorandum of point and authorities gain (or lose) significance for your case depending upon their facts.
- Stay cool. *Do not argue with opposing counsel.* Address your remarks to the court. If opposing counsel addresses a comment or question to you, *ask the court* if it wishes you to respond.
- *Be prepared to be interrupted by the court.* Listen patiently and carefully to the judge's questions and address them directly. You should welcome the opportunity to respond to issues raised by the court, rather than being irritated (as some lawyers are) at the interruption.
- Avoid demeaning opposing counsel or his or her client. Doing so makes you appear unprofes-

sional and detracts from the merit of your argument.

- Avoid "last minute" citations of authority during oral argument. Instead, if the citations are really important, ask for leave to submit a supplemental memorandum.
- If you feel you are *losing* the argument, also ask for leave to file supplemental declarations or points and authorities on what appear to be the key issues. This sometimes will set the stage for the judge to reconsider and come to a different conclusion.
- Show respect for the court. Address the judge as "Your Honor" (not simply, "Judge"). Do not argue with the judge after he or she has ruled.

d. [9:171] **Court reporters:** Although some courts still provide court reporters at all civil law and motion hearings and trials, courts are increasingly opting not to do so.

If the court does not provide a reporter, its local rules must so state and spell out the procedure for obtaining a reporter (see CRC 3.1310). In such cases, parties are entitled to arrange for a reporter at their own expense (fees may be recoverable as court costs). [CRC 2.956(c); see *Fasuyi v. Permatex, Inc.* (2008) 167 CA4th 681, 690, 84 CR3d 351, 357, fn. 5 (citing text)]

[9:171.1] ***PRACTICE POINTER:*** Check with the court to determine whether there are any special procedures associated with providing your own court reporter. For example, the Los Angeles Superior Court requires that the parties and court reporter sign a stipulation, which is entered as an order appointing the reporter as the official reporter for the proceeding. The stipulation form may be obtained on the court's website (*www.lacourt.org*) under the link "Court Reporter Information."

(1) [9:171.2] **Verbatim record for indigent litigants:** Where local rules do not provide for court reporters for civil cases but allow litigants to arrange for reporters at their own expense, a court must provide a verbatim record for litigants who have obtained a fee waiver (Gov.C. §68631, *see* ¶*1:188*) and who request a reporter. [*Jameson v. Desta* (2018) 5 C5th 594, 599, 234 CR3d 831, 834]

(a) [9:171.3] **Courts developing policies to comply with *Jameson:*** Since July 2018, individual courts have been addressing the new *Jameson* requirement (¶*9:171.2*). The California Supreme Court recognized the significant cost of court reporters and acknowledged

© 2020 Thomson Reuters/The Rutter Group

that courts had eliminated them in some civil cases because of budgetary issues. [See *Jameson v. Desta,* supra, 5 C5th at 598, 610-611, 234 CR3d at 833, 844 & fn. 2]

Court websites should be checked to determine which procedures each court is adopting to address the *Jameson* requirement. [See L.A. Sup.Ct. Rule 2.21(a), (b)—request required 10 days in advance on form LACIV 269 in unlimited cases; electronic recording is provided for limited jurisdiction cases]

(b) [9:171.4] **Retroactive:** At least one court has held that *Jameson*'s holding (¶*9:171.2*) is retroactive to all cases not yet final, and that parties with fee waivers who had requested a court reporter and had not been provided with one could be granted a new trial if the failure to have a transcript affected the party's appellate rights. [*Dogan v. Comanche Hills Apartments, Inc.* (2019) 31 CA5th 566, 567-568, 242 CR3d 702, 703]

(2) [9:171.5] **Electronic recording in limited jurisdiction cases:** A court can provide for electronic recording in limited civil cases. [See Gov.C. §69957; CRC 2.952]

A written transcript of the electronic recording may be made "by or under the direction of" the clerk or a person designated by the court, and the person making the transcript must declare under penalty of perjury that the transcript is a "full, true, and correct" transcript. Such a transcript satisfies all requirements for a reporter's transcript. [CRC 2.952(g), (h)]

On stipulation of the parties and approval by the reviewing court, the electronic recording or copies of it may satisfy the requirements for a reporter's transcript for all purposes. [CRC 2.952(j)(1)]

(3) [9:172] **Transcript may be essential for appellate review:** Unless a court reporter is present, the losing party may have no effective way of challenging the court's ruling by writ or appeal: "In the absence of a transcript, the reviewing court will have no way of knowing . . . what grounds were advanced, what arguments were made, and what facts may have been admitted, mutually assumed or judicially noticed at the hearing. *In such a case, no abuse of discretion can be found except on the basis of speculation.*" [*Snell v. Sup.Ct. (Marshall Hosp.)* (1984) 158 CA3d 44, 49, 204 CR 200, 203 (emphasis added); see also *GT, Inc. v. Sup.Ct. (Santa Cruz Sentinel Publishers, Inc.)* (1984) 151 CA3d 748, 756, 198 CR 892, 896-897]

[9:173] ***PRACTICE POINTERS:*** If you are appearing in a court in which law and motion hearings are not regularly reported and the proceedings are not electronically recorded by court rule (*see ¶9:171.5*), and there is the slightest chance you would seek appellate review if the judge rules against you, be sure to make arrangements to have a court reporter present.

If the argument is not reported, but you wish to preserve your ability to seek review of the ruling by writ or appeal, attempt to obtain an "agreed" or "settled statement" of the proceedings. [See CRC 8.130(h); *Maria P. v. Riles* (1987) 43 C3d 1281, 1295, 240 CR 872, 881 (noting that, in absence of reporter's transcript, appellant should have augmented record with settled statement "to provide an adequate record to assess error")]

The procedure for obtaining a settled statement is set forth in CRC 8.137. [See *Mooney v. Sup.Ct. (Mooney)* (2016) 245 CA4th 523, 534, 199 CR3d 647, 656—abuse of discretion not to rule on motion for settled statement since such a motion "should be granted as a matter of course unless there is a justifiable excuse for denying it"]

Cross-refer: See detailed discussion of agreed and settled statements in Eisenberg, *Cal. Prac. Guide: Civil Appeals & Writs* (TRG), Ch. 4.

(4) [9:174] **Caution—failure to request reporter as malpractice?** If the matter is one in which a transcript may be essential for appellate review, it *may* constitute malpractice for an attorney to fail to have a court reporter present. [See *In re Christina P.* (1985) 175 CA3d 115, 128, 220 CR 525, 531—failure to request court reporter in proceeding to remove child from parental custody raised "cognizable claim" of ineffective assistance of counsel]

e. [9:175] **Oral testimony:** As stated earlier, judges usually decide motions based on evidence presented in the form of affidavits or declarations, rather than oral testimony (*see ¶9:43 ff.*).

Even so, the court *has discretion* to *receive* oral testimony, as well as exclude it. There are situations in which the judge may, in the exercise of such discretion, decide to hear witnesses or to allow cross-examination of a declarant. [*Rosenthal v. Great Western Fin'l Secur. Corp.* (1996) 14 C4th 394, 414, 58 CR2d 875, 886]

(1) [9:176] **Prehearing request:** At least 3 court days before the hearing, the party requesting leave to introduce

© 2020 Thomson Reuters/The Rutter Group

oral testimony must file a statement as to the nature and extent of the proposed testimony, and a reasonable time estimate for the hearing. [CRC 3.1306(b); *see* ¶*9:45.1*]

(2) [9:177] **Court must consider request for oral testimony:** The judge may *not* adopt a policy of outright refusal to consider oral testimony on a motion hearing. Rather, if requested by either party, the judge must exercise his or her *discretion* as to whether oral testimony would be necessary or helpful to the decision of the matter. [*Reifler v. Sup.Ct.* (1974) 39 CA3d 479, 485, 114 CR 356, 359]

(3) [9:178] **Appellate review limited to abuse of discretion:** The judge's refusal order may be reviewable by extraordinary writ, but such writs are granted only if abuse of discretion is shown (which is difficult to establish with rulings on requests to introduce live testimony). [*Eddy v. Temkin* (1985) 167 CA3d 1115, 1121, 213 CR 597, 601—no abuse shown on refusal to hear oral testimony on petition for partnership charging order where documents and depositions were more important to resolving factual issues than opportunity to examine and observe demeanor of live witnesses]

[9:178.1] ***PRACTICE POINTER:*** Don't rely on being able to present oral testimony. Even if you intend to seek permission to offer such testimony, prepare declarations in such a manner that the court's refusal to consider oral testimony will not leave gaps in your evidence. The request should specifically identify the material facts to be elicited through oral testimony. Explain why oral testimony is needed to assess credibility or to resolve factual disputes. If you cannot present written testimony, explain why not.

[9:178.2-178.4] *Reserved.*

f. [9:178.5] **Open to the public:** Civil as well as criminal proceedings must generally be open to the public (see CCP §124). This includes matters that may be heard outside the courthouse before a temporary judge or referee. [See CRC 2.834, 3.931]

First Amendment standards govern closure of any *substantive* proceeding (which may include law and motion proceedings). [*NBC Subsidiary (KNBC-TV), Inc. v. Sup.Ct. (Locke)* (1999) 20 C4th 1178, 1222, 86 CR2d 778, 812-813—trial judge improperly excluded public and press from courtroom proceedings involving celebrities without any showing that their right to fair trial could not be secured by less restrictive means] For this reason a strong, particularized showing is required to seal documents filed with the court (*see* ¶*9:416 ff.*).

5. **Judge's Ruling**

a. [9:179] **Submitted matters:** Most judges try to dispose of all matters on their calendar before leaving the bench. Occasionally, a matter will be sufficiently complicated that the judge cannot fully address it without further study; or he or she may wish to consider the impact of documents that were filed late; or he or she may have granted the parties the right to submit additional declarations or points and authorities. Under these circumstances, the judge may decline to rule from the bench, and instead take the matter under submission.

b. [9:180] **Formal rulings generally not required:** Except for appointment of referees (¶*9:183*), there is no requirement that a court make a formal, written ruling in a law and motion matter. Oral on-the-record rulings suffice to provide proper appellate review. [See *Biljac Assocs. v. First Interstate Bank of Oregon, N.A.* (1990) 218 CA3d 1410, 1419, 267 CR 819, 823 (disapproved on other grounds by *Reid v. Google, Inc.* (2010) 50 C4th 512, 532, 113 CR3d 327, 344, fn. 8); *Southwestern Law School v. Benson* (2019) 42 CA5th Supp. 1, 9, 254 CR3d 629, 634 (quoting text)]

c. [9:181] **Effect of court's failure to rule:** At least in the context of motions for summary judgment/adjudication, trial courts have a duty to rule on properly presented material evidentiary objections (CCP §437c(q)). If the court fails to rule, objections properly presented are preserved on appeal. [*Reid v. Google, Inc.*, supra, 50 C4th at 532, 113 CR3d at 343-344; *see* ¶*9:63.1*]

[9:182] *Reserved.*

d. [9:183] **Appointment of referee:** The court may appoint a referee in any case with the parties' consent (CCP §638). It may also appoint a referee *without their consent* in certain cases, including:

- "when a *question of fact*, other than upon the pleadings, arises upon motion or otherwise, in any stage of the action";
- to hear and determine *discovery disputes* under specified circumstances (*see* ¶*8:1803 ff.*). [CCP §639(a)(3), (5)]

(1) [9:184] **Not for legal issues:** Law and motion matters cannot routinely be assigned to a referee without the parties' consent. This includes motions for summary judgment; such motions do not involve "questions of fact" but rather an issue of law (i.e., whether a triable question of fact exists). [*International Jet Ski Boating Ass'n, Inc. v. Sup.Ct. (Parker)* (1991) 232 CA3d 112, 115-116, 283 CR 33, 34-35]

(2) [9:185] **Who may be appointed:** The referee may be a court commissioner, or someone entirely outside

© 2020 Thomson Reuters/The Rutter Group

the court system; e.g., retired judges, private lawyers or even nonlawyers. [See *Martino v. Denevi* (1986) 182 CA3d 553, 556, 227 CR 354, 356—accountant appointed as referee]

(3) [9:185.1] **Written order required:** All nonconsensual appointments must be in writing and state the reasons the referee is appointed. [CCP §639(d)]

(4) [9:186] **Detailed findings required for appointment of discovery referees, allocation of fees, etc.:** Detailed rules and procedures governing appointment of discovery referees, including written findings by the court as to the necessity for such appointment, must be set forth in the appointment order. [CCP §639(d); *see ¶8:742 ff.*]

(5) [9:187] **Referee's report only advisory:** Except where the parties have agreed to a general reference (covering all matters in the case), the referee's findings and report to the court are merely advisory. [CCP §644; see *Aetna Life Ins. Co. v. Sup.Ct. (Hammer)* (1986) 182 CA3d 431, 436, 227 CR 460, 464]

(6) [9:188] **Timely objection required:** A party who fails to file *written* objections to the referee's report within 10 days after it is filed may be held to have waived any objections to the report. The other party has 10 days to respond to the objections. [CCP §643(c); see *Martino v. Denevi*, supra, 182 CA3d at 557-558, 227 CR at 356-357]

(7) [9:189] **Court hearing not mandatory:** Although the court must review the referee's findings and any objections thereto, no hearing is required as a matter of law. The review may be accomplished "in whatever manner the trial court deems appropriate." [*Marathon Nat'l Bank v. Sup.Ct. (Campbell)* (1993) 19 CA4th 1256, 1258, 24 CR2d 40, 40-41]

Cross-refer: Rules and procedures governing appointment of referees are discussed in detail in Knight, Chernick, Flynn & Quinn, *Cal. Prac. Guide: Alternative Dispute Resolution* (TRG), Ch. 6.

[9:190-250] *Reserved.*

E. POSTHEARING PROCEDURES

1. Posthearing Order

a. [9:251] **Findings/statement of decision normally not required:** With a few exceptions (*¶9:252*), findings of fact are *not* required in connection with law and motion rulings. [See *Beckett v. Kaynar Mfg. Co.* (1958) 49 C2d 695, 699, 321 P2d 749, 751; *Laabs v. City of Victorville* (2008) 163 CA4th 1242, 1272, 78 CR3d 372, 398 (citing text)]

This rule applies as well to a CCP §632 *statement of decision* "even if the motion involves an evidentiary issue and even if the order is appealable." [*Lien v. Lucky United Properties Investment, Inc.* (2008) 163 CA4th 620, 623-624, 77 CR3d 707, 708]

(1) [9:252] **Exceptions:** Findings are required in a few instances, including:

— orders appointing discovery referees (*see ¶9:186*);

— orders sealing court records (*see ¶9:418 ff.*);

— if timely requested, orders ruling on petitions to compel arbitration (CCP §1291; *Metis Develop. LLC v. Bohacek* (2011) 200 CA4th 679, 687-689, 133 CR3d 585, 591-593; *see ¶9:408.31 ff.*);

— if timely requested, orders confirming arbitration awards (CCP §1291).

[9:253-254] *Reserved.*

b. [9:255] **Statement of reasons or grounds:** In ruling on certain motions, the court must state the reasons or grounds for its order. These include:

(1) [9:256] **Sustaining of demurrer:** An order sustaining a demurrer must state the "specific ground or grounds" upon which it is based (which may be by reference to appropriate pages and paragraphs of the demurrer). [CCP §472d; *see ¶7:126 ff.*]

(2) [9:257] **Grant of summary judgment:** An order granting summary judgment or summary adjudication must specify the "reasons" for the court's determination and cite both supporting and opposing evidence to show there is no triable issue of fact. [CCP §§437c(g), 437c(f), third sent.; *see ¶10:331 ff.*]

(3) [9:258] **Denial of summary judgment:** An order denying summary judgment or summary adjudication must specify one or more material facts in controversy and cite the conflicting evidence on this point. [CCP §§437c(g), 437c(f), third sent.; *see ¶10:352 ff.*]

[9:259-260] *Reserved.*

(4) [9:261] **Appointment of referee:** An order appointing a referee must state the reasons for the appointment. *See ¶9:185.1 ff.*

(5) [9:262] **Class actions:** Trial judges must state their reasons for denying class certification, which are the only grounds for denial that can be reviewed on appeal. [*McCleery v. Allstate Ins. Co.* (2019) 37 CA5th 434, 450, 249 CR3d 765, 778]

[9:263-293] *Reserved.*

© 2020 Thomson Reuters/The Rutter Group

2. [9:294] **Preparation of Order:** Unless the court orders otherwise or notice is waived, the prevailing party must, within 5 days after the ruling, serve a proposed order on opposing counsel by means authorized by law and reasonably calculated to ensure delivery by the *close of the next business day*, *without any extension* of time based on the manner of service. [CRC 3.1312(a)] (This includes *rulings on demurrers*; a demurrer is listed as a "pleadings motion"; see CRC 3.1320.)

   Opposing counsel then has 5 days after service (again, without any extension of time based on the manner of service) to notify the prevailing party's counsel of any objections to the proposed order, stating the reasons for its objections. [CRC 3.1312(a)]

   The prevailing party must then promptly transmit the proposed order to the court, together with a summary of any responses received from opposing counsel or a statement that no responses were received. [CRC 3.1312(b)]

   Special requirements apply where the proposed order is submitted to the court *electronically*. [See CRC 3.1312(c)]

   ➪ [9:295] ***PRACTICE POINTER:*** If a complex ruling is made in open court, ask the court reporter for a "same day" transcript of the order to make sure you get it *verbatim*. This helps avoid disputes with opposing counsel as to precisely what was ordered. (This is particularly important with orders granting or denying *summary judgment,* where the triable or nontriable issues have to be specified in the order, along with citations to the evidence; *see ¶10:331 ff.*)

   a. [9:296] **Compare—unopposed motions:** If the motion was unopposed and a proposed order was submitted with the moving papers, the proposed order need not again be submitted unless the court so orders. [CRC 3.1312(e)]

   [9:297-298] *Reserved.*

   b. [9:299] **Judicial Council form orders:** Where a mandatory Judicial Council form order exists (e.g., MC-053: Order Granting Attorney's Motion to be Relieved as Counsel—Civil), it must be used and the court may not order counsel to alter it. The *court itself,* however, may modify a Judicial Council form order "as necessary or appropriate to adjudicate a particular case." [CRC 1.31(e)]

   c. [9:300] **Attorney-drafted order:** Where an attorney order is required, the proposed order should be drafted as follows:

      - The *name of the lawyer* preparing the order and the *party represented* should appear in the upper left hand corner of the first page (*see ¶9:81.4*).
      - *Title* your proposed order as such: i.e., "(Proposed) Order Granting Motion . . ." The judge can strike out "Proposed"

before signing the order. This avoids the confusion created where court files contain documents denominated "Order" although never adopted or signed by the court (*see* ¶*9:81.2a*).

The title of the order should also state the result or the relief granted; e.g., "(Proposed) Order Granting Motion to Strike Affirmative Defense" or "(Proposed) Order for Further Answers to Interrogatories and for Payment of Attorney Fees."

- The *introductory paragraph* should state the date, time and department in which the hearing took place, the name of the judge presiding, and the names of each attorney present and whom they represented.
- The body of the order should set forth *findings* and *reasons* where required (*see* ¶*9:251 ff.*) and all relief granted.

FORM: Proposed Order (Posthearing), *see Form 9A:15* in Rivera, *Cal. Prac. Guide: Civ. Pro. Before Trial FORMS* (TRG).

[9:301-314] *Reserved.*

d. [9:315] **Opposing counsel's options:** The opposing party has *5 days* after the "*mailing* or delivery" to notify the prevailing counsel as to any objections *as to the form* of the proposed order, stating any reasons for disapproval. Failure to so notify the prevailing party within the 5-day period is deemed an approval as to form. [CRC 3.1312(a)]

(1) [9:316] **No extension for service by mail:** CCP §1013, which usually extends time for response where papers are served by mail or other means, does *not* extend the time for opposing counsel to respond. [CRC 3.1312(a)]

[9:317] ***PRACTICE POINTER:*** Note the very short time period allowed: 5 days after the *mailing* of the order. The result is that if you are the losing counsel, you may have to act immediately upon receipt of the proposed order.

If you have objections, email or fax them to opposing counsel. Even if fax service is not otherwise allowable (*see* ¶*9:86.10*), it would constitute "notification" for purposes of CRC 3.1312. It also avoids disputes that might arise with oral notification.

If the order is *complex* and *your objections elaborate*, follow up with mailing copies to opposing counsel and to the court. (This ensures the court will receive your full response rather than merely opposing counsel's "summary" of it.)

e. [9:318] **Delivery to court:** Upon expiration of the 5-day period for approval by opposing counsel, the prevailing party

© 2020 Thomson Reuters/The Rutter Group

must deliver the proposed order to the court together with a summary of any responses by other parties or a statement that no responses were received. [CRC 3.1312(b)]

[9:318.1] ***PRACTICE POINTER:*** Your duty of candor to the court requires disclosure of the opposing party's responses to a proposed order. Moreover, failure to do so usually results in further motions and hearings pertaining to the form of the order, involving unnecessary expense to your client.

f. [9:319] **Effect of failure to comply:** If the prevailing party fails to prepare and submit the order as above provided (¶*9:294 ff.*), any other party may do so. [CRC 3.1312(d)]

[9:319.1] ***PRACTICE POINTER:*** This is what you may need to do to seek appellate review of an adverse ruling when the prevailing party is dragging its feet on preparing the order. No appeal or writ petition (*see* ¶*9:344.25*) can be filed until an order is filed.

3. [9:320] **Notice of Ruling:** Once the order is entered, unless the court orders otherwise, the prevailing party must prepare a notice of the court's ruling and serve it on all other parties or their attorneys—unless they were present at the hearing and waived notice. [CCP §1019.5(a)]

Exceptions: When an order is entered sua sponte (on court's own motion), it is the court's responsibility to prepare and serve the notice of ruling (CCP §1019.5(b)). Similarly, when the court rules on a matter it has taken under submission, the clerk must immediately notify the parties of the ruling or order by mailing the parties a copy. [CRC 3.1109(a)]

a. [9:320.1] **Purpose of notice:** The notice is required to start the time running:
— to amend or answer after the court's ruling on demurrer (CCP §472b; *see* ¶*7:134*); *or*
— to seek reconsideration (CCP §1008(a); see *Forrest v. State of Calif. Dept. of Corps.* (2007) 150 CA4th 183, 203, 58 CR3d 466, 481 (citing text) (disapproved on other grounds by *Shalant v. Girardi* (2011) 51 C4th 1164, 1172, 126 CR3d 98, 103, fn. 3); *and* ¶*9:324 ff.*); *or*
— to file an appeal of the denial of a motion to vacate a judgment entered without notice to the parties (*Kalenian v. Insen* (2014) 225 CA4th 569, 578, 170 CR3d 755, 761—plaintiffs' appeal of denial of motion for relief to allow late appeal deemed timely where court failed to serve parties with notice of judge's dismissal orders as required by law); *or*
— to take a writ petition (see *Cal West Nurseries, Inc. v. Sup.Ct. (A.J. West Ranch, LLC)* (2005) 129 CA4th 1170, 1173-1174, 29 CR3d 170, 173).

It also assures that parties *not* present at the hearing are aware of the court's order.

b. [9:320.2] **Content of notice:** The notice of ruling should state the exact terms of the court's order as entered, and should include the date of entry.

(1) [9:320.3] **Copy of order as notice:** The prevailing party may serve a "file-stamped copy" of the order as notice of ruling: "There can be no better notice of what an order says than is provided by a file-stamped copy of the order itself." [*Parris v. Cave* (1985) 174 CA3d 292, 294, 219 CR 871, 873]

FORM: Notice of Ruling, *see Form 9A:16* in Rivera, *Cal. Prac. Guide: Civ. Pro. Before Trial FORMS* (TRG).

(2) [9:320.4] **Compare—order:** A "notice of ruling" is addressed to the other parties and is signed by counsel. An "order" is not so addressed and is signed by the court.

➪ [9:320.4a] ***PRACTICE POINTER:*** In event of any discrepancy between the two, the order is the governing document. Therefore, if an issue arises as to what action was taken by the court, refer to the appropriate formal or minute order (and supply copies thereof if appropriate), *not* to the notice of ruling.

c. [9:320.5] **Service of notice:** Notice is generally served by mail on the attorney of record for each other party who has appeared in the action. Note that if a party is being represented by a law *firm*, the firm's name must be included in the address; service is improper if addressed only to a lawyer within the firm. [See *Triumph Precision Products, Inc. v. Insurance Co. of North America* (1979) 91 CA3d 362, 365, 154 CR 120, 122]

(It is good practice to include *both* the firm name and the name of the individual attorney within the firm who is handling the matter. Indeed, this is required under some local court rules.)

[9:320.6] *Reserved.*

d. [9:320.7] **Waiver of notice:** If all parties to the action are present at the time of the ruling, they may waive notice thereof. To be effective, such waiver must be in open court and entered in the minutes. [CCP §1019.5(a)]

➪ [9:320.8] ***PRACTICE POINTER:*** If you are the losing party, do *not* automatically waive notice. If a demurrer is involved, your insisting on notice will provide you with some extra time to plead. Also, if the ruling is at all complicated, insisting on notice helps avoid confusion and misunderstandings as to the specifics involved.

© 2020 Thomson Reuters/The Rutter Group

Another reason to insist on notice is that it helps avoid slip-ups caused by failure to take accurate notes of the court's ruling (e.g., dates for filing briefs, continued hearings, etc.). This is a particular problem where more than one attorney in your firm is handling the file. Neglect in noting the court's ruling is imputed to all members of the firm, and is *not "excusable."* [*Griffis v. S.S. Kresge Co.* (1984) 150 CA3d 491, 497, 197 CR 771, 775—"The instant matter readily demonstrates *the perils of waiving notice*" (emphasis added)]

[9:321] *Reserved.*

4. [9:322] **Procedures to Change Ruling in Trial Court:** Until an order is signed and entered, the court retains power to change its mind and reverse or modify its ruling. [*Bernstein v. Consolidated American Ins. Co.* (1995) 37 CA4th 763, 774, 43 CR2d 817, 823 (disapproved on other grounds by *Vandenberg v. Sup.Ct. (Centennial Ins. Co.)* (1999) 21 C4th 815, 841, 88 CR2d 366, 384, fn. 13)]

Once the order is entered, however, the court can set aside or modify its order *only* through the procedures discussed below (¶*9:323 ff.*).

a. [9:323] **"Jurisdictional" limitation on party's motion:** No application to reconsider a prior order (¶*9:324 ff.*) or for renewal of a previous motion (¶*9:337 ff.*) may be considered except as provided below (¶*9:323.1 ff.*). [CCP §1008(e)—"This section specifies the court's *jurisdiction* with regard to applications for reconsideration . . . and renewals of previous motions" (emphasis added); see *Garcia v. Hejmadi* (1997) 58 CA4th 674, 691, 68 CR2d 228, 239—plaintiff's judgment reversed because court "lacked jurisdiction" to grant plaintiff's motion to reconsider earlier order granting summary judgment to defendant]

(1) [9:323.1] **Compare—court's inherent power to reconsider:** CCP §1008 does not, however, limit the court's *inherent power* to reevaluate its interim rulings on its own motion, and to enter a new and different order any time prior to entry of judgment. *See detailed discussion at* ¶*9:327 ff.*

(2) [9:323.2] **Compare—in limine motions:** Motions in limine are not binding and are subject to reconsideration upon full information at trial, "because the trial court has the power to reconsider, modify or set aside its order at any time prior to the submission of the cause." [*Cristler v. Express Messenger Systems, Inc.* (2009) 171 CA4th 72, 90, 89 CR3d 34, 48, fn. 6 (internal quotes omitted)]

[9:323.3-323.4] *Reserved.*

b. [9:323.5] **"Interim or final" orders:** CCP §1008 governs motions to reconsider and renewals of previous motions based on an application for an order to the court, whether the challenged order is "interim or final." [CCP §1008(e), (h); see *Baldwin v. Home Sav. of America* (1997) 59 CA4th 1192, 1199, 69 CR2d 592, 597]

c. [9:324] **Motion for reconsideration:** Under the following conditions, the losing party may make a motion before the same judge to reconsider and enter a different order (CCP §1008(a)). Such motion must be:

- brought before the *same judge* who made the order (¶*9:324.3*);
- "made *within 10 days* after service upon the party of *notice of entry* of the order" (¶*9:325*);
- based on "*new or different* facts, circumstances or law" than those before the court at the time of the original ruling (¶*9:328*);
- *supported by declaration* stating the previous order, by which judge it was made, and the new or different facts, circumstances or law claimed to exist (¶*9:331*); and
- made and *decided before* entry of judgment (¶*9:332.1*).

FORM: Motion for Reconsideration and Proposed Order, *see Form 9A:17* in Rivera, *Cal. Prac. Guide: Civ. Pro. Before Trial FORMS* (TRG).

⇨ [9:324a] ***PRACTICE POINTER:*** A motion for reconsideration is often an uphill battle because you have to persuade the judge that there has been a change in the law or there are new facts, not previously available, which require a different result. There is also a higher than normal risk of sanctions on such motions, in part because contempt sanctions are expressly authorized under §1008(d). Therefore, ensure the judge understands why you could not have discovered the new facts or law during the original motion.

(1) [9:324.1] **What constitutes "motion for reconsideration":** The name of the motion is not controlling. The above requirements (¶*9:324*) apply to any motion that asks the judge to decide the *same matter* previously ruled on. [See *R & B Auto Ctr., Inc. v. Farmers Group, Inc.* (2006) 140 CA4th 327, 373, 44 CR3d 426, 463 (citing text); *Powell v. County of Orange* (2011) 197 CA4th 1573, 1577, 129 CR3d 380, 383 (citing text); *Lennar Homes of Calif., Inc. v. Stephens* (2014) 232 CA4th 673, 681-682, 181 CR3d 638, 645-646]

(a) **Application**

[9:324.2] A motion for summary judgment or adjudication is not a CCP §1008 motion for reconsideration of an earlier demurrer that raised the same issue but was overruled. A trial court is not prevented in a motion for summary judgment/adjudication from revisiting issues of law previously raised on demurrer. [*California Pub. Records Research, Inc. v. County of Yolo* (2016) 4 CA5th 150, 189, 209 CR3d 26, 56]

- [9:324.2a] Judge A issued an order staying the action. Judge B subsequently set the case for trial (implicitly revoking the stay order). Judge B's order was invalid because not made pursuant to CCP §1008 procedures governing motion for reconsideration. [*Morite of Calif. v. Sup.Ct. (Grayson)* (1993) 19 CA4th 485, 490, 23 CR2d 666, 669]

- [9:324.2b] A demurrer to a cause of action as to which an *earlier demurrer was overruled* is in effect a motion for reconsideration of the earlier demurrer ruling, and therefore subject to CCP §1008. [*Bennett v. Suncloud* (1997) 56 CA4th 91, 96, 65 CR2d 80, 83, fn. 1; *see* ¶*7:140*]

- [9:324.2c] Judge A issued minute orders denying access to court reporter transcripts of involuntary conservatorship proceedings, following the District Attorney's informal request to the court reporter and a newspaper's two sentence letter request to the court clerk. After reassignment, Judge B heard a formal "motion for reconsideration" and granted access to the transcripts. CCP §1008 did not preclude this ruling, since the original orders "were not the result of a motion process involving submission of formal requests to the court upon noticed motions supported by appropriate points and authorities and declarations" and thus did not seek modification or revocation of an order that had resulted from "an application for an order . . . made . . . to a court." [*Sorenson v. Sup.Ct. (People)* (2013) 219 CA4th 409, 420-421, 161 CR3d 794, 803-804 & fn. 13]

- [9:324.2d] Judge granted an anti-SLAPP motion as to all Ds. P filed a "Motion to Request Ruling on or Clarification of (the Prior Order)." Despite its name, the motion was a motion for reconsideration, as it was "largely a vehicle for rehashing and expanding arguments previously made, and citing authority that either was, or could have been, presented to the trial court previously." [*Lennar Homes of Calif., Inc. v. Stephens*, supra,

232 CA4th at 681-682, 181 CR3d at 645-646 & fn. 7]

[9:324.2e] *Reserved.*

(b) [9:324.2f] **Compare—motion for relief under CCP §473(b):** Section 1008 deals with the general subject of motions to reconsider previous orders and renewals of previous motions. CCP §473(b) governs applications for relief from a default or default judgment entered as a result of "mistake, surprise, inadvertence or excusable neglect." [*Even Zohar Const. & Remodeling, Inc. v. Bellaire Townhouses, LLC* (2015) 61 C4th 830, 838, 189 CR3d 824, 830]

1) [9:324.2g] **Renewed motion for CCP §473(b) relief:** If a CCP §473(b) motion for relief from default is denied, a renewed motion for relief must meet the requirements of CCP §1008(b). Rationale: "Section 1008 expressly applies to all renewed applications for orders the court has previously refused." [*Even Zohar Const. & Remodeling, Inc. v. Bellaire Townhouses, LLC,* supra, 61 C4th at 842, 189 CR3d at 832 (disapproving contrary authority)—second §473(b) motion properly denied where attorney affidavit of fault failed to show new or different information as required by §1008; *see also* ¶*5:414.5*]

(2) [9:324.3] **Same judge or court:** The statute says the motion may be addressed to the "same judge *or court*" that made the order. [CCP §1008(a)]

(a) [9:324.4] **"Or court":** The words "or court" mean simply that if the original judge is *unavailable*, another judge of the same court can hear a motion for reconsideration. There was no legislative intent to overrule earlier case law holding the motion *must be addressed to the same judge if available:* "[O]ne trial court judge may not reconsider and overrule a ruling by another trial court judge." [*Davcon, Inc. v. Roberts & Morgan* (2003) 110 CA4th 1355, 1361, 2 CR3d 782, 788; *International Ins. Co. v. Sup.Ct. (Rhone-Poulenc Basic Chemicals Co.)* (1998) 62 CA4th 784, 786, 72 CR2d 849, 850, fn. 2—where first judge unavailable due to retirement, new judge authorized to rule on reconsideration motion; *Marriage of Oliverez* (2015) 238 CA4th 1242, 1247-1249, 190 CR3d 436, 439-444]

(3) [9:325] **10-day time limit:** A formal notice of ruling (*see* ¶*9:320*) is required to set the time limit running on a motion for reconsideration. The 10-day time limit runs

© 2020 Thomson Reuters/The Rutter Group

from *service of notice of entry* of the order. [CCP §1008(a); *Forrest v. State of Calif. Dept. of Corps.* (2007) 150 CA4th 183, 203, 58 CR3d 466, 481 (disapproved on other grounds by *Shalant v. Girardi* (2011) 51 C4th 1164, 1172, 126 CR3d 98, 103, fn. 3); *Novak v. Fay* (2015) 236 CA4th 329, 335-336, 186 CR3d 451, 456—10-day limit did not apply where no notice of entry of order served]

(a) [9:326] **Effect of waiver of notice?** The wording of the statute suggests there is no time limit when notice is waived. But this seems contrary to the statutory purpose, and judges may therefore hold the 10-day period runs from the date of waiver. (In any case, the longer the delay, the less receptive the court may be to the motion.)

(b) [9:326.1] **Extension of time for service by mail or other means:** The 10-day deadline for seeking reconsideration is extended under CCP §1013 for service by mail, fax, electronic service or overnight delivery (*see* ¶*9:87.1 ff.*), which applies "in the absence of a specific exception provided for by this section or other statute or rule of court." [CCP §1013(a), (c), (e)]

Some pre-1995 cases held that CCP §1013 was not intended to apply to "jurisdictional deadlines," similar to notices of appeal. However, CCP §1013 was amended in 1995 to clarify that the extension of time provided by the statute applies "in the absence of a specific exception provided for by this section or other statute or rule of court." [CCP §1013; Stats. 1995, Ch. 576, §3.8; see *California Business Council for Equal Opportunity v. Sup.Ct. (Wilson)* (1997) 52 CA4th 1100, 1107, 62 CR2d 7, 13]

Because CCP §1008 does not contain an express exception, the extensions provided by §1013 apply to motions under §1008.

[9:326.2-326.4] *Reserved.*

(c) [9:326.5] **Compare—nonparty not subject to deadline:** News Organization, a *nonparty* to the original proceedings, brought a motion for reconsideration of an order to seal court records entered *six years* earlier. News Organization's motion was timely because, since it was not a party to the original proceedings, it was never served with notice of entry of the challenged order. Thus, the 10-day period had not commenced running at the time News Organization made its motion. [*Wilson v. Science Applications Int'l Corp.* (1997) 52 CA4th 1025, 1033, 60 CR2d 883, 887]

© 2020 Thomson Reuters/The Rutter Group

(4) [9:327] **Reconsideration after 10 days under court's inherent power:** Although parties may move for reconsideration only as authorized by §1008, that statute "does not limit the court's ability, on its own motion, to reconsider its prior interim orders so it may correct its own errors." [*Le Francois v. Goel* (2005) 35 C4th 1094, 1107, 29 CR3d 249, 260; see *Pinela v. Neiman Marcus Group, Inc.* (2015) 238 CA4th 227, 237, 190 CR3d 159, 168; *Boschetti v. Pacific Bay Investments Inc.* (2019) 32 CA5th 1059, 1070, 244 CR3d 480, 488—terms of CCP §1008 do not limit *court's* ability to reconsider]

[9:327.1-327.4] *Reserved.*

(a) [9:327.5] **Court must act sua sponte:** The court must act on its own motion, either as the result of its own second thoughts or in response to a party's request (¶*9:327.6 ff.*). [*Le Francois v. Goel*, supra, 35 C4th at 1108, 29 CR3d at 261]

Thus, in spite of the fact that a motion to reconsider is filed in violation of §1008, the court has inherent power to correct its own errors when they are called to the court's attention by way of an improperly filed motion. [*Marriage of Barthold* (2008) 158 CA4th 1301, 1308, 70 CR3d 691, 695; see also *Marriage of Herr* (2009) 174 CA4th 1463, 1468-1470, 95 CR3d 464, 469-470; *Nieto v. Blue Shield of Calif. Life & Health Ins. Co.* (2010) 181 CA4th 60, 73, 103 CR3d 906, 916-917] And prompted by arguments on a related motion, the court may on its own decide to reconsider an earlier motion. [*Boschetti v. Pacific Bay Investments Inc.* (2019) 32 CA5th 1059, 1070, 244 CR3d 480, 488]

(b) [9:327.6] **Manner of request:** It is not improper for a party to ask the court informally (e.g., at a status conference) to reconsider an earlier ruling as long as opposing counsel is present (*ex parte* communication with the court is improper). [*Le Francois v. Goel*, supra, 35 C4th at 1108, 29 CR3d at 261 (citing text)]

1) [9:327.7] **Motion asking court to reconsider improper:** A party's motion asking the court to reconsider a ruling on its own motion after the 10-day period is ineffective. The court is not obliged to rule on it and opposing counsel need not respond. [*Le Francois v. Goel*, supra, 35 C4th at 1108, 29 CR3d at 261; *Farmers Ins. Exch. v. Sup.Ct. (Wilson)* (2013) 218 CA4th 96, 102, 159 CR3d 580, 586, fn. 10]

© 2020 Thomson Reuters/The Rutter Group

☞ [9:327.8] ***PRACTICE POINTER:*** Absent changed facts or circumstances, do not make a formal motion to reconsider. The judge may impose *sanctions* for an improper motion (*see ¶9:333*). The best approach is to follow *Le Francois v. Goel*, supra, 35 C4th at 1108, 29 CR3d at 261, and make an *oral suggestion* (in the presence of opposing counsel) that the court reconsider its prior ruling.

[9:327.9] *Reserved.*

(c) [9:327.10] **Notice and hearing required:** *Before reconsidering* an earlier ruling on its own motion, the court must notify the parties that it may do so, solicit briefing and conduct a hearing. [*Le Francois v. Goel*, supra, 35 C4th at 1108, 29 CR3d at 261; see *Paramount Petroleum Corp. v. Sup.Ct. (Building Materials Corp. of America)* (2014) 227 CA4th 226, 238, 173 CR3d 518, 528]

(d) [9:327.11] **Compare—no inherent power to grant new trial:** In contrast to grants of reconsideration, courts have no inherent power to grant a new trial. Thus, the court cannot sua sponte reject evidence adduced at a hearing and order the parties to *submit new evidence.* "Whatever the court called it, the order was for a new trial." [*Marriage of Herr*, supra, 174 CA4th at 1470-1471, 95 CR3d at 470-471]

(5) [9:328] **"New or different facts, circumstances or law":** The legislative intent was to *restrict* motions for reconsideration to circumstances where a party offers the court some fact or circumstance not previously considered, and *some valid reason* for not offering it earlier. [*Gilberd v. AC Transit* (1995) 32 CA4th 1494, 1500, 38 CR2d 626, 629-630; *Mink v. Sup.Ct. (Arnel Develop. Co., Inc.)* (1992) 2 CA4th 1338, 1342, 4 CR2d 195, 197; *Baldwin v. Home Sav. of America* (1997) 59 CA4th 1192, 1198, 69 CR2d 592, 597]

The burden under §1008 "is *comparable to that of a party seeking a new trial* on the ground of newly discovered evidence: the information must be such that the moving party *could not*, with reasonable diligence, have discovered or produced it at the trial." [*New York Times Co. v. Sup.Ct. (Wall St. Network, Ltd.)* (2005) 135 CA4th 206, 212-213, 37 CR3d 338, 343 (emphasis added)]

(a) [9:329] **Reasonable diligence required:** A party seeking reconsideration of a prior order based on "new or different facts, circumstances or law" must provide a satisfactory explanation for failing to present the information at the first hearing; i.e., a showing of *reasonable diligence.* [*Garcia v. Hejmadi* (1997) 58 CA4th 674, 690, 68 CR2d 228, 238; *California Correctional Peace Officers Ass'n v. Virga* (2010) 181 CA4th 30, 47, 103 CR3d 699, 714, fn. 15 (collecting cases)—renewal motion also subject to reasonable diligence requirement (*see* ¶*9:339.6*)]

(b) **Application**

- [9:329.1] A motion to reconsider was properly granted where supported by *newly-produced documents* which had been requested but not produced at the time of the earlier hearing. [*Hollister v. Benzl* (1999) 71 CA4th 582, 585, 83 CR2d 903, 904]

- [9:329.2] "New circumstances" were shown by evidence the court *failed to consider a timely-filed memorandum* of points and authorities in its prior ruling. [*Johnston v. Corrigan* (2005) 127 CA4th 553, 556, 25 CR3d 657, 659 (citing text)]

  [9:330] *Reserved.*

- [9:330.1] A later-enacted statute that is not retroactive does *not* constitute a "new or different law" under §1008. [See CCP §1008(f)]

- [9:330.2] Reconsideration cannot be granted based on claims the court *misinterpreted* the law in its initial ruling (as opposed to a change in the law in the interim). That is *not* a "new" or "different" matter. [*Gilberd v. AC Transit*, supra, 32 CA4th at 1500, 38 CR2d at 630]

- [9:330.3] Reconsideration cannot be granted based on the moving party's claims that it had not intended to waive oral argument on the initial motion. Again, that is not a "new" or "different" matter. [*Gilberd v. AC Transit*, supra, 32 CA4th at 1500, 38 CR2d at 630]

- [9:330.4] Lack of a chance for oral argument is "clearly collateral to the merits" and therefore not ground for reconsideration. [*Garcia v. Hejmadi*, supra, 58 CA4th at 691, 68 CR2d at 238-239]

- [9:330.5] Counsel's *mistake* based on ignorance of the law is *not* a proper basis for reconsideration. [*Pazderka v. Caballeros Dimas Alang, Inc.* (1998) 62 CA4th 658, 670, 73 CR2d 242, 248]

- [9:330.6] A motion for reconsideration was properly denied where based on evidence that *could have been* presented in connection with

© 2020 Thomson Reuters/The Rutter Group

the original motion. [*Morris v. AGFA Corp.* (2006) 144 CA4th 1452, 1460, 51 CR3d 301, 308; *Hennigan v. White* (2011) 199 CA4th 395, 406, 130 CR3d 856, 865]

- [9:330.7] Deposition testimony obtained after a motion for summary judgment was granted was not ground for reconsideration where there was *no showing why the deposition could not have been taken earlier.* [*Jones v. P.S. Develop. Co., Inc.* (2008) 166 CA4th 707, 725, 82 CR3d 882, 900 (disapproved on other grounds by *Reid v. Google, Inc.* (2010) 50 C4th 512, 532, 113 CR3d 327, 343, fn. 7)]

- [9:330.8] When an order is based on a case that is later depublished, reconsideration is proper because depublication constitutes a change in the law under §1008. [*Farmers Ins. Exch. v. Sup.Ct. (Wilson)* (2013) 218 CA4th 96, 108-112, 159 CR3d 580, 590-593—"When a court decision is made on the basis of an opinion that is subsequently depublished, the law justifying that decision has necessarily changed"]

(6) [9:331] **Declaration required:** The motion for reconsideration must be accompanied by an affidavit (declaration) from the moving party stating:

— what application was made previously;

— when and to what judge the application was made;

— what order or decisions were made; and

— what new or different facts, circumstances or law are claimed to be shown. [CCP §1008(a); see *Branner v. Regents of Univ. of Calif.* (2009) 175 CA4th 1043, 1048, 96 CR3d 690, 693—motion filed and served without supporting affidavit was *invalid* (affidavit filed later insufficient)]

For example, if a demurrer is sustained without leave to amend and counsel wants "one more chance," a motion for reconsideration must be accompanied by a declaration explaining what "new or different" facts, etc. are "claimed" in the proposed amended pleading; and a satisfactory explanation for not presenting them at the time of the initial hearing (¶*9:328*).

(7) [9:332] **Ruling on motion:** If the statutory requirements above (¶*9:331*) are not met, the motion for reconsideration may be denied. Conversely, where the requirements are met, reconsideration should be granted. That does not mean, however, that the court must change its mind. Upon reconsideration, it may simply reaffirm its original order. [*Corns v. Miller* (1986) 181 CA3d 195,

202, 226 CR 247, 251; *Blake v. Ecker* (2001) 93 CA4th 728, 739, 113 CR2d 422, 430—trial court "bound to grant such reconsideration" where change in law shown (disapproved on other grounds by *Le Francois v. Goel* (2005) 35 C4th 1094, 1107, 29 CR3d 249, 260)]

(a) [9:332.1] **Ruling must precede entry of judgment:** The court loses jurisdiction to rule on a pending motion for reconsideration *after* entry of judgment. [*APRI Ins. Co. v. Sup.Ct. (Schatteman)* (1999) 76 CA4th 176, 181, 90 CR2d 171, 174—immaterial that motion to reconsider filed before entry of judgment; *Branner v. Regents of Univ. of Calif.*, supra, 175 CA4th at 1048, 96 CR3d at 693—"A motion to reconsider is not valid if it is filed after the final judgment is signed"]

- [9:332.2] An order of *dismissal* is a judgment (see CCP §581d); and therefore, a motion for reconsideration does not lie after a dismissal. [*APRI Ins. Co. v. Sup.Ct. (Schatteman)*, supra, 76 CA4th at 181, 90 CR2d at 173-174]

- [9:332.3] Once a judgment has been entered, the proper challenge is a motion for new trial (CCP §657), which may be based on various grounds including *errors of law*. [See *Ramon v. Aerospace Corp.* (1996) 50 CA4th 1233, 1237-1238, 58 CR2d 217, 219]

(b) [9:332.4] **Compare—certain postjudgment motions subject to reconsideration:** A court may reconsider orders it is *statutorily authorized to make* after entry of judgment (e.g., motions to vacate, or for relief from a default judgment). [*D.R.S. Trading Co., Inc. v. Barnes* (2009) 180 CA4th 815, 820, 103 CR3d 329, 332-333]

(8) [9:333] **Contempt and sanctions:** Any violation of CCP §1008 (e.g., motion filed after the 10-day period) may be punished as a *contempt* of court. [CCP §1008(d)]

In addition, if the motion is found to lack evidentiary support or legal merit, sanctions may be imposed against the moving party and/or counsel under CCP §128.7 (*see* ¶*9:1135 ff.*). [CCP §1008(d)]

- [9:333.1] But a party cannot be sanctioned for attempting to persuade a court its order was erroneous *if it was in fact erroneous*. If the order is set aside on appeal, the sanctions must also be set aside. [*Tutor-Saliba-Perini Joint Venture v. Sup.Ct. (San Diego Unified Port Dist.)* (1991) 233 CA3d 736, 738, 285 CR 1, 5]

[9:334] *Reserved.*

© 2020 Thomson Reuters/The Rutter Group

(9) [9:335] **Time for appeal extended?** Once a judgment or order having the effect of a judgment is entered, the court loses jurisdiction to rule on a motion for reconsideration (*see* ¶*9:332.1*). Therefore, a *postjudgment* motion for reconsideration does *not* extend the time to appeal from the judgment. [*Passavanti v. Williams* (1990) 225 CA3d 1602, 1605-1606, 275 CR 887, 889-890; *APRI Ins. Co. v. Sup.Ct. (Schatteman)* (1999) 76 CA4th 176, 181, 90 CR2d 171, 174; *Safeco Ins. Co. of Ill. v. Architectural Facades Unlimited, Inc.* (2005) 134 CA4th 1477, 1480, 36 CR3d 754, 756-757]

(a) [9:335.1] **Rationale:** After judgment is entered, a trial court can only correct judicial error in accordance with certain statutory proceedings (e.g., motions for new trial and motions to vacate the judgment). Since a motion for reconsideration is not such a proceeding, it does not extend the time to appeal the order. [*Passavanti v. Williams*, supra, 225 CA3d at 1607-1608, 275 CR at 890-891; *Crotty v. Trader* (1996) 50 CA4th 765, 770-771, 57 CR2d 818, 820-821]

(b) [9:335.2] **Compare—treated as motion for new trial:** But under certain circumstances, the court may treat a postjudgment motion for reconsideration as a motion for new trial (which does extend the time for appeal). [See *20th Century Ins. Co. v. Sup.Ct. (Ahles)* (2001) 90 CA4th 1247, 1259-1260, 109 CR2d 611, 621]

Cross-refer: For detailed discussion of how reconsideration motions affect the appeal period, see Eisenberg, *Cal. Prac. Guide: Civil Appeals & Writs* (TRG), Ch. 3.

(10) [9:336] **No reversal absent "miscarriage of justice":** Even if a motion for reconsideration was procedurally improper, the reconsidered ruling will not be reversed on appeal unless it is also wrong on the merits. [Cal. Const. Art. VI, §13 (prejudicial error rule); *People v. Edward D. Jones & Co.* (2007) 154 CA4th 627, 634, 65 CR3d 130, 136; *Paramount Petroleum Corp. v. Sup.Ct. (Building Materials Corp. of America)* (2014) 227 CA4th 226, 238, 173 CR3d 518, 528-529]

(11) [9:336.1] **Denial of motion for reconsideration not separately appealable:** The denial of a motion for reconsideration itself is not separately appealable. However, if the order that was the subject of the reconsideration motion is appealable, denial of the reconsideration motion is reviewable on appeal of the underlying order. [CCP §1008(g)]

d. [9:337] **Renewal motions:** When a motion has been denied in whole or in part, the moving party (only) may apply again for the same relief at a later time, but only on the following conditions:

- The motion must be based on "new or different facts, circumstances or law" (¶*9:340*);
- The motion must be supported by declaration showing the previous order, by which judge it was made, and what new or different facts, circumstances or law are claimed to exist (¶*9:341*). [CCP §1008(b); see *Graham v. Hansen* (1982) 128 CA3d 965, 969-970, 180 CR 604, 607-608]

FORM: Renewal Motion and Proposed Order, *see Form 9A:17.1* in Rivera, *Cal. Prac. Guide: Civ. Pro. Before Trial FORMS* (TRG).

(1) [9:338] **Exception for denials "without prejudice"?** The denial of a motion "without prejudice" evidences the court's intent to allow the motion to be renewed at a later time, potentially without the necessity of showing new facts. However, CCP §1008(b) creates no exception for such orders. Thus, the effect of a "without prejudice" denial is unclear given the jurisdictional nature of §1008.

Comment: The phrase "without prejudice" is often used to mean the matter is not ripe, such as an issue that should be raised later in a motion in limine. Use of "without prejudice" in this type of situation might be harmful. For example, where an appealable order is denied "without prejudice" and then renewed *after* the time for appeal has passed, it is possible that no timely appeal could thereafter be filed.

[9:338.1-338.4] *Reserved.*

(2) [9:338.5] **No time limit:** Unlike a motion for reconsideration, there is *no* time limit under §1008 for the renewal of a previous motion. [See CCP §1008(b), (e); *Stephen v. Enterprise Rent-A-Car of San Francisco* (1991) 235 CA3d 806, 816, 1 CR2d 130, 136]

(3) [9:339] **Different judge:** Unlike a motion for reconsideration, which must be heard by the same judge, a different judge may hear the renewal motion. [*Deauville Restaurant, Inc. v. Sup.Ct. (Taylor)* (2001) 90 CA4th 843, 849-851, 108 CR2d 863, 867-869]

But the supporting declaration must disclose the prior motion, its resolution and the judge who heard it. [CCP §1008(b)]

(a) [9:339.1] *Comment:* Judges do not like being asked to overrule another judge. Some judges routinely *transfer* renewal motions to the judge who heard the matter originally.

[9:339.2-339.4] *Reserved.*

© 2020 Thomson Reuters/The Rutter Group

(4) [9:339.5] **"Same order" means same relief sought:** An "application for the same order" as used in CCP §1008(b) means a motion seeking the *same relief* as in an earlier motion. [*California Correctional Peace Officers Ass'n v. Virga* (2010) 181 CA4th 30, 43, 103 CR3d 699, 711]

- [9:339.6] After an earlier motion for attorney fees under a *state* statute was denied, D moved for the identical relief under a *federal* statute. Although different grounds were asserted, the second motion was subject to CCP §1008(b)'s reasonable diligence requirement (¶*9:329*): "Defendants may not make *seriatim* motions that seek the same relief; rather Defendants were obligated to put forth all of their reasons for an award of attorneys' fees when they made their initial request." [*California Correctional Peace Officers Ass'n v. Virga*, supra, 181 CA4th at 45, 103 CR3d at 712-713 (emphasis in original)]

(5) [9:340] **"New or different facts, circumstances or law":** This terminology gives the court very broad power. [*Farmers Ins. Exch. v. Sup.Ct. (Wilson)* (2013) 218 CA4th 96, 106-107, 159 CR3d 580, 589 (citing text)]

There is no real limit on what the court may consider *except* that:

— it may not consider *matters presented at the earlier hearing* (such matters are neither "new" nor "different"); and

— a *later-enacted statute* that is *not retroactive* does not constitute a "new or different law" (see CCP §1008(f)).

(a) **Application**

- [9:340.1] D renewed a motion for summary judgment almost one year after the court had denied its earlier motion. D disclosed the earlier rulings and showed recent deposition admissions by P, which constituted "new facts." The renewed motion was properly granted. [*Graham v. Hansen* (1982) 128 CA3d 965, 971, 180 CR 604, 608]

- [9:340.2] P renewed its application for a right to attach order several months after its earlier application had been denied. A full showing of the facts was made at the time of the original application. Hence, there were no "new facts." But depositions obtained during the interim *explained the meaning* of the facts: "Nothing truly new is offered in terms of *substantive* facts . . . [but] there are many subtle nuances and subjective impressions . . . none of which could be read from the earlier declarations." Based thereon, it was proper for the court to grant the second application. [*Film Packages v. Brandywine Film Productions, Ltd.* (1987) 193 CA3d 824, 827, 238 CR 623, 625, fn. 3 (emphasis added)]

- [9:340.3] D's motion to compel arbitration of a consumer class action was denied on the ground that, under California law, the class action waivers in the underlying consumer contracts were unenforceable. Three years later, the U.S. Supreme Court held that the Federal Arbitration Act preempted California's rule and that class action waivers in consumer contracts provisions are enforceable. This intervening change in law permitted the trial court to revisit its prior order and issue a new order compelling arbitration. [*Phillips v. Sprint PCS* (2012) 209 CA4th 758, 768-769, 147 CR3d 274, 281-282]

[9:340.4] *Reserved.*

(b) [9:340.5] **Exception for later-enacted statutes:** Later-enacted statutes are not "new or different" laws if not retroactive in effect. [CCP §1008(f)]

Comment: Few statutes contain express nonretroactivity clauses. Thus, *until* a case determines a new law to be nonretroactive, that law may be ground for reconsideration or renewal of motions.

However, unless the language of the statute or the legislative history indicates otherwise, statutes are *presumed* to operate only *prospectively*. [*Interinsurance Exchange of Auto. Club of Southern Calif. v. Ohio Cas. Ins. Co.* (1962) 58 C2d 142, 149, 23 CR 592, 595; *Marriage of Bouquet* (1976) 16 C3d 583, 587, 128 CR 427, 429]

(c) [9:340.6] **Effect of judicial decisions:** By contrast to later-enacted statutes, "[o]rdinarily, judicial decisions apply retrospectively . . . Although prospective application may be appropriate in some circumstances when our decision alters a settled rule upon which parties justifiably relied, ordinarily this is only when a decision constitutes a clear break with decisions of *this* court or with practices we have sanctioned by implication, or when we disapprove[] a longstanding and widespread practice expressly approved by a near-unanimous body of lower-court authorities." [*Grafton Partners L.P. v. Sup.Ct. (PriceWaterhouseCoopers L.L.P.)* (2005) 36 C4th 944, 967, 32 CR3d 5, 20-21 (emphasis and second

© 2020 Thomson Reuters/The Rutter Group

brackets in original; internal quotes omitted); *Frlekin v. Apple Inc.* (2020) 8 C5th 1038, 1057, 258 CR3d 392, 407]

Comment: Even if a new appellate opinion does not technically qualify as a new law, it may sufficiently clarify the law as to qualify as a new circumstance, counseling a trial judge to revisit the ruling in question.

(6) [9:341] **Declaration required:** The renewal motion must be supported by an affidavit (declaration) stating:
— what motion or application was previously made;
— when it was made;
— the judge before whom it was made;
— what order or decision was then made; and
— what new or different facts, circumstances or law are claimed to exist. [CCP §1008(b)]

(7) [9:342] **Effect of failure to comply:** If the statutory requirements above (¶*9:341*) are not met, the renewal motion must be denied. If for any reason an order granting relief is made, that order may be revoked on ex parte application. [CCP §1008(b)]

(8) [9:343] **Contempt and sanctions:** As with motions for reconsideration, violations of CCP §1008 may be punished as a *contempt* of court. [CCP §1008(d)]

In addition, where the motion violates the attorney's certificate of merit under CCP §128.7, sanctions may be imposed. [CCP §1008(d)]

[9:344-344.19] *Reserved.*

5. [9:344.20] **Enforcement of Sanctions Orders:** A sanctions order is enforceable in the same way as a "money judgment": i.e., a writ of execution may be issued and levied on the property of the person sanctioned. [See CCP §§680.230, 680.270 & 699.510; *Newland v. Sup.Ct. (Sugasawara)* (1995) 40 CA4th 608, 615, 47 CR2d 24, 28 (citing text)]

a. [9:344.21] **Comment:** Many attorneys seem unaware that a sanctions order can be enforced by execution. Some request instead that the sanctioned party be held in contempt for failure to pay. Most judges prefer that the execution procedures be used, and will refuse to entertain contempt proceedings for collection purposes (at least until after execution has been attempted).

[9:344.22] ***PRACTICE POINTER:*** Another possibility is to obtain and record an *abstract of judgment,* creating a judgment lien on the sanctioned party's or counsel's home or other real property. To obtain an abstract of judgment, a specific *order directing issuance of a judgment* is required in some courts (to prevent harassing opposing parties in situations in which the sanctions are likely to be paid).

Cross-refer: For detailed discussion of writs of execution and judgment liens, see Ahart, *Cal. Prac. Guide: Enforcing Judgments & Debts* (TRG), Ch. 6.

[9:344.23-344.24] *Reserved.*

6. [9:344.25] **Appellate Review:** Law and motion rulings are generally not appealable orders, but the losing party may seek appellate review by petition for *extraordinary writ* (e.g., mandamus or prohibition). However, appellate courts deny such petitions in the vast majority of cases.

   Cross-refer: For detailed discussion of extraordinary writs, see Eisenberg, *Cal. Prac. Guide: Civil Appeals & Writs* (TRG), Ch. 15.

   ☞ [9:344.26] ***PRACTICE POINTER:*** To enhance prospects for appellate review, the losing party should *ask the trial court to include in its order* a statement to the effect that "there is a controlling question of law as to which there are substantial grounds for difference of opinion, appellate resolution of which may materially advance the conclusion of the litigation" (see CCP §166.1).

F. EX PARTE APPLICATIONS

1. [9:345] **Judicial Policy re Ex Parte Applications:** In this context "ex parte" motions are those heard on shortened time. Due process requires adequate notice and opportunity to be heard on any motion that affects the rights of the opposing party (*see ¶9:349*). Some statutes require fully noticed motions (e.g., 16 court days notice, *see ¶9:87 ff.*), which may be shortened on a showing of "good cause" (*see ¶9:364*). In other situations, due process is met by giving ex parte notice on shortened time (*see ¶9:347 ff.*). There are rare exceptions to these notice requirements, where, e.g., great or irreparable harm might result if notice were given (*see, e.g., ¶9:699*).

   Judges are usually reluctant to act on shortened notice in civil actions. There is always a concern that the opposing party has not had an adequate opportunity to present evidence and argument and the court does not have all the facts. In doubtful cases, the court usually will require the matter to be presented on statutory notice.

   ☞ [9:346] ***PRACTICE POINTER:*** In view of this policy, don't ask a judge for an ex parte order unless it is *clear* that such relief is proper. If there are any serious factual issues involved, don't expect the court to resolve them ex parte. You'll save a lot of time and effort by avoiding ex parte applications and filing a noticed motion. [*People ex rel. Allstate Ins. Co. v.*

© 2020 Thomson Reuters/The Rutter Group

Suh (2019) 37 CA5th 253, 257, 249 CR3d 500, 503 (citing text)]

a. [9:346.1] **Standards for professionalism:** Some courts have adopted the following guidelines as "civility in litigation recommendations to the bar":

- "Even where applicable laws or rules permit an *ex parte* application or communication to the Court . . . a lawyer should make diligent efforts to notify the opposing party . . . and should make reasonable efforts to *accommodate the schedule of such lawyer* to permit the opposing party to be represented on the application." [L.A. Sup.Ct. Rule 3.26, Appendix 3.A(j)(2) (emphasis added)]
- "Where the Rules permit an *ex parte* application or communication to the Court in an emergency situation, a lawyer should make such an application or communication (including an application to shorten an otherwise applicable time period) only where there is a *bona fide emergency* such that the lawyer's client will be seriously prejudiced by a failure to make the application or communication on regular notice." [L.A. Sup.Ct. Rule 3.26, Appendix 3.A(j)(3) (emphasis added)]

2. [9:347] **When Proper:** Only limited forms of relief are available ex parte. For the most part, these are authorized by statutes. (Very few statutes actually use the term "ex parte" relief; most authorize relief "upon application" or "for good cause shown.") The following are the most common situations in which ex parte orders may be obtained:

- to *shorten* or *extend* time to plead or for service of notice;
- to appoint a guardian ad litem;
- to amend a pleading by substituting the name of a fictitiously-named party (¶*6:612 ff.*);
- to amend a pleading by adding or deleting parties, or *correcting a mistake* in a party's name or in any other respect (¶*6:618 ff.*);
- to authorize service by publication (¶*4:247*) or substitute service on a corporation;
- to exceed page limits for memoranda of law (e.g., CRC 3.1113(e));
- to authorize discovery by plaintiff during the "hold" on discovery at the outset of the case (see CCP §§2025.210(b), 2030.020(b), (d); *and* ¶*8:444*);
- to control *deposition scheduling* (CCP §2025.270; *see* ¶*8:493.3*);

(Caution: Most other orders extending or shortening time for discovery require a noticed motion; *see* ¶*9:349.1*.)

©2020 Thomson Reuters/The Rutter Group

- dismissal for failure to amend complaint after demurrer sustained (CCP §581(f)(2); CRC 3.1320(h); *see* ¶*11:277.3*).

a. [9:348] **Not where statute requires notice:** Statutes affording relief upon "notice" or a "noticed motion" are not the proper subject of an ex parte application and cannot be satisfied by compliance with CRC 3.1200's notice requirements for ex parte relief.

☞ [9:348.1] ***PRACTICE POINTER:*** No matter how dire the emergency, the court cannot grant ex parte relief where a statute requires a noticed motion. The court can, however, *shorten the amount of notice required* for hearing the motion; *see* ¶*9:364*.

b. [9:349] **Compare—statutes not specifically requiring notice; due process limitation:** Many statutes refer only to an "application" or a "motion" and do not specifically require notice of hearing. Even so, courts may *not* grant ex parte relief that would affect the opposing party's rights: "The general rule is that notice of motion must be given whenever the order sought *may affect the rights of an adverse party*." [*McDonald v. Severy* (1936) 6 C2d 629, 631, 59 P2d 98, 99 (emphasis added)]

In such cases, therefore, a statute silent on the question of notice will *not* be interpreted to permit ex parte relief. Rather, use of the term "motion" rather than "ex parte application" implies that regular notice and hearing requirements are generally applicable to motions. [*St. Paul Fire & Marine Ins. Co. v. Sup.Ct. (Borak)* (1984) 156 CA3d 82, 86, 202 CR 571, 573 (disapproved on other grounds by *Wilcox v. Birtwhistle* (1999) 21 C4th 973, 983, 90 CR2d 260, 267, fn. 12)]

(1) [9:349.1] **Application:** Thus, for example, regular notice requirements apply to motions:
— to extend the time to plead after it has already expired (*see* ¶*6:386*);
— to shorten or extend the time for responding to discovery requests (e.g., interrogatories, RFAs, and demands for documents) (see CCP §§2030.260(a), 2031.260 & 2033.250);
— to permit discovery after the discovery "cut-off" date (CCP §2024.050);
— for a protective order to terminate deposition (*St. Paul Fire & Marine Ins. Co. v. Sup.Ct. (Borak)*, supra, 156 CA3d at 86, 202 CR at 573);
— to certify a class action (*Carabini v. Sup.Ct. (King)* (1994) 26 CA4th 239, 243, 31 CR2d 520, 523).

(2) [9:349.2] **Compare—where opposing party's rights not affected:** But ex parte relief may be allowed where the motion has no effect on the opposing party's rights or liability. For example, a motion:

© 2020 Thomson Reuters/The Rutter Group

— to *substitute parties* on death or transfer of interest of one of the original parties. [CCP §377.33; *see* ¶*2:500 ff.*]

3. [9:350] **Procedure:** Before presentation to the court, the application must be filed in the court clerk's office and appropriate filing fees paid.

In cases assigned to an independent calendar judge, it may be necessary to contact that judge's clerk to schedule a hearing.

Some courts have local rules governing ex parte application forms and procedures and scheduling of such matters. [See L.A. Sup.Ct. Rule 3.6(d); S.F. Sup.Ct. Rule 9.0] (Although CRC 3.20 preempts local rules relating to ex parte matters, rules that "relate only to the internal management of the court" are not affected; see CRC 10.613.)

a. [9:351] **Notice requirement:** No application for ex parte relief may be made unless the applicant provides a declaration showing compliance with the notice requirements of CRC 3.1204. [See CRC 3.1204(b)]

(1) [9:351.1] **Distinguish—statutory notice requirements:** Do not confuse the above (¶*9:351*) with statutory notice requirements. Where statutes require that a motion be made "upon notice," it *cannot* be granted ex parte. The notification to opposing counsel described below (¶*9:352 ff.*) is *not* the equivalent of statutory notice (¶*9:348*).

(2) [9:352] **Minimum notice:** Absent a showing of exceptional circumstances, the applicant is required to give all other parties notice no later than 10:00 a.m. the court day before the ex parte appearance. [CRC 3.1203(a)]

Exception—unlawful detainer proceedings: A party seeking an ex parte order in an unlawful detainer proceeding may provide shorter notice; the notice given need only be "reasonable." [CRC 3.1203(b)]

(3) [9:353] **Content of notice:** The person giving notice is required to state with specificity the nature of the relief to be requested and the date, time and place the application will be made. [CRC 3.1204(a)(1)]

He or she must also "attempt to determine" whether the opposing party and/or counsel will appear to oppose the ex parte application. [CRC 3.1204(a)(2)]

(4) [9:353.1] **Form of notice:** The notification may be either in writing or oral. The manner of notice must be disclosed in the declaration of notice (¶*9:357 ff.*).

[9:353.2] ***PRACTICE POINTER:*** Where permissible, use electronic service (¶*9:86.25 ff.*) or fax service (¶*9:86.10 ff.*). If the parties have not agreed to use an electronic service provider, fax service may be preferable because it provides a written record of receipt if notice is disputed.

(5) [9:354] **Parties to be notified:** Notice must be given to *all* parties (not just opposing parties). [CRC 3.1203(a)]

[9:354.1-354.4] *Reserved.*

(6) [9:354.5] **Compare—statutes excusing notice:** Although the matter is unclear, CRC 3.1203-3.1204 apparently do not apply where statutes authorize court orders *without notice* to the opposing party:

(a) [9:354.6] **Minor amendments to pleadings; extensions of time to plead:** CCP §473(a)(1) authorizes courts to:

— enlarge the time for answer or demurrer; or

— allow minor amendments to a party's pleadings ("by adding or striking out the name of any party, or by correcting a mistake in the name of a party, or a mistake in any other respect") (e.g., *"Doe" amendments*).

Although the statute does not expressly state such relief may be granted *without* notice to the adverse party, that is implicit in the statute's requirement for notice for *other amendments* to the pleadings and for orders allowing tardy answers. [See CCP §473(a)(1), 2nd sent.]

(b) [9:354.7] **Dismissal following failure to amend:** CCP §581(f)(2) authorizes dismissal *without a noticed motion* where, after a demurrer is sustained with leave to amend, plaintiff fails to amend within the permitted time (*see* ¶*11:277.3*). However, the CRC 3.1203 requirement of informal notice to opposing counsel before making an ex parte application to the court *does* apply. [*Datig v. Dove Books, Inc.* (1999) 73 CA4th 964, 977, 87 CR2d 719, 728-729 (superseded by rule on other grounds)]

(c) [9:354.8] **Application for appointment of guardian ad litem:** Notice of a guardian ad litem application is not required in most circumstances. [See *Alex R. v. Sup.Ct. (Mirian R.)* (2016) 248 CA4th 1, 8-9, 203 CR3d 251, 255-256]

[9:354.9] *Reserved.*

(7) [9:354.10] **Compare—OSCs:** In the past, courts routinely granted ex parte applications for OSCs without advance notification to opposing counsel. However, this is apparently no longer permissible; CRC 3.1203 apparently requires advance notice to opposing counsel

© 2020 Thomson Reuters/The Rutter Group

even where the only "relief" sought is setting a hearing date on an OSC. (Such relief may be obtained without a personal appearance, however; *see* ¶*9:370.6.*)

b. [9:355] **Form of application:** Ex parte applications must be in writing and include all of the following:

- *Application:* An application containing the case caption and stating the relief requested (¶*9:356*);
- *Declaration showing factual basis for emergency or other statutory basis for ex parte relief* (*see* ¶*9:358 ff.*);
- *Declaration of notice* (which may be combined with the declaration showing cause for ex parte relief) (*see* ¶*9:357*);
- *Points and authorities;* and
- *Proposed order.* [CRC 3.1201]

[9:355.1] ***PRACTICE POINTER:*** It is common practice to combine the application and declarations.

FORM: Ex Parte Motions, *see Form 9A:18* in Rivera, *Cal. Prac. Guide: Civ. Pro. Before Trial FORMS* (TRG).

(1) [9:356] **Application:** The request for an ex parte order must be in writing (CRC 3.1201) and conform to the form and format requirements of court papers generally (CRC 2.100 ff.).

(a) [9:356.1] **Identify opposing counsel/party:** The application must state the name, address, email address and telephone number of any attorney known to be representing the opposing party (or the party's name, address, email address and telephone number if there is no known attorney). [CRC 3.1202(a)]

(b) [9:356.2] **Disclose any prior application:** If the same ex parte relief was previously refused in whole or in part, the application must include a "full disclosure" of the prior application and the court's actions thereon. [CRC 3.1202(b)]

(2) [9:357] **Declaration of notice:** An application for ex parte relief must be accompanied by a declaration of notice based on personal knowledge, setting forth:

(a) [9:357.1] **Attempts to inform opposing party:** Within the required time (no later than 10:00 a.m., one court day before the hearing; *see* ¶*9:352*), the applicant either:

— informed the opposing party when and where the application would be made; *or*

— attempted in good faith to inform the opposing party but was unable to do so, *specifying the efforts made* to inform the opposing party; *or*

— for reasons specified, was not required to inform the opposing party. [CRC 3.1204(b)]

If notice was given later than 10:00 a.m. on the court day before the ex parte application, the declaration regarding notice must explain the exceptional circumstances that justify the shorter notice. [CRC 3.1204(c)]

(b) [9:357.2] **Required information:** The declaration must specify the date, time, manner and name of the party informed, the relief sought, any response, and whether opposition is expected (or a statement of reasons why notice should not be required, ¶*9:357.1*). [CRC 3.1204(b)]

FORM: Ex Parte Application for Order Extending Time, *see Form 9A:18.1* in Rivera, *Cal. Prac. Guide: Civ. Pro. Before Trial FORMS* (TRG). (An optional Judicial Council form can also be used for this purpose (CM-020).)

[9:357.3] ***PRACTICE POINTER:*** A separate declaration is not required; you can combine your declaration of notice with the required declaration showing grounds for ex parte relief (¶*9:358*).

Make sure your declaration states *facts*, rather than mere conclusions. For example, if you are unable to reach opposing counsel, state the times of day you telephoned, with whom you spoke, what messages you left, etc. (Do *not* say simply, "I attempted unsuccessfully to reach opposing counsel.")

[9:357.4] *Reserved.*

(c) [9:357.5] **Clerk must accept for filing despite improper notice:** The court clerk must accept an ex parte application for filing and promptly present it to the judge for consideration, notwithstanding the applicant's failure to comply with the notice requirements above (¶*9:357 ff.*). [CRC 3.1205]

(3) [9:358] **Declaration showing "good cause" for ex parte relief:** The application for ex parte relief must be accompanied by a declaration containing an "affirmative factual showing" consisting of "competent testimony based on personal knowledge of *irreparable harm, immediate danger or any other statutory basis* for granting relief ex parte." [CRC 3.1202(c) (emphasis added)]

(As stated above (¶*9:357.3*), this declaration is usually combined with the declaration of notice.)

The following illustrate application of this requirement:

© 2020 Thomson Reuters/The Rutter Group

(a) [9:359] **Orders extending time:** On a showing of "good cause," the court may grant ex parte an extension of time to *plead* for up to an additional 30 days, without the consent of the adverse party. [CCP §1054]

1) [9:360] **Requirements:** The application should state the nature of the case, and a declaration filed in support of the application should *state any previous extension granted* (either by stipulation or court order). [CRC 2.20(b)]

2) [9:361] **Judicial attitude:** Usually, courts are quite liberal in granting at least one extension of time to plead, etc. The "good cause" requirement is satisfied simply by statements that the attorney's "press of business" prevents him or her from being able to prepare a response within the time required; and that an extension was refused by opposing counsel (or he or she could not be reached in time, etc.).

But, courts may be reluctant to extend time more than once on an ex parte basis.

3) [9:362] **Service:** If the order is granted, a copy thereof must be *served on opposing counsel within 24 hours*, unless the court expressly orders otherwise. [CRC 2.20(c)]

4) [9:363] **Limitation—no extension after time expired:** Time cannot be extended after it has already expired. (No room for nunc pro tunc orders to avoid entry of default.) [See *Coast Elec. Service, Inc. v. Jensen* (1931) 111 CA 124, 126, 295 P 346, 347—dealing with costs memo]

(b) [9:364] **Order shortening time:** Judges are usually more cautious about shortening time for notice than about extending time. An application for an order shortening time must be supported by a declaration showing "good cause" for the order. Mere lack of time for statutory notice is *not* a sufficient showing. [See CRC 3.1202(c); *Eliceche v. Federal Land Bank Ass'n* (2002) 103 CA4th 1349, 1369, 128 CR2d 200, 216—upholding order shortening 45-day notice on CCP §583.410 discretionary dismissal motion (*discussed at ¶11:134 ff.*)]

[9:365] ***PRACTICE POINTER:*** Before asking for ex parte relief, ask opposing counsel to *stipulate* to shortened time. If he or she refuses, you can state this fact in your application for ex parte relief, and it may help convince the judge that there is "good cause" for an order shortening time.

1) [9:366] **Contents of order:** If such relief is granted, the order should specify:

- The date, time and place of the court hearing (for which notice was shortened);

  Most courts are inclined to give the opposing party as much notice as reasonable under the circumstances. In some courts, hearings will not be set fewer than *7 days* after the date of application unless it is shown that action sooner is necessary.

- A deadline for service of copies of the moving papers and the court order shortening time; and for filing proof of such service with the clerk of the law and motion department; and

- The dates by which any opposition papers and any reply papers must be filed and served for consideration at the hearing, and the manner of service. To accommodate the time pressures, frequently a reply is waived.

FORM: Ex Parte Application for Order Shortening Time and Proposed Order, *see Form 9A:18.2* in Rivera, *Cal. Prac. Guide: Civ. Pro. Before Trial FORMS* (TRG).

2) [9:367] **Service:** Service by hand is usually required for both the moving and responding papers.

3) [9:368] **Limitations:** Statutes may limit the court's power to shorten time for notice of a motion hearing:

   a) [9:368.1] **Summary judgment or summary adjudication:** The court may *not* shorten the 75-day notice period required on a summary judgment or summary adjudication motion. [CCP §437c(a); see *McMahon v. Sup.Ct. (American Equity Ins. Co.)* (2003) 106 CA4th 112, 115, 130 CR2d 407, 409—statutory provision allowing court to shorten time specifically applied to procedures *other than* notice]

c. [9:369] **To whom presented:** If the ex parte application relates to a hearing or procedure then pending before a particular judge (e.g., in cases assigned for all purposes to an independent calendar judge), the application must be pre-

© 2020 Thomson Reuters/The Rutter Group

sented to that judge. [CRC 2.20(a); see *Legg v. Brody* (1960) 187 CA2d 79, 83, 9 CR 593, 596—order extending time obtained from different judge held "ineffective and of no force"]

If the judge before whom the matter is pending is unavailable, the application should be presented to the judge assigned to hear the unavailable judge's calendar, the supervising judge or the judge of the master calendar department, as appropriate.

If the case has not been assigned to a particular judge, it may be presented to any judge of the court. In larger courts, a judge or commissioner is often regularly assigned to hear ex parte applications.

[9:370] ***PRACTICE POINTERS:*** The judge may have only a few moments to read your application, so make it clear and concise:

- *At the beginning,* state (a) exactly what orders are requested; (b) the court's legal authority for making these orders ex parte; and (c) circumstances constituting "good cause" for granting such orders.
- Remember to include a proposed order (separate from the application so that it will be easy to find).
- Because the court's file may not be readily available (many are now in electronic format), consider bringing copies with you of the key documents in the file for the judge and opposing counsel.

d. [9:370.1] **Service of papers before hearing:** The parties appearing at the ex parte hearing must serve the application (and any written opposition) on all other appearing parties "at the first reasonable opportunity." Absent exceptional circumstances, no hearing will be conducted unless such service has been made. [CRC 3.1206]

Some judges have rules or policies requiring ex parte papers to be served on the opposing party well *before* the hearing—sometimes, the day preceding the hearing. Although such rules and policies are probably preempted by CRC 3.20(a) (*see ¶9:13.2*), the safer course is to comply with them.

Some e-filing procedures have deadlines for e-filing of ex parte papers. [See Los Angeles Superior Court General Order re Mandatory Electronic Filing for Civil, available on the court's website (*www.lacourt.org*)—"a) Ex parte applications and all documents in support thereof must be electronically filed no later than 10:00 a.m. the court day before the ex parte hearing. b) Any written opposition to an ex parte application must be electronically filed by 8:30 a.m. the day of the ex parte hearing. A printed courtesy copy of any opposition to an ex parte application must be provided to the court the day of the ex parte hearing"]

If the moving party intends to appear by telephone, the papers must be served no later than 10:00 a.m. two court days before the ex parte hearing. [CRC 3.670(h)(3); *see* ¶*9:159.2 ff.*]

[9:370.2] ***PRACTICE POINTER:*** The "first reasonable opportunity" contemplated by CRC 3.1206 often means serving opposing counsel *at the ex parte hearing itself.* Formal service (as required for noticed motions) rarely will be possible because ex parte matters typically are heard on as little as 24-hour notice (*see* ¶*9:352*).

If there is time to get the papers to opposing counsel in advance (i.e., by email or fax), professional courtesy suggests this be done. Don't sandbag your opponent by waiting until the matter is called before serving your papers. The judge is likely to treat this as a failure to serve before the hearing and may defer the matter.

[9:370.3-370.4] *Reserved.*

e. [9:370.5] **Appearance by applicant or counsel required at hearing:** Except as noted below (¶*3:370.6*), an ex parte application will not be "considered" without an *appearance, either in person or by telephone,* by the applicant or applicant's attorney (i.e., no sending process servers or paralegals). [See CRC 3.1207]

(1) [9:370.6] **Exceptions:** Ex parte applications will be considered without a personal appearance in the following cases only:

— applications for extensions of time to serve pleadings;
— applications to file points and authorities in excess of the applicable page limit;
— setting a hearing date on an alternative writ or order to show cause; and
— stipulations by the parties for a court order. [CRC 3.1207]

(2) [9:370.7] **Effect of failure to appear:** Subject to the above exceptions (¶*9:370.6*), if the applicant's counsel fails to appear at the time specified in the notice to opposing counsel, no ex parte relief will be granted. [See CRC 3.1207]

Any subsequent application for the same relief will require additional notice to opposing counsel; and should show "good cause" for the failure to appear. Moreover, sanctions and an award of fees and costs to opposing counsel may be available under CRC 2.30 after notice and an opportunity to be heard.

© 2020 Thomson Reuters/The Rutter Group

f. [9:370.8] **Ruling on application:** The judge often will grant or deny the application without a formal hearing (see CCP §166(a)(1)), sometimes by minute order. In that case, it is presumed that the court considered both the moving and opposition papers. [See *Barboni v. Tuomi* (2012) 210 CA4th 340, 352, 148 CR3d 581, 591—trial court's failure to mention opposition papers in minute order did not require reversal of ex parte order: "We decline to impose on the trial bench an unduly burdensome requirement that any order issued without a hearing must specifically state that an opposition was considered"]

G. MOTIONS REGULATING COUNSEL

[9:371] There is a strong judicial interest in regulating who appears as attorney of record. As a practical matter, it is the only means the court has for retaining effective control of the case. Among other important purposes, an attorney's appearance provides the court and parties with the name and address of the person with whom they must communicate with respect to the party represented.

Some changes involving the status of counsel as attorneys of record may be made unilaterally; others require a motion. In all cases, however, the court must be apprised of the identity of all counsel of record.

1. [9:371a] **Designation of Attorneys of Record:** The first page of the pleadings identifies "the attorney for the party in whose behalf the paper is presented . . ." (CRC 2.111(1)). When a law firm is listed as "attorneys of record," the court will permit any attorney from that firm (who is a member of the California Bar) to appear for the client without the need to file an association or substitution of attorneys. [*Ellis Law Group, LLP v. Nevada City Sugar Loaf Properties, LLC* (2014) 230 CA4th 244, 258, 178 CR3d 490, 500-501]

2. [9:371.1] **Association of Counsel:** Counsel often ask other counsel to make appearances for them. If they are not members of the same law firm, a formal association of counsel is technically required. Some courts are strict in enforcing this requirement; others are not.

   An association of counsel constitutes a formal appearance in the action. That counsel cannot limit the effect by claiming to be appearing "specially." This has no effect (it is a misuse of a term applicable to personal jurisdiction over parties).

3. [9:372] **Changing Attorney of Record:** The attorney of record for a party may be changed either by mutual consent of the party and counsel, or by court order. [CCP §284]

   a. [9:373] **Ethical considerations:** While the client has the right to discharge the lawyer at any time, there are ethical limitations on the lawyer's right to withdraw.

      The Rules of Professional Conduct (CRPC) allow a lawyer to withdraw if, among other things:

- the client *insists upon presenting* a claim or defense in a litigation matter, or asserting a position or making a demand in a nonlitigation matter, that is *not warranted* and cannot be supported by good faith argument for extension, modification or reversal of the law; or
- the client either seeks to pursue a criminal or fraudulent course of conduct or has used the lawyer's services to pursue a criminal or fraudulent course of conduct; or
- the client insists that the lawyer pursue a course of conduct that is criminal or fraudulent; or
- the client breaches a material term of an agreement with or obligation to the lawyer regarding the representation and the lawyer gives a reasonable warning after the breach that the lawyer will withdraw unless the client fulfills the agreement or performs the obligation (e.g., pay fees or expenses); or
- *other conduct* by the client "renders it *unreasonably difficult* for the lawyer to carry out the representation effectively." [CRPC 1.16(b) (formerly CRPC 3-700(C)) (emphasis added)]

(1) **Application**

- [9:374] A motion to be relieved is apparently proper simply because of a *personality clash* with the client. The *breakdown* in the attorney-client relationship is ground for allowing the attorney to withdraw. [See *Estate of Falco v. Decker* (1987) 188 CA3d 1004, 1014, 233 CR 807, 813]

[9:375-377] *Reserved.*

b. [9:378] **By signed substitution of attorneys:** Where the change is by consent, it can be effected at any time (even on the eve of trial, but do not expect the trial to be postponed as a result) simply by filing and serving a signed *substitution of attorneys.* Permission of court is not required. [CCP §284(1); see *Hock v. Sup.Ct. (Woodside Business Park)* (1990) 221 CA3d 670, 671, 270 CR 579, 580 (invalidating local rule that required leave of court to substitute after trial set)]

FORM: Substitution of Attorney—Civil (Judicial Council form MC-050), *see Form 9A:20* in Rivera, *Cal. Prac. Guide: Civ. Pro. Before Trial FORMS* (TRG).

(1) [9:379] **In pro per:** If a party is being substituted in propria persona, the substitution form must include the mailing address and telephone of the party.

© 2020 Thomson Reuters/The Rutter Group

(2) [9:380] **Limitation—attorney retained by guardian ad litem:** The attorney of record for a minor appearing through a guardian ad litem can be substituted out in favor of other qualified counsel. But court approval is required (*see ¶9:381*). The guardian ad litem *cannot* be substituted *in pro per* because this could jeopardize the rights of the minor whom the guardian represents. [*Torres v. Friedman* (1985) 169 CA3d 880, 888, 215 CR 604, 609; *J.W. v. Sup.Ct.* (1993) 17 CA4th 958, 963-965, 22 CR2d 527, 529-530; *see ¶2:84*]

c. [9:381] **By court order:** If mutual consent is not obtainable, a court order is required. Either the client or attorney may seek such order upon noticed motion served on the other and upon all other parties who have appeared in the case. [CCP §284(2); CRC 3.1362]

Compare—limited scope representation: Different rules apply where the attorney was retained for only a limited scope representation (e.g., to appear at a specific hearing, etc.). [CRC 3.36; *see ¶1:192 ff.*]

(1) [9:381.1] **Opposing party's motion to disqualify counsel:** The opposing party may move to disqualify counsel for conflicts of interest based on former representation of that party, or to prevent disclosure of confidential information obtained in the course of such representation. *See discussion at ¶9:406.5 ff.*

(2) [9:382] **Client's motion to recuse counsel:** A party has the right to be represented by counsel of his or her choice. Therefore, the client's right to recuse (substitute out) existing counsel is *absolute.* I.e., on proper notice to the existing counsel and to all other parties, the client is entitled to a court order substituting new counsel, or substituting the client in propria persona.

(a) [9:383] **Client's files:** Existing counsel must turn over the client's files to new counsel immediately. It is unethical to withhold the client's files until fees or other disputes are settled. (*See discussion at ¶1:449 ff.*)

(b) [9:384] **Right to fees:** Whether or not there was "cause" for discharge, the attorney is entitled to the *reasonable value* of services rendered before the discharge. Where the case was being handled on a contingency fee basis, such fees are payable only when the recovery is obtained. But the attorney may be given a lien on the cause of action to secure such payment. (*See discussion at ¶1:421 ff.*)

(3) [9:385] **Attorney's motion to be relieved as attorney of record:** If the attorney is the moving party, the right to withdraw is conditioned on proper notice and a showing of why a court order is required (i.e., why substitution by mutual consent not obtained). [CRC 3.1362]

The attorney must disclose enough information to satisfy the court that grounds exists for relieving the attorney. (Grounds most often asserted are the client's breach of the retainer agreement, the client's refusal to follow the attorney's advice or other conduct showing a breakdown of the attorney-client relationship.)

Where the ground claimed is a "conflict of interest" with the client, the attorney must describe the *general nature* of the conflict as fully as possible, within the confines of the attorney-client privilege. [*Manfredi & Levine v. Sup.Ct. (Barles)* (1998) 66 CA4th 1128, 1134, 78 CR2d 494, 498—trial court need not accept attorney's claim that he had received "unsolicited and confidential information" which prevented him from providing further representation to client]

☞ [9:385.1] ***CAUTION:*** CRC 3.1362 contains a number of technical requirements for a motion to be relieved as counsel that are frequently overlooked, resulting in these motions having to be continued for compliance. Counsel should carefully read the rule and comply with each of its requirements when preparing the motion. Also note that counsel is not relieved as attorney of record until the order so providing has been served on the client *and* proof of such service has been filed with the court.

(a) [9:385.2] **Limitations:** The court may exercise its discretion not to permit withdrawal on the eve of trial or under other circumstances that pose obvious risk of prejudice to the client.

Compare—consensual substitution on eve of trial: Even a consensual substitution that would not require court approval might require explanation in light of an impending trial date. [See *Filbin v. Fitzgerald* (2012) 211 CA4th 154, 170, 149 CR3d 422, 435 (citing text)—judge might require "information to justify terminating the attorney-client relationship" where withdrawal hearing only 17 days before scheduled trial]

1) [9:385.3] **Where counsel representing minor:** An attorney must obtain court approval prior to withdrawing as attorney of record for a minor appearing through a guardian ad litem. [*Torres v. Friedman* (1985) 169 CA3d 880, 887, 215 CR 604, 608]

© 2020 Thomson Reuters/The Rutter Group

The court has a duty to see that the minor's interests are not prejudiced by those appointed to represent him or her, and may *refuse* to relieve the attorney until other qualified counsel has been obtained. If, due to extenuating circumstances, the court allows the attorney to withdraw, it must apprise the guardian of the need to obtain qualified replacement counsel and that the guardian may not proceed in propria persona. [*Torres v. Friedman*, supra, 169 CA3d at 888, 215 CR at 609]

2) [9:385.4] **Where dispositive motion pending:** It may be error for the court to permit counsel for a minor to withdraw when a dispositive motion (e.g., motion for summary judgment) is pending and a new attorney has not yet been retained. [*Mossanen v. Monfared* (2000) 77 CA4th 1402, 1409-1410, 92 CR2d 459, 463-464]

- [9:385.5] Plaintiff's counsel should not be permitted to withdraw from representing a minor where a new attorney has not yet been retained and defendant's motion for summary judgment is imminent. [*Mossanen v. Monfared*, supra, 77 CA4th at 1409-1410, 92 CR2d at 463-464]

[9:385.6-385.9] *Reserved.*

(b) [9:385.10] **Judicial Council forms:** Forms adopted by the Judicial Council must be used for the notice of motion and motion to be relieved as counsel, supporting declaration and order. [CRC 3.1362(a); *see ¶9:386, 9:387 & 9:392*]

Compare—limited scope representation: Different forms must be used where the attorney was retained for only a limited scope representation. [CRC 3.36; *see ¶1:192 ff.*]

[9:385.11] ***PRACTICE POINTER:*** Failure to use these forms is a common error in seeking to be relieved as counsel. Judges should never grant the motion if it is not on the Judicial Council forms.

The second most common error is failure to check all the applicable boxes and to provide all the information required by the forms. If these forms are completed properly, no other papers are ordinarily required.

1) [9:386] **Notice of motion:** The notice of motion must be directed to the client and must be on the Judicial Council form. [CRC 3.1362(a)]

- ***FORM:*** Notice of Motion and Motion to be Relieved as Counsel—Civil (MC-051), *see Form 9A:21* in Rivera, *Cal. Prac. Guide: Civ. Pro. Before Trial FORMS* (TRG).

2) [9:387] **Supporting declaration:** The notice must be accompanied by counsel's declaration showing why a substitution of attorneys by consent could not be obtained. Such declaration must be stated "in general terms and without compromising the confidentiality of the attorney-client relationship." [CRC 3.1362(c)]

   - ***FORM:*** Declaration in Support of Attorney's Motion to be Relieved as Counsel—Civil (MC-052), *see Form 9A:22* in Rivera, *Cal. Prac. Guide: Civ. Pro. Before Trial FORMS* (TRG).

   [9:387.1-387.4] *Reserved.*

3) [9:387.5] **No memorandum of points and authorities:** Unlike other motions, no memorandum of points and authorities need be filed or served with a motion to be relieved as counsel. [CRC 3.1362(b)]

(c) [9:388] **Service:** The notice of motion, declaration and proposed order must be served on the client and all other parties who have appeared in the case. [CRC 3.1362(d)]

1) [9:389] **Special requirements where client served by mail:** When the client is served by mail, the attorney's declaration must show that the client's address was *confirmed within the last 30 days* and *how* it was confirmed (i.e., by conversation, telephone, or mail with return receipt requested). [CRC 3.1362(d)]

   Merely stating the papers were sent to the client's last known address and were not returned will *not* itself be sufficient to demonstrate that the address is current. [CRC 3.1362(d)]

   [9:390] *Reserved.*

2) [9:391] **Where client's address unknown:** If the attorney is unable to confirm that the client's address is current, the attorney's declaration must state what was done in attempting to obtain a current address, such as:
   — mailing the motion papers to the client's last known address with return receipt requested;
   — calling the client's last known telephone number(s);

© 2020 Thomson Reuters/The Rutter Group

— contacting persons familiar with the client (specify);
— conducting a search (describe); and
— other efforts, which must be specified. [CRC 3.1362(d)]

Counsel must also justify why he or she should be relieved even if the client cannot be served with the moving papers.

If the attorney's declaration establishes that the client's residence address is unknown despite reasonable efforts to locate the client, the client can be served by delivering the moving papers to the *court clerk.* [CCP §1011(b)(3); CRC 3.1362(d) (last sent.)]

a) [9:391.1] **Special requirements where client served by electronic service:** When the client is served by electronic service, the attorney's declaration must show that the client's electronic address was *confirmed within 30 days.* [CRC 3.1362(d)]

"Merely demonstrating that the notice was sent to the client's last known address and was not returned or no electronic delivery failure message was received is not, by itself, sufficient to demonstrate that the address is current." [CRC 3.1362(d)]

b) [9:391.2] **Service on court clerk:** The papers must be placed in an envelope addressed to the clerk and prepared in accordance with CRC 3.252.

(d) [9:392] **Order:** A copy of the proposed order must be lodged with the court clerk and served on the client with the moving papers. [CRC 3.1362(e)]

The order must be prepared on the Judicial Council form.

It must specify all hearing dates scheduled in the action or proceeding, including the trial date, if known. If no hearing date is presently scheduled, the court may set one and specify the date in the order. [CRC 3.1362(d), (e)]

FORM: Order Granting Attorney's Motion to be Relieved as Counsel—Civil (MC-053), *see Form 9A:23* in Rivera, *Cal. Prac. Guide: Civ. Pro. Before Trial FORMS* (TRG).

1) [9:392.1] **Warnings to client:** The Official Form Order provides warnings to the client of

adverse results that may occur if the client fails to obtain representation.

(e) [9:393] **Service of order:** A copy of the signed order must be served on the client and on all parties who have appeared in the action. [CRC 3.1362(e)]

The court may delay the effective date of the order until proof of service of a copy of the signed order on the client has been filed with the court. [CRC 3.1362(e); *Gamet v. Blanchard* (2001) 91 CA4th 1276, 1286, 111 CR2d 439, 446—lack of proper service rendered order inoperative]

[9:394-400] *Reserved.*

4. [9:401] **Out-Of-State Attorneys; Admission Pro Hac Vice:** An out-of-state lawyer, not admitted to practice in California, may be admitted *pro hac vice*—i.e., to appear and take part in a particular action only. Applications for such admission are generally heard as law and motion matters. [CRC 9.40]

The rule applies to individual lawyers, not law firms. Out-of-state law firms cannot be admitted *pro hac vice*. It is sufficient that the *firm member handling the case* is either a California lawyer or has been admitted *pro hac vice*. [*Daybreak Group, Inc. v. Three Creeks Ranch, LLC* (2008) 162 CA4th 37, 42, 75 CR3d 365, 367—firm member of Montana law firm was admitted to practice in California]

If permission is granted, the out-of-state attorney is admitted to practice on the same terms as a local attorney, and is subject to the same professional standards and sanctions and to the jurisdiction of California courts. [See CRC 9.40(f)]

a. [9:402] **Requirements:** To be eligible for admission *pro hac vice:*

- The applicant must be admitted to practice before a U.S. court, or the highest court of any state or territory; and
- He or she must *not* be a California resident, nor regularly engaged in practice or other business here; and
- A member of the California Bar must be associated as attorney of record in the case. [CRC 9.40(a)]

Absent special circumstances, *repeated appearances* by out-of-state counsel in California lawsuits is cause for *denial* of his or her application. [*Walter E. Heller Western, Inc. v. Sup.Ct.* (1980) 111 CA3d 706, 709, 168 CR 785, 786; see *Golba v. Dick's Sporting Goods, Inc.* (2015) 238 CA4th 1251, 1266, 190 CR3d 337, 348—application denied where attorney had appeared 12 times in California state courts within prior 11 months]

b. [9:403] **Application:** The applicant must file a verified application (often a declaration) stating: (1) the applicant's

© 2020 Thomson Reuters/The Rutter Group

residence and office addresses; (2) the court or courts in which he or she is admitted to practice and the dates of admission; (3) that he or she is currently in good standing in such courts; (4) that he or she is not currently suspended or disbarred in any court; (5) the title and case number of any action in this state (presumably whether state or federal) in which he or she has applied to appear *pro hac vice* during the preceding two years; and (6) the name, address and telephone number of the active member of the State Bar who is attorney of record. [CRC 9.40(d)—filing fee must accompany application]

FORM: Application for Admission Pro Hac Vice, *see Form 9A:24* in Rivera, *Cal. Prac. Guide: Civ. Pro. Before Trial FORMS* (TRG).

[9:403.1] ***PRACTICE POINTER:*** Because the notion of "regularly" practicing law within the meaning of CRC 9.40(a) is not fully defined, applicants should state in their applications the number of times they have been admitted pro hac vice in the last two years and be prepared to respond to inquiries from the court on how much time in those last two years has been spent on California cases.

Many judges handle these applications without a hearing. But in the event of an issue, those judges will either issue an order requiring further information or set a hearing.

c. [9:404] **Service:** Copies of the application must be served by mail upon all parties who have appeared in the action, and also upon the *State Bar* at its San Francisco office at least 16 court days before the hearing (notice governed by CCP §1005). A fee (currently $50) must be paid to the State Bar. [CRC 9.40]

[9:405] *Reserved.*

d. [9:406] **Distinguish—registered foreign legal consultants:** Lawyers licensed in foreign countries may register as foreign legal consultants in California. (Application is made to the State Bar.) [CRC 9.44]

Such registration permits the foreign lawyer to consult and advise regarding laws of the country in which he or she is licensed. It does *not*, however, entitle the foreign lawyer to represent anyone in court; nor to prepare court papers or other documents affecting personal or property rights or status in the U.S.; nor to render legal advice on the law of the State of California, any other state, the District of Columbia, the United States or any jurisdiction other than the one for which the lawyer is registered. [See CRC 9.44(d)]

e. [9:406a] **Distinguish—international arbitration:** Non-California lawyers may represent parties in California in international arbitration. [CCP §1297.185]

f. [9:406.1] **Sanctioning pro hac vice counsel:** The court has *inherent power* to *revoke* an out-of-state attorney's pro hac vice status for conduct that would be ground for *disqualification* of a California lawyer (e.g., fraud on court). The court's power to impose *sanctions,* however, is *limited to those authorized by statute* against California lawyers. [*Sheller v. Sup.Ct. (Farmers New World Life Ins. Co.)* (2008) 158 CA4th 1697, 1716, 71 CR3d 207, 220—no inherent power to order payment of opposing party's fees or to impose reprimand]

[9:406.2-406.4] *Reserved.*

5. [9:406.5] **Motion to Recuse (Disqualify) Opposing Counsel:** A party may move to recuse (disqualify) counsel for the opposing party on grounds recognized by law, including mandatory disqualification for conflict of interest based on a prior (successive) or current representation. It may also be possible to disqualify counsel who had a "confidential nonclient relationship." [*Lynn v. George* (2017) 15 CA5th 630, 638, 223 CR3d 407, 414]

a. [9:406.6] **Court's power:** A court has inherent power "[t]o control in furtherance of justice, the conduct of its ministerial officers, and of all other persons in any manner connected with a judicial proceeding before it, in every manner pertaining thereto." [CCP §128(a)(5)]

This includes the power to disqualify counsel in appropriate cases. [*In re Complex Asbestos Litig.* (1991) 232 CA3d 572, 575, 283 CR 732, 739]

b. [9:406.7] **Procedure:** A recusal motion is made in the same manner as other motions and subject to the requirements discussed in this Chapter (¶*9:19 ff.*). *See also* ¶*1:90 ff.*

c. [9:406.8] **Factors considered:** Ruling on the motion requires the court to weigh:
- — the party's right to counsel of choice;
- — the attorney's interest in representing a client;
- — the financial burden on a client of changing counsel;
- — any tactical abuse underlying a disqualification motion; and
- — the principle that the fair resolution of disputes requires vigorous representation of parties by independent counsel. [*Mills Land & Water Co. v. Golden West Refining Co.* (1986) 186 CA3d 116, 126, 230 CR 461, 465 (superseded by rule on other grounds)]

© 2020 Thomson Reuters/The Rutter Group

(1) [9:406.8a] **Proof required in successive representation cases:** In successive representation cases, where a lawyer's duty of confidentiality is the focus, if the moving party establishes that a "substantial relationship" exists between the former representation and current litigation, a presumption arises that the attorney has obtained confidential information from the former client (*see* ¶*1:66 ff.*). [*Fiduciary Trust Int'l of Calif. v. Sup.Ct. (Brown)* (2013) 218 CA4th 465, 481, 160 CR3d 216, 227-228; *National Grange of Order of Patrons of Husbandry v. California Guild* (2019) 38 CA5th 706, 716, 250 CR3d 705, 715—if attorney previously worked on case substantially related to current case, or on same case, "it is *conclusively* presumed that attorney knows confidential information adverse to his or her former client" (emphasis added)]

Absent such a showing, the moving party must prove the lawyer in fact obtained such information—i.e., "some showing of the nature of the communications or a statement of how they relate to the current representation." [*Elliott v. McFarland Unified School Dist.* (1985) 165 CA3d 562, 570-572, 211 CR 802, 808—conclusory statements ("I have confided in attorney") insufficient to establish lawyer's receipt of confidential information; *Med-Trans Corp., Inc. v. City of Calif. City* (2007) 156 CA4th 655, 668, 68 CR3d 17, 27; *Khani v. Ford Motor Co.* (2013) 215 CA4th 916, 922, 155 CR3d 532, 536—bare-bones statement that lawyer represented former client in cases brought under same statute not sufficient to raise presumption that lawyer obtained confidential information material to new case]

(2) [9:406.8b] **Proof required in concurrent representation cases:** The primary attorney duty at stake is that of loyalty, and generally disqualification in concurrent representation cases is "automatic." [*Flatt v. Sup.Ct. (Daniel)* (1994) 9 C4th 275, 284, 36 CR2d 537, 542; *M'Guinness v. Johnson* (2015) 243 CA4th 602, 614, 196 CR3d 662, 671]

Cross-refer: Recusal motions are discussed further in Tuft, Peck & Mohr, *Cal. Prac. Guide: Professional Responsibility* (TRG), Ch 4.

d. [9:406.9] **Effect of delayed motion:** Disqualification motions are *equitable* in nature and therefore subject to equitable defenses. Last-minute recusal motions that appear to be "trial tactics" may be denied on the ground of laches. [*River West, Inc. v. Nickel* (1987) 188 CA3d 1297, 1304, 234 CR 33, 38; *Liberty Nat'l Enterprises, L.P. v. Chicago Title Ins. Co.* (2011) 194 CA4th 839, 847, 123 CR3d 498, 504—proper for trial court to deny motion brought "as a tactical device to delay the litigation"; see also *City & County of San Francisco v. Cobra Solutions, Inc.* (2014) 232 CA4th 468, 474-475, 181 CR3d 430, 435-436 (motion to restrict access to disqualified counsel's work product)—delay in moving to restrict access unreasonable, and prejudice from delay extreme, resulting in waiver of right to restrict access to disqualified counsel's work product]

When the party opposing the motion shows unreasonable delay causing prejudice, the burden shifts to the moving party to justify the delay. [*Liberty Nat'l Enterprises, L.P. v. Chicago Title Ins. Co.*, supra, 194 CA4th at 845, 123 CR3d at 502; *Fiduciary Trust Int'l of Calif. v. Sup.Ct. (Brown)*, supra, 218 CA4th at 490, 160 CR3d at 235 (finding rule inapplicable based on opposing party's failure to demonstrate extreme prejudice resulting from delay)]

(1) [9:406.10] **Motion by former client:** Where the motion is made by a former client to disqualify counsel from representing his or her present client, the following factors are usually considered in determining whether the former client is guilty of laches:

— how long the former client has known of the potential conflict of interest;

— whether the former client has been represented by counsel since such discovery;

— whether the former client was prevented from making the motion earlier (and if so, how); and

— whether an earlier motion would have been inappropriate or futile and why. [*River West, Inc. v. Nickel*, supra, 188 CA3d at 1309, 234 CR at 41]

[9:406.11-406.14] *Reserved.*

e. [9:406.15] **Ruling immediately appealable:** Since a recusal motion is in effect a request for injunctive relief (to restrain opposing counsel from participating in the case), the court's order granting or denying the motion is immediately appealable. [See CCP §904.1(a)(6); *Machado v. Sup.Ct. (Atherton)* (2007) 148 CA4th 875, 882, 55 CR3d 902, 906-907; *Gregori v. Bank of America* (1989) 207 CA3d 291, 300, 254 CR 853, 858]

Note: Such an appeal does *not* automatically stay the action. If such a stay is desired, the appellant may ask the trial court to stay the proceeding until the appeal is decided; if the trial court denies the request, the appellant may seek a stay from the appellate court. [*Reed v. Sup.Ct. (Case Fin'l, Inc.)* (2001) 92 CA4th 448, 452-455, 111 CR2d 842, 845-847]

However, an appeal does automatically stay enforcement of an order of attorney disqualification. [*URS Corp. v. Atkinson/Walsh Joint Venture* (2017) 15 CA5th 872, 887, 223 CR3d 674, 684]

Cross-refer: Recusal motions are discussed further in Tuft, Peck & Mohr, *Cal. Prac. Guide: Professional Responsibility* (TRG), Ch. 4.

© 2020 Thomson Reuters/The Rutter Group

H. MOTIONS RELATING TO CONTRACTUAL ARBITRATION

[9:407] The conduct of contractual arbitration proceedings is beyond the scope of this Practice Guide because most of it occurs outside court. (It is discussed in detail in Knight, Chernick, Flynn & Quinn, *Cal. Prac. Guide: Alternative Dispute Resolution* (TRG), Ch. 5.) The discussion here outlines the typical issues handled in court; e.g., motions or petitions to compel arbitration (*see ¶9:407.3 ff.*), motions to confirm or vacate arbitration awards (*see ¶9:412 ff.*), some of the most common defenses (*see ¶9:407.9 ff.*), and special issues pertaining to possible preemption of state law relating to arbitration (*see ¶9:408.39 ff.*).

1. [9:407.1] **Who Decides Threshold Issues:** The trial court typically decides the threshold issues of enforceability of the arbitration agreement and the scope of issues to be arbitrated. [*Aanderud v. Sup.Ct. (Vivint Solar Developer, LLC)* (2017) 13 CA5th 880, 891, 221 CR3d 225, 234—courts presume parties intend courts rather than arbitrators to decide disputes about arbitrability]

   However, the parties may delegate resolution of these issues *to the arbitrator* as long as there is clear and unmistakable evidence they intended to do so and the delegation clause is not revocable on state law grounds such as fraud, duress or unconscionability. [*Pinela v. Neiman Marcus Group, Inc.* (2015) 238 CA4th 227, 239-240, 190 CR3d 159, 169-170; *Tiri v. Lucky Chances, Inc.* (2014) 226 CA4th 231, 250, 171 CR3d 621, 636—trial court precluded from deciding enforceability of arbitration agreement where explicit provision delegating issue to arbitrator was clear, unmistakable and not unconscionable; compare *Ajamian v. CantorCO2e, L.P.* (2012) 203 CA4th 771, 787-788, 137 CR3d 773, 787—contract language requiring arbitration of "[a]ny disputes, differences or controversies arising under" contract in circumstances of that case did not clearly state that arbitrator would decide enforceability of arbitration clause itself (brackets in original; internal quotes omitted)]

   Previous cases have held that when the arbitration agreement clearly and unmistakably delegated the arbitrability issue to the arbitrators, "then the court should perform a second, more limited inquiry to determine whether the assertion of arbitrability is wholly groundless" (*Smythe v. Uber Technologies, Inc.* (2018) 24 CA5th 327, 332, 233 CR3d 895, 898 (internal quotes omitted)). However, at least to the extent the agreement is subject to the Federal Arbitration Act (FAA), the "wholly groundless" exception is inconsistent with the text of the FAA, so the arbitrator should decide the arbitrability issue. [*Henry Schein, Inc. v. Archer & White Sales, Inc.* (2019) — US —, —, 139 S.Ct. 524, 529]

   a. [9:407.1a] **Compare—who decides challenges to delegation clause:** Where there is a specific challenge to the enforceability of the delegation clause, the court must decide that issue. [*Nielsen Contracting, Inc. v. Applied Underwriters, Inc.* (2018) 22 CA5th 1096, 1107-1108, 232 CR3d 282, 288-289]

b. [9:407.2] **Compare—who decides *class* arbitration issues:** The threshold issue of who decides whether the arbitration agreement provides for *class* arbitration—the court or the arbitrator—depends on state law as applied to the contract language. [*Sandquist v. Lebo Automotive, Inc.* (2016) 1 C5th 233, 244-248, 205 CR3d 359, 366-369—availability of class arbitration decided by arbitrator where as matter of state law broad delegation language in arbitration agreement did not reserve issue for court; see also *Lamps Plus, Inc. v. Varela* (2019) — US —, —, 139 S.Ct. 1407, 1417-1418—class arbitration not available where contract is ambiguous; ¶*14:7.5*]

2. [9:407.3] **Motion (Petition) to Compel Arbitration:** A party to an arbitration agreement may seek a court order compelling the parties to arbitrate a dispute covered by the agreement. [CCP §1281.2] (For sample petition/motion forms, see Knight, Chernick, Flynn & Quinn, *Cal. Prac. Guide: Alternative Dispute Resolution* (TRG), App. D.)

   Absent a viable defense to enforcement (such as unconscionability or waiver—*see* ¶*9:407.9 ff., 9:408.15 ff.*), the court must grant the motion if it determines there is an agreement to arbitrate that has not been rescinded. [CCP §1281.2(a), (b); *Cinel v. Barna* (2012) 206 CA4th 1383, 1389, 142 CR3d 329, 334; *Ruiz v. Moss Bros. Auto Group, Inc.* (2014) 232 CA4th 836, 844, 181 CR3d 781, 788—motion to compel arbitration properly denied where employer failed to authenticate employee's electronic signature on arbitration agreement and therefore did not show valid arbitration agreement existed; *Cruise v. Kroger Co.* (2015) 233 CA4th 390, 399-400, 183 CR3d 17, 24-25—arbitration clause in employment application enforceable, despite employer's inability to establish contents of its arbitration policy]

   a. [9:407.4] **Burden on motion to compel arbitration:** The party seeking arbitration has the "burden of proving the existence of a valid arbitration agreement by a preponderance of the evidence, while a party opposing the petition bears the burden of proving by a preponderance of the evidence any fact necessary to its defense." The trial court "sits as the trier of fact, weighing all the affidavits, declarations, and other documentary evidence, and any oral testimony the court may receive at its discretion, to reach a final determination." [*Ruiz v. Moss Bros. Auto Group, Inc.* (2014) 232 CA4th 836, 842, 181 CR3d 781, 786; *Engalla v. Permanente Med. Group, Inc.* (1997) 15 C4th 951, 972, 64 CR2d 843, 856]

      A party seeking to compel arbitration pursuant to CCP §1281.2 must "plead and prove a prior demand for arbitration under the parties' arbitration agreement and a refusal to arbitrate under the agreement." [*Mansouri v. Sup.Ct. (Fleur Du Lac Estates Ass'n)* (2010) 181 CA4th 633, 640-641, 104 CR3d 824, 830; *HM DG, Inc. v. Amini* (2013) 219 CA4th 1100, 1114, 162 CR3d 412, 423; *Espejo v. Southern Calif. Permanente*

Med. Group (2016) 246 CA4th 1047, 1060, 201 CR3d 318, 327-328—moving party meets initial burden by showing agreement exists, and need only establish its validity on challenge by opponent]

In certain circumstances, the opposing party's refusal to arbitrate may be demonstrated by its filing of a lawsuit rather than commencing arbitration proceedings, as required by the parties' agreement. [*Hyundai Amco America, Inc. v. S3H, Inc.* (2014) 232 CA4th 572, 577, 181 CR3d 470, 473—statute does not require that petitioning party have made demand for arbitration, only that other party has refused to arbitrate]

b. [9:407.5] **Existence of agreement to arbitrate:** A court faced with a petition to arbitrate may consider whether the parties actually entered into a contract agreeing to arbitrate. [*Pinnacle Museum Tower Ass'n v. Pinnacle Market Develop. (US), LLC* (2012) 55 C4th 223, 236, 145 CR3d 514, 523]

If challenged, the petitioner must prove the contract is authentic, including the authenticity of the signatures. [*Ruiz v. Moss Bros. Auto Group, Inc.* (2014) 232 CA4th 836, 845-846, 181 CR3d 781, 789-790]

Doubts are resolved in favor of arbitrability and ordinary rules of contract interpretation (e.g., resolve doubts against the drafter) apply. [*Sandquist v. Lebo Automotive, Inc.* (2016) 1 C5th 233, 248, 205 CR3d 359, 369; *Greenspan v. LADT, LLC* (2010) 185 CA4th 1413, 1437, 111 CR3d 468, 486]

- [9:407.5a] Employee handbook, welcome letter and policy acknowledgement were not sufficient to show an agreement to arbitrate. [*Esparza v. Sand* & Sea, *Inc.* (2016) 2 CA5th 781, 792, 206 CR3d 474, 483]
- [9:407.5b] Trial court correctly denied motion to compel arbitration where plaintiff relied on translated version of agreement which did not contain arbitration clause. [*Ramos v. Westlake Services LLC* (2015) 242 CA4th 674, 690, 195 CR3d 34, 47]
- [9:407.5c] Consumer did not agree to website's terms of use containing an arbitration clause in a hyperlink because the terms of use were not conspicuous. [*Long v. Provide Commerce, Inc.* (2016) 245 CA4th 855, 867, 200 CR3d 117, 126-127]
- [9:407.5d] Defendant failed to establish plaintiff electronically signed contract because defendant did not explain "DocuSign" process. [*Fabian v. Renovate America, Inc.* (2019) 42 CA5th 1062, 1069, 255 CR3d 695, 701]
- [9:407.5e] *Compare:* An employee agrees to arbitration if he or she continues employment after notice that arbitration is condition of continued employment. [*Diaz*

v. Sohnen Enterprises (2019) 34 CA5th 126, 130, 245 CR3d 827, 830]

c. [9:407.6] **Court may order arbitration of less than all claims:** The court may decide that some, but not all, claims are subject to arbitration and evaluate the specific wording of the contract's arbitration clause. [See *Lane v. Francis Capital Mgmt. LLC* (2014) 224 CA4th 676, 684, 168 CR3d 800, 806; *Rice v. Downs* (2016) 248 CA4th 175, 186-187, 203 CR3d 555, 563-564 (discussion of broad and narrow arbitration clauses)]

(1) [9:407.7] **Effect of nonseverability clause:** However, if some claims are not arbitrable *and* the arbitration agreement contains a *valid nonseverability clause*, the court should deny the petition to compel arbitration. [*Montano v. Wet Seal Retail, Inc.* (2015) 7 CA5th 1248, 1258, 213 CR3d 649, 656; *Securitas Security Services USA, Inc. v. Sup.Ct. (Edwards)* (2015) 234 CA4th 1109, 1126, 184 CR3d 568, 582-583—nonseverable PAGA claims required denial of motion to compel arbitration as to all claims]

Likewise, if unconscionable terms (*see* ¶*9:407.9 ff.*) can be severed from the rest of the contract, including the arbitration provision, claims may be arbitrable; but if the contract would in effect have to be rewritten, severance is not available. [*Subcontracting Concepts (CT), LLC v. De Melo* (2019) 34 CA5th 201, 216, 245 CR3d 838, 848-849—systematic unconscionability shows "there is no single provision that can be stricken" to remove unconscionable taint from agreement and so severance not required; *Baxter v. Genworth North America Corp.* (2017) 16 CA5th 713, 738, 224 CR3d 556, 577; compare *Farrar v. Direct Commerce, Inc.* (2017) 9 CA5th 1257, 1275, 215 CR3d 785, 799-800—court severed unconscionable provisions relating to claims arising from confidentiality agreement]

d. [9:407.8] **Nonsignatories:** Generally, one must be a party to the arbitration agreement in order to enforce it or be bound by it, but there are exceptions.

(1) [9:407.8a] **Nonsignatories seeking to arbitrate:** Defendants who are not signatories may seek to enforce the arbitration agreement against a signatory under such theories as: incorporation by reference, assumption, agency, veil-piercing or alter ego, and third-party beneficiary. [*Jenks v. DLA Piper Rudnick Gray Cary U.S. LLP* (2015) 243 CA4th 1, 9-10, 196 CR3d 237, 243-244—exceptions generally based on a relationship between nonsignatory and signatory, such as principal and agent or employer and employee, where there is sufficient identity of parties; see also *UFCW & Employers Benefit Trust v. Sutter Health*

(2015) 241 CA4th 909, 919, 194 CR3d 190, 198; *Jensen v. U-Haul Co. of Calif.* (2017) 18 CA5th 295, 300-301, 226 CR3d 797, 802]

(2) [9:407.8b] **Compelling nonsignatories to arbitrate:** Where a signatory attempts to enforce an arbitration agreement against a nonsignatory, an arbitrator has no authority to join a nonsignatory over that party's objection; the court must make that decision. [*Benaroya v. Willis* (2018) 23 CA5th 462, 467, 474, 232 CR3d 808, 812, 817-818—despite JAMS rules giving arbitrator power to determine arbitrability, arbitrator had no power to determine defendant was a party under alter ego theory where nonsignatory defendant never voluntarily submitted to arbitrator's jurisdiction; *Williams v. Atria Las Posas* (2018) 24 CA5th 1048, 1053, 235 CR3d 341, 346—wife bringing loss of consortium claim resulting from injury to husband who had signed an arbitration agreement is not required to arbitrate, because "she is not bound by an arbitration agreement which she did not sign"]

A nonsignatory parent corporation can be compelled to arbitrate pursuant to an agreement signed by the subsidiary if the subsidiary was the "mere agent or instrumentality of the parent" and the claims against the parent arose out of the agency relationship. [*Cohen v. TNP 2008 Participating Notes Program, LLC* (2019) 31 CA5th 840, 863-865, 243 CR3d 340, 361-363]

e. [9:407.9] **Unconscionability defense:** "Unconscionability" is one of the principal defenses to a request for arbitration. It is a generally applicable contract defense under California law (Civ.C. §1670.5). Two elements must be shown: (1) "procedural" unconscionability, which focuses on the *manner* in which the contract was negotiated (e.g., adhesion contracts); and (2) "substantive" unconscionability, which concerns whether the contract's terms are unreasonably one-sided. [*Armendariz v. Foundation Health Psychcare Services, Inc.* (2000) 24 C4th 83, 113-115, 99 CR2d 745, 766-768; *OTO, L.L.C. v. Kho* (2019) 8 C5th 111, 125-126, 251 CR3d 714, 725-726]

The issue is decided as of the time of the contract's signing. [*Bakersfield College v. California Comm. College Athletic Ass'n* (2019) 41 CA5th 753, 762, 254 CR3d 470, 479]

(1) [9:407.10] **Procedural unconscionability:** Procedural unconscionability pertains to the *making* of the agreement; it examines the "oppression that arises from unequal bargaining power and the surprise to the weaker party that results from hidden terms or the lack of informed choice." [*Ajamian v. CantorCO2e, L.P.* (2012) 203 CA4th 771, 795, 137 CR3d 773, 793]

For example, "oppression" was shown where, among other factors, the agreement was not explained to employee, time spent reviewing the agreement was docked from employee's pay, and employee was under the impression immediate signature was required. "Surprise" was demonstrated where the agreement was "a paragon of prolixity, only slightly more than a page long but written in an extremely small font," which was "visually impenetrable," with complex sentences and "legal jargon." [*OTO, L.L.C. v. Kho,* supra, 8 C5th at 127-128, 251 CR3d at 727-728]

(a) [9:407.11] **Typical procedurally unconscionable contracts:** The U.S. Supreme Court has noted that most consumer contracts are adhesive (*AT & T Mobility LLC v. Concepcion* (2011) 563 US 333, 346-347, 131 S.Ct. 1740, 1750). As a result, they present some procedural unconscionability. [*Sanchez v. Valencia Holding Co., LLC* (2015) 61 C4th 899, 915, 190 CR3d 812, 824; *Gatton v. T-Mobile USA, Inc.* (2007) 152 CA4th 571, 582, 61 CR3d 344, 352]

Employment contracts provided on a "take-it-or-leave-it" basis are also procedurally unconscionable to some extent, except for those which have been negotiated. [*Farrar v. Direct Commerce, Inc.* (2017) 9 CA5th 1257, 1266, 215 CR3d 785, 792; *Baltazar v. Forever 21, Inc.* (2016) 62 C4th 1237, 1243-1244, 200 CR3d 7, 12-13—sliding scale for procedural and substantive unconscionability]

(2) [9:407.12] **Substantive unconscionability:** Substantive unconscionability refers to agreement terms which are "overly harsh," "unduly oppressive," "unreasonably unfavorable," or "so one-sided as to shock the conscience," all of which mean the same thing. [*Sanchez v. Valencia Holding Co., LLC*, supra, 61 C4th at 910-911, 190 CR3d at 821 (internal quotes omitted)—an "old-fashioned bad bargain" or a contract term which "merely gives one side a greater benefit" insufficient; *OTO, L.L.C. v. Kho*, supra, 8 C5th at 136-137, 251 CR3d at 735—substantive unconscionability where employee gave up rights to relatively inexpensive and informal proceeding before labor commissioner for more formal and costly arbitration process]

The test is whether the terms impair the integrity of the bargaining process or otherwise contravene public policy, or the terms "attempt to alter in an impermissible manner fundamental duties otherwise imposed by the law" or "negate the reasonable expectations of the nondrafting party." [*Sonic-Calabasas A, Inc. v. Moreno* (2013) 57 C4th 1109, 1145, 163 CR3d 269, 291 (internal quotes omitted); see also *Carbajal v. CWPSC, Inc.* (2016) 245

© 2020 Thomson Reuters/The Rutter Group

CA4th 227, 247, 199 CR3d 332, 348—term "outside the reasonable expectation of the nondrafting party or is unduly oppressive" (internal quotes omitted)]

(3) [9:407.13] **Caution—unconscionability as a defense post-*Concepcion:*** The Federal Arbitration Act (FAA) *preempts* a categorical rule invalidating as unconscionable provisions in employment contacts that waive employees' rights to an administrative hearing. [*AT & T Mobility LLC v. Concepcion* (2011) 563 US 333, 342-343, 131 S.Ct. 1740, 1747-1748 (*Concepcion*); *see* ¶*14:7.10b*]

But unconscionability "remains a valid defense" in California following *Concepcion.* The presence of such a waiver can be considered as a factor in a totality-of-circumstances test to determine whether the agreement is "unreasonably one-sided" and thus unconscionable. [*Sonic-Calabasas A, Inc. v. Moreno*, supra, 57 C4th at 1125, 1142-1143, 1145, 163 CR3d at 274, 289, 291-292]

f. [9:408] **Determining enforceability of arbitration agreement:** Typically, the facts regarding the existence or enforceability of an agreement to arbitrate "are to be proven by affidavit or declaration and documentary evidence with oral testimony taken only in the court's discretion . . . With respect to claims of fraud, where factual differences may be difficult to resolve without making credibility determinations, oral testimony is generally appropriate." [*Sonic-Calabasas A, Inc. v. Moreno*, supra, 57 C4th at 1157, 163 CR3d at 301 (internal quotes and citations omitted)]

Where the facts are in dispute or credibility issues are involved (such as when fraud is alleged), "the better course would normally be for the trial court to hear oral testimony and allow the parties the opportunity for cross-examination." [*Rosenthal v. Great Western Fin'l Secur. Corp.* (1996) 14 C4th 394, 413-414, 58 CR2d 875, 885-886; see *Ashburn v. AIG Fin'l Advisors, Inc.* (2015) 234 CA4th 79, 98, 183 CR3d 679, 693—evidentiary hearing to resolve factual dispute required before ruling on motion to compel arbitration; *Hotels Nevada v. L.A. Pac. Ctr., Inc.* (2006) 144 CA4th 754, 765, 50 CR3d 700, 708—court should hold evidentiary hearing when confronted with credibility issues re fraud in execution]

(1) [9:408.1] **Moving party cannot challenge:** Because the moving party must "allege the existence of a written agreement to arbitrate" (CCP §1281.2), it *cannot contest* the existence or validity of an arbitration agreement and at the same time move to compel arbitration. [*Brodke v. Alphatec Spine Inc.* (2008) 160 CA4th 1569, 1574, 73 CR3d 554, 557]

(2) [9:408.2] **Effect of party's inability to pay arbitration costs:** Where the arbitration agreement requires the parties to share the costs of arbitration, but one or more parties claims an inability to pay, the trial court must calculate the estimated costs of arbitration and evaluate the parties' ability to pay. If any party is unable to pay its share, the moving party can elect either to pay that portion of the arbitration cost or to waive its right to arbitrate that party's claim. [*Roldan v. Callahan & Blaine* (2013) 219 CA4th 87, 96, 161 CR3d 493, 499]

When a party arbitrates in good faith but the cost of the arbitration becomes too much for the party, it may petition the court for relief. If the court "concludes the party's financial status is not a result of the party's intentional attempt to avoid arbitration, the court may issue an order specifying: (1) the arbitration shall continue so long as the other party to the arbitration agrees to pay, or the arbitrator orders it to pay, all fees and costs of the arbitration; and (2) if neither of those occur, the arbitration shall be deemed 'had' and the case may proceed in the superior court." [*Weiler v. Marcus & Millichap Real Estate Investment Services, Inc.* (2018) 22 CA5th 970, 981, 232 CR3d 155, 164]

g. [9:408.3] **Effect of plaintiff dismissing complaint:** There is nothing to preclude plaintiff from voluntarily dismissing a complaint after the case has been ordered to arbitration but before the arbitration has commenced. In that event, the trial court no longer has jurisdiction to order the parties to complete the arbitration. [*Cardiff Equities, Inc. v. Sup.Ct. (O'Neel)* (2008) 166 CA4th 1541, 1544, 83 CR3d 699, 702; compare *Mesa Shopping Center-East, LLC v. Hill* (2014) 232 CA4th 890, 906, 181 CR3d 791, 804-805—plaintiff not entitled to voluntarily dismiss action without prejudice once arbitration on the merits has commenced]

[9:408.4-408.14] *Reserved.*

h. [9:408.15] **Waiver of right to arbitrate:** As a contractual right, the right to arbitrate may be waived, either expressly or by implication. [*Saint Agnes Med. Ctr. v. PacifiCare of Calif.* (2003) 31 C4th 1187, 1195, 8 CR3d 517, 523]

A party may waive its right to arbitrate by failing to perform an act required of it, "*regardless of the party's intent* to relinquish the right to arbitration." [*Cinel v. Barna* (2012) 206 CA4th 1383, 1389, 142 CR3d 329, 334 (emphasis added)—defendants waived right to arbitrate by failing to resolve dispute over payment of arbitrator's fees (*see ¶9:412.3*)]

A party to a construction contract containing an arbitration clause waives any right to arbitration by seeking to enforce

© 2020 Thomson Reuters/The Rutter Group

a mechanic's lien without seeking a stay as required by CCP §1281.5. [*Von Becelaere Ventures, LLC v. Zenovic* (2018) 24 CA5th 243, 249-251, 234 CR3d 217, 222-223]

(1) [9:408.16] **Waiver by litigation:** Participating in litigation of an arbitrable claim does not by itself waive the right to later seek arbitration; however, at some point, continued litigation may be deemed a waiver. [*Saint Agnes Med. Ctr. v. PacifiCare of California*, supra, 31 C4th at 1201, 8 CR3d at 528—mere filing of lawsuit insufficient]

Relevant factors in determining whether there has been a waiver include:

— "whether the party's actions are inconsistent with the right to arbitrate";
— "whether the litigation machinery has been substantially invoked and the parties were well into preparation of a lawsuit before the party notified the opposing party of an intent to arbitrate";
— "whether a party either requested arbitration enforcement close to the trial date or delayed for a long period before seeking a stay";
— "whether a defendant seeking arbitration filed a counterclaim without asking for a stay of the proceedings";
— "whether important intervening steps (e.g., taking advantage of judicial discovery procedures not available in arbitration) had taken place"; and
— "whether the delay affected, misled, or prejudiced the opposing party." [*Saint Agnes Med. Ctr. v. PacifiCare of Calif.*, supra, 31 C4th at 1196, 8 CR3d at 524 (internal quotes omitted)]

(2) **Application**

- [9:408.17] Waiver was found where a party delayed filing the motion to compel arbitration until just four months before trial, *after* taking advantage of discovery that would not have been available in the arbitration, thereby prejudicing the opposing party. [*Zamora v. Lehman* (2010) 186 CA4th 1, 17, 111 CR3d 335, 346; see *Burton v. Cruise* (2010) 190 CA4th 939, 951, 118 CR3d 613, 622—waiting to pursue arbitration until "virtual eve of trial" was deemed waiver; compare *Khalatian v. Prime Time Shuttle, Inc.* (2015) 237 CA4th 651, 660-663, 188 CR3d 113, 119-122—no waiver despite 14-month delay in demanding arbitration where little discovery had occurred and trial was over a year away; *Sprunk v. Prisma LLC* (2017) 14 CA5th 785, 798, 222 CR3d 339, 351—attempt to gain strategic advantage through court litigation, such as waiting until after ruling on class certification before moving to compel arbitration, is waiver, "a paradigm of conduct that is inconsistent with the right to arbitrate"]

- [9:408.18] Propounding classwide discovery and engaging in a months-long effort to settle claims outside the scope of arbitration was deemed inconsistent with and a waiver of the right to arbitrate. [*Bower v. Inter-Con Security Systems, Inc.* (2014) 232 CA4th 1035, 1043-1049, 181 CR3d 729, 736-741; see *Oregel v. PacPizza, LLC* (2015) 237 CA4th 342, 355-356, 360-361, 187 CR3d 436, 446-447, 450-451—employer waived right to arbitrate by participating in extensive litigation and waiting 17 months before bringing motion to compel, causing employee to incur significant expense]

- [9:408.19] After trial court denied defendant's motion for trial stay on the eve of trial, defendant demanded arbitration and had the court sign an order denying arbitration in order to file an immediate appeal which would in effect provide the stay of trial originally sought. Such actions, together with filing a summary judgment motion and engaging in discovery, constituted a waiver of defendant's right to arbitrate. [*Diaz v. Professional Comm. Mgmt., Inc.* (2017) 16 CA5th 1190, 1214-1217, 225 CR3d 39, 58-61—actions also warranted sanctions for bad faith and filing frivolous appeal]

- [9:408.19a] Even with a one-year delay, there was no waiver where defendants consistently asserted their intention to arbitrate, served no discovery, only attended case management conferences, and merely waited for demurrer against another party to be resolved. [*Gloster v. Sonic Automotive, Inc.* (2014) 226 CA4th 438, 449, 171 CR3d 648, 656]

  But "[u]nreasonable delay in seeking arbitration may, standing alone, constitute a waiver of a right to arbitrate." [*Spracher v. Paul M. Zagaris, Inc.* (2019) 39 CA5th 1135, 1138-1139, 252 CR3d 417, 420—waiver found where defendants delayed 21 months and also filed "multiple demurrers, engaged in extensive discovery, and filed a motion for summary judgment"]

- [9:408.19b] There was a waiver where party twice missed court-imposed deadlines to file a motion to compel arbitration (prompting the court to stay litigation), then stated it would not file petition to arbitrate and conducted discovery, and opposing party was prejudiced by spending money on discovery, discovery motions, notice to putative class members, and

© 2020 Thomson Reuters/The Rutter Group

retaining an expert for class issues. [*Nunez v. Nevell Group, Inc.* (2019) 35 CA5th 838, 845, 848, 247 CR3d 595, 600, 602]

i. [9:408.20] **Denial of motion proper when possibility of conflicting rulings:** The court may deny a motion to compel arbitration when a party to the arbitration agreement is also a party to a pending court action with a third party that:

— "[arises] out of the same transaction or series of related transactions," *and*

— "[presents] a possibility of conflicting rulings on a common issue of law or fact." [CCP 1281.2(c); *Ruiz v. Podolsky* (2010) 50 C4th 838, 841, 114 CR3d 263, 266; see *Los Angeles Unified School Dist. v. Safety Nat'l Cas. Corp.* (2017) 13 CA5th 471, 484, 220 CR3d 546, 555; *Bush v. Horizon West* (2012) 205 CA4th 924, 929, 140 CR3d 258, 262; *see also* ¶*12:353*]

A "third party" for these purposes is someone who is not bound by the arbitration agreement. [*Bush v. Horizon West*, supra, 205 CA4th at 929, 140 CR3d at 262]

(1) [9:408.21] **Compare—stay of arbitration:** The court has discretion to stay arbitration where pending litigation between the parties involves overlapping nonarbitrable issues that may render the arbitration unnecessary. [CCP §1281.2(c); compare *Association for L.A. Deputy Sheriffs v. County of Los Angeles* (2015) 234 CA4th 459, 468-469, 183 CR3d 854, 861-862—no basis for stay where no nonarbitrable issues]

[9:408.22-408.24] *Reserved.*

j. [9:408.25] **Renewed motion based on change in law:** When an intervening change in law affects a party's right to arbitration, a previously denied motion may be renewed (CCP §1008(b); *see* ¶*9:337 ff.*). [*Phillips v. Sprint PCS* (2012) 209 CA4th 758, 768, 147 CR3d 274, 281—renewal motion proper based on change in law re enforceability of class action waivers in consumer contract arbitration agreements following *AT&T Mobility LLC v. Concepcion* (2011) 563 US 333, 131 S.Ct. 1740]

(1) [9:408.26] **Compare—motion for reconsideration:** Even without a change in law, a trial court has inherent "authority to reconsider orders compelling or denying arbitration." [*Pinela v. Neiman Marcus Group, Inc.* (2015) 238 CA4th 227, 237, 190 CR3d 159, 168; *see* ¶*9:327 ff.*]

[9:408.27-408.30] *Reserved.*

k. [9:408.31] **Statement of decision following ruling on motion:** If timely requested by any party, the court must issue a CCP §632 statement of decision following the ruling on a petition to compel arbitration. [CCP §1291; *Metis Develop. LLC v. Bohacek* (2011) 200 CA4th 679, 689, 131 CR3d 585, 592 & fn. 5]

The request for a statement of decision *must* specify the principal controverted issues. [CRC 3.1590(d)] But the trial court ultimately decides what those issues are. [*Vukovich v. Radulovich* (1991) 235 CA3d 281, 295, 286 CR 547, 555]

Caution: The deadline for requesting a statement of decision will not necessarily commence upon denial of the petition; if the hearing lasted less than one day (and most of them do), the request must be made *before* submission of the matter for decision. [See CRC 3.1590(d), (n)]

(1) [9:408.32] **Effect of failure to request statement of decision:** Failure to request a statement of decision waives any objection on appeal to the trial court's failure to make all findings necessary to support its decision and the appellate court will presume the trial court made all such findings supported by substantial evidence. [*Acquire II, Ltd. v. Colton Real Estate Group* (2013) 213 CA4th 959, 970-971, 153 CR3d 135, 145—based on defendant's failure to request statement of decision, only question on appeal was whether implied findings were supported by substantial evidence; *Ruiz v. Moss Bros. Auto Group, Inc.* (2014) 232 CA4th 836, 842, 181 CR3d 781, 786]

Cross-refer: For further discussion of the consequences of failing to request a statement of decision, see Eisenberg, *Cal. Prac. Guide: Civil Appeals & Writs* (TRG), Ch. 8.

l. [9:408.33] **Appellate review of order:** An order *compelling* arbitration is not appealable but may be reviewed by writ petition. [*Laymon v. J. Rockcliff, Inc.* (2017) 12 CA5th 812, 825, 219 CR3d 185, 196; *Zembsch v. Sup.Ct. (Health Net of Calif., Inc.)* (2006) 146 CA4th 153, 160, 53 CR3d 69, 74-75 (discussing when writ review available)]

An order *denying* arbitration is appealable. [CCP §1294(a); *Esparza v. Sand & Sea, Inc.* (2016) 2 CA5th 781, 787, 206 CR3d 474, 479]

[9:408.34-408.36] *Reserved.*

m. [9:408.37] **Compare—motion to compel judicial reference:** CCP §638 "authoriz[es] courts to transfer a dispute to a referee" pursuant to a written agreement between the parties. [*Grafton Partners L.P. v. Sup.Ct. (PriceWaterhouseCoopers L.L.P.)* (2005) 36 C4th 944, 960-961, 32 CR3d 5, 15] Where the parties' agreement calls for all disputes to be resolved

© 2020 Thomson Reuters/The Rutter Group

by a referee, a party may bring a motion to enforce the reference if one or more parties refuses to agree after a demand for a reference is made. The motion is handled much the same way as a motion to compel contractual arbitration (*see ¶9:407 ff.*), with the court deciding the threshold issues of enforceability of the agreement and the scope of issues to be resolved by the reference. [See *O'Donoghue v. Sup.Ct. (Performing Arts, LLC)* (2013) 219 CA4th 245, 256-257, 161 CR3d 609, 618-619 & fn. 5 (relying on "cases interpreting arbitration agreements" to decide enforceability of judicial reference agreement)]

3. [9:408.37a] **Response to Petition to Compel Arbitration:** Unlike oppositions to most motions (*see ¶9:104*), a response to a petition to compel arbitration must be served and filed within 10 days after service of the petition, unless extended by an agreement in writing between the parties or by court order. [CCP §1290.6; *Correia v. NB Baker Electric, Inc.* (2019) 32 CA5th 602, 612-613, 244 CR3d 177, 182—but courts are authorized to consider late-filed opposition papers for good cause if there is no prejudice to moving party]

   However, it is not clear whether CCP §1290.6, rather than the general motions statute (CCP §1005(b), *see ¶9:104*), governs the timing requirements for filing an opposition to a motion (petition) to compel arbitration when the motion (petition) to compel arbitration is filed in an action that is already pending. [*Correia v. NB Baker Electric, Inc.*, supra, 32 CA5th at 613, 244 CR3d at 182]

   [9:408.38] *Reserved.*

4. **Special Issues Pertaining to Arbitration**

   a. [9:408.39] **Preemption:** State law refusing to enforce arbitration agreements in contracts may be preempted by a variety of federal laws, *discussed below at ¶9:408.40 ff.*

      (1) [9:408.40] **Federal preemption of conflicting state law by the Federal Arbitration Act:** The Federal Arbitration Act (FAA) governs arbitration in written contracts involving interstate commerce (9 USC §1). Conflicting state law, such as that which refuses to enforce certain kinds of arbitration agreements, may be preempted. [See *Southland Corp. v. Keating* (1984) 465 US 1, 12, 104 S.Ct. 852, 859; see also *AT & T Mobility LLC v. Concepcion* (2011) 563 US 333, 341, 131 S.Ct. 1740, 1747; *Saheli v. White Memorial Med. Ctr.* (2018) 21 CA5th 308, 332-333, 230 CR3d 258, 277]

      The party asserting FAA preemption has the burden to present evidence establishing a contract *affecting interstate commerce*. [*Carbajal v. CWPSC, Inc.* (2016) 245 CA4th 227, 238, 199 CR3d 332, 340-341; see *Scott v. Yoho* (2016) 248 CA4th 392, 401-402, 204 CR3d 89, 95—interstate commerce, broadly construed, covered dispute over liposuction procedure because supplies and procedure originated out of state, and defendant advertised on Internet and communicated with out-of-state patients; see also *Lane v. Francis Capital Mgmt. LLC* (2014) 224 CA4th 676, 688, 168 CR3d 800, 809-810—admissible evidence to support interstate commerce claim required]

(a) [9:408.41] **Contract defenses generally *not* preempted:** Even if subject to the FAA, arbitration agreements may be denied enforcement "upon such grounds as exist at law or in equity for the revocation of any contract" (9 USC §2). That is, although the FAA preempts conflicting state law, its saving clause "permits agreements to arbitrate to be invalidated by *generally applicable* contract defenses, such as fraud, duress, or unconscionability." [*AT & T Mobility LLC v. Concepcion*, supra, 563 US at 339, 131 S.Ct. at 1746 (emphasis added; internal quotes omitted); see also *Perry v. Thomas* (1987) 482 US 483, 492, 107 S.Ct. 2520, 2527; *McGill v. Citibank, N.A.* (2017) 2 C5th 945, 962, 216 CR3d 627, 638-639; *Avila v. Southern Calif. Specialty Care, Inc.* (2018) 20 CA5th 835, 840-841, 230 CR3d 42, 46—federal preemption does not apply to FAA's procedural rules unless parties have expressly so agreed in arbitration agreement]

On the other hand, if the agreement is subject to the FAA, defenses *uniquely and only applicable to arbitration* are *preempted* by the FAA. [*AT & T Mobility LLC v. Concepcion*, supra, 563 US at 341, 131 S.Ct. at 1747; *Kindred Nursing Ctrs. Ltd. Partnership v. Clark* (2017) __ US __, __, 137 S.Ct. 1421, 1426-1427—state requirement that agreements to arbitrate be express, whereas other agreements need not be, discriminated against arbitration and thus preempted; *Epic Systems Corp. v. Lewis* (2018) __ US __, __, 138 S.Ct. 1612, 1628—NLRA's protection of collective action (29 USC §157) does not make a contractual agreement to waive class arbitrability unenforceable]

(b) [9:408.42] **Waiver of right to seek public injunctive relief under certain consumer laws:** The statutory remedies available for a violation of the Consumers Legal Remedies Act (CLRA, Civ.C. §1750 et seq.), unfair competition law (UCL, Bus. & Prof.C. §17200 et seq.), and false advertising law (FAL, Bus. & Prof.C. §17500 et seq.) "include public injunctive relief, i.e.,

© 2020 Thomson Reuters/The Rutter Group

injunctive relief that has the primary purpose and effect of prohibiting unlawful acts that threaten future injury to the general public." According to the California Supreme Court, provisions in an arbitration agreement attempting to waive such a remedy and prohibit a plaintiff from seeking public injunctive relief in any forum are *unenforceable* and *not preempted* by the FAA under the FAA's saving clause, which permits arbitration agreements to be declared unenforceable "upon such grounds as exist at law or in equity for the revocation of any contract." [*McGill v. Citibank, N.A.*, supra, 2 C5th at 951, 961-963, 216 CR3d at 630, 637-639 (internal quotes omitted)]

But a "UCL claim for *private* injunctive relief or restitution" may be subject to arbitration. [*Clifford v. Quest Software Inc.* (2019) 38 CA5th 745, 748, 251 CR3d 269, 272 (emphasis added)]

Cross-refer: The FAA is discussed in detail in Knight, Chernick, Flynn & Quinn, *Cal. Prac. Guide: Alternative Dispute Resolution* (TRG), Ch. 5.

(2) [9:408.43] **Preemption under Labor Management Relations Act (LMRA):** State claims which require the interpretation of a collective bargaining agreement (CBA) are generally preempted by section 301 of the LMRA (29 USC §185(a)) and are arbitrable under the terms of the CBA. There is no preemption where "[t]he collective bargaining agreement must be consulted or referenced, but not interpreted." [*Melendez v. San Francisco Baseball Assocs. LLC* (2019) 7 C5th 1, 12-13, 246 CR3d 287, 295-296]

(3) [9:408.44] **No preemption of PAGA claims:** Because claims under the Private Attorneys General Act (PAGA, Lab.C. §2698 et seq.) are not those of the plaintiff but *of the state* (an employee brings such claims on behalf of the government), a plaintiff's arbitration agreement with an employer does not require arbitration of PAGA claims, nor does the FAA preempt the state's policy banning arbitration of PAGA claims. [*Iskanian v. CLS Transp. Los Angeles, LLC* (2014) 59 C4th 348, 386-387, 173 CR3d 289, 315]

For the same reason, the issue of whether a plaintiff is an "aggrieved employee" under PAGA is not arbitrable. [*Perez v. U-Haul Co. of Calif.* (2016) 3 CA5th 408, 421, 207 CR3d 605, 614]

b. [9:408.45] **Consumer arbitration agreements with banks:** CCP §1281.2(d) bars enforcement of a written arbitration agreement between consumers and a state- or federally-chartered depository institution if the agreement was created by the institution's fraud without the consumer's consent and

© 2020 Thomson Reuters/The Rutter Group

by unlawfully using the consumer's personal identifying information.

c. [9:408.46] **Employment agreements:** For contracts entered into after January 1, 2020, employers are prohibited from requiring (such as in an arbitration agreement) as a "condition of employment" an applicant or employee to "waive any right, forum, or procedure" for alleged violations of the Fair Employment and Housing Act (FEHA, Gov.C. §12900 et seq.) or the Labor Code. [Lab.C. §432.6(a) (added eff. 1/1/20)] "[A]n agreement that requires an employee to opt out of a waiver or take any affirmative action in order to preserve their rights is deemed a condition of employment." [Lab.C. §432.6(c) (added eff. 1/1/20)]

These provisions do not invalidate a written arbitration agreement otherwise enforceable under the FAA, post-dispute settlement agreements, or negotiated severance agreements. [Lab.C. §432.6(f),(g) (added eff. 1/1/20)]

d. [9:408.47] **Dealing with consumer or employment "arbitration limbo":** Effective January 1, 2020, the postponement of an arbitration as result of a party (usually the drafter of the arbitration clause) failing to pay the arbitration fee and costs is prohibited. If the costs are not paid within 30 days of the due date, the drafting party is in breach of the arbitration agreement, waives arbitration, and the consumer or employee may either withdraw the arbitration claim and proceed in court, or compel arbitration and have the defaulting party pay attorney fees and costs related to the arbitration. [CCP §§1280 (amended eff. 1/1/20), 1281.96 (amended eff. 1/1/20), 1281.97 (added eff. 1/1/20), 1281.98 (added eff. 1/1/20), 1281.99 (added eff. 1/1/20); *see ¶9:412.4*]

Cross-refer: For a detailed discussion of these arbitration procedures, along with applicable forms, see Knight, Chernick, Flynn & Quinn, *Cal. Prac. Guide: Alternative Dispute Resolution* (TRG), Ch. 5 and Appendix D (ADR Forms).

5. [9:409] **Motion (Petition) to Stay Pending Litigation:** A party may seek a stay of pending litigation either by itself or in conjunction with a petition to compel contract arbitration. A stay must be granted where a court has previously ordered arbitration of the dispute, or an application for such an order has been made but not yet ruled upon. [CCP §1281.4; see *Twentieth Century Fox Film Corp. v. Sup.Ct. (Lottermoser)* (2000) 79 CA4th 188, 192, 93 CR2d 896, 898; *Heritage Provider Network, Inc. v. Sup.Ct. (Eastland Med. Group, Inc.)* (2008) 158 CA4th 1146, 1152, 70 CR3d 645, 649]

Compare—stay of arbitration: See discussion at ¶9:408.21.

a. [9:409.1] **Notice of stay required:** The party who requested the stay must immediately serve and file a Notice of Stay of Proceedings with a copy of the stay order attached. [CRC 3.650]

© 2020 Thomson Reuters/The Rutter Group

6. [9:410] **Motion (Petition) for Appointment of Arbitrator:** Where the parties' agreement fails to name an arbitrator or a procedure for selection of the arbitrator, or the designated procedure cannot be followed, the court may appoint the arbitrator. [CCP §1281.6]

7. [9:411] **Motion (Petition) to Consolidate Separate Arbitrations:** Where several separate arbitration proceedings are pending or likely, a party to one or more of them may petition the court for an order consolidating proceedings involving disputes arising from the same transaction or series of transactions and involving common issues of fact or law. [CCP §1281.3]

8. [9:412] **Motion (Petition) to Confirm Arbitration Award:** If the arbitration award is not voluntarily paid, the party prevailing in the arbitration proceedings may file a motion to confirm the arbitration award and to enter a judgment thereon within four years after service of the award. [CCP §1288] (For sample petition/motion forms, see Knight, Chernick, Flynn & Quinn, *Cal. Prac. Guide: Alternative Dispute Resolution* (TRG), App. D.)

   a. [9:412.1] **Burden on moving party:** The party seeking judicial enforcement of a private arbitration award has the burden of proving the award as well as the *existence of a valid arbitration agreement.* [*Toal v. Tardif* (2009) 178 CA4th 1208, 1223, 101 CR3d 97, 108—burden not met by submitting copy of contract with arbitration provision signed by party's attorney rather than by party personally]

   b. [9:412.2] **Includes award made pursuant to Federal Arbitration Act:** The Federal Arbitration Act (FAA) provides for judicial confirmation of arbitral awards only upon consent of the parties (9 USC §9). But this provision is procedural rather than substantive and applies only in federal court proceedings. Thus, a state court can confirm an FAA arbitration award even without the parties' agreement. [*Swissmex-Rapid S.A. de C.V. v. SP Systems, LLC* (2012) 212 CA4th 539, 546-547, 151 CR3d 229, 234-235]

   c. [9:412.3] **Compare—order terminating arbitration for failure to pay fees:** An order terminating an arbitration for nonpayment of required fees is not an arbitration *award*, and a motion to confirm the "award" thus must be denied. [*Cinel v. Christopher* (2012) 203 CA4th 759, 767, 136 CR3d 763, 769—court properly denied petition to confirm where "there was no substantive award to confirm, correct or vacate"; see also *Kaiser Found. Health Plan, Inc. v. Sup.Ct. (Prime Healthcare La Palma, LLC)* (2017) 13 CA5th 1125, 1138-1139, 221 CR3d 278, 288—court may not confirm intermediate or "partial" awards]

   d. [9:412.4] **Compare—breach of arbitration agreement for failure to pay fees:** If the drafting party (usually the company or employer) in a consumer or employment arbitration agreement fails to pay arbitration fees pursuant to a mandatory arbitration provision, this is a breach of the arbitration agreement and allows the non-breaching party to bring a claim in court. [CCP §§1281.97 (added eff. 1/1/20), 1281.98 (added eff. 1/1/20), 1281.99 (added eff. 1/1/20) (sanctions may be imposed on breaching party); *see ¶9:408.47*]

9. [9:413] **Motion (Petition) to Vacate or Correct Award:** Parties dissatisfied with the arbitration award may move to vacate or correct the award within 100 days after service of the award (CCP §1288). But *only limited grounds* are available (and these are narrowly construed):

- Award "procured by corruption, fraud or other undue means" or "corruption in any of the arbitrators" (*Baker Marquart LLP v. Kantor* (2018) 22 CA5th 729, 740, 231 CR3d 796, 804—confidential brief submitted ex parte and considered by arbitrator constituted "undue means" and thus required that award be vacated);
- Arbitrators "exceeded their powers" and the award cannot be corrected without affecting the merits of their decision (see *Emerald Aero, LLC v. Kaplan* (2017) 9 CA5th 1125, 1142-1143, 215 CR3d 5, 19—arbitrator exceeded powers by awarding punitive damages without notice to absent defendant);
- Rights of party challenging the award were substantially prejudiced by arbitrator's misconduct, refusal to postpone the hearing, refusal to hear evidence "or by other conduct . . . contrary to provisions of this title";
- Arbitrator failed timely to *disclose ground for disqualification* or to disqualify himself or herself upon receipt of timely demand for disqualification as required by law (see CCP §1281.91). [CCP §1286.2(a); *Honeycutt v. JPMorgan Chase Bank, N.A.* (2018) 25 CA5th 909, 930-931, 236 CR3d 255, 269-270—failure to disclose party's offer to have arbitrator conduct additional arbitrations for party during arbitration justified vacating award] (For sample petition/motion forms, see Knight, Chernick, Flynn & Quinn, *Cal. Prac. Guide: Alternative Dispute Resolution* (TRG), App. D.)

Compare—errors of law: Generally, errors of law committed by the arbitrator are *not* grounds for challenging the arbitration award. [*Moncharsh v. Heily & Blase* (1992) 3 C4th 1, 11, 10 CR2d 183, 188; see *Singerlewak LLP v. Gantman* (2015) 241 CA4th 610, 615-616, 193 CR3d 672, 675]

But if the parties' arbitration agreement provides otherwise, the arbitrator's decision may be subject to review to determine if it complied with the applicable law. [*Cable Connection, Inc. v. DIRECTV, Inc.* (2008) 44 C4th 1334, 1340, 82 CR3d 229, 233—arbitration agreement provided award may be vacated or corrected on appeal for arbitrator "errors of law or legal reasoning"; see also *Harshad & Nasir Corp. v. Global Sign Systems, Inc.* (2017) 14 CA5th 523, 535-536, 222 CR3d 282, 293-294—agreement constrained arbitrator's

© 2020 Thomson Reuters/The Rutter Group

authority by requiring disputes be resolved according to applicable law and "ma[d]e plain their intention that the award is reviewable for legal error"]

Compare—partial award: If the arbitrator's award does not resolve all issues submitted to the arbitrator, the superior court lacks jurisdiction to confirm or vacate the award and the petition must be dismissed. [*Maplebear, Inc. v. Busick* (2018) 26 CA5th 394, 407, 237 CR3d 98, 107—"In the face of [CCP] section 1283.4, which defines 'award' as 'a determination of all the questions submitted to the arbitrators the decision of which is necessary in order to determine the controversy,' parties to an arbitration agreement cannot confer jurisdiction on courts to review arbitrator's rulings by agreeing to proceed under a private organization's rules that purport to allow immediate review of some interim awards"]

a. [9:413.1] **Service of motion:** The petition to vacate or correct an award, with notice of time and place of the hearing, must be served in the manner provided in the arbitration agreement. But if the arbitration agreement does not dictate the manner of service, and the person to be served has not yet appeared in the action, service must be made in the same manner as service of a summons and complaint (¶*4:110 ff.*). [CCP §1290.4; *Abers v. Rohrs* (2013) 217 CA4th 1199, 1205-1207, 159 CR3d 414, 418-420—service of petition by mail not sufficient to confer jurisdiction over parties who had not appeared in action]

b. [9:413.2] **Time limit jurisdictional:** The 100-day limitation for service of a petition to vacate or correct an arbitration award is jurisdictional, and the court has no power to extend that mandatory deadline. [*Abers v. Rohrs*, supra, 217 CA4th at 1211, 159 CR3d at 422-423; *Douglass v. Serenivision, Inc.* (2018) 20 CA5th 376, 384-385, 229 CR3d 54, 61—petition to vacate filed in response to petition to confirm untimely if filed after 100-day period]

10. [9:414] **Compare—Continuing Jurisdiction:** Granting such relief (e.g., to have the case arbitrated) does not divest the court of jurisdiction: "[T]he court . . . retains jurisdiction to determine any subsequent petition involving the same agreement to arbitrate and the same controversy." [CCP §1292.6]

➪ [9:415] ***PRACTICE POINTER:*** Bring this to the court's attention when a petition is granted. Otherwise, some judges routinely *dismiss* proceedings in order to "chalk up" one more disposition. Dismissal creates problems if you thereafter need court orders to replace the arbitrator, enforce discovery, etc.

But note: generally "once a dispute has been sent to arbitration, the courts may not act on that dispute absent an agreement to withdraw" the case from arbitration. [*Bucur v. Ahmad* (2016) 244 CA4th 175, 188, 198 CR3d 127, 137]

Cross-refer: For a detailed discussion of these procedures, along with applicable forms, see Knight, Chernick, Flynn & Quinn, *Cal. Prac. Guide: Alternative Dispute Resolution* (TRG), Ch. 5 and Appendix D (ADR Forms).

I. MOTION TO SEAL COURT RECORDS

[9:416] Unless confidentiality is required by law, court records are presumed to be open to the public (CRC 2.550(c)). Therefore, pleadings, motions, evidence (including that obtained in discovery), and other papers may not be filed under seal merely by stipulation of the parties. A prior court order must be obtained. [CRC 2.551(a); see *H.B. Fuller Co. v. Doe* (2007) 151 CA4th 879, 888, 60 CR3d 501, 507]

The judge who ordered the sealing (or a judge to whom the case is subsequently assigned) may order sealed documents unsealed. [*Marriage of Nicholas* (2010) 186 CA4th 1566, 1577, 113 CR3d 629, 637]

Compare—discovery motions: The criteria and procedures for sealing records (CRC 2.550 et seq.) do not apply to discovery motions. *See ¶9:418.25 ff.*

⇨ [9:416.1] ***PRACTICE POINTER:*** Many, if not most, motions to seal are unnecessary because the judge does not need to review the confidential material in order to decide the underlying motion. In such cases, simply file the redacted document in the public file and explain the redaction in, e.g., the accompanying memorandum of points and authorities.

1. [9:417] **Moving Papers:** A written motion or application is required, accompanied by points and authorities and by declarations stating facts supporting the findings required for a sealing order (*¶9:418*). [CRC 2.551(b); see *H.B. Fuller Co. v. Doe*, supra, 151 CA4th at 894, 60 CR3d at 512—moving party must present "specific enumeration of the facts sought to be withheld and specific reasons for withholding them"]

   Admissible evidence is required to support a sealing motion; generally, declarations of counsel relating to trade secrets or other overriding interest to justify sealing are inadmissible hearsay. The evidence must support the sealing of *all* materials or facts in issue.

   FORM: Motion to File Records Under Seal and Proposed Order, *see Form 9A:25* in Rivera, *Cal. Prac. Guide: Civ. Pro. Before Trial FORMS* (TRG).

   a. [9:417.1] **Parties' agreement not enough:** Parties sometimes operate under an informal arrangement pursuant to which documents are "deemed filed under seal" unless an objection is made. Such an arrangement "is entirely inconsistent with the mandatory requirements of rules 2.550 and 2.551 and the constitutional values informing those requirements." [*Savaglio v. Wal-Mart Stores, Inc.* (2007) 149 CA4th 588, 600, 57 CR3d 215, 223, fn. 8; *McNair v. National Collegiate Athletic Ass'n* (2015) 234 CA4th 25, 29, 35-36, 183 CR3d 490, 492, 497-

498—prelawsuit confidentiality agreement insufficient to support sealing order]

b. [9:417.2] **Actions pending before temporary judge or referee:** A motion to seal records in actions pending before a temporary judge or referee must be heard by the trial judge to whom the case is assigned; or, if no trial judge has been assigned, by the presiding judge or the presiding judge's designee. [CRC 2.835, 3.932]

c. [9:417.3] **Lodging documents:** The documents at issue must be lodged with the clerk, in a separate envelope sealed and labeled "CONDITIONALLY UNDER SEAL" if lodged in paper form. If transmitted electronically, a cover sheet must be affixed to the electronic transmission indicating they are subject to a motion to file the documents under seal. If the motion or application is denied, the moving party may notify the court within 10 days after denial that the documents may be filed unsealed. If such a notification is not received within 10 days of the order denying the motion, the clerk must return the lodged documents to the moving party if they are in paper form, or permanently delete the lodged documents if in electronic form. If the motion or application is granted, the sealed documents remain sealed until further order of the court. [See CRC 2.551(b)(6), (d), (e)]

➪ [9:417.4] ***PRACTICE POINTER:*** Some judges appreciate the lodging of a document that shows the proposed redactions to the publicly filed document in context, such as by red-lining. Also, consider filing the motion to seal before the underlying motion; if the sealing request is denied and the materials are withdrawn as a result, the record for the underlying motion may differ.

d. [9:417.5] **Filing before order obtained waives confidentiality:** If the party seeking the sealing order files the documents with the court *before the motion to seal is granted*, the right to move for an order sealing the documents is waived. The court cannot entertain a later motion to seal documents that are already a matter of public record. [*Savaglio v. Wal-Mart Stores, Inc.*, supra, 149 CA4th at 601, 57 CR3d at 224]

e. [9:417.6] **Sanctions for overbroad sealing request:** Sanctions may be imposed for overbroad requests to seal. [*Overstock.Com, Inc. v. Goldman Sachs Group, Inc.* (2014) 231 CA4th 471, 500, 180 CR3d 234, 259—trial court should view "overly inclusive sealing efforts with a jaundiced eye, and impose sanctions as appropriate"]

[9:417.7-417.9] *Reserved.*

(1) [9:417.10] **Compare—material already subject to confidentiality agreement or protective order:** Distinct rules apply where a party seeks to use another party's materials already covered by a confidentiality agreement or protective order at trial or for other adjudication purposes *without* requesting a sealing order. *See discussion at ¶9:420.*

2. [9:418] **Findings Required:** To grant such an order, the court must expressly find that:
   — an overriding interest exists that overcomes the right of public access to the record;
   — the overriding interest supports sealing the records;
   — a substantial probability exists that the overriding interest will be prejudiced if the record is not sealed;
   — the proposed sealing is narrowly tailored; and
   — no less restrictive means exist to achieve the overriding interest. [CRC 2.550(d); see *McGuan v. Endovascular Technologies, Inc.* (2010) 182 CA4th 974, 988, 106 CR3d 277, 290]

   These findings embody *constitutional* requirements for a request to seal court records, protecting the First Amendment right of public access to civil trials. [See *NBC Subsidiary (KNBC-TV), Inc. v. Sup.Ct. (Locke)* (1999) 20 C4th 1178, 1217-1218, 86 CR2d 778, 809; *Huffy Corp. v. Sup.Ct. (Winterthur Swiss Ins. Co.)* (2003) 112 CA4th 97, 104, 4 CR3d 823, 830; *People v. Jackson* (2005) 128 CA4th 1009, 1026-1027, 27 CR3d 596, 608—in determining whether to seal records, courts must weigh constitutional requirements for disclosure against such factors as privacy rights]

   If the trial court fails to make the required findings, the order is deficient and cannot support sealing. [*Overstock.Com, Inc. v. Goldman Sachs Group, Inc.* (2014) 231 CA4th 471, 487, 180 CR3d 234, 249]

   a. [9:418a] **Compare—sealed records on appeal:** Similar findings are required in connection with motions to seal records on appeal. [CRC 8.46(d)(6)—court may order sealing only if it makes findings required by CRC 2.550(d)-(e); see *McNair v. National Collegiate Athletic Ass'n* (2015) 234 CA4th 25, 29, 183 CR3d 490, 492—party's interest in confidentiality of proceedings (based on its bylaws and contracts) insufficient to override constitutional right of access and justify sealing of appellate record]

   Cross-refer: For detailed discussion of sealed records on appeal, see Eisenberg, *Cal. Prac. Guide: Civil Appeals & Writs* (TRG), Ch. 5.

3. [9:418.1] **Sealing Order:** A sealing order must (a) specifically *state facts* supporting the above findings (*¶9:418*) and (b) be *narrowly tailored*—i.e., the order should direct sealing of only those documents and pages that contain the material that needs

to be placed under seal; all other portions of each document or page must remain in the public file. [CRC 2.550(e)(1); *Glassdoor, Inc. v. Sup.Ct. (Machine Zone, Inc.)* (2017) 9 CA5th 623, 638, 215 CR3d 395, 408—trial court's "boilerplate findings" that sealing order was "narrowly tailored" are insufficient]

a. [9:418.2] **Alternative order to strike:** Where the material that is the subject of the sealing motion is irrelevant, the court should simply strike it. [*Overstock.Com, Inc. v. Goldman Sachs Group, Inc.* (2014) 231 CA4th 471, 510, 180 CR3d 234, 267]

[9:418.3-418.4] *Reserved.*

4. **Application**

a. [9:418.5] **Matters that may qualify for sealing:** Only the specific words of documents that constitute the sensitive material should be sealed; generally, it is not permissible to seal the entire document. Examples of documents that may include information that may warrant sealing are:

- [9:418.6] Documents containing trade secrets. [*In re Providian Credit Card Cases* (2002) 96 CA4th 292, 300, 116 CR2d 833, 839 (dictum); *McGuan v. Endovascular Tech., Inc.* (2010) 182 CA4th 974, 988, 106 CR3d 277, 289—quality control records and complaint handling procedures]

- [9:418.7] Documents containing material protected by a privilege. [*Huffy Corp. v. Sup.Ct. (Winterthur Swiss Ins. Co.)*, supra, 112 CA4th at 108, 4 CR3d at 834—attorney-client privilege (dictum)]

- [9:418.8] Confidential settlement agreement. [*Universal City Studios, Inc. v. Sup.Ct. (Unity Pictures Corp.)* (2003) 110 CA4th 1273, 1283, 2 CR3d 484, 493 (dictum)]

[9:418.9-418.14] *Reserved.*

b. [9:418.15] **Where sealing not permitted:** Examples of documents that were ordered *not* to be sealed are:

- [9:418.16] That litigants are celebrities and subject to media attention does not justify closing the proceedings (so presumably the mere fact that the documents pertain to a celebrity would not support sealing the document). [*NBC Subsidiary (KNBC-TV), Inc. v. Sup.Ct. (Locke)* (1999) 20 C4th 1178, 1217-1218, 86 CR2d 778, 809]

- [9:418.17] Documents containing material that has been disclosed to the public cannot contain trade secrets and may not be sealed on that basis. [*In re Providian Credit Card Cases* (2002) 96 CA4th 292, 304, 116 CR2d 833, 842]

- [9:418.18] That a document contains admissions of wrongdoing does not, solely for that reason, entitle a party to a sealing order. [*Huffy Corp. v. Sup.Ct. (Winterthur Swiss Ins. Co.)*, supra, 112 CA4th at 108, 4 CR3d at 834]

- [9:418.19] That a document contains the identity of witnesses to violations of law does not, solely for that reason, entitle a party to a sealing order. [*Huffy Corp. v. Sup.Ct. (Winterthur Swiss Ins. Co.)*, supra, 112 CA4th at 108, 4 CR3d at 834]

- [9:418.20] A settlement agreement that contains a confidentiality clause does not qualify for sealing after all references to financial and other confidential data have been redacted. [*Universal City Studios, Inc. v. Sup.Ct. (Unity Pictures Corp.)*, supra, 110 CA4th at 1284, 2 CR3d at 494; see also *Huffy Corp. v. Sup.Ct. (Winterthur Swiss Ins. Co.)*, supra, 112 CA4th at 107, 4 CR3d at 833—denying overbroad request to seal entire settlement agreement including "routine verbiage which appears in most settlement agreements"]

- [9:418.21] Online review of an employer that described conditions of employment such as workload, office sizes, employment perquisites, "work-life balance" and complaints about such matters protected by the Labor Code should not be sealed. [*Glassdoor, Inc. v. Sup.Ct. (Machine Zone, Inc.)* (2017) 9 CA5th 623, 638, 215 CR3d 395, 408]

[9:418.22-418.24] *Reserved.*

c. [9:418.25] **Discovery materials:** There is no right of public access to, and hence no need to seal, discovery materials exchanged between civil litigants (e.g., pretrial depositions and interrogatories). Nor do the sealing rules of court apply to discovery motions or materials filed or lodged in court in connection with discovery motions or proceedings (e.g., confidential material subject to a protective order). [CRC 2.550(a)(3)]

The sealed records rules' presumption of public access applies only to court-filed discovery materials *used at trial* or *submitted as a basis for adjudication of matters other than discovery motions or proceedings.* [CRC 2.550(a)(3); see *Mercury Interactive Corp. v. Klein* (2007) 158 CA4th 60, 100-101, 70 CR3d 88, 118-119]

Discovery materials "submitted as a basis for adjudication" refers to materials submitted in support of and in opposition to substantive pretrial motions, regardless of whether those materials play any role in the trial court's ultimate ruling on the motion. [*Overstock.Com, Inc. v. Goldman Sachs Group, Inc.* (2014) 231 CA4th 471, 496, 180 CR3d 234, 256]

However, there is no public right of access to documents that are irrelevant to the motion or as to which evidentiary objections

© 2020 Thomson Reuters/The Rutter Group

are sustained. [*Overstock.Com, Inc. v. Goldman Sachs Group, Inc.*, supra, 231 CA4th at 492, 180 CR3d at 253]

(1) [9:418.26] **Routine discovery motions; exception for questions of public importance?** Although discovery motions and materials lodged or filed with the court in connection with discovery motions are generally exempt from the sealing rules (¶*9:418.25*), a right of public access may exist where the discovery motion involves "questions of great significance to members of the public." [*H.B. Fuller Co. v. Doe* (2007) 151 CA4th 879, 893, 60 CR3d 501, 511—motion to quash subpoena affecting First Amendment right to speak anonymously]

A protective order may require certain information or documents to be maintained confidentially and may address how they are to be handled in connection with discovery and other motions. However, the court may modify those orders in appropriate circumstances where a right of public access exists.

☞ [9:418.27] ***PRACTICE POINTER:*** Some judges require the parties to file papers related to discovery motions in the public file, redacting matter only as determined by counsel in good faith to protect confidentiality, and to simultaneously file unredacted papers under seal.

5. [9:419] **Compare—Motion to Unseal Records:** Any party or member of the public may, upon notice to the parties, file a motion, application or petition to unseal a record. In ruling on the motion, the court must consider the same matters as on a motion to seal (*see* ¶*9:418*). [CRC 2.551(h); see *In re Providian Credit Card Cases,* supra, 96 CA4th at 302, 116 CR2d at 840-841—but express findings *not* required in unsealing order] The rules do not provide a time limit for making such a motion.

   If the *court* proposes to *unseal* a record on its own motion, it must mail notice to the parties stating the reasons for the proposed unsealing. Any party may file an opposition to the unsealing within 10 days thereafter, and any other party may file a response to the opposition within five days after filing of the opposition. [CRC 2.551(h)(3)]

   An order unsealing records must state whether the records are unsealed entirely or in part. If the records are only unsealed in part or are unsealed only as to certain persons, the order must specify the portion unsealed and identify the persons entitled to access. [CRC 2.551(h)(5)]

6. [9:420] **Compare—Procedure to Use Documents Subject to Confidentiality Agreement or Protective Order:** Where a party wants to use at trial (or with a motion) documents that are subject to a confidentiality agreement or protective order, and has no interest in sealing them, he or she must:

— lodge the unredacted documents with the court clerk as required on a motion to seal (¶*9:417*);
— file redacted copies of the documents (redacted so as to conceal the protected portions); and
— give notice to opposing parties that the documents will become part of the public court file unless they file a timely motion to seal. [CRC 2.551(b)(3); see *Savaglio v. Wal-Mart Stores, Inc.*, supra, 149 CA4th at 601, 57 CR3d at 224]

J. MOTION TO EXPUNGE LIS PENDENS

1. [9:421] **Lis Pendens—In General:** A lis pendens is a *recorded instrument* ("Notice of Pending Action"), recorded in the office of the county recorder where land is located, that gives *constructive notice* of a pending lawsuit affecting title to described real property. The pleadings in the lawsuit to which the lis pendens refers must describe a specific parcel of real property. [*Gale v. Sup.Ct. (Gale)* (2004) 122 CA4th 1388, 1395, 19 CR3d 554, 559]

Anyone who acquires an interest in the described property (purchaser, mortgagee, etc.) takes that interest subject to any judgment that may be entered in the lawsuit. The practical effect is to cloud the property's title and prevent its transfer until the litigation is resolved or the lis pendens is expunged or released. [See *Kirkeby v. Sup.Ct. (Fascenelli)* (2004) 33 C4th 642, 651, 15 CR3d 805, 811; *Bishop Creek Lodge v. Scira* (1996) 46 CA4th 1721, 1733, 54 CR2d 745, 751; *Mira Overseas Consulting Ltd. v. Muse Family Enterprises, Ltd.* (2015) 237 CA4th 378, 383-384, 187 CR3d 858, 862]

FORM: Lis Pendens, *see Form 9A:26* in Rivera, *Cal. Prac. Guide: Civ. Pro. Before Trial FORMS* (TRG).

Cross-refer: Lis pendens is also discussed in Greenwald & Bank, *Cal. Prac. Guide: Real Property Transactions* (TRG), Ch. 11.

a. [9:421.1] **Required in certain actions:** There are some actions in which recordation of a lis pendens is *required* by statute, including:
— actions to quiet title; [CCP §761.010]
— actions for partition; [CCP §872.250]
— eminent domain proceedings; [CCP §§1250.130, 1250.150]
— claim to escheated property; [CCP §§1355, 1410]
— action to declare building uninhabitable; [CCP §405.7]
— forfeiture proceedings. [Fin.C. §5321(b); Health & Saf.C. §11488.4; Pen.C. §186.4]

Note: A lis pendens is not the exclusive remedy in such cases. Plaintiff may also seek an injunction, attachment or other provisional remedy. [CCP §405.8]

b. [9:421.2] **Permitted in other actions affecting title, possession or easement:** Recordation of a lis pendens is permitted in any action by a "claimant" who has a "real property claim." [CCP §405.1]

© 2020 Thomson Reuters/The Rutter Group

A "real property claim" is any cause of action which, if meritorious, would affect:

— *title to, or the right to possession of*, specific real property; or

— the *use of an easement* identified in the pleading (other than an easement obtained pursuant to statute by any regulated public utility). [CCP §405.4; *see* ¶*9:431*]

[9:421.3-421.4] *Reserved.*

c. [9:421.5] **Not permitted where action pending in another state:** Even though the property is located in California, there is no statutory authority for recording a lis pendens in California relating to an action pending in another state. [*Formula Inc. v. Sup.Ct. (iStar Fin'l Inc.)* (2008) 168 CA4th 1455, 1462, 86 CR3d 341, 346]

d. [9:421.6] **Not permitted for arbitration:** There must be an action pending in state or federal court in order for a lis pendens to be filed. A lis pendens may not be filed based on a pending arbitration involving a real property claim. [*Manhattan Loft, LLC v. Mercury Liquors, Inc.* (2009) 173 CA4th 1040, 1051, 93 CR3d 457, 464]

[9:421.7] ***PRACTICE POINTER FOR PLAINTIFFS:*** To protect your client's rights in the property while arbitrating a real property dispute, first file an action in court that will support a lis pendens and then move to stay the litigation pending the arbitration.

2. [9:422] **Procedures to "Expunge" Lis Pendens—In General:** Because of the potential for abuse and injustice to the property owner, the Legislature has provided statutory procedures (CCP §405.30 et seq.) by which a lis pendens may be removed ("expunged"). [See *Shah v. McMahon* (2007) 148 CA4th 526, 529, 55 CR3d 792, 795—lis pendens procedure "provides a means by which a court may dispose of meritless real estate claims at the preliminary stage of a case"]

a. [9:423] **Grounds for expungement:** A lis pendens may be ordered removed from the record title ("expunged") on any of the following grounds:

- *Improper lis pendens:* The lis pendens is improper because:
  — the complaint does not contain a "real property claim" [CCP §405.31]; or
  — plaintiff cannot establish its "probable validity" by a "preponderance of the evidence." [CCP §405.32]

- *Lis pendens proper, but bond provides adequate security:* Even if the "real property claim" has "probable validity," a lis pendens will be expunged if the court finds "adequate relief" can be "secured to the claimant by the giving of an undertaking." [CCP §405.33]

- *Defect in service or filing:* Alternatively, defects in statutory service and filing requirements are ground for expungement. [See CCP §405.23; and *McKnight v. Sup.Ct. (Faber)* (1985) 170 CA3d 291, 303, 215 CR 909, 915]

b. [9:424] **Compare—voluntary withdrawal:** The lis pendens claimant may voluntarily withdraw it at any time by recording an acknowledged "notice of withdrawal." [CCP §405.50] (An acknowledgment before a notary public is required; see Civ.C. §1181 et seq.)

⇨ [9:424.1] ***PRACTICE POINTER:*** Voluntary withdrawal is generally required as part of any settlement or dismissal. It should also be considered by plaintiff if serious weaknesses develop in plaintiff's case. Withdrawing the lis pendens may *mitigate whatever damages* the property owner may later claim in a malicious prosecution, slander of title or contract action.

c. [9:425] **Moving party:** Normally, defendant (property owner) is the moving party. But anyone else having an interest in the property (e.g., mortgagee, tenant, etc.) has standing *even if not named as a party*. [CCP §405.30]

A nonparty, however, must seek leave to *intervene* before the motion to expunge can be filed. [CCP §405.30]

d. [9:426] **Timing:** A motion to expunge may be filed "at any time" after the lis pendens is recorded. [CCP §405.30]

(1) [9:426.1] **While judgment on appeal:** If grounds for expungement exist (CCP §§405.31, 405.32), the motion may be made in the trial court even while an appeal is pending. [*Peery v. Sup.Ct. (Beneficial Standard Properties)* (1981) 29 C3d 837, 842, 176 CR 533, 536]

If the *claimant lost* at trial, the lis pendens *must* be expunged *unless* the trial court is willing to find *its own decision will probably be reversed* on appeal (a highly unlikely situation). [*Mix v. Sup.Ct.* (*Behniwal*) (2004) 124 CA4th 987, 996, 21 CR3d 826, 833]

e. [9:427] **Moving papers:** Requirements applicable to noticed motions generally apply to a motion to expunge—i.e., notice of motion, supporting evidence, points and authorities and proof of service (*see* ¶*9:28 ff.*).

- ***FORM:*** Motion to Expunge Lis Pendens and Proposed Order, *see Form 9A:27* in Rivera, *Cal. Prac. Guide: Civ. Pro. Before Trial FORMS* (TRG).

f. [9:428] **Discovery:** The court may make any orders necessary to provide for discovery by any party "affected" by the motion to expunge. [CCP §405.30]

© 2020 Thomson Reuters/The Rutter Group

Comment: Although the matter is unclear, "affected" party presumably means *either* the moving party (defendant) or the opposing party (plaintiff).

(1) [9:428.1] **Effect of defendant claiming privilege?** If defendant refuses to provide discovery on key issues (e.g., by invoking the privilege against self-incrimination), plaintiff's evidentiary burden (*see ¶9:429 ff.*) arguably should be excused. But the point is unsettled. [See *Klein v. Sup.Ct. (Thomas)* (1988) 198 CA3d 894, 915, 244 CR 226, 239]

3. [9:429] **Motion to Expunge *Improper* Lis Pendens:** A lis pendens will be expunged *without a bond* if the court finds either:

- Plaintiff's complaint does not contain a "*real property claim*" (i.e., one affecting title or possession of specific real property or use of an easement, etc.; CCP §405.4). [CCP §405.31 (emphasis added)]
- Or, the claimant "has *not established by a preponderance of the evidence the probable validity* of the real property claim." [CCP §405.32 (emphasis added)]

a. [9:430] **Burden of proof on lis pendens claimant (plaintiff):** Unlike most other motions, the burden of proof is on the party *opposing* the motion to expunge. The lis pendens claimant (plaintiff) bears the burden of establishing the existence of a "real property claim" and that it is "probably valid." [CCP §405.32]

Plaintiff thus has the burden of producing sufficient evidence to support a finding that plaintiff will "probably" win at trial.

b. [9:431] **Proving existence of "real property claim":** The allegations of the complaint determine whether a "real property claim" is involved; no independent evidence is required. [*Urez Corp. v. Sup.Ct. (Keefer)* (1987) 190 CA3d 1141, 1149, 235 CR 837, 842—decided under former law, but principle probably still valid]

A "real property claim" is any cause of action which, if meritorious, would affect:

— *title to, or the right to possession of*, specific real property; or

— the *use of an easement* identified in the pleading (other than an easement obtained pursuant to statute by any regulated public utility). [CCP §405.4]

(1) [9:432] **Application:** The following are actions which may "affect title or possession" of real property for lis pendens purposes:

- [9:432.1] *Specific performance:* A buyer's suit to compel specific performance of a contract for sale of real property. [*Hilberg v. Sup.Ct. (Mendrin)* (1989) 215 CA3d 539, 542, 263 CR 675, 677]

- [9:432.2] *Declaratory relief:* A suit for declaratory relief as to rights in real property. [*Mason v. Sup.Ct. (Bond)* (1985) 163 CA3d 989, 996, 210 CR 63, 67—whether ambiguous provision in deed created a condition subsequent or was merely a covenant (decided under former law)]

- [9:432.3] *Easements:* Suits to enforce or determine easement rights in real property. [CCP §405.4(b); *Woodcourt II Ltd. v. McDonald Co.* (1981) 119 CA3d 245, 247-248, 173 CR 836, 837—lis pendens on servient tenement; *Park 100 Investment Group II v. Ryan* (2009) 180 CA4th 795, 809, 103 CR3d 218, 227—easement dispute is real property claim affecting title and right to possession of both dominant and servient properties]

- [9:432.4] *Leaseholds:* A lis pendens may be filed in an action to enforce or determine ownership of a leasehold interest in real property. [*Parker v. Sup.Ct. (Dwight)* (1970) 9 CA3d 397, 399-400, 88 CR 352, 353-354—marriage dissolution involving leasehold in real property]

- [9:432.5] *Fraudulent conveyances:* A suit to set aside a fraudulent conveyance of real property. [*Kirkeby v. Sup.Ct. (Fascenelli)* (2004) 33 C4th 642, 649, 15 CR3d 805, 809-810; *Hunting World, Inc. v. Sup.Ct. (Bogar)* (1994) 22 CA4th 67, 72, 26 CR2d 923, 926 (citing text)]

- [9:432.6] *Marriage dissolution:* A marriage dissolution proceeding in which ownership of real property is at issue. [*Kane v. Huntley Fin'l* (1983) 146 CA3d 1092, 1096, 194 CR 880, 882—Wife's failure to record lis pendens allowed Husband to encumber home held in both names but which was her separate property; *Mabie v. Hyatt* (1998) 61 CA4th 581, 589, 71 CR2d 657, 661, fn. 5—same]

  Cross-refer: For further discussion of lis pendens in marriage dissolution actions, see Hogoboom & King, *Cal. Prac. Guide: Family Law* (TRG), Ch. 3.

- [9:432.7] *Mechanic's lien foreclosure:* A lis pendens is expressly authorized by statute in suits to foreclose mechanics' liens (including material suppliers, contractors, etc.; see Civ.C. §9100). [Civ.C. §8461]

  — [9:432.8] The lis pendens creates a lien only for the *amounts due under the mechanic's lien*, not for attorney fees or other amounts claimed

© 2020 Thomson Reuters/The Rutter Group

under a contract cause of action joined in the mechanic's lien foreclosure action. [*Abbett Elec. Corp. v. California Fed. Sav. & Loan Ass'n* (1991) 230 CA3d 355, 362, 281 CR 362, 366]

(2) [9:433] **Compare—actions *not* affecting title or possession:** It is not enough that the action merely relates to real property. The following are illustrative:

- [9:433.1] To satisfy a debt, defendant promised to convey property to plaintiff if certain contingencies occurred. They never occurred. Plaintiff's claimed "investment" in the property was merely a contract debt and could not support a lis pendens. [*Deane v. Sup.Ct. (Fischer)* (1985) 164 CA3d 292, 296, 210 CR 406, 408]

- [9:433.2] Several limited partners sued general partners for breach of fiduciary duty in transferring partnership real property. Plaintiffs' interest was in the partnership, not the property, and therefore their suit did *not* affect "title or possession" of the property for lis pendens purposes. [*North Coast Business Park v. Sup.Ct. (Jones)* (1984) 158 CA3d 858, 860, 205 CR 81, 82]

(3) [9:434] **Compare—actions seeking equitable lien to enforce monetary claim:** Although there are earlier cases to the contrary, it is now well established that a lis pendens is *not* proper in a creditor's action to impose a constructive trust or equitable lien on real property *solely as a means of enforcing a debt.* The action does not "affect title" because the creditor *claims no present interest* in the property. [*BGJ Assocs., LLC v. Sup.Ct. (M2B2, LLC)* (1999) 75 CA4th 952, 972, 89 CR2d 693, 706; *Lewis v. Sup.Ct. (Folksam Gen. Mut. Ins. Soc.)* (1994) 30 CA4th 1850, 1864, 37 CR2d 63, 73; *Campbell v. Sup.Ct. (La Barrie)* (2005) 132 CA4th 904, 911, 34 CR3d 68, 72]

[9:435] *Reserved.*

c. [9:436] **Proving "probable validity" of claim:** To avoid a motion to expunge under CCP §405.32, the burden is on the lis pendens claimant (plaintiff) to establish the "probable validity" of the real property claim "by a preponderance of the evidence." [CCP §405.32]

Plaintiff may offer documentary or testimonial evidence. (This is one of the few motions on which oral evidence is normally received.)

(1) [9:436.1] **"Probable validity":** "Probable validity" means "it is *more likely than not* that the [plaintiff] will obtain a judgment against the defendant on the claim." [CCP §405.3 (emphasis added)]

©2020 Thomson Reuters The Rutter Group

(2) [9:436.2] **Judge weighs evidence:** If conflicting evidence is presented, the judge must weigh the evidence in deciding whether plaintiff has sustained its burden.

d. [9:437] **Ruling on motion:** Expungement of an *improper* lis pendens is mandatory, not discretionary. Thus, if the court finds the underlying claim is not a "real property claim" or that its "probable validity" has not been established "by a preponderance of the evidence," it must order the lis pendens expunged. [CCP §§405.31, 405.32]

(1) [9:437.1] **No bond if expungement granted:** The court may not order defendant to give an undertaking before expunging an improper lis pendens. [CCP §§405.31, 405.32]

(2) [9:437.2] **Bond may be ordered if expungement denied:** If the lis pendens is proper (i.e., underlying claim is a "real property claim" and its "probable validity" is established by a "preponderance" of evidence), the court still has discretion to order an undertaking as a condition of allowing the lis pendens to remain of record. [CCP §405.34; *see* ¶*9:448*]

(3) [9:438] **Compare—judgment against claimant on appeal:** Where a judgment has been entered against the claimant on the underlying real property claim, but the claimant has filed an appeal, the motion to expunge must be granted unless the court finds it more likely than not that the appellate court will *reverse* the judgment. [*Amalgamated Bank v. Sup.Ct. (Corinthian Homes)* (2007) 149 CA4th 1003, 1015, 57 CR3d 686, 693-694]

[9:439] *Reserved.*

4. [9:440] **Motion to Expunge *Proper* Lis Pendens Where Undertaking Provides Adequate Relief:** Although the lis pendens is proper (i.e., court finds the real property claim has probable validity), it may still be expunged if the court finds "adequate relief can be secured to the claimant by the giving of an undertaking" (bond). [CCP §405.33]

[9:440.1] ***PRACTICE POINTER:*** This motion should always be made *as an alternative* to a motion to expunge on the ground the lis pendens is improper (CCP §§405.31, 405.32, ¶*9:437*). Doing so avoids unnecessary return trips to court. More importantly, it gives the court some flexibility; i.e., the court has no discretion to deny expungement when CCP §405.31 (lack of "real property claim") or CCP §405.32 (lack of "probable validity") grounds are established. But it does have discretion in fixing the amount of the bond upon which expungement can be ordered under CCP §405.33.

a. [9:440.2] **Purpose:** The bond "allows the defendant to dispose of the property subject to suit while remaining capable

© 2020 Thomson Reuters/The Rutter Group

of responding in damages to the plaintiff's claim." [*On v. Cow Hollow Properties* (1990) 222 CA3d 1568, 1573, 272 CR 535, 537—decided under former law]

b. [9:440.3] **Burden of proof on moving party (defendant):** The statute does not say which party has the burden of proving whether a bond would be "adequate relief." But the Code Comment to §405.30 expressly states the burden is on the moving party. [See *Stewart Develop. Co. IV v. Sup.Ct. (Property Investments West, Inc.)* (1980) 108 CA3d 266, 272, 166 CR 450, 453—decided under former law]

c. [9:441] **Whether undertaking "adequate relief":** Expungement will not be ordered unless a bond will secure "adequate relief" to plaintiff (CCP §405.33). A bond is "adequate relief" if it will indemnify plaintiff against all resulting damage from removing the lis pendens should he or she win or lose the lawsuit. [See *Sheets v. Sup.Ct. (Devcorp)* (1978) 86 CA3d 68, 70-71, 149 CR 912, 914—decided under former law]

(1) [9:441.1] **Single family residences:** Theoretically, every parcel of land is "unique" and money cannot compensate for loss of an interest therein (see Civ.C. §3387). But for purposes of determining whether a bond will provide "adequate" security for expungement, the presumption that land is "unique" applies only to a single family residence that plaintiff intends to occupy. [CCP §405.33]

With regard to a single family residence that plaintiff intends to occupy, the presumption is *conclusive*. [Civ.C. §3387]

(2) [9:442] **Other property:** In all other cases, the adequacy of a bond must be determined by extrinsic factors, such as:

— the nature and extent of plaintiff's claim;
— *plaintiff's purpose* in acquiring the property;
— whether the property has unique characteristics (beyond the legal "uniqueness" of all real property);
— whether the property is likely to be transferred or encumbered during litigation; and
— whether any such purchaser or encumbrancer is likely to take without notice of plaintiff's claim. [See *Stewart Develop. Co. IV v. Sup.Ct. (Property Investments West, Inc.)* (1980) 108 CA3d 266, 274, 166 CR 450, 454—expungement denied where buyer was interested in property for development purposes, rather than for just monetary gain (decided under former law)]

d. [9:443] **Amount of undertaking:** Expungement may be ordered upon posting an undertaking "of such nature and in such amount" that will indemnify plaintiff "for all damages proximately *resulting from the expungement*" that plaintiffs may incur if they win the case. [CCP §405.33 (emphasis added)]

(1) [9:443.1] **Effect:** Only those damages "resulting from the expungement" need be considered. The value of the land itself and plaintiff's claimed interest therein are only factors in determining what damages would result from the expungement if plaintiff ultimately prevails in establishing an interest in the property. [See CCP §405.33]

(2) [9:443.2] **Damages on other claims not covered:** If plaintiff loses on the lis pendens claim but wins on another cause of action (that does not support recordation of a lis pendens), the judgment cannot be satisfied out of the undertaking. Such damages do not proximately result from the expungement. [See *CMSH Co., Inc. v. Antelope Develop., Inc.* (1990) 223 CA3d 174, 272 CR 605, 609—decided under former law]

e. [9:444] **Form of undertaking:** The undertaking must be in a form sufficient under the "Bond and Undertaking Law" (CCP §995.010 et seq.). That law requires generally either a bond or undertaking from an admitted surety insurer or personal sureties (with sufficient qualifications), or a cash deposit in lieu thereof. [See CCP §§995.510, 995.610, 995.710]

(1) [9:444.1] **No other security:** The court has no power to "waive" these requirements—e.g., by allowing defendant to execute a trust deed in favor of plaintiff in lieu of an undertaking. It makes no difference that defendant has no other security and is therefore unable to obtain an undertaking. [*Markley v. Sup.Ct. (Samuels)* (1992) 5 CA4th 738, 752, 7 CR2d 328, 336]

f. [9:445] **Procedural considerations:** An expungement ordered under §405.33 is conditioned on the moving party posting the designated undertaking by a specified "return date." On that day, the moving party must show the required undertaking has been provided. Otherwise, the motion to expunge will be denied "without further notice or hearing." [CCP §405.33]

(1) [9:445.1] **Continuance?** Whether this permits a continuance of the hearing is unclear.

➪ [9:445.2] ***PRACTICE POINTER:*** To avoid any question, ask the court to set a "return date" far enough out to permit hearing on any objections to the sufficiency of the undertaking.

(2) [9:445.3] **Objections to sufficiency of undertaking:** Objections to the sufficiency of the undertaking must be resolved as provided in CCP §995.010 et seq.

Cross-refer: See detailed discussion in Ahart, *Cal. Prac. Guide: Enforcing Judgments & Debts* (TRG), Ch. 6H.

© 2020 Thomson Reuters/The Rutter Group

[9:446-447] *Reserved.*

5. [9:448] **Compare—Motion for Undertaking as Condition of Lis Pendens:** Instead of posting a bond itself to obtain expungement, defendant may move the court to require plaintiff to provide an undertaking as a condition of keeping the lis pendens in effect. [CCP §405.34]

   Any party having an interest in the property (e.g., lenders, tenants, etc.) may seek such security. However, nonparties must seek leave to intervene before filing the motion. [CCP §405.34]

   a. [9:448.1] **Burden of proof on moving party (defendant):** *See discussion at ¶9:440.3.*

   b. [9:449] **Amount of undertaking:** The undertaking will be "of such nature and in such amount as the court may determine to be just." [CCP §405.34]

      The court will usually set an amount high enough to cover whatever damages the moving party is likely to suffer if the lis pendens is not removed. [See *Elder v. Carlisle Ins. Co.* (1987) 193 CA3d 1313, 1319, 238 CR 897, 901—decided under former law]

      This may include:

      - [9:449.1] *Carrying costs of property:* The taxes, interest cost and expenses of maintaining the property while lis pendens clouds title; and if property is declining in value, lost profits on resale. [See *CMSH Co., Inc. v. Antelope Develop., Inc.* (1990) 223 CA3d 174, 181, 272 CR 605, 610—decided under former law but principle still valid]

      - [9:449.2] *Attorney fees and costs:* It may also include attorney fees and costs in removing the cloud on title: "The bond would in fact have limited and uncertain value if the defendant could not use it to collect attorneys' fees and costs in the successful defense of the action." [*On v. Cow Hollow Properties* (1990) 222 CA3d 1568, 1573, 272 CR 535, 538—decided under former law]

      - [9:449.3] *Compare—no damages resulting from inflation:* But damages caused by inflation and the resulting loss of purchasing power of money may not be recoverable. Reason: The lis pendens was not the cause of inflation. [*CMSH Co., Inc. v. Antelope Develop., Inc.*, supra, 223 CA3d at 181-183, 272 CR at 610-611]

      - [9:449.4] *Compare—no malicious prosecution damages:* Similarly, damages from malicious prosecution (e.g., emotional distress, punitive damages) are not considered in assessing damages recoverable under the undertaking. [See CCP §405.34 (last sent.)]

   c. [9:450] **Procedural considerations:** The procedure for providing an undertaking is substantially the same as discussed above with respect to motions under CCP §405.33 (¶*9:445 ff.*).

[9:451-452] *Reserved.*

6. [9:453] **Motion to Expunge for Defects in Service or Filing Lis Pendens:** Although the statute does not expressly authorize expungement because of defects in service or filing of the lis pendens, these grounds are recognized by case law. [*McKnight v. Sup.Ct. (Faber)* (1985) 170 CA3d 291, 303, 215 CR 909, 915] (The Code Comment to CCP §§405.23 and 405.30 also states expungement may be ordered for such defects.)

   However, a lis pendens need not be expunged to be deemed "void and invalid" under CCP §405.23 due to defects in service or filing. [*Carr v. Rosien* (2015) 238 CA4th 845, 857, 190 CR3d 245, 253 (lis pendens declared void due to lack of mail notice)—"Legislature did not intend to require that a void lis pendens be expunged"; see *Rey Sanchez Investments v. Sup.Ct. (Pch Enterprises, Inc.)* (2016) 244 CA4th 259, 263, 197 CR3d 575, 578—lis pendens without proof of service may be deemed void without expungement motion]

   a. [9:453.1] **Compare—technical defects:** However, it may be an abuse of discretion to expunge a lis pendens solely for a "technical" defect in service, at least where defendant has actual notice of the lis pendens. [*Biddle v. Sup.Ct. (Paulson)* (1985) 170 CA3d 135, 137, 215 CR 848, 849]

      - [9:453.2] P mailed a copy of lis pendens to D's business address, but not his residence address, by first class mail (violating the requirement that notice be mailed with return receipt requested to "all known addresses"; see CCP §405.22). But D had actual notice and moved to expunge (on other grounds) within 5 days after the lis pendens was recorded. It was an abuse of discretion to expunge at a later date for technical defects in the original service of lis pendens. [*Biddle v. Sup.Ct. (Paulson)*, supra, 170 CA3d at 137, 215 CR at 849]

   b. [9:454] **Compare—defects waived by delay:** Moreover, procedural defects may be waived where the moving party unreasonably delays asserting these grounds. [*Biddle v. Sup.Ct. (Paulson)*, supra, 170 CA3d at 137, 215 CR at 849—ground first raised more than one year after notice received; compare *Rey Sanchez Investments v. Sup.Ct. (Pch Enterprises, Inc.)*, supra, 244 CA4th at 265, 197 CR3d at 579—78-day delay did not warrant refusal to expunge void lis pendens]

   c. [9:455] **Supporting material; burden of proof; filing and service requirements, etc.:** The rules applicable to motions and evidentiary hearings in general apply. [CCP §405.30, Code Comment, para. 3; CCP §1005 et seq.; Ev.C. §500]

   d. [9:456] **Refiling after expungement:** Once a lis pendens has been expunged for any reason (including defects in service

© 2020 Thomson Reuters/The Rutter Group

or filing), *leave of court* is required to re-record the lis pendens (CCP §405.36; see *Ward v. Sup.Ct. (Beverlywood Homes Ass'n)* (1997) 55 CA4th 60, 66, 63 CR2d 731, 734, fn. 3).

7. [9:457] **Expungement Order:** An attorney order will be required because the expungement order must be drafted in form suitable for recording.

➡ [9:457.1] ***PRACTICE POINTER:*** Make sure your expungement order identifies all parties and the litigation, and the recording information on the lis pendens being expunged. Title insurance companies can "nit-pick" any ambiguity and refuse to insure.

If your client has a sale or transfer pending, show the title company a draft of your order before presenting it to the court for execution. Ask the title officer whether any additional language is required to satisfy the title company so that the lis pendens will not be shown as an "exception" in the title policy.

a. [9:458] **When recordable:** The expungement order is not effective and may not be recorded "until the time within which a petition for writ of mandate may be filed . . . has expired." [CCP §405.35 (20 days after service of notice of order, unless extended for up to 10 days)]

➡ [9:458.1] ***PRACTICE POINTER:*** Ask opposing counsel to waive notice on the record. If he or she refuses, serve your notice of order immediately upon entry of the order to start the 20-day period running.

Unless there is clear authority to challenge the expungement order, plaintiff's counsel should consider executing an immediate *voluntary* withdrawal of the lis pendens. Doing so may mitigate the damages defendant may later seek against plaintiff; *see* ¶*9:424 ff.*

(1) [9:458.2] **Effect of premature recordation?** Whether an expungement order is effective if recorded before expiration of the 20-day period is unclear.

b. [9:459] **Effect of recording expungement order:** Upon recordation of a certified copy of the expungement order, the lis pendens ceases to have any effect. It no longer provides actual or constructive notice of the matters stated therein or a duty of inquiry to anyone dealing with the property. [CCP §405.60]

Thereafter, and until the ultimate judgment in the action is recorded, *no one other than the named parties* to the action takes subject to plaintiff's claims in the lawsuit. [See CCP §405.61—"It is the intent of the Legislature that this section shall provide for the *absolute and complete free transfer-*

ability of real property after the expungement or withdrawal of a notice of pendency of action" (emphasis added)]

The effect is that a subsequent purchaser takes title unencumbered by the judgment ultimately rendered in the action in which the lis pendens was recorded. [*FDIC v. Charlton* (1993) 17 CA4th 1066, 1069-1070, 21 CR2d 686, 689]

(1) [9:459.1] **Actual knowledge irrelevant:** Except for named parties, CCP §405.61 provides for "absolute and complete free transferability" of property after expungement of the lis pendens. Nonparty purchasers take free and clear of the claims involved in the lawsuit, even if they had actual knowledge thereof and would have been subject thereto had a lis pendens not been filed. [CCP §405.61; *Knapp Develop. & Design v. Pal-Mal Properties, Ltd.* (1987) 195 CA3d 786, 790, 240 CR 920, 923—decided under former law but same rule under present statute]

- [9:459.2] For example, Buyer 1 sues Vendor for specific performance and records a lis pendens. Vendor has the lis pendens expunged. Vendor may freely convey the subject property to Buyer 2, *even though Buyer 2 knows of the underlying lawsuit* and has been "waiting in the wings" to purchase the property for more money.
- [9:459.3] *Compare—if no lis pendens filed:* This is one of the main disadvantages of a lis pendens because if Buyer 1 had never recorded the lis pendens, Buyer 2 would be subject to the judgment in the underlying action because he or she had actual knowledge of the lawsuit. [See CCP §1908(a)(2)—judgment binding on successors in interest who have actual or constructive notice of action]

(2) [9:460] **No basis for claiming fraud:** CCP §405.61 relieves purchasers of "actual knowledge" following expungement of a lis pendens only for purposes of transferability of title. It does not permit a purchaser to sue for fraudulent misrepresentations or nondisclosure of matters as to which he or she had actual knowledge at the time of purchase. [*Bishop Creek Lodge v. Scira* (1996) 46 CA4th 1721, 1735, 54 CR2d 745, 752-753]

[9:461-462] *Reserved.*

8. [9:463] **Attorney Fees and Costs to Prevailing Party:** The court is required to "direct" an award to the prevailing party of the reasonable attorney fees and costs of making or opposing the motion *unless* it finds that either:

— "the other party acted with *substantial justification*"; or

— "*other circumstances* make the imposition of attorney's fees and costs unjust." [CCP §405.38 (emphasis added)]

© 2020 Thomson Reuters/The Rutter Group

. This is the same standard applicable to rulings on discovery motions. *See discussion at ¶8:1960 ff.*

a. [9:463.1] **Prevailing party:** The "prevailing party" is determined with the motion's objective in mind:

(1) [9:463.2] **Improper lis pendens:** A motion to expunge under CCP §§405.31 or 405.32 places in issue whether the lis pendens was proper. The court's ruling on this issue automatically decides who is the "prevailing party" for purposes of fees and costs. [See *Trapasso v. Sup.Ct. (Majdali)* (1977) 73 CA3d 561, 570, 140 CR 820, 825—decided under former law]

(2) [9:463.3] **Bond adequate security:** But a defendant moving to expunge under §405.33 (bond as adequate security) is the "prevailing" party only if the court orders a bond in the same amount or less than offered by defendant. If the court orders a greater amount, plaintiff is the "prevailing" party. [See *Trapasso v. Sup.Ct. (Majdali)*, supra, 73 CA3d at 570, 140 CR at 825—decided under former law]

b. [9:464] **Against losing party, not counsel:** The prevailing party on a motion to expunge is entitled to an award only against the losing party. There is no provision for an award against the losing party's attorneys as sanctions or otherwise. [*Doyle v. Sup.Ct. (Jacinth Develop., Inc.)* (1991) 226 CA3d 1355, 1359, 277 CR 630, 632]

c. [9:465] **Effect of withdrawing lis pendens before hearing on motion to expunge:** A "practical approach" is followed in determining the "prevailing party" when a lis pendens is withdrawn before the hearing on the expungement motion. The court must determine the *merits* of the motion and the extent to which each party has *realized its litigation objective.* Thus, even if the expungement motion was meritorious, attorney fees may be denied if the court finds the lis pendens claimant acted with "substantial justification" in withdrawing the lis pendens (e.g., following settlement) or other circumstances render imposition of sanctions "unjust." [*Castro v. Sup.Ct. (California Sav.)* (2004) 116 CA4th 1010, 1024-1025, 10 CR3d 865, 875-876]

9. [9:466] **Appellate Review:** The only remedy to challenge an order made in expungement proceedings, including fee awards, is to petition for a writ of mandate within 20 days of notice of the order. Such orders are *not* appealable. [CCP §405.39; *Shah v. McMahon* (2007) 148 CA4th 526, 529, 55 CR3d 792, 794—fee award not appealable as sanction under CCP §904.1]

[9:467-499] *Reserved.*

CHAPTER 9

PART II

PROVISIONAL REMEDIES

CONTENTS

© 2020 Thomson Reuters/The Rutter Group

© 2020 Thomson Reuters/The Rutter Group

© 2020 Thomson Reuters/The Rutter Group

© 2020 Thomson Reuters/The Rutter Group

© 2020 Thomson Reuters/The Rutter Group

© 2020 Thomson Reuters/The Rutter Group

© 2020 Thomson Reuters/The Rutter Group

RESERVED

PART II
PROVISIONAL REMEDIES

A. INJUNCTIONS

[9:500] **OVERVIEW**

- **Brief History:** Injunctions—i.e., orders that an act be done or not be done—were first granted in English courts of chancery when the (then strict) forms of action in the common law courts provided no remedy. While the distinction between common law and chancery courts never existed in California, and the common law forms of action were long ago abolished, injunction practice is still governed by certain rules developed in the chancery courts. For example:
  - — Injunctions will not issue unless the legal remedy (usually money damages) is inadequate.
  - — The maxims and standards originally developed by the English chancellors still guide and limit the conditions upon which injunctive relief is available: e.g., "irreparable injury," "balancing equities," "doing equity," "laches," "multiplicity of actions," etc.
- **Types of Injunctions:** Injunctions may be issued:
  - — on a temporary, emergency basis via a temporary restraining order (TRO) (¶*9:538*, *9:560 ff.*);
  - — via a preliminary injunction (PI), which usually lasts through the end of trial (¶*9:539*, *9:621 ff.*); and
  - — via a permanent injunction issued after trial and as part of the judgment (¶*9:540*).
- **Purpose:** Injunctions are equitable in nature and the general purpose of prejudgment injunctive relief is to preserve the status quo pending a determination on the merits. The grant or denial of a temporary restraining order or preliminary injunction "does not amount to an adjudication of the ultimate rights in a controversy. It merely determines that the court, balancing the respective equities of the parties, concludes that, pending a trial on the merits," exercise of the right claimed by the defendant should or should not be restrained. [*Jamison v. Department of Transp.* (2016) 4 CA5th 356, 361, 208 CR3d 610, 613-614]
- **Balancing Test:** While the court has broad discretion in ruling on an application for a TRO or PI, such discretion must be exercised in light of two related factors (¶*9:506 ff.*):
  - — **Who will suffer greater injury:** Are plaintiffs likely to suffer greater injury from denial of the injunction than defendants are likely to suffer if it is granted?

© 2020 Thomson Reuters/The Rutter Group

> — **Probable outcome at trial:** Is there a reasonable probability that plaintiffs will prevail on the merits?
>
> However, *permanent* injunctions only issue on success of the claims, and do not involve the balancing of equities commonly at the heart of motions for preliminary injunctions and TROs (¶*9:505 ff.*).

1. [9:501] **Authority for Injunctive Relief:** The primary statutory authority for injunctions pending trial is CCP §§525-533, and particularly CCP §527, which, together with CRC 3.1150-3.1152, provide the basic injunction-seeking procedure. (Any local court rules or policies in this area are preempted by CRC 3.20(a); *see* ¶*9:13.2.*)

   Injunctive relief may be granted based on a verified complaint or cross-complaint (or declarations) showing sufficient factual grounds for relief. [CCP §527(a), (h)]

   ⇨ [9:501.1] ***PRACTICE POINTER:*** Because pleadings are supposed to contain ultimate rather than evidentiary facts (*see* ¶*6:123*), a pleading may not establish the facts necessary to support an injunction. Therefore, it is better practice to rely on declarations when seeking injunctive relief.

   a. [9:502] **Grounds provided by case law:** CCP §527(a) authorizes issuance of injunctions before trial if "sufficient grounds exist therefor." In most cases, the grounds are those developed by case law, although some of these have been codified. [See CCP §526, setting forth 7 grounds upon which injunctions may be granted]

   b. [9:503] **Statutory injunctions:** An increasing number of statutes specifically authorize issuance of injunctions according to criteria specified in the statutes—i.e., *without having to satisfy* the rules developed by case law. For example, injunctions are authorized by statute in the following cases:

      - Harassment [CCP §527.6; *see* ¶*9:697 ff.*]
      - Domestic violence [Fam.C. §6200 et seq.; *see* ¶*9:683*]
      - Workplace violence [CCP §527.8; *see* ¶*9:678 ff.*]
      - Group violence [CCP §527.7]
      - Restraint of trade [Bus. & Prof.C. §16753]
      - Unfair practices [Bus. & Prof.C. §17070 et seq.]
      - Unfair competition [Bus. & Prof.C. §17203; *see* ¶*9:684 ff.*]
      - Consumers Legal Remedies Act [Civ.C. §1780]
      - Illegal expenditure of public funds [CCP §526a; *see* ¶*9:514*]

- Misappropriation of trade secrets [Civ.C. §3426 et seq.; *see ¶9:691.5 ff.*]
- Fraudulent transfer of assets [Civ.C. §3439.07; *see ¶9:707.20*]

2. Equitable Considerations for Injunctions

a. [9:504] **Legal remedy must be inadequate:** CCP §526(a) lists many of the traditional equity considerations and requirements re granting of injunctions. Inadequacy of the legal remedy is listed only 4th and 5th ("(4) when pecuniary compensation would not afford adequate relief"; and "(5) where it would be extremely difficult to ascertain the amount of compensation which would afford adequate relief"). But the placement should not be misread. Injunctions will rarely be granted (absent specific statutory authority) where a suit for damages provides an adequate remedy. [See *Thayer Plymouth Ctr., Inc. v. Chrysler Motors Corp.* (1967) 255 CA2d 300, 307, 63 CR 148, 152; *Pacific Decision Sciences Corp. v. Sup.Ct. (Maudlin)* (2004) 121 CA4th 1100, 1110, 18 CR3d 104, 111]

Conversely, injunctive relief is more likely to be granted where a damages remedy is *precluded* by law. [*Department of Fish & Game v. Anderson-Cottonwood Irrig. Dist.* (1992) 8 CA4th 1554, 1564, 11 CR2d 222, 228—statute prohibited damages award against State for activity enjoined (operating water diversion facility in manner destroying endangered fish)]

(1) [9:504.1] **Solvency of defendant as factor:** In considering the "adequacy" of damages as a remedy, the court may consider whether the party against whom the judgment is sought is able to respond in damages. I.e., if the defendant is shown to be insolvent, a monetary judgment may be inadequate. [*West Coast Const. Co. v. Oceano Sanitary Dist.* (1971) 17 CA3d 693, 700, 95 CR 169, 173]

(2) [9:504.2] **No injunction where claim and delivery available:** In general, *claim and delivery* is the proper remedy for repossessing personal property (*see discussion at ¶9:784 ff.*). Thus, where title to personal property is in dispute, courts will not issue a preliminary injunction to change possession of property pending trial. [*Simms v. NPCK Enterprises, Inc.* (2003) 109 CA4th 233, 243, 134 CR2d 557, 563-564; see *Voorhies v. Greene* (1983) 139 CA3d 989, 997-998, 189 CR 132, 137]

b. [9:505] **Balancing factors:** While the statute makes no reference to the traditional equitable concern of "balancing equities," it is a crucial factor in the judge's determination: i.e., the court must exercise its discretion "in favor of the party most likely to be injured . . . If denial of an injunction would result in great harm to the plaintiff, and the defendants would

© 2020 Thomson Reuters/The Rutter Group

suffer little harm if it were granted, then it is an *abuse of discretion* to *fail to grant* the preliminary injunction." [*Robbins v. Sup.Ct. (County of Sacramento)* (1985) 38 C3d 199, 205, 211 CR 398, 401 (emphasis added)]

"A superior court must evaluate two interrelated factors when ruling on a request for a preliminary injunction: (1) the likelihood that the plaintiff will prevail on the merits at trial and (2) the interim harm that the plaintiff would be likely to sustain if the injunction were denied as compared to the harm the defendant would be likely to suffer if the preliminary injunction were issued." [*Smith v. Adventist Health System/West* (2010) 182 CA4th 729, 749, 106 CR3d 318, 335-336; see *Brown v. Pacifica Found., Inc.* (2019) 34 CA5th 915, 925, 246 CR3d 822, 828-829]

(1) [9:506] **Two-prong test:** While the court has broad discretion in ruling on an application for PI, such discretion must be exercised in light of the following interrelated factors:

- **Who will suffer greater injury:** Are plaintiffs likely to suffer *greater* injury from denial of the injunction than defendants are likely to suffer if it is granted? [*Shoemaker v. County of Los Angeles* (1995) 37 CA4th 618, 633, 43 CR2d 774, 784]
- **Probable outcome at trial:** Is there a reasonable probability that plaintiffs will prevail on the merits? [*Robbins v. Sup.Ct. (County of Sacramento)*, supra, 38 C3d at 206, 211 CR at 402]

The court's determination must be guided by a "mix" of the potential-merit and interim-harm factors; the greater plaintiff's showing on one, the less must be shown on the other to support an injunction. [*Butt v. State of Calif.* (1992) 4 C4th 668, 678, 15 CR2d 480, 486; *King v. Meese* (1987) 43 C3d 1217, 1226-1228, 240 CR 829, 834-835—court has discretion to issue preliminary injunction where plaintiff demonstrates high likelihood of success on merits even if plaintiff unable to show balance of harm tips in his or her favor; *SB Liberty, LLC v. Isla Verde Ass'n, Inc.* (2013) 217 CA4th 272, 280, 158 CR3d 105, 111]

But the trial court may not issue an injunction, regardless of the amount of interim harm, "unless there is some possibility" that plaintiff will ultimately prevail on the merits of the claim. [*Jamison v. Department of Transp.* (2016) 4 CA5th 356, 362, 208 CR3d 610, 614; *Association of Orange County Deputy Sheriffs v. County of Orange* (2013) 217 CA4th 29, 49, 158 CR3d 135, 150; see *Yu v. University of La Verne* (2011) 196 CA4th 779, 787, 793, 126 CR3d 763, 769, 774—appellate court need not reach issue of whether balance of harms favors granting preliminary injunction where trial court correctly determined moving party failed to show any likelihood of succeeding on merits]

(a) [9:507] **Compare—test where government seeking to enjoin statutory violation:** The two-prong test (¶*9:506*) does not apply when a governmental entity is suing to enjoin violation of a statute or ordinance that *specifically authorizes* injunctive relief and the government shows a "reasonable probability" of prevailing on the merits. In such cases, a *rebuttable presumption* arises that the potential harm to the public *outweighs* the potential harm to the defendant. The *burden*, therefore, is on the *defendant* to prove that it would suffer "grave or irreparable harm" from issuance of the preliminary injunction. Only if such harm can be shown will the court proceed to examine the relative actual harms to the parties. [*IT Corp. v. County of Imperial* (1983) 35 C3d 63, 69, 196 CR 715, 719; *Water Replenishment Dist. of Southern Calif. v. City of Cerritos* (2013) 220 CA4th 1450, 1461, 1464, 163 CR3d 754, 761, 764; *People v. FXS Mgmt., Inc.* (2016) 2 CA5th 1154, 1158-1159, 206 CR3d 819, 822-823]

Rationale: By enacting the statute or ordinance, the legislative body has already determined that the proscribed activity is contrary to the public interest, that significant public harm will result from the activity and that injunctive relief is appropriate to protect against that harm. [*IT Corp. v. County of Imperial*, supra, 35 C3d at 70-71, 196 CR at 720]

(2) [9:508] **Irreparable harm:** CCP §526(a)(2) lists the traditional consideration of "irreparable harm." Irreparable harm is often related to the "inadequate legal remedy" (i.e., the damages remedy is inadequate *because* some immeasurable harm is threatened). But it is also a separate consideration. Relief is unlikely unless someone will be significantly hurt in a way that cannot later be repaired. [*People ex rel. Gow v. Mitchell Brothers' Santa Ana Theater* (1981) 118 CA3d 863, 870-871, 173 CR 476, 479]

Moreover, the threat of "irreparable harm" must be *imminent* as opposed to a mere possibility of harm sometime in the future: "An injunction cannot issue in a vacuum based on the proponents' fears about something that may happen in the future. It must be supported by actual evidence that there is a realistic prospect that the party enjoined intends to engage in the prohibited activity." [*Korean Philadelphia Presbyterian Church v. California Presbytery* (2000) 77 CA4th 1069, 1084, 92 CR2d 275, 285]

© 2020 Thomson Reuters/The Rutter Group

But plaintiffs need not wait until they have suffered actual harm before applying for an injunction; they may seek injunctive relief against *threatened* infringement of their rights. [*Maria P. v. Riles* (1987) 43 C3d 1281, 1292, 240 CR 872, 878; *Costa Mesa City Employees' Ass'n v. City of Costa Mesa* (2012) 209 CA4th 298, 305-306, 146 CR3d 677, 683]

[9:508.1] ***PRACTICE POINTER:*** Set forth the irreparable harm to your client, in detail, at the *beginning* of your memorandum of points and authorities, and emphasize why injunctive relief is necessary and appropriate in your case. Make sure you provide admissible evidence of the harm (*see ¶9:574 ff.*).

(a) [9:509] **Land:** Real property is usually deemed "unique," so that injury or loss cannot be compensated in damages, and injunctive relief is therefore more readily granted. [See Civ.C. §3387—damages presumed inadequate for breach of agreement to convey real property; *Aspen Grove Condominium Ass'n v. CNL Income Northstar LLC* (2014) 231 CA4th 53, 62-64, 179 CR3d 429, 436-438—invasion of plaintiff's land by continuous trespass of water warranted injunction regardless of damages]

However, where the real property consists of *condominium units* being held for *investment* purposes, and having an *established market price*, damages are an *adequate remedy* warranting denial of injunctive relief. [*Jessen v. Keystone Sav. & Loan Ass'n* (1983) 142 CA3d 454, 458, 191 CR 104, 106-107—refusing preliminary injunction to restrain foreclosure sale]

(b) [9:510] **Money:** Normally, an injunction will *not* issue where only money is involved. The rationale is that there is no threat of irreparable harm, because monetary losses are compensable in damages. Moreover, statutes governing *prejudgment attachment* limit the conditions on which payment of money may be restrained (*see ¶9:853 ff.*). [*Doyka v. Sup.Ct. (Lord)* (1991) 233 CA3d 1134, 1136, 285 CR 14, 15—injunction against party "*using funds* on deposit *in any bank* . . . for any purpose whatsoever" voided: this was in effect a *prejudgment attachment* without complying with attachment statute]

1) [9:510.1] **Compare—preventing obtaining funds:** But a party may be enjoined from *obtaining* funds to which it is not entitled. [See *Mitsui Manufacturers Bank v. Texas Commerce Bank-Fort Worth* (1984) 159 CA3d 1051, 1057-

1058, 206 CR 218, 222—beneficiary of letter of credit enjoined from negotiating the instrument to obtain funds to which it was not entitled]

2) [9:511] **Compare—preventing dissipation of specific funds:** In a suit to impose a *constructive trust* on specific, identifiable funds separately held by defendant, an injunction may issue to prevent dissipation of those funds pending the suit. The owner is entitled to the funds *intact*, rather than a "naked claim for damages" against the wrongdoer, or having to "trace" the assets into the hands of third parties. [See *Heckmann v. Ahmanson* (1985) 168 CA3d 119, 136, 214 CR 177, 189]

- [9:511.1] In a suit to impose a constructive trust on funds wrongfully obtained by defendant auto insurer (illegal profits on a stock transaction), the insurer was enjoined from using such funds to pay claims. Otherwise, the funds would be dissipated and "[p]laintiffs would be left with a constructive trust on the fender of a Buick in Ypsalanti [sic]." [*Heckmann v. Ahmanson*, supra, 168 CA3d at 137, 214 CR at 190]

- [9:511.2] The trial court properly issued a TRO requiring Law Firm to temporarily deposit funds received in settlement of a class action into a secure account based on evidence that Law Firm delayed disclosing the settlement to class members and attempted to mislead the court as to its terms. [*Lofton v. Wells Fargo Home Mortg.* (2014) 230 CA4th 1050, 1067, 179 CR3d 254, 269—trial court itself had "substantial interest" in preserving settlement proceeds for allocation and approval]

(c) [9:512] **Public officer or agency as defendant:** Public policy considerations come into play when a preliminary injunction is sought against a public agency or officer. A "significant" showing of irreparable injury is required because there is a "general rule against enjoining public officers or agencies from performing their duties." [*Tahoe Keys Prop. Owners Ass'n v. State Water Resources Control Bd.* (1994) 23 CA4th 1459, 1471, 28 CR2d 734, 740; *O'Connell v. Sup.Ct. (Valenzuela)* (2006) 141 CA4th 1452, 1464, 47 CR3d 147, 155-156—"principles of comity and separation of powers place significant restraints on courts' authority to order or ratify acts

© 2020 Thomson Reuters/The Rutter Group

normally committed to the discretion of other branches or officials" (internal quotes omitted)]

(d) [9:513] **Constitutional rights:** Irreparable injury is presumed where plaintiff's *First Amendment* rights are threatened: "The loss of First Amendment freedoms, for even minimal periods of time, unquestionably constitutes irreparable injury." [*Elrod v. Burns* (1976) 427 US 347, 373, 96 S.Ct. 2673, 2690]

But this does not automatically apply to other constitutional rights. For example, the court may refuse to enjoin governmental invasions of *privacy* where plaintiff shows no threat of irreparable harm. [See *Loder v. City of Glendale* (1989) 216 CA3d 777, 786, 265 CR 66, 70]

1) [9:513.1] **Past infringement not enough:** It is not enough to show merely that defendant's illegal acts have impaired plaintiff's free speech rights. There must be a showing that those acts are *likely to recur* unless enjoined. [*Choice-in-Education League v. Los Angeles Unified School Dist.* (1993) 17 CA4th 415, 431, 21 CR2d 303, 313—improper to issue preliminary injunction against school district's broadcasting partisan political messages absent evidence further broadcasts were contemplated]

(e) [9:514] **Compare—taxpayer suits:** A California taxpayer has standing to enjoin illegal expenditures of public funds (see CCP §526a). But this applies to *permanent* injunctive relief. Injury to a taxpayer's pocketbook is *not* a substitute for the high degree of existing or threatened injury required for *prejudgment* injunctive relief (preliminary injunctions). [*Cohen v. Board of Supervisors of City & County of San Francisco* (1986) 178 CA3d 447, 454, 225 CR 114, 117; see *White v. Davis* (2003) 30 C4th 528, 554-556, 133 CR2d 648, 669-671 (collecting cases)]

(f) [9:515] **Effect of delay in seeking relief:** Delay in moving for a preliminary injunction may be considered in determining whether the claimed injury is "irreparable." [*O'Connell v. Sup.Ct. (Valenzuela)*, supra, 141 CA4th at 1481, 47 CR3d at 169-170—plaintiffs' claim of imminent injury from not receiving high school diplomas, raised shortly before graduation, could have been made earlier in the school year thereby avoiding the urgency of their situation]

But other factors may explain the delay; e.g., the time required for discovery, investigation and obtaining proof. [See *Nutro Products, Inc. v. Cole Grain Co.* (1992) 3 CA4th 860, 866, 5 CR2d 41, 44—15-month delay between discovery and application for injunction did not preclude irreparable injury]

[9:515.1] ***PRACTICE POINTER:*** File your application for injunctive relief as *quickly as possible* after learning about the need for such relief. Delay may be fatal.

(3) [9:516] **Probability of success:** If convinced plaintiff is likely to lose in the end, the judge will not issue the injunction because it does not appear "that the *plaintiff is entitled* to the relief demanded." [CCP §526(a)(1) (emphasis added); see *SB Liberty, LLC v. Isla Verde Ass'n, Inc.* (2013) 217 CA4th 272, 280, 158 CR3d 105, 111]

(a) [9:517] **"Reasonable" probability or "some possibility" of success required:** A preliminary injunction *must not* issue unless it is "reasonably probable that the moving party will prevail on the merits." [*San Francisco Newspaper Printing Co., Inc. v. Sup.Ct. (Miller)* (1985) 170 CA3d 438, 442, 216 CR 462, 464—abuse of discretion to grant injunction where plaintiff lacked standing to sue; see *Costa Mesa City Employees' Ass'n v. City of Costa Mesa* (2012) 209 CA4th 298, 309, 146 CR3d 677, 685—no injunction may issue unless there is at least "some possibility" of success; *City of Pasadena v. Cohen* (2014) 228 CA4th 1461, 1467, 176 CR3d 729, 733—injunction improperly granted pending ruling on merits of declaratory relief claim where plaintiff not entitled to declaratory relief as matter of law]

(b) **Application**

- [9:517.1] To halt D's construction of a house that would block P's view, P had to show an enforceable equitable servitude or CCRs. Absent such evidence, there was no "reasonable probability" P could prevail at trial and a preliminary injunction could not issue. [*Scaringe v. J.C.C. Enterprises, Inc.* (1988) 205 CA3d 1536, 1543, 253 CR 344, 348 (disapproved on other grounds in *Citizens for Covenant Compliance v. Anderson* (1995) 12 C4th 345, 47 CR2d 898)]

- [9:517.2] A complaint challenging the validity of an ordinance adopted pursuant to the Subdivision Map Act is subject to the Act's 90-day statute of limitations (Gov.C. §66499.37). Because

© 2020 Thomson Reuters/The Rutter Group

P's action, filed five months after adoption of the ordinance, was time barred, P could not show a likelihood of success on the merits, and a preliminary injunction staying enforcement of the ordinance should not have issued. [*Aiuto v. City & County of San Francisco* (2012) 201 CA4th 1347, 1355, 135 CR3d 617, 623]

[9:517.3-517.4] *Reserved.*

[9:517.5] ***PRACTICE POINTER:*** This is an extremely important determination. Cases often settle when a judge finds either (i) plaintiff is likely to prevail on the merits and issues a preliminary injunction or (ii) the case likely has no merit. Even if there is no settlement, future rulings may be influenced by the judge's earlier determination on the preliminary injunction. It is important for a defendant in this situation to attempt to establish *additional facts* to undermine plaintiff's case on the merits, and for plaintiff to rebut those facts.

(4) **Application of balancing factors**

- [9:518] Welfare recipients sued to invalidate County program requiring them to live in a county facility in lieu of cash welfare payments. It was an *abuse of discretion* to *deny* a preliminary injunction because (1) the plaintiffs were likely to prevail on the merits because the program was of "doubtful constitutionality"; and (2) the great interim harm to plaintiffs' rights of privacy outweighed the relatively slight injury to the County in restraining the program. [*Robbins v. Sup.Ct. (County of Sacramento)* (1985) 38 C3d 199, 206-209, 211 CR 398, 402-404]
- [9:518.1] Hospital was notified it would lose accreditation for its residency training program in emergency medicine unless Doctor was replaced as chief of its emergency medicine department. Hospital replaced Doctor. Doctor sued for reinstatement. The balance of hardships favored *denying* interim relief because Doctor was still employed at Hospital and could pursue administrative remedies for reinstatement; whereas, if an injunction was issued, Hospital's residency program would be put in jeopardy and the health of the community put at risk. [*Shoemaker v. County of Los Angeles* (1995) 37 CA4th 618, 634, 43 CR2d 774, 785]
- [9:518.2] Employer sued former Employee for breach of contract, including a noncompete agreement. Issue sanctions imposed against Employee for his discovery

abuse established that Employee knowingly breached the employment contract, including the noncompete clause. As a result, on Employer's motion for PI, the likelihood that Employer would prevail was strong enough to justify issuance of the injunction even though the balance of hardships tipped in Employee's favor. [*NewLife Sciences v. Weinstock* (2011) 197 CA4th 676, 688, 128 CR3d 538, 548]

- [9:518.3] Ed.C. §99161.5 prohibits the sponsor of the LSAT from reporting test scores in a manner that reveals that a test-taker received extra testing time as a disability accommodation. Sponsor sued the State of California for declaratory and injunctive relief, challenging the constitutionality of Ed.C. §99161.5. Granting of PI ordering the State to refrain from enforcing the statute was an abuse of discretion where the likelihood of Sponsor prevailing on its claim was uncertain and the balance of interim harm favored law school applicants with disabilities. [*Law School Admission Council, Inc. v. State of Calif.* (2014) 222 CA4th 1265, 1297, 1299-1300, 166 CR3d 647, 673, 675-676]

c. [9:519] **Multiplicity of actions:** CCP §526(a)(6) sets forth the usual equity ground of preventing unnecessary legal actions. As a practical matter, this ground is usually used to require parties to collect their disputes into one lawsuit.

d. [9:520] **Laches:** The equitable defense of laches normally does not rate serious consideration at the temporary restraining order or preliminary injunction stage because it is an affirmative defense requiring a showing of prejudice (in addition to delay). Even so, a long wait before filing suit or applying for injunctive relief may convince the trial court that there is no irreparable harm. Occasionally, the term "laches" is applied to this consideration. [See *Youngblood v. Wilcox* (1989) 207 CA3d 1368, 1376, 255 CR 527, 531]

e. [9:521] **"Unclean hands":** Likewise, the doctrine of "unclean hands" plays little part at the preliminary injunction stage, since the court may not know with confidence which party's hands are "unclean." But the issue remains within the trial court's discretion. [*California Satellite Systems, Inc. v. Nichols* (1985) 170 CA3d 56, 70, 216 CR 180, 187-188]

General bad conduct is not sufficient; to bar relief, the unclean hands must relate *directly* to the transaction concerning which the complaint is made. [*Kendall-Jackson Winery, Ltd. v. Sup.Ct. (E. & J. Gallo Winery)* (1999) 76 CA4th 970, 974, 90 CR2d 743, 746]

f. [9:522] **Doing equity:** Contrasted with unclean hands, the requirement that a party seeking an injunction do equity

© 2020 Thomson Reuters/The Rutter Group

is a frequent consideration with temporary restraining orders and preliminary injunctions. Preliminary injunctions are frequently issued with conditions that plaintiff do certain acts for continued vitality of the injunction (e.g., pay appropriate expenses to preserve contested property). [*Dickson, Carlson & Campillo v. Pole* (2000) 83 CA4th 436, 445, 99 CR2d 678, 685]

g. [9:523] **Preserving status quo:** The purpose of a preliminary injunction is to preserve the status quo pending a trial on the merits. [*Continental Baking Co. v. Katz* (1968) 68 C2d 512, 528, 67 CR 761, 771; *SB Liberty, LLC v. Isla Verde Ass'n, Inc.* (2013) 217 CA4th 272, 280, 158 CR3d 105, 111]

Comment: Often, however, granting or denying a preliminary injunction tends to dispose of the controversy, so that it never reaches a trial on the merits.

[9:523.1] ***PRACTICE POINTER:*** Your chances for obtaining a preliminary injunction are better if you *limit* the relief requested to what is necessary to preserve the status quo. Don't ask at the preliminary injunction stage for all the relief in the prayer of the complaint. [See *Yee v. American Nat'l Ins. Co.* (2015) 235 CA4th 453, 458, 185 CR3d 363, 367—court may not provide permanent injunctive relief under guise of issuing preliminary injunction]

h. [9:524] **Continuing supervision:** There is a strong tendency to avoid injunctions requiring continuing court proceedings to enforce them (e.g., to complete construction of a building). The court will usually be reluctant to involve itself deeply in regulating the relationship among the parties over a sustained length of time. Rather, it will be inclined to deny the injunction and force the parties to look for other solutions. [See *Ellison v. Ventura Port Dist.* (1978) 80 CA3d 574, 581-582, 145 CR 665, 669-670; *Oceanside Comm. Ass'n v. Oceanside Land Co.* (1983) 147 CA3d 166, 176-177, 195 CR 14, 19 (disapproved on other grounds in *Citizens for Covenant Compliance v. Anderson* (1995) 12 C4th 345, 47 CR2d 898)—court properly declined to supervise reconstruction of golf course]

(1) [9:524.1] **Compare—judicial abstention:** Generally, a court will abstain from granting injunctive relief when doing so "would be unnecessarily burdensome for the trial court to monitor and enforce given the availability of more effective means of redress." [*Klein v. Chevron U.S.A., Inc.* (2012) 202 CA4th 1342, 1362, 137 CR3d 293, 309 (internal quotes omitted)]

[9:524.2] ***PRACTICE POINTER:*** A possible alternative in such "continuing supervision" cases is the *appointment of a receiver* to act as agent of the court. *See ¶9:733 ff.*

i. [9:525] **Enforceability:** A court, mindful of its own dignity and credibility, is unlikely to issue injunctions that, as a practical matter, cannot be enforced. This consideration has several ramifications:

- [9:525.1] Mandatory preliminary injunctions are automatically stayed by an appeal (*see* ¶*9:534*), and thus are rarely issued at the preliminary injunction stage.
- [9:525.2] Overbroad, vague or generally phrased injunctions are avoided because contempt will not lie. [*Evans v. Evans* (2008) 162 CA4th 1157, 1169, 76 CR3d 859, 869—enjoining "defamatory" comments]
- [9:525.3] Injunctions as to acts not subject to objective verification are looked on with suspicion (e.g., enjoining codefendants in an unfair competition case from "passing information to each other" about plaintiff's business). [See *ReadyLink Healthcare v. Cotton* (2005) 126 CA4th 1006, 1023, 24 CR3d 720, 732—injunction prohibiting former employee from soliciting anyone "associated with" or "in a business relationship with" former employer was "vague, ambitious and overbroad"]

  [9:525.4-525.6] *Reserved.*

j. [9:526] **Combination of considerations:** Few cases involve only one of the above considerations (¶*9:504 ff.*). Instead, the judge will consider all relevant factors.

[9:527-529] *Reserved.*

3. [9:530] **Classification of Injunctions as Prohibitory or Mandatory:** Injunctions may be classified as either "*prohibitory*" or "*mandatory*." This classification affects whether the injunction, if granted, is automatically stayed during appeal. [*URS Corp. v. Atkinson/Walsh Joint Venture* (2017) 15 CA5th 872, 884, 223 CR3d 674, 682]

a. [9:531] **Test:** "[A]n injunction is prohibitory if it requires a person to refrain from a particular act and mandatory if it compels performance of an affirmative act *that changes the position of the parties*." [*Davenport v. Blue Cross of Calif.*, supra, 52 CA4th at 446-448, 60 CR2d at 646-647 (emphasis added) (rejecting "preservation of status quo" as test for prohibitory injunction); see *Oiye v. Fox* (2012) 211 CA4th 1036, 1048, 151 CR3d 65, 75—order directing plaintiff not to encumber or dispose of assets was prohibitory: "It directs affirmative inaction by defendant, not affirmative action"; *URS Corp. v. Atkinson/Walsh Joint Venture*, supra, 15 CA5th at 884, 223 CR3d at 682—order prohibitory if its effect is to leave parties in same position]

Some courts look to whether the order changes the "the last actual peaceable, uncontested status which preceded the pending controversy" to determine whether the status quo is changed

© 2020 Thomson Reuters/The Rutter Group

by the order, rendering the injunction mandatory. [*People v. Hill* (1977) 66 CA3d 320, 331, 136 CR 30, 36 (internal quotes omitted); see *People v. iMERGENT, Inc.* (2009) 170 CA4th 333, 343, 87 CR3d 844, 852]

(1) [9:532] **Mandatory injunctions rarely granted:** Mandatory preliminary injunctions are *rarely* granted (and if granted, are subject to stricter scrutiny on appeal): "The granting of a mandatory injunction pending trial is not permitted except in *extreme* cases where the right thereto is *clearly* established." [*Teachers Ins. & Annuity Ass'n v. Furlotti* (1999) 70 CA4th 1487, 1493, 83 CR2d 455, 458 (emphasis added; internal quotes omitted); *Integrated Dynamic Solutions, Inc. v. VitaVet Labs, Inc.* (2016) 6 CA5th 1178, 1184, 211 CR3d 873, 877; *Brown v. Pacifica Found., Inc.* (2019) 34 CA5th 915, 925, 246 CR3d 822, 829]

b. **Impact on appeal**

(1) [9:533] **Prohibitory injunctions not stayed by appeal:** While a preliminary injunction is appealable (CCP §904.1(a)(6)), the enforcement of a prohibitory injunction is *not* automatically stayed pending appeal. (A stay order must be sought in the trial court; in rare cases, a writ of supersedeas may issue from an appellate court.) [See, e.g., *Rubin v. American Sportsmen Television Equity Soc., Inc.* (1951) 102 CA2d 288, 290, 227 P2d 303, 305]

(2) [9:534] **Mandatory injunctions automatically stayed by appeal:** Enforcement of mandatory injunctions *is* automatically stayed by the filing of an appeal. [See *URS Corp. v. Atkinson/Walsh Joint Venture* (2017) 15 CA5th 872, 884, 223 CR3d 674, 682]

Thus, while mandatory injunctions may be issued before trial in extraordinary situations, the mere filing of the notice of appeal renders them incapable of enforcement. [CCP §916; *Agricultural Labor Relations Bd. v. Sup.Ct. (Sam Andrews' Sons)* (1983) 149 CA3d 709, 713, 196 CR 920, 922]

c. [9:535] **Effect based on substance, not form:** The *substance* of an injunction, and not its form, controls whether enforcement is stayed on appeal. Thus, an injunction "prohibiting" certain conduct will be construed as a mandatory injunction if it requires affirmative action that changes the status quo. [*Agricultural Labor Relations Bd. v. Sup.Ct. (Sam Andrews' Sons)*, supra, 149 CA3d at 713, 196 CR at 922-923—injunction restraining employer from "refusing to reinstate" certain workers was actually mandatory injunction compelling employer to *rehire*, thus automatically stayed on appeal; *Davenport v. Blue Cross of Calif.* (1997) 52 CA4th 435, 446, 60 CR2d 641, 646—order "prohibiting" Blue Cross from "denying, refusing or discontinuing" specified medical benefits was actually mandatory injunction compelling payment]

But, incidental mandatory provisions of an essentially prohibitory injunction do not render the injunction unenforceable in event of an appeal. [*Jaynes v. Weickman* (1921) 51 CA 696, 700-702, 197 P 672, 674]

Where an injunction has *both* characteristics, granting both prohibitive and mandatory relief, an appeal "will not stay the prohibitive features of the injunction, but as to its mandatory provisions said injunctions will be stayed." [*Ironridge Global IV, Ltd. v. ScripsAmerica*, Inc. (2015) 238 CA4th 259, 265, 189 CR3d 583, 587, fn. 4 (internal quotes and citation omitted)]

[9:535.1] ***PRACTICE POINTER:*** The message for practitioners is that the more a preliminary injunction strays from an uncontestably prohibitory effect, the more difficulty may be experienced in enforcing it. Moral: For best results, prohibit; don't mandate. And even though a preliminary injunction is drafted to appear "prohibitory," analyze it carefully to see if it is actually mandatory *in effect*.

[9:536-537] *Reserved.*

4. **Classification of Injunctions by Time of Issuance and Duration**

a. [9:538] **Temporary restraining order:** The temporary restraining order (TRO) is issued "ex parte" (*see ¶9:590 ff.* for meaning of "ex parte" in this context). Its purpose is to preserve the status quo, or prevent irreparable harm pending the hearing of an application for preliminary injunction on notice.

(1) [9:538.1] A TRO has the same force and effect as a preliminary or permanent injunction (i.e., enforceable by contempt). But it differs from these in that it *may* issue *without a bond* or undertaking (*¶9:603*); and it terminates automatically when a preliminary injunction either is issued or denied. [*Houser v. Sup.Ct.* (1932) 121 CA 31, 8 P2d 483, 484—TRO remains in effect until order granting or denying preliminary injunction]

(2) [9:538.2] The character of the order is determined by its effect, not the title on the document. Thus, for example, if the restraining order states that it shall be effective "until further order of the court" (rather than until determination of the OSC re preliminary injunction), the order *is* a preliminary injunction and requires a bond. [See *McManus v. KPAL Broadcasting Corp.* (1960) 182 CA2d 558, 562, 6 CR 441, 444; *Integrated Lender Services, Inc. v. County of Los Angeles* (2018) 22 CA5th 867, 872, 231 CR3d 902, 905, fn. 2 (citing text)]

b. [9:539] **Preliminary injunction:** A preliminary injunction (PI) is issued after hearing on either (1) noticed motion or

© 2020 Thomson Reuters/The Rutter Group

(2) an order to show cause. Its purpose is, at least theoretically and usually in fact, to preserve the status quo and prevent irreparable harm *pending trial* on the merits. [*White v. Davis* (2003) 30 C4th 528, 554, 133 CR2d 648, 668; *Costa Mesa City Employees' Ass'n v. City of Costa Mesa* (2012) 209 CA4th 298, 305, 146 CR3d 677, 682]

TROs and PIs are *provisional* remedies, in that both are granted prior to any final judgment or disposition in the case. [See *Costa Mesa City Employees' Ass'n v. City of Costa Mesa*, supra, 209 CA4th at 305, 146 CR3d at 682]

(1) [9:539.1] **When authorized:** Generally, the complaint must set forth a cause of action for injunctive relief to support issuance of a TRO or PI. [See, e.g., CCP §526(a)(1)-(2)]

However, the court may issue injunctions at any stage of the proceedings *to maintain the status quo* until judgment—regardless of whether the complaint seeks equitable relief. [CCP §526(a)(3); *Lenard v. Edmonds* (1957) 151 CA2d 764, 769, 312 P2d 308, 311—defendant restrained from transferring assets involved in the litigation where transfer might render him unable to pay a damages judgment; see also *Lofton v. Wells Fargo Home Mortg.* (2014) 230 CA4th 1050, 1067, 179 CR3d 254, 269—*after entry of judgment*, court retained jurisdiction to issue TRO requiring law firm to temporarily deposit settlement funds in secure account to prevent dissipation]

c. [9:540] **Permanent injunction:** Permanent injunctions are issued only after trial and as a part of the judgment. [See *Aspen Grove Condominium Ass'n v. CNL Income Northstar LLC* (2014) 231 CA4th 53, 58, 179 CR3d 429, 433]

[9:541-542] *Reserved.*

5. [9:543] **Constitutional and Statutory Prohibitions:** There are also certain cases in which courts are prohibited by law from issuing injunctions. The following are the most important:

a. [9:544] **State taxation:** No injunction may be granted to stay collection of *state taxes*. [Cal.Const. Art. XIII, §32; Rev. & Tax.C. §19081; see *Hunter-Reay v. Franchise Tax Bd.* (1983) 140 CA3d 875, 878, 189 CR 810, 812—makes no difference that tax statute may be unconstitutional]

b. [9:545] **Certain other litigation:** Nor may an injunction issue to stay proceedings in a *federal* court; nor proceedings in the courts of another state upon a judgment rendered in that state; nor in any lawsuit filed prior to the injunction action (unless necessary to prevent multiplicity). [CCP §526(b)(1)-(3); Civ.C. §3423(a)-(c)]

c. [9:546] **Enforcement of statutes:** Nor may an injunction prevent "execution of a public statute by officers of the law for the public benefit"; nor "the exercise of a public or private office, in a lawful manner by the person in possession." [CCP §526(b)(4), (6); Civ.C. §3423(d), (f); *Szold v. Medical Bd. of Calif.* (2005) 127 CA4th 591, 596, 25 CR3d 665, 668-669—State Medical Board could not be ordered to remove reference to Doctor's suspension from its website because statute required Board to post this information; *Jamison v. Department of Transp.* (2016) 4 CA5th 356, 366, 208 CR3d 610, 617—P not entitled to enjoin Caltrans's performance of its statutory duty to control encroachments on public highway]

(1) [9:547] **Exception—constitutionality challenged:** However, injunctions may issue to prevent enforcement of *unconstitutional* statutes, or valid statutes sought to be enforced *illegally* (i.e., to regulate conduct beyond the reach of the statute), where their enforcement would cause irreparable injury. [*Novar Corp. v. Bureau of Collection & Investigative Services* (1984) 160 CA3d 1, 5, 206 CR 287, 290; see *National Shooting Sports Found., Inc. v. State of Calif.* (2016) 6 CA5th 298, 306-307, 210 CR3d 867, 873 (rev'd on other grounds (2018) 5 C5th 428, 235 CR3d 54)—CCP §526(b)(4) and Civ.C. §3423(d) did not bar action to enjoin application of statute where invalidity of statute shown]

(a) [9:547.1] **Example:** State Bureau claimed "deterrent system" manufactured by P was an "alarm system" and therefore subject to regulation by State. Court found otherwise, and enjoined State interference with P's marketing its product. [*Novar Corp. v. Bureau of Collection & Investigative Services*, supra, 160 CA3d at 5, 206 CR at 290]

(b) [9:547.2] **Comment:** However, as a practical matter, trial courts are "extremely cautious" about granting preliminary injunctions on this ground. Injunctive relief is usually deferred until a trial on the merits. [See *Cohen v. Board of Supervisors of City & County of San Francisco* (1986) 178 CA3d 447, 453, 225 CR 114, 117]

(2) [9:548] **Exception—Voting Rights Act violation:** An injunction was an "appropriate remedy" to prohibit a city from certifying the results of an at-large city council election (pending implementation of a final plan) where there was uncontroverted evidence at trial of vote dilution in violation of California's Voting Rights Act (Elec.C. §14209). [*Jauregui v. City of Palmdale* (2014) 226 CA4th 781, 808, 172 CR3d 333, 351-352—§14029 is exception to CCP §526(b)(4) and Civ.C. §3423(d)]

(3) [9:549] **Exhaustion of administrative remedies:** Where an administrative remedy is provided by the statute in

© 2020 Thomson Reuters/The Rutter Group

question, that remedy usually must be exhausted before any judicial relief is sought—even where the statute is challenged on constitutional grounds. A court violating this rule acts in *excess* of its *jurisdiction*, so that any injunction will be set aside. [*Board of Police Commrs. v. Sup.Ct. (Easebe Enterprises, Inc.)* (1985) 168 CA3d 420, 431-432, 214 CR 493, 498-499]

(a) [9:549.1] **Rationale:** Otherwise, "persons subject to administrative procedures with claims of unconstitutionality . . . would clog the courts, and administrative agencies would be bypassed and become impotent." [*Board of Police Commrs. v. Sup.Ct. (Easebe Enterprises, Inc.)*, supra, 168 CA3d at 432, 214 CR at 499]

(b) [9:549.2] **When excused:** Exhaustion of administrative remedies may be excused, however, and immediate injunction relief may be proper where:

- Proceedings to enforce the allegedly unconstitutional statute have not yet begun (e.g., where investigations are pending but no formal accusation filed); and
- State and federal statutes *conflict*, thus threatening to penalize the petitioner regardless of what action it takes; or
- The administrative remedy is inadequate (e.g., where irreparable harm would result if judicial intervention were withheld). [See *Board of Police Commrs. v. Sup.Ct. (Easebe Enterprises, Inc.)*, supra, 168 CA3d at 432-433, 214 CR at 499-500; *American Indian Model Schools v. Oakland Unified School Dist.* (2014) 227 CA4th 258, 292, 173 CR3d 544, 571]

d. [9:550] **Prevent breach of contract:** In general, an injunction will not issue to prevent breach of a contract that is not specifically enforceable. However, an injunction may be granted to compel performance of a written contract to perform "unique" personal services for a specified minimum compensation (currently a graduated schedule starting at $9,000 per year). [CCP §526(b)(5); Civ.C. §3423(e)]

(1) [9:551] **Breach of personal service contracts:** Money damages are awardable for breach of a personal services contract. But courts cannot order *specific performance* of such contracts (mandatory injunction compelling parties to perform). This avoids the "friction and social costs that often result when employer and employee are reunited in a relationship that has already failed." [*Barndt v. County of Los Angeles* (1989) 211 CA3d 397, 404, 259 CR 372, 376; see Civ.C. §3390]

The rule applies both where an employer sues to compel the employee to return to work and where an employee sues to get his or her job back. In either case, "the remedy of specific performance is simply not available . . ." [*Barndt v. County of Los Angeles*, supra, 211 CA3d at 405, 259 CR at 377]

(a) [9:551.1] **Rationale:** Several reasons support the rule:

- *Involuntary servitude:* Where the employer is suing, decreeing specific performance against an unwilling employee would violate the Thirteenth Amendment prohibition on involuntary servitude;
- *Adequacy of remedy at law:* Where the employee is suing, loss of employment is usually compensable in damages (e.g., the contract rate plus any damage to employee's reputation);
- *Impracticality:* Where either sues, it would be difficult for a court to pass judgment on the quality of performance of a contract calling for special knowledge, skill or ability;
- *Public policy:* Forcing parties to work with each other after their personal relationship has failed is not sound policy, especially where the services involve mutual confidence and discretionary authority. [*Woolley v. Embassy Suites, Inc.* (1991) 227 CA3d 1520, 1533-1534, 278 CR 719, 726-727; see *Beverly Glen Music, Inc. v. Warner Communications, Inc.* (1986) 178 CA3d 1142, 1144, 224 CR 260, 261]

(b) [9:552] **What constitutes "personal service" contract:** The ban on injunctive relief applies to any contract calling for "rendition of a performance that is of a distinctly personal and *non-delegable* character." [*Woolley v. Embassy Suites, Inc.*, supra, 227 CA3d at 1534, 278 CR at 727 (emphasis added)]

This category includes "the contracts of actors and artists, managers, sales agents, school teachers, mechanics, cooks, and contracts for the furnishing of personal care and support." [*Woolley v. Embassy Suites, Inc.*, supra, 227 CA3d at 1534, 278 CR at 727 (emphasis omitted) (hotel managers)]

1) [9:553] **Includes corporations supplying "personal" services:** The ban also applies to contracts by corporations or other business entities that supply services that are essentially "personal" (i.e., nondelegable). [*Woolley v. Embassy Suites, Inc.*, supra, 227 CA3d at 1534, 278 CR at 727]

© 2020 Thomson Reuters/The Rutter Group

2) **Application**

- [9:553.1] A management agreement between Hotel Owners and corporate Hotel Manager that required "the exercise of special skill and judgment" by Manager and "call[ed] for a series of complex and delicate business decisions" based on "mutual cooperation and trust . . . between the parties" was a personal services contract. Owners therefore could not be enjoined from terminating Manager's contract without cause (though they could be sued for damages). [*Woolley v. Embassy Suites, Inc.*, supra, 227 CA3d at 1534, 278 CR at 727]

- [9:553.2] By contrast, a franchise agreement between Fast Food Franchisor and Franchisee was not a personal services contract where Franchisee was not empowered to exercise discretionary judgment and the essence of the agreement was Franchisee's adherence to Franchisor's uniform standards, policies and specifications. Consequently, the agreement *was* subject to specific enforcement, and Franchisor could be enjoined from removing Franchisee from the restaurant. [*Husain v. McDonald's Corp.* (2012) 205 CA4th 860, 867-868, 140 CR3d 370, 376-377]

(c) [9:554] **Compare—employee may be enjoined from working for another:** Although the employee cannot be compelled directly to perform the contract, such performance may be *indirectly* compelled: As long as the minimum annual compensation (*see ¶9:550*) is guaranteed, the employee can be *enjoined from working for anyone else* during the term of the contract. [CCP §526(b)(5); Civ.C. §3423(e)]

As explained by one court: "The net effect is to pressure the defendant to return voluntarily to his employer by denying him the means of earning a living. Indeed this is its only purpose, for, unless the defendant relents and honors the contract, the plaintiff gains nothing from having brought the injunction." [*Beverly Glen Music, Inc. v. Warner Communications, Inc.*, supra, 178 CA3d at 1144-1145, 224 CR at 261]

1) [9:554.1] **Monetary limitation:** Breach of a personal service contract may be enjoined only where the minimum compensation (*see ¶9:550*) is *guaranteed* to the person rendering

the services. [*Motown Record Corp. v. Brockert* (1984) 160 CA3d 123, 132, 207 CR 574, 580]

a) [9:554.2] **Option not sufficient:** However, a clause giving the employer an *option* to extend the contract by paying the statutory minimum compensation does *not* meet the requirements for injunctive relief because the payment was contingent, not guaranteed. [*Motown Record Corp. v. Brockert*, supra, 160 CA3d at 135, 207 CR at 582—recording contract gave producer option to renew annually for 6 years by paying statutory minimum]

(2) [9:555] **Breach of agency contract:** For similar reasons, and except as noted below (¶*9:555.1 ff.*), neither principal nor agent may be enjoined from breaching an agency contract: "It is a cardinal principle of agency law that a principal who employs an agent always retains the power to revoke the agency." [*Woolley v. Embassy Suites, Inc.*, supra, 227 CA3d at 1529, 278 CR at 724—hotel owners could not be enjoined from terminating contract with managing agent]

(a) [9:555.1] **Exception as to agency "coupled with interest":** The principal cannot revoke (and hence the agent can obtain specific performance) where the agent's authority is "coupled with an interest." [*Woolley v. Embassy Suites, Inc.*, supra, 227 CA3d at 1529, 278 CR at 724]

But no such interest is created by a contract for monetary *compensation* to the agent, no matter what form it takes (e.g., a percentage of profits). [*Woolley v. Embassy Suites, Inc.*, supra, 227 CA3d at 1532, 278 CR at 726]

(Agencies "coupled with an interest" are rare. They exist only where (1) the agency is created for the benefit of the agent, not the principal; and (2) to secure the performance of a duty to the agent or to protect the agent's title or right; and (3) the agency is created for consideration or at the same time the duty or title is created. See *Woolley v. Embassy Suites, Inc.*, supra, 227 CA3d at 1532, 278 CR at 726.)

e. [9:556] **Compare—family law cases:** Injunctive relief in family law cases is governed by the Family Code (Fam.C. §§231 et seq., 6300 et seq.; see CRC 5.18).

But "palimony" suits under *Marvin v. Marvin* (1981) 122 CA3d 871, 176 CR 555, are *not* family law actions, and are thus subject to rules governing injunctive relief in ordinary civil actions.

[*Schafer v. Sup.Ct. (Christopher)* (1986) 180 CA3d 305, 309, 225 CR 513, 515—invalidating interim support order]

[9:557-559] *Reserved.*

6. [9:560] **Basic Procedures for TROs and PIs:** Below are the basic procedures for obtaining a TRO or PI in civil proceedings before trial (¶*9:561 ff.*).

   Compare—harassment: Different procedural rules apply to injunctive relief in cases involving harassment or domestic violence (*see* ¶*9:697 ff.*).

   a. [9:561] **TRO/OSC procedure:** Where a temporary restraining order is sought, the court may issue the TRO and at the same time order the defendant to "show cause" why a PI should not be issued.

      (1) [9:562] **Form:** The TRO and OSC must be stated separately, with the OSC stated first. In addition, the restraining language must appear in both the TRO and the OSC; i.e., the OSC *cannot* merely incorporate the TRO by reference. [CRC 3.1150(c)]

      [9:563] *Reserved.*

      (2) [9:564] **Content:** A TRO must specifically describe the conduct sought to be enjoined pending the hearing; and an OSC must describe the terms of the injunction sought at the hearing. [See CRC 3.1150(c)]

      In addition, a proposed OSC must contain blank spaces for:

      — the time and manner of service on responding parties;
      — the date on which a proof of service must be delivered to the court hearing the OSC;
      — a briefing schedule; and
      — if applicable, the expiration date of the TRO (for completion by the court or clerk). [CRC 3.1150(c)] (The TRO will nevertheless expire on the granting or denial of the preliminary injunction; *see* ¶*9:538.1, 9:652.*)

      (a) [9:564.1] **Specific acts enjoined:** The conduct to be restrained must be set forth *with particularity.* It must be specific enough to provide defendant with adequate notice for purposes of contempt (*see* ¶*9:711*).

      ➩ [9:564.2] ***PRACTICE POINTER FOR COUNSEL SEEKING TRO:*** In drafting your proposed TRO, consider whether it might be appropriate to enjoin *attempts* to do the prohibited acts as well as the prohibited acts themselves. But be realistic in drafting the proposed order (which will often, but not always, mirror the language of a requested preliminary injunction). Most judges will grant only the *least drastic relief* possible pending a hearing on the OSC. While the court has the power to modify a proposed TRO (*see* ¶*9:606*), asking for broader restraint than necessary runs the risk the court will refuse the TRO altogether.

Also, when asking for several different types of restraint, set them out in *separate paragraphs* so that it is easier for the court to modify your proposed TRO to include the particular restraints it is willing to order.

Finally, make sure that the restraint language is sufficiently *specific and clear* to be enforceable. Keep in mind that enforcement may be through quasi-criminal *contempt* proceedings in which a "beyond a reasonable doubt" standard applies; *see* ¶*9:718.1*.

[9:564.2a] ***PRACTICE POINTER FOR COUNSEL OPPOSING TRO:*** If you are opposing a TRO application, review the language of the proposed TRO carefully for potential overbreadth and lack of specificity or clarity.

(b) [9:564.3] **Previous applications disclosed:** An application for a TRO or OSC must state whether there has been any previous application to any judicial officer for similar relief and, if so, the result of the application. [CRC 3.1150(e)]

(c) [9:565] **Persons to be enjoined:** It is a good practice to make the TRO or PI run against the defendant and against anyone else, though not a party to the action, who may be acting in concert with the defendant. Thus, injunctions usually run to classes of persons through whom the enjoined person may act, such as *agents, servants, employees, partners,* etc. Any such persons who have knowledge of the injunction and violate its terms may be held guilty of contempt. The practical effect is to prevent the prohibited action by persons acting in concert with, or aiding and abetting, the enjoined party. [*Berger v. Sup.Ct.* (1917) 175 C 719, 721, 167 P 143, 144; *see* ¶*9:656.1*]

[9:566] ***CAUTION:*** The practice described above (¶*9:565*) makes sense where the nonparties are clearly the "agents, employees, servants, etc." of the party being enjoined. (For example,

© 2020 Thomson Reuters/The Rutter Group

union members on a picket line, although not named as parties, may be served with copies of an injunction prohibiting "agents and employees" from picketing.)

However, be careful about serving nonparties "as agents, servants, employees or partners" of the defendant where you have no real proof of such relationship. (For example, in an unfair competition case, serving all of D's customers and business associates with copies of the injunction prohibiting certain competitive acts by D.)

If you are simply trying to put pressure on D, the tactic may backfire: It could lead to a cross-action for *abuse of process* (i.e., using the injunction for an ulterior purpose).

[9:567] ***PRACTICE POINTER:*** If you have reason to believe that nonparties are assisting D in continuing the acts enjoined, and they are not *clearly* "agents, servants, employees, etc.," the safer alternative is to *amend* the complaint to name them and obtain a new injunction directed to them individually. (Where tortious acts are involved, the amendment can usually be based on allegations of conspiracy.)

(d) [9:568] **Bond:** Although an undertaking is only optional on a TRO (*see ¶9:603*), provision should be made in case the court requires it.

[9:568.1] ***PRACTICE POINTER:*** In determining the amount of a TRO bond, the judge will be concerned regarding what damages may result from issuance of the TRO. Therefore, it is good practice to provide a *declaration* stating *facts* regarding this matter. (Such declaration should be made by the client or a third party with *personal knowledge* of what damage defendant may suffer as a result of the TRO.)

[9:569] *Reserved.*

b. [9:570] **Notice required for PI:** When a TRO is not requested, the moving party may give notice by serving either a notice of motion (most common) or an order to show cause (OSC). [CRC 3.1150(a)]

FORM: Motion for Preliminary Injunction and Proposed Order, *see Form 9B:2* in Rivera, *Cal. Prac. Guide: Civ. Pro. Before Trial FORMS* (TRG).

(1) [9:570.1] **Basis of motion and grounds:** The papers supporting the motion should be listed in the notice of motion and the grounds for the motion clearly stated. [CCP §1010]

(2) [9:571] **Advantages of noticed motion:** When a TRO is not required, use of the notice of motion saves a trip to court to get the OSC signed by a judge.

(3) [9:572] **Compare—OSC when TRO requested:** If a TRO is sought, the moving party *must* utilize the TRO/OSC procedure. [CRC 3.1150(a); *see* ¶*9:561*]

(4) [9:573] **Compare—OSC when responding party has not appeared:** An OSC must also be used when the responding party has not yet appeared in the action. In that case, the OSC must be served in the same manner as a summons and complaint. [CRC 3.1150(a)]

7. [9:574] **Proof Requirement:** Whether the PI is requested by OSC or notice of motion, it is a "motion" procedure. Therefore, proof of facts is ordinarily made by affidavits or declarations. [CCP §§2009, 2015.5]

(The technical requirements of affidavits and declarations are discussed in detail at ¶*9:46 ff.* The following is a brief summary.)

a. **Affidavits and declarations**

(1) [9:575] **Technical sufficiency:** Affidavits must be properly notarized, with the notary using a jurat ("Subscribed and Sworn to before me . . . .")—rather than an acknowledgment. Declarations must comply with CCP §2015.5.

(2) [9:576] **Statement of evidentiary facts:** Affidavits and declarations must state *evidentiary* facts. This requires facts showing the affiant's or declarant's *personal knowledge* of the facts set forth. Conclusions and opinions may be used only to the extent that a witness may use them in testifying in person. Hearsay is inadmissible unless an appropriate hearsay exception applies. The foundation for documents must be set forth. *See detailed discussion of declarations and affidavits at* ¶*9:46 ff.*

(3) [9:577] **Disregarding inadmissible material:** If there is no objection, an affidavit or declaration may be received although it contains hearsay or other inadmissible matter. [*Waller v. Waller* (1970) 3 CA3d 456, 464, 83 CR 533, 537-538]

But if objected to, there is usually no way to repair a defective affidavit or declaration at the hearing. The result is that many an otherwise meritorious motion is lost because the lawyer drafting the affidavits or decla-

© 2020 Thomson Reuters/The Rutter Group

rations failed to pay attention to the basic requirement of admissible, evidentiary facts.

[9:578] *Reserved.*

b. [9:579] **Verified complaint:** A verified complaint may be sufficient by itself to support an application for a TRO or PI if (and only if) it contains sufficient *evidentiary facts.* [See CCP §527(a); *Bank of America Nat'l Trust & Sav. Ass'n v. Williams* (1948) 89 CA2d 21, 29, 200 P2d 151, 156-157]

CCP §446 governs verification of pleadings; *see discussion at ¶6:309 ff.*

(1) [9:580] **Disadvantages:** However, as a practical matter, a verified complaint by itself rarely suffices. First of all, as a matter of pleading, a complaint should set forth "ultimate facts," as distinguished from "evidentiary facts" (*see ¶6:124*); and therefore, a complaint that would support injunctive relief would usually be a defective pleading. Also, the *foundation* for the averments may not be apparent from the face of the complaint, in which case the material may not be found admissible.

More importantly, when plaintiff's application is based solely upon a verified complaint, a simple *verified answer* denying the essential allegations of the complaint justifies refusal to grant the preliminary injunction, "unless the complaint sets forth a *strong case* for equitable relief." [*Jessen v. Keystone Sav. & Loan Ass'n* (1983) 142 CA3d 454, 460, 191 CR 104, 108]

⇨ [9:580.1] ***PRACTICE POINTER:*** *Never* rely solely on a verified complaint. Always submit declarations in support of an injunction application.

c. [9:581] **Depositions, interrogatories, etc.:** Sworn testimony or admissions contained in depositions, answers to interrogatories, or other discovery may also be used to prove facts supporting injunctions.

(1) [9:582] Of course, such discovery is usually not available for a TRO requested at the onset of the case. But depositions may in some circumstances be obtained in time to use them to support an application for PI.

(2) [9:583] This often requires obtaining court orders shortening notice re depositions; and permission to notice depositions within the 20-day period following service of summons. Such orders can and should be sought at the same time that plaintiff applies for the TRO.

[9:583.1-583.4] *Reserved.*

d. [9:583.5] **Matters established by issue sanctions:** Having determined certain issues against a party as an issue sanction for discovery abuse, the court may rely on those determinations in granting a preliminary injunction. [*NewLife Sciences v. Weinstock* (2011) 197 CA4th 676, 687, 128 CR3d 538, 547—in opposition to motion for PI, defendant was not permitted to present evidence contradicting issues previously determined by court as discovery sanction]

e. [9:584] **Oral testimony:** There is no *right* to present oral testimony on an application for a PI. As with law and motion matters generally, the judge may decide the issues raised entirely on declarations, without oral testimony. [*Eddy v. Temkin* (1985) 167 CA3d 1115, 1120-1122, 213 CR 597, 601; *see ¶9:45*]

A party unable to obtain declarations may take a deposition. However, the court has *discretion* to receive oral testimony on an OSC hearing. A party seeking to introduce such testimony must obtain permission in advance on a showing of "good cause." [CRC 3.1306(a); *see ¶9:45.1*]

⇨ [9:585] ***PRACTICE POINTER:*** Such permission is rarely granted due both to crowded calendars in departments hearing such matters and judges' general reluctance to take "live" testimony on motion matters. Therefore, don't count on supporting or resisting a PI with oral testimony.

f. [9:586] **Demonstrative evidence required in certain cases:** Where an injunction is sought to limit *picketing,* or restrain *real property* encroachments or protect easements, the petition must depict the premises involved by drawings, plot plans, photographs or other appropriate means; *or* must "describe [them] in detail" including, if applicable, the length and width of street frontage, width of sidewalks, and number, size and location of entrances. [CRC 3.1151]

8. **TRO Procedure**

FORM: Application for Order to Show Cause and Temporary Restraining Order; Declaration of Notice and Proposed Order, *see Form 9B:1* in Rivera, *Cal. Prac. Guide: Civ. Pro. Before Trial FORMS* (TRG).

a. [9:587] **Source references:** Before starting to write any papers, read CCP §527, CRC 3.1150 and CRC 3.1200-3.1207.

Applications for ex parte temporary restraining orders are governed by CRC 3.1200-3.1207 (rule governing ex parte motions generally; *see ¶9:345 ff.*). [CRC 3.1150(g)]

(1) [9:587.1] **Local rules preempted:** All local rules "relating to" provisional remedies are null and void. [See CRC 3.20(a), *discussed at ¶9:13.2*]

© 2020 Thomson Reuters/The Rutter Group

b. [9:588] **Filing complaint:** If the action is initiated the same day a TRO or OSC is sought, the complaint must be filed first. The moving party must provide a file-stamped copy of the complaint to the judge who will hear the application. [CRC 3.1150(b)]

If the complaint is to serve as an affidavit in applying for the TRO or PI, it must be *verified.* [See CCP §527(a), ¶*9:579*]

(1) [9:589] **After filing, take to appropriate department:** The original complaint is filed at the court clerk's filing window. Conformed copies (showing the case number and date of filing) are then brought by counsel to the courtroom or department to which such proceedings are assigned.

— *San Francisco:* In San Francisco, for all civil cases (except limited unlawful detainer cases and small claims cases) all papers must be e-filed for litigants who are not exempt from e-filing (e.g., self-represented litigants). Ex parte applications for TROs, alternative writs, appointments of receivers and the like, are heard Monday through Friday in the Law and Motion Department. Civil harassment orders are issued out of Department 514, with papers filed in the clerk's office at Civil Harassment Window #1 (see *www.sfsuperiorcourt.org*). A party presenting an ex parte application must schedule the hearing with the Court clerk at least 24 hours in advance of the proposed hearing date. Endorsed filed copies of all moving papers must be submitted to the clerk no later than two hours before the ex parte hearing. [S.F. Sup.Ct. Rules 2.11, 8.1(A), (B), 8.2(A), 9.0(A)]

In cases assigned to judges for all purposes, TROs are heard by those judges. [S.F. Sup.Ct. Rule 8.1(B)(1)]

— *Los Angeles:* In Los Angeles Superior Court, Central District, such matters (other than civil harassment or domestic violence TROs, which are heard in the Family Law Division) are brought in Depts. 82, 85 and 86 *unless* an initial status conference has been held in the all-purpose court to which the case is assigned; in the latter event, the papers are taken to that court. [See L.A. Sup.Ct. Rules 2.8(b), 2.9, 5.2, 5.3(a)(1)]

For litigants who must e-file, ex parte applications and all supporting documents must be e-filed no later than 10:00 a.m. the court day before the hearing. [First Amended General Order re Mandatory Electronic Filing for Civil, available on the court's website (*www.lacourt.org*)]

(2) [9:589.1] **Compare—existing action:** If an application for a TRO or OSC is made in an existing case, it is the

moving party's responsibility to arrange for the court file to be made available to the judge hearing the application. [CRC 3.1150(b)]

c. [9:590] **Notifying opponent before seeking TRO:** Counsel seeking a TRO generally must inform the opposing party or counsel when and where the application will be made; and a declaration showing attempts to provide such notice is generally required before a TRO may issue. [CCP §527(c)(2)]

[9:591] *Reserved.*

(1) [9:592] **Declaration re notice:** The applicant must provide a declaration showing either that:

— applicant informed the opposing party or counsel when and where the application for TRO would be made; or

— applicant made a good faith effort to inform opposing party or counsel but was unable to do so (specifying the efforts made); or

— for reasons specified (e.g., risk of harm), the party should not be required to inform opposing party or counsel. [CCP §527(c)(2); CRC 3.1204; *see ¶9:357 ff.*]

If notice was given, the declaration should also state:

— defendant's response;

— the relief sought;

— whether opposition is expected; and

— the name, address, email address and telephone number of any attorney known to represent defendant (or if defendant is not represented, the defendant's name, address, email address and telephone number). [CRC 3.1202, 3.1204; *see ¶9:356.1 ff.*]

[9:592.1] ***PRACTICE POINTER:*** Consider sending your *notice of intent to seek a TRO* and supporting papers by fax or email. It is quicker and less expensive than trying to effect personal service. Many judges will now accept either method as proof of the equivalent of actual receipt.

Be aware, however, that *service of papers by fax or email* (which is different from providing notice under CCP §527) *is permitted only if the parties agree* to such service. [CRC 2.306(a)(1), 2.251(b)]

If giving notice by email, state in the "subject" line: "Notice of Ex Parte Hearing."

If notice is given by fax, obtain and bring *written confirmation of receipt* to the hearing. If given by email, submit a declaration to that effect.

© 2020 Thomson Reuters/The Rutter Group

(a) [9:593] **Facts justifying no advance notice to opposing party:** In extraordinary cases, notice may be dispensed with where the affidavit or declaration shows that notification itself may lead to irreparable injury (e.g., opposing party likely to destroy or conceal property involved). [CCP §527(c)(2)(C); CRC 3.1204(b)(3)]

1) [9:594] **Comment:** However, counsel should expect great difficulty trying to convince a court to issue a TRO without notice to the opposing party.

Moreover, even if so convinced, the court will likely limit the TRO's duration to a few days, so that the court can consider the matter further before allowing the TRO to remain in effect to the date of the PI hearing.

(b) [9:595] **"Harassment" cases:** The Code specifically authorizes TROs without notice in "harassment" cases; see CCP §527.6 (¶*9:697*).

(2) [9:596] **Amount of notice required:** Absent a showing of exceptional circumstances, the applicant must notify all parties by 10:00 a.m. on the court day before the ex parte appearance. [CRC 3.1203(a)]

d. [9:597] **Presenting the TRO:** Counsel seeking a TRO must appear in the appropriate department, either in person or by telephone, *during ex parte hours.* [See CRC 3.1207]

(1) [9:597.1] **Telephonic appearance:** The moving party may appear by telephone provided:

— moving papers have been filed and served in a manner that ensures they will be received by the court and all parties by at least 10:00 a.m. two court days before the hearing;

— words "Telephone Appearance" appear below the title of the application; and

— copies of the papers are presented directly to the department in which the matter will be heard, if required by local rule. [CRC 3.670(h)(3)]

Even if the moving party does not comply with these requirements, the opposing party may appear by telephone by giving notice to all parties and the court of its intent to do so, orally or in writing, no later than 2:00 p.m. the day before the hearing.

— *Oral notice* must be given either in person or by telephone;

— *Written notice* must be given by a "Notice of Intent to Appear by Telephone" filed with the court and served on all parties by any authorized means reasonably calculated to assure delivery no later than the close of business on the court day before the hearing. [CRC 3.670(h)(4)]

Although the rules do not expressly address when the pleadings must be served if the moving party intends to appear in person and the opposing party intends to appear by phone, presumably the moving party must deliver the papers to the opposing party *before* the hearing commences. [See CRC 3.1206]

(2) [9:597.2] **In person appearance:** The declarations (including the declaration re notice to defendant), points and authorities, form of TRO and OSC, and file-stamped copy of the complaint should be submitted to the clerk, who will deliver them to the judge in chambers.

A copy of all such papers should be served on any appearing defendant "at the first reasonable opportunity" and at least *before* the hearing commences. [CRC 3.1206—absent exceptional circumstances, court will not conduct hearing without prehearing service]

The same rule applies to *opposing papers*. [CRC 3.1206]

☞ [9:597.3] ***PRACTICE POINTER:*** Despite the stated policy favoring telephone appearances (see CRC 3.670(a)), the moving party (or its counsel) should *appear in person*. TROs are not lightly granted, and a personal appearance is likely to be far more persuasive than a telephonic one.

e. [9:598] **TRO hearing:** The judge may decide the matter on the papers without argument or may hear argument from the bench.

☞ [9:598.1] ***PRACTICE POINTER:*** Keep in mind that *no hearing is required* when a TRO is sought on an ex parte basis (as most are). If the matter is decided based on the papers and you are dissatisfied with the decision, consider asking the clerk if the court will entertain argument.

(1) [9:599] **Court reporter:** Reporters are no longer provided in many courts, and you should consider bringing your own court-certified reporter if you think you might need a record of the proceedings. Parties with a fee waiver are entitled to a reporter provided by the court upon request. [*Jameson v. Desta* (2018) 5 C5th 594, 599, 234 CR3d 831, 834; *see discussion at ¶9:171.2 ff.*]

Parties with a fee waiver should check each court's requirements for requesting a reporter.

© 2020 Thomson Reuters/The Rutter Group

[9:599.1] ***PRACTICE POINTER:*** If in doubt about whether TRO hearings are reported in your court, check the court's website or call the courtroom clerk for verification. If they are not, be sure to arrange for a court reporter *in advance* of the hearing if you want a transcript. *See discussion at ¶9:171 ff.*

(2) [9:600] **Questioning by court:** Counsel should expect to be asked many questions by the court, including those relating to the urgency, necessity and scope of the TRO requested; conditions appropriate to its issuance; the amount of bond; and practical matters regarding the date and hearing on the OSC.

[9:601] ***PRACTICE POINTER:*** Whether you are seeking or opposing a TRO, you should expect the court to focus primarily on *what danger may exist* to the rights of the parties *between then and the date of the hearing* on the application for a PI, and only secondarily on broader questions or the ultimate right to recover.

(3) [9:602] **Not a general appearance:** Defendant's appearance at a hearing at which ex parte relief is sought, or to oppose ex parte application for TRO or other provisional remedy, is *not* a general appearance. Therefore, it does not affect defendant's right to challenge jurisdiction or service of summons. [CCP §418.11; *see* ¶*3:159*]

(4) [9:602.1] **Disclosure of prior applications:** If similar relief has been requested from another judge or court, it should be disclosed to the judge hearing the TRO. Failure to do so may be treated as a contempt of court. [CCP §1008(b), (d)]

f. [9:603] **TRO bond:** There is no Code requirement that the court must order an undertaking upon granting a TRO (unlike PIs). Whether an undertaking will be required on granting a TRO is discretionary with the judge.

Some judges issue TROs effective immediately but require that a bond be filed within a few days. This both preserves the status quo and allows time for plaintiff to get a bond.

In any event, counsel should be prepared to discuss the amount of the bond with the judge. Since the TRO will be in effect only until the PI hearing, the amount of the bond is usually limited to the damages the defendant is likely to incur during that period. If no damage seems likely during that short period, the court may not require that a bond be filed.

Some courts require a declaration stating facts from which the amount of probable damage can be determined.

➪ [9:604] ***PRACTICE POINTER:*** If a bond is required (depending on the court order), the TRO may not be effective until the bond is filed. Thus, the applicant should *make arrangements in advance* with his or her bonding company for quick issuance of the bond. Because the bonding company is likely to require security for the bond, make sure that your client understands this requirement and is able to comply.

(1) [9:605] Undertakings on *personal sureties* (which are allowed on PIs, ¶*9:645*) are *not* allowed on TROs. The reason is that the 15- or 22-day duration of the TRO does not afford the restrained party sufficient time after service to challenge sufficiency of the surety.

(2) [9:605.1] Denial of a preliminary injunction does *not* render a surety immediately liable on the TRO bond. Defendant must wait until a final judgment is rendered in the action. [CCP §996.440; *Satinover v. Dean* (1988) 202 CA3d 1298, 249 CR 277]

g. [9:606] **Issuing the TRO:** The judge, if convinced, will sign the TRO, but may substantially modify it to reflect what he or she thinks is the danger to be avoided during its effective period.

[9:607-609] *Reserved.*

h. [9:610] **Duration of TRO; setting OSC hearing date:** *See discussion at ¶9:622 ff.*

i. [9:611] **Miscellaneous matters:** Counsel should be prepared to discuss with the opponent such practical matters as the setting of depositions, date of service of reply papers, accepting service of summons and complaint and moving papers, and (in proper cases) even settlement of the case.

j. [9:612] **Service of TRO and supporting papers:** The TRO is not enforceable, and the hearing on the PI cannot proceed, unless and until the party to be enjoined has *personal notice* of the court's orders.

➪ [9:612.1] ***PRACTICE POINTER:*** If counsel for the party to be enjoined appears at the ex parte hearing, ask *on the record* if she or he will accept service of the issued TRO. If counsel accepts service, write that on the TRO before the judge signs it.

(1) [9:613] **Where TRO granted without notice to opponent:** Ordinarily, when seeking a TRO, plaintiff's counsel must inform the opposing party or counsel when and where the application will be made (*see* ¶*9:592*). If this has *not* been done (e.g., because plaintiff's counsel was unable to reach the defendant or counsel), special rules apply:

© 2020 Thomson Reuters/The Rutter Group

(a) [9:614] **Early hearing date:** The preliminary injunction hearing must be set *within 15 days* after the TRO is issued; or 22 days "if good cause appears to the court." [CCP §527(d)(1)]

(b) [9:615] **Service on opposing party:** The following papers must be served on the opposing party within *5 days* after the TRO is issued or 2 days before the hearing, whichever is earlier:

— the TRO;

— the *declarations and points and authorities supporting the application* for the TRO;

— the OSC; and

— a copy of the summons and complaint (if not yet served). [CCP §527(d)(2)]

For "good cause," the court may *shorten* the time for service of these papers on the opposing party. [CCP §527(d)(2)]

1) [9:615.1] **Effect of failure to effect timely service:** If the above papers (¶*9:615*) are not timely served on the opposing party, the TRO must be dissolved. [CCP §527(d)(3)]

But if the applicant files a declaration stating why the opposing party could not be served within the time required, the court may *reissue* the TRO and set a new preliminary injunction hearing date. [See CCP §527(d)(5)]

(c) [9:616] **Opponent's right to continuance:** The opposing party is entitled to a continuance of the preliminary injunction hearing. [CCP §527(d)(4); *see* ¶*9:625*]

[9:617-618] *Reserved.*

k. [9:619] **Motion to dissolve or modify:** The party enjoined by a TRO may move to dissolve or modify the TRO on notice to the party who obtained the TRO. The motion must be based on a showing that there has been a *material* change in the facts on which the TRO was granted, the law on which the TRO was granted has been changed, or "the ends of justice would be served" by modification or dissolution of the TRO. [CCP §533; *see discussion at* ¶*9:664 ff.*]

(1) [9:620] **Comment:** Motions to dissolve or modify are rarely necessary because the PI hearing is usually set within a very few days or weeks after issuance of a TRO, and the same showing can be made at the PI hearing.

(2) [9:620.1] **Judge hearing application:** Normally, the application is made to whichever judge or department issued the TRO.

- [9:620.2] *Compare—Los Angeles Superior Court, Central District:* In the L.A. Superior Court Central District, after the first scheduled date for an initial status conference or case management conference, direct calendar judges may hear applications for TROs, and whenever made, hear motions for preliminary injunctions. [L.A. Sup.Ct. Rules 2.8(b), 2.9]

9. **Preliminary Injunction Procedure**

a. [9:621] **Hearing date where no TRO issued:** Where no TRO is in effect, notice requirements are governed by the normal rules regarding motion proceedings. Basically, this means the PI hearing date must be set *at least 16 court days* after service of the OSC, *plus* additional time if the OSC is served by mail (e.g., 5 calendar days for mail served in California to a California address; *see ¶9:87.1*). [CCP §§527(f)(1), 1005(b)]

b. [9:622] **Hearing date where TRO issued:** The PI hearing date will be set by the court when it issues the TRO.

(1) [9:623] **Special rules where defendant not notified of TRO application:** If the defendant or its counsel was not informed beforehand that a TRO was being sought:

— the hearing must be set *within 15 days* after the TRO was issued (or if "good cause" is shown, within 22 days) (CCP §527(d)(1); *see ¶9:614*); and

— the moving papers must generally be served on the defendant *within 5 days* after the TRO is issued or 2 days before the hearing, whichever is earlier (CCP §527(d)(2); *see ¶9:615*).

Failure to meet these time requirements does *not* affect the court's power to grant a PI *provided* the moving papers were served within the time required by CCP §1005(b) (*see ¶9:621*)—i.e., *at least 16 court days* before the hearing, *plus* additional time for service by mail, fax or another method of overnight delivery (*see ¶9:87.1 ff.*). [CCP §527(f)(2)]

(2) [9:623.1] **Compare—TRO issued after notice to defendant:** The time limit applies only to TROs issued without notice to the opposing party. It does not affect the court's power to extend the duration of a TRO issued after notice to the opposing party. [*Hewlett v. Squaw Valley Ski Corp.* (1997) 54 CA4th 499, 534, 63 CR2d 118, 140]

c. **Continuances of hearing**

(1) [9:624] **Plaintiff must be prepared to proceed:** Where the TRO was issued without prior notice to defendant, plaintiff (applicant) must be prepared to proceed on the

© 2020 Thomson Reuters/The Rutter Group

date set for the PI hearing. Otherwise, the TRO will be dissolved. [CCP §527(d)(3)]

Comment: Many courts do likewise even if defendant was notified of the application for TRO before it was issued.

(2) [9:625] **Defendant's right to continuance:** Where the TRO was issued *without prior notice* to defendant, defendant is *entitled* to one continuance for a "reasonable period" of at least 15 days (less, if requested by defendant). If a continuance is requested, the TRO remains in effect until the date of the continued hearing. [CCP §527(d)(4); see *Freeman v. Sullivant* (2011) 192 CA4th 523, 529, 120 CR3d 693, 697, fn. 5 (citing text)]

[9:626] ***PRACTICE POINTER:*** Defendants should notify the court *at least a full day before the hearing* if they intend to ask for a continuance. Waiting until the hearing is a gross discourtesy to the court; the judge may have worked until midnight the night before to prepare the matter for hearing.

Also, if a continuance is granted *beyond* the 15-day statutory period, make sure the court orders the TRO to remain in effect until the continued hearing date; otherwise, the TRO will be dissolved after 15 days by operation of law (CCP §527(d)(4)). Most courts will allow defendants additional time to prepare for the hearing if they agree the TRO will remain in effect.

(3) [9:627] **Stipulated continuance:** Subject to the court's agreement, the parties can stipulate to keep the TRO in effect and continue the hearing on the preliminary injunction.

[9:628-630] *Reserved.*

d. [9:631] **Effect of demurrer:** The fact that defendant has demurred to the complaint will not prevent the court from issuing a preliminary injunction. Even if the demurrer is well taken, the court can grant the injunction as long as it appears that the complaint *can be amended* to state a cause of action. [See *Handyspot Co. of Northern Calif. v. Buegeleisen* (1954) 128 CA2d 191, 194, 274 P2d 938, 940]

e. [9:632] **Evidence at hearing:** In most cases, parties are required to present their evidence without live testimony or cross-examination: i.e., evidence is received in the form of verified pleadings, declarations, deposition transcripts, etc., or requests for judicial notice. [CRC 3.1306]

(1) [9:632.1] **Burden of proof on plaintiff:** Although an OSC directs the defendant "to show cause" why a PI should not issue, the burden is on plaintiff (moving

party) to show all elements necessary to support issuance of a preliminary injunction. [See *O'Connell v. Sup.Ct. (Valenzuela)* (2006) 141 CA4th 1452, 1481, 47 CR3d 147, 169 (citing text)]

(2) [9:633] **Oral testimony:** A party seeking to introduce oral testimony (other than in rebuttal of oral testimony presented by the opposing party) must file, at least 3 court days before the hearing, a written statement describing the evidence to be introduced and a time estimate for the hearing. If this statement is filed less than 5 court days before the hearing, opposing parties must be served in a manner that assures their receipt of the statement at least 2 days before the hearing. [CRC 3.1306(b); *see* ¶*9:45.1*]

Oral testimony is usually discretionary with the trial court. There is no constitutional problem because the enjoined party still has the safeguard of a full trial (entitled to priority in setting). [See *Schraer v. Berkeley Property Owners' Ass'n* (1989) 207 CA3d 719, 732-733, 255 CR 453, 461]

However, in case of a direct conflict of testimony that can be resolved only by accepting one witness' testimony over another's, it may be an *abuse* of discretion to *refuse* oral testimony. In such cases, it may be essential for the judge to see and hear the witnesses in order to determine their credibility. [See *Eddy v. Temkin* (1985) 167 CA3d 1115, 1121, 213 CR 597, 601—no abuse in refusing oral testimony where documentary evidence supported ruling; thus immaterial that judge had no opportunity to observe witness' demeanor]

(3) [9:634] **Declarations:** The usual practice is for the judge to receive the declarations (and verified complaint if there is one) filed in support of or in opposition to the relief sought, unless there are objections (¶*9:635 ff.*).

(4) [9:635] **Evidentiary objections:** If there is objection to all or portions of certain declarations, the court may put the matter at the end of the calendar and ask counsel to confer in an attempt to resolve as many objections as possible by agreement.

(a) [9:636] **Procedure:** Although objections may be made orally at the hearing, the best practice is to file *specific, written objections in advance* so the judge may consider them before the hearing.

FORM: Objections to Evidence, *see Form 10:6* in Rivera, *Cal. Prac. Guide: Civ. Pro. Before Trial FORMS* (TRG).

© 2020 Thomson Reuters/The Rutter Group

[9:636.1] ***PRACTICE POINTER:*** Consider using the same written format for evidentiary objections on applications for preliminary injunctions as is required on motions for summary judgment (CRC 3.1354; *see* ¶*10:210 ff.*). Doing so makes it easy for the judge to follow and rule upon your objections.

[9:637] ***PRACTICE POINTER:*** Preliminary injunctions are often won or lost on the strength of the declarations. Make sure your declarations contain *admissible* evidence from *competent* witnesses (i.e., having *personal knowledge* of the facts stated). Avoid "information and belief" allegations, as well as inadmissible opinions or conclusions.

f. **Ruling on application**

(1) [9:638] **No statement of decision required:** Although the hearing is evidentiary, it is *not* a "trial" within the meaning of CCP §632. Therefore, no statement of decision is required in granting or denying a PI. [*People v. Landlords Professional Services, Inc.* (1986) 178 CA3d 68, 70-71, 223 CR 483, 484; *Whyte v. Schlage Lock Co.* (2002) 101 CA4th 1443, 1450-1451, 125 CR2d 277, 284; see *Oiye v. Fox* (2012) 211 CA4th 1036, 1049, 151 CR3d 65, 75-76 (declining to consider court's oral statements because doing so "would, in essence, compel the trial court to prepare a statement of decision explaining its ruling")]

(2) [9:639] **Not adjudication of merits:** A ruling on an application for PI is *not* an adjudication of the ultimate rights in controversy. It merely represents the trial court's discretionary decision whether defendant should be restrained from exercising a claimed right pending trial. [*Cohen v. Board of Supervisors* (1985) 40 C3d 277, 286, 219 CR 467, 471]

Indeed, the court may not adjudicate the final merits of the case under the guise of issuing a preliminary injunction. [*Yee v. American Nat'l Ins. Co.* (2015) 235 CA4th 453, 458, 185 CR3d 363, 367]

[9:639.1-639.4] *Reserved.*

(3) [9:639.5] **Not limited by scope of TRO:** Where an application for PI includes relief in addition to that requested on a TRO, the court is not limited to the relief granted on the TRO. [*Millennium Corporate Solutions v. Peckinpaugh* (2005) 126 CA4th 352, 359, 23 CR3d 500, 504-505]

g. [9:640] **Bond requirement:** If the PI is granted, the court *must* require an undertaking (CCP §529), or allow a cash deposit in lieu thereof (CCP §995.710). A bond given for a TRO will not serve as a bond for a PI; i.e., a *new* bond is required. [See *Mangini v. J.G. Durand Int'l* (1994) 31 CA4th 214, 218, 37 CR2d 153, 155]

Because the bond requirement is mandatory, defendant's failure to request a bond does not waive the requirement. [*ABBA Rubber Co. v. Seaquist* (1991) 235 CA3d 1, 10, 286 CR 518, 521]

But the bond requirement may be waived or forfeited *by the party to be enjoined:* "Any one may waive the advantage of a law intended for his benefit." [Civ.C. §3513; see *Smith v. Adventist Health System/West* (2010) 182 CA4th 729, 740, 106 CR3d 318, 328—*implied* waiver or forfeiture found where defendant (party to be enjoined) *consciously chose not to address bond requirement* at preliminary injunction hearing, as part of a *tactical decision* to focus on arguments that would result in preliminary injunction being denied]

(1) [9:641] **Amount of bond:** The bond is to cover any damages to the defendant caused by issuance of the injunction, if it is finally determined that plaintiff was not entitled to the injunction. [CCP §529; see *Top Cat Productions, Inc. v. Michael's Los Feliz* (2002) 102 CA4th 474, 478, 125 CR2d 553, 556—purpose is to afford compensation to party wrongly enjoined or restrained]

"[T]he trial court's function is to estimate the *harmful effect* which the injunction is likely to have on the restrained party, and to set the undertaking at that sum." [*ABBA Rubber Co. v. Seaquist*, supra, 235 CA3d at 14, 286 CR at 523 (emphasis added)—$1,000 bond inadequate where defendant shows possible lost profits of $315,000]

(a) [9:642] **Factors considered:** All reasonably foreseeable damages that may be proximately caused by issuance of the injunction should be considered:

1) [9:642.1] **Defense costs:** In fixing the amount of bond, the court will have in mind that where *trial* is necessary to defeat the preliminary injunction, *costs of defense* may be recovered against the surety. [*ABBA Rubber Co. v. Seaquist*, supra, 235 CA3d at 15, 286 CR at 524]

[9:642.2-642.3] *Reserved.*

2) [9:642.4] **Effect of strength of plaintiff's case?** There is a split of authority whether the likelihood of plaintiff's prevailing on the merits is a relevant consideration in fixing the bond amount.

- [9:642.4a] One case states this factor is irrelevant, because a preliminary injunction cannot issue absent a finding that plaintiff is likely to prevail. [*ABBA Rubber Co. v. Seaquist*, supra, 235 CA3d at 16, 286 CR at 525, fn. 8]

- [9:642.4b] But another case disagrees: "The greater the likelihood of the plaintiff prevailing, the less likely a preliminary injunction will have been found to be wrongfully issued. That factor may not be controlling of the amount of the bond, but we consider it relevant." [*Oiye v. Fox* (2012) 211 CA4th 1036, 1062, 151 CR3d 65, 86 (disagreeing with *ABBA Rubber Co.*, supra)]

(b) [9:642.5] **Objections:** CCP §995.930 allows defendant to contest the amount of the bond by noticed motion filed within 10 days after service of a copy of the bond.

Even an *ex parte* written objection, rather than noticed motion, is effective if it otherwise substantially complies with the statute. [*ABBA Rubber Co. v. Seaquist*, supra, 235 CA3d at 13, 286 CR at 523]

[9:643] ***PRACTICE POINTER:*** Counsel should be prepared to argue the amount of the bond based on *declarations* filed with the court. Defense counsel should present evidence showing the types and amount of damages that will be suffered from an improvidently-issued injunction. If defendant can demonstrate a sufficient amount of damages, the size of the bond may be such that plaintiff will be financially unable to post it and the preliminary injunction will never go into effect. Of course, plaintiff's counsel should be prepared with declarations that refute defendant's damages claims.

If there are multiple plaintiffs, defense counsel should make certain the bond *names every plaintiff* who is securing the injunction. Otherwise, if defendant prevails, the right to secure indemnity from the surety will be limited to those plaintiffs named in the bond. [See *Top Cat Productions, Inc. v. Michael's Los Feliz*, supra, 102 CA4th at 478, 125 CR2d at 556]

(c) [9:643.1] **Appellate review:** The amount of the bond can be reviewed on appeal from the order granting the preliminary injunction (*see* ¶*9:667*). But if the injunction ruling is not appealed, no separate appeal lies from the order fixing the amount of the bond. [*County of Los Angeles v. City of Los Angeles* (1999) 76 CA4th 1025, 1028, 90 CR2d 799, 802]

(2) [9:644] **Exceptions—no bond required:** The court has discretion to waive the bond requirement if it finds the plaintiff is indigent and unable to obtain sufficient sureties. But the court must weigh all relevant factors, including the potential harm to the defendant if bond is waived. [CCP §995.240]

The bond requirement is also waived where the plaintiff is a governmental entity, and in domestic relations litigation. [CCP §529(b); see *City of South San Francisco v. Cypress Lawn Cemetery Ass'n* (1992) 11 CA4th 916, 921-922, 14 CR2d 323, 327; *Marriage of Guasch* (2011) 201 CA4th 942, 947-949, 134 CR3d 358, 362-363]

Nor is a bond required when the court grants an injunction based on a *final decision* on the merits of the claim. The purpose of an undertaking is to protect defendant against losses incurred if a preliminary injunction is improvidently granted (¶*9:641*).

(3) [9:645] **Bond in lieu of undertaking:** In lieu of an undertaking (by corporate sureties alone), the applicant may execute a bond personally with a corporate surety, or with two or more personal sureties. [CCP §§995.210(b), 995.310]

(4) [9:646] **Sufficiency of sureties:** Defendant can object to the undertaking or bond within 5 days after service of the injunction. If the court determines that the undertaking is insufficient, the order granting the injunction will be dissolved unless a sufficient bond or undertaking is filed. [CCP §§529(a), 996.010]

(a) [9:647] **Procedure:** The procedure for objecting to the sufficiency of sureties is set forth in CCP §§995.910-995.960.

[9:647.1] ***PRACTICE POINTER:*** Using an admitted surety insurer usually avoids any objection to the sufficiency of the surety. Very limited grounds are available to attack the sufficiency of an admitted surety; see CCP §995.660.

[9:647.2-647.4] *Reserved.*

(5) [9:647.5] **Remedy where injunction dissolved?** When a preliminary injunction is dissolved as having been improperly granted, the aggrieved defendant can only recover damages by proceeding against the injunction bond (or if no bond was required, by a malicious prosecution action). [See *Dickey v. Rosso* (1972) 23 CA3d 493, 497-498, 100 CR 358, 362]

h. [9:648] **Conditions may be imposed:** A court may issue a PI upon conditions that protect all—including the pub-

© 2020 Thomson Reuters/The Rutter Group

lic—whose interests the injunction may effect. But to be valid, such conditions must relate directly to the interests sought to be protected. [*County of Inyo v. City of Los Angeles* (1976) 61 CA3d 91, 100, 132 CR 167, 173]

(1) [9:649] For example, the court may enjoin foreclosure under the power of sale provisions of a junior trust deed, *upon condition* that payments due under the senior trust deed are kept current (*see ¶9:672 ff.*).

(2) [9:650] But it is *improper* to impose a condition designed solely to protect the enjoined party against *pecuniary damage* because that is the purpose of the injunction bond. [*Hummell v. Republic Fed. Sav. & Loan Ass'n* (1982) 133 CA3d 49, 51-52, 183 CR 708, 709]

(a) [9:651] *Example:* Plaintiff sued to enjoin Savings & Loan from enforcing due-on-sale clause in his trust deed loan. His loan had been written at 9%, and Savings & Loan wanted a higher rate (unspecified) if the property were sold. It was *improper* for the judge to condition the injunction on plaintiff increasing payments to a 15% rate while the injunction was in effect. Reason: It is the function of the injunction *bond* to protect against pecuniary damage while the injunction is in effect. [*Hummell v. Republic Fed. Sav. & Loan Ass'n,* supra, 133 CA3d at 50-52, 183 CR at 708-709]

i. [9:652] **Continuance of TRO pending signing of the PI:** The TRO remains in effect for *one court day*, or longer if ordered by the court, to permit signing of the PI and filing of the bond. [CRC 3.1150(f)]

➪ [9:653] ***PRACTICE POINTER:*** If plaintiff needs more than one day, he or she should ask the court for more time; five days is customarily granted on request. However, the court may assume one day is sufficient unless plaintiff speaks up.

j. [9:654] **Form of order:** If a PI is granted, the moving party must serve and present to the court a form of written PI in accord with the court's order. [CRC 3.1150]

(1) [9:655] **Drafting the PI:** To be enforceable by contempt, the PI must contain a *reasonably adequate description* of the conduct which is prohibited, in language giving fair notice to the defendant of the consequences of disobedience. [See *In re Berry* (1968) 68 C2d 137, 155, 65 CR 273, 285; and *Watsonville Canning & Frozen Food Co., Inc. v. Sup.Ct. (Local 912, Int'l Broth. of Teamsters)* (1986) 178 CA3d 1242, 1246, 224 CR 303, 305-306]

Where First Amendment rights are involved, the order must "be tailored as precisely as possible to the exact needs of the case . . . . [and] must be sufficiently precise to provide a person of ordinary intelligence fair notice that his contemplated conduct is forbidden." [*Parisi v. Mazzaferro* (2016) 5 CA5th 1219, 1231, 210 CR3d 574, 585-586 (internal quotes and citations omitted)]

☞ [9:656] ***PRACTICE POINTER:*** The message of *Parisi v. Mazzaferro*, supra, 5 CA5th at 1231, 210 CR3d at 585-586, is good practice for any injunctive order. Set out the conduct to be enjoined as *narrowly* as possible. Use words that can be understood by the party enjoined; avoid legalese. Make sure that it expressly runs against *all* persons sought to be enjoined (¶*9:565*).

(a) [9:656.1] **Parties bound; agents and employees of named parties:** Persons not named as parties to the action cannot be named individually in the injunction. But it is common practice and proper to enjoin not only the corporation or association, but also its *officers, employees and agents*. The effect of this is to make the injunction effective against all through whom the enjoined party may act. [*Berger v. Sup.Ct.* (1917) 175 C 719, 721, 167 P 143, 144; see also *Ross v. Sup.Ct. (Woods)* (1977) 19 C3d 899, 905-906, 141 CR 133, 137]

1) [9:656.2] **Due process right to challenge status as agent or employee?** The question of whether someone named as an agent has a due process right to a hearing before the injunction can be enforced against that party was presented to the California Supreme Court, but the Court ultimately did not decide the issue. Following a default judgment ordering Yelp (a nonparty) to take down a post, Yelp intervened to argue it had a due process right to a hearing as to whether it was acting in concert with the defendant so that the judgment containing the injunction should be set aside. The plurality did not reach that issue because Yelp's "statutory argument [was] dispositive," so there was "no need to address the due process question," but three dissenters would have enforced injunction against Yelp. [*Hassell v. Bird* (2018) 5 C5th 522, 526, 534, 234 CR3d 867, 870, 876]

[9:656.3-656.4] *Reserved.*

(b) [9:656.5] **Compare—subsequent owners:** An injunction does *not* "run with the land" and therefore cannot be made binding on subsequent owners of property re use of the property. [*People ex rel. Gwinn*

© 2020 Thomson Reuters/The Rutter Group

v. *Kothari* (2000) 83 CA4th 759, 765, 100 CR2d 29, 34—error to issue injunction under Red Light Abatement Law (Pen.C. §11225 et seq.), which by its terms applied to subsequent purchasers of property]

(2) [9:657] **Service; approval as to form:** In most courts, the proposed form of PI, if not available and served at the hearing, *must* be served on the opposition before submission to the court. If the opposition is willing to approve the PI as to form (i.e., agree that it is in accord with the court's order), the judge may sign it forthwith.

(3) [9:658] **Opposition as to form:** If the party enjoined objects to the form of the proposed injunction, he or she should communicate such objection *immediately* (i.e., on the same day) to the court; otherwise it will be routinely signed by the judge as long as it appears to comply with his or her order.

Failure to object to the form of the order amounts to a *waiver* of the objection on appeal. [*City of San Marcos v. Coast Waste Mgmt., Inc.* (1996) 47 CA4th 320, 327, 54 CR2d 588, 593]

(4) [9:659] **Filing undertaking:** The undertaking (i.e., a bond) should be delivered to the clerk along with the proposed order granting the PI. Since the injunction is conditioned upon filing the undertaking, it will not be effective until the undertaking is filed.

(5) [9:660] **Service of the PI:** The same considerations apply as regarding service of the TRO (*see ¶9:612 ff.*).

(a) [9:661] **Service on counsel may not be sufficient:** Service on the opposing attorney raises only a disputable presumption that his or her client has actual knowledge of the terms of the PI, and creates difficulty of enforcement by contempt proceedings. [*People v. Sup.Ct. (Stein)* (1965) 239 CA2d 99, 104, 48 CR 445, 447]

(6) [9:662] **Effect of judgment for defendant:** A judgment for the defendant at the trial *automatically* dissolves the preliminary injunction. No formal motion is necessary. [See *City of Oakland v. Sup.Ct. (Oakland Raiders)* (1982) 136 CA3d 565, 569, 186 CR 326, 328—on subsequent reversal of judgment, plaintiff must seek new preliminary injunction]

(7) [9:663] **Damages liability on bond:** If plaintiff loses the case at trial, defendant may seek to recover damages resulting from the improperly-issued injunction, from both the plaintiff and the surety on the bond. The procedure is by noticed motion in the main action (no separate action is necessary). [CCP §996.440; see *Wallace v. Miller* (1983)

140 CA3d 636, 643, 189 CR 637, 641—where injunction erroneously issued without bond, defendant's only remedy was suit for abuse of process or malicious prosecution]

(a) [9:663.1] **Limit of liability:** The surety's liability is limited to the sum specified in the bond. Even if the bond stipulates "damages shall *include* attorney fees," the maximum liability is the same. [*Lawrence Tractor Co., Inc. v. Carlisle Ins. Co.* (1988) 202 CA3d 949, 955-956, 249 CR 150, 153]

⇨ [9:663.2] ***PRACTICE POINTER FOR DEFENDANT:*** This highlights the importance of applying for an *adequate* bond when the PI is *issued.* Provide the court with *declarations or other evidence* showing the maximum amount (within reason) of each item of damage defendant is likely to suffer as a result of the injunction; and any interest, court costs and attorney fees defendant will be entitled to recover if it prevails.

k. [9:664] **Modification or dissolution of injunction:** A TRO or PI is by no means a final order. It is subject to modification or dissolution at any time upon a showing of:

— a *material change in the facts* upon which the PI or TRO was granted;

— the *law* upon which the PI or TRO was granted has changed; or

— "the *ends of justice* would be served" by the modification or dissolution. [CCP §533 (emphasis added); see *City of San Marcos v. Coast Waste Mgmt., Inc.* (1996) 47 CA4th 320, 327, 54 CR2d 588, 593—recognizing court's inherent power to modify or dissolve preliminary injunctions; *Loeffler v. Medina* (2009) 174 CA4th 1495, 1504, 95 CR3d 343, 350; *and ¶9:619 ff.*]

• [9:664.1] While publication (e.g., in a patent) of a trade secret would allow the dissolution of an injunction barring its use, where the secret was not in fact destroyed by publication the court properly refused to dissolve the injunction. [*Global Protein Products, Inc. v. Le* (2019) 42 CA5th 352, 367-369, 255 CR3d 310, 321-322]

(1) [9:665] **Modifying TRO granted without notice:** In any case in which an injunction has been granted *without notice* to the party enjoined (e.g., TROs), that party may move to dissolve or modify the injunction on "reasonable notice" to the opposing party. [See CCP §532(a); *¶9:619*]

[9:666] *Reserved.*

© 2020 Thomson Reuters/The Rutter Group

l. [9:667] **Appellate review:** An order granting or denying a preliminary injunction (or dissolving or refusing to dissolve one) is an appealable order. [CCP §904.1(a)(6)]

Not all orders are injunctions, however: While a "court order nearly always requires some action or inaction from one or both parties or their counsel . . . this fact does not render nearly all court orders injunctive in nature." For example, orders to confer, to refrain from contact with putative class members, and to turn over copies of improperly obtained releases are not injunctions, and so are not appealable as such. [*Brown v. Upside Gading, LP* (2019) 42 CA5th 140, 145-146, 254 CR3d 803, 807-808]

(1) **Effect of type of order**

(a) [9:668] **Denial of preliminary prohibitory injunction:** An appeal may *not* be a speedy or adequate remedy to review *denial* of a preliminary prohibitory injunction because the conduct sought to be enjoined will continue pending the appeal. Therefore, immediate review may be sought by *extraordinary writ* (mandamus or prohibition). [*Robbins v. Sup.Ct. (County of Sacramento)* (1985) 38 C3d 199, 205, 211 CR 398, 401]

Alternatively, plaintiff may seek an order from the appellate court "expediting" the appeal. [*Pacific Landmark Hotel, Ltd. v. Marriott Hotels, Inc.* (1993) 19 CA4th 615, 623, 23 CR2d 555, 560]

(b) [9:669] **Grant of preliminary injunction:** In some cases, an appeal may not be a speedy or adequate remedy to review an order *granting* a preliminary injunction. E.g., where the action is already several years old and plaintiff's chance of success at trial is "slight," interests of judicial economy favor immediate review by extraordinary writ. [*San Francisco Newspaper Printing Co., Inc. v. Sup.Ct. (Miller)* (1985) 170 CA3d 438, 441, 216 CR 462, 463]

(2) [9:670] **Standard of review:** Whether review is by appeal or extraordinary writ, appellate court review is generally limited to the question whether the trial court *abused its discretion* in granting or denying the motion for preliminary injunction. [*Robbins v. Sup.Ct. (County of Sacramento)*, supra, 38 C3d at 205, 211 CR at 401; *Law School Admission Council v. State of Calif.* (2014) 222 CA4th 1265, 1280, 166 CR3d 647, 659]

However, where plaintiff's likelihood of prevailing on the merits depends *purely upon a question of law* rather than upon evidence to be introduced at trial, the issue is reviewed *de novo* on appeal. [*Pacific Landmark Hotel, Ltd. v. Marriott Hotels, Inc.* (1993) 19 CA4th 615, 624,

23 CR2d 555, 560 (appellate court ordered PI granted); *Law School Admission Council, Inc. v. State of Calif.*, supra, 222 CA4th at 1281, 166 CR3d at 659]

In addition, when a restraining order is alleged to infringe on constitutional rights of expression, the facts and statements germane to the First Amendment challenge are reviewed de novo. And whether an injunction passes constitutional muster is a question of law considered de novo. [*Parisi v. Mazzaferro* (2016) 5 CA5th 1219, 1226-1227, 210 CR3d 574, 582]

10. [9:671] **Common Injunction Situations:** Certain requests for PIs occur more frequently than others. Examples include the following:

a. [9:672] **Power of sale foreclosures:** Attempts to enjoin foreclosures under the usual power of sale provisions in deeds of trust are common. The usual showing attempted is that there is a dispute over the right to sell or the amount necessary to reinstate.

- [9:673] The court will examine the claim carefully to make sure that there is a *bona fide dispute* as to *enforceability* or *default*, rather than a mere attempt to "stall" payment of an amount clearly due. [See *Baypoint Mortgage Corp. v. Crest Premium Real Estate Investments Retirement Trust* (1985) 168 CA3d 818, 827, 214 CR 531, 536-537—dispute as to late charges; foreclosure enjoined because contract contained no "time of the essence" clause indicating that late payment alone was ground for foreclosure]

- [9:674] If a *bona fide* dispute exists, PIs are frequently granted, but on *conditions designed to prevent prejudice to the defendant.* The common conditions are paying of amounts not in dispute, continuing payments during litigation, keeping prior liens out of default, paying taxes and insurance, and waiving any claim that accepting payments pursuant to the conditions waives the default.

  Attorneys seeking such PIs should prepare their clients for the likely conditions.

(1) [9:675] **Plaintiff must show reasonable probability of success on merits:** As with any application for PI, plaintiff must establish a "reasonable probability of success" on the merits (*see* ¶*9:516*).

To meet this burden, the borrower may show either:

- *defects* in foreclosure proceedings (e.g., no recordation of notice of default);
- *reinstatement of the loan* (e.g., by proper payment during the 90 days following notice of default); or
- *offsets* or other reasons why amounts due under

© 2020 Thomson Reuters/The Rutter Group

the note are not payable. (Caution: This is the hardest to establish, and most likely to be regarded as a "stall.")

(2) [9:676] **Plaintiff must show risk of irreparable injury:** Plaintiff must also show a risk of irreparable injury (*see ¶9:508*). This is usually easy to establish in private sale foreclosure cases because land is generally considered "unique."

But relief may be denied where the real property is being held for investment purposes and has an established market value. In such cases, it is not "unique"; the *loss can be fully compensated in money damages*. [E.g., *Jessen v. Keystone Sav. & Loan Ass'n* (1983) 142 CA3d 454, 457, 191 CR 104, 106—condo units held for resale; *see ¶9:509*]

(3) [9:677] **Timing of application:** The longer the borrower waits to seek relief, the more reluctant courts may be to intervene, and the stronger the showing that may be required.

b. [9:678] **Workplace violence:** Courts may intervene to regulate threats of violence at the workplace.

(1) [9:679] **Violence threatened against employees:** An employer may act on behalf of an affected employee to obtain a TRO and an injunction (referred to as an "order after hearing") against anyone, including another current employee, who engaged in unlawful violence or made a "credible threat" of violence at the workplace. [CCP §527.8; see *City of Los Angeles v. Animal Defense League* (2006) 135 CA4th 606, 622, 37 CR3d 632, 645 (disapproved on other grounds in *City of Montebello v. Vasquez* (2016) 1 C5th 409, 205 CR3d 499)—only natural persons, not organizations, may be enjoined]

The TRO and order after hearing are in addition to whatever other remedies the employer or affected employee may have against such violence. [*City of Palo Alto v. Service Employees Int'l Union* (1999) 77 CA4th 327, 336, 91 CR2d 500, 506; *see ¶9:679.20* (forms)]

If good cause is shown, the order after hearing may also "include" (presumably, this means as protected persons) family or household members who reside with the employee. [CCP §527.8(d)]

Compare—harassment (CCP §527.6): Alternatively, an *employee* may seek to enjoin violence or threats thereof as "harassment" under CCP §527.6 (*¶9:697 ff.*).

(a) [9:679.1] **Required threat:** The remedy is available where there is a generalized threat against employees; it is not necessary that the threat be directed at a specific, identifiable employee. [*USS-Posco Indus. v. Edwards* (2003) 111 CA4th 436, 442-443, 4 CR3d 54, 59-60; *see ¶9:679.7 ff.*]

A "credible threat" is a "knowing and wilful statement or course of conduct that would place a *reasonable person* in fear for his or her safety, or the safety of his or her immediate family, and that serves no legitimate purpose." [CCP §527.8(b)(2) (emphasis added)]

(b) [9:679.2] **Hearing:** The hearing on the petition must be held within 21 days after the petition is filed, or within 25 days if the court extends the time for good cause. [CCP §527.8(h)]

1) [9:679.3] **Continuance:** The respondent is entitled to one continuance as a matter of right for a "reasonable period, to respond to the petition" and either party may request (or the court on its own motion may order) a continuance of the hearing on a showing of good cause. If a continuance is granted, the TRO continues in effect until the continued hearing, unless the court otherwise orders. In granting the continuance, the court may modify the TRO. [CCP §527.8(o), (p)]

[9:679.4] ***PRACTICE POINTER:*** Although the law provides that the TRO continues in effect until a continued hearing on the petition, the original TRO, on its face, terminates on the original hearing date. Thus, for law enforcement to enforce the TRO after a continuance, the court must sign an order extending the TRO so that it will remain in effect until the next hearing date. Without this extension of the TRO, law enforcement will not have a valid order and will not enforce it. Also, the restrained party must be served with the order for it to be enforced by contempt. Service is usually accomplished at the hearing. *See ¶9:679.20* (forms).

[9:679.5] *Reserved.*

2) [9:679.6] **Evidence:** At the hearing, the court "shall receive *any testimony that is relevant*," including hearsay evidence. [CCP §527.8(j) (emphasis added); *Kaiser Found. Hosps. v. Wilson*

© 2020 Thomson Reuters/The Rutter Group

(2011) 201 CA4th 550, 557, 133 CR3d 830, 835; *Duronslet v. Kamps* (2012) 203 CA4th 717, 728-729, 137 CR3d 756, 765 (decided under parallel civil harassment statute (CCP §527.6))]

The judge is required to receive *oral* testimony, if offered. [CCP §527.8(j); see *Schraer v. Berkeley Property Owners' Ass'n* (1989) 207 CA3d 719, 733, 255 CR 453, 462 (decided under CCP §527.6)] (This is one of the few situations in which judges handling injunction applications hear oral testimony; *see also ¶9:707.1.*)

a) [9:679.7] **Clear and convincing standard:** The petitioner must show reasonable proof to the satisfaction of the court for a temporary restraining order (CCP §527.8(e)), but an order after hearing must be based on clear and convincing evidence of entitlement to relief. [CCP §527.8(j)]

b) [9:679.8] **Alleged threat by coworker:** If the person allegedly responsible for the violence or threat is a coworker, the judge "shall receive evidence" concerning the employer's decision to retain, terminate or otherwise discipline this person. [CCP §527.8(j)]

CCP §527.8 reflects *public policy* requiring employers to adequately address potential workplace violence. But this policy does *not* require the employer to *automatically* fire an employee who makes a "credible threat" of violence against a coworker regardless of the employee's intent or the degree of risk involved. [*City of Palo Alto v. Service Employees Int'l Union,* supra, 77 CA4th at 337, 91 CR2d at 506]

c) [9:679.9] **Irreparable harm to employee:** The "clear and convincing evidence" must show not only that defendant engaged in violence or made a credible threat of violence, but also that *great or irreparable harm* would result to an employee without issuance of the prohibitory injunction. [*Scripps Health v. Marin* (1999) 72 CA4th 324, 332, 85 CR2d 86, 92]

[9:679.10] *Reserved.*

(c) [9:679.11] **Order:** If there is "clear and convincing" evidence to support the petition, an order "shall issue" prohibiting further violence or threats of violence for a period of not more than three years (subject to renewal). The failure to state an expiration date on the face of the order creates an order with a duration of three years from date of issuance. [CCP §527.8(j), (k)(1), (2)]

A TRO or order after hearing must be issued on mandatory Judicial Council forms (*see ¶9:679.20*); but the fact that an order was not issued on such forms does not render it unenforceable. [CCP §527.8(v)]

1) [9:679.12] **Exception—constitutional speech:** The court cannot prohibit constitutionally protected speech or other activities. [CCP §527.8(c)]

[9:679.13-679.14] *Reserved.*

(d) [9:679.15] **Copies to law enforcement:** Copies of the TRO and injunction must be delivered the same day to *law enforcement agencies* designated by plaintiff. Those agencies are charged with enforcement if called to the scene of further violence or threats at the workplace. [See CCP §527.8(r)] (Intentional disobedience is a crime; see Pen.C. §273.6.)

(e) [9:679.16] **Renewal of order:** Any restraining order prohibiting further violence or threats of violence may be renewed, at the request of the protected party, for a period of not more than three years "without a showing of any further violence or threats of violence since the issuance of the original order." The request for renewal may be brought at any time within three months before expiration of the order. [CCP §527.8(k)(1)]

(f) [9:679.17] **Termination or modification of order:** Any motion to terminate or modify the protective order (i.e., the injunction) brought by someone other than the protected person must be personally served on the protected party at least 16 court days before the hearing on the motion. If the protected person is not given such notice, the court must deny the motion to modify or terminate the protective order without prejudice or continue the hearing until notice is given in the manner designated by the court. The protected party can waive notice by appearing at the hearing and not challenging service. [CCP §527.8(k)(3)]

[9:679.18-679.19] *Reserved.*

(g) [9:679.20] **Judicial Council forms:** The Judicial Council has adopted the following forms for mandatory use. [CCP §527.8(v)]

© 2020 Thomson Reuters/The Rutter Group

FORMS

- Petition for Workplace Violence Restraining Orders (WV-100); *see Form 9B:3* in Rivera, *Cal. Prac. Guide: Civ. Pro. Before Trial FORMS* (TRG).
- Confidential CLETS Information (CLETS-001); *see Form 9B:4* in Rivera, *Cal. Prac. Guide: Civ. Pro. Before Trial FORMS* (TRG).
- Notice of Court Hearing (Workplace Violence Prevention) (WV-109); *see Form 9B:5* in Rivera, *Cal. Prac. Guide: Civ. Pro. Before Trial FORMS* (TRG).
- Request to Continue Hearing Court Hearing (Temporary Restraining Order) (Workplace Violence Prevention) (WV-115).
- Order on Request to Continue Hearing (CLETS-TWH) (Workplace Violence Prevention) (WV-116).
- Temporary Restraining Order (CLETS-TWH) (Workplace Violence Prevention) (WV-110); *see Form 9B:6* in Rivera, *Cal. Prac. Guide: Civ. Pro. Before Trial FORMS* (TRG).
- Response to Petition for Workplace Violence Restraining Orders (Workplace Violence Prevention) (WV-120); *see Form 9B:7* in Rivera, *Cal. Prac. Guide: Civ. Pro. Before Trial FORMS* (TRG).
- Workplace Violence Restraining Order After Hearing (CLETS-WHO) (WV-130); *see Form 9B:8* in Rivera, *Cal. Prac. Guide: Civ. Pro. Before Trial FORMS* (TRG).
- Request to Renew Restraining Order (WV-700).
- Response to Request to Renew Restraining Order (WV-720).
- Order Renewing Workplace Violence Restraining Order (WV-730).

1) [9:679.21] **Instructions:** The Judicial Council has adopted a set of instructions to utilize in connection with these forms (WV-100-INFO and WV-120-INFO).

(2) [9:680] **Labor disputes:** CCP §527.3 and Lab.C. §1138 et seq. limit a court's power to enjoin conduct involved in a labor dispute (e.g., picketing employer's premises). The more detailed provisions of later-enacted Lab.C. §1138 et seq. control. [See *United Food & Comm'l Workers Union, AFL-CIO, CLC Local No. 324 v. Sup.Ct. (Gigante USA, Inc.)* (2000) 83 CA4th 566, 576, 99 CR2d 849, 855]

"Labor dispute" means a controversy concerning terms or conditions of workers' employment, union representation, etc. [See Lab.C. §527.3(b)(4)]

(a) [9:680.1] **Findings required:** To issue a TRO or PI in a case arising out of a labor dispute, a court must make all of the following findings:

— *unlawful acts* have been threatened and will be committed (or have been committed and will continue) unless restrained;

— *substantial and irreparable injury* to plaintiff's property will follow;

— greater injury will be inflicted upon plaintiff by denial of relief than will be inflicted upon defendants by the granting of relief;

— plaintiff has no adequate remedy at law; and

— *law enforcement officers are unable or unwilling* to furnish adequate protection. [Lab.C. §1138.1(a); see *United Food & Comm'l Workers Union, AFL-CIO, CLC Local No. 324 v. Sup.Ct. (Gigante USA, Inc.)*, supra, 83 CA4th at 576, 99 CR2d at 855—if any one factor missing, injunctive relief improper]

[9:680.2-680.4] *Reserved.*

(b) [9:680.5] **Persons who may be enjoined:** A TRO or PI may issue only against the person(s) or entity that threatened or committed the unlawful acts or who "*actually authorized* those acts." [Lab.C. §1138.1 (emphasis added)]

1) [9:680.6] **Clear proof requirement:** No officer or member of any labor union or organization involved in a labor dispute may be held responsible for the unlawful acts of other officers or members "except upon clear proof of actual participation in, or actual authorization of those acts." [Lab.C. §1138]

[9:680.7-680.9] *Reserved.*

(c) [9:680.10] **Good faith settlement effort required:** No TRO or PI may issue unless plaintiffs have made "every reasonable effort to settle [the] dispute either by negotiation or with the aid of any available governmental machinery of mediation or voluntary arbitration." [Lab.C. §1138.2]

(d) [9:680.11] **Notice requirements:** Notice of the hearing must be given (in such manner as the court may direct) to the persons sought to be enjoined and to "the chief of those public officials of the county and city within which the unlawful acts have been

© 2020 Thomson Reuters/The Rutter Group

threatened or committed charged with the duty to protect complainant's property." [Lab.C. §1138.1(b)]

No TRO may issue without obtaining testimony under oath and an adequate undertaking, and without hearing oral argument from the opposing party (except where notice to the opposing party is excused; *see* ¶*9:593*). [Lab.C. §1138.1(b)]

[9:680.12-680.14] *Reserved.*

(e) [9:680.15] **Law enforcement "unable or unwilling" to provide adequate protection:** A finding to this effect is required before a restraining order can issue (Lab.C. §1138.1(a)(5)). Although the meaning of these terms is not yet clear, there need *not* be a complete breakdown in law enforcement. [See *United Food & Comm'l Workers Union, AFL-CIO, CLC Local No. 324 v. Sup.Ct. (Gigante USA, Inc.)*, supra, 83 CA4th at 579-580, 99 CR2d at 857-858—sheriff's timely response and intervention precluded finding of "inability or unwillingness"]

(f) [9:681] **Injunction must be narrowly drawn:** Because of "free speech" considerations, TROs or PIs "must be couched in the narrowest terms that will accomplish the pin-pointed objective permitted by constitutional mandate and the essential needs of the public order." [*United Farm Workers of America, AFL-CIO v. Sup.Ct. (Calif. Retail Liquor Dealers Institute)* (1976) 16 C3d 499, 504, 128 CR 209, 212]

(g) [9:682] **Limitation—federal preemption:** State courts have no power to regulate activities actually or "arguably" protected under Sections 7 or 8 of the National Labor Relations Act (29 USC §151 et seq.) as *part of the collective bargaining process*. Such activities are within the *exclusive competence* of the National Labor Relations Board (NLRB). [*San Diego Bldg. Trades Council, Millmen's Union, Local 2020 v. Garmon* (1959) 359 US 236, 245, 79 S.Ct. 773, 779-780]

But there is no preemption of matters of only "peripheral concern" to federal labor law or of "peculiar local concern and interest" (e.g., in maintaining public order and avoiding violence). [*San Diego Bldg. Trades Council, Millmen's Union, Local 2020 v. Garmon*, supra, 359 US at 247, 79 S.Ct. at 781]

1) [9:682.1] **Test:** The test is whether the controversy presented to the state court *could have been presented to the NLRB*. If it could, state court adjudications would create a "re-

alistic risk of interference" with the NLRB's primary jurisdiction. [See *Sears, Roebuck & Co. v. San Diego County Dist. Council of Carpenters* (1978) 436 US 180, 197, 98 S.Ct. 1745, 1757-1758; *Walmart Stores, Inc. v. United Food & Comm'l Workers Int'l Union* (2016) 4 CA5th 194, 202-204, 208 CR3d 542, 548-550]

[9:682.2-682.4] *Reserved.*

2) **Application**

- [9:682.5] State *criminal laws* may be invoked and state *tort actions* may proceed where they create no "realistic risk of interference" with NLRB jurisdiction. [*Sears, Roebuck & Co. v. San Diego County Dist. Council of Carpenters*, supra, 436 US at 198, 98 S.Ct. at 1758—employer's *trespass* action against union *not* preempted; the *location* of picketing (on private property) was "completely unrelated" to its purpose (protected by federal law)]
- [9:682.6] Similarly, state court injunctions may be upheld against mass picketing accompanied by violence or threats of violence and/or obstructing access to private property. [See *Youngdahl v. Rainfair, Inc.* (1957) 355 US 131, 78 S.Ct. 206; *Kaplan's Fruit & Produce Co., Inc. v. Sup.Ct. (United Farm Workers of America, AFL-CIO)* (1979) 26 C3d 60, 70, 160 CR 745, 750]

  [9:682.7-682.9] *Reserved.*

3) [9:682.10] **Compare—public employees:** Federal labor law generally does not apply to strikes and picketing by public employees. Therefore, state courts have broader injunctive powers in labor disputes involving teachers, public nurses, etc.

[9:682.11-682.19] *Reserved.*

c. [9:682.20] **Violence on private college campuses:** Forms and procedures similar to those used to prevent workplace violence may be used where a student at a private college ("private institution of vocational, professional, or postsecondary education") has suffered an off-campus *credible threat of violence* that may reasonably be construed to be carried out at the school campus or facility. [See CCP §527.85]

FORMS

- Petition for Private Postsecondary School Violence Restraining Orders (SV-100 and SV-100-INFO)

© 2020 Thomson Reuters/The Rutter Group

- Response to Petition for Private Postsecondary School Violence Restraining Orders (SV-120 and SV-120-INFO)
- Confidential CLETS Information (CLETS-001)
- Notice of Court Hearing (Private Postsecondary School Violence Prevention) and Temporary Restraining Order (CLETS-TSV) (SV-109, SV-110)
- Private Postsecondary School Violence Restraining Order After Hearing (CLETS-SVO) (SV-130)
- Proof of Personal Service (SV-200 and SV-200-INFO, SV-250)

d. [9:683] **Domestic violence:** The Domestic Violence Prevention Act (DVPA, Fam.C. §6200 et seq.) provides for the issuance of restraining or "protective" orders, either ex parte or after noticed hearing, that enjoin specific acts of statutorily-defined "abuse" (Fam.C. §6203). [*Nakamura v. Parker* (2007) 156 CA4th 327, 337, 67 CR3d 286, 292; see also *S.A. v. Maiden* (2014) 229 CA4th 27, 36, 176 CR3d 567, 572-573—no malicious prosecution liability based on attorney's request for domestic violence restraining orders; *Rodriguez v. Menjivar* (2015) 243 CA4th 816, 820, 196 CR3d 816, 818-819—in determining whether to issue DVPA order, trial court must consider past abuse, mental abuse and controlling behavior]

Cross-refer: See detailed discussion in Hogoboom & King, *Cal. Prac. Guide: Family Law* (TRG), Ch. 5.

e. [9:684] **Unfair competition:** Requests for injunctions under Bus. & Prof.C. §17203 are increasingly frequent. ("Any person who engages, has engaged, or proposes to engage in unfair competition may be enjoined in any court of competent jurisdiction.")

In order to grant injunctive relief under the Unfair Competition Law (UCL, Bus. & Prof.C. §17200 et seq.), there must be a threat that the wrongful conduct will continue. [*Davis v. Farmers Ins. Exchange* (2016) 245 CA4th 1302, 1326-1327, 200 CR3d 315, 335—injunctive relief improper where injuries plaintiff allegedly suffered were all in the past]

(1) [9:685] **"Unfair competition" broadly defined:** As used in the Business and Professions Code, "unfair competition" includes *any business practice forbidden by law* (unless defendant is privileged, immunized by another statute, or the underlying statute bars enforcement under the UCL). [*Barquis v. Merchants Collection Ass'n* (1972) 7 C3d 94, 113, 101 CR 745, 758; see also *Stevens v. Sup.Ct. (API Auto Ins. Services)* (1999) 75 CA4th 594, 603, 89 CR2d 370, 376]

Commercial speech that is false or misleading may be the subject of an action for unfair competition. [*Kasky v. Nike, Inc.* (2002) 27 C4th 939, 964, 119 CR2d 296, 315]

(a) [9:686] **Application:** "Unfair competition" is not limited to competitive conduct. Indeed, it is given the "*broadest possible definition.*" [*Consumers Union of U.S., Inc. v. Fisher Develop., Inc.* (1989) 208 CA3d 1433, 1438, 257 CR 151, 154]

For example:

- [9:686.1] Slumlord used "overcrowding" as excuse for evicting tenants who complained to authorities re condition of premises. [*Hernandez v. Stabach* (1983) 145 CA3d 309, 314, 193 CR 350, 352]
- [9:686.2] Housing tract developer restricted sales to persons over age 55, in violation of Unruh Act forbidding age discrimination in housing. [*Consumers Union of U.S., Inc. v. Fisher Develop., Inc.*, supra, 208 CA3d at 1441, 257 CR at 155-156 & fn. 4]
- [9:686.3] Employees used their employer's customers lists to set up a competing business (immaterial whether the lists were protectible as trade secrets). [*Courtesy Temporary Service, Inc. v. Camacho* (1990) 222 CA3d 1278, 1290, 272 CR 352, 359]
- [9:686.4] Ski resort's wrongful removal of trees in violation of both statute and conditional use permit constituted an "unlawful business practice" and thus "unfair competition" under §17200. [*Hewlett v. Squaw Valley Ski Corp.* (1997) 54 CA4th 499, 520, 63 CR2d 118, 130]

(2) [9:687] **Standing to sue:** Standing to sue for injunctive relief under Bus. & Prof.C. §17203 is limited to government prosecutors or a private plaintiff "who has suffered *injury in fact* and has *lost money or property* as a result of such unfair competition." [Bus. & Prof.C. §17204 (emphasis added); *see detailed discussion at ¶14:226 ff.*]

[9:688] *Reserved.*

(3) [9:689] **Compare—traditional unfair competition:** On the other hand, preliminary injunctions are granted *infrequently* in disputes between competitors over "palming off" or "customers lists" or other traditional forms of unfair competition. The reason is that there is usually no "irreparable injury," and also because most cases have meritorious claims on both sides which must be explored fully before injunctive relief can be granted.

© 2020 Thomson Reuters/The Rutter Group

(a) [9:690] **Comment:** Plaintiffs in business tort cases often seek a preliminary injunction that would put their competitors out of business. However, they are usually disappointed. Courts recognize that parties are usually allowed to compete, although the methods of their competition may be controlled.

(b) [9:691] **Competition from former employees:** A former employee has the right to compete with his or her former employer but *not* to *solicit* new business from the former employer's customers where information about those customers is "confidential, proprietary, and/or a trade secret." [*Retirement Group v. Galante* (2009) 176 CA4th 1226, 1240, 98 CR3d 585, 595; see also *Robert L. Cloud & Assocs., Inc. v. Mikesell* (1999) 69 CA4th 1141, 1150, 82 CR2d 143, 148; *ReadyLink Healthcare v. Cotton* (2005) 126 CA4th 1006, 1015, 24 CR3d 720, 727]

Cross-refer: Unfair competition from former employees is discussed in detail in Chin, Wiseman, Callahan & Lowe, *Cal. Prac. Guide: Employment Litigation* (TRG), Ch. 14.

1) [9:691.1] **Compare—announcing availability:** But "[m]erely informing customers of one's former employer of a change of employment, without more, is not solicitation . . . Equity will not enjoin a former employee from receiving business from the customers of his former employer, even though the circumstances be such that he should be prohibited from soliciting such business." [*Aetna Bldg. Maint. Co., Inc. v. West* (1952) 39 C2d 198, 204, 246 P2d 11, 15]

[9:691.2-691.4] *Reserved.*

(c) [9:691.5] **Misappropriation of trade secrets:** Confidential business information (including customers lists) may be protectible under the Uniform Trade Secrets Act (UTSA). [Civ.C. §3426; see *Robert L. Cloud & Assocs., Inc. v. Mikesell*, supra, 69 CA4th at 1148-1150, 82 CR2d at 146-147; *Wanke, Industrial, Comm'l, Residential, Inc. v. Sup.Ct. (Keck)* (2012) 209 CA4th 1151, 1174-1175, 147 CR3d 651, 668-669; *Angelica Textile Services, Inc. v. Park* (2013) 220 CA4th 495, 504-505, 163 CR3d 192, 200]

The UTSA provides various remedies for trade secret misappropriation, including injunctive relief (see Civ.C. §3426.2). If prohibiting all future use of the trade secret would be unreasonable, the court may condition future use on payment of a reasonable royalty (Civ.C. §3426.2(b)). "In appropriate circumstances, affirmative acts to protect a trade secret may be compelled by court order." [Civ.C. §3426.2(c); *FLIR Systems, Inc. v. Parrish* (2009) 174 CA4th 1270, 1279-1280, 95 CR3d 307, 316—Civ.C. §3426.2(c) authorizes mandatory injunctions]

Common law remedies preempted: The UTSA "occupies the field in California," preempting alternative civil remedies (e.g., unfair competition) "based on the same nucleus of facts as the misappropriation of trade secrets claim for relief." [*K.C. Multimedia, Inc. v. Bank of America Tech. & Operations, Inc.* (2009) 171 CA4th 939, 958, 90 CR3d 247, 261 (internal quotes omitted)]

1) [9:692] **Test for protectible "trade secret":** A customer list may be considered a trade secret where the identity of customers itself has economic value and the owner has made reasonable efforts to preserve its secrecy. [See Civ.C. §3426.1(d)]

   [9:692.1-692.4] *Reserved.*

2) [9:692.5] **Misappropriation:** Once an employer proves that its customers list is entitled to trade secret protection, it must then prove that the former employee "misappropriated" the information to attain an unfair competitive advantage. [Civ.C. §3426.1(b)]

   - [9:692.6] "Misappropriation" includes the former employee's *using his or her knowledge of the content* of the customers list to solicit the former employer's customers. [See *Morlife, Inc. v. Perry* (1997) 56 CA4th 1514, 1523, 66 CR2d 731, 737]

3) **Application**

   - [9:693] A list of policyholders for insurance that protected businesses selling on credit terms against excessive bad debts was protectible as a trade secret because:
     — it was an "esoteric" kind of insurance;
     — potential customers were an *"elite" group difficult to ascertain;*
     — existing policyholders had a high renewal rate (the list thus had economic value to competitors); and
     — the employer had made reasonable efforts to protect its secrecy. [*American*

© 2020 Thomson Reuters/The Rutter Group

Credit Indem. Co. v. Sacks (1989) 213 CA3d 622, 630-631, 262 CR 92, 97—denial of PI held abuse of discretion]

- [9:693a] A list of employers who had used temporary help furnished by an agency was protectible as a trade secret because:
  — the list resulted from *lengthy and expensive* advertising and promotional efforts;
  — the list contained *data not readily ascertainable* by other competitors (e.g., billing rates, experience and training requirements, key contacts, etc.); and
  — the agency had kept the list confidential and all employees were so advised. [*Courtesy Temporary Service, Inc. v. Camacho* (1990) 222 CA3d 1278, 1286-1287, 272 CR 352, 357—denial of PI held abuse of discretion]

- [9:693b] Trade secret protection may extend to a general contractor's project proposals, subcontractor proposals, correspondence and bid forms that derive independent economic value from not being known by the general contractor's competitors. [*San Jose Const., Inc. v. S.B.C.C., Inc.* (2007) 155 CA4th 1528, 1538, 67 CR3d 54, 63]

- [9:693.1] However, a list of manufacturers needing shipping supplies was *not* protectible as a "trade secret" where such information was *known or readily ascertainable* to competitors in the shipping business. [*American Paper & Packaging Products, Inc. v. Kirgan* (1986) 183 CA3d 1318, 1326, 228 CR 713, 717]

[9:693.2-693.9] *Reserved.*

4) [9:693.10] **Conduct enjoinable:** *Solicitation* of former customers is enjoinable; *announcing a job change* is not: "[T]he right to announce a new affiliation, even to trade secret clients of a former employer, is basic to an individual's right to engage in fair competition." [*American Credit Indem. Co. v. Sacks* (1989) 213 CA3d 622, 636, 262 CR 92, 100]

a) [9:693.11] **Compare—receiving business vs. solicitation:** The willingness to discuss business on the invitation of another party does not, by itself, constitute solicitation. [See *Hilb, Rogal & Hamilton Ins. Services of Orange County, Inc. v. Robb* (1995) 33 CA4th 1812, 1821, 39 CR2d 887, 892]

b) [9:693.12] **Timing of announcement:** The fact the employee announces his or her job change to the employer's clients *before* terminating his or her employment by itself "does not convert otherwise lawful behavior into prohibited conduct." [*Hilb, Rogal & Hamilton Ins. Services of Orange County, Inc. v. Robb*, supra, 33 CA4th at 1822, 39 CR2d at 892, fn. 6]

[9:693.13-693.19] *Reserved.*

(4) [9:693.20] **Enforcing covenants not to compete:** Subject to the following exceptions, "every contract by which anyone is restrained from engaging in a lawful profession, trade, or business of any kind is to that extent void." [Bus. & Prof.C. §16600]

Covenants not to compete are enforceable only when given by:

- a person selling the *goodwill* of a *business*; or
- the "owner of a business entity" (partner in partnership, shareholder of corporation, member of LLC, etc.) "selling or otherwise disposing" of *all* of his or her ownership interest in the business entity;
- the "owner of a business entity" selling all or substantially all of the entity's assets and goodwill (or of any division or subsidiary) or all of the shares of a subsidiary. [See Bus. & Prof.C. §§16601-16602]
- a partner in a partnership or a member of a limited liability company (LLC) who has *agreed in advance* not to carry on a similar business in the same geographic area after leaving the partnership or LLC, so long as another partner or member (or person deriving title to the business) carries on a like business in the same area. [See Bus. & Prof.C. §§16602, 16602.5]

(a) [9:693.21] **Noncompete clauses outside employment context:** Despite Bus. & Prof.C. §16600, if "a noncompetition provision does not negatively affect the public interests, is designed to protect the parties in their dealings, and does not attempt

© 2020 Thomson Reuters/The Rutter Group

to establish a monopoly, it may be reasonable and valid." [*Quidel Corp. v. Sup.Ct. (Beckman Coulter, Inc.)* (2019) 39 CA5th 530, 542, 251 CR3d 823, 831, rev.grntd. 11/13/19 (Case No. S258283), cited for persuasive value pursuant to CRC 8.1115]

[9:693.22-693.24] *Reserved.*

(b) [9:693.25] **"Sale or other disposition" of shares:** Although the statute does not expressly say so, noncompetition agreements are valid only when the sale is of *a substantial interest in the corporation* so that the owner, in transferring "all" his or her shares, can be said to transfer the *goodwill* of the corporation. [*Bosley Med. Group v. Abramson* (1984) 161 CA3d 284, 290, 207 CR 477, 481]

1) [9:693.26] **Includes exchange of shares:** A covenant not to compete may be enforceable if given *in connection with* shares exchanged in a corporate merger. The covenant need not be part of the sale or purchase agreement; it may be contained in a separate employment contract. [See *Hilb, Rogal & Hamilton Ins. Services of Orange County, Inc. v. Robb* (1995) 33 CA4th 1812, 1826-1827, 39 CR2d 887, 895-896]

[9:693.27-693.29] *Reserved.*

(c) [9:693.30] **Limitation—reasonable scope:** To be enforceable under Bus. & Prof.C. §§16601-16602, a covenant not to compete must be reasonable in scope. It must be shown to be reasonably necessary to protect the buyer's interest in terms of *duration, activity and territory.* [*Monogram Indus., Inc. v. Sar Indus., Inc.* (1976) 64 CA3d 692, 698, 134 CR 714, 718; *Fleming v. Ray-Suzuki, Inc.* (1990) 225 CA3d 574, 581, 275 CR 150, 154; see also *Marriage of Gréaux & Mermin* (2014) 223 CA4th 1242, 1255, 167 CR3d 881, 892—family court's order restraining one spouse from competing with business awarded to other spouse in marital dissolution action *not* reasonable without geographic restrictions or findings to support unlimited geographic reach]

[9:693.31-693.34] *Reserved.*

(d) **Application**

- [9:693.35] A seller's covenant not to solicit the employees and customers of the business sold may be enforceable under Bus. & Prof.C. §16601. It prevents the seller from depriving the buyer of the full value of its acquisition, including its goodwill. [*Strategix, Ltd. v. Infocrossing West,*

Inc. (2006) 142 CA4th 1068, 1073, 48 CR3d 614, 617]

But a covenant barring the seller from soliciting *all* employees and customers of the buyer—even those who were not former employees or customers of the sold business—is *unenforceable.* It would impair the seller's fundamental right to compete for employees and customers in the marketplace. [*Strategix, Ltd. v. Infocrossing West, Inc.,* supra, 142 CA4th at 1074, 48 CR3d at 617-618—court *declined to rewrite* overly broad covenant into an enforceable covenant]

(5) [9:693.36] **False advertising:** When the claim is based on allegedly false and misleading advertising, requests for injunctive relief under Bus. & Prof.C. §17203 are often joined with requests for similar relief under the False Advertising Law (Bus. & Prof.C. §17535) and the Consumers Legal Remedies Act (Civ.C. §1780). All three statutes authorize the court to enjoin persons who have engaged in unfair competition: "Probably because false advertising and unfair business practices can take many forms, the Legislature has given the courts the power to fashion remedies to prevent their use or employment in whatever context they may occur." [*People v. JTH Tax, Inc.* (2013) 212 CA4th 1219, 1257, 151 CR3d 728, 759 (internal quotes omitted)]

f. [9:694] **Class actions:** Injunctive relief may be allowed in class actions even *prior* to class certification. [CCP §527(b)]

(1) [9:695] **Comment:** However, such relief is still discretionary; and, as a practical matter, courts are usually reluctant to grant injunctive relief until after a class action has been certified as such. The reason is that, until then, it is difficult to determine the scope and effect of the injunction; *see ¶14:97.*

g. [9:696] **Specific performance:** TROs and PIs are appropriately issued to prevent interim transfers of real and personal property pending trial on the merits of plaintiff's right to obtain such property by specific performance of contractual rights. [*Forde v. Bank of Finance* (1982) 136 CA3d 38, 40-41, 186 CR 272, 273]

h. [9:696.1] **Conditions, covenants and restrictions:** Courts may be called upon to grant preliminary injunctive relief to maintain the status quo during litigation involving the validity of CC&Rs affecting use of land. [*MaJor v. Miraverde Homeowners Ass'n, Inc.* (1992) 7 CA4th 618, 623, 9 CR2d 237, 240—where homeowners association exceeded its powers under recorded CC&Rs in restricting use of common areas,

© 2020 Thomson Reuters/The Rutter Group

trial court erred in denying preliminary injunction to homeowners]

[9:696.2-696.4] *Reserved.*

i. [9:696.5] **Boundary line disputes:** TROs and PIs are frequently sought in connection with boundary line disputes. E.g., a property owner constructs a "spite fence" which would impair his neighbor's access to his property.

"Balancing equities" (*see ¶9:505*) is usually the critical consideration in determining whether an injunction will issue. [See *Hirshfield v. Schwartz* (2001) 91 CA4th 749, 759, 110 CR2d 861, 867—injunction against encroachment denied where (i) defendant acted neither intentionally nor negligently, (ii) plaintiff would not suffer irreparable injury, (iii) hardship to defendant from granting the injunction would be *greatly disproportionate* to hardship to plaintiff from permitting the encroachment to continue]

j. [9:697] **Harassment:** Special procedures (*¶9:698 ff.*) are available to provide quick relief to persons who have suffered "harassment" at the hands of others, if great or irreparable injury is threatened. [CCP §527.6] (Injunctive relief is also available under the Domestic Violence Prevention Act, Fam.C. §6200 et seq., discussed in detail in Hogoboom & King, *Cal. Prac. Guide: Family Law* (TRG), Ch. 5.)

Although CCP §527.6 allows for an award of attorney fees to the prevailing party, many persons appearing at hearings on civil harassment petitions are self-represented. [See *Thomas v. Quintero* (2005) 126 CA4th 635, 651, 24 CR3d 619, 629]

[9:697.1-697.4] *Reserved.*

(1) [9:697.5] **"Harassment" defined:** "Harassment" means either:

- *unlawful violence* (assault, battery or stalking other than in self-defense or defense of others);
- *credible threats of violence* (statement or course of conduct willfully placing another in fear for safety of self or family member); or
- *knowing and willful course of conduct* directed at a specific person that:
  — "*seriously* alarms, annoys or harasses" that person;
  — serves no legitimate purpose; and
  — would cause a reasonable person to suffer *substantial emotional distress* and in fact causes plaintiff to suffer such distress. [CCP §527.6(b); *R.D. v. P.M.* (2011) 202 CA4th 181, 188, 135 CR3d 791, 797-798]

(a) [9:697.6] **"Person":** Only natural persons, not business entities, may complain of harassment under CCP §527.6. [*Diamond View, Ltd. v. Herz* (1986) 180 CA3d 612, 618-619, 225 CR 651, 655—limited partnership not "person" within meaning of §527.6]

1) [9:697.7] **Compare—protection of animals:** The court may order that (i) a petitioner's animal remain in petitioner's exclusive custody, and/or (ii) respondent stay away from the animal. [CCP §527.6(b)(6)(A)]

[9:697.8-697.9] *Reserved.*

(b) [9:697.10] **"Course of conduct":** Proof is required of a "pattern of conduct composed of a series of acts over a period of time, however short, evidencing a continuity of purpose . . ." other than constitutionally-protected activity. [CCP §527.6(b)(1)]

This may include following or stalking a person, making harassing telephone calls to that person, or sending harassing correspondence to a person "by any means" (e.g., email). [CCP §527.6(b)(1)]

Comment: Although not expressly mentioned in the statute, social media postings often are alleged and may be considered under the phrase "by any means."

An injunction restraining future conduct is authorized when it appears from the evidence that harassment is likely to recur in the future. [*R.D. v. P.M.*, supra, 202 CA4th at 190, 135 CR3d at 799—court was entitled to consider record of past harassment that supported prior restraining order as evidence of intention to resume harassing conduct]

1) **Application**

- [9:697.11] Former patient refused to "disengage" from her psychologist. [*Ensworth v. Mullvain* (1990) 224 CA3d 1105, 1109, 274 CR 447, 450]

(2) [9:698] **Special expedited procedures:** Expedited procedures are available in these cases:

(a) [9:699] **Notice not required:** First, a TRO may issue *with or without notice* upon an affidavit or declaration showing reasonable proof of harassment by defendant, and great or irreparable harm threatened to plaintiff. The TRO or injunction may include other family or household members residing with plaintiff. [CCP §527.6(c), (d)]

(b) [9:699.1] **Points and authorities not required:** No memorandum of points and authorities is required unless otherwise ordered. [CRC 3.1152(b)]

© 2020 Thomson Reuters/The Rutter Group

(c) [9:699.2] **Petition and response:** The *petition* for injunction and any TRO must be *personally served* on defendant at least 5 days before the hearing. (For "good cause," the court may shorten the time.) [CCP §527.6(m)]

At plaintiff's request, *law enforcement officers* summoned to the scene of an incident of harassment will serve the TRO on defendant. (Plaintiff must provide the officers with copies of the order and proof of service forms.) [CCP §527.6(r)(5), (7); see Fam.C. §6383(e)—officer's verbal notice of the terms of the order constitutes service of the order]

Any *response* must be filed and delivered to plaintiff or plaintiff's attorney *at least 48 hours* before the hearing. [CRC 3.1152(d)]

Respondent is entitled as of right to one continuance, for a "reasonable period," to respond to the petition. [CCP §527.6(o)]

Both the petition and response must be on mandatory forms adopted by the Judicial Council. [CCP §527.6(x)]

(d) [9:699.3] **No discovery:** There is no provision for discovery in §527.6 proceedings. Indeed, because the hearing date is so prompt (¶*9:700*), there is no time to conduct discovery. [See *Thomas v. Quintero* (2005) 126 CA4th 635, 650, 24 CR3d 619, 628, fn. 11]

(e) [9:700] **Hearing:** Following issuance of a TRO, the court must hold a hearing *within 21 days* after the TRO is issued; or extended to 25 days, if the court finds "good cause." [CCP §527.6(g)]

Any party may request (or the court may on its own motion order) a continuance of the hearing for "good cause." If a continuance is granted, the TRO continues in effect until the end of the continued hearing unless the court otherwise orders. In granting a continuance, the court may modify or terminate the TRO. [CCP §527.6(p)(1), (2)]

There is no full trial on the merits following a TRO. But at the hearing, the court must "receive any testimony that is relevant." [CCP §527.6(i); *see* ¶*9:707.1*]

[9:701] ***PRACTICE POINTER:*** Although the law provides that the TRO continues in effect until a continued hearing on the petition (¶*9:700*), the original TRO, on its face, terminates on the original hearing date. For law enforcement to enforce the TRO after a continuance, the court must sign an order extending the TRO so it will be in effect until the next hearing date. Without this extension of the TRO, law enforcement will not have a valid order and will not enforce it.

(f) [9:702] **Evidentiary standard:** The injunction will be granted if there is "*clear and convincing evidence*" that harassment exists. [CCP §527.6(i) (emphasis added)]

(g) [9:703] **Duration:** If an injunction is granted, it remains in effect for up to *five years*, but plaintiff can seek to have it *renewed* for up to an additional five years without a showing of any further harassment since issuance of the original order by filing a new petition within three months before its expiration. [CCP §527.6(j); *Cooper v. Bettinger* (2015) 242 CA4th 77, 90, 194 CR3d 772, 782—court has discretion whether to issue renewed order and "may rely solely on the record in the original case"]

The failure to state the expiration date on the face of the order creates an order effective for three years from the date of issuance. [CCP §527.6(j)(2)]

(h) [9:703.1] **Form of order:** A TRO or civil restraining order after hearing must be issued on forms adopted by the Judicial Council (mandatory forms). But the fact that an order was not issued on such forms does not render it unenforceable. [CCP §527.6(x)]

(i) [9:703.2] **Motion to terminate or modify:** Any motion to terminate or modify the protective order (i.e., the injunction) brought by someone other than the protected person must be personally served on the protected party at least 16 court days before the hearing on the motion. If the protected person is not given such notice, the court must deny the motion to modify or terminate the protective order without prejudice or continue the hearing until notice is given in the manner designated by the court. The protected party can waive notice by appearing at the hearing and not challenging service. [CCP §527.6(j)(3)]

FORMS

- Request for Civil Harassment Restraining Orders (CH-100); *see Form 9B:9* in Rivera, *Cal. Prac. Guide: Civ. Pro. Before Trial FORMS* (TRG).
- Temporary Restraining Order (CLETS-TCH) (CH-110); *see Form 9B:9.1* in Rivera, *Cal. Prac. Guide: Civ. Pro. Before Trial FORMS* (TRG).

© 2020 Thomson Reuters/The Rutter Group

- Proof of Personal Service (CH-200); *see Form 9B:9.2* in Rivera, *Cal. Prac. Guide: Civ. Pro. Before Trial FORMS* (TRG).
- Response to Request for Civil Harassment Restraining Orders (CH-120); *see Form 9B:10* in Rivera, *Cal. Prac. Guide: Civ. Pro. Before Trial FORMS* (TRG).
- Notice of Court Hearing (CH-109); *see Form 9B:11* in Rivera, *Cal. Prac. Guide: Civ. Pro. Before Trial FORMS* (TRG).
- Civil Harassment Restraining Order After Hearing (CLETS-CHO) (CH-130); *see Form 9B:12* in Rivera, *Cal. Prac. Guide: Civ. Pro. Before Trial FORMS* (TRG).
- Request to Renew Restraining Order (Civil Harassment Prevention) (CH-700); *see Form 9B:13* in Rivera, *Cal. Prac. Guide: Civ. Pro. Before Trial FORMS* (TRG).
- Response to Request to Renew Restraining Order (Civil Harassment Prevention) (CH-720); *see Form 9B:13.1* in Rivera, *Cal. Prac. Guide: Civ. Pro. Before Trial FORMS* (TRG).
- Order Renewing Civil Harassment Restraining Order (CLETS) (CH-730); *see Form 9B:13.2* in Rivera, *Cal. Prac. Guide: Civ. Pro. Before Trial FORMS* (TRG).

(3) **Advantages**

(a) [9:704] **No bond:** No bond or undertaking of any kind is required for issuance of either a TRO or permanent injunction. (Comment: This is because there should be no damages sustained from enjoining one person from harassing another.)

(b) [9:704.1] **No filing fee:** There is no court filing fee for petitions alleging harassment and seeking protective orders under §527.6 (or for the response to such petitions, or subpoenas filed in connection with these proceedings). [CCP §527.6(y)]

[9:704.2-704.4] *Reserved.*

(c) [9:704.5] **No service of process fees:** Upon the petitioner's application, no fee shall be charged for service of a protective order, TRO or injunction based on stalking, a credible threat of violence or sexual assault, or issued pursuant to Fam.C. §6222 (dealing with recurring acts of violence and sexual abuse of a spouse). [See CCP §527.6(z)]

(d) [9:705] **Police protection:** The court shall order petitioner or petitioner's attorney to deliver copies of the injunction to all law enforcement agencies having jurisdiction over petitioner's residence and, in the court's discretion, to additional law enforcement agencies as requested by petitioner. Alternatively, the court or its designee shall transmit the order and proof of service to the California Law Enforcement Telecommunications System (CLETS), which makes the order available to all law enforcement agencies in California. [See CCP §527.6(r)(2), (3)]

(e) [9:706] **Attorney fees:** The prevailing party (plaintiff or defendant) may be awarded court costs and attorney fees. [See CCP §527.6(s); *Krug v. Maschmeier* (2009) 172 CA4th 796, 802-803, 91 CR3d 452, 456-457—prevailing defendant entitled to costs and fees even if plaintiff brought action in good faith]

1) [9:706.1] **Effect of voluntary dismissal before hearing:** P's voluntary dismissal of the action before the injunction hearing does not deprive the court of power to award attorney fees to defendant as the "prevailing party." The dismissal is treated as a final determination on the merits in D's favor. [*Adler v. Vaicius* (1993) 21 CA4th 1770, 1776, 27 CR2d 32, 36]

(f) [9:706.2] **Enforcement:** The district attorney has primary responsibility for enforcement of these orders. An intentional and knowing violation is punishable as a misdemeanor. [Pen.C. §273.6]

(g) [9:706.3] **No risk of malicious prosecution liability:** Unsuccessful filing of a petition for an injunction under §527.6 may not form the basis for a malicious prosecution action. [*Siam v. Kizilbash* (2005) 130 CA4th 1563, 1567, 31 CR3d 368, 371-372; *Kenne v. Stennis* (2014) 230 CA4th 953, 969-970, 179 CR3d 198, 211-212; see also *S.A. v. Maiden* (2014) 229 CA4th 27, 36, 176 CR3d 567, 572-573 (same re request for restraining orders under Domestic Violence Prevention Act (¶*9:683*))]

(4) [9:707] **Constitutional limitations:** CCP §527.6 *cannot* be used to prohibit constitutionally-protected free speech or the right to petition government for redress of grievances. [*Smith v. Silvey* (1983) 149 CA3d 400, 406-407, 197 CR 15, 19—improper to enjoin trailer park resident from initiating complaints with public agencies or contacting other residents re conditions at trailer park]

There is no constitutional protection, however, for harassing speech "between purely private parties, about purely

© 2020 Thomson Reuters/The Rutter Group

private parties, and on matters of purely private interest." [*Brekke v. Wills* (2005) 125 CA4th 1400, 1409, 23 CR3d 609, 617; see *R.D. v. P.M.* (2011) 202 CA4th 181, 192, 135 CR3d 791, 801 (but noting that restraining order's "incidental infringement" of speech is justified only to extent it is "no broader or more restrictive" than necessary to prevent harassment); *Parisi v. Mazzaferro* (2016) 5 CA5th 1219, 1229-1230, 210 CR3d 574, 584-585—1st Amendment did not preclude order restricting defendant's written communications as long as limited to restraining D from "continuing what has already been judicially determined to be defamation and harassment"]

Cross-refer: See further discussion of First Amendment controversies at ¶9:708 ff.

(5) [9:707.1] **Safeguards:** While CCP §527.6 permits expedited procedures, it also provides important safeguards for what is, in effect, an expedited trial on the issue of harassment:

- The judge is required to receive *oral* testimony, if offered. [CCP §527.6(i); see *Schraer v. Berkeley Property Owners' Ass'n* (1989) 207 CA3d 719, 733, 255 CR 453, 462]
- At the hearing, the court "shall receive *any testimony that is relevant*," including hearsay evidence. [CCP §527.6(i) (emphasis added); *Duronslet v. Kamps* (2012) 203 CA4th 717, 728-729, 137 CR3d 756, 765; *Kaiser Found. Hosps. v. Wilson* (2011) 201 CA4th 550, 557, 133 CR3d 830, 835 (decided under parallel workplace violence statute (CCP §527.8(j)); *see also ¶9:679.6*]
- Any finding of harassment must be based on "*clear and convincing evidence*" of a course of conduct that was not a "constitutionally protected activity" and had "no legitimate purpose." [CCP §527.6(b), (i) (emphasis added)]
- A single act is not sufficient; an ongoing course of conduct is required. [*Leydon v. Alexander* (1989) 212 CA3d 1, 4-5, 260 CR 253, 254-255; see *Russell v. Douvan* (2003) 112 CA4th 399, 401, 5 CR3d 137, 139—single act of violence may suffice where court finds *future harm is highly probable*]
- The conduct must have actually and reasonably caused *substantial* emotional distress to the plaintiff. [CCP §527.6(b); *Schraer v. Berkeley Property Owners' Ass'n*, supra, 207 CA3d at 730, 255 CR at 459]
- The "prevailing party" is entitled to recover costs and attorney fees. [CCP §527.6(s); see *Elster v.*

Friedman (1989) 211 CA3d 1439, 1443-1444, 260 CR 148, 151—court determines who "prevailed" where cross-injunctions granted]

(6) [9:707.2] **Evidentiary requirements:** It is not enough for the trial court to find that harassment *may* occur: An injunction may not issue unless the court finds, "by *clear and convincing evidence*, that unlawful harassment *already exists* in fact." [*Schraer v. Berkeley Property Owners' Ass'n* (1989) 207 CA3d 719, 733, 255 CR 453, 462 (emphasis added)]

(a) [9:707.3] **Oral testimony:** If relevant oral testimony is offered, it should be received. It may be improper for the judge to refuse oral testimony and base its decision entirely on written declarations, newspaper articles and the argument of counsel. [*Schraer v. Berkeley Property Owners' Ass'n*, supra, 207 CA3d at 733, 255 CR at 462]

(b) [9:707.4] **Conduct causing "reasonable person" to suffer "substantial emotional distress":** CCP §527.6(b) requires evidence of conduct that would cause a "*reasonable* person" to suffer "substantial emotional distress." [*Brekke v. Wills* (2005) 125 CA4th 1400, 1413-1414, 23 CR3d 609, 620 (emphasis added)—defendant's vitriolic letters and taunting telephone calls undermined plaintiff's control of her minor daughter; compare *Schild v. Rubin* (1991) 232 CA3d 755, 763, 283 CR 533, 538—sound of neighbor playing basketball at night on adjacent driveway *not* evidence that would "cause a reasonable person to suffer substantial emotional distress" within meaning of statute]

(c) [9:707.5] **Conduct having legitimate purpose:** Conduct that has a legitimate purpose cannot be enjoined as harassment. [See *Byers v. Cathcart* (1997) 57 CA4th 805, 812, 67 CR2d 398, 402—parking car in one's own driveway has legitimate purpose and cannot be enjoined as harassment, even though parties disputed use of driveway easement]

(d) [9:707.5a] **Renewal:** Restraining orders may be renewed, and the court may then "rely solely on the record in the original case." But renewal is not automatic and the court must exercise its discretion. [*Cooper v. Bettinger* (2015) 242 CA4th 77, 90-91, 194 CR3d 772, 782]

k. [9:707.6] **Protection from certain torts:** Statutes provide a number of specific situations where injunctive relief is available to prevent tortious conduct, including:

- *Elder abuse:* Upon a declaration showing reasonable

proof of a past abuse (as defined in Welf. & Inst.C. §15610.07), an elder or dependent adult may obtain a restraining order against such abuse, with or without notice to the party to be enjoined. [See Welf. & Inst.C. §15657.03]

- *Gender violence:* See Civ.C. §52.4.
- *Domestic violence:* See Civ.C. §1708.6.
- *Stalking:* See Civ.C. §1708.7.
- *Sexual battery:* See Civ.C. §1708.5.
- *Invasion of privacy:* See Civ.C. §1708.8.

[9:707.7-707.9] *Reserved.*

l. [9:707.10] **Nuisances:** Courts have traditionally exercised injunctive power to enjoin either private or public nuisances. [See Civ.C. §3491—authorizing civil action for abatement of public nuisances]

- [9:707.11] A court may issue a PI limiting specified *activities of gang members* within a specified geographical area under its equitable power to abate a public nuisance. [*People ex rel. Gallo v. Acuna* (1997) 14 C4th 1090, 60 CR2d 277; *People v. Gonzalez* (1996) 12 C4th 804, 809, 50 CR2d 74, 77]
- [9:707.12] A court may issue a PI to abate nuisances on premises where prostitution and lewdness occur. [Pen.C. §11227; see *Mitchell v. Sup.Ct. (People)* (1989) 49 C3d 1230, 1236, 265 CR 144, 147]
- [9:707.13] A court may issue a PI preventing operation of a medical marijuana dispensary. [*City of Riverside v. Inland Empire Patients Health & Wellness Ctr., Inc.* (2013) 56 C4th 729, 762, 156 CR3d 409, 431—California's Compassionate Use Act (Health & Saf.C. §11362.5) and Medical Marijuana Program Act (Health & Saf.C. §11362.7 et seq.) do not preempt local bans on medical marijuana dispensaries; *City of Claremont v. Kruse* (2009) 177 CA4th 1153, 1166-1167, 100 CR3d 1, 12-13 (same)—medical marijuana dispensary subject to injunction as nuisance per se]

[9:707.14-707.19] *Reserved.*

m. [9:707.20] **Fraudulent transfers:** The Uniform Fraudulent Transfer Act (Civ.C. §3439 et seq.) provides that an injunction may issue to prevent the further disposition of assets by one being sued for improperly transferring assets. [Civ.C. §3439.07; see *Oiye v. Fox* (2012) 211 CA4th 1036, 1057, 151 CR3d 65, 82]

n. [9:708] **First Amendment controversies:** Free speech is protected under both the First Amendment and Art. I, §2 of the California Constitution. California's provisions are "more protective, definitive and inclusive of rights to expression of speech than their federal counterparts." [*San Diego Unified Port Dist. v. U.S. Citizens Patrol* (1998) 63 CA4th 964, 970, 74 CR2d 364, 367 (internal quotes omitted)]

Censorship and "prior restraint" of free speech and press are generally unconstitutional; thus, injunctive relief is rarely granted to restrain speech or publication.

- A preliminary injunction prohibiting distribution of a political campaign leaflet was held unconstitutional as a "prior restraint on publication." [*Wilson v. Sup.Ct. (Watson)* (1975) 13 C3d 652, 658, 119 CR 468, 472]
- A disgruntled homeowner's picketing of a developer with signs "my house leaks," "we live in hell," etc. was protected by the First Amendment. [*Paradise Hills Assocs. v. Procel* (1991) 235 CA3d 1528, 1539, 1 CR2d 514, 519 (disapproved on other grounds by *Kowis v. Howard* (1992) 3 C4th 888, 898-899, 12 CR2d 728, 733-734)]
- A prior restraint was not permitted to prevent publication of defamatory statements or disclosure of matters protected by the right of privacy, even though such publication and disclosure might be actionable in tort. [*Gilbert v. National Enquirer, Inc.* (1996) 43 CA4th 1135, 1148, 51 CR2d 91, 99]
- A preliminary injunction prohibiting Former Wife from publishing "false and defamatory" statements about Former Husband on the Internet was constitutionally invalid as a prior restraint. [*Evans v. Evans* (2008) 162 CA4th 1157, 1168, 76 CR3d 859, 868]
- An injunction that sought to restrain a newspaper from publishing asserted stolen confidential information such as police background checks and applications would be an unconstitutional prior restraint. [*Association for Los Angeles Deputy Sheriffs v. Los Angeles Times Communications LLC* (2015) 239 CA4th 808, 824, 191 CR3d 564, 577]

On the other hand, injunctions are frequently granted to *protect* the exercise of free speech and petition rights even when those rights are exercised on private property.

- Shopping centers in general are appropriate forums for peaceful, orderly speech and petitioning, including signature-gathering and leafleting. [*PruneYard Shopping Ctr. v. Robins* (1980) 447 US 74, 80-81, 100 S.Ct. 2035, 2040]
- Protection for political activities on shopping center property

© 2020 Thomson Reuters/The Rutter Group

is not limited to gathering petition signatures and registering voters: distribution of issue-oriented political materials is also protected. [*Westside Sane/Freeze v. Ernest W. Hahn, Inc.* (1990) 224 CA3d 546, 555, 274 CR 51, 56-57]

- An audience's hostility is not justification to restrain lawful conduct at an airport. [*San Diego Unified Port Dist. v. U.S. Citizens Patrol*, supra, 63 CA4th at 970, 74 CR2d at 367]

Enjoining speech that violates state law? An injunction may properly issue to prohibit the repetition or continuation of speech that the court has found to be unlawful. Such an injunction *does not* constitute an invalid prior restraint of speech. [*Aguilar v. Avis Rent A Car System, Inc.* (1999) 21 C4th 121, 140-142, 147, 87 CR2d 132, 146-147, 151—court may enjoin "pervasive use" of racial epithets in workplace that have been judicially determined to constitute racial discrimination in violation of FEHA]

(1) [9:709] **Shopping centers:** Shopping centers and malls to which the public is invited have become the functional equivalent of the "public square" and thus are deemed public forums for exercising constitutionally-protected rights of speech and assembly. [*PruneYard Shopping Ctr. v. Robins,* supra, 447 US at 80-81, 100 S.Ct. at 2040; see also *Robins v. Pruneyard Shopping Ctr.* (1979) 23 C3d 899, 910, 153 CR 854, 860]

This rule is limited, however, to "those areas that have been designed and furnished to permit and encourage the public to congregate and socialize at leisure"—e.g., the common areas. Thus, a private sidewalk in front of the customer entrance to a retail store in a shopping center does *not* constitute a public forum for purposes of expressive activity. [*Ralphs Grocery Co. v. United Food & Comm'l Workers Union Local 8* (2012) 55 C4th 1083, 1093, 1104, 150 CR3d 501, 507-508, 516; *Donahue Schriber Realty Group, Inc. v. Nu Creation Outreach* (2014) 232 CA4th 1171, 1184, 181 CR3d 577, 587—sidewalk and "apron areas" adjacent to store entrance not public forum areas]

[9:709.1] *Reserved.*

(a) [9:709.2] **Stand-alone stores?** Whether a stand-alone warehouse-type retail establishment (e.g., Home Depot, Wal-Mart, etc.) is a public forum under *Pruneyard's* reasoning is unsettled. [See *Lushbaugh v. Home Depot U.S.A., Inc.* (2001) 93 CA4th 1159, 1166, 113 CR2d 700, 704; *Costco Cos., Inc. v. Gallant* (2002) 96 CA4th 740, 754-755, 117 CR2d 344, 355-356—retailer may prohibit all expressive activity at stand-alone stores and may impose reasonable time, place and manner restrictions at facilities that share parking lot with other retail businesses; *and discussion at ¶9:710 ff.*]

(b) [9:709.3] **Reasonable restrictions on speech allowed:** Property owners may impose reasonable restrictions on the time, place and manner of expressive activity, as long as the restrictions are not based on the *content* of the regulated speech (*see ¶9:709.5*). [*Savage v. Trammell Crow Co., Inc.* (1990) 223 CA3d 1562, 1571-1572, 273 CR 302, 305-306—shopping center owner may ban leafleting in parking lot]

- [9:709.3a] Shopping mall's rules limiting areas within which individuals might engage in expressive activity, requiring prior approval of signs and literature and imposing an insurance requirement, were reasonable restrictions and justified denial of injunction. [*Union of Needletrades, Industrial & Textile Employees, AFL-CIO v. Sup.Ct. (Taubman Co.)* (1997) 56 CA4th 996, 1012-1015, 65 CR2d 838, 849-851]

(c) [9:709.4] **Compare—content-based speech regulations:** Shopping mall rules prohibiting speech *based on content* must be "narrowly drawn" to serve a "compelling state interest." [*Fashion Valley Mall, LLC v. National Labor Relations Bd.* (2007) 42 C4th 850, 869, 69 CR3d 288, 302]

- [9:709.5] Shopping Mall's rule prohibiting speech *urging customers to boycott stores* within the mall served no "compelling state interest" and could not be enforced against Union's picketing. Urging customers to boycott a store lies at the core of the right to free speech. [*Fashion Valley Mall, LLC v. National Labor Relations Bd.*, supra, 42 C4th at 869, 69 CR3d at 302]

(d) [9:709.6] **Compare—speech during labor disputes:** Under California law, specified activities during a labor dispute (including dispute-related speech, picketing and assembly) are legal and cannot be enjoined, even when they occur on the private property of another (CCP §527.3(b); see Lab.C. §1138.1 (delineating criteria for issuance of injunctions during labor disputes)). These laws are constitutional, even though "they give speech regarding a labor dispute greater protection than speech on other subjects." [*Ralphs Grocery Co. v. United Food & Comm'l Workers Union Local 8*, supra, 55 C4th at 1104, 150 CR3d at 516]

© 2020 Thomson Reuters/The Rutter Group

(2) [9:710] **Less protection for free speech in "modest retail establishments":** When the private property in question is a "modest retail establishment," (i.e., where the services provided and the invitation to enter is limited to a small segment of the public), the court may be more likely to enjoin the exercise of free speech. [See *Bank of Stockton v. Church of Soldiers of Cross of Christ* (1996) 44 CA4th 1623, 1631, 52 CR2d 429, 434; *Planned Parenthood of San Diego & Riverside Counties v. Wilson* (1991) 234 CA3d 1662, 1671, 286 CR 427, 432-433]

Rationale: The store owner's invitation to the public to visit its store is more limited than the invitation made by a shopping center. The store owner invites people to come and shop, not to "congregate" as at a shopping center. Thus, the public's interest in using a retail store as a forum for free speech and petitioning is not as strong as its interest in engaging in such activities at a large shopping center. [*Trader Joe's Co. v. Progressive Campaigns, Inc.* (1999) 73 CA4th 425, 434, 86 CR2d 442, 448]

- [9:710.1] A medical clinic's private parking lot is *not* a public forum that anti-abortion protesters may freely use to express their views to clinic patients. [See *Allred v. Shawley* (1991) 232 CA3d 1489, 1504-1505, 284 CR 140, 148; *Planned Parenthood of San Diego & Riverside Counties v. Wilson*, supra, 234 CA3d at 1668, 286 CR at 430]

- [9:710.2] Similarly, a bank's private parking lot, reserved for customers transacting business with the bank, is *not* a forum where members of a religious organization may solicit donations from passersby. [*Bank of Stockton v. Church of Soldiers of Cross of Christ*, supra, 44 CA4th at 1631, 52 CR2d at 434]

- [9:710.3] A business located in a "free standing modest retail store and parking lot" was entitled to a preliminary injunction banning defendants from handbilling and petitioning for signatures on the premises. "[T]he societal interest in using the Santa Rosa Trader Joe's as a forum for exercising free speech and petitioning activities does not outweigh Trader Joe's interest in exercising exclusive control over the use of its private property." [*Trader Joe's Co. v. Progressive Campaigns, Inc.* (1999) 73 CA4th 425, 434, 86 CR2d 442, 449]

- [9:710.4] *Compare—store in mini-mall:* A nude entertainment club in a mini-mall was more like a stand-alone store than a store within a mall. Although speech could be restricted, protesters *could not* be banned entirely from the site. Reasonable restrictions were required to protect access to other stores on the property. [*Slauson Partnership v. Ochoa* (2003) 112 CA4th 1005, 1028-1029, 5 CR3d 668, 686-687]

[9:710.5-710.9] *Reserved.*

(3) [9:710.10] **Compare—when property *not* public forum:** Restrictions on speech are likely to be upheld on premises that are not open to the public in general or are otherwise not the functional equivalent of a traditional public forum (*see ¶9:709*). [*Golden Gateway Ctr. v. Golden Gateway Tenants Ass'n* (2001) 26 C4th 1013, 1033-1034, 111 CR2d 336, 352—landlord had right to ban distribution of tenants' association's newsletter at its apartment complex to which public access was restricted; see *Ralphs Grocery Co. v. United Food & Comm'l Workers Union Local 8*, supra, 55 C4th at 1092, 150 CR3d at 506—"within a shopping center or mall, the areas outside individual stores' customer entrances and exits, at least as typically configured and furnished, are not public forums"]

[9:710.11-710.14] *Reserved.*

(4) [9:710.15] **"Content neutral" injunctions only incidentally affecting speech:** The constitutionality of an injunction that burdens speech may depend on whether it is "content neutral" or "content based." I.e., an injunction that prohibits specified utterances is "content-based" and subject to heightened scrutiny. In contrast, an injunction that limits particular conduct or activities, and only incidentally affects speech, is subject to lesser scrutiny. [*DVD Copy Control Ass'n, Inc. v. Bunner* (2003) 31 C4th 864, 877, 4 CR3d 69, 80-81]

"As speech strays further from the values of persuasion, dialogue and free exchange of ideas, and moves toward *willful threats to perform illegal acts,* the state has greater latitude to regulate expression." [*City of San Jose v. Garbett* (2010) 190 CA4th 526, 537, 118 CR3d 420, 428 (emphasis added; internal quotes omitted)—speech constituting *credible threat of violence* may be enjoined]

- [9:710.16] An injunction against wrongful conduct may be upheld although speech is incidentally involved. I.e., that the conduct is initiated, carried out or evidenced through language does not mean it cannot be enjoined. [*National Subscription Television v. Formula Int'l, Inc.* (1984) 153 CA3d 308, 312-313, 200 CR 213, 215—injunction barring defendant from selling "do it yourself" pay-TV decoder kits]
- [9:710.17] Similarly, the First Amendment did not prohibit an injunction against an Internet website

operator to prevent future disclosure of a trade secret contained in a computer program: "Because the injunction is justified *without reference to the content* of Bunner's communications, it is content neutral." [*DVD Copy Control Ass'n, Inc. v. Bunner*, supra, 31 C4th at 878, 4 CR3d at 81 (emphasis added)]

(5) [9:710.18] **Scope of injunction:** The injunction should be limited to preventing *harassing conduct*. Thus, an injunction may place reasonable "time, place and manner" restrictions on expressive activity; but the *content* of speech, standing alone, cannot support an injunction.

[9:710.19] *Reserved.*

o. [9:710.20] **Multiple actions involving same subject matter (anti-suit injunction):** Where two or more actions involving the same subject matter or the same facts or principles are pending in California courts, a TRO is appropriate to avoid the "unseemly conflict" that might arise between California courts if they were free to make contradictory awards. [See *Advanced Bionics Corp. v. Medtronic, Inc.* (2002) 29 C4th 697, 705-706, 128 CR2d 172, 178]

(1) [9:710.21] **Compare—action pending outside state:** But where the action sought to be enjoined is outside California, a TRO is proper only under an "exceptional circumstance" that outweighs the judicial restraint and comity owed to courts of separate sovereignty: "[T]he possibility of an embarrassing race to judgment or potentially inconsistent adjudications does not outweigh the *respect and deference* owed to independent foreign proceedings." [*Advanced Bionics Corp. v. Medtronic, Inc.*, supra, 29 C4th at 706, 128 CR2d at 178 (emphasis added; internal quotes omitted)—immaterial that California action filed first; *TSMC North America v. Semiconductor Mfg. Int'l Corp.* (2008) 161 CA4th 581, 590, 74 CR3d 328, 334]

[9:710.22-710.24] *Reserved.*

(2) [9:710.25] **Compare—actions in federal court:** State courts are without power to enjoin commencement or prosecution of actions in federal court, regardless of whether the prohibition is addressed to the parties or to the federal court itself. [*Donovan v. City of Dallas* (1964) 377 US 408, 412-413, 84 S.Ct. 1579, 1582; *Biosense Webster, Inc. v. Sup.Ct. (Dowell)* (2006) 135 CA4th 827, 839, 37 CR3d 759, 767-768]

p. [9:710.26] **Large development projects under CEQA:** A court may enjoin construction or operation of a large arena project subject to expedited review under the California Environmental Quality Act (CEQA, Pub.Res.C. §21050 et seq.)

upon a showing of "imminent threat" to public health and safety or adverse impact to "unforeseen important historical, archaeological, or ecological values." [Pub.Res.C. §21168.6.6(h); see *Saltonstall v. City of Sacramento* (2014) 231 CA4th 837, 857, 180 CR3d 342, 357 (required showing not made)]

11. **Enforcement of Injunctions by Contempt Proceedings**

a. [9:711] **Indirect contempt:** Most violations of injunctions involve conduct outside the presence of the court, i.e., an *"indirect* contempt" (distinguished from a "direct contempt" which is committed in the court's presence—e.g., as where counsel is held in contempt for rearguing a position after court rules on a motion). Accordingly, a declaration must be presented to the court of the facts constituting the contempt for adjudication.

Cross-refer: For discussion of direct vs. indirect contempt, see Wegner, Fairbank, Epstein & Chernow, *Cal. Prac. Guide: Civil Trials & Evidence* (TRG), Ch. 12.

b. [9:712] **Issues involved:** The substantive issues involved in an indirect contempt proceeding are fourfold:

- The rendition of a *valid order*;
- Respondent's *actual knowledge* of the order;
- Respondent's *ability to comply* with the order; and
- Respondent's *willful disobedience* of the order. [*Conn v. Sup.Ct. (Farmers Group)* (1987) 196 CA3d 774, 784, 242 CR 148, 154 (citing text)]

(1) [9:712.1] **Agents, servants and employees:** An injunction may be directed to "agents, servants and employees" of named parties (*see ¶9:656.1*). In such cases, a charge of contempt may be sustained against a person for violating the injunction upon a showing that he or she was acting as the "agent or servant of or in concert or combination with" named parties, and had actual notice of the injunction. [*Ross v. Sup.Ct. (Woods)* (1977) 19 C3d 899, 905, 141 CR 133, 137]

Compare: An injunction seeking to control "*all persons with actual knowledge* of it" is too broad to be enforced: "The order must be directed against [a] person, either by *naming* that person as an individual or by *designating a class of persons* to which that person belongs." [*Planned Parenthood Golden Gate v. Garibaldi* (2003) 107 CA4th 345, 352, 132 CR2d 46, 52 (emphasis added)]

(a) [9:712.2] **Due process right to challenge status as agent or employee?** *See ¶9:656.2.*

© 2020 Thomson Reuters/The Rutter Group

c. **Commencing contempt proceeding**

(1) [9:713] **Charging affidavit:** A contempt proceeding is commenced by the filing of an affidavit showing the facts set forth in ¶*9:712* (the "charging allegations"). [CCP §1211, 2nd para.] The affidavit frames the issues to be tried. [*Reliable Enterprises, Inc. v. Sup.Ct. (People)* (1984) 158 CA3d 604, 616, 204 CR 786, 793 (disapproved on other grounds by *Mitchell v. Sup.Ct. (People)* (1989) 49 C3d 1230, 1248, 265 CR 144, 155, fn. 13)]

The filing of a sufficient affidavit is a "jurisdictional prerequisite" to a contempt proceeding and without one, any contempt order is void. [*In re Koehler* (2010) 181 CA4th 1153, 1169, 104 CR3d 877, 889]

[9:713.1] ***PRACTICE POINTER:*** Take care to draft the charging allegations to ensure you can prove each charge of contempt *beyond a reasonable doubt* (*see* ¶*9:718.1*).

(a) [9:714] Each allegation (valid order, knowledge, ability to comply and willful disobedience) must be pleaded by *factual statements*; however, the affidavit may be amended to correct technical insufficiencies if the respondent would not be prejudiced thereby. [CCP §1211.5(b)]

(b) [9:714.1] To establish willful disobedience, the affidavit should show that the alleged contemnor had *personal notice* of the contents of the order.

(2) [9:714.2] **Notice to opposing counsel of application:** As with ex parte proceedings generally, parties requesting an OSC re Contempt must notify opposing counsel before presenting the application to the court. [CRC 3.1203; *see* ¶*9:352*]

(3) [9:715] **Order to Show Cause:** If the court is satisfied that the affidavit alleges sufficient grounds for contempt, it signs an "OSC re Contempt," setting the date and time for a hearing. [CCP §1212]

(4) [9:716] **Service of OSC and affidavit:** The citee-respondent must be formally notified of the contempt charge and of the time and place of the hearing; otherwise, the court lacks jurisdiction to proceed. For this purpose, both the OSC and affidavit ordinarily must be served on respondent *in a manner authorized for service of summons.* [*Cedars-Sinai Imaging Med. Group v. Sup.Ct. (Moore)* (2000) 83 CA4th 1281, 1286, 100 CR2d 320, 324 (citing text); *In re Koehler*, supra, 181 CA4th at 1169, 104 CR3d at 889; but see *Shibley v. Sup.Ct.* (1927) 202 C 738, 741, 262 P 332, 333—court can authorize service on attorney where party conceals self to avoid service]

FORM: Application for Order to Show Cause re Contempt; Declaration of Notice and Proposed Order, *see Form 9B:14* in Rivera, *Cal. Prac. Guide: Civ. Pro. Before Trial FORMS* (TRG).

d. **Trial of the contempt proceeding**

(1) [9:717] **Quasi-criminal proceedings:** Because of the potential for imprisonment (¶*9:726 ff.*), a contempt proceeding in the court that made the order allegedly violated is considered quasi-criminal. [*People v. Gonzalez* (1996) 12 C4th 804, 816, 50 CR2d 74, 82]

(a) [9:718] **Constitutional protections:** Because the proceedings are quasi-criminal, defendant possesses "some of the rights of a criminal defendant." [*People v. Gonzalez*, supra, 12 C4th at 816, 50 CR2d at 82]

As will be seen, most of the rights of a criminal defendant are extended to a person cited for contempt *and the court must inform* him or her of such rights. [See *In re Kreitman* (1995) 40 CA4th 750, 753, 47 CR2d 595, 597—because court failed to advise citee of right to jury trial, sentence could not exceed 180 days; *see* ¶*9:721.1*]

Included are the following constitutional protections:

1) [9:718.1] **Presumption of innocence; burden of proof:** A person cited for contempt is presumed innocent until proven guilty "beyond a reasonable doubt."

2) [9:718.2] **Evidence:** Live testimony, rather than declarations, is required from witnesses against the alleged contemner, to ensure his or her right to cross-examine. [See CCP §1217—judge "must hear any answer" which the contempt citee may make and "may examine witnesses for or against him"]

Testimonial and self-incrimination privileges apply (including the right *not* to testify *at all* and not to incriminate self).

3) [9:718.3] **Presence at hearing:** The hearing may not be held in the absence of the alleged contemner or counsel unless there is a finding (supported by evidence) that the alleged contemner is *voluntarily absent*. [*Farace v. Sup.Ct. (Hale)* (1983) 148 CA3d 915, 918, 196 CR 297, 299]

4) [9:718.4] **Assistance of counsel:** The alleged contemner is entitled to the assistance of counsel

© 2020 Thomson Reuters/The Rutter Group

and such counsel must be appointed if the alleged contemner cannot afford counsel. [See Gov.C. §27706; *County of Santa Clara v. Sup.Ct. (Rodriguez)* (1992) 2 CA4th 1686, 1697, 5 CR2d 7, 14—indigent person served with OSC re Contempt for failure to pay court-ordered child support, and who is exposed to deprivation of liberty as punishment for the alleged violation, is entitled to assistance of counsel at public expense]

5) [9:718.5] **Arraignment:** The alleged contemner must be arraigned (advised of the charges) at the beginning of the contempt hearing. This includes admonition and inquiry regarding defense counsel. A continuance is likely if the alleged contemner is indigent and unrepresented by counsel at the hearing.

[9:719-720] *Reserved.*

(b) [9:721] **No right to jury trial for civil contempt:** There is no constitutional or statutory right to a jury trial in *civil* contempt proceedings under CCP §1209 et seq., although such proceedings may result in a fine or imprisonment. [*Mitchell v. Sup.Ct. (People)* (1989) 49 C3d 1230, 1240, 265 CR 144, 149]

1) [9:721.1] **Compare—criminal contempt:** The California Constitution guarantees *every* defendant faced with misdemeanor or felony charges a right to trial by jury. Contempt is a misdemeanor (Pen.C. §166). Therefore, there is a right to a jury trial in *criminal* contempt cases. [*Mitchell v. Sup.Ct. (People)*, supra, 49 C3d at 1240, 265 CR at 150]

(2) **Particular issues at trial**

(a) [9:722] **Valid order:** The terms of the order on which the contempt charge is based usually are not in doubt. However, by way of defense, the respondent may challenge the *validity* of the order.

A valid order and judgment of indirect contempt must cover the following elements:

— the issuance of an order;
— the contemner's *knowledge* of the order (¶*9:723*);
— the contemner's *ability to obey* the order (¶*9:724*); and
— the contemner's *willful* disobedience (¶*9:725*). [*In re Koehler* (2010) 181 CA4th 1153, 1169, 104 CR3d 877, 890]

1) [9:722.1] **Void orders:** Violation of a *void* order is *not* punishable as a contempt. An order

is *void* if "in excess of the court's jurisdiction." For this purpose, "jurisdiction" means more than mere subject matter and personal jurisdiction. It extends to "*the defined power of a court in any instance*," whether such power is derived from the Constitution, statute or case law. [See *People v. Gonzalez* (1996) 12 C4th 804, 823, 50 CR2d 74, 87 (emphasis added; internal quotes omitted); see also *Davidson v. Sup.Ct. (City of Mendota)* (1999) 70 CA4th 514, 528-529, 82 CR2d 739, 747-748—order enforcing purported settlement that was unenforceable because not signed by the parties could not be basis for contempt]

a) [9:722.2] **Alternative methods to challenge:** A person may challenge such orders *either* by:

— seeking appellate review of the order when issued (direct attack); or

— waiting until a violation is charged as a contempt of court (collateral attack). [*People v. Gonzalez,* supra, 12 C4th at 823-824, 50 CR2d at 87]

Note: The rule is contra in federal courts and many states; i.e., persons must challenge an injunction directly and obey it until it is set aside; no collateral attack is permitted. [See *People v. Gonzalez,* supra, 12 C4th at 818, 50 CR2d at 83, fn. 4]

2) [9:722.3] **Compare—orders merely "erroneous":** In contrast, collateral attacks are not allowed on an injunction that is merely *erroneous*, so long as the issuing court had subject matter and personal jurisdiction. (For example, an injunction enforcing an invalid contract, the invalidity of which is *not* apparent on its face, is erroneous but not in excess of the court's jurisdiction.) [*People v. Gonzalez*, supra, 12 C4th at 822-823, 50 CR2d at 86-87]

Such injunctions must be obeyed unless and until they are subsequently set aside. Therefore, persons may be punished for violations in the interim. [*People v. Gonzalez*, supra, 12 C4th at 822-823, 50 CR2d at 86-87]

(b) [9:723] **Actual knowledge:** Respondent's personal knowledge of the order is best proved by evidence of its service on respondent. Service on respondent's attorney is also probative, but this raises only

© 2020 Thomson Reuters/The Rutter Group

a rebuttable presumption that *respondent* had actual knowledge. [See, e.g., *People v. Sup.Ct. (Stein)* (1965) 239 CA2d 99, 104, 48 CR 445, 448-449]

Other means of proving knowledge may also suffice—e.g., respondent's presence in court when the order issued; or proof that respondent previously sought relief related to the order (the inference being that he or she must have had actual knowledge).

(c) [9:724] **Ability to comply:** Ability to comply is sometimes obvious, particularly where the violation is of a strictly prohibitory injunction. But in any case, it must be proved by competent evidence. [See *In re Cassil* (1995) 37 CA4th 1081, 1088, 44 CR2d 267, 271; *In re Koehler*, supra, 181 CA4th at 1160, 104 CR3d at 882 (citing text)]

1) [9:724.1] **Burden of proof on moving party:** The burden of proof is on the *moving party* to prove the respondent's ability to comply (rather than on the respondent to prove inability). [See *In re Cassil*, supra, 37 CA4th at 1088, 44 CR2d at 271, fn. 1; *In re Koehler*, supra, 181 CA4th at 1160, 104 CR3d at 882 (citing text)]

(d) [9:725] **Willful disobedience:** The case frequently turns on the issue of whether the violation was "willful." Where the injunction is vague, broad or ambiguous, it is difficult to show beyond a reasonable doubt that a possible but incorrect interpretation led to a "willful" violation.

e. **Punishment**

(1) [9:726] **$1,000 or 5 days:** The maximum punishment for civil contempt is a $1,000 fine or 5 days in jail, or both. [CCP §1218(a)] (Community service may be ordered for contempts in family law cases. See CCP §1218(c); and detailed discussion in Hogoboom & King, *Cal. Prac. Guide: Family Law* (TRG), Ch. 18.)

(a) [9:727] **Ban on multiple punishment:** The ban on multiple punishments for the same offense (Pen.C. §654(a)) applies to civil contempt. [*Conn v. Sup.Ct. (Farmers Group)* (1987) 196 CA3d 774, 786, 242 CR 148, 156]

Thus, it is improper to impose multiple fines or jail terms for what is basically a single disobedience, although *continuing* in nature; e.g., a refusal to turn over documents or to answer questions over a period of days or weeks: "An individual might well decide that disobedience of a court order is worth a $1,000 fine. However, this is not a proper ground on which to analyze whether one or more contempts has taken place." [*Conn v. Sup.Ct. (Farmers Group)*, supra, 196 CA3d at 788, 242 CR at 156-157 (internal quotes omitted)]

[9:728-728.4] *Reserved.*

(b) [9:728.5] **Order:** A written judgment is required (a minute order is *not* sufficient). In an *indirect contempt* case, the judgment need not include the court's factual findings as a jurisdictional prerequisite, provided the court orally recited such findings on the record to provide a basis for appellate review. [See *Moss v. Sup.Ct. (Ortiz)* (1998) 17 C4th 396, 404, 71 CR2d 215, 219, fn. 3]

The rule is different in *direct contempt* cases. In a direct contempt, the court must sign a written judgment or order that recites with particularity the facts constituting the contempt. [*Boysaw v. Sup.Ct.* (2000) 23 C4th 215, 219-220, 96 CR2d 531, 534; *In re Ringgold* (2006) 142 CA4th 1001, 1014, 48 CR3d 507, 516—written direct contempt order based on violation of a prior order must describe prior order *with particularity*]

[9:729] ***PRACTICE POINTER:*** Because of the ban on multiple punishments for the same offense, sanctions may be a more effective remedy than civil contempt proceedings to force compliance with court orders. Monetary sanctions can be many times greater than the $1,000 fine for contempt; and are payable to the moving party rather than the county.

(2) [9:730] **Imprisonment until compliance:** CCP §1219 provides that where the contempt consists of failure to perform an act still within the respondent's power to perform, he or she may be imprisoned until compliance. [*In re Ricardo A.* (1995) 32 CA4th 1190, 1200, 38 CR2d 586, 592]

This applies to *mandatory* injunctions (the effect of which can be obviated, in any event, by taking an appeal; *see* ¶*9:534*).

(But it is not limited to mandatory injunctions. Many orders enforceable by contempt are not injunctions and are not appealable; e.g., orders to respond to discovery cannot be stayed by appeal.)

(a) [9:730.1] **Ability to comply must be shown:** An element of an indirect contempt is that the person subject to the order has the ability to comply with

© 2020 Thomson Reuters/The Rutter Group

the order. For example, where the alleged contempt consists of failure to turn over funds in violation of a court order, imprisonment cannot be ordered unless the moving party demonstrates that the contemner *has the financial ability to* pay those funds. [*In re Cassil* (1995) 37 CA4th 1081, 1087, 44 CR2d 267, 271]

[9:730.2-730.4] *Reserved.*

f. [9:730.5] **Costs and attorney fees:** In addition to a fine or imprisonment, parties or their agents adjudged guilty of contempt may be ordered to pay reasonable attorney fees and costs incurred by the party initiating the contempt proceeding. [CCP §1218(a)]

g. [9:731] **Appellate review:** While an appeal may be taken from conviction for criminal contempt under the Penal Code, *no* appeal lies from the judgment in civil contempt proceedings under CCP §1209. [CCP §§904.1, 1222; *Conn v. Sup.Ct. (Farmers Group)* (1987) 196 CA3d 774, 784, 242 CR 148, 154 (citing text)]

However, appellate courts can review civil contempt judgments by extraordinary writ (certiorari), and a purported appeal may be treated as a petition for such writ. [See *People v. Gonzalez* (1996) 12 C4th 804, 816, 50 CR2d 74, 82]

h. [9:732] **Further reference sources:** For further discussion of contempt proceedings, see CCP §§1209-1222; Hogoboom & King, *Cal. Prac. Guide: Family Law* (TRG), Ch. 18 (enforcement of family law judgments by contempt); and Wegner, Fairbank, Epstein & Chernow, *Cal. Prac. Guide: Civil Trials & Evidence* (TRG), Ch. 12.

B. RECEIVERSHIPS

[9:733] The following material emphasizes *practical problems* in receiverships. For detailed discussion on the substantive law, refer to:

- CCP §§564-570; Corps.C. §1803.
- CRC 3.1175-3.1184.
- Ahart, *Cal. Prac. Guide: Enforcing Judgments & Debts* (TRG), Ch. 4 (Provisional Remedies).

1. [9:734] **Statutory Authority for Appointment:** Receivers are agents of the court and may be appointed only when authorized by statute. [*Marsch v. Williams* (1994) 23 CA4th 238, 246, 28 CR2d 402, 407—*arbitrators* cannot appoint a receiver even if arbitration agreement says they can ("the power to appoint receivers is unique and cannot be extended to arbitrators in the absence of legislative action"); see *City of Chula Vista v. Gutierrez* (2012) 207 CA4th 681, 685, 143 CR3d 689, 691]

But an omnibus provision of one authorizing statute broadly extends to all cases "where necessary *to preserve the property or rights of any party*" (CCP §564(b)(9) (emphasis added)). Thus, case law authority for appointment may also be relied upon. [*Turner v. Sup.Ct. (Cooke)* (1977) 72 CA3d 804, 811, 140 CR 475, 479]

Some of the most common situations calling for appointment of a receiver, and the statutory authority, are listed below (¶*9:735 ff.*). Miscellaneous provisions in other Codes likewise provide for receivers in specific situations.

- [9:734.1] *Comment:* Some courts require an "equitable" reason for the appointment of a receiver in *every* case (i.e., parties not entitled to appointment on statutory grounds alone; *see, e.g.,* ¶*9:779.1*).

a. [9:735] Where property in which plaintiff has a "probable interest" is in danger of being lost, removed or injured. [CCP §564(b)(1)]

Examples:

- Defrauded vendor, suing to rescind, seeks to prevent property from being sold or encumbered;
- Creditor with unmatured claim (i.e., attachment presently unavailable) suing to set aside transfer in fraud of creditors;
- Spouse claiming community property interest in property which other spouse holds as partner with others. [See Ahart, *Cal. Prac. Guide: Enforcing Judgments & Debts* (TRG), Ch. 4, ¶*4:860 ff.*]

b. [9:736] Where mortgaged property is being foreclosed and either (1) is in danger of being lost, etc., or (2) is probably insufficient to pay the debt. [CCP §564(b)(2)] (Receivers to enforce an assignment of rents do not normally come under this provision.)

c. [9:736.1] In an action by a secured lender for specific performance of an *assignment of rents* provision in a trust deed, mortgage or separate assignment document. [CCP §564(b)(11)]

d. [9:737] In an action to enforce a judgment. [CCP §564(b)(3), (4); see *City & County of San Francisco v. Daley* (1993) 16 CA4th 734, 742, 20 CR2d 256, 262; *Gold v. Gold Realty Co.* (2003) 114 CA4th 791, 804, 8 CR3d 118, 128 (citing text)]

e. [9:738] On dissolution or insolvency of a corporation. [CCP §564(b)(5), (6)]

f. [9:739] In an unlawful detainer action. [CCP §564(b)(7)]

g. [9:739.1] To sell perishable property seized by attachment. [CCP §488.700]

h. [9:739.2] To bring real property into compliance with Health and Safety Code requirements. [CCP §564(b)(10), (c); see

© 2020 Thomson Reuters/The Rutter Group

City of Desert Hot Springs v. Valenti (2019) 43 CA5th 788, 793, 256 CR3d 876, 880]

i. [9:739.3] To enforce a family law judgment or order. [Fam.C. §290]

j. [9:740] All other cases where necessary to preserve the property or rights of any party. [CCP §564(b)(9)]

[9:741-742] *Reserved.*

2. **Practical Considerations**

a. [9:743] **"Drastic" nature of remedy:** A receivership is a harsh, time-consuming, expensive and potentially unjust remedy and thus is available only where a more "delicate," alternative remedy (i.e., injunction, writ of possession, attachment, provisional director, lis pendens) is inadequate. In other words, it should not be requested unless *absolutely essential* because no other remedy will do the job. [See *City & County of San Francisco v. Daley* (1993) 16 CA4th 734, 745, 20 CR2d 256, 263]

b. [9:744] **Cost of receiverships:** Receiverships are very expensive—often to both parties, since the costs are normally paid out of an estate in which both parties typically have an interest. *See ¶9:782 ff.*

(1) [9:745] The receiver is *not* merely another executive appointed to run a business or an apartment house. Rather, a receiver must proceed in a prescribed way, requiring lawyers, requests to be instructed, bonds, accounts, and the like.

(2) [9:746] Thus, e.g., for a receiver to be considered seriously, a business or apartment house must simultaneously have a sufficient margin of profit to pay the costs *and* be in immediate danger of a disaster that warrants the cost of a receiver.

Moreover, the receiver, as an agent of the court, must comply with applicable laws and regulations and cannot allow "shortcuts" (e.g., wage and hour violations) found in many small businesses. Thus, a business that was marginally profitable prior to the appointment of a receiver may no longer be profitable even before the receiver's costs of administration are paid from operation of the business.

c. [9:747] **Use of other remedies:** As stated above (¶*9:743*), the court usually prefers to regulate conduct of a business by injunctions, resorting to a receiver only when it is clear that an injunction will not work. Similarly, the appointment of a provisional director (to break deadlocks on the board of directors) is preferable to the appointment of a more costly receiver who operates as a CEO.

(1) [9:747.1] **"Exceptional cases" warranting receivership:** But appointment of a receiver is warranted in "exceptional cases." [*City & County of San Francisco v. Daley*, supra, 16 CA4th at 744-745, 20 CR2d at 263—receiver properly appointed to repair family residence maintained so poorly as to constitute a public nuisance after owners "repeatedly thumbed their noses" at efforts to compel them to correct code violations and one owner had been jailed for contempt for disobeying earlier court orders]

d. [9:748] **Limited purpose receiverships:** In circumstances where a general receivership is inappropriate, the court may consider a "limited purpose receiver" to take charge of a defined aspect of a business (hold the funds, collect the accounts, take charge of the accounting functions, prosecute and settle a lawsuit), leaving the parties to run the rest of the business. Such receiver may even be given a different title so as not to upset business relationships. [*Gold v. Gold Realty Co.* (2003) 114 CA4th 791, 802, 8 CR3d 118, 126 (citing text)]

e. [9:749] **Use in combination with other remedies:** A receivership may be used in combination with other remedies, such as injunctions, to accomplish the desired results.

⇨ [9:749.1] ***PRACTICE POINTER:*** An injunction should always be requested in connection with the appointment of a receiver to compel the parties' compliance with and to prevent their interference with the receivership order.

f. [9:750] **Court's inherent power to appoint a receiver:** The court has power to appoint a receiver on its own motion, where necessary to accomplish some other judicial objective; e.g., to hold and manage trust assets when trustee declines to act. [*McCarthy v. Poulsen* (1985) 173 CA3d 1212, 1219, 219 CR 375, 380]

[9:750.1-750.4] *Reserved.*

g. [9:750.5] **Courtroom assignments:** In larger courts, receivership proceedings may be assigned to special departments. For example:

- In L.A. Superior Court, Central District, prejudgment receivership proceedings (other than receiverships in family law cases) are heard in Depts. 82, 85 and 86. [L.A. Sup.Ct. Rules 2.8(c), 2.9]

[9:750.6-750.9] *Reserved.*

3. [9:750.10] **Procedure for Appointment:** The procedure for appointment of receivers is governed by statute and CRC rules.

a. **Ex parte appointment**

(1) [9:751] **Difficult to obtain:** Although frequently requested, ex parte appointments are rarely granted.

© 2020 Thomson Reuters/The Rutter Group

[See CRC 3.1175; *Turner v. Sup.Ct. (Cooke)* (1977) 72 CA3d 804, 809, 140 CR 475, 478, fn. 2]

[9:751.1] ***PRACTICE POINTER:*** If requesting the ex parte appointment of a receiver, include an *alternative* request for an *order shortening time* for hearing on a noticed motion. Even if this does not improve your chances for an ex parte order, it is likely to reduce the delay occasioned by a fully noticed hearing.

(2) [9:752] **Application:** The rules governing TROs are followed in applying for a receiver *ex parte* (filing complaint, notification to opposition, presentation of affidavits and declarations to the Writs and Receivers Department or judge assigned to such matters; ¶*9:588 ff.*).

(a) [9:753] **Showing required:** The applicant must show, by declarations or verified pleading:

1) The *nature* of the emergency, and the *reasons* why "irreparable injury" would be suffered if no ex parte receiver was appointed;

2) A description of the property and the names, addresses, and telephone numbers of the persons in possession of it;

3) If the property in question is used by a business, facts sufficient to show the nature and size of the business and the impact that appointment of a receiver might have on the business (affecting the amount of bond); and

4) Reasonable diligence to ascertain any of these matters if such matters have not been fully ascertained. [CRC 3.1175]

[9:753.1-753.4] *Reserved.*

(b) [9:753.5] **Amount of undertaking:** At the ex parte hearing, the applicant must propose the specific amount of any bond to be required from the applicant and the receiver for any injunction ordered in connection with the order appointing a receiver. The applicant must also state the reasons for the amount proposed. [CRC 3.1178]

[9:753.6] ***PRACTICE POINTER:*** Counsel seeking an ex parte appointment should be prepared with a *declaration* stating *facts* justifying the amount of the bond requested.

(3) [9:754] **Order appointing receiver and OSC re confirmation:** If a receiver is appointed *ex parte*, a comprehensive order should be prepared appointing and giving the receiver precise instructions, granting powers, enjoining parties from interfering, fixing a bond for the plaintiff and the receiver, and setting a hearing on OSC re Confirmation of Appointment of Receiver. [CRC 3.1176]

FORM: Ex Parte Order Appointing Receiver and Order to Show Cause and Temporary Restraining Order—Rents, Issues, and Profits (RC-200).

☞ [9:754.1] ***PRACTICE POINTER:*** The Judicial Council forms are *not* mandatory. It is wise to consult with the nominated receiver about the proposed order before its submission to the court. Many receivers can provide sample orders and suggest provisions that might help avoid future hearings or disputes.

(a) [9:755] **Comment:** In effect, the OSC re Confirmation is a noticed motion to determine continuance of the receivership past the hearing date (equivalent to an OSC re PI). The OSC must be made returnable on the earliest date that the business of the court will admit, but not later than 15 days or, if good cause is shown, 22 days from the date the order was issued. [CRC 3.1176(a)]

(b) [9:755a] **Service requirement:** All moving papers must be served as soon as reasonably practical, but no later than 5 days after the date on which the order to show cause was issued, unless the court orders another time. (If the complaint has not been previously served, personal service is required.) [CRC 3.1176(b)]

Lack of diligence in effecting service on adverse parties is ground to discharge the receiver. [CRC 3.1176(c)]

(c) [9:755.1] **Bond requirements:** Two bonds are required on any ex parte appointment of a receiver:

- *Plaintiff's bond:* Before an ex parte order can be made, the applicant must post an undertaking (in an amount to be fixed by the court) to pay any damages sustained by the defendant if the appointment is erroneous. [CCP §566]
- *Receiver's bond:* Upon appointment, the receiver must post a separate undertaking to faithfully discharge his or her duties and obey court orders. [CCP §567]

1) [9:755.2] **Timing considerations:** Note that the plaintiff's bond must be filed *before* the ex

© 2020 Thomson Reuters/The Rutter Group

parte order appointing a receiver can be made. The receiver's bond can be posted later, but the court usually holds its order until the receiver's bond is posted.

(d) [9:755.3] **OSC hearing:** After the OSC hearing the court may continue the receiver in effect.

FORM: Order Confirming Appointment of Receiver and Preliminary Injunction—Rents, Issues, and Profits (RC-210).

[9:755.4] ***PRACTICE POINTER:*** As noted above (¶*9:754.1*), the Judicial Council forms are not mandatory. The appointed receiver may be able to provide other order forms with helpful provisions.

[9:756] ***PRACTICE POINTER—Alternative TRO and OSC re Appointment of Receiver:*** An attorney applying *ex parte* for a receiver should have ready an alternative form of TRO and OSC re Appointment of Receiver in the event the receiver is not appointed. In most cases, the court will prefer to hold the status quo with a TRO and set a noticed hearing for appointment of a receiver.

b. **Appointment of receiver after noticed motion**

(1) [9:757] **OSC or motion procedure:** Either an OSC or noticed motion may be used to set a receivership application for hearing. However, the OSC is usually used when a TRO is requested at the beginning of the case; and many times the OSC re appointment of a receiver will be stated as an alternative to a preliminary injunction.

(2) [9:758] **Moving papers:** The same types of moving papers must be served and filed as in the case of an injunction: notice of motion or OSC, declarations, points and authorities, complaint (verified if it is also to serve as a declaration), and proof of service.

FORMS

- Order to Show Cause and Temporary Restraining Order—Rents, Issues, and Profits (RC-300).
- Motion for Order Appointing Receiver and for Preliminary Injunction and Proposed Order, *see Form 9B:15* in Rivera, *Cal. Prac. Guide: Civ. Pro. Before Trial FORMS* (TRG).

(3) [9:759] **Necessary showing:** The moving papers must allege facts establishing one of the statutory grounds for appointment of a receiver. [*Miller v. Oliver* (1917) 174 C 407, 410, 163 P 355, 357]

Moreover, since a receivership is an equitable remedy, the equitable considerations in an injunction proceeding apply—i.e., there must be a showing of *irreparable injury* and *inadequacy of other remedies.* [*Alhambra-Shumway Mines, Inc. v. Alhambra Gold Mine Corp.* (1953) 116 CA2d 869, 872, 254 P2d 599, 602]

(4) [9:759.1] **Hearing:** A motion for the appointment of a receiver is a "law and motion" proceeding (CRC 3.1103(a)(2)) and will be decided based on declarations or requests for judicial notice without live testimony at the hearing unless the court orders otherwise "for good cause shown." [CRC 3.1306(a); *see* ¶*9:46*]

As with other law and motion matters, an application for leave to introduce live testimony must be made in writing "no later than three court days before the hearing" and must state "the nature and extent of the evidence proposed to be introduced." [CRC 3.1306(b); *see* ¶*9:45.1*; *City of Crescent City v. Reddy* (2017) 9 CA5th 458, 464-465, 215 CR3d 351, 356-357—no abuse of discretion in denying counsel's oral request to present live testimony made for first time at hearing]

(5) [9:760] **Bond requirements:** Two separate bonds may be required:

- *Plaintiff's bond (discretionary):* Unlike ex parte appointments (*see* ¶*9:755.1*), there is no statutory requirement for a bond where a receiver is appointed on noticed motion. However, the court clearly has power to require a bond, and is likely to do so where the appointment, if erroneous, would damage the defendant.

- *Receiver's bond:* A receiver is required to post a bond before he or she enters upon performance of his or her duties (the same as where the appointment is ex parte; *see* ¶*9:755.1*). [CCP §567]

(a) [9:761] **Amount of bond:** The court relies on information obtained from counsel as to the amount of protection required under each bond. The receiver's bond is usually fixed high enough to cover the value of any cash or transferable personal property coming into the receiver's possession. It is the applicant's responsibility to propose the amount of the bond, but the opposing party may (and should where necessary) propose a higher amount and state the reasons therefor. [CRC 3.1178]

Some courts require a declaration stating facts as to the amount of probable damage from appointment of a receiver, upon which the court may rely in fixing the bond.

© 2020 Thomson Reuters/The Rutter Group

☞ [9:761a] ***PRACTICE POINTER:*** Wherever possible, counsel should submit declarations stating facts justifying the amount of bond requested *prior* to the hearing. The court may or may not be willing to accept documents filed at the time of the hearing.

(b) [9:761.1] **Form and content of bond:** The considerations applicable to undertakings for injunctions apply here as well; *see ¶9:640 ff.*

FORM: Order Appointing Receiver After Hearing and Preliminary Injunction—Rents, Issues, and Profits (RC-310).

[9:761.1a-761.1d] *Reserved.*

c. [9:761.1e] **Adverse party's right to continuance of hearing:** Where the receiver was appointed on an ex parte basis (CRC 3.1175, *¶9:751 ff.*), adverse parties have the right to obtain one continuance of the confirmation hearing to permit them to prepare opposition. If such a continuance is requested, the terms of the OSC remain in effect until the continued hearing. [CRC 3.1176(d)]

d. [9:761.2] **Appellate review:** An order appointing a receiver is immediately appealable. [CCP §904.1(a)(7)]

4. **Powers and Duties of Receiver**

a. [9:762] **Powers:** The receiver's powers are specified by the court in the appointment order. [CCP §568] The order should list the powers in some detail, which requires advance thought as to the receiver's duties.

If the receiver's powers are in doubt, the receiver should petition the court for instructions. Except in emergencies, notice to all parties will normally be required.

The receiver is the agent of the court, not of any party to the litigation, and therefore must act for the benefit of all (including non-parties) who may have an interest in the property. [CRC 3.1179(a)]

(1) [9:763] **Employment of counsel:** A receiver cannot hire an attorney without court approval. If it is known at the outset legal counsel will be required, the application for appointment of a receiver should state this fact. If the need arises later, a noticed motion may be used to obtain authority.

The application for authority to employ an attorney must be in writing, stating reasons creating the necessity for the employment and the name of the attorney sought to be employed. The application must also contain a statement that the attorney is not the attorney for, associated with, or employed by an attorney for any party to the action. [CRC 3.1180]

Because the receiver acts on behalf of the court (and not the parties), confidential communications between the receiver and his or her attorney are privileged and not discoverable by either party. [*Shannon v. Sup.Ct. (First Interstate Bank)* (1990) 217 CA3d 986, 992-994, 266 CR 242, 245-247]

⇨ [9:763.1] ***PRACTICE POINTER:*** The receiver is not a judge and may communicate with one party in the absence of other parties. But be careful about engaging in such communications, because they are *not* privileged and *are discoverable* by other parties.

b. [9:764] **Duties:** The appointment order should clearly indicate the object of the receivership. For example, is the receiver to close down the business or operate it? To maintain the machinery or sell it? To collect the rents and pay the lien obligations? To complete construction or simply maintain real property? With the duties distinctly particularized, the powers can then be drafted with specificity.

5. **Identity of the Receiver**

a. [9:765] **Statutory qualifications:** Persons who can qualify for appointment are defined by statute in negative terms. The following persons may *not* be appointed: A party, attorney to the action, person interested in the action, or person related to a judge of the court within the third degree. Any other individual can be appointed. [CCP §566]

The receiver must be a natural person in order to satisfy the bonding requirements. [CCP §567]

The receiver need not be an attorney; accountants and property managers are often appointed in rents, issues and profits (and sometimes other) receiverships (*see ¶9:777*).

[9:766] *Reserved.*

b. [9:767] **Nomination and appointment of receivers:** At the hearing on an application for appointment of receiver on noticed motion (or for confirmation of an ex parte appointment), each party may nominate in writing one or more persons for appointment as receiver (or for substitution of the receiver appointed at the ex parte hearing). [CRC 3.1177]

If substitution of a previously appointed receiver is sought, reasons for the substitution must be stated. Such a nomination does not waive the opponent's right to object to the appointment of a receiver. [CRC 3.1177]

⇨ [9:767.1] ***PRACTICE POINTER:*** In selecting a receiver to nominate for appointment, seek one with experience in similar matters. The hourly fees may

© 2020 Thomson Reuters/The Rutter Group

be greater but the learning curve may be significantly reduced. Many of California's most experienced receivers are members of the California Receivers Forum, a nonprofit organization of professional receivers, and can be identified on its website (*www.receivers.org*).

In any event, be sure you have scrutinized the proposed receiver's background and "vetted" him or her *before* seeking the appointment. Also, consider nominating more than one individual since courts appreciate having two or more names to choose from.

[9:768] *Reserved.*

(1) [9:769] **Supporting documents:** A declaration summarizing the proposed receiver's experience and background should be submitted. Also, courts may be reluctant to appoint a receiver unless the statement of nomination demonstrates that the nominee is:

— not a party to the action;
— not an attorney in the action;
— not a person interested in the action; or
— not related to any judge of the court within the third degree.

[9:769.1-769.5] *Reserved.*

(2) [9:769.6] **Prohibited agreements and arrangements:** The receiver is the *agent of the court*, not of any party, and must be neutral. [CRC 3.1179(a)]

Parties nominating receivers may not enter into a contract, agreement, arrangement, or understanding with a proposed receiver, and the receiver may not enter into any such contract, agreement, arrangement, or understanding concerning:

— the receiver's role with respect to the property following the trustee's sale or termination of the receivership, without specific permission by the court;
— how the receiver will administer the receivership or how much the receiver will charge for services or pay for services to approved third parties hired to provide services;
— who the receiver will hire or seek approval to hire to perform necessary services;
— what capital expenditures will be made on the property. [CRC 3.1179(b)]

6. **Receivership Administration**

a. [9:770] **General performance:** The receiver is obliged to perform the assigned task, *but no more than the task assigned.* If the parties' circumstances change during administration, the court—and not the receiver—should be asked to make appropriate changes in duties or to terminate the receivership.

b. [9:771] **Request for instructions:** Receivers may request instructions from the court and frequently do so when powers and duties are vaguely formulated or do not cover a point in issue.

c. [9:772] **Sale of assets:** If authorized by court order, receivers may sell any property in their possession, although the sale is not final until confirmed by the court. [CCP §§568, 568.5]

Confirmation will generally be granted if it is shown that the sale was *necessary* for the estate, and *fair* to the respective parties. [*Cal-American Income Property Fund VII v. Brown Develop. Corp.* (1982) 138 CA3d 268, 274, 187 CR 703, 706—abuse of discretion to confirm sale where no need for immediate sale shown]

CCP §568.5 states the sale must be conducted in accordance with the notice requirements and other provisions of the Enforcement of Judgments Law (CCP §701.510 et seq.). Even so, a court has the power to approve or ratify a sale conducted in a manner different from the specified statutory procedure. [*People v. Riverside Univ.* (1973) 35 CA3d 572, 582-583, 111 CR 68, 75 (decided under former version of statute); compare *Wells Fargo Fin'l Leasing, Inc. v. D & M Cabinets* (2009) 177 CA4th 59, 77-78, 99 CR3d 97, 112 (reversing sale not conducted in accordance with Enforcement of Judgments Law provisions)]

[9:772.1-772.4] *Reserved.*

d. [9:772.5] **Deposit of funds:** Receivership funds may be deposited in interest-bearing accounts that are fully insured under federal law. [See CCP §569]

e. [9:773] **Inventory and accounting:** Within 30 days after appointment or such other time as the court may order, the receiver must *file an inventory* containing a complete and detailed list of all property in the receiver's possession. If property is subsequently acquired, the receiver must promptly file a *supplemental inventory*. [CRC 3.1181]

The receiver must *provide monthly reports* to the parties (and, if requested, to nonparty lienholders). The reports are not filed with the court unless the court orders otherwise. The report must include the following information:

— a narrative of events;
— a financial report;
— a statement of all fees paid to the receiver, employees, and professionals, including itemized services, a breakdown of services by 1/10th hour increments; and the basis for the fees (hourly or otherwise). [CRC 3.1182(a)]

[9:773a-773e] *Reserved.*

f. [9:773f] **Interim fees:** Interim fees are subject to review and approval by the court. The court may increase or decrease

© 2020 Thomson Reuters/The Rutter Group

such fees in evaluating the value of the services rendered. [CRC 3.1183(a)]

[9:773g-773j] *Reserved.*

g. [9:773k] **Objections to interim accounts and reports:** Unless good cause is shown, objections to the receiver's interim reports and accountings must be made *within 10 days of notice*, must be specific, and must be delivered to the receiver and all parties entitled to receive the accounts and reports. [CRC 3.1183(b)]

➪ [9:773*l*] ***PRACTICE POINTER:*** Promptly review the receiver's interim report *with your client.* Immediately communicate any questions or concerns to the receiver. Doing so may avoid the necessity for formal objections and avoid potential disputes.

h. [9:773.1] **Suing the receiver:** Because a receiver operates under court control, plaintiffs normally must obtain court permission to sue a receiver. But failure to do so is merely ground for staying the action. The defect is waived unless the receiver raises the objection by answer or demurrer. [*Vitug v. Griffin* (1989) 214 CA3d 488, 492-493, 262 CR 588, 591]

- [9:773.2] The court may not deny leave to sue the receiver based on a summary determination that the claim is without merit. [*Jun v. Myers* (2001) 88 CA4th 117, 125, 105 CR2d 537, 543]
- [9:773.3] Dismissal of the action in which the receiver was appointed does not preclude a suit against the receiver as long as the receiver has not rendered a final accounting and been discharged. [*Jun v. Myers*, supra, 88 CA4th at 123, 105 CR2d at 542]

i. [9:774] **Termination of receivership:** A receivership terminates upon completion of the duties for which the receiver was appointed; or at any time, upon court order.

A receivership appointed to preserve the status quo pending trial terminates automatically upon entry of judgment in the action. (Thereafter, the judgment determines the parties' rights to the property held; or, in appropriate cases, a new receiver may be appointed to carry the judgment into effect.) [See *Carpenson v. Najarian* (1967) 254 CA2d 856, 861-862, 62 CR 687, 691-692]

(1) [9:775] **Receiver's final account and report:** Receivers must prepare, serve and file (by noticed motion or stipulation of all parties) a "final account and report, a request for discharge, and a request for exoneration of the receiver's surety." If the report seeks allowance for compensation to the receiver or attorneys for the receiver, it must state in detail what services were rendered and whether previous

allowances have been made. These documents must be served on all parties to the action and to any others whom the receiver knows have a substantial, unsatisfied claim that will be affected by the order or stipulation. [CRC 3.1184]

(2) [9:776] **Approval of report res judicata:** Upon approval of the receiver's report and accounting, the receiver is normally discharged, and the bond exonerated. The order discharging the receiver and settling the account is res judicata as to all claims against the receiver. [*Aviation Brake Systems, Ltd. v. Voorhis* (1982) 133 CA3d 230, 234, 183 CR 766, 768]

(Compare: The discharge is *not* res judicata where the receiver *failed to disclose* a pending lawsuit against him or her in his or her final account or to notify the plaintiffs in that lawsuit of the discharge proceedings. See *Vitug v. Griffin* (1989) 214 CA3d 488, 494-495, 262 CR 588, 592-593.)

(3) [9:776.1] **Appeal:** To preserve claims against the receiver, "a party must immediately appeal from the order approving the final accounting because issues with the receiver concern matters collateral to the underlying lawsuit." [*Southern Calif. Sunbelt Developers, Inc. v. Banyan Ltd. Partnership* (2017) 8 CA5th 910, 926, 214 CR3d 719, 730]

But the question of who is ultimately responsible for paying the court-appointed receiver's fee does not have to be decided as part of the final accounting. [*Southern Calif. Sunbelt Developers, Inc. v. Banyan Ltd. Partnership,* supra, 8 CA5th at 930, 214 CR3d at 733; *see ¶9:782 ff.*]

7. [9:777] **Assignment-of-Rents Receivers:** The usual reluctance to appoint a receiver may not apply where a receiver is sought to enforce an assignment-of-rents provision in a trust deed. This is because the parties have agreed in advance to the appointment (the trust deed usually contains an express provision authorizing the appointment). Moreover, there is usually (not always) less potential for harm in an assignment-of-rents receivership. As a result, such receiverships are quite common, outnumbering all other types of receiverships combined.

Such agreements are made under CCP §564(b)(11); *see ¶9:736.1.*

a. [9:778] **Adequacy of other security:** Trust deed provisions usually authorize appointment of an assignment-of-rents receiver *without regard* to the adequacy of the security already held by the beneficiary (the value of the land and buildings, etc.). Such provisions create a *prima facie* (rebuttable) showing of entitlement to the appointment of a receiver;

© 2020 Thomson Reuters/The Rutter Group

i.e., no independent proof is required that the property is worth less than the mortgage debt. [*Barclays Bank of Calif. v. Sup.Ct. (K.V.E. Shelters, Inc.)* (1977) 69 CA3d 593, 602, 137 CR 743, 748]

(1) [9:779] **Appointment discretionary:** But the appointment is still discretionary and the court may properly decline to appoint a receiver where there are strong countervailing equities. [See *Barclays Bank of Calif. v. Sup.Ct. (K.V.E. Shelters, Inc.)*, supra, 69 CA3d at 602, 137 CR at 748]

(2) [9:779.1] **Appointment where nonjudicial foreclosure pending?** Some judges deny rents-and-profits receivership applications if the evidence presented by the applicant-lender indicates that nonjudicial foreclosure will make the lender whole (principal plus interest, etc.), and there is no showing of any other equitable reason for a receivership (e.g., waste, failure to maintain insurance, etc.). The rationale is that the lender will be made whole shortly (the owner has only 4 months to cure and save the property under nonjudicial foreclosure procedures; see Civ.C. §2924), and that equitable procedures are designed to achieve equity, not help a lender reap a windfall.

Other judges disagree and routinely appoint receivers upon default strictly on the basis of the presence of a rents-and-profits clause in the trust deed, even if there is no indication that the lender will be damaged at all by allowing the owner the time to cure specified in Civ.C. §2924.

The fact the trust deed specifically authorizes appointment of a receiver is immaterial. Parties cannot by private contract force a court to exercise its inherent equity powers. [See *Barclays Bank of Calif. v. Sup.Ct. (K.V.E. Shelters, Inc.)*, supra, 69 CA3d at 600, 137 CR at 747]

b. [9:780] **Limited right to possession:** A receiver appointed under an assignment-of-rents provision has the right to possession only of the "rents and profits" from the property in question. An order authorizing the receiver to take possession of rents and profits from *other* property (i.e., property *not* covered by the deed of trust) is beyond the court's jurisdiction. [See *Turner v. Sup.Ct. (Cooke)* (1977) 72 CA3d 804, 813-815, 140 CR 475, 480-482]

c. [9:781] **Practical considerations:** An assignment-of-rents receivership is usually relatively easy to obtain (assuming an "equitable" reason or need is shown). But plaintiff should not make such request unless the subject building (usually an apartment house) generates enough rent to pay all the costs, liens, etc., and leaves enough left over to pay the receiver.

8. [9:782] **Paying Receivership Costs:** Receivers are entitled to compensation for their own and their attorneys' services. [*City of Chula Vista v. Gutierrez* (2012) 207 CA4th 681, 685, 143 CR3d 689, 691]

   a. [9:782.1] **Payment by estate:** In the usual case, the receiver's costs are paid from the receivership estate. [*City of Chula Vista v. Gutierrez*, supra, 207 CA4th at 685, 143 CR3d at 691]

   b. [9:783] **Payment by parties:** Courts have discretion to impose the receiver's costs on the party who sought appointment of the receiver or to apportion the costs among the parties based on the circumstances. E.g., "[a] court may require one or more parties to pay for receiver fees where the property subject to the receivership is inadequate to compensate the receiver and/or where other equitable circumstances support imposing fees on a party." [*City of Chula Vista v. Gutierrez*, supra, 207 CA4th at 685-686, 143 CR3d at 691-692; *Southern Calif. Sunbelt Developers, Inc. v. Banyan Ltd. Partnership* (2017) 8 CA5th 910, 933-934, 214 CR3d 719, 736—trial court has discretion to award costs of receivership to prevailing party under CCP §1033.5(c)(4)]

C. WRIT OF POSSESSION ("CLAIM AND DELIVERY")

[9:784] This section overviews the procedure in applying for, and resisting an application for, a writ of possession (W/P) of tangible personal property prior to trial, commonly known as a writ of "claim and delivery." This statutory remedy is governed by CCP §512.010 et seq.

Cross-refer: Claim and delivery is discussed in greater detail in Ahart, *Cal. Prac. Guide: Enforcing Judgments & Debts* (TRG), Ch. 4.

1. [9:785] **Substantive Law Requirements:** Plaintiff's right to a writ of possession depends on applicable substantive law. To obtain the writ, plaintiff must show that he or she:

   — has the *right to immediate possession* of *tangible* personal property; and

   — the property is being *wrongfully withheld* by defendant. [See CCP §512.010; *Englert v. IVAC Corp.* (1979) 92 CA3d 178, 184, 154 CR 804, 807]

   a. [9:786] **Tangible property:** The property sought to be recovered must exist in some concrete or tangible form, capable of identification and seizure. [*Lamus v. Engwicht* (1919) 39 CA 523, 529, 179 P 435, 437]

      (1) [9:787] **Compare—intangibles:** A W/P cannot be used to levy on intangibles—e.g., bank accounts, accounts receivable, etc. (Intangibles, however, are subject to attachment; *see ¶9:872.*)

      (2) [9:788] **Compare—shares of corporate stock:** If a certificate has been issued representing shares of stock, the stock *certificate* is subject to seizure under a W/P. [See Comm'l C. §8112(a)]

© 2020 Thomson Reuters/The Rutter Group

- [9:788.1] But claim and delivery is not the proper remedy for either compelling the corporation to issue the stock to a party claiming to own it or determining which of two or more adverse claimants of the stock is entitled to have the certificate thereof issued and delivered to him or her. [*Lamus v. Engwicht*, supra, 39 CA at 529, 179 P at 437; see also Comm'l C. §8112(b)]

Cross-refer: See further discussion in Ahart, *Cal. Prac. Guide: Enforcing Judgments & Debts* (TRG), Ch. 4.

b. [9:789] **Wrongful withholding:** Absent a possessory lien, a defendant has no right to withhold possession of property from its owner even if the owner is indebted to the defendant. [*RCA Service Co. v. Sup.Ct. (Bullock)* (1982) 137 CA3d 1, 3, 187 CR 602, 603—lessor entitled to reclaim leased equipment notwithstanding lessee's damages claim]

2. [9:790] **Application:** The claim and delivery procedure is often used:

- to obtain possession of *tangible property* that is *security for a debt* in default (e.g., a debt secured by a chattel mortgage);
- to reclaim chattels that have been *loaned, leased or bailed* to another and not returned;
- to obtain property whose *ownership is in dispute*.

[9:791] *Reserved.*

3. [9:792] **Procedure:** The principal procedural requirements are to show that the claim of right to possession "is probably valid" [CCP §512.040(b)], and to post a bond [CCP §515.010].

a. **Overview of procedure**

(1) [9:793] **Ex parte issuance of W/P:** The ex parte W/P will issue only if:

(a) The property was stolen, or

(b) The property is a credit card, or

(c) The property was acquired by defendant for *commercial* purposes, is not necessary for support, will not be available for levy by reason of removal, or destruction, and immediate seizure is necessary to protect it. [CCP §512.020(b)]

The ex parte W/P *cannot issue in any other circumstances.* [CCP §512.020(a); *Sea Rail Truckloads, Inc. v. Pullman, Inc.* (1982) 131 CA3d 511, 514-515, 182 CR 560, 562]

(2) [9:794] **Noticed hearing:** The usual method of obtaining the W/P is by order following noticed hearing. [CCP §512.020(a)] The substantive prerequisites for issuance of the W/P must be shown at the hearing, and

defendant must be given an opportunity to oppose its issuance.

(3) [9:795] **TRO:** Once an application for W/P is filed, plaintiff may seek a temporary restraining order (TRO) to prevent defendant from concealing, removing or transferring the property or any interest therein, or otherwise impairing its value "either by acts of destruction or by failure to care for the property in a reasonable manner." [CCP §513.020]

The TRO remains in effect only until a W/P issues. At that time, the court may issue a *preliminary injunction* with the same terms as the TRO, to remain in effect until the property is seized by the levying officer. [CCP §513.010(c)]

(a) [9:795.1] **Showing required:** To obtain a TRO, plaintiff must show:

- the *probable validity* of his or her claim to possession of the property (under applicable substantive law); and
- a *probability* of "immediate danger" that the property will be transferred, concealed or removed, or may become substantially impaired in value; and
- that an *undertaking* has been filed pursuant to CCP §515.010 (*see* ¶*9:796*). [CCP §513.010(b)]

1) [9:795.2] **"Probable validity":** "Probable validity" means it is "more likely than not" that plaintiff will obtain judgment against defendant on the claim to possession of the property. [CCP §511.090; see *People v. Sup.Ct. (Ghilotti)* (2002) 27 C4th 888, 919, 119 CR2d 1, 25]

(4) [9:796] **Undertaking:** To obtain either a TRO or W/P, plaintiff must post a bond of *twice the value of defendant's interest* in the property—i.e., market value, less amounts of liens or balances due under conditional sales contracts or security agreements. [CCP §515.010]

The levying officer will deliver the undertaking to defendant (together with a copy of the W/P and of the order for issuance of the writ) upon seizure of the property. [CCP §514.020(a)]

(a) [9:796.1] **Waived if defendant has no interest:** If the court finds that defendant has *no interest* in the property, no undertaking is required. [CCP §515.010(b)]

In that event, the W/P must state the amount of any counterbond defendant must post to prevent plaintiff

© 2020 Thomson Reuters/The Rutter Group

from taking or regaining possession (*see* ¶*9:796.6*). [CCP §515.010(b)]

[9:796.2-796.4] *Reserved.*

[9:796.5] ***PRACTICE POINTER:*** If you represent plaintiff, be sure to include enough facts in your application for a W/P to allow the court to set the amount of the bond ("*not less than twice the value* of defendant's interest in the property").

If you represent defendant, be prepared to respond with declarations establishing the value of defendant's interest in the property. If the court finds a sufficiently high valuation, plaintiff may be unable to furnish a bond and a W/P will never issue. (On the other hand, it may be in defendant's interest to accept a bond in a *low* amount because defendant can *counterbond* and thus defeat the W/P.)

(5) [9:796.6] **Defendant can prevent seizure by counterbonding:** Defendant may prevent plaintiff from taking possession of the property under a W/P or may regain possession of the property seized, by posting a bond in the same amount as plaintiff's bond. [CCP §515.020(a); *see further discussion at* ¶*9:847*]

b. [9:797] **Use of Judicial Council forms:** Pursuant to instructions from the Legislature (CCP §516.020), the Judicial Council has adopted a series of mandatory forms to implement the Claim and Delivery (C/D) law (Judicial Council forms CD-100 through CD-200).

(1) [9:798] **Purpose of forms:** Aside from implementing the applicable Code provisions to which they pertain, the forms serve two practical purposes:

- To simplify C/D practice for the attorney; and
- To enable the court to process a volume of applications efficiently.

(2) [9:799] **Use as a checklist:** In addition, the forms can be used as a practical checklist, to safeguard against dangerous pitfalls at the hearing. For instance, if counsel finds the meaning and effect of a particular item on a form to be obscure, he or she is likely to ignore an essential matter at the hearing. The form can thus serve as a cautionary reminder to go back to the applicable Code section to ascertain why the information is being demanded.

[9:800] ***PRACTICE POINTER:*** While the forms greatly simplify practice under the C/D law, they cannot be used without an understanding of the *purpose* of each form and the reason for the information requested. In short, you cannot simply hand the forms to an untrained assistant and direct that they be completed without experienced supervision and review. If you are unfamiliar with the statutory scheme, the Code references at the bottom right corner of each form should be consulted.

c. **Complaint**

(1) [9:801] **Prerequisite to application:** An application for a W/P cannot be made unless a complaint is filed (commencing the action). [CCP §512.010(a)]

The complaint usually seeks, among other things, a W/P. But it is unclear whether such a claim is essential because CCP §512.010(a) does not require that the complaint seek recovery of the property. On the other hand, CCP §511.090 (defining "probable validity") refers to the probability of plaintiff securing a "judgment against the defendant on *that claim*."

(2) [9:802] **Use of verified complaint to prove facts:** The complaint, if verified, may also serve the purpose of proving facts for issuance of the W/P. However, if so used, facts must be stated as they would be in a declaration (rather than broad "ultimate facts"). [See CCP §516.030; and discussion in connection with Injunctions, ¶*9:579*]

d. **Application for Writ of Possession**

FORM: Application for Writ of Possession (Claim and Delivery) (CD-100).

[9:803] **Requisite information:** Although much of the form is self-explanatory, counsel will have to make the following decisions:

(1) [9:804] **Ex parte?** The proper box at item 2.b. must be checked, depending on whether the application is being made ex parte. Different forms are subsequently used if the application is for a W/P after noticed hearing.

➪ [9:805] ***PRACTICE POINTER:*** There is no point in checking the ex parte box just because it is there. Unless an ex parte case can be made out under the terms of the statute (¶*9:793*), apply for a W/P after noticed hearing (box 2.a).

(2) [9:806] **Statement of facts:** Facts establishing the right to possession are set forth at item 3. Since the space is limited, the statement is usually made by *reference to the verified complaint*, attached declarations, or both. Note that the declarations must be stated in terms of admissible evidence (i.e., not by hearsay). [CCP §516.030]

© 2020 Thomson Reuters/The Rutter Group

(3) [9:807] **Description and value of property:** Item 4 of the form is used to set forth a "particular description of the property and a statement of its value." [CCP §512.010(b)(3)]

(a) [9:808] The description must be specific enough so that the sheriff can identify the property.

(b) [9:809] Value is essential for purposes of the bond. The W/P cannot issue without posting of bond, the size of which depends on the property's value (¶*9:796*).

[9:810] ***PRACTICE POINTER:*** If you represent plaintiff, don't understate the value of the property. Keep in mind that defendant can retain the property by counterbonding in an amount equal to plaintiff's bond. [CCP §515.020(a); ¶*9:847*]

(4) [9:811] **Detention and manner of acquisition:** Defendant's wrongful detention, the reason for it, and the manner in which he or she acquired the property (item 5) are usually easy to allege. These items are essential, however; omission will defeat the application. [CCP §512.010(b)(2)]

(5) [9:812] **Location:** Items 6 and 7 require facts showing location of the property. Location accuracy is *imperative*, because the order and W/P are the sheriff's only authority to enter private property to seize the chattel. [CCP §512.080(c)] There cannot be a seizure without designation of an accurate location and further proceedings will be necessary. [CCP §512.090]

[9:812.1] ***PRACTICE POINTER:*** Make sure you identify where the property is *actually* located. For example, in seeking repossession of a car, some plaintiff's counsel give the location as an office address (e.g., 301 South Main, *Suite 300*). The car is certainly *not* in an office suite. You need to state where the car will be found by the levying officer (e.g., in the parking lot beneath 301 South Main in the parking spot on the first parking level, "Level P-1," which has a sign stating "RESERVED—SUITE 300").

(6) [9:813] **Number of pages attached:** This form (at item 10), as well as other forms, contemplates attachments—primarily declarations and exhibits. The pages attached should be numbered serially and the total number entered at the applicable space on the form.

e. **Ex Parte Application**

(1) **General considerations in making ex parte application**

(a) [9:814] **Disfavored:** As indicated earlier, ex parte applications for a W/P are looked upon with suspicion by some judges, particularly since a TRO is more readily available.

➪ [9:815] ***PRACTICE POINTER:*** Bring an *alternative set of forms* with you, applying for a TRO and noticed hearing. Then, in the event that your application for an ex parte W/P is denied, you may be able to get a TRO notwithstanding.

Give *both* sets to the judge at the outset, so that he or she will realize what you're doing, and won't feel that your ex parte application for a W/P was presented in bad faith.

(b) [9:816] **Notice:** The court will usually require the same notice procedure to be followed as with any TRO (¶*9:590 ff.*).

If any of the CCP §512.020(b) factors are present (*see* ¶*9:793*), the court may issue the W/P without notice.

(2) **Information necessary for application**

FORM: Declaration for Ex Parte Writ of Possession (Claim and Delivery) (CD-180).

(a) [9:817] **Substantive showing:** Items 1, 2 and 3 of the Declaration track the Code requirements. [CCP §512.020(b)(1), (2) or (3)]

1) Items 1 (felonious taking) and 2 (credit card) are unusual. Most applications are made under item 3 (property acquired for a commercial purpose, etc.).

2) Where item 3 is the applicable declaration, be sure that the danger of imminent destruction, concealment or other harm is alleged by *facts*, in the form of first-hand knowledge by the declarant. Conclusions, beliefs or worries and hearsay will be ignored by the court.

(b) [9:818] **Undertaking:** Check the box at item 4 and hand the undertaking to the judge if one has been prepared prior to the hearing.

© 2020 Thomson Reuters/The Rutter Group

(3) **Vacating the ex parte order**

(a) [9:819] **Noticed motion:** A defendant whose property has been seized by ex parte W/P can apply, by noticed motion, for the writ to be quashed and the property released. If defendant is successful on the motion, damages sustained by the levy and loss of possession can also be awarded. [CCP §512.020(b)]

FORM: Application and Notice of Application and Hearing for Order to Quash Ex Parte Writ of Possession (Claim and Delivery) (CD-160).

[9:820] *Note item 1.c of the form:* If the motion to quash will not come on for hearing before the property is delivered to plaintiff by the sheriff, defendant must apply ex parte for an *order staying delivery.* (A specially prepared order is necessary.) [See CCP §512.020(b), last para.]

f. **Temporary Restraining Order**

(1) [9:821] **When available:** A TRO may issue if:

(a) Plaintiff has established the *probable validity* of the claim; and

(b) An *undertaking* is filed; and

(c) There is a "probability" that the property will disappear or "become *substantially impaired in value.*" [CCP §513.010(b)]

(2) [9:822] **Distinction from ex parte W/P:** While the TRO statutory language is, for the most part, similar to that of the ex parte section, in practice it may be easier to obtain a TRO than an ex parte W/P:

(a) [9:823] A TRO can issue on a showing of a "probability" of disappearance or damage. [CCP §513.010(b)(3)] An ex parte writ, however, requires a *finding of fact* of "immediate danger." [CCP §512.020(b)(3)(ii)]

(b) [9:824] The risk of damage to defendant is far greater with seizure of the property than it is with an order that the property merely "stand still" and not be harmed.

(c) [9:825] The TRO is the only ex parte remedy available where the chattel was not used for commercial purposes.

But an ex parte W/P may be used where the property was obtained *feloniously* or is a *credit card.* [CCP §512.020(b)(1)-(2)]

(3) **Declaration**

FORM: Application for Temporary Restraining Order (Claim and Delivery) (CD-190).

(a) [9:826] **Property description:** Items 2.a., b. or c. must be completed because of the difference in the TRO depending on the type of property involved.

(b) [9:827] **Acts to be "enjoined":** Item 3 covers the scope of the TRO requested. Facts supporting each of the TROs requested must be set forth in supporting documents.

(c) [9:828] **Danger, disappearance or harm:** Item 5 is crucial. Facts complying with the Code requirements must be alleged or the TRO will be denied.

(4) **The Temporary Restraining Order**

FORM: Temporary Restraining Order (Claim and Delivery) (CD-200).

(a) [9:829] **Findings:** Since CCP §513.010(b) requires findings, item 1 must be appropriately completed.

(b) [9:830] **Order:** Item 2 of the form is the restraining order. Note the following:

1) Item 2.a.(1) is used where the order restrains transfer of the property under all circumstances.

2) Items 2.a.(2) and (3) are used to restrain transfer of property (farm products or inventory) other than in the ordinary course of business. [See CCP §513.020(a)]

3) Items 2.b. and c. are self-explanatory; but remember that the moving papers must allege facts justifying the order.

4) Item 2.d. is used to freeze funds resulting from ordinary business sales of farm products or inventory.

(c) [9:831] **Duration:** The TRO can remain in effect for a maximum 15 days, unless the court authorizes a 22-day duration for good cause shown. [CCP §§513.010(a), 527(d)(1)]

Accordingly, item 4 must be completed to coincide with the hearing on the application, while satisfying the statutory time limits.

☞ [9:831.1] ***PRACTICE POINTER FOR PLAINTIFF:*** First of all, when applying for the TRO, be sure to include facts constituting *good cause* for a *22-day* TRO rather than only 15 days. Otherwise, it may

© 2020 Thomson Reuters/The Rutter Group

expire before the PI hearing because *at least 16 court days'* notice of hearing is required (CCP §1005(b); *see ¶9:87 ff.*).

Second, make plans to serve the TRO and other moving papers on defendant *immediately*, because defendant is entitled to at least 16 court days' notice of the hearing (CCP §1005(b)). Otherwise the 22-day TRO will expire before the hearing date. (Alternatively, ask the court for an order shortening time on the hearing date.)

g. [9:832] **Notice of Application for W/P:** This form is used to give notice of the hearing on a noticed application for W/P.

- ***FORM:*** Notice of Application for Writ of Possession and Hearing (Claim and Delivery) (CD-110).

h. **Service and proof of service**

(1) [9:833] **Necessity for service:** As with any proceeding, the court cannot go ahead unless the complaint, the moving papers, and all the supporting documents are timely served (CCP §1005, *¶9:31*). Any TRO already issued will be *dissolved* if the hearing is thwarted due to lack of service. [CCP §527(d)(3)]

(2) [9:834] **Filing proof of service:** The Claim and Delivery forms do not provide a space for affidavits of service. Therefore, proof of service must be *specially drafted.*

i. **Hearing and Order**

(1) [9:835] **Hearing:** Except in rare cases where special permission is granted, the hearing will normally be conducted only on declarations (*cf. ¶9:632 ff.*). After resolving objections, the court will admit into evidence the declarations and (if applicable) the verified complaint.

[9:836] ***PRACTICE POINTER:*** It is good practice to have the form of order (*¶9:836.1 ff.*) prepared and with you at the hearing, so that if the application is granted the order can be signed the same day.

(2) [9:836.1] **Order:** A writ of possession shall issue if the court finds plaintiff has established the *probable validity* of the claim to possession of the property; and plaintiff posts an undertaking as described below (*¶9:838 ff.*). [CCP §512.060]

FORM: Order for Writ of Possession (Claim and Delivery) (CD-120).

[9:837] ***PRACTICE POINTER:*** Be careful when completing this form. Errors may prevent prompt issuance of the W/P.

(a) [9:838] **Findings:** Item 3 of the form tracks the requisite findings. [See CCP §512.060(a)]

1) [9:839] **"Has" vs. "has not" box:** Unless the bond is filed at the time the order is proffered, item 3.b. should be checked "has not." The "has" box may be checked, however, if a bond was posted when a TRO issued since, unlike an injunction situation, a TRO bond also covers the subsequently issued W/P. [CCP §515.010(a)]

2) [9:840] **"Location":** Item 3.d. (probable cause re location of property) should track the information set forth on the application (¶*9:812*).

(b) [9:841] **Order:** Item 5 of the form is the order to issue the writ of possession.

1) Items 5.b. and c. are alternatives (check only one). Item 5.b. is used only when the bond already has been filed; 5.c. is used to fix the amount of a bond not yet filed.

2) Item 5.f. is the sheriff's authority to enter private real property to seize the chattel. (Be inclusive here, as the sheriff cannot enter any realty not listed.)

3) Item 5.g. is a "turnover order"—i.e., a mandatory injunction (authorized by CCP §512.070), directing defendant to surrender the chattel to the plaintiff. The order is discretionary, but is frequently used.

j. [9:842] **Undertaking:** No TRO or W/P can issue until plaintiff has filed an undertaking, running in favor of the defendant, if return of the property is ordered. [CCP §515.010(a)]

The bond requirement does not apply, however, if the court finds defendant has no interest in the property. [CCP §515.010(b); *see* ¶*9:796.5*]

(1) [9:843] **Amount:** The undertaking must be in an amount equal to twice the value of the defendant's interest in the property (market value less all liens, etc.). [CCP §515.010(a); *see* ¶*9:796*]

(2) [9:844] **Attachment to writ:** A copy of the undertaking must be attached to the W/P (presumably to facilitate a challenge to the sufficiency of the sureties by the other party).

(3) [9:845] **Corporate bond or individual sureties?** Either may be used. Corporate surety bonds are costly. But

© 2020 Thomson Reuters/The Rutter Group

they have the advantage of avoiding surety justification proceedings, which are a matter of right where individual freeholders execute the surety undertaking. [CCP §515.030]

(4) [9:846] **Justification proceedings:** "Justification" proceedings follow a party's taking exception to the surety. See CCP §515.030 and Judicial Council form CD-140.

k. [9:847] **Counterbonding:** Defendant may defeat the W/P by filing an undertaking (before or after levy) in an amount equal to that required of plaintiff (or if a bond was excused based on finding defendant has no interest in the property, in the amount specified by the court; *see* ¶*9:796.1*). [CCP §515.020(a)]

(1) [9:848] **Effect on plaintiff's rights:** Sufficient counterbonding completely thwarts plaintiff's application for possession before trial. Plaintiff must obtain a *judgment* for possession of the property after trial. [*Edwards v. Sup.Ct. (Walters)* (1991) 230 CA3d 173, 178, 281 CR 30, 32-33—defendant's filing "counterbond" excused compliance with turnover order issued in aid of writ of possession]

(2) [9:849] **Timing:** If defendant waits until after the sheriff seizes the chattel, he or she must file the bond (and give the sheriff notice thereof) within 10 days of the seizure to prevent delivery to plaintiff. [CCP §514.030(a)(1)] Once notice of the counterbond filing is given, the sheriff holds the property another 10 days (to wait out any justification proceedings) and then redelivers the property to defendant. [CCP §514.030(a)(2)]

l. **Writ of Possession**

FORM: Writ of Possession (Claim and Delivery) (CD-130).

(1) [9:850] **Issuance:** The W/P is issued by the clerk. (In the Los Angeles Superior Court, Central District, it is also *prepared* by the clerk; but other courts may require counsel to prepare the writ. Be sure to check local rules.)

(2) [9:851] **Levy:** The W/P can only be executed by the sheriff or marshal, who will require written instructions and a deposit to cover estimated costs of levy. (Costs vary, and may be high, depending on the size of the chattel.) [See CCP §§514.010-514.050 for levy procedures and time limits]

⇨ [9:852] ***PRACTICE POINTER:*** Levies posing potential practical problems should be discussed with the levying officer in advance. And of course, the client should make advance plans for what is to be done with the chattel if he or she actually gets it.

D. ATTACHMENT

[9:853] Attachment is a prejudgment remedy that allows a creditor to have a lien on the debtor's assets until final adjudication of the claim sued upon (see CCP §481.010 et seq.). The creditor must follow statutory guidelines in applying for the attachment and establish a *prima facie* claim; and the court is required to make a preliminary determination of the merits of the dispute. [*Lorber Indus. of Calif. v. Turbulence, Inc.* (1985) 175 CA3d 532, 535, 221 CR 233, 235 (citing text); *Kemp Bros. Const., Inc. v. Titan Elec. Corp.* (2007) 146 CA4th 1474, 1476, 53 CR3d 673, 674]

The following sections provide an overview of the concepts and procedures involved in obtaining a Writ of Attachment. For detailed treatment, see CCP §§481.010-493.060, and Ahart, *Cal. Prac. Guide: Enforcing Judgments & Debts* (TRG), Ch. 4.

[9:853.1] **STRATEGY CONSIDERATIONS RE ATTACHMENTS**

Advantages: Where the conditions below (¶*9:858 ff.*) are met, attachments permit an unsecured creditor (plaintiff) to become a *secured* creditor, gaining priority over defendant's other creditors. Moreover, if a plaintiff gains this advantage, defendants will often reevaluate their position, facilitating early settlement of the case.

Disadvantages: However, there are burdens and risks to consider:

- Obtaining an attachment is usually time-consuming and expensive for plaintiff, particularly if defendant vigorously resists the attempt to attach its assets;
- Attaching defendant's assets may precipitate bankruptcy or an assignment for benefit of creditors (even if defendant is solvent). If this occurs *within 90 days* after the writ is levied, the attachment lien terminates automatically and plaintiff is relegated to unsecured status. [CCP §§493.010, 493.030]
- If defendant owes federal taxes or wage claims, it may be able to defeat the attachment by arranging an IRS levy on the property plaintiff has attached or having the unpaid employees file verified preferred wage claims. (Attachment liens are *subordinate* to later-arising federal tax liens and preferred wage claims; see CCP §1206.)
- *Election of remedies?* In the past, when the *same operative facts* gave rise to both contract and tort claims (e.g., D's non-performance alleged to be both a breach of contract and fraud), plaintiff's obtaining an attachment could constitute an "election" of the contract remedy, barring later recovery on the tort claim. [See *Baker v. Sup.Ct. (San Diego Best Builders, Inc.)* (1983) 150 CA3d

© 2020 Thomson Reuters/The Rutter Group

STRATEGY CONSIDERATIONS RE ATTACHMENTS (Cont'd)

140, 145, 197 CR 480, 482—because attachment lies only on contract claims, obtaining writ of attachment "waives" alternative tort claims based on same operative facts; *and* ¶*9:861 ff.*]

However, later authority rejects this result. The operative facts underlying a tort claim are *not* the same as those underlying a contract claim. Moreover, due to procedural protections for defendants now built into the attachment law (¶*9:857.5 ff.*), "it is doubtful that the doctrine of election of remedies has any continuing viability in the attachment context." [*Waffer Int'l Corp. v. Khorsandi* (1999) 69 CA4th 1261, 1278-1279, 82 CR2d 241, 252-253]

- Where the debt is secured by a mortgage on real property, attaching the borrower's nonpledged personal assets violates the "one form of action rule" (CCP §726(a)), and forfeits the lender's right to foreclose the mortgage. [See *Shin v. Sup.Ct. (Korea First Bank)* (1994) 26 CA4th 542, 548-549, 31 CR2d 587, 591-592]
- If plaintiffs *lose* the claim on which the attachment was based, they can be sued for wrongful attachment (in addition to possible claims of malicious prosecution or abuse of process), including for all fees and costs expended (*see* ¶*9:957*).

  Indeed, even if plaintiffs *win*, they can be sued for wrongful attachment if they failed to follow the technical procedures below (¶*9:854 ff.*) (e.g., by levying on exempt property). [See CCP §490.010]

1. [9:854] **Constitutional Considerations:** Statutory procedures for attachment of property are subject to the strictures of the Fourteenth Amendment Due Process Clause. Due process generally requires a notice and hearing *prior* to seizure of property. [*Sniadach v. Family Finance Corp. of Bay View* (1969) 395 US 337, 342, 89 S.Ct. 1820, 1823]

   Due process issues thus arise in connection with *ex parte* prejudgment attachments (no preattachment hearing; *see* ¶*9:882*). To pass constitutional muster, some "*exigent circumstance*" must be shown to justify such attachments. [*Connecticut v. Doehr* (1991) 501 US 1, 17, 111 S.Ct. 2105, 2116; *Tri-State Develop., Ltd. v. Johnston* (9th Cir. 1998) 160 F3d 528, 530—bond requirement no substitute for due process]

2. [9:855] **Statutory Nature of Attachment:** As with claim and delivery, attachment is purely a statutory remedy. Note the following consequences:

   a. [9:856] **Strict construction:** The Attachment Law is subject to strict construction: i.e., unless specifically provided for by the Attachment Law, no attachment procedure may be ordered by the court. [*Pacific Decision Sciences Corp. v. Sup.Ct. (Maudlin)* (2004) 121 CA4th 1100, 1106, 18 CR3d 104, 107]

b. [9:857] **Caution:** *A thorough reading and understanding of the relevant Code sections is essential for successful attachment practice.* In short, before starting to complete the forms, the statutory attachment law must be mastered.

[9:857.1-857.4] *Reserved.*

3. [9:857.5] **Attachment Proceedings Independent of Main Action:** Attachment proceedings are "ancillary" to the main action: i.e., the issue of whether the provisional remedy of attachment shall be granted is separate and distinct from the issues in the main action. Thus, for example:

a. [9:857.6] **Findings in attachment proceedings inadmissible in main action:** The court's findings and determinations in the attachment proceedings (e.g., the existence of a contract; the amount of the claim, etc.) have *no* effect at the trial of the action, and may not be received as evidence on any issue. [CCP §484.100; see *Loeb & Loeb v. Beverly Glen Music, Inc.* (1985) 166 CA3d 1110, 1116, 212 CR 830, 834]

b. [9:857.7] **Failure to oppose attachment not waiver of defenses:** Defendant's failure to oppose issuance of an attachment does not waive any defense to plaintiff's claim in the main action (or bar later suit for wrongful attachment if defendant wins at trial). [CCP §484.110; see *Loeb & Loeb v. Beverly Glen Music, Inc.*, supra, 166 CA3d at 1116, 212 CR at 834]

Likewise, *plaintiff's* failure to rebut evidence produced by defendant in the attachment proceedings (or to oppose reduction of the amount to be secured by the writ of attachment) does not waive any defense to defendant's claim or have any evidentiary effect at the trial of the main action. [CCP §484.110(b)]

c. [9:857.8] **Stay of main action not applicable to attachment:** An attachment may be granted even where the main action has been stayed pending mandatory arbitration. The purpose of an attachment is to insure the payment of any judgment rendered in the main action. There is no justification for denying such protection while the main action is stayed. [*Loeb & Loeb v. Beverly Glen Music, Inc.*, supra, 166 CA3d at 1118, 212 CR at 835]

[9:857.9] *Reserved.*

4. [9:857.10] **Delayed Public Disclosure of Proceeding:** On filing the complaint, plaintiff may request that the proceedings not be made public for 30 days or earlier return of service on any temporary protective order (*see ¶9:885*) or ex parte writ. (But any party named in the complaint, or his or her attorney, may obtain a copy of the file.) [See CCP §482.050]

This makes it more difficult for *other creditors* to learn of the pending action, so that plaintiff may have a head-start on obtaining a lien on defendant's property.

© 2020 Thomson Reuters/The Rutter Group

To obtain this secrecy, plaintiff must file declarations stating either (1) defendant is not a natural person, and the claim is unsecured; or (2) defendant is a natural person but the claim arises out of the defendant's trade, business or profession, and any funds involved were not used primarily for personal, family or household purposes. [CRC 2.580]

a. [9:857.11] **Constitutionality?** Although the issue has never been decided, the constitutionality of the secrecy provisions of CCP §482.050 may be questioned in light of the First Amendment right of access to the courts. [*NBC Subsidiary (KNBC-TV), Inc. v. Sup.Ct. (Locke)* (1999) 20 C4th 1178, 1210, 86 CR2d 778, 803]

b. [9:857.12] **Sealed record?** A request for delayed public disclosure under CCP §482.050 does *not* require the court findings that would be required for "sealing" a court record under CRC 2.550. By its terms, CRC 2.550 does not apply to a document that must be kept "confidential by law." [CRC 2.550(a)(2)]

5. [9:858] **Substantive Requirements—Claims Subject to Attachment:** An attachment may be issued only if the claim sued upon meets the following requirements:

- A "claim or claims for money . . . based upon a *contract, express or implied*";
- Of a "*fixed or readily ascertainable amount* not less than $500";
- That is either *unsecured* or *secured by personal property*, not real property (including fixtures) (subject to exceptions; *see ¶9:867.1 ff.*); and
- That is a *commercial* claim. [CCP §483.010 (emphasis added); see *Goldstein v. Barak Const.* (2008) 164 CA4th 845, 852, 79 CR3d 603, 608 (citing text)]

a. [9:859] **Contract, express or implied:** First, the claim must be for money, and based upon an express or implied contract. [CCP §483.010(a); see *Korea Water Resources Corp. v. Lee* (2004) 115 CA4th 389, 402, 8 CR3d 853, 861, fn. 11 (disapproved on other grounds in *Manco Contracting Co. (W.L.L.) v. Bezdikian* (2008) 45 C4th 192, 203, 85 CR3d 233, 241, fn. 7)—monetary claim based on foreign judgment deemed contractual in nature]

(1) [9:860] **Quasi-contract:** "Implied contract" covers restitutionary obligations; e.g., where defendant has acquired plaintiff's property through fraud, conversion or mistake and refuses to return it. [See *Klein v. Benaron* (1967) 247 CA2d 607, 610, 56 CR 5, 6; *Goldstein v. Barak Const.*, supra, 164 CA4th at 854, 79 CR3d at 611—claim to recover payments made to unlicensed contractor is "fundamentally contractual in nature"; *Santa*

Clara Waste Water Co. v. Allied World Nat'l Assur. Co. (2017) 18 CA5th 881, 886, 227 CR3d 257, 261—unjust enrichment and rescission claims sufficient for attachment]

(2) [9:861] **Attachment as election of remedies?** *See discussion at ¶9:853.1.*

(a) [9:862] **Compare—"separate" claims:** To the extent the election of remedies doctrine remains viable in this context, it does *not* apply if the tort and contract claims are based on *separate* acts and obligations at different points in time—e.g., fraud in the inducement of a contract and later breach of that contract. [*Baker v. Sup.Ct. (San Diego Best Builders, Inc.)* (1983) 150 CA3d 140, 146, 197 CR 480, 483]

[9:863-864] *Reserved.*

b. [9:865] **Readily ascertainable amount:** The money claim must be for a "*fixed* or *readily ascertainable* amount" of not less than $500 (excluding costs, interest, and attorney fees). [CCP §483.010(a) (emphasis added)]

(1) [9:866] **Measurable from contract:** The damages need not be liquidated. But they must be measurable *by reference to the contract* itself and the basis for computing damages must be reasonable and certain. [*CIT Group/Equipment Financing, Inc. v. Super DVD, Inc.* (2004) 115 CA4th 537, 541, 8 CR3d 927, 930—master lease and corresponding lease schedules provided clear formula for computation of damages: monthly rent multiplied by unexpired term]

c. [9:867] **Not secured by real (vs. personal) property:** Attachment is allowed on claims secured by personal property or by fixtures pursuant to the Commercial Code but *not* on claims secured by an interest in *real property*. (This bar on attachment applies both to mortgage and trust deed liens and any other statutory, common law or equitable liens on real property.) [CCP §483.010(b); see *United Central Bank v. Sup.Ct. (Chang)* (2009) 179 CA4th 212, 215, 101 CR3d 395, 397—attachment proper against *guarantors* on loans secured by real property whose obligation is *independent* from that of principal debt; *Bank of America, NA v. Stonehaven Manor, LLC* (2010) 186 CA4th 719, 723, 113 CR3d 57, 60—attachment upheld where guarantor of debt secured by real property *contractually waived* benefit of security]

(1) [9:867.1] **Exceptions—attachment on certain real property secured claims:** In some cases, attachment *may* issue even though the creditor's claim is (or was) secured by real property:

© 2020 Thomson Reuters/The Rutter Group

(a) [9:867.2] **Loss or decrease in value of security:** Attachment may issue if, *through no fault of plaintiff* or the security-holder (if different from plaintiff), the real property security has (i) become *valueless* or (ii) *decreased in value* to less than the amount owing on the claim. [CCP §483.010(b); *Doyka v. Sup.Ct. (Lord)* (1991) 233 CA3d 1134, 1137, 285 CR 14, 16]

Note: A creditor of a debt secured by real property does *not* violate the "one form of action" rule by seeking a writ of attachment against *other assets* of the debtor. [CCP §483.012]

[9:867.3] ***PRACTICE POINTER:*** When claiming security is valueless, be sure to allege sufficient facts in your Application for Right to Attach Order (*see ¶9:898 ff.*).

Otherwise, the court may exclude evidence of such matters at the attachment application hearing unless "good cause" is shown. (In this event, plaintiff would lose the right to attach because it has the burden of proof on such matters; *see ¶9:946.*) [See *Bank of America v. Salinas Nissan, Inc.* (1989) 207 CA3d 260, 273, 254 CR 748, 756]

(b) [9:867.4] **Multiple obligations:** Attachment also should be proper where defendant has made several promises in an agreement, one or more of which is secured by real property, provided at least one of the other promises is unsecured or secured by personal property (including fixtures). [See CCP §483.010(b); see also *FNB Fin'l Co. v. Sup.Ct. (Kawai Piano Corp.)* (1978) 80 CA3d 927, 930, 144 CR 496, 498 (decided under former law, not involving real property security)]

- [9:867.5] **Example:** Defendant signs a financing agreement containing both a secured guaranty and an unsecured promise to repurchase accounts receivable in default. Plaintiff may obtain attachment on the basis of breach of the agreement to purchase the accounts. [*FNB Fin'l Co. v. Sup.Ct. (Kawai Piano Corp.)*, supra, 80 CA3d at 930, 144 CR at 498]

(c) [9:867.6] **Mechanic's liens:** The holder of a mechanic's lien also may obtain a writ of attachment. [See Civ.C. §8468; *San Diego Wholesale Credit Men's Ass'n v. Sup.Ct. (Int'l Hotels Const. & Mgmt., Inc.)* (1973) 35 CA3d 458, 462, 110 CR 657, 659]

d. [9:868] **Commercial claims:** Attachment lies on any claim against a partnership or corporation; or on claims against individuals that "arise out of the conduct by the *defendant* of a *trade, business or profession*." [CCP §483.010(c) (emphasis added); see *Security Pac. Nat'l Bank v. Matek* (1985) 175 CA3d 1071, 1077, 223 CR 288, 292—"section 483.010 makes no distinction between those sued individually as partners and those sued as sole proprietors"]

(1) [9:869] **Not "consumer" claims:** Attachments are *precluded in consumer transactions.* The language "trade, business or profession" in §483.010(c) effectively limits attachments to commercial dealings. [*Kadison, Pfaelzer, Woodard, Quinn & Rossi v. Wilson* (1987) 197 CA3d 1, 4, 242 CR 595, 597—attorneys representing trustees in actions involving trust property were involved in "commercial," not "consumer" transactions; moreover, a trust is *not* a "natural person" exempt from prejudgment attachment]

Cross-refer: See further discussion in Ahart, *Cal. Prac. Guide: Enforcing Judgments & Debts* (TRG), Ch. 4.

e. [9:870] **Compare—special rule for nonresident attachments:** An attachment may also issue in actions against nonresident individuals or foreign corporations or partnerships not qualified to do business here. In such case, the attachment can be based on *any* monetary claim (not just contract claims). [CCP §492.010]

Such attachments are particularly useful in interstate and international commercial disputes where the debtor defendant may not be subject to personal jurisdiction in California but has significant assets here (including monies owed to it by companies located here).

However, if the nonresident defendant makes a personal appearance in the action, the attachment may be lifted. If so, plaintiff's attachment rights will revert to those discussed above (¶*9:858 ff.*). [CCP §492.050; see *Nakasone v. Randall* (1982) 129 CA3d 757, 760-763, 181 CR 324, 326-328—right to attach order had to be set aside when nonresident appeared because the claim against her did not arise out of a trade, business or profession]

(1) [9:871] **Constitutionality?** The Code provisions for nonresident attachments were drafted before the U.S. Supreme Court's decision in *Shaffer v. Heitner* (1977) 433 US 186, 207, 97 S.Ct. 2569, 2581. These provisions might now be considered overbroad and insufficient to support the minimum contacts required for jurisdictional purposes. [*See* ¶*3:360 ff.*; compare *Nakasone v. Randall* (1982) 129 CA3d 757, 760-761, 181 CR 324,

© 2020 Thomson Reuters/The Rutter Group

326 (contrasting personal jurisdiction with the *in rem* jurisdiction obtained by nonresident attachment procedures)]

[9:871.1-871.9] *Reserved.*

f. [9:871.10] **Compare—financial abuse of elder or dependent adult:** An attachment may be issued in an action for damages under Welf. & Inst.C. §15657.5 against a defendant for *financial abuse* of an elder or dependent adult, whether or not any other relief is demanded. [Welf. & Inst.C. §15657.01]

6. [9:872] **Property Subject to Attachment:** *All* property within California held by a *corporation, partnership or unincorporated association* is subject to attachment if there is a statutory method of levy for the property (¶*9:876*). [CCP §487.010(a), (b)]

a. [9:873] **Compare—property held in trust:** Property held in trust is subject to attachment in an action based on contract entered into by the trustees. [*Kadison, Pfaelzer, Woodard, Quinn & Rossi v. Wilson* (1987) 197 CA3d 1, 4, 242 CR 595, 597]

b. [9:874] **Compare—property exempt from execution:** All property exempt from execution is also exempt from attachment. And so are the defendant's *wages* and *any other property "necessary for support"* of defendant or his or her family. [CCP §487.020]

Cross-refer: Exempt property is listed in CCP §704.010 et seq. See detailed discussion in Ahart, *Cal. Prac. Guide: Enforcing Judgments & Debts* (TRG), Ch. 6.

⇨ [9:875] ***PRACTICE POINTER:*** It is *not* enough for defendant merely to submit a declaration stating that the property is "necessary for support" of his or her family. Defendant's claim of exemption must include a *financial statement* meeting the requirements of CCP §703.530 (detailing earnings of all members of family, list of assets and obligations, etc.).

(1) [9:875.1] **May be exempt by agreement:** When an agreement provides that certain categories of assets are exempt from a personal guaranty, the parties' contract will be enforced. [*Series AGI West Linn of Appian Group Investors DE, LLC v. Eves* (2013) 217 CA4th 156, 163-164, 158 CR3d 193, 199-200]

But *proceeds from the sale* of such assets are *not* exempt unless the contract so states. [*Series AGI West Linn of Appian Group Investors DE, LLC v. Eves,* supra, 217 CA4th at 169, 158 CR3d at 204]

c. [9:876] **Method of levy:** The Code specifies the precise method of levy of attachment on different types of property. [See CCP §§488.300-488.485]

Note: *No property* (corporate, partnership, or individual) *may be attached unless the code provides a method of levy for that type of property.* [CCP §§487.010, 487.020(d)]

7. [9:877] **Procedural Requirements:** The requirements for obtaining a writ of attachment are:

- the *claim* upon which the attachment is based is one upon which an attachment may issue (*¶9:858 ff.*);
- plaintiff has established the *probable validity* of the claim (*see ¶9:947 ff.*);
- the attachment is not sought for a *purpose* other than recovery of the claim upon which the attachment is based; and
- the amount to be secured by the attachment is greater than zero. [CCP §484.090(a); see *California Retail Portfolio Fund GmbH & Co. KG v. Hopkins Real Estate Group* (2011) 193 CA4th 849, 856, 122 CR3d 614, 619, fn. 3]

[9:878-879] *Reserved.*

a. [9:880] **Right to attach order:** No W/A may issue without a Right to Attach Order (RTAO). In a sense, it is a sort of "declaratory relief" order, determining for purposes of the action that plaintiff's claim is one for which a W/A may issue then or later. The order is based on a finding that the substantive prerequisites for an attachment exist and that plaintiff will probably prevail in the action. [See CCP §§484.010, 484.050 & 484.090]

(1) [9:881] **After noticed hearing:** An RTAO may be issued after notice and hearing. [CCP §484.040; *see ¶9:914 ff.*]

(2) [9:882] **Ex parte RTAO:** An RTAO or writ of attachment may issue without notice if "it appears from facts shown by affidavit that *great or irreparable injury* would result to the plaintiff if issuance of the order were delayed until the matter could be heard on notice." [CCP §485.010(a) (emphasis added); see *California Retail Portfolio Fund GmbH & Co. KG v. Hopkins Real Estate Group,* supra, 193 CA4th at 857-858, 122 CR3d at 621]

(a) [9:883] **Constitutional limitation:** A showing of "great or irreparable injury" satisfies the due process of law requirement that an "exigent circumstance" exist to justify attachment of property without prior notice or hearing (*see ¶9:854*).

(b) [9:884] **"Great or irreparable injury" inferred:** "Great or irreparable injury" is inferred where *plaintiff's declarations show*:

1) [9:884.1] *Danger of property loss:* The property sought to be attached may be "concealed, substantially impaired in value, or otherwise made unavailable to levy." [See CCP §485.010(b)(1)]

© 2020 Thomson Reuters/The Rutter Group

2) [9:884.2] *Certain asset transfers pending:* A *bulk sales* notice has been recorded and published; or an escrow has been opened for sale of defendant's *liquor license*. [See CCP §485.010(b)(3), (4)]

3) [9:884.3] *Defendant insolvent:* Defendant has failed to pay the debt on which the attachment is based *and* is "insolvent" in the bankruptcy sense (general failure to pay *undisputed* debts as they become due in ordinary course of business). [See CCP §485.010(b)(2); see also *California Retail Portfolio Fund GmbH & Co. KG v. Hopkins Real Estate Group*, supra, 193 CA4th at 859-860, 122 CR3d at 622-623]

If the court issues an ex parte writ, defendant may demand a hearing on whether it is "insolvent." The hearing must be held within 5 court days after plaintiff is served with notice of the demand. [CCP §485.010(c)]

[9:884.4-884.9] *Reserved.*

[9:884.10] ***PRACTICE POINTER:*** If you seek an ex parte RTAO, prepare a *separate declaration* showing "great and irreparable" injury to the plaintiff. The court will want to determine this question before considering the merits of your application.

However, don't count on obtaining an ex parte RTAO. They are *rarely* issued (except in cases involving liquor license or bulk sale escrows; *see* ¶*9:884.2*).

On the other hand, courts usually are more willing to grant ex parte temporary protective orders (TPOs); *see* ¶*9:885*. Thus, if you apply for an ex parte RTAO, be sure to include a request for TPO *in the alternative*.

If you represent defendant and a TPO seems likely, be prepared to *propose alternative orders or terms* to make sure the obligations of the TPO are not too onerous for your client.

b. [9:885] **Temporary Protective Order:** As with the claim and delivery law, "temporary protective orders" (TPO) are used to maintain the status quo, where necessary, pending the hearing. (TPOs are no different than TROs, despite the difference in terminology.)

c. [9:886] **"All-purpose" hearing:** CCP §484.090 contemplates one hearing where all of the issues may be thrashed out at once. Thus, the initial noticed hearing can resolve, *inter alia:*

(1) Whether plaintiff has a right to attach, in general;

(2) Whether plaintiff may attach particular property;

(3) Whether plaintiff will probably prevail in the action;

(4) Whether an individual defendant has a right to exemption as to certain property.

d. [9:887] **Exemption claims:** Exemptions are available only to natural persons, not business entities. The defendant must file and serve on plaintiff a written claim of exemption (supported by declarations) at least 5 court days before the hearing. Failure to do so constitutes a *waiver* of any otherwise available exemptions for personal property described in plaintiff's application. [CCP §484.070(a), (e)] (However, a later claim of exemption may be based on changed circumstances; see CCP §482.100.)

(1) [9:888] **Compare—real property:** But the waiver applies only to *personal* property exemptions. Failure to claim a homestead or dwelling house exemption at the time of the hearing does *not* affect the owner's right to assert the exemption later. [CCP §484.070(a); and see *Martin v. Aboyan* (1983) 148 CA3d 826, 831, 196 CR 266, 270]

(2) [9:889] **Claim re other exempt property:** A defendant may also (but is not required to) obtain a declaration that other assets *not listed* by the plaintiff are exempt from attachment. [CCP §484.070(b)]

(3) [9:890] **Supporting declarations required:** A bare claim of exemption, without evidentiary support, will usually fail in the face of written opposition. Supporting declarations must adequately identify the property claimed exempt, and state whatever foundational facts are necessary to establish the exemption as a matter of law. [CCP §484.070(c)]

[9:891-894] *Reserved.*

8. [9:895] **Procedure to Obtain RTAO and Writ of Attachment:** As with the claim and delivery statutes, the Legislature directed the Judicial Council to promulgate forms to implement the attachment law. [CCP §482.030]

[9:895.1] ***PRACTICE POINTER:*** The Judicial Council optional forms track the complex requirements of the attachment law and thus are themselves complex. *Do not attempt to use these forms* without first reading the statutes that they implement.

a. [9:896] **Complaint:** The action is started by filing a complaint—a prerequisite to application for a W/A. [CCP §484.010]

© 2020 Thomson Reuters/The Rutter Group

(1) [9:897] **Verified complaint as affidavit:** A verified complaint, if it states evidentiary facts, may be used in lieu of or in addition to an affidavit. [CCP §482.040]

Exception: A verified complaint by a *corporation* (signed by corporation, verified by a corporate officer on information and belief) "shall *not* . . . be considered as an affidavit or declaration establishing the facts therein alleged." [CCP §446(a) (emphasis added); *Lorber Indus. of Calif. v. Turbulence, Inc.* (1985) 175 CA3d 532, 536, 221 CR 233, 236 (citing text)]

b. **Application for RTAO and W/A**

FORM: Application for Right to Attach Order, Temporary Protective Order, Etc. (Attachment) (AT-105). (Note: This is a multipurpose form, designed for initial applications, subsequent applications, ex parte or noticed hearings, and TPOs.)

See Form 9B:22 in Rivera, *Cal. Prac. Guide: Civ. Pro. Before Trial FORMS* (TRG).

(1) [9:898] **Title of document; boxes:** In the title (top part of form), check only the boxes pertaining to the procedures intended to be used.

(2) [9:899] **Item 1:** Item 1 is used to designate what the application is for. Item 1.d. pertains to "turnover orders" (i.e., to deliver property to the levying officer). [See CCP §482.080]

(a) [9:899.1] **Property subject to turnover:** The only types of property that can be the subject of a turnover order are:

— tangible personal property in the debtor's control or possession, which includes chattel paper, instruments, negotiable documents and certain types of securities; and

— documentary evidence of title to property or of a debt owed to defendant (e.g., an automobile's "pink slip" or a negotiable instrument). [See CCP §482.080(a); *Pacific Decision Sciences Corp. v. Sup.Ct. (Maudlin)* (2004) 121 CA4th 1100, 1108-1109, 18 CR3d 104, 109-110]

(b) [9:899.2] **Compare—intangibles:** Bank accounts and accounts receivable (intangibles) are attached by service of the writ on the bank or account debtor, not by taking any property into custody. [CCP §§488.455(a), 488.470(a); *Pacific Decision Sciences Corp. v. Sup.Ct. (Maudlin)*, supra, 121 CA4th at 1109, 18 CR3d at 110]

(3) [9:900] **Item 2:** Item 2 calls for the capacity of defendant (corporation, partnership, etc.), which determines the scope of the W/A.

[9:901] ***PRACTICE POINTER:*** If you plan to attach assets held in the name of an "a.k.a.," or "d.b.a.," be sure to provide *supporting declarations* containing facts showing that the defendant is so known or is the same person that owns the property.

[9:901.1-901.4] *Reserved.*

(4) [9:901.5] **Item 3:** Check "Code of Civil Procedure section 483.010" for attachments involving claims *other than* those alleging financial abuse of an elder or dependent adult. The conditions for qualifying for a writ of attachment under CCP §483.010 are spelled out in item 6a.

For attachments in connection with claims of financial abuse of an elder or dependent adult, check "Welfare and Institutions Code section 15657.01." The conditions for qualifying for a writ of attachment under this statute are spelled out in item 6b.

(5) [9:902] **Items 4 and 5:** Items 4 and 5 are statutory requirements and typically do not require additional comment. Any potential issue regarding these items should be the subject of a proper evidentiary showing in attached declarations or discussion in additional points and authorities.

[9:903] *Reserved.*

(6) [9:904] **Item 6:** Item 6 is completed if the claim is against an individual. It should not be completed if defendant is a partnership or corporation.

Item 6a. should be checked for *all claims* other than financial abuse of an elder or dependent adult. Item 6b. should be checked for the latter claims.

[9:905] ***PRACTICE POINTERS:*** If you check the box claiming that the defendant is engaged in a business, trade or profession, you *must* attach supporting declarations showing:

— That the defendant is in fact so engaged; and

— That the claim sued upon arose out of that business, trade or profession (so as to render defendant personally liable for the debt; *see ¶9:868*).

- Without such declarations, invoices or billings to the defendant's trade or business name by themselves will *not* support an RTAO.
- Example: The complaint alleges defendant, John Jones, is "doing business under the

© 2020 Thomson Reuters/The Rutter Group

fictitious name, XYZ Co." But all the billings are simply to "XYZ Co." To obtain an RTAO, you will need supporting declarations showing that John Jones is the owner of "XYZ Co." (e.g., business licenses, leases, etc. in Jones' name); *and* that the debt was incurred in connection with his business operations.

- Likewise, allegations that the debtor's *spouse* is also engaged in the "trade, business or profession" are often insufficient as a matter of law. There have to be additional allegations to show co-ownership, agency, etc.
- Moreover, don't expect to obtain an RTAO against an individual based solely on allegations that he or she is an "officer" or "shareholder" of the business entity that incurred the debt. There would have to be allegations sufficient to establish alter ego liability as a matter of law (very hard to do).
- Even allegations that the defendant "guaranteed" the debt of the business entity may not support an RTAO against an individual defendant. There would have to be additional proof that the defendant executed the guarantee *in connection with* his or her business, occupation or profession. [See *Advance Transformer Co. v. Sup.Ct. (Shapiro)* (1974) 44 CA3d 127, 143-144, 118 CR 350, 361]

(7) [9:906] **Item 7:** Check whichever box is applicable (i.e., "verified complaint" or "attached affidavit or declaration" or "following facts").

[9:906.1] ***PRACTICE POINTER:*** Checking the third box under item 7 ("following facts") can be problematic because there is not enough room in the small area provided to include many facts. Because you must provide evidence sufficient to *prove* the amount you are entitled to recover, it is usually better to check the second box ("attached affidavit or declaration") and prepare and attach separate declarations (*see ¶9:912*).

(8) [9:907] **Item 8:** Fill in the amounts and check the boxes for estimated costs and fees as applicable.

[9:907.1] ***PRACTICE POINTER:*** Be sure to include the *exact amount* claimed to be due. The court won't do mathematical calculations for you.

If you are claiming accrued *interest*, your supporting declaration must include a breakdown as between principal and interest, and show your calculations in computing the amount shown as the interest due.

Likewise, if *attorney fees* are being claimed (e.g., pursuant to contract), you must allege facts in your declaration showing the work performed and the amounts claimed to be due (consult local court rules as to amounts allowable; e.g., L.A. Sup.Ct. Rule 3.214).

(9) [9:908] **Item 9:** The first box should be checked if the action is against a corporation or partnership; the second, if against a nonresident defendant. (No need to identify the property to be attached.)

The third box is checked if the action is against an individual defendant. But here, the property to be attached *must* be identified. Plaintiff must describe the property *and* cite the statute under which levy may be made. The writ will issue only for the items so identified. [See CCP §484.020]

(a) [9:909] **General vs. specific description:** Where defendant is a corporation or partnership, the attachment application may simply request attachment of all corporate or partnership property subject to attachment pursuant to CCP §487.010. [CCP §484.020(e)]

But where defendant is a *natural person*, "the description of the property *shall be reasonably adequate to permit the defendant to identify the specific property* sought to be attached." [CCP §484.020(e) (emphasis added)]

1) [9:909.1] **Purpose:** This is to enable an individual defendant to determine whether to file a claim of exemption. I.e., if the application describes only nonexempt property, a claim of exemption is unnecessary; and court hearings are avoided. [*Bank of America v. Salinas Nissan, Inc.* (1989) 207 CA3d 260, 268, 254 CR 748, 753]

2) [9:909.2] **All-inclusive categories sufficient:** An overly inclusive description in the attachment application does *not* invalidate it: "We do not understand [the requirement of specificity] to prohibit a plaintiff from *targeting for attachment everything an individual defendant owns* . . . [CCP §484.020(e)] allows for the possibility that a plaintiff may want to make such a comprehensive attempt, possibly in order to

© 2020 Thomson Reuters/The Rutter Group

provoke and resolve an individual defendant's exemption claims all at once." [*Bank of America v. Salinas Nissan, Inc.*, supra, 207 CA3d at 267-268, 254 CR at 753 (emphasis added)]

a) [9:909.3] **Example:** P applied to attach "real property, personal property, equipment, motor vehicles, chattel paper, negotiable and other instruments, securities, deposit accounts, safe deposit boxes, accounts receivable, general intangibles, property subject to pending actions, final money judgments, and personalty in estates of decedents." This was a sufficient description to support an order granting the right to attach *whatever assets* defendant owned that fell in those *categories*. [*Bank of America v. Salinas Nissan, Inc.*, supra, 207 CA3d at 267-268, 254 CR at 753]

b) [9:909.4] **Effect:** *Bank of America v. Salinas Nissan* is the first case interpreting the description requirement of §484.020(e). It drastically changes the burden in attachment proceedings: The attaching creditor does not have to "telegraph" its punches by stating in the application for RTAO what property it proposes to attach. It can simply list each of the *categories* of attachable assets set forth in CCP §487.010(c). This *forces defendant to identify* whatever property he or she intends to claim as exempt; and, unless defendant does so, the claim of exemption may be waived (CCP §484.070).

Thus, the first *specific* description of the assets to be attached may not appear until a *writ of attachment* form is completed (*see ¶9:959*), which is usually *after* the RTAO is issued.

c) [9:909.5] **Comment:** Due process challenges may be raised, however. Arguably, failure to identify the *specific* property to be attached *before* seizure may deprive a defendant of the prior notice and hearing required under *Sniadach v. Family Finance Corp. of Bay View* (1969) 395 US 337, 342, 89 S.Ct. 1820, 1823.

(10) [9:910] **Item 11:** Item 11 is used where an RTAO has already been obtained, and a further W/A is requested.

(11) [9:911] **Item 13:** Item 13 is used where an ex parte W/A and RTAO is sought, or where a TPO is sought.

An ex parte RTAO and W/A requires allegation of *facts* showing irreparable injury (usually on an attached declaration). [CCP §485.010(a)]

For the TPO, however, irreparable injury may be shown on information and belief. [CCP §486.010(b)]

[9:912] ***PRACTICE POINTERS RE DECLARATIONS GENERALLY:*** Various sections of the Official Form make reference to the "verified complaint" or "attached affidavits." Here are some suggestions:

- First, do NOT rely on a verified complaint to allege the facts necessary to obtain an RTAO. The reason is that an attachment order must be based on *evidentiary* facts, not the ultimate facts as usually set forth in your pleadings.

  For example, your complaint may allege that defendant "became indebted to plaintiff in the sum of $ . . . for goods, wares and merchandise delivered." But these are *not* evidentiary facts. You need proof of the dates, amounts, place of delivery, types of merchandise, etc. If documentary evidence is involved (promissory note, purchase orders, ledger sheets, etc.), a proper foundation has to be laid; but copies are admissible unless a "genuine issue" is raised as to material terms of the original or it would be "unfair" to admit the copy in lieu of the original. [Ev.C. §§1270-1272, 1400-1454, 1521]

  Also, a verified complaint cannot support an application for an RTAO where the *plaintiff* is a *corporation*. This is because CCP §446 *prohibits* use of a complaint verified on information and belief by an officer of a corporate plaintiff to be used in an evidentiary hearing.

- *Caution:* Declarations in support of an application for RTAO must be admissible. Further, conclusory or generalized statements do not suffice. The Code requires that the facts stated in each affidavit "be set forth *with particularity*"; and, except as to matters that may be stated on information and belief, "that the affiant, if sworn as a witness, can testify *competently* to the facts stated therein." [CCP §482.040 (emphasis added)]

  Therefore, make sure your declarations are executed by someone with *personal knowledge* of the facts stated; and contain a *detailed* account of the transaction. In general, your declarations should comply with the standards required on a Motion for Summary Judgment (*see* ¶*10:107 ff.*).

© 2020 Thomson Reuters/The Rutter Group

Don't count on being able to remedy "gaps" in your declarations by filing supplemental declarations. You may not have time to do so. CCP §484.040 requires service of the application *and any supporting papers* at least 16 court days before the hearing (extended for service by mail under CCP §1005(b), *see* ¶*9:87*). Therefore, most courts refuse to consider plaintiff's "supplemental" declarations or "reply" papers filed after the time limit for service of the original papers.

To remedy defective declarations, you can ask the court to receive additional evidence at the hearing. But "good cause" must be shown (and if additional evidence is allowed, defendant would almost certainly be entitled to a continuance). [See CCP §484.090(d)]

Alternatively, you could request a continuance of the hearing for the purpose of serving supplemental declarations.

- Make sure the declaration is signed and verified correctly. [CCP §2015.5]

[9:913] ***PRACTICE POINTERS RE SIGNATURE AND VERIFICATION:*** Mistakes are frequently made as to signatures of *corporate* plaintiffs. The Application must be *signed* by the corporation itself ("XYZ Corp. by John Jones, President"). But, it must be *verified* by an *individual* ("John Jones" . . . *not* "John Jones, President" or "XYZ Corp. by John Jones").

If the person signing the Application is someone other than the officer signing on behalf of the corporation, a separate declaration is required to explain why such person has personal knowledge and the signing officer does not.

An attorney should *not* verify an Application for RTAO unless he or she has personal knowledge of *every* fact in the Application (a rare event).

c. **Notice**

(1) [9:914] **Form of notice:** Notice of the application and hearing must be given on the following form:

FORM: Notice of Application and Hearing for Right to Attach Order and Writ of Attachment (Attachment) (AT-115), *see Form 9B:23* in Rivera, *Cal. Prac. Guide: Civ. Pro. Before Trial FORMS* (TRG).

(a) [9:914.1] **Notice:** Consult local rules to verify the department in which to notice the hearing.

In some courts, attachment matters are heard on law and motion calendars; in others, by the direct calendar judge to whom the case is assigned.

In still others, attachment hearings are assigned to special departments (for example, in Los Angeles Superior Court, Central District, Depts. 82, 85 and 86).

[9:914.2-914.5] *Reserved.*

(b) [9:914.6] **Item 4:** *See discussion at ¶9:902.*

(c) [9:915] **Item 6:** Plaintiff has the burden of giving defendant the required information (and of checking the appropriate boxes to do so).

(d) [9:915.1] **Item 6h:** The notice must also inform defendant that the *amount* to be secured by attachment will be determined by CCP §§482.110, 483.010, 483.015 and 483.020, "which statutes shall be summarized in the notice." [CCP §484.050(c)]

(2) [9:916] **Service and proof of service:** *Prior to the hearing date (¶9:917 ff.)*, plaintiff must serve defendant with the summons, complaint and all moving papers for attachment.

(a) [9:917] **Amount of notice required:** Notice of the RTAO hearing must be served on defendant at least 16 court days before the hearing. [CCP §§484.040, 1005(a)(1) & (b)]

If the required papers are served by *mail* or substitute service, the notice period is *increased* as provided by statute. [See CCP §§1005(b), 415.20; *and ¶9:87.1*]

(b) [9:918] **Proof of service filing deadline:** A proof of service must be filed with the court clerk at least *5 court days* before the hearing. [CRC 3.1300; *see ¶9:100*] (A separate proof of service is required; the attachment forms do not have space for a proof of service.)

[9:918.1] ***PRACTICE POINTER:*** Bring an extra copy of the proof of service to the hearing just in case the proof of service filed in the clerk's office or electronically does not make it to the courtroom in time for the hearing.

d. Ex parte applications for RTAO and W/A

FORMS: Ex Parte Right to Attach Order and Order for Issuance of Writ of Attachment (Resident) (Attachment) (AT-125); (Nonresident) (Attachment) (AT-130).

(1) [9:919] **Use of forms:** The ex parte forms are self-explanatory. In each case, findings must be made (item

2). Counsel should understand the significance of the various findings, keeping in mind that the form is for multi-purpose use and only appropriate boxes should be checked. The order (item 3) is largely devoted to items applicable only to individuals. Item 3.c. is a "turnover order."

(2) [9:920] **Procedure:** Applications for ex parte RTAO and W/A should be made during ex parte hours.

Ex parte RTAOs are rarely issued. Counsel will have to convince the court that a TPO will not do as well.

Ordinarily, a showing of "great or irreparable injury" sufficient to justify an ex parte RTAO will excuse notice to opposing counsel that ex parte relief is being sought. [CRC 3.1204(b)(3); see *Datig v. Dove Books, Inc.* (1999) 73 CA4th 964, 976, 87 CR2d 719, 728 (superseded by rule on other grounds)]

However, if prior notice is not given to opposing counsel, and it appears such notice would not likely cause great or irreparable harm, counsel may be required to give telephone notice and return on the next court day. (This is often the case where the assets to be attached could not easily be concealed or disbursed overnight.)

The moral, however, is this: When in doubt, give appropriate notice to opposing counsel *before* seeking an ex parte RTAO.

(3) [9:921] **No appellate review of whether ex parte relief necessary:** The debtor may not challenge whether the RTAO should have been issued ex parte. [CCP §485.240(b)—"It shall not be grounds to set aside an order that the plaintiff would not have suffered great or irreparable injury . . . if issuance of the order had been delayed until the matter could have been heard on notice"]

[9:922] *Reserved.*

(4) [9:923] **Terminating ex parte RTAO and W/A:** Upon noticed motion, an ex parte RTAO can be set aside and the W/A quashed, and any property levied upon ordered released. [CCP §485.240(a)]

Defendant can use this procedure to claim the property levied upon is exempt, or to challenge the facts or legal basis upon which the attachment was issued. (Note, however, that defendant *cannot* challenge an ex parte RTAO on the ground that plaintiff would not have suffered "great or irreparable injury" if the order had been delayed until after a noticed hearing.) [CCP §485.240(b)]

FORM: Application to Set Aside Right to Attach Order and Release Attached Property, Etc. (AT-170). (Note:

© 2020 Thomson Reuters/The Rutter Group

This form also can be used to reduce the attachment allowed against a nonresident defendant to the type allowed against a resident defendant by defendant's making a general appearance.)

(a) [9:924] **Comment:** The motion to set aside a RTAO is available only for *ex parte* RTAOs. There is no equivalent procedure available for setting aside a RTAO or writ of attachment issued after noticed hearing.

e. **Temporary Protective Orders**

FORM: Temporary Protective Order (Attachment) (AT-140), *see Form 9B:24* in Rivera, *Cal. Prac. Guide: Civ. Pro. Before Trial FORMS* (TRG).

(1) [9:925] **Procedure:** Prepare the TPO in advance and present it with the application (which must state grounds for a TPO) during ex parte hours, after notice. (Consult local rules for the time and place of hearing.)

[9:926] ***PRACTICE POINTER:*** *Many* judges are *reluctant* to grant an ex parte RTAO where a TPO is sufficient to *preserve the status quo.* This is so even though the showings for a RTAO and TPO are the same. Therefore, if you are requesting an ex parte RTAO, prepare a TPO as an *alternative* in the event the ex parte RTAO request is denied.

(2) [9:927] **Lien created by TPO:** As a practical matter, a TPO may be just as effective as a W/A. Service of the TPO upon defendant creates a lien upon his or her property described therein (provided it is otherwise subject to attachment). [CCP §486.110; see *Profile Structures, Inc. v. Long Beach Building Material Co.* (1986) 181 CA3d 437, 443, 226 CR 192, 195—failure to serve TPO prevented creation of lien and barred enforcement by contempt]

[9:928] ***PRACTICE POINTER:*** In dealing with real property, be sure to include in the TPO both the street address and the *legal description* of the property. Recording the TPO in the county recorder's office will give constructive notice of the lien and effectively prevent defendant from selling or transferring the property while the TPO remains in effect.

(3) [9:929] **Termination of TPO:** The Code authorizes termination or modification of a TPO by *ex parte* application, unless the court orders a noticed hearing. [CCP §486.100] (Compare: Termination of a W/A cannot be made by ex parte application; ¶*9:923.*)

© 2020 Thomson Reuters/The Rutter Group

FORMS

- Application and Notice of Hearing for Order to Terminate, Modify or Vacate Temporary Protective Order (AT-145).
- Order to Terminate, Modify or Vacate Temporary Protective Order (AT-150).

f. **Opposing the RTAO, W/A or claiming exemptions**

FORM: Notice of Opposition to Right to Attach Order and Claim of Exemption (AT-155), *see Form 9B:25* in Rivera, *Cal. Prac. Guide: Civ. Pro. Before Trial FORMS* (TRG).

(1) [9:930] **Nature of opposition:** The opposition may consist of challenges to the factual or legal basis of the claim upon which attachment is sought, or an asserted offset, or claim of exemption. [See CCP §484.060(a); *Goldstein v. Barak Const.* (2008) 164 CA4th 845, 852, 79 CR3d 603, 608]

(a) [9:931] **Offset:** Defendant may challenge the amount to be secured by W/A by showing that:

- A money judgment held by defendant against plaintiff remains unsatisfied;
- A cross-complaint based on an attachable claim has been filed against plaintiff;
- An attachable claim has been asserted as a defense in the answer pursuant to CCP §431.70; or
- Plaintiff holds a *nonattachable* security interest in defendant's property, and/or the underlying security has been devalued through plaintiff's acts (or those of the security-holder if different from plaintiff). [CCP §483.015(b)]

Comment: Of course, the mere fact defendant *claims* an offset does not necessarily defeat plaintiff's Application for a RTAO. The court has the power to determine disputed factual issues in an attachment proceeding; *see* ¶*9:948*.

(b) [9:932] **Claim of exemption:** Any claim of exemption as to the property sought to be attached may be asserted in the opposition papers *or separately*. But if not timely asserted, it is waived. [See CCP §§484.060(b), 484.070(a)] (However, a later claim of exemption may be based on changed circumstances; see CCP §482.100.)

Defendant may also seek a declaration of exemption as to property *other* than that described in the RTAO. [CCP §484.070(b)]

(2) [9:933] **Evidentiary requirements:** The same requirements of *evidentiary* facts are required to oppose an Application for RTAO as to support it (*see* ¶*9:912*).

(a) [9:934] Defendant's *verified* cross-complaint may be used as an affidavit of matters therein alleged (CCP §482.040), *except* if defendant is a *corporation*. [CCP §446; *Lorber Indus. of Calif. v. Turbulence, Inc.* (1985) 175 CA3d 532, 536, 221 CR 233, 236 (citing text)]

(b) [9:935] Also, if defendant claims an *offset* (to reduce or eliminate the claim subject to attachment), verified pleadings are usually too general and conclusionary to establish the offset. Instead, defendant should produce detailed, factual declarations showing the nature and extent of the claimed offset.

(c) [9:936] The same evidentiary requirements also apply to claims of exemption. [CCP §484.070(d) (often overlooked)]

(3) [9:937] **Time limit re opposition papers:** Any opposition (which may include claims of exemption, *see* ¶*9:932*) must be served *at least 5 court days before the hearing*. Otherwise, defendant will not be permitted to oppose issuance of the RTAO and W/A. [CCP §484.060(a)]

(a) [9:938] **Waived if no objection:** However, the time limit is not jurisdictional. Therefore, if plaintiff fails to object, the court may consider late-filed opposition papers. [*Lorber Indus. of Calif. v. Turbulence, Inc.* (1985) 175 CA3d 532, 534, 221 CR 233, 235, fn. 2]

(4) [9:939] **Time limit re claims of exemption:** As stated above (¶*9:932*), a claim of exemption may be filed separately from the opposition papers. In that event, it must be filed and served on plaintiff at least 5 court days before the hearing date. [CCP §484.070(e)]

g. **Plaintiff's reply to defendant's opposition or claim of exemption**

(1) [9:940] **Time limit for reply papers:** Plaintiff may file and serve a reply to defendant's opposition *2 court days* before the hearing date. [CCP §484.060(c)]

(2) [9:941] **Plaintiff's opposition to defendant's claim of exemption:** If plaintiff desires to contest any of the exemptions claimed by defendant, he or she must file and serve a "Notice of Opposition to Claim of Exemption," together with declarations supporting any factual issues and points and authorities on any legal issues showing the property is not exempt. Failure to serve and

© 2020 Thomson Reuters/The Rutter Group

file such notice waives plaintiff's right to contest the exemption. [CCP §484.070(f)]

(a) [9:942] **Time limit:** The statute says such notice must be served and filed "not less than two days" before the hearing date. [CCP §484.070(f)]

Comment: This probably means *two court days* before the hearing, the deadline for *reply papers* (CCP §484.060(c); *see* ¶*9:940*). Although the statutes are worded differently, it seems doubtful that a different deadline was intended for oppositions to claims of exemption.

☞ [9:943] ***CAUTION:*** This is a real malpractice trap for plaintiffs' lawyers: A writ of attachment cannot issue against property claimed to be exempt unless such Notice of Opposition is *timely* filed. Thus, if defendant has claimed exemptions as to *all* property listed on plaintiff's Application, and plaintiff fails to file a timely Notice of Opposition, no RTAO hearing can be held, and any temporary protective order automatically expires. [CCP §484.070(f)]

[9:944] *Reserved.*

h. **Hearing and order; undertaking**

FORM: Right to Attach Order After Hearing and Order for Issuance of Writ of Attachment (Attachment) (AT-120), *see Form 9B:26* in Rivera, *Cal. Prac. Guide: Civ. Pro. Before Trial FORMS* (TRG).

(1) [9:945] **Hearing:** Conduct of the hearing is similar to that on any motion matter; i.e., the matter ordinarily will be decided on declarations alone (although the court has discretion to receive oral testimony). [CCP §484.090(d); see *Loeb & Loeb v. Beverly Glen Music, Inc.* (1985) 166 CA3d 1110, 1120, 212 CR 830, 837]

In courts having court commissioners, the hearing may be before a court commissioner (except that a contested claim of exemption must be before a judge unless the parties stipulate otherwise). [CCP §482.060; see *Loeb & Loeb v. Beverly Glen Music, Inc.*, supra, 166 CA3d at 1121, 212 CR at 837]

(a) [9:946] **Burden of proof on plaintiff:** To obtain a RTAO, the plaintiff has the burden of proving:

- That the claim is one on which an attachment may be issued (¶*9:858*);
- The *probable validity* of such claim; and
- That the attachment is not sought for any purpose

other than to secure recovery on the claim. [CCP §484.090; see *Loeb & Loeb v. Beverly Glen Music, Inc.*, supra, 166 CA3d at 1116, 212 CR at 834; *Chino Comm'l Bank, N.A. v. Peters* (2010) 190 CA4th 1163, 1169, 118 CR3d 866, 870-871]

1) [9:947] **"Probable validity" of claim:** A claim has "probable validity" where "it is more likely than not that the plaintiff will obtain a judgment against the defendant on that claim." [CCP §481.190; see *Santa Clara Waste Water Co. v. Allied World Nat'l Assur. Co.* (2017) 18 CA5th 881, 885, 227 CR3d 257, 260]

2) [9:947.1] **Burden where security given has become worthless:** An attachment may issue where security originally given for the debt has become worthless through no fault of the attaching creditor (CCP §483.010(b); *see ¶9:867.2*).

In such cases, it is plaintiff's burden to prove (1) the security has diminished in value and (2) plaintiff was not responsible for the diminution. [*Bank of America v. Salinas Nissan, Inc.* (1989) 207 CA3d 260, 271, 254 CR 748, 755]

3) [9:947.2] **Burden to oppose claim of exemption:** It is plaintiff's burden to *oppose* any claim of exemption filed by defendant. Absent opposition, defendants are not required to prove the property is exempt; and it is error for the court to grant a right to attach order. [CCP §484.070(f); *Bank of America v. Salinas Nissan, Inc.*, supra, 207 CA3d at 270, 254 CR at 754-755]

[9:947.3-947.4] *Reserved.*

(b) [9:947.5] **Admissibility of evidence:** The evidence presented must be admissible under applicable rules of evidence; i.e., no inadmissible hearsay, opinions, conclusions, etc.

A proper foundation must be established for declarations and affidavits showing the declarant had *personal knowledge* of each fact stated. [*Generale Bank Nederland, N.V. v. Eyes of the Beholder Ltd.* (1998) 61 CA4th 1384, 1390, 72 CR2d 188, 192—declarations by "bank officer" did not show personal knowledge of transaction with bank]

(c) [9:948] **Determination of disputed facts:** The court has the power to determine disputed facts on the basis of a *preponderance* of the evidence as disclosed in the affidavits and declarations (unlike summary judgment motions, for example, in which

© 2020 Thomson Reuters/The Rutter Group

the court has no power to weigh the evidence). [*Hobbs v. Weiss* (1999) 73 CA4th 76, 80, 86 CR2d 146, 149—court must "consider the relative merits of the positions of the respective parties and make a determination of the probable outcome of the litigation"]

1) [9:948.1] **Undisputed affidavits:** The trial court is *not* required to accept as true the sworn testimony of any witness or undisputed affidavit testimony. It may make contrary findings based on inferences drawn from other evidence. [*Bank of America v. Salinas Nissan, Inc.*, supra, 207 CA3d at 273, 254 CR at 756]

   Example: D's affidavit blamed P for the diminution in value of security given for the debt. P did not respond to these charges. But P's affidavits indicated other persons were responsible for the diminution in value. [*Bank of America v. Salinas Nissan, Inc.*, supra, 207 CA3d at 273-274, 254 CR at 756-757]

2) [9:949] **Determination of no effect in main action:** However, determinations of fact made by the court in the attachment proceedings have no effect on the issues in the main action, and are inadmissible at time of trial. [CCP §484.100; see *Loeb & Loeb v. Beverly Glen Music, Inc.*, supra, 166 CA3d at 1117, 212 CR at 834; *see ¶9:857.6*]

(d) [9:950] **Renewed application:** The court has power to issue an RTAO after denying an earlier application. Ordinarily, "different facts" must be shown to justify the renewed application (CCP §1008(a), *see ¶9:324 ff.*). But this does not always require new operative facts; i.e., new declarations or discovery may cast *new meaning* on facts disclosed on the original application. [*Film Packages, Inc. v. Brandywine Film Productions, Ltd.* (1987) 193 CA3d 824, 828, 238 CR 623, 626]

(2) [9:951] **Order:** The official Judicial Council form (AT-120) may require counsel to add riders or attachments—particularly as to itemization of exempt property (items 2.f. and 2.g.). Since the form is multi-purpose, be very careful that the correct boxes are selected.

(a) Note that item 3.a. is the RTAO and item 3.c. is the order for issuance of the W/A.

(b) Many of the sub-items at item 3.c. are for attachment of an *individual's* property. Use item 3.c.(1) for corporations or partnerships.

(c) Item 3.d. is for the discretionary "turnover order." Note particularly, the box for a defendant who is personally present (item 1.b.); if it can be used, later proof of notice of the order will be facilitated.

(d) Item 3.f. is used to prevent later forgeries or surreptitious box-checkers.

(3) [9:951.1] **Amount of attachment:** The writ will issue for the amount of the claimed indebtedness, plus an amount to cover costs and allowable attorney fees as determined by the court. [CCP §483.015(a); *Goldstein v. Barak Const.* (2008) 164 CA4th 845, 852, 79 CR3d 603, 609]

But this amount must be *reduced* by:

- Any unsatisfied and enforceable money judgment in defendant's favor against plaintiff; plus
- Any indebtedness of plaintiff claimed by defendant in a cross-complaint filed in the action *if a writ of attachment could issue on the claim*; plus
- Any claim asserted as a defense in the answer upon which a writ of attachment could issue (tort claims cannot be used to reduce the attachment amount); plus
- Any security interest held by plaintiff in defendant's property, together with any decrease in value of the underlying security caused by plaintiff (or the security-holder if different from plaintiff). [CCP §483.015]
- *Compare—unlawful detainer proceedings:* For attachments ordered in unlawful detainer proceedings, the amount to be secured by attachment is *not reduced* by rent prepayments or lease deposits held by plaintiff. [CCP §483.020(e)]

The court must specifically find that the amount to be secured by attachment is *greater than zero.* [CCP §§484.090(a)(4), 485.220(a)(6) & 492.030(a)(6)]

(4) [9:952] **Undertaking:** A flat amount undertaking of $10,000 is provided for by statute. [CCP §489.220]

A writ of attachment issued without the mandated bond is *void.* [*Vershbow v. Reiner* (1991) 231 CA3d 879, 882, 282 CR 684, 686]

(a) [9:953] **Court may increase amount:** A defendant whose damages would be larger than the statutory amount may object to the statutory amount. The objection must be supported by declarations showing why the statutory amount is insufficient. If the court is convinced, it may order the undertaking increased

© 2020 Thomson Reuters/The Rutter Group

to the "probable recovery for wrongful attachment if it is ultimately determined that the attachment was wrongful." [CCP §489.220(b)]

- [9:954] Defendant cannot force plaintiff to post a massive undertaking simply because it (defendant) is in a precarious financial condition. The court may properly consider the *probability that plaintiff will prevail* in fixing the amount of bond. [*North Hollywood Marble Co., Inc. v. Sup.Ct. (Globe Marble & Title, Inc.)* (1984) 157 CA3d 683, 690-691, 204 CR 55, 60—defendant's request to increase $7,500 bond to $225,000 properly denied because evidence strongly indicated plaintiff would prevail]
- [9:955] In addition, the court has inherent jurisdiction, apart from statutory authority, to increase the amount of an attachment undertaking *on its own motion.* (Such increase is particularly likely to be ordered in ex parte attachments because of the greater danger of a "wrongful" attachment.) [See *North Hollywood Marble Co., Inc. v. Sup.Ct. (Globe Marble & Title, Inc.)*, supra, 157 CA3d at 691, 204 CR at 61]

[9:955.1] ***PRACTICE POINTER FOR DEFENDANT:*** When opposing an application for an RTAO, if you present evidence showing your client may suffer extensive costs and losses as a result of the attachment, the court may require a high enough bond that plaintiff will be unable to post it and no writ will issue. On the other hand, if the bond amount is set too high, and plaintiff does post it, your client may not be financially able to file a counterbond to release the writ (¶*9:956*).

If there is a possibility of defeating plaintiff's claim entirely, defendant should consider asking the court to increase the bond amount *based upon the anticipated costs of defense* (which may be recoverable if that is the only way to defeat the attachment; *see* ¶*9:957*). This is usually a "hard sell" but it can be worth the effort if issuance of the writ is a close call.

(5) [9:956] **Counterundertaking:** For release of the W/A by counterbonding, see CCP §489.310.

(6) [9:957] **Liability on bond:** If the attachment is wrongful (see CCP §490.010), plaintiff is liable for all damages proximately caused thereby, *plus* the costs of defeating the attachment, including reasonable attorneys' fees. [CCP §490.020(a)]

If the attachment is valid and regular on its face, and it is necessary to defend the entire action in order to defeat the attachment, defendant may recover *all expenses incurred* in its successful defenses. [*Reachi v. National Auto. & Cas. Ins. Co. of Los Angeles* (1951) 37 C2d 808, 812-813, 236 P2d 151, 153—attorney fees plus travel and hotel expenses; *Stiner v. Travelers Indem. Co.* (1964) 226 CA2d 128, 131, 37 CR 813, 814]

No separate lawsuit is necessary. Defendant may proceed by noticed motion in the main action for a judgment on the attachment undertaking against the plaintiff and the sureties on the attachment bond. But the maximum judgment would be the amount of the undertaking. [CCP §490.020(b)]

(a) [9:958] **Common law recovery:** Proceeding on the attachment undertaking does not affect defendant's right to file a separate suit against plaintiff for abuse of process or malicious prosecution. [CCP §490.060]

i. **Writ of Attachment**

FORM: Writ of Attachment (AT-135), *see Form 9B:27* in Rivera, *Cal. Prac. Guide: Civ. Pro. Before Trial FORMS* (TRG).

(1) [9:959] **Procedure:** The writ is issued by the clerk, who prepares the form from the order. Multiple and "alias" writs may be issued. [See CCP §482.090] The sheriff or marshal will, in addition, require written instructions as to levy and a deposit of fees. (Some levies are more difficult than others, and fees can be substantial in these situations.)

(2) [9:960] **Notice of Attachment:** The levying officer serves a "Notice of Attachment" along with the W/A and order for issuance of W/A. This form gives the various required notices on defendants or third parties in possession of defendant's property. Depending on the levying officer, the form may need to be prepared by plaintiff.

- ***FORM:*** Notice of Attachment (AT-165), *see Form 9B:28* in Rivera, *Cal. Prac. Guide: Civ. Pro. Before Trial FORMS* (TRG).

j. [9:961] **Defendant's motions:** A multi-purpose form is available for various defense orders—from setting aside the RTAO to releasing attached property upon filing an appeal bond.

- ***FORM:*** Order to Set Aside Attachment, to Substitute Undertaking, Etc. (AT-175).

k. [9:962] **Appellate review:** Orders *granting* an RTAO (or discharging or refusing to discharge an attachment already executed) are appealable. [CCP §§904.1(a)(5), 904.2(f)]

© 2020 Thomson Reuters/The Rutter Group

However, orders simply *denying* RTAOs are *not* appealable. [See *International Typographical Union Negotiated Pension Plan v. Ad Compositors, Inc.* (1983) 142 CA3d 733, 735, 191 CR 227, 228] (Appellate review can still be sought by petition for mandamus or prohibition, but is rarely granted.)

l. [9:963] **Third party debtor examinations:** After an RTAO has been granted, the creditor can apply for an order to compel the appearance of any third person (nonparty) for purposes of identifying assets of the debtor that are subject to attachment. [CCP §491.110 et seq.]

This procedure can be used to discover obligations owing to the debtor, or to determine whether the debtor has an interest in property held in the name of a third person (or jointly with such third person). It may even be used to "trace" assets which have been fraudulently conveyed by the debtor to avoid creditor claims.

Upon conclusion of the examination, the court is authorized to make findings respecting the debtor's interest in assets held by such third persons, or existence of enforceable obligations owing to the debtor. And, if the court finds such interests and obligations exist, it may then issue a writ of attachment as to those assets. [CCP §§491.170, 491.190]

However, such findings and order are authorized only in formal proceedings conducted before the court ("in the same manner as upon the trial of an issue"; see CCP §491.120). Where, as is often the case, the third party is examined informally (or before a court commissioner absent a *pro tem* stipulation), the court *cannot* make findings as to the debtor's interest in assets, or issue an attachment as to such assets. (The creditor's only remedy to reach such assets would be a separate creditor's suit under CCP §491.310 et seq.)

- ***FORM:*** Application and Order for Appearance and Examination (AT-138).

m. [9:964] **Third party claims:** A lienholder or other third party who claims ownership or right to possession of attached property may file a third party claim with the levying officer, and may give an undertaking to release the property. The plaintiff or creditor has 15 days from the filing of the third party claim within which to request a hearing to determine the validity of the claim and disposition of the property; otherwise, the property may be released to the third party claimant. Alternatively, plaintiff may prevent release by posting an undertaking or depositing the amount claimed due by the third party. [See CCP §720.010 et seq.]

9. [9:965] **Duration of Lien:** An attachment lien expires 3 years from the date the writ was issued, and property levied upon under such writ is automatically released. [CCP §488.510(a)]

(Death of the defendant whose property was attached does *not* terminate the lien; see CCP §488.510(e).)

a. [9:966] **Extension of lien:** If a judgment has not yet been obtained, plaintiff can obtain an extension of the attachment lien from year to year (up to 8 years from the date of the original writ). A noticed motion must be made not less than 10 nor more than 60 days before expiration of the current lien period. [CCP §488.510(b), (d)]

   To be effective, notice of the order extending the lien must be filed or recorded *prior to expiration* of the current lien period. If real property is involved, the notice must be timely recorded in the county recorder's office (mere filing with county clerk insufficient). [CCP §488.510(c); see *Arcata Publications Group v. Beverly Hills Publishing Co.* (1984) 154 CA3d 276, 280, 201 CR 223, 225]

10. [9:967] **Final Cautionary Note:** No brief summary such as this can prepare counsel to practice in attachments. A thorough study of the applicable Code sections is imperative before the proceedings are commenced, and before counsel starts to complete the forms. While the forms help make this complicated procedural law "bearable," they should not be used under the impression that attachment law practice is a mere matter of box-checking. Do not turn the forms over to an inexperienced assistant without careful supervision; *and in all cases read the code first.*

[9:968-999] *Reserved.*

© 2020 Thomson Reuters/The Rutter Group

RESERVED

CHAPTER 9

PART III

NONDISCOVERY SANCTIONS

CONTENTS

© 2020 Thomson Reuters/The Rutter Group

© 2020 Thomson Reuters/The Rutter Group

© 2020 Thomson Reuters/The Rutter Group

PART III

NONDISCOVERY SANCTIONS

[9:1000] ***PRACTICE POINTERS:*** There are several important practical considerations regarding motions for sanctions in law and motion matters:

- ***Conflict of interest with client:*** The more tenuous a position you take on a client's behalf, the more you expose both the client and yourself to a risk of sanctions. And if hit with a sanctions motion, your duty of loyalty to the client may require you to exculpate the client—even if this means taking the full blame yourself. *See further discussion at ¶9:1074.*

- ***Complicating dealing with opposing counsel:*** If you are considering seeking sanctions against the opposing party, make sure that doing so is in your client's interest. Requesting sanctions against the opposing party or counsel is likely to heighten antagonism and impede future dealings or cooperation. It may lead to a flurry of counter-motions that could cost your client far more than any amount the court is likely to award. *Avoid "boilerplate" requests for sanctions,* which won't be granted because of the strong showing required to justify sanctions. Save your sanctions battles for crucially important cases involving particularly egregious conduct, where the costs and risks can be justified.

- ***State Bar must be notified:*** An attorney against whom sanctions (*other than* sanctions for failure to make discovery) of more than $1,000 are imposed must report the matter to the State Bar. [See Bus. & Prof.C. §6068(o)(3)] (The judge imposing the sanctions must also report the matter to the State Bar; Bus. & Prof.C. §6086.7.)

  The State Bar is required to investigate each such report to determine whether disciplinary action should be instituted against the attorney. [Bus. & Prof.C. §6086.7]

  Note: A distinction is drawn between sanctions for "failure to make discovery," which need not be reported, and other sanctions such as for *disobedience* to court orders and frivolous actions under, e.g., CCP §128.5, which must be reported. [Bus. & Prof.C. §6086.7(a)(3)—court must report "any judicial sanctions against an attorney, except sanctions for failure to make discovery or monetary sanctions of less than one thousand dollars ($1,000)"]

- ***If sanctions imposed, ask judge to recommend no State Bar action:*** If you are assessed sanctions that the judge must report, consider asking the judge to add a recommendation against

© 2020 Thomson Reuters/The Rutter Group

State Bar disciplinary action. Some judges may be willing to do this depending on the facts.

A. SOURCES OF SANCTIONS POWER

1. [9:1001] **Inherent Power:** California courts have inherent power to punish for contempt and to control proceedings before the court (see CCP §128(a)(4), (5)), and to preclude evidence and dismiss actions in extreme situations as noted below (¶*9:1003.1 ff.*).

   However, courts have *no inherent power* to impose *monetary sanctions* against parties or their counsel. [*Bauguess v. Paine* (1978) 22 C3d 626, 638-639, 150 CR 461, 468 (superseded by statute on other grounds); *Andrews v. Sup.Ct. (Thomas)* (2000) 82 CA4th 779, 782, 98 CR2d 426, 429; *Clark v. Optical Coating Lab., Inc.* (2008) 165 CA4th 150, 165-166, 80 CR3d 812, 829—no inherent power to award attorney fees as sanctions for violation of *in limine* order; *Vidrio v. Hernandez* (2009) 172 CA4th 1443, 1455, 92 CR3d 178, 186—no inherent power to sanction nonparty insurer for failure to negotiate in good faith at mandatory settlement conference; *Interstate Specialty Marketing, Inc. v. ICRA Sapphire, Inc.* (2013) 217 CA4th 708, 717, 158 CR3d 743, 750—no "common law" authority to sanction plaintiff for errors in verified complaint]

   a. [9:1002] **Rationale:** Absent statutory authority, awarding attorney fees to punish misconduct "may imperil the independence of the bar and thereby undermine the adversary system." [*Bauguess v. Paine*, supra, 22 C3d at 638, 150 CR at 468]

      (1) [9:1002.1] **Contempt available:** An attorney whose conduct is disruptive of court processes or disrespectful of the court itself may be punished for contempt. Contempt proceedings, however, are subject to strict procedural safeguards and the penalty for civil contempt is limited to 5 days in jail or a $1,000 fine (*see* ¶*9:726*). [See *Clark v. Optical Coating Lab., Inc.*, supra, 165 CA4th at 163-164, 80 CR3d at 827] (Typically, judges prefer to avoid contempt in favor of trying other approaches first.)

   b. [9:1003] **Compare—federal courts:** Federal courts have broader inherent power. They may sanction attorneys and parties monetarily for "bad faith" conduct in litigation or willful disobedience of a court order. [*Chambers v. NASCO, Inc.* (1991) 501 US 32, 43, 111 S.Ct. 2123, 2132]

      Cross-refer: Sanctions in federal practice are discussed in detail in Phillips & Stevenson, *Rutter Group Prac. Guide: Federal Civ. Pro. Before Trial* (TRG), Ch. 17.

   c. [9:1003.1] **Evidence preclusion:** California courts have *inherent power* to preclude evidence to prevent abuses of the litigation process. [*Peat, Marwick, Mitchell & Co. v. Sup.Ct. (People)* (1988) 200 CA3d 272, 287, 245 CR 873, 883]

- [9:1003.2] If a party's expert witness examines critical evidence and then *destroys* it, preventing the opposing party from conducting its own examination, the court has inherent power to bar that expert's testimony about his or her examination. [See *Peat, Marwick, Mitchell & Co. v. Sup.Ct. (People),* supra, 200 CA3d at 289, 245 CR at 884]

- [9:1003.3] Where a party's expert witness has disclosed *confidential information* to the opposing party, the court has inherent power to disqualify the expert and enjoin use of the information so obtained. [See *Peat, Marwick, Mitchell & Co. v. Sup.Ct. (People),* supra, 200 CA3d at 289, 245 CR at 885]

- [9:1003.4] ABC was employed as an expert in plaintiff's accounting malpractice action against XYZ. ABC assured plaintiff it had no ties to XYZ and no merger was pending. After plaintiff had spent huge sums preparing the case, ABC and XYZ merged their firms. The court had discretion to preclude XYZ from controverting plaintiff's evidence of malpractice. [*Peat, Marwick, Mitchell & Co. v. Sup.Ct. (People),* supra, 200 CA3d at 292, 245 CR at 886]

[9:1003.5-1003.9] *Reserved.*

d. [9:1003.10] **Dismissal with prejudice:** A trial court has "limited, inherent discretionary power to dismiss claims with prejudice." [*Lyons v. Wickhorst* (1986) 42 C3d 911, 915, 231 CR 738, 739]

The court's inherent power to dismiss an action is recognized by statute. [See CCP §§581(m), 583.150]

(1) [9:1003.11] **Extreme situations:** Such power should be exercised in "extreme situations" such as:
— when the conduct was clear and deliberate;
— where no lesser alternatives would remedy the situation;
— where the fault lies with the client and not the attorney; and
— when the court issues a directive that the client fails to obey. [*Del Junco v. Hufnagel* (2007) 150 CA4th 789, 799, 60 CR3d 22, 29]

(2) **Application**

- [9:1003.12] Courts have inherent power to dismiss an action with prejudice "[w]hen a plaintiff's deliberate and egregious misconduct in the course of the litigation renders any sanction short of dismissal inadequate to protect the fairness of the trial." [*Stephen Slesinger, Inc. v. Walt Disney Co.* (2007) 155 CA4th 736, 762, 66 CR3d 268, 289—among

© 2020 Thomson Reuters/The Rutter Group

other misconduct, plaintiff illicitly obtained confidential information from defendant by breaking into dumpster locations and taking copies of documents]

- [9:1003.13] Imposition of a terminating sanction was consistent with the court's "inherent authority to compel obedience to its judgments, orders and process" and an appropriate response to plaintiff's flagrant misconduct and violation of court orders at trial—e.g., mentioning excluded matters in the opening statement and repeatedly attempting to solicit testimony that had been excluded. [*Osborne v. Todd Farm Service* (2016) 247 CA4th 43, 54-55, 202 CR3d 84, 95 (internal quotes and citation omitted)—in multi-defendant case, misconduct need not relate to specific defendant for that defendant to get benefit of terminating sanction against plaintiff]

- [9:1003.14] Dismissal with prejudice was proper where plaintiff repeatedly refused to submit a default judgment in compliance with the court's order. [*Moorer v. Noble L.A. Events, Inc.* (2019) 32 CA5th 736, 743-744, 244 CR3d 219, 225]

- [9:1003.15] *Compare:* Dismissal with prejudice as a sanction for refusing to participate in mandatory judicial arbitration was too drastic a remedy. Unless the court's authority cannot possibly be otherwise vindicated, the court should have considered and used lesser sanctions. [*Lyons v. Wickhorst,* supra, 42 C3d at 917-918, 231 CR at 741]

[9:1003.16-1003.19] *Reserved.*

e. [9:1003.20] **Default:** A court has inherent power to *strike defendant's answer and enter its default* for defendant's misconduct in the "extreme situations" that justify dismissal for plaintiff's misconduct (¶*9:1003.11*). [*Del Junco v. Hufnagel,* supra, 150 CA4th at 796, 60 CR3d at 26]

- [9:1003.21] Defendant filed an answer in propria persona that did not follow proper form, was lengthy, contained irrelevant information, and violated court rules. She filed documents without serving them. She failed to comply with an injunction. She did not pay sanctions when ordered. Her actions were willful and deliberate, caused unnecessary delay, wasted the trial court's resources, and caused the opposing party to incur unnecessary expense. "Under these circumstances the trial court had the jurisdiction to strike [Defendant's] answer and enter default." [*Del Junco v. Hufnagel,* supra, 150 CA4th at 800, 60 CR3d at 29]

2. [9:1004] **Statutes, Court Rules—In General:** Despite limitations on a court's inherent power, numerous statutes and court

rules give California courts the power to impose both monetary and nonmonetary sanctions:

- CCP §128.5 sanctions for bad-faith actions or tactics that are frivolous or solely intended to cause unnecessary delay; *see ¶9:1010 ff.*
- CCP §128.7 sanctions for violation of certificate of merit created by signing or presenting papers to the court; *see ¶9:1135 ff.*
- CCP §2023.010 et seq. discovery sanctions; *see ¶9:1263.*
- CCP §396b sanctions for improper venue; *see ¶9:1264.*
- CCP §437c(j) sanctions for "bad faith" declarations on summary judgment motions; *see ¶10:336.*
- CCP §1038 sanctions for unfounded tort actions against governmental entities; *see ¶9:1265 ff.*
- CCP §1218(a) civil contempt fines of up to $1,000 payable to the court, five days in jail, or both; *see ¶9:726.*
- CCP §177.5 sanctions payable to the court for violation of court orders; *see ¶9:1270 ff.*
- CCP §575.2 sanctions for violation of local court rules; *see ¶9:1275 ff.*
- CRC 2.30 sanctions for violation of CRC pretrial and trial rules; *see ¶9:1279.*
- CCP §907 and CRC 8.276 sanctions for frivolous appeals; *see ¶9:1284.11.*
- Gov.C. §68608(b) sanctions to achieve the purposes of the Trial Court Delay Reduction Act.
- CCP §1008(d) sanctions for improperly seeking reconsideration; *see ¶9:333.*

[9:1005] ***PRACTICE POINTER:*** It is essential to determine *which* sanctions power is being relied upon in the particular case. These statutes and court rules *vary considerably* in their scope and procedural requirements. Importantly, *attorney fees* are awardable as sanctions under some of these statutes and not others. [See *Collins v. State Dept. of Transp.* (2003) 114 CA4th 859, 866, 8 CR3d 132, 137]

Sanctions improperly granted under one statute cannot be upheld under a different statute. [*Kane v. Hurley* (1994) 30 CA4th 859, 863-864, 35 CR2d 809, 812 & fn. 8—sanctions improperly ordered under CCP §128.5 could have been based on CCP §177.5; see also *Marriage of Reese & Guy* (1999) 73 CA4th 1214, 1221, 87 CR2d 339, 343-344—court could not award sanctions under CCP §128.5 where sanction motion was based on §128.7]

© 2020 Thomson Reuters/The Rutter Group

3. [9:1006] **Multiple Awards for Same Misconduct?** Some sanctions provisions specifically authorize sanctions "[i]n addition to any other sanctions permitted by law." [CRC 2.30; see also CCP §177.5, authorizing sanctions "notwithstanding any other provision of law"]

   Comment: Even so, multiple awards for the same misconduct may violate public policy behind sanctions awards generally—i.e., that the "punishment fit the crime," and that the award be *no more than necessary to secure compliance* with the rule or order involved (*see* ¶*8:2212 ff.*).

   a. [9:1006.1] **Additional sanctions for failure to pay earlier award:** An attorney or party who fails to pay a sanctions award may be punished for violating the court's order. Additional monetary sanctions of up to $1,500 may be imposed for each violation. Such sanctions are *payable to the court* (not the opposing party). [CCP §177.5; *20th Century Ins. Co. v. Choong* (2000) 79 CA4th 1274, 1277-1278, 94 CR2d 753, 755; *see also* ¶*9:1272.1*]

4. [9:1007] **Compare—Disciplinary Proceedings:** Counsel who violate court orders may face discipline beyond judicial sanctions. Willful disobedience of a court order is cause for disbarment or suspension. [See Bus. & Prof.C. §6103]

   A judge must notify the State Bar if it appears a final contempt order involves grounds for discipline, or when a sanction of $1,000 or more is imposed (except for failure to make discovery). [Bus. & Prof.C. §6086.7(a)(1), (3)]

5. [9:1008] **Compare—Sanctions in Contractual Arbitration Proceedings:** By voluntarily appearing for clients in contractual arbitration, attorneys subject themselves to the jurisdiction of the arbitrator, and become subject to the arbitrator's rulings, including sanctions orders. Those rulings are generally not subject to judicial review for errors of fact or law. [*Bak v. MCL Fin'l Group, Inc.* (2009) 170 CA4th 1118, 1126, 88 CR3d 800, 806—arbitration panel had power to sanction party's counsel for copying privileged material]

   ⇨ [9:1009] ***PRACTICE POINTER:*** Be careful how you act in front of a private arbitrator. If the arbitrator decides to sanction you, for whatever reason, you may have no appellate recourse.

B. SANCTIONS UNDER CCP §128.5

1. [9:1010] **In General:** In all civil cases, the judge may order a party or counsel, or both, "to pay the reasonable expenses, including attorney's fees, incurred by another party as a result of actions or tactics, made in bad faith, that are frivolous or solely intended to cause unnecessary delay." [CCP §128.5(a)]

   [9:1010.1] ***Caution re prior versions of statute:*** The Legislature's 2017 amendments changed the version of CCP §128.5 which had become effective on January 1, 2015; that version, in turn, was based on another version of the statute which was only applicable to cases commenced before 1995. Therefore, caution should be exercised in citing cases construing earlier versions of §128.5.

a. [9:1010.1a] **Effect of 2017 amendments:** The latest amendments to CCP §128.5, together with the legislative history, reflect the following changes from the 2015 version of the statute:

(1) [9:1010.1b] **Bad faith standard:** The legislative history states that the standard for bad faith is a subjective rather than an objective one. [See 7/20/17 Assembly Floor Analysis of AB 984, available on the California Legislative Information website (*https://leginfo.legislature.ca.gov*)—"This bill clarifies that the standard applied in CCP Section 128.5 is a subjective bad faith standard"; *Marriage of Sahafzadeh-Taeb & Taeb* (2019) 39 CA5th 124, 134-135, 251 CR3d 610, 618; *and discussion at ¶9:1020 ff.*]

(2) [9:1010.1c] **Application of safe harbor provisions:** The *safe harbor provisions* of CCP §128.7 (*see ¶9:1196 ff.*) do not apply to most of CCP §128.5 (thereby removing an ambiguity in prior versions); however, under the 2017 amendment to CCP §128.5, a safe harbor procedure almost identical to that in §128.7 *is* available for making or opposing a written motion or the filing and service of a complaint, cross-complaint, answer or other responsive pleading that can be withdrawn or appropriately corrected. [CCP §128.5(f)(1)(B), (D); *Nutrition Distribution, LLC v. Southern Sarms, Inc.* (2018) 20 CA5th 117, 127-130, 228 CR3d 737, 744-746; *see ¶9:1090*]

(3) [9:1010.1d] **Moving party's due diligence:** Judges must consider "whether a party seeking sanctions has exercised due diligence." [CCP §128.5(f)(1)]

(4) [9:1010.1e] **Liability of law firm:** "Absent exceptional circumstances, a law firm shall be held jointly responsible for violations committed by its partners, associates, and employees." [CCP §128.5(f)(1)(C)]

(5) [9:1010.1f] **Deterrence:** Sanctions "shall be limited to what is sufficient to deter repetition of the action or tactic or comparable action or tactic by others similarly situated." [CCP §128.5(f)(2)]

(6) [9:1010.1g] **Sanctions may be nonmonetary:** The sanction "may consist of, or include, directives of a nonmonetary nature." [CCP §128.5(f)(2)]

(7) [9:1010.1h] **Bad faith motion for sanctions:** A motion for sanctions brought "primarily for an improper purpose, such as to harass or to cause unnecessary delay or

© 2020 Thomson Reuters/The Rutter Group

needless increase in the cost of litigation," may *itself* be subject to a sanctions motion. [CCP §128.5(g)]

- [9:1010.2] **Compare—anti-SLAPP statute incorporates CCP §128.5:** CCP §128.5 also applies to CCP §425.16 anti-SLAPP motions (*see ¶7:500 ff.*). Under that statute, if the court finds a special motion to strike is "frivolous or is solely intended to cause unnecessary delay," it *must* award attorney fees and costs to the prevailing plaintiff "pursuant to Section 128.5." This means a court "must use the procedures and apply the substantive standards of §128.5 in deciding whether to award attorney fees under the anti-SLAPP statute." [*Decker v. U.D. Registry, Inc.* (2003) 105 CA4th 1382, 1392, 129 CR2d 892, 898 (superseded by statute on other grounds); *Doe v. Luster* (2006) 145 CA4th 139, 143, 51 CR3d 403, 405; *see further discussion at ¶7:1165 ff.*]

b. [9:1010.3] **Nonexclusive:** Sanctions under §128.5 may be imposed in addition to any other liability resulting from the sanctioned conduct. [CCP §128.5(h)]

c. [9:1010.4] **Not dependent on outcome of suit:** For purposes of imposing CCP §128.5 sanctions, it is immaterial who ultimately wins or loses the case. I.e., the prevailing party may end up having to pay sanctions for "frivolous" tactics during the course of the suit. [*Magnolia v. Fields* (1987) 191 CA3d Supp. 1, 6-7, 236 CR 900, 903-904]

d. [9:1010.5] **Constitutionality:** Judge-imposed sanctions under CCP §128.5 do not deprive the sanctioned party of the right to jury trial guaranteed by Art. I, §16 of the California Constitution. While CCP §128.5 may reach the same conduct as an action for malicious prosecution (in which there is a right to jury trial), it is a different remedy. It is a "much more efficient method of addressing the misuse of the legal system." [*Andrus v. Estrada* (1995) 39 CA4th 1030, 1038, 46 CR2d 300, 304; see also *Lavine v. Hospital of the Good Samaritan* (1985) 169 CA3d 1019, 1028, 215 CR 708, 715]

e. [9:1010.6] **Not applicable to discovery:** By its terms, CCP §128.5 does not apply to disclosures and discovery requests, responses, objections and discovery motions. [CCP §128.5(e)]

f. [9:1010.7] **Not applicable to appeals:** CCP §128.5 does not authorize sanctions on appeals, unlike CCP §907 and CRC 8.276(a)(1), which do. [*de la Carriere v. Greene* (2019) 39 CA5th 270, 278-279, 251 CR3d 795, 802]

g. [9:1011] **Application of statute—timing:** CCP §128.5 applies to "actions or tactics that were part of a civil case filed on or after January 1, 2015." [CCP §128.5(i)]

[9:1012] *Reserved.*

2. Sanctionable Misconduct

a. [9:1013] **Bad faith "actions or tactics":** "Actions or tactics" sanctionable under CCP §128.5 specifically include:

— making or opposing motions (CCP §128.5(b)(1));

— the filing and service of a complaint, cross-complaint, answer or other pleading (but not "the mere filing of a complaint without service thereof") (CCP §128.5(b)(1); *see discussion at ¶9:1037*); and

— bad faith actions or tactics in judicial arbitration proceedings (CCP §128.5(a)).

(1) [9:1014] **Comment:** As a practical matter, *any* conduct in the course of litigation (other than in connection with "disclosures and discovery requests, responses, objections and motions") may be sanctionable if the court finds it to be "frivolous" or "solely intended to cause unnecessary delay." [See CCP §128.5(a); *Ellis v. Roshei Corp.* (1983) 143 CA3d 642, 649, 192 CR 57, 61; *but see ¶9:1037*]

[9:1015-1016] *Reserved.*

b. [9:1017] **"Frivolous" actions:** "Frivolous" means either: (1) "*totally* and completely without merit"; or (2) "for the *sole* purpose of *harassing* an opposing party." [CCP §128.5(b)(2) (emphasis added); see *Marriage of Flaherty* (1982) 31 C3d 637, 649-650, 183 CR 508, 516 (sanctions for "frivolous" appeal)]

"Harassing" conduct includes vexatious tactics which, although literally authorized by statute or rule, go *beyond that which is appropriate* under any reasonable standard. [See *West Coast Develop. v. Reed* (1992) 2 CA4th 693, 702, 3 CR2d 790, 795]

[9:1018-1019] *Reserved.*

(1) [9:1020] **Subjective bad faith standard:** Under a former version of CCP §128.5, it was not clear whether "frivolousness" (lack of merit) by itself was enough for CCP §128.5 sanctions, or whether subjective "bad faith" also had to be proved. Some earlier cases held an objective standard was proper. [E.g., *Finnie v. Town of Tiburon* (1988) 199 CA3d 1, 12, 244 CR 581, 587] The court in *San Diegans for Open Government v. City of San Diego* (2016) 247 CA4th 1306, 1318, 203 CR3d 34, 41-42, also held that the standard was objective, but the legislative history of the most recent (2017) statutory amendments reflects that one of the purposes of the amendments was to clarify that the standard applied in CCP §128.5 is a "subjective bad faith standard." [*Marriage of Sahafzadeh-Taeb & Taeb* (2019) 39 CA5th 124, 135, 251 CR3d 610, 618; *see ¶9:1010.1b*]

Therefore, caution should be exercised in citing cases construing earlier versions of the statute, including cases

© 2020 Thomson Reuters/The Rutter Group

holding that either an objective or a subjective standard will suffice.

(a) [9:1021] **Comment:** However, many cases, including those noted below (¶*9:1025 ff.*), in which sanctions were imposed under an objective standard of "frivolous," may remain persuasive because courts have *inferred* subjective bad faith from the objective circumstances. Indeed, absent counsel's admission of subjective bad faith, a rare occurrence, the moving party generally will ask the court to draw such an inference. [*Summers v. City of Cathedral City* (1990) 225 CA3d 1047, 1073, 275 CR 594, 610—court may, but need not, draw inference of subjective bad faith from objective lack of merit; see also *Gemini Aluminum Corp. v. California Custom Shapes, Inc.* (2002) 95 CA4th 1249, 1263, 116 CR2d 358, 369—subjective bad faith inferred from circumstantial evidence]

[9:1022-1024] *Reserved.*

c. [9:1025] **Conduct held sanctionable:** The following are examples of conduct held to justify imposition of sanctions under earlier versions of CCP §128.5:

(1) [9:1026] **Motion or opposition totally devoid of merit:** A motion is "frivolous" and in "bad faith" where "any reasonable lawyer would agree it is totally devoid of merit" (i.e., lacking any basis in statutory or case law, or without any necessary evidence to support it). [*Karwasky v. Zachay* (1983) 146 CA3d 679, 681, 194 CR 292, 293]

(a) **Application**

- [9:1027] Filing a motion for summary judgment on the basis of "undisputed facts" that are *clearly* in dispute. [*Monex Int'l, Ltd. v. Peinado* (1990) 224 CA3d 1619, 1626, 274 CR 667, 671]
- [9:1028] Moving for reconsideration of a matter previously ruled upon without complying with statutory requirements governing reconsideration (*see* ¶*9:324 ff.*). [*Fegles v. Kraft* (1985) 168 CA3d 812, 816, 214 CR 380, 382]

  Cross-refer: Reconsideration motions in violation of CCP §1008 are also punishable as a contempt and with sanctions under CCP §128.7 (CCP §1008(d)); *see* ¶*9:333.*
- [9:1029] Attempting to mislead the trial court by "citation to large quantities of material which does not support, directly or indirectly, the alleged facts for which they are cited." [*580 Folsom Assocs. v. Prometheus Develop. Co.* (1990) 223

CA3d 1, 23-26, 272 CR 227, 239-241—"a deliberate, patent effort at obfuscation intended to overwhelm the trial judge"]

- [9:1030] Filing declarations the court found to be "an out-and-out lie." [*Young v. Rosenthal* (1989) 212 CA3d 96, 127, 260 CR 369, 388]

- [9:1031] Continuing to file pleadings after the right to appear in the action has terminated. [*McFarland v. City of Sausalito* (1990) 218 CA3d 909, 911-912, 267 CR 412, 413—after demurrer to complaint-in-intervention sustained without leave to amend, would-be intervenor filed declarations opposing relief sought by other parties]

(b) [9:1032] **Sanctions for *partially* frivolous motions?** It is unclear whether CCP §128.5 sanctions may be imposed where a motion is made (or opposed) on *several* grounds, some (but not all) of which are "frivolous."

Comment: Presumably, sanctions could be imposed in such a case, at least where the frivolous grounds are a "significant and material part" of the motion or opposition. [See *Bach v. McNelis* (1989) 207 CA3d 852, 875, 255 CR 232, 245]

(2) [9:1033] **Dilatory motions:** Sanctions may be imposed where motions are made for purposes of delay—for example, waiting until the eve of trial to move for an order compelling contractual arbitration without valid excuse. [See *Zimmerman v. Drexel Burnham Lambert Inc.* (1988) 205 CA3d 153, 159, 252 CR 115, 117-118]

(3) [9:1034] **Frivolous pleadings:** Under previous law, sanctions were considered appropriate where any reasonable person would conclude the claims (or defenses) asserted are totally and completely without merit. [*Simonian v. Patterson* (1994) 27 CA4th 773, 785, 32 CR2d 722, 729]

(a) **Application**

- [9:1035] P, a lawyer, sued his ex-fiancee's *father* on various contract and tort claims relating to personal property the ex-fiancee took when she broke up with P. Sanctions were properly imposed: "Like the trial court, we know a sham pleading when we see one." [*Simonian v. Patterson,* supra, 27 CA4th at 776, 32 CR2d at 724]

- [9:1036] After several demurrers had been sustained with leave to amend, and warnings

© 2020 Thomson Reuters/The Rutter Group

from the court, P filed an amended complaint that was only superficially different. Sanctions for "frivolous" pleadings were properly imposed. [*Wilhelm v. Pray, Price, Williams & Russell* (1986) 186 CA3d 1324, 1334, 231 CR 355, 360]

(b) [9:1037] **Limitation—complaints filed but not served:** No matter how "frivolous" the complaint, sanctions cannot be imposed if the complaint is filed but not served (CCP §128.5(b)(1)). The purpose is to protect plaintiffs and their counsel from sanctions when they file suit without sufficient opportunity to investigate the case (e.g., to avoid the statute of limitations). Thus, a defendant who appears voluntarily in the action without being served is not able to obtain sanctions.

(4) [9:1038] **Causing "unnecessary" hearings:** Sanctions may also be awarded under CCP §128.5 where counsel *refuses to stipulate* to relief sought in an obviously well-taken motion; or counsel for the moving party insists that the motion be heard notwithstanding opposing counsel's offer to stipulate that the motion be granted. In either case, the court may find that counsel's conduct is not in "good faith" and has caused "unnecessary delay." [*Ellis v. Roshei Corp.* (1983) 143 CA3d 642, 649, 192 CR 57, 61-62; *Lavine v. Hospital of the Good Samaritan* (1985) 169 CA3d 1019, 1027, 215 CR 708, 714 (going forward on motion after relief sought voluntarily provided)]

- [9:1039] D filed a technically correct demurrer, although the defect challenged was minor and clearly amendable. P offered to stipulate to an amendment that would cure the defect. But D's lawyer insisted that the demurrer be heard because he was "suspicious" of opposing counsel. Although the demurrer was sustained, sanctions were awarded against D's counsel under CCP §128.5 for causing an "unnecessary" hearing. [*Ellis v. Roshei Corp.*, supra, 143 CA3d at 649, 192 CR at 61]

- [9:1040] P caused a writ of execution to be levied against D's assets. D moved to quash on the ground that it was a public entity and its assets therefore were exempt from execution. P's counsel said he would release the levy if D supplied him with proof of D's public entity status. D did so. However, instead of releasing the levy, P filed an opposition to the motion, calling on the court to determine D's status. D was therefore compelled to go forward with its motion. Sanctions of $1,000 were upheld. [*De Vera v. Long Beach Pub. Transp. Co.* (1986) 180 CA3d

782, 798-799, 225 CR 789, 796-797—no basis for relief from sanctions under CCP §473]

(5) [9:1041] **Failing to advise opposing counsel or court of inability to appear:** Sanctions may be imposed against an attorney who is aware of his or her inability to appear at the time set for hearing, but fails to notify opposing counsel and the court of that fact. Such discourteous conduct constitutes "delaying tactics" within the meaning of CCP §128.5. [*Marriage of Gumabao* (1984) 150 CA3d 572, 573-574, 198 CR 90, 92; *Wong v. Davidian* (1988) 206 CA3d 264, 271-272, 253 CR 675, 680]

(a) **Application**

- [9:1042] Attorney knew he would be late for a scheduled hearing because he was in trial elsewhere, but did not call opposing counsel. Instead, on the date of the hearing, Attorney telephoned the court clerk to state he would be late. The matter was put over for a few hours, but Attorney called again to say he was still engaged. Opposing counsel had wasted the better part of a day, justifying sanctions of $450. [*Marriage of Gumabao,* supra, 150 CA3d at 577, 198 CR at 94]

(b) [9:1043] **Willfulness not required:** Under cases construing prior versions of the statute, sanctions under CCP §128.5 (unlike contempt proceedings); were proper even though counsel's misconduct was not willful. [See *Marriage of Gumabao,* supra, 150 CA3d at 577, 198 CR at 94]

(c) [9:1044] **Secretary's inefficiency charged to counsel:** It is no excuse that the attorney's secretary failed to deliver messages as instructed. Any failure to communicate is chargeable to counsel. [*Marriage of Gumabao,* supra, 150 CA3d at 575, 198 CR at 93]

(6) [9:1045] **Reneging on stipulation:** "Bad faith" may be found when counsel have reneged or "dragged their feet" on a stipulation. [See *M.E. Gray Co. v. Gray* (1985) 163 CA3d 1025, 1034-1035, 210 CR 285, 290-291]

- [9:1046] D moved for a continuance of trial beyond the 5-year statute. In granting the motion, the court required D to prepare a stipulation waiving the 5-year statute and circulate it to all counsel. Due to D's "dragging his feet," the stipulation was not executed and returned within the 5-year period. Attempting to take advantage of the situation, D filed a motion to dismiss under the 5-year statute. D's

© 2020 Thomson Reuters/The Rutter Group

motion was found to be "a product of tactics and actions undertaken in bad faith." [*M.E. Gray Co. v. Gray*, supra, 163 CA3d at 1034-1035, 210 CR at 290-291]

(7) [9:1047] **Unauthorized defaults:** Plaintiff's counsel caused entry of default before defendant's time to respond expired; obtained a judgment and writ of possession based on the invalid default; and refused to set them aside upon request, necessitating motions and writs. Plaintiff's counsel was guilty of "frivolous" tactics *as a matter of law.* [*Magnolia v. Fields* (1987) 191 CA3d Supp. 1, 5-6, 236 CR 900, 903]

(8) [9:1048] **Scheduling motions, discovery, as harassment:** CCP §128.5 sanctions were imposed under older law where counsel attempted to *take advantage of an opposing counsel's absence* to schedule discovery or motions. [See *Tenderloin Housing Clinic, Inc. v. Sparks* (1992) 8 CA4th 299, 304-305, 10 CR2d 371, 373—counsel purposefully set depositions and discovery motions while opposing counsel on vacation and refused to change or modify the dates]

Comment: It is unclear whether this type of bad faith conduct in connection with discovery is covered by the newly amended statute, which now specifically states the statute "*shall not apply to disclosures and discovery requests, responses, objections, and motions.*" [CCP §128.5(e) (emphasis added)]

(9) [9:1049] **Misrepresentations to opposing counsel or court:** A motion or opposition that misrepresents material facts may be sanctionable under CCP §128.5. [*Young v. Rosenthal* (1989) 212 CA3d 96, 128, 260 CR 369, 389—attorneys "willfully and knowingly made false declarations and statements in an attempt to deceive the court"]

(10) [9:1050] **Frivolous attempt to disqualify judge:** If designed for delay or obfuscation, challenges to the judge for cause may be sanctioned under CCP §128.5. The delay involved in hearing the challenge may *remove* the judge from the pool of available judges, thus accomplishing the purpose of the challenge although it is meritless. [*Estate of Di Grazia* (1993) 13 CA4th 681, 685-686, 16 CR2d 621, 622-623 (disapproved on other grounds in *Curle v. Sup.Ct.* (*Gleason*) (2001) 24 C4th 1057, 1068-1069, 103 CR2d 751, 759-760 & fn. 6)—sanctions ordered paid to county for representing judge in disqualification proceeding]

d. [9:1051] **Conduct held *not* sanctionable:** The fact the motion lacks merit is not enough by itself to justify an award of CCP §128.5 sanctions. It is error to award sanctions if:

— it is *not unreasonable* for the moving party's attorney to think the issues raised were *arguable;* and

— there is *no evidence of subjective bad faith or improper motive.* [*Garcia v. Sterling* (1985) 176 CA3d 17, 20, 221 CR 349, 351; see *Bruno v. Sup.Ct.* (*Gridley*) (1990) 219 CA3d 1359, 1365, 269 CR 142, 146—attorney cannot be sanctioned for raising issue of first impression]

(1) [9:1052] **Misstatements of law but arguable merit shown:** P's motion relied on cases for a certain point. The court held those cases "misstated" or "misapplied" the law. This was not enough to make the motion "frivolous" for sanctions purposes: "[T]here was no evidence of subjective bad faith or improper motive and it was *not unreasonable for appellant's attorney to think the issues were arguable."* [*Garcia v. Sterling,* supra, 176 CA3d at 22-23, 221 CR at 352 (emphasis added)]

[9:1053-1056] *Reserved.*

3. [9:1057] **Who May Recover Sanctions:** CCP §128.5 sanctions can be awarded in favor of any *party.* But there is no authority for a §128.5 award to a *nonparty.* [*Rabbitt v. Vincente* (1987) 195 CA3d 170, 174, 240 CR 524, 526 (reversing award to nonparty deponent against her own attorney for misconduct that exposed her to contempt proceedings)]

a. [9:1058] **Defendant who has been dismissed:** Although dismissed from the action, a *former defendant* may obtain CCP §128.5 sanctions for bad faith tactics suffered while a party. Rationale: Otherwise, plaintiffs could avoid CCP §128.5 sanctions by dismissing without prejudice before the matter could be heard. [*Annino & Sons Const., Inc. v. McArthur Restaurants, Inc.* (1989) 215 CA3d 353, 358-359, 263 CR 592, 596]

b. [9:1059] **Sanctions payable to court:** According to cases construing prior versions of CCP §128.5, sanctions could not be ordered payable to the trial court (see *Kane v. Hurley* (1994) 30 CA4th 859, 862-863, 35 CR2d 809, 811-812). However, the version of the statute that became effective in August of 2017 permits "an order to pay a penalty into court." [CCP §128.5(f)(2)]

(1) [9:1060] **Compare—CCP §177.5:** Sanctions payable to the court can be granted under CCP §177.5 for violation of a court order; *see ¶9:1270.* [*Kane v. Hurley,* supra, 30 CA4th at 863, 35 CR2d at 812]

4. [9:1061] **Who May be Sanctioned:** CCP §128.5 sanctions may be imposed only against parties or their attorneys. [See *Midwife v. Bernal* (1988) 203 CA3d 57, 65, 249 CR 708, 712—parties appearing in pro per held to same standard as if represented by counsel]

© 2020 Thomson Reuters/The Rutter Group

And, "[a]bsent exceptional circumstances, a law firm shall be held jointly responsible for violations committed by its partners, associates, and employees." [CCP §128.5(f)(1)(C)]

a. [9:1062] **Attorneys *not* of record?** There is a split of authority whether an attorney who has *not* appeared of record in the action is subject to sanctions under CCP §128.5. [See *Rush v. Weinzettl* (1993) 14 CA4th 66, 68-69, 17 CR2d 354, 355-356—attorney who failed to file substitution of attorneys was subject to sanctions as "party's attorney" although not attorney of record; compare *Capotosto v. Collins* (1991) 235 CA3d 1439, 1442, 1 CR2d 470, 471-472—attorneys not of record cannot be sanctioned even if they advise party to the action]

- [9:1063] Attorney attempted to settle matter for Client but never appeared as attorney of record. The settlement fell through. Attorney was not subject to CCP §128.5 sanctions because he was neither a "party (n)or a party's attorney." [*Capotosto v. Collins,* supra, 235 CA3d at 1442, 1 CR2d at 471-472—immaterial that Attorney had wrongfully sought sanctions against opposing party]

b. [9:1064] **Parties dismissed from action:** The court retains jurisdiction to award sanctions under CCP §128.5 against a person who has been involuntarily dismissed from the action for frivolous acts prior to the dismissal. [*West Coast Develop. v. Reed* (1992) 2 CA4th 693, 706, 3 CR2d 790, 798]

Likewise, plaintiffs may be sanctioned under §128.5 for filing a frivolous action notwithstanding their voluntary dismissal of the action prior to the sanctions hearing. [*Abandonato v. Coldren* (1995) 41 CA4th 264, 266, 48 CR2d 429, 430 (disapproved on other grounds in *Musaelian v. Adams* (2009) 45 C4th 512, 520, 87 CR3d 475, 481)]

(1) [9:1064.1] **Frivolous tactics following dismissal:** Moreover, CCP §128.5 sanctions *may* be awarded for frivolous motions or tactics *after* a party's right to appear in the action has terminated (e.g., party who has been dismissed continues to file pleadings and declarations). [*McFarland v. City of Sausalito* (1990) 218 CA3d 909, 912, 267 CR 412, 414]

c. [9:1065] **Compare—coparties not joining in sanctionable conduct:** Even if represented by the same counsel, a coparty cannot be sanctioned for sanctionable conduct to which *he or she was not a party.* [*Optical Surplus, Inc. v. Sup.Ct.* (*Niskar*) (1991) 228 CA3d 776, 785, 279 CR 194, 199, fn. 4]

- [9:1065.1] Defendant A and Defendant B are represented by the same counsel. If Defendant A (only) makes a "bad faith" motion (e.g., to quash service of summons), sanctions may be imposed against A and its counsel but *not* against

Defendant B. [*Optical Surplus, Inc. v. Sup.Ct.* (*Niskar*), supra, 228 CA3d at 785, 279 CR at 199, fn. 4]

d. [9:1066] **Compare—party's insurer:** The court is not empowered to amend a judgment to add a defendant's insurer as a party to the action, in order to sanction it for refusing to settle the action. [*Triplett v. Farmers Ins. Exch.* (1994) 24 CA4th 1415, 1420, 29 CR2d 741, 743—no such thing as "malicious defense" or bad faith refusal to settle]

e. [9:1067] **Attorney or client?** CCP §128.5 specifically authorizes the court to sanction the "party, the party's attorney, *or both.*" [CCP §128.5(a) (emphasis added)]

Sanctions against the client can usually be justified on the basis that the attorney was acting as the client's agent. In some circumstances, sanctions can also be justified against the *attorney individually* (i.e., ordering the attorney to pay directly, and *not* to charge client).

(1) [9:1068] **Procedural violations:** Courts have little hesitation in sanctioning the attorney *alone* when the misconduct consists of violating some procedural rule for which the client bears no responsibility. Possible examples:

- Failure to appear at a hearing (see *Wong v. Davidian* (1988) 206 CA3d 264, 272, 253 CR 675, 680 (citing text));
- Briefs that mislead the court as to the facts or law (see *580 Folsom Assocs. v. Prometheus Develop. Co.* (1990) 223 CA3d 1, 21-22, 272 CR 227, 238);
- Arguing claims already made and rejected by the court without complying with rules governing motions for reconsideration. [See *Dwyer v. Crocker Nat'l Bank* (1987) 194 CA3d 1418, 1434-1345, 240 CR 297, 305-306—failure to appear at pretrial conferences, tardiness at trial, improper trial conduct, etc.]

(2) [9:1069] **Improper motive or purpose:** Where the issue is whether a pleading or motion has been filed for an improper motive or purpose, sanctions are generally proper *only against the client,* and *not* against the attorney individually. [See *Luke v. Baldwin-United Corp.* (1985) 167 CA3d 664, 669, 213 CR 654, 657-658]

(a) [9:1070] **Rationale:** "Without invading the attorney-client privilege, we have no available means of determining whether it was the client or counsel who was responsible . . . [I]f the fault lies with counsel the client can obtain relief in another forum [i.e., a suit for malpractice]. Thus, we conclude that *the appropriate course of action is to impose the sanctions*

© 2020 Thomson Reuters/The Rutter Group

on the party . . . . which in the final analysis was the beneficiary of the delay and disruption [caused by counsel's conduct]." [*Luke v. Baldwin-United Corp.*, supra, 167 CA3d at 670, 213 CR at 657 (internal quotes omitted)]

(b) **Application**

- [9:1071] Attorneys moved to quash service of summons on the ground Client had no California "contacts" and therefore was not subject to jurisdiction here. Later, during deposition, Client admitted it had California contacts. Attorneys promptly withdrew the motion to quash. Even so, the trial court sanctioned Attorneys (not Client) for filing the motion, on the theory they "must have known" or "should have known" the facts. This was *reversed* on appeal; sanctions cannot be "based upon impermissible speculation and conjecture as to facts [Attorneys] *could* have or *should* have discovered." [*Luke v. Baldwin-United Corp.,* supra, 167 CA3d at 669, 213 CR at 657]
- [9:1072] *Compare:* But an attorney was ordered to pay opposing counsel $250 in sanctions for refusing to stipulate to a minor amendment of a pleading that would have obviated the necessity for a demurrer hearing. The attorney *said* he refused because his client was "suspicious" of the opposing party. But the court found he acted for purposes of delay or harassment: "As an officer of the court, [Attorney] *simply could not blindly follow his client's instructions* based upon his client's suspicion of defendants." [*Ellis v. Roshei Corp.* (1983) 143 CA3d 642, 650, 192 CR 57, 62 (emphasis added); *see ¶9:1039*]
- [9:1072.1] Sanctions against an attorney individually were also held proper for (among other acts) "*participation in the filing of a complaint* that itself had no meritorious basis in law or fact." [*Dwyer v. Crocker Nat'l Bank* (1987) 194 CA3d 1418, 1438, 240 CR 297, 308 (emphasis added); see also *Young v. Rosenthal* (1989) 212 CA3d 96, 128, 260 CR 369, 389—attorney filed false declarations; *580 Folsom Assocs. v. Prometheus Develop. Co.* (1990) 223 CA3d 1, 23, 272 CR 227, 239—attorney continued to assert validity of client's claims after it was clear claims were invalid]

(3) [9:1073] **Comment:** The question whether to sanction the attorney or client, or both, is one of the most dif-

ficult facing the judge. The cases above (¶*9:1071 ff.*) are merely the tip of the iceberg. Standards continue to evolve.

To avoid placing counsel in an impossible conflict situation, it may be better practice for the court to sanction the client; and leave it to the client and attorney to work out the ultimate responsibility between themselves. [See *Wong v. Davidian* (1988) 206 CA3d 264, 272, 253 CR 675, 680 (citing text)]

Other courts may choose to sanction *both* attorney and client, leaving it up to them to determine "how responsibility for the expenses should be allocated between client and counsel." [See *580 Folsom Assocs. v. Prometheus Develop. Co.* (1990) 223 CA3d 1, 28, 272 CR 227, 242, fn. 6]

[9:1074] ***CAUTION—RISK OF CONFLICT:*** The important point here is for counsel to recognize the potential conflict of interest with the client, and to *discuss the risk of sanctions with the client* before taking tenuous positions in law and motion matters. Otherwise, you'd better be prepared to pay out of your own pocket any sanctions awarded against your client. (*See* ¶*9:1000.*)

Keep in mind that it is no defense to sanctions that you were "merely carrying out the client's instructions." If a client insists on a course of action that you *know* has no merit and is in bad faith, it is your duty to *withdraw from the case.* [Bus. & Prof.C. §6068(c); CRPC 1.16(a)(1), (b)(1) (formerly CRPC 3-700(B)(1), (C)(1)); see *Young v. Rosenthal* (1989) 212 CA3d 96, 128, 260 CR 369, 389; and *580 Folsom Assocs. v. Prometheus Develop. Co.*, supra]

Your duty of loyalty to the client obligates you (1) to *avoid blaming the client* for whatever sanctionable conduct is involved; and (2) even if you get sanctioned personally, *to continue to assert arguably meritorious contentions* in order to protect the client's interests. [See *Optical Surplus, Inc. v. Sup.Ct. (Niskar)* (1991) 228 CA3d 776, 789, 279 CR 194, 199]

You must also *avoid revealing client communications*, even if it means accepting full responsibility for the sanctionable conduct. [See *Manzetti v. Sup.Ct. (Fitzgerald)* (1993) 21 CA4th 373, 381, 25 CR2d 857, 862]

Where the sanctions motion creates a *conflict of interest* with the client (e.g., imposing financial burden if sanctions awarded), the attorney may not continue to represent the client without the client's informed written consent. [CRPC 1.7 (formerly CRPC 3-310(B)(4)); see Cal. State Bar Form.Opn. 1997-151—not required in

© 2020 Thomson Reuters/The Rutter Group

"routine" discovery motions where attorney and client agree to take a common position]

In opposing the sanctions motion, the attorney must represent only the client's interests, unless they *agree* to take different positions. [See Cal. State Bar Form.Opn. 1997-151]

If attorney and client *agree* to present competing positions, the client must have *independent counsel* to oppose the motion. [See Cal. State Bar Form.Opn. 1997-151]

If the attorney insists on exonerating himself or herself from liability for sanctions and the *client does not agree* with such an approach, the attorney must *withdraw from the case*. [See Cal. State Bar Form.Opn. 1997-151]

(4) [9:1075] **Apportionment between attorney and client:** Where sanctions are imposed against attorney and client *jointly and severally*, whoever pays the full amount is entitled to pro rata contribution from the other. Absent a different apportionment by the court, *as between themselves,* the attorney and the client must share the burden equally. [*Young v. Rosenthal* (1989) 212 CA3d 96, 128, 260 CR 369, 389]

5. [9:1076] **Amount Awardable as Sanctions:** Sanctions may be awarded under CCP §128.5 for "reasonable expenses, including attorney's fees, incurred by another party as a result of" the sanctionable conduct. [CCP §128.5(a)]

These sanctions are intended both to compensate *and to deter improper conduct:* "The statute permits the award of attorney fees, not simply as appropriate compensation to the prevailing party, but *as a means of controlling* burdensome and unnecessary legal tactics." [*Childs v. PaineWebber Inc.* (1994) 29 CA4th 982, 995-996, 35 CR2d 93, 101 (emphasis added)]

In determining the amount of the sanction, the order for sanctions "shall be limited to what is sufficient to deter repetition of the action or tactic or comparable action or tactic by others similarly situated." [CCP §128.5(f)(2)] (This might result in a penalty payable to the court in *addition* to the reasonable attorney fees and costs incurred on the motion in an amount sufficient to actually deter; or it might result in an award of only some of the reasonable attorney fees and costs if that amount is sufficient to deter the sanctionable conduct.)

The trial court's decision to award or deny sanctions under CCP §128.5, and the amount of any award, is reviewable only for abuse of discretion. [*Childs v. PaineWebber Inc.*, supra, 29 CA4th at 997, 35 CR2d at 102]

a. [9:1077] **Attorney fees:** Attorney fees *incurred* by a party are a proper measure of sanctions even if not yet actually paid, absent evidence that the fees were not warranted or the services rendered were inappropriate. [*West Coast Develop. v. Reed* (1992) 2 CA4th 693, 707, 3 CR2d 790, 798]

(1) [9:1078] **Need not be attorney of record:** Sanctions may be awarded for legal fees incurred before the party's attorney appeared in the action. It is sufficient that the party had to *retain* an attorney as a result of the "bad faith" actions by the opposing party. [*West Coast Develop. v. Reed*, supra, 2 CA4th at 706, 3 CR2d at 798]

(2) [9:1078.1] **No attorney fees sanctions to parties appearing *in pro per*:** Because a pro per litigant does not "incur" attorney fees, he or she may not recover an award of attorney fees as sanctions. This includes attorneys who appear *in pro per* in response to a filing abuse. [*Musaelian v. Adams* (2009) 45 C4th 512, 520, 87 CR3d 475, 481 (overruling earlier court of appeal cases allowing fee awards to attorney pro per litigants under CCP §128.5 and §128.7)]

(a) [9:1078.2] **Similar rule for discovery sanctions:** Similarly, parties appearing in pro per may not recover attorney fees through discovery sanctions (*see ¶8:835.2a*). [*Kravitz v. Sup.Ct. (Milner)* (2001) 91 CA4th 1015, 1020, 111 CR2d 385, 389—but such parties may recover reasonably identifiable litigation costs (e.g., photocopying, transportation to and from court, etc.) even if those costs would ordinarily be included in a lawyer's hourly rate]

(3) [9:1078.3] **Award in favor of contingency fee attorney:** The requirement that fees be "incurred by a party" does not preclude an award in favor of a party who is being represented on a contingency fee basis: "Just because a client does not become liable to pay an attorney for services rendered if a settlement is not reached or a favorable judgment rendered does not preclude imposition of sanctions for an attorney's egregious behavior." [*Marriage of Adams* (1997) 52 CA4th 911, 913, 60 CR2d 811, 814]

b. [9:1079] **Other "expenses":** The statute's wording makes clear that sanctions may *exceed* the attorney fees incurred by the prevailing party in opposing the frivolous motion. [*580 Folsom Assocs. v. Prometheus Develop. Co.* (1990) 223 CA3d 1, 27-28, 272 CR 227, 242]

- [9:1080] CCP §128.5 sanctions may reimburse the prevailing party for its *personnel costs*, as well as its attorney fees, in defending against a "frivolous" pleading. [*580 Folsom Assocs. v. Prometheus Develop. Co.*, supra, 223 CA3d at 25-26, 272 CR at 240-241]

[9:1081] *Reserved.*

© 2020 Thomson Reuters/The Rutter Group

c. [9:1082] **Causal relationship required:** It must be shown that the attorney fees and expenses were incurred "as a result of" the other party's sanctionable conduct. [CCP §128.5(a)]

(1) **Application**

- [9:1083] D cross-complained against a frivolous complaint. Although it defeated the complaint, D lost on its cross-complaint. An award of fees under §128.5 was upheld even though there was *no apportionment* for services on the complaint vs. the cross-complaint. It was enough that a causal relationship existed: "The filing of the cross-complaint was occasioned solely by the filing of appellant's bad faith complaint . . . Therefore, the expenses incurred were 'as a result of' the frivolous complaint." [*On v. Cow Hollow Properties* (1990) 222 CA3d 1568, 1578, 272 CR 535, 540]

  [9:1083.1-1083.4] *Reserved.*

(2) [9:1083.5] **Entire course of conduct:** When a party or counsel has engaged in dilatory tactics over the course of litigation, the entire pattern of conduct may be considered. Past conduct that has already been punished cannot justify additional sanctions. But prior conduct that has not been punished can contribute to a later award of sanctions for continuing misconduct. [*Andrus v. Estrada* (1995) 39 CA4th 1030, 1042-1043, 46 CR2d 300, 307-308—counsel's conduct in different court before change of venue properly considered; see also *Abandonato v. Coldren* (1995) 41 CA4th 264, 267, 48 CR2d 429, 431 (disapproved on other grounds in *Musaelian v. Adams* (2009) 45 C4th 512, 520, 87 CR3d 475, 481) (upholding sanctions against attorney who twice filed and voluntarily dismissed complaints raising issues that should have been litigated in already-pending declaratory relief action)]

(3) [9:1084] **Strict accounting not necessary:** An award of attorney fees under §128.5 is *not* subject to strict scrutiny by appellate courts. I.e., the trial court is not bound by such traditional factors as hours spent, results attained, etc. [*On v. Cow Hollow Properties* (1990) 222 CA3d 1568, 1577, 272 CR 535, 540]

[9:1085] ***PRACTICE POINTER:*** Don't rely on this if you're the party seeking sanctions. Be sure to provide the court with *detailed* documentation of your hours, billings, etc. and a showing how each was the result of the opposing party's "frivolous" and "bad faith" conduct.

However, if you are going to submit to the court copies of your client's billing statements, make sure you *redact* any attorney-client or work product information. Failure to redact such information may be deemed to be a waiver of attorney-client privilege and work product protection.

(4) [9:1086] **"Comparative fault" principles?** Previously, it was unclear whether sanctions should be reduced to reflect "comparative fault" by the opposing party (e.g., failing to cooperate in investigation prior to lawsuit). [See *Abbett Elec. Corp. v. Sullwold* (1987) 193 CA3d 708, 711, 238 CR 496, 498, fn. 4]

However, the newest version of CCP §128.5 requires the court to consider the "due diligence" of the party *seeking* sanctions in fixing the amount (CCP §128.5(f)(1)), suggesting that some apportionment may be appropriate.

[9:1087] *Reserved.*

d. [9:1088] **Limitation—not a substitute for damages:** Whatever "expenses" are awarded as CCP §128.5 sanctions must be directly related to and *in furtherance* of the litigation. Consequential damages suffered by a party as a result of the litigation *cannot* be awarded in the guise of "reasonable expenses." [*Brewster v. Southern Pac. Transp. Co.* (1991) 235 CA3d 701, 711-712, 1 CR2d 89, 95; see *Crowley v. Katleman* (1994) 8 C4th 666, 688, 34 CR2d 386, 398—CCP §128.5 sanctions no substitute for malicious prosecution action]

- [9:1089] Railroad was forced to close down operations when served with a copy of what Attorney represented to be a valid temporary restraining order (TRO). In fact, no TRO had ever been issued. Sanctions were properly awarded against Attorney for Railroad's *legal fees* in having the TRO declared invalid. But Attorney could not be sanctioned for Railroad's costs in closing down operations. Such damages were recoverable only in a separate civil suit against Attorney. [*Brewster v. Southern Pac. Transp. Co.*, supra, 235 CA3d at 712, 1 CR2d at 94]

e. [9:1090] **Safe harbor provision:** For motions and pleadings (and oppositions to motions and responses to pleadings) that can be "appropriately corrected" by withdrawing or correcting them, the complaining party must follow a safe harbor procedure, giving the opposing party a 21-day opportunity to withdraw the offending document before filing a motion for sanctions. [CCP §128.5(f)(1)(D); *Nutrition Distribution, LLC v. Southern Sarms, Inc.* (2018) 20 CA5th 117, 129-130, 228 CR3d 737, 745-746]

On its own motion the court may provide a 21-day safe harbor period after which, if the offending document is not cor-

© 2020 Thomson Reuters/The Rutter Group

rected or withdrawn, sanctions may be imposed. [CCP §128.5(f)(1)(D), (f)(2)(B)—court order must issue before voluntary dismissal or settlement made by or against party or attorney to be sanctioned]

Note that this safe harbor provision is virtually identical to that of CCP §128.7 (*see ¶9:1210 ff.*). Therefore, cases construing CCP §128.7(c), (d) and (h) may be useful in evaluating procedures under CCP §128.5(f)(1)(B) and (D).

f. [9:1091] **Special rule allowing punitive damages for suits by convicted felons against their victims:** In addition to other CCP §128.5 sanctions, the court may "assess" *punitive damages* against *convicted felons* who sue their victims (or the victim's heirs, relatives, estate or personal representative) for injuries suffered by the felon in commission of the crime, provided the court finds that the plaintiff-felon "is guilty of fraud, oppression or malice in *maintaining* the action." [CCP §128.5(d) (emphasis added)]

Comment: Since many felons have neither assets nor insurance, this statute is not likely to have wide application.

6. **Procedural Considerations**

a. [9:1092] **Due process considerations:** Adequate *notice* and *opportunity to be heard* on a motion for monetary sanctions is mandated by constitutional due process requirements. [*O'Brien v. Cseh* (1983) 148 CA3d 957, 961-962, 196 CR 409, 411; *Marriage of Reese & Guy* (1999) 73 CA4th 1214, 1221, 87 CR2d 339, 343]

(1) [9:1092.1] **Notice requirement:** No award of sanctions can be made under CCP §128.5 unless a request for them is contained in a party's moving or opposing papers; or the award is made on the court's own motion after notice and opportunity to be heard. [CCP §128.5(c); *Lesser v. Huntington Harbor Corp.* (1985) 173 CA3d 922, 932, 219 CR 562, 567—includes sanctions imposed on court's own motion; *Kleveland v. Siegel & Wolensky, LLP* (2013) 215 CA4th 534, 540, 155 CR3d 599, 604—request for attorney fees and costs set forth in opposition to anti-SLAPP motion complies with notice requirements of CCP §128.5(c)]

The sanctions request need not be made in the first round of papers, and can be based on frivolous opposition or reply papers: "Bad faith tactics in supplemental and reply papers are equally as repugnant to the orderly conduct of legal proceedings . . ." [*Sherman v. Kinetic Concepts, Inc.* (1998) 67 CA4th 1152, 1164, 79 CR2d 641, 648-649]

FORM: Motion for Sanctions Under Code of Civil Procedure Section 128.5, *see Form 9C:3* in Rivera, *Cal. Prac. Guide: Civ. Pro. Before Trial FORMS* (TRG).

(a) [9:1093] **Must precede sanctions decision:** The notice must be given *before* findings are made and at a time preceding the trial judge's decision whether, in fact, to impose sanctions. [*Bergman v. Rifkind & Sterling, Inc.* (1991) 227 CA3d 1380, 1387, 278 CR 583, 587—error for court sua sponte to find sanctionable conduct has occurred and then offer counsel a hearing on the matter]

(b) [9:1094] **Must specify against whom sanctions sought:** If sanctions are being sought against the opposing *attorney*, the notice must so state: i.e., the attorney must be put on notice of the need to prove his or her own blamelessness in the matters in question. [*Corralejo v. Quiroga* (1984) 152 CA3d 871, 874, 199 CR 733, 735] Sanctions against partners, associates, and employees of law firms usually must also be imposed jointly against the law firm. [CCP §128.5(f)(1)(C)]

(c) [9:1094a] **Must specify type of sanction sought:** The notice of motion should also specify the type of sanction requested (e.g., dismissal or default, monetary award to moving party, etc.). Where monetary sanctions are sought, counsel should provide declarations specifying the amount requested and the manner of calculation; *see ¶9:1085.* (And recall that under the new amendment to CCP §128.5, "nonmonetary" sanctions and penalties payable to the court may be available; *see ¶9:1010.1g, 9:1059.*)

(d) [9:1094.1] **Must specify basis for sanctions:** In order for the offending party to respond to the sanctions motion, it must be on notice as to the *basis* for imposing the sanctions. [*Childs v. Paine-Webber Inc.* (1994) 29 CA4th 982, 996, 35 CR2d 93, 102]

- [9:1094.2] Notice that sanctions were being sought *under CCP §128.7* was *not* sufficient to warn the opposing party and counsel that sanctions might be awarded under CCP §128.5. [*Marriage of Reese & Guy* (1999) 73 CA4th 1214, 1221, 87 CR2d 339, 343; *Levy v. Blum* (2001) 92 CA4th 625, 628, 112 CR2d 144, 147]

(e) [9:1095] **Ex parte notice insufficient:** Notice requirements for ex parte hearings (e.g., telephone notice by 10:00 a.m. the court day before the hearing) are *not* sufficient for an award of sanctions.

(f) [9:1096] **Waiver by failure to object:** By contesting a motion for sanctions on its merits, without raising alleged inadequate notice, the responding party waives any objection on this ground. [*M.E. Gray Co. v. Gray* (1985) 163 CA3d 1025, 1034, 210 CR 285, 290]

© 2020 Thomson Reuters/The Rutter Group

- [9:1097] P's notice of motion stated sanctions were sought against D. But the court imposed sanctions against D's *attorney.* The attorney waived the lack of notice by failing to object or seek a continuance or move for reconsideration. [*Jansen Assocs., Inc. v. Codercard, Inc.* (1990) 218 CA3d 1166, 1170, 267 CR 516, 518]

(g) [9:1098] **Compare—sanctions for misconduct during hearing:** Due process does *not* necessarily require written notice and a *separate* hearing to sanction dilatory conduct during the course of a court hearing. But the attorney must still receive "adequate" notice and an opportunity to be heard before sanctions are imposed. [*Marriage of Quinlan* (1989) 209 CA3d 1417, 1422, 257 CR 850, 853—attorney deliberately dragged out hearing in order to force mistrial]

1) [9:1099] **Nature of warning required:** Adequacy of notice depends on the conduct involved and the amount of sanctions imposed. A *clear warning* from the bench (or by the opposing party) of the anticipated grounds for sanctions suffices where "the substantive basis for sanctions was very narrow, the amount of the request was small, the need to prepare a defense was minimal, and no request for a separate hearing was made." [*Marriage of Quinlan,* supra, 209 CA3d at 1423, 257 CR at 853]

[9:1100-1102] *Reserved.*

b. [9:1103] **Proof requirements:** Arbitrary imposition of sanctions could chill the valid assertion of a litigant's rights. Therefore, sanctions should be imposed only for the "most egregious conduct" and in the "clearest of cases." [*Luke v. Baldwin-United Corp.* (1985) 167 CA3d 664, 669, 213 CR 654, 657]

(1) [9:1104] **Declarations:** Most courts require declarations or other evidence establishing the expenses incurred by the party seeking sanctions—e.g., where attorney fees have been incurred, the nature of the work done, the time expended, and the amount deemed the reasonable hourly fee for the services performed.

(2) [9:1105] **Factual allegations required:** It is an abuse of discretion to impose sanctions on the basis of impermissible speculation and conjecture as to an attorney's knowledge or motives in filing a motion or pleading. [See *Luke v. Baldwin-United Corp.*, supra, 167 CA3d at 669, 213 CR at 657; *and ¶9:1071*]

(3) [9:1106] **Burden of proof on motion:** As in motion proceedings generally, the burden of proof on a motion

for sanctions is usually on the moving party. [See generally, Ev.C. §500]

(4) [9:1107] **Respondent's right to subpoena witnesses?** The scope of the hearing is within the trial court's discretion. But *due process* may require that the party against whom sanctions are sought be permitted to subpoena witnesses and produce evidence to defend against the request. [See *Lavine v. Hospital of the Good Samaritan* (1985) 169 CA3d 1019, 1028, 215 CR 708, 715]

c. [9:1108] **Order must state reasons:** An order imposing sanctions must be in writing and "recite in detail the conduct or circumstances justifying the order." [CCP §128.5(c)]

(1) [9:1109] **Writing required:** A trial judge's on-the-record oral recitation of reasons for imposing sanctions is insufficient. [*Childs v. PaineWebber Inc.* (1994) 29 CA4th 982, 995-996, 35 CR2d 93, 101-102]

(2) [9:1110] **Separate order required?** CCP §128.5(c) requires that the order be "in writing and . . . recite in detail" the sanctionable conduct. But it is unclear whether a separate written order signed by the judge is necessary.

(a) [9:1111] **View requiring separate order:** Several cases hold a formal order signed by the judge is required. A clerk's minute order is insufficient; so also is the judge's on-the-record oral recitation of reasons at the hearing. [*Jansen Assocs., Inc. v. Codercard, Inc.* (1990) 218 CA3d 1166, 1171, 267 CR 516, 518; *County of Imperial v. Farmer* (1988) 205 CA3d 479, 486, 252 CR 382, 386]

- [9:1112] However, the order may *incorporate by reference* specifications of sanctionable conduct in a statement of decision. [*On v. Cow Hollow Properties* (1990) 222 CA3d 1568, 1576, 272 CR 535, 539]

- [9:1113] Alternatively, the court may incorporate by reference other papers (e.g., moving party's declarations) setting forth the conduct, circumstances and legal arguments underlying the court's conclusions. [*Childs v. PaineWebber Inc.*, supra, 29 CA4th at 996-997, 35 CR2d at 102]

(b) [9:1114] **View allowing clerk's minute order:** Some cases hold CCP §128.5(c) is satisfied by a judge's on-the-record statement at the hearing, *summarized in the minute order*, since the only purpose of the order is to provide a record for appellate review. [*Olson Partnership v. Gaylord Plating Lab, Inc.* (1990) 226 CA3d 235, 240-241, 276 CR 493, 496; see also *Kleveland v. Siegel & Wolensky, LLP* (2013) 215

© 2020 Thomson Reuters/The Rutter Group

CA4th 534, 555, 155 CR3d 599, 616—minute order sufficient where it "stated that the motion was frivolous and/or intended to harass" plaintiff, "explain[ed] its reasoning for this conclusion," with reference to supporting facts and case law, and cited to CCP §425.16(b) as authorizing sanctions]

(3) [9:1115] **Specificity required:** To impose sanctions pursuant to CCP §128.5, the trial court must (a) state *specific circumstances* giving rise to the award of attorney fees, and (b) articulate with particularity the basis for finding the sanctioned party's conduct reflected tactics or actions performed in "bad faith." [*Childs v. PaineWebber Inc.*, supra, 29 CA4th at 996, 35 CR2d at 101]

- [9:1116] An order stating merely "Motion granted. Following sanctions ordered . . ." violates both CCP §128.5 and due process principles. [*Corralejo v. Quiroga* (1984) 152 CA3d 871, 874, 199 CR 733, 735]
- [9:1117] An order merely reciting the words of the statute (e.g., "Plaintiff's motion is frivolous and not based in good faith") is likewise insufficient. [*Fegles v. Kraft* (1985) 168 CA3d 812, 817, 214 CR 380, 382; see also *Lavine v. Hospital of the Good Samaritan* (1985) 169 CA3d 1019, 1028-1029, 215 CR 708, 715; *Garcia v. Sterling* (1985) 176 CA3d 17, 23, 221 CR 349, 353; *Childs v. PaineWebber Inc.*, supra, 29 CA4th at 996, 35 CR2d at 102]
- [9:1118] Although a trial court made no express findings on bad faith, the order "recited in detail the factual circumstances leading to its imposition of sanctions," which sufficed. [*Marriage of Sahafzadeh-Taeb & Taeb* (2019) 39 CA5th 124, 143, 251 CR3d 610, 625]
- [9:1119] An order granting sanctions under CCP §128.5 was upheld where it stated the motion was "frivolous" and not made in good faith because it had no basis in law, and the party had no standing to bring the action. [*Karwasky v. Zachay* (1983) 146 CA3d 679, 681, 194 CR 292, 294]

(4) [9:1120] **Effect of insufficient order:** Several cases hold failure to specify sanctionable conduct constitutes reversible error: "The insufficiency of the order requires that we reverse it." [*Caldwell v. Samuels Jewelers* (1990) 222 CA3d 970, 976, 272 CR 126, 131; *Jansen Assocs., Inc. v. Codercard, Inc.* (1990) 218 CA3d 1166, 1171, 267 CR 516, 519; *Lavine v. Hospital of the Good Samaritan,* supra, 169 CA3d at 1030, 215 CR at 716]

(a) [9:1121] **Harmless error doctrine inapplicable:** The "harmless error" doctrine *cannot* be invoked to avoid reversal of an order that fails to detail the conduct justifying sanctions. [*West Coast Develop. v. Reed* (1992) 2 CA4th 693, 705-706, 3 CR2d 790, 797]

(b) [9:1122] **May be cured on rehearing:** However, even if a deficient order is reversed on appeal, the sanctioned party is *not* exonerated. On remand, the trial court has the power to reenter its order in compliance with §128.5, at which point the sanctions originally awarded take effect. [*Lavine v. Hospital of the Good Samaritan*, supra, 169 CA3d at 1030, 215 CR at 716; and see *I.J. Weinrot & Son, Inc. v. Jackson* (1985) 40 C3d 327, 341, 220 CR 103, 112, fn. 10]

[9:1123] *Reserved.*

d. [9:1124] **Denial of sanctions no bar to malicious prosecution action:** The court's refusal to award CCP §128.5 sanctions, and specifically its finding that there was no "bad faith," is *not* an adjudication on the substantive merits of the case, and therefore is no bar to a later action for malicious prosecution by the party denied sanctions. [*Wright v. Ripley* (1998) 65 CA4th 1189, 1194, 77 CR2d 334, 337]

The statute itself provides that the liability imposed is "*in addition to* any other liability imposed by law for acts or omissions within the purview of this section" (CCP §128.5(h)); and recovery is limited to "reasonable" out-of-pocket litigation expenses (*see* ¶*9:1076*) rather than damages. [*Wright v. Ripley*, supra, 65 CA4th at 1194, 77 CR2d at 337]

[9:1125-1134] *Reserved.*

C. SANCTIONS UNDER CCP §128.7

1. [9:1135] **In General:** An attorney or unrepresented party who *presents* a pleading, motion or similar paper to the court makes an implied "certification" as to its legal and factual merit; and is subject to sanctions for violation of this certification. [CCP §128.7; see *Murphy v. Yale Materials Handling Corp.* (1997) 54 CA4th 619, 623, 62 CR2d 865, 867—statute inapplicable to pre-1995 cases]

The purpose of the statute is "to check abuses in the filing of pleadings, petitions, written notices of motions or similar papers." [*Musaelian v. Adams* (2009) 45 C4th 512, 514, 87 CR3d 475, 476]

a. [9:1136] **Scope of certification:** The person presenting the paper to the court impliedly certifies that:

- It is not being presented primarily for an improper purpose, such as to harass or to cause unnecessary delay or needless increase in the cost of litigation;

© 2020 Thomson Reuters/The Rutter Group

- The claims, defenses and other legal contentions asserted are warranted by existing law or by a nonfrivolous argument for the extension or change in existing law;
- Any factual contentions have "evidentiary support" or, if specifically so identified, are likely to have evidentiary support after reasonable opportunity for further investigation or discovery;
- The denials of factual allegations are warranted on the evidence or, if identified as such, are reasonably based on a lack of information or belief. [CCP §128.7(b); *see discussion at ¶9:1157 ff.*]

b. [9:1136.1] **Motion by party or by court sua sponte:** The CCP §128.7 sanctions process is usually commenced by party motion. Less frequently, a court may issue an order to show cause sua sponte. [CCP §128.7(c); *see discussion at ¶9:1186 ff.*]

c. [9:1137] **Two-step procedure:** A CCP §128.7 motion involves a two-step process. The moving party first *serves* the sanctions motion on the offending party *without filing it*. The opposing party then has *21 days* to withdraw the improper pleading and avoid sanctions (the so-called "safe harbor" waiting period). At the end of the waiting period, if the pleading is not withdrawn, the moving party may then file the motion. [CCP §128.7(c)(1); *Primo Hospitality Group, Inc. v. Haney* (2019) 37 CA5th 165, 173-174, 249 CR3d 601, 607-608; *Martorana v. Marlin & Saltzman* (2009) 175 CA4th 685, 698-699, 96 CR3d 172, 182; see *Marriage of Falcone & Fyke* (2008) 164 CA4th 814, 826, 79 CR3d 588, 599; *and further discussion at ¶9:1196 ff.*]

d. [9:1138] **Not applicable to discovery papers:** By its terms, CCP §128.7 does not apply to disclosures and discovery requests, responses, objections and discovery motions. [CCP §128.7(g)]

e. [9:1139] **Statute based on Federal Rule 11:** CCP §128.7 is based in large part on Rule 11 of the Federal Rules of Civil Procedure. Therefore, federal case law interpreting Rule 11 is likely to be instructive in construing §128.7. (However, as discussed below (*¶9:1150 ff.*), there are some differences between CCP §128.7 and Federal Rule 11.) [See *Bucur v. Ahmad* (2016) 244 CA4th 175, 190, 198 CR3d 127, 138—"federal case law construing Rule 11 is persuasive authority on the meaning of section 128.7"]

[9:1140-1149] *Reserved.*

2. [9:1150] **Sanctionable Conduct:** Sanctionable conduct under CCP §128.7 is limited to "presenting" a "pleading, petition, written notice of motion, or other similar paper" to the court. [CCP §128.7(b)]

A motion for sanctions shall itself be subject to sanctions if brought for an improper purpose. [CCP §128.7(h)]

a. [9:1151] **"Presenting" papers to court:** "Presenting" includes "signing, filing, submitting, or *later advocating*" described papers to the court. [CCP §128.7(b) (emphasis added)] Thus it is possible that opposing a motion for summary judgment where the action is frivolous might be sanctionable conduct. [See *Primo Hospitality Group, Inc. v. Haney* (2019) 37 CA5th 165, 175-176, 249 CR3d 601, 609—no sanctions for opposing summary judgment because sanctions motion based on complaint, which targeted attorney did not file]

(1) [9:1152] **Compare—misconduct unrelated to presenting papers:** Because §128.7 has no application to tactics not embodied in papers presented to the court, no sanctions are available under CCP §128.7 for any of the following:

- *Oral misconduct* during trial (e.g., violating in limine orders). [*Trans-Action Comm'l Investors, Ltd. v. Jelinek* (1997) 60 CA4th 352, 368-369, 70 CR2d 449, 459]
- Statements made during *oral argument* that do not involve "advocating" a paper previously presented to the court. [See *Trans-Action Comm'l Investors, Ltd. v. Jelinek*, supra, 60 CA4th at 368-369, 70 CR2d at 459; *see also* ¶*9:1161*]
- Advocating meritless claims to an *arbitrator.* [*Optimal Markets, Inc. v. Salant* (2013) 221 CA4th 912, 922-923, 164 CR3d 901, 908—prosecution of meritless claim to arbitrator is not presentation of claim "to the court" as required by §128.7]

[9:1153] *Reserved.*

b. [9:1154] **Which papers:** CCP §128.7 expressly applies to "petitions" and "pleadings"; the latter term includes allegations and defenses contained in complaints, cross-complaints, answers *and demurrers.* [CCP §§420, 422.10]

CCP §128.7 also applies to a "written notice of motion" and to "*other similar papers.*" This clearly covers grounds set forth in a notice of motion and (presumably) matters contained in other documents attached to the motion; e.g., declarations and points and authorities. [CCP §128.7(b)]

(1) [9:1155] **"Other similar papers"?** This phrase is vague, but the word "similar" presumably refers to all court papers relating to a motion hearing, thus including opposition or reply papers.

(2) [9:1156] **Compare—federal rule:** The federal rule does not use the word "similar" and thus avoids this ambiguity. The federal rule applies to "a pleading, written motion *or other paper*" presented to the court. [FRCP 11(b)]

© 2020 Thomson Reuters/The Rutter Group

3. [9:1157] **Scope of Certification—In General:** By "presenting" the above-described papers (¶*9:1154 ff.*) to the court, an attorney or unrepresented party certifies that it has read the paper, and "to the best of the person's knowledge, information, and belief, formed after an inquiry reasonable under the circumstances":

- *Proper purpose:* "It is not being *presented primarily for an improper purpose*, such as to harass or to cause unnecessary delay or needless increase in the cost of litigation" (CCP §128.7(b)(1) (emphasis added); *see* ¶*9:1181 ff.*);
- *Legal merit:* "The claims, defenses, and other legal contentions therein are *warranted by existing law* or by a nonfrivolous argument for the extension, modification, or reversal of existing law or the establishment of new law" (CCP §128.7(b)(2) (emphasis added); *see* ¶*9:1176 ff.*);
- *Evidentiary support:* "The allegations and other factual contentions have *evidentiary support* or, if specifically so identified, are likely to have evidentiary support after a reasonable opportunity for further investigation or discovery" (CCP §128.7(b)(3) (emphasis added)); and

  "The *denials* of factual contentions are *warranted on the evidence* or, if specifically so identified, are reasonably based on a lack of information or belief" (CCP §128.7(b)(4) (emphasis added)).

Violation of *any* of these certifications may give rise to sanctions. [*Eichenbaum v. Alon* (2003) 106 CA4th 967, 976, 131 CR2d 296, 302]

a. [9:1158] **Purpose:** This certification is designed to create an *affirmative duty of investigation* as to both law and fact, and thus to deter frivolous actions and costly meritless maneuvers. [See *Business Guides, Inc. v. Chromatic Communications Enterprises, Inc.* (1991) 498 US 533, 550, 111 S.Ct. 922, 929—interpreting Federal Rule 11]

b. [9:1159] **Objective standard:** Whether the certificate is violated is tested *objectively*—i.e., whether the paper filed is frivolous, legally unreasonable or without factual foundation. "The actual belief standard . . . requires a *well-founded* belief. We measure the truth-finding inquiry's reasonableness under an objective standard and apply this standard both to attorneys and to their clients." [*Bockrath v. Aldrich Chem. Co., Inc.* (1999) 21 C4th 71, 82, 86 CR2d 846, 853-854 (emphasis added); *Marriage of Sahafzadeh-Taeb & Taeb* (2019) 39 CA5th 124, 135, 251 CR3d 610, 618, fn. 6; *Peake v. Underwood* (2014) 227 CA4th 428, 440, 173 CR3d 624, 635—"A claim is objectively unreasonable if any reasonable attorney would agree that [it] is totally and completely without merit" (brackets in original; internal quotes omitted)]

Under §128.7, "it is not necessary to show the party acted with an improper motive or subjective bad faith. But the fact that a party does not actually believe in the merits of his or her claim is relevant to the issue whether sanctions are warranted in the particular case." [*Peake v. Underwood*, supra, 227 CA4th at 449, 173 CR3d at 642]

Compare—CCP §128.5: See discussion at ¶9:1020 ff.

(1) **Application**

[9:1159.1] *Reserved.*

- [9:1159.2] The court handling a marital dissolution proceeding was authorized to impose CCP §128.7 sanctions against Wife and her attorney for filing a separate lawsuit against Husband and his accountants over *matters clearly within the jurisdiction of the family law court.* [*Burkle v. Burkle* (2006) 144 CA4th 387, 400, 50 CR3d 436, 446]

- [9:1159.3] Where evidence showed Home Buyer had actual notice of defects in the home she purchased, Buyer's statutory claims against Seller's agent for breach of duty for failing to disclose defects were inconsistent with the facts and well-settled law, and Buyer's counsel could have had no honest or reasonable belief in the validity of Buyer's claim. Moreover, Buyer declined to dismiss her action during the statutory safe harbor period and instead amended her complaint to *add* common law fraud claims similar to claims she had previously dismissed. Given these facts, the trial court was within its discretion in imposing CCP §128.7 sanctions against Buyer and her counsel. [*Peake v. Underwood*, supra, 227 CA4th at 449, 173 CR3d at 642]

- [9:1159.4] The trial court did not abuse its discretion in imposing sanctions where it was obvious that plaintiffs' claims were barred by res judicata, judicial admissions and judicial estoppel. Filing a new complaint based on the same facts to evade a ruling made in previous litigation is sanctionable under §128.7. [*Bucur v. Ahmad* (2016) 244 CA4th 175, 191, 198 CR3d 127, 139]

[9:1159.5-1159.9] *Reserved.*

[9:1159.10] ***PRACTICE POINTER:*** Where plaintiff *lacks* sufficient evidence to support particular allegations but *believes such evidence is likely to be discovered* through further investigation or discovery, the complaint must "specifically identify" those al-

© 2020 Thomson Reuters/The Rutter Group

legations (see CCP §128.7(b)(3), *discussed at ¶9:1169 ff.*). [*Bockrath v. Aldrich Chem. Co., Inc.*, supra, 21 C4th at 82, 86 CR2d at 854]

c. [9:1160] **Duty to reevaluate:** The certificate is not limited to the signing or filing of papers. Rather, sanctions are imposed for "presenting" a pleading or other paper in violation of the statute. As discussed (¶*9:1151*), a party "presents" a pleading or paper if it *signs, files, submits or later advocates* the positions set forth in the original document. [See CCP §128.7(b)]

The statute thus imposes a *continuing obligation* on party and counsel to insure that claims, defenses and arguments are factually and legally sound.

(1) [9:1161] **Later "advocacy" of prior papers:** A litigant's obligations with respect to the contents of papers are not measured solely as of the time the papers are filed with the court. The same certification applies when the litigant "advocates" claims or defenses previously pleaded. [See CCP §128.7(b)]

Thus, sanctions may be awarded where an attorney or unrepresented party argues positions contained in earlier-filed papers after learning such positions are without evidentiary support or legal merit. E.g., an attorney at a pretrial conference orally argues ("presents" to the court) the merits of a claim or defense previously pleaded; whether the argument is objectively reasonable is measured *at the time it is made* rather than when the pleading was filed.

[9:1161.1-1161.4] *Reserved.*

d. [9:1161.5] **Duty owed by attorneys substituted in pending lawsuit?** Attorneys who substitute in a pending lawsuit should *reevaluate* the merits of the client's case and, if necessary, conduct further investigation and research. Advocating a meritless pleading filed by another lawyer likely falls within the provisions of CCP §128.7(b). [See *Primo Hospitality Group, Inc. v. Haney* (2019) 37 CA5th 165, 176, 249 CR3d 601, 609]

However, §128.7 sanctions cannot be imposed unless the successor counsel presented a "petition" or "pleading" to the court. [*Optimal Markets, Inc. v. Salant* (2013) 221 CA4th 912, 921, 164 CR3d 901, 907—court without jurisdiction to impose §128.7 sanctions where counsel substituted into lawsuit after it had been stayed and referred to binding arbitration]

4. [9:1162] **Certification re Evidentiary Support:** The attorney or party presenting a pleading or other paper to the court certifies that, to the best of that person's knowledge and belief "formed after an inquiry reasonable under the circumstances," the allegations and other factual contentions have evidentiary support or, "*if specifically so identified*, are likely to have evidentiary support

after a reasonable opportunity for further investigation or discovery." [CCP §128.7(b)(3) (emphasis added)]

The same basic standard governs *denials* of factual contentions: i.e., the denials must be "warranted on the evidence or, if specifically so identified, are reasonably based on a lack of information or belief." [CCP §128.7(b)(4)]

a. [9:1163] **Factors affecting whether inquiry "reasonable":** What constitutes a *reasonable* inquiry may depend on such factors as:

- how much time for investigation was available before filing (see *Cooter & Gell v. Hartmarx Corp.* (1990) 496 US 384, 401-402, 110 S.Ct. 2447, 2459—interpreting FRCP 11);
- whether the attorney had to rely on a client for information as to the facts underlying the pleading, motion or other paper;
- whether the attorney depended on forwarding counsel or another member of the bar (see *Business Guides, Inc. v. Chromatic Communications Enterprises, Inc.* (1991) 498 US 533, 550, 111 S.Ct. 922, 933 (interpreting Federal Rule 11));
- *complexity* of the factual issues and the massiveness of the threatened liability;
- whether the *opposing party controls* the relevant facts (in which case, a pleader must have leeway at least in the early stages of litigation to make allegations that may not be well-grounded);
- whether the allegations relate to the *opposing party's knowledge, intent or purpose* (in which case, again the pleader must be allowed leeway);
- whether prudent lawyers, "to be safe," would include the claims asserted or make the allegations made (see *Townsend v. Holman Consulting Corp.* (9th Cir. 1990) 929 F2d 1358, 1364 (interpreting FRCP 11)).

b. [9:1164] **Reliance on information supplied by client:** An attorney may normally rely on information obtained from the client *as to which the client has first-hand knowledge.* I.e., an attorney is not required to pass judgment on the credibility of his or her client under threat of a monetary sanction.

- [9:1165] But reliance on the client's statement must be *reasonable.* Counsel cannot blindly accept statements that are implausible or hearsay without investigating or seeking corroboration. [*Childs v. State Farm Mut. Auto. Ins. Co.* (5th Cir. 1994) 29 F3d 1018, 1026 (interpreting FRCP 11)—P's counsel made adequate prefiling inquiry but later ignored facts indicating P's claim was fraudulent]

© 2020 Thomson Reuters/The Rutter Group

c. [9:1166] **Reliance on hearsay:** The attorney's certification re evidentiary support presumes the attorney has personal knowledge of facts sufficient to support the certification. An attorney may rely on hearsay information only to the extent it is *reasonable* to do so. [See *Unioil, Inc. v. E.F. Hutton & Co., Inc.* (9th Cir. 1986) 809 F2d 548, 558 (interpreting FRCP 11)—unreasonable to rely entirely on facts provided by forwarding counsel; *Garr v. U.S. Healthcare* (3rd Cir. 1994) 22 F3d 1274, 1278-1279 (interpreting FRCP 11)—unreasonable to rely entirely on information reported in newspaper]

(1) [9:1167] **"Shot in the dark" sanctionable:** The fact the hearsay turns out to be correct does not insulate the attorney from sanctions: "A shot in the dark is a sanctionable event, even if it somehow hits the mark." [*Garr v. U.S. Healthcare*, supra, 22 F3d at 1279 (interpreting FRCP 11)]

d. [9:1168] **Impact of summary judgment motion:** The fact a judge grants summary judgment does not by itself establish that the opposing party violated its CCP §128.7(a) certification. [See Committee Notes on 1993 Amendments to Federal Rules of Civil Procedure (1993) 146 FRD 401, 586 (interpreting FRCP 11)]

On the other hand, if a party has sufficient evidence with respect to a contention to *defeat* a summary judgment motion, that contention clearly has sufficient evidentiary support for purposes of §128.7.

e. [9:1169] **Allegations requiring further investigation:** The statute requires that allegations lacking evidentiary support be "specifically so identified." [CCP §128.7(b)(3); see *Cole v. Patricia A. Meyer & Assocs., APC* (2012) 206 CA4th 1095, 1113, 142 CR3d 646, 661, fn. 6 (citing text)]

(1) [9:1170] **When proper:** Such allegations are proper where the pleader:

— is unable to confirm a factual allegation before filing *despite reasonable investigation*;

— specifically identifies the allegations in question (¶*9:1171*); and

— *has a reasonable belief* that the allegations *will* have evidentiary support after further investigation or discovery. [See Committee Notes on 1993 Amendments to Federal Rules of Civil Procedure (1993) 146 FRD 401, 585 (interpreting FRCP 11)]

(2) [9:1171] **"Specifically identified":** The meaning of this phrase is not entirely clear (under FRCP 11 as well).

Under the Federal Rule, it appears to be enough that the allegations are made "on information and belief." [See Committee Notes on 1993 Amendments to Federal

Rules of Civil Procedure (1993) 146 FRD 401, 585 (interpreting FRCP 11)]

However, to avoid any question regarding the "specifically identified" requirement, the pleader can allege as follows:

> "The following are facts for which (plaintiff/defendant) lacks evidentiary support at the present time but which (plaintiff/defendant) is informed and believes are likely to have evidentiary support after a reasonable opportunity for further investigation or discovery."

(3) [9:1172] **Effect of failure to obtain evidentiary support:** Pleaders need not amend their pleadings to delete allegations for which they cannot obtain evidentiary support. But they risk sanctions if they continue to advocate claims or defenses which they *know* (or should know) are lacking in evidentiary support. [See *Childs v. State Farm Mut. Auto. Ins. Co.* (5th Cir. 1994) 29 F3d 1018, 1026 (interpreting FRCP 11)]

f. [9:1173] **Comment—impact on pleadings generally:** The certification re evidentiary support is likely to have dramatic impact on "blunderbuss pleadings"; i.e., complaints and answers that raise every conceivable claim or defense known to the pleader regardless of any facts to support them.

(1) [9:1174] **Examples:**
- "alter ego" allegations in lawsuits against corporations (to justify naming its officers and directors as codefendants) where there is no evidence to support such allegations;
- "bad faith" claims in every complaint for insurance proceeds;
- answers containing every conceivable affirmative defense ("laches," "estoppel," "waiver," "public policy," etc.) even though there are no facts to support them. Recall that affirmative defenses must be pled with as much factual specificity as a cause of action. [*Department of Finance v. City of Merced* (2019) 33 CA5th 286, 294, 244 CR3d 831, 838]

☞ [9:1175] ***PRACTICE POINTER:*** Omit claims or defenses for which you have no reasonable likelihood of obtaining evidentiary support. It is safer to seek leave to amend your pleadings after investigations and discovery to allege additional claims or defenses.

5. [9:1176] **Certification re Legal Contentions:** The attorney or unrepresented party also certifies that "[t]he claims, defenses, and other legal contentions therein are warranted by existing law or by a *nonfrivolous argument* for the extension, modification,

© 2020 Thomson Reuters/The Rutter Group

or reversal of existing law or the establishment of new law." [CCP §128.7(b)(2) (emphasis added)]

a. [9:1177] **"Nonfrivolous" argument required:** A "nonfrivolous" argument presupposes reasonable research and investigation. Again, this is an objective standard and bars any excuse for patently frivolous arguments. [See Committee Notes on 1993 Amendments to Federal Rules of Civil Procedure (1993) 146 FRD 401, 587 (interpreting FRCP 11)]

(1) [9:1178] **Reasonable research:** "[T]he extent to which a litigant has researched the issues and found some support for its theories even in minority opinions, in law review articles, or through consultation with other attorneys, should be taken into account in determining whether [the certification] has been violated." [Committee Notes on 1993 Amendments to Federal Rules of Civil Procedure (1993) 146 FRD 401, 587 (interpreting FRCP 11)]

b. [9:1179] **Frivolous argument in support of otherwise valid motion:** Sanctions are proper only if the "*pleading, motion or paper*" is without merit. Therefore, if the pleading or motion is otherwise meritorious, the fact that one of the supporting arguments is frivolous does *not* justify sanctions. [*Golden Eagle Distributing Corp. v. Burroughs Corp.* (9th Cir. 1986) 801 F2d 1531, 1540-1541 (interpreting FRCP 11)]

c. [9:1180] **Concern re "chilling" advocacy:** Several federal cases caution against "chilling" an attorney's enthusiasm or creativity in pursuing new theories, at least in areas of the law that cannot be regarded as settled. [*Hudson v. Moore Business Forms, Inc.* (9th Cir. 1987) 836 F2d 1156, 1160 (interpreting FRCP 11)]

6. [9:1181] **Certification re Purpose:** The signer also certifies that the pleading, motion or paper "is not being presented *primarily* for an improper purpose, such as to harass or to cause unnecessary delay or needless increase in the cost of litigation." [CCP §128.7(b)(1) (emphasis added)]

a. [9:1182] **"Primarily":** There is no violation of the certification unless the "primary" purpose is to harass or cause needless delay or expense. If a claim is "nonfrivolous," then as a matter of law it is "not presented for an improper purpose." [*Ponce v. Wells Fargo Bank* (2018) 21 CA5th 253, 265, 230 CR3d 236, 246]

(1) [9:1183] **Compare—federal rule:** This is another area in which the California statute differs from Federal Rule 11. Under FRCP 11, the certificate is violated if the attorney or party has "*any* improper purpose" (FRCP 11(b)(1)), which could lead to sanctions for even an incidental intent to harass.

b. [9:1184] **Frivolous claims as evidence of improper purpose:** Although the "proper purpose" and "nonfrivolous claims" certifications are separate and distinct, they often *overlap* because "frivolousness" is evidence of an improper purpose. Indeed, with respect to *complaints*, a finding of frivolousness is a prerequisite to a finding of improper purpose. [*Townsend v. Holman Consulting Corp.* (9th Cir. 1990) 929 F2d 1358, 1362 (interpreting FRCP 11)]

[9:1184.1-1184.4] *Reserved.*

- [9:1184.5] Any claim against a *deceased person* (instead of his or her representative) is deemed frivolous and sanctionable under CCP §128.7. [*Eichenbaum v. Alon* (2003) 106 CA4th 967, 976, 131 CR2d 296, 302—amended complaint contained fraud claim against decedent despite court orders striking such claims from previous complaints]

c. [9:1185] **No violation where valid claim or defense shown:** There is no "improper purpose" in filing a complaint or other paper that is well-grounded in fact and warranted by existing law. Such a paper cannot be sanctioned regardless of the subjective intent of the attorney or party to harass the opposing party. [See *Zaldivar v. City of Los Angeles* (9th Cir. 1986) 780 F2d 823, 830 (interpreting FRCP 11) (overruled on other grounds in *Cooter & Gell v. Hartmarx Corp.* (1990) 496 US 384, 110 S.Ct. 2447)]

7. **Procedural Considerations**

a. [9:1186] **Motion by party or by court sua sponte:** Normally, sanctions are awarded on motion of a party (CCP §128.7(c)(1)); although the court is also empowered to impose sanctions "[o]n its own motion" (CCP §128.7(c)(2)). (But court-initiated sanctions cannot include monetary awards to a party; *see ¶9:1209.5.*)

Two-step procedure: A party seeking sanctions, or the court on its own initiative, must follow a two-step procedure:

- First, the offending party must be *served* with a motion for sanctions (or, where the court is acting sua sponte, an OSC why sanctions should not be imposed). This starts the 21-day "safe harbor" period during which the offending party may withdraw the improper pleading and thereby avoid sanctions (*see ¶9:1196*).
- If the offending pleading is not withdrawn during the "safe harbor" period, the motion for sanctions may then be filed. [*Malovec v. Hamrell* (1999) 70 CA4th 434, 440, 82 CR2d 712, 717]

© 2020 Thomson Reuters/The Rutter Group

➪ [9:1186.1] ***PRACTICE POINTER:*** Where the violation is blatant, *ask the court to set a §128.7 hearing on its own motion.* This is likely to cause the opposing party to withdraw the offending pleading, saving you and your client the effort and cost of a sanctions hearing. You may also ask the court to shorten the 21-day safe harbor period if you bring the motion (*see ¶9:1202*).

Where the offense is not so blatant, give opposing counsel *informal* notice of the potential violation *before* serving a CCP §128.7 motion. This may avoid unnecessary expense for both parties. It also displays tact because it enables opposing counsel to back down from untenable positions with less "loss of face" than after being served with a sanctions motion. (Informal notice, however, will *not* satisfy the 21-day "safe harbor" requirement; a formal sanctions motion is required. *See ¶9:1193, 9:1196.*)

b. [9:1187] **Timeliness:** Although there is no time limit on a party's motion for sanctions, the court may consider whether the moving party exercised "due diligence." [CCP §128.7(c)]

- [9:1188] Ordinarily, the motion should be served *promptly* after the violation occurs. (It cannot be delayed until after trial because this would defeat the "safe harbor" provision below (*¶9:1196 ff.*).)

[9:1189-1189.4] *Reserved.*

c. [9:1189.5] **Notice:** Constitutional principles of due process require a notice of motion to identify the persons against whom monetary sanctions are being sought. [*Cromwell v. Cummings* (1998) 65 CA4th Supp. 10, 13, 76 CR2d 171, 173; *see discussion at ¶9:1092 ff.*]

d. [9:1190] **Separate motion required:** A party motion for sanctions under §128.7 must be made *separately* from any other motion or request to the court. [CCP §128.7(c)(1); see *Martorana v. Marlin & Saltzman* (2009) 175 CA4th 685, 699, 96 CR3d 172, 182—including request for sanctions in demurrer did not satisfy CCP §128.7(c)(1)]

FORM: Motion for Sanctions Under Code of Civil Procedure Section 128.7, *see Form 9C:1* in Rivera, *Cal. Prac. Guide: Civ. Pro. Before Trial FORMS* (TRG).

(1) [9:1191] **Effect:** First of all, this prevents the moving party from simply adding a sanctions request to every motion or opposition.

It also prevents the moving party from seeking sanctions both under §128.7 and *some other source* of sanctions power (e.g., sanctions for contempt or violation of court orders) in the "same motion."

(2) [9:1192] **Fees and expenses to prevailing party:** The court may award to the party prevailing on the sanctions motion its reasonable expenses and attorney fees in presenting *or opposing* the motion. [CCP §128.7(c)(1); *see ¶9:1220*]

(3) [9:1193] **Compare—correspondence stating intent to seek sanctions:** Informal notice of an intent to seek sanctions cannot serve as a substitute for a formal motion. The latter must be served on the offending party to commence the 21-day "safe harbor" period (¶*9:1196*). [*Martorana v. Marlin & Saltzman* (2009) 175 CA4th 685, 699, 96 CR3d 172, 182]

[9:1194-1195] *Reserved.*

e. [9:1196] **Waiting period on sanctions motion (21-day "safe harbor" provision):** A party's motion for sanctions *may not be filed* until *21 days* ("or any other period as the court may prescribe") after it is *served*. This allows the party against whom sanctions are sought an opportunity—i.e., a "safe harbor"—to withdraw or correct the challenged paper and thereby avoid sanctions. [See CCP §128.7(c)(1); *Primo Hospitality Group, Inc. v. Haney* (2019) 37 CA5th 165, 173-174, 249 CR3d 601, 607-608; *Barnes v. Department of Corrections* (1999) 74 CA4th 126, 130, 87 CR2d 594, 596 (citing text)]

The same 21-day "safe harbor" applies when the court issues an order to show cause re sanctions sua sponte. I.e., the targeted attorney can avoid sanctions by withdrawing or appropriately correcting the challenged paper within the 21-day period. [CCP §128.7(c)(2); *Malovec v. Hamrell* (1999) 70 CA4th 434, 440, 82 CR2d 712, 716; *Interstate Specialty Marketing, Inc. v. ICRA Sapphire, Inc.* (2013) 217 CA4th 708, 710, 715-716, 158 CR3d 743, 745, 749—court erred in issuing sanctions on same day it set OSC; *Moofly Productions, LLC v. Favila* (2018) 24 CA5th 993, 999, 234 CR3d 769, 772—court erred in scheduling OSC hearing re sanctions at same time as denying P's motion for reconsideration, making P's later attempt to withdraw motion before OSC hearing "meaningless"]

Rationale: CCP §128.7's purpose is not to punish the offender but to *promote compliance* and *deter frivolous filings.* "To this end, the statute permits withdrawal of a challenged pleading." [*Malovec v. Hamrell,* supra, 70 CA4th at 442, 82 CR2d at 718; see *Marriage of Falcone & Fyke* (2008) 164 CA4th 814, 826, 79 CR3d 588, 599]

Compare—pre-2003 cases: The safe harbor period was reduced from 30 to 21 days effective 1/1/03. Therefore, cases dealing with sanctions imposed prior to that date may refer to a "30-day safe harbor period."

(1) [9:1196a] **Extended for service by mail?** It is not clear whether CCP §1013, which generally extends the

© 2020 Thomson Reuters/The Rutter Group

time to do an act following service by mail (¶*9:87.4 ff.*), applies to the §128.7 safe harbor period. [See *Marriage of Falcone & Fyke*, supra, 164 CA4th at 825-826, 79 CR3d at 599-600 (declining to reach issue)]

☞ [9:1196.1] ***PRACTICE POINTERS:*** This may cause you to think twice about making a sanctions motion because the costs and fees incurred in preparing the motion *cannot be recovered* if your opponent withdraws the offending paper during the "safe harbor" period.

Further, the 21-day "safe-harbor" provision may preclude CCP §128.7 sanctions based on frivolous pleadings where you also *demur or move to strike* those pleadings. Once the demurrer or motion has been ruled upon, it is not possible to withdraw or correct the challenged pleading (*see* ¶*9:1206*).

If you decide to proceed with the motion, it may be safer to wait until at least the 22nd day after service before filing it. Because a party has 21 days to withdraw the offending document, a judge may decide that filing the motion on the 21st day is *premature.*

(2) [9:1197] **Compare—other sanctions:** This "safe harbor" provision applies only to sanctions under CCP §128.7. It does not apply to other rules and statutes authorizing sanctions (e.g., discovery sanctions).

(3) [9:1198] **Compare—federal rule:** There is no "safe harbor" under FRCP 11 where the court acts sua sponte to impose sanctions. [FRCP 11(c); see *Malovec v. Hamrell*, supra, 70 CA4th at 440, 82 CR2d at 716]

(4) [9:1199] **Hearing date:** All moving and supporting papers must be served *and filed* at least *16 court days* before the hearing date, *plus* additional time where service is by mail. [CCP §1005(b); *see* ¶*9:87 ff.*]

(a) [9:1200] **Effect—approximate 40-day delay:** Absent an order shortening time, this means there will be at least an approximate 40-day delay (21 calendar days' "hold" plus 16 *court* days after filing) between service and hearing of the §128.7 motion. [*Cromwell v. Cummings* (1998) 65 CA4th Supp. 10, 13, 76 CR2d 171, 173, fn. 3 (decided under prior law requiring 15 days' minimum notice)]

Comment: This strongly suggests that the violation should be pretty important to justify the effort and delay.

(b) [9:1201] **Notice served must contain hearing date:** A notice served on the party against whom sanctions is sought must comply with all of the requirements of CCP §1010, including the time and place of the motion hearing. Otherwise, it does not satisfy the "safe harbor" requirement even if a second notice stating the time and place is served when the motion is filed. [*Galleria Plus, Inc. v. Hanmi Bank* (2009) 179 CA4th 535, 538, 101 CR3d 803, 805—document served stating sanctions motion would be filed "on or after" specified date (more than 21 days later) did not provide notice of hearing date and thus did not satisfy "safe harbor" requirement]

Comment: Some have questioned whether having a hearing date on the originally-served motion is necessary because what is important is giving notice of the date on which the motion will be *filed* (the last date in the "safe harbor" period within which the offending document may be withdrawn). But since the statute says the notice must be served as provided in CCP §1010 (CCP §128.7(c)(1)), which requires a hearing date, the safest course is to include the hearing date on the original notice.

➪ [9:1201.1] ***PRACTICE POINTER:*** This assumes you can set or obtain a hearing date from the court without filing your motion until 21 days later. Depending on the procedure for obtaining a hearing date in the court in which your matter is pending, if you are unable to set a date without filing the motion, you may need to make an ex parte request to obtain a hearing date to commence the CCP §128.7 procedures.

(5) [9:1202] **Orders shortening time:** On a *party's* motion for sanctions, the court may shorten (or extend) the 21-day "safe harbor" period. [See CCP §128.7(c)(1)—"or any other period as the court may prescribe"]

But the rule is different where the court moves for sanctions sua sponte; i.e., the statute apparently does *not* permit the court to shorten (or extend) the 21-day period. [See CCP §128.7(c)(2)]

➪ [9:1203] ***PRACTICE POINTERS:*** Seeking an order shortening the 21-day "safe harbor" period makes sense when sanctionable *motion papers* are filed by the opposing party and only 16 court days' notice of motion is given. Without an order shortening the safe harbor period, your CCP §128.7

© 2020 Thomson Reuters/The Rutter Group

motion cannot be heard at the same time as the noticed motion. The same is true, of course, where sanctionable conduct appears in *opposition* or *reply* papers. (But an order shortening time should be unnecessary to attack frivolous matters in a motion for *summary judgment or summary adjudication* because there is a minimum 75-day notice requirement.)

Alternatively, you can move to *continue* the hearing date on the offending motion so as to allow the 21-day safe harbor period to expire. [See *Li v. Majestic Industry Hills, LLC* (2009) 177 CA4th 585, 594, 99 CR3d 334, 340 (quoting text)]

Requests to shorten the 21-day safe harbor period or to continue the hearing on the allegedly improper motion can be made *ex parte.* [CRC 3.1200-3.1207; *see ¶9:347*]

(a) [9:1203.1] **Effect of opposition to continuance:** If the party serving a sanctions motion seeks to continue the hearing on the offending motion and the other party *unreasonably opposes* the continuance, making compliance with CCP §128.7's safe harbor period impossible, "it might be appropriate to conclude the right to the full safe harbor period has been *waived or forfeited.*" [*Li v. Majestic Industry Hills, LLC,* supra, 177 CA4th at 594, 99 CR3d at 340, fn. 7 (emphasis added)]

(6) [9:1204] **"Appropriate" correction:** To avoid sanctions, the party need only "appropriately" correct the violation. [CCP §128.7(c)(1)]

Normally, this means the party must *withdraw* the challenged pleading or paper or at least *acknowledge* its lack of factual or legal merit at the present time.

This can be done either *formally or informally*; e.g., by filing amendments to challenged pleadings or declarations, or formally withdrawing a challenged motion, or simply writing a letter to opposing counsel stating the challenged argument is withdrawn, etc. [See Committee Notes on 1993 Amendments to Federal Rules of Civil Procedure (1993) 146 FRD 401, 591 (interpreting FRCP 11)]

➪ [9:1205] ***PRACTICE POINTER:*** Most judges or lawyers probably will not accept "informal" agreements to correct or withdraw a claim or defense. They will insist on a dismissal or written stipulation withdrawing the challenged pleading or allegations; or at the very least, an interlineation on the pleading in question signed by counsel.

Also, if leave of court is required to amend or correct your pleading, in addition to telling opposing counsel, you should obtain the necessary court approval.

[9:1205.1-1205.4] *Reserved.*

(a) [9:1205.5] **Notice of compliance required:** Parties who comply by dismissing the complaint or otherwise withdrawing papers that are the subject of a CCP §128.7 motion must notify the moving party of such compliance before the end of the "safe harbor" period to avoid the imposition of sanctions. Without such notice, the moving party may not realize the problem has been resolved and may incur the expense and effort of filing the sanctions motions. [*Liberty Mut. Fire Ins. Co. v. McKenzie* (2001) 88 CA4th 681, 692, 105 CR2d 910, 917]

(7) [9:1206] **Sanctions barred if offending motion resolved during "safe harbor" period:** Because compliance with the "safe harbor" is a prerequisite to recovery of sanctions under CCP §128.7, the opposing party must have the full 21 days to correct or withdraw an offending pleading or motion. Thus, where a frivolous motion is involved, if the court *denies the motion* before the 21-day period has expired, no sanctions can be awarded. To avoid this result, the party seeking sanctions should either request an order shortening the "safe harbor" period or a continuance of the hearing (¶*9:1202 ff.*). [*Li v. Majestic Industry Hills, LLC,* supra, 177 CA4th at 595, 99 CR3d at 341]

[9:1206.1-1206.9] *Reserved.*

(8) [9:1206.10] **Sanctions barred where motion filed before expiration of "safe harbor":** No sanctions can be imposed under a motion filed before expiration of the 21-day "safe harbor" *no matter how improper* the conduct sought to be sanctioned. [*Goodstone v. Southwest Airlines Co.* (1998) 63 CA4th 406, 418-419, 73 CR2d 655, 673]

(a) [9:1206.11] **"Substantial compliance" not sufficient:** The 21-day "safe harbor" provision is *strictly* enforced. "Substantial compliance" is *not* enough. [See *Cromwell v. Cummings* (1998) 65 CA4th Supp. 10, 15, 76 CR2d 171, 174—"Correspondence to opposing counsel which threatens sanctions of an unknown nature at an unspecified time against unidentified persons, and which lacks citation to controlling authority, does not fulfill these statutory purposes"]

© 2020 Thomson Reuters/The Rutter Group

(b) [9:1206.12] **Motion filed must be same as motion served:** Where the sanctions motion filed with the court differs from that previously served on the opponent, the 21-day safe harbor period runs from the filing date, not the date of service. [*Hart v. Avetoom* (2002) 95 CA4th 410, 413, 115 CR2d 511, 513—"new and improved" sanctions motion violated safe harbor requirement]

[9:1206.13-1206.19] *Reserved.*

(9) [9:1206.20] **Sanctions barred where motion served after action terminated:** The 21-day safe harbor provision precludes a party or the court from initiating efforts to obtain CCP §128.7 sanctions after a case has been dismissed or judgment rendered. [*Malovec v. Hamrell*, supra, 70 CA4th at 441, 82 CR2d at 717—court may not issue order to show cause after case dismissed; *Barnes v. Department of Corrections* (1999) 74 CA4th 126, 130, 87 CR2d 594, 598—may not file motion for sanctions after conclusion of case]

[9:1206.21-1206.29] *Reserved.*

[9:1206.30] ***PRACTICE POINTER:*** If you're seeking §128.7 sanctions, *serve your sanctions motion before* demurring, moving for summary judgment, etc. After the 21-day hold, if the opposing party has not withdrawn or cured the offense voluntarily, you can then file your sanctions motion concurrently with your demurrer or summary judgment motion.

(a) [9:1206.31] **Compare—motion served after demurrer sustained without leave to amend:** An order sustaining a demurrer without leave to amend does not bar an award of §128.7 sanctions *unless the order is reduced to a judgment* before the sanctions motion is served and filed. [*Banks v. Hathaway, Perrett, Webster, Powers & Chrisman* (2002) 97 CA4th 949, 954, 118 CR2d 803, 806-807 (citing text)]

[9:1206.32-1206.34] *Reserved.*

(b) [9:1206.35] **Compare—motion *served* but not filed before judgment entered:** As long as the CCP §128.7 motion is *served* in compliance with the "safe harbor" provision before a judgment was entered, the court retains jurisdiction to grant it even if it was filed after entry of the judgment: "Section 128.7 does not require that a motion for sanctions be filed before the court renders a dispositive ruling on the pleading or motion as to which sanctions are sought." [*Day v. Collingwood* (2006) 144 CA4th 1116, 1126, 50 CR3d 903, 910 (emphasis omitted)]

[9:1206.36-1206.39] *Reserved.*

f. [9:1206.40] **Judge hearing motion:** Sanctions motions are usually brought before the judge before whom the allegedly sanctionable conduct occurred. But there is no jurisdictional requirement preventing an award by a different judge—e.g., because of illness, retirement or reassignment of the original judge.

An award may also be appropriate in cases assigned for all purposes to a single judge (e.g., in family law cases) for sanctionable conduct before a different judge—e.g., where a party has improperly instituted a separate action on the same claims or defenses before a different judge. [See *Burkle v. Burkle* (2006) 144 CA4th 387, 400, 50 CR3d 436, 446 (*discussed at ¶9:1159.2*)]

(1) [9:1206.41] **Compare—where subjective bad faith finding required:** When it is necessary for the judge awarding sanctions to make a subjective finding of bad faith to justify the sanctions order (e.g., for conduct constituting contempt), the judge in whose court the sanctionable conduct occurred is the only appropriate judicial officer to award sanctions. [See *Burkle v. Burkle*, supra, 144 CA4th at 402, 50 CR3d at 447]

g. [9:1207] **Sua sponte motions:** The court may impose sanctions sua sponte but only after (a) entering an order describing the sanctionable conduct; (b) directing the offending party to show cause why it has not violated the statute; and (c) after expiration of the 21-day "safe harbor" period. [CCP §128.7(c)(2)]

(1) [9:1208] **Limitation—effect of dismissal:** The court cannot impose *monetary* sanctions (e.g., attorney fees to opposing party) where the case settles or is voluntarily dismissed before the court's order to show cause is issued. [CCP §128.7(d)(2); see *Malovec v. Hamrell* (1999) 70 CA4th 434, 443, 82 CR2d 712, 718-719]

(a) [9:1209] **Rationale:** Parties settling a case should not subsequently be faced with an unexpected order from the court leading to monetary sanctions that might have affected their willingness to settle or voluntarily dismiss the case. [See *Malovec v. Hamrell*, supra, 70 CA4th at 442, 82 CR2d at 718]

[9:1209.1-1209.4] *Reserved.*

(2) [9:1209.5] **Limitation—no monetary sanctions to opposing party:** A monetary sanction imposed after a court-initiated order to show cause is limited to a penalty payable to the court and may not include or consist of sanctions payable to a party. [See CCP §128.7(d); *Malovec*

© 2020 Thomson Reuters/The Rutter Group

v. Hamrell, supra, 70 CA4th at 443-444, 82 CR2d at 718; *Interstate Specialty Marketing, Inc. v. ICRA Sapphire, Inc.* (2013) 217 CA4th 708, 710-711, 717, 158 CR3d 743, 745, 750]

[9:1209.6-1209.9] *Reserved.*

h. [9:1209.10] **Effect of dismissal filed after sanctions motion:** If the "safe harbor" period has *expired* and a sanctions motion filed, plaintiff cannot avoid CCP §128.7 sanctions by voluntarily dismissing the action: "The availability of section 128.7 sanctions against an offending plaintiff that has voluntarily dismissed its action *depends upon whether the sanctions motion was filed before or after the dismissal.*" [*Eichenbaum v. Alon* (2003) 106 CA4th 967, 975-976, 131 CR2d 296, 301 (emphasis added)—dismissal with prejudice filed after sanctions motion heard and taken under submission]

(1) [9:1209.11] **Compare—dismissal during "safe harbor period":** Plaintiff can avoid §128.7 sanctions by voluntarily dismissing the action (with or without prejudice) *before* expiration of the "safe harbor" period. [See *Hart v. Avetoom* (2002) 95 CA4th 410, 414, 115 CR2d 511, 514—dismissal before sanctions motion served and filed]

8. [9:1210] **Sanctions Awardable:** If the CCP §128.7 certification is violated, the court may impose an "appropriate" sanction upon the attorneys, law firms or parties responsible for the violation. [CCP §128.7(c)]

a. [9:1211] **Sanctions discretionary:** Sanctions under CCP §128.7 are discretionary. The court is *not* required to impose a monetary sanction or any sanction at all. [See CCP §128.7(c); *Kojababian v. Genuine Home Loans, Inc.* (2009) 174 CA4th 408, 421, 94 CR3d 288, 298]

[9:1212] *Reserved.*

(1) [9:1213] **Different rule as to improperly motivated sanctions motion?** A motion for sanctions brought by a party *primarily* for an improper purpose—such as to harass or cause unnecessary delay or needless expense—is itself subject to a motion for sanctions. [CCP §128.7(h)]

In this situation, sanctions seem required: "It is the intent of the Legislature that courts shall vigorously use [their] sanctions authority to deter that improper conduct or comparable conduct by others similarly situated." [CCP §128.7(h)]

b. [9:1214] **Limited to deterrence:** CCP §128.7 is not designed as a fee-shifting provision or to compensate innocent litigants. Its primary purpose is to deter sanctionable conduct: "A sanction imposed for violation . . . *shall be limited* to what is sufficient to *deter repetition* of this conduct or comparable conduct by others similarly situated." [CCP §128.7(d) (emphasis added); see *Trans-Action Comm'l Investors, Ltd. v. Jelinek* (1997) 60 CA4th 352, 368, 70 CR2d 449, 459]

c. [9:1215] **What constitutes "appropriate" sanction:** Subject to the above limitations (¶*9:1214*), CCP §128.7 expressly authorizes both monetary and nonmonetary sanctions. [CCP §128.7(d)]

(1) [9:1216] **Nonmonetary:** "Directives of a nonmonetary nature" may include:
— striking the offending pleading;
— issuing a reprimand;
— requiring participation in continuing legal education programs; or
— referring the matters to disciplinary authorities. [See Committee Notes on 1993 Amendments to Federal Rules of Civil Procedure (1993) 146 FRD 401, 587 (interpreting FRCP 11)]

(a) [9:1217] **Striking pleadings; alternative to summary judgment?** Where a party's claims or defenses are stricken for lack of evidentiary support, the effect may be the same as a summary judgment or summary adjudication (*see* ¶*10:1*).

[9:1218] *Reserved.*

(2) [9:1219] **Monetary:** Monetary sanctions include both:
— *fines or penalties* payable to the court; and
— an *award* to the opposing party for some or all of the "reasonable attorney's fees and other expenses incurred as a direct result of the violation." [CCP §128.7(d)]

(a) [9:1219.1] **Policy favoring fines rather than fee awards?** Under Federal Rule 11, monetary sanctions "for effective deterrence" are ordinarily imposed by fine payable to the court rather than by fee awards to the opposing party. [See Adv. Comm. Notes on 1993 Amendments to FRCP 11 at 146 FRD 401, 587-588]

Whether the same policy applies under CCP §128.7(d) is unclear.

d. [9:1220] **Fee awards as sanctions:** Attorney fees may be awarded as CCP §128.7 sanctions for:

(1) [9:1221] **Expenses incurred on sanctions motion:** "If warranted," the court may award the *prevailing party* its reasonable expenses and attorney fees "incurred in *presenting or opposing the motion.*" [CCP §128.7(c)(1) (emphasis added); see *Eichenbaum v. Alon* (2003) 106 CA4th 967, 977, 131 CR2d 296, 303—fee awards under §128.7(c) *limited to fees on the sanction motion itself*]

© 2020 Thomson Reuters/The Rutter Group

But an award of fees incurred in *opposing* an unsuccessful CCP §128.7 sanctions motion is not "warranted" unless the motion was frivolous, unfounded, filed for an improper purpose or otherwise unreasonable. [*Musaelian v. Adams* (2011) 197 CA4th 1251, 1258, 130 CR3d 32, 37—attorney fee award for opposing §128.7 motion not warranted because motion was not frivolous]

(2) [9:1222] **Expenses incurred as result of CCP §128.7 violation:** If "warranted for effective deterrence" the court may also award the moving party some or all of the attorney fees and other expenses "incurred as a *direct result* of the violation." [CCP §128.7(d) (emphasis added); see *Eichenbaum v. Alon*, supra, 106 CA4th at 977, 131 CR2d at 303]

(a) [9:1222.1] **Causal relationship required:** Sanctions under §128.7(d) are limited to fees and expenses incurred as a "direct" result of the violation. Thus, for example, sanctions could not be imposed for proceedings bearing only an "attenuated" relation to the sanctionable conduct (e.g., a motion to amend a frivolous complaint). [See *Lloyd v. Schlag* (9th Cir. 1989) 884 F2d 409, 415 (interpreting FRCP 11)]

(3) [9:1223] **Compare—no sua sponte fee awards after settlement or dismissal:** As previously stated, a court may not impose *monetary* sanctions (fines or fee awards) sua sponte on the basis of an OSC issued after a case has been settled or dismissed. [CCP §128.7(d)(2); *see* ¶*9:1208*]

e. [9:1224] **Who may be sanctioned:** Sanctions may be awarded against the persons—whether attorneys, law firms, or parties—who have violated CCP §128.7(b) or who are responsible for the violation. [CCP §128.7(c)]

(1) [9:1225] **Law firm:** "Absent exceptional circumstances," a law firm must be held jointly responsible for violations by its partners, associates or employees, and sanctioned accordingly. [CCP §128.7(c)(1)]

(2) [9:1226] **Allocation as between attorney and client:** Courts may allocate sanctions between the client and attorney based on their relative responsibility where this is ascertainable. [*Business Guides, Inc. v. Chromatic Communications Enterprises, Inc.* (1991) 498 US 533, 550, 111 S.Ct. 922, 933 (interpreting FRCP 11)]

- [9:1227] Where the record does not indicate that one should be regarded as less blameworthy than the other, sanctions may be imposed against the attorney and client jointly and severally. [*Kendrick v. Zanides* (ND CA 1985) 609 F.Supp. 1162, 1173 (interpreting FRCP 11)]

- [9:1228] Where the attorney's personal responsibility is apparent to the court, it may specifically order the attorney to pay the sanction personally and not seek reimbursement from the client. [*Derechin v. State Univ. of New York* (2nd Cir. 1992) 963 F2d 513, 518 (interpreting FRCP 11)]
- [9:1229] But an attorney should not be sanctioned for the client's refusal to comply with a valid court order if the attorney has attempted in good faith to secure the client's compliance. [*Universal Cooperatives, Inc. v. Tribal Cooperative Marketing Develop. Federation of India, Ltd.* (8th Cir. 1995) 45 F3d 1194, 1197]

(3) [9:1230] **Limitation—no sanctions against client for meritless legal contentions:** Where the violation consists of meritless contentions of law (see CCP §128.7(b)(2)), no *monetary sanctions* may be awarded against the client. [CCP §128.7(d)(1); see *Cromwell v. Cummings* (1998) 65 CA4th Supp. 10, 13, 76 CR2d 171, 173, fn. 4—"Monetary responsibility for such violations is more properly placed *solely* on the party's attorneys" (emphasis added); *Burkle v. Burkle* (2006) 144 CA4th 387, 407, 50 CR3d 436, 447—"sanctions cannot be awarded against her for a violation of subdivision (b)(2)"]

(a) [9:1230.1] **Compare—frivolous pleadings:** Where the court finds that the client caused the filing of a frivolous complaint ("presented primarily for an improper purpose, such as to harass or to cause unnecessary delay or needless increase in the cost of litigation"), the client may be sanctioned despite his or her contention that the ultimate decision to file the offending pleading was made by his or her lawyers. [*Burkle v. Burkle*, supra, 144 CA4th at 402-403, 50 CR3d at 447-448—sanctions upheld against both attorney and client]

[9:1230.2-1230.4] *Reserved.*

(4) [9:1230.5] **No attorney fees sanctions to self-represented attorney:** *See ¶9:1078.1.*

f. [9:1231] **Moving party's diligence:** In evaluating the amount of sanctions, the court must consider "whether a party seeking sanctions has exercised due diligence." [CCP §128.7(c) (last sent.)]

(1) [9:1232] **Effect:** This apparently permits the court to consider to what extent any fees incurred by the party seeking sanctions were self-inflicted due to failure to mitigate or resulted from his or her own misconduct.

(2) [9:1233] **Compare—federal rule:** Federal Rule 11 does not contain a similar provision. But federal courts

© 2020 Thomson Reuters/The Rutter Group

have generally held that Rule 11 sanctions are not "appropriate" for any fees or other expenses provoked by the moving party's own misconduct. [See *Mossman v. Roadway Express, Inc.* (9th Cir. 1986) 789 F2d 804, 806]

g. [9:1234] **Punitive damages for claims by felon against victim:** In addition to any award above (¶*9:1210 ff.*), the court may "assess" *punitive damages* against a convicted felon who sues his or her victim (or the victim's heirs) for injuries suffered in the course of committing the crime, if the court finds the suit is maintained with "fraud, oppression, or malice." [CCP §128.7(f)]

Comment: There is no comparable provision under Federal Rule 11. *See further discussion at ¶9:1139.*

9. [9:1235] **Requirements re Sanctions Order:** When *imposing* sanctions, the court must:
— "describe" the sanctionable conduct; and
— "*explain the basis* for the sanction imposed." [CCP §128.7(e) (emphasis added)]

FORM: Proposed Order Granting Motion for Sanctions, *see Form 9C:2* in Rivera, *Cal. Prac. Guide: Civ. Pro. Before Trial FORMS* (TRG).

a. [9:1236] **Oral or written?** The statute does not specifically require a written order. Therefore, presumably, an oral statement on the record suffices. However, the moving party is required to prepare an order after hearing (CRC 3.1312; *see* ¶*9:294 ff.*) and should ensure that the order describes the sanctionable conduct and explains the reasons for the sanctions imposed as required by CCP §128.7(e).

Alternatively, even if the court does not give an oral explanation for the sanctions at the hearing, it may, after the hearing, sign an order prepared by the moving party, explaining the basis for the order. [*Hopkins & Carley v. Gens* (2011) 200 CA4th 1401, 1418, 135 CR3d 1, 15]

b. [9:1237] **Explanation:** Where monetary sanctions are imposed, they must be "quantifiable with some precision." I.e., the award must be properly itemized in terms of the perceived misconduct and the fees and expenses incurred as a direct result thereof. [See *In re Yagman* (9th Cir. 1986) 796 F2d 1165, 1184 (interpreting FRCP 11)]

c. [9:1238] **Compare—order denying sanctions:** The statute mentions only orders *imposing* sanctions, implying that no explanation is required in an order denying sanctions.

- [9:1239] However, some federal cases require a court denying a sanctions motion to make findings as to whether a Rule 11 violation has occurred; and if so, why imposition of sanctions is inappropriate. [*Warren v. Guelker* (9th Cir. 1994) 29 F3d 1386, 1389-1390]

[9:1240-1262] *Reserved.*

D. OTHER SANCTIONS STATUTES AND RULES

1. [9:1263] **Discovery Sanctions:** The losing party on a discovery motion and/or his or her lawyer may be ordered to pay the prevailing party's attorney fees and expenses, unless the court finds the losing party acted with "substantial justification" or that imposition of sanctions would otherwise be "unjust." [CCP §2023.030(a)]

   Cross-refer: Discovery sanctions are discussed in detail in *Ch. 8M.*

2. [9:1264] **Change of Venue Sanctions:** Where a motion for change of venue is made upon the ground the action was filed in the "wrong court," the court may, in its discretion, order the losing party to pay the prevailing party's attorney fees and expenses in making (or resisting) the motion. The losing party's *attorney* is *personally liable* for any such award (because the attorney, rather than the party, is presumed to know the venue rules). [CCP §396b; *see* ¶*3:583*]

3. [9:1265] **Defense Costs for Unfounded Tort Action Against Governmental Entity (CCP §1038):** CCP §1038 provides a separate basis for the award of "defense costs" in *tort* actions against a governmental entity. This provides public entities, which are barred from filing malicious prosecution actions, with a way to recover the costs of defending against unmeritorious and frivolous tort claims. [*Kobzoff v. Los Angeles County Harbor/UCLA Med. Ctr.* (1998) 19 C4th 851, 857, 80 CR2d 803, 807]

   However, defense costs under §1038 can be assessed only against a *party.* No award can be made against the party's counsel, "even if counsel lacked reasonable cause and good faith in filing or maintaining" the action. [*Settle v. State of Calif.* (2014) 228 CA4th 215, 219, 174 CR3d 925, 928; *Suarez v. City of Corona* (2014) 229 CA4th 325, 328-329, 177 CR3d 244, 247]

   a. [9:1265.1] **Judgments subject to award:** An award of defense costs under CCP §1038 is authorized only on granting of:

      — a motion for summary judgment; or

      — at trial, upon granting a motion for nonsuit, directed verdict or motion under CCP §631.8 (at close of plaintiff's case in nonjury trial). [CCP §1038(d)]

   b. [9:1265.2] **Separate motion required:** An award of defense costs under §1038 may be made only on notice and an opportunity to be heard. [*Kobzoff v. Los Angeles County Harbor/UCLA Med. Ctr.*, supra, 19 C4th at 856, 80 CR2d at 806]

      (1) [9:1265.3] **Before same judge:** The CCP §1038 motion must be noticed for hearing before the same judge who

© 2020 Thomson Reuters/The Rutter Group

hears the summary judgment motion, unless that judge is unavailable. [See *Gamble v. Los Angeles Dept. of Water & Power* (2002) 97 CA4th 253, 259, 118 CR2d 271, 275]

c. [9:1266] **Proof requirements—lacking "good faith"** ***or*** **"reasonable cause":** Defendant may not recover CCP §1038 costs simply because it won a summary judgment or other dispositive motion. To support such an award, the court must find that plaintiff lacked *both* good faith and "reasonable (probable) cause." [CCP §1038(a); *Kobzoff v. Los Angeles County Harbor/UCLA Med. Ctr.*, supra, 19 C4th at 854, 80 CR2d at 806—award based on lack of reasonable cause even though action maintained in "good faith"; *Laabs v. City of Victorville* (2008) 163 CA4th 1242, 1272, 78 CR3d 372, 397—denial of City's motion for CCP §1038 fees *implies findings* that plaintiff acted in good faith and with reasonable cause]

These requirements apply both to *commencing* the action and to its *continued maintenance*. [*Kobzoff v. Los Angeles County Harbor/UCLA Med. Ctr.*, supra, 19 C4th at 854, 80 CR2d at 806, fn. 1]

(1) [9:1266.1] **"Good faith":** An award may be based on finding plaintiffs lacked a good faith belief in the action's "justifiability." [*Kobzoff v. Los Angeles County Harbor/UCLA Med. Ctr.*, supra, 19 C4th at 862, 80 CR2d at 810]

Courts often use the terms "good faith" and "reasonable cause" interchangeably, *inferring a lack of good faith* from a finding that the lawsuit was brought or maintained without reasonable cause. [*Kobzoff v. Los Angeles County Harbor/UCLA Med. Ctr.*, supra, 19 C4th at 862, 80 CR2d at 810]

(2) [9:1267] **"Reasonable cause":** This term means the same as "probable cause" for malicious prosecution purposes. It calls for an *objective* determination of whether a reasonable attorney would have thought the claim tenable when the action was filed or maintained; i.e., whether plaintiff (or plaintiff's attorney) had *facts sufficient to conclude* defendant was liable. [*Kobzoff v. Los Angeles County Harbor/UCLA Med. Ctr.*, supra, 19 C4th at 857, 80 CR2d at 807]

(a) [9:1267.1] **Investigation required:** "[P]laintiff must bear a *burden of investigation* sufficient to establish at least a basis for reasonable belief that all elements exist. Abstract hope is not reasonable belief . . . [plaintiff] cannot simply name every conceivable defendant and rely on what future discovery may turn up." [*Kobzoff v. Los Angeles County Harbor/UCLA Med. Ctr.,* supra, 19 C4th at 858, 80 CR2d at 807 (emphasis added; internal quotes omitted)]

[9:1267.2-1267.4] *Reserved.*

(b) **Application**

- [9:1267.5] P was advised before filing suit that neither County nor State had jurisdiction over the intersection where the accident occurred. Despite this, P named County and State as defendants and repeatedly refused to dismiss them, forcing them to move for summary judgment. CCP §1038 sanctions were imposed because P showed *no facts to support naming of these defendants* in the first place. [*Carroll v. State of Calif.* (1990) 217 CA3d 134, 141, 265 CR 753, 757]
- [9:1267.6] P sued County Hospital for wrongful death based on medical malpractice. P refused to dismiss despite being advised that County was statutorily immune from liability (Gov.C. §856.2(a)(2)). P lacked "reasonable cause" for maintaining the action. [*Kobzoff v. Los Angeles County Harbor/UCLA Med. Ctr.*, supra, 19 C4th at 863, 80 CR2d at 811]
- [9:1267.7] P received conflicting information on whether City or County was responsible for condition of street on which he was injured. Being unsure, he sued both. Later, he discovered County had nothing to do with the street in question, but he refused to dismiss County. Even if the action was brought "in good faith and with reasonable cause" originally, §1038 sanctions were proper for *continuing* the action against County after its hopelessness became apparent. [*Curtis v. County of Los Angeles* (1985) 172 CA3d 1243, 1250, 218 CR 772, 776]

d. [9:1268] **"Defense costs":** Recoverable "defense costs" include reasonable attorney fees, expert witness fees, and even fees paid to advisors and consultants "reasonably and necessarily incurred in defending the proceeding." [CCP §1038(b)]

[9:1268.1-1268.4] *Reserved.*

e. [9:1268.5] **Ruling on motion:** The court must determine as a matter of law whether plaintiff brought the underlying proceeding in "good faith" and with "reasonable cause." [CCP §1038(a); *Kobzoff v. Los Angeles County Harbor/UCLA Med. Ctr.*, supra, 19 C4th at 856, 80 CR2d at 807]

(1) [9:1268.6] **Timing:** The court's ruling must be made "*at the time of the granting* of . . . summary judgment [or other judgment subject to §1038] . . . or at a later time set forth by rule of the Judicial Council." [CCP §1038(a) (emphasis added)]

© 2020 Thomson Reuters/The Rutter Group

No such rule has yet been adopted by the Judicial Council. [See *Gamble v. Los Angeles Dept. of Water & Power* (2002) 97 CA4th 253, 256, 118 CR2d 271, 273 (citing text)]

The statute has been interpreted *liberally* to allow filing of a CCP §1038 motion "at the earliest *practical* time prior to the discharge of the jury or entry of judgment." [*Gamble v. Los Angeles Dept. of Water & Power,* supra, 97 CA4th at 259, 118 CR2d at 275 (emphasis added)]

[9:1268.7-1268.9] *Reserved.*

f. [9:1268.10] **Waiver of malicious prosecution action:** In seeking CCP §1038 costs, defendant waives its right to malicious prosecution damages to the extent the right exists. Conversely, failure to make the motion will not be deemed a waiver of the right to pursue a malicious prosecution action. [CCP §1038(c); *Kobzoff v. Los Angeles County Harbor/UCLA Med. Ctr.* (1998) 19 C4th 851, 857, 80 CR2d 803, 806—public entities are barred from suing for malicious prosecution; *see ¶9:1265*]

4. [9:1269] **Defense Costs in Unfounded Actions for Indemnity or Contribution (CCP §1038):** CCP §1038 also authorizes the award of "defense costs" in *any* civil action for indemnity or contribution. Such awards are subject to the same rules and procedures discussed above (¶*9:1265.2 ff.*) (including the required showing of lack of good faith and reasonable cause).

a. [9:1269.1] **Compare—CCP §1021.6:** In indemnity actions, attorney fees may be recoverable under *either* CCP §1038 or CCP §1021.6, which authorizes an attorney fee award to the prevailing party in an action for implied indemnity. [See CCP §1021.6]

Recovering under §1021.6 is easier than under §1038 because the proof requirements are lower ("good faith" and "reasonable cause" are *not* required). [See *Wilson, McCall & Daoro v. American Qualified Plans, Inc.* (1999) 70 CA4th 1030, 1037-1038, 83 CR2d 192, 196-197]

5. [9:1270] **Sanctions to Court for Violation of Court Order (CCP §177.5):** In addition to other sanctions, the court may impose monetary sanctions up to $1,500 against a party or counsel (or witness) for violation of a lawful court order without good cause or substantial justification. [CCP §177.5] However, the scope of CCP §177.5 is not limited to parties, counsel, or witnesses. [*People v. Hooper* (2019) 40 CA5th 685, 692-693, 253 CR3d 369, 377-378—sanctions imposed against Department of State Hospitals for failure to follow standing order; *People v. Kareem A.* (2020) 46 CA5th 58, 70-71, 259 CR3d 545, 555 (same)]

Sanctions may be imposed for a *knowing* violation of a valid court order without good cause or substantial justification. [*Winikow v.*

Sup.Ct. (Schroeder) (2000) 82 CA4th 719, 726, 98 CR2d 413, 418; see *Seykora v. Sup.Ct.* (1991) 232 CA3d 1075, 1081, 283 CR 857, 860—all that need be shown is that there was *no valid excuse* for the violation]

CCP §177.5 does *not* authorize monetary sanctions for misconduct other than violation of a specific court order. [*People v. Muhammad* (2003) 108 CA4th 313, 323-324, 133 CR2d 308, 317—no authorization under §177.5 for monetary sanctions where counsel's misconduct caused a mistrial; *People v. Hundal* (2008) 168 CA4th 965, 970, 86 CR3d 166, 170]

CCP §177.5 expressly states the court's sanctions power "does not apply to *advocacy of counsel* before the court" (emphasis added). Even so, sanctions may be imposed for a lawyer's use of certain terms in argument to a jury, or questions posed to a witness at trial, in *direct violation of a court order*. [*People v. Ward* (2009) 173 CA4th 1518, 1530-1531, 93 CR3d 871, 880—sanctions upheld for public defender's use of term "prosecutorial misconduct" in deliberate violation of court order; *Scott C. Moody, Inc. v. Starr Surgical Co.* (2011) 195 CA4th 1043, 1049, 128 CR3d 89, 94—sanctions upheld for lawyer inquiring into topic in direct violation of court order that he not do so (lawyer's questions did not constitute "advocacy" but rather "calculated decision to violate the court's order")]

a. [9:1271] **Comment:** The main advantage to §177.5 is that it offers an alternative to more cumbersome contempt proceedings. But, the monetary sanctions are payable to the *court*, so the aggrieved party usually has no incentive to seek this sanction. Rather, it is usually imposed by the court *on its own motion*.

b. **Application**

- [9:1272] Where *both* counsel are guilty of misconduct, the court can impose monetary sanctions against each counsel under §177.5. Because such sanctions are payable *to the court* rather than the opposing party, the awards do *not* offset each other. [See *Caldwell v. Samuels Jewelers* (1990) 222 CA3d 970, 977, 272 CR 126, 130]

- [9:1272.1] Where a party or attorney has failed to pay an earlier sanctions award, additional monetary sanctions of up to $1,500 can be imposed under CCP §177.5 for violation of the earlier order. [*20th Century Ins. Co. v. Choong* (2000) 79 CA4th 1274, 1277-1278, 94 CR2d 753, 755]

  It is no excuse that the opposing party could have obtained payment by levying a writ of execution on the sanctioned party's property. [*20th Century Ins. Co. v. Choong*, supra, 79 CA4th at 1277, 94 CR2d at 755]

- [9:1272.2] Where Department of State Hospitals violated standing court order that it admit defendants to state

© 2020 Thomson Reuters/The Rutter Group

hospital within 60 days of commitment order, sanctions of $1,500 as to each of 11 defendants (for a total of $16,500) were proper. [*People v. Hooper* (2019) 40 CA5th 685, 688, 692-694, 253 CR3d 369, 375, 377-379]

c. [9:1273] **Due process required:** As with sanctions proceedings generally, notice and opportunity to be heard are prerequisites to any sanction award. [*Barrientos v. City of Los Angeles* (1994) 30 CA4th 63, 70, 35 CR2d 520, 524; *People v. Hundal*, supra, 168 CA4th at 970, 86 CR3d at 170; *People v. Whitus* (2012) 209 CA4th Supp. 1, 6, 146 CR3d 823, 827]

However, the scope of the sanctions hearing is within the trial court's discretion. There is no absolute right to present oral testimony. [*Seykora v. Sup.Ct.*, supra, 232 CA3d at 1081-1082, 283 CR at 860-861]

d. [9:1274] **Form of order:** The sanctions order must "recite in detail the conduct or circumstances justifying the order." [CCP §177.5; *People v. Hundal*, supra, 168 CA4th at 970, 86 CR3d at 170]

Specification is required both for due process purposes and to enable the reviewing court to determine whether there has been an abuse of discretion. [*Caldwell v. Samuels Jewelers* (1990) 222 CA3d 970, 977-978, 272 CR 126, 131—order stating "good cause appears" to impose sanctions held insufficient]

[9:1274.1-1274.4] *Reserved.*

6. [9:1274.5] **Defense Costs in Frivolous False Claims Act (FCA) Case:** Under the FCA, where the action is objectively frivolous or the complaint is "bereft of any objective factual support" and "clearly has no chance of success," attorney fees are recoverable. [*County of Kern v. Jadwin* (2011) 197 CA4th 65, 72, 127 CR3d 837, 843]

7. [9:1275] **Sanctions for Violation of Local Court Rules (CCP §575.2):** Sanctions may be imposed for violation of local court rules if they contain adequate warnings of the consequences of failure to comply. [CCP §575.2; *see* ¶*9:9.1a*]

Where the local rules so provide, the court may:

- strike all or any part of the pleadings of the party violating the rules; or
- dismiss the action or enter judgment by default against such party; or
- impose "penalties of a lesser nature as otherwise provided by law" (see *Rietveld v. Rosebud Storage Partners, L.P.* (2004) 121 CA4th 250, 256, 16 CR3d 791, 796—*monetary sanctions* are "penalties of a lesser nature"); and
- (in addition to any of the above) order the offending party *or*

his or her counsel to pay the moving party's reasonable expenses, including attorney fees, incurred in seeking enforcement of the local rules. [CCP §575.2(a); *see* ¶*9:9*]

Caution re local rule preemption: CRC 3.20(a) preempts certain local rules relating to pretrial proceedings (*see* ¶*9:13.2 ff.*). Since such local rules are void, judges cannot impose sanctions for violating those rules. Other local rules, however, (e.g., case management conference rules) are not preempted and may be enforced by CCP §575.2 sanctions. [*Lee v. An* (2008) 168 CA4th 558, 565, 85 CR3d 620, 625]

a. [9:1276] **Examples:** The following are examples of local rules authorizing sanctions for violations:

- [9:1276.1] *Case management rules:* Local rules may authorize "appropriate sanctions" for failure to comply with the court's time standards or other case management rules and orders. [L.A. Sup.Ct. Rule 3.10; Orange Sup.Ct. Rule 381; S.D. Sup.Ct. Rule 2.5.12; *see discussion at* ¶*12:91*]

  [9:1276.2] *Reserved.*

- [9:1276.3] *Conduct relating to court-ordered mediation:* The court may impose sanctions for failure to participate in *court-ordered* mediation. [See CRC 3.894(a); *Ellerbee v. County of Los Angeles* (2010) 187 CA4th 1206, 1216-1217, 114 CR3d 756, 762-763—mediation confidentiality rule did not preclude imposition of sanctions where defendant failed to have persons with authority to settle present during mediation]

b. [9:1277] **Innocent clients protected:** Where the failure to comply is the *fault of counsel* and not of the party, "any penalty shall be imposed on counsel and shall not adversely affect the party's cause of action or defense." [CCP §575.2(b); *see* ¶*9:9.2*]

- [9:1277.1] It is error to exclude Wife's evidence as punishment for her *counsel's* noncompliance with local rules requiring pretrial exchange of information. [*Marriage of Colombo* (1987) 197 CA3d 572, 578, 242 CR 100, 104]

- [9:1277.2] It is error to strike a party's demand for jury trial because of his attorney's failure to submit proposed jury instructions within the time required by local rules. [*Cooks v. Sup.Ct. (Cruz)* (1990) 224 CA3d 723, 727, 274 CR 113, 116]

- [9:1277.3] A court may not dismiss the complaint for failure to comply with local "fast track" rules where the failure is the responsibility of plaintiff's counsel rather than that of plaintiff. [*Garcia v. McCutchen* (1997) 16

© 2020 Thomson Reuters/The Rutter Group

C4th 469, 475-476, 66 CR2d 319, 323-324; *Tliche v. Van Quathem* (1998) 66 CA4th 1054, 1063, 78 CR2d 458, 462-463; *see* ¶*12:94*; *Franklin Capital Corp. v. Wilson* (2007) 148 CA4th 187, 211, 55 CR3d 424, 442—attorney failed to attend mandatory settlement conference]

c. [9:1278] **Notice and hearing required:** No sanctions may be imposed under this provision without prior notice to, and an opportunity to be heard by, the party against whom the sanctions are sought to be imposed. [CCP §575.2; see *Annex British Cars, Inc. v. Parker-Rhodes* (1988) 198 CA3d 788, 792-793, 244 CR 48, 50—hearing not sufficient where court considered only its authority to impose sanctions and did not allow counsel to address whether sanctions should be imposed or the amount thereof; *Lee v. An,* supra, 168 CA4th at 565, 85 CR3d at 625—error to strike answer and enter default for failure to attend case management conference where notice did not state these penalties for failure to attend]

8. [9:1279] **Sanctions for Violation of CRC:** Unless good cause is shown, the court may impose monetary sanctions against a party or counsel, or both, or against a witness, an *insurer or any other person or entity* whose approval is necessary for settlement of a case, for failure to comply with CRC pretrial and trial rules (e.g., rules requiring sending claims representatives with settlement authority to MSC). [CRC 2.30(b)]

a. [9:1280] **Who may be sanctioned; party or counsel:** Whether the party or counsel (or both) may be sanctioned for violating the CRC rules is determined by the nature of the violation:

(1) [9:1280.1] **Violation of pretrial rules:** Sanctions for violation of pretrial rules must be imposed *only on counsel* if the violation is counsel's responsibility. Sanctions must *not* adversely affect the client's case. [*Levitz v. The Warlocks* (2007) 148 CA4th 531, 535-536, 55 CR3d 800, 803—error to dismiss complaint for counsel's violation of pretrial rule]

b. [9:1281] **Types of sanctions:** The court may order "reasonable monetary sanctions" payable to the court or to the opposing party or counsel, "*[i]n addition to any other sanctions permitted by law.*" [CRC 2.30(b) (emphasis added)]

(1) [9:1281.1] **Plus expenses:** In addition, the court may order payment of the opposing parties' reasonable expenses, including reasonable attorney fees and costs, incurred in connection *with the sanctions motion.* [CRC 2.30(d); *Sino Century Develop. Ltd. v. Farley* (2012) 211 CA4th 688, 698, 149 CR3d 866, 873—recovery limited to fees incurred in connection with sanctions motion, not all fees incurred as result of rule violation]

(2) [9:1282] **Amount of monetary sanctions:** There is no limitation on the amount of monetary sanctions that can be imposed under Rule 2.30 for violation of CRC rules. [See *Caldwell v. Samuels Jewelers* (1990) 222 CA3d 970, 976, 272 CR 126, 131 (compared to $1,500 limit on sanctions for violation of *court order, and* ¶*9:1270*)]

c. [9:1283] **Procedural requirements:** Rule 2.30 sanctions may be imposed either on a party's motion or by the court on its own motion, if written notice and opportunity to be heard are provided. [CRC 2.30(c)]

(1) [9:1283.1] **Party's motion:** A party's motion for sanctions must:

— set forth the applicable CRC pretrial or trial rule that has been violated;

— describe the specific conduct that is alleged to have violated the rule; and

— identify the attorney, law firm, party, witness or other person against whom sanctions are sought. [CRC 2.30(c)]

(2) [9:1283.2] **Court may act sua sponte:** The court may also impose sanctions under CRC 2.30 on its own motion. To do so, the court must issue an *order to show cause* that sets forth the same information required on a party motion (¶*9:1283.1*). [CRC 2.30(c); see also *Bergman v. Rifkind & Sterling, Inc.* (1991) 227 CA3d 1380, 1387, 278 CR 583, 587—error for court sua sponte to find sanctionable conduct occurred and then offer counsel a hearing on the matter]

A court may also issue an OSC re sanctions for *failure to timely serve pleadings and file proofs of service.* Responsive papers must be filed 5 calendar days before the scheduled hearing. [CRC 3.110(f), (i)]

(3) [9:1283.3] **Findings required if sanctions imposed:** An order imposing sanctions must be in writing and "recite in detail the conduct or circumstances justifying the order." [CRC 2.30(e)]

d. [9:1284] **Rules of Professional Conduct not included:** The Rules of Professional Conduct are not part of the California Rules of Court, and violations of those rules cannot be sanctioned under CRC 2.30(b). [*Marriage of Bianco* (2013) 221 CA4th 826, 829, 164 CR3d 785, 787—trial court erred in sanctioning counsel under CRC 2.30(b) for violation of former CRPC 1-300 and 1-311 (hiring person ineligible to practice law to assist in trial)]

[9:1284.1-1284.9] *Reserved.*

© 2020 Thomson Reuters/The Rutter Group

9. [9:1284.10] **Sanctions for Bad Faith Declaration on Summary Judgment:** If the court finds that a declaration filed in connection with a motion for summary judgment or summary adjudication was "presented in bad faith or solely for the purpose of delay," the court must order the party who presented the declaration to pay the opposing party's reasonable expenses caused by the filing of the declaration. [CCP §437c(j); *see ¶10:336 ff.*]

10. [9:1284.11] **Sanctions on Appeal:** On a party's motion or the court's own motion, an appellate court may impose sanctions on a party or an attorney for "[t]aking a frivolous appeal or appealing solely to cause delay." [CRC 8.276(a)(1); *Workman v. Colichman* (2019) 33 CA5th 1039, 1061-1065, 245 CR3d 636, 655-658—where court found appeal of denial of anti-SLAPP motion to be frivolous and solely for delay, court issued sanctions of more than $35,000 to P for attorney fees on appeal and $8,500 to court for costs of processing appeal]

    Cross-refer: For detailed discussion of appellate sanctions, see Eisenberg, *Cal. Prac. Guide: Civil Appeals & Writs* (TRG), Ch. 11.

E. ENFORCEMENT OF SANCTIONS ORDERS

[9:1285] A sanctions order is enforceable in the same way as a "money judgment"; i.e., a *writ of execution* may be issued by the court and levied on the property of the person sanctioned. [See CCP §§680.230, 680.270, 699.510; *Newland v. Sup.Ct. (Sugasawara)* (1995) 40 CA4th 608, 615, 47 CR2d 24, 28 (citing text)]

Another alternative is to ask the court for a *judgment* based on the sanctions order, and then record an *abstract of judgment.* This will create a judgment lien on the sanctioned party's (or counsel's) home or other assets. *See discussion at ¶9:344.22.*

F. APPELLATE REVIEW OF SANCTIONS

1. [9:1286] **Limited Right of Appeal:** Except in a "limited civil case," an immediate appeal lies from superior court sanctions orders or interlocutory judgments against a *party or counsel* exceeding $5,000. [CCP §904.1(a)(11), (12); *see ¶8:2040 ff.*]

    Appellate review of lesser superior court sanctions may be obtained only on appeal from the final judgment in the action or by petition for extraordinary writ. [See CCP §§904.1(b), 904.2] (But an immediate appeal is allowed where sanctioned counsel is no longer counsel of record (*see ¶9:1291*) or the action is dismissed; see *Eichenbaum v. Alon* (2003) 106 CA4th 967, 974, 131 CR2d 296, 300.)

    Compare—limited civil cases: In a *limited* civil case, any appeal is to the appellate division of the superior court (CCP §904.2). A sanctions award (not involving discovery) in a limited civil case, *regardless of amount*—i.e., whether or not it exceeds $5,000—is *immediately appealable* as a "collateral order." [*Drum v. Sup.Ct.*

(2006) 139 CA4th 845, 850-851, 43 CR3d 279, 283-284—failure to file timely notice of appeal precludes review of sanctions award on appeal from final judgment]

It is an open question whether a sanctions order for less than $5,000 made *before a case is transferred* from an unlimited civil court to a limited civil court is immediately appealable. [*Drum v. Sup.Ct.*, supra, 139 CA4th at 852, 43 CR3d at 284-285]

[9:1287] *Reserved.*

a. [9:1288] **Effect:** Unless the sanctions against parties or their counsel exceed $5,000, the only possibility for *immediate* appellate review in an *unlimited* civil case is by petition for extraordinary writ (which is rarely granted).

Conversely, if the sanctions exceed $5,000, any appeal *must* be taken immediately.

☞ [9:1289] ***PRACTICE POINTER:*** Don't wait until the final judgment to appeal superior court sanctions exceeding $5,000 that are imposed against you or your client. And if the sanction award is imposed against you as counsel individually (whether also imposed against your client or not), you should be listed as an appellant in the notice of appeal. [*K.J. v. Los Angeles Unified School Dist.* (2020) 8 C5th 875, 889, 257 CR3d 850, 860—in some circumstances, the attorney may be considered an appellant even if not listed on the notice, but the "better practice" is to list attorney as appellant on notice of appeal]

Because an immediate appeal lies from such sanctions, the right to appeal will be *waived* unless notice of appeal is filed within 60 days after notice of entry of the order or judgment (CRC 8.104(a)). [See *Imuta v. Nakano* (1991) 233 CA3d 1570, 1578-1579, 285 CR 681, 686]

b. [9:1290] **No aggregation of sanctions:** *Unrelated* sanctions, each less than $5,000, may not be aggregated to reach the appealability threshold even if payable to the same person and awarded at the same time. [See *Champion/L.B.S. Assocs. Develop. Co. v. E-Z Serve Petroleum Marketing, Inc.* (1993) 15 CA4th 56, 59, 18 CR2d 726, 728 (decided under former statute with $750 threshold)]

Nor may sanctions of less than $5,000 payable to several parties be aggregated for purposes of appeal. [*Calhoun v. Vallejo City Unified School Dist.* (1993) 20 CA4th 39, 44, 24 CR2d 337, 340 (disapproved on other grounds by *K.J. v. Los Angeles Unified School Dist.*, supra, 8 C5th at 887-888, 257 CR3d at 859 & fn. 6) (also decided under former law with $750 threshold)]

c. [9:1290.1] **Discovery sanctions:** Although there was at one time a split of authority, courts now agree that orders

© 2020 Thomson Reuters/The Rutter Group

imposing monetary *discovery* sanctions are directly appealable if they meet the $5,000 threshold. *See* ¶*8:2041*.

Cross-refer: See further discussion in Eisenberg, *Cal. Prac. Guide: Civil Appeals & Writs* (TRG), Ch. 2.

[9:1290.2-1290.4] *Reserved.*

2. [9:1290.5] **Law Firm's Standing to Appeal Sanctions Against Member:** Because a law firm (employer) must indemnify its employee-associate for sanctions ordered to be paid by the latter (Lab.C. §2802), the firm is an "aggrieved party" and thus has standing to appeal the sanction order. [*20th Century Ins. Co. v. Choong* (2000) 79 CA4th 1274, 1278, 94 CR2d 753, 754-755]

3. [9:1291] **Compare—Sanctions Against Nonparties:** The statutes limiting the right to appeal do *not* apply to sanctions against nonparty witnesses (e.g., for refusing to answer deposition questions; CCP §2025.480, *see* ¶*8:842*). A sanction against someone who is neither a party nor counsel in the action is treated as a final judgment on a collateral matter, and hence *immediately appealable*. [*Marriage of Lemen* (1980) 113 CA3d 769, 778, 170 CR 642, 646; *Barton v. Ahmanson Develops., Inc.* (1993) 17 CA4th 1358, 1361, 22 CR2d 56, 58—sanctions imposed against *former* attorney; *Diepenbrock v. Brown* (2012) 208 CA4th 743, 746, 145 CR3d 659, 661-662 (citing text)]